# The United States

CANADA

MINNESOTA
Winnipeg
Lake of the Woods
International Falls
Fargo
Duluth
Huron
Sioux Falls
Sioux City

WISCONSIN
Lake Superior
Sault Ste. Marie
Minneapolis
St. Paul
Green Bay
Lake Winnebago
Oshkosh
Madison
Milwaukee
Traverse City

MICHIGAN
Lake Michigan
Lake Huron
Lansing
Port Huron
Detroit
Lake St. Clair

IOWA
Cedar Rapids
Des Moines
Chicago
Gary
Fort Wayne

ILLINOIS
Peoria
Springfield
Hannibal

INDIANA
Indianapolis
Cincinnati

OHIO
Columbus
Akron
Cleveland
Toledo
Lake Erie
Erie

NEW YORK
Lake Ontario
Toronto
Buffalo
Watertown
Albany

Ottawa
Montréal
Québec
Burlington
Montpelier
Lake Champlain

MAINE
Bangor
Augusta
Portland
Gulf of Maine

NH
Concord
VT
MA
Boston
Providence
Hartford
New Haven

RHODE ISLAND
CONNECTICUT

PENNSYLVANIA
Pittsburgh
Harrisburg
Philadelphia
Newark
New York
Trenton

NEW JERSEY
Atlantic City

WEST VIRGINIA
Charleston

VIRGINIA
Richmond
Roanoke
Washington, D.C.
Baltimore
Annapolis
Dover
Delaware Bay

DELAWARE
MARYLAND
Chesapeake Bay
Norfolk

MISSOURI
Kansas City
Independence
Topeka
St. Louis
Jefferson City
Lake of the Ozarks
Springfield
Wichita

KENTUCKY
Louisville
Frankfort
Lexington

TENNESSEE
Nashville
Knoxville
Chattanooga
Memphis

NORTH CAROLINA
Raleigh
Charlotte
Asheville
Wilmington

SOUTH CAROLINA
Columbia
Charleston

OKLAHOMA
Oklahoma City
Tulsa

ARKANSAS
Little Rock
Jonesboro

MISSISSIPPI
Jackson
Tupelo

ALABAMA
Birmingham
Montgomery
Columbus

GEORGIA
Atlanta
Macon
Savannah

LOUISIANA
Baton Rouge
Lafayette
New Orleans
Mobile
Biloxi
Pensacola
Lake Pontchartrain
Breton Sound
Mississippi River Delta
Atchafalaya Bay

FLORIDA
Tallahassee
Jacksonville
Apalachee Bay
Orlando
Tampa
Lake Okeechobee
Fort Lauderdale
Miami
Key West

Texarkana
Shreveport
Natchitoches
Dallas
Fort Worth
Waco
Austin
Houston
Beaumont
Galveston
Galveston Bay
Corpus Christi
Brownsville

Omaha
Lincoln

Gulf of Mexico

Atlantic Ocean

Nassau
BAHAMAS

## Puerto Rico & U.S. Virgin Islands

Atlantic Ocean
San Juan
PUERTO RICO
St. Thomas
British Virgin Islands
Tortola
St. John
U.S. Virgin Islands
St. Croix
Caribbean Sea

0    50 mi
0    50 km

0    150    300 mi
0    150    300 km

NINTH TEXAS EDITION

# We the People

## AN INTRODUCTION TO AMERICAN POLITICS

**Benjamin Ginsberg**
THE JOHNS HOPKINS UNIVERSITY

**Theodore J. Lowi**
CORNELL UNIVERSITY

**Margaret Weir**
UNIVERSITY OF CALIFORNIA AT BERKELEY

**Caroline J. Tolbert**
UNIVERSITY OF IOWA

**Anthony Champagne**
UNIVERSITY OF TEXAS AT DALLAS

**Edward J. Harpham**
UNIVERSITY OF TEXAS AT DALLAS

 W. W. NORTON & COMPANY
NEW YORK   LONDON

*To Sandy, Cindy, and Alex Ginsberg*

*Angele, Anna, and Jason Lowi*

*Nicholas Ziegler*

*Dave, Jackie, Eveline, and Eddie Dowling*

W. W. Norton & Company has been independent since its founding in 1923, when William Warder Norton and Mary D. Herter Norton first published lectures delivered at the People's Institute, the adult education division of New York City's Cooper Union. The firm soon expanded its program beyond the Institute, publishing books by celebrated academics from America and abroad. By mid-century, the two major pillars of Norton's publishing program—trade books and college texts—were firmly established. In the 1950s, the Norton family transferred control of the company to its employees, and today—with a staff of four hundred and a comparable number of trade, college, and professional titles published each year—W. W. Norton & Company stands as the largest and oldest publishing house owned wholly by its employees.

*Editor:* Ann Shin
*Associate Editor:* Jake Schindel
*Associate Editor, Ancillaries:* Lorraine Klimowich
*Manuscript Editor:* Jenna Dolan
*Project Editor:* Christine D'Antonio
*Electronic Media Editor:* Peter Lesser
*Editorial Assistant:* Sarah Wolf
*Editorial Assistant, Media:* Jennifer Barnhardt
*Marketing Manager, Political Science:* Sasha Levitt
*Associate Director of Production, College:* Benjamin Reynolds
*Photo Editor:* Stephanie Romeo
*Photo Researcher:* Elyse Rieder
*Permissions Manager:* Megan Jackson
*Text Design:* Lissi Sigillo and Chris Welch
*Information Graphics Design:* Kiss Me I'm Polish LLC, New York
*Art Director:* Hope Miller Goodell
*Composition:* Jouve International—Brattleboro, VT
*Manufacturing:* R.R. Donnelley & Sons—Jefferson City, MO

Library of Congress Cataloging-in-Publication Data has been applied for.

978-0-393-92111-3

W. W. Norton & Company, Inc., 500 Fifth Avenue, New York, N. Y. 10110
www.wwnorton.com

W. W. Norton & Company Ltd., Castle House, 75/76 Wells Street, London W1T 3QT

1 2 3 4 5 6 7 8 9 0

# contents

## 4 ● Civil Liberties   112

# PART II   Politics

# 9 ● Political Parties   338

# PART III   Institutions

## 12 ● Congress   468

## 13 ● The Presidency   514

## 14 ● Bureaucracy in a Democracy   554

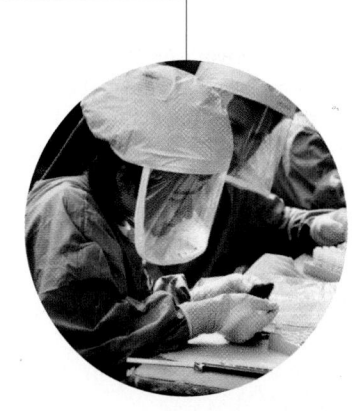

# 15 ● The Federal Courts   600

# PART IV  Policy

# 18 ● Foreign Policy and Democracy   726

# PART V  Texas Politics

# 21 ● Parties and Elections in Texas   830

# preface

This book has been and continues to be dedicated to developing a satisfactory response to the question more and more Americans are asking: Why should we be engaged with government and politics? Through the first eight editions, we sought to answer this question by making the text directly relevant to the lives of the students who would be reading it. As a result, we tried to make politics interesting by demonstrating that students' interests are at stake and that they therefore need to take a personal, even selfish, interest in the outcomes of government. At the same time, we realized that students needed guidance in how to become politically engaged. Beyond providing students with a core of political knowledge, we needed to show them how they could apply that knowledge as participants in the political process. The Get Involved/Go Online sections in each chapter help achieve that goal.

As events from the last several years have reminded us, "what government does" can be a matter of life and death. Recent events have reinforced the centrality of government in citizens' lives. The U.S. government has fought two wars abroad, while claiming sweeping new powers at home that could compromise the liberties of its citizens. America's role in the world is discussed daily both inside and outside the classroom. Moreover, the Internet has opened up new avenues to participation and mobilization. Reflecting all of these trends, this new Ninth Edition shows more than any other book on the market (1) how students are connected to government; (2) how digital media are changing (or not changing) the way Americans experience politics; and (3) why students should think critically about government and politics. These themes are incorporated in the following ways:

- **New Digital Citizens boxes explore how new information technologies— especially the Internet—are changing the way we experience politics.** These boxes draw on recent scholarship to get students thinking critically about the rise of online politics. Examples include "The Digital Divide" (Chapter 5: Civil Rights), "Social Media, Crowdsourcing, and the 2012 Election" (Chapter 10: Campaigns and Elections), and "E-Government" (Chapter 14: Bureaucracy).

- **New Get Involved/Go Online units show students how to make a difference in politics.** These full-page boxes use contemporary examples to explain how young people (even those with busy lives!) can get involved in politics using the Internet, smart phones, and social media. Specific, step-by-step instructions guide students through a range of possible political activities related to each chapter's topic.

- **Who Are Americans? and Who Are Texans? infographics ask students to think critically about how Americans from different backgrounds experience politics.** These sections use bold, engaging graphics to present a statistical snapshot of the nation related to each chapter's topic. Critical-thinking questions in each unit and related exercises on the StudySpace website give students a chance to compare their own views and experiences and consider the political implications. The Who Are Americans? and Who Are Texans? PowerPoint slides include enhanced versions of the graphics for use in lectures.

- **Chapter introductions focus on "What Government Does and Why It Matters."** In recent decades, cynicism about "big government" has dominated the political zeitgeist. But critics of government often forget that governments do a great deal for citizens. Every year, Americans are the beneficiaries of billions of dollars of goods and services from government programs. Government "does" a lot, and what it does matters a great deal to everyone, including college students. At the start of each chapter, this theme is introduced and applied to the chapter's topic. The goal is to show students that government and politics mean something to their daily lives.

- **America in the World boxes show students how American government is connected to the world.** These one-page boxes in every chapter illustrate the important political role the United States plays abroad. Topics include "Should America Export Democracy?" "Human Rights and International Politics," "The American Health Care System in Comparison," and "What Is Congress's Role in Foreign Policy?" These boxes exemplify the critical-analytical approach that characterizes the text and include "For Critical Analysis" questions.

- **For Critical Analysis questions are incorporated throughout the text.** For Critical Analysis questions in the margins of every chapter prompt students' own critical thinking about the material in the chapter, encouraging them to engage with the topic. The two For Critical Analysis questions that conclude each America in the World box get students to think more deeply about America's role in the world. The questions at the end of each Digital Citizens box ask students to think critically about the intersection of politics and digital media. And the questions that accompany each Who Are Americans? unit ask students to consider how Americans from various backgrounds experience politics.

We continue to hope that our book will itself be accepted as a form of enlightened political action. This Ninth Edition is another chance. It is an advancement toward our goal. We promise to keep trying.

# acknowledgments

W e are pleased to acknowledge the many colleagues who had an active role in criticism and preparation of the manuscript. Our thanks go to:

**First Edition Reviewers**

Sarah Binder, Brookings Institution
Kathleen Gille, Office of Representative David Bonior
Rodney Hero, University of Colorado at Boulder
Robert Katzmann, Brookings Institution
Kathleen Knight, University of Houston
Robin Kolodny, Temple University
Nancy Kral, Tomball College
Robert C. Lieberman, Columbia University
David A. Marcum, University of Wyoming
Laura R. Winsky Mattei, State University of New York at Buffalo
Marilyn S. Mertens, Midwestern State University
Barbara Suhay, Henry Ford Community College
Carolyn Wong, Stanford University
Julian Zelizer, State University of New York at Albany

**Second Edition Reviewers**

Lydia Andrade, University of North Texas
John Coleman, University of Wisconsin at Madison
Daphne Eastman, Odessa College
Otto Feinstein, Wayne State University
Elizabeth Flores, Delmar College
James Gimpel, University of Maryland at College Park
Jill Glaathar, Southwest Missouri State University
Shaun Herness, University of Florida
William Lyons, University of Tennessee at Knoxville
Andrew Polsky, Hunter College, City University of New York
Grant Reeher, Syracuse University
Richard Rich, Virginia Polytechnic
Bartholomew Sparrow, University of Texas at Austin

**Third Edition Reviewers**

Bruce R. Drury, Lamar University
Andrew I. E. Ewoh, Prairie View A&M University
Amy Jasperson, University of Texas at San Antonio
Loch Johnson, University of Georgia

Mark Kann, University of Southern California
Robert L. Perry, University of Texas of the Permian Basin
Wayne Pryor, Brazosport College
Elizabeth A. Rexford, Wharton County Junior College
Andrea Simpson, University of Washington
Brian Smentkowski, Southeast Missouri State University
Nelson Wikstrom, Virginia Commonwealth University

**Fourth Edition Reviewers**

M. E. Banks, Virginia Commonwealth University
Lynn Brink, North Lake College
Mark Cichock, University of Texas at Arlington
Del Fields, St. Petersburg College
Nancy Kinney, Washtenaw Community College
William Klein, St. Petersburg College
Dana Morales, Montgomery College
Christopher Muste, Louisiana State University
Larry Norris, South Plains College
David Rankin, State University of New York at Fredonia
Paul Roesler, St. Charles Community College
J. Philip Rogers, San Antonio College
Greg Shaw, Illinois Wesleyan University
Tracy Skopek, Stephen F. Austin State University
Don Smith, University of North Texas
Terri Wright, Cal State, Fullerton

**Fifth Edition Reviewers**

Annie Benifield, Tomball College
Denise Dutton, Southwest Missouri State University
Rick Kurtz, Central Michigan University
Kelly McDaniel, Three Rivers Community College
Eric Plutzer, Pennsylvania State University
Daniel Smith, Northwest Missouri State University
Dara Strolovitch, University of Minnesota
Dennis Toombs, San Jacinto College–North
Stacy Ulbig, Southwest Missouri State University

## Sixth Edition Reviewers

Janet Adamski, University of Mary Hardin–Baylor
Greg Andrews, St. Petersburg College
Louis Bolce, Baruch College
Darin Combs, Tulsa Community College
Sean Conroy, University of New Orleans
Paul Cooke, Cy Fair College
Vida Davoudi, Kingwood College
Robert DiClerico, West Virginia University
Corey Ditslear, University of North Texas
Kathy Dolan, University of Wisconsin, Milwaukee
Randy Glean, Midwestern State University
Nancy Kral, Tomball College
Mark Logas, Valencia Community College
Scott MacDougall, Diablo Valley College
David Mann, College of Charleston
Christopher Muste, University of Montana
Richard Pacelle, Georgia Southern University
Sarah Poggione, Florida International University
Richard Rich, Virginia Tech
Thomas Schmeling, Rhode Island College
Scott Spitzer, California State University–Fullerton
Dennis Toombs, San Jacinto College–North
John Vento, Antelope Valley College
Robert Wood, University of North Dakota

## Seventh Edition Reviewers

Molly Andolina, DePaul University
Nancy Bednar, Antelope Valley College
Paul Blakelock, Kingwood College
Amy Brandon, San Jacinto College
Jim Cauthen, John Jay College
Kevin Davis, North Central Texas College
Louis DeSipio, University of California–Irvine
Brandon Franke, Blinn College
Steve Garrison, Midwestern State University
Joseph Howard, University of Central Arkansas
Aaron Knight, Houston Community College
Paul Labedz, Valencia Community College
Elise Langan, John Jay College
Mark Logas, Valencia Community College
Eric Miller, Blinn College
Anthony O'Regan, Los Angeles Valley College
David Putz, Kingwood College
Chis Soper, Pepperdine University
Kevin Wagner, Florida Atlantic University
Laura Wood, Tarrant County College

## Eighth Edition Reviewers

Andrea Aleman, University of Texas at San Antonio
Stephen Amberg, University of Texas at San Antonio
Steve Anthony, Georgia State University
Brian Arbour, John Jay College, CUNY
Greg Arey, Cape Fear Community College
Ellen Baik, University of Texas–Pan American

David Birch, Lone Star College–Tomball
Bill Carroll, Sam Houston State University
Ed Chervenak, University of New Orleans
Gary Church, Mountain View College
Adrian Stefan Clark, Del Mar College
Casey Clofstad, University of Miami
Annie Cole, Los Angeles City College
Greg Combs, University of Texas at Dallas
Cassandra Cookson, Lee College
Brian Cravens, Blinn College
John Crosby, California State University–Chico
Scott Crosby, Valencia Community College
Courtenay Daum, Colorado State University, Fort Collins
Paul Davis, Truckee Meadows Community College
Peter Doas, University of Texas–Pan American
Vida Davoudi, Lone Star College–Kingwood
John Domino, Sam Houston State University
Doug Dow, University of Texas–Dallas
Jeremy Duff, Midwestern State University
Heather Evans, Sam Houston State University
Hyacinth Ezeamii, Albany State University
Bob Fitrakis, Columbus State Community College
Brian Fletcher, Truckee Meadows Community College
Paul Foote, Eastern Kentucky University
Frank Garrahan, Austin Community College
Jimmy Gleason, Purdue University
Steven Greene, North Carolina State University
Jeannie Grussendorf, Georgia State University
M. Ahad Hayaud-Din, Brookhaven College
Virginia Haysley, Lone Star College–Tomball
Alexander Hogan, Lone Star College–CyFair
Glen Hunt, Austin Community College
Mark Jendrysik, University of North Dakota
Krista Jenkins, Fairleigh Dickinson University
Carlos Juárez, Hawaii Pacific University
Melinda Kovas, Sam Houston State University
Paul Labedz, Valencia Community College
Boyd Lanier, Lamar University
Jeff Lazarus, Georgia State University
Jeffrey Lee, Blinn College
Alan Lehmann, Blinn College
Julie Lester, Macon State College
Steven Lichtman, Shippensburg University
Mark Logas, Valencia Community College
Fred Lokken, Truckee Meadows Community College
Shari MacLachlan, Palm Beach Community College
Guy Martin, Winston-Salem State University
Fred Monardi, College of Southern Nevada
Vincent Moscardelli, University of Connecticut
Jason Mycoff, University of Delaware
Sugmaran Narayanan, Midwestern State University
Adam Newmark, Appalachian State University
Larry Norris, South Plains College
Anthony Nownes, University of Tennessee, Knoxville

Elizabeth Oldmixon, University of North Texas
Anthony O'Regan, Los Angeles Valley College
John Osterman, San Jacinto College–Central
Mark Peplowski, College of Southern Nevada
Maria Victoria Perez-Rios, John Jay College, CUNY
Sara Rinfret, University of Wisconsin, Green Bay
Andre Robinson, Pulaski Technical College
Paul Roesler, St. Charles Community College
Susan Roomberg, University of Texas at San Antonio
Ryan Rynbrandt, Collin County Community College
Mario Salas, Northwest Vista College
Michael Sanchez, San Antonio College
Mary Schander, Pasadena City College
Laura Schneider, Grand Valley State University
Ronee Schreiber, San Diego State University
Subash Shah, Winston-Salem State University
Mark Shomaker, Blinn College
Roy Slater, St. Petersburg College
Scott Spitzer, California State University–Fullerton
Debra St. John, Collin College
John Vento, Antelope Valley College
Eric Whitaker, Western Washington University
Clay Wiegand, Cisco College
Walter Wilson, University of Texas at San Antonio
Kevan Yenerall, Clarion University
Rogerio Zapata, South Texas College

**Ninth Edition Reviewers**

Amy Acord, Lone Star College–CyFair
Milan Andrejevich, Ivy Tech Community College
Steve Anthony, Georgia State University
Phillip Ardoin, Appalachian State University
Gregory Arey, Cape Fear Community College
Joan Babcock, Northwest Vista College
Evelyn Ballard, Houston Community College
Robert Ballinger, South Texas College
Mary Barnes-Tilley, Blinn College
Robert Bartels, Evangel University
Nancy Bednar, Antelope Valley College
Annie Benifield, Lone Star College–Tomball
Donna Bennett, Trinity Valley Community College
Amy Brandon, El Paso Community College
Mark Brewer, The University of Maine
Gary Brown, Lone Star College–Montgomery
Joe Campbell, Johnson County Community College
Dewey Clayton, University of Louisville
Jeff Colbert, Elon University
Amanda Cook-Fesperman, Illinois Valley Community College
Kevin Corder, Western Michigan University
Kevin Davis, North Central Texas College
Paul Davis, Truckee Meadows Community College
Terri Davis, Lamar University
Jennifer De Maio, California State University, Northridge
Christopher Durso, Valencia College

Ryan Emenaker, College of the Redwoods
Leslie Feldman, Hofstra University
Glen Findley, Odessa College
Michael Gattis, Gulf Coast State College
Donna Godwin, Trinity Valley Community College
Precious Hall, Truckee Meadows Community College
Sally Hansen, Daytona State College
Tiffany Harper, Collin College
Todd Hartman, Appalachian State University
Virginia Haysley, Lone Star College–Tomball
David Head, John Tyler Community College
Rick Henderson, Texas State University–San Marcos
Richard Herrera, Arizona State University
Thaddaus Hill, Blinn College
Steven Holmes, Bakersfield College
Kevin Holton, South Texas College
Robin Jacobson, University of Puget Sound
Joseph Jozwiak, Texas A & M–Corpus Christi
Casey Klofstad, University of Miami
Samuel Lingrosso, Los Angeles Valley College
Mark Logas, Valencia College
Christopher Marshall, South Texas College
Larry McElvain, South Texas College
Elizabeth McLane, Wharton County Junior College
Eddie Meaders, University of North Texas
Rob Mellen, Mississippi State University
Jalal Nejad, Northwest Vista College
Adam Newmark, Appalachian State University
Stephen Nicholson, University of California, Merced
Cissie Owen, Lamar University
Suzanne Preston, St. Petersburg College
David Putz, Lone Star College–Kingwood
Auksuole Rubavichute, Mountain View College
Ronnee Schreiber, San Diego State University
Ronald Schurin, University of Connecticut
Jason Seitz, Georgia Perimeter College
Jennifer Seitz, Georgia Perimeter College
Shannon Sinegal, The University of New Orleans
John Sides, George Washington University
Thomas Sowers, Lamar University
Jim Startin, University of Texas at San Antonio
Robert Sterken, University of Texas at Tyler
Bobby Summers, Harper College
John Theis, Lone Star College–Kingwood
John Todd, University of North Texas
Delaina Toothman, The University of Maine
David Trussell, Cisco College
Ronald Vardy, University of Houston
Linda Veazey, Midwestern State University
John Vento, Antelope Valley Community College
Clif Wilkinson, Georgia College
John Wood, Rose State College
Michael Young, Trinity Valley Community College
Tyler Young, Collin College

Students at several schools around the country participated in small focus groups that helped shape the book's pedagogical program. They included Brittany Boyle, Luan Do, Brent Harvey, Jorge Hernandez, Tiara Jackson, Josh Jacobs, Jimmy Johnson, Laura Konisek, Gabriela Maddox, Taylor Marcantel, Anna Mearidy, Lori Mendel, Jacob Minter, Mayela Montano, Diana Ortega, Natalie Pereira, Michael Rocca, Christine Sanders, Kirk Sharma, Andrea Soto-Innes, Mary Storey, Joe Street, Jamie Sula, and Mia Williams. We are grateful for their smart and candid feedback.

We are also grateful for the talents and hard work of several research assistants, whose contributions can never be adequately compensated. In particular, for his work on the Eighth Edition, we thank Peter Ryan.

Perhaps above all, we wish to thank those at W.W. Norton. For its first five editions, editor Steve Dunn helped us shape the book in countless ways. Our current editor, Ann Shin, has carried on the Norton tradition of splendid editorial work. We thank Elyse Rieder for devoting an enormous amount of time to finding new photos. For our student website and other media resources for the book, Peter Lesser has been an energetic and visionary editor, and Lorraine Klimowich has efficiently managed the test bank and instructor's manual. Michael Fleming was a thorough and thoughtful developmental editor. Jenna Dolan copyedited the manuscript, and project editor Christine D'Antonio devoted countless hours keeping on top of myriad details. Ben Reynolds has been dedicated in managing production. Finally, we wish to thank Roby Harrington, the head of Norton's college department.

Benjamin Ginsberg
Theodore J. Lowi
Margaret Weir
Caroline J. Tolbert
Anthony Champagne
Edward J. Harpham

*January 2013*

NINTH TEXAS EDITION

# We the People

## AN INTRODUCTION TO AMERICAN POLITICS

Most Americans share the core political values of liberty, equality, and democracy and want their government and its policies to reflect these values. However, people often disagree on the meaning of these values and what government should do to protect them.

# American Political Culture

**WHAT GOVERNMENT DOES AND WHY IT MATTERS** Americans sometimes appear to believe that the government is an institution that does things *to* them and from which they need protection. Business owners complain that federal health and safety regulations threaten their ability to make a profit. Farmers and ranchers complain that federal and state environmental rules intrude on their property rights. Motorists allege that municipal "red light" cameras, designed to photograph traffic violators, represent the intrusion of "Big Brother" into their lives. Civil libertarians express concern over what they view as sometimes overly aggressive police and prosecutorial practices. And almost everyone complains about federal, state, and local taxes.

Yet many of the same individuals who complain about what the government does *to* them also want the government to do a great deal *for* them. For example, most members of the Tea Party movement believe that the federal government has gotten too big and that government spending should be cut back. Even so, in poll after poll, the majority of those who identify with the Tea Party express support for two of the largest and fastest-growing federal programs, Social Security and Medicare.[1] Whatever they say about big government, most Americans expect to collect Social Security benefits when they retire and to obtain their health care from Medicare after they turn 65. In a similar vein, after the September 11, 2001, terrorist attacks on the World Trade Center and the Pentagon, Americans demanded government action. President George W. Bush responded by mobilizing powerful military forces and creating an Office of Homeland Security (later reorganized as a cabinet department). Congress authorized tens of billions of dollars in new federal expenditures to combat terrorism and to repair the damage already caused by terrorists. The states mobilized their own police and national guard forces, and local police and public safety departments were placed on high alert.

Americans also look to government for assistance with more routine matters. Farmers are the beneficiaries of billions in federal subsidies and research programs. Motorists would have no roads on which to be photographed by those hated cameras if not for the tens of billions of dollars spent each year on road construction and maintenance by federal, state, and municipal authorities. Individuals accused of crimes benefit from procedural safeguards and state-funded defense attorneys. Most Americans would not be here at all if it were not for federal immigration policies, which set the terms for entry into the United States and for obtaining citizenship. And, as for those detested taxes, without them there would be no government benefits at all.

**government** institutions and procedures through which a territory and its people are ruled

**Government** is the term generally used to describe the formal institutions through which a land and its people are ruled. As the government seeks to help and protect its citizens, it faces the challenge of doing so in ways that are true to the key American political values of liberty, equality, and democracy. Most Americans find it easy to affirm all three values in principle. In practice, however, matters are not always so clear; these values mean different things to different people, and they often seem to conflict. This is where politics comes in. **Politics** refers to conflicts and struggles over the leadership, structure, and policies of governments. As we will see in this chapter and throughout this book, much political conflict concerns policies and practices that seem to affirm one of the key American political values but appear to contradict another.

**politics** conflict over the leadership, structure, and policies of governments

## chaptergoals

- **Explore how Americans see their government** (pages 5–8)
- **Describe the role of the citizen in politics** (pages 9–11)
- **Define government and forms of government** (pages 11–16)
- **Show how the American people have changed over time** (pages 16–23)
- **Analyze whether the system of government upholds American political values** (pages 23–30)

# What Americans Think about Government

**Explore how Americans see their government**

Since the United States was established as a nation, Americans have been reluctant to grant government too much power, and they have often been suspicious of politicians. But over the course of the nation's history, Americans have also turned to government for assistance in times of need and have strongly supported the government in periods of war. In 1933 the power of the government began to expand to meet the crises created by the stock market crash of 1929, the Great Depression, and the run on banks of 1933. Congress passed legislation that brought the government into the businesses of home mortgages, farm mortgages, credit, and relief of personal distress. More recently, when the economy threatened to fall into a deep recession in 2008 and 2009, the federal government stepped in to shore up the financial system, oversee the restructuring of the ailing auto companies, and to inject hundreds of billions of dollars into the faltering economy. Today the national government is an enormous institution with programs and policies reaching into every corner of American life. It oversees the nation's economy; it is the nation's largest employer; it provides citizens with a host of services; it controls the world's most formidable military; and it regulates a wide range of social and commercial activities.

Much of what citizens have come to depend on and take for granted as somehow part of the natural environment is in fact created by government. Take the example of a typical college student's day, throughout which that student relies on a host of services and activities organized by national, state, and local government agencies. The extent of this dependence on government is illustrated by Table 1.1 on page 6.

## Trust in Government

Ironically, even as popular dependence on the government has grown, the American public's view of government has turned more sour. Public trust in government has declined, and Americans are now more likely to feel that they can do little to influence the government's actions. The decline in public trust among Americans is striking. In the early 1960s, three-quarters of Americans said they trusted government most of the time. By 1994, only 21 percent of Americans expressed trust in government; three-quarters stated that they did not trust government most of the time.[2] Different groups vary somewhat in their levels of trust: African Americans and Latinos express more confidence in the federal government than do whites. But even among the most supportive groups, considerably more than half do not trust the government.[3] These developments are important because politically engaged citizens and public confidence in government are vital for the health of a democracy.

*Public approval of government hit a record low in 2011 when Republicans and Democrats came into sharp conflict over the federal debt limit. While House Speaker John Boehner (a Republican) and President Barack Obama (a Democrat) struggled to find a compromise, many Americans worried that the delay in settling on a solution was harming the economy.*

## TABLE 1.1

### The Presence of Government in the Daily Life of a Student at "State University"

| TIME OF DAY | SCHEDULE |
| --- | --- |
| 7:00 A.M. | Wake up. Standard time set by the national government. |
| 7:10 A.M. | Shower. Water courtesy of local government, either a public entity or a regulated private company. Brush your teeth with toothpaste whose cavity-fighting claims have been verified by a federal agency. Dry your hair with an electric dryer manufactured according to federal government agency guidelines. |
| 7:30 A.M. | Have a bowl of cereal with milk for breakfast. "Nutrition Facts" on food labels are a federal requirement, pasteurization of milk required by state law, freshness dating on milk based on state and federal standards, recycling the empty cereal box and milk carton enabled by state or local laws. |
| 8:30 A.M. | Drive or take public transportation to campus. Air bags and seat belts required by federal and state laws. Roads and bridges paid for by state and local governments, speed and traffic laws set by state and local governments, public transportation subsidized by all levels of government. |
| 8:45 A.M. | Arrive on campus of large public university. Buildings are 70 percent financed by state taxpayers. |
| 9:00 A.M. | First class: Chemistry 101. Tuition partially paid by a federal loan (more than half the cost of university instruction is paid for by taxpayers), chemistry lab paid for with grants from the National Science Foundation (a federal agency) and smaller grants from business corporations made possible by federal income tax deductions for charitable contributions. |
| Noon | Eat lunch. College cafeteria financed by state dormitory authority on land grant from federal Department of Agriculture. |
| 2:00 P.M. | Second class: American Government 101 (your favorite class!). You may be taking this class because it is required by the state legislature or because it fulfills a university requirement. |
| 4:00 P.M. | Third class: Computer Lab. Free computers, software, and Internet access courtesy of state subsidies plus grants and discounts from IBM and Microsoft, the costs of which are deducted from their corporate income taxes; Internet built in part by federal government. Duplication of software prohibited by federal copyright laws. |
| 6:00 P.M. | Eat dinner: hamburger and french fries. Meat inspected for bacteria by federal agencies. |
| 7:00 P.M. | Work at part-time job at the campus library. Minimum wage set by federal government, books and journals in library paid for by state taxpayers. |
| 10:00 P.M. | Go home. Street lighting paid for by county and city governments, police patrols by city government. |
| 10:15 P.M. | Watch TV. Networks regulated by federal government, cable public-access channels required by city law. Weather forecast provided to broadcasters by a federal agency. |
| Midnight | Put out the garbage before going to bed. Garbage collected by city sanitation department, financed by "user charges." |

In the aftermath of the September 11, 2001, terrorist attacks, a number of studies reported a substantial increase in popular trust in government. For example, in 2000, 44 percent of those surveyed said they trusted the government to "do the right thing" all or most of the time. After September 11, 2001, trust had jumped to 56 percent.[4] This view, expressed during a period of national crisis, may have been indicative less of a renewed *trust* in government to do the right thing than of a fervent *hope* that it would. And, indeed, by 2004, trust in government had neared its pre–September 11 level, with only 47 percent of Americans indicating that they trusted the government all or most of the time (see Figure 1.1).[5] Several fac-

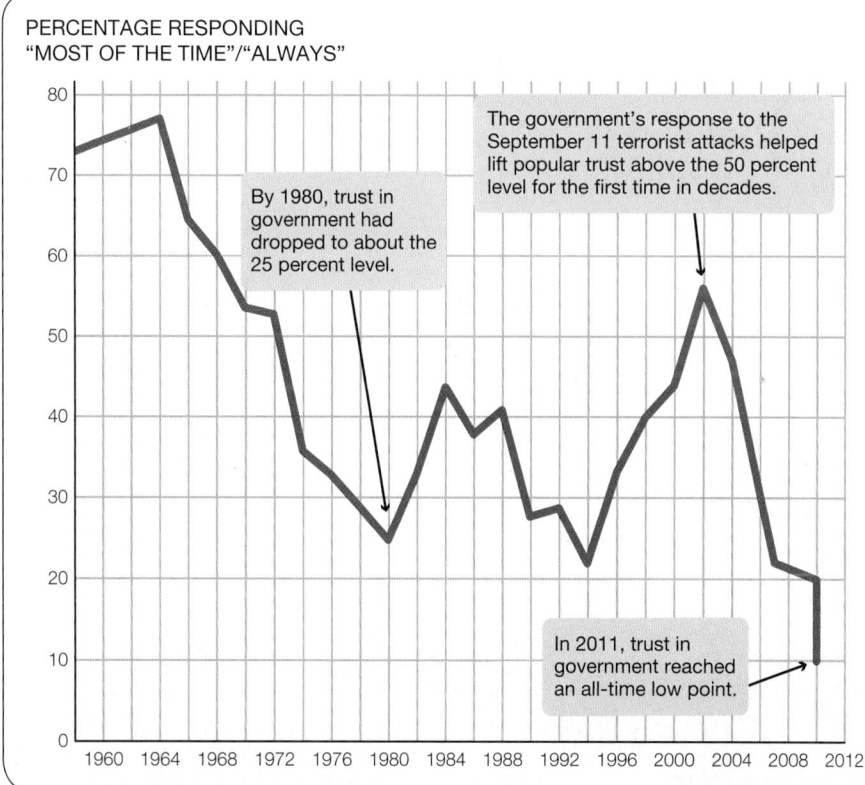

PERCENTAGE RESPONDING
"MOST OF THE TIME"/"ALWAYS"

By 1980, trust in government had dropped to about the 25 percent level.

The government's response to the September 11 terrorist attacks helped lift popular trust above the 50 percent level for the first time in decades.

In 2011, trust in government reached an all-time low point.

**FIGURE 1.1**

## Trust in Government, 1958–2011

Participants in these polls were asked if they trusted the government to "do the right thing" always, most of the time, or only some of the time.

Since the 1960s, general levels of public trust in government have declined. What factors might help to account for changes in the public's trust in government? Why has confidence in government dropped again since September 11, 2001?

SOURCES: *The National Election Studies*, 1958–2004, and CBS News/New York Times Poll, October 2010 and October 2011, iPoll Databank, www.ropercenter .uconn.edu (accessed 6/8/12).

tors contributed to the decline in trust. Revelations about the faulty information that led up to the war in Iraq and ongoing concern about the war had increased Americans' distrust of government. In March 2007, 54 percent of those surveyed believed that the Bush administration had deliberately misled the American public about whether Iraq had weapons of mass destruction.

By 2012 the government's inability to get the economy moving had further undermined trust in government. Intense partisan conflict over the government's role in the economy fueled public discontent. The public watched with dismay as political differences over taxing and spending ended in repeated threats to shut down the federal government. By the fall of 2011, after a bitter congressional battle over raising the national debt limit—usually a routine matter—only 10 percent of Americans trusted government to do the right thing always or most of the time, the lowest level of trust ever recorded.[6]

Does it matter if Americans trust their government? For the most part, the answer is yes. As we have seen, most Americans rely on government for a wide range of services and laws that they simply take for granted. But long-term distrust in government can result in public refusal to pay taxes adequate to support such widely approved public activities. Low levels of confidence may also make it difficult for government to attract talented and effective workers to public service.[7] The weakening of government as a result of prolonged levels of distrust may ultimately harm the United States' capacity to defend its national interest in the world economy and may jeopardize its national security. Likewise, a weak government can do little to assist citizens who need help in weathering periods of sharp economic or technological change.

**for critical analysis**

What recent events have affected Americans' trust in government? Have the U.S. government's efforts to address the economic downturn since 2008 increased the public's trust in government?

*In response to the terrorist attacks of September 11, 2001, Americans rallied around government officials and offered unprecedented support. Is support for the government during times of crisis at odds with Americans' distrust of government at other times?*

## Political Efficacy

**political efficacy** the ability to influence government and politics

Another important trend in American views about government has been a declining sense of **political efficacy**, the belief that ordinary citizens can affect what government does, that they can make government listen to them. In 2012, 62 percent of Americans said that elected officials don't care what people like them think; in 1960, only 25 percent felt so shut out of government. Accompanying this sense that ordinary people can't get heard is a growing belief that government is not run for the benefit of all the people. In 2012, 57 percent of the public disagreed with the idea that the "government is really run for the benefit of all the people."[8] These views are widely shared across the age spectrum.

This widely felt loss of political efficacy is bad news for American democracy. The feeling that you can't affect government decisions can lead to a self-perpetuating cycle of apathy, declining political participation, and withdrawal from political life. Why bother to participate if you believe it makes no difference? Yet the belief that you can be effective is the first step needed to influence government. Not every effort of ordinary citizens to influence government will succeed, but without any such efforts, government decisions will be made by a smaller and smaller circle of powerful people. Such loss of broad popular influence over government actions undermines the key feature of American democracy—government by the people.

*Following the 2003 Iraq War and the ongoing fighting in Afghanistan, Americans' trust in government declined sharply. Why do you think so many Americans were critical of the government's handling of these conflicts?*

# ● Citizenship: Knowledge and Participation

**Describe the role of the citizen in politics**

The first prerequisite for achieving an increased sense of political efficacy is knowledge. Political indifference is often simply a habit that stems from a lack of knowledge about how your interests are affected by politics and from a sense that you can do nothing to affect politics. But political efficacy is a self-fulfilling prophecy: if you think you cannot be effective, chances are you will never try. Most research suggests that people active in politics have a high sense of their own efficacy. This means they believe they can make a difference—even if they do not win all the time. Most people do not want to be politically active every day of their lives, but it is essential to American political ideals that all citizens be informed and able to act.

Even though the Internet has made it easier than ever to learn about politics, the state of political knowledge in the United States today is spotty. Most Americans know little about current issues or debates. Numerous surveys indicate that the majority of Americans have significant gaps in their political knowledge. For example, in 2011 only 43 percent of those surveyed knew that Republicans held the majority in the House of Representatives, and only 47 percent knew that Chief Justice John Roberts Jr. is generally considered a conservative. On the other hand, the public is more knowledgeable about politicians and policy makers who have been prominent in the national media. For example, when shown pictures of public figures, 82 percent could identify Hillary Clinton as Secretary of State and 70 percent could identify Ben Bernanke as head of the Federal Reserve (see Table 1.2). But rather than dwell on the widespread political ignorance of many Americans, we

## TABLE 1.2

## What Americans Know about Government

| RESPONDENTS WHO | PERCENTAGE |
| --- | --- |
| Knew that only citizens can vote in federal elections | 48 |
| Could identify two members of the president's cabinet and name their department | 46 |
| Knew how much of a majority is required for the U.S. Senate and House to override a presidential veto | 38 |
| Knew that Chief Justice John Roberts Jr. is generally considered a conservative | 47* |
| Felt that the government spends more on Social Security than on foreign aid | 18 |
| Could identify Secretary of State Hillary Clinton (from a picture) | 82* |
| Could identify House Speaker John Boehner | 56* |
| Could identify Ben Bernanke's position as Federal Reserve chairman (when shown his picture) | 70* |

SOURCES: Center for Information and Research on Civic Learning and Engagement, www.civicyouth.org (accessed 2/4/08); and Pew Research Center for People and the Press, http://people-press.org (accessed 2/4/08).

*Pew Research Center for the People and the Press, "What the Public Knows—in Words and Pictures," November 7, 2011, www.people-press.org/files/legacy-pdf/11-7-11%20Knowledge%20Release.pdf (accessed 6/8/12)

prefer to view this as an opportunity for the readers of this book. Those of you who make the effort to become more knowledgeable will be much better prepared to influence the political system regarding the issues and concerns that you care most about.

After September 11, many commentators noted a revival in Americans' sense of citizenship, as manifested by ubiquitous flag displays and other demonstrations of patriotic sentiment. There seems to be little doubt that millions of Americans experienced a renewed sense of identification with their nation. Citizenship, however, has a broader meaning than just patriotism.

**citizenship** informed and active membership in a political community

Beginning with the ancient Greeks, citizenship has meant membership in one's community. Citizenship entailed involvement in public discussion, debate, and activity designed to improve the welfare of the community. Our meaning for **citizenship** derives from the Greek ideal: enlightened political engagement.[9] To be politically engaged in a meaningful way, citizens require resources, especially political knowledge and information. Democracy functions best when citizens are informed. But citizenship in the full sense, as understood first by the ancient Greeks, goes beyond an occasional visit to a voting booth. A good citizen must be politically engaged and have the knowledge needed to participate in political debate.

## The Necessity of Political Knowledge

Political knowledge means more than having a few opinions to offer the pollster or to guide your decisions in a voting booth. It is important to know the rules and strategies that govern political institutions and the principles on which they are based, but it is more important to know them in ways that relate to your own interests. Citizens need knowledge in order to assess their interests and to know when to act on them. Knowledgeable citizens are more attentive to and engaged in politics because they understand how and why politics is relevant to their lives.

Without political knowledge, no citizen can be aware of her interests or her stake in a political dispute. In the year preceding the 2012 presidential election, for example, the prospective Republican candidates presented a diverse set of proposals on how to return the American economy to prosperity. These proposals could be easily accessed on the candidates' websites. How many voters paid enough attention to the discussion to be able to distinguish meaningfully among the various proposals and their implications? How many citizens attempted to ascertain whether they and their families would be better off under the tax proposals envisioned by Cain, Perry, or Romney, rather than the system favored by Obama? How could a voter participate intelligently without this knowledge? Various public and private interest groups devote enormous time and energy to understanding alternative policy proposals and their implications so they will know whom to support. Interest groups understand something that every citizen should also understand: effective participation requires knowledge.

Citizens need political knowledge also to identify the best ways to act on their interests. If your street is rendered impassable by snow, what can you do? Is snow removal the responsibility of the federal government? Is it a state or municipal responsibility? Knowing that you have a stake in a clear road does not help much if you do not know that snow removal is a city or a county responsibility and if you cannot identify the municipal agency that deals with the problem. Americans are fond of complaining that government is not responsive to their needs, but in some cases, it is possible that citizens simply lack the information they need to present their problems to the appropriate government officials.

Citizens need political knowledge also to ascertain what they cannot or should not ask of politicians and the government. We need to balance our need for protection and service with our equally pressing need for liberty. Particularly during periods when the nation's safety is threatened, Americans may be inclined to accept increased governmental intrusion into their lives in the name of national security. Since 2001, for example, Americans have accepted unprecedented levels of governmental surveillance and the erosion of some traditional restrictions on police powers in the name of preventing terrorism. It remains to be seen whether this exchange of liberty for the promise of security was a wise choice. Political knowledge, therefore, includes knowing the limits on (as well as the possibilities for) pursuing one's own individual interests through political action. This is, perhaps, the most difficult form of political knowledge to acquire.

**for critical analysis**

Many studies seem to show that most Americans know very little about government and politics. Can we have democratic government without knowledgeable and aware citizens?

## ● Government

**Define government and forms of government**

As we saw in the introduction to this chapter, government refers to the formal institutions through which a land and its people are ruled. To govern is to rule. A government may be as simple as a tribal council that meets occasionally to advise the chief, or as complex as the vast establishments, with their procedures, laws, and bureaucracies, found in many large countries today. In

# Digital Citizens

**As society and politics have migrated** online, Americans have become "digital citizens." Digital citizens are daily Internet users. They go online for work, the news, communication with friends and family, entertainment, and information about politics, health, transportation, and more. Young people spend more time online than watching television, and many observers believed that the 2012 presidential election would be the first in which online politics trumps the television. In 2012, 80 percent of Americans used the Internet and 7 in 10 Americans went online daily. The Internet has become the backbone of a global digital infrastructure and an integral part of the information economy.

Digital citizenship is the ability to participate in society online, and it is increasingly important in politics. A 2012 Pew survey found that over 90 percent of Internet users in the United States use e-mail or have used a search engine, and 66 percent use a social networking site such as Facebook. Eight in 10 Internet users check the weather online, 75 percent read the news online (up from 61 percent in 2011), and more than six in 10 look up political information online. They also seek out government information; 67 percent visit a local, state, or federal government website (up from 56 percent in 2011). Economic activity online is widespread; 60 percent do banking online, 71 percent have purchased a product online, and 56 percent

look for information about a job. Online information even affects where you live; 4 in 10 Internet users look for a place to live online.

What does it take to become a digital citizen? Home access and high-speed access to the Internet are necessary for digital citizenship. Regular access and effective use enable full participation in society online. Research has shown that home access is important for activities connected with jobs, education, finances, politics, and community engagement.

Digital citizenship is beneficial to individuals, but it also has spillover benefits that provide advantages to society as a whole. Digital citizens are likely to be "good" citizens. They are more likely to be interested in politics and to discuss politics with friends, family, and coworkers than individuals who do not use online political information. They are also more likely to vote and participate in other ways in elections. When defined as those using the Internet at work, digital citizens earn higher wages (controlling for other factors), even among those with only a high school degree. Thus the Internet can encourage participation in politics and economic productivity.

However, individuals without Internet access or the skills to participate in politics and the economy online are being left further behind. Exclusion from

participation online is referred to as the digital divide (which we discuss further in Chapters 5 and 8).

Internet access and digital literacy are critical for full participation in American society in the twenty-first century. In much the same way that higher levels of education and literacy promoted democracy and economic growth in the nineteenth century, the Internet has the potential to benefit society as a whole and to facilitate political participation of individuals within society. At the same time, the rise of the Internet raises new questions about who is able to participate and whether digital politics is changing the traditional dynamics of American politics. Throughout this book, Digital Citizens boxes like this one will explore these questions.

SOURCES: Pew Internet and American Life, 2012, "What Internet Users Do Online," February 2012 Survey, http://pewinternet.org/Trend-Data-(Adults)/Online-Activites-Total.aspx (accessed 6/25/12). Karen Mossberger, Caroline Tolbert, and Ramona McNeal, *Digital Citizenship: The Internet, Society and Participation* (Cambridge, MA: MIT Press, 2008).

## for critical analysis

1. Just as all Americans have the right to a public education and to be taught to read and write, should all Americans have access to the Internet and be taught skills to use information online?

2. Does the prevalence of economic and political activities online justify government intervention in providing broadband Internet access? Why or why not?

the history of civilization, governments have not been difficult to establish. There have been thousands of them. The hard part is establishing a government that lasts. Even more difficult is developing a stable government that is compatible with liberty, equality, and democracy.

## Is Government Needed?

Americans have always harbored some suspicion of government and have wondered how extensive a role it should play in their lives. Thomas Jefferson famously observed that the best government was one that "governed least." Generally speaking, a government is needed to provide those services, sometimes called "public goods," that all citizens need but are not likely to be able to provide adequately for themselves. These might include defense against foreign aggression, maintenance of public order, enforcement of contractual obligations and property rights, and a guarantee of some measure of social justice. The precise extent to which government involvement in American society is needed has been debated throughout the nation's history and will continue to be a central focus of political contention.

## Forms of Government

Governments vary in their structure, their size, and the way they operate. Two questions are of special importance in determining how governments differ: Who governs? And how much government control is permitted?

Some nations are governed by a single individual—a king or dictator, for example. This state of affairs is called **autocracy**. Where a small group—perhaps landowners, military officers, or wealthy merchants—controls most of the governing decisions, that government is said to be an **oligarchy**. If more people participate and have some influence over decision making, that government is a **democracy**.

Governments also vary considerably in terms of how they govern. In the United States and a small number of other nations, governments are limited as to what they are permitted to control (substantive limits) and how they go about it (procedural limits). Governments that are limited in this way are called **constitutional governments**, or liberal governments. In other nations, including many in Latin America, Asia, and Africa, though the law imposes few real limits, the government is nevertheless kept in check by other political and social institutions that it is unable to control and must come to terms with—such as autonomous territories, an organized religion, organized business groups, or organized labor unions. Such governments are generally called **authoritarian**. In a third group of nations, including the Soviet Union under Joseph Stalin, Nazi Germany, perhaps prewar Japan and Italy, and North Korea today, governments not only are free of legal limits but also seek to eliminate those organized social groups that might challenge or limit their authority. These governments typically attempt to dominate or control every sphere of political, economic, and social life and, as a result, are called **totalitarian**.

Americans have the good fortune to live in a nation in which limits are placed on what governments can do and how they can do it. Many of the world's people do not live in a constitutional democracy. By one measure, just 45 percent of the global population (those living in 87 countries) enjoy sufficient levels of political and personal freedom to be classified as living in a constitutional democracy.[10] And constitutional democracies were unheard of before the modern era. Prior to the eighteenth and nineteenth centuries, governments seldom sought—and rarely received—the support of their subjects. The available evidence strongly suggests

**autocracy** a form of government in which a single individual—a king, queen, or dictator—rules

**oligarchy** a form of government in which a small group—landowners, military officers, or wealthy merchants—controls most of the governing decisions

**democracy** a system of rule that permits citizens to play a significant part in the governmental process, usually through the election of key public officials

**constitutional government** a system of rule in which formal and effective limits are placed on the powers of the government

**authoritarian government** a system of rule in which the government recognizes no formal limits but may nevertheless be restrained by the power of other social institutions

**totalitarian government** a system of rule in which the government recognizes no formal limits on its power and seeks to absorb or eliminate other social institutions that might challenge it

that the ordinary people often had little love for the government or for the social order. After all, they had no stake in it. They equated government with the police officer, the bailiff, and the tax collector.[11]

Beginning in the seventeenth century, in a handful of Western nations, two important changes began to take place in the character and conduct of government. First, governments began to acknowledge formal limits on their power. Second, a small number of governments began to provide ordinary citizens with a formal voice in public affairs—through the vote. Obviously, the desirability of limits on government and the expansion of popular influence were at the heart of the American Revolution in 1776. "No taxation without representation," as we shall see in Chapter 2, was fiercely asserted from the beginning of the Revolution through the Founding in 1789. But even before the Revolution, a tradition of limiting government and expanding participation in the political process had developed throughout western Europe.

## Limiting Government

America's Founders were influenced by the English thinker John Locke (1632–1704). Locke argued that governments need the consent of the people.

The key force behind the imposition of limits on government power was a new social class, the bourgeoisie, which became an important political force in the sixteenth and seventeenth centuries. *Bourgeois* is a French word for "freeman of the city," or *bourg*. Being part of the bourgeoisie later became associated with being "middle class" and with involvement in commerce or industry. In order to gain a share of control of government, joining or even displacing the kings, aristocrats, and gentry who had dominated government for centuries, the bourgeoisie sought to change existing institutions—especially parliaments—into instruments of real political participation. Parliaments had existed for centuries, but were generally aristocratic institutions. The bourgeoisie embraced parliaments as means by which they could exert the weight of their superior numbers and growing economic advantage on their aristocratic rivals. At the same time, the bourgeoisie sought to place restraints on the capacity of governments to threaten these economic and political interests by placing formal or constitutional limits on governmental power.

Although motivated primarily by the need to protect and defend their own interests, the bourgeoisie advanced many of the principles that would define the central underpinnings of individual liberty for all citizens—freedom of speech, freedom of assembly, freedom of conscience, and freedom from arbitrary search and seizure. The work of political theorists such as John Locke (1632–1704) and, later, John Stuart Mill (1806–73) helped shape these evolving ideas about liberty and political rights. However, it is important to note that the bourgeoisie generally did not favor democracy as we know it. They were advocates of electoral and representative institutions, but they favored property requirements and other restrictions so as to limit participation to the middle and upper classes. Yet once these institutions of politics and the protection of the right to engage in politics were established, it was difficult to limit them to the bourgeoisie.

## Access to Government: The Expansion of Participation

John Stuart Mill (1806–73) presented a ringing defense of individual freedom in his famous treatise On Liberty. Mill's work influenced Americans' evolving ideas about the relationship between government and the individual.

The expansion of participation from the bourgeoisie to ever-larger segments of society took two paths. In some nations, popular participation was expanded by the Crown or the aristocracy, which ironically saw common people as potential political allies against the bourgeoisie. Thus in nineteenth-century Prussia, for example, it was the emperor and his great minister Otto von Bismarck who expanded popular participation in order to build political support among the lower orders.

In other nations, participation expanded because competing segments of the bourgeoisie sought to gain political advantage by reaching out and mobilizing the support of working- and lower-class groups that craved the opportunity to take part in politics—"lining up the unwashed," as one American historian put it.[12] To be sure, excluded groups often agitated for greater participation. But seldom was such agitation by itself enough to secure the right to participate. Usually, expansion of voting rights resulted from a combination of pressure from below and help from above.

The gradual expansion of voting rights by groups hoping to derive some political advantage has been typical of American history. After the Civil War, one of the chief reasons that Republicans moved to enfranchise newly freed slaves was to use the support of the former slaves to maintain Republican control over the defeated southern states. Similarly, in the early twentieth century, upper-middle-class Progressives advocated women's suffrage because they believed that women were likely to support the reforms espoused by the Progressive movement.

## Influencing the Government through Participation: Politics

Expansion of participation means that more and more people have a legal right to take part in politics. *Politics* is an important term. In its broadest sense, it refers to conflicts over the character, membership, and policies of any organization to which people belong. As Harold Lasswell, a famous political scientist, once put it, politics is the struggle over "who gets what, when, how."[13] Although politics is a phenomenon that can be found in any organization, our concern in this book is narrower. Here, **politics** will be used to refer only to conflicts and struggles over the leadership, structure, and policies of governments. The goal of politics, as we define it, is to have a share or a say in the composition of the government's leadership, how the government is organized, or what its policies are going to be. Having a share is called having **power** or influence.

Politics can take many forms, including everything from blogging and posting opinion pieces online, sending e-mails to government officials, voting, lobbying legislators on behalf of particular programs, and participating in protest marches and even violent demonstrations. A system of government that gives citizens a regular opportunity to elect the top government officials is usually called a **representative democracy**, or **republic**. A system that permits citizens to vote directly on laws and policies is often called a **direct democracy**. At the national level, America is a representative democracy in which citizens select government officials but do not vote on legislation. Some states and cities, however, have provisions for direct legislation through popular initiative and ballot referendum. These procedures allow citizens to collect petitions requiring an issue to be brought directly to the voters for a decision. In 2012, more than 188 initiatives appeared on state ballots, dealing with matters that ranged from taxes and education to animal cruelty and affirmative action. Many hot-button issues are decided by initiatives. For example, in 2006, Michigan voters approved a measure that prohibits public institutions such as the University of Michigan from giving preferential treatment on the basis of race; in Colorado in 2010, voters passed a referendum that called on the state to sue the federal government to enforce immigration laws. Often, broad public campaigns promote controversial referenda, attempting to persuade voters to change existing laws. For example, in 2012 voters in Massachusetts approved the use of medical

**politics** conflict over the leadership, structure, and policies of governments

**power** influence over a government's leadership, organization, or policies

**representative democracy/ republic** a system of government in which the populace selects representatives, who play a significant role in governmental decision making

**direct democracy** a system of rule that permits citizens to vote directly on laws and policies

marijuana while voters in Arkansas defeated a similar measure. Voters in Colorado, Oregon, and Washington state enacted initiatives to legalize the recreational use of marijuana, a development that puts them at odds with federal law. Voters in Maryland, Maine, and Washington state approved same-sex marriage, the first victory for this issue at the ballot box.

Groups and organized interests do not vote (although their members do), but they certainly do participate in politics. Their political activities usually consist of such endeavors as providing funds for candidates, lobbying, and trying to influence public opinion. The pattern of struggles among interests is called group politics, or **pluralism**. Americans have always been ambivalent about pluralist politics. On the one hand, the right of groups to press their views and compete for influence in the government is the essence of liberty. On the other hand, Americans often fear that organized groups may sometimes exert too much influence, advancing special interests at the expense of larger public interests. (We will return to this problem in Chapter 11.)

Sometimes, of course, politics does not take place through formal channels at all but instead involves direct action. Direct-action politics can include either violent politics or civil disobedience, both of which attempt to shock rulers into behaving more responsibly. Direct action can also be a form of revolutionary politics, which rejects the system entirely and attempts to replace it with a new ruling group and a new set of rules. In recent years in the United States, groups ranging from animal-rights activists to right-to-life advocates to the Occupy Wall Street protesters have used direct action to underline their demands. Many forms of peaceful direct political action are protected by the U.S. Constitution. The country's Founders knew that the right to protest is essential to the maintenance of political freedom, even where the ballot box is available.

**pluralism** the theory that all interests are and should be free to compete for influence in the government; the outcome of this competition is compromise and moderation

## ● Who Are Americans?

**Show how the American people have changed over time**

While American democracy aims to give the people a voice in government, the meaning of "we the people" has changed over time. Who are Americans? Through the course of American history, politicians, religious leaders, prominent scholars, and ordinary Americans have puzzled over and fought about the answer to this fundamental question. Since the Founding, the American population has grown from 3.9 million in 1790, the year of the first official census, to 314 million in 2012. As the American population has grown, it has become more diverse on nearly every dimension imaginable.[14]

At the time of the Founding, when the United States consisted of 13 states arrayed along the Eastern Seaboard, 81 percent of Americans counted by the census traced their roots to Europe, mostly England and northern Europe; nearly 20 percent were of African origin, the vast majority of whom were slaves.[15] Only 1.5 percent of the black population was free. There was also an unknown number of Native Americans, the original inhabitants of the land, not counted by the census because the government did not consider them Americans. The first estimates

# An Increasingly Diverse Nation

Since the Founding, the American people have become increasingly diverse. This diversity and the changes in the population have frequently raised challenging questions in American politics.

## Race

|  | 1790* | 1900* | 2010 |
|---|---|---|---|

👤 = 1 million people

| 1790* | 1900* | 2010 |
|---|---|---|
| White 81% | White 88% | White 64% |
| Black 19% | Black 12% | Black 13% |
|  | Other 0.5% | Hispanic 16% |
|  |  | Asian 5% |
|  |  | Native American 1% |
|  |  | Other 1% |
|  |  | 2 or more races 2% |

**TOTAL POPULATION =**  3,929,214     75,994,575     308,745,538

## Geography

| 1790 | 1900 | 2010 |
|---|---|---|
| 50% | 28% | 18% |
| 50% | 6% 35% 33% | 23% 22% 37% |

| | 1790 | 1900 | 2010 |
|---|---|---|---|
| Northeast | 50% | 28% | 18% |
| South | 50% | 33% | 37% |
| Midwest | | 35% | 22% |
| West | | 6% | 23% |

## for critical analysis

1. The 2010 census showed that the populations of the South and the West continued to grow more rapidly than the Northeast and Midwest. What are some of the political implications of this trend?

2. Today, Americans over age 37 outnumber Americans under 37—and older adults are more likely to participate in the political process. What do you think this means for the kinds of issues and policies taken up by the government?

## Age

| 1900 | | 2010 | |
|---|---|---|---|
| 0 - 19 | 44% | 0 - 19 | 27% |
| 20 - 44 | 38% | 20 - 44 | 34% |
| 45 - 64 | 14% | 45 - 64 | 26% |
| 65 + | 4% | 65 + | 13% |

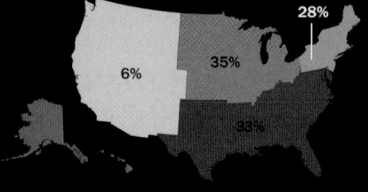
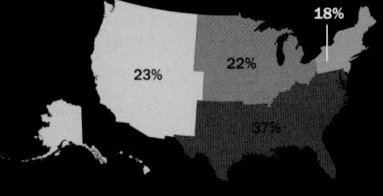

* The 1790 census does not accurately reflect the population because it only counted blacks and whites. It did not include Native Americans or other groups. The 1900 census did not count Hispanic Americans.

SOURCE: U.S. Census Bureau, www.census.gov (accessed 8/16/12).

*Native American societies, with their own forms of government, existed for thousands of years before the first European settlers arrived. By the time this photo of Red Cloud and other Sioux warriors was taken, around 1870, Native Americans made up about 1 percent of the American population.*

of Native Americans and Hispanics in the mid-1800s showed that each group made up less than 1 percent of the total population.[16]

Flash forward to 1900. The country now stretched out across the continent, and waves of immigrants, mainly from Europe, boosted the population to 76 million. In 1900 the United States was predominantly composed of whites of European ancestry, but this number now included many from southern and eastern as well as northern Europe; the black population stood at 12 percent. Residents who traced their origin to Latin America or Asia each accounted for less than 1 percent of the entire population (see the infographic on page 17).[17] The large number of new immigrants was reflected in the high proportion of foreign-born people in the United States: the foreign-born population reached its height at 14.7 percent in 1910.[18]

## Immigration and Ethnic Diversity

As the European-origin population grew more diverse, anxiety about Americans' ethnic identity mounted. In 1900 the author of a *New York Times* front-page article answered his own question—"Are the Americans an Anglo-Saxon People?"—in the affirmative.[19] But the growing numbers of immigrants from southern and eastern Europe who were crowding into American cities spurred heated debates about how long Anglo-Saxons could dominate. Much as today, politicians and scholars argued about whether the country could absorb such large numbers of immigrants. Concerns ranged from whether their political and social values were compatible with American democracy, to whether they would learn English, to alarm about the diseases they might bring into the United States.

The distinct ethnic backgrounds and language differences of the new immigrants were not the only characteristics that worried the Anglo-Saxon natives; immigrant religious affiliations also aroused concern. The first immigrants to the United States were overwhelmingly Protestant, many of them fleeing religious persecution. The arrival of Germans and Irish in the mid-1800s began to shift that balance with increasing numbers of Catholics. Even so, in 1900, four in five Americans were still Protestants. The large-scale immigration of the early twentieth century threatened

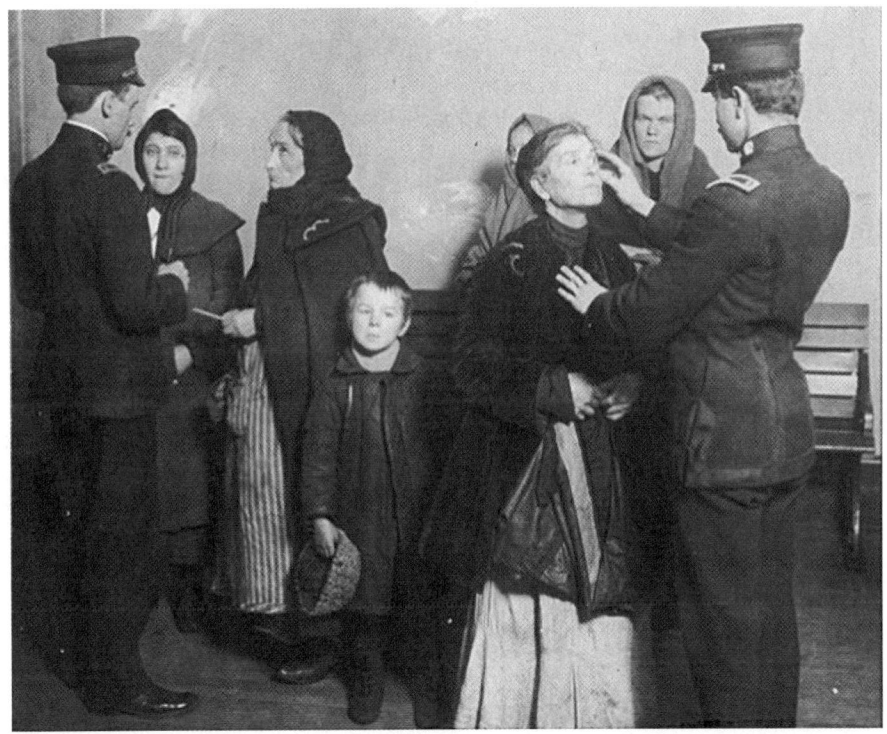

*Millions of immigrants from Europe came to the United States in the early 1900s. Most passed through New York's Ellis Island, where they were checked for diseases before being admitted. Today many Americans trace their ancestry to immigrants who passed through Ellis Island.*

to reduce the proportion of Protestants significantly. The eastern European immigrants pouring into the country, especially those from Russia, were heavily Jewish; the southern Europeans, especially Italians, were Catholic. A more religiously diverse country challenged the implicit Protestantism embedded in many aspects of American public life. For example, religious diversity introduced new conflicts into public schooling, as Catholics sought public funding for parochial schools and dissident Protestant sects lobbied to eliminate Bible reading and prayer in the schools.

Anxieties about immigration sparked intense debate. Should the numbers of immigrants entering the country be limited? Should restrictions be placed on the types of immigrants to be granted entry? After World War I, Congress responded to the fears swirling around immigration with new laws that sharply limited the number who could enter the country each year. It also established a new National Origins quota system, based on the nation's population in 1890, before the wave of immigrants from eastern and southern Europe arrived.[20] Supporters of ethnic quotas hoped to turn back the clock and revert to an earlier America in which northern Europeans dominated. The new system set up a hierarchy of admissions: northern European countries received generous quotas for new immigrants, whereas eastern and southern European countries were granted very small quotas. These restrictions ratcheted down the numbers of immigrants so that by 1970, the foreign-born population in the United States reached an all-time low of 5 percent.

## Immigration and Race

Official efforts to use racial and ethnic criteria to restrict the American population were not new but had been used to draw boundaries around the American community from the start. The very first census, as just mentioned, did not count

*Although the number of immigrants from Asia increased sharply in the 1970s, the number of Asian Americans who hold elected office is relatively small. When Nikki Haley (right) was elected governor of South Carolina in 2010, she became the second Indian American governor in the United States.*

Native Americans; in fact, no Native Americans became citizens until 1924. Although the Constitution infamously declared that each slave would count as three-fifths of a person for purposes of apportioning representation among the states, most people of African descent were not officially citizens until 1868, when the Fourteenth Amendment to the Constitution conferred citizenship on the freed slaves.

Over half a century earlier, the federal government had sought to limit the nonwhite population with a 1790 law stipulating that only free whites could become naturalized citizens. Not until 1870 did Congress lift the ban on the naturalization of nonwhites. In addition to the restrictions on blacks and Native Americans, restrictions applied to Asians as well. The Chinese Exclusion Act of 1882 outlawed the entry of Chinese laborers to the United States. These provisions were not lifted until 1943, when China became America's ally during World War II. Additional barriers enacted after World War I meant that virtually no Asians entered the country as immigrants until the 1940s. People of Hispanic origin do not fit simply into the American system of racial classification. In 1930, for example, the census counted people of Mexican origin as nonwhite but reversed this decision a decade later—after protests by the Mexican-origin population and the Mexican government. Only in 1970 did the census officially begin counting persons of Hispanic origin, noting that they could be any race.[21]

## Twenty-First-Century Americans

By 2000, immigration had profoundly transformed the nation's racial and ethnic profile once again. The primary cause was Congress's decision in 1965 to lift the tight restrictions of the 1920s, allowing for much-expanded immigration from Asia and Latin America (see Figure 1.2). One consequence of the shift has been the growth in the Hispanic, or Latino, population. Census figures for 2010 show that the total Hispanic proportion of the population is now 16 percent; the black, or African American, population is 12 percent of the total population. Asians made up 5 percent of the population. European Americans accounted for less than two-thirds of the population in 2010—their lowest share ever. Moreover, 2 percent of the population now identified itself as of "two or more races," a new category that the census added in 2000.[22] Although it is only a small percentage of the population, the multiracial category points toward a future in which the traditional labels of racial identification may be blurring, marking a major shift in the long-standing American tradition of strict racial categorization. The blurring of racial categories poses challenges to a host of policies—many of them put in place to remedy past discrimination—that rely on racial counts of the population.

Large-scale immigration means that many more residents are foreign born. In 2010, 12.36 percent of the population was born outside the United States, a figure comparable to foreign-born rates at the turn of the previous century.[23] Over half of the foreign born came from Latin America and the Caribbean—almost 1 in 10 from the Caribbean, nearly 4 in 10 from Central America (including Mexico), and 6.8 percent from South America. Those born in Asia constituted the next-largest group, making up over one-quarter of foreign-born residents. In sharp contrast to the immigration patterns of a century earlier, fewer immigrants came from

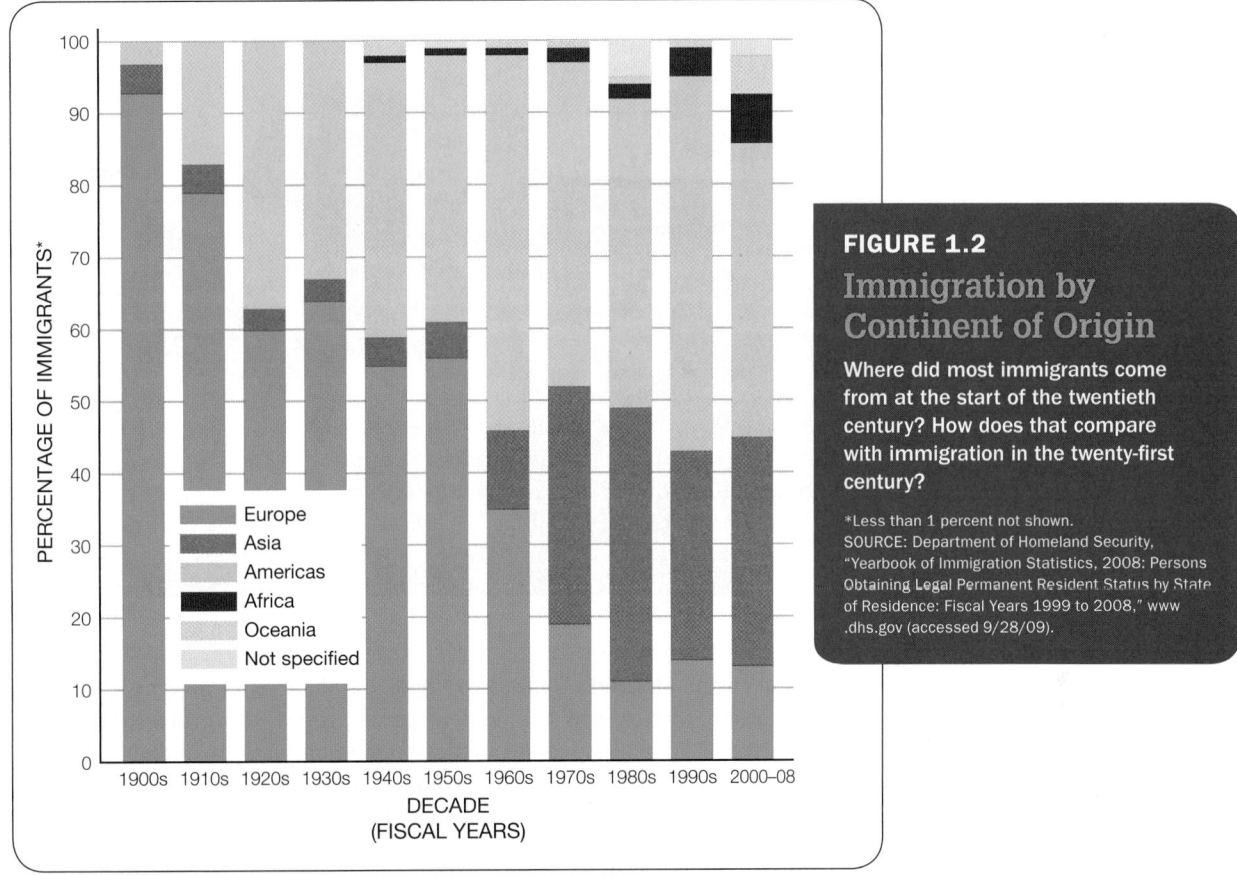

FIGURE 1.2

Immigration by Continent of Origin

Where did most immigrants come from at the start of the twentieth century? How does that compare with immigration in the twenty-first century?

*Less than 1 percent not shown.
SOURCE: Department of Homeland Security, "Yearbook of Immigration Statistics, 2008: Persons Obtaining Legal Permanent Resident Status by State of Residence: Fiscal Years 1999 to 2008," www .dhs.gov (accessed 9/28/09).

Europe. By 2010 only 12 percent of those born outside the United States came from Europe.[24]

These figures represent only legally authorized immigrants. One new feature of American society in recent years is the very large number of immigrants who live in the country without legal authorization. Estimates put the number of undocumented immigrants at 11 million, the majority of whom are from Mexico and Central America.[25] The large unauthorized population has become a flashpoint for controversy as states and cities have passed a variety of conflicting laws. Some states have offered driver's licenses to undocumented immigrants, while others have sought to bar them from public services, such as education and emergency health care, both of which are constitutionally guaranteed to unauthorized immigrants.[26] In 1982 the Supreme Court ensured access to education when it ruled in *Plyler v. Doe* that Texas could not deny funding for undocumented students.[27] In 1986, Congress guaranteed emergency medical care to all people regardless of immigration status when it passed the Emergency Medical Treatment and Active Labor Act (EMTALA).

The new patterns of immigration combined with differences in birth rates and underlying social changes to alter the religious affiliations of Americans. In 1900, 80 percent of the American adult population was Protestant; by 2008 only a little over half of Americans identified themselves as Protestants.[28] Catholics now made up a quarter of the population, and Jews accounted for 1.2 percent. A small Muslim population had also grown, with over one-half of 1 percent of the population.

*In 1965, Congress loosened restrictions on immigration, allowing millions of people from Latin America and Asia to enter the country in the decades that followed. By 2002, Hispanics were the largest minority group in the United States. Here, Antonio Villaraigosa campaigns to become the first Latino mayor of Los Angeles in 130 years.*

One of the most important shifts in religious affiliation during the latter half of the twentieth century was the percentage of people who professed no organized religion: in 2008, 15 percent of the population was not affiliated with an organized church. These changes suggest an important shift in American religious identity; although the United States thinks of itself as a "Judeo-Christian" nation—and indeed was 95 percent Protestant, Catholic, or Jewish from 1900 to 1968—by 2008, this number had fallen to only 77 percent of the adult population.[29]

As America grew and its population expanded and diversified, the country's age profile shifted with it. In 1900 only 4 percent of the population was over age 65. As life expectancy increased, the number of older Americans grew with it: by 2010, 13 percent of the population was over 65. The percentage of children under the age of 18 also changed; in 1900 this group comprised 43 percent of the American population; by 2010, children 18 and under had fallen to just over a quarter of the population.[30] Another way to think about the age of Americans is that in 1800, the median age of the population was 16 years; by 1900 it was 22.9 years, and by 2010 it was 37.2 years. Even though the median age of Americans has increased, Americans tend to be younger than citizens of many industrialized countries, mainly because of the large immigrant population in the United States. In most European countries, the median age was above 40 in 2000.[31] But an aging population poses challenges to the United States as well. As the elderly population grows and the working-age population shrinks, questions arise about how we will fund programs for the elderly, such as Social Security.

Over the nation's history, Americans have changed in other ways, moving from mostly rural settings and small towns to large urban areas. The idealization of country life in American culture traces its roots to the long period in which the majority of Americans lived in rural areas. Before 1920, less than half the population lived in urban areas; today 83.7 percent of Americans do.[32] Critics charge that the American political system—created when America was a largely rural society—underrepresents urban areas. The constitutional provision allocating each state two senators, for example, overrepresents sparsely populated rural states and underrepresents urban states, where the population is far more concentrated. In addition to becoming more urban over time, the American population has shifted regionally. During the past 50 years especially, many Americans left the Northeast and Midwest and moved to the South and Southwest. As congressional seats have been reapportioned to reflect the population shift, many problems that particularly plague the Midwest and Northeast, such as the decline in manufacturing jobs, receive less attention in national politics.

The shifting contours of the American people have regularly raised challenging questions about our politics and governing arrangements. Population growth has spurred politically charged debates about how the population should be apportioned among congressional districts. These conflicts have major implications for the representation of different regions of the country and for the balance of representation between urban and rural areas. Population growth has also transformed the close democratic relationship between congressional representatives and their constituents envisioned by the framers. For example, the framers stipulated that the number of representatives in the House of Representatives "shall not exceed one for every thirty Thousand" constituents; today the average member of Congress represents 710,767 constituents.[33] Immigration and the cultural and religious changes it entails provoked heated disputes 100 years ago and still spark passionate debate today. The different languages and customs that immigrants bring to the United States trigger fears that the country is changing in ways that may undermine American values and alter fundamental identities. The large number of unauthorized immigrants in the country today makes these anxieties even more acute. Yet a changing population has been one of the constants of American history. Indeed, each generation has confronted the myriad political challenges associated with answering anew "Who are Americans?"

# ● Thinking Critically about American Political Culture

> **Analyze whether the system of government upholds American political values**

Underlying and framing political life in the United States are agreements on basic political values but disagreements over the ends or goals of government. Most Americans affirm the values of liberty, equality, and democracy. Values shape citizens' views of the world and define their sense of what is right and wrong, just and unjust, possible and impossible. If Americans shared no values, they would have difficulty communicating, much less agreeing on a common system of government and politics. However, sharing broad values does not guarantee political consensus. We can agree on principles but disagree over their application or how they are to be balanced. Much of the debate over the role of government has been over what government should do and how far it should go to reduce the inequalities within our society and political system while still preserving essential liberties.

Even though Americans have disagreed over the meaning of such political ideals as equality, they still agree on the importance of those ideals. The values, beliefs, and attitudes that form our **political culture** and hold together the United States and its people date back to the time of the founding of the Union.

**political culture** broadly shared values, beliefs, and attitudes about how the government should function. American political culture emphasizes the values of liberty, equality, and democracy

The essential documents of the American Founding—the Declaration of Independence and the Constitution—enunciated a set of political principles about the purposes of the new republic. In contrast with many other democracies, in the United States these political ideals did not just remain words on dusty documents. Americans actively embraced the principles of the Founders and made them central to the national identity. Let us look more closely at three of these ideals: liberty, equality, and democracy.

## Liberty

No ideal is more central to American values than liberty. The Declaration of Independence defined three inalienable rights: "Life, Liberty and the pursuit of Happiness." The preamble of the Constitution likewise identified the need to secure "the Blessings of Liberty" as one of the key reasons for drawing up the Constitution. For Americans, **liberty** means both personal freedom and economic freedom. Both are closely linked to the idea of **limited government**.

The Constitution's first 10 amendments, known collectively as the Bill of Rights, above all preserve individual personal liberties and rights. In fact, the word *liberty* has come to mean many of the freedoms guaranteed in the Bill of Rights: freedom of speech and writing, the right to assemble freely, and the right to practice religious beliefs without interference from the government. Over the course of American history, the scope of personal liberties has expanded, as laws have become more tolerant and as individuals have successfully used the courts to challenge restrictions on their individual freedoms. Far fewer restrictions exist today on the press, political speech, and individual moral behavior than in the early years of the nation. Even so, conflicts persist over how personal liberties should be extended and when personal liberties violate community norms. For example, a number of cities have recently passed "sit-lie" ordinances, which limit the freedom of individuals to sit or lie down on sidewalks. Designed to limit the presence of the homeless and make city streets more attractive to pedestrians, the ordinances have also been denounced as infringements on individual liberties.

*Patrick Henry's famous "Give me liberty or give me death" speech demanded freedom at any cost and has resonated with Americans throughout the nation's history.*

The central historical conflict regarding liberty in the United States was about the enslavement of blacks. The facts of slavery and the differential treatment of the races have cast a long shadow over all of American history. In fact, scholars today note that the American definition of freedom has been formed in relation to the concept of slavery. The right to control one's labor and the right to receive rewards for that labor have been central elements of our definition of freedom precisely because these freedoms were denied to slaves.[34]

In addition to personal freedom, the American concept of liberty means economic freedom. Since the Founding, economic freedom has been linked to capitalism, free markets, and the protection of private property. Free competition, unfettered movement of goods, and the right to enjoy the fruits of one's labor are all essential aspects of economic freedom and American capitalism.[35] In the first century of the republic, support for capitalism often meant support for the doctrine of laissez-faire (literally, "leave alone" in French). **Laissez-faire capitalism** allowed very little room for the national government to regulate trade or restrict the use of private property, even in the public interest. Americans still strongly support capitalism and economic liberty, but they now also endorse some restrictions on economic freedoms to protect the public. Today, federal and state governments deploy a wide array of regulations in the name of public protection. These include health and safety laws, environmental rules, and workplace regulations.

Not surprisingly, fierce disagreements often erupt over what the proper scope of government regulation should be. What some people regard as protecting the public, others see as an infringement on their own freedom to run their businesses and use their property as they see fit. For example, in September 2009 the Food and Drug Administration banned the sale of flavored cigarettes under the terms of the Family Smoking Prevention and Tobacco Control Act passed by Congress three months earlier. The FDA and health care professionals argue that such cigarettes are manufactured primarily to lure children and teenagers into smoking. It is estimated that 3,600 children and teenagers start smoking each day; by banning flavored cigarettes, the agency hopes to reduce that number. Manufacturers of these products, however, are averse to such regulations, feeling that the government is limiting their freedom and their ability to make a profit.[36]

More recently, concerns about liberty have arisen in relation to the government's efforts to combat terrorism. In the months following September 11, hundreds of individuals, mainly of Middle Eastern origin, were arrested by federal authorities and held on immigration charges or by material witness warrants that allowed the government to incarcerate them without having to show any evidence they were linked to terrorist activities. Also in the immediate aftermath of September 11, President George W. Bush issued secret orders to the National Security Agency, authorizing the agency to monitor domestic phone traffic in search of possible communications among terrorist groups. This program meant that the calls of millions of Americans were secretly intercepted without a court warrant. Concerns about terrorism leave us with an extraordinary dilemma. On the one hand, we treasure liberty, but on the other hand, we recognize that the lives of thousands of Americans have already been lost and countless others are threatened by terrorism. Can we reconcile liberty and security? Liberty and order? In previous national emergencies, Americans accepted restrictions on liberty with the understanding that these would be temporary. But because the threat of terrorism has no clear end point, doubts have grown about whether special government powers that infringe on liberties should be continued.

## Equality

The Declaration of Independence declares as its first "self-evident" truth that "all men are created equal." As central as it is to the American political creed, however, equality has been an even less well-defined ideal than liberty, because people interpret "equality" in different ways. Few Americans have wholeheartedly embraced the ideal of full equality of results, but most Americans share the ideal of **equality of opportunity**—that is, the notion that each person should be given a fair chance to go as far as his or her talents will allow. Yet it is hard for Americans to reach agreement on what constitutes equality of opportunity. Must *past* inequalities be remedied in order to ensure equal opportunity in the *present*? Should inequalities in the legal, political, and economic spheres be given the same weight? In contrast to liberty, which requires limits on the role of government, equality implies an *obligation* of the government to the people.[37]

Americans do make clear distinctions between political equality and social or economic equality. **Political equality** means that members of the American political community have the right to participate in politics on equal terms. Beginning from a very restricted definition of political community, which originally included only propertied white men, the United States has moved much closer to an ideal of political equality that can be summed up as "one person, one vote." Broad support

**equality of opportunity** a widely shared American ideal that all people should have the freedom to use whatever talents and wealth they have to reach their fullest potential

**political equality** the right to participate in politics equally, based on the principle of "one person, one vote"

for the ideal of political equality has helped expand the American political community and extend to all the right to participate. Although considerable conflict remains over whether the political system makes participation in it harder for some people and easier for others, and whether the role of money in politics has drowned out the public voice, Americans agree that all citizens should have an equal right to participate and that government should enforce that right.

In part because Americans believe that individuals are free to work as hard as they choose, they have always been less concerned about social or economic inequality. Many Americans regard economic differences as the consequence of individual choices, virtues, or failures. Because of this, Americans tend to be less supportive than most Europeans of government action to ensure economic equality. Yet when major economic forces, such as the Great Depression of the 1930s, affect many people, or when systematic barriers appear to block equality of opportunity, Americans support government action to promote equality. Even then, however, they have endorsed only a limited government role designed to help people get back on their feet or to open up opportunity.

Because equality is such an elusive concept, many conflicts have arisen over what it should mean in practice. Americans have engaged in three kinds of controversies about the public role in addressing inequality. The first is determining what constitutes equality of access to public institutions. In 1896 the Supreme Court ruled in *Plessy v. Ferguson* that "separate but equal" accommodation for blacks and whites was constitutional.[38] In 1954, in a major legal victory for the civil rights movement, the Supreme Court's decision in *Brown v. Board of Education* overturned the "separate but equal" doctrine (see Chapter 5).[39] Today, new questions have been raised about what constitutes equal access to public institutions. Some argue that the unequal financing of public schools in cities, suburbs, and rural districts is a violation of the right to equal education. To date, these claims have not been supported by the federal courts, which have rejected the notion that the unequal economic impacts of public policy outcomes are a constitutional matter.[40] Lawsuits arguing a right to "economic equal protection" stalled in 1973 when the Supreme Court ruled that a Texas school-financing law did not violate the Constitution even though the law affected rich and poor students differently.[41]

A second debate concerns the public role in ensuring equality of opportunity in private life. Although Americans generally agree that discrimination should not be tolerated, people disagree over what should be done to ensure equality of opportunity (see Table 1.3). Controversies about affirmative-action programs reflect these disputes. Supporters of affirmative action claim that such programs are necessary to compensate for past discrimination in order to establish true equality of opportunity today. Opponents maintain that affirmative action amounts to reverse discrimination and that a society that espouses true equality should not acknowledge gender or racial differences. The question of the public responsibility for private inequalities is central to gender issues. The traditional view, still held by many today, sees the special responsibilities

*Opponents of gay marriage have proposed amending the Constitution to define marriage as a union between one man and one woman. Supporters of gay rights argue that same-sex couples should have an equal right to marry.*

## TABLE 1.3

## Equality and Public Opinion

Americans believe in some forms of equality more than others. How do these survey results reflect disagreement about what equality means in practice?

| STATEMENT | PERCENTAGE WHO AGREE |
| --- | --- |
| Male and female citizens of the United States have equal rights. | 97 |
| Our society should do what is necessary to make sure that everyone has an equal opportunity to succeed. | 86 |
| Homosexuals should have equal rights in terms of job opportunities. | 87 |
| It should be legal for gay and lesbian couples to get married. | 50 |
| The fact that some are rich and some are poor is an acceptable part of the economic system. | 52 |
| We should make every possible effort to improve the position of blacks and other minorities even if it means preferential treatment (according to whites). | 22 |
| We should make every possible effort to improve the position of blacks and other minorities even if it means preferential treatment (according to blacks). | 62 |

SOURCES: Pew Global Attitudes Project Poll, April 2010. Retrieved June 9, 2012 from the iPOLL Databank, The Roper Center for Public Opinion Research, University of Connecticut. www.ropercenter.uconn.edu/data_access/ipoll/ipoll.html. Pew Research Center for the People and the Press and for the Public, "Trends in American Values, 1987–2012, Partisan Polarization Surges in Bush, Obama Years," June 4, 2012, p. 104. Princeton Survey Research Associates International/Newsweek Poll, December 2008. Retrieved June 9, 2012 from the iPOLL Databank, The Roper Center for Public Opinion Research, University of Connecticut. www.ropercenter.uconn.edu/data_access/ipoll/ipoll.html. Polling Report.com, Gallup, May 3–June 12, 2012, pollingreport.com/civil.htm. Pew Research Center for the People and the Press and for the Public, "It's Not about Class Warfare, but Fairness Poll Analysis," March 2, 2012, www.peoplepress.org/2012/03/02/for-the-public-its-not-about-class-warfare-but-fairness/. (All accessed 6/9/12.)

of women in the family as falling outside the range of public concern. Indeed, from this perspective, the role of women within families is essential to the functioning of a democratic society. In the past 30 years especially, these traditional views have come under fire as advocates for women have argued that women occupy a subordinate place within the family and that such private inequalities *are* a topic of public concern.[42]

A third debate about equality concerns differences in income and wealth. Unlike in other countries, income inequality has not been an enduring topic of political controversy in the United States, which currently has the largest gap in income and wealth between rich and poor citizens of any developed nation. But Americans have generally tolerated great differences among rich and poor citizens, in part because of a pervasive belief that mobility is possible and that economic success is the product of individual effort.[43] This tolerance for inequality is reflected in America's tax code, which is more advantageous to wealthy taxpayers than that of almost any other Western nation. Indeed, tax changes enacted in recent years

Beginning in 2011, the Occupy movement drew attention to increasing inequality in the United States, arguing that the gap between the top 1 percent of earners and the other 99 percent was unfair.

**for critical analysis**

Economic inequality among Americans is now as high as it was 100 years ago. Many politicians and news commentators say that inequality is threatening the middle class. Is there any evidence that the American public is worried about the growth in inequality?

have sharply reduced the tax burdens of upper-income Americans. Debate about taxes surfaced throughout the Obama presidency and during the 2012 election. President Obama defended the need to raise the tax rate of Americans earning more than $250,000 a year to support programs that benefit the middle class.[44] Even so, opposition among Republicans—and some Democrats—meant that tax rates remained untouched. The issue of inequality emerged in a new dramatic way in late 2011, when the Occupy Wall Street movement mounted protests across the country. Motivated by concerns about inequality, the movement did not develop a clear policy agenda, but concerns about inequality received new prominence. Polls showed that Americans are split in their views about whether government should aim to reduce economic inequality. In 2012, 52 percent viewed the gap between the rich and the poor as an acceptable part of the economic system while 45 percent considered it a problem that needs to be fixed. More Americans expressed concern about the power of the rich, with 77 percent agreeing that there was too much power in the hands of a few rich people and large corporations.[45]

## Democracy

The essence of democracy is the participation of the people in choosing their rulers and the people's ability to influence what those rulers do. In a democracy, political power ultimately comes from the people. The idea of placing power in the hands of the people is known as **popular sovereignty**. In the United States, popular sovereignty and political equality make politicians accountable to the people. Ideally, democracy envisions an engaged citizenry prepared to exercise its power over rulers. As we noted earlier, the United States is a representative democracy, meaning that the people do not rule directly but instead exercise power through elected representatives. Forms of participation in a democracy vary greatly, but voting is a key element of the representative democracy that the American Founders established.

American democracy rests on the principle of **majority rule** with **minority rights**. Majority rule means that the wishes of the majority determine what government does. The House of Representatives—a large body elected directly by

**popular sovereignty** a principle of democracy in which political authority rests ultimately in the hands of the people

**majority rule, minority rights** the democratic principle that a government follows the preferences of the majority of voters but protects the interests of the minority

# Should America Export Democracy?

**Americans are justifiably proud** of their democratic political institutions and often believe that the people of all nations would benefit from living under American-style democratic rule. Indeed, on a number of occasions Americans have sought to transform other nations into democracies—a policy called "democratization." In the aftermath of World War II, American military forces occupied Japan and the western portion of Germany, imposing new democratic governments to replace the dictatorial regimes blamed for launching the war. More recently, after successful American military campaigns to overthrow the governments of Afghanistan and Iraq, the United States has undertaken an effort to build democratic governments in those nations.

Exporting democracy might be seen as a desirable goal for three reasons. The first of these is humanitarian. Generally speaking, individuals are better off when they possess civil liberties and political rights. Indeed, former president George W. Bush asserted that one of the main purposes of American policy in the Middle East was to bring democracy to the people of the region. "It is the calling of our country," Bush said.

A second reason sometimes given in support of American efforts to export democracy is the promotion of political stability. In a democracy, competing economic and social forces have a chance to work out their differences through lawful political struggle. Dictatorial regimes, by contrast, seldom provide opportunities for lawful political activity and usually seek to quash expressions of political dissent or opposition. Lacking lawful channels, political grievances in nations ruled by dictatorships usually manifest themselves in such forms as public protest, political violence, and terrorism. The uprisings of the "Arab Spring," including the prolonged struggle in Libya, overthrew dictators across the Arab world in 2011. Whether these major political shifts also build stable democratic regimes remains to be seen. A third reason Americans might wish to support policies of democratization is that the spread of democracy may promote world peace. In his famous 1795 essay "Toward Perpetual Peace," the German philosopher Immanuel Kant observed that democratic regimes seldom made war on each other. Thus, he argued, the expansion of democracy would enhance the prospects for world peace. In recent years, a good deal of empirical research has supported Kant's hypothesis.

Although a more democratic world might, indeed, be more humane, stable, and peaceful, a policy of democratization faces daunting prospects. First, a huge percentage of the world's population lives in nations that are not democracies. It seems unlikely that America could actually democratize so much of the globe. Second, many nations might not be capable of sustaining democratic regimes even if they were established. Democracy is most likely to flourish where there are vigorous social institutions and a stable economy—conditions that do not exist in many regions of the world. Finally, the process of democratization can itself be dangerous for American interests because it may lead to political instability or the election of hostile governments. By 2009 some observers were questioning whether it would be possible to build democracies in Iraq and Afghanistan, where corruption and security challenges were undermining government stability. With the threat from the Taliban mounting in Afghanistan, the British ambassador there went so far as to suggest that it would take "an acceptable dictator" to unite the country.

## for critical analysis

1. What are some of the factors that might help determine whether democratic politics can take root in a country that has not previously experienced democracy?

2. Is it appropriate for America to try to shape the governments and political arrangements of other countries?

the people—was designed in particular to ensure majority rule. But the Founders feared that popular majorities could turn government into a "tyranny of the majority" in which individual liberties would be violated. Concern for individual rights has thus been a part of American democracy from the beginning. The rights enumerated in the Bill of Rights and enforced through the courts provide an important check on the power of the majority.

Despite Americans' deep attachment to the *ideal* of democracy, many questions can be raised about our *practice* of democracy. The first is the restricted definition of the political community during much of American history. Property restrictions on the right to vote were eliminated by 1828; in 1870 the Fifteenth Amendment to the Constitution granted African Americans the vote, although later exclusionary practices denied them that right; in 1920 the Nineteenth Amendment guaranteed women the right to vote; and in 1965 the Voting Rights Act finally secured the right of African Americans to vote.

Just securing the right to vote does not end concerns about democracy, however. The organization of electoral institutions can have a significant impact on access to elections and on who can get elected. During the first two decades of the twentieth century, states and cities enacted many reforms, including strict registration requirements and scheduling of elections, that made it harder to vote. The aim was to rid politics of corruption, but the consequence was to reduce participation. Other institutional decisions affect which candidates stand the best chance of getting elected (see Chapter 10).

A further consideration about democracy concerns the relationship between economic power and political power. Money has always played an important role in elections and governing in the United States. Many argue that the pervasive influence of money in American electoral campaigns today undermines democracy. With the decline of locally based political parties that depend on party loyalists to turn out the vote, and the rise of political action committees, political consultants, and expensive media campaigns, money has become the central fact of life in American politics. Money often determines who runs for office; it can exert a heavy influence on who wins; and some argue that it affects what politicians do once they are in office.[46]

Low turnout for elections and a pervasive sense of apathy and cynicism characterized American politics for much of the past half-century. The widespread interest in the 2008 election and the near-record levels of voter turnout, which, at 61.7 percent, was the highest turnout since 1980, reversed this trend.[47] Nine million voters registered and voted for the first time in 2008, including near-record numbers of voters under the age of 24.[48] Volunteers found ways to become personally involved in politics. Although turnout in 2012 did not match 2008, these developments were a hopeful sign for those wishing to revitalize American democracy.

*Although most barriers to voting have been removed for Americans aged 18 and up, many people do not vote. In the 2012 election only only about 60 percent of eligible citizens turned out at the polls.*

# Explore American Politics Online

## Inform Yourself

**Keep up-to-date on political news.** Political information websites are numerous and useful for checking on a daily or at least weekly basis to keep up-to-date on what is happing in terms of legislation, elections, and other political news. Websites for general political information include the Huffington Post (www.huffingtonpost .com) and Politico (www.politico.com). The Real Clear Politics website (www .realclearpolitics.com) focuses on elections and public opinion polling. Under the Polls tab there are opinion polls on hundreds of different upcoming races.

**Find out what's happening in Congress.** To find out specifically what is happening in Washington, D.C., visit Roll Call (www.rollcall.com). The website features information on proposed legislation, the legislative process, and "who's who" on Capitol Hill. Visit the website and see what the headlines are in each of the drop-down categories.

**See what the public across the country is thinking.** The Pew Research Center offers some of the highest-quality public opinion surveys available. At www.pewresearch .org you will find public opinion polls on a plethora of topics related to American politics. There is even a poll on the costs and benefits of a college education and student debt, with opinions of college students and their parents (http://pewresearch .org/pubs/2261/college-university-education-costs-student-debt). How should this information be used by politicians when making education policy? Do you think elected officials in Washington, D.C., will pay attention to this public opinion poll?

## Express Yourself

**Visit the Rock the Vote website.** Rock the Vote (www.rockthevote.org) was created to help young people express their political power. Its website offers opportunities to register to vote, find your polling place, volunteer for a campaign, contribute money, read blog posts and press releases, and more. Consider joining Rock the Vote for one of its "Road Trips" to mobilize and register young voters across the country. Summer 2012 music tours included the Vans Warped Tour, the Rock the Bells festival, and the band Blink-182. There are opportunities to volunteer for the shows and get free tickets.

## Connect with Others

**Join the discussion on American Politics 411's Facebook page.** This is a page linked to a bipartisan group of students "dedicated to redefining transparency in politics and the media." You can also find American Politics 411 on Twitter. Skim through the items on its Facebook time line or Twitter feed and determine what materials are "bipartisan" and what materials still have a clear political slant. Consider joining the discussion on one of its posts.

*Find links to the sites listed above as well as related activities on wwnorton.com/studyspace.*

# study guide

 **Practice online with:** Chapter 1 Diagnostic Quiz ▪ Chapter 1 Key Term Flashcards

## What Americans Think about Government

◼ **Explore how Americans see their government (pp. 5–8)**

While Americans have always been hesitant about granting government too much power, they have frequently relied on it during times of national crisis and have become increasingly dependent on it to provide important services. Over the last few decades, the public's trust in government and their sense of political efficacy have declined significantly. Low levels of trust and efficacy may threaten American democracy by weakening the government and reducing the public's willingness to participate in political life.

**Key Terms**

**government** (p. 4)

**politics** (p. 4)

**political efficacy** (p. 8)

**Practice Quiz**

1. Political efficacy is the belief that (*p. 8*)
   a) government is wasteful and corrupt.
   b) government operates efficiently.
   c) government has grown too large.
   d) government cannot be trusted.
   e) one can influence what government does.

2. American's trust in their government (*pp. 5–7*)
   a) rose significantly between 1964 and 1980.
   b) increased immediately following September 11, 2001, but declined shortly thereafter.
   c) declined immediately after the September 11 attacks but has risen dramatically since 2004.
   d) has never been studied.
   e) has remained the same over the last 50 years.

 **Practice Online**
Video exercise: *Democracy Is . . .*

## Citizenship: Knowledge and Participation

◼ **Describe the role of the citizen in politics (pp. 9–11)**

Citizenship requires political knowledge. When citizens know about politics, they are better able to understand their interests and to identify the best way to act on those interests. Most Americans, however, do not know much about politics.

**Key Term**

**citizenship** (p. 10)

**Practice Quiz**

3. Generally speaking, Americans (*p. 9*)
   a) know very little about current political issues but are able to identify high-profile political leaders.
   b) know a great deal about current political issues but are not able to identify high-profile political leaders.
   c) know very little about current political issues and are not able to identify high-profile political leaders.
   d) know a great deal about current political issues and are able to identify high-profile political leaders.
   e) are extremely engaged with politics and trust the government to do what is right.

4. According to the authors, good citizenship requires (*p. 10*)
   a) political knowledge and political engagement.
   b) political knowledge but not political engagement.
   c) a good education.
   d) a significant amount of money.
   e) political engagement but not political knowledge.

 **Practice Online**
"Get Involved" exercise: *Political News in the Digital Age*

# Government

 **Define government and forms of government (pp. 11–16)**

There are many different kinds of government. Prior to the modern era, governments accepted almost no limits on their behavior and provided citizens with few opportunities to participate in public affairs. Today, numerous countries, including the United States, are constitutional democracies. America's democracy provides citizens with the chance to elect top officials at all levels of government and even allows them to vote directly on laws in many states and localities.

## Key Terms

**autocracy** (p. 13)

**oligarchy** (p. 13)

**democracy** (p. 13)

**constitutional government** (p. 13)

**authoritarian government** (p. 13)

**totalitarian government** (p. 13)

**politics** (p. 15)

**power** (p. 15)

**representative democracy/republic** (p. 15)

**direct democracy** (p. 15)

**pluralism** (p. 16)

## Practice Quiz

5. What is the basic difference between autocracy and oligarchy? (*p. 13*)
   a) the extent to which the average citizen has a say in government affairs
   b) the means of collecting taxes and conscripting soldiers
   c) the number of people who control governing decisions
   d) the size and political influence of the military
   e) They are fundamentally the same thing.

6. The famous political scientist Harold Lasswell defined politics are the struggle over (*p. 15*)
   a) who gets elected.
   b) who is most popular.
   c) who gets what, when, how.
   d) who protests.
   e) who gets to vote.

7. Although not present at the national level, a number of states and cities permit citizens to vote directly on laws and policies. What is this form of rule called? (*p. 15*)
   a) a republic
   b) representative democracy
   c) direct democracy
   d) pluralism
   e) laissez-faire capitalism

8. *Pluralism* is a theory that says (*p. 16*)
   a) the means of economic production should be privately owned and operated without interference from the government.
   b) all interests in a society should be free to compete for influence over governmental decisions.
   c) government should always follow the preferences of the majority while also protecting the rights of those in the minority.
   d) american political culture should emphasize the values of liberty, equality, and democracy.
   e) one ruler should dominate all spheres of social, political, economic and cultural life.

# Who Are Americans?

 **Show how the American people have changed over time (pp. 16–23)**

The United States is defined, in part, by its ever growing and changing population. During the last 200 years, America has become more racially, ethnically, geographically, and religiously diverse. Immigration has been an important reason for the country's shifting demographics, and it has frequently sparked intense debate about the nature of American identity and American democracy.

## Practice Quiz

9. Since 1900, which of the following groups has increased as a percentage of the overall population in the United States? (*p. 20*)
   a) black, Hispanic, and Asian
   b) Hispanic only
   c) Asian only
   d) black only
   e) Hispanic and Asian only

10. The percentage of foreign-born individuals living in the United States (*pp. 19–20*)
   a) has increased significantly since reaching its low point in 1970.
   b) has decreased significantly since reaching its high point in 1970.
   c) has remained the same since 1970.
   d) has not been studied since 1970.
   e) has never been less than the percentage of native born individuals living in the United States.

 **Practice Online**
"Who Are Americans?" interactive exercise:
*An Increasingly Diverse Nation*

# Thinking Critically About American Political Culture

■ **Analyze whether the system of government upholds American political values (pp. 23–30)**

Most Americans espouse strong support for liberty, equality, and democracy. Agreement on these basic values does not mean, however, that political debate in the United States is without conflict. Questions about how to apply and balance the different elements of American political culture have motivated disagreements throughout the country's history.

## Key Terms

**political culture** (p. 23)

**liberty** (p. 24)

**limited government** (p. 24)

**laissez-faire capitalism** (p. 24)

**equality of opportunity** (p. 25)

**political equality** (p. 25)

**popular sovereignty** (p. 28)

**majority rule, minority rights** (p. 28)

## Practice Quiz

11. The principle of political equality can be best summed up as *(p. 25)*
    a) "equality of results."
    b) "equality of opportunity."
    c) "one person, one vote."
    d) "equality between the sexes."
    e) "leave everyone alone."

12. Which of the following is an important principle of American democracy? *(pp. 28–30)*
    a) popular sovereignty
    b) majority rule
    c) limited government
    d) minority rights
    e) All of the above are important principles of American democracy.

13. Which of the following is *not* related to the American conception of liberty? *(pp. 24–25)*
    a) freedom of speech
    b) free enterprise
    c) freedom of religion
    d) freedom of assembly
    e) All of the above are related to liberty.

14. Which of the following is *not* part of American political culture? *(p. 25)*
    a) belief in equality of results
    b) belief in democracy
    c) belief in individual liberty
    d) belief in free competition
    e) belief in equality of opportunity

15. Which of the following restrictions on voting have been repealed over the last 182 years of American history? *(p. 30)*
    a) property, gender, and race
    b) gender only
    c) race only
    d) property only
    e) race and gender only

 **Practice Online**
Interactive simulation: *Liberty vs. Security*

# For Further Reading

Dahl, Robert. *Democracy and Its Critics*. New Haven, CT: Yale University Press, 1989.

Dalton, Russell. *The Good Citizen: How a Younger Generation Is Reshaping American Politics*. Rev. ed. Washington, DC: CQ Press, 2008.

Delli Carpini, Michael X., and Scott Keeter. *What Americans Know about Politics and Why It Matters*. New Haven, CT: Yale University Press, 1996.

Fischer, Claude S., and Michael Hout. *A Century of Difference: How America Changed in the Last One Hundred Years*. New York: Russell Sage Foundation, 2006.

Hibbing, John R., and Elizabeth Theiss-Morse. *Stealth Democracy: Americans' Belief about How Government Should Work*. New York: Cambridge University Press, 2002.

Huntington, Samuel. *Who Are We: The Challenges to America's National Identity*. New York: Simon & Schuster, 2004.

Lasswell, Harold. *Politics: Who Gets What, When, How*. New York: Meridian Books, 1958.

McCarty, Nolan, Keith T. Poole, and Howard Rosenthal, *Polarized America: The Dance of Ideology and Unequal Riches*. Cambridge, MA: MIT Press, 2008.

Page, Benjamin I., and Lawrence R. Jacobs. *Class War? What Americans Really Think about Economic Inequality*. Chicago: University of Chicago Press, 2009.

Tocqueville, Alexis de. *Democracy in America*. Translated by Phillips Bradley. New York: Knopf, Vintage Books, 1945; orig. published 1835.

Zakaria, Fareed. *The Future of Freedom*. New York: W.W.Norton, 2003.

# Recommended Websites

**American Democracy Project**
www.aascu.org/programs/adp/
> This is an effort by the Association of State Colleges and Universities to increase political engagement among college students. See what opportunities are available for you to become politically active.

**Americans for Informed Democracy**
www.aidemocracy.org
> A nonpartisan organization that promotes democracy and seeks to build a new generation of globally conscious leaders. Find out how you can be politically active and coordinate a town hall meeting on campus, attend a leadership retreat, or publish your opinions on democracy.

**DiversityInc**
http://diversityinc.com
> This site is dedicated to the promotion of American diversity and education. Here you can read about the issues that directly affect American minorities.

**For Democracy**
www.fordemocracy.com
> Most Americans know little about our government. Log on to this independent site to find a plethora of information on the history of American democracy and related current events.

**Future of Freedom Foundation**
www.fff.org
> This organization promotes individual liberty, free markets, private property, and limited government. Find out how some people are trying to protect freedom in the United States.

**Institute for Learning Technologies**
www.ilt.columbia.edu/publications/digitext.html#
> Columbia University's Institute for Learning Technologies provides general information on early political thinkers such as Aristotle, Hobbes, Locke, and Rousseau. Take a moment to read some of the writings on topics such as popular sovereignty, democracy, and limited government.

**Mobilize.org**
http://mobilize.org
> This all-partisan network is dedicated to educating, empowering, and energizing young people. Find out how politics affects America's youth and what they are doing about it by being engaged and active.

**U.S. Census Bureau**
www.census.gov
> The website for the Bureau of the Census offers a statistical look at our country's population and economy. Check out some of the statistics to get a better idea of American diversity.

When the framers of the Constitution met in 1787, they set out to establish a political system that would protect liberty and place limits on government. They also believed a powerful government required a broad popular base. However, they debated how best to protect liberty and how to balance democracy with other concerns.

# The Founding and the Constitution

**WHAT GOVERNMENT DOES AND WHY IT MATTERS** The framers of the U.S. Constitution knew why government mattered. In the Constitution's preamble, the framers tell us that the purposes of government are to promote justice, to maintain peace at home, to defend the nation from foreign foes, to provide for the welfare of the citizenry, and, above all, to secure the "blessings of liberty" for Americans. The remainder of the Constitution spells out a plan for achieving these objectives. This plan includes provisions for the exercise of legislative, executive, and judicial powers and a recipe for the division of powers among the federal government's branches and between the national and state governments. The framers' conception of why government matters and how it is to achieve its goals has been America's political blueprint for more than two centuries.

Today, some question the continuing value of the Constitution. Critics blame the constitutional division of powers for the gridlock that often seems to block legislation in the Congress. In 2011, when the United States very nearly defaulted on its debts because the president and Congress could not reach an agreement, the Constitution seemed more a hindrance to a solution than a recipe for effective governance. But, eventually, a decision was reached and the constitutional formula prevailed.

The story of America's Founding and the Constitution is generally presented as something both inevitable and glorious: it was inevitable that the American colonies would break away from Great Britain to establish their own country; and it was glorious in that the country established the best of all possible forms of government under a new constitution, which was easily adopted and quickly embraced, even by its critics. In reality, though, America's successful breakaway from Britain was by no means assured, and the Constitution was in fact highly controversial. Moreover, its ratification and durability were often in doubt. George Washington, the man chosen to preside over the Constitutional Convention of 1787, thought the document produced that hot summer in Philadelphia would probably last no more than 20 years, at which time leaders would have to convene again to come up with something new.

That Washington's expectation proved wrong is, indeed, a testament to the enduring strength of the Constitution. America's long-standing values of liberty, equality, and democracy were all major themes of the founding period and are all elements of the U.S. Constitution. However, the Constitution was a product of political bargaining and compromise, formed in very much the same way political decisions are made today. This fact is often overlooked because of what the historian Michael Kammen has called the "cult of the Constitution"—a tendency of Americans, going back more than a century, to venerate, sometimes to the point of near worship, the Founders and the document they created.[1] As this chapter will show, the Constitution reflects high principle as well as political self-interest, and also defines the relationship between American citizens and their government.

## chaptergoals

- Describe the events that led to the Declaration of Independence and the Articles of Confederation (pages 39–43)

- Explain how the Constitution attempted to improve America's governance (pages 43–49)

- Outline the major institutions and rules established by the Constitution (pages 49–56)

- Present the controversies involved in the struggle for ratification (pages 56–62)

- Trace how the Constitution has changed over time through the amendment process (pages 62–66)

# ● The First Founding: Interests and Conflicts

**Describe the events that led to the Declaration of Independence and the Articles of Confederation**

Competing ideals and principles often reflect competing interests, and so it was in Revolutionary America. The American Revolution and the American Constitution were outgrowths and expressions of a struggle among economic and political forces within the colonies. Five sectors of society had interests that were important in colonial politics: (1) the New England merchants; (2) the southern planters; (3) the "royalists"—holders of royal lands, offices, and patents (licenses to engage in a profession or business activity); (4) shopkeepers, artisans, and laborers; and (5) small farmers. Throughout the eighteenth century, these groups were in conflict over issues of taxation, trade, and commerce. For the most part, however, the southern planters, the New England merchants, and the royal office and patent holders—groups that together made up the colonial elite—were able to maintain a political alliance that held in check the more radical forces representing shopkeepers, laborers, and small farmers. After 1760, however, by seriously threatening the interests of New England merchants and southern planters, British tax and trade policies split the colonial elite, permitting radical forces to expand their political influence, and set in motion a chain of events that culminated in the American Revolution.[2]

## British Taxes and Colonial Interests

Beginning in the 1760s, the debts and other financial problems confronting the British government forced it to search for new revenue sources. This search rather quickly led to the Crown's North American colonies, which, on the whole, paid remarkably little in taxes to their parent country. The British government reasoned that a sizable fraction of its debt was, in fact, attributable to the expenses it had incurred in defense of the colonies during the French and Indian War, which ended in 1763, driving France from North America. The British also considered the cost of the continuing protection that British forces were giving the colonists from Indian attacks and that the British navy was providing for colonial shipping. Thus, during the 1760s, Britain sought to impose new, though relatively modest, taxes on the colonists.

Like most governments of the period, the British regime had limited ways in which to collect revenues. The income tax, which in the twentieth century became the single most important source of governmental revenues, had not yet been developed. In the mid-eighteenth century, governments relied mainly on tariffs, duties, and other taxes on commerce, and it was to such taxes, and to the Stamp Act, that the British turned during the 1760s.

The Stamp Act, and other taxes on commerce, such as the Sugar Act of 1764, which taxed sugar, molasses, and other commodities, most heavily affected the two groups in colonial society whose commercial interests and activities were most extensive—the New England merchants and the southern planters. United under

*British colonists in America shipped many goods back to England, such as furs obtained by trading with Native Americans. The British government claimed that the colonists should pay more in taxes in light of the protection their shipments received from the British navy and the expenses Britain incurred defending the colonies.*

the famous slogan "no taxation without representation," the merchants and planters sought to organize opposition to these new taxes. In the course of the struggle against British tax measures, the planters and merchants broke with their royalist allies and turned to their former adversaries—the shopkeepers, small farmers, laborers, and artisans—for help. With the assistance of these groups, the merchants and planters organized demonstrations and a boycott of British goods that ultimately forced the Crown to rescind most of its hated new taxes.

From the perspective of the merchants and planters, this was a victorious conclusion to their struggle with the mother country. They were anxious to end the unrest they had helped arouse, and they supported the British government's efforts to restore order. Indeed, most respectable Bostonians supported the actions of the British soldiers involved in the Boston Massacre—the 1770 killing of five colonists by British soldiers attempting to repel an angry mob gathered outside the Town House, the seat of the colonial government. In their subsequent trial, the soldiers were defended by John Adams, a pillar of Boston society and a future president of the United States. Adams asserted that the soldiers' actions were entirely justified, provoked by "a motley rabble of saucy boys, negroes and mulattoes, Irish teagues and outlandish Jack tars." All but two of the soldiers were acquitted.[3]

Despite the efforts of the British government and the better-to-do strata of colonial society, it proved difficult to bring an end to the political strife. The more radical forces representing shopkeepers, artisans, laborers, and small farmers, who had been mobilized and energized by the struggle over taxes, continued to agitate for political and social change. These radicals, whose leaders included Samuel Adams, a cousin of John Adams, asserted that British power supported an unjust political and social structure within the colonies, and began to advocate an end to British rule.[4]

## Political Strife and the Radicalizing of the Colonists

The political strife within the colonies was the background for the events of 1773–74. In 1773 the British government granted the politically powerful East India Company a monopoly on the export of tea from Britain, eliminating a lucrative form of trade for colonial merchants. To add to the injury, the East India Com-

*The British helped radicalize colonists through bad policy decisions in the years before the Revolution. For example, Britain gave the ailing East India Company a monopoly on the tea trade in the American colonies. Colonists feared that the monopoly would hurt colonial merchants' business and protested by throwing East India Company tea into Boston Harbor in 1773.*

pany sought to sell the tea directly in the colonies instead of working through the colonial merchants. Tea was an extremely important commodity during the 1770s, and these British actions posed a serious threat to the New England merchants. Together with their southern allies, the merchants once again called on their radical adversaries for support. The most dramatic result was the Boston Tea Party. In three other colonies, anti-tax Americans succeeded in blocking the unloading of taxed tea, which then had to be returned to Britain. The royal governor of Massachusetts, however, refused to allow three shiploads of unsold tea to leave Boston Harbor. Anti-British radicals seized this opportunity: on the night of December 16, 1773, a group led by Samuel Adams, some of them hastily "disguised" as Mohawk Indians, boarded the three vessels and threw the entire cargo of 342 chests of tea into the harbor.

**for critical analysis**
Conflicts over taxes did not end with the American Revolution. Why is tax policy almost always controversial?

This event was of decisive importance in American history. The merchants had hoped to force the British government to rescind the Tea Act, but they did not support any further demands and did not seek independence from Britain. Samuel Adams and the other radicals, however, hoped to provoke the British government to take actions that would alienate its colonial supporters and pave the way for a rebellion. This was precisely the purpose of the Boston Tea Party, and it succeeded. By dumping the East India Company's tea into Boston Harbor, Adams and his followers goaded the British into enacting a number of harsh reprisals. Within five months after the incident in Boston, the House of Commons passed a series of acts that closed the port of Boston to commerce, changed the provincial government of Massachusetts, provided for the removal of accused persons to Britain for trial, and, most important, restricted movement to the West—further alienating the southern planters, who depended on access to new western lands. These acts of retaliation confirmed the worst criticisms of British rule and helped radicalize Americans. Radicals such as Samuel Adams and Christopher Gadsden (of South Carolina) had been agitating for more-violent measures against the British. But ultimately they needed Britain's political repression to create widespread support for independence.

Thus, the Boston Tea Party set in motion a cycle of provocation and retaliation that in 1774 resulted in the convening of the First Continental Congress—an assembly of delegates from all parts of the country—that called for a total boycott of British goods and, under the prodding of the radicals, began to consider the possibility of independence from British rule. The eventual result was the Declaration of Independence.

## The Declaration of Independence

In 1776, more than a year after open warfare had commenced in Massachusetts, the Second Continental Congress appointed a committee consisting of Thomas Jefferson of Virginia, Benjamin Franklin of Pennsylvania, Roger Sherman of Connecticut, John Adams of Massachusetts, and Robert Livingston of New York to draft a statement of American independence from British rule. The Declaration of Independence, written by Jefferson and adopted by the Second Continental Congress, was an extraordinary document both philosophically and politically. In philosophic terms,

*Britain eventually sent troops to subdue the American colonists. Grant Wood's* Midnight Ride of Paul Revere *(1931) depicts Revere alerting colonists to the British army's arrival. The subsequent battle between colonial and British forces at Concord and Lexington began the Revolutionary War.*

THE DECLARATION OF INDEPENDENCE.
JULY 4TH 1776.

*The year after fighting began between American colonists and the British army, the Continental Congress voted for independence on July 2, 1776, and approved the Declaration of Independence two days later, on July 4.*

the Declaration was remarkable for its assertion that certain rights—the "unalienable rights" that include life, liberty, and the pursuit of happiness—could not be abridged by governments. In the world of 1776, a world in which some kings still claimed to rule by divine right, this was a dramatic statement. In political terms, the Declaration was remarkable because, despite the differences of interest that divided the colonists along economic, regional, and philosophical lines, it identified and focused on grievances, aspirations, and principles that might unify the various colonial groups. The Declaration was an attempt to identify and articulate a history and set of principles that might help forge national unity.[5]

## The Articles of Confederation

Having declared their independence, the colonies needed to establish a governmental structure. In November 1777 the Continental Congress adopted the **Articles of Confederation**—the United States' first written constitution. Although it was not ratified by all the states until 1781, it was the country's operative constitution for almost 12 years, until March 1789.

The first goal of the Articles had been to limit the powers of the central government. The relationship between the national government and the states was called a **confederation**; as provided under Article II, "each state retains its sovereignty, freedom, and independence," much like the contemporary relationship between the United Nations and its member states. The central government was given no president or any other presiding officer. The entire national government was vested in a Congress, with execution of its few laws to be left to the individual states. And the Articles gave Congress very little power to exercise. Its members were not much more than delegates or messengers from the state legislatures: their salaries were paid out of the state treasuries; they were subject to immediate recall by state

**Articles of Confederation**
America's first written constitution; served as the basis for America's national government until 1789

**confederation** a system of government in which states retain sovereign authority except for the powers expressly delegated to the national government authorities; and each state, regardless of its size, had only one vote. All 13 states had to agree to any amendments to the Articles.

Under the Articles of Confederation, Congress was given the power to declare war and make peace, to make treaties and alliances, to coin or borrow money, and to regulate trade with the Native Americans. It could also appoint the senior officers of the U.S. Army, but the national government had no army for those officers to command, because the nation's armed forces were composed of the state militias. Moreover, the central government could not prevent one state from discriminating against other states in the competition for foreign commerce. These extreme limits on the power of the national government made the Articles of Confederation hopelessly impractical.[6]

# The Second Founding: From Compromise to Constitution

> **Explain how the Constitution attempted to improve America's governance**

The Declaration of Independence and the Articles of Confederation were not sufficient to hold the new nation together as an independent and effective nation-state. A series of developments following the armistice with the British in 1783 highlighted the shortcomings of the Articles of Confederation.

## International Standing and Balance of Power

There was a special concern for the country's international position. Competition among the states for foreign commerce allowed the European powers to play the states off one another, which created confusion on both sides of the Atlantic. At one point during the winter of 1786–87, John Adams of Massachusetts, a leader in the independence struggle, was sent to negotiate a new treaty with the British, one that would cover disputes left over from the war. The British government responded that since the United States under the Articles of Confederation was unable to enforce existing treaties, it would negotiate with each of the 13 states separately.

At the same time, the United States faced a threat from Spain, which still held vast territories in North and South America. Well-to-do Americans—in particular the New England merchants and southern planters—were especially troubled by the influence that "radical" forces exercised in the Continental Congress and in the governments of several of the states. The colonists' victory in the Revolutionary War had not only ended British rule but also significantly changed the balance of political power within the new states. As a result of the Revolution, one key segment of the colonial elite—the royal land, office, and patent holders—was stripped of its economic and political privileges. In fact, many of these individuals, along with tens of thousands of other colonists who considered themselves loyal British subjects, left for Canada after the British surrender. And although the prerevolutionary elite was weakened, the prerevolutionary radicals were better organized than ever and now controlled such states as Pennsylvania and Rhode Island, where they pursued economic and political policies that struck terror in the hearts of the prerevolutionary political establishment. In Rhode Island, for example, between 1783 and 1785, a legislature dominated by representatives of small farmers, artisans, and shopkeepers had instituted economic policies, including drastic currency inflation, that frightened business and property owners throughout the country. Of course, the central government under the Articles of Confederation was powerless to intervene. Similarly, the Pennsylvania government engaged in land redistribution, to the chagrin of property owners.

## The Annapolis Convention

The continuation of international weakness and domestic economic turmoil led many Americans to consider whether their newly adopted form of government might not already require revision. In the fall of 1786, many state leaders accepted an invitation from the Virginia legislature for a conference of representatives of all the states, to be held in Annapolis, Maryland. Delegates from only five states actually attended, so nothing substantive could be accomplished. Still, this conference was the first step toward what is now known as the second founding. The one positive thing that came out of the Annapolis Convention was a carefully worded resolution calling on the Congress to send commissioners to Philadelphia at a later time "to devise such further provisions as shall appear to them necessary to render the Constitution of the Federal Government adequate to the exigencies of the Union."[7] But the resolution did not necessarily imply any desire to do more than improve and reform the Articles of Confederation.

## Shays's Rebellion

*In the winter of 1787, Daniel Shays led a makeshift army against the federal arsenal at Springfield to protest heavy taxes levied by the Massachusetts legislature. The rebellion proved the Articles of Confederation too weak to protect the fledgling nation.*

It is quite possible that the Constitutional Convention of 1787 in Philadelphia would never have taken place at all except for a single event that occurred during the winter following the Annapolis Convention: Shays's Rebellion.

Daniel Shays, a former army captain, led a mob of farmers in a rebellion against the government of Massachusetts. The purpose of the rebellion was to prevent foreclosures on their debt-ridden land by keeping the county courts of western Massachusetts from sitting until after the next election. The state militia dispersed the mob, but for several days in February 1787, Shays and his followers terrified the state government by attempting to capture the federal arsenal at Springfield, provoking an appeal to the Congress to help restore order. Within a few days, the state government regained control and captured 14 of the rebels. Later that year, a newly elected Massachusetts legislature granted some of the farmers' demands.

The effects of the incident lingered and spread. Washington summed it up: "I am mortified beyond expression that in the moment of our acknowledged independence we should by our conduct verify the predictions of our transatlantic foe, and render ourselves ridiculous and contemptible in the eyes of all Europe."[8]

The Congress under the Confederation had been unable to act decisively in a time of crisis. This provided critics of the Articles of Confederation with precisely the evidence they needed to push the Annapolis resolution through the Congress. Thus, the states were asked to send representatives to Philadelphia to discuss constitutional revision. Seventy-four delegates were chosen. Of these, 55 would actually attend the convention, representing every state except Rhode Island, and 39 would eventually sign the newly drafted Constitution.

# The Constitutional Convention

The delegates who convened in Philadelphia in May 1787 had political strife, international embarrassment, national weakness, and local rebellion fixed in their minds. Recognizing that these issues were symptoms of fundamental flaws in the Articles of Confederation, the delegates soon abandoned the plan to revise the Articles and committed themselves to a second founding—a second, and ultimately successful, attempt to create a legitimate and effective national system of government. This effort would occupy the convention for the next five months.

**A Marriage of Interest and Principle** For years, scholars have disagreed about the motives of the Founders in Philadelphia. Among the most controversial views of the framers' motives is the "economic interpretation" put forward by the historian Charles Beard and his disciples.[9] According to Beard's account, America's Founders were a collection of securities speculators and property owners whose only aim was personal enrichment. From this perspective, the Constitution's lofty principles were little more than sophisticated masks behind which the most venal interests sought to enrich themselves.

Contrary to Beard's approach is the view that the framers of the Constitution *were* concerned with philosophical and ethical principles. Indeed, they sought to devise a system of government consistent with the dominant philosophical and moral principles of the day. But in fact, these two views belong together; the Founders' interests were reinforced by their principles. The convention that drafted the American Constitution was chiefly organized by the New England merchants and southern planters. Although the delegates representing these groups did not all hope to profit personally from an increase in the value of their securities, as Beard would have it, they did hope to benefit in the broadest political and economic sense by breaking the power of their radical foes and establishing a system of government more compatible with their long-term economic and political interests. Thus, the framers sought to create a new government capable of promoting commerce and protecting property from radical state legislatures and populist forces hostile to the interests of the commercial and propertied classes.

**The Great Compromise** The proponents of a new government fired their opening shot on May 29, 1787, when Edmund Randolph of Virginia offered a resolution that proposed corrections and enlargements in the Articles of Confederation. The proposal was no simple motion but instead provided for virtually every aspect of a new government.

The portion of Randolph's motion that became most controversial was called the **Virginia Plan**. This plan provided for a system of representation in the national legislature based on the population of each state or the proportion of each state's revenue contribution to the national government, or both. (Randolph also proposed a second chamber of the legislature, to be elected by the members of the first chamber.) Since the states varied enormously in size and wealth, the Virginia Plan was thought to be heavily biased in favor of the large states.

While the convention was debating the Virginia Plan, opposition to it began to mount as more delegates arrived in Philadelphia. William Paterson of New Jersey introduced a resolution known as the **New Jersey Plan**. Its main proponents were delegates from the less-populous states, including Delaware, New Jersey, Connecticut, and New York, who asserted that the more populous states—Virginia, Pennsylvania, North Carolina, Massachusetts, and Georgia—would dominate the

**Virginia Plan** a framework for the Constitution, introduced by Edmund Randolph, that called for representation in the national legislature based on the population of each state

**New Jersey Plan** a framework for the Constitution, introduced by William Paterson, that called for equal state representation in the national legislature regardless of population

*When the framers of the Constitution met in 1787, they set out to establish a political system that would protect liberty and place limits on government. They also believed that a powerful government required a broad popular base. However, they debated how best to protect liberty and how to balance democracy with other concerns.*

new government if representation were to be determined by population. The smaller states argued that each state should be equally represented in the new regime regardless of that state's population.

The issue of representation threatened to wreck the entire constitutional enterprise. Delegates conferred, factions maneuvered, and tempers flared. James Wilson of Pennsylvania told the small-state delegates that if they wanted to disrupt the union, they should go ahead. The separation, he said, could "never happen on better grounds." Small-state delegates were equally blunt. Gunning Bedford of Delaware declared that the small states might, if forced, look elsewhere for friends. "The large states," he said, "dare not dissolve the confederation. If they do the small ones will find some foreign ally of more honor and good faith, who will take them by the hand and do them justice." These sentiments were widely shared. The union, as Oliver Ellsworth of Connecticut put it, was "on the verge of dissolution, scarcely held together by the strength of a hair."

The outcome of this debate was the Connecticut Compromise, also known as the **Great Compromise**. Under the terms of this compromise, in the first chamber of Congress—the House of Representatives—the representatives would be apportioned according to the population in each state. This, of course, was what delegates from the large states had sought. But in the second branch—the Senate—each state would have equal representation regardless of its size; this provision addressed the concerns of small states. This compromise was not immediately satisfactory to all the delegates. Indeed, two of the most vocal members of the small-state faction, John Lansing and Robert Yates of New York, were so incensed by the concession that their colleagues had made to the large-state forces that they stormed out of the convention. In the end, however, most of the delegates preferred compromise to the breakup of the Union, and the plan was accepted.

**The Question of Slavery: The Three-Fifths Compromise** Many of the conflicts that emerged during the Constitutional Convention were reflections of the fundamental differences between the slave and the nonslave states—differences that

**Great Compromise** the agreement reached at the Constitutional Convention of 1787 that gave each state an equal number of senators regardless of its population, but linked representation in the House of Representatives to population

# Who Benefits from the Great Compromise?

The Great Compromise attempted to balance power between large and small states in the new Congress. The charts show the difference in representation for states in the House and Senate in the first Congress (1789–91). In the Senate each state has equal representation, which in the first Congress meant each had 1/13 of all seats. In the House the number of seats apportioned to each state is based on population; thus, the larger states have more representation.

## Representation in the First Congress

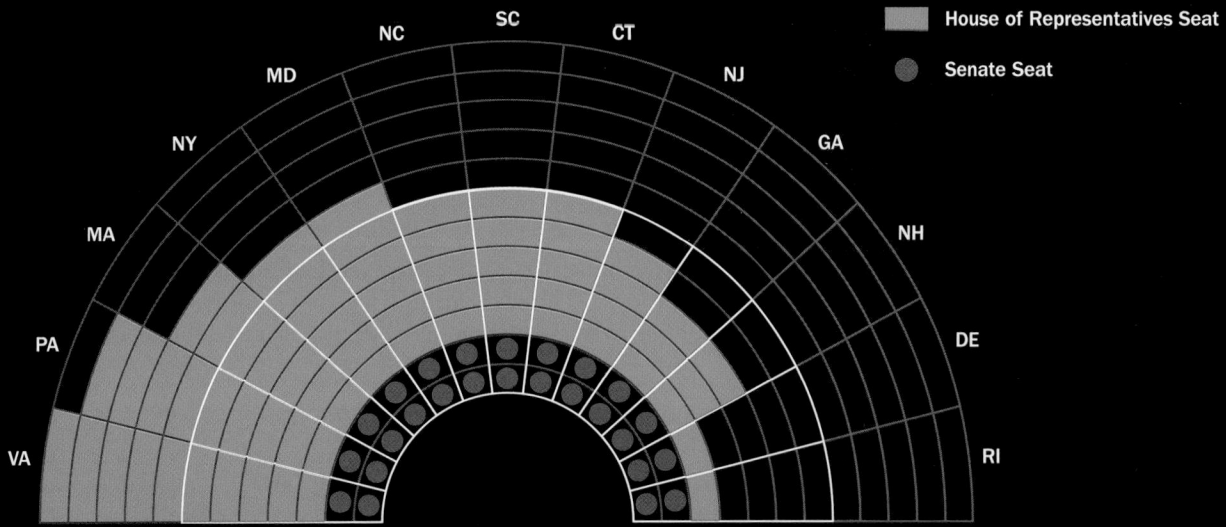

House of Representatives Seat

Senate Seat

## State Populations, 1790*

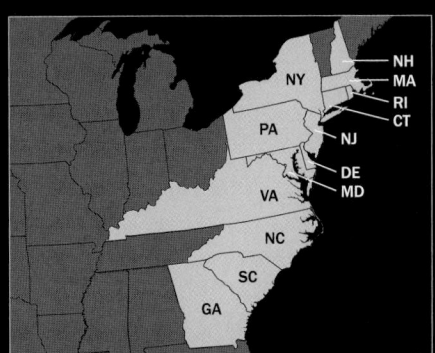

| | | |
|---|---|---:|
| 1. | Virginia | 747,610 |
| 2. | Pennsylvania | 433,373 |
| 3. | Massachusetts | 378,787 |
| 4. | New York | 340,120 |
| 5. | Maryland | 319,728 |
| 6. | North Carolina | 393,751 |
| 7. | South Carolina | 249,073 |
| 8. | Connecticut | 237,946 |
| 9. | New Jersey | 184,139 |
| 10. | Georgia | 82,548 |
| 11. | New Hampshire | 141,885 |
| 12. | Delaware | 59,096 |
| 13. | Rhode Island | 68,825 |

* The framers calculated the number of representatives per state in 1787 using population estimates. The first census was not taken until 1790. Total state population includes slave population. Slaves were counted as 3/5 of a person for purposes of apportioning seats in the House.

SOURCE: U.S. Census Bureau, www.census.gov (accessed 8/16/12).

## for critical analysis

1. At the Constitutional Convention, large states supported the Virginia Plan, which would have made the whole Congress look like the House. Small states supported the New Jersey Plan, which would have made the whole Congress look like the Senate. How would each group have benefited from its favored plans?

2. What are the advantages of equal representation by states? What are the drawbacks? In your opinion, do the advantages outweigh the disadvantages?

pitted the southern planters and New England merchants against one another and would almost destroy the Republic in later years. In the midst of debate over large versus small states, James Madison observed,

> The great danger to our general government is the great southern and northern interests of the continent, being opposed to each other. Look to the votes in Congress, and most of them stand divided by the geography of the country, not according to the size of the states.[10]

More than 90 percent of the country's slaves resided in five states—Georgia, Maryland, North Carolina, South Carolina, and Virginia—where they accounted for 30 percent of the total population. In some places, slaves outnumbered nonslaves by as much as 10 to 1. If the Constitution were to embody any principle of national supremacy, some basic decisions would have to be made about the place of slavery in the general scheme. Madison hit on this point on several occasions as different aspects of the Constitution were being discussed. For example, he observed,

> It seemed now to be pretty well understood that the real difference of interests lay, not between the large and small but between the northern and southern states. The institution of slavery and its consequences formed the line of discrimination. There were five states on the South, eight on the northern side of this line. Should a proportional representation take place it was true, the northern side would still outnumber the other: but not in the same degree, at this time; and every day would tend towards an equilibrium.[11]

**Three-Fifths Compromise**
the agreement reached at the Constitutional Convention of 1787 that stipulated that for purposes of the apportionment of congressional seats, every slave would be counted as three-fifths of a person

Northerners and southerners eventually reached agreement through the **Three-Fifths Compromise.** The seats in the House of Representatives would be apportioned according to a "population" in which five slaves would count as three

*Despite the Founders' emphasis on liberty, the new Constitution allowed slavery, counting each slave as three-fifths of a person in apportioning seats in the House of Representatives. In this 1792 painting,* Liberty Displaying the Arts and Sciences, *the books, instruments, and classical columns at the left contrast with the kneeling slaves at the right— illustrating the divide between America's rhetoric of liberty and equality and the realities of slavery.*

free persons. The slaves would not be allowed to vote, of course, but the number of representatives would be apportioned accordingly.

The issue of slavery was the most difficult one faced by the framers, and it nearly destroyed the Union. Although some delegates believed slavery to be morally wrong, an evil and oppressive institution that made a mockery of the ideals and values espoused in the Constitution, morality was not the issue that caused the framers to support or oppose the Three-Fifths Compromise. Whatever they thought of the institution of slavery, most delegates from the northern states opposed counting slaves in the distribution of congressional seats. Wilson of Pennsylvania, for example, argued that if slaves were citizens, they should be treated and counted like other citizens. If, on the other hand, they were property, then why should not other forms of property be counted toward the apportionment of representatives? But southern delegates made it clear that they would never agree to the new government if the northerners refused to give in. William R. Davie of North Carolina heatedly said that it was time "to speak out." He asserted that the people of North Carolina would never enter the Union if slaves were not counted as part of the basis for representation. Without such agreement, he asserted ominously, "the business was at an end." Even southerners such as Edmund Randolph of Virginia, who conceded that slavery was immoral, insisted on including slaves in the allocation of congressional seats. Pierce Butler of South Carolina declared that the North and South were as different as Russia and Turkey. Eventually, the North and South compromised on the issue of slavery and representation. Indeed, northerners even agreed to permit a continuation of the odious slave trade in order to keep the South in the Union. But in due course, Butler proved to be correct, and a bloody war resulted when the disparate interests of the North and the South could no longer be reconciled.

## ● The Constitution

**Outline the major institutions and rules established by the Constitution**

The political significance of the Great Compromise and the Three-Fifths Compromise was to reinforce the unity of the mercantile and planter forces that sought to create a new government. The Great Compromise reassured those who feared that a new governmental framework would reduce the importance of their own local or regional influence. The Three-Fifths Compromise temporarily defused the rivalry between the merchants and planters. Their unity secured, members of the alliance supporting the establishment of a new government moved to fashion a constitutional framework consistent with their economic and political interests.

In particular, the framers sought a new government that, first, would be strong enough to promote commerce and protect property from radical state legislatures such as Rhode Island's. This became the constitutional basis for national control over commerce and finance, and for the establishment of national judicial supremacy and the effort to construct a strong presidency. Second, the framers sought to prevent what they saw as the threat posed by the "excessive democracy" of the state and national governments under the Articles of Confederation. This led to such constitutional principles as bicameralism (division of the Congress into two chambers), **checks and balances**, staggered terms in office, and indirect election

**checks and balances**
mechanisms through which each branch of government is able to participate in and influence the activities of the other branches; major examples include the presidential veto power over congressional legislation, the power of the Senate to approve presidential appointments, and judicial review of congressional enactments

## TABLE 2.1

## The Seven Articles of the Constitution

1. The Legislative Branch
   House: two-year terms, elected directly by the people.
   Senate: six-year terms (staggered so that only one-third of the Senate changes in any given election), appointed by state legislature (changed in 1913 to direct election).
   Expressed powers of the national government: collecting taxes, borrowing money, regulating commerce, declaring war, and maintaining an army and a navy; all other power belongs to the states, unless deemed otherwise by the elastic (necessary and proper) clause.
   Exclusive powers of the national government: states are expressly forbidden to issue their own paper money, tax imports and exports, regulate trade outside their own borders, and impair the obligation of contracts; these powers are the exclusive domain of the national government.

2. The Executive Branch
   Presidency: four-year terms (limited in 1951 to a maximum of two terms), elected indirectly by the electoral college.
   Powers: can recognize other countries, negotiate treaties, grant reprieves and pardons, convene Congress in special sessions, and veto congressional enactment.

3. The Judicial Branch
   Supreme Court: lifetime terms, appointed by the president with the approval of the Senate.
   Powers: include resolving conflicts between federal and state laws, determining whether power belongs to the national government or the states, and settling controversies between citizens of different states.

4. National Unity and Power
   Reciprocity among states: establishes that each state must give "full faith and credit" to official acts of other states and guarantees citizens of any state the "privileges and immunities" of every other state.

5. Amending the Constitution
   Procedure: requires approval by two-thirds of Congress and adoption by three-fourths of the states.

6. National Supremacy
   The Constitution and national law are the supreme law of the land and cannot be overruled by state law.

7. Ratification
   The Constitution became effective when approved by nine states.

**electoral college** the presidential electors from each state who meet after the popular election to cast ballots for president and vice president

**Bill of Rights** the first 10 amendments to the U.S. Constitution, ratified in 1791; they ensure certain rights and liberties to the people

**separation of powers** the division of governmental power among several institutions that must cooperate in decision making

**federalism** a system of government in which power is divided, by a constitution, between a central government and regional governments

(selection of the president by an **electoral college** rather than directly by voters and election of senators by state legislatures). Third, the framers, lacking the power to force the states or the public at large to accept the new form of government, sought to identify principles that would help secure support. This became the basis of the constitutional provision for direct popular election of representatives and, subsequently, for the addition of the **Bill of Rights** to the Constitution. Finally, the framers wanted to be certain that the government they created did not pose an even greater threat to its citizens' liberties and property rights than did the radical state legislatures they feared and despised. To prevent the new government from abusing its power, the framers incorporated principles such as the **separation of powers** and **federalism** into the Constitution. Let us assess the major provisions of the Constitution's seven articles (listed in Table 2.1) to see how each relates to these objectives.

## The Legislative Branch

In Article I, Sections 1–7, the Constitution provided for a Congress consisting of two chambers: a House of Representatives and a Senate. Members of the House of Representatives were given two-year terms in office and were to be elected directly by the people. Members of the Senate were to be appointed by the state legislatures (this was changed in 1913 by the Seventeenth Amendment, which instituted direct election of senators) for six-year terms. These terms were staggered so that the appointments of one-third of the senators would expire every two years. The Constitution assigned somewhat different tasks to the House and Senate. Though the approval of each body was required for the enactment of a law, the Senate alone was given the power to ratify treaties and approve presidential appointments. The House, on the other hand, was given the sole power to originate revenue bills.

The character of the legislative branch was directly related to the framers' major goals. The House of Representatives was designed to be directly responsible to the people in order to encourage popular consent for the new Constitution and to help enhance the power of the new government. At the same time, to guard against "excessive democracy," the power of the House of Representatives was checked by the Senate, whose members were to be appointed by the states for long terms rather than elected directly by the people. The purpose of this provision, according to Alexander Hamilton, was to avoid "an unqualified complaisance to every sudden breeze of passion, or to every transient impulse which the people may receive."[12] Staggered terms of service in the Senate, moreover, were intended to make that body even more resistant to popular pressure. Since only one-third of the senators would be selected at any given time, the composition of the institution would be protected from changes in popular preferences transmitted by the state legislatures. This would prevent what James Madison called "mutability in the public councils arising from a rapid succession of new members."[13] Thus, the structure of the legislative branch was designed to contribute to governmental power, to promote popular consent for the new government, and at the same time to place limits on the popular political currents that many of the framers saw as a radical threat to the economic and social order.

*Article I of the Constitution establishes the structure of Congress and lists certain specific powers of Congress. The language of the Constitution reflects the framers' desire to create a government that was powerful enough to be effective but not so powerful that it would threaten individual liberty.*

The issues of power and consent were important throughout the Constitution. Section 8 of Article I specifically listed the powers of Congress, which include the authority to collect taxes, borrow money, regulate commerce, declare war, and maintain an army and navy. By granting Congress these powers, the framers indicated very clearly that they intended the new government to be far more influential than its predecessor. At the same time, by defining the new government's most important powers as belonging to Congress, the framers sought to promote popular acceptance of this critical change by reassuring citizens that their views would be fully represented whenever the government exercised its new powers.

As a further guarantee to the people that the new government would pose no threat to them, the Constitution implied that any powers not listed were not granted at all. This is the doctrine of **expressed powers**: the Constitution grants only those powers specifically expressed in its text. But the framers intended to create an active and powerful government, and so they included the necessary and proper clause, sometimes known as the **elastic clause**, which signified that the enumerated powers were meant to be a source of strength to the national government, not a limitation on it. In response to the charge that they intended to give the national government too much power, the framers included language in the Tenth Amendment stipulating that powers not specifically granted by the Constitution to the federal government were reserved to the states or to the people. As we will see in Chapter 3, the resulting tension between the elastic clause and the Tenth Amendment has been at the heart of constitutional struggles between federal and state powers.

**expressed powers** specific powers granted by the Constitution to Congress (Article I, Section 8) and to the president (Article II)

**elastic clause** Article I, Section 8, of the Constitution (also known as the necessary and proper clause), which enumerates the powers of Congress and provides Congress with the authority to make all laws "necessary and proper" to carry them out

THE CONSTITUTIONAL CONVENTION · 1787

*According to Alexander Hamilton (left), the Constitution aimed toward "energy in the Executive." The framers wanted the president to be capable of timely and decisive action. This painting depicts Hamilton, James Wilson, James Madison, and Benjamin Franklin meeting in Franklin's garden.*

**bicameral** having a legislative assembly composed of two chambers or houses; distinguished from *unicameral*

**for critical analysis**

The framers sought to create an "energetic" presidency, but some observers believe that the presidency has become too powerful. Has the presidency become too powerful?

## The Executive Branch

The Constitution provided for the establishment of the presidency in Article II. As Alexander Hamilton commented, the presidential article aimed toward "energy in the Executive." It did so in an effort to overcome the natural tendency toward stalemate that was built into the **bicameral** legislature and into the separation of powers among the three branches. The Constitution afforded the president a measure of independence from the people and from the other branches of government—particularly the Congress.

In line with the framers' goal of increased power to the national government, the president was granted the unconditional power to accept ambassadors from other countries; this amounted to the power to "recognize" other countries. The president was also given the power to negotiate treaties, although their acceptance required the approval of the Senate by a two-thirds vote. The president was given the unconditional right to grant reprieves and pardons, except in cases of impeachment. And the president was provided with the power to appoint major departmental personnel, convene Congress in special session, and veto congressional enactments. (The veto power is formidable, but it is not absolute, since Congress can override it by a two-thirds vote.)

The framers hoped to create a presidency that would make the federal government rather than the states the agency capable of timely and decisive action to deal with public issues and problems—hence the "energy" that Hamilton hoped to impart to the executive branch.[14] At the same time, however, the framers sought to help the presidency withstand excessively democratic pressures by creating a system of indirect rather than direct election through a separate electoral college.

# The Judicial Branch

In establishing the judicial branch in Article III, the Constitution reflected the framers' preoccupations with nationalizing governmental power and checking radical democratic impulses while preventing the new national government itself from interfering with liberty and property.

Under the provisions of Article III, the framers created a court that was literally a supreme court of the United States, and not merely the highest court of the national government alone. The most important expression of this intention was granting the Supreme Court the power to resolve any conflicts that might emerge between federal and state laws. In particular, the Supreme Court was given the right to determine whether a power was exclusive to the national government, concurrent with the states, or exclusive to the states. In addition, the Supreme Court was assigned jurisdiction over controversies between citizens of different states. The long-term significance of this provision was that as the country developed a national economy, it came to rely increasingly on the federal judiciary, rather than on the state courts, for the resolution of disputes.

Judges were given lifetime appointments to protect them from popular politics and from interference by the other branches. This, however, did not mean that the judiciary would remain totally impartial to political considerations or to the other branches, for the president was to appoint the judges, and the Senate to approve the appointments. Congress would also have the power to create inferior (lower) courts, change the jurisdiction of the federal courts, add or subtract federal judges, and even change the size of the Supreme Court.

No explicit mention is made in the Constitution of **judicial review**—the power of the courts to render the final decision when there is a conflict of interpretation of the Constitution or of laws between the courts and Congress, the courts and the executive branch, or the courts and the states. The Supreme Court eventually assumed the power of judicial review. Its assumption of this power, as we shall see in Chapter 15, was based not on the Constitution itself but on the politics of later decades and the membership of the Court.

**judicial review** the power of the courts to review and, if necessary, declare actions of the legislative and executive branches invalid or unconstitutional; the Supreme Court asserted this power in *Marbury v. Madison*

# National Unity and Power

Various provisions in the Constitution addressed the framers' concern with national unity and power, including Article IV's provisions for comity (reciprocity) among states and among citizens of all states. Each state was prohibited from discriminating against the citizens of other states in favor of its own citizens. The Supreme Court was charged with deciding in each case whether a state had discriminated against goods or people from another state. The Constitution restricted the power of the states in favor of ensuring enough power to the national government to give the country a free-flowing national economy.

The framers' concern with national supremacy was also expressed in Article VI, in the **supremacy clause**, which provided that national laws and treaties "shall be the supreme Law of the Land." This meant that all laws made under the "Authority of the United States" would be superior to all laws adopted by any state or any other subdivision, and the states would be expected to respect all treaties made under that authority. The supremacy clause also bound the officials of all governments— state and local as well as federal—to take an oath of office to support the national Constitution. This meant that every action taken by the U.S. Congress would have to be applied within each state as though the action were in fact state law.

**supremacy clause** Article VI of the Constitution, which states that laws passed by the national government and all treaties are the supreme law of the land and superior to all laws adopted by any state or any subdivision

## Amending the Constitution

The Constitution established procedures for its own revision in Article V. Its provisions are so difficult that Americans have successfully availed themselves of the amending process only 17 times since 1791, when the first 10 amendments were adopted. Many other amendments have been proposed in Congress, but fewer than 40 of them have even come close to fulfilling the Constitution's requirement of a two-thirds vote in Congress, and only a fraction have gotten anywhere near adoption by three-fourths of the states. Article V also provides that the Constitution can be amended by a constitutional convention. Occasionally, proponents of particular measures, such as a balanced-budget amendment, have called for a constitutional convention to consider their proposals. Whatever the purpose for which it were called, however, such a convention would presumably have the authority to revise America's entire system of government.

## Ratifying the Constitution

The rules for the ratification of the Constitution were set forth in Article VII. Nine of the 13 states would have to ratify, or agree on, the terms in order for the Constitution to be formally adopted.

## Constitutional Limits on the National Government's Power

Although the framers sought to create a powerful national government, they also wanted to guard against possible misuse of that power. To that end, the framers incorporated two key principles into the Constitution—federalism and the separation of powers. A third set of limitations, in the form of the Bill of Rights, was added to the Constitution to help secure its ratification when opponents of the document charged that it paid insufficient attention to citizens' rights.

**The Separation of Powers**  No principle of politics was more widely shared at the time of the 1787 Founding than the principle that power must be used to balance power. The French political theorist Baron de la Brède et de Montesquieu (1689–1755) believed that this balance was an indispensable defense against tyranny. His writings, especially his major work, *The Spirit of the Laws*, "were taken as political gospel" at the Philadelphia Convention.[15] Although the principle of the separation of powers was not explicitly stated in the Constitution, the entire structure of the national government was built precisely on Article I, the legislature; Article II, the executive; and Article III, the judiciary (see Figure 2.1).

However, separation of powers is nothing but mere words on parchment without a method to maintain that separation. The method became known by the popular label "checks and balances" (see Figure 2.2). Each branch is given not only its own powers but also some power over the other two branches. Among the most familiar checks and balances are the president's veto as power over Congress and Congress's power over the president through its control of appointments to high executive posts and to the judiciary. Congress also has power over the president with its control of appropriations and (by the Senate) the right of approval of treaties. The judiciary was assumed to have the power of judicial review over the other two branches.

Another important feature of the separation of powers is the principle of giving each of the branches a distinctly different constituency. Theorists such as Montes-

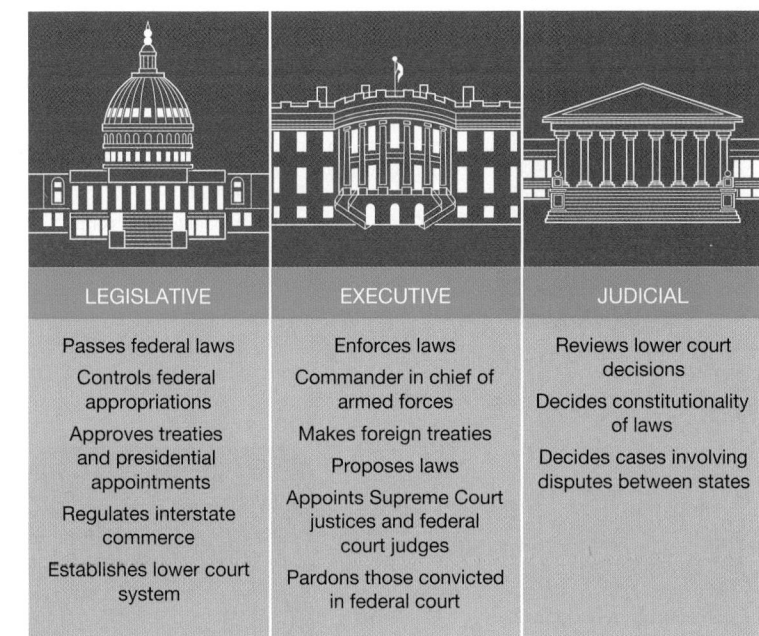

FIGURE 2.1
The Separation of Powers

| LEGISLATIVE | EXECUTIVE | JUDICIAL |
| --- | --- | --- |
| Passes federal laws | Enforces laws | Reviews lower court decisions |
| Controls federal appropriations | Commander in chief of armed forces | Decides constitutionality of laws |
| Approves treaties and presidential appointments | Makes foreign treaties | Decides cases involving disputes between states |
| Regulates interstate commerce | Proposes laws | |
| Establishes lower court system | Appoints Supreme Court justices and federal court judges | |
| | Pardons those convicted in federal court | |

quieu called this a "mixed regime," with the president chosen, indirectly, by electors; the House, by popular vote; the Senate (originally), by state legislatures; and the judiciary, by presidential appointment. By these means, the occupants of each branch would tend to develop very different outlooks on how to govern, different definitions of the public interest, and different alliances with private interests.

**Federalism** Compared with the confederation principle of the Articles of Confederation, federalism was a step toward greater centralization of power. The delegates agreed that they needed to place more power at the national level, without completely undermining the power of the state governments. Thus, they devised a system of two sovereigns—the states and the nation—with the hope that competition between the two would be an effective limitation on the power of both.

**The Bill of Rights** Late in the Philadelphia Convention, a motion was made to include a list of citizens' rights in the Constitution. After a brief debate in which hardly a word was said in its favor and only one speech was made against it, the motion was almost unanimously turned down. Most delegates sincerely believed that since the federal government was already limited to its expressed powers, further protection of citizens was not needed. The delegates argued that the states should adopt bills of rights because their greater powers needed greater limitations. But almost immediately after the Constitution was ratified, a movement arose to adopt a national bill of rights. This is why the Bill of Rights, adopted in 1791, comprises the first 10 amendments to the Constitution rather than being part of the body of it. (We will have a good deal more to say about the Bill of Rights in Chapter 4.)

Executive over Legislative

Can veto acts of Congress

Can call Congress into a special session

Carries out, and thereby interprets, laws passed by Congress

Vice president casts tie-breaking vote in the Senate

LEGISLATIVE

Legislative over Judicial

Can change size of federal court system and the number of Supreme Court justices

Can propose constitutional amendments

Can reject Supreme Court nominees

Can impeach and remove federal judges

Legislative over Executive

Can override presidential veto

Can impeach and remove president

Can reject president's appointments and refuse to ratify treaties

Can conduct investigations into president's actions

Can refuse to pass laws or to provide funding that president requests

Judicial over Legislative

Can declare laws unconstitutional

Chief justice presides over Senate during hearing to impeach the president

JUDICIAL

Executive over Judicial

Nominates Supreme Court justices

Nominates federal judges

Can pardon those convicted in federal court

Can refuse to enforce Court decisions

Judicial over Executive

Can declare executive actions unconstitutional

Power to issue warrants

Chief justice presides over impeachment of president

EXECUTIVE

**FIGURE 2.2**
Checks and Balances

# ● The Fight for Ratification

**Federalists** those who favored a strong national government and supported the Constitution proposed at the American Constitutional Convention of 1787

**Antifederalists** those who favored strong state governments and a weak national government and who were opponents of the Constitution proposed at the American Constitutional Convention of 1787

**Present the controversies involved in the struggle for ratification**

The first hurdle faced by the Constitution was ratification by state conventions of delegates elected by the people of each state. This struggle for ratification was carried out in 13 separate campaigns. Each involved different people, moved at a different pace, and was influenced by local and national considerations. Two sides faced off throughout the states, however, calling themselves **Federalists** and **Antifederalists** (see Table 2.2). The Federalists (who more accurately should have called themselves "Nationalists," but who took their name to appear to follow in the revolutionary tradition) supported the Constitution and preferred a strong national government.

**TABLE 2.2**

## Federalists versus Antifederalists

| | FEDERALISTS | ANTIFEDERALISTS |
| --- | --- | --- |
| Who were they? | Property owners, creditors, merchants | Small farmers, frontiersmen, debtors, shopkeepers, some state government officials |
| What did they believe? | Believed that elites were most fit to govern; feared "excessive democracy" | Believed that government should be closer to the people; feared concentration of power in hands of the elites |
| What system of government did they favor? | Favored strong national government; believed in "filtration" so that only elites would obtain governmental power | Favored retention of power by state governments and protection of individual rights |
| Who were their leaders? | Alexander Hamilton, James Madison, George Washington | Patrick Henry, George Mason, Elbridge Gerry, George Clinton |

The Antifederalists opposed the Constitution and preferred a federal system of government that was decentralized; they took their name by default, in reaction to their better-organized opponents. The Federalists were united in their support of the Constitution, whereas the Antifederalists were divided over possible alternatives to the Constitution.

During the struggle over ratification of the Constitution, Americans argued about great political issues and principles. How much power should the national government be given? What safeguards would most likely prevent the abuse of power? What institutional arrangements could best ensure adequate representation for all Americans? Was tyranny of the many to be feared more than tyranny of the few?

## Federalists versus Antifederalists

During the ratification struggle, thousands of essays, speeches, pamphlets, and letters were presented in support of and in opposition to the proposed Constitution. The best-known pieces supporting ratification were the 85 essays written between the fall of 1787 and the spring of 1788 under the name of "Publius," by Alexander Hamilton, James Madison, and John Jay. These *Federalist Papers*, as they are collectively known today, defended the principles of the Constitution and sought to dispel fears of a national authority. The Antifederalists published essays of their own, arguing that the new Constitution betrayed the Revolution and was a step toward monarchy. Among the best of the Antifederalist works were the essays, usually attributed to the New York State Supreme Court justice Robert Yates, that were written under the name of "Brutus" and published in the *New York Journal* at the same time the *Federalist Papers* appeared. The Antifederalist view was also ably presented in the pamphlets and letters written by a former delegate to the Continental Congress and future U.S. senator, Richard Henry Lee of Virginia, using the pen name "The Federal Farmer." These essays highlight the major differences of opinion between Federalists and Antifederalists. Federalists appealed to basic

*Federalist Papers* a series of essays written by Alexander Hamilton, James Madison, and John Jay supporting ratification of the Constitution

# The American Constitution: A Model for the World?

**The U.S. Constitution is often said** to be both the world's oldest written constitution and a continuing model for the nations of the world. These assertions are *partly* accurate. Nearly two millennia before the delegates to America's Constitutional Convention met in Philadelphia, Greek city-states produced written constitutions.[a] And closer to home, all the first American states possessed written constitutions. Nevertheless, it might be said that the U.S. Constitution is the world's oldest written document that formally organizes the governmental processes of an entire nation.

As to the second assertion, the U.S. Constitution has indeed frequently been a model for others, but other nations' constitution writers often consciously sought to avoid rather than imitate American-style institutions and practices. One important American idea that has been widely copied is that of having a written constitution. After America wrote its constitution in 1789, both Poland and France adopted written constitutions in 1791. The French became so enamored of constitution writing that they put forth four different constitutions during the 1790s alone, as successive revolutionary

governments seized power.[b] As revolutions swept Europe during the nineteenth and early twentieth centuries, every new government viewed a written constitution both as an important legitimating instrument and as a declaration that the new regime categorically rejected the despotic and arbitrary practices of its predecessor. Today, virtually all the world's democracies have written constitutions. Britain, Israel, and New Zealand remain important exceptions.[c] Ironically, possession of a written constitution has become such an important attribute of political legitimacy and a symbol of freedom that even some despotic regimes have sham constitutions to provide the appearance, albeit not the substance, of popular government. For example, the former Soviet Union often boasted that it possessed the world's most democratic constitution.

Among the world's constitutional democracies, some have copied elements of the U.S. Constitution, but most have chosen patterns of government quite different from the American model. Judicial review of statutes, an American politi-

cal innovation, has been adopted by most democracies. In a number of instances, too, new constitutions have incorporated the principle of federalism to deal with the problem of ethnic or regional divisions. For example, with American encouragement, both Iraq and Afghanistan have made federalism an important principle in their new constitutional documents. However, it remains to be seen if these constitutions will survive after American troops leave those countries. Few democracies have copied the American system of checks and balances and separation of powers, with most opting, instead, for parliamentary government. Even the Japanese and German constitutions, written under the supervision of American occupation authorities following World War II, created parliamentary systems.

In addition to providing for parliamentary government, most of the world's constitutions have departed from the American model by specifying extensive lists of rights. For example, the constitution of the Czech Republic includes a lengthy "Charter of Fundamental Rights and Freedoms."

Thus, although the U.S. Constitution inspired many other nations to develop a written constitution, the precise form that national constitutions take can diverge considerably from the American model.

[a]Kim Lane Scheppele, "Constitutions around the World," www.constitutioncenter.org (accessed 2/9/08).
[b]Scheppele, "Constitutions."
[c]Scheppele, "Constitutions."

**for critical analysis**

1. Is America's Constitution appropriate for every nation? Which elements might have universal validity? Which features might be relevant mainly to the United States?

2. The U.S. Constitution is a brief document, whereas many new constitutions are lengthy documents. What are the advantages and disadvantages of America's constitutional model?

principles of government in support of their nationalist vision. Antifederalists cited equally fundamental precepts to support their vision of a looser confederacy of small republics.

**Representation** One major area of contention between the two sides was the question of representation. The Antifederalists asserted that representatives must be "a true picture of the people . . . [possessing] the knowledge of their circumstances and their wants."[16] This could be achieved, argued the Antifederalists, only in small, relatively homogeneous republics such as the existing states. In their view, the size and extent of the entire nation precluded the construction of a truly representative form of government. As Brutus put it, "Is it practicable for a country so large and so numerous . . . to elect a representation that will speak their sentiments? . . . It certainly is not."[17]

Federalists, for their part, saw no reason that representatives should be precisely like those they represented. In the Federalist view, one of the great advantages of representative government over direct democracy was precisely the possibility that the people would choose as their representatives individuals possessing ability, experience, and talent superior to their own. In Madison's words, rather than serving as a mirror or reflection of society, representatives must be "[those] who possess [the] most wisdom to discern, and [the] most virtue to pursue, the common good of the society."[18]

**Tyranny of the Majority** A second important issue dividing Federalists and Antifederalists was the threat of **tyranny**—unjust rule by the group in power. Both opponents and defenders of the Constitution frequently affirmed their fear of tyrannical rule. Each side, however, had a different view of the most likely source of tyranny and, hence, of the way in which to forestall the threat.

From the Antifederalist perspective, the great danger was the tendency of all governments—including republican governments—to become gradually more and more "aristocratic" in character, wherein the small number of individuals in positions of authority would use their stations to gain more and more power over the general citizenry. In essence, the few would use their power to tyrannize the many. For this reason, Antifederalists were sharply critical of those features of the Constitution that divorced governmental institutions from direct responsibility to the people—institutions such as the Senate, the executive, and the federal judiciary. The last, appointed for life, presented a particular threat: "I wonder if the world ever saw . . . a court of justice invested with such immense powers, and yet placed in a situation so little responsible," protested Brutus.[19]

The Federalists, too, recognized the threat of tyranny, but they believed that the danger particularly associated with republican governments was not aristocracy but majority tyranny. The Federalists were concerned that a popular majority, "united and actuated by some common impulse of passion, or of interest, adverse to the rights of other citizens," would endeavor to "trample on the rules of justice."[20] From the Federalist perspective, it was precisely those features of the Constitution that the Antifederalists attacked as potential sources of tyranny that actually offered the best hope of averting the threat of oppression. The size and extent of the nation, for instance, was for the Federalists a bulwark against tyranny, because a majority would have difficulty uniting in a large and populous nation.

**Governmental Power** A third major difference between Federalists and Antifederalists was the issue of governmental power. Both opponents and proponents of the Constitution agreed on the principle of **limited government**. They differed,

**tyranny** oppressive government that employs cruel and unjust use of power and authority

**limited government** a principle of constitutional government; a government whose powers are defined and limited by a constitution

# The Constitution, the U.S. Postal System, and the Internet

**Imagine living in a world where, in** order to send a message to someone, you had to find a person willing to travel the distance to deliver the message personally, and you had to pay him for the time and effort it took to do this. Before the postal system was developed, this was the norm for people living in the British colonies that eventually became the United States.

The Founders knew the importance of the postal system, and thus wrote it into the Constitution, which gives Congress the power to "To establish post offices and post roads." Following the Founding, the postal service was the first major department created for the new United States of America, because it was one necessity all states could agree upon. The first postal system was founded in 1775, and the first postmaster was Benjamin Franklin. Until 1970 the U.S. Postal Service (USPS) was headed by a cabinet appointee and funded by tax dollars. After 1970 it became an independent agency, responsible for raising revenue through selling stamps and mailing packages to cover its expenses each year and (at least try to) to break even.

The U.S. post office was a cornerstone of many small rural towns over the past two centuries, a gathering place where citizens would meet to discuss local and national events. The invention of the Internet has changed this. In terms of volume of mail delivered, the peak year for the USPS was 2001; volume has declined almost 30 percent over the past decade. As e-mail, online bill paying, and competitors such as FedEx and UPS have reduced the volume of mail, operating costs (including salaries for employees, retirement benefits, health care, and gasoline) have risen. The USPS now spends more than it raises in revenue. Since 2007 the USPS has been running a deficit, and in 2010 its shortfall reached $8.3 billion. The government has responded by closing 2,500 post offices in small towns since 2010. Plans include the closing of as many as 12,000 others, which would result in the layoff of more than 10,000 postal workers.

Even as more and more Americans turn to e-mail instead of letters and to online banking and online greeting cards, and as businesses rely on FedEx or UPS, the postal system remains one of the top five employers in America. It is the only publicly controlled method of delivering packages or mail. If the postal system collapsed, private companies such as FedEx and UPS could charge more, because they would not have to compete with the publicly controlled prices of the USPS. Moreover, e-mail and the other Internet services used for correspondence are generally controlled by private companies. The Founders could not have conceived of the ability to pay bills, talk to friends, or apply for jobs through the medium of the Internet. The decline of the postal system is in effect privatizing a service the Founders saw as important enough to write into the U.S. Constitution.

SOURCES: Josh Sanburn, "How the U.S. Postal Service Fell Apart," *Time*, May 11, 2011, www.time.com/time/nation/article/0,8599,2099187,00.html (accessed 6/11/12). United States Postal Service, "The United States Postal Service: An American History 1775–2006," http://about.usps.com/publications/pub100/welcome.htm (accessed 6/11/12).

## for critical analysis

1. Does the closing of small-town post offices and the possible privatization of mail and package delivery violate the U.S. Constitution? Why or why not?

2. Should the federal government continue to deliver the mail to the homes of all Americans in an era of digital communication, or should it focus on operating post offices only?

however, on the fundamentally important question of how to place limits on governmental action. Antifederalists favored limiting and enumerating the powers granted to the national government in relation both to the states and to the people at large. To them, the powers given the national government ought to be "confined to certain defined national objects."[21] Otherwise, the national government would "swallow up all the power of the state governments."[22] Antifederalists bitterly attacked the supremacy clause and the elastic clause of the Constitution as unlimited and dangerous grants of power to the national government.[23] Antifederalists also demanded that a bill of rights be added to the Constitution to place limits on the government's exercise of power over the citizenry.

Federalists favored the construction of a government with broad powers to defend the nation against foreign foes, guard against domestic strife and insurrection, promote commerce, and expand the nation's economy. Antifederalists shared some of these goals but still feared governmental power. In reply, Federalists such as Hamilton acknowledged that every power could be abused but argued

*Although there was much acrimonious debate and necessary compromise as the new Constitution was written, this print suggests that farmers, artisans, and "gentlemen" alike supported it after its ratification.*

that the way to prevent misuse of power was not by depriving the government of the powers needed to achieve national goals but by adopting the Constitution's internal checks and controls. As Madison put it, "the power surrendered by the people is first divided between two distinct governments (state and national), and then the portion allotted to each subdivided among distinct and separate departments. Hence, a double security arises to the rights of the people. The different governments will control each other, at the same time that each will be controlled by itself."[24] The Federalists' concern with avoiding unwarranted limits on governmental power led them to oppose a bill of rights, which they saw as nothing more than a set of unnecessary restrictions on the government.

The Federalists acknowledged that abuse of power remained a possibility but felt that the risk had to be taken because of the goals to be achieved. "The very idea of power included a possibility of doing harm," said the Federalist John Rutledge during the South Carolina ratification debates. "If the gentleman would show the power that could do no harm," Rutledge continued, "he would at once discover it to be a power that could do no good."[25] This aspect of the debate between the Federalists and the Antifederalists, perhaps more than any other, continues to reverberate through American politics. Should the nation limit the federal government's power to tax and spend? Should Congress limit the capacity of federal agencies to issue new regulations? Should the government endeavor to create new rights for minorities, the disabled, and others? Though the details have changed, these are the same great questions that have been debated since the Founding.

## Reflections on the Founding

The final product of the Constitutional Convention would have to be considered an extraordinary victory for the groups that had most forcefully called for the creation of a new system of government to replace the Articles of Confederation. Antifederalist criticisms did force the Constitution's proponents to accept the addition of a bill of rights designed to limit the powers of the national government. In general, however, it was the Federalist vision of America that triumphed. The Constitution adopted in 1789 created the framework for a powerful national government that for more than 200 years has defended the nation's interests, promoted its commerce, and maintained national unity. In one notable instance, the national government fought and won a bloody war to prevent the nation from breaking apart. And despite this powerful government, the system of internal checks and balances has functioned reasonably well, as the Federalists predicted, to prevent the national government from tyrannizing its citizens.

Of course, the groups whose interests were served by the Constitution in 1789, mainly the merchants and planters, are not the same groups that benefit from the Constitution's provisions today. Once incorporated into law, political principles often take on lives of their own and have consequences that were never anticipated by their original champions. Indeed, many of the groups that benefit from constitutional provisions today did not even exist in 1789. Who would have thought that the principle of free speech would influence the transmission of data on the Internet? Who would have predicted that commercial interests that once sought a powerful government might come, two centuries later, to denounce governmental activism as "socialistic"? Perhaps one secret of the Constitution's longevity is that it did not confer permanent advantage on any one set of economic or social forces.

Although they were defeated in 1789, the Antifederalists present us with an important picture of a road not taken and of an America that might have been. Would the Americans have been worse off if they had been governed by a confederacy of small republics linked by a national administration with severely limited powers? Were the Antifederalists correct in predicting that a government given great power in the hope that it might do good would, through "insensible progress," inevitably turn to evil purposes? Two hundred years of government under the federal Constitution are not necessarily enough to answer these questions definitively.

# The Citizen's Role and the Changing Constitution

**Trace how the Constitution has changed over time through the amendment process**

The Constitution has endured for more than two centuries as the framework of government. But it has not gone unchanged. Without change, the Constitution might have become merely a sacred text, stored under glass.

## Amendments: Many Are Called; Few Are Chosen

**amendment** a change added to a bill, law, or constitution

The inevitable need for change was recognized by the framers of the Constitution, and provisions for **amendment** were incorporated into Article V. Four methods of amendment are described:

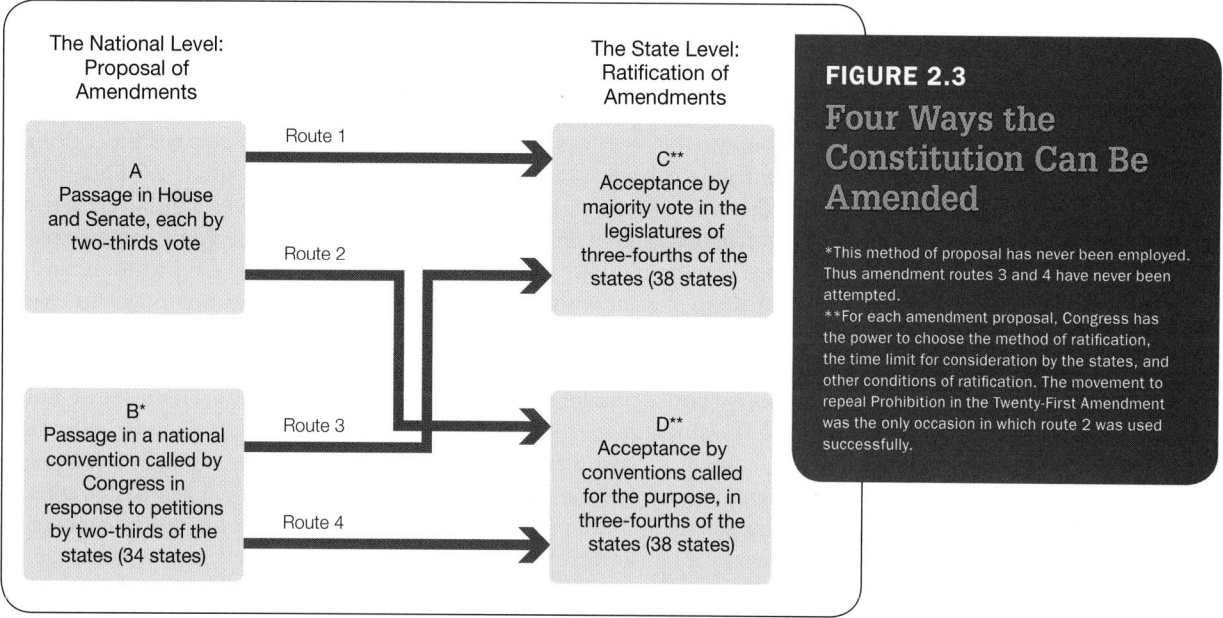

The National Level: Proposal of Amendments

**A**
Passage in House and Senate, each by two-thirds vote

**B***
Passage in a national convention called by Congress in response to petitions by two-thirds of the states (34 states)

Route 1
Route 2
Route 3
Route 4

The State Level: Ratification of Amendments

**C****
Acceptance by majority vote in the legislatures of three-fourths of the states (38 states)

**D****
Acceptance by conventions called for the purpose, in three-fourths of the states (38 states)

**FIGURE 2.3**

**Four Ways the Constitution Can Be Amended**

*This method of proposal has never been employed. Thus amendment routes 3 and 4 have never been attempted.
**For each amendment proposal, Congress has the power to choose the method of ratification, the time limit for consideration by the states, and other conditions of ratification. The movement to repeal Prohibition in the Twenty-First Amendment was the only occasion in which route 2 was used successfully.

1. Passage in House and Senate by two-thirds vote; then ratification by majority vote of the legislatures of three-fourths (now 38) of the states.

2. Passage in House and Senate by two-thirds vote; then ratification by conventions called for the purpose in three-fourths of the states.

3. Passage in a national convention called for by Congress in response to petitions by two-thirds of the states; ratification by majority vote of the legislatures of three-fourths of the states.

4. Passage in a national convention (as in method 3); then ratification by conventions called for the purpose in three-fourths of the states.

Figure 2.3 illustrates each of these possible methods. Since no amendment has ever been proposed by national convention, however, methods 3 and 4 have never been employed. And method 2 has been employed only once (the Twenty-First Amendment, which repealed the Eighteenth Amendment, or Prohibition). Thus, method 1 has been used for all the others.

The Constitution has proved to be extremely difficult to amend. In the history of efforts to amend it, the most appropriate characterization is "many are called, few are chosen." Since 1789, more than 11,000 amendments have been formally offered in Congress. Of these, Congress officially proposed only 29, and 27 of these were eventually ratified by the states. Two of these—Prohibition and its repeal—cancel each other out, so that for all practical purposes, only 25 amendments have been added to the Constitution since 1791.

**for critical analysis**

It is very difficult to amend the Constitution. Should it be made easier? Would the American system of government be more democratic if the Constitution could be revised more easily?

## Which Were Chosen? An Analysis of the Twenty-Seven

There is more to the amending difficulties than the politics of campaigning and voting. It would appear that only a limited number of changes can actually be made to the Constitution. Most efforts to amend the Constitution have failed because they were simply attempts to use the Constitution as an alternative to legislation for dealing directly with a specific public problem.

The 25 successful amendments, on the other hand, are concerned with the structure or composition of government (see Table 2.3). This is consistent with the dictionary, which defines *constitution* as the makeup or composition of something. And it is consistent with the concept of a constitution as "higher law," because the whole point and purpose of a higher law is to establish a framework within which government and the process of making ordinary law can take place. Even those who would have preferred more changes to the Constitution have to agree that there is great wisdom in this principle. A constitution ought to enable legislation and public policies to be enacted, but it should not determine what that legislation or those public policies ought to be.

For those whose hopes for change center on the Constitution, it must be emphasized that the amendment route to social change is, and always will be, extremely limited. Through a constitution it is possible to establish a working structure of government, and through a constitution it is possible to establish basic rights of citizens by placing limitations on the powers of that government. Of course, the Constitution cannot enforce itself. But it can and does have a real influence on everyday life because a right or an obligation set forth in the Constitution can become a cause of action in the hands of an otherwise powerless person.

Private property is an excellent example. Property is one of the most fundamental and well-established rights in the United States; but it is well established not because it is recognized in so many words in the Constitution, but because legislatures and courts, working within an agreed-upon constitutional framework, have made it a crime for anyone, including the government, to trespass or to take away property without compensation. A constitution is good if it produces the cause of action that leads to good legislation, good case law, and appropriate police behavior. A constitution cannot eliminate power. But its principles can be a citizen's dependable defense against the abuse of power.

## The Supreme Court and Constitutional Amendment

Although the process of constitutional amendment outlined in Article V has seldom been used successfully, another form of constitutional revision is constantly at work in the United States. This is, of course, judicial interpretation of the Constitution and its amendments by the Supreme Court as it reviews cases. In some instances, the Court may give concrete definition to abstract constitutional principles. For example, the Constitution's Fifth Amendment asserts in general terms that individuals accused of crimes are entitled to procedural rights. The Supreme Court, in a series of decisions, established principles giving effect to those rights. Every viewer of television crime programs knows that, upon being arrested, individuals must receive Miranda warnings informing them of their right to refuse to speak and their right to counsel. These required warnings are the result of a 1966 Supreme Court decision interpreting the meaning and implications of the Fifth Amendment.

In some instances, the Supreme Court does more than interpret or flesh out constitutional provisions: it seems to modify or augment the text itself. For example, in decisions in 1965 and 1973 on birth control and abortion, respectively, the Court said that Americans were constitutionally entitled to a right of privacy. No such right is mentioned anywhere in the Constitution. Similarly, the Court has held that the First Amendment prohibits many forms of government support for

TABLE 2.3

## Amendments to the Constitution

| AMENDMENT | PURPOSE | YEAR PROPOSED | YEAR ADOPTED |
|---|---|---|---|
| I | *Limits on Congress:* Congress is not to make any law establishing a religion or abridging speech, press, assembly, or petition freedoms. | | |
| II, III, IV | *Limits on Executive:* The executive branch is not to infringe on the right of people to keep arms (II), is not arbitrarily to take houses for a militia (III), and is not to engage in the search or seizure of evidence without a court warrant swearing to belief in the probable existence of a crime (IV). | | |
| V, VI, VII, VIII | *Limits on Courts:*\* The courts are not to hold trials for serious offenses without provision for a grand jury (V), a petit (trial) jury (VII), a speedy trial (VI), presentation of charges (VI), confrontation of hostile witnesses (VI), immunity from testimony against oneself (V), and immunity from more than one trial for the same offense (V). Neither bail nor punishment can be excessive (VIII), and no property can be taken without just compensation (V). | | |
| IX, X | *Limits on National Government:* All rights not enumerated are reserved to the states or the people. | | |
| XI | Limited jurisdiction of federal courts over suits involving the states. | 1794 | 1798 |
| XII | Provided separate ballot for vice president in the electoral college. | 1803 | 1804 |
| XIII | Eliminated slavery and eliminated the right of states to allow property in persons. | 1865\*\* | 1865 |
| XIV | (Part 1) Provided a national definition of citizenship.† | 1866 | 1868 |
| XIV | (Part 2) Applied due process of Bill of Rights to the states. | 1866 | 1868 |
| XV | Extended voting rights to all races. | 1869 | 1870 |
| XVI | Established national power to tax incomes. | 1909 | 1913 |
| XVII†† | Provided direct election of senators. | 1911 | 1913 |
| XIX | Extended voting rights to women. | 1919 | 1920 |
| XX | Eliminated "lame duck" session of Congress. | 1932 | 1933 |
| XXII | Limited presidential term. | 1947 | 1951 |
| XXIII | Extended voting rights to residents of the District of Columbia. | 1960 | 1961 |
| XXIV | Extended voting rights to all classes by abolition of poll taxes. | 1962 | 1964 |
| XXV | Provided presidential succession in case of disability. | 1965 | 1967 |
| XXVI | Extended voting rights to citizens aged 18 and over. | 1971 | 1971† |
| XXVII | Limited Congress's power to raise its own salary. | 1789 | 1992 |

\*These amendments also impose limits on the law-enforcement powers of federal (and especially) state and local executive branches.

\*\*The Thirteenth Amendment was proposed on January 31, 1865, and adopted less than a year later, on December 18, 1865.

†In defining *citizenship*, the Fourteenth Amendment actually provided the constitutional basis for expanding the electorate to include all races, women, and residents of the District of Columbia. Only the "eighteen-year-olds' amendment" should have been necessary, since it changed the definition of citizenship. The fact that additional amendments were required following the Fourteenth suggests that voting is not considered an inherent right of U.S. citizenship. Instead, it is viewed as a privilege.

††The Eighteenth Amendment, ratified in 1919, outlawed the sale and transportation of liquor. It was repealed by the Twenty-First Amendment, ratified in 1933.

†The Twenty-Sixth Amendment holds the record for speed of adoption. It was proposed on March 23, 1971, and adopted on July 5, 1971.

religion and many forms of religious exercise in public institutions, such as schools. By doing this, the Court was saying that the framers of the First Amendment simply meant that the government was prohibited from declaring one religion to be the nation's official faith. They did not intend to prohibit nondenominational school prayer.

Of course, much of the Supreme Court's power is itself based on constitutional interpretation rather than on the text of the document. The Supreme Court claims the power of judicial review—the power to render the final decision when there is a conflict of interpretations of the Constitution or federal law among the courts, Congress, the executive branch, or the states. Nowhere does the Constitution mention this power. In a number of early cases, however, the Supreme Court asserted that the Constitution gave it the power of judicial review, and this interpretation has prevailed, enhancing the Court's power. Some commentators denounce constitutional amendment by the judiciary and demand that judges limit themselves to "strict construction" of the Constitution, adhering closely to the words of the document's text. Proponents of the idea of the *living Constitution*, on the other hand, assert that the Constitution is subject to change as conditions warrant, and they argue that the judiciary is the institution best qualified to adjust the Constitution's principles to new problems and times. Advocates of strict construction and champions of the living Constitution disagree about the desirability of constitutional amendment by the courts, but both acknowledge its reality.

*The Equal Rights Amendment (ERA) is an example of an amendment that almost succeeded. The proposed amendment guaranteed equality under the law for women and made gender discrimination illegal. The ERA was ratified by 35 state legislatures but failed to get the 38 necessary to equaly three-fourths of the states.*

# Thinking Critically about Liberty, Equality, and Democracy in the Constitution

The Constitution's framers placed individual liberty ahead of all other political values, a concern that led many of the framers to distrust both democracy and equality. They feared that democracy could degenerate into a majority tyranny in which the populace, perhaps led by rabble-rousing demagogues, trampled on liberty. As for equality, the framers were products of their time and place; our contemporary ideas of racial and gender equality would have been foreign to them. The framers were concerned primarily with another manifestation of equality: they feared that those without property or position might be driven by what some called a "leveling spirit" to infringe on liberty in the name of greater economic or social equality. Indeed, the framers believed that this leveling spirit was most likely to produce demagoguery and majority tyranny. As a result, the basic structure of the Constitution—separated powers, internal checks and balances, and federalism—was designed to safeguard liberty, and the Bill of Rights created further safeguards for liberty. At the same time, however, many of the Constitution's other key provisions, such as indirect election of senators and the president, and the appointment of judges for life, were designed to limit democracy and, hence, the threat of majority tyranny.

By championing liberty, however, the framers virtually guaranteed that democracy and even a measure of equality would sooner or later evolve in the United States. For liberty promotes the growth of political activity and the expansion of political participation. In James Madison's famous phrase, "Liberty is to faction as air is to fire."[26] Where they have liberty, more and more people, groups, and interests will almost inevitably engage in politics and gradually overcome whatever restrictions might have been placed on participation. Indeed, this is precisely what happened in the early years of the American republic. During the Jeffersonian period, political parties formed. During the Jacksonian period, many state suffrage restrictions were removed and popular participation greatly expanded. Over time, liberty is conducive to democracy.

Liberty does not guarantee that everyone will be equal. It does, however, reduce the threat of inequality in one very important way. Historically, the greatest inequalities of wealth, power, and privilege have arisen where governments have used their power to allocate status and opportunity among individuals or groups. From the aristocracies of the early modern period to twentieth-century despotisms, the most extreme cases of inequality are associated with the most tyrannical regimes.

The other side of the coin, however, is that the absence of government intervention in economic affairs—in the name of liberty—may mean that there is no antidote to the inevitable inequalities of wealth produced by the marketplace. Economic inequalities, in turn, may lead to inequalities in political power as wealthy groups and individuals use their superior resources to elect politicians friendly to them and their aims and to influence the legislative process. Thus, liberty is a complex matter. In the absence of liberty, inequality is virtually certain. The existence of liberty, however, poses its own threat to political equality. Can we fully reconcile liberty and equality? Doing so remains a constant challenge in a democratic society.

Another limitation of liberty as a political principle is that limits on government action can also inhibit effective government. Consider, for example, one of the basic tasks of government, the protection of citizens' lives and property. A government limited by concerns over the rights of those accused of crimes may therefore

**for critical analysis**

What are the U.S. Constitution's greatest strengths? What are its most pronounced weaknesses? If you were a framer, what would you change in the Constitution? Why?

*The Eighteenth Amendment was passed in 1919 and prohibited the manufacture, transportation, and sale of alcoholic beverages. Repealed in 1933 by the Twenty-First Amendment, the Prohibition Amendment can be seen as an attempt to legislate through the amendment process.*

be limited in its ability to maintain public order. Recently, the U.S. government has asserted that protecting the nation against terrorists requires law-enforcement measures that seem at odds with legal and constitutional formalities.

Liberty is sometimes confused with the absence of government. The framers of the Constitution, though, saw liberty as a purpose or goal of government, not the result of governmental absence. The government they created was designed to "secure the Blessings of Liberty" by maintaining order, keeping the peace, and intervening where necessary to allow citizens to conduct their affairs in safety and freedom. Every generation of Americans ponders and reconsiders the work of the men who framed the Constitution.

# Madison's Notes and the U.S. Constitution

## Inform Yourself

 **Read the Constitution.** Visit the Library of Congress's "The Making of the U.S. Constitution" page (http://memory.loc.gov/ammem/amlaw/ac001/lawpres.html) to read a brief account of the Constitutional Convention followed by the text of the Constitution as originally adopted (that is, without the Bill of Rights and other amendments). The text of the Constitution also appears at the end of this book. Are you surprised by how short the document is? Does the text sound familiar? What did you not expect to find?

 **Dip into James Madison's notes from the Constitutional Convention.** To read what happened on those hot summer days in 1787 in Philadelphia, click on a day in the calendar on "The Debates in the Federal Convention of 1787" page to read that day's entry in Madison's journal (www.constitution.org/dfc/dfc_0000.htm). After reading the notes for any day, answer the following questions: What did the members of the Convention agree on? What issues did they disagree on? Can you find evidence of the debates between the small and large population states? Can you find evidence of the debates between slave-owning and non-slave-owning states? Can you find debate over the power of the presidency?

 **Watch a slide show on the Bill of Rights.** "Jump Back in Time" is also presented by the Library of Congress (www.americaslibrary.gov/jb/nation/jb_nation_bofright_1.html). Four short slides walk you through the adoption of the Bill of Rights.

## Connect with Others

 **Visit the United States Constitution page on Facebook.** The U.S. Constitution has more than 200,000 Facebook fans. What type of posts appear on this page? Do the messages reflect different interpretations of the Constitution? What does this tell us about the Constitution? Is the Constitution a living document, or is it fixed in stone?

*Find links to the sites listed above as well as related activities on wwnorton.com/studyspace.*

# study guide

## The First Founding: Interests and Conflicts

■ Describe the events that led to the Declaration of Independence and the Articles of Confederation (pp. 39–43)

Dissatisfaction with British tax policies and discontent over retaliatory acts of political repression radicalized many colonists during the 1770s to push for independence from British rule. By identifying widely shared grievances, aspirations, and principles, the Declaration of Independence helped forge a sense of national unity among diverse elements in colonial society. The first written constitution of the United States, the Articles of Confederation, lefts most governmental responsibilities in the hands of states and placed serious limits on the powers of the national government.

### Key Terms

**Articles of Confederation** (p. 42)

**confederation** (p. 42)

### Practice Quiz

1. In their fight against British taxes such as the Stamp Act and the Sugar Act of 1764, New England merchants allied with which of the following groups? *(pp. 39–40)*
   a) artisans, southern planters, and laborers
   b) southern planters only
   c) laborers only
   d) artisans only
   e) southern planters and laborers only

2. How did the British attempt to raise revenue in the North American colonies? *(p. 39)*
   a) income tax
   b) taxes on commerce
   c) expropriation and government sale of land
   d) government asset sales
   e) requests for voluntary donations

3. The first governing document in the United States was *(p. 42)*
   a) the Declaration of Independence.
   b) the Articles of Confederation.
   c) the Constitution.
   d) the Bill of Rights.
   e) the Virginia Plan.

4. Where was the execution of laws conducted under the Articles of Confederation? *(p. 42)*
   a) the presidency
   b) the Congress
   c) the states
   d) the federal bureaucracy
   e) the federal judiciary

 **Practice Online**
Video exercise: South Park, *"I'm a Little Bit Country"*

## The Second Founding: From Compromise to Constitution

■ Explain how the Constitution attempted to improve America's governance (pp. 43–49)

International weakness, domestic economic problems and the national government's inability to act decisively in response to Shays's Rebellion led to a constitutional convention to replace the Articles of Confederation. The convention's delegates were deeply divided on the issues of slavery and representation in the national government. The Great Compromise and the Three-Fifths Compromise temporarily reconciled these divisions and allowed the Founders to move forward with creating a new constitutional framework for the United States.

### Key Terms

**Virginia Plan** (p. 45)

**New Jersey Plan** (p. 45)

**Great Compromise** (p. 46)

**Three-Fifths Compromise** (p. 48)

### Practice Quiz

5. Which of the following was *not* a reason that the Articles of Confederation seemed inadequate *(pp. 43–44)*
   a) the lack of a single voice in international affairs
   b) weakness of the national government

c) persistent economic turmoil among states

d) the power of radical forces in several states

e) the power of radical forces in Congress

6. Which event led directly to the Constitutional Convention by providing evidence that the government created under the Articles of Confederation was unable to act decisively in times of national crisis? *(p. 44)*
   a) the Boston Tea Party
   b) the Boston Massacre
   c) Shays's Rebellion
   d) the Annapolis Convention
   e) the War of 1812

7. The draft constitution that was introduced at the start of the Constitutional Convention was authored by *(p. 45)*
   a) Edmund Randolph.
   b) Benjamin Franklin.
   c) James Madison.
   d) George Clinton.
   e) Thomas Jefferson.

8. Which state's proposal embodied a principle of representing states in the Congress according to their size and wealth? *(p. 45)*
   a) New Jersey
   b) Maryland
   c) Rhode Island
   d) Virginia
   e) Connecticut

9. The agreement reached at the Constitutional Convention that determined that every slave would be counted as a fraction of a person for the purposes of taxation and representation in the House of Representatives was called the *(pp. 48–49)*
   a) Connecticut Compromise.
   b) Three-Fifths Compromise.
   c) Great Compromise.
   d) Virginia Plan.
   e) New Jersey Plan.

 **Practice Online**
Interactive simulation: *The Role of a Delegate at the Constitutional Convention*

# The Constitution

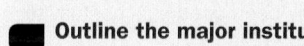 **Outline the major institutions and rules established by the Constitution (pp. 49–56)**

The Founders sought to create a stronger national government than existed under the Articles of Confederation. In particular, they hoped that the new constitution would promote commerce, protect private property, and avoid the perils of "excessive democracy." The Founders' concern with national power was expressed most clearly in the supremacy clause of Article VI. The national government, however, did not have unlimited power, and there were significant limits placed on it through the separation of powers, federalism, and the Bill of Rights.

## Key Terms

**checks and balances** (p. 49)

**electoral college** (p. 50)

**Bill of Rights** (p. 50)

**separation of powers** (p. 50)

**federalism** (p. 50)

**expressed powers** (p. 51)

**elastic clause** (p. 51)

**bicameral** (p. 52)

**judicial review** (p. 53)

**supremacy clause** (p. 53)

## Practice Quiz

10. What mechanism was instituted in the Congress to guard against "excessive democracy"? *(pp. 49–50)*
    a) bicameralism
    b) staggered terms in office
    c) checks and balances
    d) selection of senators by state legislatures
    e) all of the above

11. Which of the following best describes the Supreme Court as understood by the Founders? *(p. 53)*
    a) the highest court of the national government
    b) arbiter of disputes within the Congress
    c) the body that would choose the president
    d) a figurehead commission of elders
    e) a supreme court of the nation and its states

12. Theorists such as Montesquieu referred to the principle of giving each branch of government a distinctly different constituency as *(pp. 54–55)*
    a) laissez-faire.
    b) mixed regime.
    c) confederation.
    d) limited government.
    e) federalism.

 **Practice Online**
Video exercise: *Happy Constitution Day*

# The Fight for Ratification

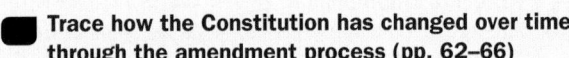

**Present the controversies involved in the struggle for ratification (pp. 56–62)**

Before the Constitution could go into effect, it had to be ratified by 9 of the 13 states. In the debate over ratification, the Federalists supported the Constitution and the Antifederalists opposed it. The three major areas of disagreement between Federalists and Antifederalists were the quality of representation, the threat of tyranny of the majority, and the extent of government power.

## Key Terms

**Federalists** (p. 56)

**Antifederalists** (p. 56)

*Federalist Papers* (p. 57)

**tyranny** (p. 59)

**limited government** (p. 59)

## Practice Quiz

13. Which of the following were the Antifederalists most concerned with? *(p. 59)*
    a) interstate commerce
    b) the protection of property
    c) the distinction between principles and interests
    d) abolishing slavery
    e) the potential for tyranny in the central government

# The Citizen's Role and the Changing Constitution

**Trace how the Constitution has changed over time through the amendment process (pp. 62–66)**

The amendment process outlined in Article V of the Constitution creates significant hurdles to change that have rarely been cleared in American history. Attempts to solve specific social problems through the use of a constitutional amendment have been particularly unsuccessful at winning the support required to change the country's basic governing document. The Supreme Court, however, has provided new meaning and new substance to the Constitution on countless occasions during the last 200 years through their decisions on important cases.

## Key Term

**amendment** (p. 62)

## Practice Quiz

14. Which of the following best describes the process of amending the Constitution? *(pp. 62–63)*
    a) It is difficult and has rarely been used successfully to address specific public problems.
    b) It is difficult and has frequently been used successfully to address specific public problems.
    c) It is easy and has rarely been used successfully to address specific public problems.
    d) It is easy and has frequently been used successfully to address specific public problems.
    e) It is easy, but it has never been used for any purpose.

 **Practice Online**
"You Decide" exercise: *A Federal Marriage Amendment?*

# For Further Reading

Amar, Akhil Reed. *America's Constitution: A Biography*. New York: Random House, 2006.

Beard, Charles. *An Economic Interpretation of the Constitution of the United States*. New York: Macmillan, 1913.

Beeman, Richard. *Plain, Honest Men: The Making of the American Constitution*. New York: Random House, 2010.

Breyer, Stephen G. *Active Liberty: Interpreting Our Democratic Constitution*. New York: Knopf, 2005.

Dahl, Robert A. *How Democratic Is the American Constitution?* 2nd ed. New Haven, CT: Yale University Press, 2002.

Ellis, Joseph. *American Creation: Triumphs and Tragedies at the Founding of the Republic*. New York: Knopf, 2007.

Hamilton, Alexander, James Madison, and John Jay. *The Federalist Papers*. Edited by Isaac Kramnick. New York: Viking, 1987.

Holton, Woody. *Unruly Americans and the Origins of the Constitution*. New York: Hill and Wang, 2007.

Jensen, Merrill. *The Articles of Confederation*. Madison: University of Wisconsin Press, 1963.

Keller, Morton. *America's Three Regimes*. New York: Oxford University Press, 2009.

Lewis, Anthony. *Freedom for the Thought That We Hate: A Biography of the First Amendment*. New York: Basic Books, 2008.

Main, Jackson Turner. *The Social Structure of Revolutionary America*. Princeton, NJ: Princeton University Press, 1965.

Rossiter, Clinton. *1787: Grand Convention*. New York: Macmillan, 1966.

Storing, Herbert, ed. *The Complete Anti-Federalist*. 7 vols. Chicago: University of Chicago Press, 1981.

Winik, Jay. *The Great Upheaval: America and the Birth of the Modern World, 1788–1800*. New York: HarperCollins, 2007.

# Recommended Websites

**The American Civil Liberties Union**
**www.aclu.org**
>The ACLU is committed to protecting, for all individuals, the freedoms found in the Bill of Rights. This sometimes controversial organization constantly monitors the government for violations of liberty and encourages its members to take political action.

**Archiving Early America**
**www.earlyamerica.com**
>Revolutionary Americans were motivated by a variety of competing ideals, principles, and interests. Visit this website to learn more about the early colonists and the founding of our government.

**Constitution Finder**
**http://confinder.richmond.edu**
>Is the American Constitution a model for the world? Explore the constitutions of many different nations and see what elements of the U.S. Constitution can be found in the governing documents of other countries.

**Find Law**
**http://findlaw.com/casecode/state.html**
>The Find Law website provides all fifty states' constitutions. Click on your state and try to identify such constitutional principles as bicameralism, staggered terms of office, checks and balances, and separation of powers.

**The National Archives**
**www.archives.gov**
>This government site provides information about and actual digital images of such founding documents as the Declaration of Independence, the U.S. Constitution, and the Bill of Rights.

**The National Constitution Center**
**www.constitutioncenter.org**
>The National Constitution Center in Philadelphia maintains a website that provides in-depth instructional analysis of the U.S. Constitution. Check out the Interactive Constitution function and follow the document from its Preamble through the Twenty-Seventh Amendment.

**Oyez**
**www.oyez.org**
>This website for U.S. Supreme Court Media has an excellent search engine for finding information on Supreme Court cases. See how the Court has interpreted the Constitution over time.

**The PBS Liberty! Series**
**www.pbs.org/ktca/liberty**
>The PBS *Liberty!* series on the American Revolution offers an in-depth look at the Revolutionary War and includes information on historical events such as the Constitutional Convention.

**The Supreme Court of the United States**
**www.supremecourtus.gov**
>The website for the U.S. Supreme Court provides information on recent decisions. Take a moment to read some oral arguments, briefs, or opinions

Federalism was at the center of the controversy concerning the Affordable Care Act, as 26 states sued the federal government over the health care reform law. When the Supreme Court heard arguments in the case in 2012, groups on both sides of the issue demonstrated outside the Court.

# Federalism

**WHAT GOVERNMENT DOES AND WHY IT MATTERS** Few laws have attracted as much controversy as the Affordable Care Act, the Obama administration's signature legislation that aimed to make health care available to all Americans. From the time it was enacted in 2010, the law became the target of opponents in the states who charged that the federal government exceeded its constitutional powers in enacting the measure. The new law would require states to comply with federal rules on matters that had previously been decided by the states, such as who was eligible for Medicaid in the state. Twenty-six states sued the federal government, and the case made its way to the Supreme Court. In the Court's 2012 decision, Chief Justice John Roberts surprised many when he broke with the Court's conservative majority, penning an opinion that declared the main provisions of the Affordable Care Act constitutional.[1] Yet, the Court's ruling raised fundamental questions about federal power and about the relationship of the federal government to the states.

Although it upheld most of the Affordable Care Act and the federal government's power to force states to comply with the act, the decision also introduced the potential for significant new restrictions on federal power in two main ways. First, it limited the reach of the commerce clause, the main constitutional provision under which federal power has expanded for the past 80 years. Although the Court found the controversial "individual mandate"—the requirement that uninsured individuals buy health insurance—constitutional, it ruled that this provision could not be justified under the commerce clause. Instead, the decision stated, it was Congress's taxing power that justified the mandate.

Even more surprising was the Court's ruling that the federal government could not cut off all Medicaid funding to states that declined to expand the program as required in the Affordable Care Act.

Expanding Medicaid, the federal–state program that provides health care to low-income Americans, was one of the main ways the new law sought to reduce the number of uninsured. The Court's decision on Medicaid raises new questions far beyond the domain of health care. The federal government has long attached conditions to federal funding as a way to achieve national goals. For example, in 1984 the federal government pressured state governments to change the laws governing the age at which a person could legally drink alcohol to 21. It did so by threatening states with the loss of federal highway funds if they did not adopt the new drinking age. Eventually, all 50 states fell into line. The ruling on health care is likely to unleash challenges to the many federal laws that seek to influence what states do by attaching conditions to federal funds.

The debates about the Affordable Care Act engaged one of the oldest questions in American government: What is the responsibility of the federal government and what is the responsibility of the states? When should there be uniformity across the states and when is it better to let states adopt a diverse set of laws? Which approach serves the common good?

The United States is a federal system, in which the national government shares power with lower levels of government. Throughout American history, lawmakers, politicians, and citizens have wrestled with questions about how responsibilities should be allocated across the different levels of government. Some responsibilities, such as international relations, clearly lie with the federal government. Others, such as divorce laws, are controlled by state governments. In fact, most of the rules and regulations that Americans face in their daily lives are set by state and local governments. However, many government responsibilities are shared in American federalism and require cooperation among local, state, and federal governments. The debate about "who should do what" remains one of the most important discussions in American politics.

## chaptergoals

- **Describe what the Constitution says about the powers of the national government and of the states (pages 77–81)**

- **Trace how the federal government became much stronger over time (pages 82–89)**

- **Analyze major developments in the federal framework since the 1930s (pages 89–105)**

# Federalism in the Constitution

**Describe what the Constitution says about the powers of the national government and of the states**

The Constitution has had its most fundamental influence on American life through **federalism**. Federalism can be defined as the division of powers and functions between the national government and the state governments. Governments can organize power in a variety of ways. One of the most important distinctions is between unitary and federal governments. In a **unitary system**, the central government makes the important decisions, and lower levels of government have little independent power. In such systems, lower levels of government primarily implement decisions made by the central government. In France, for example, the central government was once so involved in the smallest details of local activity that the minister of education boasted that by looking at his watch he could tell what all French schoolchildren were learning at that moment because the central government set the school curriculum. In a **federal system**, by contrast, the central government shares power or functions with lower levels of government, such as regions or states. Nations with diverse ethnic or language groupings, such as Switzerland and Canada, are most likely to have federal arrangements. In federal systems, lower levels of government often have significant independent power to set policy in some areas, such as education and social programs, and to impose taxes. Yet the specific ways in which power is shared vary greatly: no two federal systems are exactly the same.

The United States was the first nation to adopt federalism as its governing framework. With federalism, the framers sought to limit the national government by creating a second layer of state governments. By granting a few "expressed powers" to the national government and reserving all the rest to the states, the original Constitution recognized two sovereigns, the principle of American federalism reinforced in the Bill of Rights.

**federalism** a system of government in which power is divided, by a constitution, between a central government and regional governments

**unitary system** a centralized government system in which lower levels of government have little power independent of the national government

**federal system** a system of government in which the national government shares power with lower levels of government, such as states

**expressed powers** specific powers granted by the Constitution to Congress (Article I, Section 8) and to the president (Article II)

**implied powers** powers derived from the necessary and proper clause of Article I, Section 8, of the Constitution. Such powers are not specifically expressed, but are implied through the expansive interpretation of delegated powers

**necessary and proper clause** Article I, Section 8, of the Constitution, which provides Congress with the authority to make all laws "necessary and proper" to carry out its expressed powers

## The Powers of the National Government

As we saw in Chapter 2, the **expressed powers** granted to the national government are found in Article I, Section 8, of the Constitution. These 17 powers include the power to collect taxes, to coin money, to declare war, and to regulate commerce. Article I, Section 8, also contains another important source of power for the national government: the **implied powers** that enable Congress "to make all Laws which shall be necessary and proper for carrying into Execution the foregoing Powers." Not until several decades after the Founding did the Supreme Court allow Congress to exercise the power granted in this **necessary and proper clause**, but as we shall see later in this chapter, this doctrine allowed the national government to expand considerably the scope of its authority, although the process was a slow one. In addition to these expressed and implied powers, the Constitution affirmed the power of the national government in the supremacy clause (Article VI), which made all national laws and treaties "the supreme Law of the Land."

*Especially since the mid-1990s, Republican Party leaders have contended that the national government has grown too powerful at the expense of the states and that the Tenth Amendment should restrict the growth of national power.*

## The Powers of State Government

One way in which the framers sought to preserve a strong role for the states was through the Tenth Amendment to the Constitution. The Tenth Amendment states that the powers that the Constitution does not delegate to the national government or prohibit to the states are "reserved to the States respectively, or to the people." The Antifederalists, who feared that a strong central government would encroach on individual liberty, repeatedly pressed for such an amendment as a way of limiting national power. Federalists agreed to the amendment because they did not think it would do much harm, given the powers of the Constitution already granted to the national government. The Tenth Amendment is also called the "**reserved powers** amendment," because it aims to reserve powers to the states.

**reserved powers** powers, derived from the Tenth Amendment to the Constitution, that are not specifically delegated to the national government or denied to the states

The most fundamental power that the states retain is that of coercion—the power to develop and enforce criminal codes, to administer health and safety rules, to regulate the family via marriage and divorce laws. The states have the power to regulate individuals' livelihoods; if you're a doctor or a lawyer or a plumber or a barber, you must be licensed by the state. Even more fundamentally, the states have the power to define private property—private property exists because state laws against trespass define who is and is not entitled to use a piece of property. If you own a car, your ownership isn't worth much unless the state is willing to enforce your right to possession by making it a crime for anyone else to drive your car without your consent. These are fundamental matters, and the powers of the states regarding these domestic issues are much greater than the powers of the national government, even today.

**police power** power reserved to the state government to regulate the health, safety, and morals of its citizens

A state's authority to regulate these fundamental matters is commonly referred to as the **police power** of the state and encompasses the state's power to regulate the health, safety, welfare, and morals of its citizens. Policing is what states do—they coerce you in the name of the community in order to maintain public order. And this was exactly the type of power that the Founders intended the states, not the federal government, to exercise.

**concurrent powers** authority possessed by *both* state and national governments, such as the power to levy taxes

In some areas, the states share **concurrent powers** with the national government, whereby they retain and share some power to regulate commerce and affect the currency—for example, by being able to charter banks, grant or deny corporate charters, grant or deny licenses to engage in a business or practice a trade, regulate the quality of products or the conditions of labor, and levy taxes (see the Digital Citizens box on page 81). Wherever there is a direct conflict of laws between the federal and the state levels, the issue will most likely be resolved in favor of national supremacy.

## State Obligations to One Another

The Constitution also creates obligations among the states. These obligations, spelled out in Article IV, were intended to promote national unity. By requiring the states to recognize actions and decisions taken in other states as legal and proper, the framers aimed to make the states less like independent countries and more like components of a single nation.

Article IV, Section 1, calls for "Full Faith and Credit" among states, meaning that each state is normally expected to honor the "public Acts, Records, and judicial Proceedings" that take place in any other state. So, for example, if a couple is married in Texas—marriage being regulated by state law—in most cases, Missouri must also recognize that marriage, even though the couple was not married under Missouri state law.

This **full faith and credit clause** notwithstanding, if a practice is against their "strong public policy," states are not obligated to recognize it—even if it has been sanctioned by other states. A look at the history of interracial marriage, for example, offers some perspective on how much leeway states have to recognize marriages performed in other states. In 1952, 30 states prohibited interracial marriage. In 1967, when the Supreme Court struck down such laws as unconstitutional, 16 states still had these statutes on the books. Many of the states that prohibited interracial marriage also refused to recognize such marriages performed in other states. But many states that outlawed interracial marriage did recognize out-of-state marriages, depending on the circumstances.[2] In the case of same-sex marriage, the states that allow same-sex marriage (Connecticut, Iowa, Maine, Maryland, Massachussets, New Hampshire, New York, Vermont, and Washington) recognize same-sex marriages performed out of state, as does Rhode Island. In California, the governor signed a law in 2009 granting recognition of gay and lesbian marriages that were performed out of state during the five-month period in 2008 that these marriages were legal in California.[3]

Most states, however, do not recognize same-sex marriages performed in other states. And to underscore their opposition to same-sex marriage, a large majority of states have enacted provisions against gay marriage. By 2011, 38 states had passed "defense of marriage acts" or had adopted constitutional amendments that defined marriage as a union between one man and one woman only. Most of these states also outlaw recognition of gay marriages performed in other states. Anxious to show its disapproval of gay marriage, Congress passed the Defense of Marriage Act in 1996, which declared that states will *not* have to recognize a same-sex marriage, even if it is legal in one state. The act also said that the federal government will not recognize gay marriage—even if it is legal under state law—and that gay marriage partners will not be eligible for the federal benefits, such as Medicare and Social Security, normally available to spouses.[4]

Same-sex marriage is not the only issue in which the "full faith and credit" clause has come into play. It has played a role also in conflicts over gay adoption. In these cases, however, the courts have so far ruled that the full faith and credit clause requires states to accept the legal decisions of other states. Two states, Mississippi and Utah, explicitly ban gay adoption, and several other states sharply restrict it. An Oklahoma law banned state agencies from recognizing adoption orders to gay and lesbian couples approved in other states. Effectively, this meant that Oklahoma refused to issue birth certificates for children born in Oklahoma but legally adopted by same-sex couples in other states. In 2007 a federal appeals court struck down the Oklahoma law, ruling that the full faith and credit clause required Oklahoma to honor adoption orders approved by courts in other states.[5]

Article IV, Section 2, known as the "comity clause," also seeks to promote national unity. It provides that citizens enjoying the **privileges and immunities** of one state should be entitled to similar treatment in other states. What this has come to mean is that a state cannot discriminate against someone from another state or give special privileges to its own residents. For example, in the 1970s, when Alaska passed a law

*Should same-sex marriages performed in one state be legally recognized in another state? State laws vary, and despite the Constitution's full faith and credit clause, these differences can lead to debate over controversial issues.*

**full faith and credit clause**
provision, from Article IV, Section 1, of the Constitution, requiring that the states normally honor the public acts and judicial decisions that take place in another state

**privileges and immunities clause**
provision, from Article IV, Section 2, of the Constitution, that a state cannot discriminate against someone from another state or give its own residents special privileges

that gave residents preference over nonresidents in obtaining work on the state's oil and gas pipelines, the Supreme Court ruled the law illegal because it discriminated against citizens of other states.[6] The comity clause also regulates criminal justice among the states by requiring states to return fugitives to the states from which they have fled. Thus, in 1952, when an inmate escaped from an Alabama prison and sought to avoid being returned to Alabama on the grounds that he was being subjected to "cruel and unusual punishment" there, the Supreme Court ruled that he must be returned according to Article IV, Section 2.[7] This example highlights the difference between the obligations among states and those among different countries. In 2011, Portugal refused to return an American fugitive captured after more than 30 years on the run because he had become a Portuguese national and had a family in Portugal.[8] The Constitution clearly forbids states from doing something similar.

States' relationships with one another are also governed by the interstate compact clause (Article I, Section 10), which states that "No State shall, without the Consent of Congress . . . enter into any Agreement or Compact with another State." The Court has interpreted the clause to mean that states may enter into agreements with each other, subject to congressional approval. Compacts are a way for two or more states to reach a legally binding agreement about how to solve a problem that crosses state lines. In the early years of the republic, states turned to compacts primarily to settle border disputes. Today compacts are used for a wide range of issues but are especially important in regulating the distribution of river water, addressing environmental concerns, and operating transportation systems that cross state lines.[9] One unusual use of the interstate compact is the effort to enact the National Popular Vote compact. Initiated after George W. Bush won the presidency without winning the popular vote, the compact aims to make the popular vote, not the electoral college results, the criterion for victory. In signing onto the compact, a state agrees to award all its electoral college votes to the winner of the popular vote. By 2011, with eight states and the District of Columbia supporting the compact, the movement had obtained 49 percent of the 270 electoral votes needed for it to be effective.[10]

**home rule** power delegated by the state to a local unit of government to manage its own affairs

## Local Government and the Constitution

Local government occupies a peculiar but very important place in the American system. In fact, the status of American local government is probably unique in world experience. First, it must be pointed out that local government has no status in the U.S. Constitution. *State* legislatures created local governments, and *state* constitutions and laws permit local governments to take on some of the responsibilities of the state governments. Local governments have always been subject to ultimate control by the states. This imbalance of power means that state governments could legally dissolve local governments or force multiple local governments to consolidate into one large locality. Most states amended their own constitutions to give their larger cities **home rule**—a guarantee of noninterference in various areas of local affairs. But local governments enjoy no such recognition and have no protected standing at all in the federal Constitution.[11]

Local governments became administratively important in the early years of the Republic because the states possessed little administrative capability. They relied on local governments—cities and counties—to implement state laws. Local government was an alternative to a statewide bureaucracy (see Table 3.1).

## TABLE 3.1

### 89,527 Governments in the United States

| TYPE | NUMBER |
| --- | --- |
| National | 1 |
| State | 50 |
| County | 3,033 |
| Municipal | 19,492 |
| Townships | 16,519 |
| School districts | 13,051 |
| Other special districts | 37,381 |

SOURCE: U.S. Census Bureau, www.census.gov/govs/cog/GovOrgTab03ss.html (accessed 11/21/11).

# E-Commerce and State Taxes

**Where you buy a product can significantly** affect how much it costs. Similar products in local stores often cost more than buying online, even after accounting for shipping costs. Have you ever wondered why? One reason is online stores don't have to pay rent for physical space, or hire sales clerks, or pay electrical bills. This allows them to share the cost savings with consumers. What began as an online bookstore, Amazon.com, for example, became the world's largest online retailer.

But a large part of the reason for the difference in cost is that we don't pay state sales tax on what we buy online unless the location the product is shipping from is in the same state as the shipping address (or the company has a warehouse in the state). We also do not pay local sales taxes on items bought online. This is one reason many people prefer to purchase expensive items, such as computers, online.

In our federal system, each state establishes its own state-level tax policies. Tax policies and rates vary from state to state, but most states collect a sales tax on items

that are not considered basic needs (such as food items). The rule that taxes are not charged for online purchases unless the business has a physical presence in the buyer's state dates back to a Supreme Court case in the 1990s that had nothing to do with online commerce. The decision concerned mail-order items and established the rules that now extend to Internet purchases.

This is not to say we do not technically owe the state taxes on items purchased online. Each year, when we file our state tax forms, we are supposed to report whether we bought items online, and if so, how much those items cost. But it is up to individuals to self-report purchases, and many people do not even know they are supposed to pay sales taxes on online purchases. In the majority of cases, the taxes are never paid.

The nonpayment of state sales taxes online has become a significant issue. Why? Traditional retailers have to collect state (and sometimes local) sales tax, which makes their items seem more expensive to consumers, which in turn hurts their business. More important, the sales tax is the leading source of revenue for state governments, so collectively, the states are missing out on billions of dollars in sales tax because of e-commerce. According to one estimate, over the last six years, the states lost more than $52 billion in sales taxes that went uncollected on online purchases. The year 2011 was the lowest collection year since 1967 because of the difficulty in collecting online sales taxes.

In response, more than 40 states have signed an agreement that simplifies and streamlines the various state taxes. Some major online sellers have agreed to start collecting state sales tax in a few years; others have not. For example, Amazon.com sued the state of Illinois in 2012 after the state government passed a law requiring all online vendors (regardless of where they were based) selling to residents of Illinois to collect Illinois sales taxes. Amazon has no physical presence in the state, and it fought the law, arguing that it violated the Internet Tax Freedom Act. The court ruled

that because Amazon does not have a presence in the state, the state government cannot force the company to collect taxes from the state's citizens for online purchases.

The Amazon case did not fully settle the question of whether the states can regulate e-commerce. Some observers argue that the patchwork of state and national laws threatens the growth of e-commerce, as many state laws place additional burdens on out-of-state commerce. The commerce clause in the U.S. Constitution gives the power to regulate commerce among the states to the federal government. However, while the states have been aggressive in collecting state taxes from online retailers, Congress is loath to be seen as raising taxes, and might not force retailers to collect the tax. Do the states have a right to force online retailers to collect sales taxes from consumers, or must Congress address this issue?

SOURCES: Dennis Cauchon, "Tax-Free Internet Sales, Exemptions Erode State Revenue." *USA Today*, February 28, 2012, www.usatoday.com/money/economy/story/2012-02-27/sales-tax-rate/53274224/1 (accessed 6/12/12). Jim Brunner, "States Fight Back against Amazon.com's Tax Deals." *Seattle Times*, April 2, 2012, http://seattletimes.nwsource.com/html/localnews/2017895493_amazonsalestax03.html (accessed 6/12/12). Rich Stim, "Sales Tax on the Internet: When Sales Tax Must Be Charged for Online Purchases," 2012, NOLO Law for ALL, www.nolo.com/legal-encyclopedia/sales-tax-internet-29919.html (accessed 6/12/12).

## for critical analysis

1. What are the benefits of having the states (rather than the federal government) determine the rules for Internet sales to their residents? What are the possible disadvantages?

2. As commerce moves online and collecting sales taxes becomes more difficult, how can states replace lost revenue? What other taxes might state governments use to generate revenue?

# The Changing Relationship between the Federal Government and the States

**Trace how the federal government became much stronger over time**

At the time of the Founding, the states far outstripped the federal government in their power to influence the lives of ordinary Americans. In the system of shared powers between the states and the federal government, the states were most active in economic and social regulation, while Washington took a much more hands-off approach. Even so, the federal government gradually expanded its powers in the wake of important Supreme Court decisions. However, it was not until the New Deal in the 1930s that the federal government gained vast new powers.

## Restraining National Power with Dual Federalism

**dual federalism** the system of government that prevailed in the United States from 1789 to 1937, in which most fundamental governmental powers were shared between the federal and state governments

As we have noted, the Constitution created two layers of government: the national government and the state governments. The consequences of this **dual federalism** are fundamental to the American system of government in theory and in practice; they have meant that states have done most of the fundamental governing. For evidence, look at Table 3.2, which lists the major types of public policies by which Americans were governed for the first century and a half under the Constitution. We call it the "traditional system" because it prevailed for much of American history and because it closely approximates the intentions of the framers of the Constitution.

Under the traditional system, the national government was quite small compared with both the state governments and the governments of other Western nations. Not only was it smaller than most governments of that time, but in fact it was also very narrowly specialized in the functions it performed. The national government built or sponsored the construction of roads, canals, and bridges (internal improvements). It provided cash subsidies to shippers and shipbuilders and distributed free or low-priced public land to encourage western settlement and business ventures. It placed relatively heavy taxes on imported goods (tariffs), not only to raise revenues but also to protect "infant industries" from competition from the more advanced European enterprises. It protected patents and provided for a common currency, which encouraged and facilitated enterprises and to expand markets.

What do these functions of the national government reveal? First, virtually all the functions were aimed at assisting commerce. It is quite appropriate to refer to the traditional American system as a "commercial republic." Second, virtually none of the national government's policies directly coerced citizens. The emphasis of governmental programs was on assistance, promotion, and encouragement—the allocation of land or capital to meet the needs of economic development.

Meanwhile, state legislatures were actively involved in economic regulation during the nineteenth century. In the United States, then and now, private property exists only in state laws and state court decisions regarding property, trespass, and real estate. American capitalism took its form from state property and trespass laws, and from state laws and court decisions regarding contracts, markets, credit, banking, incorporation, and insurance. Laws concerning slavery were a subdivision of property law in states where slavery existed. The practice of important

## TABLE 3.2

## The Federal System: Specialization of Governmental Functions in the Traditional System (1800–1933)

| NATIONAL GOVERNMENT POLICIES (DOMESTIC) | STATE GOVERNMENT POLICIES | LOCAL GOVERNMENT POLICIES |
|---|---|---|
| Internal improvements | Property laws (including slavery) | Adaptation of state laws to local conditions |
| Subsidies | Estate and inheritance laws | Public works |
| Tariffs | Commerce laws | Contracts for public works |
| Public land disposal | Banking and credit laws | Licensing of public accommodation |
| Patents | Corporate laws | Assessible improvements |
| Currency | Insurance laws | Basic public services |
| | Family laws | |
| | Morality laws | |
| | Public health laws | |
| | Education laws | |
| | General penal laws | |
| | Eminent domain laws | |
| | Construction codes | |
| | Land-use laws | |
| | Water and mineral laws | |
| | Criminal procedure laws | |
| | Electoral and political party laws | |
| | Local government laws | |
| | Civil service laws | |
| | Occupations and professions laws | |

professions, such as law and medicine, was (and is) illegal except as provided for by state law. To educate or not to educate a child has been a decision governed more by state laws than by parents. It is important to note also that virtually all criminal laws—regarding everything from trespass to murder—have been state laws. Most of the criminal laws adopted by Congress are concerned only with the District of Columbia and other federal territories.

All this (and more, as shown in the middle column of Table 3.2) demonstrates that most of the fundamental governing in the United States was done by the states. The contrast between national and state policies, as shown by Table 3.2, demonstrates the difference in the power vested in each. The list of items in the middle column could actually have been made longer. Moreover, each item on the list is a category of law that fills many volumes of statutes and court decisions.

This contrast between national and state governments is all the more impressive because it is basically what the framers of the Constitution intended. Since the 1930s the national government has expanded into local and intrastate matters far beyond what anyone could have foreseen in 1790, 1890, or even in the 1920s.

In 1815, President James Madison called for a federally funded program of "internal improvements," which was one of the few policy roles for the national government during the first half of the nineteenth century. By improving transportation through the construction of roads and canals, the government fostered the growth of the market economy and boosted federal power.

But this significant expansion of the national government did not alter the basic framework. The national government has become much larger, yet the states have continued to be central to the American system of government.

Herein lies probably the most important point of all: the fundamental impact of federalism on the way the United States is governed comes not from any particular provision of the Constitution but from the framework itself, which has determined which level of government does what and, through that, the political development of the country. By allowing state governments to do most of the fundamental governing, the Constitution saved the national government from many policy decisions that might have proven too divisive for a large and very young country. There is little doubt that if the Constitution had provided for a unitary rather than a federal system, the war over slavery would have come in 1789 or not long thereafter rather than in 1861; and if it had come that early, the South might very well have seceded and established a separate, slaveholding nation.

In helping the national government remain small and aloof from the most divisive issues of the day, federalism contributed significantly to the political stability of the nation, even as the social, economic, and political systems of many of the states and regions of the country were undergoing tremendous, profound, and sometimes violent, change.[12] As we shall see, some important aspects of federalism have changed, but the federal framework has survived two centuries and a devastating civil war.

## Federalism and the Slow Growth of the National Government's Power

Having created the national government, and recognizing the potential for abuse of power, the states sought through federalism to constrain it. The "traditional system" of a weak national government prevailed for over a century, despite economic forces favoring its expansion and despite Supreme Court cases giving a pro-national interpretation to Article I, Section 8, of the Constitution.

That article delegates to Congress the power "to regulate commerce with foreign nations, and among the several States and with the Indian tribes." This **commerce clause** was consistently interpreted *in favor* of national power over the economy by the Supreme Court for most of the nineteenth century. The first and most important such case was *McCulloch v. Maryland* (1819), which involved the question of whether Congress had the power to charter a national bank—an explicit grant of power nowhere to be found in Article I, Section 8.[13] Chief Justice John Marshall answered that this power could be "implied" from other powers that were expressly delegated to Congress, such as the "powers to lay and collect taxes; to borrow money; to regulate commerce; and to declare and conduct a war."

By allowing Congress to use the necessary and proper clause to interpret its delegated powers expansively, the Supreme Court created the potential for an unprecedented increase in national government power. Marshall also concluded that whenever a state law conflicted with a federal law (as in the case of *McCulloch v. Maryland*), the state law would be deemed invalid since the Constitution states that "the Laws of the United States . . . shall be the supreme Law of the Land." Both parts of this great case are pro-national, yet Congress did not immediately seek to expand the policies of the national government.

Another major case, *Gibbons v. Ogden* (1824), reinforced this nationalistic interpretation of the Constitution. The important but relatively narrow issue was whether the state of New York could grant a monopoly to Robert Fulton's steamboat company to operate an exclusive service between New York and New Jersey. Chief Justice Marshall argued that New York state did not have the power to grant this particular monopoly, and so Marshall had to define what Article I, Section 8, meant by "commerce among the several states." He insisted that the definition was "comprehensive," extending to "every species of commercial intercourse." However, this comprehensiveness was limited "to that commerce which concerns more states than one." *Gibbons* is important because it established the supremacy of the national government in all matters affecting what later came to be called "interstate commerce."[14] But the precise meaning of interstate commerce would remain uncertain during several decades of constitutional discourse. Backed by the implied-powers decision in *McCulloch* and by the broad definition of "interstate commerce" in *Gibbons*, Article I, Section 8, was a source of power for the national government as long as Congress sought to facilitate commerce through subsidies, services, and land grants. Later in the nineteenth century, though, any effort of the national government to *regulate* commerce in such areas as fraud, the production of substandard goods, the use of child labor, or the existence of dangerous working conditions or long hours was declared unconstitutional by the Supreme Court as a violation of the concept of interstate commerce. Such legislation meant that the federal government was entering the factory and the workplace—local areas—and was attempting to regulate goods that had not yet passed into interstate commerce. To enter these local workplaces was to exercise police power—a power reserved to the states. No one questioned the power of the national government to regulate businesses that intrinsically involved interstate commerce, such as railroads, gas pipelines, and waterway transportation. But well into the twentieth century the Supreme Court used the concept of interstate commerce as a barrier against most efforts by Congress to regulate local conditions.

This aspect of federalism prevailed during an epoch of tremendous economic development, the period between the Civil War and the 1930s. It gave the American economy a freedom from federal government control that closely approximated the ideal of free enterprise. The economy was never entirely free, of course; in

**commerce clause** Article I, Section 8, of the Constitution, which delegates to Congress the power "to regulate commerce with foreign nations, and among the several States and with the Indian tribes." This clause was interpreted by the Supreme Court in favor of national power over the economy

fact, entrepreneurs themselves did not want complete freedom from government. They needed law and order. They needed a stable currency. They needed courts and police to enforce contracts and prevent trespass. They needed roads, canals, and railroads. But federalism, as interpreted by the Supreme Court for 70 years after the Civil War, made it possible for business to have its cake and eat it, too: entrepreneurs enjoyed the benefits of national policies facilitating commerce and were protected by the courts from policies regulating commerce by protecting the rights of consumers and workers.[15]

All this changed after 1937, when the Supreme Court issued a series of decisions that laid the groundwork for a much stronger federal government. Most significant was the Court's dramatic expansion of the commerce clause. By throwing out the old distinction between interstate and intrastate commerce, the Court converted the commerce clause from a source of limitations to a source of power for the national government. The Court upheld acts of Congress protecting the rights of employees to organize and engage in collective bargaining, regulating the amount of farmland in cultivation, extending low-interest credit to small businesses and farmers, and restricting the activities of corporations dealing in the stock market. The Court also upheld many other laws that contributed to the construction of

*In 1916 the national government passed the Keating-Owen Child Labor Act, which excluded from interstate commerce all goods manufactured by children under age 14. The act was ruled unconstitutional by the Supreme Court, and the regulation of child labor remained in the hands of state governments until the 1930s.*

the "welfare state."[16] With these rulings, the Court decisively signaled that the era of dual federalism was over. In the future, Congress would have very broad powers to regulate activity in the states.

## The Changing Role of the States

As we have seen, the Constitution's commerce clause contained the seeds of a very expansive national government. For much of the nineteenth century, federal power remained limited. The Tenth Amendment was used to bolster arguments in favor of **states' rights**, which in their extreme version claimed that the states did not have to submit to national laws whenever they believed the national government had exceeded its authority. Prior to the Civil War, sharp differences between the North and the South over tariffs and slavery gave rise to arguments supporting nullification. Most fully articulated by John C. Calhoun, vice president under Andrew Jackson and later a senator from South Carolina, the doctrine of nullification proposed that states were not bound by federal laws that they considered unconstitutional. Such arguments were voiced less often after the Civil War, but the Supreme Court continued to use the Tenth Amendment to strike down laws that it thought exceeded national power, including the Civil Rights Act passed in 1875.

In the early twentieth century, however, reformers began to press for national regulations to limit the power of large corporations and to preserve the health and welfare of citizens. The Supreme Court approved some of these laws, but it struck down others, including a law combating child labor. The Court stated that the law violated the Tenth Amendment because only states should have the power to regulate conditions of employment. By the late 1930s, however, the Supreme Court had approved such an expansion of federal power that the Tenth Amendment appeared irrelevant. The desire to promote equal working conditions across the country had elevated the federal government over the states. In fact, in 1941, Justice Harlan Fiske Stone declared that the Tenth Amendment was simply a "truism," that it had no real meaning.[17]

**states' rights** the principle that the states should oppose the increasing authority of the national government. This principle was most popular in the period before the Civil War

*States' rights have been embraced by many causes in the past 50 years. Governor George Wallace of Alabama, a vocal supporter of states' rights, defiantly turned away U.S. attorney general Nicholas Katzenbach, who tried to enroll two black students at the University of Alabama at Tuscaloosa in 1963.*

# International Trade Agreements and the States

**The Constitution reserves for the** federal government the power to make foreign policy and to enter into treaties. Yet the expansion of the global economy over the past three decades has increased the importance of the international arena for state and local governments. For states, the expansion of international trade offers new opportunities to promote economic development but also presents frustrations. This is because international trade agreements may tie the hands of states and because states have little formal voice in these agreements.

One of the most important such trade agreements is the North American Free Trade Agreement (NAFTA), a treaty signed by Canada, the United States, and Mexico in 1992 to open trade across the national borders of these three countries. It also created new trade rules that each national government is obligated to follow. Although U.S. state governments were not involved in creating these trade rules, the rules may significantly restrict their own policies. Other trade agreements, such as those negotiated through the World Trade Organization (WTO), also may limit what American states can do.

Trade agreements that have recently aroused concern in the states are proposed rulings that would label many common state procurement policies as barriers to trade and therefore unenforceable. Procurement policies determine who can sell goods and provide services to the state. States often impose conditions on the companies with which they do business. For example, some states have policies requiring them to buy local or American-made products in an effort to reduce the offshoring of jobs. Other states impose requirements aimed at improving the environment, including provisions for buying goods with recycled content or doing business with firms that use renewable energy sources. These conditions vary from state to state. As Maine's then-governor John Baldacci noted in a 2006 letter to the U.S. trade

representative, "The state of Maine's procurement laws have been developed to protect the interests of Maine's citizens and businesses and to reflect the state's commitment to spend its citizens' tax dollars in a socially and environmentally responsible way."[a]

The states have challenged the proposed national rules in international trade agreement as an infringement on state sovereignty. And some states have started to pass legislation to ensure that trade agreements are scrutinized by the state legislature. In 2007 the Hawaii state legislature passed legislation to ensure that only the state legislature could approve or reject the terms relating to procurement in international trade agreements. It became the third state to pass such legislation, joining Rhode Island and Maryland.

One of the major complaints that states have is that they have no voice in the process of formulating trade agreement provisions even when such agreements significantly limit their sovereignty and regulatory authority. Five state legislatures (California, Maine, Minnesota, North Carolina, and Washington) have created formal committees on international trade and federalism. These committees assess the impact of trade agreements and gain expert and constituency views about the policies. They are also a point of contact for the state legislatures, the U.S. Trade Representative, and the members of Congress on issues related to trade and economic development. The potential for trade agreements to restrict the traditional decision-making powers of the states means that, in the future, states will have to consider the international repercussions of their actions as a normal part of state lawmaking.

[a]www.citizens.org (accessed 9/25/07).

## for critical analysis

1. How do international treaties such as NAFTA and international organizations such as the World Trade Organization (WTO) affect the sovereign powers of the states?

2. What are states doing to ensure that their interests are considered when the federal government enters into international trade agreements?

Yet the idea that some powers should be reserved to the states did not go away. One reason is that groups with substantive policy interests often support states' rights as a means for achieving their policy goals. For example, in the 1950s, southern opponents of the civil rights movement revived the idea of states' rights to support racial segregation. In 1956, 96 southern members of Congress issued a "Southern Manifesto" in which they declared that southern states were not constitutionally bound by Supreme Court decisions outlawing racial segregation. They believed that states' rights should override individual rights to liberty and formal equality. With the eventual triumph of the civil rights movement, the slogan of "states' rights" became tarnished by its association with racial inequality.

The 1990s saw a revival of interest in the Tenth Amendment and important Supreme Court decisions limiting federal power. Much of the interest in the Tenth Amendment stemmed from conservatives who believed that a strong federal government encroached on individual liberties. They believed such freedoms were better protected by returning more power to the states through the process of devolution. In 1996, Bob Dole, the Republican presidential candidate, carried a copy of the Tenth Amendment in his pocket as he campaigned, pulling it out to read it aloud at rallies.[18] The Supreme Court's 1995 ruling in *United States v. Lopez* fueled further interest in the Tenth Amendment.[19] In that case, the Court, stating that Congress had exceeded its authority under the commerce clause, struck down a federal law that barred handguns near schools. This was the first time since the New Deal that the Court had limited congressional powers in this way. In 1997 the Court again relied on the Tenth Amendment to limit federal power in *Printz v. United States*.[20] The decision declared unconstitutional a provision of the Brady Handgun Violence Prevention Act that required state and local law-enforcement officials to conduct background checks on handgun purchasers. The Court declared that this provision violated state sovereignty guaranteed by the Tenth Amendment because it required state and local officials to administer a federal regulatory program.

The expansion of the power of the national government has not left the states powerless. State governments continue to make important laws. No better demonstration of the continuing influence of the federal framework can be offered than that the middle column of Table 3.2 is still a fairly accurate characterization of state government today. In each of these domains, however, states must now share power with the federal government.

> **for critical analysis**
>
> How have Supreme Court decisions affected the balance of power between the federal government and the states? Has the Supreme Court favored the federal government or the states?

# Who Does What? Public Spending and the Federal Framework

> **Analyze major developments in the federal framework since the 1930s**

Questions about how to divide responsibilities between the states and the national government first arose more than 200 years ago, when the framers wrote the Constitution to create a stronger union. But they did not solve the issue of who should do what. There is no "right" answer to that question; each generation of Americans has provided its own answer. In recent decades, many Americans have grown distrustful of the federal government and have supported giving more responsibility to the states.[21] Even so, they still want the federal government to set standards, promote equality, and provide security.

In political debates about the division of responsibility, some people argue for a strong federal role to set national standards, whereas others say the states should do more. These two goals are not necessarily at odds. The key is to find the right balance. In this section we will look at how the balance has shifted, and then we will consider current efforts to reshape the relationship between the national government and the states.

## The New Deal

The door to increased federal action opened when states proved unable to cope with the demands brought on by the depression. Before the Great Depression of the 1930s, states and localities took responsibility for addressing the needs of the poor, usually through private charity. But the extent of the need created by the depression quickly exhausted local and state capacities. By 1932, 25 percent of the workforce was unemployed. The jobless lost their homes and settled into camps all over the country, called "Hoovervilles," after President Herbert Hoover. Elected in 1928, the year before the depression hit, Hoover steadfastly maintained that the federal government could do little to alleviate the misery caused by the depression. It was a matter for state and local governments, he said.

Yet demands mounted for the federal government to take action. In Congress, some Democrats proposed that the federal government finance public works to aid the economy and put people back to work. Other members of Congress introduced legislation to provide federal grants to the states to assist them in their relief efforts. Most of these measures failed to win congressional approval or were vetoed by President Hoover.

When Franklin Delano Roosevelt took office in 1933, he energetically threw the federal government into the business of fighting the depression through a number

*The vast new programs created as part of the New Deal expanded the federal government's power. Programs like the Works Progress Administration (WPA), which provided jobs for the unemployed, were established to address the Great Depression, but the overall expansion of the national government lasted even after the depression ended.*

of proposals known collectively as the New Deal. He proposed a variety of temporary measures to provide federal relief and work programs. Most of the programs he proposed were to be financed by the federal government but administered by the states. In addition to these temporary measures, Roosevelt presided over the creation of several important federal programs designed to provide future economic security for Americans. The New Deal signaled the rise of a more active national government.

## Federal Grants

For the most part, the new national programs that the Roosevelt administration developed did not directly take power away from the states. Instead, Washington typically redirected states by offering them **grants-in-aid**, whereby Congress appropriates money to state and local governments on the condition that the money be spent for a particular purpose defined by Congress (see Figure 3.1). Franklin Roosevelt's New Deal expanded the range of grants-in-aid into social programs, providing grants to the states for financial assistance to poor children. Congress added more grants after World War II, creating new programs to help states fund activities such as providing school lunches and building highways. Sometimes the national government required state or local governments to match the national contribution dollar for dollar, but in some programs, such as the development of the interstate highway system, the congressional grants provided 90 percent of the cost of the program.

**grants-in-aid** programs through which Congress provides money to state and local governments on the condition that the funds be employed for purposes defined by the federal government

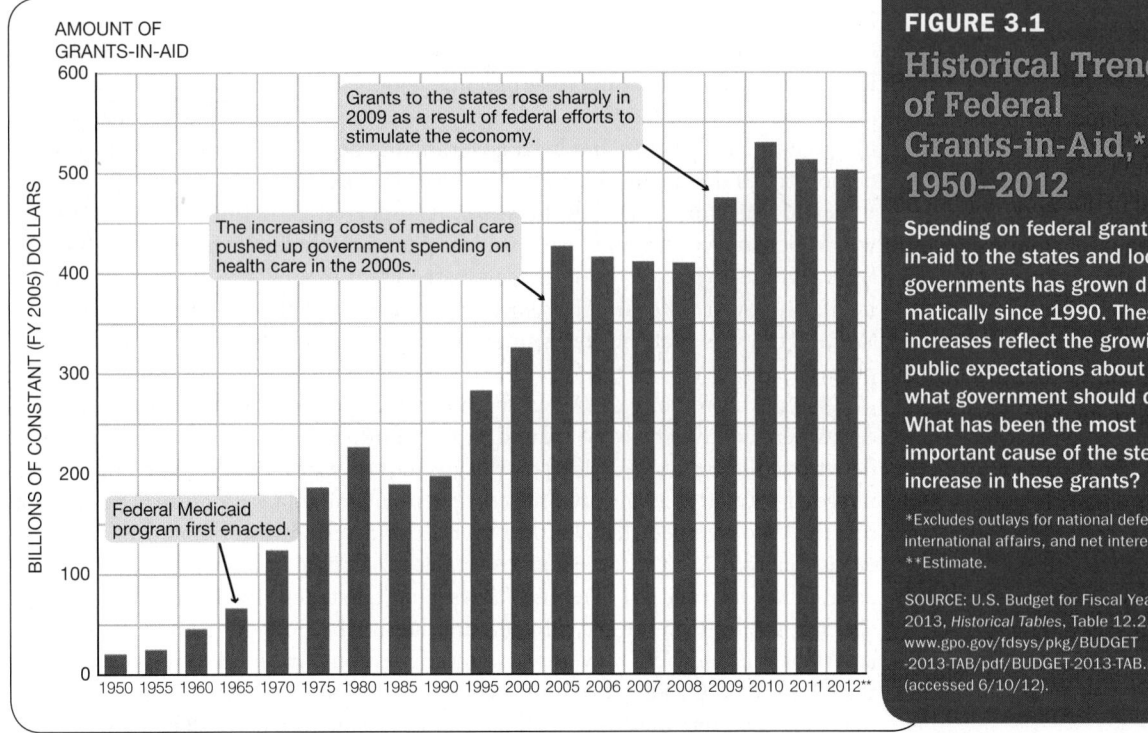

AMOUNT OF GRANTS-IN-AID

BILLIONS OF CONSTANT (FY 2005) DOLLARS

Grants to the states rose sharply in 2009 as a result of federal efforts to stimulate the economy.

The increasing costs of medical care pushed up government spending on health care in the 2000s.

Federal Medicaid program first enacted.

### FIGURE 3.1
### Historical Trend of Federal Grants-in-Aid,* 1950–2012

Spending on federal grants-in-aid to the states and local governments has grown dramatically since 1990. These increases reflect the growing public expectations about what government should do. What has been the most important cause of the steady increase in these grants?

*Excludes outlays for national defense, international affairs, and net interest.
**Estimate.

SOURCE: U.S. Budget for Fiscal Year 2013, *Historical Tables*, Table 12.2, www.gpo.gov/fdsys/pkg/BUDGET-2013-TAB/pdf/BUDGET-2013-TAB.pdf (accessed 6/10/12).

**categorical grants** congressional grants given to states and localities on the condition that expenditures be limited to a problem or group specified by law

These types of federal grants-in-aid are also called **categorical grants** because the national government determines the purposes, or categories, for which the money can be used. For the most part, the categorical grants created before the 1960s simply helped the states perform their traditional functions.[22] During the 1960s, however, the national role expanded and the number of categorical grants increased dramatically. For example, during the 89th Congress (1965–66) alone, the number of categorical grant-in-aid programs grew from 221 to 379.[23] The *value* of categorical grants also has risen dramatically, increasing from $2.3 billion in 1950 to an estimated $467 billion in 2008. The grants authorized during the 1960s announced national purposes much more strongly than did earlier grants. One of the most important—and expensive—was the federal Medicaid program, which provides states with grants to pay for medical care for the poor, the disabled, and many nursing home residents.

**project grants** grant programs in which state and local governments submit proposals to federal agencies and for which funding is provided on a competitive basis

**formula grants** grants-in-aid in which a formula is used to determine the amount of federal funds a state or local government will receive

Many of the categorical grants enacted during the 1960s were **project grants**, which require state and local governments to submit proposals to federal agencies. In contrast to the older, **formula grants**, which used a formula (composed of such elements as need and state and local capacities) to distribute funds, the project grants made funding available on a competitive basis. Federal agencies would give grants to the proposals they judged to be the best. In this way, the national government acquired substantial control over which state and local governments got money, how much they got, and how they spent it.

## Cooperative Federalism

**cooperative federalism** a type of federalism existing since the New Deal era in which grants-in-aid have been used strategically to encourage states and localities (without commanding them) to pursue nationally defined goals. Also known as "intergovernmental cooperation"

The growth of categorical grants created a new kind of federalism. If the traditional system of two sovereigns performing highly different functions could be called dual federalism, historians of federalism suggest that the system since the New Deal could be called **cooperative federalism**. The political scientist Morton Grodzins characterized this as a move from "layer cake federalism" to "marble cake federalism,"[24] in which intergovernmental cooperation and sharing have blurred a once-clear distinguishing line, making it difficult to say where the national government ends and the state and local governments begin (see Figure 3.2). Figure 3.3 demonstrates the financial basis of the "marble cake" idea.

For a while in the 1960s, however, it appeared as if the state governments would become increasingly irrelevant to American federalism. Many of the new federal grants bypassed the states and instead sent money directly to local governments and even to local nonprofit organizations. The theme heard repeatedly in Washington was that the states simply could not be trusted to carry out national purposes.[25]

One of the reasons that Washington distrusted the states was the way African American citizens were treated in the South. The southern states' forthright defense of segregation, justified on the grounds of states' rights, helped tarnish the image of the states as the civil rights movement gained momentum. The national officials who planned the War on Poverty during the 1960s pointed to the racial exclusion practiced in the southern states as a reason for bypassing state governments. The political scientist James Sundquist described how this thinking affected the War on Poverty: "In the drafting of the Economic Opportunity Act, an 'Alabama syndrome' developed. Any suggestion within the poverty task force that the states be given a role in the administration of the act was met with the question, 'Do you want to give that kind of power to [then–Alabama governor] George Wallace?'"[26]

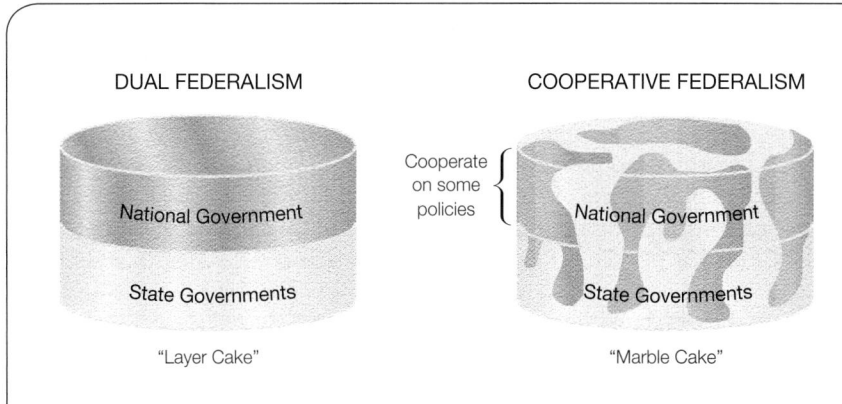

DUAL FEDERALISM

National Government

State Governments

"Layer Cake"

Cooperate on some policies

COOPERATIVE FEDERALISM

National Government

State Governments

"Marble Cake"

**FIGURE 3.2**

Dual versus Cooperative Federalism

In layer cake federalism, the responsibilities of the national government and state governments are clearly separated. In marble cake federalism, national policies, state policies, and local policies overlap in many areas.

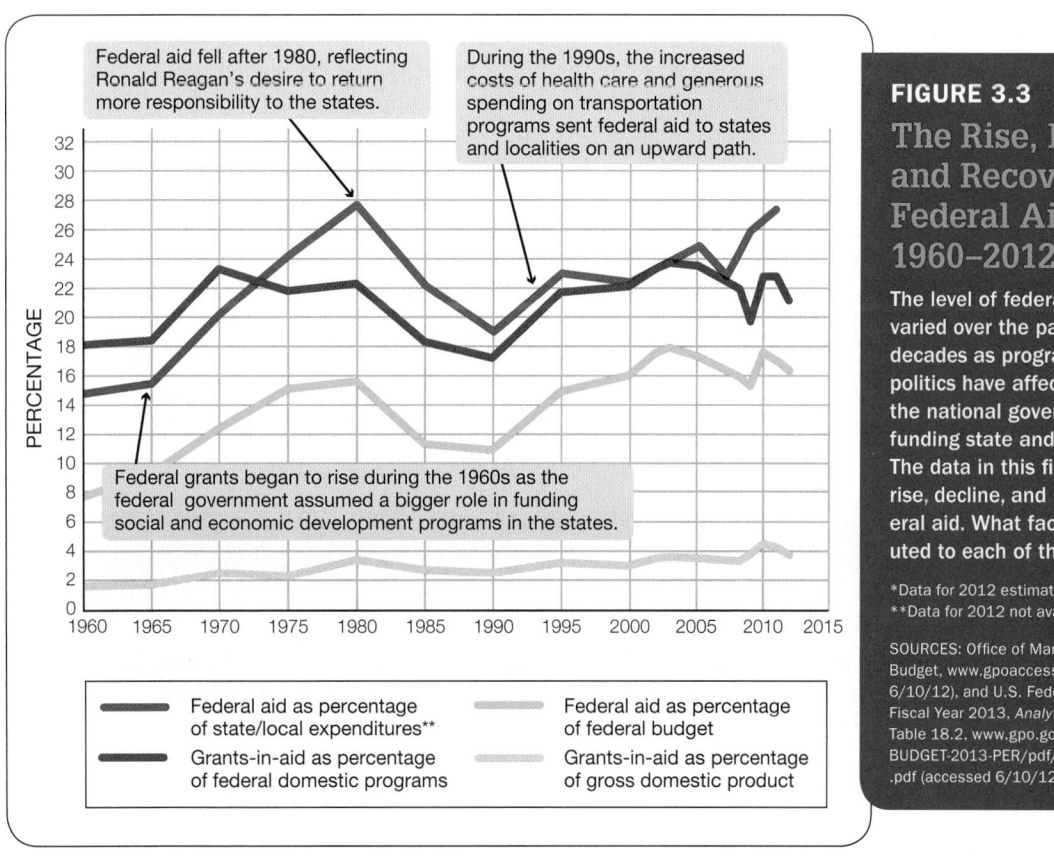

Federal aid fell after 1980, reflecting Ronald Reagan's desire to return more responsibility to the states.

During the 1990s, the increased costs of health care and generous spending on transportation programs sent federal aid to states and localities on an upward path.

Federal grants began to rise during the 1960s as the federal government assumed a bigger role in funding social and economic development programs in the states.

PERCENTAGE

1960 1965 1970 1975 1980 1985 1990 1995 2000 2005 2010 2015

Federal aid as percentage of state/local expenditures**

Grants-in-aid as percentage of federal domestic programs

Federal aid as percentage of federal budget

Grants-in-aid as percentage of gross domestic product

**FIGURE 3.3**

The Rise, Decline, and Recovery of Federal Aid, 1960–2012*

The level of federal aid has varied over the past several decades as program costs and politics have affected the role the national government plays in funding state and local services. The data in this figure show a rise, decline, and recovery of federal aid. What factors contributed to each of these trends?

*Data for 2012 estimated.
**Data for 2012 not available.

SOURCES: Office of Management and Budget, www.gpoaccess.gov (accessed 6/10/12), and U.S. Federal Budget for Fiscal Year 2013, *Analytical Perspectives*, Table 18.2, www.gpo.gov/fdsys/pkg/BUDGET-2013-PER/pdf/BUDGET-2013-PER.pdf (accessed 6/10/12).

Yet even though many national policies of the 1960s bypassed the states, other new programs, such as Medicaid—the health program for the poor—relied on state governments for their implementation. In addition, as the national government expanded existing programs run by the states, states had to take on more responsibility. These new responsibilities meant that the states were playing a very important role in the federal system.

## Regulated Federalism and National Standards

The question of who decides what each level of government should do goes to the very heart of what it means to be an American citizen. How different should things be when one crosses a state line? In what policy areas is it acceptable for states to differ? In what areas should states be similar? How much inequality among the states is acceptable? Supreme Court decisions about the fundamental rights of American citizens provide the most important answers to these questions. Over time, the Court has pushed for greater uniformity across the states. In addition to legal decisions, the national government uses two other tools to create similarities across the states: grants-in-aid and regulations.

Grants-in-aid, as we have seen, are incentives: Congress gives money to state and local governments if they agree to spend it for the purposes Congress specifies. But as Congress began to enact legislation in new areas, such as environmental policy, it also imposed additional regulations on states and localities. Some political scientists call this a move toward **regulated federalism**.[27] The national government began to set standards of conduct or to require the states to set standards that met national guidelines. The effect of these national standards is that state and local policies in the areas of environmental protection, social services, and education are more uniform from coast to coast than are other nationally funded policies.

Some national standards require the federal government to take over areas of regulation formerly overseen by state or local governments. Such **preemption** occurs when state and local actions are found to be inconsistent with federal requirements. In some cases, federal laws and regulations are more stringent than state laws. For example, as federal regulations proliferated after the 1970s, Washington increasingly preempted state and local action in many different policy areas. These preemptions required the states to abide by tougher federal rules in policies as diverse as air and water pollution, occupational health and safety, and access for the handicapped. The regulated industries often oppose such laws because they increase the cost of doing business. After 1994, when Republicans retook control

**regulated federalism** a form of federalism in which Congress imposes legislation on states and localities, requiring them to meet national standards

**preemption** the principle that allows the national government to override state or local actions in certain policy areas; in foreign policy, the willingness to strike first in order to prevent an enemy attack

*In 2005 the Supreme Court ruled that the federal government had the right to prosecute individuals for using medical marijuana, even in states that had made such use legal. Despite the Court's ruling, some states have continued to permit the dispensing and use of medical marijuana.*

of Congress, the federal government used its preemption power in business's favor, limiting the ability of states to tax and regulate industry. For example, the Internet Tax Freedom Act (ITFA), first enacted by Congress in 1998 and subsequently renewed, prohibits states and localities from taxing Internet access services.

Congress is not the only federal body that can preempt the states; federal regulatory agencies can also issue rules that override state law. One controversial case involved a 2006 Food and Drug Administration drug-labeling rule preempting state laws that allow individuals to sue drug companies in state courts. Opponents—many of them trial lawyers—charged that such rules amounted to "stealth preemption" that "will deprive consumers of their right to hold negligent corporations accountable for injuries caused by defective products."[28] Supporters claimed that the rules were a proper use of federal authority. Although the Republicans came to power promising to grant more responsibility to the states, they ended up reducing state control in many areas by preemption.

State and local governments often contest federal preemptions. For example, in 2001, Attorney General John Ashcroft declared that Oregon's law permitting doctor-assisted suicide was illegal under federal drug regulations. In January 2006 the Supreme Court ruled in a 6–3 vote that the attorney general did not have the authority to outlaw the Oregon law.[29] Individuals have also challenged federal preemption. In 2009 the Supreme Court ruled against a drug manufacturer and in favor of a woman whose arm had to be amputated after she was improperly injected with a drug designed to counter nausea.[30] Although the drug company knew that such complications could arise, it argued that it was not responsible for the amputation because federal regulations did not require it to warn against this danger in labeling the drug. The Court, however, found the company liable for the damage. In its decision, the Court made it clear that federal regulations could not preempt state consumer protections and that states had the power to adopt stricter protections than those of the federal government.

In 2009, after only a few months in office, President Obama reversed the Bush administration's use of federal regulations to limit state laws. Under the new policy, federal regulations should preempt state laws only in extraordinary cases. The president directed agency leaders to review the regulations that had been put in place over the past ten years and consider amending them if they interfered with the "legitimate prerogatives of the states."[31] But as we will see below, the Obama administration did use its power of preemption to challenge state immigration laws, charging that states were making laws in a domain reserved for federal authority.

The growth of national standards has created some new problems and has raised questions about how far federal standardization should go. One problem that emerged in the 1980s was the increase in **unfunded mandates**—the product of a Democratic Congress that wanted to achieve liberal social objectives and Republican presidents who opposed increased social spending. Between 1983 and 1991, Congress mandated standards in many policy areas, including social services and environmental regulations, without providing additional funds to help the states meet those standards. Altogether, Congress enacted 27 laws that imposed new regulations or required states to expand existing programs.[32] For example, in the late 1980s, Congress ordered the states to extend the coverage provided by Medicaid, the medical insurance program for the poor. The aim was to make the program serve more people, particularly poor children, and to expand services. But Congress did not supply additional funding to help states meet these new requirements; the states had to shoulder the increased financial burden themselves.

**for critical analysis**

Is federal preemption of local laws desirable? Is preemption justified for some issues more than for others?

**unfunded mandates** regulations or conditions for receiving grants that impose costs on state and local governments for which they are not reimbursed by the federal government

States and localities quickly began to protest the cost of unfunded mandates. Although it is very hard to determine the exact cost of federal regulations, the Congressional Budget Office estimated that between 1983 and 1990, new federal regulations cost states and localities between $8.9 and $12.7 billion.[33] States complained that mandates took up so much of their budgets that they were not able to set their own priorities. These burdens became part of a rallying cry to reduce the power of the federal government—a cry that took center stage when a Republican Congress was elected in 1994. One of the first measures the new Congress passed was an act to limit the cost of unfunded mandates, the Unfunded Mandates Reform Act (UMRA). Under this law, Congress must estimate the cost of any proposal it believes will require more than $50 million.

New national problems inevitably raise the question of "who pays?" Recently, concern about unfunded mandates has arisen around health care reform. The major health care reform enacted during Obama's first two years as president, the Affordable Care Act of 2010 called for a major expansion of Medicaid. But because Medicaid is partly funded by the states, any major increase in the number of Medicaid recipients could impose a significant fiscal burden on the states. Although the law provided additional federal aid to support the new requirements, the Medicaid provisions became a target for state challenges to the health care law. One of the central claims in the 26 states' lawsuits charged that the federal government did not have the power to withhold Medicaid funds from states that did not implement the new expansions. Although a lower court rejected the states' arguments, the Supreme Court included the Medicaid challenge when it agreed to hear the case.[34] As we saw in the introduction to this chapter, the Court ultimately ruled that states could decline to expand Medicaid coverage without losing their existing Medicaid funds. After the Court's decision, a handful of Republican governors announced that they would not implement the expanded coverage. Whatever they decide to do, it is clear that the Court's decision has injected a whole new set of issues into the question of "who pays."

## New Federalism and State Control

In 1970 the mayor of Oakland, California, told Congress that his city had 22 separate employment and training programs but that few poor residents were being trained for jobs that were available in the local labor market.[35] National programs had proliferated as Congress enacted many small grants, but little effort was made to coordinate or adapt programs to local needs. Today many governors argue for more control over such national grant programs. They complain that national grants do not allow for enough local flexibility and instead take a "one size fits all" approach.[36] These criticisms point to a fundamental challenge in American federalism: how to get the best results for the money spent. Do some divisions of responsibility between states and the federal government work better than others? Since the 1970s, as states have become more capable of administering large-scale programs, the idea of **devolution**—transferring responsibility for policy from the federal government to the states and localities—has become popular.

Proponents of more state authority have looked to **block grants** as a way of reducing federal control. Block grants are federal grants that allow the states considerable leeway in spending federal money. President Nixon led the first push for block grants in the early 1970s, as part of his **New Federalism**. Nixon's approach consolidated programs in the areas of job training, community development, and social services into three large block grants. These grants imposed some conditions on states and localities as to how the money should be spent, but not the narrow

**devolution** a policy to remove a program from one level of government by delegating it or passing it down to a lower level of government, such as from the national government to the state and local governments

**block grants** federal grants-in-aid that allow states considerable discretion in how the funds are spent

**New Federalism** attempts by Presidents Nixon and Reagan to return power to the states through block grants

regulations contained in the categorical grants. In addition, Congress provided an important new form of federal assistance to state and local governments, called **general revenue sharing**. Revenue sharing provided money to local governments and counties with no strings attached; localities could spend the money as they wished. In enacting revenue sharing, Washington acknowledged both the critical role that state and local governments play in implementing national priorities and their need for increased funding and enhanced flexibility in order to carry out that role (see Figure 3.4). Reagan's version of New Federalism also looked to block grants. Like Nixon, Reagan wanted to reduce the national government's control and return power to the states. But unlike Nixon, whose block grants increased federal spending, Reagan's block grants cut federal funding by 12 percent. His view was that the states could spend their own funds to make up the difference, if they chose to do so. Revenue sharing was also eliminated during the Reagan administration, leaving localities to fend for themselves. In all, Congress created 12 new block grants between 1981 and 1990.[37]

The Republican Congress elected in 1994 took this strategy even further, making substantial cuts in federal programs as well as supporting block grants. Their biggest success was the 1996 welfare reform law, which delegated to states important new responsibilities. Most of the other major proposed block grants or spending reductions, however, failed to pass Congress or were vetoed by President Clinton. The Republican congressional leadership had found that it was much easier to promise a "devolution revolution" than to deliver on that promise.[38]

Neither block grants nor reduced federal funding have proven to be magic solutions to the problems of federalism. For one thing, there is always a trade-off between accountability—that is, whether the states are using funds for the purposes intended—and flexibility. If the objective is to have accountable and efficient government, it is not clear that state bureaucracies are any more efficient or more capable than national agencies. In Mississippi, for example, the state Department of Human Services spent money from the child care block grant for office furniture

**general revenue sharing** the process by which one unit of government yields a portion of its tax income to another unit of government, according to an established formula. Revenue sharing typically involves the national government providing money to state governments

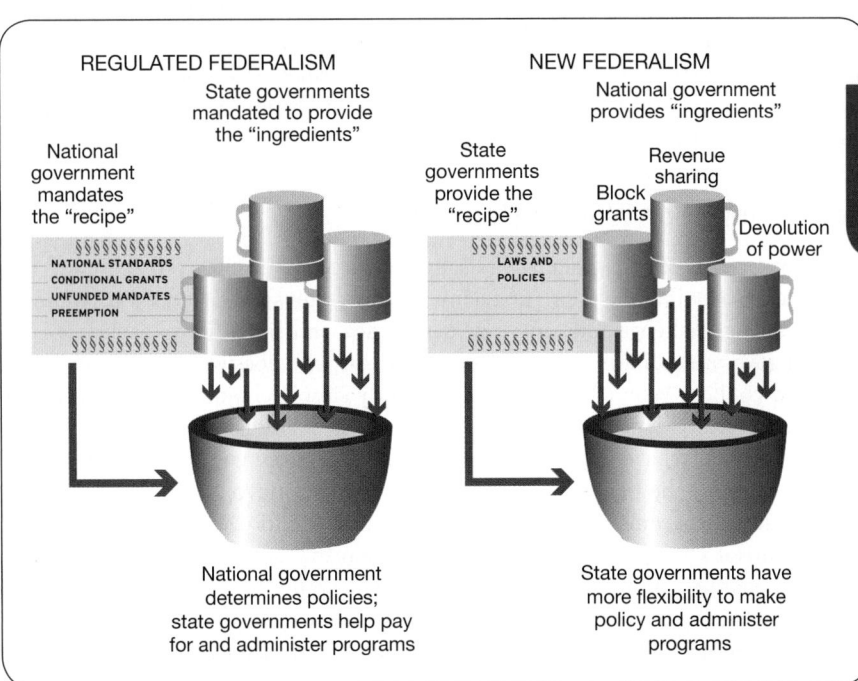

REGULATED FEDERALISM

State governments mandated to provide the "ingredients"

National government mandates the "recipe"

§§§§§§§§§§§
NATIONAL STANDARDS
CONDITIONAL GRANTS
UNFUNDED MANDATES
PREEMPTION
§§§§§§§§§§§

National government determines policies; state governments help pay for and administer programs

NEW FEDERALISM

National government provides "ingredients"

State governments provide the "recipe"

Revenue sharing

Block grants

Devolution of power

§§§§§§§§§§§
LAWS AND POLICIES
§§§§§§§§§§§

State governments have more flexibility to make policy and administer programs

**FIGURE 3.4**
Regulated versus New Federalism

*The debate over national-versus-state control of speed limits arose in 1973, when gas prices skyrocketed and supplies became scarce. Drivers nationwide were forced to wait in long lines at gas stations. The federal government responded to the gas crisis by instituting a national 55-mile-per-hour speed limit.*

and designer salt and pepper shakers that cost $37.50 a pair. As one Mississippi state legislator said, "I've seen too many years of good ol' boy politics to know they shouldn't [transfer money to the states] without stricter controls and requirements."[39] Even after block grants were created, Congress reimposed regulations in order to increase the states' accountability.

At times the federal government has also moved to limit state discretion over spending in cases where it thinks states are too generous. For example, in 2007, President Bush issued regulations that prevented states from providing benefits under the State Children's Health Insurance Program (SCHIP) to children in families well above the poverty line. The Bush administration also barred states from providing chemotherapy to illegal immigrants, who are guaranteed emergency medical treatment under Medicaid.[40] These new rules embroiled states and the federal government in sharp conflicts over state discretion in spending decisions, once the hallmark of New Federalism.

## Devolution: For Whose Benefit?

As Figure 3.5 indicates, federalism has changed dramatically over the course of American history. Finding the right balance among states and the federal government is an evolving challenge for American democracy, and since the expansion of the national government in the 1930s, questions about "who does what" have frequently provoked conflict. Why does such an apparently simple choice set off such highly charged political debate? One reason is that many decisions about federal-versus-state responsibility have implications for who benefits from government action.

Let's consider the benefits of federal control versus devolution in the realm of **redistributive programs**—programs designed primarily for the benefit of the poor. Many political scientists and economists maintain that states and localities should not be in charge of redistributive programs. They argue that since states and local governments have to compete with one another, they do not have the incentive to spend their money on the needy people in their areas. Instead, they want to keep

**redistributive programs** economic policies designed to control the economy through taxing and spending, with the goal of benefiting the poor

taxes low and spend money on things that promote economic development.[41] In this situation, states might engage in a "race to the bottom": if one state cuts assistance to the poor, neighboring states will institute similar or deeper cuts both to reduce expenditures and to discourage poorer people from moving to their states. As one New York legislator put it, "The concern we have is that unless we make our welfare system and our tax and regulatory system competitive with the states around us, we will have too many disincentives for business to move here. Welfare is a big part of that."[42]

In 1996, when Congress enacted major welfare reform, it followed a different logic. By changing welfare from a combined federal-state program into a block grant to the states, Congress gave the states more responsibility for programs that serve the poor. Supporters of the change hoped to reduce welfare spending and argued that states could act as "laboratories of democracy" by experimenting with many different approaches in order to find those that best met the needs of their citizens.[43] As states altered their welfare programs in the wake of the new law, they did indeed design diverse approaches. For example, Minnesota adopted an incentive-based approach that offers extra assistance to families that take low-wage jobs, while six other states imposed very strict time limits on receiving benefits, allowing welfare recipients less than the five-year limit in the federal legislation. After the passage of the law, welfare rolls declined dramatically. On average, they declined by more than half from their peak in 1994; in 12 states the decline was 70 percent or higher. Politicians have cited these statistics to claim that the poor have benefited from greater state control of welfare, yet most studies have found that the majority of those leaving welfare remain in poverty.

In some decisions about federalism, local concerns are overridden in the name of the national interest. The question of speed limits, traditionally a state and local responsibility, provides an example. In 1973, at the height of the oil shortage, Congress passed legislation to withhold federal highway funds from states that did not adopt a maximum speed limit of 55 miles per hour (mph) in order to reduce fuel consumption. Although Congress had not formally taken over the authority to set speed limits, the power of its purse was so important that every state adopted the new speed limit. As the crisis faded, concern about energy conservation diminished. The national speed limit lost much of its support, even though it was found to have reduced the number of traffic deaths. In 1995, Congress repealed the penalties for higher speed limits, and states once again became free to set their own speed limits. Many states with large rural areas raised their maximum to 75 mph; Montana initially set unlimited speeds in its rural areas during daylight hours. Research indicates that the number of highway deaths has indeed risen in the states that increased the limits.[44]

Because the division of responsibility in the federal system has important implications for who benefits, few conflicts over state-versus-national control will ever be settled once and for all. New evidence about the costs and benefits of different arrangements provides fuel for ongoing debates about what are properly the states' responsibilities and what the federal government should do. Likewise, changes in the political

In 1995, Congress removed its speed limit restrictions and allowed states to raise the limit above 55 miles per hour without losing federal highway funds. As a result, speed limits went up on many highways.

**FIGURE 3.5**

**The Changing
Federal Framework**

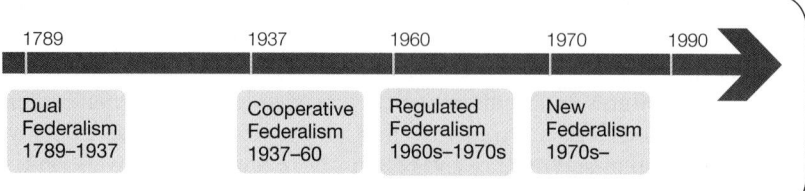

| 1789 | 1937 | 1960 | 1970 | 1990 |

Dual Federalism 1789–1937

Cooperative Federalism 1937–60

Regulated Federalism 1960s–1970s

New Federalism 1970s–

control of the national government usually provoke a rethinking of responsibilities as new leaders seek to alter federal arrangements for the benefit of the groups they represent.

## Federalism since 2000

During the past 13 years, many of the most controversial issues in American politics—including the appropriate size of public social spending, the rights and benefits of immigrants (legal as well as undocumented), government response to global climate change, and questions about whether and how government should regulate business and moral behavior—have been fought through the federal system. Politicians of all stripes regularly turn to the federal government to override decisions made by states. Likewise, when the federal government proves unable or unwilling to act, activists and politicians try to achieve their goals in states and localities. In many cases, it is up to the courts to decide which level of government should have the final say.

Although conservatives proclaim their preference for a small federal government and their support for more state autonomy, in fact they often expand the federal government and limit state autonomy. During the presidency of George W. Bush, the growth of government, the activist, free-spending Republican Congress, and a series of Supreme Court rulings supporting federal power over the states made it clear that conservatives do not always support small government; nor do they always favor returning power to the states. Once in power, many conservatives discovered not only that they needed a strong federal government to respond to public demands but also that they could use federal power to advance conservative policy goals.

For President Bush, the importance of a strong federal government dawned with force after the terrorist attacks in 2001. Aware that the American public was looking to Washington for protection, Bush worked with Congress to pass the Patriot Act, which greatly increased the surveillance powers of the federal government. A year later he created the enormous new federal Department of Homeland Security.

President Bush also expanded federal control and increased spending in policy areas far removed from concerns about security. The 2001 No Child Left Behind Act introduced unprecedented federal intervention in public education, traditionally a state and local responsibility. New, detailed federal testing requirements and provisions stipulating how states should treat failing schools were major expansions of federal authority in education. When a number of states threatened to defy some of the new federal requirements, Bush's Department of Education relaxed its tough stance and became more flexible in enforcing the act. The Obama administration increased flexibility even more by granting waivers to 19 states. The waivers released the states from the federal mandates around school accountability and performance, replacing them with state measures.

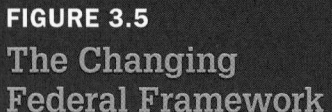

**for critical analysis**

The role of the national government has changed significantly from the Founding era to the present. Do you think the framers of the Constitution would be pleased with the current balance of power between the national government and the state governments?

In the Supreme Court, too, many decisions began to support a stronger federal role over the states. This was surprising to many observers, because in the 1990s it had appeared that the Rehnquist Court was embarked on a "federalism revolution" designed to return more power to the states. Instead, in several key decisions, the Court reaffirmed the power of the federal government. Decisions to uphold the federal Family and Medical Leave Act and the Americans with Disabilities Act asserted federal authority against state claims of immunity from the acts. In one important 2005 case, the Court upheld the right of Congress to ban medical marijuana, even though 11 states had legalized its use. Overturning a lower court ruling that said Congress did not have authority to regulate marijuana when it had been grown for noncommercial purposes in a single state, the Supreme Court ruled that the federal government did have the power to regulate use of all marijuana under the commerce clause. Even so, by 2011, 15 states had legalized medical marijuana. Amid this legal confusion, a medical marijuana industry began to flourish in states that allowed medical use of the drug. However, when the federal government unexpectedly began to crack down on marijuana dispensaries in 2011, some states began to reconsider their laws.[45]

One closely watched federalism case in 2006 was the challenge to Oregon's "right to die" law, which allows doctors to prescribe lethal doses of medicine for terminally ill patients who request it. Challengers claimed the law was illegal because Congress has the right to outlaw such use of drugs under the Controlled Substances Act, which regulates prescription drugs. In a 6–3 decision, the Court ruled in Oregon's favor.[46] Despite the ruling, only Washington state followed in Oregon's footsteps to make physician-assisted suicide legal. When challenged, other states, including Florida and Alaska, have upheld state prohibitions on physician-assisted suicide.

In other policy areas, states and localities have forged their own policies because the federal government has not acted. One of the most controversial of these issues is immigration legislation. In the first half of 2011, for example, state legislatures introduced more than 1,592 bills related to immigration.[47] Many state and local laws that govern immigration are not controversial, but some raise critical questions about what is the federal role and what are the responsibilities of state and local governments. In April 2010, Arizona enacted an extremely controversial immigration measure requiring immigrants to carry identity documents and requiring police to ask about immigration status when they stop drivers they suspect of being illegal immigrants. The federal Department of Justice joined several other groups in challenging the law, and the courts struck down the strongest provisions of the law. Even so, several states enacted similar laws. By 2012 the Department of Justice had sued three additional states—Alabama, South Carolina, and Utah—charging that their immigration laws were preempted by federal law. In the words of Attorney General Eric Holder, "It is clearly unconstitutional for a state to set its own immigration policy."[48] The Alabama law attracted national attention for its sweeping provisions, which made the failure to carry immigration papers a crime, gave police broad powers to stop suspected illegal immigrants, required employers and landlords to verify immigration status, and forced schools to check the legal status of students and their parents. In 2012 the Supreme Court ruled that Arizona's law did not preempt federal authority to make immigration law.[49] The decision allowed states to enact tough measures including immigration checks by local law enforcement officials. Even so, these laws will continued to be challenged on other grounds, such as racial profiling.

The presence of an estimated 11 million unauthorized immigrants in communities across the country is an especially volatile issue affecting many aspects of state lawmaking. In 2007 the federal Department of Homeland Security enlisted state and local officials in the effort to enforce federal immigration law. Under the program, state and local law-enforcement agencies can be deputized to arrest suspected unauthorized immigrants and to check the immigration status of those apprehended on unrelated offenses. Yet the aggressive use of these powers in some localities has led to calls for ending the program. In 2009 the Justice Department stripped Joe Arpaio, sheriff of Maricopa County (Phoenix), Arizona, of the authority to make immigration sweeps. Arpaio had gained national attention for his harsh treatment of those rounded up in immigration raids, which included housing the immigrants in tent cities in the Arizona desert and putting female inmates in chain gangs. The Justice Department launched a series of investigations into Arpaio's actions, including one charging that his department discriminated against Latinos. However, the federal government did not eliminate the program. Instead, it vowed to exercise greater oversight over local actions.[50]

In fact, the federal government launched an additional program, Secure Communities, which allows state and local authorities to check the fingerprints of people being booked into jail against a Homeland Security database. If the fingerprints find a match in the database, it is up to the federal Immigration and Customs Enforcement agents to take further action. The law led to a record number of deportations in 2009 and 2010. Some states have objected to the program, and Illinois pulled out of the agreement with the federal government on the grounds that the law was detaining too many undocumented immigrants who had never committed a crime. Despite these objections, the federal government has declared that participation of state and local law-enforcement authorities is mandatory.[51]

As the cases of immigration and medical marijuana show, the Obama administration signaled a much stronger role for the federal government on some dimensions. The stronger federal role was also evident in measures to jump-start the failing economy. In February 2009, Congress enacted the American Recovery and Reinvestment Act (ARRA), a $787 billion measure that, in addition to tax cuts, offered states substantial one-time funds for a variety of purposes, including education, road building, unemployment insurance, and health care. Many governors, strapped for cash, welcomed the new funds. Others, however, worried that the

In 2010, Arizona passed a controversial law that required police to check the immigration status of people stopped for even minor matters. Opponents of the law called on the federal government to intervene. In 2012 the Supreme Court upheld the main part of the law.

# Who Opposed the Affordable Care Act?

Prior to the passage of the Affordable Care Act (ACA) in 2010, the states set the eligibility requirements for Medicaid, the government's health insurance program for lower-income Americans. States set various thresholds for Medicaid eligibility, which is shown below as a percentage of the federal poverty level (FPL); a lower number means it is harder to qualify for Medicaid benefits. The ACA would have required states to set Medicaid eligibility at 133% of the FPL. However, in June 2012, the U.S. Supreme Court struck the ACA's requirement of a national standard for Medicaid eligibility.

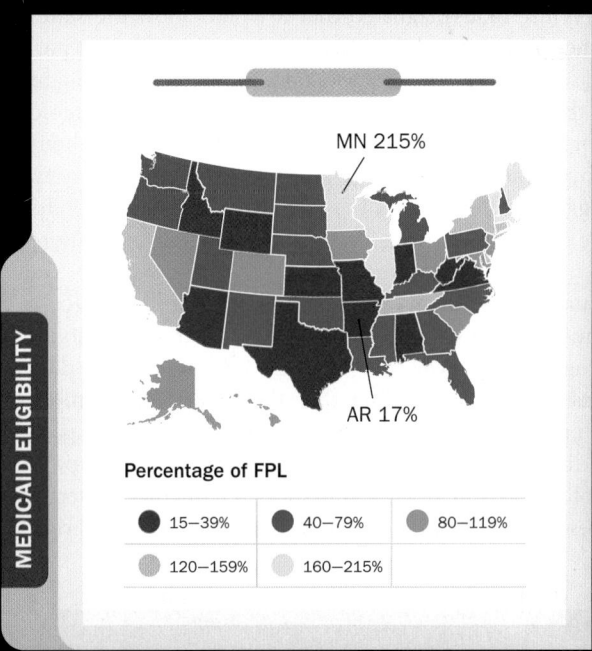

**MEDICAID ELIGIBILITY**

MN 215%

AR 17%

**Percentage of FPL**

- 15–39%
- 40–79%
- 80–119%
- 120–159%
- 160–215%

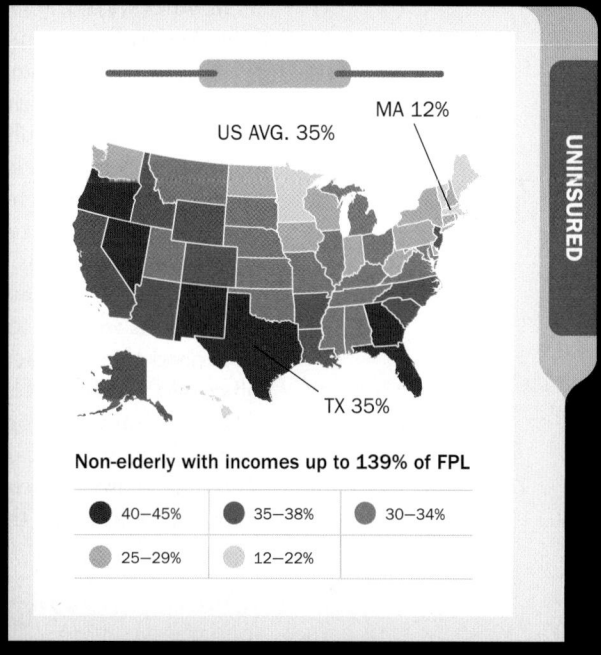

**UNINSURED**

MA 12%

US AVG. 35%

TX 35%

**Non-elderly with incomes up to 139% of FPL**

- 40–45%
- 35–38%
- 30–34%
- 25–29%
- 12–22%

## States That Challenged the ACA

*Iowa is both a plaintiff and a supporter of the ACA. The attorney general filed a brief in support of the legislation while the governor, Terry Branstad, filed a motion to join the suit against it.

SOURCES: U.S. Census Bureau, www.census.gov; Kaiser Family Foundation, 50 State Comparisons, Health Coverage & Uninsured, www.statehealthfacts.org (both accessed 7/25/11); *National Federation of Independent Business v. Sebelius*, 567 U.S. ___ (2012).

| AL | CA | DC | ID | KS | MD | MS | NV | NY | OK | SC | UT | WV |
| AK | CO | FL | IL | KY | MA | MO | NH | NC | OR | SD | VT | WI |
| AZ | CT | GA | IN | LA | MI | MT | NJ | ND | PA | TN | VA | WY |
| AR | DE | HI | IA* | ME | MN | NE | NM | OH | RI | TX | WA | |

## for critical analysis

1. Why do you think the states highlighted in green challenged the ACA? In general, were these states where the ACA made it easier or harder to get Medicaid?

2. In 2009, a family of four in Minnesota could earn up to $47,408 (215% of FPL) and still qualify for Medicaid benefits, while the same size family in Texas would be ineligible if they earned more than $5,733 (26% of FPL). Is it more important to provide equal access to health care or to preserve state choices?

federal government was using ARRA to dictate state spending priorities. Some of these governors sought to use the funds for purposes not allowed in the legislation or refused parts of the funds that they believed would tie their hands in the future. For example, former governor Mark Sanford of South Carolina, a Republican, asked the federal government for a waiver that would permit his state to use approximately $700 million of its estimated $2.8 billion ARRA allocation to pay down the state's debt. When the waiver was denied, Sanford vowed to reject the federal funds; however, the state legislature overrode his decision.[52] Several states objected to the unemployment funds, which required states to expand eligibility for unemployment insurance to many part-time and temporary workers. A handful of Republican southern governors refused to accept the funds on the grounds that expanded eligibility would place a future burden on employers. A majority of states, however, did change their laws in response to the federal requirements.[53]

In other ways, the Obama White House signaled that it would allow the states more leeway for action than they had under the Bush administration. This was particularly true in the domains of social policy and the environment when states sought to enact laws more stringent than those of the federal government. In the memo reversing the Bush policy of preemption, the White House noted, "Throughout our history, State and local governments have frequently protected health, safety, and the environment more aggressively than has the national Government."[54] Its new policy aimed to keep the federal government from infringing on these more aggressive state actions.

The most significant Obama law to affect the states was the 2010 health care overhaul. As we have seen, one controversial part of that legislation required states to expand their Medicaid programs to cover more low-income residents and to offer them additional services. The Court's ruling that the federal government could not impose all or nothing conditions on the states—implement the expansion or lose all Medicaid funding—represented a sharp departure from the past. The ruling has far-reaching potential to change the federal government's power to impose conditions on the states when it supplies the funds. The other controversial

*The Affordable Care Act asserted federal power over the states by imposing new expansions of the Medicaid program in exchange for expanded funding. When the Supreme Court ruled that this "all or nothing" approach was too coercive, some states vowed to opt out of the law's Medicaid provisions.*

provision of the Affordable Care Act was the "individual mandate," the requirement that individuals without health care insurance be required to purchase such insurance. The 26 states suing the federal government charged that Congress exceeded its power under the commerce clause when it enacted the mandate. They charged that Congress had no power to force individuals to purchase a product and argued that the act set up a "slippery slope" in which Congress could force individuals to make other purchases. As one judge (who upheld the law) asked, "Would it be unconstitutional to require people to buy broccoli?" In defending the law, the federal government argued that the complex interactions of the health care market made the individual mandate constitutional under Congress's power to regulate commerce among the states.[55] From the moment a person is born, he or she is part of the health care economy. Even if a person does not have health insurance, federal law requires that hospitals provide treatment in an emergency. Those costs are borne by all of the people who do pay for health insurance. Taking a more narrow view of the health care market, the Court rejected this argument on the grounds that the federal government cannot regulate economic inactivity, that is, the failure to purchase health insurance. Instead, it found that the Affordable Care Act could be justified by Congress's power to tax. The law requires individuals who do not receive insurance from their employers or their parents, and are not eligible for Medicaid, to purchase insurance or pay a penalty. The Court reasoned that the penalty could be considered a tax, and in that sense, passed constitutional muster. The complex and surprising decision marked a new era in American federalism. The Court placed limits on two of the key powers that have expanded the reach of the federal government since the New Deal—the power to regulate commerce and the power to spend for the general welfare. The decision will surely invite challenges to federal power in diverse areas, possibly including education programs, the drinking age, and environmental regulations.

## ● Thinking Critically about the Federal System

It is often argued that liberals prefer a strong federal government because they value equality more than liberty. Conservatives are said to prefer granting more power to states and localities because they care most about liberty. Although this greatly oversimplifies liberal and conservative views, such arguments underscore the reality that ideas about federalism are linked to different views about the purposes of government. For what ends should government powers be used? What happens when widely shared national values conflict in practice? The connections between federalism and our fundamental national values have made federalism a focus of political contention throughout our nation's history.

The Constitution limited the power of the federal government in order to promote liberty. This decision reflected the framers' suspicions of centralized power, based on their experience with the British Crown. The American suspicion of centralized power lives on today in widespread dislike of "big government,"

*Under the No Child Left Behind Act, schools can lose federal funding if students perform poorly on standardized tests. The Supreme Court's decision on the Affordable Care Act may open the door to new challenges from the states in areas such as education.*

*Will states attempt to change the drinking age in the future? The federal government required states to set the drinking age at 21 or risk losing federal highway funds, but some people feel this decision should be left to the states.*

**for critical analysis**

What would be the advantages and disadvantages of a unitary system in which the federal government had all the power? What would be the advantages and disadvantages of a fully decentralized system in which the states had all the power?

which generally evokes a picture of a bloated federal government. But over the course of our history we have come to realize that the federal government is also an important guarantor of liberty. As we'll see in Chapter 4, it took enhanced federal power to ensure that local and state governments adhered to the fundamental constitutional freedoms in the Bill of Rights.

One of the most important continuing arguments for a strong federal government is its role in ensuring equality. A key puzzle of federalism is deciding when differences across states represent the proper democratic decisions of the states and when such differences represent inequalities that should not be tolerated. Sometimes a decision to eliminate differences is made on the grounds of equality and individual rights, as in the Civil Rights Act of 1964, which outlawed legally instituted racial segregation. At other times, a stronger federal role is justified on the grounds of national interest, as in the case of the oil shortage and the institution of a 55-mph speed limit in the 1970s. Yet advocates of a more limited federal role often point to the value of democracy. Public actions can more easily be tailored to fit distinctive local or state desires if states and localities have more power to make policy. Viewed this way, variation across states can be an expression of democratic will.

In recent decades, many Americans have grown disillusioned with the federal government and have supported efforts to give the states more responsibilities. After the terrorist attacks of 2001, however, support for the federal government soared. With issues of security topping the list of citizens' concerns, the federal government, which had seemed less important with the waning of the Cold War, suddenly reemerged as the central actor in American politics. As one observer put it, "Federalism was a luxury of peaceful times."[56] Yet polls show that trust in the federal government gradually dropped over the decade. In 2002, 64 percent of Americans expressed a positive view of the federal government; by 2008, only 37 percent did. Although approval of the federal government climbed to 42 percent after Obama's election in 2008, it fell as the economy stagnated. After the 2010 elections brought a Republican majority to the House of Representatives, political stalemate reduced approval of the federal government to new lows. By 2011, 89 percent of Americans did not trust the federal government to do the right thing.[57] Public views about state governments are generally more positive and more stable. However, the long recession took a toll: the proportion of those expressing a favorable view of states dropped from 62 percent in 2002 to 52 percent in 2012. Local governments remain most popular, with positive ratings of 67 percent in 2002 and 61 percent in 2012.[58]

American federalism remains a work in progress. As public problems shift and as local, state, and federal governments change, questions about the relationship between American values and federalism naturally emerge. The different views that people bring to this discussion suggest that federalism will remain a central issue in American democracy.

# Mapping Federalism

## Inform Yourself

 **Review the levels of government and their roles**. The White House has a valuable website that discusses how states share power with the federal government and local governments (www.whitehouse.gov/our-government/state-and-local -government), in what is known as federalism.

 **Watch the cartoon "Federal Powers vs. State Powers"** (www.youtube.com/watch? v=WQMZ2PT7kr0&feature=related). Consider what powers were reserved to the states. How has the federal government restricted these reserved powers over the last 50 years? When has the U.S. Supreme Court upheld laws that have taken power from the states? Do you believe this is constitutional?

## Express Yourself

 **Go to the Patchwork Nation website** (www.patchworknation.org/) to see hundreds of maps broken down by county, congressional district, and state government. Find the percentage of children who are on foods stamps by county. (Above the map of the United States, click on the "County Map" tab, and then on the "Latest Data" tab. Under "Select a Category," choose "Food Stamps." Click on a state to zoom in.) In South Dakota, for example, in some areas almost no children qualify for a free lunch, while in other counties over 80 percent of children qualify. How do state governments make one set of policies for areas as different as these?

The federal government faces similar issues when providing grant money to states. Consider the stimulus money provided for highway repairs. (Follow the directions just given by choosing the "County Map" and "Latest Data" tabs, but click on "Stimulus [via ProPublica].") If the money is broken down by number of people in the counties (per capita), the region receiving the most federal dollars for highway repairs is the Midwest. These maps offer many examples of how the federal government grants money to the states. What region of the country appears to benefit the most from federal tax dollars? Do populous states benefit more, or do the least-populated states? Looking at the data, do you think the current system is fair, or would you make changes in how money is allocated?

 **Consider texting or e-mailing your members of Congress** your views about how federal government tax dollars should be spent and allocated. You can find your representatives and their contact information by using the tools "Find Your Senators" (www.senate.gov) and "Find Your Representative" (www.house.gov). Or send a letter (or e-mail) to the editor of your state/local newspaper expressing your views.

*Find links to the sites listed above as well as related activities on wwnorton.com/studyspace.*

# study guide

## Federalism in the Constitution

■ **Describe what the Constitution says about the powers of the national government and of the states (pp. 77–81)**

While the Founders wanted a national government that was stronger than it had been under the Articles of Confederation, they also wanted to preserve the autonomy of the states. The necessary and proper clause, supremacy clause, and the specific powers granted to Congress in Article I demonstrate the nation-centered focus of the Constitution. The Tenth Amendment, which grants all undelegated powers to the states, shows the state-centered focus of the Constitution. The Constitution also includes some concurrent powers that are shared by both the federal government and state governments.

### Key Terms

**federalism** (p. 77)

**unitary system** (p. 77)

**federal system** (p. 77)

**expressed powers** (p. 77)

**implied powers** (p. 77)

**necessary and proper clause** (p. 77)

**reserved powers** (p. 78)

**police power** (p. 78)

**concurrent powers** (p. 78)

**full faith and credit clause** (p. 79)

**privileges and immunities clause** (p. 79)

**home rule** (p. 80)

### Practice Quiz

1. Which term describes the sharing of powers between the national government and the state governments? *(p. 77)*
   a) home rule
   b) separation of powers
   c) federalism
   d) checks and balances
   e) unitary system

2. Which amendment to the Constitution stated that the powers not delegated to the national government or prohibited to the states were "reserved to the states"? *(p. 78)*
   a) First Amendment
   b) Fifth Amendment
   c) Tenth Amendment
   d) Fourteenth Amendment
   e) Twenty-Sixth Amendment

3. A state government's authority to regulate the health, safety, and morals of its citizens is frequently referred to as *(p. 78)*
   a) the reserved power.
   b) the police power.
   c) the expressed power.
   d) the concurrent power.
   e) the implied power.

4. Which constitutional clause has been central in debates over gay and lesbian marriage because it requires that states normally honor the public acts and judicial decisions of other states? *(p. 79)*
   a) privileges and immunities clause
   b) necessary and proper clause
   c) interstate commerce clause
   d) preemption clause
   e) full faith and credit clause

5. Many states have amended their constitutions to guarantee that large cities will have the authority to manage local affairs without interference from state government. This power is called *(p. 80)*
   a) home rule.
   b) devolution.
   c) preemption.
   d) states' rights.
   e) new federalism.

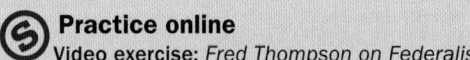
**Practice online**
Video exercise: *Fred Thompson on Federalism*

# The Changing Relationship between the Federal Government and the States

■ **Trace how the federal government became much stronger over time (pp. 82–89)**

The relative importance of states and the federal government has changed significantly over time. During the first 100 years of American history, the national government was small and focused entirely on assisting commerce. Beginning in the 1930s, the Supreme Court dramatically expanded the power of the federal government through its expansive interpretation of the commerce clause. The growing power of the national government has not, however, left the states powerless and state governments continue to make important laws.

## Key Terms

**dual federalism** (p. 82)

**commerce clause** (p. 85)

**states' rights** (p. 87)

## Practice Quiz

6. The system of federalism that allowed states to do most of the fundamental governing from 1789 to 1937 was *(p. 82)*
   a) new federalism.
   b) home rule.
   c) regulated federalism.
   d) dual federalism.
   e) cooperative federalism.

7. In which case did the Supreme Court create the potential for increased national power by ruling that Congress could use the necessary and proper clause to interpret its delegated powers broadly? *(p. 85)*
   a) *United States v. Lopez*
   b) *Printz v. United States*
   c) *Marbury v. Madison*
   d) *McCulloch v. Maryland*
   d) *Gibbons v. Ogden*

8. In 1937 the Supreme Court laid the groundwork for a stronger federal government by *(p. 86)*
   a) issuing a number of decisions that dramatically narrowed the definition of the commerce clause.
   b) issuing a number of decisions that dramatically expanded the definition of the commerce clause.
   c) issuing a number of decisions that struck down the supremacy clause.
   d) issuing a number of decisions that struck down the privileges and immunities clause.
   e) issuing a number of decision that struck down the full faith and credit clause.

 **Practice Online**
Interactive simulation: *Power Distribution among Federal, State, and Local Governments*

# Who Does What? Public Spending and the Federal Framework

■ **Analyze major developments in the federal framework since the 1930s (pp. 89–105)**

The Great Depression effectively ended the traditional system of dual federalism in which the states and the federal government performed very different functions. Today, American federalism includes elements of cooperative, coercive and "new" federalism. Most of the important public policy issues in recent years, including controversies about government spending, immigration, climate change and economic regulation, are debated and addressed through the United States' unique system of federalism.

## Key Terms

**grants-in-aid** (p. 91)

**categorical grants** (p. 92)

**project grants** (p. 92)

**formula grants** (p. 92)

**cooperative federalism** (p. 92)

**regulated federalism** (p. 94)

**preemption** (p. 94)

**unfunded mandates** (p. 95)

**devolution** (p. 96)

**block grants** (p. 96)

**New Federalism** (p. 96)

**general revenue sharing** (p. 97)

**redistributive programs** (p. 98)

## Practice Quiz

9. One of the most powerful tools by which the federal government has attempted to get the states to act in ways that are desired by the federal government is by *(p. 91)*
   a) defending states' rights.
   b) general revenue sharing.
   c) providing grants-in-aid.
   d) requiring licensing.
   e) granting home rule.

10. The form of regulated federalism that allows the federal government to take over areas of regulation formerly overseen by states or local governments is called *(p. 94)*
    a) project grants.
    b) preemption.
    c) devolution.
    d) categorical grants.
    e) formula grants.

11. When state and local governments must conform to costly regulations or conditions in order to receive grants but do not receive reimbursements for their expenditures from the federal government it is called *(p. 95)*
    a) a reciprocal grant.
    b) an unfunded mandate.
    c) general revenue sharing.

    d) a concurrent grant.
    e) a counterfunded mandate.

12. The process of returning more of the responsibilities of governing from the national level to the state level is known as *(p. 96)*
    a) devolution.
    b) dual federalism.
    c) incorporation.
    d) home rule.
    e) preemption.

13. To what does the term *New Federalism* refer? *(p. 96)*
    a) the era of federalism initiated by President Roosevelt during the late 1930s
    b) the national government's regulation of state action through grants-in-aid
    c) the type of federalism relying on categorical grants
    d) efforts to return more policy-making discretion to the states through the use of block grants
    e) the recent emergence of local governments as important political actors

14. A recent notable example of the process of giving the states more responsibility for administering government programs is *(p. 99)*
    a) campaign finance reform.
    b) prison reform.
    c) Social Security.
    d) welfare reform
    e) trade reform.

 **Practice Online**
"Who Are Americans" interactive exercise: *Who Opposed the Affordable Health Care Act?*

# For Further Reading

Bensel, Richard. *Sectionalism and American Political Development: 1880–1980.* Madison: University of Wisconsin Press, 1984.

Bowman, Ann O'M., and Richard C. Kearney. *The Resurgence of the States.* Englewood Cliffs, NJ: Prentice-Hall, 1986.

Derthick, Martha. *Keeping the Compound Republic: Essays on American Federalism.* Washington, DC: Brookings Institution Press, 2001.

Donahue, John D. *Disunited States.* New York: Basic Books, 1997.

Elazar, Daniel. *American Federalism: A View from the States.* 3rd ed. New York: Harper & Row, 1984.

Feiock, Richard C., and John T. Scholz, *Self-Organizing Federalism: Collaborative Mechanisms to Mitigate Institutional Collective Action Dilemmas.* New York: Cambridge University Press, 2009.

Gerston, Larry N. *American Federalism: A Concise Introduction.* Armonk, NY: M.E. Sharpe, 2007.

Grodzins, Morton. *The American System.* Chicago: Rand McNally, 1974.

Johnson, Kimberly S. *Governing the American State: Congress and the New Federalism, 1877–1929.* Princeton, NJ: Princeton University Press, 2007.

Kettl, Donald. *The Regulation of American Federalism.* Baltimore: Johns Hopkins University Press, 1987.

Robertson, David Brian. *Federalism and the Making of America.* New York: Routledge, 2011.

Van Horn, Carl E. *The State of the States.* 4th ed. Washington, DC: CQ Press, 2005.

# Recommended Websites

**Constitution Finder**
http://confinder.richmond.edu

Governments can organize power in either unitary or federal systems. Examine the constitutions of different countries throughout the world and try to identify how those governments organize power.

**Council of State Governments**
www.csg.org

This organization provides information on a variety of state-federal policy areas. See what current issues concerning federalism are of prime importance to the state governments on this site.

**Governing.com**
www.governing.com

See what state-federal issues are important to your local government officials on the website for *Governing* magazine.

**National Conference of State Legislatures**
www.ncsl.org

**National Governors Association**
www.nga.org

These are two of the largest organizations dedicated to representing state and local government interests at the federal level.

**Oyez: U.S. Supreme Court Media**
www.oyez.org

Read here about one of the most important U.S. Supreme Court decisions regarding the division of federal and state power in the case of *McCulloch v. Maryland.*

**Pew Center for the States**
www.pewstates.org

The Pew Center on the States provides nonpartisan reporting and research, advocacy, and technical assistance to help states deliver better results and achieve long-term fiscal health by investing in programs that provide the strongest returns.

**Urban Institute**
www.newfederalism.urban.org

New Federalism gives state governments more flexibility to make public policy and administer programs. The Urban Institute's "Assessing the New Federalism" policy center takes a statistical look at the success and failure of recent government programs.

**U.S. Census Bureau**
www.census.gov

The Census Bureau maintains one of the largest collections of data about social and economic conditions of the nation's 50 states.

**World Federalist Movement**
www.wfm.org

This international organization is dedicated to the division of power and authority among all local, state, and international governmental agencies. Generally, it promotes federalism and constitutional democracy throughout the world.

Freedom of speech is one of the liberties protected by the First Amendment. Even speech that is hostile or offensive—such as the views expressed by these Ku Klux Klan members—cannot be prohibited so long as they do not incite illegal action.

# Civil Liberties

**WHAT GOVERNMENT DOES AND WHY IT MATTERS** Today in the United States, we often take for granted the liberties contained in the Bill of Rights. In fact, few people in recorded history, including many American citizens before the 1960s, have enjoyed such protections. For more than 170 years after its ratification by the states in 1791, the Bill of Rights meant little to most Americans. As we shall see in this chapter, guaranteeing the liberties articulated in the Bill of Rights to all Americans required a long struggle. As recently as the early 1960s, criminal suspects in state cases did not have to be informed of their rights, some states required daily Bible readings and prayers in their public schools, and some communities regularly censored books that they deemed to be obscene.

Today, many Americans regard searches and, especially, full-body scans at airports as infringements upon their civil liberties, most notably their right to privacy. This right is mentioned nowhere in the Constitution but, instead, was invoked by the Supreme Court in its decisions striking down state restrictions on birth control and abortion. No court has yet been persuaded that airport searches violate the Constitution.

Thomas Jefferson said that a bill of rights "is what people are entitled to against every government on earth." Note the wording: *against government.* Civil liberties are *protections from* improper government action. Some of these restraints are substantive liberties, which put limits on *what* the government shall and shall not have power to do—such as establishing a religion, quartering troops in private homes without consent, or seizing private property without just compensation. Other restraints are procedural liberties, which deal with *how* the government is supposed to act. Civil liberties require a delicate balance between governmental power and governmental restraint. The government must be kept in check, with strict limits on its powers; yet, at the same time, the government must be given enough power to defend liberty and its benefits from those who seek to deprive others of them. This chapter will explore how this balance is struck. We will see how the Supreme Court, an inherently undemocratic institution, is especially important in establishing the balance. Civil liberties also reflect how well the democratic principle of majority rule with minority rights works. The rights enumerated in the Bill of Rights and enforced through the courts can provide an important check on the power of the majority.

## chaptergoals

- Explain how the civil liberties included in the Bill of Rights were "nationalized" (pages 115–19)

- Describe how the First Amendment protects freedom of religion (pages 119–22)

- Describe how the First Amendment protects free speech (pages 122–32)

- Explore whether the Second Amendment means people have a right to own guns (pages 132–33)

- Explain the major rights that people have if they are accused of a crime (pages 133–43)

- Assess whether people have a right to privacy under the Constitution (pages 143–47)

# A Brief History of the Bill of Rights

**Explain how the civil liberties included in the Bill of Rights were "nationalized"**

When the first Congress under the newly ratified Constitution met in late April of 1789, the most important item of business was the consideration of a proposal to add a bill of rights to the Constitution. Such a proposal had been turned down with little debate in the waning days of the Philadelphia Constitutional Convention in 1787, not because the delegates were against rights, but because, as the Federalists, led by Alexander Hamilton, later argued, it was "not only unnecessary in the proposed Constitution but would even be dangerous."[1] First, according to Hamilton, a bill of rights would be irrelevant to a national government that was given only delegated powers in the first place. To put restraints on "powers which are not granted" could provide a pretext for governments to claim more powers than were in fact granted: "For why declare that things shall not be done which there is no power to do?"[2] Second, the Constitution was to Hamilton and the Federalists a bill of rights in itself, containing provisions that amounted to a bill of rights without requiring additional amendments (see Table 4.1). For example, Article I, Section 9, included the right of **habeas corpus**, which prohibits the government from depriving a person of liberty without an open trial before a judge.

Despite the power of Hamilton's arguments, when the Constitution was submitted to the states for ratification, Antifederalists, most of whom had not been delegates in Philadelphia, picked up on the argument of Thomas Jefferson (who also had not been a delegate) that the omission of a bill of rights was a major imperfection of the new Constitution. The Federalists conceded that in order to gain ratification they would have to make an "unwritten but unequivocal pledge" to add a bill of rights that would include a confirmation (in what would become the Tenth Amendment) of the understanding that all powers not expressly delegated to the national government or explicitly prohibited to the states were reserved to the states.[3]

**habeas corpus** a court order demanding that an individual in custody be brought into court and shown the cause for detention

**TABLE 4.1**

## Rights in the Original Constitution (Not in the Bill of Rights)

| CLAUSE | RIGHT ESTABLISHED |
| --- | --- |
| Article I, Sec. 9 | guarantee of habeas corpus |
| Article I, Sec. 9 | prohibition of **bills of attainder** |
| Article I, Sec. 9 | prohibition of **ex post facto laws** |
| Article I, Sec. 9 | prohibition against acceptance of titles of nobility, etc., from any foreign state |
| Article III | guarantee of trial by jury in state where crime was committed |
| Article III | treason defined and limited to the life of the person convicted, not to the person's heirs |

**bill of attainder** a law that declares a person guilty of a crime without a trial

**ex post facto laws** laws that declare an action to be illegal after it has been committed

**Bill of Rights** the first 10 amendments to the U.S. Constitution, ratified in 1791; they ensure certain rights and liberties to the people

**civil liberties** areas of personal freedom with which governments are constrained from interfering

"After much discussion and manipulation . . . at the delicate prompting of Washington and under the masterful prodding of Madison," the House of Representatives adopted 17 amendments; of these, the Senate adopted 12. Ten of the amendments were ratified by the necessary three-fourths of the states on December 15, 1791; from the start, these 10 were called the **Bill of Rights** (see Table 4.2).[4] The protections against improper government action contained in the Constitution and the Bill of Rights represent important **civil liberties**.

## Nationalizing the Bill of Rights

The First Amendment provides that "Congress shall make no law . . ." But this is the only amendment in the Bill of Rights that addresses itself exclusively to the national government. For example, the Second Amendment provides that "the right of the people to keep and bear Arms, shall not be infringed." And the Fifth Amendment says, among other things, that "no person shall . . . be twice put in jeopardy of life or limb" for the same crime. Since the First Amendment is the only part of the Bill of Rights that is explicit in its intention to put limits on Congress and therefore on the national government, a fundamental question inevitably arises: Do the remaining provisions of the Bill of Rights put limits only on the national government, or do they limit the state governments as well?

The Supreme Court first answered this question in 1833 by ruling that the Bill of Rights limited only the national government and not the state governments.[5] But in 1868, when the Fourteenth Amendment was added to the Constitution, the question arose once again. The Fourteenth Amendment reads as if it were meant to impose the Bill of Rights on the states:

> No *State* shall make or enforce any law which shall abridge the privileges or immunities of citizens of the United States; nor shall any *State* deprive any person of life, liberty, or property, without due process of law; nor deny to any person within its jurisdiction the equal protection of the laws [emphasis added].

This language sounds like an effort to extend the Bill of Rights in its entirety to all citizens, wherever they might reside.[6] Yet this was not the Supreme Court's interpretation of the amendment for nearly 100 years. Within five years of ratification of the Fourteenth Amendment, the Court was making decisions as though the amendment had never been adopted.[7]

The only change in civil liberties during the first 50-odd years following the adoption of the Fourteenth Amendment came in 1897, when the Supreme Court held that the due process clause of the Fourteenth Amendment did in fact prohibit states from taking property for a public use without just compensation.[8] However, the Supreme Court had selectively "incorporated" into the Fourteenth Amendment only the property protection provision of the Fifth Amendment and no other clause of the Fifth or any other amendment of the Bill of Rights. In other words, although according to the Fifth Amendment, "due process" applied to the taking of life and liberty as well as property, only property was incorporated into the Fourteenth Amendment as a limitation on state power.

*Although the Bill of Rights specifies certain rights and liberties, the interpretation and protection of those rights and liberties has evolved over time. The government's fight against terrorism has raised numerous civil liberties issues, such as whether suspected terrorists and "enemy combatants" are entitled to due process rights, such as a fair trial.*

## TABLE 4.2

## The Bill of Rights

| | |
|---|---|
| Amendment I: Limits on Congress | Congress cannot make any law establishing a religion or abridging freedoms of religious exercise, speech, assembly, or petition. |
| Amendments II, III, IV: Limits on the Executive | The executive branch cannot infringe on the right of the people to keep arms (II), cannot arbitrarily take houses for militia (III), and cannot search for or seize evidence without a court warrant swearing to the probable existence of a crime (IV). |
| Amendments V, VI, VII, VIII: Limits on the Judiciary | The courts cannot hold trials for serious offenses without provision for a grand jury (V), a trial jury (VII), a speedy trial (VI), presentation of charges and confrontation by the accused of hostile witnesses (VI), and immunity from testimony against oneself and immunity from trial more than once for the same offense (V). Furthermore, neither bail nor punishment can be excessive (VIII), and no property can be taken without "just compensation" (V). |
| Amendments IX, X: Limits on the National Government | Any rights not enumerated are reserved to the state or the people (X), and the enumeration of certain rights in the Constitution should not be interpreted to mean that those are the only rights the people have (IX). |

No further expansion of civil liberties via the Fourteenth Amendment occurred until 1925, when the Supreme Court held that freedom of speech is "among the fundamental personal rights and 'liberties' protected by the due process clause of the Fourteenth Amendment from impairment by the states."[9] In 1931 the Court added freedom of the press to that short list of freedoms protected by the Bill of Rights from state action; in 1939 it added freedom of assembly.[10]

But that was as far as the Court was willing to go. As late as 1937 the Supreme Court was still unwilling to nationalize civil liberties beyond the First Amendment. The Constitution, as interpreted by the Supreme Court in *Palko v. Connecticut*, left standing the framework in which the states had the power to determine their own laws on a number of fundamental issues. The *Palko* case (described in more detail later in the chapter) established the principle of **selective incorporation**, by which the provisions of the Bill of Rights were to be considered one by one and selectively applied as limits on the states through the Fourteenth Amendment. In order to make clear that "selective incorporation" should be narrowly interpreted, Justice Benjamin Cardozo, writing for an 8–1 majority, asserted that although many rights have value and importance, some rights do not represent a "principle of justice so rooted in the traditions and conscience of our people as to be ranked as fundamental." He went on to remark that if the Fourteenth Amendment has absorbed such rights as freedom of thought and speech, "the process of absorption has had its source in the belief that neither liberty nor justice would exist if they were

**selective incorporation** the process by which different protections in the Bill of Rights were incorporated into the Fourteenth Amendment, thus guaranteeing citizens protection from state as well as national governments

## TABLE 4.3

## Incorporation of the Bill of Rights into the Fourteenth Amendment

| SELECTED PROVISIONS AND AMENDMENTS | INCORPORATED | KEY CASE |
| --- | --- | --- |
| Eminent domain (V) | 1897 | *Chicago, Burlington, and Quincy R.R. v. Chicago* |
| Freedom of speech (I) | 1925 | *Gitlow v. New York* |
| Freedom of press (I) | 1931 | *Near v. Minnesota* |
| Free exercise of religion (I) | 1934 | *Hamilton v. Regents of the University of California* |
| Freedom of assembly (I) and freedom to petition the government for redress of grievances (I) | 1937 | *DeJonge v. Oregon* |
| Freedom of assembly (I) | 1939 | *Hague v. CIO* |
| Nonestablishment of state religion (I) | 1947 | *Everson v. Board of Education* |
| Freedom from unnecessary search and seizure (IV) | 1949 | *Wolf v. Colorado* |
| Freedom from warrantless search and seizure (IV) ("exclusionary rule") | 1961 | *Mapp v. Ohio* |
| Freedom from cruel and unusual punishment (VIII) | 1962 | *Robinson v. California* |
| Right to counsel in any criminal trial (VI) | 1963 | *Gideon v. Wainwright* |
| Right against self-incrimination and forced confessions (V) | 1964 | *Mallory v. Hogan Escobedo v. Illinois* |
| Right to counsel and to remain silent (V) | 1966 | *Miranda v. Arizona* |
| Right against double jeopardy (V) | 1969 | *Benton v. Maryland* |
| Right to bear arms (II) | 2010 | *McDonald v. Chicago* |

sacrificed."[11] *Palko* left states with most of the powers they had possessed even before the adoption of the Fourteenth Amendment, including the power to pass laws segregating the races—a power, in fact, that the 13 former Confederate states chose to continue to exercise on into the 1960s, despite *Brown v. Board of Education* in 1954. The constitutional framework also left states with the power to engage in searches and seizures without a warrant, to indict accused persons without a grand jury, to deprive accused persons of trial by jury, to deprive persons of their right not to have to testify against themselves, to deprive accused persons of their right to confront adverse witnesses, and to prosecute accused persons more than once for the same crime.[12] Few states chose to use these kinds of powers, but some states did, and the power to do so was available for any state whose legislative majority or courts so chose.

So, until 1961, only the First Amendment and one clause of the Fifth Amendment had been clearly incorporated into the Fourteenth Amendment as binding on the states as well as on the national government.[13] After that, one by one, most of the important provisions of the Bill of Rights were incorporated into the Fourteenth Amendment and applied to the states. Table 4.3 shows the progress of this revolution in the interpretation of the Constitution.

The final provision of the Bill of Rights to be incorporated by the Supreme Court was the Second Amendment, which protects the right to bear arms. In the 2010 case of *McDonald v. Chicago*, the Court held that the right of an individual "to keep and bear arms" is incorporated by the due process clause of the Fourteenth Amendment and applies to the states.[14]

The best way to examine the Bill of Rights today is the simplest way: to take the major provisions one at a time. Some of these provisions are settled areas of law; others are not. The Court can reinterpret any one of them at any time.

# ● The First Amendment and Freedom of Religion

**Describe how the First Amendment protects freedom of religion**

Congress shall make no law respecting an establishment of religion, or prohibiting the free exercise thereof; or abridging the freedom of speech, or of the press; or the right of the people peaceably to assemble, and to petition the Government for a redress of grievances.

The Bill of Rights begins by guaranteeing freedom, and the First Amendment provides for that freedom in two distinct clauses: "Congress shall make no law [1] respecting an establishment of religion, or [2] prohibiting the free exercise thereof." The first clause is called the "establishment clause," and the second is called the "free exercise clause."

## Separation between Church and State

The **establishment clause** and the idea of "no law" regarding the establishment of religion could be interpreted in several possible ways. One interpretation, which probably reflects the views of many of the First Amendment's authors, is that the government is prohibited from establishing an official church. Official state churches, such as the Church of England, were common in the eighteenth century and were viewed by many Americans as inconsistent with a republican form of government. Indeed, many American colonists had fled Europe to escape persecution for having rejected state-sponsored churches. A second possible interpretation is the view that the government may not take sides among competing religions but is not prohibited from providing assistance to religious institutions or ideas as long as it shows no favoritism. The United States accommodates religious beliefs in a variety of ways, from the reference to God on U.S. currency to the prayer that begins every session of Congress. These forms of religious establishment have never been struck down by the courts. The third view regarding religious

**establishment clause** the First Amendment clause that says that "Congress shall make no law respecting an establishment of religion." This law means that a "wall of separation" exists between church and state

*The First Amendment affects everyday life in a multitude of ways. Because of the amendment's ban on state-sanctioned religion, the Supreme Court ruled in 2000 that student-initiated public prayer in school is illegal. Pregame prayer at public schools violates the establishment clause of the First Amendment.*

**Lemon test** a rule articulated in *Lemon v. Kurtzman* that government action toward religion is permissible if it is secular in purpose, neither promotes nor inhibits the practice of religion, and does not lead to "excessive entanglement" with religion

establishment, which for many years dominated Supreme Court decision making in this realm, is the idea of a "wall of separation" between church and state—Jefferson's formulation—that cannot be breached by the government. For two centuries, Jefferson's words have had a powerful impact on our understanding of the proper relationship between church and state in America.

Despite the seeming absoluteness of the phrase "wall of separation," there is ample room to disagree on how high the wall is or of what materials it is composed. For example, the Court has been consistently strict in cases of school prayer, striking down such practices as Bible reading,[15] nondenominational prayer,[16] a moment of silence for meditation, and pregame prayer at public sporting events.[17] In each of these cases, the Court reasoned that school-sponsored religious observations, even of an apparently nondenominational character, are highly suggestive of school sponsorship and therefore violate the prohibition against establishment of religion. On the other hand, the Court has been quite permissive (and, some would say, inconsistent) about the public display of religious symbols, such as city-sponsored nativity scenes in commercial or municipal areas.[18] And although the Court has consistently disapproved of government financial support for religious schools, even when the purpose has been purely educational and secular, it has permitted certain direct aid to students of such schools in the form of busing, for example. In 1971, after 30 years of cases involving religious schools, the Court attempted to specify some criteria to guide its decisions and those of lower courts, indicating, for example, in a decision invalidating state payments for the teaching of secular subjects in parochial schools, circumstances under which the Court might allow certain financial assistance. The case was *Lemon v. Kurtzman*; in its decision, the Supreme Court established three criteria to guide future cases—what came to be called the ***Lemon*** test. The Court held that government aid to religious schools would be accepted as constitutional if (1) it had a secular purpose, (2) its effect was neither to advance nor to inhibit religion, and (3) it did not entangle government and religious institutions in each other's affairs.[19]

Although these restrictions make the *Lemon* test hard to pass, imaginative authorities are finding ways to do so, and the Supreme Court has demonstrated a willingness to let them. For example, in 1995 the Court narrowly ruled that a student religious group at the University of Virginia could not be denied student activities funds merely because it was a religious group espousing a particular viewpoint about a deity. The Court called the denial "viewpoint discrimination" that violated the free speech rights of the group.[20]

In 2004 the question of whether the phrase "under God" in the Pledge of Allegiance violated the establishment clause was brought before the Court. Written without any religious references in 1892, the pledge had long been used in schools. But in 1954, in the midst of the Cold War, Congress voted to change the pledge in response to the "godless Communism" of the Soviet Union. The conversion was made by adding two key words, so that the revised version read, "I pledge allegiance to the flag of the United States of America and to the Republic for which it stands, one nation *under God*, indivisible, with liberty and justice for all."

Ever since the change was made, there has been a steady murmuring of discontent from those who object to an officially sanctioned profession of belief in a deity as a violation of the establishment clause of the First Amendment. When saying the pledge, those who object to the phrase have often simply stayed silent during the two key words and then resumed for the rest of the pledge. In 2003, Michael A. Newdow, the atheist father of a kindergarten student, forced the issue to the surface when he brought suit against the local California school district. Newdow argued that the reference to God turned the daily recitation of the pledge into a religious exercise. A federal court ruled that although students were not required to recite the pledge at all, having to stand and listen to "under God" still violated the First Amendment's establishment clause. The case was appealed to the Supreme Court, and on June 14, 2004—exactly 50 years to the day

after the adoption of "under God" in the pledge—the Court ruled that Newdow lacked a sufficient personal stake in the case to bring the complaint. This inconclusive decision by the Supreme Court left "under God" in the pledge while keeping the issue alive for possible resolution in a future case.

In 2005 the Supreme Court ruled, again inconclusively, on government-sponsored displays of religious symbols. Two 2005 cases involved displays of the Ten Commandments. In *Van Orden v. Perry*, the Court decided by a 5–4 margin that a display of the Ten Commandments outside the Texas state capitol did not violate the Constitution.[21] However, in *McCreary County v. American Civil Liberties Union of Kentucky*, decided at the same time and also by a 5–4 margin, the Court determined that a display of the Ten Commandments inside two Kentucky courthouses was unconstitutional.[22] Justice Stephen Breyer, the deciding vote in the two cases, said that the display in *Van Orden* had a secular purpose, whereas the displays in *McCreary* had a purely religious purpose. The key difference between the two cases is that the Texas display had been exhibited in a large park for 40 years with other monuments related to the development of American law without any objections raised until this case, whereas the Kentucky display was erected much more recently and initially by itself, suggesting to some justices that its posting had a religious purpose. But most observers saw little difference between the two cases. Even Breyer was hard-pressed to explain his shifting votes, except to say that *Van Orden* was a "borderline" case. Obviously, the issue of government-sponsored displays of religious symbols has not been settled.

## Free Exercise of Religion

The **free exercise clause** protects the right to believe and to practice whatever religion one chooses; it also protects the right to be a nonbeliever. The precedent-setting case involving free exercise is *West Virginia State Board of Education v. Barnette* (1943), which involved the children of a family of Jehovah's Witnesses who refused to salute and pledge allegiance to the American flag on the grounds that their religious faith did not permit it. Three years earlier, the Court had upheld such a requirement and had permitted schools to expel students for refusing to salute the flag. But the entry of the United States into a war to defend democracy,

**free exercise clause** the First Amendment clause that protects a citizen's right to believe and practice whatever religion he or she chooses

**for critical analysis**

Despite the establishment clause, the United States still uses the motto "In God We Trust" and calls itself "one nation, under God." This Indiana license plate was introduced in 2007. Do you think its reference to God is a violation of the separation of church and state?

coupled with the ugly treatment to which the Jehovah's Witnesses' children had been subjected, induced the Court to reverse itself and to endorse the free exercise of religion even when it may be offensive to the beliefs of the majority.[23]

Although the Supreme Court has been fairly consistent and strict in protecting the free exercise of religious belief, it has taken pains to distinguish between religious beliefs and *actions* based on those beliefs. The 1940 case of *Cantwell v. Connecticut* established the "time, place and manner" rule. Americans are free to adhere to any religious beliefs, but the time, place, and manner of their exercise are subject to regulation in the public interest.[24]

In one case, for example, two Native Americans had been fired from their jobs for ingesting peyote, a cactus banned as an illegal drug. They claimed that they had been fired from their jobs unlawfully because the use of peyote was a religious sacrament protected by the free exercise clause. The Court disagreed with their claim in an important 1990 decision,[25] but Congress supported the claim and went on to engage in an unusual controversy with the Court, involving the separation of powers and the proper application of the separation of church and state. Congress literally reversed the Court's 1990 decision with the enactment of the Religious Freedom Restoration Act of 1993 (RFRA), forbidding any federal agency or state government from restricting a person's free exercise of religion unless the federal agency or state government demonstrates that its action "furthers a compelling government interest" and "is the least restrictive means of furthering that compelling governmental interest." One of the first applications of RFRA was to a case brought by St. Peter's Catholic Church against the city of Boerne, Texas, which had denied permission to the church to enlarge its building because the building had been declared a historic landmark. The case went to federal court on the argument that the city had violated the church's religious freedom as guaranteed by Congress in RFRA. The Supreme Court declared RFRA unconstitutional, but on grounds rarely utilized, if not unique to this case: Congress had violated the separation of powers principle, infringing on the powers of the judiciary by going so far beyond its lawmaking powers that it ended up actually expanding the scope of religious rights rather than just enforcing them. The Court thereby implied that questions requiring a balancing of religious claims against public policy claims were reserved strictly to the judiciary.[26]

## ● The First Amendment and Freedom of Speech and of the Press

**Describe how the First Amendment protects free speech**

Congress shall make no law . . . abridging the freedom of speech, or of the press.

Freedom of speech and of the press have a special place in American political thought. To begin with, democracy depends on the ability of individuals to talk to each other and to disseminate information and ideas. It would be difficult to conceive how democratic politics could function without free and open debate. Such debate, moreover, is seen as an essential mechanism for determining the quality or validity of competing ideas. As Justice Oliver Wendell Holmes said in 1919, "The best test of truth is the power of the thought to get itself accepted in the competition of the market. . . . That at any rate is the theory of our Constitution."[27] What is sometimes called the "marketplace of ideas" receives a good deal of protection from the courts. In 1938 the Supreme Court held that any legislation that attempts to restrict speech "is to be subjected to a more exacting judicial scrutiny . . . than are most other types of legislation."[28] This higher standard of judicial review came to be called "strict scrutiny."

The doctrine of strict scrutiny places a heavy burden of proof on the government if it seeks to regulate or restrict speech. Americans are assumed to have the right to speak and to broadcast their ideas unless some compelling reason can be identified to stop them. But strict scrutiny does not mean that speech can never be regulated. Over the past 200 years, the courts have scrutinized many different forms of speech and constructed different principles and guidelines for each. According to the courts, although virtually all speech is protected by the Constitution, some forms of speech are entitled to a greater degree of protection than others. Let us examine what the federal courts have said about some of the major forms of speech.

## Political Speech

Political speech was the activity of greatest concern to the framers of the Constitution, even though some found it the most difficult form of speech to tolerate. Within seven years of the ratification of the Bill of Rights in 1791, Congress adopted the infamous Alien and Sedition Acts, which, among other things, made it a crime to say or publish anything that might tend to defame or bring into disrepute the government of the United States.

The first modern free speech case arose immediately after World War I. It involved persons who had been convicted under the federal Espionage Act of 1917 for opposing U.S. involvement in the war. The Supreme Court upheld the Espionage Act and refused to protect the speech rights of the defendants on the grounds that their activities—appeals to draftees to resist the draft—constituted a "**clear and present danger**" to national security.[29] This is the first and most famous "test" for when government intervention or censorship can be permitted.

It was only after the 1920s that real progress toward a genuinely effective First Amendment was made. Since then, political speech has been consistently protected by the courts even when it has been deemed "insulting" or "outrageous." Here is the way the Supreme Court put it in one of its most important statements on the subject:

> The constitutional guarantees of free speech and free press do not permit a State to forbid or proscribe advocacy of the use of force or of law violation *except where such advocacy is directed to inciting or producing imminent lawless action and is likely to incite or produce such action* [emphasis added].[30]

In other words, as long as speech falls short of actually inciting action, it cannot be prohibited, even if it is hostile to or subversive of the government and its policies. This statement was made in the case of a Ku Klux Klan leader, Charles Brandenburg, who had been arrested and convicted of advocating "revengent" action against the president, Congress, and the Supreme Court, among others, if they continued "to suppress the white, Caucasian race." Although Brandenburg was not carrying a weapon, some of the members of his audience were. Nevertheless, the Supreme Court reversed the state courts and freed Brandenburg while also

**"clear and present danger" test** test to determine whether speech is protected or unprotected, based on its capacity to present a "clear and present danger" to society

declaring Ohio's Criminal Syndicalism Act unconstitutional because it punished persons who "advocate, or teach the duty, necessity, or propriety [of violence] as a means of accomplishing industrial or political reform"; or who publish materials or "voluntarily assemble . . . to teach or advocate the doctrines of criminal syndicalism." The Supreme Court argued that the statute did not distinguish "mere advocacy" from "incitement to imminent lawless action." It would be difficult to go much further in protecting freedom of speech.

Another area of recent expansion of political speech, the participation of wealthy persons and corporations in political campaigns, was opened up in 1976 with the Supreme Court's decision in *Buckley v. Valeo.* Campaign finance reform laws of the early 1970s, arising out of the Watergate scandal, sought to put severe limits on campaign spending. In the *Buckley* case, a number of important provisions were declared unconstitutional on the basis of a new principle that spending money by or on behalf of candidates is a form of speech protected by the First Amendment. (For more details, see Chapter 10.)

The issue came up again in 2003, with passage of a new and still more severe campaign finance law, the Bipartisan Campaign Reform Act (BCRA). In *McConnell v. Federal Election Commission*, the 5–4 majority seriously reduced the area of speech protected by the *Buckley v. Valeo* decision by holding that Congress was well within its power to put limits on campaign spending. The Court argued that "the selling of access . . . has given rise to the appearance of undue influence [that justifies] regulations impinging on First Amendment rights . . . in order to curb corruption or the appearance of corruption."[31] In the *McConnell* case, the Court also upheld BCRA's limitations on "issue advertising." The act prohibited political advocacy groups from running ads that mentioned a candidate within 30 days of a primary election and 60 days of a general election. This ban was justified with the argument that wealthy special interests could affect election outcomes with last-minute ad campaigns. However, in its 2007 decision in the case of *Federal Election Commission v. Wisconsin Right to Life*, the Court reversed itself, declaring that such ads were protected speech and could not be prohibited so long as they focused mainly on issues and were not simply appeals to vote for or against a specific candidate.[32]

In the 2008 case of *Davis v. Federal Election Commission*, the Supreme Court struck down another element of BCRA, the so-called millionaire's amendment, which had increased contribution limits for opponents of wealthy, self-funded candidates.[33] Even more recently, in the 2010 case of *Citizens United v. Federal Election Commission*, the Supreme Court declared that the First Amendment prohibited BCRA's ban on corporate funding of independent political broadcasts aimed at electing or defeating particular candidates.[34] The case arose in 2008 when Citizens United, a conservative nonprofit organization, sought to show its film *Hillary: The Movie*, a documentary aimed at attacking Hillary Clinton's presidential bid during the 2008 Democratic primaries. In its 5–4 decision, the Supreme Court ruled that the Constitution prohibits the government from regulating political speech and that therefore the government could not ban this type of political spending by corporations. The Court's decision in this case has been controversial. Republicans, seeing themselves as the main beneficiaries of corporate ads, hailed the decision as a victory for free speech. Democrats denounced the decision, with President Obama calling it "a major victory for big oil, Wall Street banks, health insurance companies, and the other powerful interests that marshal their power every day in Washington to drown out the voices of everyday Americans."[35] Congressional Democrats vowed to rewrite the law to circumvent the Court's decision.

## Symbolic Speech, Speech Plus, and the Rights of Assembly and Petition

The First Amendment treats the freedoms of religion and political speech as equal to the freedoms of assembly and petition—speech associated with action. Freedom of speech and freedom of assembly are closely related by the "public forum doctrine." In the 1939 case of *Hague v. Committee for Industrial Organization*, the Court declared that the government may not prohibit speech-related activities such as demonstrations or leafleting in public areas traditionally used for that purpose, though, of course, the government may impose rules designed to protect the public safety so long as these rules do not discriminate against particular viewpoints.[36]

Generally, the Supreme Court has sought to protect actions that are designed to send a political message. (Usually the purpose of a symbolic act is not only to send a direct message but also to draw a crowd—to do something spectacular in order to strengthen the message by attracting spectators. Therefore the Court held unconstitutional a California statute making it a felony to display a red Communist flag "as a sign, symbol or emblem of opposition to organized government."[37] Although today there are limits on how far one can go with actions that convey a message symbolically, the protection of such actions is very broad. Thus, although the Court upheld a federal statute making it a crime to burn draft cards to protest the Vietnam War, on the grounds that the government had a compelling interest in preserving draft cards as part of the conduct of the war itself, the Court also deemed the wearing of black armbands to school a protected form of assembly for symbolic action.

Another example is the burning of the American flag as a protest. In 1984, at a political rally held during the Republican National Convention in Dallas, Texas, a political protester burned an American flag, thereby violating a Texas statute that prohibited desecration of a venerated object. In a 5–4 decision, the Supreme Court declared the Texas law unconstitutional on the grounds that flag burning was expressive conduct protected by the First Amendment.[38] Congress reacted immediately with a proposal for a constitutional amendment reversing the Court's Texas decision, and when the amendment failed to receive the necessary two-thirds majority in the Senate, Congress passed the Flag Protection Act of 1989. Protesters promptly violated this act, and their prosecution moved quickly into the federal district court, which declared the new law unconstitutional. The Supreme Court, in another 5–4 decision, affirmed the lower court decision.[39] A renewed effort began in Congress to propose a constitutional amendment that would reverse the Supreme Court and place flag burning outside the realm of protected speech or assembly. Since 1995 the House of Representatives has four times passed a resolution for a constitutional amendment to ban this form of expressive conduct, but each time, the Senate has failed to go along.[40] In a 2003 decision, the Supreme Court struck down a Virginia cross-burning statute. In that case, the Court ruled that states could criminalize cross burning—typically an

*The Supreme Court has interpreted the freedom of speech as extending to symbolic acts of political protest, such as flag burning. On several occasions—most recently in 2006—a resolution for a constitutional amendment to ban flag burning has passed in the House of Representatives but has never found enough support in the Senate.*

expression of hatred of African Americans—as long as the statute required prosecutors to prove that the act of setting fire to the cross was intended to intimidate. Former justice Sandra Day O'Connor wrote for the majority that the First Amendment permits the government to forbid cross burning as a "particularly virulent form of intimidation," but not when the act was "a form of symbolic expression."[41] This decision will almost inevitably become a more generalized First Amendment protection of any conduct, including flag burning, that can be shown to be a form of symbolic expression.

In the 2011 case of *Snyder v. Phelps*, the Court sought to protect another form of symbolic speech. Members of the Westboro Baptist Church had frequently demonstrated at military funerals, claiming that the deaths of the soldiers were a sign that God disapproved of the acceptance of homosexuality in the United States. The father of a soldier killed in Iraq brought suit against the church and its pastor, claiming that the demonstrators had caused him and his family severe emotional distress. The Supreme Court ruled, however, that the First Amendment protected free speech in a public place against such suits.[42]

Closer to the original intent of the assembly and petition clause is the category of "**speech plus**"—following speech with physical activity such as picketing, distributing leaflets, and other forms of peaceful demonstration or assembly. Such assemblies are consistently protected by courts under the First Amendment; state and local laws regulating such activities are closely scrutinized and frequently overturned. But the same assembly on private property is quite another matter, and can in many circumstances be regulated. For example, the directors of a shopping center can lawfully prohibit an assembly protesting a war or supporting a ban on abortion. Assemblies in public areas can also be restricted under some circumstances, especially when the assembly or demonstration jeopardizes the health, safety, or rights of others. This condition was the basis of the Supreme Court's decision to uphold a lower court order that restricted the access that abortion protesters had to the entrances of abortion clinics.[43]

An unusual "speech plus" case, decided in 2006, was *Rumsfeld v. Forum for Academic and Institutional Rights*.[44] A number of law schools had banned military recruiters from their campuses to protest the military's antigay policies. The government responded by threatening to cut off federal funding to schools that joined the ban. The schools argued, in turn, that the government was violating their constitutional right to voice opposition to its policies. The Supreme Court ruled that the government could require schools to host recruiters as a condition for funding. Banning recruitment, said the Court, was not a form of expression protected by the Constitution; the schools remained completely free to voice their opposition to the military's policies even as they hosted the recruiters.

## Freedom of the Press

For all practical purposes, freedom of speech implies and includes freedom of the press. With the exception of the broadcast media, which are subject to federal regulation, the press is protected under the doctrine against **prior restraint**. Beginning with the landmark 1931 case of *Near v. Minnesota*, the U.S. Supreme Court has held that, except under the most extraordinary circumstances, the First Amendment of the Constitution prohibits government agencies from seeking to prevent newspapers or magazines from publishing whatever they wish.[45] Indeed, in the case of *New York Times v. United States* (the so-called Pentagon Papers case), the Supreme Court ruled that the government could not block publication of secret

**"speech plus"** speech accompanied by conduct such as sit-ins, picketing, and demonstrations. Protection of this form of speech under the First Amendment is conditional, and restrictions imposed by state or local authorities are acceptable if properly balanced by considerations of public order

**prior restraint** an effort by a governmental agency to block the publication of material it deems libelous or harmful in some other way; censorship. In the United States, the courts forbid prior restraint except under the most extraordinary circumstances

*Journalists often claim that the right to protect the names of their sources is essential to a free press. In 2005 a* New York Times *reporter, Judith Miller, went to jail rather than reveal the name of a confidential source in court.*

Defense Department documents furnished to the *New York Times* by an opponent of the Vietnam War who had obtained the documents illegally.[46] In a 1990 case, however, the Supreme Court upheld a lower court order restraining Cable News Network (CNN) from broadcasting tapes of conversations between the former Panamanian dictator Manuel Noriega and his lawyer, supposedly recorded by the U.S. government. By a vote of 7 to 2, the Court held that CNN could be restrained from broadcasting the tapes until the trial court in the Noriega case had listened to the tapes and decided whether their broadcast would violate Noriega's right to a fair trial.[47]

Another press freedom issue that the courts have often been asked to decide is the question of whether journalists can be compelled to reveal their sources of information. Journalists assert that if they cannot ensure their sources' confidentiality, the flow of information will be reduced and press freedom effectively curtailed. Government agencies, however, aver that names of news sources may be relevant to criminal or even national security investigations. More than 30 states have "shield laws," which, to varying degrees, protect journalistic sources. There is, however, no federal shield law. The Supreme Court has held that the press has no constitutional right to withhold information in court.[48] In 2005 a *New York Times* reporter, Judith Miller, was jailed for contempt of court for refusing to tell a federal grand jury the name of a confidential source in a case involving the leaked identity of the CIA analyst Valerie Plame. Plame's husband, Joseph Wilson, had been critical of the Bush administration's Iraq policies.

**Libel and Slander** Some speech is not protected at all. If a written statement is made in "reckless disregard of the truth" and is considered damaging to the victim because it is "malicious, scandalous, and defamatory," it can be punished as **libel**. If such a statement is made orally, it can be punished as **slander**.

Most libel suits today involve freedom of the press, and the realm of free press is enormous. Historically, newspapers were subject to the law of libel, which provided that newspapers that printed false and malicious stories could be compelled to pay damages to those they defamed. In recent years, however, American courts

**libel** a written statement made in "reckless disregard of the truth" that is considered damaging to a victim because it is "malicious, scandalous, and defamatory"

**slander** an oral statement made in "reckless disregard of the truth" that is considered damaging to the victim because it is "malicious, scandalous, and defamatory"

have greatly narrowed the meaning of libel and made it extremely difficult, particularly for politicians or other public figures, to win a libel case against a newspaper. In the important 1964 case of *New York Times v. Sullivan*, the Court held that to be deemed libelous, a story about a public official not only had to untrue, but also had to result from "actual malice" or "reckless disregard" for the truth.[49] In other words, the newspaper had to print false and malicious material deliberately. In practice, it is nearly impossible to prove that a paper *deliberately* printed maliciously false information, and it is especially difficult for a politician or other public figure to win a libel case. Essentially, the print media have been able to publish anything they want about a public figure.

However, the Court has opened up the possibility for public officials to file libel suits against the press. The Court has held that the press was immune to libel suits only when the printed material was "a matter of public concern."[50] In other words, a newspaper would have to show that the public official was engaged in activities that were indeed *public*. This principle has made the press more vulnerable to libel suits, but it still leaves an enormous realm of freedom for the press. For example, the Reverend Jerry Falwell, the leader of the Moral Majority, lost his libel suit against *Hustler* magazine even though the magazine had published a cartoon of Falwell showing him having drunken intercourse with his mother in an outhouse. A unanimous Supreme Court rejected a jury verdict in favor of damages for "emotional distress" on the grounds that parodies, no matter how outrageous, are protected because "outrageousness" is too subjective a test and thus would interfere with the free flow of ideas protected by the First Amendment.[51]

With the emergence of the Internet as an important communications medium, the courts have had to decide how traditional libel law applies to Internet content. In 1995 the New York courts held that an online bulletin board could be held responsible for the libelous content of material posted by a third party. To protect Internet service providers, Congress subsequently enacted legislation absolving them of responsibility for third-party posts. The federal courts have generally upheld this law and declared that service providers are immune from suits regarding the content of material posted by others.[52]

**Obscenity and Pornography** If libel and slander cases can be difficult because of the problem of determining the truth of statements and whether those statements are malicious and damaging, cases involving pornography and obscenity can be even stickier. It is easy to say that pornography and obscenity fall outside the realm of protected speech, but it is impossible to draw a clear line between protected and unprotected speech. Not until 1957 did the Supreme Court confront this problem, and it did so with a definition of obscenity that may have caused more confusion than it cleared up. In writing the Court's opinion, Justice William Brennan defined obscenity as speech or writing that appeals to the "prurient interest"—that is, books, magazines, films, and other material whose purpose is to excite lust, as this appears "to the average person, applying contemporary community standards." Even so, Brennan added, the work should be judged obscene only when it is "utterly without redeeming social importance."[53] Instead of clarifying the Court's view, Brennan's definition actually caused more confusion. In 1964, Justice Potter Stewart confessed that, although he found pornography impossible to define, "I know it when I see it."[54]

All attempts by the courts to define pornography and obscenity have proved impractical, because each instance required courts to screen thousands of pages of print material and feet of film alleged to be pornographic. The vague and impractical standards that had been developed meant ultimately that almost nothing could be banned on the grounds that it was pornographic and obscene. An effort was made to strengthen the restrictions in 1973, when the Supreme Court expressed its willingness to define pornography as a work that (1) as a whole, is deemed prurient by the "average person" according to "community standards"; (2) depicts sexual conduct "in a patently offensive way"; and (3) lacks "serious literary, artistic, political, or scientific value." This definition meant that pornography would be determined by local rather than national standards. Thus, a local bookseller might be prosecuted for selling a volume that was a best seller nationally but that was deemed pornographic locally.[55] This new definition of standards did not help much either, and not long after 1973, the Court began again to review all such community antipornography laws, reversing most of them.

In recent years, the battle against obscene speech has targeted "cyberporn"—pornography on the Internet. Opponents of this form of expression argue that it should be banned because of the easy access children have to the Internet. The first major effort to regulate the content of the Internet occurred in 1996, when the 104th Congress passed the Telecommunications Act. Attached to it was an amendment, called the Communications Decency Act (CDA), designed to regulate the online transmission of obscene material. The constitutionality of the CDA was immediately challenged in court by a coalition of interests led by the American Civil Liberties Union (ACLU). In the 1997 case of *Reno v. ACLU*, the Supreme Court struck down the CDA, ruling that it suppressed speech that "adults have a constitutional right to receive," and that governments may not limit the adult population to messages that are fit for children. Supreme Court justice John Paul Stevens described the Internet as the "town crier" of the modern age and said that the Internet was entitled to the greatest degree of First Amendment protection possible.[56] Congress again tried limiting children's access to Internet pornography with the 2001 Children's Internet Protection Act, which required public libraries to install antipornography filters on all library computers with Internet access. Though the act made cooperation a condition for receiving federal subsidies, it did permit librarians to unblock a site at the request of an adult patron. The law was challenged, but in 2003 the Court upheld it, asserting that its provisions did not violate library patrons' First Amendment rights.[57] In 2003, Congress enacted the PROTECT Act, which outlawed efforts to sell child pornography via the Internet. The Supreme Court upheld this act in the 2008 case of *United States v. Williams*, in which the majority said that criminalizing efforts to purvey child pornography did not violate free speech guarantees.[58]

In 2000 the Supreme Court extended the highest degree of First Amendment protection to cable (not broadcast) television. In *United States v. Playboy Entertainment Group*, the Court struck down a portion of the 1996 Telecommunications Act that required cable TV companies to limit the broadcast of sexually explicit programming to late-night hours. In its decision, the Court noted that the law already provided parents with the means to restrict access to sexually explicit cable channels through various blocking devices. Moreover, such programming could come into the home only if parents decided to purchase such channels in the first place.[59]

Closely related to the issue of obscenity is the matter of violent broadcast content. Can a state or the federal government prohibit broadcasts or publications deemed to be excessively violent? Here, too, the Court has generally upheld freedom of speech. For example, in the 2011 case of *Brown v. Entertainment Merchants Association*, the Court struck down a California law banning the sale of violent video games to children, saying that the law violated the First Amendment.[60]

One of the more visible issues of free speech has been the banning of certain books in public schools. For example, in recent years, one of the most frequently banned books has been Twilight, *a vampire saga by Stephenie Meyer.*

**Fighting Words and Hate Speech** Speech can also lose its protected position when it moves toward the sphere of action. "Expressive speech," for example, is protected until it moves from the symbolic realm to the realm of actual conduct—to direct incitement of damaging conduct with the use of so-called **fighting words**. In 1942 a man called a police officer a "goddamned racketeer" and "a damn Fascist," and was arrested and convicted of violating a state law forbidding the use of offensive language in public. When his case reached the Supreme Court, the arrest was upheld on the grounds that the First Amendment provides no protection for such offensive language because such words "are no essential part of any exposition of ideas."[61] This decision was reaffirmed in the important 1951 case of *Dennis v. United States* when the Supreme Court held that

> there is no substantial public interest in permitting certain kinds of utterances: the lewd and obscene, the profane, the libelous, and the insulting or "fighting" words—those which by their very utterance inflict injury or tend to incite an immediate breach of the peace.[62]

**forcriticalanalysis**

Should hate speech be protected? Is it contradictory that many who strongly support free thought and expression draw the line at protecting "thought we hate"?

Since that time, however, the Supreme Court has reversed almost every conviction based on arguments that the speaker had used "fighting words." But again, it does not mean this is an absolutely settled area. In recent years, the increased activism of minority and women's groups has prompted a movement against words that might be construed as offensive to members of a particular group. But how should we determine what words are "fighting words" and therefore fall outside the protections of the freedom of speech?

Scores of universities have attempted to develop speech codes to suppress utterances deemed to be racial or ethnic slurs. Similar developments have taken place in large corporations, both public and private, with many successful complaints and lawsuits alleging that the words of employers or their supervisors created a "hostile or abusive working environment." The Supreme Court has held that a "hostile working environment" results from "sexual harassment," including "unwelcome sexual advances, requests for sexual favors, and other *verbal* or physical conduct of a sexual nature [emphasis added]."[63] A fundamental free speech issue is involved in these regulations of hostile speech.

Many jurisdictions have drafted ordinances banning hate speech—forms of expression designed to assert hatred toward one or another group, be they African Americans, Jews, Muslims, or others. Such ordinances seldom pass constitutional muster. The leading Supreme Court case in this realm is the 1992 decision in *R.A.V. v. City of St. Paul*.[64] Here, a white teenager was arrested for burning a cross on the lawn of a black family in violation of a municipal ordinance that banned cross burning. The Court ruled that such an ordinance must be *content neutral*—that is, it must not prohibit actions directed at some groups but not others. The statute in question prohibited only cross burning—which is typically directed at African Americans. Since a statute banning all forms of hateful expression would be deemed overly broad, the *R.A.V.* standard suggests that virtually all hate speech is constitutionally protected.

One category of conditionally protected speech is the speech of high school students in public schools. In 1986 the Supreme Court backed away from a broad protection of student free speech rights by upholding the punishment of a high school student for making a sexually suggestive speech. The Court opinion held that such speech interfered with the school's goal of teaching students the limits of socially acceptable behavior.[65] Two years later the Supreme Court took another conser-

The Supreme Court has ruled that high school students' speech can be restricted. In a 2007 case involving a student who displayed the banner at left, the Court found that the school principal had not violated the student's right to free speech by suspending him.

vative step by restricting students' speech and press rights even further, defining them as part of the educational process and not to be treated with the same standard as adult speech in a regular public forum.[66] A later case involving high school students is the 2007 case of *Morse v. Frederick*.[67] This case dealt with the policies of Juneau-Douglas High School in Juneau, Alaska. In 2002 the Olympic torch relay had passed through Juneau on its way to Salt Lake City for the opening of the Winter Olympics. As the torch passed Juneau-Douglas High, a senior, Joseph Frederick, unfurled a banner reading "Bong Hits 4 Jesus." The school's principal promptly suspended Frederick, who then brought suit for reinstatement, alleging that his free speech rights had been violated. Like most of America's public schools, Juneau High prohibits assemblies or expressions on school grounds that advocate illegal drug use, saying that some federal aid is contingent on this policy. Civil libertarians, of course, see such policies as restricting students' right to free speech. Speaking for the Court's majority, Chief Justice Roberts said that the First Amendment did not require schools to permit students to advocate illegal drug use.

**Commercial Speech** Commercial speech, such as newspaper or television advertisements, does not have full First Amendment protection because it cannot be considered political speech. Initially considered to be entirely outside the protection of the First Amendment, commercial speech is still subject to some regulation. For example, the prohibition of false and misleading advertising by the Federal Trade Commission is an old and well-established power of the federal government. The Supreme Court long ago approved the constitutionality of laws prohibiting the electronic media from carrying cigarette advertising.[68] It has upheld city ordinances prohibiting the posting of all commercial signs on public property (as long as the ban is total, so that there is no hint of selective censorship).[69] And the Supreme Court, in a contentious 5–4 decision written by Chief Justice William

Rehnquist, upheld Puerto Rico's statute restricting gambling advertising aimed at residents of Puerto Rico.[70]

However, the gains far outweigh the losses in the effort to expand the protection of commercial speech under the First Amendment. "In part, this reflects the growing appreciation that commercial speech is part of the free flow of information necessary for informed choice and democratic participation."[71] For example, in 1975 the Supreme Court struck down a state statute making it a misdemeanor to sell or circulate newspapers encouraging abortions; the Court ruled that the statute infringed on constitutionally protected speech and on the right of the reader to make informed choices.[72] On a similar basis, the Court reversed its own earlier decisions upholding laws that prohibited dentists and other professionals from advertising their services. For the Court, medical service advertising was a matter of health that could be advanced by the free flow of information.[73] In 1996 the Court struck down Rhode Island laws and regulations banning the advertisement of liquor prices as a violation of the First Amendment.[74] And in a 2001 case, the Court ruled that a Massachusetts ban on all cigarette advertising violated the First Amendment right of the tobacco industry to advertise its products to adult consumers.[75] These instances of commercial speech, significant in themselves, are all the more significant because they indicate the breadth and depth of the freedom existing today to direct appeals to a large public, not only to sell goods and services but also to mobilize people for political purposes.

## ● The Second Amendment and the Right to Bear Arms

*A loophole in gun purchase laws allowed a student at Virginia Tech with a history of mental illness to purchase the handguns he used to kill 32 people, including instructors and fellow students, and wound many others. Following the tragedy, both the state of Virginia and the national government strengthened the requirements for background checks on gun buyers.*

**Explore whether the Second Amendment means people have a right to own guns**

A well regulated Militia, being necessary to the security of a free State, the right of the people to keep and bear Arms, shall not be infringed.

The point and purpose of the Second Amendment is the provision for militias; they were to be the backing of the government for the maintenance of local public order. "Militia" was understood at the time of the Founding to be a military or police resource for state governments, and militias were specifically distinguished from armies and troops, which came within the sole constitutional jurisdiction of Congress.

Thus, the right of the people "to keep and bear Arms" is based on and associated with participation in state militias. The reference to citizens keeping arms underscored the fact that in the 1700s, state governments could not be relied on to provide firearms to militia members, so citizens eligible to serve in militias (white males between the ages of 18 and 45) were expected to keep their own firearms at the ready. In the late nineteenth century, some citizens sought to form their own *private* militias, but

*The Second Amendment arouses as much controversy as the First. The right to bear arms is constitutionally guaranteed, although an estimated 80 percent of Americans support some form of gun control.*

the Supreme Court cut that short with a ruling that militias are a military or police resource of state governments.[76] In 2008 the U.S. Supreme Court declared that the Second Amendment also protected an individual's right to possess a firearm for private use.[77] In the case of *District of Columbia v. Heller*, the Court struck down a Washington, D.C., law that was designed to make it nearly impossible for private individuals to purchase firearms legally. The District of Columbia is an entity of the federal government, and the Court did not indicate that its ruling applied to state firearms laws. However, in the 2010 case of *McDonald v. Chicago*, the Court struck down a Chicago firearms ordinance and applied the Second Amendment to the states as well,[78] making this the first new incorporation decision by the Court in 40 years.

# ● Rights of the Criminally Accused

**Explain the major rights that people have if they are accused of a crime**

Except for the First Amendment, most of the battle to apply the Bill of Rights to the states has been fought over the various protections granted to individuals who are accused of a crime, who are suspects in the commission of a crime, or who are brought before the court as a witness to a crime (Table 4.4). The Fourth, Fifth, Sixth, and Eighth amendments, taken together, are the essence of the **due process of law**, even though these precise words for this fundamental concept do not appear until the end of the Fifth Amendment. In the next sections, we will look at specific cases that illuminate the dynamics of this important constitutional issue. The procedural safeguards that we will discuss may seem remote to most law-abiding citizens, but they help define the limits of government action against the personal liberty of every citizen. Many Americans believe that "legal

**due process of law** the right of every citizen against arbitrary action by national or state governments

technicalities" are responsible for setting many actual criminals free. In many cases, this is absolutely true. In fact, setting defendants free is the very purpose of the requirements that constitute due process. One of America's traditional and most strongly held juridical values is that "it is far worse to convict an innocent man than to let a guilty man go free."[79] In civil suits, verdicts rest on "the preponderance of the evidence," but in criminal cases, guilt has to be proven "beyond a reasonable doubt"—a far higher standard. The provisions for due process in the Bill of Rights were added in order to improve the probability that the standard of "reasonable doubt" would be respected.

## The Fourth Amendment and Searches and Seizures

> The right of the people to be secure in their persons, houses, papers, and effects, against unreasonable searches and seizures, shall not be violated, and no Warrants shall issue, but upon probable cause, supported by Oath or affirmation, and particularly describing the place to be searched, and the persons or things to be seized.

The purpose of the Fourth Amendment is to guarantee the security of citizens against unreasonable (i.e., improper) searches and seizures. In 1990 the Supreme Court summarized its understanding of the Fourth Amendment brilliantly and succinctly: "A search compromises the individual interest in privacy; a seizure deprives the individual of dominion over his or her person or property."[80] But how are we to define what is reasonable and what is unreasonable?

The 1961 case of *Mapp v. Ohio* illustrates one of the most important of the principles that have grown out of the Fourth Amendment—the **exclusionary rule**, which prohibits evidence obtained during an illegal search from being introduced in a trial. Acting on a tip that Dollree (Dolly) Mapp was harboring a suspect in a bombing incident, several policemen forcibly entered Mapp's house, claiming they had a warrant to look for the bombing suspect. The police did not find the bombing suspect but did find some materials connected to a local numbers racket (an illegal gambling operation) and a quantity of "obscene materials," in violation of

**exclusionary rule** the ability of courts to exclude evidence obtained in violation of the Fourth Amendment

*Under what circumstances can the police search an individual's car? The Fourth Amendment protects against "unreasonable searches and seizures," but the Supreme Court has had to interpret what is unreasonable.*

## TABLE 4.4

### The Rights of the Accused from Arrest to Trial

No improper searches and seizures (Fourth Amendment)

No arrest without probable cause (Fourth Amendment)

Right to remain silent (Fifth Amendment)

No self-incrimination during arrest or trial (Fifth Amendment)

Right to be informed of charges (Sixth Amendment)

Right to counsel (Sixth Amendment)

No excessive bail (Eighth Amendment)

Right to grand jury (Fifth Amendment)

Right to open trial before a judge (Article I, Section 9)

Right to speedy and public trial before an impartial jury (Sixth Amendment)

Evidence obtained by illegal search not admissible during trial (Fourth Amendment)

Right to confront witnesses (Sixth Amendment)

No double jeopardy (Fifth Amendment)

No cruel and unusual punishment (Eighth Amendment)

an Ohio law banning possession of such materials. Although no warrant was ever produced, the evidence that had been seized was admitted by a court, and Mapp was charged and convicted of illegal possession of obscene materials.

By the time Mapp's appeal reached the Supreme Court, the issue of obscene materials had faded into obscurity, and the question before the Court was whether any evidence produced under the circumstances of the search of her home was admissible. The Court's opinion affirmed the exclusionary rule: under the Fourth Amendment (applied to the states through the Fourteenth Amendment), "all evidence obtained by searches and seizures in violation of the Constitution . . . is inadmissible."[81] This means that even people who are clearly guilty of the crime of which they are accused must not be convicted if the only evidence for their conviction was obtained illegally. This idea was expressed by Supreme Court justice Benjamin Cardozo nearly a century ago, when he wrote that "the criminal is to go free because the constable has blundered."

The exclusionary rule is the most dramatic restraint imposed by the courts on police behavior because it rules out precisely the evidence that produces a conviction; it frees those people who are *known* to have committed the crime of which they have been accused. Thus, in recent years the Court has softened the application of the exclusionary rule, and federal courts have relied on its discretionary use, whereby they make a judgment as to the "nature and quality of the intrusion." It is thus difficult to know ahead of time whether a defendant will or will not be protected from an illegal search under the Fourth Amendment.[82] In 2006, in the case of *United States v. Grubbs*, the Supreme Court ruled that the police could conduct searches using such "anticipatory warrants"—warrants issued when the police know that incriminating material is not yet present but have reason to believe that it will eventually arrive at a particular premises.[83] The warrants are held until the police are ready to conduct their search. In some instances, such as during an arrest, the authorities can conduct searches without obtaining any warrants at all.

The Fourth Amendment is also at issue in the controversy over mandatory drug testing. Such tests are most widely applied to public employees, and in 1989 the Supreme Court upheld the U.S. Customs Service's drug-testing program for its employees.[84] That same year, the Court approved drug and alcohol tests for railroad workers if they were involved in serious accidents.[85] Since then, more than 40 federal agencies have initiated mandatory employee drug tests, giving rise to public appeals against the general practice of "suspicionless testing" of employees, in violation of the Fourth Amendment. A 1995 case, in which the Court upheld a public school district's policy requiring all students participating in interscholastic sports to submit to random drug tests, surely contributed to the efforts of federal, state, and local agencies to initiate random and suspicionless drug and alcohol testing.[86]

The most recent cases suggest, however, that the Court is beginning to consider limits on the war against drugs. In 2001 the Court found it unconstitutional for police to use trained dogs in roadblocks set up to look for drugs in cars. Unlike drunk-driving roadblocks, where public safety is directly involved, narcotics roadblocks "cannot escape the Fourth Amendment's requirement that searches be based on suspicion of individual wrongdoing."[87] In a decisive 8–1 decision in 1997, the Court applied the Fourth Amendment as a shield against "state action that diminishes personal privacy" in cases that do not involve high-risk or safety-sensitive tasks.[88] That same year, the Court extended protection against unlawful searches to passengers in cars that have been stopped by the police, giving passengers the same right as drivers to challenge the validity of a search.[89] The Court also ruled that a public hospital cannot constitutionally test maternity patients for illegal drug use without their consent,[90] and that the police may not use thermal imaging devices to detect suspicious patterns of heat emerging from private homes without obtaining the usual search warrant.[91] In 2009 the Court ruled against an Arizona school district that conducted a strip search of a thirteen-year-old student suspected of hiding ibuprofen in her underwear.[92]

## The Fifth Amendment

No person shall be held to answer for a capital, or otherwise infamous crime, unless on a presentment or indictment of a Grand Jury, except in cases arising in the land or naval forces, or in the Militia, when in actual service in time of War or public danger; nor shall any person be subject for the same offence to be twice put in jeopardy of life or limb; nor shall be compelled in any criminal case to be a witness against himself, nor be deprived of life, liberty, or property, without due process of law; nor shall private property be taken for public use, without just compensation.

**grand jury** jury that determines whether sufficient evidence is available to justify a trial; grand juries do not rule on the accused's guilt or innocence

**Grand Juries** The first clause of the Fifth Amendment, the right to a **grand jury** to determine whether a trial is warranted, is considered "the oldest institution known to the Constitution."[93] Grand juries play an important role in federal criminal cases. However, the provision for a grand jury is the one important civil liberties provision of the Bill of Rights that was not incorporated into the Fourteenth Amendment to apply to state criminal prosecutions. Thus, some states operate without grand juries. In such states, the prosecuting attorney simply files a "bill of information" affirming that there is sufficient evidence available to justify a trial. If the accused person is to be held in custody, the prosecutor must take the available information before a judge to determine that the evidence shows probable cause.

# Who Is in Prison?

Despite the many freedoms protected by the Bill of Rights, the United States imprisons more of its people than any other country. Although African Americans make up only about 13 percent of the total U.S. population, they make up 38 percent of the prison population. People convicted of violent crimes make up the majority of prison inmates, with drug offenders as the second largest group.

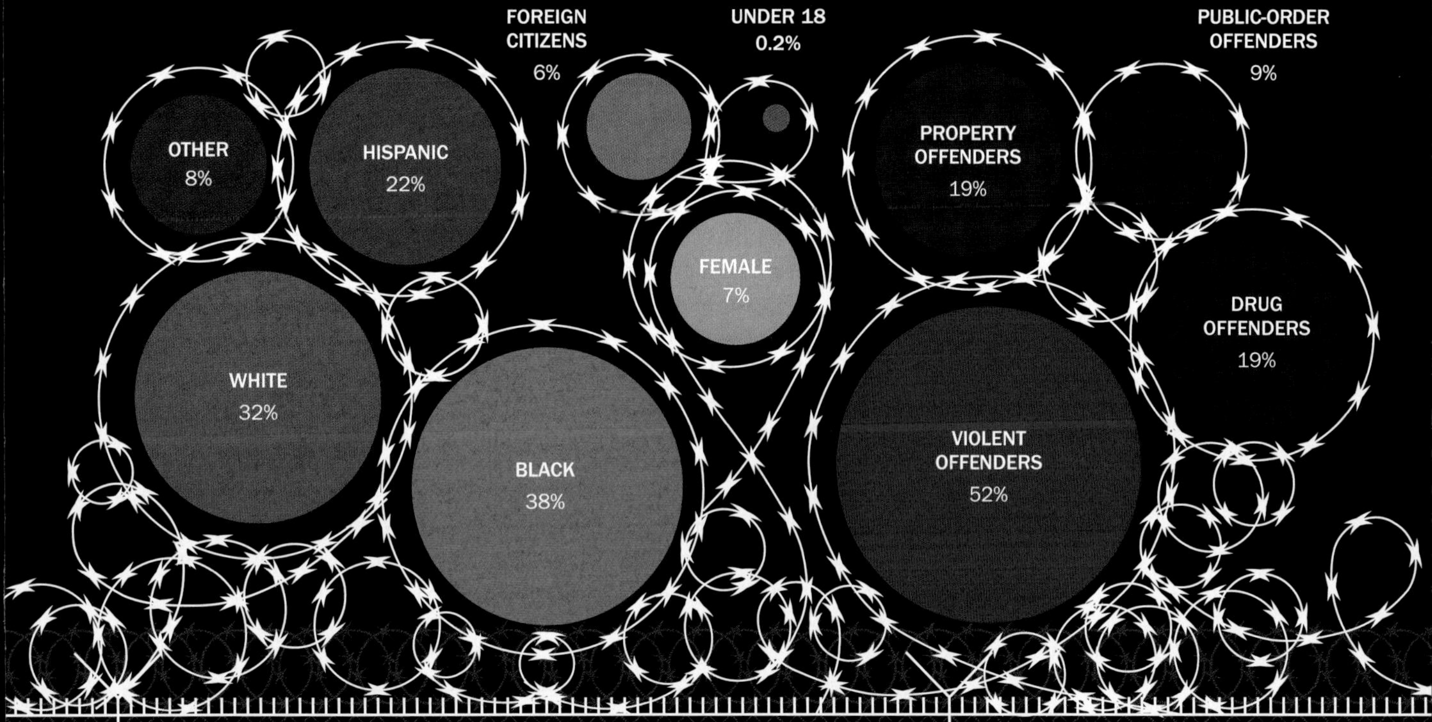

FOREIGN CITIZENS 6%

UNDER 18 0.2%

PUBLIC-ORDER OFFENDERS 9%

OTHER 8%

HISPANIC 22%

PROPERTY OFFENDERS 19%

FEMALE 7%

DRUG OFFENDERS 19%

WHITE 32%

BLACK 38%

VIOLENT OFFENDERS 52%

## Incarceration Rates around the World
per 100,000 of the national population

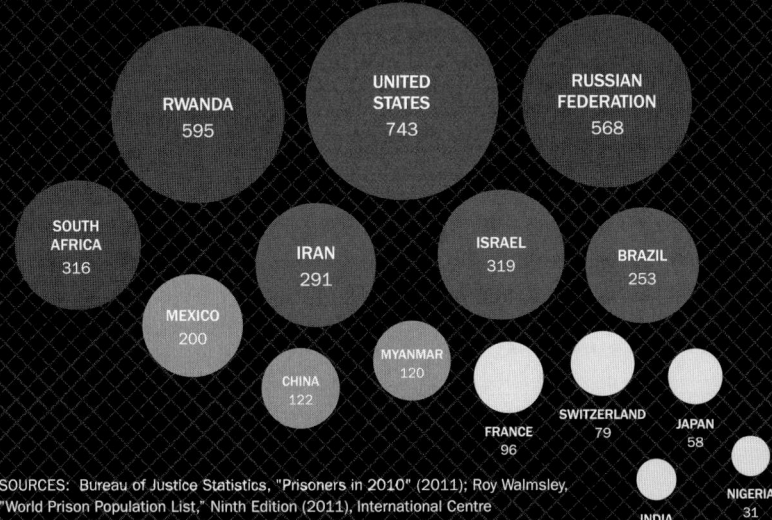

RWANDA 595
UNITED STATES 743
RUSSIAN FEDERATION 568
SOUTH AFRICA 316
IRAN 291
ISRAEL 319
BRAZIL 253
MEXICO 200
MYANMAR 120
CHINA 122
FRANCE 96
SWITZERLAND 79
JAPAN 58
INDIA 32
NIGERIA 31

SOURCES: Bureau of Justice Statistics, "Prisoners in 2010" (2011); Roy Walmsley, "World Prison Population List," Ninth Edition (2011), International Centre for Prison Studies, School of Law, King's College, London.

## for critical analysis

1. Due process guarantees the same legal protections to anyone accused of a crime. However, studies have shown that African Americans and Hispanics are more likely to be jailed—and jailed for longer—than whites convicted of similar crimes. Is this a violation of civil liberties?

2. Some people have argued that prison terms for relatively minor drug offenses violate the Eighth Amendment's ban on cruel and unusual punishment. What do you think?

**double jeopardy** the Fifth Amendment right providing that a person cannot be tried twice for the same crime

**Double Jeopardy** "Nor shall any person be subject for the same offence to be twice put in jeopardy of life or limb" is the constitutional protection from **double jeopardy**, or being tried more than once for the same crime. The protection from double jeopardy was at the heart of the *Palko* case in 1937, which, as we saw earlier in this chapter, also established the principle of selective incorporation of the Bill of Rights. In that case, a Connecticut court had found Frank Palko guilty of second-degree murder and sentenced him to life in prison. Unhappy with the verdict, the state of Connecticut appealed the conviction to its highest court, won the appeal, got a new trial, and then succeeded in getting Palko convicted of first-degree murder. Palko appealed to the Supreme Court on what seemed an open-and-shut case of double jeopardy. Yet, although the majority of the Court agreed that this could indeed be considered a case of double jeopardy, they decided that double jeopardy was *not* one of the provisions of the Bill of Rights incorporated into the Fourteenth Amendment as a restriction on the powers of the states. It took more than 30 years for the Court to nationalize the constitutional protection against double jeopardy. Because Frank Palko lived in the state of Connecticut rather than in a state whose constitution included a guarantee against double jeopardy, he was eventually executed for the crime.

**Self-Incrimination** Perhaps the most significant liberty found in the Fifth Amendment, and the one most familiar to the many Americans who watch television crime shows, is the guarantee that no citizen "shall be compelled in any criminal case to be a witness against himself." The most famous case concerning self-incrimination is one of such importance that Chief Justice Earl Warren assessed its results as going "to the very root of our concepts of American criminal jurisprudence."[94] Twenty-three-year-old Ernesto Miranda was sentenced to between 20 and 30 years in prison for the kidnapping and rape of an eighteen-year-old woman. The woman had identified him in a police lineup, and after two hours of questioning, Miranda confessed, subsequently signing a statement that his confession had been made voluntarily, without threats or promises of immunity. These confessions were admitted into evidence, served as the basis for Miranda's conviction, and also served as the basis for the appeal of his conviction all the way to the Supreme Court. Following

*The case of Ernesto Miranda resulted in the creation of Miranda rights, which must be read to those arrested to make them aware of their constitutional rights.*

| DEFENDANT | LOCATION |
|---|---|

### SPECIFIC WARNING REGARDING INTERROGATIONS

1. YOU HAVE THE RIGHT TO REMAIN SILENT.

2. ANYTHING YOU SAY CAN AND WILL BE USED AGAINST YOU IN A COURT OF LAW.

3. YOU HAVE THE RIGHT TO TALK TO A LAWYER AND HAVE HIM PRESENT WITH YOU WHILE YOU ARE BEING QUESTIONED.

4. IF YOU CANNOT AFFORD TO HIRE A LAWYER ONE WILL BE APPOINTED TO REPRESENT YOU BEFORE ANY QUESTIONING, IF YOU WISH ONE.

| SIGNATURE OF DEFENDANT | DATE |
|---|---|
| WITNESS | TIME |

☐ REFUSED SIGNATURE   SAN FRANCISCO POLICE DEPARTMENT   PR.9.1.4

one of the most intensely and widely criticized decisions ever handed down by the Supreme Court, Ernesto Miranda's case produced the rules the police must follow before questioning an arrested criminal suspect. The reading of a person's "Miranda rights" became a standard scene in every police station and on virtually every dramatization of police action on television and in the movies. *Miranda* advanced the civil liberties of accused persons not only by expanding the scope of the Fifth Amendment clause covering coerced confessions and self-incrimination but also by confirming the right to counsel (discussed later). The Supreme Court under Burger and Rehnquist considerably softened the *Miranda* restrictions, but the **Miranda rule** still stands as a protection against egregious police abuses of arrested persons. The Supreme Court reaffirmed *Miranda* in *Dickerson v. United States* (2000). However, in the 2010 case of *Berghuis v. Thompkins*, the Supreme Court introduced an important qualification to the Miranda rule.[95] In a 5–4 decision, the Court said that statements made by suspects who did not expressly waive their rights (usually by signing a form) could be used against them. The dissenting justices feared that this decision might open the way for police abuses and misleading claims.

**Eminent Domain** The other fundamental clause of the Fifth Amendment is the "takings clause," which extends to each citizen a protection against the "taking" of private property "without just compensation." Although this part of the Fifth Amendment is not specifically concerned with protecting persons accused of crimes, it is nevertheless a fundamentally important instance where the government and the citizen are adversaries. The power of any government to take private property for public use—a power essential to the very concept of sovereignty—is called **eminent domain**. The Fifth Amendment neither invents eminent domain nor takes it away; its purpose is to put limits on that inherent power through procedures that require a showing of a public purpose and the provision of fair payment for the taking of someone's property. This provision is now universally observed in all U.S. principalities, but it has not always been meticulously observed.

The first modern case confronting the issue of public use involved a mom-and-pop grocery store in a run-down neighborhood on the southwest side of the District of Columbia. In carrying out a vast urban redevelopment program, the city government of Washington, D.C., took the property as one of a large number of privately owned lots to be cleared for new housing and business construction. The owner of the grocery store, and his successors after his death, took the government to court on the grounds that it was an unconstitutional use of eminent domain to take property from one private owner and eventually to turn that property back, in altered form, to another private owner. In 1945 the store owners lost their case. The Supreme Court's argument was a curious but very important one: the "public interest" can mean virtually anything a legislature says it means. In other words, since the overall slum clearance and redevelopment project was in the public interest, according to the legislature, the eventual transfers of property were justified.[96] This principle was reaffirmed in the 2005 case of *Kelo v. City of New London*, where the Court held that the city could seize land from one private owner and transfer it to another as part of a redevelopment plan.[97]

## The Sixth Amendment and the Right to Counsel

In all criminal prosecutions, the accused shall enjoy the right to a speedy and public trial, by an impartial jury of the State and district wherein the crime shall have been committed, which district shall have been previously ascertained by law, and

**Miranda rule** the requirement, articulated by the Supreme Court in *Miranda v. Arizona*, that persons under arrest must be informed prior to police interrogation of their rights to remain silent and to have the benefit of legal counsel

**eminent domain** the right of government to take private property for public use

to be informed of the nature and cause of the accusation; to be confronted with the witnesses against him; to have compulsory process for obtaining witnesses in his favor, and to have the Assistance of Counsel for his defence.

Like the exclusionary rule of the Fourth Amendment and the self-incrimination clause of the Fifth Amendment, the "right to counsel" provision of the Sixth Amendment is notable for sometimes freeing defendants who seem to be guilty as charged. Other provisions of the Sixth Amendment, such as the right to a speedy trial and the right to confront witnesses before an impartial jury, are less controversial in nature.

*Gideon v. Wainwright* (1963) is the perfect case study because it involved a disreputable person who seemed patently guilty of the crime of which he was convicted. In and out of jails for most of his 51 years, Clarence Earl Gideon received a five-year sentence for breaking and entering a poolroom in Panama City, Florida. While serving time in jail, Gideon became a fairly well-qualified "jailhouse lawyer," made his own appeal on a handwritten petition, and eventually won the landmark ruling on the right to counsel in all felony cases.[98]

The right to counsel has been expanded during the past few decades, even as the courts have become more conservative. For example, although at first the right to counsel was met by judges assigning lawyers from the community as a formal public obligation, now most states and cities have created an office of public defender; these state-employed professional defense lawyers typically provide poor defendants with much better legal representation. And although these defendants cannot afford to hire their own defense attorney, they do have the right to appeal a conviction on the grounds that the counsel provided by the state was deficient. For example, in 2003 the Supreme Court overturned the death sentence of a Maryland death row inmate, holding that the defense lawyer had failed to inform the jury fully of the defendant's history of "horrendous childhood abuse."[99] Moreover, the right to counsel extends beyond serious crimes to any trial, with or without a jury, that holds the possibility of imprisonment.[100] In the 2006 case of *United States v. Gonzalez-Lopez*, the Court held that a defendant had been deprived of his Sixth Amendment rights because the trial court had refused to allow him to make use of the particular counsel of his own choosing.[101]

## The Eighth Amendment and Cruel and Unusual Punishment

Excessive bail shall not be required, nor excessive fines imposed, nor cruel and unusual punishment inflicted.

Virtually all the debate over Eighth Amendment issues focuses on the last clause of the amendment: one of the greatest challenges in interpreting this provision consistently is that what is considered "cruel and unusual" varies from culture to culture and from generation to generation.

In 1972 the Supreme Court overturned several state death-penalty laws, not because they were cruel and unusual but because they were being applied unevenly—that is, blacks were much more likely than whites to be sentenced to death, and the poor more likely than the rich, and men more likely than women.[102] Very soon after that decision, a majority of states revised their capital punishment provisions to meet the Court's standards, and the Court reaffirmed that the death penalty could be used if certain standards were met.[103] Since 1976, the Court

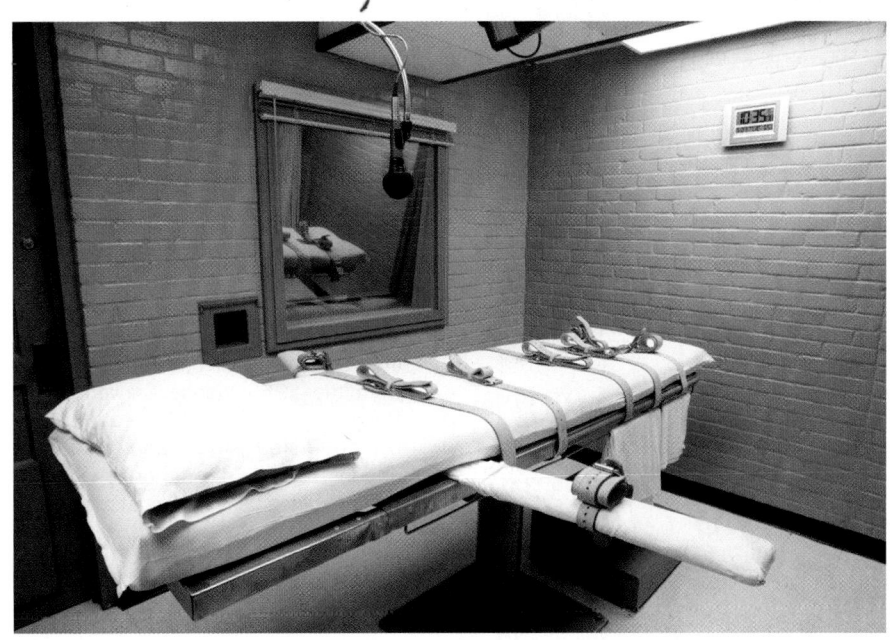

*Thirty-seven states currently have the death penalty for the most serious crimes. Although a majority of Americans support the death penalty, it has always been controversial and is sometimes seen as a violation of the Eighth Amendment.*

has consistently upheld state laws providing for capital punishment, although the Court also continues to review numerous death-penalty appeals each year.

Between 1976 and 2012, states executed 1,307 people. Most of those executions occurred in southern states, with Texas leading the way at 489. As of 2012, 33 states had statutes providing for capital punishment for specified offenses, a move approved of by about three-quarters of all Americans. And criminal conduct is traditionally defined by the states. In recent years, though, Congress has expanded federal criminal law, even imposing capital punishment for more than 50 federal crimes.

Despite the seeming popularity of the death penalty, the debate has become, if anything, more intense. Many death-penalty supporters assert its deterrent effects on other would-be criminals. Although studies of capital crimes usually fail to demonstrate any direct deterrent effect, this failure may be due to the lengthy delays—typically years and even decades—between convictions and executions. A system that eliminates undue delays might enhance deterrence. And deterring even one murder or other heinous crime, proponents argue, is ample justification for such laws. Beyond that, the death penalty is seen by proponents as a proper expression of retribution, embodying the biblical phrase "an eye for an eye": people who commit vicious crimes deserve to forfeit their lives in exchange for the suffering they have inflicted.

Death-penalty opponents are quick to counter that the death penalty has not been proved to deter crime, either in the United States or abroad. In fact, America is the only Western nation that still executes criminals. If the government is to serve as an example of proper behavior, say foes of capital punishment, it has no business sanctioning killing when incarceration will similarly protect society. Furthermore, execution is time-consuming and expensive—more expensive than life imprisonment—precisely because the government must make every effort to ensure that it is not executing an innocent person. Curtailing legal appeals would make the possibility of a mistake too great. And although most Americans do support the death penalty, people also support life imprisonment without the possibility of parole as an alternative. Race also intrudes in death-penalty cases: people of

# AMERICA IN THE WORLD

# The Death Penalty

**The United States is the only** Western democracy that continues to make use of capital punishment as a form of criminal sanction. Thirty-seven of the 50 states provide for the death penalty, as do the federal government and the military. Since 1976 the states have executed more than 1,000 convicted criminals. In 2011 alone, 43 individuals were put to death by state authorities. Though this is a small number compared with, say, China, which executed several thousand persons for a variety of crimes in 2011, it was enough executions to rank the United States fifth, just behind Yemen, in its use of execution as a form of punishment.

Though a majority of Americans support capital punishment, America's continuing use of the death penalty has put the United States at odds with its European allies and with Canada and Mexico, which have all abolished capital punishment. One area of conflict concerns the extradition of criminals. If an individual charged with or convicted of a crime flees to another country, the fugitive's home country may ask that he or she be returned home to face trial or punishment. The United States has extradition treaties with many nations. In recent years, however, a number of European nations have resisted extraditing fugitives to the United States if there has been a possibility that

those fugitives might face a death sentence upon their return.

One of the most important of these cases involved Jens Soering. Soering was arrested in the United Kingdom in 1986 on a U.S. extradition warrant charging that he and his girlfriend had murdered her parents in Virginia. The European Court of Human Rights ruled that Soering's extradition to the United States would violate the European Convention on Human Rights, which prohibited torture or other degrading forms of punishment, because, if convicted in Virginia, he could be sentenced to death. To obtain Soering's extradition, the United States had to assure Britain that he would not be prosecuted for capital murder. Subsequently, Soering was returned, tried, and sentenced to 99 years in prison. Since the Soering case, European authorities have generally made extradition to the United States conditional on American assurances that the individual sought by American

authorities not face capital charges if he or she is returned.

A second realm in which America's continuing use of capital punishment has created conflict with other nations stems from the 1963 Vienna Convention on Consular Relations. This treaty, signed by the United States and 162 other nations, requires the authorities to notify foreign nationals in their custody of their right to contact their own consulates for assistance before they are brought to trial. Police and courts in the United States often fail to comply with this obligation. As a result, a number of foreigners have been convicted of capital crimes and sentenced to death without having been allowed to contact their consulates for help. In 2001 the International Court of Justice ruled that the United States had violated its treaty obligations with Germany by executing a German citizen, Walter LaGrand, without notifying him of his treaty rights. In recent years, the Mexican government has challenged the convictions and death sentences of several Mexican nationals in the United States on the grounds that the individuals in question were not allowed to contact the Mexican consulate in a timely manner. In 2003, Mexico won a judgment against the United States in the International Court of Justice, but the U.S. Supreme Court ruled that Texas courts were not bound by this decision. Generally, U.S. courts have not been particularly hospitable to Vienna Convention claims.

SOURCE: William A. Schabas, "Indirect Abolition: Capital Punishment's Role in Extradition Law and Practice," *Loyola Los Angeles International and Comparative Law Review* 25 (2003): 581–604.

## for critical analysis

1. America's continued use of capital punishment has complicated its relations with its neighbors and allies. Should the United States adjust its laws to accommodate the wishes of other nations?

2. What might explain why the United States continues to use capital punishment, whereas other Western nations have abandoned the practice?

color are disproportionately more likely than whites charged with identical crimes to be given the ultimate punishment.

The Supreme Court has long struggled to establish principles to govern executions. In recent years, the Court has issued a number of death-penalty opinions, declaring that death was too harsh a penalty for a child rapist[104] and invalidating a death sentence for a black defendant after the prosecutor improperly excluded African Americans from the jury.[105] On the other hand, in a decision that received worldwide attention, the Court ruled that the International Court of Justice had no authority to order a Texas court to reopen a death-penalty case involving a foreign national.[106] The Court also upheld Kentucky's policy of execution by lethal injection despite arguments that this form of execution was likely to cause considerable pain.[107]

# ● The Right to Privacy

> **Assess whether people have a right to privacy under the Constitution**

A **right to privacy** was not granted in the Bill of Rights, but a clause in the Fourth Amendment provides for "the right of the people to be secure in their persons, houses, papers, and effects, against unreasonable searches and seizures." In a 1928 case, Justice Louis Brandeis argued in a dissent that the Fourth Amendment should be extended to a more general principle of "privacy in the home."[108] Another step in this direction was taken when several Jehovah's Witnesses directed their children not to salute the flag or say the Pledge of Allegiance in school because the first of the Ten Commandments prohibits the worship of "graven images." They lost their case in 1940, but the Supreme Court, reversing itself in 1943, held that the 1940 case had been "wrongly decided" and recognized "a right to be left alone" as part of the free speech clause of the First Amendment.[109] Another small step was taken in 1958, when the Supreme Court recognized "privacy in one's association" in its decision that the state of Alabama could not use the membership list of the National Association for the Advancement of Colored People (NAACP) in state investigations.[110]

**right to privacy** the right to be left alone, which has been interpreted by the Supreme Court to entail individual access to birth control and abortions

> **for critical analysis**
> Read the Third, Fourth, Fifth, and Ninth amendments in the appendix at the end of this book. In your opinion, do American citizens have a right to privacy?

## Birth Control

The sphere of privacy was formally recognized in 1965, when the Court ruled that a Connecticut statute forbidding the use of contraceptives violated the right of marital privacy. Estelle Griswold, the executive director of the Planned Parenthood League of Connecticut, was arrested by the state of Connecticut for providing information, instruction, and medical advice about contraception to married couples. She and her associates were found guilty as accessories to the crime and fined $100 each. The Supreme Court reversed the lower court decisions and declared the Connecticut law unconstitutional because it violated "a right of privacy older than the Bill of Rights—older than our political parties, older than our school system."[111] Justice William O. Douglas, author of the majority decision in the *Griswold* case, argued that this right of privacy is also grounded in the Constitution, because it fits into a "zone of privacy" created by a combination of the Third, Fourth, and Fifth amendments. A concurring opinion, written by Justice Arthur Goldberg, attempted to strengthen Douglas's argument by adding that "the concept of liberty . . . embraces the right of marital privacy though that right is not mentioned explicitly in the Constitution [and] is supported by numerous decisions of this Court . . . and *by the language and history of the Ninth Amendment* [emphasis added]."[112]

## Abortion

The right to privacy was confirmed and extended in 1973 in one of the most important Supreme Court decisions in American history: *Roe v. Wade*. This decision established a woman's right to seek an abortion and prohibited states from making abortion a criminal act.[113] The Burger Court's decision in *Roe* took a revolutionary step toward establishing the right to privacy. It is important to emphasize that the preference for privacy rights and for their extension to include the rights of women to control their own bodies was not something the Supreme Court invented in a vacuum. Most states did not regulate abortions in any fashion until the 1840s, at which time only 6 of the 26 existing states had any regulations governing abortion. In addition, many states had begun to ease their abortion restrictions well before the 1973 *Roe* decision, although in recent years a number of states have reinstated some restrictions on abortion.

By extending the umbrella of privacy, this sweeping ruling dramatically changed abortion practices in America. In addition, it galvanized and nationalized

*One of the most important cases related to the right to privacy was* Roe v. Wade, *which established a woman's right to seek an abortion. However, the decision has remained highly controversial, with opponents arguing that the Constitution does not guarantee this right.*

the abortion debate. Groups opposed to abortion, such as the National Right to Life Committee, organized to fight the liberal new standard, while abortion rights groups have sought to maintain that protection. In recent years, the legal standard shifted against abortion rights supporters in two key Supreme Court cases. In *Webster v. Reproductive Health Services* (1989), the Court narrowly upheld (by a 5–4 majority) the constitutionality of restrictions on the use of public medical facilities for abortion.[114] And in the 1992 case of *Planned Parenthood of Southeastern Pennsylvania v. Casey*, another 5–4 majority of the Court upheld *Roe* but narrowed its scope, refusing to invalidate a Pennsylvania law that significantly limits freedom of choice. The Court's decision defined the right to an abortion as a "limited or qualified" right subject to regulation by the states as long as the regulation does not constitute an "undue burden."[115] In the 2000 case of *Stenberg v. Carhart*, the Court, by a vote of 5 to 4, struck down Nebraska's ban on partial-birth abortions because the law had the "effect of placing a substantial obstacle in the path of a woman seeking an abortion."[116] However, in the 2006 case of *Ayotte v. Planned Parenthood of Northern New England*, the Court held that a law requiring parental notification before a minor could obtain an abortion was not an undue burden.[117] And in *Gonzales v. Carhart*, the Court effectively reversed its earlier *Carhart* decision by upholding the federal partial-birth abortion ban, which was virtually identical to the Nebraska law it had struck down in 2000.[118]

## Homosexuality

In the last two decades, the right to be left alone began to include the privacy rights of homosexuals. One morning in Atlanta, Georgia, in the mid-1980s, a police officer came to the home of Michael Hardwick to serve a warrant for Hardwick's arrest for failure to appear in court to answer charges of drinking in public. One of Hardwick's unknowing housemates invited the officer to look in Hardwick's room, where he found Hardwick and another man engaging in "consensual sexual behavior" and then proceeded to arrest him under Georgia's laws against heterosexual and homosexual sodomy. Hardwick filed a lawsuit against

*The right to privacy has also included the rights of gay men and lesbians. Here, supporters of gay rights celebrate the repeal in 2011 of the military's "don't ask don't tell" policy, which was seen as discriminatory in part because a service member could be dismissed based on his or her private sexual conduct.*

# A Right to Privacy Online?

**While the right to privacy is not** explicitly written into the Constitution, the common understanding is that Americans do enjoy a right to privacy. The Courts have wavered in terms of how far to extend this right. Many observers predict that in the coming years the major cases in this area will involve individuals seeking protection of their privacy online.

Currently it is not illegal for a potential employer to ask for an individual's password and Facebook login to see what that person has been doing. Companies will often Google an individual they are considering hiring to see if his or her behavior online can inform hiring decisions. A 2012 survey found that 46 percent of company executives said their company does and will continue to consider an individual's "online profiles" (including Facebook, Twitter, blogs, and the like) in hiring decisions. Almost half of those surveyed consider inappropriate content on social networking sites also as a legitimate reason for termination of a current employee.

What we post online affects more than our economic opportunities. If, for example, you share a picture in which you are keying an ex-boyfriend's car or committing another crime, the police can use that as evidence against you. No warrant is needed, and the image is not protected by a right to privacy. Government agencies ranging from local police to the FBI routinely check Facebook, Twitter, and other online social media sites for evidence of illegal activities, as individuals who commit crimes often post pictures of their crimes or other evidence online. Even street gangs now have Facebook pages where fans can "like" their photos and comments. Headline news was made when the Justice Department sought Twitter account information from individuals working with WikiLeaks, the website that spills government secrets. Twitter went to court to fight for permission to notify its subscribers that the government had requested their account information.

Other concerns about online privacy involve the tracking of Internet users. Google and other large technology companies have admitted to tracking user habits, data, and personal information and selling this information to outside marketing companies without the users' permission. This practice, and other instances of companies using individuals' information without permission, led to the Consumer Privacy Bill of Rights promoted by the Obama administration in 2012. The Consumer Privacy Bill of Rights is a blueprint for giving citizens more control over

how their personal information is used on the Internet. The Commerce Department will begin convening companies' representatives, privacy advocates, and other stakeholders to develop and implement enforceable privacy policies based on the Consumer Privacy Bill of Rights. However, these guidelines are not yet law.

While the White House, Congress, and many state legislatures are considering how to protect people's personal information online, there is still no formal right to privacy online. What you post can and likely will be used to determine whether you've committed any crimes and your suitability for hiring by a potential employer. Even if the Consumer Privacy Bill of Rights or some comparable law is eventually passed, the police, the FBI, and others involved in law enforcement will still be able to use what you post as evidence if you are charged with a crime. The proposed "privacy bills" are aimed at stopping companies from tracking your usage and selling your information, not at protecting you from the consequences of sharing information online.

SOURCES: Stan Finger, "Police: Street Gangs Embrace Social Media, Too," *Wichita Eagle*, June 10, 2012, www.kansas.com/2012/06/10/2366765/police-street-gangs-embrace-social.html (accessed 6/14/12). David Goldman, David, "White House Pushes Online Privacy Bill of Rights." CNN Money, February 23, 2012, http://money.cnn.com/2012/02/23/technology/privacy_bill_of_rights/index.htm (accessed 6/14/12). Daniel Hong, "Your Facebook Profile Could Affect Your Hiring Potential," PRWeb, May 31, 2012, www.prweb.com/releases/prweb2012/5/prweb9556895.htm (accessed 6/14/12).

## for critical analysis

1. With the migration of more personal information online via social networking sites, should Congress pass a law to protect citizens' privacy online? Why or why not?

2. How does a right to privacy differ from our other constitutionally protected rights?

the state, challenging the constitutionality of the Georgia law, and won his case in the federal court of appeals. The state of Georgia, in an unusual move, appealed the court's decision to the Supreme Court. The majority of the Court reversed the lower court decision, holding against Hardwick on the grounds that "the federal Constitution confers [no] fundamental right upon homosexuals to engage in sodomy," and that therefore there was no basis to invalidate "the laws of the many states that still make such conduct illegal and have done so for a very long time."[119]

Seventeen years later, and to almost everyone's surprise, in *Lawrence v. Texas* (2003) the Court overturned *Bowers v. Hardwick* with a dramatic pronouncement that gays are "entitled to respect for their private lives"[120] as a matter of constitutional due process. Drawing from the tradition of negative liberty, the Court maintained, "In our tradition the State is not omnipresent in the home. And there are other spheres of our lives and existence outside the home, where the State should not be a dominant presence." Explicitly encompassing lesbians and gay men within the umbrella of privacy, the Court concluded that the "petitioners are entitled to respect for their private lives. The State cannot demean their existence or control their destiny by making their private sexual conduct a crime."[121] This decision added substance to the "right of privacy."[122]

## The Right to Die

Another area ripe for litigation and public discourse is the so-called right to die. A number of highly publicized physician-assisted suicides in the 1990s focused attention on whether people have a right to choose their own death and to receive assistance in carrying it out. Can this become part of the privacy right? Or is it a new substantive right? The Supreme Court has not definitively answered this question. However, the Court refused to intervene in the well-publicized case of Terri Schiavo, a woman who suffered irreversible brain damage and was kept alive in a vegetative state via a feeding tube for 15 years. During this period, Schiavo's husband wanted to withdraw life support, citing his wife's wishes, while her parents wanted support continued indefinitely. The case was heard multiple times in the Florida state courts and the federal courts. In 2005, Schiavo's husband finally prevailed, and she was removed from life support and subsequently died. In the 2006 case of *Gonzales v. Oregon*, however, the Supreme Court did intervene to uphold a law allowing doctors to use drugs to facilitate the deaths of terminally ill patients who requested such assistance.[123] Thus, although the Court has not ruled definitively on the right-to-die question, it does not seem hostile to the idea.

## ● Thinking Critically about the Future of Civil Liberties

In the months after the September 11 terrorists attacks against the United States, President George W. Bush issued a series of executive orders to combat the threat of terrorism. He authorized the indefinite detention at the Guantánamo Bay military prison in Cuba of individuals whom he designated enemy combatants, the creation of special military tribunals to try enemy combatants, and the initiation of a massive warrantless surveillance program by the National Security Agency (NSA) to monitor communications into and out of the United States. The president averred that these policies were necessary to protect the nation, but each

*The dilemma of balancing liberty and security has continued during the Obama administration. The introduction of full-body scanners at some airports was criticized as an intrusion on individual rights but also has been defended as a necessary step to prevent terrorist attacks.*

of his orders was denounced by civil libertarians as an intrusion on constitutional rights and was challenged in the courts.

In the 2004 case of *Hamdi v. Rumsfeld*, the Supreme Court ruled that those declared enemy combatants could challenge their detention before a judge, but the Court affirmed the president's power to declare even U.S. citizens to be enemy combatants.[124] In 2006, in the case of *Hamdan v. Rumsfeld*, the Court invalidated the military tribunals established by presidential order, because their procedures did not accord with current law. The Court, however, accepted the principle that the president could order the creation of such tribunals as long as their procedures had some statutory basis. Congress provided that basis in the 2006 Military Commissions Act, which mainly reaffirmed the procedures that had been devised by the president.[125] The act also seemed partially to reverse the *Hamdi* decision by declaring that prisoners at Guantánamo could not present habeas corpus petitions to the federal courts to challenge their detention. The legality of that portion of the act is currently being debated in the federal courts.

As for the NSA surveillance program, in 2007 the Sixth Circuit Court of Appeals upheld the program's validity, but the ACLU has appealed the decision to the Supreme Court. Under new rules established by President Bush, the NSA requests warrants from the Foreign Intelligence Surveillance (FISA) Court, a secretive panel established to hear top-secret cases. The president, however, reserved the right to order warrantless searches if he deemed them to be necessary. The Obama administration took the same position and sent government lawyers to defend the program. As these "war on terrorism" cases illustrate, battles over civil liberties are not abstract, historical matters. They are part of our lives today.

When President Obama took office in 2009, civil libertarians were confident that the new administration would move quickly to curb what many saw as the civil liberties abuses of the Bush years, primarily those associated with the war on terrorism. After Obama's first year in office, however, civil libertarians gave the president a mixed review. Anthony Romero, director of the ACLU, declared that the Obama administration had "made some significant strides toward restoring civil liberties and the rule of law."[126] Nevertheless, the ACLU took the Obama administration to task for continuing a number of Bush's policies. Thus, while Obama issued executive orders closing the Guantánamo Bay prison, which housed a number of terrorism suspects, the prison actually remained open, holding detainees without charge or trial while the administration considered what to do with them. Similarly, although Obama ordered an end to the harsh interrogation of terrorist suspects countenanced by the Bush administration, he showed little interest in investigating charges of prisoner abuse by the military and intelligence agencies. The ACLU criticized Obama for not bringing an end to government spying on Americans, the monitoring of political activists, and the continued use of secret detentions and removals of terrorist suspects to overseas facilities.

Many Americans believe that America's reputation in the world has been hurt by the image of prisoners being held without proper legal process, and they are eager to find ways to restore America's reputation as a bastion of liberty. At the same time, of course, no president wishes to see dangerous foes of the United States do harm to Americans. The dilemma of liberty versus security is rarely easy to resolve.

# Freedom of Speech, the Right to Privacy, and Digital Media

## Inform Yourself

 **Know your rights and protect your information online.** Visit the Electronic Frontier Foundation's (EFF) website (www.eff.org), which is dedicated to protecting freedom on the Internet. Since there is no established right to privacy online, the EFF works to defend digital rights, including privacy, free speech, innovation, and consumer rights. Click on the "Our Work" tab to see the EFF's "Whitepapers" (reports). Your computer, phone, and other digital devices hold vast amounts of personal information about you and your family. Read the "Know Your Rights" (June 2011) white paper to learn how to protect your personal documents.

 **Understand current issues in digital rights.** The EFF's Deeplink Blog provides up-to-the-minute reporting on current political issues and issues of civil liberties that may affect you and others you know. There are posts on online video privacy, drones, bloggers' rights, coders' rights, free speech, surveillance self-defense, worldwide Internet censorship, cell phone tracking data from wireless carriers, personal data and social media, patent problems, and much more.

 **Think critically about civil liberties issues.** The American Civil Liberties Union (www.aclu.org) is one of the country's oldest and most active groups working to protect civil liberties. Visit its website and select a "Key Issue," such as Internet privacy, rights of individuals accused of a crime, immigration, religion, reproductive freedom, or flag burning. Read the arguments for protecting these rights. Do you agree or disagree with the ACLU's position on the issue? Why?

## Express Yourself

 **Read and consider signing the petitions** available at the EFF's website to defend digital rights online, by clicking the "Take Action" tab. Do you believe in a free and open Internet? What about the rights of bloggers who are the victims of frivolous lawsuits for legitimate online content? How do you feel about criminal penalties for online streaming of copyrighted videos? (Congress is considering such a law.)

 **Would you burn a virtual flag?** The Flag Burning Page (www.esquilax.com/flag/index2.shtml) gives visitors the opportunity to burn a virtual flag, and points out that if the Constitution were amended to ban flag desecration (as has been proposed), the page would be illegal. The Supreme Court considers burning the American flag an act protected by the First Amendment right to free speech. Do you agree or disagree?

*Find links to the sites listed above as well as related activities on wwnorton.com/studyspace.*

# study guide

 **Practice online with:** Chapter 4 Diagnostic Quiz ■ Chapter 4 Key Term Flashcards

## A Brief History of the Bill of Rights

■ **Explain how the civil liberties included in the Bill of Rights were "nationalized" (pp. 115–19)**

Although some believed that a bill of rights was unnecessary and potentially dangerous, the Federalists made a pledge to add one in order to secure support for the Constitution during the ratification process. During the first hundred years of American history, the Bill of Rights was interpreted to limit only the actions of the federal government. One by one, most of the important provisions of the first 10 amendments have eventually been incorporated into the Fourteenth Amendment and applied to the states.

### Key Terms

**habeas corpus** (p. 115)

**bill of attainder** (p. 115)

**ex post facto laws** (p. 115)

**Bill of Rights** (p. 116)

**civil liberties** (p. 116)

**selective incorporation** (p. 117)

### Practice Quiz

1. From 1789 until the end of the nineteenth century, the Bill of Rights put limits on *(pp. 116–19)*
   a) the national government only.
   b) the state government only.
   c) both the national and state governments.
   d) neither the national nor the state government.
   e) political parties and interest groups.

2. Which of the following rights were *not* included in the original Constitution? *(p. 115)*
   a) prohibition of bills of attainder
   b) prohibition of ex post facto laws

c) guarantee of habeas corpus
d) guarantee of trial by jury in the state where the crime was committed
e) None—they were all included in the original Constitution.

3. Which of the following provided that all of the protections contained in the Bill of Rights applied to the states as well as national government? *(pp. 116–19)*
   a) the First Amendment
   b) the Fourteenth Amendment
   c) *Palko v. Connecticut*
   d) *Gitlow v. New York*
   e) none of the above

4. The process by which some of the liberties in the Bill of Rights were applied to the states (or nationalized) is known as *(p. 117)*
   a) preemption.
   b) selective incorporation.
   c) judicial activism.
   d) civil liberties.
   e) establishment.

5. Which of the following provisions of the Bill of Rights was incorporated in 2010? *(p. 119)*
   a) the right to counsel in any criminal trial
   b) the right against self-incrimination
   c) freedom from unnecessary searches and seizures
   d) freedom to petition the government for redress of grievance
   e) the right to bear arms

 **Practice Online**
Video exercise: *Where Do Civil Liberties Come From?*

## The First Amendment and Freedom of Religion

■ **Describe how the First Amendment protects freedom of religion (pp. 119–22)**

Two parts of the First Amendment touch on religious freedom: the establishment clause and the free exercise clause. The courts have been somewhat inconsistent in determining how porous the establishment clause's "wall of separation" between church and state actually is in practice. While the courts have been more consistent in protecting the free exercise of religious beliefs, they have

taken pains to distinguish between religious beliefs and actions based on those beliefs.

### Key Terms

**establishment clause** (p. 119)

***Lemon* test** (p. 120)

**free exercise clause** (p. 121)

## Practice Quiz

6. Which of the following protections are *not* contained in the First Amendment? *(pp. 119–32)*
   a) the establishment clause
   b) the free exercise clause
   c) freedom of the press
   d) the right to peaceably assemble
   e) All of the above are First Amendment protections.

7. The so-called *Lemon* test, derived from the Supreme Court's ruling in *Lemon v. Kurtzman*, concerns the issue of *(p. 120)*
   a) school desegregation.
   b) aid to religious schools.
   c) cruel and unusual punishment.
   d) obscenity.
   e) prayer in school.

 **Practice Online**
Video exercise *Religious Freedom and Contraception*

# The First Amendment and Freedom of Speech and of the Press

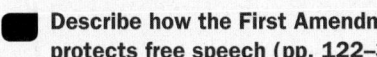 **Describe how the First Amendment protects free speech (pp. 122–32)**

Given the importance of freedom of speech and of the press to the functioning of democratic government, Americans are assumed to have the right to speak and broadcast their ideas unless there is some compelling reason to stop them. According to the courts, although virtually all speech is protected by the Constitution, some forms of speech are entitled to a greater degree of protection than others. Libel, slander, and speech that incites lawless action are examples of speech that can be limited by the government.

## Key Terms

**"clear and present danger" test** (p. 123)

**"speech plus"** (p. 126)

**prior restraint** (p. 126)

**libel** (p. 127)

**slander** (p. 127)

**fighting words** (p. 130)

## Practice Quiz

8. The judicial doctrine that places a heavy burden of proof on the government when it seeks to regulate or restrict speech is called *(p. 123)*
   a) judicial restraint.
   b) judicial activism.
   c) habeas corpus.
   d) prior restraint.
   e) strict scrutiny.

9. Which of the following describes a written statement made in "reckless disregard of the truth" that is considered damaging to a victim because it is "malicious, scandalous, and defamatory"? *(p. 137)*
   a) slander
   b) libel
   c) speech plus
   d) fighting words
   e) expressive speech

 **Practice Online**
Video exercise: The Daily Show with Jon Stewart, *Headlines—Flame Retarded*

# The Second Amendment and the Right to Bear Arms

**Explore whether the Second Amendment means people have a right to own guns (pp. 132–33)**

The Second Amendment granted Americans the right "to keep and bear Arms" in order to provide for state militias. Prior to 2010, the Second Amendment was not incorporated. In *McDonald v. Chicago*, the Supreme Court asserted that the right to bear arms applies to both state governments and the federal government.

## Practice Quiz

10. In *McDonald v. Chicago*, the Supreme Court ruled that *(p. 133)*
    a) states can require citizens to own firearms.
    b) federal grants can be used to support the formation of state militias.
    c) felons can be prevented from purchasing assault rifles.
    d) the Second Amendment applies to states as well as the federal government.
    e) the Second Amendment applies only to the federal government and not to states.

# Rights of the Criminally Accused

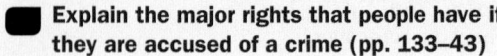 **Explain the major rights that people have if they are accused of a crime (pp. 133–43)**

The essence of the Constitution's due process of the law is found in the Fourth, Fifth, Sixth, and Eighth amendments. The Fourth Amendment protects individuals from unreasonable searches and seizures. The Fifth Amendment provides individuals with the right to a grand jury, protection from double jeopardy, and a guarantee against self-incrimination. The Sixth Amendment provides the right to legal counsel, the right to a speedy trial, and the right to confront witnesses before an impartial jury. The Eighth Amendment protects individuals against "cruel and unusual" punishment.

## Key Terms

**due process of law** (p. 133)

**exclusionary law** (p. 134)

**grand jury** (p. 136)

**double jeopardy** (p. 138)

**Miranda rule** (p. 139)

**eminent domain** (p. 139)

## Practice Quiz

11. The Fourth, Fifth, Sixth, and Eighth amendments, taken together, define *(p. 133)*
    a) freedom of religion.
    b) due process of law.
    c) free speech.
    d) the right to bear arms.
    e) civil rights of minorities.

12. In *Mapp v. Ohio,* the Supreme Court ruled that *(p. 134)*
    a) evidence obtained from an illegal search could not be introduced in a trial.
    b) the government must provide legal counsel for defendants who are too poor to provide it for themselves.
    c) persons under arrest must be informed prior to police interrogation of their rights to remain silent and to have the benefits of legal counsel.
    d) the government has the right to take private property for public use if just compensation is provided.
    e) a person cannot be tried twice for the same crime.

13. Which famous case deals with Sixth Amendment issues? *(p. 140)*
    a) *Roe v. Wade*
    b) *Mapp v. Ohio*
    c) *Gideon v. Wainwright*
    d) *Terry v. Ohio*
    e) *Miranda v. Arizona*

 **Practice Online**
"You Decide" exercise: *The USA PATRIOT Act*

# The Rights to Privacy

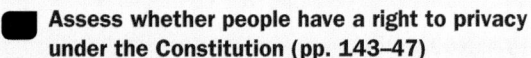 **Assess whether people have a right to privacy under the Constitution (pp. 143–47)**

A right to privacy is never explicitly mentioned in the Constitution. In fact, it was not until 1965 that the Supreme Court interpreted the Third, Fourth, Fifth, and Ninth amendments to create a constitutional "zone of privacy." The right to privacy has since been used to strike down laws limiting access to birth control, outlawing abortion, and criminalizing gay and lesbian sexual activity.

## Key Term

**right to privacy** (p. 143)

## Practice Quiz

14. In what case was a right to privacy first found in the Constitution? *(p. 152)*
    a) *Griswold v. Connecticut*
    b) *Roe v. Wade*
    c) *Lemon v. Kurtzman*
    d) *Planned Parenthood v. Casey*
    e) *Baker v. Carr*

15. In which case did the Supreme Court rule that state governments no longer had the authority to make private sexual behavior a crime? *(p. 147)*
    a) *Texas v. Johnson*
    b) *Webster v. Reproductive Health Services*
    c) *Gonzales v. Oregon*
    d) *Lawrence v. Texas*
    e) *Bowers v. Hardwick*

 **Practice Online**
Video exercise: *Stop the Spying! People for the American Way and the Electronic Frontier Foundation*

# For Further Reading

Barendt, Eric. *Freedom of Speech.* 2nd ed. New York: Oxford University Press, 2007.

Brandon, Mark. *The Constitution in Wartime.* Durham, NC: Duke University Press, 2005.

Cash, Arthur. *John Wilkes: The Scandalous Father of Civil Liberties.* New Haven, CT: Yale University Press, 2007.

Cook, Byrne. *Reporting the War: Freedom of the Press from the American Revolution to the War on Terror.* New York: Palgrave Macmillan, 2007.

Domino, John. *Civil Rights and Liberties in the 21st Century.* 3rd ed. New York: Longman, 2009.

Dworkin, Ronald. *Justice in Robes.* Cambridge, MA: Belknap Press, 2006.

Fisher, Louis. *Military Tribunals and Presidential Power.* Lawrence: University Press of Kansas, 2005.

Friendly, Fred W. *Minnesota Rag: The Dramatic Story of the Landmark Supreme Court Case that Gave New Meaning to Freedom of the Press.* New York: Vintage, 1982.

Glendon, Mary Ann. *Rights Talk: The Impoverishment of Political Discourse.* New York: Free Press, 1991.

Hentoff, Nat. *The First Freedom: The Tumultuous History of Free Speech in America.* New York: Basic Books, 1994.

Lewis, Anthony. *Gideon's Trumpet.* New York: Random House, 1964.

David M O'Brien, *Constitutional Law and Politics: Civil Rights and Civil Liberties.* 8th ed. Vol. 2. New York: W. W. Norton, 2011.

Sundby, Scott. A Life and Death Decision: A Jury Weighs the Death Penalty. New York: Palgrave Macmillan, 2007.

# Recommended Websites

**The American Civil Liberties Union (ACLU)**
www.aclu.org

The ACLU is committed in protecting for all individuals the freedoms found in the Bill of Rights. This sometimes controversial organization constantly monitors the government for violations of liberty and encourages its members to take political action.

**Electronic Privacy Information Center**
http://epic.org/privacy

For an extensive list of privacy issues, go to the Web page for the Electronic Privacy Information Center. Here you will find civil liberties concerns as they relate to all forms of information technology, including the Internet.

**The Free Expression Network**
www.freeexpression.org

The Free Expression Network is an organization "dedicated to preserving the right to free expression." On its website you can find links to important First Amendment issues and organizations.

**Freedom Forum**
www.freedomforum.org

Freedom of speech and freedom of the press are considered critical in any democracy; however, only some kinds of speech are fully protected against restrictions. Freedom Forum is a nonpartisan agency that investigates and analyzes such First Amendment restrictions.

**National Abortion and Reproductive Rights Action League**
www.naral.org

**National Right to Life Committee**
www.HRIC.org

The National Abortion and Reproductive Rights Action League and the National Right to Life Committee are two of the nation's largest interest groups weighing in on the abortion issue. See what these opposing groups have to say about privacy rights.

**Religious Freedom Page**
http://religiousfreedom.lib.virginia.edu

The establishment clause of the U.S. Constitution has been interpreted to mean a "wall of separation" between government and religion. On the Religious Freedom Page you can find information on a variety of issues pertaining to religious freedom in the United States and around the world.

**U.S. Supreme Court Media**
www.oyez.org

This website for U.S. Supreme Court media has a great search engine for finding information on cases affecting civil liberties, such as *Lemon v. Kurtzman*, *Miranda v. Arizona*, *Mapp v. Ohio*, and *New York Times v. Sullivan*, to name a few.

Today, many conflicts about civil rights relate to immigration law and Latinos. In 2011 the debate over the rights of immigrants erupted into mass protests after Arizona and Georgia passed controversial laws targeting Latino immigrants.

# 5 Civil Rights

**WHAT GOVERNMENT DOES AND WHY IT MATTERS** In 2011 the federal Department of Justice accused the Maricopa County Sheriff's Office in Phoenix, Arizona, of violating the civil rights of Latinos. The results of a three-year investigation showed that the Sheriff's Department had routinely used racial profiling to detain and arrest Latinos and that county jails discriminated against people who spoke limited English. Both practices, Justice officials declared, were unconstitutional. At the same time, however, advocates charged that the federal government itself violated the Constitution in implementing the Secure Communities program. A centerpiece of the Obama administration's immigration policy, Secure Communities connects local police with the Department of Homeland Security to identify and deport undocumented residents who break the law. However, studies show that the program also has detained American citizens, who have been held illegally for days at a time.[1] The presence of an estimated 11 million undocumented immigrants in the United States presents the government with a thorny set of questions about civil rights. How aggressively should the government seek out and deport undocumented immigrants? How can the civil rights of Americans and legal residents be protected as the government enforces immigration laws?

Today, many conflicts about civil rights relate to immigration laws and Latinos. Fifty years ago, the African American struggle for equal rights took center stage. Many goals of the civil rights movement that once aroused bitter controversy are now widely accepted as part of the American commitment to equal rights. But even today the question of what is meant by "equal rights" is hardly settled. Although most Americans reject the idea that government should create equal outcomes for its citizens, they do widely endorse government action to prohibit public and private discrimination, and they do support the idea of equality of opportunity. However, even these concepts are elusive. When immigration law leads to civil rights violations and discrimination against Latinos, should the enforcement efforts be abandoned? When past denial of rights creates unequal starting points for some groups, should government take additional steps to ensure equal opportunity? What kinds of groups should be specially protected against discrimination? Should the disabled receive special protection? Should lesbians and gay men? What about individuals who identify as bisexual and transgender? Finally, what kinds of steps are acceptable to remedy discrimination, and who should bear the costs? These questions are at the heart of contemporary debates over civil rights.

The answers that Americans give to these questions have shifted dramatically over the course of our nation's history. But ideas about civil rights did not change easily; advocates who challenged barriers to civil rights often struggled against strong resistance. The election of Barack Obama as the nation's first black president is a testament to the successes of those struggles but does not by itself alter persistent social and economic differences across racial lines. The black civil rights movement inspired a new wave of movements for equality, as groups including women, gay men and lesbians, Native Americans, Latinos, and the disabled launched campaigns for equal rights.

This chapter will show how inequalities between races and genders were tolerated and even enforced by law during much of our country's history. Although the United States was founded on the ideals of liberty, equality, and democracy, its history of civil rights reveals a gap between these principles and actual practice. This history also demonstrates how the struggle to attain those ideals has helped narrow this gap. More recently, the ongoing struggle for political and social equality also shows how liberty and equality are not mutually supportive. In fact, these principles are often in conflict with each other. This chapter's concluding discussion of affirmative action illustrates this conflict.

## chaptergoals

- Trace the legal developments and social movements that expanded civil rights (pages 157–76)

- Describe how different groups have won protection of their rights (pages 176–90)

- Contrast arguments for and against affirmative action (pages 190–95)

# The Struggle for Civil Rights

In the United States the history of slavery and legalized racial **discrimination** against African Americans coexists uneasily with a strong tradition of individual liberty. Indeed, for much of our history Americans have struggled to reconcile such exclusionary racial practices with our notions of individual rights. With the adoption of the Fourteenth Amendment in 1868, **civil rights** became part of the Constitution, guaranteed to each citizen through "equal protection of the laws." This **equal protection clause** launched a century of political movements and legal efforts to press for racial equality.

For African Americans, the central fact of political life for most of American history has been a denial of full citizenship rights. By accepting the institution of slavery, the Founders embraced a system fundamentally at odds with the "Blessings of Liberty" promised in the Constitution. Their decision set the stage for two centuries of African American struggles to achieve full citizenship. For women as well, electoral politics was a decidedly masculine world. Until 1920, not only were women barred from voting in national politics, but electoral politics was closely tied to such male social institutions as lodges, bars, and clubs. Yet the exclusion of women from this political world did not prevent them from engaging in public life. Instead, women carved out a "separate sphere" for their public activities. Emphasizing female stewardship of the moral realm, women became important voices in social reform well before they won the right to vote.[2] Prior to the Civil War, women played leading roles in the abolitionist movement.

**discrimination** the use of any unreasonable and unjust criterion of exclusion

**civil rights** obligation imposed on government to take positive action to protect citizens from any illegal action of government agencies and of other private citizens

**equal protection clause** provision of the Fourteenth Amendment guaranteeing citizens "the equal protection of the laws." This clause has been the basis for the civil rights of African Americans, women, and other groups

*African American men won the right to vote after the Civil War, and many former slaves began registering and voting in state elections as early as 1867. This political influence soon evaporated in the face of Jim Crow laws and the end of Reconstruction.*

## Slavery and the Abolitionist Movement

No issue in the nation's history so deeply divided Americans as that of slavery. The importation and subjugation of Africans kidnapped from their native lands was a practice virtually as old as the country itself: the first slaves brought to what became the United States arrived in 1619, a year before the Plymouth colony was established in Massachusetts. White southerners built their agricultural economy (especially cotton production) on a large slave labor force. By 1840 nearly half of the populations of Alabama and Louisiana consisted of black slaves. Even so, only about a quarter of southern white families owned slaves.

Slavery was so much a part of southern culture that efforts to restrict or abolish the institution were met with fierce resistance. Despite the manifest cruelties of the slave system, southerners referred to it merely as the "peculiar institution." This quaint label meant little to slavery's opponents, however, and an abolitionist movement grew and spread among northerners in the 1830s (although abolitionist sentiment could be traced back to the prerevolutionary era). Slavery had been all but eliminated in the North by this time, but few northerners favored outright abolition. In fact, most whites held attitudes toward blacks that would be considered racist today.

The abolitionist movement spread primarily through local organizations in the North. Antislavery groups coalesced in New York, Ohio, New Hampshire, Pennsylvania, New Jersey, and Michigan. In addition, the movement spawned two political parties: the staunchly antislavery Liberty Party and the larger but more moderate Free Soil Party, which sought primarily to restrict slavery from spreading into new western territories. In 1857 the infamous case of *Dred Scott v. Sandford* "roused passions as never before"[3] by splitting the country deeply, with the U.S. Supreme Court holding that Scott had no due process rights because, as a slave, he was his master's permanent property, regardless of his master's having taken him to a free state or territory.[4]

Some opponents of slavery took matters into their own hands, aiding in the escape of runaway slaves along the Underground Railroad. Even today, private homes and churches scattered throughout the Northeast, once used to hide blacks on their trips to Canada, still attest to the involvement of local citizenry. In the South, a similar, if contrary, fervor prompted mobs to break into post offices in order to seize and destroy antislavery literature.

The emotional power of the slavery issue was such that it precipitated the nation's bloodiest conflict, the Civil War. From the ashes of the Civil War came the Thirteenth, Fourteenth, and Fifteenth amendments, which would redefine civil rights from that time on.

## The Link to the Women's Rights Movement

The quiet upstate New York town of Seneca Falls played host to what would later come to be known as the starting point of the modern women's movement. Convened in July 1848 and organized by the activists Elizabeth Cady Stanton and Lucretia Mott, the Seneca Falls Convention drew 300 delegates to formulate plans for advancing the political and social rights of women.

The centerpiece of the convention was its Declaration of Sentiments and Resolutions. Patterned after the Declaration of Independence, the Seneca Falls document declared, "We hold these truths to be self-evident: that all men and women are created equal" and "The history of mankind is a history of repeated injuries and usurpations on the part of man toward woman, having in direct object the establishment of an absolute tyranny over her." The most controversial provision of the declaration, nearly rejected as too radical, was the call for the right to vote for

*Although a few women could vote in the early American republic, such as these New Jersey women who satisfied state property qualifications, laws were soon enacted to block women from the ballot box. At the beginning of the nineteenth century, no American woman could legally vote.*

women. Although most of the delegates were women, about 40 men participated, including the renowned abolitionist Frederick Douglass.

The link to the antislavery movement was not new. Stanton and Mott had attended the World Anti-Slavery Convention in London in 1840 but had been denied delegate seats because of their sex. This rebuke helped precipitate the 1848 convention in Seneca Falls. The movements for women's rights and the abolition of slavery were also closely linked with the temperance movement (because alcohol abuse was closely linked to male abuses of women). The convergence of the antislavery, temperance, and suffrage movements was reflected in the views and actions of some women's movement leaders, such as Susan B. Anthony.

The convention and its participants were subjected to widespread ridicule, but similar conventions were organized in other states, and in the same year as the Seneca Falls Convention, New York State passed the Married Women's Property Act in order to restore the right of married women to own property.

## The Civil War Amendments to the Constitution

The hopes of African Americans for achieving full citizenship rights initially seemed fulfilled when three constitutional amendments were adopted after the Civil War: the **Thirteenth Amendment** abolished slavery, the **Fourteenth Amendment** guaranteed equal protection under the law, and the **Fifteenth Amendment** guaranteed voting rights for blacks. Protected by the presence of federal troops, African American men were able to exercise their political rights immediately after the war. Between 1869 and 1877, blacks were elected to many political offices: two black senators were elected from Mississippi and a total of 14 African Americans were elected to the House of Representatives. African Americans also held many state-level political offices. As voters and public officials, black citizens found a home in the Republican Party, which had secured the ratification of the three constitutional amendments guaranteeing black rights. After the war, the Republican Party continued to reach out to black voters as a means to build party strength in the South.[5]

This political equality was short-lived, however. The national government withdrew its troops from the South and turned its back on African Americans in 1877,

**Thirteenth Amendment** one of three Civil War amendments; it abolished slavery

**Fourteenth Amendment** one of three Civil War amendments; it guaranteed equal protection and due process

**Fifteenth Amendment** one of three Civil War amendments; it guaranteed voting rights for African American men

when Reconstruction ended. In the Compromise of 1877, southern Democrats agreed to allow the Republican candidate, Rutherford B. Hayes, to become president after a disputed election. In exchange, northern Republicans dropped their support for the civil liberties and political participation of African Americans. After that, southern states erected a "Jim Crow" system of social, political, and economic inequality that made a mockery of the promises in the Constitution. The first **Jim Crow laws** were adopted in the 1870s, in each southern state, to criminalize intermarriage of the races and to segregate trains and depots. These were promptly followed by laws segregating all public accommodations, and within 10 years all southern states had adopted laws segregating the schools.

Immediately after the Civil War, when male ex-slaves won the franchise, some women pressed for the right to vote at the national level, but politicians in both parties rejected women's suffrage as disruptive and unrealistic. Women also started to press for the vote at the state level in 1867, when a referendum to give women the vote in Kansas failed. Frustration with the general failure to win reforms in other states accelerated suffrage activism. In 1872, Susan B. Anthony and several other women were arrested in Rochester, New York, for illegally registering and voting in that year's national election. (The men who allowed the women to register and vote were also indicted; Anthony paid their expenses and eventually won presidential pardons for them.) At Anthony's trial, Judge Ward Hunt ordered the jury to find her guilty without deliberation. Yet Anthony was allowed to address the court, saying, "Your denial of my citizen's right to vote is the denial of my right of consent as one of the governed, the denial of my right of representation as one of the taxed, the denial of my right to a trial of my peers as an offender against the law."[6] Hunt assessed Anthony a fine of $100 but did not sentence her to jail. She refused to pay the fine.

## Civil Rights and the Supreme Court: "Separate but Equal"

Resistance to equality for African Americans in the South led Congress to adopt the Civil Rights Act of 1875, which attempted to protect blacks from discrimination by proprietors of hotels, theaters, and other public accommodations. But

*The 1896 Supreme Court case of* Plessy v. Ferguson *upheld legal segregation and created the "separate but equal" rule, which fostered national segregation. Overt discrimination in public accommodations was common.*

the Court declared the legislation unconstitutional on the grounds that the act sought to protect blacks against discrimination by *private* businesses, whereas the Fourteenth Amendment, according to the Court's interpretation, was intended to protect individuals from discrimination only against actions by *public* officials of state and local governments.

In the infamous case of *Plessy v. Ferguson* (1896), the Court went still further by upholding a Louisiana statute that *required* segregation of the races on trolleys and other public carriers (and, by implication, in all public facilities, including schools). Homer Plessy, a man defined as "one-eighth black," had violated a Louisiana law that provided for "equal but separate accommodations" on trains and levied a $25 fine on any white passenger who sat in a car reserved for blacks or on any black passenger who sat in a car reserved for whites. The Supreme Court held that the Fourteenth Amendment's equal protection clause was not violated by racial distinction as long as the facilities were equal, thus establishing the **"separate but equal" rule** that prevailed through the mid-twentieth century. People generally pretended that segregated accommodations were equal as long as some accommodation for blacks existed. The Court said that although "the object of the [Fourteenth] Amendment was undoubtedly to enforce the absolute equality of the two races before the law, . . . it could not have intended to abolish distinctions based on color, or to enforce social, as distinguished from political, equality, or a commingling of the two races upon terms unsatisfactory to either."[7] What the Court was saying in effect was that the use of race as a criterion of exclusion in public matters was not unreasonable.

> **"separate but equal" rule** doctrine that public accommodations could be segregated by race but still be considered equal

## Organizing for Equality

**The National Association for the Advancement of Colored People** The creation of a Jim Crow system in the southern states and the lack of a legal basis for "equal protection of the laws" prompted the beginning of a long process in which African Americans built organizations and devised strategies for asserting their constitutional rights.

One such strategy sought to win political rights through political pressure and litigation. This approach was championed by the National Association for the Advancement of Colored People (NAACP), established in 1909 by a group of black and white reformers that included W. E. B. Du Bois, one of the twentieth century's most influential and creative thinkers on racial issues. Because the northern black vote was so small in the early 1900s, the NAACP relied primarily on the courts to press for black political rights. After the 1920s it built a strong membership base, with some strength in the South, which would be critical when the civil rights movement gained momentum in the 1950s.

The great migration of blacks to the North beginning around World War I enlivened a protest strategy. Although protest organizations had existed in the nineteenth century, the continuing migration of blacks made protest an increasingly useful tool. The black labor leader A. Philip Randolph forced the federal government to address racial discrimination in hiring practices during World War II by threatening a massive march on Washington. The federal government also grew more attentive to blacks as their voting strength increased as a result of the northward migration. By the 1940s the black vote had swung away from Republicans, but the Democratic hold on black votes was by no means absolute.

**Women's Organizations and the Right to Suffrage** The 1886 unveiling in New York Harbor of the Statue of Liberty, depicting liberty as a woman, prompted

*People had been agitating for women's right to vote since the 1830s, especially during the Civil War era. Here, early twentieth-century suffragists protest in front of the White House. Women gained the constitutional right to vote in 1920.*

women's rights advocates to call it "the greatest hypocrisy of the nineteenth century," in that "not one single woman throughout the length and breadth of the Land is as yet in possession of political Liberty."[8] Suffragists used the occasion of the Constitution's centennial in 1887 to protest the continued denial of their rights. For these women, the centennial represented "a century of injustice."

The climactic movement toward suffrage had been formally launched in 1878 with the introduction of a proposed constitutional amendment in Congress. Parallel efforts were made in the states. Many states granted women the right to vote before the national government did; western states with less entrenched political systems opened politics to women earliest. When Wyoming became a state in 1890, it was the first state to grant full suffrage to women. Colorado, Utah, and Idaho all followed suit in the next several years. Suffrage organizations grew— the National American Woman Suffrage Association (NAWSA), formed in 1890, claimed 2 million members by 1917—and staged mass meetings, parades, petitions, and protests. NAWSA organized state-by-state efforts to win the right for women to vote. Members of a more militant group, the National Woman's Party, staged pickets and got arrested in front of the White House to protest President Wilson's opposition to a constitutional amendment granting women this right. When the Nineteenth Amendment was ratified in 1920, women were finally guaranteed the right to vote.

## Litigating for Equality after World War II

The shame of discrimination against black military personnel during World War II, plus revelations of Nazi racial atrocities, moved President Harry S. Truman finally to bring the problem of racial discrimination to the White House and national attention, with the appointment in 1946 of the President's Commission on Civil Rights. In 1948 the commission submitted its report, *To Secure These Rights*, which laid bare the extent of the problem and its consequences. The report also revealed the success of experiments with racial integration in the armed forces during

World War II, to demonstrate to southern society that it had nothing to fear. But the commission recognized that the national government had no clear constitutional authority to pass and implement civil rights legislation. It proposed tying such legislation to the commerce power described in Article I of the Constitution, which allows Congress to regulate interstate commerce, although it was clear that discrimination was not itself related to the flow of interstate commerce.[9] The committee even suggested using the treaty power as a source of constitutional authority for civil rights legislation.[10]

The Supreme Court had begun to change its position on racial discrimination before World War II by being stricter about the criterion of equal facilities in the "separate but equal" rule. In 1938, for example, the Court rejected Missouri's policy of paying the tuition of qualified blacks to out-of-state law schools rather than admitting them to the University of Missouri Law School.[11]

After the war, modest progress resumed. In 1950 the Court rejected Texas's claim that its new "law school for Negroes" afforded education equal to that of the all-white University of Texas Law School, anticipating its future civil rights rulings by opening the question of whether *any* segregated facilities could be truly equal.[12] But in ordering the admission of blacks to all-white state law schools, the Supreme Court did not directly confront the "separate but equal" rule, because the Court needed only to recognize the absence of *any* equal law school for blacks. The same had been true in 1944, when the Supreme Court struck down the southern practice of "white primaries," which legally excluded blacks from participation in the nominating process. Here the Court simply recognized that primaries could no longer be regarded as the private affairs of the parties but were an integral aspect of the electoral process, making parties "an agency of the State." Therefore any practice of discrimination against blacks was "state action within the meaning of the Fifteenth Amendment."[13] The most important pre-1954 decision was probably *Shelley v. Kraemer*, in which the Court ruled against the widespread practice of "restrictive covenants" whereby the seller of a home added a clause to the sales contract requiring the buyer to agree never to sell the home to any non-Caucasian, non-Christian, and so on. The Court ruled that such covenants could not be judicially enforced, since the Fourteenth Amendment prohibits any organ of the state, including the courts, from denying equal protection of its laws.[14]

Although none of those pre-1954 cases confronted "separate but equal" and the principle of racial discrimination as such, they were extremely significant to black leaders in the 1940s and gave them encouragement to believe that at last they had an opportunity and enough legal precedent to change the constitutional framework itself. Much of this legal work was done by the Legal Defense and Educational Fund of the NAACP. Until the late 1940s, lawyers working for the Legal Defense Fund had concentrated on winning small victories within the existing framework. Then, in 1948, the Legal Defense Fund upgraded its approach by simultaneously filing suits in different federal districts and through each level of schooling, with complaints ranging from unequal provision of kindergarten for blacks to unequal sports and science facilities in all-black high schools. After nearly two years of these mostly successful equalization suits, the lawyers decided the time was ripe to confront the "separate but equal" rule head-on, but they felt they needed some heavier artillery to lead the attack. Their choice was the African American lawyer Thurgood Marshall, who had been fighting, and often winning, equalization suits since the early 1930s. Marshall was pessimistic about the readiness of the Supreme Court for a full confrontation with segregation itself and the constitutional principle sustaining it. But the unwillingness of Congress after the 1948 election to consider fair-employment legislation seems to have convinced Marshall that the courts were the only hope.

*The NAACP was formed in 1909 to promote the political rights of blacks. In the decades following the 1920s, the NAACP expanded its membership significantly and played an important role in the civil rights movement of the 1950s and '60s.*

**Brown v. Board of Education**
the 1954 Supreme Court decision that struck down the "separate but equal" doctrine as fundamentally unequal. This case eliminated state power to use race as a criterion of discrimination in law and provided the national government with the power to intervene by exercising strict regulatory policies against discriminatory actions

During the next four years there emerged a clear indication that the Supreme Court itself was willing to take more civil rights cases on appeal. Yet this was no guarantee that the Court would reverse *on principle* the separate-but-equal precedent of *Plessy v. Ferguson*. All through 1951 and 1952, as cases were winding slowly through the lower-court litigation maze, intense discussions and disagreements arose among NAACP lawyers as to whether a full-scale assault on *Plessy* was good strategy, or whether it might not be better to continue with specific cases alleging unequal treatment and demanding relief with a Court-imposed policy of equalization.[15] For some lawyers, including Marshall, such victories could amount to a defeat. For example, under the leadership of Governor James F. Byrnes, a former Supreme Court justice, South Carolina had undertaken a strategy of large-scale equalization of school services, both to satisfy the *Plessy* rule and to head off or render moot any litigation against the principle of separate but equal.

In the fall of 1952, the Court had on its docket cases from Delaware, Kansas, South Carolina, Virginia, and the District of Columbia challenging the constitutionality of school segregation. Of these, the case filed in Kansas became the one chosen by the NAACP. It seemed to be ahead of the pack in its district court, and it had the advantage of being located in a state outside the Deep South.[16]

Oliver Brown, the father of three girls, lived "across the tracks" in a low-income, racially mixed Topeka neighborhood. Every school day, Linda Brown took the school bus to the Monroe Elementary School, for black children, about a mile away. In September 1950, Oliver Brown took Linda to the all-white Sumner School, which was closer to home, to enter her into the third grade, in defiance of state law and local segregation rules. When they were refused, Brown took his case to the NAACP, and soon thereafter, the case **Brown v. Board of Education** was born. In mid-1953 the Court announced that the several cases on their way up would be re-argued within a set of questions having to do with the intent of the Fourteenth Amendment. Almost exactly a year later, the Court responded to those questions in one of the most important decisions in its history.

In deciding the *Brown* case, the Court, to the surprise of many, basically rejected as inconclusive all the learned arguments about the intent and the history of the Fourteenth Amendment and committed itself instead to considering only the consequences of segregation:

> Does segregation of children in public schools solely on the basis of race, even though the physical facilities and other "tangible" factors may be equal, deprive the children of the minority group of equal educational opportunities? We believe that it does. . . . We conclude that in the field of public education the doctrine of "separate but equal" has no place. Separate educational facilities are inherently unequal.[17]

The *Brown* decision altered the constitutional framework in two fundamental respects. First, after *Brown*, the states no longer had the power to use race as a criterion of discrimination in law. Second, the national government from then on had the power (and eventually the obligation) to intervene with strict regulatory policies against the discriminatory actions of state or local governments, school boards, employers, and many others in the private sector.

## Civil Rights after *Brown v. Board of Education*

*Brown v. Board of Education* withdrew all constitutional authority to use race as a criterion of exclusion, and it signaled more clearly the Court's determination to use the **strict scrutiny** test in cases related to racial discrimination. This meant that the burden of proof would fall on the government to show that the law in question *was* constitutional—not on the challengers to show the law's *unconstitutionality*.[18] Although the use of strict scrutiny would give an advantage to those attacking racial discrimination, the historic decision in *Brown v. Board of Education* was merely a small opening move. First, most states refused to cooperate until sued, and many ingenious schemes were employed to delay obedience (such as paying the tuition for white students to attend newly created "private" academies). Second, even as southern school boards began to cooperate by eliminating their legally enforced (**de jure**) school segregation, extensive actual (**de facto**) school segregation remained, in the North as well as in the South, as a consequence of racially segregated housing that could not be addressed by the 1954–55 *Brown* principles. Third, discrimination in employment, public accommodations, juries, voting, and other areas of social and economic activity were not directly touched by *Brown*.

**School Desegregation, Phase One**  Although the District of Columbia and some of the school districts in the border states began to respond almost immediately to court-ordered desegregation, the states of the Deep South responded with a

**strict scrutiny** a test used by the Supreme Court in racial discrimination cases and other cases involving civil liberties and civil rights that places the burden of proof on the government rather than on the challengers to show that the law in question is constitutional

**de jure** literally, "by law"; refers to legally enforced practices, such as school segregation in the South before the 1960s

**de facto** literally, "by fact"; refers to practices that occur even when there is no legal enforcement, such as school segregation in much of the United States today

*"Massive resistance" among white southerners attempted to block the desegregation efforts of the national government. For example, at Little Rock Central High School in 1957, an angry mob of white students prevented black students from entering the school.*

carefully planned delaying tactic commonly called "massive resistance" by the more demagogic southern leaders and "nullification" and "interposition" by the centrists. Either way, southern politicians stood shoulder to shoulder to declare that the Supreme Court's decisions and orders were without effect. The legislatures in these states enacted statutes ordering school districts to maintain segregated schools and state superintendents to terminate state funding wherever there was racial mixing in the classroom. Some southern states violated their own long traditions of local school autonomy by centralizing public school authority under the governor or the state board of education, and they gave themselves the power to close the schools and to provide alternative private schooling wherever local school boards might be inclined to obey the Supreme Court.

Most of these plans of "massive resistance" were tested in the federal courts and were struck down as unconstitutional.[19] But southern resistance was not confined to legislation. For example, in Arkansas in 1957, Governor Orval Faubus mobilized the Arkansas National Guard to intercede against enforcement of a federal court order to integrate Little Rock Central High School, and President Eisenhower was compelled to deploy U.S. troops and place the city under martial law. The Supreme Court considered the Little Rock confrontation so historically important that the opinion it rendered in that case was not only agreed to unanimously but was, unprecedentedly, signed personally by every one of the justices.[20] The end of massive resistance, however, became simply the beginning of still another southern strategy. "Pupil placement" laws authorized school districts to place each pupil in a school according to a variety of academic, personal, and psychological considerations, never mentioning race at all. This put the burden of transferring to an all-white school on the nonwhite children and their parents, making it almost impossible for a single court order to cover a whole district, let alone a whole state. This delayed desegregation awhile longer.[21]

**Social Protest after *Brown*** Ten years after *Brown*, fewer than 1 percent of black school-age children in the Deep South were attending schools with whites.[22] A decade of frustration made it fairly obvious to all observers that adjudication alone would not succeed. The goal of "equal protection" required positive, or affirmative, action by Congress and by administrative agencies. And given massive southern resistance and a generally negative national public opinion toward racial integration, progress would not be made through courts, Congress, or federal agencies without intense, well-organized support. Figure 5.1 shows the increase in the number of civil rights demonstrations for voting rights and public accommodations during the years following *Brown*. The number of organized demonstrations began to mount slowly but surely after *Brown v. Board of Education*. Only a year after *Brown*, black citizens in Montgomery, Alabama, challenged the city's segregated bus system with a yearlong boycott. The boycott began with the arrest of Rosa Parks, who refused to give up her seat for a white man. A seamstress who worked with civil rights groups, Parks eventually became a civil rights icon, as did one of the ministers leading the boycott, Martin Luther King Jr. But the boycott was a group effort, a carefully planned

The 1955–56 Montgomery bus boycott began with the arrest of Rosa Parks, who refused to give up her seat for a white man. The boycott lasted a year and drew national attention to the cause of civil rights.

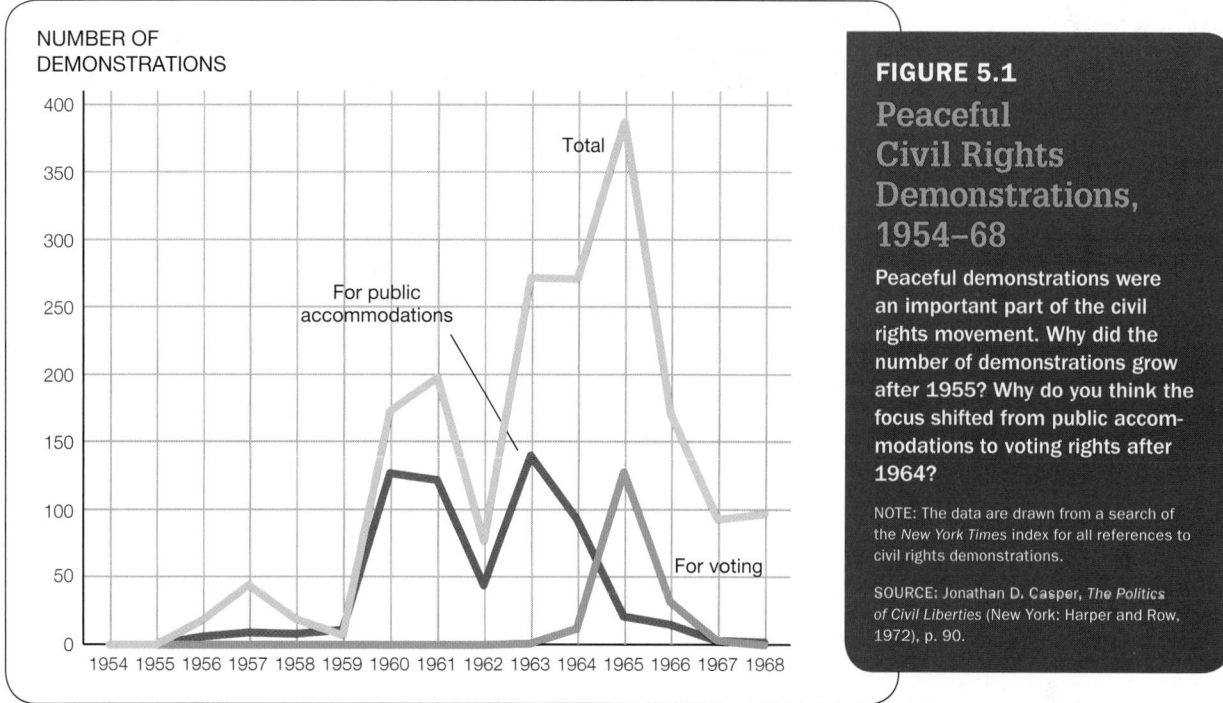

NUMBER OF DEMONSTRATIONS

**FIGURE 5.1**

**Peaceful Civil Rights Demonstrations, 1954–68**

Peaceful demonstrations were an important part of the civil rights movement. Why did the number of demonstrations grow after 1955? Why do you think the focus shifted from public accommodations to voting rights after 1964?

NOTE: The data are drawn from a search of the *New York Times* index for all references to civil rights demonstrations.

SOURCE: Jonathan D. Casper, *The Politics of Civil Liberties* (New York: Harper and Row, 1972), p. 90.

campaign in which nearly all the black citizens of Montgomery took part. After a year of private carpools and walking, Montgomery's bus system desegregated, but only after the Supreme Court ruled the system unconstitutional. The lengthy boycott and the white violence that accompanied it riveted national attention on the emerging civil rights movement. By the 1960s the many organizations that made up the civil rights movement had accumulated experience and built networks capable of launching large-scale direct-action campaigns against southern segregationists. The Southern Christian Leadership Conference, the Student Nonviolent Coordinating Committee, and many other organizations had built a movement that stretched across the South, using the media to attract nationwide attention and support. The image of protesters being beaten, attacked by police dogs, and set upon with fire hoses did much to win broad sympathy for the cause of black civil rights and to discredit state and local governments in the South. In the massive March on Washington in 1963, the Reverend Martin Luther King Jr. staked out the movement's moral claims in his famous "I Have a Dream" speech. Steadily, the movement created intense pressure for a reluctant federal government to take more assertive steps to defend black civil rights.

## The Civil Rights Acts

It is important to observe here the mutual dependence of the courts and legislatures: the legislatures need constitutional authority to act, and the courts need legislative assistance to implement court orders and focus political support. Consequently, even as the U.S. Congress finally moved into the field of school desegregation (and other areas of "equal protection"), the courts continued to exercise their powers, not only by placing court orders against recalcitrant school districts but also by extending

## TABLE 5.1

## Cause and Effect in the Civil Rights Movement

Political action and government action worked in tandem to produce dramatic changes in American civil rights policies.

| JUDICIAL AND LEGAL ACTION | POLITICAL ACTION |
| --- | --- |
| **1954** *Brown v. Board of Education* | **1955** Montgomery, Alabama, bus boycott |
| **1956** Federal courts order school integration; of special note is one ordering Autherine Lucy admitted to the University of Alabama, with Governor Wallace officially protesting | |
| **1957** Civil Rights Act creating Civil Rights Commission; President Eisenhower sends 101st Airborne Division paratroops to Little Rock, Arkansas, to enforce integration of Central High School | **1957** Southern Christian Leadership Conference (SCLC) formed, with Martin Luther King Jr. as president |
| **1960** First substantive Civil Rights Act, primarily voting rights | **1960** Student Nonviolent Coordinating Committee formed to organize protests, sit-ins, freedom rides |
| **1961** Interstate Commerce Commission orders desegregation on all buses and trains, and in terminals | |
| **1961** JFK favors executive action over civil rights legislation | |
| **1963** JFK shifts, supports strong civil rights law; JFK's assassination; LBJ asserts strong support for civil rights | **1963** Nonviolent demonstrations in Birmingham, Alabama, lead to King's arrest and his "Letter from Birmingham Jail" |
| | **1963** March on Washington |
| **1964** Congress passes historic Civil Rights Act covering voting, employment, public accommodations, education | |
| **1965** Voting Rights Act | **1965** King announces drive to register 3 million blacks in the South |
| **1966** War on Poverty in full swing | **Late 1960s** Movement diverges: part toward litigation, part toward community action programs, part toward war protest, part toward more militant "Black Power" actions |

and reinterpreting aspects of the equal protection clause to support legislative and administrative actions (see Table 5.1). But after a decade of very frustrating efforts, the courts and Congress ultimately came to the conclusion that the federal courts alone were not adequate to the task of changing the social rules, and that legislation and administrative action would be needed.

Three civil rights acts were passed during the first decade after the 1954 Supreme Court decision in *Brown v. Board of Education*. But these acts were of only marginal importance. The first one, in 1957, created the U.S. Commission on Civil Rights, to study abuses. The second, in 1960, established that the Fourteenth Amendment to the Constitution, adopted almost a century earlier, could no longer be disregarded, particularly with regard to voting. The third, the Equal Pay Act of 1963, was more important, but it was concerned with women, did not touch the question of racial discrimination, and, like the 1960 legislation, had no enforcement mechanisms.

By far the most important piece of legislation passed by Congress concerning equal opportunity was the Civil Rights Act of 1964. It not only put some teeth in the voting rights provisions of the 1957 and 1960 acts but also went far beyond voting to attack discrimination in public accommodations, segregation in the schools, and, at long last, the discriminatory conduct of employers in hiring, promoting, and laying off their employees. Discrimination against women was also included, extending the important 1963 provisions. The 1964 act seemed bold at the time, but it was enacted 10 years after the Supreme Court had declared racial discrimination "inherently unequal" under the Fifth and Fourteenth amendments. And it was enacted long after blacks had demonstrated that discrimination was no longer acceptable. The choice in 1964 was not between congressional action or inaction but between legal action and expanded violence.

**Public Accommodations** After the passage of the 1964 Civil Rights Act, public accommodations quickly removed some of the most blatant forms of racial discrimination. Signs defining "colored" and "white" restrooms, water fountains, waiting rooms, and seating arrangements were removed, and a host of other practices that relegated black people to separate and inferior arrangements was ended. In addition, the federal government filed more than 400 antidiscrimination suits in federal courts against hotels, restaurants, taverns, gas stations, and other "public accommodations."

Many aspects of legalized racial segregation—such as separate Bibles in the courtroom—seem like ancient history today. But the issue of racial discrimination in public settings is by no means over. In 1993, six African American Secret Service agents filed charges after a Denny's restaurant in Annapolis, Maryland, failed to serve them; white Secret Service agents at a nearby table had received prompt service. Similar charges citing discriminatory service at Denny's restaurants surfaced across the country. Faced with evidence of a pattern of systematic discrimination and numerous lawsuits, Denny's paid $45 million in damages to plaintiffs in Maryland and California in what is said to be the largest settlement ever in a public accommodations case.[23] In addition to the settlement, the chain vowed to expand employment and management opportunities for minorities in its restaurants. Other forms of racial discrimination in public accommodations are harder to challenge, however. For example, there is considerable evidence that taxicabs often refuse to pick up black passengers.[24] Such practices may be common, but they are difficult to prove and remedy through the law.

**School Desegregation, Phase Two** The 1964 Civil Rights Act also declared discrimination by private employers and state governments (school boards, etc.) illegal, and then went further to provide for administrative agencies to help the courts implement these laws. Title IV of the act, for example, authorized the executive branch, through the Justice Department, to implement federal court orders to desegregate schools, and to do so without having to wait for individual parents to bring complaints. Title VI of the act vastly strengthened the role of the executive branch and the credibility of court orders by providing that federal grants-in-aid to state and local governments for education must be withheld from any school system practicing racial segregation. Title VI became the most effective weapon for desegregating schools outside the South because the situation in northern communities was subtler and more difficult to address. In the South, the problem was segregation by law coupled with overt resistance to the national government's efforts to change the situation. In contrast, outside the South, segregated facilities were the outcome of hundreds of thousands of housing choices made by individuals and families. Once racial residential patterns emerged, racial homogeneity, property values, and neighborhood schools and churches were defended by real estate agents, neighborhood organizations, and the like. Thus, in order to eliminate discrimination nationwide, the 1964 Civil Rights Act gave (1) the president, through the Justice Department's Office for Civil Rights, the power to withhold federal education grants,[25] and (2) the attorney general of the United States the power to initiate suits (rather than having to await complaints) wherever there was a "pattern or practice" of discrimination.[26]

In the decade following the 1964 Civil Rights Act, the Justice Department brought legal action against more than 500 school districts. During the same period, administrative agencies filed lawsuits against 600 school districts, threatening to suspend federal aid to education unless real desegregation steps were taken.

**Busing** One step taken toward desegregation was busing children from poor urban school districts to wealthier suburban ones. In 1971 the Supreme Court held that state-imposed desegregation could be brought about by busing children across school districts:

> If school authorities fail in their affirmative obligations, judicial authority may be invoked. Once a right and a violation have been shown, the scope of a district court's equitable powers to remedy past wrongs is broad. . . . Bus transportation [is] a normal and accepted tool of educational policy.[27]

But the decision went beyond that, adding that under certain limited circumstances even racial quotas could be used as the "starting point in shaping a remedy to correct past constitutional violations," and that pairing or grouping schools and reorganizing school attendance zones would also be acceptable.

Three years later, however, this principle was severely restricted when the Supreme Court determined that only cities found guilty of deliberate and de jure racial segregation would have to desegregate their schools,[28] effectively exempting most northern states and cities from busing because school segregation in northern

*The 1964 Civil Rights Act made desegregation a legal requirement. The policy of busing from black neighborhoods to white schools bitterly divided the black and white communities in Boston. In 1976 a protester waved an American Flag threateningly at an innocent black bystander—a lawyer on his way to his office—as another white man sought to help him get out of the way.*

cities is generally the de facto result of segregated housing and thousands of acts of private discrimination against blacks and other minorities.

Boston provides a good illustration of the agonizing problem of making further progress in civil rights in the schools under the constitutional framework established by these decisions. Boston school authorities were found guilty of deliberately building school facilities and drawing school districts "to increase racial segregation." After vain efforts by Boston school authorities to draw up an acceptable plan to remedy the segregation, federal judge W. Arthur Garrity ordered an elaborate desegregation plan of his own, involving busing between the all-black neighborhood of Roxbury and the nearby white, working-class community of South Boston. The city's schools were so segregated and uncooperative that even the conservative administration of President Richard Nixon had already initiated a punitive cutoff of funds. But even many liberals criticized Judge Garrity's plan as being badly conceived for involving two neighboring communities with a history of tension and mutual resentment. The plan did work well at the elementary school level but proved explosive at the high school level, generating a continuing crisis for the city of Boston and for the whole nation.[29]

The prospects for further school integration diminished with a 1991 Supreme Court decision holding that lower federal courts could end supervision of local school boards if they could show "good faith" compliance with court orders to desegregate and could show that "vestiges of past discrimination" had been eliminated "to the extent practicable."[30] It is not necessarily easy for a school board to prove that the new standard has been met, but this was the first time since *Brown* and the 1964 Civil Rights Act that the Court had opened the door at all to retreat.

That door was opened further by a 1995 Court ruling that the remedies being applied in Kansas City, Missouri, were improper.[31] In accordance with a lower-court order, the state was pouring additional funding into salaries and remedial programs for Kansas City schools, which had a history of segregation. The aim of the spending was to improve student performance and to attract white students from the suburbs into the city schools. The Supreme Court declared the interdistrict goal improper, and reiterated its earlier ruling that states can free themselves of court orders by showing a good-faith effort. This decision indicated the Court's new willingness to end desegregation plans even when predominantly minority schools continued to lag significantly behind white suburban schools. In 2007 the Court's ruling in *Parents Involved in Community Schools v. Seattle School District No. 1* limited school integration measures still further. By making race one factor in assigning students to schools, the cities of Seattle and Louisville had hoped to achieve greater racial balance across the public schools. The Court ruled that these plans (even though the cities had voluntarily adopted them) were unconstitutional because they discriminated against white students on the basis of race. Many observers described the decision as the end of the *Brown* era because it eliminated one of the few public strategies left to promote racial integration. Others argued that Justice Anthony Kennedy's concurring opinion, which recognized the harm of racial isolation, may provide the basis for new efforts to promote integration in the future.[32]

### Outlawing Discrimination in Employment

Despite the agonizingly slow progress of school desegregation, some progress was made in other areas of civil rights during the 1960s and '70s. Voting rights were established and fairly quickly began to revolutionize southern politics. Service on juries was no longer denied to minorities.

But progress in the right to participate in politics and government dramatized the relative lack of progress in the economic domain, where battles over civil rights were increasingly being fought.

The federal courts and the Justice Department entered this area through Title VII of the Civil Rights Act of 1964, which outlawed job discrimination by all private and public employers, including governmental agencies (such as fire and police departments) that employed more than 15 workers. We have already seen (in Chapter 3) that the Supreme Court gave "interstate commerce" such a broad definition that Congress had the constitutional authority to cover discrimination by virtually any local employers.[33] Title VII makes it unlawful to discriminate in employment on the basis of color, religion, sex, or national origin, as well as race.

Title VII delegated some of the powers to enforce fair-employment practices to the Justice Department's Civil Rights Division and others to a new agency created in the 1964 act, the Equal Employment Opportunity Commission (EEOC). By executive order, these agencies had the power of the national government to revoke public contracts for goods and services and to refuse to engage in contracts with any private company that could not guarantee that its rules for hiring, promotion, and firing were nondiscriminatory. Executive orders in 1965, 1967, and 1969, by Presidents Johnson and Nixon, extended and reaffirmed nondiscrimination practices in employment and promotion in the federal government service. And in 1972, President Nixon and a Democratic Congress cooperated to strengthen the EEOC by giving it authority to initiate suits rather than wait for grievances.

But one problem with Title VII was that the complaining party had to show that deliberate discrimination was the cause of the failure to get a job or a training opportunity. Rarely, of course, does an employer explicitly admit discrimination on the basis of race, sex, or any other illegal reason. Recognizing this, the courts have allowed aggrieved parties (the plaintiffs) to make their case if they can show that an employer's hiring practices had the *effect* of exclusion. A leading case in 1971 involved a "class action" by several black employees in North Carolina attempting to show with statistical evidence that blacks had been relegated to only one department in the Duke Power Company, which involved the least desirable manual-labor jobs, and that they had been kept out of contention for better jobs because the employer had added attainment of a high school education and the passing of specially prepared aptitude tests as qualifications for higher jobs. The Supreme Court held that although the statistical evidence did not prove intentional discrimination, and although the requirements were race-neutral in appearance, their effects were sufficient to shift the burden of justification to the employer to show that the requirements were a "business necessity" that bore "a demonstrable relationship to successful performance."[34] The ruling in this case was subsequently applied to other hiring, promotion, and training programs.[35]

**Voting Rights** Although 1964 was the *most* important year for civil rights legislation, it was not the only important year. In 1965, Congress significantly strengthened legislation protecting voting rights by barring literacy and other tests as a condition for voting in six southern states[36] by setting criminal penalties for interference with efforts to vote and by providing for the replacement of local registrars with federally appointed registrars in counties designated by the attorney general as significantly resistant to registering eligible blacks to vote. The right to vote was further strengthened with ratification in 1964 of the Twenty-Fourth Amendment, which abolished the poll tax, and in 1975 with legislation permanently outlawing literacy tests in all 50 states and mandating bilingual ballots or oral assistance for Spanish speakers; Chinese, Japanese, Korean, and Native Americans; and Alaska natives.

In the long run, the laws extending and protecting voting rights could prove to be the most effective of all the great civil rights legislation because the progress in black political participation produced by these acts has altered the shape of American politics. In 1965, in the seven states of the Old Confederacy covered by the Voting Rights Act (VRA), 29.3 percent of the eligible black residents were registered to vote, compared with 73.4 percent of the white residents (see Table 5.2). Mississippi was the extreme case, with 6.7 percent black and 69.9 percent white registration. By 1971–72, 56.6 percent of the eligible blacks in the seven states were registered, compared with 67.8 percent of the eligible whites, a gap of 11.2 points. By 1972 the gap between black and white registration in the seven states was only 11.2 points, and in Mississippi the gap had been reduced to 9.4 points. At one time, white leaders in Mississippi had attempted to dilute the influence of this growing black vote by **gerrymandering** districts to ensure that no blacks would be elected to Congress. But the black voters changed Mississippi before Mississippi could change them. In 1988, 11 percent of all elected officials in Mississippi were black, a figure closely approximating the size of the national black electorate, which at the time was just over 11 percent of the American voting-age population. Mississippi's blacks had made significant gains (as they had in other Deep South states) as elected state and local representatives, and Mississippi was one of only

**gerrymandering** the apportionment of voters in districts in such a way as to give unfair advantage to one racial or ethnic group or political party

## TABLE 5.2

### Registration by Race and State in Southern States Covered by the Voting Rights Act (VRA)

The VRA had a direct impact on the rate of black voter registration in the southern states, as measured by the gap between white and black voters in each state. Further insights can be gained by examining changes in white registration rates before and after passage of the Voting Rights Act and by comparing the gaps between white and black registration. Why do you think registration rates for whites increased significantly in some states and dropped in others? What impact could the increase in black registration have had on public policy?

| | BEFORE THE ACT* | | | AFTER THE ACT* 1971–72 | | |
|---|---|---|---|---|---|---|
| | WHITE % | BLACK % | GAP** % | WHITE % | BLACK % | GAP % |
| Alabama | 69.2 | 19.3 | 49.9 | 80.7 | 57.1 | 23.6 |
| Georgia | 62.6 | 27.4 | 35.2 | 70.6 | 67.8 | 2.8 |
| Louisiana | 80.5 | 31.6 | 48.9 | 80.0 | 59.1 | 20.9 |
| Mississippi | 69.9 | 6.7 | 63.2 | 71.6 | 62.2 | 9.4 |
| North Carolina | 96.8 | 46.8 | 50.0 | 62.2 | 46.3 | 15.9 |
| South Carolina | 75.7 | 37.3 | 38.4 | 51.2 | 48.0 | 3.2 |
| Virginia | 61.1 | 38.3 | 22.8 | 61.2 | 54.0 | 7.2 |
| TOTAL | 73.4 | 29.3 | 44.1 | 67.8 | 56.6 | 11.2 |

*Available registration data as of March 1965 and 1971–72.
**The gap is the percentage-point difference between white and black registration rates.

SOURCE: U.S. Commission on Civil Rights, *Political Participation* (1968), Appendix VII: Voter Education Project, attachment to press release, October 3, 1972.

eight states in the country in which a black judge presided over the highest state court. (Four of the eight were Deep South states.)[37]

Several provisions of the 1965 act were scheduled to expire in 2007. However, in 2006, responding to charges that black voters still faced discrimination at the polls, Congress renewed the act for another 25 years. Pressure for renewal of the act had been intense since the disputed 2000 presidential election. The U.S. Commission on Civil Rights conducted hearings on the election in Florida, at which black voters testified about being turned away from the polls and wrongly purged from the voting rolls, and about the unreliable voting technology in their neighborhoods. On the basis of this testimony and after an analysis of the vote, the commission charged that there had been extensive racial discrimination.[38] Most recently, Texas has come under fire for gerrymandering congressional districts that discriminate against Latino voters. Due to population growth, most of it among Latinos, Texas gained four new congressional seats after the 2010 census. The heavily Republican state legislature drew a map designed to ensure that three of the new seats would go to Republican candidates. However, a coalition of minority groups and the Justice Department contested the map in court, charging that it failed to create a sufficient number of majority-minority districts. After extensive legal wrangling, the new redistricting plan included three majority-minority districts.[39]

**Housing** The Civil Rights Act of 1964 did not address housing, but in 1968, Congress passed another civil rights act specifically to outlaw housing discrimination. Called the Fair Housing Act, the law prohibited discrimination in the sale or rental of most housing—eventually covering nearly all the nation's housing. Housing was among the most controversial of discrimination issues because of deeply entrenched patterns of residential segregation across the United States. Such segregation was not simply a product of individual choice. Local housing authorities deliberately segregated public housing, and federal guidelines had sanctioned discrimination in Federal Housing Administration mortgage lending, effectively preventing blacks from joining the exodus to the suburbs in the 1950s and '60s. Nonetheless, Congress had been reluctant to tackle housing discrimination, fearing the tremendous controversy it could arouse. But just as the housing legislation was being considered in April 1968, the civil rights leader Martin Luther King Jr. was assassinated; this tragedy brought the measure unexpected support in Congress.

Although it pronounced sweeping goals, the Fair Housing Act had little effect on housing segregation, because its enforcement mechanisms were so weak. Individuals who believed they had been discriminated against had to file suit themselves. The burden was on the individual to prove that housing discrimination had occurred, even though such discrimination is often subtle and difficult to document. Although local fair-housing groups emerged to assist individuals in their court claims, the procedures for proving discrimination constituted a formidable barrier to effective change. These procedures were not altered until 1988, when Congress passed the Fair Housing Amendments Act. This new law put more teeth in the enforcement procedures and allowed the Department of Housing and Urban Development (HUD) to initiate legal action in cases of discrimination.[40]

Other attempts to challenge residential segregation had similarly mixed success. HUD tried briefly in the early 1970s to create racially "open communities" by withholding federal funds to suburbs that refused to accept subsidized housing. Confronted with charges of "forced integration" and bitter local protests, however, the administration quickly backed down. Efforts to prohibit discrimination in lending have been somewhat more promising. Several laws passed in the 1970s

*The mortgage crisis that led to foreclosures on many homes in 2008 and 2009 hit minority communities especially hard. Civil rights organizations argued that some lenders discriminated against African American and Latino home buyers, making it harder for them to get a fair deal on a mortgage.*

required banks to report information about their mortgage lending patterns, making it more difficult for them to engage in **redlining**, the practice of refusing to lend to entire neighborhoods. The 1977 Community Reinvestment Act required banks to lend in neighborhoods in which they do business. Through vigorous use of this act, many neighborhood organizations have reached agreements with banks that, as a result, have significantly increased investment in some poor neighborhoods.

Even so, racial discrimination in home mortgage lending remains a significant issue. In 2007 the issue of predatory lending—offering loans well above market rates, often with complex provisions that borrowers do not understand—attracted nationwide attention as the number of home foreclosures skyrocketed. Several lawsuits charged that these loans were particularly targeted at minority borrowers. In 2009, civil rights organizations; several states, including California, Illinois, Massachusetts, and New York; and some cities, including Baltimore, filed charges against banks and other lenders claiming they had illegally discriminated against African American and Latino home buyers. Minority home buyers, the suits charged, had been offered subprime mortgage products, with higher interest rates, in contrast to whites with similar income levels, who were offered loans at lower interest rates. By 2012 some of these lawsuits had resulted in the largest financial settlements ever issued for lending discrimination. In announcing one settlement, the Justice Department vowed to "vigorously pursue those who would take advantage of certain Americans because of their race, national origin, gender or disability," noting that such discrimination "betrays the promise of equal opportunity that is enshrined in our Constitution and our legal framework."[41]

**Marriage** The Civil Rights Act of 1964 was also silent on the question of interracial marriage, which 16 states continued to outlaw in 1967. In that year, the Supreme Court ruled in *Loving v. Virginia* that such state laws were unconstitutional. The case concerned a Virginia couple, a white man and a black woman, who married in Washington, D.C., where such unions were legal. When they moved back to Virginia, which outlawed interracial marriage, authorities charged

**redlining** a practice in which banks refuse to make loans to people living in certain geographic locations

the couple with violating Virginia law. The Lovings moved back to Washington, D.C., and challenged the Virginia law. Nine years later the Supreme Court struck down state laws banning marriage on the basis of racial classifications. In so doing, the Court declared marriage "one of the 'basic civil rights of man,' fundamental to our very existence and survival."[42]

# Extending Civil Rights

**Describe how different groups have won protection of their rights**

Even before equal-employment laws began to have a positive effect on the economic situation of blacks, something far more dramatic began happening: the extension of civil rights to other groups. The right not to be discriminated against was being successfully claimed by the other groups listed in Title VII of the 1964 Civil Rights Act, those defined by sex, religion, or national origin, and eventually by still other groups defined by age or sexual preference. This extension of civil rights has become the new frontier of the civil rights struggle.

Once gender discrimination began to be seen as an important civil rights issue, other groups rose to demand recognition and active protection of their civil rights. Under Title VII, any group or individual can try, and in fact is encouraged to try, to convert goals and grievances into questions of rights and of the deprivation of those rights. A plaintiff must establish only that his or her membership in a group is an unreasonable basis for discrimination—that is, that the unequal treatment cannot be proven to be a "job-related" or otherwise clearly reasonable and relevant decision. In the United States today, the list of individuals and groups claiming illegal discrimination is lengthy.

## Women and Gender Discrimination

Title VII provided a valuable tool for the growing women's movement in the 1960s and '70s. In fact, in many ways the law fostered the growth of the women's movement. The first major campaign of the National Organization for Women (NOW)

*Political equality did not end discrimination against women in the workplace or in society at large. African Americans' struggle for civil rights in the 1950s and '60s spurred a parallel equal rights movement for women in the 1960s and '70s.*

# Have Women Achieved Equal Rights?

Title VII of the 1964 Civil Rights Act prohibits gender discrimination, and the Supreme Court has consistently upheld the principle that women should have the same rights as men. Since 1960, the United States has made great strides toward gender equality in some areas but, as the data show, still has a long way to go in other areas.

## Education

**% of college students**

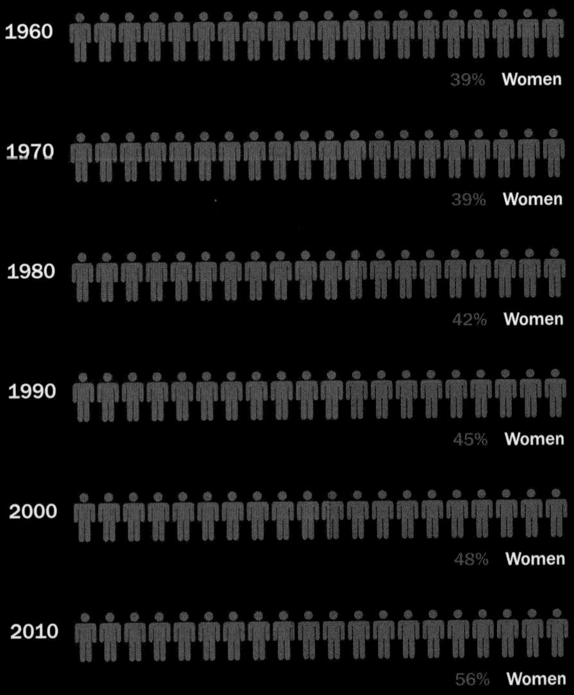

| Year | Women |
|---|---|
| 1960 | 39% |
| 1970 | 39% |
| 1980 | 42% |
| 1990 | 45% |
| 2000 | 48% |
| 2010 | 56% |

## Politics

**% of members of Congress and state legislatures**

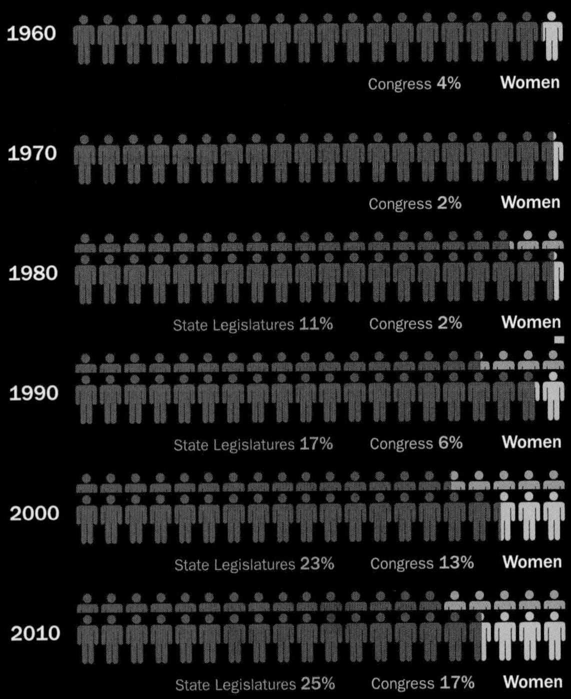

| Year | State Legislatures | Congress |
|---|---|---|
| 1960 | | 4% |
| 1970 | | 2% |
| 1980 | 11% | 2% |
| 1990 | 17% | 6% |
| 2000 | 23% | 13% |
| 2010 | 25% | 17% |

*Women*

## Women's Income as a Percentage of Men's

**Weekly earnings, by occupation, 2010**

**81%**

Educators
Men: **$1,065**
Women: **$862**

**74%**

Professional
Men: **$1,256**
Women: **$923**

**81%**

Office/Sales
Men: **$736**
Women: **$597**

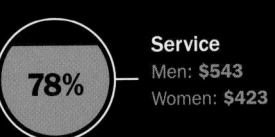

**78%**

Service
Men: **$543**
Women: **$423**

**74%**

Production
Men: **$640**
Women: **$473**

SOURCES: U.S. Census Bureau, census.gov; Center for American Women and Politics, cawp.rutgers.edu (accessed 7/18/12).

## for critical analysis

1. How much do each of these factors—education, political office holders, and income—say about gender equality in the United States?

2. While most Americans support the principle of equal opportunity for all groups, there is disagreement over how much the government should do to ensure equal outcomes. Discuss the difference between equal opportunity and equal outcomes in the context of women's rights.

involved picketing the EEOC for its refusal to ban sex-segregated employment advertisements. NOW also sued the *New York Times* for continuing to publish such ads after the passage of Title VII. Another organization, the Women's Equity Action League (WEAL), pursued legal action on a wide range of sex-discrimination issues, filing lawsuits against law schools and medical schools for discriminatory admission policies, for example.

Building on these victories and the growth of the women's movement, feminist activists sought an "Equal Rights Amendment" (ERA) to the Constitution. The proposed amendment was short: its substantive passage stated that "equality of rights under the law shall not be denied or abridged by the United States or by any State on account of sex." The amendment's supporters believed that such a sweeping guarantee of equal rights was a necessary tool for ending all discrimination against women and for making gender roles more equal. Opponents charged that the amendment would be socially disruptive and would introduce changes (such as unisex restrooms) that most Americans did not want. The amendment easily passed Congress in 1972 and won quick approval in many state legislatures, but it fell three states short of the 38 needed to ratify it by the 1982 deadline.[43]

Despite the failure of the ERA, efforts to stop gender discrimination expanded dramatically as an area of civil rights law. In the 1970s the conservative Burger Court (under Chief Justice Warren Burger) helped establish gender discrimination as a major and highly visible civil rights issue. Although the Supreme Court refused to treat gender discrimination as the equivalent of racial discrimination,[44] it did make it easier for plaintiffs to file and win suits on the basis of gender discrimination by applying an "intermediate" level of review to these cases.[45] This **intermediate scrutiny** is midway between traditional rules of evidence, which put the burden of proof on the plaintiff, and the doctrine of strict scrutiny, which requires the defendant to show that unequal treatment is both reasonable and necessary. Intermediate scrutiny shifts the burden of proof partially onto the defendant.

One major step was taken in 1992, when the Court decided in *Franklin v. Gwinnett County Public Schools* that violations of Title IX of the 1972 Education Act could be remedied with monetary damages.[46] Title IX forbade gender discrimination in education, but it initially sparked little litigation because of its weak enforcement provisions. The Court's 1992 ruling that monetary damages could be awarded for gender discrimination opened the door for more legal action in the area of education. The greatest impact has been in the areas of sexual harassment (the subject of the *Franklin* case) and in equal treatment of women's athletic programs. The potential for monetary damages has made universities and public schools take the problem of sexual harassment more seriously. And in the two years after the *Franklin* case, complaints to the Education Department's Office for Civil Rights about unequal treatment of women's athletic programs nearly tripled. In several high-profile legal cases, some prominent universities were ordered to create more women's sports programs, prompting many other colleges and universities to follow suit in order to avoid potential litigation.[47] In 1997 the Supreme Court refused to hear a petition by Brown University challenging a lower-court order that the university establish strict sex equity in its athletic programs. The Court's decision meant that in colleges and universities across the country, varsity athletic positions for men and women must reflect the schools' overall enrollment numbers.[48] By 2012, 40 years after Title IX was first enacted, it was clear that the had a major impact on college athletic programs. But advocates for gender equality noted that many differences between men and women students continued to exist. They pointed to gender barriers in important fields such as science, technology, engineering, and math, which women students are much less likely to enter.[49]

**intermediate scrutiny** a test used by the Supreme Court in gender discrimination cases that places the burden of proof partially on the government and partially on the challengers to show that the law in question is unconstitutional

*Kim Messer, pictured here with a group of male cadets, was one of the first women admitted to the Citadel, a military college in South Carolina. The Supreme Court ruled in 1996 that state-sponsored schools must be open to both men and women.*

In 1996 the Supreme Court made another important decision about gender and education by putting an end to all-male schools supported by public funds. It ruled that the Virginia Military Institute's (VMI) policy of not admitting women was unconstitutional.[50] Along with the Citadel, an all-male military college in South Carolina, VMI had never admitted women in its 157-year history. VMI argued that the unique educational experience it offered (including intense physical training and the harsh treatment of freshmen) would be destroyed if women students were admitted. The Court, however, ruled that the male-only policy denied "substantial equality" to women. Two days after the ruling, the Citadel announced that it would accept women. VMI considered becoming a private institution in order to remain all-male, but in September 1996, the school's board finally voted to admit women. Even without formal barriers to entry, the experience of the new female cadets at these schools was not easy. The first female cadet at the Citadel, Shannon Faulkner, won admission in 1995 under a federal court order but quit after four days. Of the four women admitted to the Citadel after the Supreme Court decision, two quit within months. They charged harassment from male students, including attempts to set the female cadets on fire.[51]

Courts began to find sexual harassment to be a form of sex discrimination during the late 1970s. Although sexual harassment law applies to education, most such law has been developed by courts through interpretation of Title VII of the 1964 Civil Rights Act. In 1986 the Supreme Court recognized two forms of sexual harassment. One type is "quid pro quo" harassment, which involves an explicit or strongly implied threat that submission is a condition of continued employment. The second is harassment that creates offensive or intimidating employment conditions amounting to a "hostile environment."[52]

Employers and many employees have complained that "hostile environment" sexual harassment is too ambiguous. When can an employee bring charges? When is the employer liable? In 1986 the Court said that sexual harassment may be legally actionable even if the employee did not suffer tangible economic or job-related losses in relation to it. In 1993 the Court said that sexual harassment may be legally actionable even if the employee did not suffer tangible psychological costs as a result of it.[53] In two 1998 cases, the Court further strengthened the law when it said that whether or not sexual harassment results in economic harm to the employee, an employer is liable for the harassment if it was committed by someone with authority over the employee—by a supervisor, for example. But the Court also said that an employer may defend itself by showing that it had a sexual harassment prevention and grievance policy in effect.[54]

The fight against gender discrimination as an important part of the civil rights struggle has coincided with the rise of women's politics as a discrete movement in American politics. As with the struggle for racial equality, the relationship between changes in government policies and political action suggests that, to a great degree, changes in government policies produce political action. Today, the existence of a powerful women's movement derives in large measure from the enactment of Title VII of the Civil Rights Act of 1964 and from the Burger Court's vital steps in applying that law to protect women. The recognition of women's civil rights has become an issue that in many ways transcends the usual distinctions of American political discourse. In the heavily partisan debate over the federal crime bill enacted in 1994, for instance, the section of the bill that enjoyed the widest support was the Violence Against Women Act, whose most important feature was that it defined gender-biased violent crimes as a matter of civil rights, with a civil rights remedy for women, the crimes' victims. The Supreme Court's 2000 decision ruling the act unconstitutional signaled a defeat for women's rights.[55] Another setback occurred in 2007, when the Court ruled against a claim of pay discrimination at work. The case, *Ledbetter v. Goodyear Tire and Rubber Co.*, involved a woman supervisor named Lily Ledbetter, who learned late in her career that she was being paid up to 40 percent less than male supervisors, including those with less seniority. Ledbetter filed a grievance with the EEOC, charging sex discrimination.[56] The Supreme Court denied her claim, ruling that according to the law, workers must file their grievance 180 days after the discrimination occurs. Many observers found the ruling unfair because workers often do not know about pay differentials until well after the initial decision to discriminate has been made. Justice Ruth Bader Ginsburg, the only female member of the Court, marked her disagreement by reading her dissent aloud, a rare occurrence. In January 2009 the Lily Ledbetter Fair Pay Act became the first bill that President Obama signed into law. The new law gave workers expanded rights to sue in cases, such as Ledbetter's, when an employee learns of discriminatory treatment well after it has started.

## Latinos

The labels *Latino* and *Hispanic* encompass a wide range of groups with diverse national origins, distinctive cultural identities, and particular experiences. As a result, civil rights issues for them have varied considerably by group and by place. For example, the early political experiences of Mexican Americans were shaped by race and by region. For the earliest Mexican Americans in the Southwest, the United States came to them, rather than the other way around. In 1848, under the Treaty of Guadalupe Hidalgo, Mexico ceded to the United States territory that now comprises Arizona, California, New Mexico, and parts of Colorado, Nevada, and Utah, as well as extending the Texas border to the Rio Grande. Although the treaty guaranteed full civil rights to the residents of these territories, Mexican Americans in fact experienced ongoing discrimination, which they sought to remedy through the courts. In 1898 the courts reconfirmed Mexican Americans' formal political rights, including the right to vote. In many places, however, and especially in Texas, Mexican Americans were segregated and prevented from voting through such means as the white primary and the poll tax.[57]

There were regional differences, too. In contrast to the northeastern and midwestern cities to which most European ethnics immigrated, the Southwest did not have a tradition of ethnic mobilization associated with machine politics. Particularly after the political reforms enacted in the first decade of the twentieth century, city politics in the Southwest was dominated by small groups of Anglo elites. In the countryside, when Mexican Americans participated in politics, it was often as part of a political organization dominated by a white landowner, or *patrón*. Texas established separate schools for Mexicans, a practice also common in Southern California. In the housing markets, Mexicans were often banned by restrictive covenants from buying or renting houses in many neighborhoods.

*The 1947* Mendez v. Westminster *case challenged segregation of Mexican American students in California and was an important precursor to later school segregation cases. In 2007 a U.S. postal stamp was issued to commemorate the* Mendez *case.*

The earliest Mexican American independent political organizations included the League of United Latin American Citizens (LULAC), founded in 1929, and the GI Forum, created in 1948. Both groups worked to stem discrimination against Mexican Americans. LULAC pursued a legal strategy like the NAACP's to eliminate the segregation of Mexican American students. One of its earliest victories came in 1931, when it successfully challenged a Texas school district's decision to establish separate schools for Anglos and Mexicans.[58] LULAC also litigated the 1947 *Mendez v. Westminster* case, which overturned school segregation in Orange County, California. This case was an important precursor to *Brown v. Board of Education*, and many of the same actors were involved. For example, Thurgood Marshall of the NAACP, the lead attorney on *Brown* (and later a Supreme Court justice), filed a brief supporting desegregation in the *Mendez* case. Moreover, Earl Warren, the California governor who signed the legislation outlawing school segregation there after the *Mendez* decision, served as chief justice when the Supreme Court ruled on *Brown* seven years later. By the late 1950s the first Mexican American was elected to Congress, and four others followed in the 1960s.

In the 1960s a new kind of Mexican American political movement was born. A central inspiration for political mobilization emerged from the United Farm Workers union and its charismatic leader, César Chávez. In an era of unprecedented economic prosperity, California's farmworkers, mainly Mexican migrants, remained poorly paid and lacked basic rights for fair treatment on the job. Employing novel tactics such as the national grape boycott, the union drew Americans' attention to the plight of farmworkers and the injustices that confronted Mexican migrants and Mexican Americans in the fields. Chávez, whose hunger strikes and inspirational speeches kept the movement in the public eye, came to symbolize the quest for Mexican American civil rights more broadly.[59] The fields were not the only focus of conflict. In the late 1960s, Mexican American students, inspired by the black civil rights movement, launched boycotts of high school classes in East Los Angeles, Denver, and San Antonio. Students in colleges and universities across California joined in as well. Among their demands were bilingual education, an end to discrimination, and more cultural recognition. In Crystal City, Texas, which had been dominated by Anglo politicians despite a population that was overwhelmingly Mexican American, the newly formed La Raza Unida Party took over the city government.[60]

*Cesar Chavez, a leader of the United Farm Workers, advocated for the rights of Mexican Americans. During the 1960s, Chavez and his supporters used hunger strikes and other protests to draw attention to the discriminatory treatment of Mexican Americans.*

Since that time, Latino political strategy has developed along two tracks. One is a traditional ethnic group path of voter registration and voting along ethnic lines. The second is a legal strategy using the various civil rights laws designed to ensure fair access to the political system. The Mexican American Legal Defense and Education Fund (MALDEF), founded in 1968, has played a key role in designing and pursuing the latter strategy.

**Immigrants and Civil Rights** Since the 1960s, rights for Latinos have been intertwined with immigrant rights. Latino organizations opposed the Immigration Reform and Control Act of 1986 because it imposed sanctions on employers who hire undocumented workers. Such sanctions, they feared, would lead employers to discriminate against Latinos. These suspicions were confirmed in a 1990 report by the General Accounting Office that found employer sanctions had created a "widespread pattern of discrimination" against Latinos and others who appear foreign.[61] Organizations such as MALDEF monitor and challenge such discrimination. These groups have turned their attention to the rights of legal and illegal immigrants, as anti-immigrant sentiment has grown in recent years.

For much of American history, legal immigrants were treated much the same as citizens. But growing immigration—including an estimated 300,000 unauthorized immigrants per year—and mounting economic insecurity have undermined this sense of equality. Groups of voters across the country now strongly support drawing a sharper line between immigrants and citizens. The Supreme Court has ruled that unauthorized immigrants are eligible for education and emergency medical care but can be denied other social benefits. The movement to deny benefits to noncitizens gathered steam in California, which experienced sharp economic distress in the early 1990s and has the highest levels of immigration of any state. In 1994, California voters approved Proposition 187, denying unauthorized immigrants all services except emergency medical care. Supporters of the measure hoped to discourage unauthorized immigration and to pressure those already in the country to leave. Opponents contended that denying basic services to unauthorized immigrants risked creating a subclass of residents in the United States whose poor health and lack of education would threaten all Americans. In 1994 and 1997 a federal court declared most of Proposition 187 unconstitutional, affirming previous rulings that unauthorized immigrants should be granted public education. A booming economy helped reduce public concern about unauthorized immigration, but these worries soon emerged again.

Questions about the rights of unauthorized immigrants became especially contentious in 2007. That year, Congress considered a complex compromise bill—running some 761 pages long—that attempted to accomplish three goals: increase border security to reduce illegal immigration; provide unauthorized immigrants who had been in the country for at least five years with a pathway to legal citizenship; and ensure employers an adequate supply of temporary immigrant workers through a guest worker program. The compromise failed in the face of opposition from the Right, which disliked the provision for creating a path to legal citizenship, and from the Left, which opposed the proposed guest worker program.

*Some states and cities have tried to address illegal immigration by enacting stricter laws than those under consideration by Congress. This worker protested one such law with a sign reading, "I am a day laborer, not a criminal."*

In the aftermath of the failed legislation, unauthorized immigration has continued to be a hot-button political issue with important repercussions for civil rights. Antagonism against undocumented immigrants has spilled over into violence against Latinos. One priority for civil rights groups is to ensure that such violence is classified as a hate crime by the federal Justice Department, thus carrying significantly heavier penalties than would otherwise be the case. In 2009 a Shenandoah, Pennsylvania, jury imposed a very light sentence on three teenage defendants who had beaten a Mexican man to death while shouting ethnic slurs. The National Council of La Raza (a Latino civil rights advocacy organization) and MALDEF collected 50,000 signatures on a petition urging the Justice Department to declare the murder a hate crime.[62]

Another ongoing issue is federal cooperation with local and state law enforcement agencies to enforce federal immigration laws. Programs first initiated by the Department of Homeland Security in the final years of the George W. Bush administration led to immigrant "sweeps," which rounded up Latinos, many of whom were legal immigrants or even American citizens. A broad coalition of civil rights organizations opposed the program for engaging in racial profiling and violating civil rights, and the congressional Hispanic Caucus called on the new president to end it. Yet, as we saw in the introduction to this chapter, the Obama administration's Secure Communities program, which initially sought to focus on major drug offenders, violent criminals, and those already in prison, has come under fire for illegally detaining citizens and legal immigrants. In the case of Maricopa County (Phoenix) sheriff Joe Arpaio, the federal government took strong measures to limit local discriminatory behavior. Charging that the Sheriff's Office had "a pervasive culture of discriminatory bias against Latinos," the Justice Department threatened to withdraw all federal money from the county if it did not agree to change its practices.[63]

Finally, as we saw in Chapter 3, a number of states, including Arizona, Utah, South Carolina, Indiana, Georgia, and Alabama passed very strict immigration laws. Civil rights groups have contested the laws in court, and the federal Justice Department has instituted its own legal challenges. Arizona's 2010 law provided the inspiration for these far-reaching state measures. Arizona's law required immigrants to carry identity documents with them at all times, made it a crime for an undocumented immigrant to apply for a job, gave the police greater powers to stop anyone they suspected of being an unauthorized immigrant, and required them to check the immigration status of a person they detain if they suspect that person is an unauthorized immigrant. The Justice Department challenged the law on the grounds that the federal government was responsible for making immigration law, not the states. The Supreme Court's 2012 decision was a partial victory for the federal government. The court struck down three parts of the Arizona law on the grounds that they preempted federal responsibility. These included the provision that immigrants carry identity papers, that undocumented immigrants cannot apply for jobs, and that police can stop persons they suspect of being undocumented immigrants. The Court let stand the provision that required local police to check the immigration status of an individual detained for other reasons, if they had grounds to suspect that the person was in the country illegally. Opponents of the police checks vowed to challenge that part of the law on the grounds that it led to illegal racial profiling.[64]

## for critical analysis

In 2012 the Supreme Court let stand the portion of Arizona's immigration law that requires police to check the immigration status of anyone they detain. Why are immigration and the rights of immigrants so controversial?

## Asian Americans

Like the term *Latino*, the label *Asian American* encompasses a wide range of people from very different national backgrounds who came to the United States at different moments in history. As a consequence, Asian Americans have had very diverse experiences.

The early Asian experience in the United States was shaped by a series of naturalization laws dating back to 1790, the first of which declared that only white aliens were eligible for citizenship. Chinese immigrants began arriving in California in the 1850s, drawn by the boom of the gold rush, but they were immediately met with virulent antagonism. In 1870, Congress declared Chinese immigrants ineligible for citizenship; in 1882 the first Chinese Exclusion Act suspended the entry of Chinese laborers.

At the time of the Exclusion Act, the Chinese community was composed predominantly of single male laborers, with few women and children. The few Chinese children in San Francisco were initially denied entry to the public schools; only after parents of American-born Chinese children pressed legal action were the children allowed to attend public school. Even then, however, they were segregated into a separate Chinese school. American-born Chinese children could not be denied citizenship, however; this right was confirmed by the Supreme Court in 1898, when it ruled in *United States v. Wong Kim Ark* that anyone born in the United States was entitled to full citizenship.[65] Still, new Chinese immigrants were barred from the United States until 1943, after China had become a key wartime ally and Congress repealed the Chinese Exclusion Act and permitted Chinese residents to become citizens.

The earliest Japanese immigrants, who came to California in the 1880s, at the height of the anti-Chinese movement, faced similar discrimination. Like Chinese immigrants, Japanese immigrants were ineligible to become citizens because of their race. During the first part of the twentieth century, California and several other western states enacted laws that denied Japanese immigrants the right to own property. The denial of basic civil rights to Japanese Americans culminated in the decision to

*Asian immigrants faced discrimination throughout much of American history. During World War II, Americans of Japanese descent were forced from their homes and confined in internment camps. At the time, the Supreme Court supported this denial of civil rights as a necessary security measure.*

forcibly remove Americans of Japanese descent as well as Japanese noncitizen residents from their homes and confine them in internment camps during World War II. Despite a vigorous legal challenge, the Supreme Court ruled that the internment was constitutional on the grounds of military necessity.[66] Not until the Civil Liberties Act of 1988 did the federal government formally acknowledge this denial of civil rights as a "grave injustice" that had been "motivated largely by racial prejudice, wartime hysteria, and a failure of political leadership."[67] Along with a formal apology from the president, Congress issued each surviving internee a $20,000 check.

Asian immigration increased rapidly after the 1965 Immigration Act, which lifted discriminatory quotas. In spite of this and other developments, limited English proficiency barred many new Asian American and Latino immigrants from full participation in American life. Two developments in the 1970s, however, established rights for language minorities. In 1974 the Supreme Court ruled in *Lau v. Nichols*, a suit filed on behalf of Chinese students in San Francisco, that school districts have to provide education for students whose English is limited.[68] It did not mandate bilingual education, but it established a duty to provide instruction that the students could understand. As we saw earlier, the 1970 amendments to the Voting Rights Act permanently outlawed literacy tests in all 50 states and mandated bilingual ballots or oral assistance for those who speak Chinese, Japanese, Korean, Spanish, or Native American or Alaskan languages.

# The Digital Divide

**Digital inequality**, or the **digital** *divide*, refers to the gap between Internet users and individuals or groups who do not have access to the Internet. Those least likely to be online and use the Internet daily are the poor, racial and ethnic minorities, non-English speakers, the less educated, and the elderly. The same groups are also less likely to have digital literacy skills. Thus, addressing the divide requires both access and skills, the two components necessary for digital citizenship, or full participation in today's increasingly digital politics and society.

It is hard to image that less than 20 years ago (1995) only one in 10 adults in the United States was online. In contrast, in 2012 almost 8 out of 10 adults were online. When the Pew Research Center first began tracking the role of the Internet in American life (in 1995) there were stark demographic differences between who was on- and offline. Today, these differences still exist, especially when it comes to broadband access at home.

While the overall number of Internet users has increased dramatically, almost 4 in 10 don't have high-speed access at home. As we discussed in Chapter 1, home access and high-speed access are necessary for digital citizenship and full participation in society online. A 2011 Pew survey found that two-thirds (66 percent) of whites have high-speed Internet at home, but only half of African Americans (49 percent) and Hispanics (51 percent) have such access. The 2011 survey also found gaps based on age, income, and educational attainment. Among those who earn less than $30,000 per year, only 41 percent have such access. This compares with 89 percent of those making at least $75,000 per year. Thus

Internet access follows a similar socio-economic pattern as voter turnout (see Chapter 8), potentially reinforcing political inequalities as some groups participate more than others in politics.

The ways in which people connect to the Internet are more varied today than they were a decade ago. Some people argue that mobile access will solve the digital divide. Mobile access on smartphones is a primary way the poor and racial and ethnic minorities go online. Among smartphone users, the groups that are more likely than other groups to say that their phone is their main source of Internet access are young adults, minorities, those with no college experience, and those with lower household income levels. In 2012 over 40 percent of Americans used a smartphone that could connect to the Internet, while over 60 percent went online wirelessly using a laptop, tablet, or cell phone.

However, in a 2011 *New York Times* editorial, Yeshiva University law school Professor Susan Crawford argued that although smartphones have many benefits, they provide "second-class access" compared with high-speed broadband. There are significant gaps in the activities online for broadband users versus for individuals with mobile access only. A 2009 Federal Communications Commission (FCC) survey found that only 52 percent of the less connected read national or international news online, compared to 77 percent of those with broadband at home. Of the less connected, only 57 percent used state, local, or federal government websites compared with

79 percent with broadband a home. The growth in mobile phone use has not erased inequalities in participation online and seems unlikely to do so.

What are the reasons people give for remaining offline? For rural residents, broadband is often not available. But the number one reason people report for not having home broadband is price. Despite President Obama's promise to build a digital highway across America and despite the adoption of the National Broadband Plan, the United States lags behind numerous other countries in broadband investment, ranking 15th in the percentage of broadband subscribers in 2010. Government spending has focused on subsidizing rural broadband wiring rather than addressing the high cost of access. In 2012 the FCC began experimenting with subsidizing broadband access for the poor. At this point it is a pilot project, but future government policy may help provide Internet access for those who are unable to afford it.

SOURCES: Karen Mossberger, Caroline Tolbert, and Mary Stansbury, *Virtual Inequality: Beyond the Digital Divide* (Washington, DC: Georgetown University Press, 2003). Karen Mossberger, Caroline Tolbert, and William Franko, *Digital Cities: The Internet and the Geography of Opportunity* (New York: Oxford University Press, 2012). Pew Internet and American Life, *Digital Differences*, April 2012.

## for critical analysis

1. In 2011 the United Nations declared that access to the Internet is a human right Do you think the government has an obligation to provide Internet access to all Americans?

2. The Internet has the potential to increase participation in politics, but does this matter if the same groups that have historically been underrepresented in politics also have less access to digital politics?

## Native Americans

The political status of Native Americans was left unclear in the Constitution. But by the early 1800s the courts had defined each of the Indian tribes as a nation. As members of Indian nations, Native Americans were thus declared noncitizens of the United States. The political status of Native Americans changed in 1924, when congressional legislation granted citizenship to all persons born in the United States. A variety of changes in federal policy toward Native Americans during the 1930s paved the way for a later resurgence of their political power. Most important was the federal decision to encourage Native Americans on reservations to establish local self-government.[69] Since the 1920s and '30s, Native American tribes have sued the federal government for illegal land seizures; both monetary reparations and land have been awarded as damages, but only in small amounts. Native American tribes have been more successful in winning federal recognition of their sovereignty. Sovereign status has, in turn, allowed them to exercise greater self-determination.

The Native American political movement gathered force in the 1960s as Native Americans began to use protest, litigation, and assertion of tribal rights to improve their situation. In 1968, Dennis Banks, Herb Powless, and Clyde Bellecourt cofounded the American Indian Movement (AIM), the most prominent Native American rights organization. AIM won national attention in 1969 when 200 of its members, representing 20 different tribes, took over the famous prison island of Alcatraz in San Francisco Bay, claiming it for Native Americans. The federal government responded to the rise in Native American activism with the Indian Self-Determination and Education Assistance Act, which began to give Native Americans more control over their own land.[70]

As a language minority, Native Americans also benefited from the 1975 amendments to the Voting Rights Act and the *Lau* decision, which established the right of Native Americans to be taught in their own languages. This marked quite a change from the boarding schools by the Bureau of Indian Affairs, where members of Native American tribes were forbidden to speak their own languages until reforms began in the 1930s. In addition to these language-related issues, Native Americans have sought to expand their rights on the basis of their sovereign status. Most significant in economic terms was a 1987 Supreme Court decision that freed Native American tribes from most state regulations prohibiting gambling. The establishment of casino gambling on Native American lands has brought a substantial flow of new income onto desperately poor reservations.

## Disabled Americans

The concept of rights for the disabled began to emerge in the 1970s as the civil rights model spread to other groups. The seed was planted in a little-noticed provision of the 1973 Rehabilitation Act, which outlawed discrimination against individuals on the basis of disabilities. As in many other cases, the law itself helped give rise to the movement demanding rights for the handicapped.[71] Inspired by the NAACP's use of a Legal Defense Fund, the disability movement founded a Disability Rights Education and Defense Fund to press its legal claims. The movement achieved its greatest success with the passage of the Americans with Disabilities Act (ADA) of 1990, which guarantees equal employment rights and access to public businesses for the disabled and prohibits discrimination in employment, housing, and health care. Claims of discrimination in violation of this act are considered by the EEOC. The impact of the law has been far-reaching, as businesses and public facilities have installed ramps, elevators, and other devices to meet the act's requirements.[72] In 1998 the Supreme Court interpreted the ADA to apply not only to people with AIDS but to those with HIV as well. The case arose when a dentist refused to fill a cavity for a woman with HIV unless the procedure were done in a hospital setting. The woman sued on the grounds that HIV had already disabled her because it was discouraging her from having children. Despite widespread concerns that the ADA was being applied too broadly and that costs were becoming too burdensome, corporate America did not seem to be disturbed by the Court's ruling. Stephen Bokat, general counsel of the U.S. Chamber of Commerce, said businesses in general had already been accommodating people with HIV as well as those with AIDS and that the case presented no serious problem.[73]

## Older Americans

The 1967 federal Age Discrimination in Employment Act (ADEA) makes age discrimination illegal when practiced by employers with at least 20 employees. Many states have added to the federal provisions with their own age discrimination laws, and some such state laws are stronger than the federal provisions. The major lobbyist for seniors, AARP, formerly the American Association of Retired Persons (see Chapter 11), with its claim to more than 30 million members, has been active in pushing for these laws and making sure that they are vigorously implemented. Rights for older workers received a setback, however, in a 2009 Supreme Court decision in the case of *Gross v. FBL Financial Services*.[74] The Court ruled that a 54-year-old employee who had challenged his demotion on the grounds of age discrimination would have to show that this action was a direct result of discrimination. This was a major change in the law: in the past, the burden of proof had been on employers to demonstrate that they had valid reasons other than age for demoting or terminating one of their employees.

## Gay Men and Lesbians

In less than 30 years, the lesbian, gay, bisexual, and transgender (LGBT) movement has become one of the largest civil rights movements in contemporary America. From its beginnings with the Stonewall Riots in New York City's Greenwich Village in 1969, the movement has grown into a sophisticated and well-financed lobby. The Human Rights Campaign is the primary national political action committee (PAC) focused on gay rights; it provides campaign financing and volunteers to work for political candidates endorsed by the group. The movement has also formed legal-rights organizations, including the Lambda Legal Defense and Education Fund.

Gay rights drew national attention in 1993, when President Bill Clinton confronted the question of whether gays should be allowed to serve in the military. As a candidate, Clinton had said he favored lifting the ban on homosexuals in the military. The issue set off a huge controversy in the first months of Clinton's presidency. After nearly a year of deliberation, the administration enunciated a compromise: its "Don't Ask, Don't Tell" policy allowed gay men and lesbians to serve in the military as long as they did not openly proclaim their sexual orientation or engage in homosexual activity. The administration maintained that the ruling would protect gay men and lesbians against witch hunt investigations, but many advocates of gay men and lesbians expressed disappointment, charging the president with reneging on his campaign promise. After nearly 20 years of challenges, President Obama signed an executive order repealing "Don't Ask, Don't Tell," and beginning in September 2011, gay men and lesbians could serve openly in the military.

But until 1996, there was no Supreme Court ruling or national legislation explicitly protecting gay men and lesbians from discrimination. In the first gay rights case it decided, *Bowers v. Hardwick*, the Court ruled against a right to privacy that would protect consensual homosexual activity.[75] After the *Bowers* decision, the gay rights movement sought suitable legal cases to test the constitutionality of discrimination against gay men and lesbians, much as the black civil rights movement had done in the late 1940s and '50s. As one advocate put it, "lesbians and gay men are looking for their *Brown v. Board of Education*."[76] Test cases stemmed from local ordinances restricting gay rights (including the right to marry), allowing job discrimination, and affecting family law issues such as adoption and parental rights. In 1996 the Supreme Court, in *Romer v. Evans*, explicitly extended fundamental civil rights protections to gay men and lesbians by declaring unconstitutional a 1992 amendment to the Colorado state constitution that prohibited local governments from passing ordinances to protect gay rights.[77] In its decision, the Court highlighted the connection between gay rights and civil rights.

In *Lawrence v. Texas* (2003), the Court overturned *Bowers* and struck down a Texas statute criminalizing certain intimate sexual conduct between consenting partners of the same sex.[78] A victory for gay men and lesbians every bit as significant as *Roe v. Wade* was for women, *Lawrence v. Texas* extends the right to privacy to sexual minorities. However, this decision does not undo the various exclusions that deprive gay men and lesbians of full civil rights, including the right to marry, which became a hot-button issue in the 1990s and remains one today. In 1993, Hawaii's supreme court declared the state's ban on same-sex marriage discriminatory, raising the possibility that such marriages could become legal. In Washington, D.C., the Republican congressional majority responded with the Defense of Marriage Act, which defined marriage as the union of a man and a woman for purposes of federal law and benefits, such as Social Security.

Although Hawaii's voters and its legislature eventually outlawed same-sex marriage, other states took up the issue. A significant victory came in 2004, when the Supreme Judicial Court of Massachusetts ruled that under that state's constitution, same-sex couples were entitled to marry. After that, 10 other states and the District of Columbia passed laws that allowed such couples to marry, including Maryland and Washington state, which passed laws approving same-sex marriage in 2012. Some of these laws, however, have faced challenges. In California, voters repealed the law five months after its passage, although lower courts subsequently declared the California vote as unconstitutional discrimination. In 2012 voters for the first time approved same-sex marriage at the ballot box, with measures winning a majority in Maine, Maryland, and Washington state. Voters in Minnesota blocked an effort to place a ban on same-sex marriage in the state constitution. Gay rights

*In 2008, California voters passed Proposition 8, which restricted marriage to couples consisting of a man and woman. Opponents of the proposition argued that same-sex couples should be treated equally under the law and allowed the right to marry.*

## for critical analysis

Political conflicts over same-sex marriage have been carried out in the courts, in state legislatures, in Congress, and in elections. What are some of the decisions that have been reached in each of these different decision-making arenas? Where should decision about same-sex marriage be made?

advocates won a significant victory of a different kind in national politics. New legislation extended the definition of hate crimes to include crimes against gay and transgender people. Such legislation had been sought since the 1998 murder of Matthew Shepard, a Wyoming college student who was brutally slain because of his sexual orientation. The new law allows for tougher penalties when a crime is designated a hate crime.

# Affirmative Action

> **Contrast arguments for and against affirmative action**

The politics of rights has spread to increasing numbers of groups in American society since the 1960s. The relatively narrow goal of equalizing opportunity by eliminating discriminatory barriers evolved into the far broader goal of **affirmative action**, compensatory action to overcome the consequences of past discrimination. Affirmative action policies take race or some other status into account in order to provide greater opportunities to groups that have previously been at a disadvantage due to discrimination.

**affirmative action** government policies or programs that seek to redress past injustices against specified groups by making special efforts to provide members of those groups with access to educational and employment opportunities

President Lyndon Johnson put the case emotionally in 1965: "You do not take a person who, for years, has been hobbled by chains . . . and then say you are free to compete with all the others, and still just believe that you have been completely fair."[79] Johnson issued executive orders directing agency heads and personnel officers vigorously to pursue a policy of minority employment in the federal civil service and in companies doing business with the national government. But affirmative action did not become a prominent goal of the national government until the 1970s.

Affirmative action also took the form of efforts by the agencies in the Department of Health, Education, and Welfare to shift their focus from "desegregation" to "integration."[80] Federal agencies, sometimes with court orders and sometimes without them, required school districts to present plans for busing children across district lines, for pairing schools, for closing certain schools, and for redistributing faculties as well as students, or face the loss of grants-in-aid from the federal government. The guidelines constituted preferential treatment to compensate for past discrimination, and without this legislatively assisted approach to integration, there would certainly not have been the dramatic increase in the number of black children attending integrated classes. The yellow school bus became a symbol of hope for many and defeat for others.

Affirmative action was also initiated in the area of employment opportunity. The EEOC has often required plans whereby employers must attempt to increase the number of their minority employees, and the Department of Labor's Office of Federal Contract Compliance Programs has used the threat of contract revocation for the same purpose. These programs did not require the use of formal quotas.

## The Supreme Court and the Burden of Proof

Efforts by the executive, legislative, and judicial branches to shape the meaning of affirmative action today tend to center on one key issue: What is the appropriate level of review in affirmative action cases—that is, on whom should the burden of proof be placed, the plaintiff or the defendant? Affirmative action was first addressed

## TABLE 5.3

## Supreme Court Rulings on Affirmative Action

| CASE | COURT RULING |
|---|---|
| *Regents of the University of California v. Bakke*, 438 U.S. 265 (1978) | Affirmative action upheld, but quotas and separate admission for minorities rejected; burden of proof on defendant |
| *Wards Cove v. Atonio*, 490 U.S. 642 (1989) | All affirmative action programs put in doubt: burden of proof shifted from defendant to plaintiff (victim), then burden of proof shifted back to employers (defendants) |
| *St. Mary's Honor Center v. Hicks*, 113 S. Ct. 2742 (1993) | Required victim to prove discrimination was intentional |
| *Adarand Constructors v. Peña*, 515 U.S. 200 (1995) | All race-conscious policies must survive "strict scrutiny," with burden of proof on government to show the program serves "compelling interest" to redress past discrimination |
| *Hopwood v. Texas*, 78 F3d 932 (5th Cir., 1996) | Race can *never* be used as a factor in admission, even to promote diversity (Supreme Court refusal to review limited application to the Fifth Circuit—Texas, Louisiana, Mississippi) |
| *Gratz v. Bollinger*, 123 S. Ct. 2411 (2003) | Rejection of a "mechanical" point system favoring minority applicants to University of Michigan as tantamount to a quota; *Bakke reaffirmed* |
| *Grutter v. Bollinger*, 123 S. Ct. 2325 (2003) | Upheld race-conscious admission to Michigan Law School, passing strict scrutiny with diversity as a "compelling" state interest, as long as admission was "highly individualized" and not "mechanical," as in *Gratz* |

formally by the Supreme Court in the case of Allan Bakke (see Table 5.3). Bakke, a white male, brought suit against the University of California at Davis Medical School on the grounds that, in denying him admission, the school had discriminated against him on the basis of his race. (That year, the school had reserved 16 of 100 available slots for minority applicants.) Bakke argued that his grades and test scores had ranked him well above many students who had been accepted at the school and that the only possible explanation for his rejection was that he was white, whereas those others accepted were black or Latino. In 1978, Bakke won his case before the Supreme Court and was admitted to the medical school, but the Court stopped short of declaring affirmative action unconstitutional. The Court rejected the procedures at the University of California because its medical school had used both a quota *and* a separate admissions system for minorities. The Court accepted the argument that achieving "a diverse student body" was a "compelling public purpose," but found that the method of a rigid quota of student slots assigned on the basis of race was incompatible with the Fourteenth Amendment's equal protection clause. Thus,

Allan Bakke sued the University of California at Davis Medical School after he was denied admission. The school had reserved 16 of 100 available slots for minority students. The Supreme Court ordered the school to admit Bakke, who is shown here on his first day of classes in 1978.

the Court permitted universities (and presumably other schools, training programs, and hiring authorities) to continue to take minority status into consideration, but severely limited the use of quotas to situations (1) in which previous discrimination had been shown, and (2) where quotas were used more as a guideline for social diversity than as a mathematically defined ratio.[81]

For nearly a decade after *Bakke*, the Supreme Court was tentative and permissive about efforts by universities, corporations, and governments to experiment with affirmative action programs.[82] But in 1989, with the case of *Wards Cove Packing Co. v. Atonio*, the Court backed away further from affirmative action by easing the way for employers to prefer white males, holding that the burden of proof of unlawful discrimination should be shifted from the defendant (the employer) to the plaintiff (the person claiming to be the victim of discrimination).[83] Congress responded with the Civil Rights Act of 1991, which shifted the burden of proof in employment discrimination cases back to employers.

In 1995 the Supreme Court's ruling in *Adarand Constructors v. Peña* further weakened affirmative action. This decision stated that race-based policies, such as preferences given by the government to minority contractors, must survive strict scrutiny, placing the burden on the government to show that such affirmative action programs serve a compelling government interest and are narrowly tailored to address identifiable past discrimination.[84] President Clinton responded to the *Adarand* decision by ordering a review of all government affirmative action policies and practices, and adopted an informal policy of trying to "mend, not end" affirmative action.

This betwixt-and-between status of affirmative action was how things stood in 2003, when the Supreme Court took two cases against the University of Michigan that were virtually certain to clarify, if not put closure on, affirmative action. The first suit, *Gratz v. Bollinger* (Lee Bollinger, the university president), challenged the University of Michigan's undergraduate admissions policy and practices, alleging that by using a point-based ranking system that automatically awarded 20 points (out of 150) to African American, Latino, and Native American applicants, the university discriminated unconstitutionally against white students of otherwise equal or superior academic qualifications. The Supreme Court agreed, 6–3, arguing that something tantamount to a quota was involved because undergraduate admissions lacked the necessary "individualized consideration" and had employed instead a "mechanical one," based too much on the favorable minority points.[85] The Court's ruling in *Gratz v. Bollinger* was not surprising, given *Bakke*'s (1978) holding against quotas and given recent decisions calling for strict scrutiny of all racial classifications, even those that are intended to remedy past discrimination or promote future equality.

The second case, *Grutter v. Bollinger*, broke new ground. Barbara Grutter sued the law school on the grounds that it had discriminated in a race-conscious way against white applicants with equal or superior grades and law boards. A precarious 5–4 decision for the first time aligned the majority of the Supreme Court with Justice Powell's lone plurality opinion in *Bakke*. Powell had argued that (1) diversity in education is a compelling state interest, and (2) race could be constitutionally considered as a plus factor in admissions decisions. In *Grutter*, the Court reiterated Powell's holding and, applying strict scrutiny to the law school's policy, found that the law school's admissions process was narrowly tailored to the school's compelling state interest in diversity because it gave a "highly individualized, holistic review of each applicant's file" in which race counted but was not used in a "mechanical" way.[86] The Court's ruling that racial categories can be deployed to serve a compelling state interest put affirmative action on stronger ground. But in 2012 the Court agreed to hear a case that might spell the end of affirmative action in higher education. In *Fisher v. University of Texas*, a white student challenged the use of race as one factor among many in the admissions decision.[87] Many observers believed that the Court's decision to hear the case suggested it was ready to revisit the Grutter decision.

## Referenda on Affirmative Action

The courts have not been the only center of action: during the 1990s, challenges to affirmative action also emerged in state and local politics. One of the most significant state actions was the passage by referendum in 1996 of the California Civil Rights Initiative, also known as Proposition 209. Proposition 209 outlawed affirmative action programs in the state and local governments of California, thus prohibiting those governments from using race or gender preferences in their decisions about hiring, contracting, or university admissions. Following a heated political battle, the measure passed with 54 percent of the vote, including 27 percent of the black vote, 30 percent of the Latino vote, and 45 percent of the Asian American vote.[88] In 1997 the Supreme Court refused to hear a challenge to the new law. Proposition 209 was framed as a civil rights initiative: "the state shall not discriminate against, or grant preferential treatment to, any individual or group on the basis of race, sex, color, ethnicity, or national origin."

Different wording can produce quite different outcomes. A 1997 ballot initiative asked Houston voters whether they wanted to ban affirmative action in city contracting and hiring, not whether they wanted to end preferential treatment. Fifty-five percent of Houston voters decided in favor of affirmative action.[89] In 2006, 58 percent of Michigan voters supported a measure, modeled after California's Proposition 209, to amend the state constitution by outlawing affirmative action in public education, contracting, and employment. Although University of Michigan officials initially declared that they would continue to use affirmative action criteria in the admissions process until all legal appeals were exhausted, in early 2007 the university announced

*The election of Barack Obama as the country's first black president raised questions about whether America's racial problems had been solved and whether policies such as affirmative action were still needed. Does the election of an African American as president mean we are closer to achieving racial equality?*

# Human Rights and International Politics

**When Barack Obama entered** office, many observers expected the United States to place a stronger emphasis on human rights in its international engagement. In some respects, the new administration has fulfilled those expectations, but in other ways, it has pursued international policies that some view as hostile to the goal of promoting human rights around the world.

In March 2009 the new administration signaled that it would engage international concerns about human rights when it sought and won a seat on the UN Human Rights Council. The Bush administration had refused to join the council on the grounds that the United Nations was biased and that the United States could better protect international human rights by remaining outside the council.

However, when it comes to foreign policy, the Obama administration has made it clear that advancing human rights is not its sole goal. Instead, the administration has balanced support for human rights with the recognition that the United States often has to work with countries that may violate those rights. For example, concerned with offending the Chinese president before their November 2009 meeting, Obama delayed a meeting with the Dalai Lama, who has long led resistance to Chinese rule in Tibet. This was in sharp contrast to the

approach taken by President George W. Bush, who presented the Dalai Lama with the Congressional Gold Medal. Both decisions were mainly symbolic. Bush wanted to send a message that the United States opposed violations of human rights in Tibet and elsewhere. Obama's decision was seen as part of a broader effort by the administration to cultivate Chinese support, an approach that has been called "strategic reassurance." On her visit to China soon after becoming secretary of state, Hillary Clinton suggested that concern for human rights should not "interfere with the global economic crisis, the global climate-change crisis, and the security crisis"—a reference to the U.S. desire for North Korean nuclear disarmament—all of which required the Chinese to work with the United States.[a]

The Obama administration's stance toward Myanmar (also known as Burma)

provides another example of its effort to balance human rights advocacy with foreign policy realism. Myanmar is ruled by a military junta that seized power almost five decades ago and has blocked democratic elections ever since. The United States long imposed sanctions on Myanmar for its failure to hold elections and for its continued imprisonment of opposition leaders, most notably Nobel Peace Prize–winner Aung San Suu Kyi. However, the Obama administration concluded that sanctions alone haven't worked. Therefore, in late September 2009, the administration announced that it would start talks with the country's military junta for the first time. At the same time, it declared that it would increase humanitarian assistance to the country. In response to Myanmar's return to civilian rule in 2010 and its implementation of some reforms, Hillary Clinton became the first American leader to visit Myanmar in more than 55 years. In 2012 after Myanmar had released hundreds of political prisoners, Washington restored diplomatic ties. Soon after the country held its first elections in two decades.

Striking the right balance between human rights and achieving America's other international interests is not simple. As the Obama administration seeks to advance America's interests in the world, it will have to determine how best to reconcile those interests with its support for international human rights.

[a]John Pomfret, "Obama's Meeting with the Dalai Lama Is Delayed," *Washington Post*, October 5, 2009, www.washingtonpost.com (accessed 10/24/09).

## for critical analysis

1. How has the Obama administration sought to balance support for human rights and the United States' international interests?

2. Are symbolic meetings, such as that with the Dalai Lama, important for advancing international human rights? Will better relations with Chinese leaders lead to stronger human rights in the long run or will they compromise the United States' ability to serve as a leader in this field?

that it would stop using affirmative action procedures in admissions. Buoyed by their success in Michigan, affirmative action opponents planned to place similar initiatives on the ballot in other states. However, in 2008 they succeeded in gaining sufficient signatures to bring the measure before voters only in Colorado, where the initiative failed to obtain voter approval, and Nebraska, where voters approved the measure.

## ● Thinking Critically about Civil Rights and Affirmative Action

The election of Barack Obama as the nation's first black president fueled discussions about whether America's racial problems had been solved. Polls taken just before Obama's inauguration revealed a sharp upturn in positive views about progress toward racial equality, but the euphoria about racial equality did not last for long. A Gallup poll in October 2009 revealed that broad attitudes about America's racial divisions remained remarkably stable. When asked whether they were hopeful that a solution to problems between blacks and whites would be worked out, 56 percent responded positively. This response was nearly identical to that in 1963, when 55 percent indicated that they were hopeful. After Obama's election, the proportion of those believing that racism against blacks was widespread dropped somewhat. Even so, in October 2009, nearly three-quarters of blacks and close to half of all whites continued to view racism against blacks as a widespread problem.[90]

Such beliefs indicate that the election of a black president will not make the debate about civil rights and affirmative action disappear, because Americans hold fundamentally different views about whether and how the government should recognize racial distinctions. At the risk of gross oversimplification, we can divide those with differing views into two groups, and label them liberals and conservatives.[91] Conservatives argue, first, that rights in the American tradition are *individual* rights, and affirmative action violates this concept by concerning itself with "group rights," an idea said to be alien to the American tradition. Second, conservatives argue that the Constitution is "color blind" and that any discrimination, even if it is called positive or benign, must inevitably rely on quotas and thus ultimately violate the equal protection clause.

Liberals agree that rights ultimately come down to individuals but argue that since the essence of discrimination is the unreasonable and unjust exclusion of *an entire group* from something valuable the society has to offer, discrimination itself has to be attacked on a group basis. Despite progress toward racial equality (see Table 5.4), liberals argue that race still matters. They can also cite Supreme Court history, because the first definitive interpretation of the Fourteenth Amendment by the Court, in 1873, stated that

> the existence of laws in the state where the newly emancipated Negroes resided, which discriminated with gross injustice and hardship against them *as a class*, was the evil to be remedied by this clause [emphasis added].[92]

As to the conservative argument concerning quotas, the liberal response is that the Supreme Court has already accepted ratios (a form of quota) that are admitted as evidence to prove a "pattern or practice of discrimination" sufficient to reverse the burden of proof—to obligate the employer to show that there was *not* an intent to discriminate. Further, benign quotas have often been used by Americans

TABLE 5.4

## Americans' Opinions on Racial Equality

"How much of a role, if any, do you think the government should have in trying to improve the social and economic position of blacks and other minority groups in this country: a major role, a minor role, or no role at all?"

| | MAJOR ROLE % | MINOR ROLE % | NO ROLE % | UNSURE % |
|---|---|---|---|---|
| All | 27 | 46 | 26 | 1 |
| Blacks | 59 | 32 | 8 | 1 |
| Whites | 19 | 50 | 30 | 1 |

SOURCE: USA Today/Gallup Poll, August 4–7, 2011, www.pollingreport.com/race.htm (accessed 6/23/12).

both to compensate for some bad action in the past or to provide some desired distribution of social characteristics—that is, diversity. For example, a long-respected policy in the United States is the "veterans' preference" by which the government automatically gives extra consideration in hiring to persons who have served in the country's armed forces. And the goal of social diversity has long justified "positive discrimination," especially in higher education—the very institution where conservatives have most adamantly argued against positive quotas for blacks and women. For example, all the Ivy League schools and many other private colleges and universities regularly and consistently reserve admissions places not only for students from minority groups but also for the children of loyal alumni and of their own faculty, even when, in a pure competition based solely on test scores and high school records, many of those same students would not have been admitted. These practices certainly underscore the liberal argument that affirmative or compensatory action for minorities is not alien to American experience.

If we think of the debate about affirmative action in terms of American political values, it is clear that conservatives emphasize liberty, whereas liberals stress equality. Conservatives believe that actively using government to promote equality for minorities and women infringes on the rights of white men. Lawsuits challenging affirmative action often cite this "reverse discrimination" as a justification. Liberals, on the other hand, traditionally have defended affirmative action as the best way to achieve equality. In recent years, however, the debate over affirmative action has become more complex and has divided liberals. One study of public opinion found that many self-identified liberals were angry about affirmative action, feeling that in the name of equality, affirmative action actually violates norms of fairness and equality of opportunity by giving special advantages to some.[93] Moreover, it is argued, affirmative action is broadly unpopular, making it questionable in terms of democratic values. Because our nation has a history of slavery and legalized racial discrimination, and because discrimination continues to exist (although it has declined), the question of racial justice, more than any other issue, highlights the difficulty of reconciling our values to our practice.

# Explore Civil Rights Online

## Inform Yourself

**Watch video of key moments in the struggle to end racial discrimination.** The Gettysburg Address in 1863, during the height of the Civil War, is considered a turning point in Americans' understanding of equality and freedom. Read the text of the speech at www.gettysburg.com/bog/address.htm. Next, watch a video of Martin Luther King Jr.'s famous "I Have a Dream" speech during the March on Washington at www.youtube.com/watch?v=1UV1fs8lAbg&feature=related, and consider how far the country had come since the Gettysburg address a century earlier. Finally, watch a video of Barack Obama's speech as he accepted the Democratic Party's nomination for president in 2008 (www.youtube.com/watch?v=tQGsP8mnHsg) and consider that, just 45 years after Martin Luther King Jr., an African American is president of the United States. Will African Americans achieve full equality with whites in the years to come?

**Learn about the women's suffrage movement.** The fight for equality in the political sphere was also a long one for women seeking the right to vote in elections, and continues today in the fight for policy representation and political influence in government. Visit the Library of Congress's photo collection of the women's suffrage movement (http://memory.loc.gov/ammem/vfwhtml/vfwhome.html).

**Hear an argument for LGBT rights.** Secretary of State Hillary Clinton released a video in 2011 stating that LGBT (lesbian, gay, bisexual, and transgender) individuals deserve equal rights, and that LGBT rights are human rights. Learn more about her argument by clicking the video link at www.state.gov/secretary/rm/2011/12/178368.htm.

## Connect with Others

**Connect with rights organizations.** The objective of the Leadership Conference, an organization with more than 200 subsidiary organizations, is "to promote and protect the civil and human rights of all persons in the United States." Go to its "Action Center" page (www.civilrights.org/action_center/action-center.html) and read through the current issues. Consider signing one of its online petitions to show your support for the issues relating to you.

*Find links to the sites listed above as well as related activities on wwnorton.com/studyspace.*

# study guide

## The Struggle for Civil Rights

■ **Trace the legal developments and social movements that expanded civil rights (pp. 157–76)**

Discrimination against individuals on the basis of their race and gender was tolerated and even enforced by government policy throughout much of American history. With the adoption of the Fourteenth Amendment in 1868, civil rights became a part of the Constitution. The political struggles of African Americans and women have narrowed the gap between Americans' belief in equality and the reality of life in the United States, but they have not eliminated it.

### Key Terms

**discrimination** (p. 157)

**civil rights** (p. 157)

**equal protection clause** (p. 157)

**Thirteenth Amendment** (p. 159)

**Fourteenth Amendment** (p. 159)

**Fifteenth Amendment** (p. 159)

**Jim Crow laws** (p. 160)

**"separate but equal" rule** (p. 161)

***Brown v. Board of Education*** (p. 164)

**strict scrutiny** (p. 165)

**de jure** (p. 165)

**de facto** (p. 165)

**gerrymandering** (p. 173)

**redlining** (p. 175)

### Practice Quiz

1. When did civil rights become part of the Constitution? *(p. 157)*
   a) in 1789 at the Founding
   b) with the adoption of the Fourteenth Amendment in 1868
   c) in 2008 when Barack Obama was elected president
   d) with the adoption of the Nineteenth Amendment in 1920
   e) in the 1954 *Brown v. Board of Education* case

2. Which of the following could be described as a Jim Crow law? *(p. 160)*
   a) a law forcing blacks and whites to ride on separate trains
   b) a law criminalizing interracial marriage

c) a law requiring blacks and whites to attend different schools
   d) a law segregating all public accommodations, such as hotels, restaurants, and theaters
   e) all of the above

3. Which civil rights case established the "separate but equal" rule? *(p. 161)*
   a) *Plessy v. Ferguson*
   b) *Grotter v. Bollinger*
   c) *Brown v. Board of Education*
   d) *Regents of the University of California v. Bakke*
   e) *Adarand Constructors v. Peña*

4. Which of the following organizations established a Legal Defense Fund to challenge segregation? *(p. 163)*
   a) the Association of American Trial Lawyers
   b) the National Association of Evangelicals
   c) the National Association for the Advancement of Colored People
   d) the Student Nonviolent Coordinating Committee
   e) the Southern Christian Leadership Council

5. The judicial test that places the burden of proof on government to show that a race-based policy serves a compelling government interest and is narrowly tailored to address identifiable past discrimination is called *(p. 165)*
   a) strict scrutiny.
   b) intermediate scrutiny.
   c) limited scrutiny.
   d) de facto segregation.
   e) de jure segregation.

6. "Massive resistance" refers to efforts by southern states during the late 1950s and early 1960s to *(p. 165)*
   a) build public housing for poor blacks.
   b) defy federal mandates to desegregate public schools.
   c) give women the right to have an abortion.
   d) bus black students to white schools.
   e) stage large-scale protests against Jim Crow laws.

7. Which of the following made discrimination by private employers and state governments illegal? *(pp. 168–69)*
   a) the Fourteenth Amendment
   b) the Fifteenth Amendment
   c) *Brown v. Board of Education*
   d) the 1964 Civil Rights Act
   e) *Regents of the University of California v. Bakke*

8. The Voting Rights Act of 1965 significantly extended and protected voting rights by doing which of the following? *(p. 172)*
   a) barring literacy tests as a condition for voting in six southern states
   b) requiring all voters to register two weeks before any federal election
   c) eliminating all federal-level registration requirements
   d) allowing voters to sue election officials for monetary damages in civil court
   e) all of the above

 **Practice Online**
Video exercise: *John F. Kennedy—Address on Civil Rights*

# Extending Civil Rights

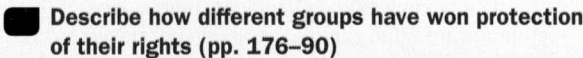 **Describe how different groups have won protection of their rights (pp. 176–90)**

In the 1970s the civil rights model created by African Americans began to spread beyond racial and ethnic groups to include groups defined by sex, religion, national origin, age, and sexual preference. For many of these groups, government polices played an important role in giving rise to movements that demanded equal treatment.

## Key Term

**intermediate scrutiny** (p. 178)

## Practice Quiz

9. In what way does the struggle for gender equality most resemble the struggle for racial equality? *(p. 180)*
   a) There has been very little political action in realizing the goal.
   b) Changes in government policies to a great degree produced political action.
   c) The Supreme Court has not ruled on the issue.
   d) The Constitution has not been invoked by proponents of the movement.
   e) No legislation has passed adopting the aims of the movement.

10. Which of the following is *not* an example of an area in which women have made progress since the 1970s in guaranteeing certain civil rights? *(pp. 176–80)*
    a) sexual harassment
    b) integration into all-male publicly supported universities
    c) more equal funding for college women's varsity athletic programs
    d) the passage of the Equal Rights Amendment
    e) None—these are all examples of areas in which women have made progress.

11. The Supreme Court's decision in *Mendez v. Westminster* was significant because it *(p. 181)*
    a) served as a precursor for *Brown v. Board of Education* by ruling that the segregation of Anglos and Mexican Americans into separate schools was unconstitutional.
    b) determined that anyone born in the United States was entitled to full citizenship.
    c) allowed school districts to achieve racial integration through busing.
    d) held that public accommodations could be segregated by race but still be equal.
    e) eliminated state power to use race as a criterion for discrimination in law.

12. Which of the following civil rights measures dealt with access to public businesses and accommodations? *(p. 187)*
    a) the 1990 Americans with Disabilities Act and the 1964 Civil Rights Act
    b) the 1964 Civil Rights Act only
    c) the 1990 Americans with Disabilities Act only
    d) the Equal Rights Amendment only
    e) the Equal Rights Amendment and the 1964 Civil Rights Act

13. Which of the following cases represents the *Brown v. Board of Education* case for lesbians and gay men? *(p. 189)*
    a) *Bowers v. Hardwick*
    b) *Lau v. Nichols*
    c) *Romer v. Evans*
    d) *Regents of the University of California v. Bakke*
    e) There has not been a Supreme Court ruling explicitly protecting gay men and lesbians from discrimination.

 **Practice Online**
"Get Involved" exercise: *Online Activism and Contemporary Civil Rights*

# Affirmative Action

■ **Contrast arguments for and against affirmative action (pp. 190–95)**

Affirmative action policies take race or some other status into account in order to provide greater educational and employment opportunities to groups that have been discriminated against. The Supreme Court has ruled that the government must show evidence that affirmative action programs serve a compelling government interest and are narrowly tailored to address identifiable past discrimination in order to be ruled constitutional. In recent years, challenges to affirmative action have also emerged at the state and local levels.

## Key Term

**affirmative action** (p. 190)

## Practice Quiz

14. In what case did the Supreme Court find that rigid quotas are incompatible with the equal protection clause of the Fourteenth Amendment? *(p. 191)*
    a) *Regents of the University of California v. Bakke*
    b) *Korematsu v. United States*
    c) *Brown v. Board of Education*
    d) *United States v. Nixon*
    e) *Immigration and Naturalization Service v. Chadha*

15. The Supreme Court's decision in *Grutter v. Bollinger* was significant because *(p. 193)*
    a) it stated that race can never be used as a factor in university admissions.
    b) it stated that diversity is a compelling state interest and that university admissions that take racial categorized into account are constitutional as long as they are highly individualized.
    c) it outlawed quotas and separate university admission standards for members of minority groups.
    d) it rejected mechanical point systems that favor minority applicants in university admissions.
    e) it declared that affirmative action policies would no longer be subject to strict scrutiny from the courts.

 **Practice Online**
"You Decide" exercise: *Affirmative Action*

# For Further Reading

Chen, Anthony S. *The Fifth Freedom: Jobs, Politics, and Civil Rights in the United States, 1941–1972.* Princeton, NJ: Princeton University Press, 2009.

Garrow, David J. *Bearing the Cross: Martin Luther King and the Southern Christian Leadership Conference: A Personal Portrait.* New York: Morrow, 1986.

Greenberg, Jack. *Crusaders in the Courts: How a Dedicated Band of Lawyers Fought for the Civil Rights Revolution.* New York: Basic Books, 1994.

Katznelson, Ira. *When Affirmative Action Was White: The Untold Story of Racial Inequality in Twentieth-Century America.* New York: W.W. Norton, 2006.

Klinkner, Philip A., with Rogers M. Smith. *The Unsteady March: The Rise and Decline of Racial Equality in America.* Chicago: University of Chicago Press, 1999.

McClain, Paula D., and Joseph Stewart Jr. *"Can We All Get Along?" Racial Minorities in American Politics.* 4th ed. Boulder, CO: Westview Press, 2005.

Mink, Gwendolyn. *Hostile Environment: The Political Betrayal of Sexually Harassed Women.* Ithaca, NY: Cornell University Press, 2000.

Nava, Michael. *Created Equal: Why Gay Rights Matter to America.* New York: St. Martin's, 1994.

Rosales, Francisco. *Chicano! The History of the Mexican American Civil Rights Movement.* Houston: Arte Público Press, 1997.

Rosenberg, Gerald N. *The Hollow Hope: Can Courts Bring About Social Change?* Chicago: University of Chicago Press, 1991.

Russell, Nancy. *Freedom Is Not Enough: The Opening of the American Workplace.* Cambridge, MA: Harvard University Press, 2006.

Valelly, Richard. *The Voting Rights Act.* Washington, DC: CQ Press, 2005.

# Recommended Websites

**ADA Home Page**
www.ada.gov

The Americans with Disabilities Act (ADA), enacted in 1990, guarantees equal employment rights and access to public businesses for the physically disabled. The U.S. Department of Justice maintains this website, which offers general information on ADA standards, changes in regulation, and policy enforcement.

**The Martin Luther King, Jr., Research and Education Institute**
http://mlk-kpp01.stanford.edu

Dr. Martin Luther King Jr. was a key leader in the fight for civil rights and desegregation. At this website you can find Dr. King's important speeches and papers, as well as other information about social injustice.

**Equal Employment Opportunity Commission (EEOC)**
www.eeoc.gov

This website provides information on the federal agency and current employment laws. At this site you can even find out how someone might file a harassment or discrimination charge against an employer.

**Equality Now**
www.equalitynow.org

This is an organization dedicated to ending gender discrimination around the world. Read about how this group is fighting for the rights of women in Africa or campaigning against female genital mutilation and sex trafficking.

**Federal Bureau of Investigation**
www.fbi.gov/hq/cid/civilrights/hate.htm

Civil rights violations fall under the jurisdiction of the Federal Bureau of Investigation. Find out what steps the FBI is taking to combat the problem of hate crimes and view some comprehensive statistical data.

**Human Rights Campaign (HRC)**
www.hrc.org

**Gay and Lesbian Alliance against Defamation (GLAAD)**
www.glaad.org

These two prominent interest groups are dedicated to equal rights for lesbians and gay men and ending gender discrimination.

**League of United Latin American Citizens (LULAC)**
www.lulac.org

LULAC has worked to stem discrimination against Mexican Americans since World War II and is now the largest and oldest Hispanic organization in the United States. See what this group is doing to guarantee racial equality based on the Fourteenth Amendment's equal protection clause.

**Mexican American Legal Defense and Education Fund (MALDEF)**
www.maldef.org

MALDEF is the leading nonprofit Latino litigation, advocacy, and educational outreach institution in the United States. At this site, you will learn about litigation and other activities that MALDEF has initiated related to the rights of Latinos and of immigrants more generally.

**NAACP**
www.naacp.org

The NAACP is one of the oldest and largest civil rights organizations that is dedicated to equal rights and putting an end to racial discrimination. This group was particularly influential in the landmark case *Brown v. Board of Education,* which led to the desegregation of public schools.

**National Organization for Women**
www.now.org

**Feminist Majority Foundation**
www.feminist.org

These leading women's rights groups continue to fight for gender equality and equal rights.

**U.S. Commission on Civil Rights**
www.usccr.gov

The U.S. Commission on Civil Rights was created by Congress in the late 1950s and continues to investigate complaints of discrimination in American society.

**U.S. Supreme Court Media**
www.oyez.org

This website has a good search engine for finding information on such landmark civil rights cases as *Plessy v. Ferguson, Brown v. Board of Education, Lawrence v. Texas,* and *United States v. Wong Kim Ark*, to name only a few.

How closely should the government follow public opinion? Public opinion is sometimes sharply divided over policies or even over the role of government. In other cases, citizens seem to lack the political knowledge necessary for informed opinions. These circumstances can make it difficult for lawmakers to follow the will of the people.

# Public Opinion

**WHAT GOVERNMENT DOES AND WHY IT MATTERS** The "consent of the governed"—demanded in the Declaration of Independence—is critical for the functioning of a democracy. We expect the government to pay attention to public opinion, and research has shown that public opinion does indeed have a significant impact on public policy, especially foreign policy.[1] However, many Americans have very little knowledge about government, and their opinions about what government should do are often shifting and inconsistent.

More than halfway through Barack Obama's first presidential term, nearly one in five Americans believed he was a Muslim or had been born outside the United States and thus, as a noncitizen, was ineligible for the presidency. Among Republicans, those doubting the president's citizenship numbered more than two in five.[2] This belief persisted even as the verified details of Obama's personal life were widely available and included ample evidence of his American citizenship. To counter the widespread misperception, the White House eventually posted to the Internet a photograph of President Obama's "long-form" birth certificate, showing that he was born in a hospital in Honolulu, Hawaii, on August 4, 1961, at 7:24 P.M.[3] In over two centuries since the Founding, a sitting president had never before been forced to prove his citizenship publicly. Why did this happen? If public opinion did not matter, why would President Obama have released his birth certificate?

In 2008, as many as 40 percent of voters said they were unsure when asked about Obama's religion. Before Obama was elected president, about 12 percent of Americans believed he was a Muslim, when in fact he and his family are practicing Christians.[4] To be sure, Hussein, Obama's middle name, is a common name in Muslim countries. Obama's unusual background (Kenyan black father; American white mother; raised in Indonesia, Kansas, and Hawaii) was highlighted by both his supporters and opponents. But why did the misperception that he was a Muslim or noncitizen *increase* among some groups after he became president? We would expect that as Americans learned more about Obama over time, these misperceptions would decrease.

In the decade following the September 11, 2001, terrorist attacks and the beginning of the Iraq War in 2003, anti-Muslim sentiment in the United States grew substantially.[5] During the 2008 election some of Obama's opponents waged a media attack insinuating that he had ties to the Muslim community. For example, photographs of Obama with his extended family in Indonesia, some wearing turbans, were widely circulated online. Political scientist Tali Mendelberg has found that nonverbal campaign messages (such as the photos in this case) can be used to exploit discriminatory attitudes among the public.[6] From a base of uncertainty laid by this media campaign, misperceptions of Obama's religion grew.

Are people who believe that Obama was not born in the United States or is a Muslim simply ill-informed, despite the substantial media coverage of the facts? Research shows that facts do not mean much to those who believe that Obama is not American.[7] This disregard of evidence is not unique to those who dislike Obama. Individuals often ignore or discount new information that goes against their feelings about an individual or issue.[8] Emotions in part color how we process information about politics. Moreover, studies have shown that Americans have little interest in politics and political information. Can we have government by the people if the people are not well informed?

## chaptergoals

- Define public opinion and identify broad types of values and beliefs Americans have about politics (pages 205–19)

- Explain the major factors that shape specific individual opinions (pages 219–28)

- Describe basic survey methods and other techniques researchers use to measure public opinion (pages 228–41)

- Analyze the relationship between public opinion and government policies (pages 241–43)

# ● Defining Public Opinion

Define public opinion and identify broad types of values and beliefs Americans have about politics

The term **public opinion** is used to denote the attitudes that people have about issues, events, elected officials, and, of course, politics and policy. It is useful to distinguish between values and beliefs on the one hand and attitudes and opinions on the other. **Values (or beliefs)** constitute a person's basic orientation to politics. Values underlie deep-rooted goals, aspirations, and ideals that shape an individual's perceptions of political issues and events. Liberty, democracy, and equality of opportunity, for example, are basic political values held by most Americans. Another useful term for understanding public opinion is *ideology*. **Political ideology** refers to a complex set of beliefs and values that, as a whole, form a general philosophy about government.

For example, many Americans believe that governmental solutions to problems are inherently inferior to solutions offered by the private sector. The Tea Party movement, for example, advocates private-sector solutions to the problems that face society. Such a general belief may, in turn, lead individuals to form negative views of specific government programs even before they know much about them. An **attitude (or opinion)** is a specific view about a particular issue, person, or event. An individual may have an attitude toward American policy in Iraq or an opinion about Barack Obama's citizenship. The attitude or opinion may have emerged from a broad belief about military intervention or about Democrats, but the opinion itself is very specific. Some attitudes may be short-lived and can change based on changing circumstances or new information.

When we think of public opinion, we often think in terms of differences of opinion. The media are fond of reporting political differences between Democrats and Republicans, blacks and whites, men and women, the young and the old, and so on. Certainly Americans differ on many issues, and often these differences do seem to be associated with race, religion, gender, age, or other social characteristics. For example, opinion polls show that roughly half of Americans sympathize with

**public opinion** citizens' attitudes about political issues, leaders, institutions, and events

**values (or beliefs)** basic principles that shape a person's opinions about political issues and events

**political ideology** a cohesive set of beliefs that forms a general philosophy about the role of government

**attitude (or opinion)** a specific preference on a particular issue

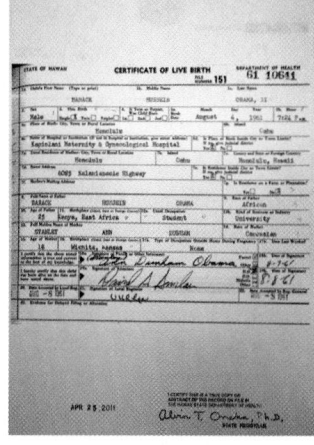

*Attitudes may change over time based on new information, but many Americans who doubted President Obama's U.S. citizenship did not change their views even as ample evidence of his citizenship became available. Finally, the White House published the president's "long-form" birth certificate.*

the Tea Party movement and half with the Occupy Wall Street movement. Those who support the Wall Street protestors have very different beliefs regarding the cause of the poor economy (the banks and elected officials are held captive by corporate interests) from those of people supporting the Tea Party (government regulation is strangling the private sector, preventing an economic rebound). While both Occupy Wall Street and the Tea Party are populist economic movements, they have very different underlying opinions, attitudes, and ideologies about the economy and government.

Differences of political opinion are often associated with income, education, and occupation. Similarly, factors such as race, gender, ethnicity, age, religion, and region—which not only influence individuals' interests but also shape their experiences and upbringing—have enormous influence on their beliefs and opinions. For example, individuals whose incomes differ substantially have correspondingly different views on the desirability of any number of important economic and social programs. In general, the poor, who are the chief beneficiaries of these programs, support them more strongly than do those who are wealthier and pay more of the taxes that fund the programs. Religious individuals are much more likely to oppose allowing gays and lesbians to wed than citizens who do not regularly attend church. Blacks and whites have different views on issues that touch upon civil rights and race relations (such as affirmative action)—presumably reflecting differences of interest and historical experience. In recent years, many observers have begun to take note of various differences between the views expressed by men and those expressed by women, especially on foreign policy questions, where women appear to be much more concerned with the dangers of war. Political attitudes are also strongly influenced by partisanship (Republican versus Democrat; see Chapter 9) and ideology (conservative versus liberal).

Today there is a renewed understanding that opinions about issues and politics have emotional underpinnings as well.[9] Emotional responses to candidates or policies run the gamut from strongly positive to strongly negative, and these emotions are traditionally measured by survey questions asking if a candidate (or individual, event, or issue) makes the respondent feel fearful, anxious, hopeful, or enthusiastic. Contrary to the idea that public opinion is purely rational, feelings are complicated and often irrational; once individuals become emotionally attached to particular beliefs, they tend to hold on to them even in the face of contradictory information. Using emotions as a guide, individuals will form opinions quickly in response to current events.[10]

## Political Values

Most Americans share a common set of values, including a belief in the principles, if not always the actual practice, of liberty, equality, and democracy. The United States was founded on the principle of individual **liberty**. Americans have always voiced strong support for the idea of liberty, and typically support the notion that governmental interference with individuals' lives and property should be kept to a minimum. (Although, in recent years, Americans have grown accustomed to greater levels of governmental intervention than would have been deemed acceptable by the founders of liberal theory.) Liberty was highlighted in Republican Ron Paul's campaign for president in 2012.

Concerns about liberty have increased since the September 11 terrorist attacks, with the Patriot Act and policies adopted under President George W. Bush. In 2012, President Obama signed into law the National Defense Authorization Act

**liberty** freedom from governmental control

*Most Americans share certain basic political values, including a belief in equality of opportunity. For example, most people believe that all individuals should be allowed to pursue success based on their own efforts and abilities—and not on their social background.*

(NDAA), which was overwhelmingly approved by Congress. Under the law, even an American citizen on U.S. soil can be held in military prison indefinitely without charge or a trial. Proponents contend that the law is necessary to prevent another terrorist attack on the United States. Critics, such as the American Civil Liberties Union (ACLU), argue the law is unconstitutional, in that it violates the rights of the accused to a trial and can be used to militarily detain people captured far from a battlefield.[11] Concerns about due process are rooted in the value of liberty.

Similarly, **equality of opportunity** has always been an important theme in American society. Most Americans believe that all individuals should be allowed to seek personal and material success. Moreover, Americans generally believe that such success should be the result of individual effort and ability, rather than family connections or other forms of special privilege. Quality public education is one of the most important mechanisms for obtaining equality of opportunity in that it allows individuals, regardless of personal or family wealth, a chance to get ahead. Today, Internet access is emerging as an important form of equality of opportunity by providing online access to news, politics, jobs, the economy, health care, and other benefits of digital citizenship.[12] Economic opportunity, defined as a good job and a decent standard of living, is a core value in American politics.

Most Americans also believe in **democracy**. They presume that every person should have the opportunity to take part in the nation's governmental and policy-making processes and to have some say in determining how they are governed, including the right to vote in elections.[13] (See Chapter 8 for a discussion of rules affecting voting in elections.) Figure 6.1 shows there is consensus among Americans on fundamental values: for instance, 88 percent believe the government should support equality of opportunity with public policy, and 71 percent believe government censorship is a bigger threat than illegal downloading.

Obviously, the principles that Americans espouse have not always been put into practice. For 200 years, Americans embraced the principles of equality of opportunity and individual liberty while denying them in practice to generations of African Americans. Yet the strength of the principles ultimately helped overcome practices that deviated from those principles. This is echoed in speeches by President Lincoln leading up to the Civil War. Proponents of slavery and, later, of segregation

**equality of opportunity** a widely shared American ideal that all people should have the freedom to use whatever talents and wealth they have to reach their fullest potential

**democracy** a system of rule that permits citizens to play a significant part in the governmental process, usually through the election of key public officials

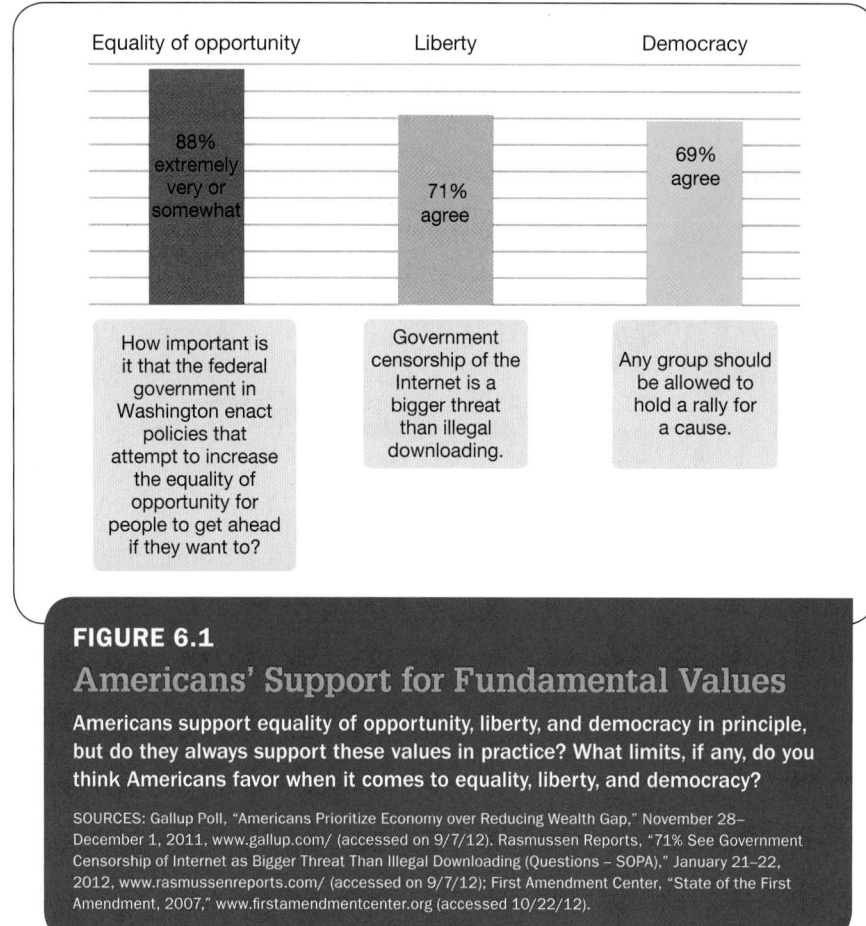

Equality of opportunity | Liberty | Democracy

88% extremely very or somewhat

71% agree

69% agree

How important is it that the federal government in Washington enact policies that attempt to increase the equality of opportunity for people to get ahead if they want to?

Government censorship of the Internet is a bigger threat than illegal downloading.

Any group should be allowed to hold a rally for a cause.

**FIGURE 6.1**

## Americans' Support for Fundamental Values

Americans support equality of opportunity, liberty, and democracy in principle, but do they always support these values in practice? What limits, if any, do you think Americans favor when it comes to equality, liberty, and democracy?

SOURCES: Gallup Poll, "Americans Prioritize Economy over Reducing Wealth Gap," November 28–December 1, 2011, www.gallup.com/ (accessed on 9/7/12). Rasmussen Reports, "71% See Government Censorship of Internet as Bigger Threat Than Illegal Downloading (Questions – SOPA)," January 21–22, 2012, www.rasmussenreports.com/ (accessed on 9/7/12); First Amendment Center, "State of the First Amendment, 2007," www.firstamendmentcenter.org (accessed 10/22/12).

were defeated in the arena of public opinion because their practices differed so sharply from the fundamental principles accepted by most Americans.

Yet even when there is broad agreement over principles, practical *interpretations* of principles can differ. For example, in contemporary politics Americans' fundamental commitment to equality of opportunity has led to divisions over racial policy, with both proponents and opponents of affirmative action programs citing their belief in equality of opportunity as the justification for their position. Proponents of these programs see them as necessary to ensure equality of opportunity, whereas opponents believe that affirmative action is a form of preferential treatment that violates basic American values.[14]

## Political Socialization and Public Opinion

People's attitudes about political issues and elected officials tend to be shaped by their underlying political beliefs and values. For example, an individual who has negative feelings about government intervention into America's economy and society would probably be predisposed to oppose the development of new social and health care programs. Similarly, someone who distrusts the military would likely be suspicious of any call for the use of U.S. troops. The processes through which these underlying political beliefs and values are formed are collectively called **political socialization**.

**political socialization** the induction of individuals into the political culture; learning the underlying beliefs and values on which the political system is based

Probably no nation, and certainly no democracy, could survive if its citizens did not share some fundamental beliefs. If Americans had few common values or perspectives, it would be very difficult for them to reach agreement on particular issues. In contemporary America, some elements of the socialization process tend to produce differences in outlook, whereas others promote similarities. Four of the most important **agents of socialization** that foster differences in political perspectives are the family and social networks, membership in social groups, education, and political environment.

Of course, no brief list of the agents of socialization can fully explain the development of a given individual's basic political beliefs. In addition to the factors that are important for everyone, experiences and influences that are unique to each individual also play a role in shaping political orientation. An early encounter with a single member of another racial group, for example, can have a lasting impact on an individual's view of the entire group. A highly salient political event, such as the Vietnam War or September 11, can leave an indelible mark on a person's political consciousness. And some deep-seated personality characteristic, such as paranoia, may strongly influence the formation of someone's political beliefs. One recent experiment revealed that individuals displaying measurably higher physiological reactions to sudden noises and threatening visual images were more likely to favor defense spending, capital punishment, patriotism, and the Iraq War. That is, people who are more fearful appear to support policies that protect the existing social structure from both external and internal threats.[15] Nevertheless, even if we cannot fully explain the development of any given individual's political outlook, let us look at some of the most important agencies of socialization that do affect one's beliefs.

**The Family and Social Networks** Most people acquire their initial orientation to politics from their families. As might be expected, differences in family background tend to produce divergent political perspectives. Although relatively few parents spend much time directly teaching their children about politics, political conversations occur in many households, and children tend to absorb the political views of parents and other caregivers, often without realizing it. Studies find, for example, that party preferences are initially acquired at home. Children raised in households in which the primary caregivers are Democrats tend to become Democrats, whereas children raised in homes where their caregivers are Republicans tend to favor the Republican Party.[16] Similarly, children reared in politically liberal households are more likely than not to develop a liberal outlook, whereas children raised in politically conservative settings are likely to see the world through conservative lenses. (Obviously not all children absorb their parents' political views. Two of the late conservative Republican president Ronald Reagan's three children, for instance, rejected their parents' conservative values and became active on behalf of Democratic candidates.) Moreover, even those children whose views are initially shaped by parental values may change their minds as they mature and experience political life for themselves.

Nevertheless, family, friends, coworkers, and neighbors are an important source of political orientation for nearly everyone. Political scientist Betsy Sinclair argues that people are "social citizens" whose political opinion and behavior are significantly shaped by peer influence.[17] Sinclair shows that social networks can and do have the power to change public opinion, including the decision to declare oneself a Democrat or

**agents of socialization** social institutions, including families and schools, that help to shape individuals' basic political beliefs and values

*The terrorist attacks of September 11, 2001, certainly influenced public opinion in the months immediately following the attacks and likely also had a long-term effect on many Americans' basic political beliefs.*

a Republican. When members of a social network express a particular political opinion or belief, Sinclair finds, others notice and conform, particularly if their conformity is likely to be highly visible. The conclusion is that basic political acts are surprisingly subject to social pressures. Online social networks such as Facebook and Twitter likely increase the role of peers in shaping public opinion.

**Social Groups** Another important source of political values are the social groups to which individuals belong. Social groups include those to which individuals belong involuntarily (national, religious, gender, and racial groups, for example) as well as those they join willingly (political parties, labor unions, the military, and environmental, educational, and occupational groups).

Membership in a particular group can give individuals experiences and perspectives that shape their view of political and social life. In American society, for example, the experiences of blacks and whites can differ significantly. Blacks are a minority and have been victims of persecution and discrimination throughout American history. Blacks and whites also have different educational and occupational opportunities, often live in separate communities, and may attend separate schools. Such differences tend to produce distinctive political outlooks. For example, blacks and whites differ considerably in their perceptions of the extent of racism in America (see Figure 6.2). Indeed, according to a CNN poll, 47 percent of white respondents thought racism fairly or very common, while almost half (49 percent) thought it was rare in the United States, according to a survey. Among African Americans, on the other hand, fully 86 percent thought racism was common and only 12 percent said it was rare, almost a 40 point difference between blacks and whites.[18] Interestingly, Hispanic Americans, who have also been victims of racism in the United States, are less likely than African Americans to see America as a racist society; in a 2008 survey, 52 percent of Hispanic Americans and 55 percent of white Americans said that race relations in the United States were generally good. Only 29 percent of black Americans agreed.[19]

Men and women have important differences of opinion as well. Reflecting differences in social roles and occupational patterns, women tend to oppose military intervention more than men, are more likely than men to favor policies to protect the environment, and are more likely to support government social and health care programs (see Table 6.1). Perhaps because of these differences on issues, women are more likely than men to vote for Democratic candidates. This tendency of men's and women's opinions to differ is known as the **gender gap**.

**gender gap** a distinctive pattern of voting behavior reflecting the differences in views between women and men

**Party Affiliation** Political party membership—that is, voluntary membership of a social group—is one of the most important factors affecting political orientation.[20] We can think of partisanship as red-tinted or blue-tinted glasses that color public opinion on a vast array of issues. Partisans tend to rely on party leaders and the media for cues on the appropriate positions to take on major political issues.[21] Walter Lippmann, an influential political commentator of the mid-twentieth century, argued that public opinion is but an echo of elite positions on policy issues, and many others studying public opinion agree.

In recent years, partisan realignment in the South and congressional redistricting have reduced the number of conservative Democrats and all but eliminated liberal Republicans from the Congress and from positions of prominence in the party. As a result, the leadership of the Republican Party has become increasingly conservative, whereas that of the Democratic Party has become somewhat more liberal. Polarization among party leaders has been reflected in the views of party adherents

## RACE RELATIONS IN THE UNITED STATES

### Racism is a very serious problem.

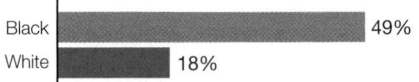

Black 49%
White 18%

### Percentages who think only a few white people dislike blacks, many white people dislike blacks, or just about all white people dislike blacks.

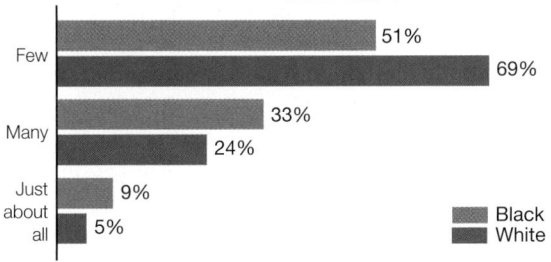

Few 51%
69%

Many 33%
24%

Just about all 9%
5%

■ Black
■ White

## EDUCATIONAL OPPORTUNITY

### Do black children have as good a chance as white children to get a good education?

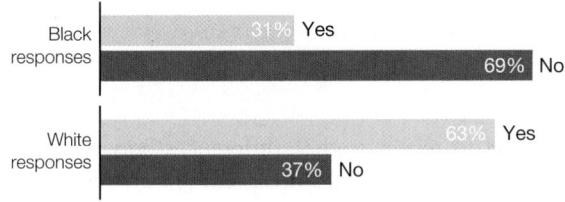

Black responses 31% Yes
69% No

White responses 63% Yes
37% No

## TREATMENT BLACKS RECEIVE

### Discrimination against blacks is rare today.

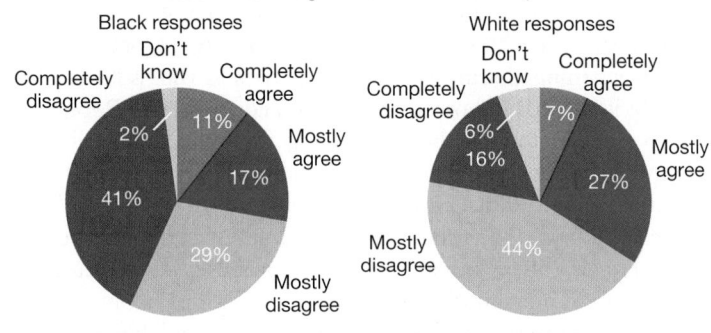

Black responses
Don't know
Completely disagree
Completely agree
2%
11%
Mostly agree
41%
17%
29%
Mostly disagree

White responses
Don't know
Completely disagree
Completely agree
6%
7%
16%
Mostly agree
27%
44%
Mostly disagree

### Percent who favor affirmative action programs.

Blacks 93%
Whites 65%

**FIGURE 6.2**

## Disagreement among Blacks and Whites

In the United States, racial and ethnic groups may not perceive race relations in precisely the same way. How, according to the data in this figure, do blacks and whites differ in their views on race relations? Which group is more likely to think that race relations are good? What factors help to account for these differences in perception?

SOURCES: CNN, www.cnn.com; Gallup, Inc., www.gallup.com; and Pew Research Center Publications, http://pewresearch.org (accessed 4/1/08).

## TABLE 6.1

## Disagreements among Men and Women on National Security Issues

For the most part, fewer women than men favor the use of military force as an instrument of foreign policy. Is this pattern reflected consistently in the data? What might explain gender differences in this realm?

| GOVERNMENT ACTION | PERCENTAGE APPROVING OF ACTION | |
| --- | --- | --- |
| | MEN | WOMEN |
| Agree that torture of terrorism suspects is acceptable | 50 | 31 |
| Favor withdrawing troops from Iraq within a year | 43 | 55 |
| Agree that NSA surveillance program is needed | 60 | 50 |
| Oppose sending more troops to Iraq | 52 | 69 |
| Favor cutting off funding for Iraq War | 48 | 57 |
| Believe United States should send more troops to Afghanistan (2009) | 49 | 36 |

SOURCES: ABC, 2009; *Ms.*, 2006; UPI/Zogby, 2007; *USA Today*, 2007; *Washington* Post/ABC, 2007; CBS, 2009.

and the general public. According to recent studies, differences between Democratic and Republican partisans on a variety of political and policy questions are greater today than during any other period for which data are available. On issues of national security, for example, Republicans have become very "hawkish," whereas Democrats have become quite "dovish." In an October 2003 survey, 85 percent of Republicans but only 39 percent of Democrats thought that America's war against Iraq was a good idea.[22] Gaps on social and economic issues are just as broad. Some refer to the ever-widening chasm between the parties as the "politics of extremism." An example is the 2011 showdown between congressional Republicans and Democrats as to whether to raise the debt ceiling. Republicans initially refused to raise the amount the federal government could borrow, which would have caused the government to default on its loans and prevent it from operating.[23] The "debt ceiling fiasco" led to a lowering of the federal government's credit rating (so it pays a higher interest rate to borrow money), but a compromise was eventually reached and the government did not shut down.

Despite the rift between the "red" (Republican-leaning) and "blue" (Democratic-leaning) states that seems deeper than ever, political scientist Morris Fiorina and colleagues refute the common belief that Americans are deeply divided in their fundamental political views, showing that on a broad range of issues, ranging from homosexuality to abortion, most Americans hold moderate opinions.[24] While political elites and members of Congress may be highly polarized, there is general agreement among most Americans—even on those issues thought to be most divisive. Fiorina and colleagues argue that relatively small differences are often magnified by the rhetoric used to present policy issues. For example, survey data showed that the average opinions of self-identified liberals and conservatives regarding abortion differ only regarding the specific conditions under which they think abortion should be legal, not the legality of abortion in general (which is generally accepted). Overall, in fact, the so-called culture war appears to be between polarized political parties and their activists, with the mass public in the middle being forced to choose between them. Fiorina and colleagues' study suggests that America divides itself because we have little choice when presented with highly divided political parties and elected officials. (See Chapter 9 on why we have a two-party system.) However, contemporary debates over abortion and birth control that emerged in the 2012 Republican presidential primaries may further widen the gap between liberals and conservatives over social issues. As of 2012, 53 percent of Americans believe abortion should be legal in all or most cases, and 41 percent say that abortion should be illegal in all or most cases.[25]

**Other Social Groups** Other kinds of social affiliations affect individuals' political attitudes. Different religions, for example, provide unique historical experiences and philosophical perspectives that lead their members to see the world in different ways. And social groups can affect individuals' political orientations through the direct efforts of the groups themselves to influence their members. Environmental groups may shape the opinions of their members on issues ranging from public open space and recycling to the wisdom of producing energy from wind power. Labor unions often use meetings, rallies, and literature to shape their members' understanding of politics and to make them more amenable to supporting the political positions favored by union leaders. Women's groups, minority groups, religious groups, and the like often endeavor to structure their members' political views through intensive educational programs. Women who belong to women's organizations, for example, are likely to differ from men in their political views to a greater extent than women without such affiliations.[26] Some analysts have found that African Americans who belong to black organizations are likely to differ more from whites in their political orientations than are blacks who don't belong to such organizations.[27]

**Self-Interest and Public Opinion** Another way that membership in social groups can affect political beliefs is through what might be called objective political interests. On many economic issues, for example, the interests of the rich and the poor differ significantly. Inevitably, these differences in interests will produce differences in political outlook. The framers of the Constitution thought that the inherent gulf between the rich and the poor would always be the most important source of conflict in political life. More recently, the Occupy Wall Street protesters have decried the chasm between the 99 percent of income earners and the top 1 percent. Struggles over welfare, minimum wage, job creation, health care policy, Social Security, the bailout of the banks, and so forth are fueled by differences in interest between wealthier and poorer Americans. Latinos consider the issue of immigration to be significantly more important than non-Latinos, while African Americans are more supportive of affirmative action programs than non-blacks. Difference in public opinion on these issues is influenced by group self-interest.

However, some researchers find little evidence that economic self-interest has much effect on public opinion, and most people don't translate broad concerns about inequality or their own economic self-interest into specific policy preferences.[28] The public, both rich and poor, is far from demanding redistribution, for example, and has actually become more conservative even as economic inequality in the United States has increased over the past two decades.[29] Political scientist Larry Bartels found that when asked if the income difference between the rich and poor had changed

*Is there a culture war between the "red" states of "middle America" and the liberal "blue" states? The television program* King of the Hill *took a more nuanced perspective on middle American values, showing that most individuals are less rigid and extreme in their opinions than party leaders. Recent political science research supports this view.*

*During the Vietnam War era, public opinion was sharply divided over the war and numerous other issues. Anti–Vietnam War protestors staged passionate demonstrations.*

in recent decades, nearly 75 percent of the Americans asked believed that the difference had increased.[30] Of those who stated that the gap between the rich and the poor had grown, over half said that this was a "bad thing." Only 5 percent of the respondents thought it was a "good thing"; the rest said they had not thought about whether rising inequality was good or bad. Despite this concern about inequality, two-thirds of Americans favored the 2000 federal tax cuts supported by President George W. Bush, even though the tax disproportionately benefited the very wealthy, and would therefore likely increase economic inequality. The poor, middle class, and affluent alike favored the tax cuts. Bartels concludes that the public does not seem able to translate a concern for economic self-interest into policy preferences that would benefit average citizens.

Differences in interest also exist among the generations, not just among economic classes. Senior citizens and younger Americans have very different views on such diverse issues as the war on drugs, Social Security, and criminal justice. The young, for example, are much more accepting of allowing same-sex couples to marry legally than are those who are older. And in recent decades major differences in opinion and political orientation have developed between American civilians and members of the armed services. Military officers, in particular, are far more conservative in their domestic and foreign policy views than the public at large and are heavily Republican in their political leanings.[31] Support for the Republican Party among military officers climbed sharply during the 1980s and '90s, decades in which the GOP championed large military budgets.

Nevertheless, group membership can never fully explain a given individual's political views. One's unique personality and life experiences may produce political views very different from those of the group to which one might nominally belong. Some African Americans are conservative Republicans, and the occasional wealthy businessperson is also very liberal. Group membership is conducive to particular outlooks, but it is not determinative.

**Education** After family and social groups, education can be a third important source of differences in political perspectives. Indeed, education may be the great equalizer. Governments use public education to try to teach all children a common set of civic values; it is mainly in school that Americans acquire their basic belief in liberty, equality, and democracy. In history classes, students are taught that the Founders fought for the principle of liberty. In the course of studying such topics as the Constitution, the Civil War, and the civil rights movement, students are taught the importance of equality. Research finds education to be a strong predictor of tolerance for racial minorities.[32] Through participation in class elections and student government, students are taught the virtues of democracy. These lessons are repeated in every grade, and in a variety of contexts. It is no wonder they constitute such an important element in Americans' beliefs.

At the same time, differences in formal education are strongly associated with differences in political outlook. In particular, those who attend college are often exposed to modes of thought that will distinguish them from their friends and neighbors who do not pursue college diplomas. One of the major differences between college graduates and other Americans can be seen in levels of political participation. Table 6.2 outlines some general differences of opinion found between college graduates and other Americans. College graduates vote, join campaigns, take part in protests, and generally make their voices heard.[33]

**TABLE 6.2**

## Education and Public Opinion

The figures show the percentage of respondents in each category who agree with the statement. Are college graduates generally more or less liberal than other Americans? Which data support your claim? Can you think of economic or political explanations for these findings?

| | PERCENTAGE WHO AGREE, BY EDUCATION LEVEL | | | |
|---|---|---|---|---|
| ISSUE | GRADE SCHOOL | HIGH SCHOOL | SOME COLLEGE | COLLEGE GRADUATE |
| Women and men should have equal roles. | 38 | 75 | 83 | 86 |
| Abortion should never be allowed. | 21 | 10 | 7 | 4 |
| The government should adopt national health insurance. | 35 | 47 | 42 | 49 |
| The United States should not concern itself with other nations' problems. | 45 | 26 | 20 | 8 |
| Government should see to fair treatment in jobs for African Americans. | 49 | 28 | 30 | 45 |
| Government should provide fewer services to reduce government spending. | 8 | 17 | 19 | 27 |

SOURCE: The American National Election Studies, 2004 data, provided by the Inter-University Consortium for Political and Social Research, University of Michigan.

**Political Environment** A fourth set of factors that shape political attitudes and values are the conditions under which individuals and groups are recruited into and become involved in political life. Although political beliefs are influenced by family background and group membership, the content and character of these views is, to a large extent, determined by political circumstances. For example, the baby-boom generation that came of age in the 1960s was exposed to both the Vietnam War itself and also widespread antiwar protests on college campuses and in urban areas throughout the nation. This experience fundamentally shaped the opinions of this age cohort, just as September 11 and the war on terrorism helped shape the political lives of those who came of age in the 1990s and 2000s.

Similarly, the views held by members of a particular group can shift drastically over time, as political circumstances change. For example, American white southerners were staunch members of the Democratic Party from the Civil War through the 1960s. As Democrats, they became key supporters of liberal New Deal and post–New Deal social programs that greatly expanded the size and power of the American national government. The 1960s mark the beginning of the South's move from the Democratic to the Republican camp—mainly because of white southern opposition to the Democratic Party's integrationist racial policies and because of determined Republican efforts to win white southern support. Since the 1960s a majority of southern whites has shifted to the Republican Party. Now southern whites provide a solid base of support for efforts to scale back social programs and sharply reduce the size and power of the national government—hence the popularity of the Tea Party movement in the South.[34] It was not a change in the character of white southerners but a change in the political environment in which they found themselves that induced this major shift in partisanship in the South.

Another example of partisan realignment due to an evolving political environment can be seen in the West. California's Republican governor in the 1970s, Ronald Reagan, went on in the 1980s to become one of the most admired Republican presidents, ushering in the tax revolt and regulating many government policies. But since the 1990s, California, once a Republican stronghold, has become solidly Democratic. Some argue that the realignment began with a series of ballot measures targeting racial and ethnic minorities endorsed by the Republican Party in the 1990s, including immigration, affirmative action, and bilingual education. These ballot measures triggered a backlash, especially among Latinos, who had previously voted in very low numbers. In the 1990s, registration and voting by Latinos increased dramatically, and favored Democratic political candidates. With Latinos and blacks combined making up more than 50 percent of California's population, this demographic environmental change moved California to a solid Democratic state.[35]

In sum, public opinion cannot be inferred simply from the character of groups or the political climate of an era. Any group's political outlooks and orientations are shaped by the political circumstances in which that group finds itself, and those outlooks can change as circumstances change. The generation of American students now coming of political age after the September 11 terrorist attacks will have a very different view of the use of American military power from that of their parents—members of a generation that reached political consciousness during the 1960s, when opposition to the Vietnam War and military conscription was, for many, a defining political stance.

## Political Ideology

As we have seen, people's beliefs about government can vary widely. But for some individuals, a set of beliefs can fit together into a coherent philosophy about government. The set of underlying orientations, ideas, and beliefs through which we come to understand and interpret politics is called a *political ideology*. Ideologies take many different forms. Some people may view politics primarily in religious terms. During the course of European political history, for example, Protestantism and Catholicism were often political ideologies as much as they were religious creeds. Each set of beliefs included not only elements of religious practice but also distinct ideas about secular authority and political action. Other people may see politics through a racial lens. In mid-twentieth-century Germany, Nazi ideology placed race at the center of political life and sought to interpret politics in terms of racial categories.

In America today, a variety of ideologies compete for attention and support. **Libertarianism**, for example, argues that government is wasteful and interferes with free markets and society, and so it should be limited to as few spheres of activity as possible. In 2012, Republican presidential candidate Ron Paul, a staunch libertarian, gained support among many young voters for his opposition to foreign wars and his support of civil liberties and smaller government. While Libertarians believe in less government intervention in economic and social realms, **socialists**, on the other hand, argue that more government is necessary to promote justice and to reduce economic and social inequality. Although many Americans subscribe to libertarianism, socialism, and other ideologies in part, most Americans describe themselves as either liberals or conservatives, or some shade of the two. Like the political ideologies already described, liberalism and conservatism comprise beliefs about the role of the government, preferences regarding specific public policies, and ideas about which groups in society should exercise power and how they should do so (see Boxes 6.1 and 6.2).

The definitions of both *liberal* and *conservative* have changed over time. To some extent, contemporary liberalism and conser-

**libertarianism** a political ideology that emphasizes freedom and voluntary association with small government

**socialism** a political ideology that emphasizes social ownership or collective government ownership and strong government

*Although liberalism and conservatism are the most common political ideologies in the United States today, other ideologies, such as libertarianism, offer different perspectives on the role of government, policy issues, and society. For example, libertarians advocate a smaller role for government, less involvement overseas, and more freedom for businesses.*

vatism can be seen as differences in emphasis with regard to the fundamental American political values of liberty and equality. For liberals, equality is the most important of the core values. Liberals encourage government action in such areas as college admissions and business practices to enhance race, class, and gender equality, or in terms of social programs and redistributive taxation that promote equality. For conservatives, on the other hand, liberty is the core value. Conservatives oppose many efforts of the government, however well intentioned, to interfere in private life and the marketplace.

**Liberalism** In classical political theory, a **liberal** was someone who favored individual initiative and was suspicious of the motives of government and of its ability to manage economic and social affairs—a definition akin to that of today's libertarian. Liberals saw government as a foe of freedom. The proponents of a larger and more active government, on the other hand, called themselves progressives. In the early twentieth century, though, many liberals and progressives coalesced around the doctrine of "social liberalism," which represented recognition that government action might be needed to preserve individual liberty. Today's liberals are social liberals rather than classical liberals.

In contemporary politics being a liberal has come to imply supporting political and social reform, government intervention in the economy, the expansion of federal social services and health care, more vigorous efforts on behalf of the poor and minorities, and greater concern for consumers and the environment. Liberals generally support abortion rights and rights for gay men and lesbians, and are concerned with protecting the rights of people accused of crimes. Liberals oppose state involvement in religious institutions and state sanction of religious expression. In international affairs, liberals often support arms control, aid to poor nations, and international organizations such as the United Nations and the European Union; liberals generally oppose the development and testing of nuclear weapons, and the use of American troops to influence the affairs of developing nations. Many liberals are opposed to military wars. Under the broad umbrella of liberalism, some liberals have a specific focus: Occupy Wall Street groups, for instance, demonstrate for greater economic equality, and environmentalists view global warming and other ecological threats as the most important issues facing humanity today.

**liberal** today this term refers to those who generally support social and political reform; extensive governmental intervention in the economy; the expansion of federal social services; more vigorous efforts on behalf of the poor, minorities, and women; and greater concern for consumers and the environment

## BOX 6.1

## Profile of a Liberal: Representative Nancy Pelosi

- Supports abortion rights and birth control.
- Opposes prayer in the public schools.
- Supports affirmative action.
- Supports same-sex marriage.
- Favors expanded health coverage for all Americans.
- Advocates increased funding for education.
- Supports further increases in the minimum wage.

## Profile of a Conservative: House Speaker John Boehner

- Wants to trim the size of the federal government.
- Wants to diminish government regulation of business.
- Favors prayer in the public schools.
- Opposes gay rights legislation.
- Favors making most abortions illegal.
- Supports harsher treatment of criminals.
- Opposes many affirmative action programs.
- Favors tax cuts.

**conservative** today this term refers to those who generally support the social and economic status quo and are suspicious of efforts to introduce new political formulae and economic arrangements. Conservatives believe that a large and powerful government poses a threat to citizens' freedom

**Conservatism**  By contrast, **conservatives** believe strongly that a large and powerful government poses a threat to the freedom of individual citizens. Ironically, today's conservatives espouse the views of classical liberalism. Premodern conservatives were the defenders of monarchy and aristocracy—doctrines that seem completely antiquated today. Today, in the domestic arena, conservatives generally oppose the expansion of governmental activity, asserting that solutions to social and economic problems can and should be developed in the private sector. Conservatives particularly oppose efforts to impose government regulation on business, maintaining that regulation frequently leads to economic inefficiency, is costly, and can ultimately lower the entire nation's standard of living. In terms of social policy, many conservatives support school prayer and traditional family arrangements, and are concerned about law and order; conservatives generally oppose abortion, same-sex marriage, and the use of mandatory school busing to achieve the racial integration of schools. In international affairs, conservatism has come to mean support for military intervention and the maintenance of American military power.

**Mixing Ideologies**  Both liberalism and conservatism are far from monolithic ideologies, and most Americans consider themselves moderates, with shades of liberal or conservative values. Figure 6.3 shows that the percentage of Americans who consider themselves moderates has declined slightly since 2008, but overall Americans' ideology has been fairly stable. Many conservatives support at least some government social programs. Republican president George W. Bush called himself a "compassionate conservative," to indicate that he favored programs that assist the poor and needy. Other conservatives dismissed Bush as a "big government" Republican, and therefore not a true conservative. Many staunch conservatives joined the rising Tea Party movement in 2009 to protest President Obama's efforts to expand the role of the federal government, especially in health care. And while President Obama is liberal in supporting health care reform and other social programs, he has been criticized by those on the left for extending the tax policies of his Republican predecessor, Bush, which benefited the affluent, and for expanding U.S. military involvement in Afghanistan and other countries. In short, some

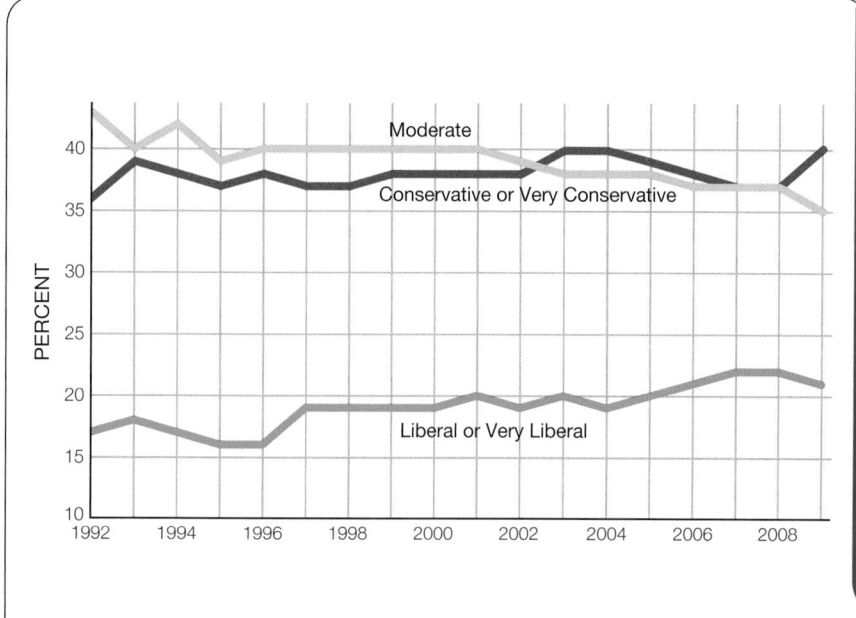

**Americans' Ideology, 1972–2012**

Over the past two decades, more Americans have identified themselves as "conservatives" than "liberals." During this same period, however, Americans have elected two Democratic presidents and have, several times, elected Democratic majorities in Congress. What might account for this apparent discrepancy between ideology and partisanship?

SOURCE: Gallup Poll, "Conservatives Remain the Largest Ideological Group in U.S." January 12, 2012, www.gallup.com/poll/152021/conservatives-remain-largest-ideological-group.aspx (accessed 9/7/12).

of Obama's economic and foreign policies are associated with conservatives, and some with liberals. The real political world is far too complex to be seen simply in terms of a struggle between liberals and conservatives.

Sometimes political ideologies provide little guidance in a crisis. At the root of the financial collapse in 2008 was a sudden collapse in real estate values and an accompanying breakdown in the home mortgage system, one that has been blamed for wiping out much of the wealth of American families. The ensuing bailout of the home mortgage industry, including the federally backed mortgage institutions Freddie Mac and Fannie Mae, is estimated to have cost taxpayers hundreds of billions of dollars.[36] In October 2008 many conservatives in Congress, and some liberals, voted against the Bush administration's emergency plan to address the nation's financial crisis because they opposed the partial government takeover of banks and other financial institutions as a massive government intervention in the nation's economy; they believed that even the risk of a catastrophic financial meltdown did not justify the expansion of government power in the marketplace, or the high cost to taxpayers. Some conservatives, though, strongly favored actions designed to rescue American capitalism in a time of crisis. Reducing the national debt, creating jobs, improving the economy, and keeping American safe are "valence principles"—that is, unifying because they are deemed important by conservatives and liberals alike.

# How We Form Political Opinions

**Explain the major factors that shape specific individual opinions**

Few individuals possess ideologies so cohesive that they will automatically shape all their opinions. Most people have at least some conflicting underlying attitudes. Most conservatives support some federal programs—defense, national security, or tax deductions for businesses, for example—and wish to see them, and hence the government, expanded. Many liberals favor American military intervention in other nations for what they deem to be humanitarian purposes but generally oppose American military intervention in the affairs of other nations. For most individuals, attitudes on specific issues are not shaped by ideological predispositions. Let's explore what we know about how public opinion is formed.

One of the most important studies of public opinion is by political scientist John Zaller, who argues that the public relies on elite cues, or bits of information from the media and political leaders, when forming opinions about complex policies.[37] Opinions on survey questions are often derived from the individual's feeling on the issue at the time the question is asked. Individuals form opinions from the most recent news or media coverage they have remembered, responding to survey questions with whatever information happens to be at the "top of the head," which is mentally sampled when an individual is asked to take a stance on an issue. Responses to questions about policy positions are based largely on the way survey questions are asked. The answer to a question about a specific policy is usually determined by the framing of the question, or by relevant events being discussed by political elites and mass media at that time. Opinions are often unreliable, primarily because these elite sources provide competing information, causing public opinion polls to measure whatever recent elite message (or media story) an individual has stored in his or her short-term memory. One should thus expect a fair amount of variability in people's responses to survey questions.

Zaller's work tells us that most people don't hold consistent opinions for every policy issue. Individuals are often ambivalent or have many different opinions about most issues. Zaller suggests that more general aspects of political awareness—best proxied with political knowledge—are critical for shaping public opinion. Political knowledge is what allows individuals to connect underlying attitudes with opinions on politics and policy. But other research has shown that individuals are quite stable and rational in their policy attitude formation. Individuals do not just guess about their policy preferences on foreign policy issues, for example, but tend to have fairly constrained and structured attitudes.[38]

## Political Knowledge and Public Opinion

What best explains whether citizens are generally consistent in their political views or inconsistent and open to the influence of others? In general, knowledgeable citizens are better able to evaluate new information and determine if it is relevant to and consistent with their beliefs and opinions.[39] As a result, better-informed individuals can recognize their political interests and act consistently to further those interests. But political knowledge is generally low in America.[40]

Using public opinion surveys, political scientist Adam Berinsky has found that certain segments of the population may lack sufficient knowledge of public policy to give informed opinions. When asked about preferences toward social welfare policy, disadvantaged groups are more likely than any other group to abstain from giving answers—mainly due to the lack of politically relevant information available to those with few resources. This not only leads to a potential underreporting of support for welfare policy among the poor, but also limits the political voice of those who are most likely to support social welfare policies.[41]

This raises the question of how much political knowledge is necessary for one to act as an effective citizen. In an important study of political knowledge in the United States, the political scientists Michael X. Delli Carpini and Scott Keeter found that

# How Americans View the World and Vice Versa

**When they are not being accused** of seeking to conquer the world, Americans are often charged with failing to pay enough attention to international affairs. It is true that many Americans lack a basic knowledge of world history and geography and have considerable difficulty naming the leaders of other nations. Several surveys have indicated that some Americans think Canada is one of the 50 states.

Nevertheless, Americans do have strong opinions about which foreign nations are America's friends in the world and which are its foes. Topping the list of friends is Great Britain, seen by 74 percent of recent poll respondents as a "close ally." Curiously, 2 percent of those surveyed viewed Britain as an enemy. Perhaps they have not forgotten King George's mistreatment of the colonists in 1775. When it comes to China, now one of America's most important trading partners, only 9 percent of Americans believe China is a close ally, whereas 54 percent think China is not friendly or even is America's enemy. It is interesting to note also that France, traditionally an American ally, came to be viewed less favorably than Russia, America's Cold War adversary, in the wake of vocal French opposition to America's Middle East policy.

Just as Americans have opinions about the world, citizens of other nations have their own opinions about America. Americans sometimes complain that their efforts on behalf of other nations are not properly appreciated and feel envied and disliked by the rest of the world. Only Kenyan, Nigerian, and Filipino respondents to a recent survey had an overwhelmingly positive view of America. Even normally friendly Europeans seem to have developed a negative view of the United States.

During the American occupation of Iraq, antagonism toward American foreign policy has hardened even more in most Muslim countries. An overwhelming majority of those polled in the Middle East expressed strongly anti-American senti-

ment. The enduring popularity of Osama bin Laden in these countries also reinforces Muslim attitudes generally toward the United States. Worldwide, a majority of people believed that the United States' war on terror is actually an attempt to control the Middle East's oil or to dominate the world. The Bush administration's foreign policies earned few converts abroad and lost support at home as well.

## for critical analysis

1. What are the factors shaping the ways Americans view other nations and how others view America?

2. Should Americans care about how they are seen around the world? Why or why not?

the average American exhibits little knowledge of political institutions, processes, leaders, or policy debates.[42] Many Americans cannot even name their own congressional representatives. Does this ignorance of key political facts matter? Delli Carpini and Keeter also found that political knowledge is not evenly distributed throughout the population. Those with higher education, income, and occupational status, and who are members of social or political organizations, are more likely to know about and be active in politics. As a result, individuals with a disproportionate share of income and education also have a disproportionate share of knowledge and influence and thus are better able to get what they want from government.

Presidential elections provide ample illustration of the relationship between political knowledge and public opinion. Despite the obvious fact that most Republicans prefer Republican candidates and most Democrats prefer Democratic candidates (see Chapter 9 for a discussion of party identification), some voters are swayed by the information they receive during a campaign. During the 2008 presidential campaign, for instance, voters weighed the arguments of Barack Obama against those of John McCain to determine who was more qualified to oversee the U.S. economy. Many independents and Republican voters turned to Obama because they held the GOP responsible for the nation's financial crisis and found Obama's economic proposals more credible than McCain's. In the 2012 presidential campaign, both candidates campaigned aggressively on their ability to improve the nation's economy. In exit polls, voters said the economy was the most important issue in the election. The polls found that voters were evenly divided as to whether they blamed Obama or his predecessor, George W. Bush, for the poor economic conditions. In this close presidential race, Obama was re-elected with the highest unemployment rate since Franklin Delano Roosevelt.[43]

Latino voters provide another example. Republican president George W. Bush made a concerted effort to attract Latino voters, and was rewarded with about 40 percent of the Latino vote in the 2004 elections. Latino support helped Bush win battleground

*Members of various social groups may see political issues in different ways. After a racially-charged incident in 2009 involving Harvard professor Henry Louis Gates Jr. (second from left) and police officer James Crowley (second from right), President Obama tried to address the tensions surrounding the incident by bringing the two men together for a "beer summit" at the White House.*

states such as Colorado, Florida, Nevada, and New Mexico, which all have large Latino electorates. In the 2012 election, Republican presidential candidate Romney had the support of only 3 in 10 Latinos, in part due to his opposition to immigration and his promise to repeal the Patient Protection and Affordable Care Act.[44] Romney's harsh rhetoric on these subjects did not resonate with this large and growing minority population. In a June 2011 Latinos Decisions tracking poll, three-quarters of Latinos want the president to "stop deporting immigrants who are married to U.S. citizens and have families here in the U.S. and two-thirds of Latino voters support executive orders to stop the deportation of youth who would be eligible for the Dream Act" (Development, Relief, and Education for Alien Minors).[45] Obama took a step in this direction with an Executive Order implementing parts of the Dream Act in 2012. Clearly, Latinos have a high level of political knowledge about the issue of immigration, and the president's policies may shape their voting behavior in the 2012 elections.

**Shortcuts and Cues** Because being informed politically requires a substantial investment of time and energy, most Americans seek to acquire political information and to make political decisions "on the cheap" by making use of shortcuts for political evaluation and decision making rather than engaging in a lengthy process of information gathering. Researchers have found that the public relies on cues and heuristics (problem-solving strategies) from party elites and the media to aid in attitude formation.[46] Other "inexpensive" ways to become informed involve taking cues from trusted friends, relatives, colleagues, and perhaps religious leaders. Political scientists Richard Lau and David Redlawsk argue that most public opinion is formed by taking cues from trusted political elites: elected officials, the media, and interest groups.[47] By means of these informational shortcuts, average citizens can form political opinions that are, in most instances, consistent with their underlying preferences. They call this "voting correctly." Results find that even individuals with low levels of political knowledge are able to make relatively informed political choices by relying on these voter cues. It is generally accepted by scholars in political science that people are cognitive misers and rely on shortcuts in forming public opinion on politics and public policy.[48]

Even the best-informed citizens often assess new issues and events through the lens of their more general beliefs and orientations, and sometimes the outcome is less than optimal. Partisanship and general ideological orientations can often be poor guides to decision making. For example, few Americans read the details of the health care reform proposals debated in the House and Senate in 2009, and instead took their cues from politicians whose views, they assumed, were similar to their own. Yet many liberals who took their cues from President Obama might have preferred no bill at all to a bill without the "public option"—a comprehensive, nationalized system of financing health care coverage—which the president agreed to drop. And many conservatives who took their cues from House and Senate Republican leaders might have found much to like in the legislation these same politicians castigated. Surveys have consistently shown strong public approval of ideas such as maintaining health care coverage for young adults on their parents' insurance, and prohibiting insurance companies from denying coverage due to "preexisting conditions"—ideas contained in the bill that eventually became law.

**Costs to Democracy?** If political scientists are correct in their findings that so many citizens base their opinions (and votes) on inadequate knowledge and an overreliance on cues from political elites, this raises a critical question: If political

*In 2012 the billionaire Warren Buffett argued that is was not right that he—one of the richest people in the world—paid a lower tax rate than his secretary, Debbie Bosanek (pictured here). However, many Americans may not understand how changes in the tax code will affect them.*

knowledge is necessary for effective citizenship, how does a general lack of such knowledge affect the way we govern ourselves?

Although understandable and, perhaps, inevitable, low levels of political knowledge and engagement weaken American democracy in two ways. First, those who lack political information cannot effectively defend their own political interests and can easily become losers in political struggles. The presence of large numbers of politically inattentive or ignorant individuals means that political power can more easily be manipulated by political elites, the media, and wealthy special interests that seek to shape public opinion.

Second, if knowledge is power, then a lack of knowledge can contribute to growing political and economic inequality. When individuals are unaware of their interests or how to pursue them, it is virtually certain that political outcomes will not favor them. One of the most important areas of government policy is taxation. America has the largest gap between the super rich and the poor than any other nation in the world. But rather than raise taxes, over the past several decades, the United States has substantially reduced the rate of taxation levied on its wealthiest citizens. Most recently, tax cuts signed into law by George W. Bush in 2001, and extended by President Obama in 2010, provided a substantial tax break mainly for the top 1 percent of the nation's wage earners. Political scientist Larry Bartels shows that, surprisingly, most Americans favored the tax cuts, including millions of middle- and lower-middle-class citizens who did not stand to benefit from the tax policy. Additionally, 40 percent of Americans had no opinion at all regarding the Bush tax cuts. The explanation for this odd state of affairs appears to be a lack of political knowledge. Millions of individuals who were unlikely to derive benefit from President Bush's tax policy thought they would. Since most Americans think they pay too much in taxes, they favored the policy, even if the wealthy benefited much more than the middle class.

Bartels has employed the cartoon character Homer Simpson to explain how people don't realize what is in their economic interest: Homer wants a tax cut, and even if he gets only $1 and Mr. Burns, his boss, takes $1,000, Homer still wants his dollar in savings.[49] Homer is a fool to want his dollar in tax savings: the overall lost tax revenues, collected mainly from the wealthy, would have funded programs that benefit middle-class taxpayers like Homer. Upper-bracket taxpayers, who are more informed and knowledgeable, are more likely to see to it that their economic self-interest aligns with government policy—and vice versa. This example illustrates that basic political knowledge matters in American politics.

## The Media, Government, and Public Opinion

When individuals attempt to form opinions about particular political issues, events, and personalities, they seldom do so in isolation. Typically, they are confronted with—sometimes bombarded by—the efforts of a host of individuals and groups seeking to persuade them to adopt a particular point of view. In the approach to the 2012 presidential election, someone trying to decide what to think about Barack Obama or Mitt Romney could hardly avoid an avalanche of opinions expressed through the media, in meetings, or in conversations with friends. The **marketplace of ideas** is the interplay of opinions and views that takes place as competing forces attempt to persuade as many people as possible to accept a particular position on a particular issue. Given this constant exposure to the ideas of others, it is virtually impossible for most individuals to resist some modification of their own beliefs. Three forces that play important roles in shaping opinions in the marketplace are the government, private groups, and the news media.[50]

**marketplace of ideas** the public forum in which beliefs and ideas are exchanged and compete

**Government and the Shaping of Public Opinion** All governments try to influence, manipulate, or manage their citizens' beliefs. But the extent to which public opinion is actually affected by governmental public relations can be limited. Often, governmental claims are disputed by the media, by interest groups, and at times even by opposing forces within the government itself.

This hasn't stopped modern presidents from focusing a great deal of attention on shaping public opinion to boost support for their policy agendas. Franklin Delano Roosevelt promoted his policy agenda directly to the American people through his famous "fireside chats" radio broadcasts. A hallmark of the Clinton administration was the employment of techniques such as those used in election campaigns to bolster popular enthusiasm for White House initiatives. The president established a political "war room" similar to the one that operated in his campaign headquarters, where representatives from all departments met daily to discuss and coordinate the president's public-relations efforts. Many of the same consultants and pollsters who had directed the successful Clinton election campaign then became employed in the selling of the president's programs.[51]

The George W. Bush administration developed an extensive public-relations program to bolster popular support for the president's policies. Working with the conservative TV personality Mary Matalin, the White House worked to maintain popular support for the administration's war against terrorism. These efforts included presidential speeches, media appearances by administration officials, numerous press conferences, and thousands of press releases presenting the administration's views.[52] Using the runway of an aircraft carrier as his stage, a confident Commander in Chief Bush, dressed in military fatigues, proclaimed the end of the Iraq War. His statement was premature by nearly half a decade, but it effectively maintained public support for the Iraq War effort. His speech proved hollow compared to President Reagan's command that Mikhail Gorbachev "tear down this wall!" (referring to the Berlin Wall)—a tearing down that actually occurred—dramatically calling an end to the Cold War.

Like its predecessors, the Obama administration has sought to shape public opinion in the United States and abroad, relying upon the power of the president's oratorical skills to build support for his administration's initiatives in domestic and foreign policy. But Obama's White House is unique in using social media to promote the president's policy agenda. President Obama has been as theatrical as Bush and Reagan, but largely through the digital media. In spring 2012, Barack Obama's Facebook page had 26 million "likes" and counting, compared to 1.7 million fans for his 2012 challenger, Romney.[53] Hourly posts on Facebook promote his policies, campaign, and serve to personalize the president. In one of the most humanizing publicly available photographs in the history of the American presidency, a young boy touches the hair of Obama, who has bowed down to accommodate the child's request to see what his hair feels like. The photograph hangs in the White House and was widely shared online and via social media. Obama's adept use of e-mail, Twitter, Facebook, online videos, and other methods helped to solidify his re-election in 2012.

**Private Groups and the Shaping of Public Opinion** The ideas that become prominent in political life are developed and spread not only by government officials but also by important economic and political groups searching for issues that will advance their causes. One especially notable example is the abortion issue, which has inflamed American politics over the past 30 years. The notion of a fetal "right to life," whose proponents seek to outlaw abortion and overturn the Supreme Court's 1973 *Roe v. Wade* decision, was developed by conservative politicians who saw the issue of abortion as a means of uniting Catholic and Protestant conservatives and linking both groups to the Republican Party.[54] To advance their cause, leaders of the right-to-life movement sponsored well-publicized Senate hearings at which testimony, photographs, and other exhibits were presented to illustrate the violent results of abortion procedures. At the same time, publicists for the movement produced leaflets, articles, books, and films such as *The Silent Scream* to highlight the agony and pain ostensibly felt by the "unborn" when they were being aborted. All this underscored the movement's claim that abortion was nothing more or less than the murder of more than a million innocent human beings annually in the United States. Finally, Catholic and evangelical Protestant religious leaders were organized to denounce abortion from their church pulpits and, increasingly, from their electronic pulpits on the Christian Broadcasting Network (CBN) and the various other television forums available for religious programming. Religious leaders have also organized demonstrations, pickets, and disruptions at abortion clinics throughout the nation.[55] The abortion rights issue remains a potent one.

In recent years, the issue of same-sex marriage has played out in much the same way as the abortion debate, and with many of the same opposing constituencies. In 2009, Iowa's seven-member supreme court ruled unanimously that the state's constitution guarantees gay men and lesbians the right to wed, as in a handful of other states with similar laws. At the time, polls showed about a third of Iowans supporting gay marriage, a third opposing gay marriage but supporting legalized civil unions, and a third opposing both gay marriage and civil unions. In the 2010 midterm elections, Iowa's incumbent Democratic governor Chet Culver was attacked by his Republican opponents not only for the state's poor economy but also the court's decision to legalize same-sex marriage. Hundreds of thousands of dollars poured in from out-of-state religious and "527" organizations (see Chapter 10) such as the National Organization for Marriage to fund negative campaign ads denouncing same-sex marriage and the Iowa Supreme Court, and encouraging voters to vote against retaining the justices who had ruled that same-sex marriage is constitutional. Polls conducted after the election revealed that many people turned out to vote because of the judicial retention elections, not the midterm elections for public office.[56] That is, the judicial elections became a referendum, akin to the politics of direct democracy, on the court's ruling to legalize gay marriage. And the 527 groups were key to shaping public opinion about the issue.[57] The headline story of the Iowa 2010 elections was not Culver's loss to his Republican challenger, but the fact that Iowans had

*Opponents and proponents of a woman's right to choose often clash with one another. Large well-financed groups on both sides of the debate try to influence public opinion and government policy.*

overwhelmingly voted not to retain three state supreme court judges who had ruled to legalize same-sex marriage a year earlier. Never in the 60 years since retention elections were instituted in the state had supreme court judges not been retained.

Ideas are marketed most effectively by groups with access to financial resources, public or private institutional support, and sufficient skill or education to select, develop, and draft ideas that will attract interest and support. The development and promotion of conservative themes and ideas in recent years have been greatly facilitated by the millions of dollars that conservative corporations and business organizations such as "super PACs" (see Chapter 10), the U.S. Chamber of Commerce, and the Public Affairs Council spend each year on public information. In addition, conservative business leaders have contributed millions of dollars to such conservative institutions as the Heritage Foundation, the Hoover Institution, and the American Enterprise Institute.[58] Many of the ideas that helped those on the right influence political debate were first developed and articulated by scholars associated with institutions such as these.

In much the same way, liberal organizations vie for public attention armed with ample financial assets, access to the media, and well-honed skills in creating, communicating, and using ideas. In recent decades, various left-leaning public-interest groups, relying heavily on voluntary contributions of time, effort, and money from their members, have organized in parallel with the rise of such institutions on the right. Through groups such as Common Cause, the National Organization for Women, the Sierra Club, the World Wildlife Federation, and Friends of the Earth, liberal intellectuals and professionals have been able to apply their organizational skills and educational resources to developing and promoting their ideas.[59] Often, research conducted in universities and in liberal "think tanks" such as the Brookings Institution provides the ideas that ultimately become law through the efforts of liberal politicians.

**The News Media and the Shaping of Public Opinion** The media are among the most powerful forces operating in the marketplace of ideas. As we shall see in Chapter 7, the mass media are not simply neutral messengers for ideas developed by others. Instead, the media are very much opinion makers in their own right and have an enormous impact on popular attitudes. For example, for the past 40 years since the publication of the Pentagon Papers by the *New York Times* and the exposure of the Watergate scandal led by the *Washington Post*, the national news media have relentlessly investigated personal and official wrongdoing on the part of politicians and public officials. The continual media presentation of corruption in government and venality in politics has undoubtedly contributed to the cynicism toward and distrust of government that prevails in much of the general public. Approval of Congress reached a new record low in 2011, with just 11 percent of Americans approving of the job Congress is doing. It is the lowest single rating in Gallup's history of asking this question since 1974.[60] In 1964, on the eve of the Vietnam War, 77 percent of Americans expected their government to "do the right thing" always or most of the time, according to opinion polls. Ten years later, after Vietnam and Watergate, 77 percent had become 36. Today, just one in five Americans has that confidence in the federal government.[61] Very low trust in government is a defining feature of contemporary American politics.

At the same time, the ways in which media coverage interprets or "frames" specific events can have a major impact on popular responses and opinions about these events.[62] Given the critical importance of media framing to the way the public perceives the news, the Bush administration went to great lengths to persuade broadcasters to follow its lead in their coverage of both terrorism and America's response to terrorism in the months following the September 11, 2001, attacks. For the most part, the media acquiesced, presenting the administration's military campaigns in Afghanistan and Iraq, as well as its domestic antiterrorist efforts, in a positive light. Even supposedly liberal newspapers such as the *New York Times*, which had strongly opposed Bush in the 2000 election, praised his leadership and published articles supportive of the president's bellicose rhetoric against the Iraqi regime prior to March 2003, when President Bush ordered the invasion of Iraq.

# ● Measuring Public Opinion

> **Describe basic survey methods and other techniques researchers use to measure public opinion**

As recently as 50 years ago, American political leaders gauged public opinion by the presence of crowds at meetings and their applause. This direct exposure to the people's views did not necessarily produce accurate knowledge of public opinion. It did, however, give political leaders confidence in their public support—and therefore confidence in their ability to govern by consent.

Abraham Lincoln and Stephen Douglas debated each other seven times during the summer and autumn of 1858, two years before they became presidential nominees. Their debates took place before audiences in parched cornfields and courthouse squares. A century later, the presidential debates, although seen by millions, take place in television studios, before a few reporters, technicians, and audiences instructed not to applaud or make noise. Only rarely, such as in the grassroots or "retail" politics of the Iowa caucuses or New Hampshire presidential primary, can politicians gauge the public's response directly.[63] Retail politics is where candidates meet citizens face-to-face to discuss politics.[64]

As Chapter 7 on the media illustrates, the media convey information to millions of people, but the media are not yet as efficient at getting information back to leaders, although the rise of social media, such as Facebook and Twitter, has created improved feedback for elected officials. Today public officials make extensive use of **public-opinion polls** to help them decide whether to run for office, what policies to support, how to vote on important legislation, and what types of appeals to make in their campaigns. All recent presidents and other major political figures have worked closely with polls and pollsters.

**public-opinion polls** scientific instruments for measuring public opinion

## Measuring Public Opinion from Surveys

It is not feasible to interview the 311 million-plus Americans residing in the United States on their opinions of who should be the next president or what should be done about important policy issues such as how to improve the economy and create jobs. Instead, pollsters take a **sample** of the population and use it to make inferences (i.e., extrapolations and educated guesses) about the preferences of the population as a whole. For a political survey to be an accurate representation of the population, it must meet certain requirements, including an appropriate sampling method, a sufficient sample size, and the avoidance of selection bias.[65]

**sample** a small group selected by researchers to represent the most important characteristics of an entire population

# Political Knowledge and Opinion in a "Scan-and-Skim" Culture

**The transformation of political** information in the digital era has had a profound effect on the way the news is reported and how citizens obtain information about politics. A 2012 survey conducted by the Pew Internet and American Life Project found that 36 percent of social networking site users say those sites are important for their political information, and more than three in four Americans read the news online or seek political information online. Recent research also indicates a trend in journalism toward shorter articles and flashier headlines, as the number of articles published by reputable newspapers such as *The Wall Street Journal* have doubled within the last decade. Americans today are likely to read the news by scanning and skimming multiple headlines online, in bits and bytes, rather than by reading long news articles. They also learn about politics in online discussion with family and friends.

Has the rise of digital politics and online news affected mass public opinion? *Newsweek's* July 2012 cover story

by Tony Dokoupil asked the question "Is the Web Driving Us Mad?" And Nicholas Carr's best-selling book, *The Shallows: What the Internet Is Doing to Our Brains,* asks, "Is Google making us stupid?" The answer from a review of scientific data conducted by both authors is, in part, yes.

Nicholas Carr's carefully researched study details the decline in the deep processing that underpins "mindful knowledge acquisition, inductive analysis, critical thinking, imagination, and reflection." He argues that although the Internet may seem to be making us smarter by virtue of giving us access to more data faster than ever, it also seriously threatens the type of intelligence that is measured by depth of thought rather than sheer speed. The Internet has encouraged "cursory reading, hurried and distracted thinking, and superficial learning"; a scan-and-skim culture rather than one practicing deep and reflectful thought. The habits of browsing, scanning, and reading in a nonlinear fashion have undermined the capacity to immerse oneself in longer works of writing, such as books. A study conducted by University College London found that people tend to go online to avoid reading in the traditional sense, and instead rely on new forms of reading to "power browse" horizontally through titles, contents pages, and abstracts. In order to maintain their profits, magazine and newspaper editors have yielded to this tendency by offering brief capsules of news instead of longer stories.

Carr argues that throughout the history of human evolution the ways in which we obtain information have actually changed our brain processes. He explains how human thought has been shaped over time by "tools of the mind"—from the alphabet to maps, to the printing press, the clock, and the computer. Our brains change in response to our experiences. The technologies we employ to find, store, and share information can literally

reroute our neural pathways. The rise of digital media is actually changing the way we think.

Extending this logic to politics, the implications are that public opinion will be less rational and more erratic, as individuals will lack a carefully developed understanding on which to base their opinions, despite the overwhelming volume of information about politics online. This trend might explain the significant percentage of Americans who believe political stories that are untrue or based on misinformation, such as the claim that President Obama is not a U.S. citizen (as discussed in the introduction to this chapter). However, as we've seen in this chapter, some research indicates that most individuals use simple cues and shortcuts to process political information. If this is correct, scanning and skimming headlines might provide a reasonable way to be informed about politics without extensive time or effort.

SOURCE: Nicholas Carr, *The Shallows: What the Internet Is Doing to Our Brains* (New York: W.W. Norton, 2011).

## for critical analysis

1. Will the Internet have a positive or negative impact on how we process political information and form opinions about politics? Why?

2. While the Internet provides less depth of information, it also offers a more interactive environment for discussing politics. Will the use of social media and other online forums to share political information and opinions help increase political knowledge as well as interest in politics in general?

**probability sampling** a method used by pollsters to select a representative sample in which every individual in the population has an equal probability of being selected as a respondent

**random digit dialing** a polling method in which respondents are selected at random from a list of ten-digit telephone numbers, with every effort made to avoid bias in the construction of the sample

**Representative Sample** The most representative sample is what statisticians call a **simple random sample** (or **probability sample**). To draw such a sample, one would need a complete list of all the people in the United States, and individuals would be randomly selected from that list. Imagine that everyone's name were entered into a lottery, with names then drawn blindly from an enormous box. If everyone had an equal chance of selection, we would have a truly random sample. Since we don't have a complete list of all Americans, pollsters use census data, lists of households (for in-person or telephone surveys), and telephone numbers (telephone surveys) to create lists, drawing samples from regions and then neighborhoods within regions. Just as in a simple random sample, everyone has an equal chance of being selected for the survey. Rolls of registered voters are often used in political surveys designed to predict the outcome of an election.

Another method of drawing samples of the national population is a technique called **random digit dialing** of landline and cell phone numbers, but not business phones or inoperative home telephones. A computer random number generator is used to produce a list of 10-digit telephone numbers. Given that 95 percent of Americans have telephones (cell phones or landlines), this technique usually results in a random national sample. Until recently, opinion polls did not include cell phone numbers, but because so many young people, urban residents, and other demographic groups (the poor) don't have landlines, cell phone numbers are included in many opinion polls. It allows almost every citizen a chance of being included in the survey. Telephone surveys are fairly accurate, cost-effective, and flexible in the type of questions that can be asked. Websites such as RealClearPolitics.com list the results of every political survey released each day; during elections, this can be as many as 20 different surveys daily. Every week, the opinions of Americans regarding candidates and public policies are measured, but also opinions on a vast array of products (toothpaste), entertainment (movie star romances), and even college political science textbooks!

**Sample Size** A sample must be large enough to provide an accurate representation of the population. Surprisingly, though, the size of the population being measured doesn't matter, only the size of the *sample*. A survey of 1,000 people is just as effective for measuring the opinions of all Texans (25 million residents) as the opinions of all Americans (over 300 million residents).

Flipping a coin shows how this works. After tossing a coin ten times, the number of heads and tails may not be close to five and five. After 100 tosses of the coin, though, the percentage of heads should be close to 50 percent, and after 1,000 tosses, very close to 50 percent (assuming it is a fair coin). In fact, after 1,000 tosses there is a 95 percent chance that the number of heads will be somewhere between 46.9 percent and 53.1 percent. This 3.1 percent variation from 50 percent is called the sampling error or margin of error. The chance that the sample used does not accurately represent the population from which it is drawn is called the **sampling error** (or **margin of error**). It is the amount of error we can expect with a typical 1,000-person survey. Normally, samples of 1,000 people are considered sufficient for accurately measuring public opinion through the use of surveys.

Larger sample sizes can yield more accurate predictions of the opinions of a population, but there is a trade-off in terms of cost, since it is also more expensive to poll more people. Why is a sample size of only 1,000 generally accepted as adequately representative of much larger populations? Consider the "diminishing returns" of sampling more and more people. The sample error from a sample of 500 people is 4.4 percent. With 1,000 respondents, it drops to 3.1 percent, and

**sampling error (or margin of error)** polling error that arises based on the small size of the sample

# Who Thinks Economic Inequality Is a Problem?

Percentage who said there are "strong" or "very strong" conflicts between rich and poor

An individual's ideology and party identification may influence his or her opinions on specific issues. As this study showed, the percentage of Americans concerned about economic inequality was rougly similar for all income groups. However, the differences between liberals and conservatives, and between Democrats and Republicans, were more significant.

## By income

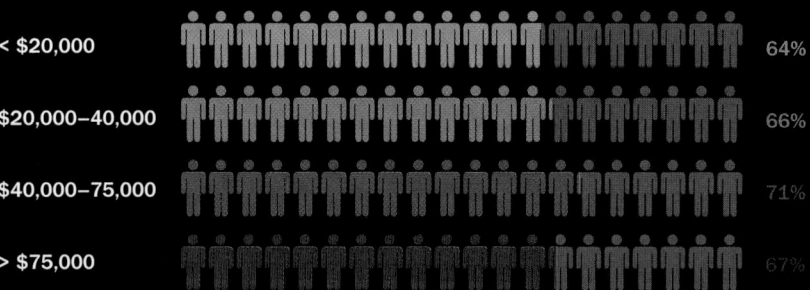

| < $20,000 | 64% |
| $20,000–40,000 | 66% |
| $40,000–75,000 | 71% |
| > $75,000 | 67% |

## By ideology

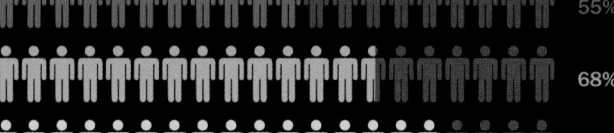

| Conservative | 55% |
| Moderate | 68% |
| Liberal | 79% |

## By party

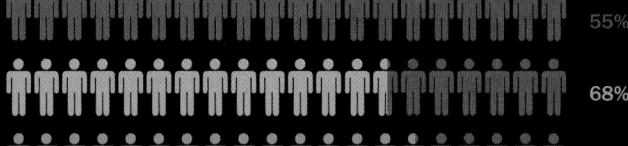

| Republican | 55% |
| Independent | 68% |
| Democrat | 73% |

SOURCE: Pew Research Center, "Rising Share of Americans See Conflict between Rich and Poor," January 11, 2012, www.pewsocialtrends.org/2012/01/11/rising-share-of-americans-see-conflict-between-rich-and-poor/ (accessed 5/10/12).

### for critical analysis

1. Do the findings in this study show that opinions are shaped by economic self-interest? Why or why not?

2. Which ideological group and which party are most likely to support government action to address inequality? Are the other groups not concerned about inequality? Use the data to explain your answers.

with 1,500 to 2.5 percent. That is, the smaller and smaller gains in accuracy have to be weighed against the steadily increasing costs of polling more and more people. The consensus among statisticians and pollsters is that the optimal trade-off point is 1,000—hence 1,000 is the "gold standard."

When an election poll of 1,000 people indicates that 51 percent of voters surveyed favor the Republican candidate, say, Mitt Romney, and 49 percent support the Democratic candidate, Barack Obama, the outcome is considered too close to call because the difference, 2 percent, is within the margin of error. That is, a figure of 51 percent really means that between 48 and 54 percent of voters in the population *probably* favor the Republican, while a figure of 49 percent indicates that between 46 and 52 percent of all voters *probably* support the Democrat. Thus, in this example, a 52-to-48 percent Democratic victory would still be consistent with polls predicting a 51-to-49 percent Republican triumph. Table 6.3 shows how accurate two of the major national polling organizations, Gallup and Harris, have been in predicting the outcomes of presidential elections. As you can see, the two firms have mostly been correct in their predictions. When the media refer to a "scientific poll" conducted by a highly respected polling firm such as Gallup or Harris, they actually mean a poll that has followed the steps just outlined: a poll based on a random (representative) sample of the population that is sufficiently large and avoids selection bias.

**Survey Design and Question Wording** Even with reliable sample procedures and a large sample, surveys may fail to reflect the true distribution of opinion within a target population. One frequent source of measurement error is the wording of survey questions. The precise words used in a question can have an enormous impact on the answers it elicits. The reliability of survey results can also be adversely affected by poor question format, faulty ordering of questions, poor vocabulary, ambiguity of questions, or questions with built-in biases.

Often, seemingly minor differences in the wording of a question can convey vastly different meanings to respondents and thus produce quite different response

**TABLE 6.3**

## Two Pollsters and Their Records, 1948–2012

Since their poor showing in 1948, the major pollsters have been close to the mark in every national presidential election. In 2000, though, neither Gallup nor Harris accurately predicted the outcome. From what you have learned about polling, what were some of the possible sources of error in these two national polls?

|  | HARRIS (%) | GALLUP (%) | ACTUAL OUTCOME (%) |
|---|---|---|---|
| **2012** | | | |
| Obama | NA | 49 | 50 |
| Romney | | 50 | 48 |
| **2008** | | | |
| Obama | 50 | 51 | 53 |
| McCain | 44 | 43 | 46 |
| **2004** | | | |
| Bush | 49 | 49 | 51 |
| Kerry | 48 | 49 | 48 |
| Nader | 1 | 1 | 0 |

| | HARRIS (%) | GALLUP (%) | ACTUAL OUTCOME (%) |
|---|---|---|---|
| **2000** | | | |
| Bush | 47 | 48 | 48 |
| Gore | 47 | 46 | 49 |
| Nader | 5 | 4 | 3 |
| **1996** | | | |
| Clinton | 51 | 52 | 49 |
| Dole | 39 | 41 | 41 |
| Perot | 9 | 7 | 8 |
| **1992** | | | |
| Clinton | 44 | 44 | 43 |
| Bush | 38 | 37 | 38 |
| Perot | 17 | 14 | 19 |
| **1988** | | | |
| Bush | 51 | 53 | 54 |
| Dukakis | 47 | 42 | 46 |
| **1984** | | | |
| Reagan | 56 | 59 | 59 |
| Mondale | 44 | 41 | 41 |
| **1980** | | | |
| Reagan | 48 | 47 | 51 |
| Carter | 43 | 44 | 41 |
| Anderson | | 8 | |
| **1976** | | | |
| Carter | 48 | 48 | 51 |
| Ford | 45 | 49 | 48 |
| **1972** | | | |
| Nixon | 59 | 62 | 61 |
| McGovern | 35 | 38 | 38 |
| **1968** | | | |
| Nixon | 40 | 43 | 43 |
| Humphrey | 43 | 42 | 43 |
| Wallace | 13 | 15 | 14 |
| **1964** | | | |
| Johnson | 62 | 64 | 61 |
| Goldwater | 33 | 36 | 39 |
| **1960** | | | |
| Kennedy | 49 | 51 | 50 |
| Nixon | 41 | 49 | 49 |
| **1956** | | | |
| Eisenhower | NA | 60 | 58 |
| Stevenson | | 41 | 42 |
| **1952** | | | |
| Eisenhower | 47 | 51 | 55 |
| Stevenson | 42 | 49 | 44 |
| **1948** | | | |
| Truman | NA | 44.5 | 49.6 |
| Dewey | | 49.5 | 45.1 |

NOTE: All figures except those for 1948 are rounded. NA = Not asked.

SOURCES: Data from the Gallup Poll and the Harris Survey, *Chicago Tribune*–New York News Syndicate, various press releases 1964–2012. Courtesy of the Gallup Organization and Louis Harris Associates.

patterns (see Box 6.3). For example, for many years the University of Chicago's National Opinion Research Center has asked respondents whether they think the federal government is spending too much, too little, or about the right amount of money on "assistance for the poor." Answering the question posed this way, about two-thirds of all respondents seem to believe that the government is spending too little. However, the same survey also asks whether the government spends too much, too little, or about the right amount for welfare. When the word *welfare* is substituted for "assistance for the poor," about half of all respondents indicate that too much is being spent.[66]

## BOX 6.3

## It Depends on How You Ask

**THE SITUATION**
The public's desire for tax cuts can be hard to measure. In 2000, pollsters asked what should be done with the nation's budget surplus and got different results depending on the specifics of the question.

**THE QUESTION**
President Clinton has proposed setting aside approximately two-thirds of an expected budget surplus to fix the Social Security system. What do you think the leaders in Washington should do with the remainder of the surplus?

**VARIATION 1**
Should the money be used for a tax cut, or should it be used to fund new government programs?

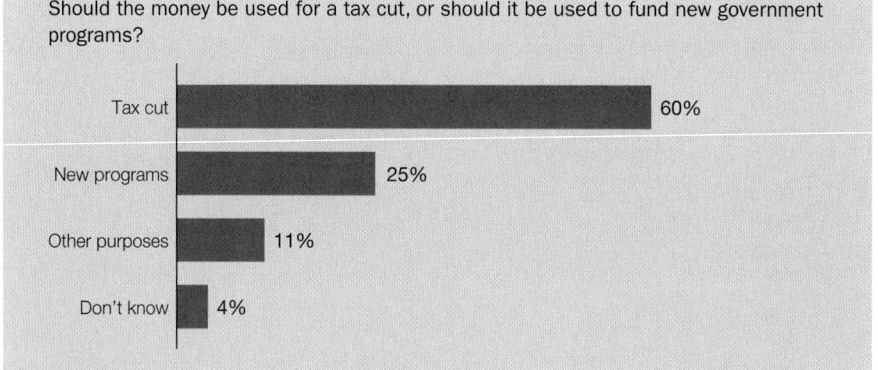

| | |
|---|---|
| Tax cut | 60% |
| New programs | 25% |
| Other purposes | 11% |
| Don't know | 4% |

**VARIATION 2**
Should the money be used for a tax cut, or should it be spent on programs for education, the environment, health care, crime fighting, and military defense?

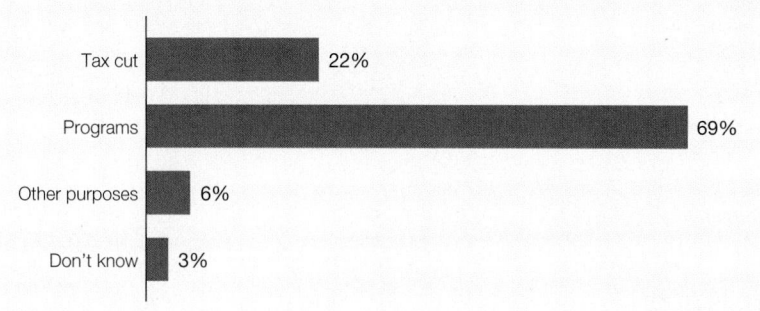

| | |
|---|---|
| Tax cut | 22% |
| Programs | 69% |
| Other purposes | 6% |
| Don't know | 3% |

SOURCE: Pew Research Center, reported in the *New York Times*, January 30, 2000, p. WK 3.

**Internet Surveys** Today, pollsters are increasingly turning to the use of online surveys, often using similar techniques to those of telephone surveys. But Internet surveys can be more efficient, less costly, and more accurate than standard phone surveys, and they include larger samples of young people and yield more accurate results within age cohorts. Many surveys you will find online do not use probability sampling (random sampling), and thus are not representative of the American population. Instead, they reflect those willing to take a quiz online, or on Facebook.

Knowledge Networks (KN) and YouGov are leaders in Internet polling using random sampling methods in which respondents complete surveys online instead of being interviewed on the phone. KN has a large population of respondents (hundreds of thousands of individuals) identified using probability sampling, so the sample is representative of the American population in terms of age, education, income, gender, race, political interest, region, partisanship, and other attributes. Individuals without Internet access are given free subscriptions and, if necessary, a computer or WebTV; those with Internet access are given free subscriptions to complete the surveys. If a client commissions a survey, KN randomly draws a sample of, say, 1,000 respondents from its population of online respondents. Because respondents have agreed to complete a number of surveys in exchange for free Internet access, they are more likely to complete the surveys.

Other polling companies, such as YouGov, use other methods for conducting Internet surveys, often by using statistical weights to make the surveys generally representative of the American population.[67] Internet surveys such as the Cooperative Congressional Election Study (CCES) can have very large samples, up to 50,000 people. In the future, Internet surveys may be more representative of the American population than traditional telephone surveys, and may replace telephone surveys entirely, especially given falling response rates and the growing number of households without landline phones but using cell phones exclusively.

Critics of Internet surveys contend that the samples may still be biased by not including enough respondents from groups that are more likely to be offline, especially non–English speakers, Latinos, African Americans, the elderly, and the poor.

*Because not everyone has Internet access at home, obtaining a representative sample for an online survey can be difficult. However, polling companies such as YouGov are developing methods to improve accuracy, and online surveys may eventually offer a more efficient and affordable alternative to telephone surveys.*

Online surveys may include more "politicos," or respondents who are interested in politics, than the normal population. Proponents contend that minorities and the poor are increasingly online, but via mobile access, and that the samples are representative of the American population. Because Internet surveys have proved to be accurate in forecasting elections, and some argue they are more accurate than random digital telephone surveys, Internet surveys are likely here to stay.

**Face-to-Face Surveys** With more than 60 years' experience studying American politics, the American National Election Studies (ANES) is the premier omnibus survey. The ANES traditionally has conducted surveys using face-to-face interviews, but because interviewing respondents in person is very costly, the ANES uses a multi-stage, stratified probability sample of 2,000-plus respondents from regions of the country (what they call primary sampling units). While this method approximates a simple random sample of the entire population, it does not guarantee random samples within states; all respondents from Iowa may be from Des Moines, for example. This can cause problems for generalizing the results for individual states. Even the ANES has begun experimenting with adding Internet surveys to its traditional face-to-face surveys. However, in-person surveys remain one of the most valuable and accurate ways to conduct interviews, and thus the ANES is an important source of survey data in political science.

## Framing Experiments within Surveys

Surveys are increasingly drawing on experimental techniques in which one group of respondents is given a treatment, or unique question wording, and responses are compared to a control group of respondents that does not receive the treatment. For example, the widespread tendency to base survey responses on the way questions are worded or "framed" provides a way to measure public opinion—through what are called framing experiments. Because of the media's power to shape public opinion, framing experiments are an important tool for measuring how the media and government shape political attitudes. Let us return to the opening example of this chapter. For more people to have become convinced that Obama is Muslim during his presidency than when he was running for office, there must have been some underlying misperception in the first place; that is, citizens were unsure enough about Obama to consider and ultimately embrace the idea.

Researchers often use framing experiments (in surveys or laboratory experiments) to understand how subtle changes in the structure of political information can result in the expression of different political opinions. In one experiment, individuals in one group were exposed to a frame arguing that affirmative action is necessary to correct past discrimination, while those in a second group received a competing frame arguing that affirmative action gives African Americans special treatment. Not surprisingly, those in the first group showed greater support for affirmative action than did those in the second group for the same policies. By using a treatment and control group design, framing experiments provide more leverage in assessing cause and effect in measuring changes in public opinion.

Dennis Chong and Jamie Druckman have extended how we measure framing effects on public opinion by testing the effect of multiple countervailing frames to create more realistic models of real-world political debate, where citizens are exposed to multiple perspectives on candidates and political issues.[68] Such competing frames can be expected to have different effects in shaping public opinion on a policy. In the marketplace of ideas, it matters crucially whether, say, the wealthiest

Americans are characterized as "the super-rich" and "1-percenters," or "business leaders" and "job creators." Framing experiments help researchers understand how public opinion changes in the face of new information. John Zaller's work shows that framing by the media, political groups, or candidates is important because individuals form opinions based on the latest information and arguments they are exposed to—what is "on the top of their heads"—and as a result, public opinion polls often merely measure whatever recent elite cues (or media stories) individual respondents happen to have stored in their short-term memory.[69] Thus framing experiments are an important way to understand how public opinion moves in response to political elites and the mass media.

## When Polls Are Wrong

The history of polling over the past century contains many instances of getting it wrong and learning valuable lessons in the process. As a result, polling techniques have grown more and more sophisticated, and pollsters have a more and more nuanced understanding of how public opinion is formed and how it is revealed.

**Social Desirability Effects and List Experiments** Political scientists have found that survey results can be inaccurate when the surveys include questions about sensitive issues for which individuals do not wish to share their true preferences. For example, respondents tend to overreport voting in elections and the frequency of their church attendance. Why? These activities are deemed socially appropriate, so even if the respondents did not vote or do not attend church regularly, they may feel social pressure to do so, and thus they may respond inaccurately on a survey. Political scientist Adam Berinsky calls this the **social desirability effect**, whereby respondents report what they expect the interviewer wishes to hear or whatever they think is socially acceptable, rather than what they actually believe or know to be true.[70] Additionally, surveys tend to report a high degree of nonresponse to questions about income; researchers have found that those most likely not to report their income in surveys are the poor.

**social desirability effect**
the effect that results when respondents in a survey report what they expect the interviewer wishes to hear rather than what they believe

Questions that ask directly about race or gender are particularly problematic. New research finds that social desirability makes it difficult to learn voters' true opinions about touchy subjects such as racial attitudes, because respondents hide their preferences from the interviewer for fear of social retribution (against what might be deemed "politically incorrect"). However, surveys using experiments can be designed to tap respondents' latent or hidden feelings about sensitive issues without directly asking them to express overt opinions. For example, one such survey examined support for a generic black presidential candidate; the study was conducted in mid-2007, well before Barack Obama became president. The survey was designed to tap underlying attitudes toward a black candidate, allowing researchers to compare openly expressed support for such a candidate with unvoiced hidden attitudes toward the same candidate. Results show that 30 percent of Americans exhibited reluctance about voting for a generic black presidential candidate, even though, when asked directly, nearly 85 percent had claimed they would support such a candidate.[71] However, there may be a significant difference between expressing support for a generic candidate and supporting a real candidate in the heat of an actual campaign. Yet, in 2008, another study found that 30 percent of white Americans were "troubled" by the prospect of "Obama as the first black president," almost the identical percentage as the previous study.[72] The fact that both studies found that roughly one-third of Americans had misgivings about a black president suggests that racism may be a factor.

Both of the studies just described made use of so-called list experiments, which rely on comparisons between subsamples (a treatment and a control group) that receive slightly different survey questions (see Box 6.4). List experiments work like this: One randomly assigned control group receives a list of items to which they are asked to respond by indicating how many of those items "trouble" them. The treatment group receives the same list, with one different "target item," and is similarly asked to report how many items are troubling. The respondents are not asked to share which statements bother them, only how many. The simple difference in the average number of statements between the treatment and control groups provides a measure of the percentage of the treatment group that is troubled by the target item, since otherwise all items are the same for both groups. And because the treatment group is a random subset of the full sample, results can be generalized to the larger population from which the random sample is drawn.

In examining the emotional underpinnings of attitudes about Obama as the first black president, David Redlawsk and his colleagues found that anxiety and enthusiasm were driving hidden racial opinions. Their study's results suggest that Obama's victory in the 2008 presidential election, despite a high level of concern about his race, was at least partly a result of the intense enthusiasm his campaign generated. This makes sense, given that Obama's campaign message focused on hope. Their

---

**BOX 6.4**

## Measuring Opinion about Obama's Race

In this experiment, half the participants were given Version A, which included the target item ("he is the first black president") and the other half were given Version B, which didn't include that statement. By comparing the average responses from the two groups, researchers were able to measure opinion on Obama's race.

**VERSION A (TREATMENT GROUP)**

Some people approve of the job Barack Obama is doing as president, and some people do not. Regardless of your overall feelings toward him, please indicate how many of the following facts about President Obama trouble you. We are not interested in WHICH ONES, only HOW MANY. Just enter a number from 0 to 5.

1. As a child, he spent several years in Indonesia.
2. He is the first black president.
3. He sometimes smokes cigarettes.
4. He is a former law professor.
5. He was a community organizer.

**VERSION B (CONTROL GROUP)**

Some people approve of the job Barack Obama is doing as president, and some people do not. Regardless of your overall feelings toward him, please indicate how many of the following five facts about President Obama trouble you. We are not interested in WHICH ONES, only HOW MANY. Just enter a number from 0 to 5.

1. As a child, he spent several years in Indonesia.
2. He has two children.
3. He sometimes smokes cigarettes.
4. He is a former law professor.
5. He was a community organizer.

enthusiasm for Obama may have allowed some white voters to overcome latent concerns about his race. The lesson here, once again, is that public opinion cannot be understood without understanding the public's underlying emotions.

Other racial attitude surveys conducted during the 2008 election—many of which do reveal substantial prejudice even when obscured by social desirability effects—tend to estimate that closer to 5 percent of Americans hold such attitudes.[73] List experiments were also employed to reveal that a quarter of Americans would not vote for a female president, and that it is common to hide true opinions about race and racial policies, such as affirmative action.[74] The list experiment provides a way to measure public opinion on sensitive issues and does so without respondents knowing what information is being sought.

**Selection Bias** The importance of accurate sampling was brought home early in the history of political polling. A 1936 *Literary Digest* poll predicted that the Republican candidate, Alf Landon, would defeat the Democratic incumbent, Roosevelt, in that year's presidential election. The actual election, of course, ended in a Roosevelt landslide. The main problem with the survey was what is called **selection bias** in drawing the sample. The pollsters had relied on telephone directories and automobile registration rosters to produce the survey sample. During the Great Depression, though, only wealthier Americans owned telephones and automobiles. Thus, the millions of working-class Americans who constituted Roosevelt's principal base of support were excluded from the sample.

> **selection bias (surveys)** polling error that arises when the sample is not representative of the population being studied, which creates errors in overrepresenting or underrepresenting some opinions

A more recent instance of polling error caused by selection bias was the 1998 Minnesota gubernatorial election. A poll conducted by the *Minneapolis Star Tribune* just six weeks before the election showed independent candidate and former professional wrestler Jesse Ventura running a distant third behind the Democratic candidate, Hubert Humphrey III, who seemed to have the support of 49 percent of the electorate, and the Republican candidate, Norm Coleman, whose support stood at 29 percent. Only 10 percent of those polled said they were planning to vote for Ventura. Yet on Election Day, Ventura garnered more votes than either Humphrey or Coleman. Analysis of exit poll data showed why the polls had been so wrong. In an effort to be more accurate, preelection pollsters often take into account the likelihood that respondents will actually vote, and so the *Star Tribune* poll was conducted only among individuals who had voted in the previous election. Ventura, however, attracted to the polls not only individuals who had not voted in the last election but also many people who had never voted before in their lives; in fact, a full 12 percent of Minnesota's voters in 1998 said they came to the polls only because Ventura was on the ballot. This surge in turnout was facilitated by the fact that Minnesota permits same-day voter registration. (See Chapter 8 for a discussion of the effects of registration rules.) Thus, the pollsters were wrong because Ventura changed the composition of the electorate.[75]

In recent years, the issue of selection bias has been complicated by the fact that growing numbers of individuals refuse to answer pollsters' questions, or they use such devices as answering machines and caller ID to screen unwanted callers. As noted previously, the increasing number of Americans who use cell phones (including many who do not have a landline at all) may be a problem in surveys that only include landline phone numbers. Individuals most likely to rely on cell phones alone include the young, urban residents, the poor, and minorities. These individuals would be less likely to be contacted if a telephone survey did not include cell phone numbers.

Additionally, response rates for surveys—the percentage of calls attempted that are completed—have been falling steeply. Response rates for the Pew Research

*Though public opinion is important, it is not always easy to interpret, and polls often fail to predict accurately how Americans will vote. In 1948, election-night polls showed Thomas Dewey defeating Harry S. Truman for the presidency.*

Center's highly respected surveys, for example, are less than one in five individuals called, or 20 percent. If pollsters could be certain that those who responded to their surveys simply reflected the views of those who refused to respond, there would be no problem. Some studies, however, suggest that the views of respondents and non-respondents can differ, especially along social class lines. Upper-class individuals are often less willing to respond to surveys or less likely to be at home than their working-class counterparts, which can bias telephone surveys. And women are significantly more likely to answer telephone surveys than men. Additionally, as discussed, most young people (ages 18–25) and a majority of minorities do not have landline phones, only cell phones, and are often excluded from telephone surveys. This can lead to incorrect inferences of public opinion.

**push polling** a polling technique in which the questions are designed to shape the respondent's opinion

**Push Polling** Push polling introduces a different type of bias into public opinion polling. Push polls are not scientific polls, as just discussed, and are not intended to yield accurate information about a population. Instead, they involve asking a respondent a loaded question about a political candidate designed to elicit the response sought by the pollster and, simultaneously, to shape the respondent's perception of the candidate in question. One of the most notorious uses of push polling occurred in the 2000 South Carolina Republican presidential primary, in which George W. Bush defeated John McCain and went on to win the presidency. Callers working for Bush supporters asked conservative white voters if they would be more or less likely to vote for McCain if they knew he had fathered an illegitimate black child. Because McCain often campaigned with a daughter whom he and his wife had adopted from Mother Teresa's orphanage in Bangladesh, many voters accepted the premise of the "poll." This push poll was often cited by McCain as one of the political smear tactics that made him reluctant to expose his family to the stresses of the 2008 presidential race. More than 100 consulting firms across the nation now specialize in push polling.[76] Calling push polling the "political equivalent of a drive-by shooting," Representative Joe Barton (R-Tex.)

launched a congressional investigation into the practice.[77] Push polls may be one reason Americans are becoming increasingly skeptical about the practice of polling and increasingly unwilling to answer pollsters' questions.[78]

**The Bandwagon Effect** By influencing perceptions, public opinion polls can even influence political realities. In fact, sometimes polling can even create its own reality. The so-called **bandwagon effect** occurs when polling results influence people to support the candidate marked as the probable victor. This is especially true in the presidential nomination process, where there may be multiple candidates within one party vying to be the party's nominee. Todd Donovan and his coauthors found that the change in national media coverage received by a candidate before and after the Iowa caucuses, the first nominating event, was a major predictor of how well the candidate would do in the New Hampshire primary (the second nominating event) and in presidential primaries nationwide, controlling for other factors, including money and standing in the polls.[79] A candidate who has "momentum"—that is, one who demonstrates a lead in the polls—usually finds it considerably easier to raise campaign funds than a candidate whose poll standing is poor. And with these additional funds, poll leaders can often afford to pay for television time and other campaign activities that will generate positive media attention and thus cement their advantage.

> **bandwagon effect** a shift in electoral support to the candidate whom public opinion polls report as the front-runner

# ● Public Opinion and Government Policy

> **Analyze the relationship between public opinion and government policies**

In 1960, Angus Campbell and the other authors of the *American Voter* argued that few Americans think about politics ideologically or consistently, so one would naturally expect public opinion to vary, as discussed earlier.[80] In fact, one of the reasons elected officials sometimes do not follow public opinion is that it tends to be unpredictable. Given the general lack of political knowledge among voters, the sometimes volatile nature of public opinion, and the difficulty of measuring the public will accurately, it's little wonder that politicians are sometimes unable, or unwilling, to act solely on the basis of public opinion. In fact, John Zaller's work on how Americans form specific opinions calls into question whether government leaders should consult public opinion at all when they make policy decisions—but consulting public opinion is their democratic duty. So how responsive is government policy to public opinion?

## Government Responsiveness to Public Opinion

Even though there is no one-to-one correlation between public opinion and the policy decisions made on the public's behalf, studies generally do suggest that elected officials are constrained by the preferences of the public. For example, political scientists Benjamin Page and Robert Shapiro have studied the relationship between macro-level changes in opinion toward various political issues and the policy outcomes that most closely correspond to the issues.[81] The results show that shifts in public opinion on particular issues do in fact tend to lead to changes in public policy. This is especially true when there are wide swings in opinion regarding particularly high-profile issues that are relatively simple. Other researchers have

*Professional polling companies gather extensive information about public opinion, but do politicians do what the public wants? In general, policies appear to follow the broad preferences of the public, but specific policies may not always align with what the majority of constituents want.*

**median voter theorem**
a proposition predicting that when policy options can be arrayed along a single dimension, majority rule will pick the policy most preferred by the voter whose ideal policy is to the left of half of the voters and to the right of exactly half of the voters

found similar evidence that government policy generally does track public opinion. By measuring public opinion over time, political scientists Gerald Wright, Robert Erikson, and John McIver have found, unsurprisingly, that states where conservative opinions predominate tend to adopt more conservative laws, and states with more liberal public opinion adopt more liberal policies.[82]

In order to maintain their positions in public office—that is, in order to be re-elected or reappointed—politicians will naturally attempt to create policies that align with the preferences of their constituents. One of the most important theories of how legislators make policy is the **median voter theorem**, proposed by Anthony Downs in 1957. This view suggests that, in order for a politician to get re-elected, the most reliable strategy for him or her to take is to adopt the preferences of the median voter. Representing centrist opinion will allow politicians to garner the largest number of votes, even though this approach also has the potential to alienate supporters holding more extreme opinions.

However, not only do public officials know how unreliable public opinion can be, it's also true that voters may not know exactly what positions the officials actually support. So the fact that voters and government leaders will not always be certain about each other's preferences provides elected officials some latitude in which to pursue their own goals—so long as they do not stray so far from centrist opinion as to jeopardize their position of power.[83] Sometimes officials act on their own preferences if they believe it will benefit government or society, and studies have indeed shown that lawmakers typically do use their own judgment when making policy choices.[84] The bailout of the banks in 2008, for example, was carried out despite polls showing that a majority of Americans opposed this policy. When elected officials pursue policies not aligned with centrist opinion, it is often because they view particular groups of the electorate as more important than others. Inevitably, loyal voting blocs or interest groups that regularly contribute to a candidate may have their interests more closely represented than the general public.[85]

## Does Everyone's Opinion Count Equally?

In a democracy, it is assumed that elected representatives should implement the policies favored by the people, and in a general sense this happens in the United States. But when policy issues are more complicated, the public is likely to have less of a voice. Further, citizens who are more affluent and more educated may have a disproportionate influence over politics and public-policy decisions. This has been shown when comparing the responsiveness of elected officials to low- and high-income individuals, voters and nonvoters, and whites and minorities. The view that some groups in a society have more influence over the political process is not new, but it is quite different from the traditional pluralist view of all citizens having equal access to the political sphere—the democratic ideal outlined by Robert Dahl. By contrast, E. E. Schattschneider's famous critique argues that "the flaw in the pluralist heaven is that the heavenly chorus sings with a strong upper-class accent."

How do more affluent and educated citizens manage to wield outsize influence over policy makers? One way is obvious: they vote and they are more likely to contribute money to political campaigns. As we will discuss in Chapter 8, voters and individuals making political contributions tend to be more affluent and educated than nonvoters. Indeed, there is some evidence supporting the common, but generally untested, assumption that voters are better represented than nonvoters. In a comparative study of the roll call votes of U.S. senators, political scientists John Griffin and Brian Newman demonstrate that elected officials are indeed responsive to the policy preferences (and public opinion) of voters, but not to those of non-voters.[86] Political scientist Larry Bartels finds that U.S. senators from both the Republican and Democratic parties are less likely to respond to the opinions of low-income constituents than to those of constituents with higher incomes.[87] Senate roll call votes on such varied issues as the minimum wage, civil rights, and abortion are more likely to reflect the opinions of the upper-income constituency. Additionally, Bartels's study shows that, when weighing the opinions of those who vote and have high levels of political knowledge, senators are still more responsive to the rich. Bartels argues that government policies such as tax cuts for the ultra-wealthy, failure to increase the minimum wage, and the elimination of the inheritance tax have created greater inequality between the ultra-rich and average Americans than at any other time in American history.[88]

*Because of the importance of public opinion, most presidents have made major efforts both to ascertain the public's views and to promote opinions favorable to themselves and their policies. Bill Clinton was often criticized for retaining a number of pollsters to chart shifts in public opinion on a daily basis.*

As an alternative to analyzing legislative roll call votes, political scientist Martin Gilens uses survey results to confirm that those with higher incomes are more likely to have their policy preferences represented by actual policies.[89] He considers public opinion surveys on a wide variety of policy issues conducted over 20 years and compares the responses of upper- and lower-income groups to related federal policy outcomes. Gilens finds a moderately strong relationship between what the public wants and what the government actually does, albeit with a strong bias toward the status quo. But when Americans with different income levels differ in their policy preferences, actual policies strongly reflect the preferences of the most affluent and show little or no relationship to the preferences of poor or middle-income Americans. Robert Dahl may be right when he argues that every American citizen has an equal right to voice opinions in the political arena, but his critics are also right to point out that some voices receive a very attentive listening while others are hardly heard at all.

## ● Thinking Critically about Public Opinion and Democracy

This chapter has focused on the role of public opinion in American politics. A major purpose of democratic government, with its participatory procedures and representative institutions, is to ensure that political leaders will heed the public will. And, indeed, a good deal of evidence suggests that they do. There are many instances in which public policy and public opinion do not coincide, but often the government's actions are consistent with citizens' preferences, at least in the most general sense.[90]

Some political scientists argue, however, that government policy is much less responsive to public opinion on the issues that really count, and that when the interests of elites are at stake, government officials are much more likely to represent the opinions of the affluent than the poor.[91] There is often a disconnect between public opinion and policy. For example, most Americans oppose U.S. military intervention in

*Wealthy people, groups, and corporations have more access to policy makers and may have greater influence on government. Here, Vice President Joe Biden (who was a senator at the time) poses for a photo with two lobbyists at a gala dinner.*

other nations' affairs in the principle, yet such interventions continue to take place in the Middle East and Africa, often winning public approval—at least at first. The overwhelming majority of Americans supported the Bush administration's decision to attack Afghanistan after September 11, and a year and a half later, most Americans were persuaded that invading Iraq and toppling the regime of Saddam Hussein was necessary for U.S. national security and to prevent a repeat of September 11.

The migration of politics online has greatly expanded the amount of information available and the ease of becoming informed. And as we will see in Chapter 7, online media are more diverse than traditional media. Given this new media environment, we might expect public opinion to be more accurate, even about the nuances of public policy. Digital citizenship offers the promise of a more informed electorate, with citizens having multiple venues in which to translate their opinions into political action and demand improved representation from political leaders.

At the same time, the Internet raises the same concerns about the accuracy and consistency of public opinion that were a central focus of the pre-Internet-era work on public opinion by John Zaller. As Chapter 7 will show, Americans may become trapped in a "filter bubble" in which they are exposed only to news consistent with their political preferences. There are Internet vandals, or "bomb-throwers," who defame other people and their opinions in ways that may negatively color public opinion. Misinformation—rumor masked as legitimate news—may be more common, especially in blogs, as the confusion regarding Barack Obama's religion illustrates. Some research finds that the gap between the haves and the have-nots in terms of political knowledge actually increases with more information. The implications are significant, given the explosion of political coverage online. The research suggests that with more information, public opinion may actually be less consistent.[92]

In a recent book, *The Shallows*, author Nicholas Carr poses another concern: "Is Google making us stupid?"[93] That is, as we enjoy the endless information available online, are we sacrificing our ability to read closely and think deeply, to evaluate competing claims and draw reasoned conclusions? Carr argues that human thought has been shaped through the centuries by "tools of the mind"—from the earliest alphabets and maps to the printing press, the clock, and the computer. Our brain structure changes in response to our experiences. Using the Internet to find, store, and share information can literally reroute our neural pathways. While the printed book served to focus our attention, promoting in-depth thought, the Internet, in contrast, encourages the rapid, distracted sampling of small bits of information from multiple sources, such as updates in Facebook, Twitter, or Google News. While we are becoming ever more adept at scanning and skimming, Carr wonders if we are losing our capacity for concentration, contemplation, and reflection.

The Internet may be reshaping what is public opinion. The effects of new media—vast and still unfolding—include the wide dissemination of public opinion polls and the rise of Internet polling. Do new media make public opinion more or less important? Do they make elected officials more or less responsive to the citizens? Time will tell.

# Measuring Public Opinion—Including Your Own

## Inform Yourself

**Consider opinion on current issues.** Visit the Polling Report (www.pollingreport .com) and click on a topic. For example, what percentage of Americans approve of the president's job performance? How has that figure changed over the last year? Next look for polls on same-sex marriage. What percentage of Americans approves of allowing gay men/lesbians to marry and what percentage opposes?

**Compare multiple surveys on the same topic.** An important clearinghouse for election polls is Real Clear Politics (www.realclearpolitics.com). Click "Polls" and then "Latest Polls." Each day, you can find the results of opinion polls that have been conducted, often including several on the same topic. This website has become increasingly important because it aggregates the results of so many surveys. How much do the results of different polls on the same topic vary? Does aggregating the results from many surveys make the findings more reliable?

**Watch a video about opinion on the economy.** Watch the Pew Research Center's video on "The Lost Decade of the Middle Class" (www.pewsocialtrends .org/2012/08/22/video-lost-decade-of-the-middle-class/). Then click on the report with the same name on the top right of the page. Who do Americans blame for the economic losses of the middle class? Which groups are most optimistic about their future economic prospects? Which are least optimistic?

## Connect with Others

**What is your political ideology?** First take the very short political quiz at www .theadvocates.org/quiz. What was your result? Next take the Pew Research Center's political typology quiz (www.people-press.org/typology/quiz). How are your results for the two quizzes similar or different? Were you surprised by the findings? How would you redesign the questions to better measure political ideology? Share the political quizzes on your Facebook page or on Twitter.

*Find links to the sites listed above as well as related activities on wwnorton.com/studyspace.*

# study guide

## Defining Public Opinion

■ **Define public opinion and identify broad types of values and beliefs Americans have about politics (pp. 205–19)**

Public opinion refers to the attitudes that people have about issues, events, elected officials, and public policy. Individuals' attitudes are shaped by their underlying political beliefs and values. A number of factors, including the family, membership in social groups, education, and political conditions, help form people's underlying political beliefs and values in a process called *political socialization*. Despite differences in opinion on many issues, most Americans share a common set of values, including a belief in the principles of liberty, equality, and democracy.

### Key Terms

**public opinion** (p. 205)

**values (or beliefs)** (p. 205)

**political ideology** (p. 205)

**attitude (or opinion)** (p. 205)

**liberty** (p. 206)

**equality of opportunity** (p. 207)

**democracy** (p. 207)

**political socialization** (p. 208)

**agents of socialization** (p. 209)

**gender gap** (p. 210)

**libertarianism** (p. 216)

**socialist** (p. 216)

**liberal** (p. 217)

**conservative** (p. 218)

### Practice Quiz

1. The term *public opinion* is used to describe *(p. 205)*
   a) the collected speeches and writings made by a president during his or her term in office.
   b) the analysis of events broadcast by news reporters during the evening news.
   c) the beliefs and attitudes that people have about issues.
   d) decisions of the Supreme Court.
   e) any political statement that is made by a citizen outside of their private residencies or places of employment.

2. Variables such as income, education, race, gender, and ethnicity *(p. 206)*
   a) often create differences of political opinion in America.
   b) have consistently been a challenge to America's core political values.
   c) have little impact on political opinions.
   d) help explain why public opinion polls are so unreliable.
   e) matter only for people's opinions on moral issues but not for their opinions on economic issues.

3. The process by which Americans learn political beliefs and values is called *(p. 208)*
   a) brainwashing.
   b) propaganda.
   c) indoctrination.
   d) political socialization.
   e) political development.

4. Which of the following is an agency of socialization? *(p. 209)*
   a) the family
   b) social groups
   c) education
   d) political conditions
   e) all of the above

5. When men and women respond differently to issues of public policy, they are demonstrating an example of *(p. 210)*
   a) liberalism.
   b) educational differences.
   c) the gender gap.
   d) party politics.
   e) feminism.

6. A politician who opposes abortion, government regulation of business, and gay rights legislation would be best described as a *(p. 218)*
   a) liberal.
   b) conservative.
   c) libertarian.
   d) socialist.
   e) communist.

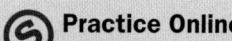 **Practice Online**
"Get Involved" exercise: *Public-Opinion Polls*

# How We Form Political Opinions

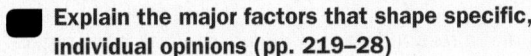 **Explain the major factors that shape specific, individual opinions (pp. 219–28)**

As a result of the fact that being politically informed requires a substantial investment of time and energy, most Americans know relatively little about the political world. In fact, most people acquire political information and make political decisions by relying on cues and heuristics from party elites, trusted acquaintances, and the mass media. These informational shortcuts can allow average citizens to from political opinions that are, in most instances, consistent with their underlying preferences and interests.

## Key Term

**marketplace of ideas** (p. 224)

## Practice Quiz

7. The fact that the public is inattentive to politics and must frequently rely on informational shortcuts has which of the following effects on American democracy? *(p. 224)*
   a) It strengthens it by providing politicians with more freedom to act on a wider variety of issues.
   b) It strengthens it by increasing the number of people who participate in politics.
   c) It weakens it by making it easier for various institutions and political actors to manipulate the political process.
   d) It weakens it by making every citizen equally empowered to produce outcomes that are consistent with their interests on every issue.
   e) It has no effect on it.

8. Which of the following are the most important external influences on how political opinions are formed in the marketplace of ideas? *(p. 224)*
   a) the government, private groups, and the news media
   b) the unemployment rate, the Dow Jones industrial average, and the NASDAQ composite
   c) random digit dialing surveys, push polls, and framing experiments
   d) the Constitution, the Declaration of Independence, and the Federalist Papers
   e) the legislative branch, the executive branch, and the judicial branch

 **Practice Online**
Video exercise: *Constructing Public Opinion—Media Education Foundation*

# Measuring Public Opinion

**Describe basic survey methods and other techniques researchers use to measure public opinion (pp. 228–41)**

Politicians frequently use public-opinion surveys to decide whether to run for office, what policies to support, how to vote on important pieces of legislation, and what types of appeals to make in their campaigns. Surveys can provide a very accurate description of the true distribution of opinion on an issue if they employ an appropriate sampling method and include a sufficient sample size. In addition to the characteristics of the sample, the reliability of surveys is also determined by the ordering and wording of the questions pollsters choose to ask.

## Key Terms

**public-opinion polls** (p. 228)

**sample** (p. 228)

**simple random sample (or probability sample)** (p. 230)

**random digit dialing** (p. 230)

**sampling error (or margin of error)** (p. 230)

**social desirability effect** (p. 237)

**selection bias (surveys)** (p. 239)

**push polling** (p. 240)

**bandwagon effect** (p. 241)

## Practice Quiz

9. Which of the following is the term used in public-opinion polling to denote the small group representing the opinions of the whole population? *(p. 228)*
   a) control group
   b) sample
   c) micropopulation
   d) respondents
   e) median voters

10. A poll that includes many poorly worded or ambiguous questions has a high degree of *(p. 232)*
    a) sampling error.
    b) measurement error.
    c) selection bias.
    d) validity error.
    e) attribution error.

11. A push poll is a poll in which *(p. 240)*
    a) the questions are designed to shape the respondent's opinion rather than measure the respondent's opinion.
    b) the questions are designed to measure the respondent's opinion rather than shape the respondent's opinion.
    c) the questions are designed to reduce measurement error.

d) the sample is chosen to include only undecided or independent voters.

e) the sample is not representative of the population it is drawn from.

12. A familiar polling problem is the "bandwagon effect," which occurs when *(p. 241)*

 a) the same results are used over and over again.

 b) polling results influence people to support the candidate marked as the probable victor in a campaign.

c) polling results influence people to support the candidate who is trailing in a campaign.

d) background noise makes it difficult for a pollster and a respondent to communicate with each other.

e) a large number of people refuse to answer a pollster's questions.

 **Practice Online**
Video exercise: *What Do You Do for a Living? with Andrew Kohut*

# Public Opinion and Government Policy

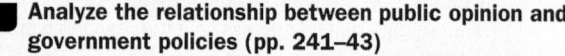 **Analyze the relationship between public opinion and government policies (pp. 241–43)**

In a democracy, elected officials should pursue policies that are favored by the public. Although there are many instances where government policy differs from the desires of the public, academic research has shown that there is generally a strong connection between what government does and what people want. Academic research has also shown, however, that the government is less responsive to the public on complex issues and that more affluent and more educated citizens have a disproportionate influence over policy decisions.

## Key Term

**median voter theorem** (p. 242)

## Practice Quiz

13. The median voter theorem suggests that *(p. 242)*

 a) the most reliable strategy for a politician to take in winning reelection is to adopt policies that are consistent with the preferences of ideologically extreme voters.

b) the most reliable strategy for a politician to take in winning re-election is to adopt policies that are consistent with the preferences of centrist voters.

c) the average American voter is uninformed about the details of most government policies.

d) the average American voter is well informed about the details of most government policies.

e) government policy should always reflect what a majority of Americans want.

 **Practice Online**
"You Decide" exercise: *School Prayer*

# For Further Reading

Althaus, Scott. *Collective Preferences in Democratic Politics.* New York: Cambridge University Press, 2003.

Bartels, Larry. *Unequal Democracy.* Princeton, NJ: Princeton University Press, 2008.

Berinsky, Adam. *Silent Voices: Public Opinion and Political Participation in America.* Princeton, NJ: Princeton University Press, 2005.

Bishop, George. *The Illusion of Public Opinion.* New York: Rowman and Littlefield, 2004.

Clawson, Rosalee, and Zoe Oxley. *Public Opinion: Democratic Ideals and Democratic Practice.* Washington, DC: CQ Press, 2008.

Erikson, Robert, and Kent Tedin. *American Public Opinion.* 7th ed. New York: Longman, 2004.

Fiorina, Morris. *Culture War: The Myth of a Polarized America.* New York: Longman, 2005.

Gallup, George. *The Pulse of Democracy.* New York: Simon and Schuster, 1940.

Ginsberg, Benjamin. *The Captive Public: How Mass Opinion Promotes State Power.* New York: Basic Books, 1986.

Glynn, Carol et al., ed. *Public Opinion.* Boulder, CO: Westview, 2004.

Jacobs, Lawrence R., and Robert Y. Shapiro. *Politicians Don't Pander: Political Manipulation and the Loss of Democratic Responsiveness.* Chicago: University of Chicago Press, 2000.

Lee, Taeku. *Mobilizing Public Opinion.* Chicago: University of Chicago Press, 2002.

Lippman, Walter. *Public Opinion.* New York: Harcourt, Brace, 1922.

Norrander, Barbara, and Clyde Wilcox. *Understanding Public Opinion.* Washington, DC: CQ Press, 2009.

Zaller, John. *The Nature and Origins of Mass Opinion.* New York: Cambridge University Press, 1992.

# Recommended Websites

**American Association for Public Opinion Research**
www.aapor.org

This website is one of the premier academic sites for public opinion data on a host of political and social topics.

**eTalkinghead**
http://directory.etalkinghead.com

Political blogs have become an increasingly popular way for Americans to express and discuss political opinions. This Web page provides a directory of political blogs by ideology and issue.

**Gallup**
www.gallup.com

The Gallup Organization has been involved in the scientific study of public opinion for more than 70 years and is very highly regarded. This website contains public-opinion data archives, video archives, and international polls.

**The Political Compass**
www.politicalcompass.org

A political ideology is a cohesive set of beliefs that form a general philosophy about government; however, people are often unsure if they are liberal, moderate, or conservative. Go to the website for the Political Compass and take the test to see if it helps you identify your ideology.

**Polling Report**
http://pollingreport.com

This independent, nonpartisan resource tracks trends in American public opinion. On this site you will find countless political opinion polls by all the major media outlets, all in one place.

**Public Agenda**
www.publicagenda.org

Measuring public opinion from surveys can be problematic. Often samples contain selection bias, or surveys have measurement error. Public Agenda is an organization that studies public opinion on major policy issues. Its website contains critiques of public opinion.

**ThisNation.com**
www.thisnation.com/socialization.html

The process through which underlying political beliefs and values are formed is called political socialization. This civic-minded Web page offers a brief discussion of political socialization with some related Web links.

Political candidates who receive positive news coverage gain momentum, which helps them attract campaign contributions and endorsements and eventually win votes. The influence of the media on political campaigns is just one example of its important role in American democracy.

# The Media

**WHAT GOVERNMENT DOES AND WHY IT MATTERS** One area in which our government's role is intended to be minimal is the realm of the news media. The Constitution's First Amendment guarantees freedom of the press, and most Americans believe that a free press is an essential condition for both liberty and democratic politics. Today the media (new and old) play a central role in American politics, not only in setting the agenda of topics that Americans think about and discuss, but often in swaying opinions on political issues and candidates.

Political candidates who receive positive news coverage gain momentum, pick up political endorsements, attract campaign contributions, and win support from voters.[1] In the 2008 campaign for the Democratic Party's presidential nomination, Barack Obama exceeded the media's expectations with his early win in the Iowa caucuses, in which he upset the front-runner, Hillary Clinton. Obama's unexpected victory earned him greatly increased press attention and eventually led him to the White House.[2] But candidates who disappoint media expectations see their political endorsements, campaign contributions, and polling numbers dwindle.

The influence of the media on political campaigns is just one example of the media's vitally important role in American democracy. Without the media's investigations, citizens would be forced to rely entirely on the information provided by politicians and the government, and would be deprived of an indispensable opportunity to evaluate issues carefully and form reasoned opinions.

The rise of the Internet has brought important changes to the media industry and its influence in politics. In fact, the Internet is fundamentally altering the media's role in politics and American democracy. Just 20 years ago the majority of Americans got their political news from a daily newspaper, from radio, or by watching the local evening news and the national evening news from one of the three major networks (ABC, CBS, NBC). In the twenty-first century, America is becoming a nation of "digital citizens"—daily Internet users who turn to the Internet for politics and news.[3] Overall 80 percent of Americans have used the Internet, although just under 7 in 10 have high-speed home access.[4] Among Internet users in 2012, 3 in 4 read the news online and 6 in 10 go online for information about politics.[5] In fact, more Americans now read the news online than read a print newspaper, and those reading online news are more likely to vote and participate in politics in other ways.[6] Today mainstream media must compete with niche media outlets that tailor news to their readers and viewers, and Americans increasingly find political content via blogs and social media such as Facebook and Twitter.

The sharing of information and opinions is critical to democracy. Discussing the right of press freedom, Thomas Jefferson wrote, "The basis of our government being the opinion of the people, the very first object should be to keep that right; and were it left to me to decide whether we should have a government without newspapers or newspapers without a government, I should not hesitate a moment to prefer the latter." In the twenty-first century, newspapers and other traditional media have been joined by today's electronic and digital media as an essential component of American democracy.

## chaptergoals

- Describe the role of print and broadcast media in providing political information (pages 253–56)

- Explain how the Internet has transformed the news media (pages 256–68)

- Describe trends in who owns mass media companies (pages 268–70)

- Analyze the ways the media can influence public opinion and politics (pages 270–77)

- Explain how politicians and others try to shape the news (pages 278–83)

- Trace the evolution of rules that govern broadcast media (pages 283–85)

# ● Traditional Media

**Describe the role of print and broadcast media in providing political information**

The American news media are among the world's freest and most diverse. Americans have literally thousands of available options in political reporting. The wide variety of newspapers, newsmagazines, broadcast media, and online sources regularly present information that is at odds with the government's claims, and editorial opinions sharply critical of high-ranking officials. The freedom to speak one's mind is one of the most cherished of American political values.

Americans get their news from three main sources: **broadcast media** (radio and television), print media (newspapers and magazines), and, increasingly, the Internet. Each of these sources has distinctive characteristics. We discuss the first two in this section, and in the next section, we will take a close look at the emergence of the Internet and how it is changing the media industry and the way Americans get political news.

**broadcast media** television, radio, or other media that transmit audio and/or video content to the public

## Broadcast Media

Television news reaches more Americans than any other single news source. It is estimated that over 95 percent of Americans have a television, although the percentage of Americans with cable television may be dropping among the young, as the Internet becomes the preferred vehicle for news, communication, and entertainment. The 2012 presidential elections may be the first time digital media trumped television media. Yet tens of millions of people watch national and local news programs every day. Television news, however, covers relatively few topics and provides little depth of coverage. It serves the extremely important function of alerting viewers to issues and events, but generally doesn't provide much more than a series of sound bites—brief quotes

*When Rick Perry made a major gaffe in a 2012 Republican primary debate, the scene was broadcast on national television—and then viewed millions of times on YouTube.*

and short characterizations of the day's events, often little more than a few seconds in length. Because they are aware of the character of television news coverage, politicians and others often seek to manipulate the news by providing the media with sound bites that will dominate news coverage for at least a few days. Twenty-four-hour news stations such as Cable News Network (CNN) offer more detail and commentary than the networks' half-hour evening news shows. Even CNN and the others, however, offer more headlines and sound bites than analysis, especially during their prime-time broadcasts. Politicians generally consider local broadcast news a friendlier venue than the national news. National reporters are often inclined to criticize and question, whereas local reporters are more likely to accept the pronouncements of national leaders at face value.

Radio news is also essentially a headline service. In the short time they devote to news (usually five minutes per hour), radio stations announce the day's major events without providing much detail. All-news stations such as WTOP in Washington, D.C., and New York's WCBS assume that most listeners are in their cars and that, as a result, the people in the audience change throughout the day as listeners reach their destinations. Thus, rather than use their time to flesh out a given set of stories, they repeat the same stories each hour to present them to new listeners. In the 1990s, radio talk shows became important sources of commentary and opinion. A number of conservative radio hosts such as Rush Limbaugh and Sean Hannity have huge audiences and have helped to mobilize support for conservative political causes and candidates. In the political center or left center, National Public Radio is a coveted source for moderate talk radio and provides in-depth political reporting, while the now-defunct Air America hoped to achieve on the left what Limbaugh had achieved on the right.

*Comedy talk shows with political content, like* The Colbert Report, *have become a significant source of political information for some Americans.*

Comedy talk shows with political content, such as *The Daily Show* or *The Colbert Report*, have become increasingly important, attracting millions of television viewers. Comedian Stephen Colbert went so far as to establish a political action committee during the 2012 presidential primaries and to enter the Republican primary in his home state of South Carolina in an effort to draw attention to problems with current campaign finance laws. *Colbert, The Daily Show,* and other late-night talk shows use cutting-edge humor, sarcasm, and social criticism to cover almost every major political event. Yet talk shows that cover political topics are not just for fun. They have become increasingly important sources of political news, especially for younger viewers. Pew surveys show that many Americans get political news from these shows and that followers of comedic talk shows are well informed about politics.[7]

The broadcast media are also diversifying as they adapt to changes in the American population, especially the growing number of Latinos. California and Texas are both projected to become majority Hispanic by the middle of the twenty-first century. In both states, as well as others, the Latino-oriented television channels Telemundo, Univision, and MSN Latino attract large audiences. These channels have Spanish-language programming, including political reporting and other news. They also may focus on topics or perspectives of particular interest to their audience. Coverage of the Arizona and Alabama illegal immigration laws, for example, in Hispanic media outlets was significantly different from that of mainstream media. News outlets aimed at other ethnic groups have also become common in many areas. As America has become more multicultural, multiethnic television—a form of niche media—has broadened news media.

## Print Media

Newspapers, though no longer the primary news source for most Americans, remain important nevertheless, because they are influential among the political elite. The broadcast media also rely on leading newspapers such as the *New York Times* and the *Washington Post* to set their news agenda. In fact, the broadcast media engage in very little actual reporting; they primarily cover stories that have been "broken," or initially reported, by the print media or online media. For example, sensational charges that President Bill Clinton had had an affair with a White House intern were reported first by the Drudge Report, a popular news aggregation website, and then picked up by the *Washington Post* and *Newsweek* before being trumpeted around the world by the broadcast media. Print and online media, as written text, also provide more detailed and complete information than radio or television media, offering a better context for analysis. The nation's economic, social, and political elite tend to rely on the detailed coverage provided by the print media to inform and influence their views about important public matters. The print media may have a smaller audience than their cousins in broadcasting, but they have an especially influential audience.

For most traditional newspapers, though, recent decades have been ruinous. Competition from broadcast media and, more recently, free content online, combined with simultaneous declines in advertising revenue and circulation levels, have undermined the traditional business model of newspapers, bringing financial disaster to traditional print media.[8] Daily newspaper print circulation has declined from 62 million to 49 million nationwide over the past 20 years. Circulation for the *New York Times*, for example, dropped more than 10 percent from 2010 to 2011, and in 2011 alone the paper lost 25 percent of its revenue.[9] For the first time, advertisers prefer online media; advertising revenue at print newspapers has dropped by 25 percent since 2006.[10] Major newspapers such as the *Chicago Tribune*, the *Minneapolis Star Tribune*, and the *Philadelphia Inquirer* have all sought bankruptcy protection. Many newspapers, such as the *Rocky Mountain News*, have gone out of business altogether. The *Los Angeles Times* has reduced its news staff by half over the past decade. Newspapers have cut costs by closing their foreign bureaus and their offices in Washington, D.C.

To counter these trends, traditional media organizations have been forced to adapt, and most now have a significant online presence, blurring the distinction between old media and new. Faced with shrinking revenues from their print versions, a few news organizations, such as the *Washington Post*, the *New York Times*, and the *Economist*, have begun to charge customers for reading the news online, while others, such as the *Seattle Post-Intelligencer* and the *Christian Science Monitor*, have become online only. If this approach succeeds, we may see more online subscription newspapers in the future, and a more viable business model for the digital press.

## ● New Media and Online News

**Explain how the Internet has transformed the news media**

The twenty-first century has already experienced a profound transformation of the media. The impact of the Internet in communications technology parallels that of the printing press in nineteenth-century America, which saw the rise of the **penny press** and widespread literacy.[11] Today, even as the newspaper business struggles for its life, readership of online news has soared. Nielsen estimates that 75 million Americans read the news online, a number higher than that for print newspapers.[12] Beside online-only newspapers, other forums include news websites, blogs, Facebook, YouTube, and Twitter. **News aggregators**, such as Google News and Real Clear Politics, provide links to thousands of stories covered in the news each day, as well as the latest public opinion polls and their own synthesis of the headline news. Younger Americans are more likely to rely on the Internet than any other news source, which suggests that this trend will continue in the future.[13] One great advantage of online news is that it is frequently updated. After the September 11, 2001, terrorist attacks, many Americans relied on the Internet for news about terrorism, bioterrorism, and the wars in Iraq and Afghanistan, as well as for viewing video of the Twin Towers falling. In general, news watchers have quickly grown accustomed to following world events unfolding in real time. Online media are more diverse and have created a more democratic and participatory press, one in which citizens and nonprofit organizations now play a prominent role. No longer relegated to the letters-to-the-editor section found in most print publications, readers can now post comments online and participate in a community providing feedback on almost all online news articles. Online media, by representing a wider range of political views than traditional media, have created a more democratic press.

The term *digital citizenship* refers to the ability to participate in society and politics online. In much the same way that education and literacy promoted democracy and economic growth in the nineteenth century, today's Internet has the potential to benefit society as a whole and to facilitate political participation by individuals within society. Like education, the Internet helps provide the information and skills needed for democratic engagement and economic opportunity.[14] It facilitates social inclusion through greater access to political information and news.[15]

However, regular and effective use of the Internet requires high-speed access, technical skills, and literacy to evaluate and use information online.[16] Individuals

**penny press** cheap, tabloid-style newspaper produced in the nineteenth century, when mass production of inexpensive newspapers first became possible due to the steam-powered printing press; a penny press cost one cent compared to other papers, which cost more than five cents

**news aggregator** an application or feed that collects Web content such as news headlines, blogs, podcasts, online videos, and more in one location for easy viewing

*The rise of new media has made it easier for Americans with Internet access to get political news, but 1 in 5 Americans is still completely offline. For example, there are neighborhoods in large cities like Chicago where over 80 percent of households lack broadband access.*

# Who Gets Political Information Online?

## Percentage of Internet Users Who Go Online to Find...

In a democracy like the United States, people need political information to understand current issues and their government's actions. With the rise of the Internet as a news source, Americans are increasingly likely to get political and other important information online. However, not everyone has the same level of access to the Internet and thus to information.

| News | Political news | Health/medical information |
|------|----------------|----------------------------|
| 76% | 61% | 80% |

| Job information | A government website | Housing information |
|-----------------|----------------------|---------------------|
| 56% | 67% | 39% |

## Who Has High-Speed Internet at Home?

SOURCES: Pew Internet and American Life Project, "Trend Data: Adults" 2011, http://pewinternet.org/Trend-Data-(Adults)/Online-Activites-Total.aspx; National Telecommunications & Information Administration, "Digital Nation: Understanding Internet Usage," February 2011, www.ntia.doc.gov/files/ntia/publications/ntia_internet_use_report_february_2011.pdf (both accessed 5/23/12).

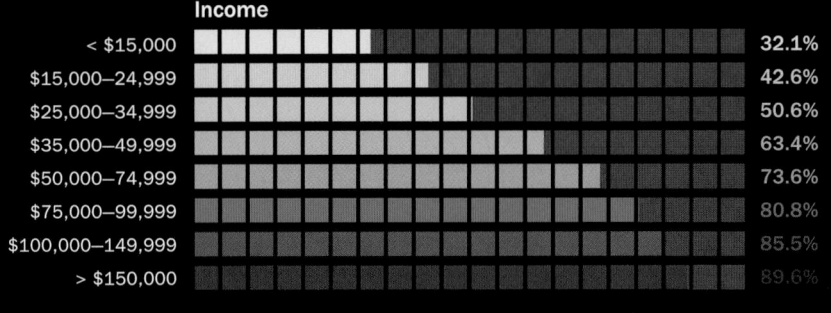

### Income

| Income | Percentage |
|--------|-----------|
| < $15,000 | 32.1% |
| $15,000–24,999 | 42.6% |
| $25,000–34,999 | 50.6% |
| $35,000–49,999 | 63.4% |
| $50,000–74,999 | 73.6% |
| $75,000–99,999 | 80.8% |
| $100,000–149,999 | 85.5% |
| > $150,000 | 89.6% |

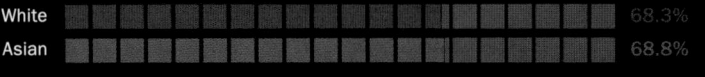

### Race/Ethnicity

| Race/Ethnicity | Percentage |
|----------------|-----------|
| Hispanic | 45.2% |
| Black | 49.9% |
| White | 68.3% |
| Asian | 68.8% |

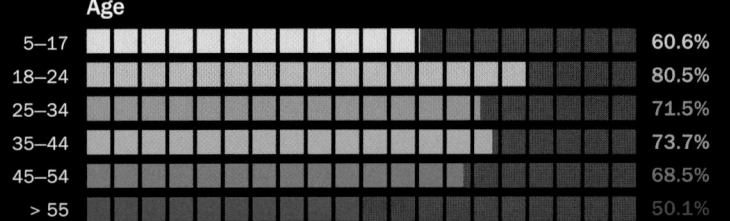

### Age

| Age | Percentage |
|-----|-----------|
| 5–17 | 60.6% |
| 18–24 | 80.5% |
| 25–34 | 71.5% |
| 35–44 | 73.7% |
| 45–54 | 68.5% |
| > 55 | 50.1% |

## for critical analysis

1. Which groups are less likely to have access to high-speed Internet? Why might this be a concern in American politics?

2. In the past, young people have been less likely than older Americans to use news sources, like newspapers or television news programs. Will digital politics change this pattern?

**digital citizen** a daily Internet user with high-speed home Internet access and the technology and literacy skills to go online for employment, news, politics, entertainment, commerce, and other activities

**niche journalism** news reporting devoted to a targeted portion (subset) of a journalism market sector or for a portion of readers/ viewers based on content or ideological presentation

without the access or skills to use the Internet may be increasingly uninformed and excluded from the world of politics online. As of 2011, almost 7 in 10 Americans were **digital citizens**, individuals with high-speed access at home (beyond mobile access), and nearly 8 in 10 Americans used the Internet in some location (e.g., home, school, library). However, 1 in 5 Americans are completely offline. Moreover, just half of African Americans, Latinos, and the poor are digital citizens by this definition (home access), as well as the poor, which suggests that there are significant inequalities in access to digital media.[17] Additionally, up to 20 percent of adult Americans fall into the lowest literacy category. Although most people in this category were not illiterate (completely unable to read or write), they lacked the basic skills necessary to read a simple newspaper article.[18] Digital citizenship requires literacy skills for reading and understanding printed information, as well as regular Internet access.

In this section we look at the major types of online news available to citizens today. While many traditional news sources, such as newspapers, now publish online, other Web news outlets tend to be smaller and more specialized, and have lower personnel and overhead costs than mainstream publishers. Sharing videos online through sites such as YouTube is fundamentally altering broadcast news, as dedicated channels provide analysis, commentary, and comedy, just as podcasts are restructuring radio news. Beyond news aggregation websites, online news sources include niche journalism, citizen journalism and blogs, nonprofit journalism, and social media.

## Niche Journalism

In the gap opened by the decline of traditional print media, the last decade has seen the rise of **niche journalism** and specialty publications. Bloomberg News, one of the most successful specialty online sources, has hundreds of thousands of readers paying a large annual fee for detailed business-related news. In politics, Roll Call, The Hill, the National Journal, Congressional Quarterly, Salon, the Huffington Post, Real Clear Politics, and Politico, the niche leader, have detailed political reporting inside the Beltway (that is, in Washington, D.C., which is encircled by freeways). *The Onion*, a satiric publication also available in print, has an avid following among the young and liberals. Niche journalism feeds citizens' interest in politics from the full range of the political spectrum. These niche outlets are supplemented by a rich array of international and foreign online news sources.

News consumers have shifted from a few general-purpose sources, such as the evening television news and a local newspaper, to a large number of niche publications and specialized new sources: business news from one source; weather from another; sport, politics and commentary from others. Just 10 years ago Americans tuned to local evening news for weather; today many Americans use Weather. com or Weather Channel applications on smartphones. Two-thirds of Americans go online wirelessly using a laptop, tablet computer, or smartphone, while 46 percent of Americans have a smartphone that connects to the Internet as of 2012.[19] The radio has long been a primary medium for information about local traffic, but today Google Maps on smartphones provides up-to-the-minute traffic information and routing with the touch of a screen. Sports fans once depended on local evening news for information about their favorite teams but now find it online through a variety of niche media outlets, including EPSN online. The rise of niche journalism has fundamentally changed how Americans consume news and what they read.

## Citizen Journalism and Blogs

The old media system was dominated by professional journalists, trained in journalism schools, who served as gatekeepers in determining what was front-page news and how political events were to be interpreted. This system had benefits and costs: the quality was high, but the diversity of opinions was relatively low. The media's gatekeeper role continues, but the diversity of online media is changing traditional journalism and the very nature of "news coverage." Even five years ago, most establishment journalists took their cues exclusively from a small handful of outlets (such as the Drudge Report), but now many of them use a much more extensive and diversified roster of sources, including blogs, Twitter, and independent political commentators, such as Nate Silver's FiveThirtyEight blog on elections (now published on the *New York Times* website). Online news is creating a new generation of whistle-blowers, enhancing the media's traditional role as a watchdog for the people against government corruption, and it is creating new venues for the political activism of ideological conservatives, liberals, and moderates.

A distinguishing feature of the digital media is **citizen journalism**, which is interactive and participatory. Citizen journalism includes news reporting and political commentary by ordinary citizens, and even crisis coverage from eyewitnesses on the scene. If the September 11 attacks had occurred in 2011 instead of 2001, the Web would be populated by citizen videos of the devastating terrorist attack on U.S. soil. In just 10 years, news reporting has dramatically changed. Because it involves a wider range of voices in gathering news and interpreting political events, contemporary news reporting and commentary are more democratic. Magnifying the power of the Internet is the near-universal availability of digital cameras and camera-equipped cell phones, which gives millions of Americans the capacity to photograph or film events. At the same time, Internet sites such as YouTube permit users to upload photos and video clips that are then viewed by hundreds of thousands of subscribers or relayed by the mainstream media for even wider dissemination. When a citizen using a mobile phone captured video of police pepper-spraying peaceful Occupy Wall Street demonstrators at the University of California–Davis in November 2011, it became headline news; the video was viewed by millions and fueled mounting concerns about police brutality toward the Occupy protesters.

A growing number of readers turn to online blogs (short for "Web logs"). There are thousands of blogs, covering virtually every topic imaginable, and a large share of these include political news and commentary on local, national, and world events. Many blogs are citizen-run and are more interactive and representative of the diversity of American views than traditional news, which generally reflects the priorities of political elites. A number of blogs, such as the Daily Kos, Nate Silver's FiveThirtyEight, and Salon's Glen Greenwald, have thousands of loyal readers who regularly critique stories presented by the print and broadcast media. These online discussion and comment forums create a community for readers, further interpreting the news.

Citizen journalism supplements the work of professional journalists in many important ways. The diversity of online media has created new opinion leaders, new voices, and even, at times, improved information. In recent years, for example, bloggers have uncovered major factual errors in media reports and forced the networks and newspapers to issue corrections. Sharp-eyed bloggers have proven adept at recognizing faked or Photoshopped photographs in news stories—for example, pointing out that major news outlets, including the *New York Times*, the *Los Angeles*

**citizen journalism** news reported and distributed by citizens, rather than professional journalists and for-profit news organizations

*In 2011 an ordinary citizen recorded video of police pepper-spraying peaceful Occupy protesters at the University of California–Davis. This video was widely shared on the Internet and the story became headline news.*

*Times*, Reuters, and the Associated Press, had presented doctored photos in their reports from Iraq, Afghanistan, and the Israeli-Palestinian conflict.[20] Because bloggers do not have strict editorial boards, they can post a story within minutes. This ability to scoop the mainstream media often means that bloggers are now the ones framing stories about political candidates, and candidates have only minutes to respond to accusations before the story breaks in the mainstream media.[21] By sharply lowering the technological and financial barriers that previously prevented all but a few individuals and interests from reaching mass audiences, blogs (at least potentially) increase the ability of ordinary people to engage in effective political action. (In Chapter 8, we will take a closer look at the Internet's effects on political participation.)

To be sure, the open, freewheeling nature of blogging often means that there's little of the traditional quality control employed by "respectable," institutional old media. Many of the claims found in blogs are unsupported or simply untrue. And because they do not face the burden of fact-checking required for the mainstream media, even well-meaning bloggers can post false information. This could be one reason why misinformation about political issues is higher among blog readers than those reading online news from the mainstream press.[22] Moreover, niche bloggers may not be subject to the moderating influences felt by mainstream publications, which try to appeal to the widest possible readership. In 2008, for example, bloggers were responsible for some of the harshest attacks of the presidential campaign, often focusing on negative stories and even scurrilous rumors. Republican bloggers circulated the unfounded claim that Barack Obama was a Muslim intent on subverting the U.S. government, or that Obama was a noncitizen. (This false rumor is covered in detail in Chapter 6.) Democratic bloggers, for their part, circulated unflattering stories about John McCain's personal history and made much of an allegation that Sarah Palin's infant son was actually her daughter's baby. These blog-driven rumors became widespread enough to receive attention in the mainstream media.

## Nonprofit Journalism

As traditional news organizations have cut budgets and especially investigative journalism, political information is increasingly emanating from universities, think tanks, nonprofit organizations, and private foundations. Think tanks such as the Brookings Institution, the Cato Institute, the Hoover Institution, the Heritage Foundation, the Center for American Progress, and the American Enterprise Institute provide information and analysis on current events in order to influence public debate. Universities have expended their public outreach, encouraging faculty to explain their findings for a general audience; as a result, university faculty are increasingly cited in the mainstream media. Universities have even constructed television studios and entire networks, such as the Big Ten Network, which includes athletic and academic programming, and polling during presidential elections. Community-based nonprofit newspapers are supported by local foundations seeking to fill the void in local news as local papers close their doors. Corporations are players, too. The Bill and Melinda Gates Foundation, established by Microsoft founder Bill Gates, provides extensive funding to National Public Radio. The Pew Research Center's 2010 report entitled the "State of the Media 2010" estimates that, in the past four years, $14 million in nonprofit funding has been spent in new media. But this represents only one-tenth of the $1.6 billion in print newspaper revenue lost during this same period.[23]

## Social Media

**Social media**, such as Twitter and Facebook, are the most recent players in news and political communication. Nearly half of the U.S. population of 311 million is registered as users on Facebook. Pew surveys show that 15 percent of Americans who use the Internet use Twitter, and this figure has been rising over the past few years; 8 percent use Twitter on a typical day.[24] Young adults, African Americans, and mobile users have the highest rates of using Twitter. Both Facebook and Twitter are online networking forums that allow users to share content, news stories, photos, and videos with others, from a handful of close friends to thousands of people. Because they are more personalized and interactive than anonymous news organizations, social media are becoming increasing popular means for Americans to receive political information from the candidates and interest groups they support. In turn, candidates for political office, elected officials, political organizations, and interest groups have been quick to adopt Facebook and Twitter as means of communicating with their supporters and providing them a continual feed of new information. For example, in 2007, Chris Hughes, one of the founders of Facebook, helped the Obama presidential campaign establish a Facebook site that allowed Obama supporters to "like" the senator's page. At the site's resource center, visitors could download flyers, videos, and other campaign materials, and could create or join online groups to

**social media** Web-based and mobile-based technologies that are used to turn communication into interactive dialogue between organizations, communities, and individuals; social media technologies take on many different forms including blogs, Wikis, podcasts, pictures, video, Facebook, Twitter, and more

*Barack Obama's Facebook page was an important tool in his 2008 and 2012 campaigns, offering a way to inform and organize supporters. As of summer 2012, Obama had 26 million friends on Facebook.*

share ideas and organize events. The site's fund-raising section allowed visitors to set personal fund-raising goals and to invite other registered friends to help them reach those goals. The Obama site attracted more than a million visitors during the campaign for the 2008 Democratic presidential nomination,[25] and as of 2012, Obama's Facebook page has 26 million friends.

Both Facebook and Twitter have contributed to political mobilization and information sharing by creating virtual social networks where groups of like-minded individuals, or individuals with shared interests, can quickly and easily share information. Twitter was the communication tool of choice for organizing the Occupy Wall Street demonstrations in 2011, as thousands of Americans camped out in cities across the United States to protest growing income inequality between the top 1 percent of American income earners and the bottom 99 percent. In another example, from outside the United States, bloggers and Twitter users helped organize protests around the Middle East during the 2010 "Arab Spring," bringing down the Egyptian dictator Hosni Mubarak and other governments.

## Benefits of Online News

So why have new media become so popular? We have just touched on many of the reasons: Americans may prefer online news because of (1) the convenience of getting the news online; (2) the up-to-the-moment currency of the information available online; (3) the depth of the information available online; and (4) the diversity of online viewpoints.[26] At the same time, changes to the media arising from the rapid proliferation of the Internet have raised a multitude of concerns, as we will see in the section "Concerns about Online News."

**Convenience** Information online is convenient and always available for those who have regular access to the Internet at home or, increasingly, through mobile devices such as smartphones. Pew surveys show that nearly half of those who use online news and political information cite its convenience.[27] Finding specific information is simplified by search engines, links, and search functions within Web pages. Google News, for example, reports the headline news (domestic and international) from thousands of sources updated by the minute, with 24-hour-a-day convenience, providing access to information with much more depth than that found when tuning into the national evening news on television. Twitter, Facebook, Google News, and Weather Channel applications provide news updates on smartphones. Because political knowledge is central to the formation of political attitudes, the convenience of online political news may lead to a more informed and engaged citizenry. Use of online political information is associated with more interest in politics, greater knowledge of politics, and a greater likelihood of discussing politics with friends and family.[28]

**Currency** One of the fundamental changes ushered in by an era of online news is the speed with which local, national, and international events are covered, as well as the scope of coverage. Major news stories regularly break first online, and are later reported through print newspapers and television. Social media have accelerated even further the speed with which news travels around the globe. News of Osama bin Laden's death in May 2011 spread rapidly through text-messaging, smartphones, and social media outlets such as Facebook and Twitter even before it could be verified by traditional media. When the Twin Towers fell on September 11, online videos spread rapidly, with the most updated information about the terrorist attack found online. Likewise, many Americans watched online videos of millions of gallons of crude oil gushing into the Gulf of Mexico in 2010. Viewership peaked with "top kill" efforts by British Petroleum (BP) to stop the leak on the *Deepwater Horizon* rig.

**Depth** Online news provides more information than the 60-second sound bites found in television and radio news. By blending more-detailed treatment of topics with the visual and emotive appeal of streaming videos, the Internet shares qualities both of print media (promoting knowledge) and of the visual aspects of television (promoting interest and engagement).[29] Online news covers events and issues with the same immediacy as television, but with the in-depth treatment that is typical of newspapers. The multimedia capacity of the Internet notwithstanding, most websites still rely heavily upon written text, and most political "Web surfing" consists mainly of reading, which facilitates greater recall of information and, in turn, encourages the acquisition of political knowledge.[30]

**Diversity** Like the myriad products sold in a modern grocery store or available for purchase on Amazon.com, the American media industry is now highly fragmented, with hundreds of thousands of sources presenting political information. Online sources are much more diverse than those found in the traditional media, and this diversity may lead to an increase in political knowledge and interest.[31] While major players online certainly do include mainstream outlets (such as websites sponsored by television networks and major newspapers in the United States),[32] the Internet remains populated by a wide range of information sources. By making foreign media such as the British Broadcasting Company (BBC) and Al Jazeera television easily available, the Internet has reduced the importance of physical proximity and created a truly global shared culture. Millions went online to watch live broadcasts of Egyptian citizens protesting for democratic freedoms in 2011. News aggregators provide links to a broad international array of sources; Google News, for example, draws from more than 25,000 publishers around the world and offers its services in two dozen languages. Sites such as RealClearPolitics .com focus on politics, presenting links to commentary, the latest polling results, and

# Traditional Media vs. Social Media

**The Internet, especially Twitter, has** transformed how political campaigns interact with the media, and how Americans get campaign news. Before the rise of the Internet, news reached the public through television, radio, or newspapers. Each of these sources required journalists (to find stories), editors, and researchers (to ensure the information was accurate), as well as time to distribute the story. Stories used to take hours if not days to reach the public, and controversial or scandalous stories sometimes did not appear at all because journalists had trouble verifying the information. To publish a story based on hearsay opens the publisher to a libel charge if the information turns out to be false. Today, blogs, Twitter, and other sites repeat rumors (as well as breaking news) at lightning speed, while political campaigns and journalists are forced to play catchup.

The changing standards of the news have become evident in presidential elections. Campaigns used to hire strategists who were friendly with reporters, in the hope that tips about forthcoming stories would give the campaign team time to prepare a response to a negative story. Since the 2000 presidential election, however, the 24-hour news cycle has meant that campaign staffers have had to scour the Internet for any possible negative information about their candidate and respond immediately. Campaigns cannot afford to take an entire day to respond to negative information.

Another trend is that traditional media tend to focus on campaign strategy among the candidates, while social media focus more on the likability of the candidates, their positions on issues, and the candidates' personal lives. One study analyzed more than 20 million tweets in the run-up to the 2012 primary election, and researchers found that the discourse on Twitter was much more opinionated and candidate-biased than mainstream media coverage. There is also more of it on Twitter. Discussions

of the 2012 presidential candidates on Twitter outnumbered those found in blogs by nine to one.

The content of traditional and social media also differs. In 2012, coverage of Republican presidential candidate Ron Paul was virtually nonexistent in the mainstream news, but Paul had a loyal following of supporters online who posted their "news" daily. Paul enjoyed the most favorable tone on Twitter of all candidates; 55 percent of the statements made about him were positive. However, the study found that overall political discussion on Twitter is slightly more negative than that in the mainstream news.

In recent years, there is evidence that individuals have become more skeptical of major news outlets and have increasingly turned to Twitter, blogs, social media, and other online sources for information. A National Journal/Heartland Monitor poll conducted in the summer of 2012 found that input from personal relationships was more important than information from major newspapers in voting decisions in the 2012 presidential election. Three in four Americans relied on conversations and information shared

by friends, family, and acquaintances. Only 6 in 10 relied on editors' opinions in news magazines and major newspapers. Social media allows information from individuals' social networks to loom large in political decisions.

As news consumers increasingly turn to social networks, they need to be mindful of where the information has come from and whether it is a reputable news source or an unregulated rumor. While there are still some restraints on major outlets, bloggers and tweeters have free rein to write whatever they want. Bloggers have been known to fabricate entire stories about candidates they do not like. Candidates and parties, in turn, must be ready at a second's notice to refute claims made on these unregulated "news" sites.

SOURCES: Jeff Howe, "The Next Economy: The Dialogue Economy, Social Media and the Marketplace," *A Special Supplement to the Atlantic Monthly* (a joint project with the National Journal) (Summer 2012). Tom Rosenstiel, Mark Jurkowitz, and Tricia Sartor. "How the Media Covered the 2012 Primary Campaign," Pew Research Center, April 23, 2012, www.journalism.org/analysis _report/romney_report?src=prc-headline (accessed 6/23/12). Tom Rosenstiel, Mark Jurkowitz, et al. "Twitter and the Campaign: How the Discussion on Twitter Varies from Blogs and News Coverage and Ron Paul's Twitter Triumph." Pew Research Center, December 8, 2011, www .journalism.org/analysis_report/twitter_and_campaign" (accessed 6/23/12).

## for critical analysis

1. Do you think today's 24-hour news cycle and multitude of news sources create a more informed citizenry? Why or why not?
2. What are some of the benefits of getting political information from trusted friends or family members? What are some of the possible drawbacks?

*The Egyptian Revolution in 2011 showed how new media—from citizen journalism to social media—can empower citizens. The Egyptian government shut down Internet access and cell phone service in an effort to keep the protesters from organizing and publicizing their cause.*

news analysis from newspapers nationwide. By including links to columns by ideological liberals, moderates, conservatives, and libertarians, such sites highlight the diversity of political news online. Such a vast array of voices, of course, means that online sources also can provide questionable information, misinformation, or outright lies—just as can happen in mainstream media and even presidential debates. To verify media reports found in both traditional and online media, there are new websites, such as FactCheck.org and PolitiFact.com, devoted exclusively to checking the veracity of political claims.

**Decentralization and Local News** A long-standing concern of scholars of traditional media has been the "nationalization of the news" that results when most political news emanates from inside the Washington, D.C., Beltway, to the detriment of local news coverage. Ten years ago the dominance of national wire services, such as the Associated Press, and budget constraints by local newspapers resulted in a dearth of relevant local news reporting. As the seat of national government, Washington has been the focus for traditional print and television media. New media have decentered the political news. In 2010 the Pew Research Center's Project for Excellence in Journalism found that many traditional national news outlets were in irreversible decline, and when unavoidable belt-tightening meant cuts in overall staff numbers and news-gathering bureaus, the first to go were often the D.C. offices. NBC and CBS cut their Washington bureaus by 50 percent over the past five years, while the number of newspaper reporters based in Washington bureaus declined by 50 percent.[33] And many newspapers, including the *Chicago Tribune* and the *Los Angeles Times*, closed their Washington bureaus altogether. While the cost to traditional journalism is apparent, the decentralization of online news may have a silver lining resulting in a revival of local news coverage. Online local newspapers; blogs; city and local government websites and Facebook pages; community newsletters; email listservs; social media; and other new sources have made local news and local political news more available than in previous decades. Almost every city government has a Facebook page and website, which publish news and events, as well as offer services. A 2011 survey from the Pew Internet and American Life found 67 percent of American adult Internet users had visited a local, state, or federal government website; over 50 percent of Americans use the Internet to get community or neighborhoods news.[34] Readily available local news coverage may engage citizens in politics in their communities.

## Concerns about Online News

While online news holds significant promise for improving access to the political information citizens need, the shift toward online media has also given rise to several major concerns. These potential disadvantages include a decline in investigative journalism, uneven quality in news content, and negative effects on knowledge and tolerance.

**Loss of Investigative Power**  In a democracy, the press is expected to be a watchdog for the people and to inform citizens about government abuses of power. Stated another way, democracies depend upon news organizations to inform the people about current events and to help citizens hold their leaders accountable for their actions. The greatest challenge for contemporary news organizations is to generate enough revenue to finance traditional investigative journalism.[35] This activity requires more time and resources than other aspects of the news, and it may be the most important. When readers paid subscription fees to read the news, circulation was high and advertising provided sufficient revenue to allow newspapers and, later, broadcasters to cover both basic news (weather, sports, business) and political events. Revenue from publishing basic news would subsidize political analysis and investigative journalism. By breaking apart mainstream news organizations, online news may actually reduce the media's ability to engage in the kind of sustained, in-depth reporting that is critical to the media's watchdog role and thus to the health of American democracy.

**More Variation in the Quality of News**  As already noted, the growing diversity of online news has led to substantial variation in the quality of available information. Multiple perspectives certainly do provide citizens with a well-stocked marketplace of ideas, but the freewheeling nature of the Internet also means that hate speech, unsubstantiated rumors, and outdated information can overwhelm thoughtful, original, and civic-oriented voices. And while viral media may elevate the watchdog function of the media, the misinformation and unsubstantiated rumors that are part of viral media can substitute for objective truth as claims are widely repeated. This is especially so in anonymous online forums, where sexism and racism can be freely communicated in unedited form. Political scientist Dianne Bystrom has noted that "the online universe of political commentary operates outside traditional media editorial boundaries and is sometimes incisive but often offensive and unsubstantiated."[36]

Political candidates and political leaders are particularly susceptible to attack when negative stories go viral and spread quickly without the traditional media filters of fact-checking and respect for the privacy of public figures. This can have real consequences; for example, scholars have found that Hillary Clinton's 2008 presidential campaign was hurt by negative and arguably sexist discussion on the blogs.[37] False rumors that President Obama was not a natural-born citizen and therefore not eligible to be president under Article II of the U.S. Constitution spread rapidly on the Internet and spilled over into mainstream news. These "birther movement" conspiracy theories, promoted by real estate tycoon Donald Trump and his allies, alleged that Obama was born in Kenya, not Hawaii, or that his birth certificate was a forgery. Extensive media coverage of the birther movement allowed what many viewed as an attack against a sitting president to become the nation's headline news, something that may not have occurred in a pre-Internet era. Belief in these theories has persisted, despite Obama's pre-election release of his official long-form birth certificate from Hawaii in 2008, the posting of a copy of his birth certificate online, and confirmation by the Hawaii Department of Health based on the original documents. The birther movement is an example of a story that went viral based on claims that were proven to be untrue. (See Chapter 6 for a related discussion.)

Another case of viral media occurred when Penn State assistant football coach Jerry Sandusky was charged by a grand jury of 67 counts of child sexual abuse involving up to a dozen victims. More than 10,000 stories appeared in Google News each day for weeks as a member of America's iconic Big Ten football program was charged with an egregious crime against a number of youths and university officials were accused of not protecting children from violence. The fury caused the ouster of Hall of Fame football coach Joe Paterno and the school's longtime president. While a court would eventually determine Sandusky's innocence or guilt, viral media created a tsunami of media coverage, increasing the importance of the media in politics and society. As Sandusky's lawyer complained, "my client has been tried in the court of public opinion."[38] The implication is that Sandusky's reputation was ruined by the viral mass media even before he was convicted in a court of law.

**Potential Effects on Knowledge and Tolerance** Perhaps the greatest concern about politics in the digital age goes to the heart of modern democracy: Do online media ultimately help or hinder progress toward the ideal of a well-informed citizenry that can govern itself effectively? One study has found that while readers of online news from major websites (largely offshoots of the traditional print and broadcast media) are more knowledgeable than average citizens, those who get their political news mainly from blogs are actually worse off.[39] And the very diversity of online news, in fact, may actually *lower* tolerance for social and political diversity. Most new media do not abide by traditional media's principle of objective

*Some online news sources like Politico.com have developed a reputation for accuracy and professionalism. Here, a Politico reporter talks with Treasury Secretary Timothy Geithner. However, the quality of information from many online news sources varies and isn't always reliable.*

journalism, in which both sides of an argument are reported. Instead, the specialization of information online and on cable television means that liberals and conservatives alike can turn to specialized websites and television channels that cater to their underlying assumptions and that avoid exposing readers/viewers to information that might challenge their preconceived beliefs. Online news outlets, for their part, serve certain self-selected groups and are unlikely to cover stories that do not conform to what that group wants to hear.[40] Even the active nature of the online experience can contribute to the "balkanization," or compartmentalization, of the electorate. On the Internet, an individual must seek out information, compared with the passive process of simply watching or listening to television.[41] The natural tendency to select online news that conforms with our own beliefs is exacerbated by the way search engines cater to our individual preferences—what one scholar has called the "filter bubble," which screens out exposure to information that might challenge or broaden our worldview.[42]

The undeniable benefits and possibilities created by digital media for the American political process may well outweigh these concerns about accuracy, reliability, ethical practices, and depth of reporting. If the new media are to realize their potential as a boon to informed democratic participation, citizens must have "information literacy," or the ability to find, evaluate, and apply information.[43] Greater access to information online makes education and critical thinking among citizens more important than ever before.

## ● Mass Media Ownership

> **Describe trends in who owns mass media companies**

Ironically, and in sharp contrast to the immense diversity in online news sources, the second most significant trend in America's largely unregulated media system is the growing concentration in ownership of traditional media. The popularity of online news may in part be a response to the growing homogenization of traditional corporate media that has been occurring over the last three decades.

The United States boasts approximately 1,400 daily newspapers, 2,000 television stations, and more than 13,000 radio stations (20 percent of which are devoted to news, talk, or public affairs). Despite these substantial numbers overall, the number of traditional news-gathering sources operating nationally is actually quite small—several wire services, four broadcast networks, public radio and television, two elite newspapers, three newsmagazines, and a smattering of other sources, such as the national correspondents of a few large local papers and several small, independent radio networks. More than three-fourths of the daily newspapers in the United States are owned by large media conglomerates such as the Hearst, McClatchy, and Gannett corporations. Much of the national news that is published by local newspapers is provided by one wire service, the Associated Press, while additional coverage is provided by services run by several major newspapers, including the *New York Times* and the *Chicago Tribune*. More than 500 of the nation's television stations are affiliated with one of the four networks and carry that network's evening news programs. Dozens of others carry PBS (Public Broadcasting System) news. Several hundred local radio stations also carry network news or National Public Radio news broadcasts.

At the same time, though, there are only three truly national newspapers: the *Wall Street Journal*, the *Christian Science Monitor*, and *USA Today*; two other papers, the *New York Times* and the *Washington Post*, are read by political leaders and other influential Americans throughout the nation. National news is also carried to millions of Americans by the newsmagazine *Time*, though it is declining in readership. Beginning in the late 1980s, CNN became another major news source for Americans, especially after its coverage of the Persian Gulf War. However, the number of news sources—those doing actual news-gathering, not simply relying on news reporting by others—has remained essentially the same, or has declined. Some of the most popular online news outlets are electronic versions of the conventional print or broadcast media.

The trend toward less variety in traditional media has been accelerated by changes in media ownership, which became possible in large part due to the relaxation of government regulations in the 1980s and '90s. The enactment of the 1996 Telecommunications Act opened the way for additional consolidation in the media industry, and a wave of mergers and consolidations has further reduced the field of independent media across the country. For example, the Australian press baron Rupert Murdoch owns the Fox network plus a host of radio, television, and newspaper properties around the world, known collectively as News Corporation, the world's second-largest media conglomerate. In 2007, Murdoch won control of the *Wall Street Journal*, consolidating his position as one of the world's most powerful publishers. News Corporation owns 800 media companies in more than 50 countries and has a net worth of $5 billion. A small number of giant corporations now control a wide swath of media holdings, including television networks, movie studios, record companies, cable channels and local cable providers, book publishers, magazines, and newspapers. Clear Channel Communications, for example, a Texas-based media conglomerate, owns 850 radio stations—by far the largest number controlled by a single company. These developments have prompted questions about whether enough competition exists among the media to produce a truly diverse set of views on political and corporate matters, or even whether the United States has become a prisoner of media monopolies.[44]

As major newspapers, television stations, and radio networks fall into fewer and fewer hands, the risk increases that politicians and citizens who express less-popular or minority viewpoints will have difficulty finding a public forum. Examples include 2012 Republican presidential candidate Ron Paul, who despite favorable showing in early nominating events, such as the Iowa caucuses and the New Hampshire primary, received little national media coverage because his libertarian ideas were outside the mainstream of his political party. **Media monopolies** may also be a reason for the relatively scant mainstream media coverage of the Occupy Wall Street protests, which have sought to bring attention to the issue of income inequality. (See Chapter 8 for more discussion of the Occupy movement.) The mainstream media are often committed to the status quo, which is why they were less enthusiastic about the Occupy protests or, at the other end of the political spectrum, the Tea Party. Increasingly, these groups turn to the Internet to express their views. The Internet is an important mechanism for linking communities of adherents, but can it mitigate traditional media's homogeneous point of view in terms of what constitutes news coverage, or its treatment of opinions that challenge the status quo? Can the diversity of media sources available online, including blogs and social media, help balance the corporate concentration of media ownership?

**media monopoly** the ownership and control of the media by a few large corporations

One negative consequence of media concentration may be a steadily growing distrust of the press. Jonathan Ladd argues that from the 1950s through the 1970s, competition in American party politics and the media industry reached historic lows.[45] When competition later intensified in both of these realms, the public's distrust of the institutional media grew, leading the public to resist the mainstream press's reporting about policy outcomes and to turn toward alternative partisan media outlets—those expressly favored by Republicans or Democrats. As a result, public opinion and voting behavior are now increasingly shaped by partisan media, such as Fox News on the right and MSNBC on the left. While it is impossible to suppress party and media competition in the twenty-first century, and certainly not in a new media environment, Ladd argues that we need new ways to augment the public's political knowledge. In an age of digital media having uneven and unpredictable quality, it is more important than ever for citizens to find, evaluate, and apply information.

# ● Media Influence

Analyze the ways the media can influence public opinion and politics

The content and character of news and public affairs programming—what the media choose to present and how they present it—can have far-reaching political consequences. The media can shape and modify, if not fully form, the public's perception of events, issues, and institutions. Media coverage can rally support for, or intensify opposition to, national policies on matters as weighty as health care, the economy, or international wars. Media disclosures can greatly enhance, or fatally damage, the careers of public figures, as discussed earlier. At the same time, the media are influenced by the individuals or groups who are subjects of the news. The president, in particular, has the power to set the news agenda through speeches and actions. All politicians, for that matter, seek to shape or manipulate their media images by cultivating good relations with reporters and through news leaks and staged news events.

In recent American political history, the media have played a central role in many major events. For example, the media were a critically important factor in the civil rights movement of the 1950s and '60s. Television images showing peaceful civil rights marchers attacked by club-swinging police helped to generate sympathy among northern whites for the civil rights struggle and greatly increased the pressure on Congress to bring an end to segregation.[46] To take a second example, the media were instrumental in compelling the Nixon administration to negotiate an end to American involvement in the Vietnam War. Beginning in 1967 the national media, reacting in part to a shift in elite opinion, portrayed the war as misguided and unwinnable, and as a result helped turn popular sentiment against continued American involvement.[47]

The media were also central actors in the Watergate affair, the cluster of scandals that ultimately forced President Richard Nixon, the landslide victor in the 1972 presidential election, to resign from office in disgrace just two years later. A relentless series of investigations launched by the *Washington Post*, the *New York Times*, and the television networks led to disclosures of the various abuses of which Nixon was guilty, ultimately forcing him to choose between resignation and almost certain impeachment.

*During the 1960s, civil rights protesters learned a variety of techniques designed to elicit sympathetic media coverage. Television images of police brutality in Alabama led directly to the enactment of the 1965 Civil Rights Act.*

More recently, the media were crucial actors in the U.S. decision to invade Iraq in March 2003, despite the fact that Iraq had not invaded a neighboring country or attacked the United States. In the wake of the September 11 terrorist attacks, harsh media coverage of Iraqi leader Saddam Hussein, combined with White House claims that Iraq was harboring weapons of mass destruction (WMDs), led 70 percent of Americans to approve of the invasion of Iraq. (It was later determined that, in fact, Iraq did not have any WMDs. The news media, including the *New York Times*, issued a public apology to readers for some of its coverage of claims of Iraqi WMDs.) The Pew Research Center reported in a 2003 survey that individuals getting the news from mainstream American media were more supportive of the Iraq invasion, while those relying on foreign news coverage, political comedy shows, or online news were more likely to oppose the invasion.

Conservatives have long charged that the liberal biases of reporters and journalists result in distorted news coverage.[48] A 2004 survey conducted by the Pew Research Center found that 34 percent of national news reporters identified themselves as liberal, whereas only 7 percent said they were conservative.[49] While journalists may lean in a Democratic direction, journalists generally defend their professionalism, insisting that their personal political leanings do not affect the way they perform their jobs. Moreover, those who decry "the liberal media" seldom acknowledge the partisan or ideological leanings of media owners. Rupert Murdoch, the CEO of News Corporation (the parent company of Fox News and the *Wall Street Journal*), is a politically active conservative. Philip Anschutz, owner of the *Examiner* newspapers in San Francisco, Washington, and other cities, has been a major financial contributor to the Republican Party and to GOP candidates, including George W. Bush. As discussed in detail in the previous section, the diversity of online news sources, however, may mean that debates about liberal or conservative bias in the mainstream media are becoming less important.

## How the Media Influence Politics

Traditional and new media influence American politics in a number of important ways.[50] The power of all media collectively, both traditional and online, lies in their ability to shape what issues Americans think about (agenda setting) and what opinions Americans hold about those issues (framing and priming).

**agenda setting** the power of the media to bring public attention to particular issues and problems

**Agenda Setting and Selection Bias** The first source of media power is **agenda setting**; that is, the media help to set the agenda for political discussion. Agenda setting involves identifying the issues that will receive attention by the media, which means that some things are deemed important while others are not. Groups and forces that wish to bring their ideas before the public in order to generate support for policy proposals or political candidacies must secure media coverage. If the media are persuaded that an idea is newsworthy, then they may declare it an "issue" that must be confronted or a "problem" to be solved, thus clearing the first hurdle in the policy-making process. If, on the other hand, an idea lacks or loses media appeal, its chance of resulting in new programs or policies is diminished.

After September 11, President George W. Bush had little difficulty convincing the media that terrorism and his administration's efforts to forestall further terrorist attacks merited a dominant place on the national agenda. Not surprisingly, the American-led military campaigns in Afghanistan and Iraq dominated the news throughout 2002 and 2003. Some stories have such overwhelming significance that

*In April 2004, 60 Minutes II's broadcast of the story of American soldiers' abuse of Iraqi inmates at Abu Ghraib prison was seen around the world. Initial efforts by the Bush administration to contain the Abu Ghraib scandal and limit the blame to a handful of soldiers failed.*

the main concern of political leaders is not whether a story will receive attention—wars and natural disasters always receive attention—but whether the leaders themselves will figure prominently and positively in media accounts. This was certainly true in 2005, when Hurricane Katrina struck the Gulf Coast. There was no question that this storm and the damage it caused would be on the national agenda; the question was how the press and the public would apportion blame and credit. As the story took shape, the media found little to praise in the belated, haphazard emergency and relief efforts. Local, state, and national leaders were all faulted for the region's lack of preparedness and a botched relief plan, with the Bush administration and the Federal Emergency Management Agency (FEMA) receiving the largest share of blame for these failures In 2008 and 2009 the news agenda was dominated by the global financial crisis and the severe economic recession that ensued. Continuing media attention created enormous pressure for the government to "do something" even as the crisis began to ease, and the new Obama administration's "honeymoon period" was cut short by public frustration over the government's inability to solve economic problems quickly. In 2010 the media's focus on a massive oil spill in the Gulf of Mexico contributed to widespread anger at the Obama administration's seeming helplessness to contain the environmental disaster.

In many instances, the media serve as conduits for agenda-setting efforts by competing groups and forces. Occasionally, however, journalists themselves are instrumental in setting the agenda of political discussion. The Watergate scandal that destroyed Nixon's presidency was in some measure initiated and driven by the *Washington Post* and the national television networks.

Because the media are businesses, and because the media seek to attract the largest possible audiences, they naturally tend to cover stories with dramatic or entertainment value, giving less attention to important stories that are less compelling. News coverage often focuses on crimes and scandals, especially those involving prominent individuals. This **selection bias** means that the media may provide less information about important political issues that the public depends upon. For example, the Democratic partisan predisposition of many journalists did not prevent a media frenzy in January 1998 when reports surfaced that President Clinton (a Democrat) might have had an affair with a White House intern. It was the Republicans' turn in 2012 when the extramarital affairs of presidential candidates Herman Cain and Newt Gingrich made headlines. Partisanship and ideology notwithstanding, the age-old journalistic instinct for sensational stories to tell often trumps both the media's responsibility to inform the public about what really matters and the public's responsibility to demand that from the media.

What the mainstream media decide to report on and what they ignore has important implications. For example, the mainstream media published few stories critical of the U.S. invasion of Iraq leading up to the war in March 2003. As of 2012, the Iraq and Afghanistan wars have cost an estimated $3 trillion, with more than 6,000 American troops killed and 46,000 wounded in Iraq and Afghanistan, not to mention the hundreds of thousands of citizens of these two nations who have been killed or wounded. Both wars lasted far longer than predicted. Similarly, the press shied away from other controversial topics, including the government's failure to close the Guantánamo Bay prison camp, where suspected terrorist and alleged Al Qaeda personnel have been held without a trial since 2002. In 2009, President Obama gave orders for the detention camp to be closed by 2010, but as of 2012 the camp remains open. The media provided little coverage of the Bush tax cuts in 2001, although they dramatically increased the federal budget deficit and widened the gap between the

**selection bias (news)** the tendency to focus news coverage on only on aspect of an event or issue, avoiding coverage of over aspects

# What the Media Tell Americans about the World and the World about America

**It is often said that we live in an age** of "globalization," when events anywhere in the world affect everyone in the world. Nevertheless, the American news media are surprisingly parochial in their orientation. Few news organizations have foreign bureaus or foreign correspondents. Indeed, in the face of globalization, the number of foreign bureaus operated by major news organizations has actually decreased. One veteran CBS reporter, Tom Fenton, said that when he joined the network in 1970, "I was one of three correspondents in the Rome bureau. We had bureaus in Paris, Bonn, Warsaw, Cairo, and Nairobi. Now you can count the number of foreign correspondents on two hands and have three fingers left over."[a] Despite vital American interests in the Middle East, most reporters know very little about the history, culture, and languages of the region. U.S. correspondents sent to cover the Iraq war could not speak directly with Iraqis or understand Arabic news media.[b]

On a typical Sunday, most major American newspapers devote roughly 20 percent of their news coverage to international events. It is interesting to note that the bulk of the international news featured in these papers involved war, terrorism, and political violence. To the extent that Americans derive their understanding of the world from the newspapers, they might reasonably see much of it as a very dangerous place.

However, before we dismiss the American news media as parochial, we should compare U.S. coverage of international events with that presented on the same day by one of the world's oldest and most famous newspapers, *The Times* of London. *The Times* did, indeed, devote a considerably greater portion of its news coverage to international events than did the American newspapers. Slightly more than 44 percent of the stories in *The Times* focused on world affairs—twice the percentage found in the typical American paper.

*The Times* and other international newspapers devote enormous attention to the United States because America's economic and military power mean that American actions are likely to have important consequences throughout the world. In their news pages and editorial commentary, newspapers in Europe, Asia, Africa, Latin America, and the Middle East seek to dissect American policy to understand its intentions and significance for their own nations. Often, this coverage is less than flattering, even when American policy appears to be successful. Most European newspapers were sharply critical of the Bush administration's decision to go to war against Iraq without UN approval, and, in 2009 the president of the Czech Republic, which held the six-month rotating presidency of the European Union, called the Obama administration's economic policies "a road to Hell" that would cause global inflation. However, not all foreign news coverage of U.S. politics is critical.

[a]Michael Massing, "The Unseen War," *New York Review of Books,* May 29, 2003, p. 17.
[b]Massing, "Unseen War," p. 17.

## for critical analysis

1. In 2004, American news coverage of the abuse of Iraqi prisoners by U.S. soldiers shocked the world. Should the American media present a more positive image of the United States to foreigners?

2. American newspapers offer more coverage of local events than of world affairs. What factors might explain the local focus of the American press?

super rich and most other Americans in terms of wealth.[51] Access to the print and broadcast media is such an important political resource that political forces that lack media access, such as the Occupy Wall Street protestors, have only a very limited opportunity to influence the political process. The selection bias of traditional media run by a handful of powerful corporations, however, may be balanced out by the diversity of media sources available online, especially the growing influence of social media sites such as Twitter and Facebook.

Election campaigns are important because the officials we elect set public policy, but successful campaigners know that politics in a democracy is about not only policy issues but also spectacle and entertainment. Media coverage of election campaigns typically focuses on the "horse race" (that is, who is ahead and by how much), which sometimes deflects attention from issues and candidate records. In the year preceding the 2008 national elections, for example, it appeared that Senator Hillary Clinton was nearly certain to become the Democratic nominee. Looking for a horse race, however, the national media gave enormous publicity to Senator Barack Obama. Months of positive coverage helped transform Obama into a serious presidential contender.

**Framing** The language and context in which the media presents the news, known as **framing**, can determine how the American people interpret political events. Knowing this, politicians take care to choose language that presents their ideas in the most favorable light possible. Public opinion on politics naturally changes with facts, but few citizens read legislation, so when forming opinions about policy and politics, the public relies on media coverage. This means that arguments made by elected officials and other political actors, or frames, are critical to the process of forming opinions. Political elites have some (but certainly not complete) freedom to determine the dimensions along which policies will be debated, and the frames and arguments elites use can have a powerful influence on how the public evaluates not only candidates for elected office but also public policy.

For example, the Obama administration labeled its health care initiative the Patient Protection and Affordable Care Act, thus framing the proposal as a matter of compassionate responsibility and good economic sense. As the bill was debated in Congress, early press coverage framed it as "health care reform." Sensing that Americans generally approve of the idea of "reform," Republican opponents of the legislation chose language that framed it quite differently. The law's provisions for limiting excessive medical testing were labeled as "health care rationing," for example, and proposals to create committees to advise patients about end-of-life care were called "death panels." Public support for the legislation waned as media coverage gravitated to the Republicans' framing of the issues involved; the bill that barely passed in 2010 was a much-watered-down version of the original proposal.

One of the most important aspects of the 2008 election was that for the first time in American history an African American was a major party contender for the presidency of the United States. Political scientists Michael Tesler and David O. Sears found that the 2008 election was more polarized by racial attitudes than any other presidential election on record. There were two sides: racial opposition *to* Obama and racially liberal support *for* Obama. Obama's campaign was given a boost in the primaries from racial liberals that extended well beyond that usually offered to ideologically similar white candidates, such as Hillary Clinton.[52] The media coverage of the campaign reflected this, and regarded race as more significant than Hillary Clinton's bid to become the first woman to serve as president. Partly because they regarded the fact that Obama was America's first serious black

**framing** the power of the media to influence how events and issues are interpreted

presidential candidate as newsworthy, the media gave Obama much more attention and scrutiny than they afforded other candidates. This extra attention frequently allowed Obama to dominate the news and led his opponents constantly to charge that the media were biased in his favor. Obama was able to take advantage of the extra media attention he was given to generate popular enthusiasm for his campaign and raise tens of millions of dollars in small contributions via the Internet. By devoting enormous quantities of ink and airtime to Obama, the media were not so much exhibiting bias as reflecting what they saw as the historic importance of the story. Nevertheless, they may have contributed to Obama's presidential victory in 2008.

In the 2012 Republican presidential primaries, the media frequently framed front-runner Mitt Romney as not a "real conservative," a notion stemming either from his position as governor of Massachusetts, a northern and liberal-leaning state, or from his Mormon religion. (Evangelical Christians dominate the ranks of the strongest conservatives in the Republican Party.) This created opportunities for many Republican challengers to do better than expected in primary elections, especially Newt Gingrich and Rick Santorum. A counter media frame was that only Mitt Romney, a moderate Republican, could beat President Obama in the general election among those seeking the Republican presidential nomination, and opinion polls cited widely in the media showed the closest margin in head-to-head races between Obama and Romney in the 2012 general election. Framing Romney as able to beat President Obama may have increased support for him. The mass media framed the general election as a toss-up. Political pundits claimed that either candidate might win, predicting a 1 percent margin in the popular vote. But this widely touted media frame may have misled voters, as many pollsters predicted a decisive Obama victory. Election forecaster Nate Silver predicted an Obama win months before the election.

**Priming** A third important way the media can shape political events is known as **priming**, which is closely related to framing. This occurs when media coverage affects the way the public evaluates political leaders, issues, and events. Priming involves "calling attention to some matters while ignoring others."[53] Often candidate research is described as "priming" while research on political issues is called "framing." Both may examine subliminal priming of subjects using varying forms media frames. For example, media praise for President George W. Bush's speeches in the wake of the September 11, 2001, terrorist attacks prepared, or *primed*, the public to view Bush's subsequent response to terrorism in an extremely positive light, at least initially, even though some aspects of the administration's efforts, most notably the invasion of Iraq, eventually lost public support.

In the case of political candidates, the media have considerable influence over whether a particular individual will receive public attention and be taken seriously as a viable contender. Thus, if the media find a candidate interesting, they may treat him or her as a serious contender despite possible weaknesses and shortcomings. For example, in the 2012 Republican presidential primaries there were positive stories covering New Jersey governor Chris Christie as a possible candidate (though Christie ultimately did not run). Similarly, the media may report that a candidate has "momentum," a property that the media confer on candidates when they exceed the media's own expectations. After winning the 2008 Iowa caucuses in the Democratic primaries, the media declared that Barack Obama had momentum, as his fund-raising and poll numbers had exceeded early projections.[54] Nothing Hillary Clinton was able to do seemed to deprive Obama of

**priming** process of preparing the public to take a particular view of an event or political actor

the coveted momentum the media had granted him—momentum soon becomes a feedback loop by which media attention generates public enthusiasm, which in turn garners further media attention. Republican presidential candidate Mitt Romney was anointed with "momentum" by the media in the 2012 primaries.

In 2004, controversial measures banning same-sex marriage were placed on 13 statewide ballots as referenda by Republican state lawmakers or as initiatives by conservative interest groups sympathetic to the Republican Party. All 13 ballot measures were approved by voters. The well-coordinated, high-profile campaigns urging passage of the measures garnered extensive media coverage in these states and may have primed citizens to vote for the Republican presidential incumbent, George W. Bush. One study found that citizens residing in one of the states with such ballot measures were more likely to rank the issue of gay marriage as very important in the presidential election, tracking a higher volume of media coverage, compared with voters in the 37 states that didn't vote on this issue. When evaluating the 2004 presidential candidates, voters in these 13 states who believed that the issue of same-sex marriage was very important were more likely to vote for the Republican candidate. The research suggests that the ballot measures on a same-sex-marriage ban may have helped re-elect President Bush in the 2004 election.[55]

Media coverage of ballot measures can benefit Democratic candidates in much the same way. In 2006 coordinated ballot-measure campaigns in six states to raise the minimum wage were successful in modifying support for the policy among partisan subsamples (with Democrats becoming more likely and Republicans less likely to support the measure), thus increasing the saliency of the economy as an issue in general among these targeted populations, and priming support for Democratic candidates for Congress and governor.[56]

*In the 2012 primaries, positive media attention gave Mitt Romney momentum, helping him secure the Republican presidential nomination.*

# ● News Coverage

> **Explain how politicians and others try to shape the news**

News coverage, or the content of the news, includes information and leaks to the press. Such media leaks are key for investigative journalism, as are press releases and the tradition of adversarial journalism.

## Media Leaks

**leak** a disclosure of confidential information to the news media

The media may also report information that is leaked by government officials. A **leak** is the disclosure of confidential information to the news media. Leaks may emanate from a variety of sources, including "whistle-blowers," lower-level officials who hope to publicize what they view as their bosses' or the government's improper activities. In 1971, for example, a minor Defense Department staffer named Daniel Ellsberg sought to discredit official justifications for America's involvement in Vietnam by leaking top-secret documents to the press. The "Pentagon Papers"—the Defense Department's own secret history of the war, differing widely from the Pentagon's public pronouncements—were published by the *New York Times* and the *Washington Post* after the U.S. Supreme Court ruled that the government could not block their release.[57] Pentagon credibility was severely damaged, hastening the erosion of public support for the war. In 2005, President George W. Bush was infuriated when he learned that a still-unidentified source, presumed to be a whistle-blower, had leaked information concerning the president's secret orders authorizing the National Security Agency to conduct clandestine, warrantless surveillance of suspected terrorists. Bush ordered the Justice Department to launch a probe of the leak. In 2006 another unidentified source leaked part of a secret intelligence summary that seemed to contradict the administration's claims of progress in the war in Iraq. In 2009 a leak to journalist Bob Woodward embarrassed the Pentagon by revealing General Stanley McChrystal's secret report to the president on the failures of American military efforts in Afghanistan.

Most leaks, though, originate not with low-level whistle-blowers but rather with senior government officials, prominent politicians, and political activists. These individuals cultivate long-term relationships with journalists to whom they regularly leak confidential information, knowing that it is likely to be published on a priority basis in a form acceptable to them. In turn, of course, journalists are likely to regard high-level sources of confidential information as valuable assets whose favor must be retained. For example, during the George W. Bush administration, Lewis "Scooter" Libby, Vice President Dick Cheney's chief of staff, was apparently such a valuable source of leaks to so many journalists that his name was seldom even mentioned in the newspapers, despite his prominence in Washington and his importance as a decision maker.[58] Further, the more that recipients of leaked information strive to keep their sources secret, the more difficulty other journalists will have in checking that information's validity.

Through such tacit alliances with journalists, prominent figures can manipulate news coverage and secure the publication of stories that serve their purposes. One recent case that revealed the complexities of this culture of leaks was the 2005 Valerie Plame affair. Plame was an undercover CIA analyst who happened to be married to Joseph Wilson, a prominent career diplomat. Wilson had angered the

*In 2010 and 2011, WikiLeaks published thousands of classified documents after they were leaked by Bradley Manning (center). As a member of the military, Manning was tried for breaking the laws related to how classified information is handled. However, many observers debated whether WikiLeaks broke the law by publishing the documents.*

Bush White House by publicly questioning the president's stated rationales for threatening the invasion of Iraq. In an apparent effort to discredit Wilson, one or more administration officials informed prominent journalists that Plame had improperly used her position to help Wilson. In so doing, these officials may have violated a federal statute prohibiting disclosure of the identities of covert intelligence operatives. The subsequent investigation revealed that the story had been leaked to several journalists, including the *Washington Post*'s Bob Woodward, who did not use it, and the *New York Times*'s Judith Miller, who did. Miller initially refused to name her source and spent several weeks in jail for contempt of court. When Miller was finally compelled to testify before a federal grand jury looking into the leak, Scooter Libby was charged with having been the source of the leak, though it later emerged that the leak had actually come from a former State Department official, Richard Armitage. The leak in the Plame case came to light only because it was illegal. Thousands of other leaks each year are quietly and seamlessly incorporated into the news.

New technology and online media have taken the cat-and-mouse game of leaks to a new level. WikiLeaks, an independent nonprofit organization dedicated to publishing classified information, posts leaked documents to its website and uses an anonymous drop-box system so leakers cannot be identified. In recent years, WikiLeaks has released thousands of secret government documents involving instances of government corruption, war crimes in Afghanistan and Iraq, torture at the Guantánamo Bay detention camp, and numerous embarrassing private communiqués sent by U.S. diplomats abroad. WikiLeaks also shares its treasure trove of leaked government documents with major international papers, including the *New York Times*. In July 2007, gunners aboard two U.S. Army helicopters killed over a dozen people, including two Reuters news staffers, in the Iraqi suburb of New Baghdad. When Reuters subsequently learned that the U.S. military had video footage of the attack, it tried to obtain the video through the Freedom of Information Act, but without success. The video was leaked to WikiLeaks, however, which released it in April 2010. Shot through an Apache helicopter gunsight, the video clearly shows the slaying of a wounded Reuters employee and his would-be rescuers; it led to a worldwide storm of condemnation of U.S. military action in the Iraq War.

Critics of WikiLeaks argue that posting government documents online is not journalism, that governments must have some secrets, and that the release of some government documents may jeopardize American soldiers and their local allies by revealing their identities. The whistle-blower behind the Pentagon Papers, Daniel Ellsberg, and many others, including Congressman Ron Paul and Salon's Glenn Greenwald, defend WikiLeaks, arguing that it has played a vital role in informing the public of government wrongdoings.

## Press Releases

Also seamlessly incorporated into daily news reports each year are thousands of press releases—stories written by advocates or publicists and distributed to the media in the hope that journalists will publish them, under their own bylines, with little or no revision. The originator of the press release, or news release, was a well-known New York public-relations consultant named Ivy Lee. In 1906 a train operated by one of Lee's clients, the Pennsylvania Railroad, was involved in a serious wreck. Lee quickly wrote a story about the accident that presented the railroad in a favorable light, and he distributed the account to reporters. Many papers published Lee's slanted story as their own objective account of events, and the railroad's reputation for quality and safety remained untarnished.

Consistent with Lee's example, today's press release presents facts and perspectives that serve an advocate's interests but is written in a way that mimics the factual news style of the paper, periodical, or television news program to which the press release has been sent. A well-designed press release can be nearly impossible to distinguish from an actual news story. Newspapers, of course, understand that, in publishing press releases, they are allowing themselves to be used, but they have a strong financial incentive to publish material that, in effect, allows them to fill their pages at little cost. The White House regularly issues press releases—for example, in preparation for a State of the Union address or major legislation supported by the president. Polling companies, such as Gallup, use press releases to share the results of election surveys.

The capacity of news subjects to influence the news is hardly unlimited. Media consultants and issues managers may shape the news for a time, but it is generally not difficult for the media to penetrate the smoke screens thrown up by news sources if they have a reason to do so. Thus, for example, despite the Obama administration's media management, press accounts of continuing U.S. casualties in Afghanistan, coupled with stories about the corruption and incompetence of the Afghan government, forced the White House to declare in 2009 that America's commitment to Afghanistan was not open-ended and to indicate that there would be a timetable for the withdrawal of American forces from that country.

## Adversarial Journalism

The political power of the news media vis-à-vis the government has greatly increased in recent years through the growing prominence of "adversarial journalism," a form of reporting in which the media adopt a skeptical or even hostile posture toward the government and public officials.

During the nineteenth century, American newspapers were subordinate to the political parties. Newspapers depended on official patronage (legal notices and party subsidies) for their financial survival and were controlled by party leaders.

(A vestige of that era survived into the twentieth century in such newspaper names as the *Springfield Republican* and the *St. Louis Globe-Democrat*.) At the turn of the twentieth century, with the development of commercial advertising, newspapers became financially independent, making possible the emergence of a formally non-partisan press.

Presidents were the first national officials to make use of the opportunities presented by this development. By communicating directly to the electorate through newspapers and magazines, Theodore Roosevelt and Woodrow Wilson established political constituencies for themselves, independent of party organizations, and thereby strengthened their own power relative to that of Congress. President Franklin Delano Roosevelt used the radio, most notably in his famous fireside chats, to reach out to voters throughout the nation and to make himself the center of American political life. Roosevelt was also adept at developing close personal relationships with reporters, which enabled him to obtain favorable news coverage despite the fact that, in his day, a majority of newspaper owners and publishers were staunch conservatives. Following Roosevelt's example, subsequent presidents have all sought to use the media to enhance their popularity and power. John F. Kennedy, for example, used televised news conferences to mobilize public support for his domestic and foreign policy initiatives.

During the 1950s and early 1960s a few members of Congress also made successful use of the media, especially television, to mobilize national support for their causes. Senator Joseph McCarthy of Wisconsin made himself a powerful national figure through his well-publicized investigations of alleged Communist infiltration of key American institutions. However, through the mid-1960s, the executive branch continued to generate the bulk of news coverage, and the media became a cornerstone of presidential power.

The Vietnam War shattered this amicable relationship between the press and the presidency. During the early stages of U.S. involvement, American

*This famous photograph of the aftermath of a napalm attack was one of many media images that shaped the American public's views on the Vietnam War. Media accounts critical of the war helped to turn public opinion against it and hastened the withdrawal of American troops.*

officials in Vietnam who disapproved of the way the war was being conducted leaked to reporters information critical of administrative policy. Publication of this material infuriated the White House, which pressured publishers to block its release—on one occasion, President Kennedy went so far as to ask the *New York Times* to reassign its Saigon correspondent. However, the national broadcast media and especially the two leading national newspapers, the *Washington Post* and the *New York Times*, discovered an audience for critical coverage and investigative reporting among segments of the public skeptical of administration policy. As the Vietnam War dragged on, adverse media coverage fanned antiwar sentiment. Moreover, growing opposition to the war among liberals encouraged some members of Congress to break with the White House, by then occupied by Lyndon Johnson. In turn, these shifts in popular and congressional sentiment emboldened journalists and publishers to continue to present news reports critical of the war. Gradually a generation of journalists developed a commitment to adversarial journalism, and a constituency emerged that would rally to the defense of the media whenever it came under attack from the White House.

This pattern persisted through the 1970s and into the 1980s. Political forces opposed to presidential policies, along with many members of Congress and the national news media, began to find that their interests often overlapped. Opponents of the Nixon, Carter, Reagan, and Bush administrations welcomed news accounts detailing the failures of executive agencies and officials involved with U.S. conduct abroad and domestic matters such as race relations, the environment, and regulatory policy. In addition, many senators and representatives found it politically advantageous to champion causes favored by the antiwar, consumer, or environmental movements because, by conducting televised hearings on such issues, they were able to mobilize national constituencies, become national figures, and, in a number of instances, become serious contenders for their party's presidential nomination.

As for the national media, aggressive use of the techniques of investigation, publicity, and exposure allowed them to enhance their autonomy and carve out a prominent place for themselves in American government and politics. Without aggressive media coverage, would we have known of Bill Clinton's extramarital affair or of the illegal break-in to the Democratic Party headquarters in the Watergate Building by Nixon's "Committee to Re-elect the President" and the White House's subsequent cover-up of the scandal? Without aggressive media coverage, would important questions be raised about the conduct of American foreign and domestic policy, including drone attacks, torture, and civil liberty violations? It is easy to criticize the media for their aggressive tactics, but would our democracy function effectively without the critical role of the press? Independent media are needed as the watchdogs of American politics.

Of course, in October 2001 the adversarial relationship between the government and the media was at least temporarily transformed into a much more supportive association as the media helped rally the American people for the fight against terrorism. The *Washington Post* and the *New York Times* were complicit with the government in the buildup to the Iraq War in 2003, publishing few stories critical of the invasion. Since the September 11 terrorist attacks, the mainstream media and the government have at times prevented the release of information that may have been damaging to U.S. foreign policy. Adversarial journalism waned in the surge of "patriotism" following the September 11 terrorist attacks when it was considered unpatriotic to oppose President Bush's response to the attacks, including the war on terrorism. The adversarial relationship between the government and segments of the press partially resumed in the wake of the 2003 Iraq War. The

*Prior to the Iraq War, the Bush administration invited more than one hundred news correspondents and photographers to accompany American forces into battle. These "embedded" journalists developed considerable rapport with the soldiers and provided generally sympathetic war coverage.*

same newspapers that had been largely uncritical of the U.S. invasion (for example, the *Washington Post* and the *New York Times*) castigated President Bush for going to war without the support of some of America's major allies. When American forces failed to uncover evidence that Iraq possessed WMDs—a major reason cited by the administration for launching the war—these newspapers intimated that the war had been based on intelligence failures, if not outright presidential deceptions.

New media has ushered in a new watchdog of government wrongdoing. The release of confidential government documents by WikiLeaks showed the world that the American government and press (including the *New York Times*) sometimes concealed news, including war crimes against civilians and the use of torture by American forces. One advantage of new media is that they are less likely to be co-opted by the government, as WikiLeaks is not dependent on the U.S. government in terms of regulation or taxation. A website controlled by an Australian citizen, with Web servers in many nations worldwide, including Iceland, WikiLeaks is indicative of the lawless environment that now characterizes the new media, and of how the new media are challenging even traditional media, taking the adversarial role of the press to new heights.

**for critical analysis**

In wartime, can media criticism of government action aid the nation's enemies? Should there be limits on media criticism of the government during time of war? Or does criticism actually enhance the nation's strength?

## ● Regulation of the Media

**Trace the evolution of rules that govern broadcast media**

In many countries, such as China, the government exercises strict control over traditional media content. In others, the government owns the broadcast media (for example, the BBC in Britain) but does not tell the media what to say.

In the United States, the print and online media are essentially free from government interference. The broadcast media, on the other hand, are subject to federal regulation. American radio and television are regulated by the Federal Communications Commission (FCC), an independent agency established in 1934. Radio and TV stations must have FCC licenses, which must be renewed every five years. Licensing provides a mechanism for allocating radio and TV frequencies in order to prevent broadcasts from interfering with and garbling one another. License renewals are almost always granted automatically by the FCC. Indeed, renewal requests are now filed by postcard.

Through regulations prohibiting obscenity, indecency, and profanity, the FCC has also sought to prohibit radio and television stations from airing explicit sexual and excretory references between 6 A.M. and 10 P.M., the hours when the audience is most likely to include children. Generally speaking, FCC regulation applies only to the over-the-air broadcast media. It does not apply to cable television, the Internet, or satellite radio. As a result, explicit sexual content and graphic language that would run afoul of the rules on broadcast television are regularly available on cable channels. This explains why "shock jock" Howard Stern moved his program to satellite radio after years of incurring fines and penalties while he was on broadcast radio. A number of bills have been introduced in recent congresses to extend the rules to apply to cable TV and satellite radio, but none has succeeded so far.

For more than 60 years, the FCC sought not only to regulate but also to promote competition in the broadcast industry, but in 1996, Congress passed the Telecommunications Act, a broad effort to end most regulations in effect since 1934. The legislation loosened restrictions on media ownership and allowed telephone companies, cable television providers, and broadcasters to compete with one another to provide telecommunication services. Following the passage of the Telecommunications Act, several mergers between telephone and cable companies and among different segments of the entertainment media produced an even greater concentration of media ownership than had been possible since regulation of the industry began in 1934.

The Telecommunications Act of 1996 included an attempt to regulate the content of material transmitted over the Internet. This law, known as the Communications Decency Act, made it illegal to make "indecent" sexual material on the Internet accessible to those under age 18. The act was immediately denounced by civil libertarians and became the subject of lawsuits. In 1997 the Supreme Court ruled that the Communications Decency Act was an unconstitutional infringement of the right to freedom of speech guaranteed by the First Amendment (see Chapter 4).

Although the government's ability to regulate the content of the Internet has been curtailed, the FCC has used its licensing power to impose several regulations that can affect the political content of radio and TV broadcasts. The first of these is the **equal time rule**, under which broadcasters must provide to candidates for the same political office equal opportunities to communicate their messages to the public. If, for example, a television station sells commercial time to a state's Republican gubernatorial candidate, it may not refuse to sell time to the Democratic candidate for the same office. Under the terms of the Telecommunications Act, during the 45 days before an election, broadcasters are required to make time available to candidates at the lowest rate charged for that time slot.

The second regulation affecting the content of broadcasts is the **right of rebuttal**, which requires that individuals be given the opportunity to respond to personal attacks. In the 1969 case of *Red Lion Broadcasting Company v. FCC*, for example, the U.S. Supreme Court upheld the FCC's determination that a radio station was required to provide a liberal author with an opportunity to respond to a conservative commentator's attack that the station had aired.[59]

**equal time rule** the requirement that broadcasters provide candidates for the same political office equal opportunities to communicate their messages to the public

**right of rebuttal** a Federal Communications Commission regulation giving individuals the right to have the opportunity to respond to personal attacks made on a radio or television broadcast

For many years, a third important federal regulation was the **fairness doctrine**. Under this rule, broadcasters who aired programs on controversial issues were required to provide time for opposing views. In 1985, however, the FCC stopped enforcing the fairness doctrine on the grounds that there were so many radio and television stations—to say nothing of newspapers and newsmagazines—that in all likelihood many different viewpoints were already being presented without each station being required to try to present all sides of every argument. Critics of this FCC decision charged, and continue to charge, that in many media markets the number of competing viewpoints is actually quite small. During the past several years, Democratic members of Congress, including Nancy Pelosi, John Kerry, and Richard Durbin, have sought to revive the fairness doctrine in response to what they see as the "unfairness" of conservative talk radio.

The rise of online media requires revising our thinking about regulation of the media, as it is more difficult—some say impossible—to regulate political content online. The United Nations recently declared that access to the Internet is a human right.[60] While this declaration came in response to threats by authoritarian governments against Internet access—the Egyptian government, for example, disabled Internet access for the entire nation during protests in 2011—the UN's position demonstrates the significance of information technology in modern life. Many authoritarian countries continue to censor the Internet, sometimes blocking the transmission of stories that contain specific terms or information from specific websites.[61] In the United States, controversy erupted in 2012 over proposed congressional legislation that would have regulated content on the Internet, commonly referred to as SOPA and PIPA. In the face of mass online protests organized by Google, Wikipedia, and thousands of technology companies and websites, congressional leaders from both parties withdrew their support for the legislation. (See Chapter 8 for further discussion.) The government does have the power to regulate the Internet if a website infringes U.S. copyright law. In January 2012 the U.S. Department of Justice shut down a website, Megaupload, that ran services for file storing and viewing. The owners of the Hong Kong–based company, in operation since 2005, were arrested on charges of copyright infringement. The U.S. government claimed it had the right to shut down the website because the company used an Internet server located in Virginia.

*Federal Communications Commission (FCC) regulations prohibit obscenity, indecency, and profanity in American television and radio broadcasts. The radio personality Howard Stern incurred millions of dollars in FCC fines before moving to satellite radio, which is not regulated by the FCC.*

**fairness doctrine** a Federal Communications Commission requirement for broadcasters who air programs on controversial issues to provide time for opposing views; the FCC ceased enforcing this doctrine in 1985

# ● Thinking Critically about Digital Citizens, the Media, and Democracy

The free media comprise an institution essential to democratic government. Ordinary citizens depend on the media to investigate wrongdoing, to publicize and explain governmental actions, to evaluate programs and politicians, and to bring to light matters that might otherwise be known to only a handful of governmental insiders. In short, without free and active media, democratic government would be virtually impossible. Citizens would have few means through which to know or assess the government's actions—other than the claims or pronouncements of the government itself. Moreover, without active (indeed, aggressive) media, citizens would be hard-pressed to make informed choices among competing candidates at the polls.

Today's media are not only adversarial but also increasingly partisan. Debates about the liberalism and conservatism of the mass media make it clear that many readers and viewers perceive more and more bias in newspapers, radio, and television. Blogs, niche media, social media, and other Internet outlets, of course, are often unabashedly partisan. To some extent, increasing ideological and partisan stridency is an inevitable result of the expansion and proliferation of news sources. When the news was dominated by three networks and a handful of national papers, each sought to appeal to the entire national audience. This required a moderate and balanced tone so that consumers would not be offended and transfer their attention to a rival network or newspaper. Today, there are so many news sources that few can aim for a broad-based national audience. Instead, each targets a partisan or ideological niche and aims to develop a strong relationship with consumers in that audience segment by catering to their biases and predispositions. The end result may be to encourage greater division and disharmony among Americans.

The media can make or break reputations, help to launch or destroy political careers, and build support for or rally opposition to programs and institutions.[62] Wherever there is so much power, at least the potential exists for its abuse or overly zealous use. All things considered, free media are so critically important to the maintenance of a democratic society that Americans must be prepared to take the risk that the media will occasionally abuse their power. Governmental controls that would prevent the media from misusing their power would also certainly destroy freedom. The ultimate beneficiaries of free and active media are the American people.

Has the rise of citizen journalism and the Internet fundamentally changed how political information is gathered and distributed? As more and more Americans go online to read the news and learn about politics, even the definition of "journalist" is being challenged. Is WikiLeaks a media organization protected by First Amendment guarantees of press freedom, or is it a website engaged in illegal activity? Are Twitter feeds from protestors on the ground in Egypt or in an Occupy Wall Street camp examples of citizen journalism? In an era of online news, regular citizens create content and distribute the news through personal pages and blogs. Is this real news or just local gossip on a global scale? Wikipedia, the free online encyclopedia founded by Jimmy Wales, has millions of pages providing relatively unbiased content on virtually every political topic imaginable. The information is compiled by legions of volunteers working in teams in almost every country in the world, including China. Wikipedia is the only nonprofit among the 10 most popular websites worldwide. Social media (Facebook, Twitter, and countless others), Wikipedia, and all Wiki-type sites involve people working collaboratively to write and create information and to transmit knowledge. Is Wikimedia the future of the media?

In the twenty-first century, political campaigns are covered wall to wall by the Internet; on newspapers' sites updated throughout the day; and on blogs, tweets, social media, and cable television. There is no doubt that the new digital media are more diverse, more representative of multiple viewpoints, more interactive and participatory, and, to many, more interesting than traditional news media. Time will tell whether the shift to online news strengthens or harms American democracy.

# Become a Critical Consumer of Political News

## Inform Yourself

**Visit news sources outside the traditional mainstream media.** Many blogs and websites serve as media watchdogs and alternative voices. Have you read or heard of the Drudge Report (www.drudgereport.com"), the Huffington Post (www.huffingtonpost.com), Salon's blog (www.salon.com), the National Review (www.nationalreview.com), the Weekly Standard (www.weeklystandard.com), Truth Out (www.truthout.org), Moveon.org, or www.rightmarch.org? What about TheMonkeyCage.org? Can you tell which news sites represent the ideological left versus the right, and which are created by scholars on neither the right nor the left?

**Check the facts.** Candidates and political groups use the Internet and social media to deliver their messages directly to the public, unfiltered by editors. One downside to this process is that lies and misinformation are more common online. Visit the popular Factcheck website (www.factcheck.org) and its Viral Spiral page (from the site's top menu). What are the current Internet rumors? Who are the subjects of these rumors? Do you see a pattern?

## Express Yourself

**Share your view of the media.** HBO's *The Newsroom* is a show about how the mainstream media care more about ratings than reporting the news. Consider the clip at www.youtube.com/watch?v=og3D5UwxjU0. What does the character say that you agree with? What does he say that you disagree with? Share your thoughts on the *Newsroom* clip and the media with others and see what your friends think.

## Connect with Others

**What is news?** Go to the Drudge Report website (www.drudgereport.com) and find two articles that never became headline news. Why do you think these stories never made mainstream news? What does this tell us about what is thought of as news? Consider sharing the stories and your opinion on your Facebook page, Twitter, or in class with other students.

*Find links to the sites listed above as well as related activities on wwnorton.com/studyspace.*

# study guide

**Ⓢ Practice online with:** Chapter 7 Diagnostic Quiz ▪ Chapter 7 Key Term Flashcards

## Traditional Media

■ **Describe the role of print and broadcast media in providing political information (pp. 253–56)**

Americans have traditionally gotten their political information from broadcast media (radio and television) and print media (newspapers and magazines). Television reaches the largest audience but provides little depth of coverage. Radio news is essentially a headline service that alerts listeners to important events without providing much detail. Newspapers, by contrast, are read by political elites for their in-depth coverage and are important in setting the agenda of the broadcast media.

### Key Term

**broadcast media** (p. 253)

### Practice Quiz

1. Which of the following statements is *not* true about old-fashioned newspapers? *(p. 255)*
   a) They typically offer readers a better context for analysis by providing more detailed and complete information than other forms of media.
   b) They are the read on a daily basis by almost all Americans.
   c) They serve as the primary source of news for the nation's social and political elite.
   d) Broadcast media organizations rely heavily on newspapers to set their news agenda.
   e) Daily newspaper circulation in the United States has declined over the last 20 years.

 **Practice Online**
Interactive simulation: *Editor-in-chief of a Daily Newspaper*

## News Media and Online News

■ **Explain how the Internet has transformed the news media (pp. 256–68)**

Online political information includes news aggregation websites, niche journalism, citizen journalism, nonprofit journalism, blogs, and social media. The convenience, currency, and diversity of online news have led many Americans to prefer it to more traditional sources. Changes arising from the emergence of the Internet have also raised of concerns that online news may produce a decline in investigative journalism, a decrease in the quality of news content, and a reduction in political knowledge and tolerance.

### Key Terms

**penny press** (p. 256)

**news aggregator** (p. 256)

**digital citizen** (p. 258)

**niche journalism** (p. 258)

**citizen journalism** (p. 259)

**social media** (p. 261)

### Practice Quiz

2. *Penny press* refers to *(p. 256)*
   a) the very low wages paid to reporters.
   b) the single-page newspapers released on a weekly basis during the colonial era.
   c) the emergence of low-cost online news sources.
   d) the fact that most Americans see very little value in the information provided to them by the media.
   e) the cheap, tabloid style newspapers produced in the nineteenth century.

3. News reporting that is targeted in its content toward a narrow segment of the population is called *(p. 258)*
   a) nonprofit journalism.
   b) for-profit journalism.
   c) niche journalism.
   d) citizen journalism.
   e) adversarial journalism.

4. Which of the following is *not* a reason that Americans may prefer online news? *(pp. 262–65)*
   a) the convenience of getting news online.
   b) the up-to-the-moment currency of the information available online.
   c) the depth of the information available online.

d) the diversity of online viewpoints.

e) the accuracy and objectivity compared to traditional media outlets.

**Practice Online**
"Get Involved" interactive exercise: *Become a Critical Consumer of Political News*

# Mass Media Ownership

■ **Describe trends in who owns mass media companies (pp. 268–70)**

One of the most important trends for the American media system over the last few decades has been the growing concentration in ownership of print and broadcast media outlets. Although there are thousands of newspapers, magazines, and television and radio stations across the country, the number of traditional news-gathering sources operating nationally is quite small and may be declining. As major newspapers, television stations, and radio networks fall into fewer and fewer hands, there is a growing risk that the diversity of viewpoints heard by the public will decline.

**Key Term**

media monopoly (p. 269)

**Practice Quiz**

5. Consolidation of the media was accelerated by *(p. 269)*

a) the Supreme Court's decision in *Red Lion Broadcasting Company v. FCC.*

b) the declining number of reporters working for the major media outlets.

c) the enactment of the 1996 Telecommunications Act.

d) the purchase of influential newspapers and magazines by foreign corporations.

e) the purchase of major networks and newspapers by the federal government.

**Practice Online**
"You Decide" exercise: *Regulation of Media Ownership*

# Media Influence

■ **Analyze the ways the media can influence public opinion and politics (pp. 270–77)**

The content and character of news programming can have far-reaching political consequences. In recent American political history, the media have played a central role in numerous major events, such as the civil rights movement of the 1950s and '60s, the Vietnam War, and the Watergate affair. The power of the media lies in their ability to shape what issues Americans think about (agenda setting) and what opinions Americans hold about those issues (framing and priming).

**Key Terms**

agenda setting (p. 272)

selection bias (news) (p. 273)

framing (p. 275)

priming (p. 276)

**Practice Quiz**

6. The media's powers to determine what becomes a part of political discussion and to shape how political events are interpreted are known as *(p. 272)*

a) media consolidation and selection bias.

b) issue definition and protest power.

c) agenda setting and framing.

d) the illusion of saliency and the bandwagon effect.

e) the equal time rule and the right of rebuttal.

7. Which of the following best describes the media's role in the Watergate affair? *(p. 273)*

a) They played a central role in reporting on President Nixon's resignation but did little to reveal his abuses of power while he was president.

b) They played a central role in President Nixon's decision to resign from the presidency by revealing his abuses of power to the public.

c) They played a central role in disproving claims that President Nixon had abused his power while in office.

d) They played almost no role in the Watergate affair because they were legally prohibited from discussing ongoing police investigations.

e) They played almost no role in the Watergate affair because they refused to investigate claims that President Nixon had abused his power.

8. Media coverage of election campaigns typically focuses on which of the following? *(p. 275)*

a) the details of each candidate's domestic policy proposals

b) the details of each candidate's foreign policy proposals

c) the biography of each of the candidates

d) the records of each of the candidates

e) the "horse race" (that is, who is ahead and by how much)

**Practice Online**
Video exercise: *The Word—Media Culpa*

# News Coverage

■ **Explain how politicians and others try to shape the news (pp. 278–83)**

Leaks, press releases, and the tradition of adversarial journalism are important in determining the content of news coverage. Leaks, which are confidential pieces of information disclosed to members of the media, have driven press coverage on issues ranging from foreign policy to government corruption. Also incorporated into daily news coverage are thousands of press releases authored by advocates of influential political interests. "Adversarial journalism," a form of reporting in which the media adopt a skeptical or even hostile posture toward public officials, has increased the political power of the press in recent years.

## Key Term

**leak** (p. 278)

## Practice Quiz

9. Most leaks originate with *(p. 278)*
   a) low-level, government whistle-blowers.
   b) senior government officials, prominent politicians, and political activists.
   c) members of the public who witness misbehavior.
   d) ambassadors from foreign countries.
   e) members of the media.

10. Which of the following best describes the media's use of press releases? *(p. 280)*
   a) Press releases are never incorporated into daily news reports because it is illegal under federal law.
   b) Press releases are never incorporated into daily news reports because reporters view the information they contain as biased and politically motivated.
   c) Thousands of press releases are incorporated into daily news reports every year because press releases allow news organizations to fill their pages at little cost.
   d) Press releases are rarely incorporated into daily news reports because reporters view the information as biased and politically motivated.
   e) Every press release written by a political party, interest group, candidate, or government official is incorporated into daily news reports because reporters view the information as newsworthy.

11. *Adversarial journalism* refers to *(p. 280)*
   a) the recent shift in American society away from general purpose sources of information and toward narrowly focused niche sources.
   b) an era in American history when political parties provided all of the financing for newspapers.
   c) a form of reporting in which the media adopt a skeptical or even hostile posture toward the opinions and behaviors of their audience.
   d) a form of reporting in which the media adopt an accepting and friendly posture toward the government and public officials.
   e) a form of reporting in which the media adopt a skeptical or even hostile posture toward the government and public officials.

12. Which event shattered the amicable relationship between the press and the presidency? *(p. 281)*
   a) September 11, 2001
   b) the Vietnam War
   c) Watergate
   d) World War II
   e) the Monica Lewinsky affair

 **Practice Online**
Video Exercises: *Press Secretary's "Zumtrel Flooby" Answer May Be Attempt to Evade Question—Onion News Network*

# Regulation of the Media

■ **Trace the evolution of rules that govern broadcast media (pp. 283–85)**

Although American print and online media are free from government interference, broadcast media are subject to significant federal regulation. Radio and television stations in the United States are licensed by the Federal Communications Commission. The FCC has used its licensing power to impose several regulations, such as the equal time rule, the right of rebuttal, and the fairness doctrine, that affect the political content of radio and television broadcasts.

## Key Terms

**equal time rule** (p. 284)

**right of rebuttal** (p. 284)

**fairness doctrine** (p. 285)

## Practice Quiz

13. In general, FCC regulations apply only to *(p. 284)*
   a) cable television.
   b) Internet websites.
   c) over-the-air broadcast media.
   d) satellite radio.
   e) newspapers and magazines.

14. The now defunct requirement that broadcasters provide time for opposing views when they air programs on controversial issues was called *(p. 285)*
   a) the equal time rule.
   b) the free speech doctrine.
   c) the fairness doctrine.
   d) the right of rebuttal.
   e) the response rule.

# For Further Reading

Ansolabehere, Stephen, and Shanto Iyengar. *Going Negative*. New York: Simon & Schuster, 1997.

Carr, Nicholas. *The Shallows: What the Internet Is Doing to Our Brains*. New York: W.W. Norton & Company, 2011.

De Zengotita, Thomas. *Mediated: How the Media Shapes Our World and the Way We Live in It*. New York: Bloomsbury, 2006.

Fenton, Tom. *Bad News: The Decline of Reporting, the Business of News, and the Danger to Us All*. New York: Harper-Collins, 2005.

Fox, Richard, and Jennifer Ramos. *iPolitics: Citizens, Elections and Governing in the New Media Era*. New York: Cambridge University Press, 2011.

Hamilton, James T. *All the News That's Fit to Sell*. Princeton, NJ: Princeton University Press, 2004.

Iyengar, Shanto, and Donald Kinder. *News That Matters: Television and American Public Opinion*. Chicago: University of Chicago Press, 2010.

Jamieson, Kathleen, and Paul Waldman. *The Press Effect*. New York: Oxford University Press, 2004.

Mossberger, Karen, Caroline Tolbert, and Ramona McNeal. *Digital Citizenship: The Internet, Society and Participation*. Cambridge, MA: MIT Press, 2008.

Pariser, Eli. *The Filter Bubble: What the Internet Is Hiding from You*. New York: Penguin, 2011.

Weaver, David, et al. *The American Journalist in the 21st Century: U.S. News People at the Dawn of a New Millennium*. New York: Erlbaum, 2006.

West, Darrell. *The Next Wave: Using Digital Technology to Further Social and Political Innovation*. Washington, DC: Brookings Institution Press, 2011.

# Recommended Websites

**Accuracy in Media**
www.aim.org

This nonprofit, watchdog group attempts to ensure accuracy in media reporting by identifying botched or slanted stories and then "setting the record straight."

**Federal Communications Commission**
www.fcc.gov

The FCC is an independent regulatory agency established by the U.S. government in 1934 to regulate the broadcast media. On the official FCC website you can read about the rules and regulations that affect the media, along with other current topics of interest.

**Journalism.org**
www.journalism.org

This nonprofit, nonpolitical site, sponsored by the Project for Excellence in Journalism, examines the overall performance of the press as providers of information. Their aim is to help both consumers and producers of the news.

**National Newspaper Association**
www.nnawes.org

The NNA is one of the oldest and largest professional associations in the print media today. As ownership of major newspapers falls into fewer and fewer hands, the NNA is trying to protect, promote, and enhance America's community newspapers.

**Newseum**
www.newseum.org

Newseum is the Web page for an interactive museum of news journalism. On this site you can browse the front pages of over 500 daily national and international newspapers and explore the galleries and theaters of the news museum in Washington, D.C.

**The Pew Research Center for the People and the Press**
http://people-press.org

This independent survey research organization studies attitudes toward the press and numerous political issues.

For much of the country's history, large groups of Americans were denied the right to vote. Most restrictions on voting have been eliminated for Americans age 18 and older, but voter turnout remains relatively low, especially among young voters. Will the rise of online politics increase participation?

# 8

# Political Participation and Voting

**WHAT GOVERNMENT DOES AND WHY IT MATTERS** In many ways, Barack Obama's 2008 presidential campaign rewrote the rules for engaging supporters in electoral campaigns. Seeking to replace cynicism and apathy with idealism and hope, the Obama campaign focused on mobilizing new voters—the young in particular—and on making effective use of the Internet. The campaign linked online point-to-point communication to traditional offline opportunities to volunteer, thus engaging many who were not previously interested in politics. By opening 700 field offices across the country and developing a state-of-the-art website, the campaign made it easier for potential supporters to connect with campaign activities. Obama's team frequently communicated with supporters through e-mail, texting, and social networking sites such as Facebook and Twitter to make personal pleas for contributions, raising over $600 million in small contributions (a record) from 3 million donors.

Obama's 2008 campaign also took advantage of early-voting laws, newly adopted by many states, which allowed citizens to vote up to 40 days prior to the actual election. The campaign employed a sophisticated voter registration database to get out the vote, calling, messaging, and e-mailing supporters until it was confirmed that a ballot had been cast. The combination of excitement and mobilization (online and offline) spurred 62 percent of eligible citizens to vote, a modern record and the highest turnout since the 1960s. Participation increased among many categories of voters. African Americans turned out at historically high levels, inspired by the first major-party black presidential nominee in American history. Young voters (ages 18–29), traditionally the most apathetic segment of the electorate, increased their turnout to 51 percent, but their participation was still lower than expected.[1]

Despite the success of their 2008 campaign, however, Democrats had trouble mobilizing African Americans and young voters just two years later, for the 2010 midterm elections. Young voters, who made up 18 percent of the electorate in 2008, comprised only 10 percent in 2010. Use of the Internet for information about politics and mobilization continued to grow by leaps and bounds in 2012, but young voters still turned out at low rates.

It is not just the young who vote at low rates: nearly 40 percent of eligible American adults do not vote. Along with young adults, nonvoters are also disproportionately poor, uneducated, and nonwhite.[2] Their reasons for not voting are many: some find the process of voting and registering to vote onerous; some are not interested in politics because of uncompetitive elections without active campaigns. And for some people the decision to stay away from politics has been reinforced by a perception that politics is corrupt.[3]

So who does vote? Wealth, education, and strong partisanship are all associated with a greater likelihood of voting and other forms of political participation, such as contributing money to candidates or contacting elected officials. Political interest and knowledge are important predictors of whether an individual will vote. Some people vote because they view voting as a patriotic duty of citizenship. In fact, many people consider higher voter turnout to be an important goal in itself.[4] But many citizens, of course, vote because they want their preferred candidates, parties, and policies to win. As we will see in this chapter, who participates in politics matters because it affects the issues that candidates and elected officials put at the top of their agenda.

# chaptergoals

- Describe the major types of traditional and online participation in politics (pages 295–304)

- Examine voter turnout in American elections (pages 305–6)

- Explain the factors that influence whether individuals vote or not (pages 306–20)

- Describe the patterns of participation among major social groups (pages 320–31)

# Forms of Political Participation

**Describe the major types of traditional and online participation in politics**

We can think of political participation as falling into two major categories. Traditional participation in politics includes voting, of course, as well as attending campaign events, party business meetings, and fund-raisers. It also includes volunteering, canvassing, displaying campaign signs, and contributing to candidates and parties, or even challenging a law in court. Even protests and demonstrations can be considered age-old forms of participatory politics. Many, but not all, are face-to-face forms of participation in politics.

In addition to traditional participation there is a growing online world of digital politics—not just the exchange of information, but also fund-raising and voter mobilization. Some observers contend that digital politics is just a new way of engaging in traditional politics, while others argue that it is fundamentally different. There may be some truth to both arguments, but it is clear that digital politics is increasingly intertwined with traditional participation and is changing participation in important ways that may increase engagement in politics overall. We will see in this chapter that digital and traditional participation are combining to broaden the ways Americans participate in politics.

## Traditional Political Participation

**Traditional political participation** refers to a wide range of activities designed to influence government, politics, and policy. For most citizens today, voting is the most common form of political participation. (Voting will be discussed at length later in this chapter.) Yet ordinary people took part in politics long before the advent of the election or any other formal mechanism of popular involvement in political life. If there is any natural or spontaneous form of popular political participation, it is not the election but the riot. In fact, for much of American history, fewer Americans exercised their right to vote than participated in urban riots and rural uprisings, as voting was for a long time limited to white, male, landowning citizens. Civil unrest played an important role in American politics in the 1960s and '70s. As recently as 1999, protests helped labor unions and other opponents of trade liberalization slow the pace of change in the rules governing world trade.

**traditional political participation** activities designed to influence government including voting and face-to-face activities such as protesting or volunteering for a campaign

*Protests and rallies are forms of political participation. At this rally, demonstrators gathered in support of immigrants' rights. They hoped to draw attention to their cause and to influence the government to adopt policies that would result in better conditions for immigrant workers.*

*Volunteering for a campaign— for example, making calls on behalf of a candidate—is one traditional form of political participation.*

**protest** participation that involves assembling crowds to confront a government or other official organization

The vast majority of Americans, of course, reject rioting or violence for political ends, but peaceful **protest** is protected by the First Amendment and is generally recognized as a legitimate and important form of political activity. During the height of the civil rights movement in the 1960s, hundreds of thousands of Americans took part in peaceful protests to demand social and political rights for African Americans. More recently, peaceful marches and demonstrations have been employed by a host of groups, ranging from opponents of the war in Iraq to antiabortion activists and conservative Tea Party activists. The Occupy Wall Street movement began in September 2011 in New York City's Financial District, using peaceful demonstrations to protest high unemployment, undue corporate influence on government, and growing inequality between the super rich and the middle class—or, in the lingo of the Occupy Wall Street movement, the 1 percent versus the 99 percent of Americans. The protests in New York sparked similar Occupy movements, and their tent cities, across America. Opinion polls suggest that the movement has been especially successful in raising awareness of income inequality. For example, a Pew Research Center survey found that in 2012, two-thirds of Americans (66 percent) believed there were "very strong" or "strong" conflicts between the rich and the poor—an increase of 19 percentage points since 2009.[5]

Elections are the hallmark of political participation in a democracy, of course. In addition to voting, citizens can give money to politicians or political organizations, volunteer in campaigns, contact political officials, sign petitions, attend public meetings, join organizations, display campaign signs and pins, write letters to the editor, publish articles, attend rallies, or lobby their representatives in Congress; they can even sue the government or run for elected office. They can also join interest groups, which will be discussed in Chapter 11. These other forms of political action generally require more time, effort, or money than voting. In a 2008 survey of participation, just 22 percent of respondents said they had attended a local community meeting in the previous year; 16 percent said they had contacted a public official. Only 10 percent of those surveyed reported giving money to a candidate's campaign during the election, while 9 percent said they had attended a rally or political meeting. Fewer than 5 percent of those questioned said they had actually spent time volunteering for a political campaign.[6] (See Figure 8.1.)

Such activities differ from voting because they can communicate much more detailed information to public officials than voting can. Voters may support a can-

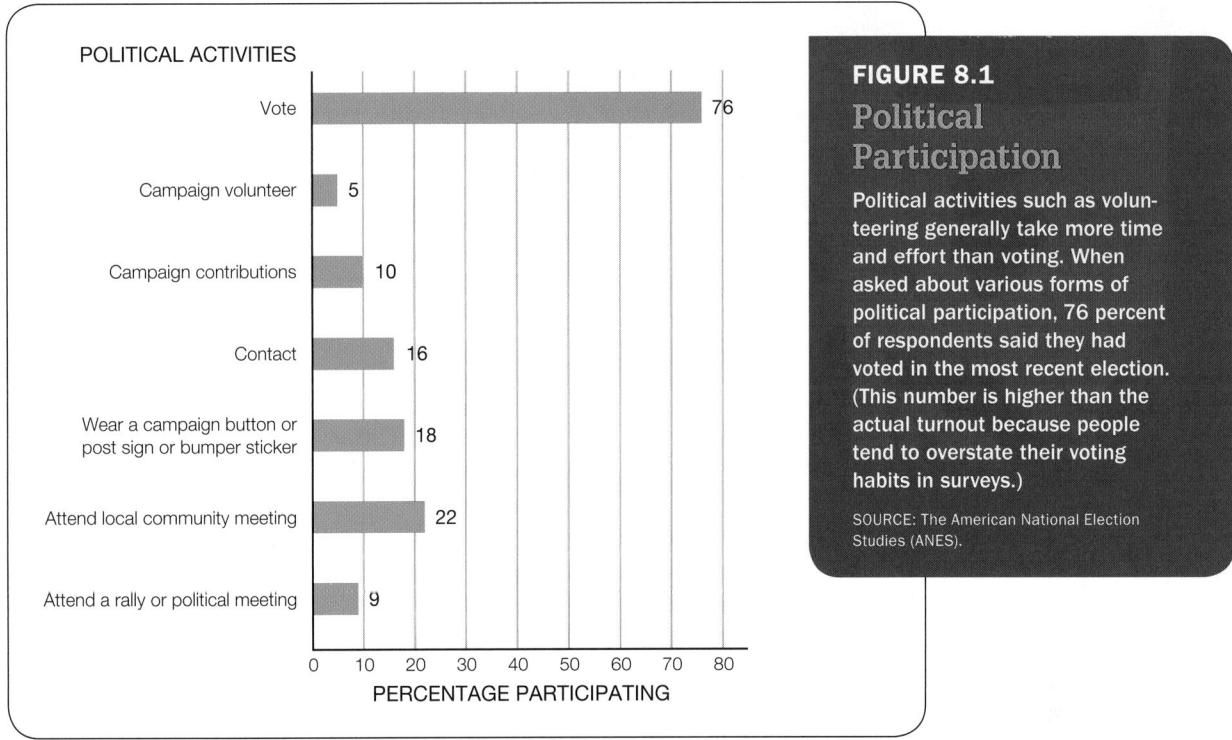

POLITICAL ACTIVITIES

| Activity | Percentage |
|---|---|
| Vote | 76 |
| Campaign volunteer | 5 |
| Campaign contributions | 10 |
| Contact | 16 |
| Wear a campaign button or post sign or bumper sticker | 18 |
| Attend local community meeting | 22 |
| Attend a rally or political meeting | 9 |

PERCENTAGE PARTICIPATING

**FIGURE 8.1**

**Political Participation**

Political activities such as volunteering generally take more time and effort than voting. When asked about various forms of political participation, 76 percent of respondents said they had voted in the most recent election. (This number is higher than the actual turnout because people tend to overstate their voting habits in surveys.)

SOURCE: The American National Election Studies (ANES).

didate for many reasons, but their actual votes do not indicate specifically what they like and don't like, nor do they tell officials how intensely voters feel about issues. By volunteering for a political campaign or writing to their member of Congress or attending a protest, people can convey much more specific information. For that reason, people often find these other political activities more satisfying than voting.[7]

## Online Political Participation

**Online political participation** is rapidly changing the way Americans experience politics. While traditional forms of participation remain important, the Internet gives citizens greater access to political information and, at least potentially, a greater role in politics than ever before. Many forms of online participation build on traditional forms of participation, but the Internet makes many of these activities easier and gives them greater potential as community-building tools. The Internet offers an active, two-way form of communication with feedback, rather than the more passive, one-way communication involved in reading printed newspapers, watching television, or listening to the radio. The Internet allows person-to-person communication as well as broadcast capability through online text, video, and visual images where information can be widely shared. For these reasons the Internet has been called a telephone, library, soapbox, storehouse of information, and channel for communication—all in one.

As of 2012, nearly 7 in 10 Americans read the news online, and nearly as many use online political information. Smartphones, or Internet-enabled mobile devices,

**online political participation**
activities designed to influence government using the Internet, including visiting a candidate's website, organizing events online, or signing an online petition

*Americans are increasingly likely to participate in politics through digital means, such as cell phones or the Internet. They may use online tools to coordinate traditional political activities such as protests or campaigning.*

which were used by 60 percent of Americans in 2012, bring the power of the Internet for politics via mobile applications to new heights. Today these online forms of participation have become more common than most of the traditional forms of participation just discussed.[8]

Online participation in elections includes discussing issues or mobilizing supporters through e-mail, electronic messaging, and Twitter; posting comments on blogs and online news stories; contributing money to candidates; visiting candidate and political party websites; creating and viewing online campaign ads and videos on sites such as YouTube; campaigning on social networking sites such as Facebook; and organizing face-to-face neighborhood meetings on sites such as Meetup.com. With each successive election, the Internet creates new platforms for communication and mobilization about politics. Digital technology brought fresh vigor to citizen participation in the 2008 and 2012 elections. While this wasn't unprecedented—after all, in 2004, presidential candidate Howard Dean made significant use of the Internet—in 2008, Democratic candidates in particular built comprehensive Internet strategies that did more than just duplicate offline efforts to mobilize supporters, and citizens made unprecedented use of the Internet to learn about candidates and issues and to participate in campaigns. While only 4 percent of likely voters went online for election information in 1996, a full 61 percent of American voters reported looking at information online or discussing politics online in 2012 according to Pew's Internet and American Life Project.[9] During the 2008 general election, over half of American adults used the Internet to learn about the candidates or to express their views.[10]

The 2012 presidential elections saw increasing sophistication of online campaigning and improved integration of online and offline participation opportunities. Facebook and Twitter, independent journalism (blogs), and political videos became critical means of organizing and communicating during the 2012 presidential elections. Many analysts believe that television, which had dominated presidential campaigns for the past half century, may have played second fiddle. Every serious presidential candidate had a Facebook page, with millions of fans who received weekly if not daily updates from the campaigns and candidates. These fans, in turn, signaled to their "friends" which candidates they supported for elected office, making politics part of everyday discussion.

The young (ages 18–29) were significantly more likely than middle-aged and older respondents to be engaged in presidential electoral activities online. Among young Americans who were registered to vote, 22 percent were highly engaged in the 2008 presidential primaries online, while another 43 percent were moderately active online (two to three activities). Thus, 65 percent of those young people registered to vote were moderately or highly active in the presidential nomination by way of online activities. In comparison, of those in the oldest age group (age 60 and older), only 5 percent were very active online, another 19 percent were moderately active online, and most (76 percent) reported little (one activity) or no political involvement online.[11] If these trends are sustained, they may result in greater overall levels of political interest and activity. Those who benefit most from online politics are likely to be those who are most active online: the young.[12]

Why is digital politics so effective with young people? Young Americans tend to move from place to place more often than citizens aged 40 years and older, so traditional "snail mail" campaigns are less likely to mobilize them. Young people are especially likely to be online, increasingly via mobile phones or smartphones rather than landlines. A 2011 survey found that the young (ages 18–29) made up 55 percent of citizens with only mobile Internet access (no Internet connection at home). In contrast, the young accounted for just 14 percent of individuals with an Internet connection at home. Similar patterns are found for blacks and Latinos and the less affluent, who disproportionately rely on mobile phones for Internet access.[13] Thus candidates and political campaigns are turning more and more to digital politics to reach young Americans, especially using mobile applications.

**Does Online Participation Lead to Offline Participation?** An important question is whether online political participation influences offline participation, especially voting. Political participation requires that people be motivated and have an interest in the outcome of the election. They must have the knowledge or capacity to understand how to participate, and they must be mobilized.[14] Digital technology encourages information-gathering and interaction between users by combining features of traditional media in content and interpersonal communication for discussion and mobilization. Because of this combination of information and interactivity, the Internet has the potential to promote interest in politics and to transform the nature of political participation. The Digital Citizens section on page 301 describes the case of the Occupy movement, in which the use of the Internet and cell phones was crucial in mobilizing participants.

A growing body of research indicates that activities such as reading online news, commenting on blogs, or sending or receiving political e-mails increase the likelihood that someone will not only vote but also contribute to political campaigns and candidates, attend campaign meetings, volunteer for campaigns, engage in community activities, and even contact elected officials.[15]

For example, one study found that participating in politics online—reading online news, commenting on blogs, or sending or receiving political e-mails—increases the likelihood of voting and participating in others ways offline. Online participation is also linked with discussing politics with friends or family, having an interest in politics, and being politically knowledgeable.

Researchers who study this subject have suggested at least six possible reasons online politics may increase participation. First, information, which is necessary for effective political participation, is easier to obtain online and is available 24 hours a day for those who have regular access to the Internet. The Internet is increasingly compared to the invention of the printing press, which stimulated the demand for greater literacy in society.[16] The Internet, like printed material, conveys information to the masses, and indeed, more Americans now read the news online than read print newspapers. Surveys show that nearly half of those who use online news and political information cite the Internet's convenience.[17]

Second, online news may "accidentally" engage individuals who otherwise would not be involved in politics at all. The political scientist Doris Graber has referred to the "accidental" mobilization of the electorate through the election news coverage that many Americans were exposed to by default when there were only a few television networks.[18] The Internet has created a new version of the "accidental mobilization" of those who are greeted by political information when they open their e-mail, check their Facebook accounts, or conduct online searches—sometimes politics finds the individual, rather than the other way around.[19] Candidates regularly place political ads on social media sites and in Google searches. Individuals may be "accidently" exposed to these ads and learn about politics, even if their motives for being online do not involve politics. Some research shows that individuals with low to moderate interest in politics, who are frequently online, are more likely to participate than individuals with low interest who are are not online.[20]

The flexibility of the Internet allows candidates to micro-target campaign ads to voters:[21] sophisticated techniques enable political campaigns to target information that will be of interest to potential supporters while those potential supporters are doing Google searches. This micro-targeting by candidates and campaigns may drive accidental political mobilization.[22]

Third, digital media have unique characteristics that enhance participation and even democratic accountability. The Internet effectively combines the qualities of print media that promote knowledge with the visual aspects of television that generate interest, engagement, and emotion.[23] Online news covers events and issues with the same immediacy as television, but with the in-depth treatment that is typical of newspapers. Emotional responses to political candidates or issues learned in online media, positive or negative, have been shown to trigger interest in politics and engagement.[24] In 2012, for example, Senate candidate Elizabeth Warren became a national sensation overnight with a video in which she passionately rebutted the idea that taxing the wealthy is "class warfare." Her campaign video was viewed more than 100,000 times on YouTube in one week.

Online readers can also post comments and participate in a community by providing feedback on news articles. A parallel experience for the print media does not exist outside of letters to the editor, a forum that can never have the potential scope of online feedback.

Fourth, online sources are more diverse than those found in the traditional media, and this diversity, too, may influence participation through its effects on political knowledge and interest. While online news is dominated by mainstream outlets available in other modes,[25] such as the websites of major newspapers or television networks, the Web is populated also by a wide range of information sources that reduce the impact of distance, making foreign media or media that appeal mainly to a narrow segment of the population easily available to anyone. This diversity matters, as surveys show that one-third of those who get their political information online believe that other information media are inadequate in comparison.[26] Many argue that the diversity of news sources online is good for democracy and that it makes debates about the purported liberal or conservative bias of the mainstream media irrelevant.

Fifth, online politics lowers the barriers for entry, making it easier for people to participate in ways that require less effort. By its very nature online political participation occurs in ways that are less location dependent than traditional politics: *community* takes on a very different meaning in an online context compared to a voter's actual neighborhood precinct or a local political party office. The Internet facilitates participation that is potentially broad, but with looser connections between participants than in more traditional networks of coworkers or neighbors.[27] The breadth of networks—for example, on Facebook or Twitter—is encouraged by the ease of sending information or appeals through hyperlinked websites, videos, and blogs as well as e-mail. While this may promote more extensive organizing efforts, it also encourages forms of participation that are low-intensity and sporadic, possibly attracting individuals with only moderate political interest.

# Occupy Wall Street

**The movement that became** known as Occupy Wall Street started with one simple e-mail sent to 90,000 individuals in July 2011. The idea was vague, but the goal was to get 20,000 people to protest economic inequality on September 17, 2011, in New York. Only 2,000 showed up. Many of those involved feared the event would fail to have an impact.

However, viral media fueled the flames of the populist economic protest, as

people around the country shared videos of young protesters being arrested by the police. After two weeks, the protesters coordinated occupations in hundreds of other cities via the Internet. The mainstream media and the rest of the country began to pay attention. When a citizen using a mobile phone captured video of police pepper-spraying peaceful Occupy demonstrators at the University of California–Davis in November 2011, it became headline news; the video was viewed by millions.

Twitter was the communication tool of choice, offering a way to connect with the thousands of Americans camped out in cities across the United States as part of the protest. One month after the movement's humble beginnings, Occupy Wall Street's Twitter account had over 85,000 followers, and in the first week of October 2011 approximately 400,000 people visited their website *per day*, making Occupy Wall Street the first mass protest in the United States built on new media.

One debate about digital politics is whether it mainly affects the people most likely to participate anyway or whether it can mobilize new groups and individuals. The Occupy movement represents a high-water mark in the use of online communications to mobilize offline political protest. But did it mobilize people who were otherwise unlikely to get involved? An in-person random sample of 200 New York protesters found that almost half were under age 30, and about half reported this event as the first time they were involved in a protest, rally, or march. Just over half had voted in the 2008 presidential election.[a] Additionally Occupy protes-

tors were economically hard pressed; a third reported they were "struggling" in the labor market. These findings suggest that the Occupy movement and the use of digital media may indeed have helped mobilize groups—such as the young, the poor, and nonvoters—who tend to have lower rates of political participation.

On Facebook, the main Occupy site had over 167,000 "likes" as of June 2012. There are four other general pages and dozens of other Occupy pages dedicated to specific cities. The Occupy protests indicate that digital politics can lead to offline participation.

[a]Douglas E. Schoen, "Occupy Wall Street Survey Topline," http://www.douglasschoen.com/pdf/Occupy_Wall_Street_Poll_Douglas_Schoen.pdf (data collected October 10 and 11, 2011).

## for critical analysis

1. Will online politics benefit those most likely to participate in politics already, such as the affluent and educated, or will digital politics help level the playing field, giving greater voice to the young, minorities, less affluent, and lower educated?

2. Does social media provide a new way to mobilize young people, a group with traditionally low voter turnout, to participate in politics? Or will the same barriers that have prevented young people from participating still apply, despite the Internet?

Thus participation online may be broader, but also less intense, possibly leading more people to participate in ways that require less effort. Forwarding an e-mail to a friend, posting a link on Facebook, or uploading a brief comment to a local newspaper website is an individual act that doesn't require commitment to organizational membership. However, it may improve political knowledge, interest, and participation. The political scientist Bruce Bimber has shown that some interest groups are responding to this new political climate of sporadic participation by focusing more outreach on the Web and by making it possible for individuals to support a specific issue or campaign without making a commitment to membership in the organization as a whole.[28] If citizens with low to moderate interest can become engaged in politics online, this will widen the pool of people participating in politics.

Finally, the Internet enables new forms of political expression through the creation of content on blogs, videos, social media, and websites.[29] This expressive capacity of the technology can lead to increased citizen involvement in politics, much of it through citizen journalism. Online news is creating a new generation of whistle blowers and citizen journalists, enhancing the media's traditional role as a watchdog for the people against government corruption. Although writing a blog is an obviously creative activity, 67 percent of those who follow blogs say that they also consider reading them an expression of their political beliefs.[30] The scholar Russell Dalton argues that, in fact, participation isn't declining at all but rather is changing by including norms of citizenship that are more expressive than voting.[31] For many citizens, becoming a "fan" of a candidate page on Facebook is a first step toward active participation in politics.

For all these reasons, digital media may foster a new kind of community-building that has the potential to reverse the trends in voter turnout and political participation, which have been declining over the past four decades. Explanations for these trends vary, but many analysts cite reduced trust in government, failures of the party system, and a diminishing stock of what Robert Putnam, author of *Bowling Alone*, calls social capital—community networks that motivate political participation.[32] By making political information, discussion, communication, and online mobilization easier, the Internet may help Americans grow a new kind of social capital, one based on shared political experiences in cyberspace.[33]

**Online Protest against SOPA and PIPA** Online protests to preserve Internet freedom provide a striking example of how new media can be used to mobilize offline participation in politics. Media "content producers" have long complained of severe economic losses due to online piracy—the illegal downloading of music, movies, TV shows, and other copyrighted material posted by foreign piracy websites. Early in 2012, at the urging of media companies and industry associations, legislation designed to clamp down on U.S.-based websites that facilitated international piracy was brought before Congress. These proposed laws, known as SOPA and PIPA,[34] represented an attempt to extend U.S. copyright laws beyond U.S. borders.

In what became characterized as a duel pitting Hollywood against Silicon Valley, proponents of the anti-piracy legislation, including the U.S. Chamber of Commerce and the motion picture industry, said that SOPA and PIPA were necessary to prevent digital thievery. While acknowledging that online piracy was a problem, the technology industry objected to provisions that would have held them liable for policing any website they linked to that might contain pirated content, such as a video or song. Google, for example, links to millions and millions

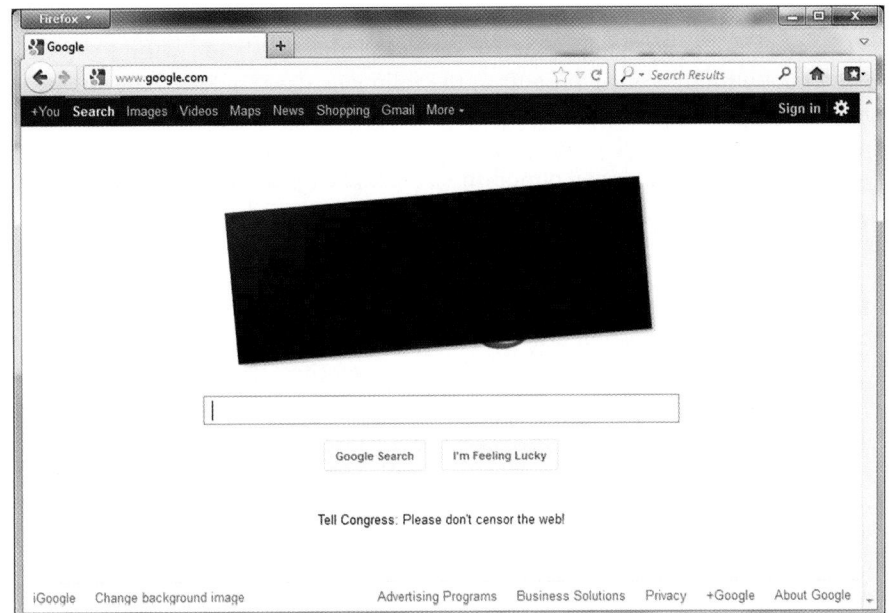

In 2012 an online protest prompted Congress to reconsider legislation designed to regulate the Internet and protect intellectual property rights. Numerous major websites "went dark" to draw attention to the issue, and Google displayed a black censorship bar along with a link to an online petition against the proposed law.

of websites. More generally, opponents of SOPA and PIPA said that the proposals would allow government censorship of the Internet and would damage free and open online communication. They argued further that the legislation could stifle innovation and job creation in the twenty-first-century economy, especially among small businesses reliant on the Internet.

At least initially, the bills had broad bipartisan support and appeared destined to be enacted into law. Then, on January 18, 2012, more than a hundred websites launched a coordinated protest—the largest online protest in history. It included a 24-hour shutdown of the online encyclopedia Wikipedia, a nonprofit organization and one of the top 10 most-visited websites worldwide. Users were redirected to a black screen providing information on the bills and links for users to click on to contact their member of Congress. According to Wikipedia, in one day there were 160 million visits to the site, and more than 4 million people accessed the information about contacting their member of Congress. (To put this figure in perspective, remember that there are 311 million citizens in the United States.). Google users, meanwhile, faced a black censorship bar blocking the Google logo and a link reading "Tell Congress: Please don't censor the web!" The search engine directed users to a petition opposing the bills; 10 million people signed the petition in 24 hours. Craigslist, Facebook, Twitter, and hundreds of other tech giants participated as well, either blacking out their content or posting information about the issue in order to raise awareness.[35] Yahoo, Microsoft, and many other major Internet companies opposed the legislation with public statements.

To be sure, this was a different form of protest: quiet compared to a traditional street rally, but loud in its impact on the media industry and government. Overnight, protest as a tool was transformed as people turned from traditional constituent lobbying techniques (scripted calls and form letters) and toward the use of new media. Mark Zuckerberg, founder and CEO of Facebook, tweeted, "Tell your congressmen you want them to be pro-Internet." Members of Congress faced a barrage of phone calls, e-mails, and tweets from concerned citizens voicing opposition to the anti-piracy laws. In response, at least eight members of Congress publicly changed their position on the legislation within the day, many more withdrew their support in the following days, and the bills' momentum was stalled. As former senator Chris Dodd said, "No Washington player can safely assume that a well-wired, heavily financed legislative program is safe from a sudden burst of Web-driven populism. . . . This is altogether a new effect."[36] The websites and citizens participating in the blackout created a grassroots backlash against Congress.

**Are There Drawbacks to Online Participation?** Traditional political participation and online participation are not mutually exclusive, of course. Many people are equally comfortable in both worlds, using websites such as Meetup.com to facilitate organizing face-to-face neighborhood meetings, using the Internet to seek out information about where to vote, or using social media for information about a local campaign event.

As we described in Chapter 1, digital citizens are daily Internet users, requiring regular and effective access to the technology, and the skills to use the technology, including language skills.[37] A barrier to participation in politics online is the digital divide—defined as the line separating citizens with Internet access from those without. Those on the wrong side of the divide tend to be poorer, lower educated, African American and Latino, and older. This creates new inequalities as the world of politics moves online.[38] Nearly one-third of Americans lack high-speed Internet access at home, although a growing number of Americans connect to the Internet through mobile devices such as cell phones, even if they lack home access, especially racial minorities and the young.[39] However, one in five Americans remains completely offline as of 2012. For some, Internet access is prohibitively costly or difficult to use, precluding online activities such as participation in politics altogether. Racial minorities and the poor are more likely to cite affordability and cost as reasons for their lacking Internet access at home compared to other groups. A lack of skills is a primary reason for being offline for Latinos, while a lack of interest is the primary reason among the elderly.[40] Inequality in access to political information online is an important public policy issue, separating the digital "haves" from the "have-nots." (See Chapter 7 for more discussion.)

**The Future of Online Participation?** Inequality in technology access notwithstanding, a growing number of voters finds the advantages of online participation to be overwhelming—and in any case, the Internet isn't going away. So what does this mean for American politics? The breakthrough success of the 2008 Obama campaign's use of the Internet to attract donations and the tidal wave of digital protest against SOPA and PIPA strongly suggest that online participation will play an increasingly important role in real-world offline politics.

Perhaps the most transformative aspect of digital media is how they affect not the participation of ordinary citizens, but rather that of candidates and officeholders. Running for office can be enormously expensive, but new media may level the playing field by reducing candidate reliance on money from corporations, special interests, and wealthy donors. Dark-horse and third-party candidates can now reach voters because of the relatively low cost and the 24-hour availability of the Internet. Despite recent Supreme Court rulings against legislative attempts to limit the influence of money in politics (*Citizens United*), new media offer the promise of reinvigorating a more grassroots and participatory American democracy.[41] But it also costs money to advertise online, which may benefit wealthy candidates.

# ● Voter Participation

**Examine voter turnout in American elections**

Whether voting is as effective or satisfying as protest (online or offline) and other forms of political action is an open question. It is clear, however, that for most Americans, voting remains one of the most important forms of political activity. The right to vote gives ordinary Americans a more equal chance to participate in politics than almost any other form of political activity. Voting is especially important because this act selects the officials who make the laws that the American people must follow, including laws compelling them to pay taxes. Voting is the single most important political act for most Americans, and it is the most common way that individuals involve themselves in politics. In the remainder of this chapter, therefore, we will turn to voting in America.

## Voting Rights

The right to vote, or **suffrage**, is a legal right. During the colonial and early national periods of American history, suffrage was generally restricted to white males over the age of 21. Many states further limited voting to those who owned property or paid more than a specified amount of annual tax. The Founders gave to the state legislatures the authority to regulate congressional elections, a decision that would have profound consequences for voting rights throughout American history. Until the early 1900s, state legislatures elected U.S. senators, and there were no direct elections for members of the Electoral College (who in turn elect the president), so elections for the U.S. House as well as state and local offices were the primary venue for citizen participation in government.

During the nineteenth and early twentieth centuries, the right to vote was not distributed equally across the American population. The states often acted to restrict expanding suffrage, initially through poll taxes (fees to vote) and literacy tests designed to curtail immigrant voting in northern cities controlled by political machines, and later imported to the southern states to disenfranchise African Americans and uneducated whites during the Jim Crow era. Voter eligibility requirements often varied greatly from state to state. Some states openly prevented the right to vote on the basis of race; others did not. Some states required property ownership for voting; others had no such restrictions. Most states mandated lengthy residency requirements, which meant that persons moving from one state to another sometimes lost their right to vote for as much as a year.[42]

Over the past two centuries of American history, a dominant trend has been federal statutes, court decisions, and constitutional amendments designed to override state voting laws and expand suffrage to non-landowners, African Americans, Asian Americans, women, young adults, and others.[43] In the South, black voting rights were established by the Fifteenth Amendment (1870), which prohibited denying the right to vote on the basis of race. Despite the Fifteenth Amendment, the voting rights of African Americans were effectively rescinded during the 1880s by the states of the former Confederacy. During the 1950s and '60s, through the civil rights movement led by Martin Luther King Jr. and others, African Americans demanded their voting rights. This goal was achieved with the enactment of the 1965 Voting Rights Act, which authorized the federal government to register voters in states that discriminated against minority citizens. The result was the reenfranchisement of southern blacks for the first time since the 1860s.

**suffrage** the right to vote; also called franchise

**for critical analysis**

Describe the expansion of suffrage in the United States since the Founding. Why might the government have denied participation to so many for so long? What forces influenced the expansion of voting rights?

Women won the right to vote in 1920, through the adoption of the Nineteenth Amendment. This amendment resulted primarily from the activism of the women's suffrage movement, led by Elizabeth Cady Stanton, Susan B. Anthony, and Carrie Chapman Catt, among others, during the late nineteenth and early twentieth centuries. The "suffragists" held rallies, demonstrations, and protest marches for more than half a century before achieving their goal. The cause of women's suffrage was ultimately advanced by World War I, when President Woodrow Wilson and members of Congress became convinced that women would be more likely to support the war effort if they were granted the right to vote.

The most recent expansion of the right to vote in the United States, the Twenty-Sixth Amendment, lowering the voting age from 21 to 18, was ratified during the Vietnam War, in 1971. Unlike black suffrage and women's suffrage, which came about in part because of the demands of groups that had been deprived of the right to vote, the Twenty-Sixth Amendment was not a response to the demands of young people to be given the right to vote. Instead, the right to vote was intended to channel the disruptive protest activities of students involved in the anti–Vietnam War movement into peaceful participation at the ballot box.

**Current Trends in Voter Turnout** Today voting rights are granted to all American citizens age 18 and older, although some states revoke this right from those who have committed a felony or are mentally incompetent. (This will be discussed in detail below.) Despite granting suffrage to women, racial minorities, and young adults, however, America's rate of voting participation, or **turnout**, is low. Only 6 in 10 eligible Americans vote in presidential elections, and turnout for midterm elections (elections that fall between presidential elections) is typically much lower, around 33 percent of eligible voters; for local elections, turnout is even lower.[44] Turnout in state and local races that do not coincide with national contests is typically much lower. (In most European countries and other Western democracies, by contrast, national voter turnout is usually between 70 and 90 percent;[45] see America in the World.)

Participation in U.S. presidential elections dropped significantly after 1960, when 64 percent of eligible voters cast ballots. In 1996, participation reached a modern low when only 52 percent of eligible voters went to the polls. Since then, though, overall trends have improved somewhat. In 2004, major efforts to get out the vote brought turnout to over 60 percent—the first significant increase in voting in 40 years. The trend continued in 2008, when nearly 62 percent of the population eligible to vote did so, a modern-day record, and in the 2006 and 2010 midterm elections, turnout rose to more than 40 percent although turnout dropped slightly in 2012 (see Figure 8.2).

**turnout** the percentage of eligible individuals who actually vote

# ● Explaining Political Participation: The Individual in Context

> **Explain the factors that influence whether individuals vote or not**

A common starting point for understanding who votes and who does not is to consider that individuals face a number of costs and benefits related to their decision to become involved in politics, just as in any other activity in life. According to such an analysis, an individual is likely to participate only if the benefits of voting in an election outweigh the costs.[46] One benefit associated with voting, for instance, may be the

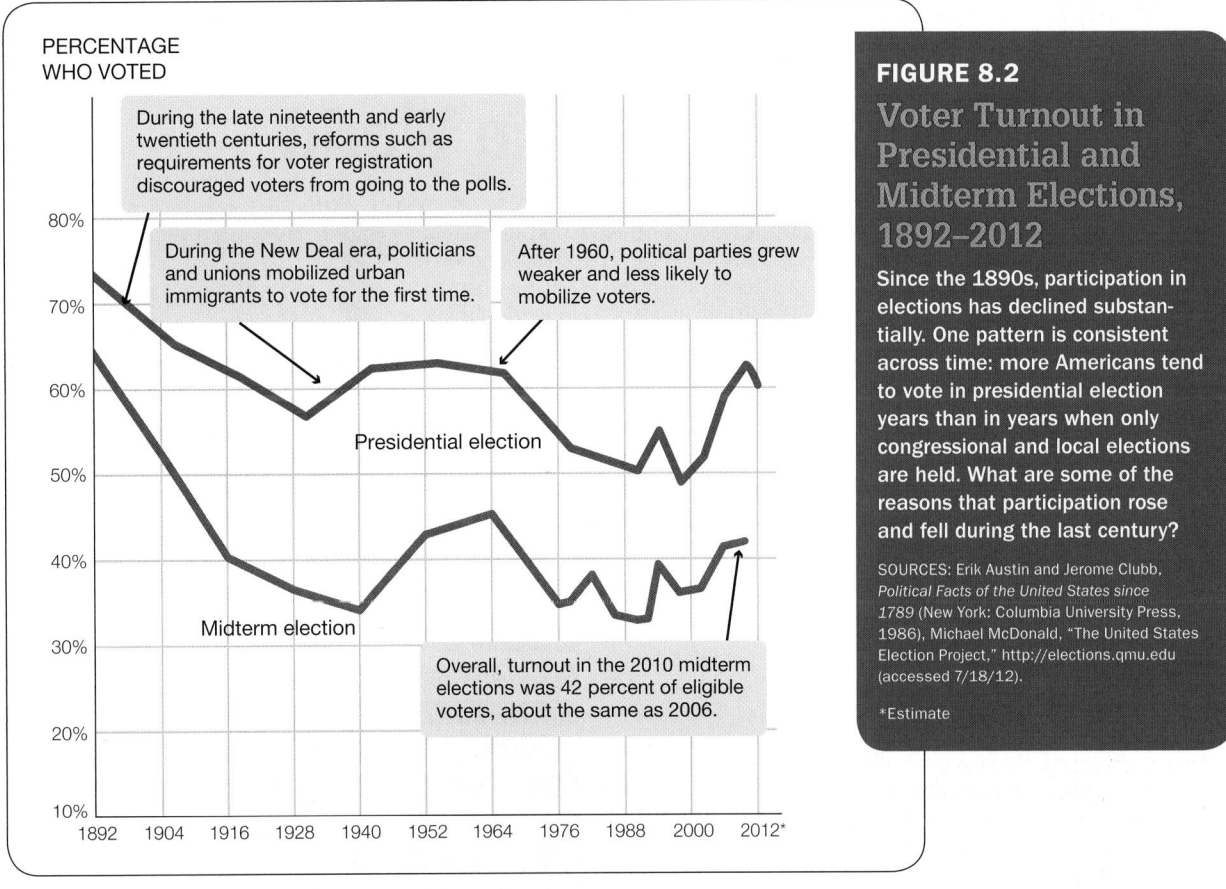

PERCENTAGE WHO VOTED

During the late nineteenth and early twentieth centuries, reforms such as requirements for voter registration discouraged voters from going to the polls.

During the New Deal era, politicians and unions mobilized urban immigrants to vote for the first time.

After 1960, political parties grew weaker and less likely to mobilize voters.

Presidential election

Midterm election

Overall, turnout in the 2010 midterm elections was 42 percent of eligible voters, about the same as 2006.

**FIGURE 8.2**

**Voter Turnout in Presidential and Midterm Elections, 1892–2012**

Since the 1890s, participation in elections has declined substantially. One pattern is consistent across time: more Americans tend to vote in presidential election years than in years when only congressional and local elections are held. What are some of the reasons that participation rose and fell during the last century?

SOURCES: Erik Austin and Jerome Clubb, *Political Facts of the United States since 1789* (New York: Columbia University Press, 1986), Michael McDonald, "The United States Election Project," http://elections.qmu.edu (accessed 7/18/12).

*Estimate

favorable policies that might result from having one's preferred candidate or party in office, which the potential voter weighs against the slim likelihood of his or her vote actually influencing the outcome of the election. Another benefit of voting is the sense of pride gained from fulfilling one's civic duty. The costs related to voting can include the time and resources needed to cast a ballot and the citizen's ability to gather political information and become informed. This may in part explain why the poor and the less educated are less likely to vote.

Beyond the costs and benefits of voting, political scientists have focused on understanding the individual in his or her political environment and how contextual factors affect whether or not that person decides to cast a ballot on Election Day. A simple example is headline news stories declaring an early winner in the exit polls in presidential elections. If a candidate is proclaimed the winner, there is little incentive for individuals to vote; in fact nonvoting is rational. This occurs every four years when voters on the West Coast, located in a time zone three hours later than that of the East Coast, learn that the presidential race is effectively over. Turnout in California and other western states naturally plummets.

The factors that organize our understanding of voting in elections can be grouped into three general categories: (1) a person's socioeconomic status and attitudes about politics, (2) the political environment in which elections take place, such as campaigns that seek to mobilize voters and whether an election is contested among two political candidates, and finally, (3) the state electoral laws that shape the political process.

# Voter Turnout around the World

**In the United States voter turnout** was 38 percent in the 2010 midterm election and about 60 percent in the 2008 presidential election; which is an average of 48 percent. Over the decades since 1945, the average in the United States was a bit higher but still lower than many other nations. The average among the other advanced democracies of the OECD is around 70 percent of the adult population, though there are considerable differences among countries. As the graph below shows, we also find a range of voting rates in developing countries like Thailand and Brazil.

Why is there so much variation in electoral participation around the world? One simple explanation is different electoral rules and electoral systems. These rules determine how the game of politics is played. In most countries citizens are automatically registered to vote when they turn a given age, based on a national ID number (like a social security number in the United States). In the United States, citizens have to register to vote. If they move residences, citizens must reregister to vote in the new district. Not being registered to vote is a primary reason people do not vote. Another reason is that many countries, including Australia, have compulsory voting laws. Citizens can be fined or ticketed for nonvoting. In the United States, there is no penalty for nonvoting. These two simple rules go a long way towards explaining why participation in elections is so low in the United States compared to other nations.

Additionally, many adults in the United States are either noncitizens (and thus denied voting rights) or are ex-felons who have been denied voting rights. The graph measures turnout as a percentage of the voting-age population. If voting rates are calculated as the percent of the population that is *eligible* to vote instead of the adult population, participation in U.S. elections is somewhat higher. Political scientist Michael McDonald's Voter Election Project calculates turnout as the number of votes for the highest office divided by the voting-eligible population (VEP), which excludes noncitizens

and the disenfranchised. Calculated this way, turnout in the 2010 elections was 42 percent, and in the 2008 presidential election was almost 62 percent of Americans. That is only 8 percentage points lower than the OECD average. The lesson is that how we count matters.

[a]www.citizens.org (accessed 9/25/07).

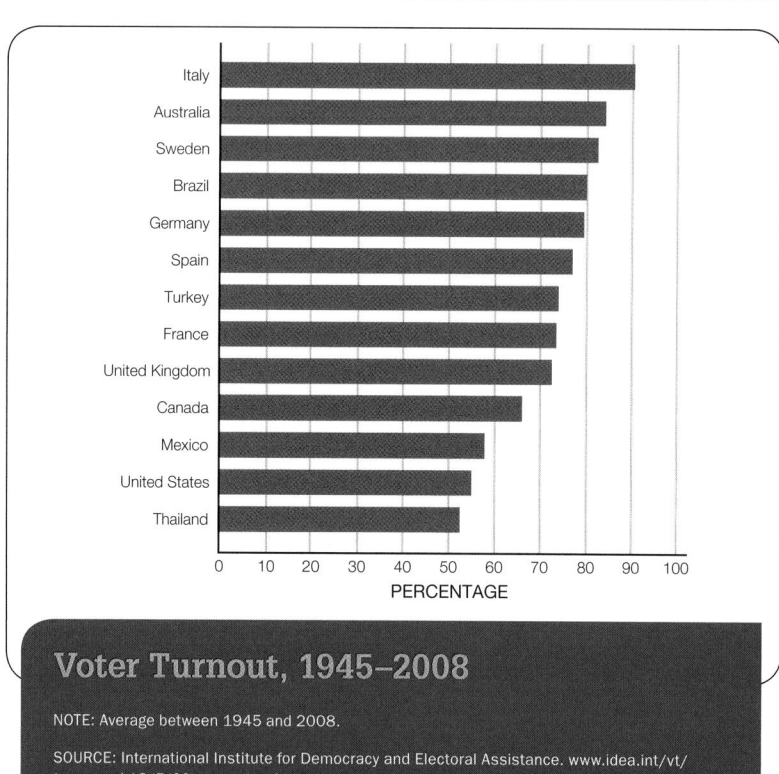

## Voter Turnout, 1945–2008

NOTE: Average between 1945 and 2008.

SOURCE: International Institute for Democracy and Electoral Assistance. www.idea.int/vt/ (accessed 12/5/09); note that for some of the countries, the most recent election data are from 2007; for Brazil the average is calculated for the period after 1989, when democracy was restored. Turnout is based on percentage of voting-age population.

## for critical analysis

1. Would compulsory voting laws and automatic voter registration laws be useful to adopt in the United States? Or should participation in elections be purely by choice?

2. Does it matter if everyone votes? Do you think ex-felons should be allowed to vote? What about permanent residents who are not citizens? Why or why not?

## Socioeconomic Status

One of the most important and consistent findings from surveys about participation is that Americans with higher levels of education, more income, and higher-level occupations—collectively, what social scientists call higher **socioeconomic status**—participate much more in politics than do those with less education and less income.[47] Education level is the single most important factor in predicting not only whether an individual will vote, but also most kinds of participation, but income is an important factor (not surprisingly) when it comes to making contributions. People who are more affluent have the money, time, education, and capacity to participate effectively in the political system. These characteristics are also related to attitudes toward politics. Higher levels of political interest and psychological involvement in politics, such as political efficacy, are associated with individuals higher on the socioeconomic scale.[48]

Figure 8.3 on next page shows the differences in voter turnout linked to ethnic group, income and education level, and age. In 2008, for example, just 54 percent of those earning under $25,000 a year voted in the presidential election, compared with 79 percent of those earning more than $100,000 a year.[49] In addition to education and income, other individual characteristics affect participation. For example, African Americans and Latinos are less likely to participate than are whites, although when differences in education and income are taken into account, African Americans participate at similar levels as do whites.[50] Finally, young people are far less likely to participate in politics than are older people. (We will take a closer look at these groups later in this chapter.) Individuals with strong partisan ties—mainly those who affiliate with the Republican or Democratic parties—are more likely to vote than nonpartisans or independents.

But individual-level factors are not the only explanations for voter turnout. Our incomplete understanding of participation is evident when we compare voting across countries. For example, if more political resources lead to a greater likelihood of voting, why does the United States, one of the most prosperous countries in the world, have such a dismal history of participation? And Americans have become more educated over the past century, with more people finishing high school and attending college; so, given the well-documented links between educational attainment and voting, why has participation declined during this period?[51] These puzzles mean we need to look beyond the socioeconomic characteristics of individuals and to the larger political environment in which participation occurs.

**socioeconomic status** status in society based on level of education, income, and occupational prestige

## Political Environment

However important such individual factors as age and socioeconomic class may be in determining political participation, political environments and state election laws have increasingly proven to be even more significant. Whether or not people have resources, feel engaged, or are recruited to participate in politics depends very much on their social setting—what their parents are like, whom they know, what associations they belong to. In the United States, churches are one important social institution for helping foster political participation. Through their church activities people learn the civic skills that prepare them to participate in the political world more broadly. However, Robert Putnam argues that, over the past five decades, America has experienced a collapse of community organizations (or social capital), which may explain low participation. Younger generations are less likely to be engaged in community organizations that are involved in politics than, say, generations that came of age during World War II.

## The Percentage of Americans Who Voted, 1976–2008

Voting rates vary substantially by race and ethnicity, education, employment status, and age. Which groups have the highest rates of voter turnout? Among which groups has participation increased the most since 1992?

SOURCES: U.S. Census Bureau, "Reported Voting and Registration by Race, Hispanic Origin, Sex, and Age Groups: November 1964 to 2008"; "Reported Voting and Registration by Region, Educational Attainment, and Labor Force: November 1964 to 2008," www .census.gov (accessed 11/24/09).

PERCENTAGE OF POPULATION
REPORTING THEY VOTED

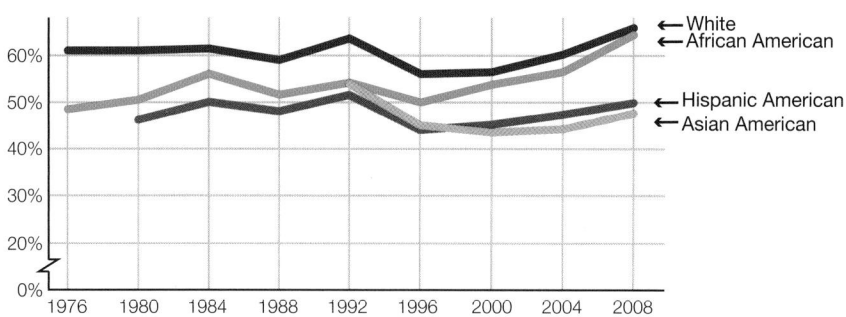

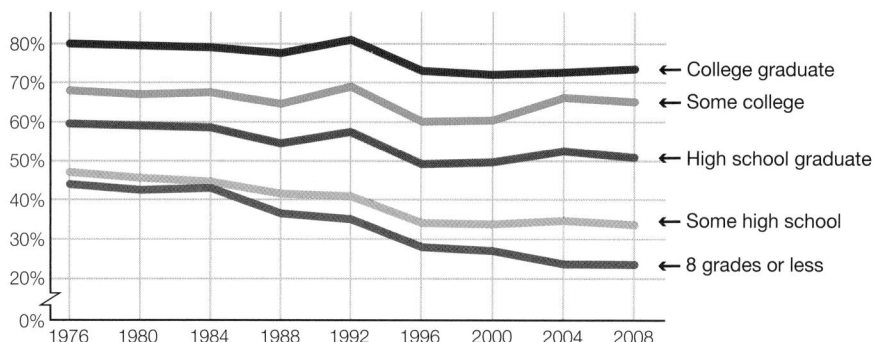

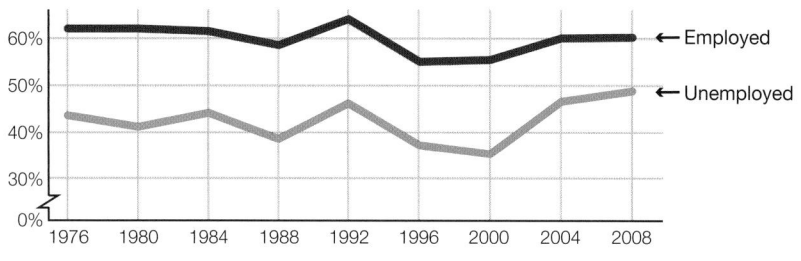

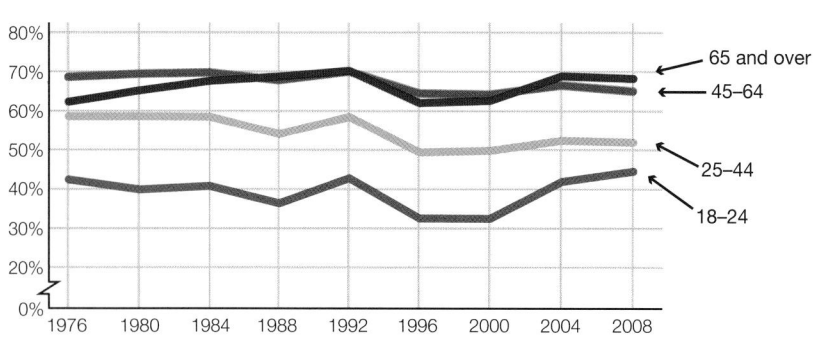

Still, arguments about long-term declines in community involvement may not give enough attention to the actual political environments where participation takes place. Participation depends not only on what people think politics has to offer them and their communities, but also on whether citizens are motivated and mobilized to participate and on whether there are formal obstacles in the political system.

**Mobilization** A critical aspect of political environments is whether people are mobilized—by parties, candidates, campaigns, interest groups, and social movements. A recent comprehensive study of the decline in political participation in the United States found that half of the drop-off could be accounted for by reduced **mobilization** efforts.[56] People become much more likely to participate when someone—preferably someone they know—asks them to get involved.

**mobilization** the process by which large numbers of people are organized for a political activity

A series of experiments conducted by the political scientists Donald Green and Alan Gerber demonstrates the importance of personal contact for mobilizing voters. Evaluating the results of several get-out-the-vote drives, Gerber and Green showed that face-to-face interaction with a canvasser greatly increased the chances that the person contacted would go to the polls. They estimated that personal contact boosted voter turnout by 9.8 percent. The impact of direct mail was much smaller, causing only a 0.6 percent increase in voting.[53] Impersonal calls from a phone bank had no measurable effect on voter turnout. Green and Gerber also evaluated the impact of mobilization on young voters by studying a series of get-out-the-vote campaigns conducted near college campuses during the 2000 election. In these campaigns, phone contacts that were chattier and more informal than standard phone-bank messages increased turnout by an estimated 5 percent. Face-to-face contact again proved even more powerful, increasing turnout by 8.5 percent.[54] Recent research has shown that text messaging has a positive impact on youth turnout. In 2008 one study showed that sending text messages to young voters on the day before a presidential primary election increased turnout by 2.1 percent; sending messages on the day of the election increased turnout by 4.6 percent.[55]

In previous decades, political parties and social movements relied on personal contact to mobilize voters. As we will see in Chapter 9, during the nineteenth century, American political party machines employed hundreds of thousands of workers to organize and mobilize voters as well as bring them to the polls. The result was an extremely high turnout rate, typically more than 90 percent

*People are more likely to turn out to vote if someone asks them face-to-face. Direct mail and impersonal phonecalls are less likely to have an effect on turnout.*

of eligible voters.[56] But political party machines began to decline in strength at the beginning of the twentieth century, and by now have, for the most part, disappeared. By the late twentieth century, political parties had become essentially fund-raising and advertising organizations rather than mobilizers of people. Without party workers to encourage eligible voters to go to the polls, and even bring them there if necessary, many of them will not participate. Nevertheless, competitive presidential elections since 2000 have once again motivated both parties to build strong grassroots organizations to reach voters and turn them out on Election Day. In the 2004 elections, Republicans were more successful in their organizational efforts than Democrats. Republicans

**for critical analysis**

Why do efforts toward direct mobilization seem to be more successful than television advertising in promoting voter turnout? How is the Internet becoming an important tool for increasing political participation?

built an organization with more than 1.4 million volunteers who were trained to make calls, go door to door to register voters, write letters to the editor in support of President Bush, post blogs online, and phone local radio call-in shows.

During the 2008 campaign, though, the Democrats built a more extensive organization to contact and turn out voters than did Republicans. Barack Obama's campaign made mobilization a centerpiece of its strategy from the start. Inspired by Obama's own experience as a community organizer, the campaign sought to organize a base of volunteers to go door to door seeking support for their candidate. Many of Obama's crucial primary victories, including his initial win in Iowa and his later success in states that, like Iowa, used the caucus system to select presidential candidates, relied on direct voter mobilization. These victories in the primaries led the Obama campaign to create a nationwide organization of paid staff and volunteers for the general election, rather than focusing on battleground states as his predecessors had done. The expansion of the electorate through mobilization became a central pillar of the Obama strategy. The campaign opened more than 700 offices in the battleground states, where paid staff coordinated the work of tens of thousands of volunteers. The Internet, as discussed earlier, played a significant role in this mobilization strategy. In contrast, the McCain campaign put less emphasis on building an organization of paid staff and volunteers, relying instead on traditional voter mobilization tactics and the battleground-state strategy that had worked four years earlier for George W. Bush.

Analyses of the 2008 election have suggested that the Democrats' organization and mobilization helped Barack Obama win the White House. By mobilizing support in places where Democrats had not seriously contended in the past, including largely Republican states such as Indiana, the Obama campaign expanded the electoral map. In 2012, Obama swept most almost all of the battleground states besides North Carolina. The marriage of technology, money, early voting, and field organization that the Obama campaign assembled for the 2008 campaign was repeated in 2012, and will surely be imitated in future elections.

In the past, social movements, such as the labor movement in the 1930s and the civil rights movement of the 1960s, played an important role in mobilizing people into politics. Since then, social movements, interest groups, and political parties have generally reduced their efforts at direct mobilization, although some—such as the labor movement, the Christian right, and the Tea Party movement—have revived direct mobilization in recent years. The number of interest groups has grown dramatically, but the connection that most members have to such groups often extends no further than their checkbooks. Rather than promoting political activity through personal contact, membership in an organization is likely to bring solicitation letters through the mail, requesting donations. And rather than providing a venue for meeting new people and widening a citizen's circle of engagement, organizational membership is more likely to land one's name on yet another mailing list, generating still more requests for funds.

**Electoral Competition** To be motivated to vote, individuals must be interested in the election and knowledgeable about the candidates. An important factor, often overlooked in analyzing political participation, is whether elections are competitive; that is, whether there are at least two parties (and their candidates) actively contesting a position in government.[57] Competitive elections, and the campaign spending and mobilization efforts that go along with them, have been identified as playing an important role in turnout rates in the United States and cross-nationally.[58] Conversely, limited exposure to competitive elections may be one reason for the lower levels of turnout recorded since the 1960s. In many congressional, statewide, and local races, a candidate (often the incumbent) runs unopposed or is expected to win by such a large margin that the challenger's chances are virtually nil. When congressional districts are drawn to favor one political party over another—what is termed *gerrymandering*—election outcomes can be highly lopsided in favor of one candidate over another. This is a primary reason why most members of Congress win elections by landslides—that is, by overwhelming margins.

One political scientist, Todd O. Donovan, uses a baseball analogy to explain the importance of competitive elections in mobilizing people to participate in politics: "People watch a game to see their team win, or because of interest in an important game. Perfect scoring is meaningless if only one team takes the field, and attendance will suffer if two teams are playing that no one can cheer for."[59] When candidates and political parties spend more effort and money to compete for an elected office, more information becomes available to voters in the form of media ads, newspaper coverage, door-to-door campaigns, online campaigns, and more. Electoral competition may reduce the cost to individuals of becoming informed, leading to higher turnout. Conversely, if elections are uncompetitive or uncontested, they generate little political information. Without active campaigns, individuals have fewer opportunities to be interested in an election, and may have less motivation to vote.[60] Under these conditions, the cost of being informed and actually voting is high.

The American states vary dramatically in the competitiveness of presidential elections, congressional elections, gubernatorial elections, and substantive ballot measures. Some U.S. House districts are so uncompetitive that a single candidate often runs in an uncontested election; in some states, up to one-third of congressional races are uncontested in some election years.[61] With only one name appearing on the election ballot, there is little incentive for a rational citizen to vote, as voting will not affect the outcome. On average over the past 40 years, only two dozen U.S. House races have been very competitive every two years, producing a

*A baseball game in which only one team competed or where neither team had many fans would not attract much interest. Similarly, an uncontested (or noncompetitive) election is unlikely to motivate citizens to participate.*

victory margin of 5 percentage points or less by the winning candidate over the losing candidate—for example, the winning candidate gets 52 percent of the vote and the losing candidate 48 percent. Many studies have shown that more electoral competition and increased campaign spending on the part of candidates lead to higher voter turnout.[62]

Beyond candidate races, ballot measures (initiatives and referenda) have been found to increase voter turnout, especially among less educated citizens.[63] Elections that include controversial initiatives on the state ballot—in which citizens vote directly on policy questions such as affirmative action, increasing the minimum wage, or bans on same-sex marriage—have also been found to increase political interest, political knowledge, and contributions to interest groups.[64] In many states, ballot measure campaigns are increasingly important for mobilizing voter turnout and can have spillover effects on candidate races.[65] In the 2004 presidential election, for example, laws prohibiting same-sex marriage appeared on the ballot in 13 states. Scholars have found that the ballot measure campaigns and media attention increased the importance of marriage as an issue when voters evaluated the 2004 presidential candidates in these states. The issue was also a more important factor in voting for the president in the 13 states where marriage was on the ballot than in the states without such ballot measures. That is, the same-sex-marriage ballot measures may have helped re-elect George W. Bush in the 2004 presidential elections by priming voters to make the issue of same-sex marriage more salient, which had the effect of benefiting the Republican candidate over the Democratic candidate.[66] These studies point to ballot measure campaigns providing the motivation to engage citizens to participate in politics.

An important source of variation in electoral competition is America's unique structure for presidential elections. No other country uses an electoral college to mediate between a national or direct vote for presidential candidates and the actual winner. To win, a U.S. presidential candidate must receive a majority of the votes in the electoral college (270), which are awarded to states based on the size of their congressional delegation. (The electoral college is covered in more detail in Chapter 10.) Some citizens reside in highly competitive battleground states, such as Ohio, Florida, and Pennsylvania. These states are defined by high levels of competition between the Democratic and Republican parties, with half the voters affiliating with the Republicans and half with the Democrats. Most Americans, however, live in non-battleground states such as California, New York, and Texas, where one or the other of the major parties, Democratic or Republican, is generally assured of victory in presidential elections. Every four years, residents of battleground states get smothered with attention from candidates and media, while citizens in states with few electoral votes or where one political party has a solid majority barely get noticed. Hence, presidential elections are often decided by a relatively small number of voters in America's dozen or so battleground states.[67] One study found that voter turnout in battleground states is higher than in non-battleground states and less skewed in terms of participation by the poor and young. Furthermore, the poor in battleground states are more interested in politics than the poor in non-battleground states.[68] Since the number of battleground states has been decreasing, fewer and fewer Americans are exposed to high-intensity presidential campaigns, which may be another reason for lower levels of turnout since the 1960s.

Even the structure for nominating presidential candidates has implications for participation in government. Selecting presidential candidates involves a sequence of statewide primary elections and caucuses; the early phase of this process is dominated by a handful of small-population states. The resulting privileged position of Iowa and New Hampshire, sites of the nation's first caucus and first primary election, respectively, can boost political participation. Similarly, studies have shown that citizens residing in early-voting states, such as Iowa, New Hampshire, or the "Super Tuesday" states (the two dozen states that hold primaries or caucuses on a single day about six weeks after the New Hampshire primary), are more likely to vote in presidential primaries and be interested in the election.[69] For residents of late-voting states, by contrast, turnout in primaries is often very low. Frequently the nomination contest is over almost before it starts, as one candidate secures a significant lead in early primaries, leaving many citizens (sometimes the majority of Americans) with no role in selecting their party's nominee. Turnout in these later states naturally plummets. For example, California's 2012 primary election was in June, well after the Republican nominee, Mitt Romney, had already been chosen; turnout in the primary was thus very low.

## State Electoral Laws

As stipulated by the Constitution, the states retain control of voter registration and voting itself. This decentralized system continues to create wide variation in the laws governing elections and voting, as well as participation in politics.[70] Voter turnout in presidential elections in the last decade ranges from a high of over 70 percent of eligible voters in Minnesota to 45 percent in Mississippi, a 25-point difference. State electoral laws can create formal barriers to voting—costs to be weighed against the potential benefits of voting—that can reduce participation.

**Registration Requirements** An important factor reducing voter turnout in the United States is our nation's unique state-by-state patchwork of registration rules. In most other democracies in the world, citizens are automatically registered to vote, but the United States requires a two-step process: registering to vote and then voting. In every American state but North Dakota, individuals who are eligible to vote must register with the state election board before they are actually allowed to vote, although a handful of states now allow this to occur on Election Day itself. Registration requirements (another voting cost) were introduced at the end of the nineteenth century in response to the demands of the Progressive movement. Historical Progressive reformers hoped to make voting more difficult, both to reduce multiple voting and other forms of corruption and to discourage immigrant and working-class voters from going to the polls so political parties would be more responsive to middle-class voters and professionals. In some states, registration requirements reduced voter turnout by as much as 50 percent. Once voters are registered, they participate at very high levels—80 to 90 percent of those registered have voted in recent elections.

Registration requirements particularly reduce voting by the young, those with low education, and those with low incomes because registration requires a greater degree of political involvement (a cost) than does the act of voting itself. Those with relatively little education may become interested in politics once the issues of a particular campaign become salient, but by then it may be too late for them to register, especially if they live in states that require registration up to a month before the election. And because young people tend to change residences more often than older people, registration requirements place a greater burden on them. As a result, registration requirements not only diminish the size of the electorate but also tend to create an electorate that is, on average, better educated, more affluent, and composed of fewer young people and minorities than the citizenry as a whole (see Figure 8.4). In Europe, there is typically no registration burden on the individual voter; voter registration is handled automatically by the government. This is one reason that voter turnout rates in Europe are higher than those in the United States.

**Other Formal Barriers** A barrier to voting that has grown more important in recent years is the restriction on the voting rights of people who have committed a felony. Forty-eight states and the District of Columbia prohibit prison inmates who are serving a felony sentence from voting.[71] In 36 states, felons on probation or parole are not permitted to vote. There are also numerous restrictions on the voting rights of felons who have served their sentences. In 11 states, a felony record can result in a lifetime ban on voting.

With the sharp rise in incarceration rates in the 1980s and '90s, these restrictions have had a significant impact on voting rights. By one estimate, 5.3 million people (2.4 percent of the voting-age population) have lost their voting rights as a result of these restrictions. Further, such restrictions disproportionately affect minorities because 60 percent of the prison population is African American or Latino, though these groups make up only roughly 25 percent of the population. One in eight black men cannot vote because of a criminal record. In the states that deny the vote to all ex-felons, nearly one in three black men has lost the right to vote.[72] The impact of felon disenfranchisement has been especially strong in the South, where Republican candidates have benefited from the reduction in the numbers of minority voters. Concern over the impact of these voting restrictions has led to campaigns to restore voting rights to people who have committed a felony. Since 1997, 19 states have reduced voting restrictions for people with a felony record.[73] Such reforms may have an important impact on politics: one study showed that if all people with felony records had been allowed to vote, Al Gore would have won the 2000 election.[74]

A relatively recent barrier is a requirement that voters provide proof of identity. Thirty-one states require all voters to show ID before voting at the polls: in 15 states a voter must provide photo identification to vote; in the remaining 16, non-photo forms of ID are acceptable. Georgia and Indiana have what the National Conference of State Legislatures (NCSL) calls strict photo identification laws, requiring government photo ID. In 2011 and 2012, six additional states (Kansas, Mississippi, South Carolina, Tennessee, Texas, and Wisconsin) passed similar laws. Voter identification laws in the states disproportionately affect minority citizens and the less affluent, reducing voter turnout of certain groups.[75]

Another barrier to voting has received less attention. In the United States, elections are held on Tuesdays—regular working days. In most European countries, by contrast, elections are held on Sundays or holidays. In some countries, such as India, polls remain open for several days. Holding elections on working days may make it difficult for some people to vote due to the demands of work and family. The United States has addressed this problem somewhat by expanding the use of absentee ballots, early voting, and voting by mail. Some reformers have called for an Election Day holiday, as is commonly used in Europe. This would underscore the importance of voting in America, making democratic participation a priority.

**Voting and Registration Reforms** Election reform efforts over the past quarter-century have focused mainly on making voter registration and voting easier and more convenient. These reforms are based on the premise that reducing the cost of voting (in the sense of cost-benefit analysis) should increase voter turnout.[76] Lever-

**for critical analysis**

Why is voter turnout so low in the United States? What are the consequences of low voter turnout?

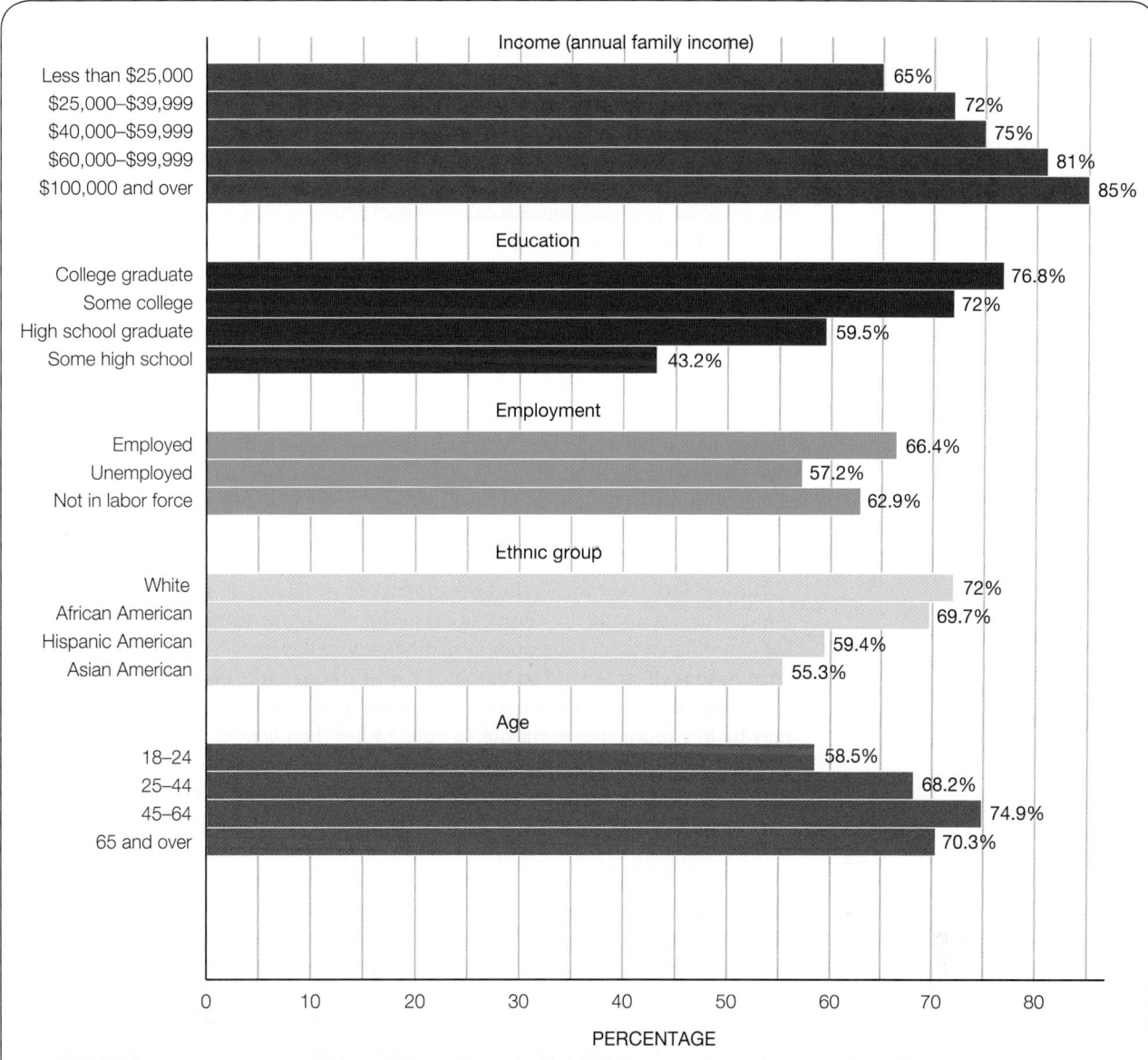

**FIGURE 8.4**

## Voter Registration Rates by Social Group, 2008

Some political analysts argue that registration requirements depress turnout. The percentage of the population that is registered to vote varies according to education level, employment status, race and ethnicity, and age. Are people with a lower income more or less likely to register to vote? Are less educated people more or less likely to register? Would the rates of participation among these groups change if registration requirements were altered?

Sources: U.S. Census Bureau, "Reported Voting and Registration by Race, Hispanic Origin, Sex, and Age Groups: November 1964 to 2008"; "Reported Voting and Registration by Region, Educational Attainment, and Labor Force: November 1964 to 2008," www.census.gov (accessed 11/24/09); U.S. Census Bureau, "Reported Voting and Registration by Region, Educational Attainment, and Labor Force: November 1964 to 2008," www.census.gov (accessed 11/24/09); Douglass R. Hess and Jody Herman, "Representational Bias in the 2008 Electorate," November 2009, www.projectvote.org (accessed 11/21/09).

**Election-Day registration** the option in some states to register on the day of the election, at the polling place, rather than in advance of the election

aging the natural variation in the American states, scholars have studied the effects of early voting, voting by mail, election-day registration, and absentee voting laws, among other such reforms.[77] **Election-Day registration** (EDR) combines the two-step process of voting—registering to vote and casting a ballot on Election Day—into one. On the same day, citizens can both register to vote and actually cast a ballot. A dozen states have EDR laws, with North Carolina and Iowa the two most recent adopters, in 2008. Proposals to adopt EDR have been considered in other states, but are often opposed because of concerns (whether legitimate or not) of Election Day fraud and noncitizens voting.

As might be expected, in states that do not require registration (North Dakota) or that allow registration on the day of the election (Idaho, Iowa, Minnesota, Maine, Montana, New Hampshire, North Carolina, Wisconsin, and Wyoming), not only is voter turnout higher than the national average, but younger and less affluent voters turn out in larger percentages.[78] On average, EDR increases turnout by 5 percent, with all other factors held constant.[79] One of the most sophisticated studies, conducted by political scientist Michael Hamner, measured change in voter turnout after the statewide adoption of EDR, comparing turnout rates with those of similar states without EDR. The study controlled for the possibility that states adopting registration reforms may have higher turnout rates in the first place and a political culture that supports citizen participation. The results of Hamner's study indicate EDR does increase turnout, but the effects are modest. The largest effects of EDR laws are in modifying the composition of the electorate; turnout among the young, the less educated, and the poor is significantly higher in the dozen states allowing citizens to register to vote on the same day as the election, compared to states with longer registration requirements.[80] Thus the real effect of state election reforms may be in altering *who* turns out to vote, rather than *how many* turn out.

New portable voter registration requirements in some states, for example, eliminate the need to reregister after changing residences and may reduce the bias of the electorate by removing one barrier to participation by young people and others

*Why is voter turnout relatively low in the United States? One reason may be that the United States requires a two-step process to vote—registering and then voting. Some states have tried to make voting easier and less time-consuming by offering Election-Day registration, early voting, or voting, by mail, and by providing ballots and other information in multiple languages.*

who tend to move frequently.[81] In 1988, Oregon voters adopted a ballot measure to create a system for voting exclusively by mail, thus eliminating polling places altogether. Individual voters fill out their ballot at home and place it in the mail or in drop-boxes throughout the state. Washington State followed suit a few years later, and the majority of Californians and citizens of other Western states now cast votes using **permanent absentee ballots**, which are mailed.[82] In Colorado, a state that promotes absentee voting, 78.6 percent of the vote was cast via absentee ballot in 2008.[83] The western states tend to have higher voter turnout than other parts of the country besides the Midwest, making it difficult to disentangle whether mail voting or regional political culture drives higher turnout.

Another reform that has been adopted by many states is **early voting**, which allows registered voters to cast a ballot at their regular polling place up to 40 days before the election. In contrast to EDR or mail voting, early voting may not significantly increase turnout or alter the demographic composition of the electorate.[84] One study from Oregon found that voting by mail increased voter turnout, but only among those groups already predisposed to vote; early voting reinforces higher turnout among the upper class and older citizens, and nonvoting among the lower class.[85]

Removing formal obstacles to voting, or reducing voting costs, may not be enough to ensure that people participate, as the example of the National Voter Registration Act passed in 1993 shows. Popularly known as the Motor Voter Act, the law aimed to increase participation by making it easier to register to vote. The law allowed people to register at the Department of Motor Vehicles when they applied for a driver's license and at other public facilities. An estimated 3.4 million people registered to vote as a result of the Motor Voter Act, but turnout in the 1996 election—the first presidential election held after the law went into effect—actually declined by 6 percent from that in 1992.[86] The limited success of the Motor Voter Act suggests that people need motivation to vote, such as active candidate campaigns and competitive elections, not simply the removal of registration barriers.

The political scientist Adam Berinksy provides an explanation for these seemingly contradictory findings that overall voter turnout has not increased despite efforts to make voting easier and more convenient. He suggests that making voting more convenient (e.g., voting by mail, early voting, and absentee voting) simply reinforces the behavior of those most likely to vote. These reforms do not lower the costs of voting enough to engage those with few political resources, but instead lower the costs enough for the upper classes to vote more consistently. One study shows that different election reforms may produce different outcomes. Reducing barriers to registration can increase the likelihood of voting among those not already a part of the electoral system, and voting that is more convenient mainly helps those most likely to vote anyway, while EDR has a relatively strong influence on turning out lower-income voters.[87]

Of all the reforms, EDR has shown the most promise for increasing turnout in general and in increasing voting among the young and those with few resources. But voter turnout isn't the only outcome that matters. One estimate put the number of early votes at one-third of the national total in 2008, with Obama outperforming his Republican opponent, John McCain, in early-voting ballots.[88] Thus state election laws allowing early voting may have helped Obama win office in 2008.[89] Obama wisely made early voting a key part of his campaign in 2008 and again in 2012, encouraging his supporters to vote early and thus avoid problems that occur on Election Day, such as long lines, poor weather, or malfunctioning voting machines.

**Recent Restrictions on Voting Rights: A Backlash?** Not everyone agrees that increasing voter turnout is a worthy goal. In recent years, despite the general trend

**permanent absentee ballots** the option in some states to have a ballot sent automatically to your home for each election, rather than having to request an absentee ballot each time

**early voting** the option in some states to cast a vote at a polling place or by mail before the election

throughout American history toward encouraging wider political participation, there have been efforts in many states to reimpose restrictions on voting rights.

As just noted, more than half of the states—31 as of 2012—have introduced requirements that would-be voters must produce proof of identity at their polling places. The issue of whether to require voters' proof of identity has become bitterly partisan. Proponents of such measures, mainly Republicans, insist that the possibility of voter fraud threatens "the sanctity of the vote"; opponents, mainly Democrats, counter that there have been almost no significant instances of voter fraud in the modern era and that the new photo ID laws are actually designed to suppress the vote of segments of the population most likely to vote for Democrats but also least likely to have photo ID—racial minorities, the elderly, and the poor.

# ● Diversity and Participation

> **Describe the patterns of participation among major social groups**

America's racial and ethnic diversity distinguishes it from many other democracies; participation by varying groups is important, as government must balance the demands of varying segments of the population. We've seen that individual characteristics, especially socioeconomic status, are associated with different levels and types of political participation.

Why does minority participation matter? One study of black political participation, for example, found that African Americans in cities run by a black mayor were more likely to vote, participate in campaigns, and contact public officials.[90] African Americans and Latinos are also more likely to vote when residing in states with increased representation in the state legislature, as measured by the percentage of black or Latino lawmakers.[91] One study found that African Americans represented by a black member of Congress are more likely to vote in elections and to have a sense of efficacy—the belief that the government is responsive to them—and have higher levels of political knowledge.[92] The same pattern is found for Latinos, with Latino representation in Congress and in state legislatures increasing Latino voting participation.[93] This phenomenon is commonly referred to as descriptive representation—when individuals are represented in government by officials of their same race, ethnicity, or gender.

When meaningful descriptive representation occurs, minority groups may have a greater ability to affect policy outcomes, thus incorporating minority populations and their concerns and interests into the political system. Descriptive representation may also confer symbolic benefits, such as reducing levels of political alienation among racial and ethnic minorities.[94] Since racial and ethnic groups generally hold different political opinions and support different political parties, elected officials disproportionately represent those who participate, which potentially leads to policies that pay little heed to nonvoters.[95] We discuss descriptive representation again in Chapter 12.

## African Americans

As we saw earlier in Chapter 5, in the South during much of the twentieth century, the widespread use of the poll tax, literacy tests, and other measures such as the white primary deprived African Americans (and many poor whites) of the right to vote. This system of legal segregation meant that black Americans in the South had few avenues for participating in politics.

Political and legal pressure, as well as protest, all played a part in the modern civil rights movement, which became a major force for change in the 1950s (see Chapter 5). The movement drew on an organizational base and network of communication rooted in black churches, the NAACP, and black colleges.

The nonviolent protest tactics adopted by local clergy members, including Reverend Martin Luther King Jr., eventually spread across the South and brought national attention to the movement. The clergy organized themselves into a group called the Southern Christian Leadership Conference (SCLC). Students also played a key role. The most important student organization was the Student Nonviolent Coordinating Committee (SNCC). In 1960, four black students in Greensboro, North Carolina, sat down at the lunch counter of a Woolworth's department store, which, like most southern establishments, did not serve African Americans. Their sit-in was the first of many. Through a combination of protest, legal action, and political pressure, the civil rights movement compelled a reluctant federal government to enforce black civil and political rights.

The victories of the civil rights movement made blacks full citizens and stimulated a tremendous growth in the number of black public officials at all levels of government as blacks exercised their newfound political rights. By voting as a cohesive bloc, African American voters began to wield considerable political power. When such legal barriers as the poll tax and the white primary were removed in the 1960s, black political participation shot up, with rates of turnout approaching those of southern whites as early as 1968.[96] Yet despite these successes, racial segregation remains a fact of life in the United States, and new problems have emerged. Most troubling is the persistence of black urban poverty, now coupled with deep social and economic isolation.[97] These conditions, often called concentrated poverty, raise new questions about African American political participation. One such question concerns black political cohesion: Will blacks continue to vote as a bloc, given the sharp economic differences that now divide a large black middle class from an equally large group of deeply impoverished African Americans? Public opinion and voting evidence indicate that African Americans have indeed continued to vote cohesively despite their economic differences.[98] Surveys of black voters show that blacks across the income spectrum believe that their fates are linked because of their race. This sense of shared experience and a common fate has united blacks at the polls and in politics.[99]

In the decades after the Civil War, newly enfranchised African American voters overwhelmingly supported Republicans, the "Party of Lincoln." When Franklin Delano Roosevelt ran for the presidency in 1932, however, most black voters joined the coalition that, through the many social programs that composed the New Deal, redefined not only the Democratic Party but also government itself. Especially since the 1960s when the Democratic Party favored the civil rights movement and white southerners began to desert the Democratic Party of Lyndon Johnson's Great Society, blacks have largely chosen Democratic candidates (roughly 90 percent of blacks vote Democratic), and black candidates have sought election under the Democratic banner. African Americans are one of the most cohesive groups in voting Democratic. Republican hostility to affirmative action and other programs of racial preference is likely to prevent any large-scale black migration to the Republican Party. At the same time, however, the black community has been considerably frustrated that their loyalty to the Democratic Party, even under African American president Barack Obama, has not been rewarded with economic opportunity. Because Republicans have not sought to win the black vote and Democrats take it for granted, neither party is willing to support bold measures to address the problems of poor African Americans.

With Barack Obama running in 2008 as the first black major-party candidate for president, African American interest in the election surged. Exit polls indicated that 95 percent of African Americans who voted cast ballots for Obama. The 2008 election also witnessed a significant increase in minority participation and marked an end to the long-standing gap in the level of black and white voter turnout. Black turnout rose 5 percent from 2004 to 2008, while there was only a 3 percent increase for Latinos. White non-Hispanic turnout was 67 percent in 2004 and 66 percent in 2008. The black-white gap went from 7 percent in 2004 to 1 percent in 2008.[100] Was this surge in minority voting merely an anomaly sparked by the Obama campaign, or was it indicative of a more general relationship between the election of minorities to public office and voter turnout?

## Latinos

For many years, analysts called the Latino vote "the sleeping giant" because Latinos as a group had relatively low levels of political mobilization. One important reason for this was the low rate of naturalization, which meant that many Latinos, as noncitizens, were not eligible to vote. Among those who were eligible to vote, registration and turnout rates were relatively low.

Today politicians and political parties view Latinos as a political group of critical importance, as they have become the largest minority group in the United States. Rapid population growth, increased political participation, and uncertain party attachment all magnify the importance of the Latino vote.[101] The Latino population stands at 50.5 million people as of 2010, or 16.3 percent of Americans, making Hispanics significantly more numerous than African Americans.[102] In large states such as California, Latinos approach 50 percent of the population. Although Latino registration and turnout are still significantly lower than those of whites and African Americans, these numbers have been steadily increasing. In 2008 a record 9.75 million Hispanics voted, accounting for 7.4 percent of the total national vote. In 2012, these numbers increased, with Latinos accounting for 10 percent of voters.[103]

Latinos have tended to favor the Democrats in national elections, though not as strongly or consistently as African Americans. Indeed, many Republicans believe that the tendency of Hispanic voters to be more socially conservative on issues of marriage, abortion, and religion than other groups within the Democratic Party provides the GOP with an opportunity to attract support from this growing constituency. President George W. Bush was especially committed to cultivating support in the Latino community, winning upwards of 44 percent of Latino votes in the 2004 presidential election, more than any other Republican presidential candidate in modern history. However, Republican opposition to immigration reform prompted Latinos to return to their more typical Democratic voting patterns in 2006 and 2008.

President Obama, much like his predecessor, has actively courted Latino voters. Nowhere was this more evident than in his nomination in May 2009 of Sonia Sotomayor to be the nation's first Latina Supreme Court justice. Obama also appointed two Latino lawmakers, Ken Salazar and Hilda Solis, to his cabinet and named a record number of Hispanics to positions within the administration. Obama's expansion of health insurance coverage was far more popular within the Latino community than the nation at large, mainly because of the high percentage of Latinos without insurance coverage.[104] The Obama administration has also aggressively reached out to Spanish-speaking media in an effort to connect to Latino voters: it held the first bilingual White House press briefing and partnered with Spanish-language networks Univision and Telemundo to broadcast White House events. Latino voters retained their strong allegiance to Democratic candidates in the 2010 midterm elections.[105]

However, Obama's failure to adopt immigration reform, combined with increased deportations of illegal immigrants during his first term, led to disaffection among some in the Latino community. Latinos were disappointed that, during the first four years of the Obama administration, more illegal immigrants were deported than during the eight years of the George W. Bush administration. However, Latinos leaned back toward the Democratic Party after the decision from the Obama administration in 2012 not to deport young people who came to the United States as children of illegal immigrants. In 2012, Obama and his challenger Mitt Romney both tried to appeal to Latino voters, but according to exit polls, Obama won 70 percent of the Latino vote.

## Asian Americans

Asian Americans are a smaller group than whites, Latinos, or African Americans, comprising 4.8 percent of the U.S. population in 2010. Yet, individuals who were Asian combined with at least one other race made up 5.6 percent of the nation's population. However, in particular states, such as California, home to 33 percent of the nation's Asian population, the group has become an important political presence. While the Asian population is just over 5 percent nationally, in California it is 13.4 percent of the population, according to the 2010 census. In terms of socioeconomic status, Asian Americans are more similar to non-Hispanic whites as

*Although Asian Americans come from diverse national backgrounds and hold diverse political opinions, efforts have been made recently to increase overall turnout among Asian American voters and increase their influence as a group. In 2008, the Center for Asian Americans United for Self-Empowerment (CAUSE) undertook a major effort to register Asian Pacific voters.*

a group, with education and income levels closer to those of whites than of Latinos or African Americans. Asians often vote similarly to whites.

No one national group dominates among the Asian American population, and their diversity has impeded the development of group-based political power. This diversity means that Asian Americans often have different political concerns, stemming from their different national backgrounds and experiences in the United States. Historically, these groups have united most effectively around common issues of ethnic discrimination or anti-Asian violence, federal immigration policies, and discriminatory mortgage loan practices.

Turnout rates among Asian Americans have been generally lower than those of other groups, though they have been gradually increasing; in 2008, 47.6 percent of Asian Americans turned out to vote, their second-highest percentage turnout since the census began tracking their participation in 1990.[106] In terms of political orientation, Asian Americans are a diverse group, but they have been moving, along with other minority groups, toward the Democratic Party in recent elections. Although a majority of Asian Americans voted Republican in the early 1990s, in the 2000s they have been voting increasingly Democratic,[107] and 73 percent of Asian Americans voted to re-elect Barack Obama in 2012.

## Gender and Participation

gender gap a distinctive pattern of voting behavior reflecting the differences in views between women and men

Today women register and vote at rates similar to or higher than those of men. The ongoing significance of gender issues in American politics is best exemplified by the **gender gap**—a distinctive pattern of male and female voting decisions—in electoral politics. Women tend to vote in higher numbers for Democratic candidates, whereas Republicans win more male votes. In 1980, men voted heavily for the Republican candidate, Ronald Reagan; women divided their votes between Reagan and the incumbent Democratic president, Jimmy Carter. Since that election, gender differences have emerged in congressional and state elections as well. In the 2004 election, George W. Bush narrowed the gender gap substantially, winning 48 percent of the female vote.[108] By 2006 the gender gap had reappeared, with 55 percent of women voting Democratic and only 43 percent Republican.[109] In the 2008 presidential election, observers expressed doubt about how women would vote, especially disappointed supporters of Democratic candidate Hillary Clinton. In fact, women voted strongly Democratic in 2008, with exit polls showing that 58 percent of women cast their ballots for the Obama-Biden ticket and 43 percent for the McCain-Palin ticket. In 2012, both parties considered women's votes as potentially decisive in the close race. However, Obama won the majority of women's votes again; according to exit polls, 55 percent of women voters cast their vote for compared to 44 percent favoring Romney.

Behind these voting patterns are differing assessments of key policy issues. Women are more likely than men to oppose military activities, especially war, and are more likely to support social spending. In 2003, 79 percent of men supported the Iraq War, for example, compared with 65 percent of women—a 14-point difference. This split continued during the debate about when to withdraw from Iraq. In 2007, 51 percent of men stated that they were in favor of keeping troops in Iraq until civil order was restored, whereas only 35 percent of women supported keeping troops there with such an indefinite time horizon.[110] On social programs, women tend to want stronger action from government: 37 percent of men express satisfaction with the Social Security and Medicare systems, whereas only 33 percent of women do; 45 percent of men were content with the quality of public education, whereas only 39 percent of women

*Women won the right to vote with the adoption of the Nineteenth Amendment in 1920, in part because many officials were convinced that women's suffrage would increase female support for American involvement in World War I. However, women have generally been less likely than men to support military activities.*

were.[111] These differences do not mean that all women vote more liberally than all men. In fact, the voting differences between women who are homemakers and women who are in the workforce are almost as large as the differences between men and women.[112]

One key development in gender politics in recent years is the growing number of women in elective office (see Figure 8.5), an increasingly significant form of descriptive representation. Journalists dubbed 1992 the "Year of the Woman" because so many women were elected to Congress: women doubled their numbers in the House and tripled them in the Senate. By 2009, women held 17.2 percent of the seats in the House of Representatives, including that held by the first female Speaker of the House, Nancy Pelosi. A total of 17 women served in the 100-member Senate in 2009–11, which represented an all-time high for an institution that had had only 38 female senators in its entire history.[113] Following the 2012 elections, 20 women served in the Senate, including 4 freshmen, notably Elizabeth Warren (D-Mass.) and Tammy Baldwin (D-Wisc.). Baldwin is also the first openly gay person elected to the senate. A record 28 women of color were elected to House, including 13 African American women, 9 Latinas, and 6 Asian/Pacific Islander Americans.

Recent research has shown that one key to increasing the number of women in political office is to encourage more women to run for election and by asking women to run for political office. Although women are just as likely to win an election as men, women are less likely to run for office, even if they are equally qualified as men. They are also disadvantaged as candidates not because they are women, but because male candidates are more likely to have the advantage of incumbency.[114] Organizations supporting female candidates have worked to encourage more women to run for office and have supported them financially. In addition to the bipartisan National Women's Political Caucus (NWPC), the Women's Campaign

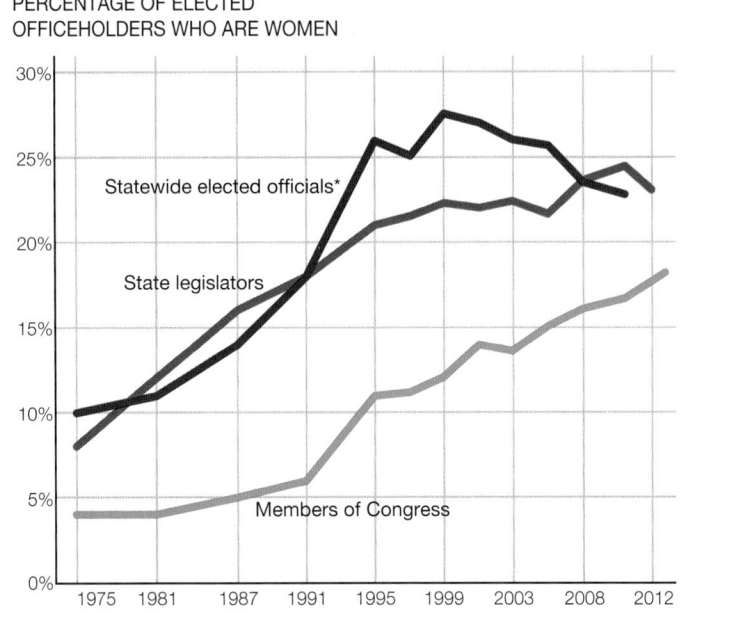

**FIGURE 8.5**

**Increase in Number of Women in Elective Office, 1975–2013**

The number of women holding elected office has always been larger in state offices than in Congress. When did the percentage of women elected to office begin to rise more rapidly?

*Governors, attorneys general, etc.

SOURCES: Cynthia Costello, Shari Miles, and Anne J. Stone, eds., *The American Woman, 2001–2002* (New York: W.W. Norton, 2002), p. 328; and Center for American Women and Politics, www.cawp.rutgers.edu (accessed 11/8/12).

PERCENTAGE OF ELECTED OFFICEHOLDERS WHO ARE WOMEN

Statewide elected officials*

State legislators

Members of Congress

Fund (WCF), and EMILY's List ("Early Money Is Like Yeast—it helps raise the dough") provide prochoice Democratic women with early campaign financing, which is critical to establishing electoral momentum.

Women candidates gained special prominence in the 2008 elections, with Senator Hillary Clinton's strong campaign for the Democratic presidential nomination and the selection of Alaska's governor Sarah Palin to run as vice president on the Republican ticket. Although neither succeeded in winning office, their campaigns marked important milestones in the road to power for women politicians. Clinton's nearmiss for the Democratic presidential nomination, in particular, is likely to make it easier for women to be considered credible presidential candidates in the future. Some research suggests that women were more likely to vote for Hillary Clinton in the 2008 presidential primaries than for the male candidates.

Why does the gender gap matter? Although women in public office by no means take uniform positions on policy issues, surveys show that, on the whole, female legislators are more supportive of women's rights and education and health care spending, and are more attentive to children's and family issues.[115] Recent surveys have shown that voters judge public officials differently on the basis of gender. While women are evaluated more positively on issues such as education and health care and are viewed as more skilled at striking compromises, the public views male officials as far more capable of dealing with national security and defense, and with crime and public safety.[116]

## Age and Participation

Older people have much higher rates of participation than young people. In the 2008 presidential elections, youth turnout was at its highest level in decades, with

51 percent of those aged 18 to 29 voting. However, this figure is still far lower than the number of older (65 and over) voters who turned out: an estimated 70 percent of those voters cast ballots in 2008.[117] Moreover, in midterm elections, youth turnout has historically been extremely low. In 2012, for example, young voters made up 19 percent of the electorate (up from 18 percent in 2008) but only slightly more than 10 percent in the midterm elections of 2010.

One reason younger people vote less is that political campaigns have rarely targeted young voters. A study of political advertising in the 2000 elections found that 64 percent of campaign television advertising was directed at people over 50. Only 14.2 percent of advertising was aimed at eighteen- to thirty-four-year-olds.[118] Another reason that political campaigns target older voters is that the elderly are better organized to participate than young people. The most important organization representing the elderly is AARP (formerly the American Association of Retired People), which has a membership of 40 million. AARP's ability to mobilize many thousands of individuals to weigh in on policy proposals has made the organization one of the most powerful in Washington. Young people have no comparable organization.

Since the early 1990s, several campaigns have been designed to increase the participation of young voters. Rock the Vote, which began in 1990, uses musicians and actors to urge young people to vote. It has spawned other initiatives aimed at young voters, including Rap the Vote and Rock the Vote a lo Latino.

The Obama campaign made young voters central to its electoral strategy in 2008 and 2012. The campaign posted videos on YouTube and used social media to reach out to young people. It sought to increase participation of young voters through a major voter registration campaign. In 2008, 22.3 million eighteen- to twenty-nine-year-olds (51 percent) turned out to vote, which represented a slight increase from 2004 and a big increase from the 2000 election, in which just

**for critical analysis**

When the Twenty-Sixth Amendment changed the voting age from 21 to 18 in 1971, observers expected that the youth vote would add a significant new voice to American politics. Why has the youth vote turned out to be less important than was hoped? What changes would engage more young people in the political system?

*Registration requirements make it harder to vote because voters have to plan ahead and register, rather than just showing up at the polls on election day. Some groups try to increase voting rates by getting more people registered in advance of elections.*

*At this 2008 Rock the Vote concert, musicians such as Pharrell Williams, from the band N\*E\*R\*D, performed to support efforts to get young people to vote. Particularly since 2000, campaigns like Rock the Vote have contributed to increases in the youth vote.*

40 percent of young voters cast ballots.[119] Exit polls showed that 66 percent of younger voters choose Barack Obama in 2008, with 60 percent supporting Obama in 2012.[120]

Relatively low voter turnout by the young has implications for the policies addressed by government at the local, state, and federal levels. Young people share older Americans' concerns about the economy and national security, but they tend to have more positive views about the role of government and express support for stronger environmental laws, funding for public education and colleges, and more tolerance for personal freedoms than older people do. They also are more likely to oppose military intervention overseas.[121] And although young people are less likely to engage in politics than older generations, they do have a strong interest in community service. One recent survey found that 19 percent of young people are involved in community service projects, with numbers higher among those with college experience.[122] Another survey found that 57 percent of young people felt that they could have a role in solving the problems in their community. Yet that same survey revealed cynicism about politics, with 61 percent of young people responding that "politics is a way for the powerful to keep themselves powerful."[123]

# Who Made Up the Electorate in 2012?

The electorate—those citizens who vote in elections—does not necessarily resemble the American population. For example, in 2012, Latinos made up at least 16 percent of the population but only 10 percent of the electorate in the 2012 presidential election (though this percentage has been steadily increasing over recent elections). Americans older than 65 made up about 13 percent of the population but 16 percent of the electorate.

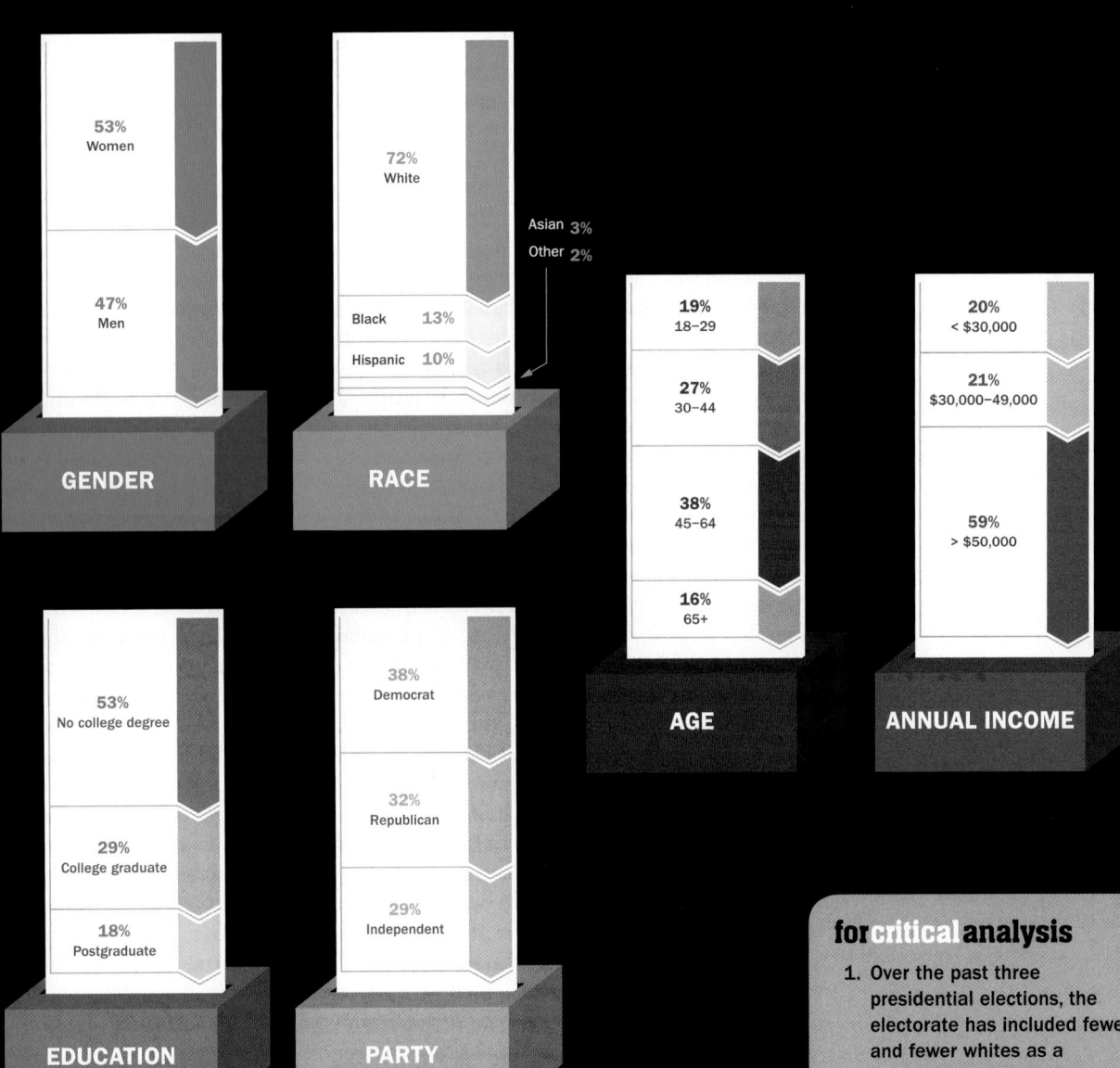

**GENDER**
- 53% Women
- 47% Men

**RACE**
- 72% White
- Black 13%
- Hispanic 10%
- Asian 3%
- Other 2%

**AGE**
- 19% 18–29
- 27% 30–44
- 38% 45–64
- 16% 65+

**ANNUAL INCOME**
- 20% < $30,000
- 21% $30,000–49,000
- 59% > $50,000

**EDUCATION**
- 53% No college degree
- 29% College graduate
- 18% Postgraduate

**PARTY**
- 38% Democrat
- 32% Republican
- 29% Independent

## for critical analysis

1. Over the past three presidential elections, the electorate has included fewer and fewer whites as a percentage of total voters. What does this mean for candidates and parties?

2. Does it matter if the electorate reflects the overall population? Why or why not?

SOURCE: Data are based on exit polls available at http://elections.nytimes.com/2012/results/president/exit-polls (accessed 11/12/12).

## Religious Identity

Religious identity plays an important role in American life and has come to the forefront with 2008 and 2012 Republican presidential candidate Mitt Romney, a Mormon, as a front-runner. For many citizens, religious groups provide an organizational infrastructure for political participation, especially around issues of special group concern. Black churches, for example, were instrumental in the civil rights movement, and black religious leaders continue to play important roles in national and local politics. Jews have also been active as a group in politics, but less through religious bodies than through a variety of social action agencies, including the American Jewish Congress, the American Jewish Committee, and the Anti-Defamation League.

For most of American history, religious language, symbols, and values have been woven deeply into the fabric of public life. Until the mid-twentieth century, public school students generally began the day with prayers or Bible readings; city halls displayed crèches during the Christmas season. But over the past 35 years, a variety of court decisions has greatly reduced this kind of overt religious influence on public life. In 1962 the Supreme Court ruled in *Engel v. Vitale* that prayer in public schools was unconstitutional—that government should not be in the business of sponsoring official prayers.[124]

These decisions helped to spawn a countermovement of religious activists seeking to roll back these decisions and restore the prominent role of religion in civic life. The mobilization of religious organizations and other groups that aim to reintroduce their moral views into the public sphere has been one of the most significant political developments of the past two and a half decades. Some of the most divisive conflicts in politics today, such as those over abortion and same-sex marriage, hinge on differences over religious and moral beliefs. These divisions have become so salient that they now constitute a major clash of cultures, with repercussions throughout the political system and across many different areas of policy.

One of the most significant drivers of this new politics has been the mobilization of white evangelical Protestants into a cohesive political force. The Moral Majority, the first broad-based political organization of evangelical Christians, was founded in 1979 and quickly rose to prominence in the 1980 election when it aligned with the Republican Party, eventually backing Ronald Reagan for president. Over the next few years, evangelicals strengthened their movement by registering voters and mobilizing them with sophisticated, state-of-the-art political techniques such as direct-mail campaigns and telephone hotlines. Their success was evident in the 1984 election, when 80 percent of evangelical Christian voters cast their ballots for Reagan. The 1988 election was a turning point in the political development of the Christian right. The televangelist Pat Robertson ran for president, and, although his candidacy was unsuccessful, his effort laid the groundwork for future political strength. Robertson's supporters gained control of some state Republican parties and won positions of power in others. With this new organizational base and sharply honed political skills, Robertson formed a new organization, the Christian Coalition, which capitalized on its ability to mobilize a large grassroots base to become one of the most important groups in American politics during the 1990s.

President George W. Bush was closely aligned with religious conservatives, and the religious right played an important role in mobilizing voters to support him in the 2000 and 2004 elections. Many analysts viewed Bush's Office of Faith-Based and Community Initiatives (whose programs were generally known as faith-based initiatives), which sought to funnel government assistance to religious groups engaged in charitable work, as a way to reward conservative Christian groups for supporting his candidacy. In fact, conservative religious groups spoke out against the initiative at first because they feared that government control would accompany federal dollars.[125]

# Thinking Critically about the Future of Political Participation

The American political community has expanded over the course of history, with new groups winning and asserting political rights. This expansion has brought American politics more closely into line with the fundamental values of liberty, equality, and democracy. But for much of the twentieth century, the electoral system in the United States failed to mobilize an active citizenry, giving rise to an uneven pattern of political participation that gives some people more of a voice in politics than others and thus goes against the American values of equality and democracy. Since 2000 a series of highly competitive presidential elections has spurred political campaigns to pay more attention to drawing greater numbers of voters into the political process, but many Americans still do not participate in politics.

Naturally enough, one of the most important factors in sustaining participation is a sense of political efficacy, the feeling that average citizens can help shape what government actually does. One important study found that elected officials respond more to the preferences of voters than nonvoters, confirming long-held assumptions that the affluent, more educated, and older citizens have more voice in politics and public policy.[126] A study by the political scientist Larry Bartels showed that senators (both Republicans and Democrats) are much less responsive to the policy preferences of low-income citizens—who are also less likely to be active voters.[127] If the voices of only the more affluent are heard during election time, the issues that concern lower-income Americans may not find a place at the top of the political agenda.

What would it take to increase political engagement among citizens of all backgrounds? For decades the conventional wisdom of reformers was to limit the role of money in politics so that the voices of ordinary Americans couldn't be easily drowned out by wealthy individuals and well-financed special interests. In 1976, however, the Supreme Court ruled that individual contributions to candidates were a form of free speech and that it would be a curtailment of liberty to forbid such spending so long as it was not formally connected with political campaigns.[128] And the Supreme Court's 2010 ruling in *Citizens United v. Federal Election Commission* increases the role of money in campaigns. Again defending campaign spending as free speech, the Court ruled that corporations and labor unions could directly spend unlimited amounts of money in favor of candidates as long as the corporations and unions did not coordinate directly with the candidates' campaign organizations. (See Chapter 10 for a discussion of this decision.) The *Citizens United* decision may increase the

*For much of American history, formal barriers restricted the right to vote and created a pattern of unequal participation in politics. Today, most of those barriers have been eliminated, but voter turnout remains relatively low, especially among young voters. In 2008, these voters cast their ballots at a polling station in a fraternity house near the UCLA campus.*

political influence of the affluent and special interests, such as corporations, potentially weakening the voice of the middle class and poor in politics.[129]

Nonetheless, other recent developments promise to give more people more of a voice in American government. Over the past few decades innovative states have led the way by reforming and modernizing America's patchwork election system, with innovations ranging from EDR to early and mail voting, and even portable registration that eliminates altogether the need to reregister after moving to a new residence. Hawaii registers all high school students to vote, while permanent voter registration, akin to voting systems used in European countries, is increasingly a popular reform at the state level. Some states, such as Iowa, use nonpartisan boards to draw legislative districts, which tend to boost competition in congressional and state legislative races. Increased competition, in turn, often results in a more informed and energized electorate, thus increasing turnout.

Drawing on the American states as laboratories of democracy allows policy makers to test what works and what does not. Reforms found to be successful at the state level may be adopted at the national level: Congress debated legislation to create early voting nationally in 2008. Eighteen states granted women's suffrage before adoption of the Nineteenth Amendment in 1920 gave women the right to vote nationally, and many states allowed the direct election of U.S. senators before the Seventeenth Amendment to the Constitution established direct election of senators by popular vote in each state. If more Americans voted, the policies adopted by their governments would be more representative of the majority preferences in this country.

The explosive growth in online communication as a means of organizing political participation has been especially apparent during recent elections. New technologies have supplied political leaders and candidates with new avenues for reaching out to citizens and have given citizens novel (and even enjoyable) ways to learn about and engage with politics. As we have learned, individuals who learn about politics online are more likely to vote and participate in politics in myriad other ways. Astonishingly diverse online news sources have given rise to new opinion leaders and new voices.

Nevertheless, the new media revolution has some drawbacks for American politics. Misinformation spreads as quickly through the Internet as good information, and false rumors and gender or racial sterotypes can proliferate. Inequality in access to the Internet remains a barrier to full participation in a digital democracy. Those most likely to be offline include the poor, the less educated, the elderly, and racial and ethnic minorities, such as Latinos and African Americans—all the same demographic groups who, along with young Americans, have been least likely to vote. It's possible, then, that these overlapping disadvantages may make the electorate even more unrepresentative. However, mobile access on cell phones is most common among racial minorities and the young, partially bridging the digital divide. Digital politics offers hope for reinvigorating American democracy and participation in politics.

Whatever promise digital politics holds for increasing political participation, it also raises the same fundamental questions that have arisen with every major new development in America's political history: How can citizens turn participation in politics into meaningful representation in government? And how, in turn, can representation result in public policies that reflect the needs of the greatest number of American citizens?

# get involved/go online

# Become a Voter

## Inform Yourself

 **Find out** *when* the next election is, and *what* is on the ballot. Go to vote411 .org (a website from the League of Women Voters), and locate "On Your Ballot." Select your state from th e drop-down menu. Either click on the link to all of your state's elections or use the form for "Personalized Ballot" to get information about what is on the ballot in the next election. *Where* do you vote? Enter your street address in the "Polling Place Finder" (on the main vote411.org page) to receive your voting location.

## Express Yourself

 **Register to vote**. Voting is one of the most important forms of expression in politics. In most states, you must be registered in order to vote. One way to do so is by visiting vote411.org and selecting "Register to Vote." Your state's page on the site also includes information on what type of ID is necessary to vote.

 **Ask about voting**. If you have questions about how to register to vote or wish to request an absentee ballot, call or e-mail the your state's secretary of state or board of elections. Contact information is provided on the state pages at vote411.org. Most states allow voting via an absentee ballot, which is mailed to your home.

## Connect with Others

 **Get involved in the next election**. If there is an election coming up, your local newspaper's website will likely have a guide to the candidates and issues. Many candidates have Facebook pages or personal websites where you can learn about upcoming campaign events and how to get involved (donating money? displaying a sign? attending a meeting?).

 **Know your current representatives**. Even if there's not an election coming up soon, it's a safe bet that some of your current representatives in government will be running for re-election in the next election. Will you support them? Find out who represents you by entering your zip code at the Project Vote Smart website (www .votesmart.org). Choose two of your representatives, and visit their personal websites or Facebook pages to see what types of messages they are posting and whether you agree with the policies they support.

*Find links to the sites listed above as well as related activities on wwnorton.com/studyspace.*

# study guide

**(S) Practice online with:** Chapter 8 Diagnostic Quiz ▪ Chapter 8 Key Term Flashcards

## Forms of Political Participation

■ **Describe the major types of traditional and online participation in politics (pp. 295–304)**

Political participation refers to a wide range of activities designed to influence government, politics, and policy. These activities fall into two major categories: traditional political participation, which refers to long-standing activities, such as voting, volunteering, and contributing to a candidate; and online political participation, which refers to a newer set of activities carried out through the Internet, such as posting comments on a blog or Twitter, or visiting a political party's website. There are many reasons to believe that the opportunities created by Internet in turn increase traditional political participation among large segments of the population.

### Key Terms

**traditional political participation** (p. 295)

**protest** (p. 296)

**online political participation** (p. 297)

### Practice Quiz

1. Which of the following is not a form of traditional political participation? *(pp. 295–97)*
   a) volunteering in a campaign
   b) attending an abortion-rights rally
   c) contributing to the Democratic Party
   d) voting in an election
   e) uploading a political video to YouTube

2. Online sources of information *(pp. 299–302)*
   a) are less diverse than those found in the traditional media.
   b) are more diverse than those found in the traditional media.
   c) are exactly the same as those found in the traditional media.
   d) do not influence political knowledge, political interest, or political participation.
   e) never "accidentally" engage individuals who otherwise would not be involved in politics at all.

3. The *digital divide* refers to *(p. 304)*
   a) the line separating citizens who watch television news from those who do not.
   b) the fact that newspapers rarely publish the same stories on their websites that they do in their print editions.
   c) the fact that few politicians maintain websites once they are elected to office.
   d) the line separating citizens with Internet access from those without.
   e) the fact that people who learn about politics online are less informed than those who learn about it through traditional media.

 **Practice Online**
"Get Involved" exercise: *Become a Voter*

## Voter Participation

■ **Examine voter turnout in American elections (pp. 305–6)**

Voting is the most important and most common form of political participation in the United States. Although suffrage was once limited to white males over age 21, numerous federal statutes, court decisions, and constitutional amendments over the last 200 years have extended voting rights to minority groups, women, and young adults. The dramatic expansion of voting rights has not, however, increased voting participation in the United States. Only 60 percent of Americans vote in presidential elections, and turnout in congressional, state, and local elections is much lower.

### Key Terms

**suffrage** (p. 305)

**turnout** (p. 306)

### Practice Quiz

4. What is the most common form of political participation? *(p. 305)*
   a) lobbying
   b) contributing money to a campaign
   c) protesting
   d) voting
   e) creating a political website

5. Which of the following best describes the composition of the electorate during the colonial and early national periods of American history? *(p. 305)*
   a) landowning white males over age 21
   b) all white males
   c) all literate males
   d) "universal suffrage"
   e) no suffrage for any citizen

6. Women won the right to vote in _____ with the adoption of the _____ Amendment. *(p. 306)*
   a) 1791; Fifth
   b) 1868; Fourteenth
   c) 1920; Nineteenth
   d) 1971; Twenty-Sixth
   e) 1965; Twenty-First

7. Voter turnout in presidential election years has *(p. 306)*
   a) been consistently higher than in years when only congressional and local elections are held.
   b) been consistently lower than in years when only congressional and local elections are held.
   c) been the same as in years when only congressional and local elections are held.
   d) consistently increased since 1892.
   e) consistently decreased since 1892.

**Practice Online**
Interactive simulation: *Getting People to the Polls*

# Explaining Political Participation: The Individual in Context

■ **Explain the factors that influence whether individuals vote or not (pp. 306–20)**

Three general sets of factors help explain why some Americans vote and others do not: (1) a person's socioeconomic status and attitudes about politics, (2) features of the political environment in which elections take place, and (3) state-level electoral laws. Research has consistently shown, for example, that people with higher levels of education, more income, and higher-level occupations participate in elections much more frequently than those with less education, less income, and lower-level occupations. Similarly, people mobilized by political parties, candidates, campaigns, interest groups, and social movements are more likely to participate than those who are not. Electoral laws passed by state governments, such as registration requirements, can create formal barriers to voting that also influence who participates and who does not.

## Key Terms

**socioeconomic status** (p. 309)

**mobilization** (p. 311)

**Election-Day registration** (p. 318)

**permanent absentee ballots** (p. 319)

**early voting** (p. 319)

## Practice Quiz

8. Americans who vote are more likely to be _____ than the population as a whole. *(p. 309)*
   a) poorer
   b) employed in lower-level occupations
   c) less educated
   d) better educated
   e) residents of states with strict registration requirements

9. On average over the last 40 years, how many U.S. House races have been very competitive in each election? *(pp. 312–15)*
   a) 0
   b) 24
   c) 100
   d) 217
   e) 435

10. Which of the following factors is not currently an obstacle to voting in the United States? *(pp. 315–16)*
    a) registration requirements
    b) that elections occur on Tuesdays
    c) the restriction of voting rights for people who have committed a felony
    d) literacy tests
    e) that many states provide for absentee voting

11. After passage of the Motor Voter Act in 1993, participation in the 1996 elections *(p. 319)*
    a) increased dramatically.
    b) increased somewhat.
    c) declined somewhat.
    d) declined dramatically.
    e) was not affected, since few people registered to vote as a result of the act.

# Diversity and Participation

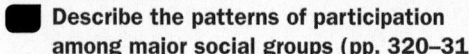 **Describe the patterns of participation among major social groups (pp. 320–31)**

Race, gender, age, and religious affiliation are associated with different levels and types of political participation. Generally speaking, whites, older people, and women vote most frequently. In recent elections, African Americans, Latinos, women and young people have been more likely to support Democratic candidates than whites, males, and older people.

## Key Term

**gender gap** (p. 324)

## Practice Quiz

12. In the decades immediately following the Civil War, African Americans voted *(p. 321)*
    a) overwhelmingly in support of the Democratic Party.
    b) overwhelmingly in support of the Republican Party.
    c) for mostly independent or third-party candidates.
    d) in nearly equal numbers for the Democratic and Republican parties.
    e) with slightly larger numbers supporting the Democratic Party.

13. Currently, African Americans *(pp. 320–22)*
    a) almost never participate in politics.
    b) consistently support the Republican Party in elections.
    c) vote at much lower rates than they did 15 years ago.
    d) vote differently from one another based on income.
    e) vote cohesively despite economic differences.

14. One reason that there are fewer women than men in elected office is that *(pp. 324–26)*
    a) there is a limit set by the Constitution on the number of women who can serve in the House of Representatives.
    b) fewer women are eligible to run for office under the rules created by state and local governments.
    c) women are less attentive to politics than men.
    d) women are less likely to run for office than men.
    e) women are less likely to win elections than men.

15. Which of the following statements most accurately characterizes the rates of political participation among different age groups? *(pp. 326–28)*
    a) Older people have much lower rates of participation than young people.
    b) Older people have much higher rates of participation than young people.
    c) Both older people and younger people participate in politics at extremely low rates.
    d) Both older people and younger people participate in politics at extremely high rates.
    e) There is no consistent pattern because sometimes younger people participate more than older people and sometimes older people participate more than younger people.

 **Practice Online**
Video exercise: *Rock the Vote*

# For Further Reading

Bimber, Bruce, and Richard Davis. *Campaigning Online: The Internet in U.S. Elections*. Oxford, UK: Oxford University Press, 2003.

Cain, Bruce E., Todd Donovan, and Caroline J. Tolbert, eds. *Democracy in the States: Experiments in Election Reform*. Washington, DC: Brookings Institution Press, 2008.

Crenson, Matthew A., and Benjamin Ginsberg. *Downsizing Democracy: How America Sidelined Its Citizens and Privatized Its Public*. Baltimore: Johns Hopkins University Press, 2004.

Dalton, Russell J. *The Good Citizen: How a Younger Generation Is Reshaping American Politics*. Washington, DC: CQ Press, 2008.

Donovan, Todd, and Shawn Bowler. *Reforming the Republic: Democratic Institutions for the New America*. Upper Saddle River, NJ: Pearson/Prentice Hall, 2004.

Green, Donald P., and Alan S. Gerber. *Get Out the Vote! How to Increase Voter Turnout*. Washington, DC: Brookings Institution Press, 2004.

Griffin, John D., and Brian Newman. *Minority Report: Evaluating Political Equality in America*. Chicago: University of Chicago Press, 2008.

Hahn, Hahrie. *Moved to Action: Motivation, Participation, and Inequality in American Politics*. Stanford, CA: Stanford University Press, 2009.

Hanmer, Michael J. *Discount Voting: Voter Registration Reforms and Their Effects*. New York: Cambridge University Press, 2009.

Lewis-Beck, Michael S., William G. Jacoby, Helmut Norpoth, and Herbert F. Weisberg. *The American Voter Revisited*. Ann Arbor: University of Michigan Press, 2008.

McDonald, Michael P., and John Samples, eds. *The Market-place of Democracy: Electoral Competition and American Politics*. Washington, DC: Brookings Institution Press, 2006.

Manza, Jeff, and Christopher Uggen. *Locked Out: Felon Disenfranchisement and American Democracy*. New York: Oxford University Press, 2006.

Mossberger, Karen, Caroline Tolbert, and Ramona McNeal. *Digital Citizenship: The Internet, Society and Participation*. Cambridge, MA: MIT Press, 2008.

Nicholson, Steven P. *Voting the Agenda: Candidates Elections and Ballot Propositions*. Princeton, NJ: Princeton University Press, 2005.

Patterson, Thomas E. *The Vanishing Voter: Public Involvement in an Age of Uncertainty*. New York: Vintage, 2003.

Piven, Frances Fox, and Richard Cloward. *Why Americans Don't Vote*. New York: Pantheon, 1988.

Putnam, Robert D. *Bowling Alone: The Collapse and Revival of American Community*. New York: Simon and Schuster, 2000.

Rosenstone, Steven J., and John Mark Hansen. *Mobilization, Participation and Democracy in America*. New York: Macmillan, 1993.

Smith, Daniel, and Caroline Tolbert. *Educated by Initiative: The Effects of Direct Democracy on Citizens and Political Organizations in the American States*. Ann Arbor: University of Michigan Press, 2004.

Verba, Sidney, Kay Lehman Schlozman, and Henry Brady. *Voice and Equality: Civic Voluntarism in American Politics*. Cambridge, MA: Harvard University Press, 1995.

# Recommended Websites

**CQ MoneyLine**
http://moneyline.cq.com/pml/home.do
Campaign contributions are a form of political participation that is both necessary and controversial. This website uses data from the Federal Election Commission (FEC) to publish the names of those who give elected officials campaign money and those who may be receiving preferential treatment.

**Declare Yourself**
http://declareyourself.com
Statistics on political participation show that older people are much more likely to vote than are young people. Declare Yourself is a national nonpartisan, nonprofit campaign dedicated to closing the intergenerational divide by energizing and empowering a new movement of young voters.

**League of Women Voters**
www.lwv.org
Established in 1920 as part of the women's suffrage movement, the League of Women Voters encourages informed and active participation in government.

**Project Vote**
www.projectvote.org
Since 1982, Project Vote has worked to increase the participation of low-income, minority, youth and other marginalized and under-represented voters. The organization sponsors voter registration drives, get-out-the-vote programs, and monitors election laws across the states. As a community organizer, Barack Obama worked for Project Vote, registering voters in Chicago.

**Project Vote Smart**
www.votesmart.org
This nonpartisan site is dedicated to providing citizens with information on political candidates and elected officials. Here you can easily view candidates' biographical information, positions on issues, and voting records, so that you can make an informed choice on Election Day.

**U.S. Census Bureau: Voting and Registration**
www.census.gov/population/www/socdemo/voting.html
The U.S. Census Bureau collects statistics on voting and registration by various demographic and socioeconomic characteristics. See if you can find differences in voter turnout by race, age, sex, or socioeconomic status.

At their 2012 national convention, Republicans formally nominated Mitt Romney as their presidential candidate. While many Americans express frustration over partisan conflict, political parties play an important role in organizing American politics and government.

# Political Parties

**WHAT GOVERNMENT DOES AND WHY IT MATTERS** In the United States, political parties force the government to concern itself with the needs of its citizens. Strong parties and energetic party competition make it more likely that the political system will support basic American values.

Liberty requires coherent and well-organized opposition to those in power. Political parties organize the collective interests of those who, as individuals, might lack the resources and knowledge to compete with elites and interest groups. Democracy is promoted when parties mobilize large numbers of individuals to participate in the political arena, and to vote.

Political parties are a core feature of the American political system. They provide guideposts for citizens and politicians alike by helping to organize the political world and simplify complex policy debates. Individual partisanship is the most important factor in predicting whom Americans vote for. In Congress, parties are key in setting the terms of policy conflict; they exercise significant influence over the votes of individual members of Congress on many important issues. Parties also play central roles in mobilizing citizens to vote and ensuring that the public voice is heard in policy making.

The importance of parties in organizing congressional debate and mobilizing citizens was evident in the 2009 debate over national health care, one of President Obama's central achievements in office. Democratic Party leaders in the House of Representatives and in the Senate worked to build support among their members for a health care reform bill. Although the bill passed the House with 84 percent support from Democrats and won all 60 Democratic votes in the Senate, crafting a compromise between the two houses of Congress presented a major challenge, and led to significant changes that diluted the final legislation. Democratic leaders had to work hard to win the support of enough Democrats in the House and Senate to send a final bill to President Obama. The role of parties was also evident in the nearly unanimous opposition of the Republican Party to the health care legislation. Republican opposition stemmed from both policy and political concerns. Most Republicans prefer policy approaches that require less government regulation of the market and less public spending. As the opposition party, however, Republicans were also aware that a major policy win would likely strengthen Democrats. Republican Party leaders mobilized staunch opposition to the Democratic health care reform proposals in both the House and the Senate. In the end, only one Republican in the House voted for the health care reform bill. Unified Republican opposition led Senate Democratic leaders to use the reconciliation process, a procedure that requires only a majority vote to pass legislation, in order to enact their health care reform.

Today, the political parties in Congress are more polarized than at any time in recent history, with over 90 percent of the votes in Congress passed with unanimous party-line voting.[1] Partisanship was also important in the 2012 elections, with most Democrats voting for the Democratic candidates and most Republicans voting for the Republican candidates, but many Americans expressed concern that "partisan politics" was distracting the candidates and the government from the real issues facing the nation. Are the major political parties fulfilling their role in American democracy?

## chaptergoals

- **Define political parties and their general role in politics** (pages 341–42)

- **Describe how the party system in the United States has changed over time and its main features today** (pages 342–55)

- **Describe how the major American parties are structured at the national, state, and local levels** (pages 355–60)

- **Identify the social groups that tend to support the Republicans and the Democrats** (pages 360–66)

- **Explain the roles parties play in elections** (pages 366–67)

- **Explain how parties organize legislative business and influence policy** (pages 367–70)

# What Are Political Parties?

**Define political parties and their general role in politics**

Political parties, like interest groups, are organizations that seek influence over government. Ordinarily, they can be distinguished from interest groups on the basis of their orientation. A party seeks to control the government by electing its members to office, thereby controlling the government. As we will see in Chapter 11, interest groups don't control the operation of government and its personnel, but rather try to influence government policies.

In the United States today, the relationship between parties and government is more complex than this basic definition suggests. Political parties have been the chief points of contact between government, on the one side, and individual citizens and interest groups, on the other. Through organized political parties, citizens and groups can gain some control over governmental policies. Simultaneously, the government often seeks to organize and influence important groups in society through political parties. All political parties have this dual character: they are instruments through which citizens and government attempt to influence each other.

**political parties** organized groups that attempt to influence the government by electing their members to important government offices

*The Democratic Party of the United States is the world's oldest political party. It can trace its history back to Thomas Jefferson's Jeffersonian Republicans and, later, to Andrew Jackson's Jacksonian Democrats. The Jacksonians expanded voter participation and ushered in the political era of the common person, as shown in this image of Jackson's inauguration celebration.*

As long as political parties have existed, they have been criticized for introducing selfish, "partisan" concerns into public debates and national policy. Yet political parties are extremely important to the proper functioning of a democracy. As we will see, parties increase participation in politics, provide a central cue for citizens to cast informed votes, and organize the business of Congress and governing. Some argue that the problem in America today is that political elites in Congress and the parties are too polarized (liberal versus conservative), whereas the majority of Americans hold moderate opinions and values, and thus Congress and the parties do a poor job representing the citizens.[2] Others argue that the problem is not that politics is too partisan but that our parties are not strong enough to function effectively—one reason that America has such low levels of political involvement and voter turnout.[3] Still others argue that the rules governing our election system need to be updated—what is called "election reform"—so that there are more than two major political parties and so representation of the citizens can be improved.[4]

## The Two-Party System in America

**Describe how the party system in the United States has changed over time and its main features today**

Over the past 200 years, Americans' conception of political parties has changed considerably. In the early years of the Republic, parties were seen as threats to the social order, and were referred to as factions. In *The Federalist Papers*, both Alexander Hamilton and James Madison condemned "factions" that pursued narrow self-interest over the broader well-being of the nation as a whole.[5] In his 1796 Farewell Address, President George Washington warned his countrymen to shun partisan politics. Nonetheless, a **two-party system** emerged early in the history of the new Republic. Beginning with the Federalists and the Jeffersonian Republicans in the late 1780s, two major parties have dominated national politics, although *which* particular two parties has changed with the times and issues. This two-party system today includes Democrats and Republicans (see Figure 9.1).

**two-party system** a political system in which only two parties have a realistic opportunity to compete effectively for control

Unlike many other countries in the world that use a proportional representation system, in which seats are allocated to political parties based on their share (percentage) of the total vote cast in the election, the United States uses geographic single-member districts combined with a winner-take-all system. It doesn't matter, for example, if the contest for a U.S. House seat is won by 1 percent or 20 percent of the total votes, the candidate (and his/her party) with the largest number of votes (plurality) in that district wins the seat in Congress. Unlike in proportional systems, runners-up do not gain representation in first-past-the-post system. In the United States, proportional representation systems are uncommon, especially above the local level, and are absent at the national level. Voters thus have an incentive not to vote for small or third parties for fear of wasting their vote, as only one party (usually one of the two largest parties) can win the election. This winner-take-all system has helped create our two-party-dominant system, and third parties have historically not won seats in Congress, or won the presidency. Third parties are discussed in more detail later in this chapter.

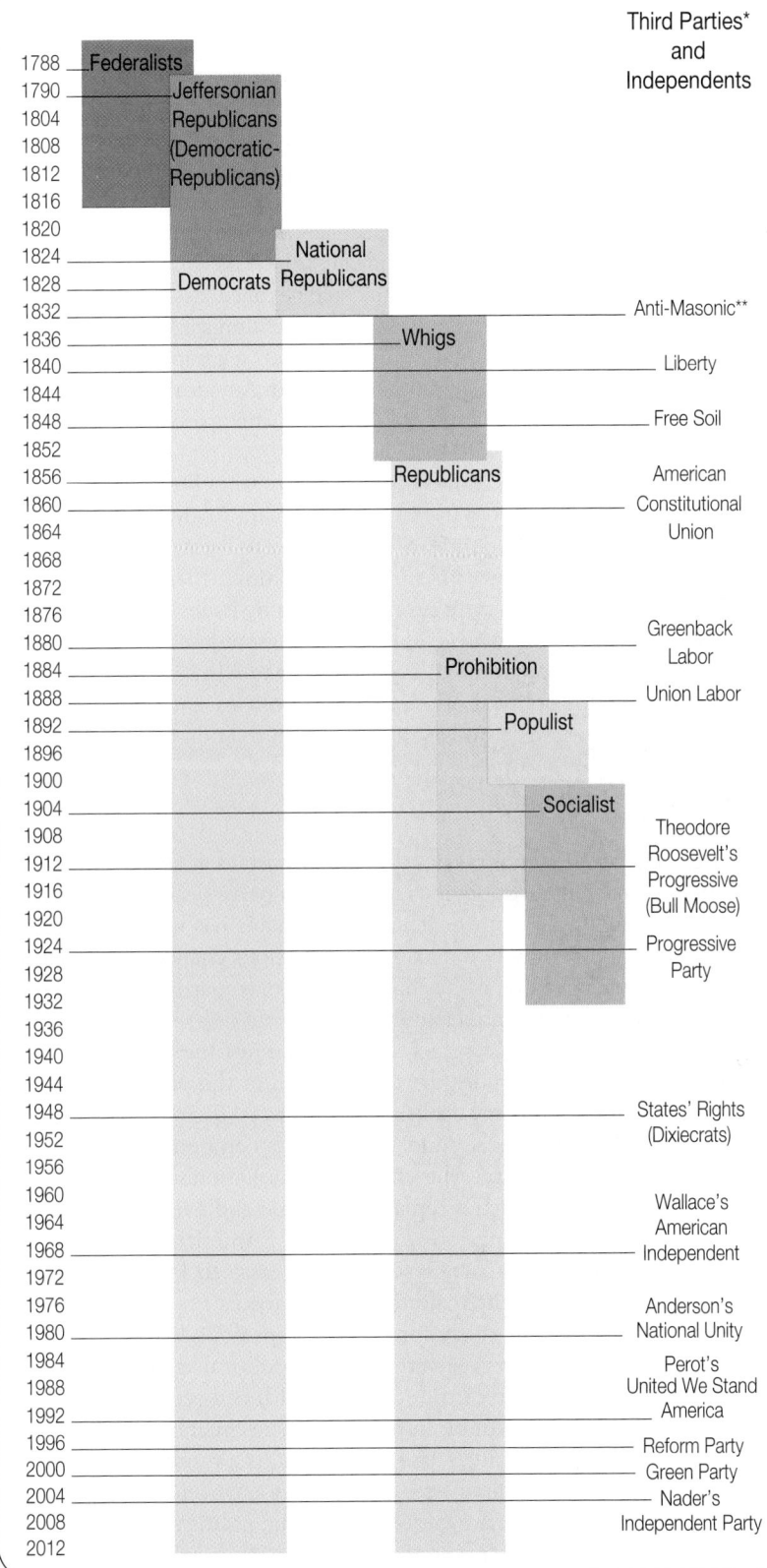

**FIGURE 9.1**

## How the Party System Evolved

During the nineteenth century, the Democrats and the Republicans emerged as the two dominant parties in American politics. As the American party system evolved, many third parties emerged, but few of them remained in existence for very long.

*Or in some cases, fourth parties; most of these parties lasted through only one term.

**The Anti-Masonics had the distinction of being not only the first third party but also the first party to hold a national nominating convention and the first to announce a party platform.

## How Do Political Parties Form?

Historically, parties form in one of two ways. The first, which could be called "internal mobilization," occurs when political conflicts prompt officials and competing factions within government to mobilize popular support. This is precisely what happened during the early years of the American Republic. Competition in the Congress between northeastern merchants and southern agricultural factions led first the southerners and then the northeasterners to attempt to organize their supporters. The result was the foundation of America's first national parties: the Jeffersonians, whose primary base was in the South, and the Federalists, whose strength was greatest in the New England states.

The second way that parties may form, which could be called "external mobilization," takes place when a group of politicians outside government organizes popular support to win governmental power. For example, during the 1850s, a group of state politicians who opposed slavery, especially the expansion of slavery in America's territorial possessions, built what became the Republican Party by constructing party organizations and mobilizing popular support in the Northeast and West.

America's two major parties now, of course, are the Democrats and the Republicans. Both trace their roots back over 150 years to the nineteenth century, and both have evolved over time. Since they were formed, the two major parties have undergone significant shifts in their positions, their goals, and their membership. These changes have been prompted both by issues and events and by demographic and social developments and population growth in the United States. Parties also change as they compete with one another to win support among voters and interest groups for political office, different policies, and enduring power. Because of this, it is important to understand parties in relation to one another.

## Party Systems

Historians often refer to the set of parties that are important at any given time as a nation's "party system." The most obvious feature of a party system is the number of major parties competing for power. The United States has usually had a two-party system, meaning that only two parties have a serious chance to win national elections. Of course, we have not always had the same two parties, and as we shall see, minor parties often put forward candidates.

The term *party system*, however, refers to more than just the number of parties competing for power. It also includes the organization of the parties, the balance of power between and within party coalitions, the parties' social and institutional bases, and the issues and policies around which party competition is organized. Seen from this broader perspective, the character of a nation's party system can change even if the number of parties remains the same and even when the same two parties seem to be competing for power. Today's American party system is very different from the country's party system of 50 years ago, but the Democrats and Republicans continue to be the major competing forces.

The character of a nation's party system can have profound consequences for the types of issues and policies that reach the nation's political agenda, and for critically important issues such as the distribution of wealth and economic inequality. For example, the contemporary American political parties mainly compete for the support of different groups of middle-class Americans. As a result, issues that concern the middle and upper-middle classes, such as the environment, health care, retirement benefits, and taxation, are very much on the political agenda, whereas issues that concern working-class and poorer Americans, such as welfare and housing, receive short shrift from both parties.[6] Some argue that the government and the political parties have become more responsive to the wealthy over the past few decades, rather than to the middle or working class.[7] Political scientist Larry Bartels shows in an important study that neither the Democrats nor the Republicans in Congress are responsive to the poor, Americans in the bottom one-third of the income distribution. Both political parties respond some of the time to the middle class (those in the middle third of the income distribution), and the Republican Party is the most responsive to the wealthy, those in the top third of incomes.[8] Bartels shows that over the past half century, income of the poor and working class grew more under Democratic Party presidents than Republican administrations.

Over the course of American history, changes in political forces and alignments have produced six distinctive party systems.

**The First Party System: Federalists and Jeffersonian Republicans** The first party system emerged in the 1790s and pitted the Federalists against the Jeffersonian Republicans. The Federalists spoke mainly for New England merchants and supported a program of protective tariffs to encourage manufacturing, assumption of the states' Revolutionary War debts, the creation of a national bank, and resumption of commercial ties with Britain. The Jeffersonians, led by southern agricultural interests, opposed these policies and instead favored free trade, the promotion of agricultural over commercial interests, and friendship with France. The Federalists sought, unsuccessfully, to use the force of law against the Jeffersonians by enacting the Alien and Sedition Acts to outlaw criticism of the government. These acts, however, proved virtually impossible to enforce, and the Jeffersonians gradually expanded their base from the South into the Middle Atlantic states. In the election of 1800, Jefferson defeated the incumbent Federalist president, John Adams, and led his party to power. Over the following years, the Federalists gradually weakened. The party disappeared altogether after the pro-British sympathies of some Federalist leaders during the War of 1812 led to charges of treason against the party.

From the collapse of the Federalists until the 1830s, America had only one political party, the Jeffersonian Republicans, who gradually came to be known as the Democrats. This period of one-party politics is sometimes known as the Era of Good Feelings, to indicate the absence of party competition. Throughout this period, however, there was intense factional conflict within the Democratic Party, particularly between the supporters and opponents of General Andrew Jackson, America's great military hero of the War of 1812. Jackson's opponents united to deny him the presidency in 1824, but Jackson won elections in 1828 and 1832. Jackson's support was in the South and West, and he generally espoused a program of free trade and policies that appealed to those regions.

**The Second Party System: Democrats and Whigs** During the 1830s, groups opposing Jackson united to form a new political force, the Whig Party—thus giving rise to the second American party system. Both the Democrats and the Whigs built party organizations throughout the nation, and both sought to enlarge their bases of support by expanding the right to vote. They increased the number of eligible voters through the elimination of property restrictions and other barriers to voting—at least voting by white males. Support for the new Whig Party

In the 1930s the Whig Party emerged as the Democrats' main rival. This drawing depicts a Whig rally and parade during the 1840 election, which became known as the "hard cider" campaign.

was stronger in the Northeast than in the South and West and stronger among merchants than among small farmers. Hence, in some measure, the Whigs were the successors of the Federalists. Yet conflict between the two parties revolved more around personalities than policies. The Whigs were a diverse group united more by opposition to the Democrats than by agreement on programs. In 1840 the Whigs won their first presidential election under the leadership of General William Henry Harrison, a military hero known as "Old Tippecanoe." The Whig campaign carefully avoided issues—since the party could agree on almost none—and emphasized the personal qualities and heroism of the candidate. The Whigs also invested heavily in campaign rallies and entertainment to win the hearts, if not exactly the minds, of the voters. The 1840 campaign came to be called the "hard cider" campaign because of the practice of using food and especially drink to win votes.

During the late 1840s and early 1850s, conflicts over slavery produced sharp divisions within both the Whig and the Democratic parties, despite the efforts of party leaders to develop compromises. By 1856 the Whig Party had all but disintegrated under the strain, and many Whig politicians and voters, along with antislavery Democrats, joined the new Republican Party, which pledged to ban slavery from the western territories. In 1860 the Republicans nominated Abraham Lincoln for the presidency. Lincoln's victory strengthened southern calls for secession from the Union and, soon thereafter, for all-out civil war.

**The Civil War and Post–Civil War Party System: Republicans and Democrats** During the course of the war, President Lincoln depended heavily on Republican governors and state legislatures to raise troops, provide funding, and maintain popular support for a long and bloody military conflict. The secession of the South had stripped the Democratic Party of many of its leaders and supporters, but the Democrats remained politically competitive throughout the war and nearly won the 1864 presidential election because of war weariness on the part of the northern public. With the defeat of the Confederacy in 1865, some congressional Republicans sought to convert the South into a Republican bastion through a program of Reconstruction that enfranchised newly freed slaves. This Reconstruction program collapsed in the 1870s as a result of disagreement within the Republican Party in Congress and violent resistance by southern whites. With the end of Reconstruction, the former Confederate states regained full membership in the Union and full control of their internal affairs. Throughout the South, African Americans were deprived of political rights, including the right to vote, despite post–Civil War constitutional guarantees to the contrary. The post–Civil War South was solidly Democratic in its political affiliation, and with a firm southern base, the national Democratic Party was able to confront the Republicans on a more or less equal basis. From the end of the Civil War to the 1890s, the Republican Party remained the party of the North, with strong business and middle-class support, while the Democrats were the party of the South, with support also from working-class and immigrant groups.

**The System of 1896: Republicans and Democrats** During the 1890s, profound and rapid social and economic changes led to the emergence of a variety of protest parties, including the Populist Party, which won the support of hundreds of thousands of voters in the South and West. The Populists appealed mainly to small farmers but also attracted western mining interests and urban workers. In the 1892 presidential election, the Populist Party carried four states and elected governors in eight. In 1896 the Populist Party effectively merged with the Democrats, who nominated William Jennings Bryan, a Democratic senator with pronounced

Populist sympathies, for the presidency. The Republicans nominated the conservative senator William McKinley. In the ensuing campaign, northern and midwestern businesses made an all-out effort to defeat what they saw as a radical threat from the Populist-Democratic alliance. When the dust settled, the Republicans had won a resounding victory. The GOP ("Grand Old Party"), or Republican Party, had carried the more heavily populated northern and midwestern states and confined the Democrats to their smaller bases of support in the South and far West. For the next 36 years, the Republicans were the nation's majority party, carrying 7 of 9 presidential elections and controlling both houses of Congress in 15 of 18 contests. The Republican Party of this era was very much the party of American business, advocating low taxes, high tariffs on imports, and a minimum of government regulation. The Democrats were far too weak to offer much opposition. Southern Democrats, moreover, were too concerned with maintaining the region's autonomy on issues of race to challenge the Republicans on other fronts.

**The New Deal Party System: Reversal of Fortune** Soon after the Republican presidential candidate Herbert Hoover won the 1928 presidential election, the nation's economy collapsed. The Great Depression, which produced unprecedented economic hardship, stemmed from a variety of causes, but from the perspective of millions of Americans, the Republican Party did not do enough to promote economic recovery. In 1932, Americans elected Franklin Delano Roosevelt and a solidly Democratic Congress. Roosevelt developed a program for economic recovery that he dubbed the "New Deal." Under the auspices of the New Deal, the size and reach of America's national government increased substantially. The federal government took responsibility for economic management and social welfare to an extent that was unprecedented in American history. Roosevelt designed many of his programs specifically to expand the political base of the Democratic Party. He rebuilt and revitalized the party around a nucleus of unionized workers, upper-middle-class intellectuals and professionals, southern farmers, Jews, Catholics, and African Americans—the so-called New Deal coalition that made the Democrats the nation's majority party for the next 36 years. Groping for a response to the New Deal, Republicans often wound up supporting popular New Deal programs such as Social Security in what was sometimes derided as "me too" Republicanism. Even the relatively conservative administration of Dwight D. Eisenhower in the 1950s left the principal New Deal programs intact.

The New Deal coalition was severely strained during the 1960s by conflicts over civil rights and the Vietnam War. The struggle over civil rights initially divided northern Democrats who supported the civil rights cause from white southern Democrats who defended the system of racial segregation. Subsequently, as the civil rights movement launched a northern campaign aimed at securing access to jobs and education and an end to racial discrimination in

*Following the Civil War, the Republican Party remained dominant in the North. This poster supporting Republican Benjamin Harrison in the 1888 election promises protective tariffs, and other policies that appealed to the industrial states in the North.*

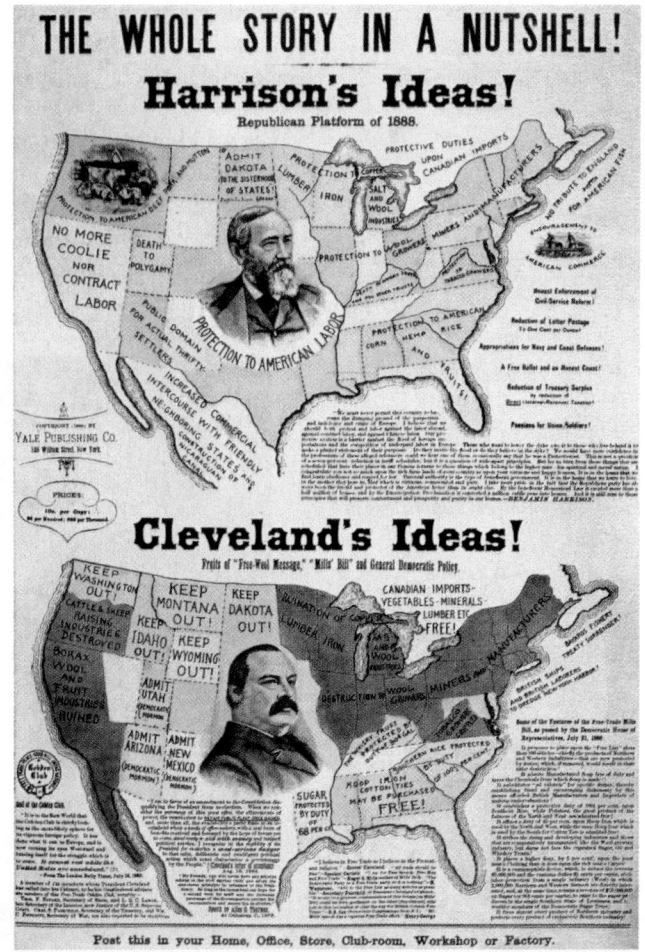

such realms as housing, northern Democrats also split, often along income lines. The struggle over the Vietnam War further divided the Democrats, with upper-income liberal Democrats strongly opposing the Johnson administration's decision to greatly expand the numbers of U.S. troops fighting in Southeast Asia. These schisms within the Democratic Party provided an opportunity for the GOP, which returned to power in 1968 under the leadership of Richard Nixon.

**The Contemporary American Party System** The Republican Party widened its appeal in the second half of the twentieth century. In 1964, for example, the Republican presidential candidate Barry Goldwater argued in favor of substantially reduced levels of taxation and spending, less government regulation of the economy, and the elimination of many federal social programs. Though Goldwater was defeated by Lyndon Johnson, the ideas he espoused continued to be major themes for the Republican Party. It took Richard Nixon's "southern strategy" to give the GOP the votes it needed to end Democratic dominance of national politics. Nixon appealed to disaffected white southerners, and with the help of the independent candidate and former Alabama governor George Wallace, he sparked the shift of voters that gave the party a strong position in all the states of the former Confederacy. The movement of white southerners to the Republican Party was in part because of opposition to desegregation of the South and to the civil rights movement supported by Democratic leaders, including President Kennedy. During the 1980s, under the leadership of President Ronald Reagan, Republicans added two additional important groups to their coalition. The first were religious conservatives who were offended by Democratic support for abortion and gay rights and by alleged Democratic disdain for traditional cultural and religious values. The second were working-class whites who were drawn to Reagan's tough approach to foreign policy and his positions against affirmative action.

While Republicans built a political base around economic and social conservatives and white southerners, the Democratic Party maintained its support among a majority of unionized workers and upper-middle-class intellectuals and professionals. Democrats also appealed strongly to racial minorities. The 1965 Voting

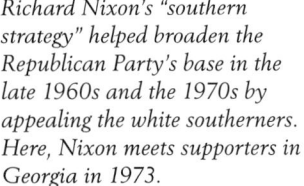

*Richard Nixon's "southern strategy" helped broaden the Republican Party's base in the late 1960s and the 1970s by appealing the white southerners. Here, Nixon meets supporters in Georgia in 1973.*

Rights Act had greatly increased black voter participation in the South and helped the Democratic Party retain some House and Senate seats in southern states. And whereas the Republicans appealed to social conservatives, the Democrats appealed strongly to Americans concerned with abortion rights, gay rights, feminism, environmentalism, and other progressive social causes.

Despite the success of Republican presidential candidates in attracting votes from groups previously associated with the Democratic Party, Republicans generally did not do as well at the state and local levels until the 1990s, when conservative religious groups made a concerted effort to expand their influence within the Republican Party. This effort led to conflict between these members of the "religious right" and more traditional "country club" Republicans, whose major concerns were economic matters such as taxes and federal regulation of business. The two factions of the party came together when the Republicans won both houses of Congress in 1994 (the first time in almost half a century). The Republicans retained control of Congress in 1996, despite President Clinton's re-election in that year. In 2000, George W. Bush united the party's centrist and right wings behind a program of tax cuts, education reform, military strength, and family values.

However, by 2006, the public's disapproval of the Bush administration and the war in Iraq led to major losses for Republicans in both houses of Congress. Campaigning during the worst financial crisis since the 1930s and burdened with a president whose approval ratings had sunk to historic lows, Republicans again fared poorly in the 2008 elections. With the party in disarray, contending factions sought to redefine a strategy that would allow Republicans to regain the influence they had enjoyed in the early days of George W. Bush's presidency.

In 2008, Democrats reached beyond their base by appealing to moderate voters in states that had once been Republican strongholds, and they won control of Congress as well as the presidency for the first time since 1995. However, the continuation of sharp partisan differences in Congress signaled that intense party conflict would continue to characterize American politics. Republicans won control of the House of Representatives in 2010, and although Obama was re-elected to the presidency in 2012, control of Congress remained divided.

## Electoral Alignments and Realignments

The points of transition between party systems in American history are sometimes called **electoral realignments**. During these periods, the coalitions that support the parties and the balance of power between the parties are redefined. In historical terms, realignments occur when new issues, combined with economic or political crises, mobilize new voters and persuade large numbers of them to reexamine their traditional partisan loyalties and permanently shift their support from one party to another. Figure 9.2 charts the sequence of party systems and realignments in American history.

Although scholars dispute the timing of realignments, there is some agreement that five have occurred since the Founding. The first took place around 1800, when the Jeffersonian Republicans defeated the Federalists and became the dominant force in American politics. The second realignment took place in about 1828, when the Jacksonian Democrats seized control of the White House and the Congress. In the third period of realignment, centered on 1860, the newly founded Republican Party, led by Abraham Lincoln, won power, in the process destroying the Whig Party, which had been one of the nation's two major parties since the 1830s. Many northern voters who had supported the Whigs or the Democrats on the basis of their economic stands shifted their support to the Republicans as slavery replaced

**electoral realignment** the point in history when a new party supplants the ruling party, becoming in turn the dominant political force; in the United States, this has tended to occur roughly every 30 years

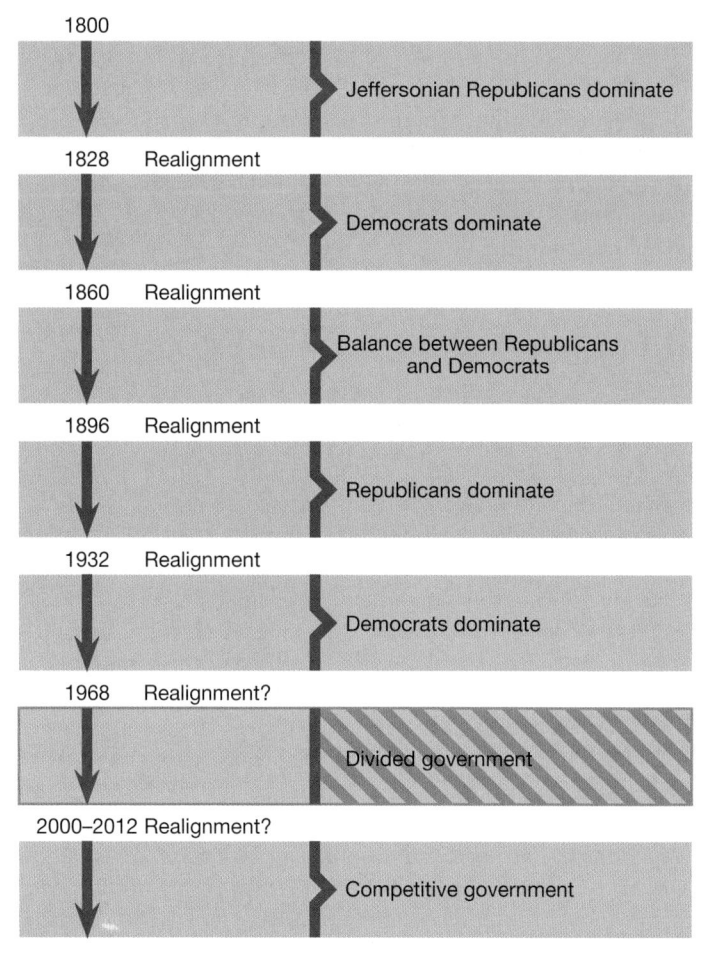

**FIGURE 9.2**

## Electoral Realignments

Political scientists disagree over whether an electoral realignment occurred in 1968, because no one party clearly dominated the national government after that election. Although Republicans dominated the federal government between 2000 and 2006, their control fell short of a full-fledged realignment: Republicans never gained a majority of party identifiers, they failed to enact many of their key policy goals, and elections remained extremely close.

1800 — Jeffersonian Republicans dominate

1828 Realignment — Democrats dominate

1860 Realignment — Balance between Republicans and Democrats

1896 Realignment — Republicans dominate

1932 Realignment — Democrats dominate

1968 Realignment? — Divided government

2000–2012 Realignment? — Competitive government

tariffs and economic concerns as the central item on the nation's political agenda. Many southern Whigs shifted their support to the Democrats. The new sectional alignment of forces that emerged was solidified by the trauma of the Civil War and persisted almost to the turn of the century.

In the 1890s, this alignment was at least partially supplanted by an alignment of political forces based on economic and cultural factors, bringing about the fourth electoral realignment. In the election of 1896, the Republican candidate, William McKinley, emphasizing business, industry, and urban interests, defeated the Democrat, William Jennings Bryan, who spoke for sectional interests, farmers, and fundamentalism.

Republican dominance lasted until the fifth realignment, during the period 1932–36, when the Democrats, led by Franklin Delano Roosevelt, took control of the White House and Congress and, despite sporadic interruptions, maintained control of both through the 1960s. Since that time, American party politics has been characterized primarily by **divided government**, wherein the presidency is controlled by one party while the other party controls one or both houses of Congress.

Such periods of electoral realignment in American politics have had extremely important policy consequences. Realignments occur when new issue concerns, coupled with economic or political crises, weaken the established political elite

**divided government** the condition in American government wherein the presidency is controlled by one party while the opposing party controls one or both houses of Congress

and permit new groups of politicians to create coalitions of forces capable of capturing and holding the reins of governmental power. The construction of new governing coalitions during these realigning periods has effected major changes in American governmental institutions and policies. Each period of realignment was a turning point in American politics. The choices made by the national electorate during these periods helped shape the course of American political history for the following generation.[9]

## Party Polarization

A distinguishing feature of the contemporary party system is **party polarization**. Polarization in Congress is measured by party unity in roll call votes. In 2010, for example, Republicans in both the House and Senate voted with their fellow Republican colleagues on 91 percent of roll call votes.[10] Similarly, Democrats in Congress voted in unity with their party over 90 percent of the time. Both parties are more unified than at any time since 1956. And frequently, the Democrats and Republicans in Congress vote in exactly the opposite ways. Legislation is often enacted by the slimmest of vote margins in Congress. While the majority of Americans hold moderate views, representatives in Congress tend to be strong conservatives among Republicans and strong liberals among Democrats; many of these members are elected from "safe" districts, where a majority of voters identify with their party, which means they have little chance of losing in the next election. Both Republicans and Democrats in Congress are usually re-elected in landslide elections. (The average winning margin of victory in the House is over 40 percentage points. That means incumbents, on average, win 70 percent of the popular vote compared with challengers' 30 percent.)[11] Of the 435 House races, only a dozen are highly contested, measured by a vote margin of 5 percent or less. Uncompetitive elections in Congress and safe seats are associated with growing party polarization.

This polarization among the parties in Congress does not match the ideology of the American public. Imagine if we could line up all 311 million Americans on a continuum from the most liberal on the left to the most conservative on the right. There would be far fewer very strong liberals and very strong conservatives than moderates. The majority of Americans would fall somewhere in between, somewhat left of center or just right of center. Opinion polls show that the distribution of ideology in the United States represents a single hump (like a one-humped camel), with the majority of Americans holding a moderate ideology. Now imagine lining up the members of Congress on the same continuum from most liberal to most conservative. Few lawmakers would fall in the middle, with the majority either to the far left (strong Democrat) or the far right (strong Republican)—essentially a two-humped camel. This suggests that party polarization in Congress has created a Congress that does not match the aggregate ideology of the American public. Approval of Congress in 2012 stood at just under 10 percent of the American public, the lowest level on record.[12] This extreme polarization has led not only to low approval of government, but also an inability of Congress to compromise and adopt policies that would benefit the majority of Americans.

Should we believe the media pundits who tell us that Americans are deeply divided between the red states and the blue states? Is the American population really polarized on hot-button moral, religious, and cultural issues? Political scientist Morris Fiorina and his colleagues debunk the commonly held myth that Americans are deeply divided in their fundamental political views, showing that on a broad range of topics from homosexuality to abortion, most Americans hold moderate opinions.[13] While political elites and members of Congress may be

**party polarization** the division between the two major parties on most policy issues, with members of each party unified around their party's positions with little crossover

**for critical analysis**

What are the principal issues dividing the two major parties today? What are the chief areas of agreement between the two parties? Doe the parties agree or disagree on questions of liberty and democracy?

highly polarized, with sharp divisions between Republicans and Democrats, most Americans are moderates in terms of public opinion. Both the Democratic and Republican parties are essentially centrist parties.

## Third Parties

Although the United States has a two-party-dominant system, the country has always had more than two parties. Typically, **third parties** in the United States have represented social and economic interests that for one or another reason were not given voice by the two major parties.[14] Such parties have had a good deal of influence on ideas and elections in the United States. The Populists, a party centered in the rural areas of the West and Midwest, and the Progressives, spokesmen for the urban middle classes in the late nineteenth and early twentieth centuries, are the most important examples in the past 100 years. More recently, Ross Perot, who ran in 1992 as an independent and in 1996 as the Reform Party's nominee, won the votes of almost one in five Americans.

Because third parties almost always lose at the national level, such parties exist as a protest movement against the two parties or to promote specific issues. Third parties profoundly affect American elections, as they steal votes from the two major parties, often swinging the election in favor of the Democrats or the Republicans. In the extremely close 2000 presidential election, for example, third-party candidate Ralph Nader won just 3 percent of the popular vote, but that was enough to swing the election to Republican George W. Bush. While the majority of Americans favored the Democratic Party in 2000, having a third party in the race split the Democratic vote, so the party lost the White House. Most Nader voters would have preferred Al Gore over George Bush, but by voting for Nader they inadvertently enabled Bush to win. The same thing happened in 1992 and 1996, but this time it was the conservative vote that was split between two parties. At times third parties have become a major force in presidential politics. H. Ross Perot's Reform Party won roughly 18.9 percent of the popular vote in 1992 (the highest third-party vote share since Roosevelt), which allowed Democrat Bill Clinton to win the presidency with just 43.0 percent of the popular vote (to Republican George H. W. Bush's 37.4 percent). In 1996, Perot won just over 8.0 percent of the popular vote, and Democrat Bill Clinton again won the White House, with less than 50 percent of the popular vote (49.2 to Republican Bob Dole's 40.7). Because of these dramatic losses, leaders in both major political parties fear third-party challenges in presidential elections. In 1912, Theodore Roosevelt made a run for the presidency on the Progressive Party, and Abraham Lincoln, our most revered president, won the presidency in a four-way race with less than 40 percent of the popular vote.

*In 2000, Ralph Nader ran as the candidate of the Green Party and won 3 percent of the vote, mainly at the expense of the Democratic candidate, Al Gore. Many observers believed that Gore would have won the 2000 election had Nader dropped out. In 2004 and 2008, Nader ran again as an independent candidate, receiving less than 1 percent of the vote.*

Table 9.1 lists the top candidates in the presidential election of 2012, including the top third-party and independent candidates who ran. In addition to the candidates listed in Table 9.1, the Socialist Party, the Prohibition Party, and several other parties nominated candidates for the presidency in 2012.

**Third Parties at the State and Local Levels** Third parties are active not only in presidential races. Third-party and independent candidacies also arise at the state and local levels. In New York, the Liberal and Conservative parties have been on the ballot for decades. In 1998, Minnesota elected a third-party governor, the former professional wrestler Jesse Ventura. During the 2002 midterm elections, third-party candidates ran for state office and for congressional seats in

## TABLE 9.1

### Parties and Candidates in 2012

| CANDIDATE | PARTY | VOTE TOTAL* | PERCENTAGE OF VOTE* |
|-----------|-------|-------------|---------------------|
| Barack Obama | Democratic | 62,088,847 | 50.5% |
| Mitt Romney | Republican | 58,783,137 | 48 |
| Gary Johnson | Libertarian | 1,198,942 | 1 |
| Jill Stein | Green | 424,676 | 0.4 |
| Virgil Goode | Constitution | 117,877 | 0.1 |

*With 99 percent of votes tallied.

SOURCE: http://elections.huffingtonpost.com/2012/results# (accessed 11/12/12).

many states. Libertarian Party gubernatorial candidates received at least 2 percent of the vote in 15 states, including a whopping 11 percent of the vote in Wisconsin. The Green Party was also active throughout the nation. The Green Party candidate for governor in Massachusetts, Jill Stein, may have affected the race between Republican Mitt Romney and his Democratic rival by drawing votes away from the Democrats in a close race. In races with razor-thin margins between the Republican and Democratic candidates, any fraction of the vote going to a third-party candidate can make a difference. In Florida in 2012, Barack Obama was .05 percent ahead of Mitt Romney, but Libertarian Party candidate Gary Johnson won .05 percent of the popular vote, likely from voters who otherwise would have supported Romney. In 2012, third party or independent candidates won Senate races in Maine and Vermont.

**Obstacles Facing Third Parties** Americans usually assume that only candidates nominated by one of the two major parties have any chance of winning an election. Thus, a vote cast for a third-party or independent candidate is often seen as a vote wasted. Voters who would prefer a third-party candidate may feel compelled to vote for the major-party candidate whom they regard as the "lesser of two evils," to avoid wasting their votes in a futile gesture.

Under federal election law, any minor party receiving more than 5 percent of the national presidential vote is entitled to federal funds. The Reform Party qualified by winning 8.2 percent in 1996. Ralph Nader, the Green Party candidate in 2000, hoped to win the 5.0 percent of the vote that would entitle the Green Party to federal funds, but failed to achieve that threshold.

As discussed earlier, third-party prospects are also hampered by America's single-member district system for allocating seats. In many other nations, several individuals can be elected to represent each legislative district—a system of multiple-member districts, which are more favorable to minor-party candidates. Add to that the plurality, or winner-take-all, system of voting discussed earlier in this chapter, where candidates need to win more votes (usually over 50 percent) than in countries using the proportional representation system. (In a proportional system, parties can earn seats in government with 15–20 percent of the popular vote.) This higher American threshold discourages minor parties.[15]

*Green Party candidate Jill Stein ran for president in 2012 and received less than 1 percent of the vote. Although minor party candidates do not have much chance of winning the presidency, their campaigns can affect the issues that the major parties put on their agendas.*

## The Influence of Third Parties

Although the Republican Party was the only American third party to make itself permanent (by replacing the Whigs), other third parties have enjoyed an influence far beyond their electoral size. This is because large parts of their programs were adopted by one or both of the major parties, which sought to appeal to the voters mobilized by the new party, and so expand their own electoral strength. The Democratic Party, for example, became a great deal more liberal when it adopted most of the Progressive program early in the twentieth century. Many socialists felt that President Roosevelt's New Deal had adopted most of their party's program, including old-age pensions, unemployment compensation, an agricultural marketing program, and laws guaranteeing workers the right to organize into unions. This kind of influence explains the short lives of third parties. Their causes are usually eliminated when the major parties absorb their programs and draw their supporters into the mainstream.

Although it is not technically a political party, the Tea Party movement had a considerable impact on the Republican Party primaries in 2010, when Tea Party candidates defeated several incumbents and candidates endorsed by Republican Party leaders. Some high-profile Tea Party candidates, including Rand Paul (R-Ky.), then went on to win office in the 2010 midterm elections, but on the whole, the Tea Party succeeded in electing only about 32 percent of their candidates. Although it took the name Tea Party and sponsored a national convention, the Tea Party movement is not a formal party. It is an organized challenge to incumbents by the most conservative wing of the Republican Party.[16]

**Election Reform and Third Parties** In part because third parties have become increasingly common in American politics, despite election rules favoring a two-party system, one-third of all winning presidential candidates since the Civil War have been elected with a plurality (simply more votes than any other candidate) but not a majority (more than 50 percent of all votes) of the national popular vote.[17] When one considers those voting for the losing major-party presidential candidate and a losing third-party candidate (e.g., Perot, Nader), a majority of Americans who cast a vote for president in recent elections are on the "losing side" about a third of the time. If the party that wins the presidency in one out of three elections is not favored by a majority of voters, that calls into question the legitimacy of our election system. Some scholars suggest that the failure to secure majorities may continue in the future with the rise of independent candidates and dissatisfaction with the two major political parties.[18]

Some proponents of election reform argue that two major parties are not sufficient to represent the varied interests of America's 311 million people, and that more political parties would improve representation. Forms of proportional representation, multiple-member districts, or instant run-off voting would increase the probability of third-party representation in American politics. State ballot access laws are another major impediment for third parties. Third parties often fail to meet criteria to get on the ballot, such as registration fees or petition requirements in which a certain number of voters must sign a petition in order for the third party or independent candidate to gain ballot access. States with lower access hurdles, such as Minnesota, have more third-party candidates. Those who favor a stronger role for third parties argue that states should make it easier to get on the ballot. Supporters of the current system, on the other hand, contend that America's two-party system creates stability in governing and prevents the need for a coalition government, where multiple small parties work together to form a majority to govern.

# ● Party Organization

> **Describe how the major American parties are structured at the national, state, and local levels**

In the United States, **party organizations** exist at virtually every level of government (see Figure 9.3). These organizations are usually committees made up of a number of active party members. State law and party rules prescribe how such committees are constituted. Usually committee members are elected at local party meetings, called **caucuses**, or as part of the regular primary election. The best-known examples of these committees are at the national level: the Democratic National Committee and the Republican National Committee.

**party organization** the formal structure of a political party, including its leadership, election committees, active members, and paid staff

**caucus (political)** a normally closed meeting of a political or legislative group to select candidates, plan strategy, or make decisions regarding legislative matters

## National Convention

At the national level, the party's most important institution is the **national convention**. The convention, held every four years, is attended by delegates from each of the states; as a group, they nominate the party's presidential and vice-presidential candidates, draft the party's campaign platform for the presidential race, and approve changes in the rules and regulations governing party procedures. Before World War II, presidential nominations occupied most of the time, energy, and

**national convention** a national party political institution that nominates the party's presidential and vice presidential candidates, establishes party rules, and writes and ratifies the party's platform

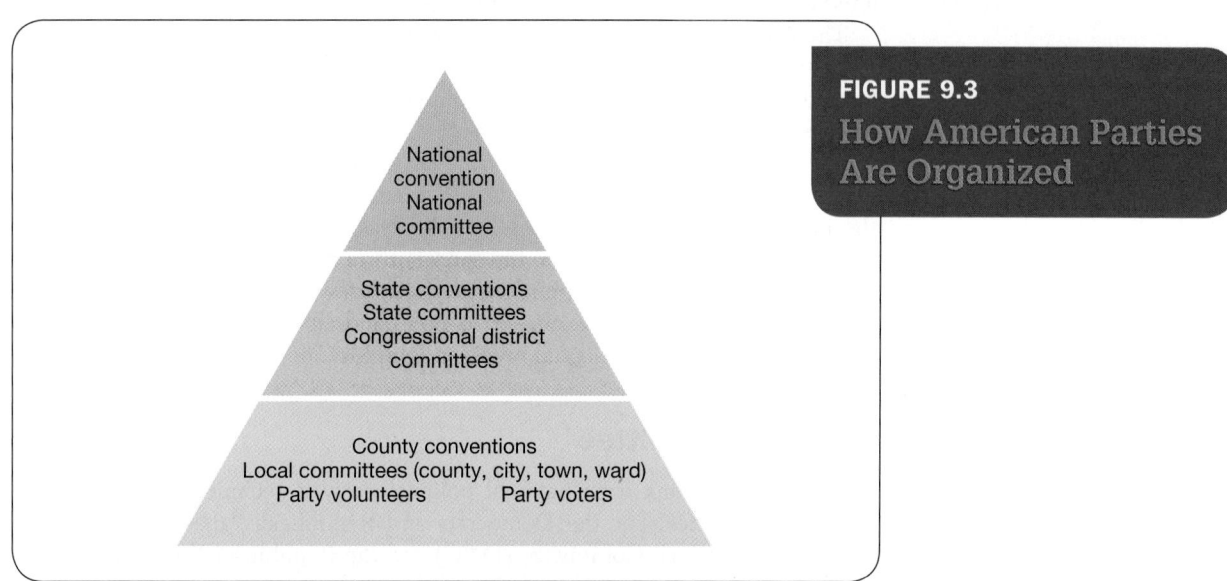

**FIGURE 9.3**
How American Parties Are Organized

National convention
National committee

State conventions
State committees
Congressional district committees

County conventions
Local committees (county, city, town, ward)
Party volunteers          Party voters

effort expended at the national convention. The nomination process required days of negotiation and compromise among state party leaders and often required many ballots before a nominee was selected. In recent years, however, presidential candidates have been chosen by winning enough delegate support in primary elections to win the official nomination on the first ballot. The actual convention has become symbolic.

The convention's other two tasks, determining the party's rules and its platform, remain important. Party rules can determine the relative influence of competing factions within the party and can also increase or decrease the party's chances for electoral success. In 1972, for example, the Democratic National Convention adopted a new set of rules favored by the party's liberal wing. Under these rules, state delegations to the Democratic Convention were required to include women and members of minority groups in rough proportion to those groups' representation among the party's membership in that state. Liberals correctly calculated that women and African Americans would generally support liberal ideas and candidates. The rules also called for the use of the proportional representation voting system, which liberals thought would give them an advantage by allowing the election of more women and minority delegates. The Republican Party used proportional representation voting for the first time in the 2012 presidential nomination.

The convention also approves the party **platform**. Platforms are often dismissed as documents filled with platitudes that voters seldom read. To some extent this criticism is well founded. Not one voter in a thousand so much as glances at the party platform, and even the news media pay little attention to the documents. Furthermore, the parties' presidential candidates make little use of the platforms in their campaigns; usually they prefer to develop and promote their own themes. Nonetheless, the platform can be an important document. The platform should be understood as a contract in which the various party groups attending the convention state their terms for supporting the ticket. For one, welfare reform may be a key issue. For another, tax reduction may be more important. For a third, the critical issue might be deficit reduction. When one of these "planks" is included in the platform, its promoters are asserting that this is what they want in exchange for their support for the ticket, while other party factions might be agreeing that the plank seems reasonable and appropriate. Thus, party platforms should be seen more as internal party documents than as public pledges.

The 2008 Democratic platform, for example, included a plank aimed at cities, promising to "strengthen the federal commitment to cities." Urban areas have long formed the backbone of Democratic political strength; a party plank pledging aid to cities and metropolitan areas rewards a key constituency whose enthusiastic support is crucial to a Democratic victory. Because party platforms are written more for the delegates than for ordinary voters, they tend to be less centrist than the presidential candidates themselves. A presidential candidate hoping to win over "swing" voters in addition to the party faithful has to stake out more moderate positions. Thus, the 2008 Republican platform presented more extreme views on issues such as the rights of same-sex couples and environmental regulation than those of Republican presidential nominee John McCain.

## National Committee

Between conventions, each national political party is technically headed by its national committee. For the Democrats and Republicans, these are called the Democratic National Committee (DNC) and the Republican National Commit-

*At the Democatic Party's 2012 national convention, the party officially confirmed the nomination of President Barack Obama as their candidate for president in 2012.*

tee (RNC), respectively. These national committees raise campaign funds, head off factional disputes within the party, and endeavor to enhance the party's media image. The actual work of each national committee is overseen by its chairperson. During every election cycle prior to the enactment of the campaign finance reforms of 2002, the DNC and RNC each raised tens of millions of dollars of so-called **soft money**, which could be used to support party candidates throughout the nation. The 2002 Bipartisan Campaign Reform Act (BCRA), sometimes known as the McCain-Feingold Act, outlawed this practice. To circumvent BCRA, however, each party has established a set of "shadow parties." These are **527 committees**, groups organized to promote and publicize political issues. As such, they can claim tax-exempt status under Section 527 of the Internal Revenue Code, which defines and provides tax-exempt status for nonprofit political advocacy groups.

Under the law, 527 committees can raise and spend unlimited amounts of money as long as their activities are not coordinated with those of the formal party organizations. Although some 527 committees are actually independent, many are directed by former Republican and Democratic party officials and run shadow campaigns on behalf of the parties.[19] In the 2008 election cycle, nonprofit organizations formed specifically to support particular candidates became an additional source of soft money. This change was the result of a 2007 Supreme Court decision that overturned parts of the BCRA, allowing corporations, including nonprofits, to run issue advertisements in the days leading up to the primaries and general elections.[20] Soft money played a less prominent role in the 2008 presidential election, in part because the presidential candidates and their parties created such successful fund-raising operations. But a diverse array of outside groups, including the U.S. Chamber of Commerce, the National Rifle Association, and Defenders of Wildlife Action Fund, continued to raise and spend large sums of money on competitive congressional races. In 2010, the Supreme Court's decision in *Citizens United v. Federal Election Committee* again changed the terms for campaigning. As we will see in Chapter 10, the amount of money spent in the 2012 presidential primaries broke new records because the 2010 Court decision allowed unlimited corporate contributions to political campaigns.[21]

**soft money** money contributed directly to political parties and other organizations for political activities that is not regulated by federal campaign spending laws; in 2002 federal law prohibited unregulated donations to national party committees

**527 committees** nonprofit independent groups that receive and disburse funds to influence the nomination, election, or defeat of candidates. Named after Section 527 of the Internal Revenue Code, which defines and grants tax-exempt status to nonprofit advocacy groups

When a party controls the White House, that party's national committee chair is appointed by the president. Typically, this means that the party's national committee becomes little more than an adjunct to the White House staff. For a first-term president, the committee devotes the bulk of its energy to the re-election campaign. The national committee chair of the party not in control of the White House is selected by the committee itself and usually takes a broader view of the party's needs, raising money and performing other activities on behalf of the party members in Congress and in the state legislatures.

## Congressional Campaign Committees

Each party also forms House and Senate campaign committees to raise funds for House and Senate election campaigns. Their efforts may or may not be coordinated with the activities of the national committees. Within the party that controls the White House, the national committee and the congressional campaign committees are often rivals, since both groups are seeking donations from the same people but for different candidates: the national committee seeks funds for the presidential race, while the congressional campaign committees approach the same contributors for support for the congressional contests. In recent years, the Republican Party has attempted to coordinate the fund-raising activities of all its committees. Republicans have also sought to give the GOP's national institutions the capacity to invest funds in those close congressional, state, and local races where they can do the most good. The Democrats soon followed suit. Their aggressive stance and party unity allowed them to win back Congress in 2006.

## State and Local Party Organizations

Each of the two major parties has a central committee in each state. The parties traditionally also have county committees and, in some instances, state senate district committees, judicial district committees, and, in the case of larger cities, citywide party committees and local assembly district "ward" committees. Congressional districts also may have party committees. Some cities also have precinct committees. Precincts are not districts from which any representative is elected but instead are legally defined subdivisions of wards that are used to register voters and set up ballot boxes or voting machines. A precinct is typically composed of 300 to 600 voters.

During the nineteenth and early twentieth centuries, many cities, counties, and occasionally even a few states had such well-organized parties that they were called **machines**, whose leaders were called "bosses." The famous old machines of New York, Chicago, and Boston relied on "precinct captains" and a fairly tight group of party members around them. Precinct captains were usually members of long standing in neighborhood party clubhouses, which were important social centers and places for distributing favors to constituents.[22] Traditional party machines depended heavily on **patronage**, their power to control government jobs. With thousands of jobs to dispense, party bosses were able to recruit armies of political workers, who in turn mobilized millions of voters.

Some of the major reform movements in American history were motivated by the excessive powers and abuses of these machines and their bosses. Few, if any, machines are left today. With civil-service reform, party leaders no longer control many positions. Nevertheless, state and local party organizations are very active in recruiting candidates and conducting voter registration drives. In addition,

**machines** strong party organizations in late-nineteenth- and early-twentieth-century American cities. These machines were led by "bosses" who controlled party nominations and patronage

**patronage** the resources available to higher officials, usually opportunities to make partisan appointments to offices and to confer grants, licenses, or special favors to supporters

# DIGITAL CITIZENS

# Party Power in a Digital Age

**Parties in the United States are** considered to be ground-up organizations, meaning that they get their power from the members of the mass public who support them at the local level. However, until fairly recently, political party bosses controlled the party platform, the party message, and often, through early money to candidates, who held elected office and who won the nomination for president. Even with the decline of party machines and the increased use of primaries in the nominations process in the twentieth century, party elites retained a great deal of control over these decisions. Local party leaders would then spread the message from the elites by word of mouth and at local events to gain new supporters and keep existing supporters in line.

While this elite-driven process still occurs today, the process of party formation and many aspects of party politics have been turned upside down with the digital revolution in communication. Four resources that political parties use to contest and win elections (time, money, expertise, and organization) have all been altered by the Internet. New

media are decentralizing party power, as citizens can volunteer and give money to the party of their choice without ever being contacted by a party official. Online fund-raising allows millions of donors to give small contributions to parties, and new media allow the party to spread its message far and wide online. This is beneficial for parties because more people are involved, but at the same time, there are more divergent opinions that must be recognized and appeased. No longer can party leaders craft their own message and relay it to the field; they must also listen to what their supporters want. If the party does not appeal to the mass public, members of the mass public will form their own groups, or even competing parties.

This is exactly what happened in the case of the Tea Party movement in 2010. A large number of Republican supporters felt the party was not listening to their concerns and decided to create their own groups. Without the Internet, the Tea Party groups may not have been able to form, let alone influence the Republican Party as they did in the 2010 elections. Fearing a major split in the party and a mass exodus of party supporters, the Republican Party was forced to change its platform to reincorporate these supporters.

The Republican Party had to move farther away from the center and become more conservative to appease a core group of supporters. As online news becomes more important, the Internet is increasingly cited as a cause for the growing polarization of the political parties, where they agree on fewer and fewer political issues. In a 2010 Pew survey, over half of those interviewed agreed that "the Internet increases the influence of those with extreme political views" while only 30 percent believed that

the Internet is decreasing the power of party extremists.

Whether the Internet increases polarization or not, it seems clear that, the days of political elites deciding the party agenda behind closed doors are gone. The term *party leader* still invokes images of powerful governors, senators, and presidents; however, with the changes to party makeup in a world of digital politics, the term more appropriately applies to the average citizen watching what the party does from his computer or smartphone, with party leaders sending out texts, tweets, e-mails, or Facebook posts.

SOURCES: Bruce Bimber, *Information and American Democracy: Technology in the Evolution of Political Power* (Cambridge, UK: Cambridge University Press, 2003). Marty Cohen, David Karol, Hans Noel, and John Zaller, *The Party Decides: Presidential Nominations before and after Reform* (Chicago: University of Chicago Press, 2008). Thomas Mann, and Norman Ornstein, *It's Even Worse Than It Looks: How the American Constitutional System Collided with the New Politics of Extremism* (Washington, DC: Brookings Institution Press, 2012). Trygve Olson, and Terry Nelson, "The Internet's Impact on Political Parties and Campaigns," International Reports, 2010, www.kas.de/wf/en/33.19706/ (accessed 6/23/12). Adam Smith, "Attitudes towards the Internet's Impact on Politics," Pew Internet and American Life Project, 2011, http://pewinternet.org/Reports/2011/The-Internet-and-Campaign-2010/Section-4.aspx (accessed 6/24/12).

## for critical analysis

1. Can you image a new political party that makes online communication its primary mode of operation? Why or why not? Why did the experiment in an online political party, Americans Elect, fail?

2. Do political elites and party bosses still control party politics in the United States, or have new media fostered a more democratic and participatory process for average Americans? Explain your answer.

*Local party offices may work in tandem with the national and state party organizations, but they also have a good deal of independence to decide which local candidates and issues to support.*

under current federal law, state and local party organizations can spend unlimited amounts of money on "party-building" activities such as voter registration and get-out-the-vote drives (though in some states such practices are limited by state law). As a result, for many years the national party organizations, which had enormous fund-raising abilities but were restricted by law in how much they could spend on candidates, transferred millions of dollars to the state and local organizations. The state and local parties, in turn, spent this soft money to promote national, state, and local political activities. In this process, local organizations became linked financially to the national parties and American political parties became somewhat more integrated and nationalized than ever before. At the same time, the state and local party organizations came to control large financial resources and play important roles in elections despite the collapse of the old patronage machines.[23]

## ● Parties and the Electorate

**party identification** an individual voter's psychological ties to one party or another

> **Identify the social groups that tend to support the Republicans and the Democrats**

One reason why parties are so important is that individual voters tend to develop **party identification** with one of the political parties. Party identification has been compared to wearing blue- or red-tinted glasses: they color voters' understanding of politics in general, and are the most important cue in how to vote in elections. That is, most Republicans vote for Republican Party candidates, and most Democrats vote for Democratic Party candidates. Although it is an emotional tie, party identification also has a rational component. Voters generally form attachments to parties that reflect their views and interests. Once those attachments are formed, however, they are likely to persist and even be handed down to children, unless some very strong factors convince individuals that their party is no longer an appropriate object of their affections. In some sense, party identification is similar to brand loyalty in the marketplace: consumers choose a

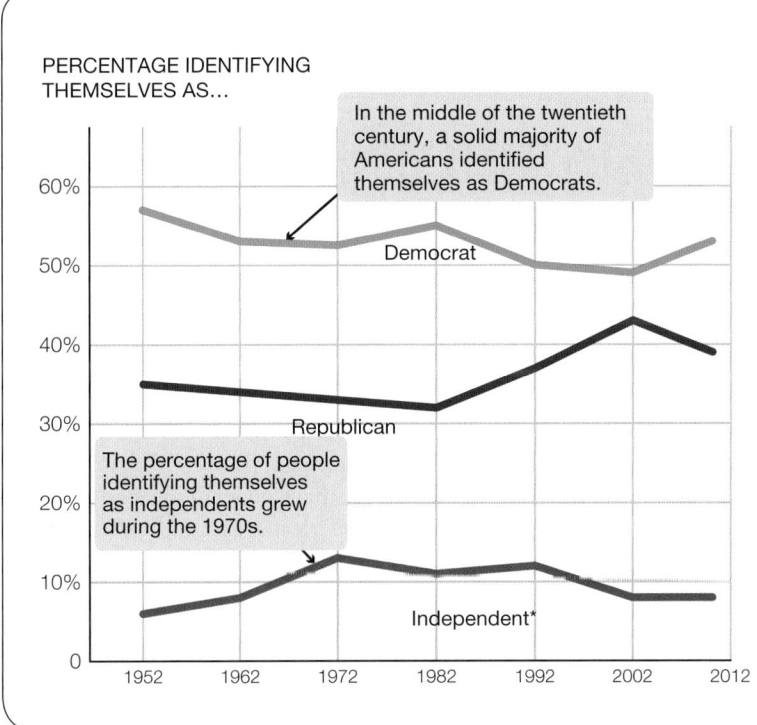

PERCENTAGE IDENTIFYING THEMSELVES AS...

In the middle of the twentieth century, a solid majority of Americans identified themselves as Democrats.

The percentage of people identifying themselves as independents grew during the 1970s.

Democrat

Republican

Independent*

**FIGURE 9.4**

## Americans' Party Identification, 1952–2010

Over time, the Democrats lost strength as more Americans identified themselves as Republicans and independents. Why do you think the percentage of people identifying themselves as independents grew during the 1970s?

SOURCES: 1952 to 2004: American National Election Studies; 2006–2008: Gallup.com (accessed 7/15/10).
*Independents who said they leaned toward one party are counted with that party.

brand of automobile for its appearance or mechanical characteristics and stick with it out of loyalty, habit, and unwillingness to reexamine their choices, but they may eventually change if the old brand no longer serves their interests.

On any general-election ballot, there are likely to be only two or three candidacies where the nature of the office and the characteristics and positions of the candidates are well known to voters. But what about the choices for judges, the state comptroller, the state attorney general, and many other elected positions? Parties and campaigns help by providing information when voters must choose among obscure candidates. Without knowledge of local races or judges, most voters fall back on their partisanship, voting for Republican candidates or Democratic candidates for these positions.

Although roughly one in three Americans is independent, roughly a third are Republican and a third Democrat, and most independents "lean" toward one major party (see Figure 9.4). Party identification gives citizens a stake in election outcomes that goes beyond the particular race at hand. This is why strong party identifiers are more likely to go to the polls and, of course, are more likely than others to support the party with which they identify. **Party activists** are drawn from the ranks of the strong identifiers. Activists are those who not only vote but also contribute their time and effort to party affairs. No party could succeed without the thousands of volunteers who undertake the tasks needed to keep the organization going. Many party activists devote their time to politics because they have strong beliefs on particular policy issues. Across a range of issues, the views of Democratic activists are more liberal than those of Democratic voters, whereas the views of Republican activists are more conservative than those of Republican voters. One study that compared the views of party activists and rank-and-file voters across a range of issues found that since the 1990s, the views of Republican Party activists have diverged most sharply from those of the average voter.[24]

**party activists** partisans who contribute time, energy, and effort to support their party and its candidates

## Group Affiliations

The Democratic and Republican parties are currently America's only truly national parties. They are the only political organizations that draw support from most regions of the country and from Americans of every racial, economic, religious, and ethnic group. The two parties do not draw equal support from members of every social stratum, however. In the United States today, a variety of group characteristics is associated with party identification. These include race and ethnicity, gender, religion, class, ideology, region, and age.

**Race and Ethnicity** Since the 1930s and Franklin Delano Roosevelt's New Deal, African Americans have been overwhelmingly Democratic in their party identification. More than 90 percent of African Americans describe themselves as Democrats and support Democratic candidates in national, state, and local elections. In 2012, over 90 percent of African Americans supported the Democrat Barack Obama for president. Latino voters are less monolithic, by contrast, but tend to support the Democratic Party. Cuban Americans, for example, have generally leaned Republican in their party affiliations, whereas Mexican Americans favored the Democrats.

This mix of partisan preferences shifted strongly toward the Democrats in 2008, when the exit polls showed that 67 percent of Latinos supported Obama. The trend continued in 2012, with over 70 percent voting for Obama. The Latino vote is particularly important because it can help alter the electoral map. In 2012 the Latino vote in swing states such as Florida and Colorado helped bring the Democrats to victory. Asian Americans have been divided in past elections, but in 2012, 73 percent of Asian Americans voted for Barack Obama, and 26 percent voted for Mitt Romney, according to exit polls.

**gender gap** a distinctive pattern of voting behavior reflecting the differences in views between women and men

**Gender** Women are somewhat more likely to support Democrats, and men are somewhat more likely to support Republicans, in surveys of party affiliation. This difference is known as the **gender gap**. The gender gap has varied between 6 and 11 percent since 1992. For example, George W. Bush's first election, in 2000, had

*In 2012 both major parties tried to appeal to Latino and Hispanic voters. Mitt Romney called on members of his family who speak Spanish to appear at campaign events with Latino groups.*

a sizable gender gap of 53 percent support among men and 43 percent among women. In 2004 the gender gap decreased slightly, with 55 percent of men voting for Bush compared with 48 percent of women. In 2008 the gap remained on the small side, with 56 percent of women and 49 percent of men supporting Barack Obama for president but it widened again in 2012, with 55 percent of women supporting Obama as compared with just 45 percent of men.[25]

**Religion** Jews are among the Democratic Party's most loyal constituent groups and have been since the New Deal. Nearly 90 percent of all Jewish Americans describe themselves as Democrats. Catholics were also once a strongly pro-Democratic group but have been shifting toward the Republican Party since the 1970s, when the party focused on abortion and other social issues deemed to be important to Catholics. Protestants are more likely to identify with the Republicans than with the Democrats. Evangelical Protestants, in particular, have been drawn to the Republicans' conservative stands on social issues, such as marriage and abortion. The importance of religious conservatives to the Republican Party became more evident after 2000, when George W. Bush awarded federal grants and contracts to religious groups. By using so-called faith-based groups as federal contractors, Bush sought to ensure that these groups would have a continuing stake in Republican success. Religious conservatives, particularly white born-again Christians, overwhelmingly supported President Bush in 2004, accounting for one-third of his votes. Almost 80 percent of white born-again Christians voted for President Bush; only 21 percent supported the Democratic candidate, Senator John Kerry. Yet the 2004 election results also revealed that religiosity, as measured by frequency of attendance at religious services, had a larger impact on voting than denominational affiliation. Voters who attended religious services weekly were more likely to vote for Bush, regardless of their religion, than were voters who were less observant. In 2008 and 2012, white evangelicals continued to vote overwhelmingly Republican.[26]

**Class** The patterns of class voting that emerged from the New Deal of the 1930s were simple: upper-income Americans were considerably more likely to affiliate with the Republicans, whereas lower-income Americans were far more likely to identify with the Democrats. This divide is reflected in the differences between the two parties on economic issues. In general, the Republicans support cutting taxes and social spending—positions that reflect the interests of the wealthy. The Democrats, however, favor increasing social spending—a position consistent with the interests of less-affluent Americans. But beginning in the 1970s, many white working-class voters, concerned about "law and order," moral issues, and racial liberalism, started voting Republican, and have remained in the Republican Party. Analysts disagree about the trend of class voting, because there is no widely accepted definition of class. When the electorate is divided into thirds on the basis of income, the relationship between lower-income voters and Democratic allegiance remains strong. When class is measured by education, however, white workers without a college degree have voted heavily for Republicans in recent elections.[27]

**Ideology** Ideology and party identification are very closely linked. Most individuals who describe themselves as conservatives identify with the Republican Party, whereas most who call themselves liberals support the Democrats. This division has increased in recent years as the two parties have taken very different positions on social and economic issues. Before the 1970s, when party differences were more blurred, it was not uncommon to find Democratic conservatives and Republican liberals. Both of these species are rare today. Yet important differences remain among conservatives and liberals. Economic conservatives care most about reducing government regulation and taxes. Social conservatives are concerned about social issues such as abortion and same-sex marriage. The Republican Party includes both groups, but at times the interests of these two kinds of conservatives conflict. Likewise, many Democrats who are economic liberals, in favor of generous social spending, are conservative when it comes to matters such as gun control.

**Region** After the 2000 election, red and blue maps appeared showing the regional distribution of the vote. Democrats, represented as "Blue America," were clustered on the coasts and the upper Midwest and across the northern states. Republicans, represented as "Red America," were concentrated in the Mountain West, the Southwest, and the South.

The explanations for these regional variations are complex. Between the Civil War and the 1960s, the "Solid South" was a Democratic bastion. Today the South is solidly Republican. Southern Republicanism has come about because conservative white southerners identify the Democratic Party with the civil rights movement, racial liberalism, and with liberal positions on abortion, school prayer, and other social issues. Republican strength in the South is also related to the weakness of organized labor in these regions, and to the dependence of the two regions on military programs supported by the Republicans. Democratic strength in the Northeast and Midwest is a function of the continuing influence of organized labor in the large cities of these regions, and of the regions' large populations of minority and elderly voters, who benefit from Democratic social programs. The coastal West, especially California, shifted toward the Democrats in the 1990s, in part because of the growing importance of the Latino vote.[28]

**for critical analysis**

What are the major components of each party's political coalition? What factors tie these groups to their respective parties?

**Age** Age is another factor associated with partisanship. In 2008 the shift toward the Democratic Party affected all age groups, but it was particularly strong among young voters. Polls showed that, while older voters preferred Democrats by 11–12 percent, those born after 1977 favored Democrats by 24 percent. There is nothing about a particular numerical age that leads to a particular party loyalty. Rather, individuals from the same age cohort are likely to have experienced a similar set of events during the period when their party loyalties were formed. Thus, Americans between the ages of 50 and 64 came of political age during the Cold War, Vietnam, and civil rights eras. Apparently, among voters whose initial perceptions of politics were shaped during this period, more responded favorably to the role played by the Democrats than to the actions of the Republicans. Young people who came of age during the Bush presidency had the strongest Democratic Party identification of any age group.

## Recent Trends in Party Affiliation

After the 1960s, many analysts began to express concern that American parties had become too weak to play their vital role in converting popular political participation into effective government. These scholars noted such trends as a decline in partisan attachment within the electorate, the growth in the numbers of voters identifying as independents, and a rise in so-called split-ticket voting. This overall trend, sometimes termed dealignment, was seen as a product of growing social diversity and educational attainment, which made voters less reliant on parties to guide their political decision making. The growth of the mass media, particularly television, also seemed to reduce the role of parties in elections, as television tends to focus on the personality of indi-

# Who Identifies with Which Party?

## Gender

| | | Rep | Ind | Dem |
|---|---|---|---|---|
| Men | | 42% | 11% | 47% |
| Women | | 34% | 11% | 55% |

## Age

| | Rep | Ind | Dem |
|---|---|---|---|
| 18-29 | 33% | 10% | 58% |
| 30-49 | 39% | 10% | 50% |
| 50-64 | 38% | 11% | 51% |
| 65 and over | 40% | 11% | 49% |

## Race

| | Rep | Ind | Dem |
|---|---|---|---|
| White | 44% | 10% | 46% |
| Black | 7% | 8% | 86% |
| Hispanic | 27% | 11% | 62% |
| All others | 15% | 12% | 73% |

## Income

| | Rep | Ind | Dem |
|---|---|---|---|
| Under $20K | 24% | 12% | 63% |
| $20K–$29,999 | 32% | 10% | 58% |
| $30K–$49,999 | 36% | 9% | 54% |
| $50K–$74,999 | 51% | 8% | 41% |
| $75K and over | 48% | 8% | 45% |

## Region

| | Rep | Ind | Dem |
|---|---|---|---|
| East | 34% | 11% | 55% |
| Midwest | 38% | 12% | 50% |
| South | 41% | 10% | 49% |
| West | 37% | 10% | 53% |

## Education

| | Rep | Ind | Dem |
|---|---|---|---|
| < High school | 27% | 13% | 60% |
| High school grad. | 38% | 11% | 52% |
| College grad. | 43% | 10% | 47% |
| Postgraduate | 38% | 9% | 53% |

Party identification varies by income, race, and gender. For example, as these statistics from 2008 show, Americans with higher incomes are significantly more likely to support the Republican Party. Women and African Americans are more likely than white men to identify with the Democratic Party.

Republican Party

Democratic Party

Independent

## for critical analysis

1. How do younger Americans differ from older Americans in their party identification? How—and how much—do regions of the country differ?

2. Do you think of yourself as a Democrat, Republican, or independent? Are other Americans of your gender, age, race, region, and income level likely to share your party preference?

SOURCE: Harold W. Stanley and Richard G. Niemi, *Vital Statistics on American Politics, 2011-2012* (Washington, DC: Congressional Quarterly Press, 2011), p. 110.

vidual candidates rather than the "institution" of the party. Today, party loyalties in America continue to be in a state of flux. On the one hand, the percentage of voters who declare no party loyalty remains at an all-time high.[29] On the other hand, party identification among a large number of the most active voters has grown stronger.[30]

The Who Are Americans? feature indicates the relationship between party identification and a number of social criteria. Race and income seem to have the greatest influence on Americans' party affiliations. Neither of these social characteristics is inevitably linked to partisan identification, however. The general party identifications just discussed are broad tendencies that both reflect and reinforce the issue and policy positions the two parties take in the national and local political arenas.

## ● Parties and Elections

> **Explain the roles parties play in elections**

Parties have always been central to the electoral process, and in recent years they have taken on a renewed role in recruiting candidates, coordinating campaigns, mobilizing voters, and raising money.[31] One of the most important but least noticed party activities is the recruitment of candidates for local, state, and national office. Each election year, candidates must be found for thousands of state and local offices as well as congressional seats. Where they do not have an incumbent running for re-election, party leaders attempt to identify strong candidates and to interest them in entering the campaign.

An ideal candidate will have an unblemished record and the capacity to raise enough money to mount a serious campaign. Party leaders are usually not willing to provide financial backing to candidates who are unable to raise substantial funds on their own. For a House seat, this can mean several hundred thousand dollars; for a Senate seat, a serious candidate must be able to raise several million dollars. Often party leaders have difficulty finding attractive candidates and persuading them to run. Candidate recruitment is problematic in an era when political candidates must assume that their personal lives will be intensely scrutinized in the press and even subjected to mudslinging campaigns by their opponents.[32]

### Nominations

Article I, Section 4, of the Constitution makes only a few provisions for elections. It delegates to the states the power to set the "times, places, and manner" of holding elections, even for U.S. senators and representatives. The Constitution has been amended from time to time to expand the right to participate in elections. Congress has also occasionally passed laws regulating elections, congressional districting, and campaign practices. But the Constitution and the laws are almost completely silent on nominations, setting only age and citizenship requirements for candidates. The president must be at least 35 years of age, a native-born citizen, and a resident of the United States for 14 years. A senator must be at least 30, a U.S. citizen for at least nine years, and a resident of the state he or she represents. A member of the House must be at least 25, a U.S. citizen for 7 years, and a resident of the state he or she represents.

**nomination** the process by which political parties select their candidates for election to public office

**Nomination** is the process by which a party selects a single candidate to run for each elective office. The nominating process can precede the election by many months, as it does when the many candidates for the presidency are eliminated from consideration through a grueling series of debates and state primaries until there is only one survivor in each party: the party's nominee.

## Mobilizing Voters

The actual election period begins immediately after the nominations. Throughout American history, this has been a time of glory for the political parties, whose popular base of support is fully displayed. All the paraphernalia of party committees (signs, bumper stickers, buttons) are on display, and all the committee members are activated into local party workforces. The first step involves voter registration. There was a time when party workers were responsible for virtually all this kind of electoral activity, but they have been supplemented by civic groups such as the League of Women Voters, unions, and Chambers of Commerce, although the parties frequently mail notices and call voters to ensure that they are registered. Those who have registered have to decide on Election Day if they will actually go to the polling place, stand in line, and vote for the various candidates and referenda on the ballot. If they are voting by mail in one of the states that allow this, they have to request the ballot, fill it out, and return it (see Chapter 8).

Political parties, candidates, and campaigning can make a big difference in persuading voters to vote. Voter mobilization, once an art, has now become a science. In recent years, each of the two major parties has developed an extensive database on hundreds of millions of potential voters, which allows the parties to bring their search for votes, contributions, and campaign help down to named individuals. The Republican Party calls its archive Voter Vault. To compete with the technologically sophisticated Republicans, in the mid-2000s the Democratic National Committee began to use a state-of-the-art Web-based system, originally called Demzilla and later renamed VoteBuilder, for collecting and sharing voter information. In the 2008 and 2012 elections, the DNC made the voter file available to state parties, and this technology became one of the keys to their successful mobilization and get-out-the-vote activities those years.

*Since the 1980s, the Republicans have appealed to "values voters" concerned about social issues like school prayer, abortion, and gay marriage with promises to enact new policies in these areas. In 2011, Mitt Romney spoke at the Values Voter Summit in Washington, D.C.*

## ● Parties and Government

> **Explain how parties organize legislative business and influence policy**

When the dust of the campaign has settled, does it matter which party has won? It does. Especially when the parties are sharply divided ideologically, as they have been in recent years, the party that controls government can make significant changes by moving policy in new directions.

### Parties and Policy

One of the most familiar complaints about American politics is that the two major parties try to be all things to all people, and are therefore indistinguishable from each other. But since the 1980s, important differences have emerged between the positions of Democratic and Republican party leaders on a number of key issues, and these differences are still apparent today.

For example, the national leadership of the Republican Party supports maintaining high levels of military spending, cuts in social programs, tax relief for upper-income voters, tax incentives for businesses, and the "social agenda" backed by members of conservative religious denominations. The national Democratic leadership, on the other hand, supports expanded social welfare spending, cuts in military spending, increased regulation of business, and a variety of consumer and environmental programs.

These differences reflect differences in philosophy and differences in the core constituencies to which the parties seek to appeal. The Democratic Party at the national level seeks to unite organized labor, the poor and working class, members of racial minorities, and liberal upper-middle-class professionals. The Republicans, by contrast, appeal to business, upper-middle- and upper-class groups in the private sector, white working-class voters, and social conservatives. Often party leaders will seek to develop issues they hope will add new groups to their party's constituent base. During the 1980s, for example, under the leadership of Ronald Reagan, the Republicans devised a series of "social issues," including support for school prayer, opposition to abortion, and opposition to affirmative action, designed to cultivate the support of white southerners. This effort was extremely successful in increasing Republican strength in the once solidly Democratic South. In the 1990s, under the leadership of Bill Clinton, who called himself a "new Democrat," the Democratic Party sought to develop new social programs designed to solidify the party's base among working-class and poor voters, and new, somewhat more conservative economic programs aimed at attracting the votes of middle- and upper-middle-class voters. In 2000, George W. Bush labeled himself a "compassionate conservative" to signal to the Republican base that he was a conservative while seeking to reassure moderate and independent voters that he was not an opponent of federal social programs.

As these examples suggest, parties do not always support policies just because their constituents already favor those policies. Instead, party leaders can play the role of **policy entrepreneurs**, seeking ideas and programs that will expand their party's base of support while eroding that of the opposition. It is one of the essential characteristics of party politics in America that a party's programs and policies often lead, rather than follow, public opinion. Like their counterparts in the business world, party leaders seek to identify and develop "products" (programs and policies) that will appeal to the public. The public, of course, has the ultimate voice. With its votes it decides whether or not to "buy" new policy offerings.

Thus, for example, in 2010 many Republican congressional candidates vowed to repeal the major health care reform act signed by President Obama earlier in the year. Republican presidential candidates in 2012 also vowed to repeal what they referred to as Obamacare, but it was not clear whether they would be able to obtain the necessary votes in Congress. There are, however, a number of legal cases that have challenged the individual mandate requiring individuals to purchase health care insurance if they are not covered by their employer. In 2012 the Supreme Court ruled arguments concerning the individual mandate was constitutional.

## Parties in Congress

Congress depends more on the party system than is generally recognized. For one thing, the speakership of the House is essentially a party office. All the members of the House take part in the election of the Speaker. But the actual selection is made

**policy entrepreneur** an individual who identifies a problem as a political issue and brings a policy proposal into the political agenda

*Within the government, parties help like-minded politicians achieve their policy goals. In Congress party members work together to try to pass legislation, and they also work with the president. Here, President Barack Obama meet with the Democrats' congressional leaders in the Oval Office.*

by the **majority party**—the party that holds a majority of seats in the House. (The other party is known as the **minority party**.) When the majority party caucus presents a nominee to the entire House, its choice is then invariably ratified in a straight vote along party lines. The committee system of both houses of Congress is also a product of the two-party system. For example, each party is assigned a quota of members for each committee, depending on the percentage of total seats held by the party. As we shall see in Chapter 12, the assignment of individual members to committees is a party decision. Each party has a "committee on committees" to make such decisions. Granting permission to transfer to another committee is also a party decision, as is advancement up the committee ladder toward the chair. Since the late nineteenth century, most advancements have been automatic—based on the length of continual service on the committee. This seniority system has existed only because of the support of the two parties, however, and either party can depart from it by a simple vote.

The importance of parties in Congress became especially evident in the months after the Republicans won control of Congress in 1994. The Republican leadership was able to maintain nearly unanimous support among party members on vote after vote as it sought to implement the GOP's legislative agenda, and Democrats were rarely able to match the Republicans' strong party discipline. After 2006, however, when Democrats won back the Congress, they showed considerably more party discipline than they had in past decades. After Obama's election, Republican members of Congress also showed remarkable party discipline in their united party-line opposition to the president's major initiatives ranging from economic stimulus to major health care reform, which led Democrats to decry the GOP as "the party of No."

## President and Party

Strong presidents with broad popular support can depend on party ties to get their legislation enacted in Congress. Yet there has been a trade-off in using the

**majority party** the party that holds the majority of legislative seats in either the House or the Senate

**minority party** the party that holds a minority of legislative seats in either the House or the Senate

party machinery to support the president's legislative agenda and building it to support the party in congressional elections. The political scientist Daniel Galvin argues that since the Eisenhower presidency, Republicans have paid much more attention to party building than have Democrats.[33] Given their minority status in the electorate for much of the past 50 years, Republican presidents have sought to enhance the party's capabilities to mobilize voters and win elections. George W. Bush's adviser Karl Rove hoped to build a strong party apparatus that would ensure a permanent Republican majority. Democratic presidents have put much less energy into building the party apparatus, focusing instead on their legislative agenda and their own re-election. It was only after their 2004 election defeat that Democrats began to pour their energies into building a stronger party. Under the chairmanship of Howard Dean, a previous presidential candidate and a former Vermont governor, the Democratic National Committee invested heavily in new technology and in creating party-mobilizing capabilities in states across the country, not just the traditionally "blue" states that have reliably voted Democratic.

The Obama campaign was able to use this party machinery as a springboard for its own mobilizing organization, Obama for America. With detailed information about Democratic Party activists, Obama for America's database became, in turn, an important political resource for the mobilizing capacities of the Democratic Party. After Obama took office, the organization was renamed Organizing for America (OFA) and became an independent project of the Democratic National Committee. During Obama's first year in office, the president used Organizing for America to mobilize grassroots support for his legislative agenda. For example, OFA took a very active part in lobbying members of Congress to support health care reform. Organizing for America provides training for volunteers to learn how to become organizers and it has established offices in nearly every state.

## ● Thinking Critically about Why Political Parties Matter

Political parties are bulwarks of liberty. The Constitution certainly provides for freedom of speech, freedom of assembly, and freedom of the press. Maintaining these liberties, though, requires more than parchment guarantees. Of course, as long as freedom is not seriously threatened, abstract guarantees suffice to protect it. If, however, those in power actually do threaten citizens' liberties, the preservation of freedom may come to depend on the presence of a coherent and well-organized opposition. As noted earlier, in the first years of the Republic, it was not the Constitution or the courts that preserved free speech in the face of Federalist efforts to silence the government's critics; it was the vigorous opposition of the Jeffersonian Republicans. To this day, the presence of an opposition party is a fundamentally important check on attempts by those in power to skirt the law and infringe on citizens' liberties.

Competition among the political parties is a key factor in stimulating voter turnout. Competition gives citizens an incentive to vote and politicians an incentive to get them to vote.[34] The origins of the American national electorate can be traced to the earliest days of the Republic. According to the historian David Fischer, "the Jeffersonians revolutionized electioneering" during the 1790s, and the Federalists, although initially reluctant, soon adopted the same techniques for mobilizing voters: "mass meetings, barbecues, stump-speaking, festivals of many kinds, processions

# Political Parties and the World

**Few Americans are aware** of the international involvements of our two major political parties. Since the mid-1980s each political party has been associated with a formal foreign policy institute. The International Republican Institute (IRI) was founded in 1983, and the National Democratic Institute for International Affairs (NDI) was established in 1985. Each party's institute is led by a cadre of the party's former officials and elected officeholders.

Both the IRI and the NDI work to encourage citizen participation and democracy throughout the world, particularly in regions that lack a historical and institutional base for democratic politics. Both party institutes work with local politicians, civic leaders, and community activists to encourage understanding of democratic political techniques and respect for democratic values.

Although the programs of the party institutes have many similarities, they diverge in ways that reflect the differences between the two American political parties. NDI programs pay special attention to women and young people—groups cultivated by the Democratic Party in the United States—and to trade unions, another bulwark of the U.S. Democratic Party. Thus, for example, an NDI program in Senegal was designed to increase the involvement of women in local government and in the leadership of the nation's political parties.

The IRI, for its part, has emphasized cultivating relationships with government officials and business leaders, and whereas the NDI's approach is decidedly grassroots in character, the IRI, like the Republican Party, emphasizes political technology. For example, in Macedonia, the IRI has taught public officials the elements of media relations, public-opinion polling, and "message development." Differences are also evident in which countries each institute emphasizes. For example, the IRI pays special attention to the issue of democracy in Cuba, reflecting the significance of the Cuban American vote to the Republican Party.

Although promoting democracy sounds uncontroversial, intervention into the affairs of other countries can lead to results that are anything but democratic. The case of the IRI's activities in Haiti provide an example. A 2006 investigative article in the *New York Times* charged that the IRI deliberately worked to destabilize democracy in Haiti in 2003–04.[a] At the time, Haiti was in a political crisis, with two opposing sides seeking to reach a political reconciliation. According to interviews and public records, the IRI's representative in Haiti provided one-sided support to the opponents of the elected president, Bertrand Aristide. Aristide was a controversial leader who was seen as a voice for Haiti's poor. Although the U.S. ambassador to Haiti at the time protested the involvement of the IRI, the group continued to operate with little accountability. Aristide's opponents launched a coup in 2004, sending the country into chaos for years to come.

Despite criticism, the IRI has grown and in 2008 employed 400 people working on democracy projects in seventy countries.[b]

[a]Walt Bogdanich and Jenny Nordberg, "Mixed U.S. Signals Helped Tilt Haiti toward Chaos," *New York Times,* January 29, 2006, p. 1.
[b]Mike McIntire, "Democracy Group Gives Donors Access to McCain," *New York Times,* July 28, 2008, p. A1.

## for critical analysis

1. What are the similarities and differences between the NDI and the IRI? Do these parallel the similarities and differences between the Democratic and Republican parties?

2. How can Americans ensure that the activities of groups such as the IRI and NDI are accountable to the taxpayers who fund them?

**for critical analysis**

Describe the factors that have contributed to the overall strength and weakness of political parties in America. What are the advantages of a political system in which political parties organize conflict?

and parades, runners and riders, door-to-door canvassing, the distribution of tickets and ballots, . . . free transportation to the polls, outright bribery and corruption of other kinds."[35] The result of this competition for votes was described by the historian Henry Jones Ford in his classic *Rise and Growth of American Politics*.[36] Ford examined the popular clamor against John Adams and Federalist policies in the 1790s that made government a "weak, shakey affair" and appeared to contemporary observers to mark the beginnings of popular insurrection.[37] Attempts by the Federalists to suppress mass discontent, Ford observed, might have "caused an explosion of force which would have blown up the government."[38] What intervened to prevent rebellion was Jefferson's creation of an opposition party that served to "open constitutional channels of political agitation" that diverted opposition to the administration into electoral channels.[39] Party competition gave citizens a sense that their votes were valuable and that it was thus not necessary to take to the streets to have a political impact.

Finally, political parties make democratic government possible. We often fail to appreciate that *democratic government* is a contradiction in terms: *government* implies policies, programs, and decisive action, while *democracy* implies an opportunity for all citizens to participate fully in the governmental process. But full participation by everyone is often inconsistent with getting anything done. At what point should participation stop and governance begin? The problem of democratic government is especially acute in the United States because of the Constitution's system of separated powers, making it very difficult to link popular participation with effective decision making. Often, after the citizens have spoken and the dust has settled, no single set of political forces has been able to win control of enough of the scattered levers of power actually to do anything. Instead of governance, we have continual political struggle. Strong political parties, then, are a partial antidote to the inherent contradiction between participation and government: they can both encourage popular involvement and convert participation into effective government.

There is an old saying that politics is the art of compromise, but politics is more than that—it is also the challenge of making choices. Parties help to crystallize a world of possible government actions into a set of distinct choices. In so doing, they make it easier for ordinary citizens to understand politics, evaluate candidates, and make their own choices.

# Connect with Political Parties

## Inform Yourself

**Learn about third (and fourth and fifth) parties.** Most people in the United States are aware of the two major political parties. Many do not know of the dozens of smaller parties that operate on a national scale. Visit the webpage: http://www .politics1.com/parties.htm and read the platforms of each of the major and minor parties. Does any of the information about these parties surprise you?

**Compare videos from a range of parties.** The Procon website (2012election .procon.org) lists the candidates who ran for office in 2012 from the major two parties and third parties, including their mission statements and platforms. Using the menu on the left side of the screen, you can watch videos of the candidates and hear their speeches. The summary chart shows the candidates' positions on 61 issues (http://2012election.procon.org/view.source-summary -chart.php?topic=64).

## Express Yourself

**Are concerns about today's major parties valid?** When parties began to form in the early 1790s, President Washington was concerned about their potential power. Read his Farewell Address at http://thehistoryprofessor.us/bin/ history/politics.html, and consider what Washington might have said about political parties today. Were his concerns valid? What would the Founders have said about the platforms and roles of the modern parties? Consider posting your opinion on the Facebook page of one of parties listed under "Connect."

## Connect

Both the Republican and Democratic national committees have Facebook pages. Dozens of third-party committees do as well. Visit their Facebook pages at www .facebook.com/#!/electdemocrats, www.facebook.com/#!/GOP, www.facebook .com/#!/GreenPartyUS, or www.facebook.com/#!/libertarians. (There are many others.) Read a few of the posts on each page and consider whether you agree with any of the comments. If one in particular stands out to you, consider commenting on the post.

*Find links to the sites listed above as well as related activities on wwnorton.com/studyspace.*

# study guide

 **Practice online with:** Chapter 9 Diagnostic Quiz ▪ Chapter 9 Key Term Flashcards

## What Are Political Parties

■ **Define political parties and their general role in politics (pp. 341–42)**

A political party is an organization that seeks influence over government by electing its members to office. Although some people are critical of political parties, they are extremely important to the functioning of a democracy because they increase participation in politics, provide a central cue for citizens to cast informed votes, and organize the business of Congress and governing.

### Key Term

**political parties** (p. 341)

### Practice Quiz

1. A political party is different from an interest group in that a political party *(p. 341)*
   a) seeks to control the entire government by electing its members to office and thereby controlling the government's personnel.
   b) seeks to control only limited, very specific functions of government.
   c) is entirely nonprofit.
   d) has a much larger membership.
   e) has a much smaller membership.

## The Two-Party System in America

■ **Describe how the party system in the United States has changed over time and its main features today (pp. 342–55)**

Historically, political parties in the United States have formed through either "internal mobilization" or "external mobilization." A nation's party system refers to the organization of the parties within the country, the balance of power between and within party coalitions, the parties' social and institutional bases, and the issues and policies around which party competition is organized. Over the course of American history, changes in political forces and alignments have produced six distinctive party systems. Although third parties have occasionally influenced election outcomes and placed new ideas on the political agenda, numerous factors limit their long-term success and they have rarely been able to win elections at the national level.

### Key Terms

**two-party system** (p. 342)

**electoral realignment** (p. 349)

**divided government** (p. 350)

**party polarization** (p. 351)

**third parties** (p. 352)

### Practice Quiz

2. External mobilization occurs when *(p. 344)*
   a) political activists from a foreign country seek to influence American politics by financing the formation of a new political party in the United States.
   b) a politician seeks to pursue a moderate course that places him or her midway between the positions of conservative Republicans and liberal Democrats.
   c) the presidency is controlled by one party while the opposing party controls one or both houses of Congress.
   d) a group of politicians outside government organizes popular support to win governmental power.
   e) political conflicts within government break out and competing factions seek to mobilize popular support.

3. A proportional-representation electoral system is *(p. 342)*
   a) a system that gives each political party representation in proportion to its percentage of the total vote.
   b) a system where a candidate needs to win at least three-fourths of the vote to win the election.
   c) a system where the candidate with the most votes wins the election.
   d) a system where every candidate that wins at least 5 percent of the overall vote is given a seat in the legislature.

e) a system that gives each political party an equal number of seats in the legislature regardless of how many votes they receive in the election.

4. Which party was founded as a political expression of the antislavery movement? *(p. 346)*
   a) American Independent
   b) Prohibition
   c) Republican
   d) Democratic
   e) Whig

5. The periodic episodes in American history in which an "old" dominant political party is replaced by a "new" dominant political party are called *(p. 349)*
   a) constitutional revolutions.
   b) party turnovers.

c) governmental realignments.
d) presidential elections.
e) electoral realignments.

6. Historically, when do realignments occur? *(p. 349)*
   a) typically, every 20 years
   b) whenever a minority party takes over Congress
   c) when large numbers of voters permanently shift their support from one party to another
   d) in even-numbered years
   e) in odd-numbered years

 **Practice Online**
Video exercise: *Time Ripe for a Third Party?*

# Party Organization

■ **Describe how the major American parties are structured at the national, state, and local levels (pp. 355–60)**

Party organizations exist at virtually every level of government in the United States, and they play an important role in structuring electoral competition. At the national level, for example, party organizations assemble conventions every four years that nominate the party's presidential and vice-presidential candidates, draft the party's campaign platform for the presidential race and approve changes in the rules governing party procedures. Similarly, at the state and local level, party organizations are active in recruiting candidates to run for office and in conducting voter registration and get-out-the-vote drives.

## Key Terms

**party organization** (p. 355)

**caucus (political)** (p. 355)

**national convention** (p. 355)

**platform** (p. 356)

**soft money** (p. 357)

**527 committees** (p. 357)

**machines** (p. 358)

**patronage** (p. 358)

## Practice Quiz

7. Which of the following is *not* determined at a party's national convention? *(p. 355)*
   a) the party's candidate for president
   b) the party's candidate for vice president

c) the party's campaign platform for the presidential race
d) the congressional committees party representatives will be assigned to
e) the rules and regulations governing party procedures.

8. The Bipartisan Campaign Reform Act *(p. 357)*
   a) outlawed patronage.
   b) outlawed caucuses.
   c) outlawed hard money.
   d) outlawed soft money.
   e) outlawed party machines.

9. An independent, nonprofit group that receives and disburses funds to influence election campaigns is called *(p. 357)*
   a) a party election committee.
   b) a 527 committee.
   c) a political machine.
   d) a party organization.
   e) a third party.

10. Through which mechanism did party leaders in the late nineteenth and early twentieth centuries maintain their control? *(p. 358)*
   a) civil service reform
   b) soft money contributions
   c) machine politics
   d) electoral reform
   e) political action committees.

 **Practice Online**
Interactive simulation: *Running for Local Office*

# Parties and the Electorate

■ **Identify the social groups that tend to support the Republicans and the Democrats (pp. 360–66)**

Party identification refers to the psychological and emotional attachments people have to one of the political parties. In contemporary American politics, a wide variety of group characteristics, including race, ethnicity, gender, religion, class, ideology, region, and age, are associated with an individual's party identification. Party loyalties in the United States are currently in a state of flux, and roughly one-third of Americans identify themselves as independents rather than as Democrats or Republicans.

## Key Terms

**party identification** (p. 360)

**party activists** (p. 361)

**gender gap** (p. 362)

## Practice Quiz

11. Which of the following best describes in the current state of Americans' party identification? (*p. 361*)
    a) Roughly one-third identify as Democrats, roughly one-third identify as Republicans and roughly one-third identify as independents.
    b) Roughly half identify as Republicans and half identify as Democrats.
    c) Roughly half identify as Democrats, roughly 25 percent identify as Republicans, and roughly 25 percent identify as independents.
    d) Roughly half identify as Republicans, roughly 25 percent identify as Democrats, and roughly 25 percent identify as independents.
    e) A majority of Americans do not identify with any party.

12. The decline in partisan attachment in the electorate is referred to as (*p. 364*)
    a) polarization.
    b) independentification.
    c) unalignment.
    d) realignment.
    e) dealignment.

 **Practice Online**
Video exercise: *Party Identification and Voting Behavior*

# Parties and Elections

■ **Explain the roles parties play in elections (pp. 366–67)**

While political parties have always been important to the electoral process, they have recently taken on a renewed role in recruiting candidates and mobilizing voters. The Constitution sets age and citizenship requirements for candidates but says nothing about who can be recruited for office or who can be nominated by the political parties. As a result, party leaders attempt to identify strong candidates and to interest them in entering the campaign. Once the party's nominee has been selected, parties devote a great deal of energy registering people to vote and convincing them to show up on election day.

## Key Term

**nomination** (p. 366)

## Practice Quiz

13. Parties today are most important in the electoral process in (*p. 366*)
    a) recruiting and nominating candidates for office.
    b) financing all of the campaign's spending.
    c) providing millions of volunteers to mobilize voters.
    d) creating a responsible party government.
    e) changing the electoral laws to make voting easier.

 **Practice Online**
Video exercise: *Pinellas County Republican Executive Committee (PCREC)*

# Parties and Government

■ **Explain how parties organize legislative business and influence policy (pp. 367–70)**

Political parties exert a great deal of influence over the content of public policy, the structure of Congress and the behavior of presidents. The sharp ideological divisions between Democrats and Republicans in recent years mean that election outcomes matter greatly for the kinds of laws that government enacts. Many of the most important organizational features of Congress, such as Speaker, the committee system, and seniority, also depend on the party system. In order to overcome their minority status in the electorate, Republican presidents have spent significantly more time mobilizing voters than Democratic presidents.

## Key Terms

**policy entrepreneur** (p. 368)

**majority party** (p. 369)

**minority party** (p. 369)

## Practice Quiz

14. Which of the following feature of the House of Representatives is determined by a vote of the whole membership rather than by decisions within each party? *(p. 368)*
    a) the assignments of individual members to particular committees.
    b) advancement up the committee ladder.
    c) the ability of individual members to transfer from one committee to another.
    d) the use of the seniority system for determining committee chairs.
    e) selection of the Speaker of the House.

15. Which of the following statements best describes party-building activities from the 1960s to 2004 *(pp. 369–70)*
    a) Party-building activities were legally allowed but both political parties chose to ignore them.
    b) Democrats and Republicans paid equally high levels of attention to party-building.
    c) Democrats paid more attention to party-building than Republicans.
    d) Republicans paid more attention to party-building than Democrats.
    e) Party-building activities were outlawed under federal law.

# For Further Reading

Aldrich, John H. *Why Parties? The Origin and Transformation of Political Parties in America.* Chicago: University of Chicago Press, 1995.

Bartels Larry. *Presidential Primaries and the Dynamics of Public Choice.* Princeton, NJ: Princeton University Press, 1988.

Burnham, Walter Dean. *Critical Elections and the Mainsprings of American Politics.* New York: W.W. Norton, 1970.

Cohen, Marty, David Karol, Hans Noel, and John Zaller. *The Party Decides: Presidential Nominations Before and After Reform.* Chicago: University of Chicago Press, 2008.

Donovan, Todd, and Shaun Bowler. *Reforming the Republic: Democratic Institutions for the New America.* Englewood Cliffs, NJ: Prentice Hall, 2003.

Green, Donald, Bradley Palmquist, and Eric Schickler. *Partisan Hearts and Minds: Political Parties and the Social Identities of Voters.* New Haven, CT: Yale University Press, 2002.

Maisel, L. Sandy. *Political Parties and Elections: A Very Short Introduction.* New York: Oxford University Press, 2007.

McCarty, Nolan, Keith Poole, and Howard Rosenthal. *Polarized America: The Dance of Ideology and Unequal Riches.* Cambridge, MA: MIT Press, 2006.

Polsby, Nelson W. *The Consequences of Party Reform.* New York: Oxford University Press, 1983.

Redlawsk, David, Caroline Tolbert, and Todd Donovan. *Why Iowa? How Caucuses and Sequential Elections Improve the Presidential Nominating Process.* Chicago: University of Chicago Press, 2011.

Schattschneider, E. E. *The Semi-sovereign People.* New York: Harcourt Brace, 1960.

Shefter, Martin. *Political Parties and the State: The American Historical Experience.* Princeton, NJ: Princeton University Press, 1994.

# Recommended Websites

**D.C.'s Political Report**
www.dcpoliticalreport.com/Disclaimer.htm
    Here you can find almost every organization that identifies itself as a political party, including such obscure groups as the American Beer Drinker's Party or the Scorched Earth Party.

**Democratic Party**
www.dnc.org

**Republican Party**
www.GOP.com, www.rnc.org
    These are the official websites for the Democrats and Republicans. Compare the platforms of the two main U.S. parties and see if there's "not a dime's worth of difference" between the two of them.

**Green Party**
www.gp.org

**Libertarian Party**
www.lp.org
    The Green Party and Libertarian Party are two of the largest and most successful third parties in recent years. Find out what these parties are trying to accomplish.

**National Annenberg Election Survey**
http://annenbergpublicpolicycenter.org
    Individual voters tend to develop psychological ties to one party or another. The National Annenberg Election Survey (NAES) uses survey data to track party identification by state every two years. Find out if your state has more Democratic or Republican identifiers.

In the 2012 elections, Barack Obama and Mitt Romney competed for the presidency, offering Americans a choice between two approaches to government and the major issues facing the nation. Elections determine who is in government and thus influence what issues and policies will be taken up by the government.

# Campaigns and Elections

**WHAT GOVERNMENT DOES AND WHY IT MATTERS** In many ways, the 2012 presidential election seemed like a repeat of 2008 but sung in a slightly lower key and with a few new notes. Barack Obama was elected to a second term as president in a close race against Republican challenger Mitt Romney. Sixty percent of eligible voters turned out to vote in the general election, down slightly from 62 percent in 2008. Obama's campaign message that he would keep the nation moving "forward" replaced his 2008 theme of "hope," but the technical aspects of Obama's ground game in swing states remained the same. Notably, Obama's efforts to mobilize Democratic voters were more important than efforts to persuade Republicans or independents to vote for him. Obama won nearly every battleground state, including Colorado, Iowa, Ohio, New Hampshire, Virginia, Wisconsin, and Florida. Republicans retained control of the House, and Democrats retained control of the Senate.

The biggest issue for voters in 2012 was the economy, with three-quarters saying that economic conditions were poor. Historically, a weak economy and high unemployment makes re-election difficult for an incumbent president. However, the electorate was evenly divided as to whether responsibility for the country's economic woes rested with Obama or his predecessor, George W. Bush. Obama was re-elected with the highest unemployment rate of any incumbent since Franklin Delano Roosevelt.

Who supported Obama in 2012? While Obama's support among young and black voters did decline slightly from 2008, he still received large majorities of the vote from both groups. Obama's biggest gains came from Asian and Latino voters. Over 70 percent of Latinos voted for Obama, up from 61 percent in 2008. Minority voters accounted for 45 percent of Obama's support, reflecting the expanded power of black, Latino, and Asian voters. While whites made up 77 percent of the electorate in 2004 and 74 percent in 2008, they accounted for just 72 percent in 2012, according to exit polls released immediately after the election. Romney won among whites, men, older people, affluent voters, evangelical Christians, and those from suburban and rural counties.

As expected, the 2012 presidential election shattered previous records for campaign spending. In the aftermath of the Supreme Court's 2010 *Citizens United* decision, which allowed unlimited political spending by unaffiliated groups, both majority party candidates opted out of the campaign financing system that imposes spending limits in return for government financing. Spending in the presidential race, including expenditures by "super PACs," was $2.6 billion, and the combined cost of congressional and presidential races, including money spent by candidates' campaigns, their parties, and super PACs, was a staggering $6 billion, up from $5.3 billion in 2008 and $4.2 billion in 2004.

Finally, the influence of digital media and political pollsters reached new heights in 2012. While many in the mass media painted the election as a too-close-to-predict nail-biter, the growing sophistication of opinion polling suggested otherwise, predicting a solid victory for Obama. By aggregating thousands of polling results, experts like Nate Silver of the FiveThirtyEight blog accurately forecast the electoral outcomes well in advance of November. Not only did the Internet continue to grow as a forum for political news, but the art of predicting election outcomes became a science.

# chaptergoals

- Describe the major rules and procedures of elections in the United States (pages 381–94)

- Explain how campaigns are typically conducted (pages 394–403)

- Identify the major factors that influence voters' decisions (pages 403–8)

- Analyze the strategies, issues, and outcomes of the 2012 elections (pages 408–18)

- Describe how candidates raise the money they need to run (pages 419–25)

# Elections in America

Describe the major
rules and procedures of
elections in the United
States

Voting in elections is the most important form of participation in American politics, and the most common. Elections allow average citizens to hold their elected representatives in government accountable. Elections are at the heart of democracy. In the United States, elections are held at regular intervals. National presidential elections take place every four years, on the first Tuesday in November; congressional elections are held every two years, also on the first Tuesday in November. Congressional elections that do not coincide with a presidential election are sometimes called **midterm elections**. Elections for state and local office also often coincide with national elections. Some state and local governments, however, prefer to schedule their local elections in years that do not coincide with national elections, to avoid having national considerations distract from or unduly influence local contests.

In the American federal system, the responsibility for running elections is highly decentralized, and rests largely with state and county governments. State laws specify how elections are to be administered, determine the boundaries of

**midterm elections** congressional elections that do not coincide with a presidential election; also called off-year elections

*Elections are the most important way that Americans participate in politics. Some of the rules for American elections have been in place since the Founding, while others have evolved over time. This painting shows election day in Philadelphia in 1815.*

electoral districts, and specify candidate and voter qualifications. Elections are administered by state, county, and city election boards that are responsible for establishing and staffing polling places and verifying the eligibility of individuals who come to vote.

## Types of Elections

Four types of elections are held in the United States: primary elections, general elections, runoff elections, and initiative and referendum elections, (in which proposed laws are placed on the ballot for a popular vote). We discuss the first three types here; we will take a closer look at ballot initiatives and referenda later in the section "Direct-Democracy Elections."

**Primary elections** are held to select each party's candidates for the general election. In the case of local and statewide offices, the winners of primary elections face one another as their parties' nominees in the general election. At the presidential level, however, primary elections are indirect; they are used to select state delegates to the national conventions, at which the major party presidential candidates are chosen. America is one of few nations in the world to hold primary elections. In most countries, nominations are controlled by party officials, as they once were in the United States. The primary system was introduced at the turn of the twentieth century by Progressive reformers who hoped to weaken the power of party leaders by taking candidate nominations out of their hands.

Under the laws of some states, only registered members of a political party may vote in a primary election to select that party's candidates. This is called a **closed primary**. Other states allow all registered voters to choose on the day of the primary in which party's primary they will participate. This is called an **open primary**. A primary election is like a prelim in a sporting event. It is used to select the best candidate to represent the political party in the general election. Thus primary elections are races where Democrats compete against Democrats and Republicans against

**primary elections** elections held to select a party's candidate for the general election

**closed primary** a primary election in which voters can participate in the nomination of candidates, but only of the party in which they are enrolled for a period of time prior to primary day

**open primary** a primary election in which the voter can wait until the day of the primary to choose which party to enroll in to select candidates for the general election

*Iowa caucus-goers were the first to vote in the 2012 presidential primaries. The United States is one of few nations in the world to hold primary elections and caucuses.*

Republicans. Today, party conventions are largely symbolic, and the delegates won by each candidate in the primary elections largely determine who the party nominee is.

The primary is followed by the **general election**, the decisive electoral contest. The winner of the general election is elected to office for a specified term. In some states, however, mainly in the Southeast, if no candidate wins an absolute majority in the primary, a **runoff election** is held before the general election. This situation is most likely to arise if there are more than two candidates, none of whom has received a majority of the votes cast. A runoff election is held between the two candidates who received the largest number of votes.

## Plurality and Winner-Take-All Electoral Rules

In some countries, to win a seat in the parliament or other governing body, a candidate must receive an absolute majority (50 percent plus 1) of all the votes cast in the relevant district. This type of electoral system is called a **majority system**. In the United States, it is used in primary elections by some southern states. Majority systems usually include a provision for a runoff election between the two top candidates, because if the initial race draws several candidates, there is little chance that any one will receive a majority.

In other nations, as in the United States, candidates for office need not win an absolute majority of the votes cast to win an election. Instead, victory is awarded to the candidate who receives the most votes, regardless of the actual percentage this represents. A candidate receiving 50 percent, or 30 percent, or even 20 percent, of the popular vote can win if no other candidate receives more votes. This type of electoral system is called a **plurality system** and is used in virtually all general elections in the United States. In part because of plurality election rules, the United States has usually had only two significant political parties, whereas with proportional representation, many European countries have developed multiparty systems. (See Chapter 9 for more on the two-party system in the United States.)

Most European nations employ a third type of electoral system, called **proportional representation**. Under proportional rules, competing political parties are awarded legislative seats in rough proportion to the percentage of popular votes that each party won. A party that wins 30 percent of the vote will receive roughly 30 percent of the seats in the parliament or other representative body. In the United States, proportional representation is used by many states in presidential primary elections, but not in general election for president or Congress. Proportional representation benefits smaller groups because it usually allows a party to win legislative seats with fewer votes than would be required under a majority or plurality system. A party that wins 10 percent of the national vote might win 10 percent of the parliamentary seats. In the United States, by contrast, a party that wins 10 percent of the vote would probably win no seats in Congress. Because they give small parties little chance of success, plurality and majority systems tend to reduce the number of competitive political parties.

## The Ballot

Before the 1890s, voters cast ballots according to political parties. Each party printed its own ballots, listed only its own candidates for each office, and employed party workers to distribute the ballots at the polls. Because voters had to choose which party's ballot to use, it was very difficult for a voter to cast anything other than a **straight-ticket vote**. The advent of a new, neutral ballot during the Progressive era

**general election** a regularly scheduled election involving most districts in the nation or state, in which voters select officeholders; in the United States, general elections for national office and most state and local offices are held on the first Tuesday following the first Monday in November in even-numbered years (every four years for presidential elections)

**runoff election** a "second round" election in which voters choose between the top two candidates from the first round

**majority system** a type of electoral system in which, to win a seat in the parliament or other representative body, a candidate must receive a majority of all the votes cast in the relevant district

**plurality system** a type of electoral system in which, to win a seat in the parliament or other representative body, a candidate need only receive the most votes in the election, not necessarily a majority of votes cast

**proportional representation** a multiple-member district system that allows each political party representation in proportion to its percentage of the total vote

**straight-ticket voting** selecting candidates from the same political party for all offices on the ballot

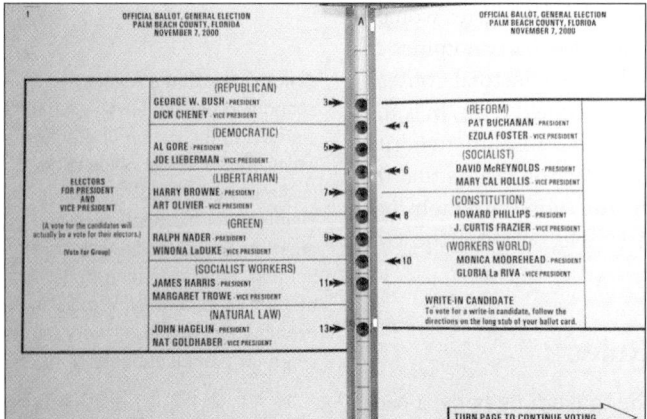

*Some of the devices that have been used to record votes in the United States are notably prone to errors that can affect election results. For example, in 2000 in Florida's Palm Beach County, some voters were confused by the "butterfly ballot" (left), which made it difficult to match candidates and votes. In the 2012 elections, many of the nation's voters cast their ballots on electronic touch-screen machines. Critics of touch-screen voting systems, however, question the machines for their accuracy and security against fraud.*

(at the turn of the twentieth century) brought a significant change to electoral procedure. The new ballot (call the Australian ballot) was prepared and administered by the government rather than the political parties. Each ballot was identical and included the names of all candidates for office. This ballot reform made it possible for voters to make their choices on the basis of the individual rather than the collective merits of a party's candidates.

Because all candidates for the same office now appeared on the same ballot, voters were no longer forced to choose straight-ticket voting. This gave rise to the phenomenon of split-ticket voting in American elections, where voters may vote for a Democrat for Congress and a Republican for governor. If a voter supports candidates from more than one party in the same election, he or she is said to be casting a split-ticket vote. Voters who support only one party's candidates are casting a straight-ticket vote. Straight-ticket voting occurs most often when a voter casts a ballot for a party's presidential candidate and then "automatically" votes for the rest of that party's candidates. The result of this voting pattern is known as the **coattail effect**.

**coattail effect** the result of voters casting their ballot for president or governor and "automatically" voting for the remainder of the party's ticket

Prior to the reform of the ballot, it was not uncommon for an entire incumbent administration to be swept from office and replaced by an entirely new set of officials. In the absence of a real possibility of split-ticket voting, the electorate could express any desire for change only as a vote against all candidates of the party in power. Because of this, the possibility always existed, particularly at the state and local levels, that an insurgent slate committed to policy change could be swept into power. The party ballot thus increased the potential impact of elections on the government's composition. Although this potential may not always have been realized, the party ballot at least increased the chance that electoral decisions could lead to policy changes. By contrast, because it permitted choice on the basis of candidates' individual appeal, ticket splitting led to increasingly divided partisan control of government.

The actual ballots used by voters vary from county to county across the United States. Some counties employ paper ballots, while most use mechanical voting machines or computerized systems. Not surprisingly, the controversy surrounding Florida's presidential vote in 2000 led to a closer look at the different balloting systems, and it became apparent that some of them produced unreliable results. When many counties moved to introduce computerized voting systems, critics warned that they might be vulnerable to unauthorized use or "hacking." During the 2008 Ohio primaries a software error was discovered that potentially affected electronic voting machines used in 34 states. The machine's manufacturer moved to correct the error before the November national elections, and the 2008, 2010, and 2012 elections produced few complaints about electronic voting.

## Legislative Elections and Electoral Districts

The boundaries for congressional and state legislative districts in the United States are usually redrawn by the states every 10 years in response to population changes determined by the U.S. Census. This redrawing of district boundaries is called **redistricting**. The geographic shape of district boundaries is influenced by several factors. Some of the most important influences have been federal court decisions. In the 1963 case of *Gray v. Sanders*, and in the 1964 cases of *Wesberry v. Sanders* and *Reynolds v. Sims*, the Supreme Court held that legislative districts within a state must include roughly equal populations, so as to accord with the principle of "one person, one vote."[1] During the 1980s the Supreme Court also declared that legislative districts should, insofar as possible, be contiguous, compact, and consistent with existing political subdivisions.[2]

Despite these legal cases, state lawmakers routinely seek to influence electoral outcomes to favor one political party over another (or incumbents over challengers) in drawing electoral districts for Congress and state legislatures. This strategy is called **gerrymandering**, named for a nineteenth-century Massachusetts governor, Elbridge Gerry, who was alleged to have designed a district in the shape of a salamander to promote his party's interests. The principle behind gerrymandering is simple: different populations of voters in districts can produce different electoral results. For example, by dispersing the members of a particular group across two or more districts, state legislators can dilute that group's voting power and prevent it from electing a representative in any district. (In the lingo of gerrymandering, this is called "cracking.") Alternatively, by concentrating the members of a party in as few districts as possible, state lawmakers can try to ensure that their opponents will elect as few representatives as possible. (This is referred to as "packing.") The widespread practice of gerrymandering has created many safe districts in Congress, where incumbents rarely face a serious challenger, even if there are elections every two years in the House. This is one reason most members of Congress are elected in landslide elections, and why 98 percent of incumbents are re-elected.

The federal government has supported congressional districts made up primarily of minority group members, a practice intended to increase the number of African Americans and Latinos elected to public office. The Supreme Court has viewed this effort as constitutionally dubious, however. Beginning with the 1993 case of *Shaw v. Reno*, the Court has generally rejected efforts to create such **majority-minority districts**.[3] The Court has asserted that districting based exclusively on racial criteria is unlawful.

## Presidential Elections

While many of the rules related to presidential elections and congressional elections are the same, presidential elections have certain special features. First, the president is technically elected by the electoral college, not by popular vote. Second, presidential candidates from the

**redistricting** the process of redrawing election districts and redistributing legislative representatives. This happens every ten years to reflect shifts in population or in response to legal challenges in existing districts

**gerrymandering** apportionment of voters in districts in such a way as to give unfair advantage to one racial or ethnic group or political party

**majority-minority district** a gerrymandered voting district that improves the chances of minority candidates by making selected minority groups the majority within the district

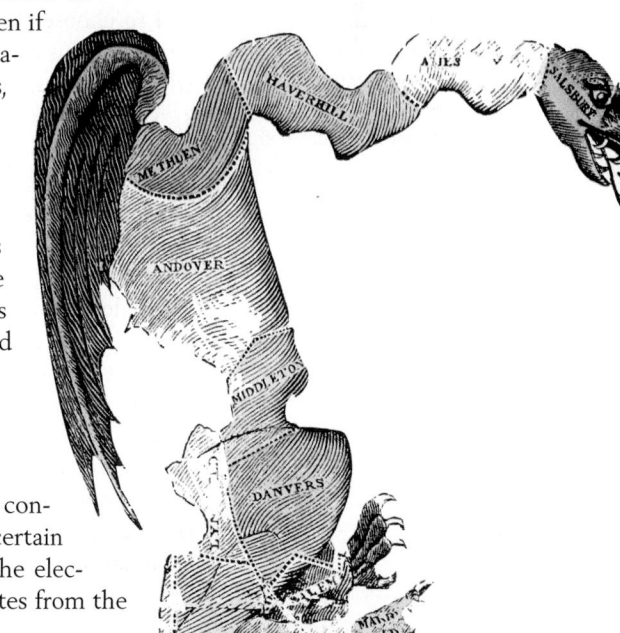

*The drawing of electoral districts is always a matter of controversy, with opponents accusing one another of "gerrymandering"— drawing district boundaries in such a way as to serve a particular group's interests. The original gerrymander was a districting plan attributed to the Massachusetts governor Elbridge Gerry (1744–1814) that had the shape of a salamander.*

*In a number of recent cases, black, white, and Hispanic voters have claimed to be the victims of racial gerrymanders. For instance, in 1995 the Supreme Court held that one Georgia district, which was 64 percent African American, was unfairly based on race. Meanwhile, no challenge was made to Texas's 6th District, which was predominantly white. In 2006, the Supreme Court rejected part of a Texas redistricting plan on the grounds that it suppressed minority votes, though the Court upheld most of the plan.*

two major parties are officially nominated at the parties' national conventions, following primary elections and caucuses to select delegates to the conventions. While primary elections are also used to select candidates in congressional and other types of elections, the national convention delegate system for nominating candidates is unique to presidential elections.

**The Electoral College** In the early history of popular voting, nations often made use of indirect elections. In these elections, voters would choose the members of an intermediate body. These members would, in turn, select public officials. The assumption underlying such a process was that ordinary citizens were not qualified to choose their leaders and could not be trusted to do so directly. The last vestige of this procedure in America is the **electoral college**, the group of electors who formally select the president and vice president of the United States.

When Americans go to the polls on Election Day, they are technically not voting directly for presidential candidates. Instead, voters within each state are choosing among slates of electors selected by each state's party and pledged, if elected, to support that party's presidential candidate. These are indirect elections. To win, a U.S. presidential candidate must receive a majority of the votes in the electoral college, which are awarded to states based on the size of their congressional delegation.[4] In each state (except Maine and Nebraska), the party candidate who wins the popular vote wins all the electoral college votes for that state, in a winner-take-all fashion.[5] Each state has electoral college votes equal to the size of its congressional delegation (House plus Senate), for a total of 538 electoral votes for the 50 states and the District of Columbia. The presidential candidate with a majority of votes in the electoral college—not necessarily the candidate with the most votes from the people—becomes president. No other country uses an electoral college to mediate between a national or direct/popular vote for presidential candidates and the winner.

**electoral college** the presidential electors from each state who meet after the popular election to cast ballots for president and vice president

Support for changing the election rules in the United States has been gaining momentum since the contested 2000 presidential election, which was followed by a lengthy legal battle in Florida that ultimately ended with the U.S. Supreme Court's decision in *Bush v. Gore*.[6] The decision resolved the dispute in Florida, which handed George W. Bush the presidency. Even though the Democratic candidate, Vice President Al Gore, had won 500,000 more votes nationwide, Republican George W. Bush won a majority of the electoral college and was elected president. Only on rare occasions in American history has the winner of the popular vote been defeated, but this controversial election created ripple effects in motivating efforts to reform American elections.

Another rare occurrence is if an elector breaks his or her pledge and votes for the other party's candidate. For example, in 1976, when the Republicans carried the state of Washington, one Republican elector from that state refused to vote for Gerald Ford, the Republican presidential nominee. Many states have now enacted statutes formally binding electors to their pledges, but some constitutional authorities doubt whether such statutes are enforceable.

Throughout history there have been a few cases where the electoral college failed to produce a majority for any candidate. In the election of 1800, Thomas Jefferson, the Jeffersonian Republican Party's presidential candidate, and Aaron Burr, that party's vice-presidential candidate, received an equal number of votes in the electoral college, throwing the election to the House of Representatives. (The electoral rules at that time made no distinction between presidential and vice-presidential candidates, specifying only that the individual receiving a majority of electoral votes would be named president, and that the individual receiving the second most votes would be the vice president.) Some members of the Federalist Party in Congress suggested that they should seize the opportunity to damage the Republican cause by supporting Burr and denying Jefferson the presidency. The Federalist leader Alexander Hamilton put a stop to this mischievous notion, however, and made certain that his party supported Jefferson. Hamilton's actions enraged Burr and helped lead to the infamous duel between the two men, in which Burr killed Hamilton. The Twelfth Amendment, ratified in 1804, was designed to prevent a repetition of such an inconclusive election by providing for separate electoral college votes for president and vice president.

In the 1824 election, four candidates—John Quincy Adams, Andrew Jackson, Henry Clay, and William H. Crawford—divided the electoral vote; no one of them received a majority. The House of Representatives eventually chose Adams over the others, even though Jackson had won more electoral and popular votes. After 1824 the two major political parties began to dominate presidential politics to such an extent that by December of each election year, only two candidates remained for the electors to choose between, thus ensuring that one would receive a majority.

On all but three occasions since 1824, the electoral vote has simply ratified the nationwide popular vote. Since electoral votes are won on a state-by-state basis, it is mathematically possible for a candidate who receives a nationwide popular plurality to fail to carry states whose electoral votes would add up to a majority. Thus, in 1876, Rutherford B. Hayes was the winner in the electoral college despite receiving fewer popular votes than his rival, Samuel Tilden. In 1888, Grover Cleveland received more popular votes than Benjamin Harrison, but received fewer electoral votes. And in 2000, Al Gore outpolled his opponent, George W. Bush, by more than 500,000 votes, but narrowly lost the electoral college by a mere four electoral votes.

Calls for eliminating the electoral college and using a national popular vote for president are widespread, as surveys show that more than three in four Americans would prefer such a direct election for the president.[7] Replacing the electoral college with another system would require a constitutional amendment that most agree would be extremely difficult to pass. However, reform is still possible, since the constitution allows states to choose the method of selecting presidential electors. One example of a recent attempt to reform the electoral college is the National Popular Vote plan, which has been introduced as a bill in a number of state legislatures.[8] Under the proposed rule change, a state's Electoral College votes would go to the candidate who won the national popular vote, not the candidate with a plurality of votes in that specific state. States would enter a compact with other states making the same change, which would go into effect when a number of states representing a majority in the electoral college (270 electoral votes) approved it. The reform would effectively bypass the electoral college without the need for an amendment to the U.S. Constitution. To date, 10 states have enacted the bill into law. Replacing the electoral college with a national popular vote would dramatically alter the influence of states and change the nature of presidential campaigns. Competition would no longer be confined to a few large battleground states, such as Florida, Ohio, and Pennsylvania, but would likely focus more on urban areas where the most votes are found.[9]

**Nominating Presidential Candidates: Primaries and Caucuses** Before the general election, the two major parties must select candidates to represent the parties in the general election. The major-party presidential nominations are quite different from the nominating process employed for other political offices. In years when an incumbent president is running for re-election, as in 2012, one party's nomination may not be contested. When the Democratic or Republican presidential nomination is contested, however, candidates typically compete to win national convention delegates in all 50 states. Most states hold primary elections to choose their delegates, but about a third of the states hold **caucuses**, essentially a party business meeting rather than an election, to choose candidates for president. Caucuses begin with precinct-level meetings throughout the state. The most famous caucuses are those in Iowa, the first state to select presidential candidates in the calendar year. Citizens attending the caucuses typically elect delegates to statewide conventions, at which delegates to the national party conventions are then chosen.

The primaries and caucuses traditionally begin in January of a presidential election year and end in June (see Table 10.1). Early voting states, such as Iowa and New Hampshire, are important because they can help candidates secure media attention, campaign contributions, and increased standing in the polls, or what is called "momentum." Candidates spend months courting voter support in these two states. A candidate who performs better than expected in Iowa and New Hampshire will usually be able to secure public support and media coverage for subsequent races. A candidate who fares poorly in these two states may be written off as a loser, and drop out of the race. Gradually, the presidential nomination has become "front-loaded," with states vying with one another to increase their political influence by holding their nominating processes earlier. But is it fair that two relatively small states (in terms of population) such as Iowa and New Hampshire should have such outsize influence in picking presidents?

**caucus (political)** a normally closed political party business meeting of citizens or law makers to select candidates elect officers, plan strategy, or make decisions regarding legislative matters

*In the election of 1800, the electoral college didn't produce a majority for any candidate; it was split between Thomas Jefferson, Aaron Burr, and John Adams, with Jefferson and Burr tied at 73 electoral votes each. The decision was put to the House of Representatives, which chose Jefferson.*

## TABLE 10.1

## The 2012 Primaries and Caucuses Calendar

| DATE | STATE | ELECTION TYPE |
| --- | --- | --- |
| January 3 | Iowa | Caucus |
| January 10 | New Hampshire | Primary |
| January 21 | South Carolina | Primary (R) |
| | Nevada | Caucus (D) |
| January 31 | Florida | Primary |
| February 4 | Nevada | Caucus (R) |
| February 4–11 | Maine | Caucus (R) |
| February 7 | Colorado, Minnesota | Caucus (R) |
| | Missouri | Primary |
| February 28 | Arizona, Michigan | Primary |
| March 3 | Washington | Caucus (R) |
| March 6 | Alaska, Idaho | Caucus (R) |
| | Minnesota | Caucus (D) |
| | North Dakota | Caucus |
| | Georgia, Massachusetts, Ohio, Oklahoma, Tennessee, Vermont | Primary |
| | Virginia | Primary (R) |
| March 6–10 | Wyoming | Caucus (R) |
| March 7 | Hawaii | Caucus (D) |
| March 10 | Kansas | Caucus (R) |
| March 11 | Maine | Caucus (D) |
| March 13 | Alabama, Mississippi | Primary |
| | Hawaii | Caucus (R) |
| | Utah | Caucus (D) |
| March 17 | Missouri | Caucus (R) |
| March 20 | Illinois | Primary |
| March 24 | Louisiana | Primary |
| April 3 | District of Columbia, Maryland, Wisconsin | Primary |
| April 9 | Alaska | Caucus (D) |
| April 14 | Idaho, Kansas, Nebraska, Wyoming | Caucus (D) |
| April 15 | Washington | Caucus (D) |
| April 24 | Connecticut, Delaware, New York, Pennsylvania, Rhode Island | Primary |
| May 8 | Indiana, North Carolina, West Virginia | Primary |
| May 19–June 1 | Colorado | Caucus (D) |
| May 15 | Nebraska, Oregon | Primary |
| May 22 | Arkansas, Kentucky | Primary |
| May 29 | Texas | Primary |
| June 5 | California, Montana, New Jersey, New Mexico, South Dakota | Primary |
| | North Dakota | Caucus (D) |
| June 26 | Utah | Primary (R) |

NOTES: Many states will not hold a Democratic nominating contest if only one candidate qualified for the ballot. The Missouri primary is non-binding. The Missouri Republican Party chose convention delegates in a March 17 caucus.

SOURCE: The United States Elections Project, http://elections.gmu.edu (accessed 8/16/12).

As we saw in Chapter 7, if Barack Obama had not won in Iowa, most commentators believe he would not have been able to go on to capture the Democratic nomination for president in 2008. One study found that the change in mass media coverage that candidates receive before and after the Iowa caucuses predicts how well they will do in the New Hampshire primary, and in presidential primaries nationwide measured by vote share.[10] It is not winning the Iowa caucuses that matters, but doing better than expected by the media. President Carter came in second (after "undecided") in the 1976 Iowa caucuses, for example, but beat media expectations and used this success to propel his nomination to the White House. With the rise of the Internet, media coverage of early nominating events is even greater, and may further increase the importance of states holding early primaries and caucuses.[11]

As noted in Chapter 9, the Democratic Party requires that state presidential primaries allocate delegates on the basis of proportional representation; Democratic candidates win delegates in rough proportion to their percentage of the primary vote. The Republican Party does not require proportional representation, but most states have now written proportional representation requirements into their election laws. A few states use the winner-take-all system, by which the candidate with the most votes wins all the party's delegates in that state. When the primaries and caucuses are concluded, it is usually clear which candidates have won their parties' nominations.

**Nominating Presidential Candidates: Party Conventions**  For more than 50 years after America's founding, presidential nominations were controlled by each party's congressional caucus—all the party's members in the House and the Senate. Critics referred to this process as the "King Caucus" and charged that it did not fairly represent the views of party members throughout the nation. In 1824 the King Caucus method came under severe attack when the Democratic Party caucus failed to nominate Andrew Jackson, the candidate with the greatest support among both party members and supporters outside the capital. In the 1830s the party convention was devised as a way of allowing party leaders throughout the nation to participate in selecting presidential candidates, although the U.S. Constitution is silent on procedures for picking presidents. The first such convention was held by the Anti-Masonic Party in 1831. The Democratic Party held its first convention in 1832, when Andrew Jackson was nominated for a second term.

As it developed during the course of the next century, the convention became the decisive institution in the presidential nominating processes of the two major parties. The convention was a deliberative body in which party groups argued, negotiated, and eventually reached a decision. The convention was composed of delegations from each state. The size of a state's delegation depended on the state's population, and each delegate was allowed one vote for the purpose of nominating the party's presidential and vice-presidential candidates. Before 1936, victory required the support of two-thirds of the delegates. Until 1968, state delegations voted according to the "unit rule," by which all the members of the state delegation would vote for the candidate favored by the majority of the state's delegates. This practice was designed to maximize a state's influence in the nominating process. In 1968 both major parties abolished the unit rule.

Between the 1830s and World War II, national convention delegates were generally selected by a state's party leaders. Usually the delegates were public officials, political activists, and party notables from all regions of the state, representing most major party factions. Some delegates would arrive at the convention having pledged in advance to give their support to a particular presidential candidate. Most delegates were uncommitted, however. This fact, coupled with the unit rule, allowed state party leaders (i.e., the delegates) to negotiate with one another and with presidential candidates for their support. Typically, many votes were needed before the nomination could be decided. Often deadlocks developed among the most powerful party factions, and state leaders would be forced to compromise, sometimes choosing a little-known candidate. Among the more famous "dark horse" nominees were James Polk in 1844 and Warren Harding in 1920. Although he was virtually unknown, Polk won the Democratic nomination when it became clear that none of the more established candidates could win. Similarly, Harding, another political unknown, won the Republican nomination after the major candidates had fought one another to a standstill.

Over time, reformers came to view the convention as a symbol of rule by party leaders. During the Progressive era, at the turn of the twentieth century, many states adopted primary elections to choose presidential candidates, at which average citizens would have a voice in picking presidents. Today, as we saw earlier in this chapter, the nomination is determined in a series of primary elections and local party caucuses held in virtually all 50 states during the months prior to the party's national convention. These primaries and caucuses determine how each state's convention delegates will vote. Candidates now arrive at the convention knowing who has enough delegate support in hand to assure a victory in the first round of balloting. State party leaders no longer serve as power brokers, and the party's presidential and vice-presidential choices are made relatively quickly.

Even though the party convention no longer controls presidential nominations, it still has a number of important tasks. The first of these is the adoption of party rules concerning such matters as convention delegate selection and future presidential primary elections. In 1972, for example, the Democratic convention accepted rules requiring convention delegates to be broadly representative of the party's membership in terms of race and gender. After those rules were passed, the convention refused to seat several state delegations that were deemed not to meet this standard. Another important task for the convention is the drafting of a party **platform**, a statement of principles and pledges around which the delegates can unite. Although the two major parties' platforms tend to contain many similar principles and platitudes, differences between their platforms can be significant. In recent years, for example, the Republican platform has advocated tax cuts and taken strong positions opposing affirmative action and abortion. The Democratic platform, on the other hand, has focused on the importance of maintaining welfare and regulatory programs. A close reading of the party platforms can reveal many of the ideological differences between the parties.

Today, convention **delegates** are generally political activists with strong positions on social and political issues. In states such as Michigan and Iowa, local party caucuses choose many of the delegates who will actually attend the national convention. In most of the remaining states, primary elections determine how a state's delegation will vote, but the actual delegates are selected by state party officials. Delegate votes won in primary elections are apportioned to candidates on the basis of proportional representation. Thus, a candidate who received 30 percent of the vote in the California Democratic primary would receive roughly 30 percent of the state's delegate votes at the party's national convention.

*Although the party's nominees for the president and the vice president are "officially" announced at the party conventions, they are actually selected much earlier through caucuses and primary elections. In 2012, Mitt Romney and Paul Ryan formally accepted the Republican nomination at the national convention.*

**platform** a party document, written at a national convention, that contains party philosophy, principles, and positions on issues

**delegate** political activist selected to vote at a party's national convention

As was mentioned earlier, the Democratic Party requires that a state's convention delegation be representative of that state's Democratic electorate in terms of race, gender, and age. Republican delegates, by contrast, are more likely to be male and white. The Democrats also reserve slots for elected Democratic Party officials, called **superdelegates**. All the Democratic governors and about 80 percent of the party's members of Congress now attend the national convention as delegates.

Once the nominations have been settled and most other party business has been resolved, the presidential and vice-presidential nominees deliver acceptance speeches. These speeches are opportunities for the nominees to begin their formal campaigns on a positive note, and they are usually meticulously crafted to make as positive an impression on the electorate as possible.

## Direct-Democracy Elections

Beyond presidential and congressional elections, 24 states also provide for the initiative process, as we saw in Chapter 1. **Ballot initiatives** allow citizens to circulate petitions to place policy change or proposed laws directly on the ballot for a popular vote. If a ballot measure receives majority support, it becomes law. Controversial issues frequently appear on the ballot of states with the initiative process—for example, proposals to ban same-sex marriage, raise the minimum wage, adopt legislative term limits, and reform the election process. In recent years, voters in several states have voted to cut taxes, to prohibit social services for illegal immigrants, to end affirmative action, to protect open space and the environment, and to prevent offshore drilling. At the turn of the twentieth century, ballot initiatives were used to grant women suffrage (the right to vote), to prevent child labor, to limit the work day to eight hours, and to allow voters to elect U.S. senators directly (rather than having them chosen by state legislatures). Ballot initiative campaigns often involve high spending by proponents and opponents, and mass media campaigns than can rival that of congressional and presidential candidates within a state. All 50 states have the legislative **referendum**, in which the state legislature refers laws to the voters for a popular vote. Referendum votes are required for changes to state constitutions.

The initiative and the referendum, both adopted by Progressive reformers at the turn of the twentieth century, are examples of what is called direct democracy. They allow voters to govern directly without intervention by government officials or the political parties. The validity of ballot measure results, however, is subject to judicial action. If a court finds that an initiative violates the state or national constitution, it can overturn the result. This happened in the case of a 1994 California initiative curtailing social services to illegal aliens and again in 2012 when the federal courts overturned California's Proposition 8 banning same-sex marriage.[12]

Ballot initiatives not only change policy but also appear to affect political engagement. One study found that states with initiatives on the ballot have higher voter turnout over time. Citizens living in direct-democracy states report more interest in politics, and are more likely to discuss politics. Why is this so? If electoral rules offer people more opportunities to participate in decisions, those institutions may have an "educative" effect on those people.[13] Representative democracy allows citizens to vote on who gets to make political decisions; ballot propositions go further, offering voters the possibility of directly making public policy. By having more opportunities to act politically, citizens may learn to participate more, and come to believe their participation has meaning.

Issue elections provide information to voters in the form of political campaigns and attention in the mass media. Ballot measures concerning controversial policy issues such as same-sex marriage, taxes for the wealthy, nonpartisan redistricting, and immigration rights generate their own campaigns, with television, newspaper, and Internet ads; professional campaign consultants; and organized interests that contact potential voters.[14] Like candidate races, issue elections generate free media coverage, paid media campaigns, and grassroots mobilization efforts. Legislative hearings, court disputes, and signature-gathering petition drives to qualify ballot measures may generate additional media attention. Initiative campaigns and the mass media provide information and appeals to the electorate that can stimulate political participation.[15]

*In 2010, voters in Missouri decided several referenda, including a proposition to block government-mandated health insurance.*

Hundreds of initiatives and referenda appear on state election ballots every two years, often with millions of dollars in campaign expenditures. Initiative campaigns can pump millions of dollars into the American states each election. In the 2002 elections, almost $9.00 per capita was spent on initiative campaigns in Arizona, more than the amount spent on any single candidate race, congressional or statewide. In the 2004 presidential elections, Oregon topped the list, with $8.98 on ballot initiative expenditure per capita, followed by Nevada ($6.65) and California ($5.95).[16] More money was spent per capita on initiatives in California in 2004 than on any of the other major candidate races in the state. Spending on ballot initiatives continues to rise with each election. Although not well recognized, ballot measures and their associated campaigns often draw more media attention and spending than prominent candidate races. For example, in 2012, Colorado and Washington voters approved measures to legalize marijuana sale and consumption. More initiatives and referenda have appeared on state ballots in the last 30 years than at any other time in American history, outside of the Progressive era.

Controversial ballot propositions can have spillover effects, shaping both the national agenda and evaluations of and voting for gubernatorial and congressional candidates.[17] The tax revolt in the late 1970s, with initiatives and referenda on many state ballots lowering taxes, may have contributed to Republican Ronald Reagan's successful bid for the White House in 1980. Ballot measures banning same-sex marriage placed on the ballot of 13 states may have primed voting for the Republican presidential candidate in the 2004 election, George W. Bush. In 2006, coordinated ballot measures in multiple state raising the minimum wage may have influenced voters to focus on the economy, and increased voting for Democrats in Congress and for Democratic governors. Placing issues on the ballot as part of an effort to influence candidate elections is a relatively new, but important strategy, for political campaigns. Such effects on candidate races highlight just how important issue elections are in American politics.

Eighteen states also have legal provisions for **recall** elections, which allow voters to remove governors and other state officials from office prior to the expiration of their terms. Generally, a recall effort begins with a petition campaign. In California, for example, if 12 percent of those who voted in the last general election

**recall** a procedure to allow voters to remove state officials from office before their terms expire by circulating petitions to call a vote

sign petitions demanding a special recall election, one must be scheduled by the state board of elections. In 2003 many California voters blamed Governor Gray Davis for the state's $38 billion budget deficit, allowing his opponents to secure enough signatures to force a vote. In October 2003, Davis became only the second governor in American history to be recalled by his state's electorate. Under California law, voters are also asked to choose a replacement for the official whom they've dismissed, and in 2003 they elected Arnold Schwarzenegger to be their governor. Federal officials, such as the president and members of Congress, are not subject to recall.

## ● Election Campaigns

**campaign** an effort by political candidates and their supporters to win the backing of donors, political activists, and voters in their quest for political office

> **Explain how campaigns are typically conducted**

A **campaign** is an effort by political candidates (and their supporters) to win the backing of donors, political activists, and voters in their quest for political office. Campaigns precede every primary and general election. Because of the complexity of the campaign process, and because of the amount of money that candidates must raise, presidential campaigns usually begin almost two years before the November presidential elections. The campaign for any office consists of a number of steps. Candidates must first organize an exploratory committee consisting of supporters who will help them raise funds and bring their names to the attention of the media and potential donors. This step is relatively easy for a candidate currently in office, known as an **incumbent**. Incumbents usually are already well known and have little difficulty attracting supporters and contributors—unless of course they have been subject to damaging publicity while in office.

**incumbent** a candidate running for reelection to a position that he or she already holds

### Advisers

The next step in a typical campaign involves recruiting advisers and creating a formal campaign organization (see Figure 10.1). Most candidates, especially for national or statewide office, will need a campaign manager, a media consultant, a pollster, a financial adviser, and a press spokesperson, as well as a staff director to coordinate the activities of volunteer and paid workers. For a local campaign, candidates generally need hundreds of workers, both professionals and volunteers. State-level campaigns call for thousands of workers, and presidential campaigns require tens of thousands of workers nationwide.

Virtually all serious contenders for national and statewide office retain the services of professional campaign consultants. Increasingly, candidates for local office, too, have come to rely on professional campaign managers. Consultants offer candidates the expertise necessary to conduct accurate opinion polls, produce television commercials, organize direct-mail campaigns, and make use of sophisticated computer analyses. Professional political consultants have taken the place of the old-time party bosses who once controlled political campaigns, and naturally they prefer to work for candidates who seem to have a reasonable chance of winning. Most consultants who direct campaigns specialize in politics, although some are drawn from the ranks of corporate advertising or public relations, and they may

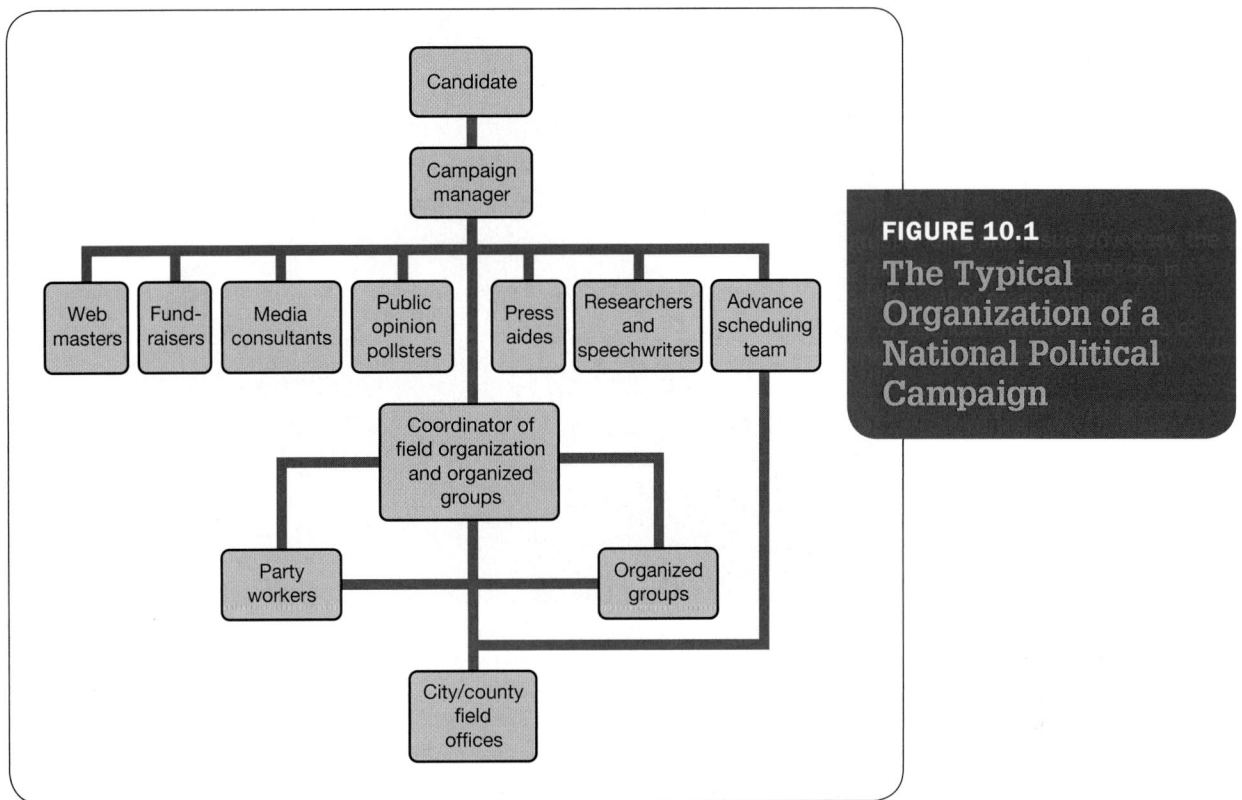

**FIGURE 10.1**
The Typical Organization of a National Political Campaign

work with commercial clients in addition to politicians. Campaign consultants conduct public opinion polls, produce television commercials, organize direct-mail campaigns, and develop the issues and advertising messages the candidate will use to mobilize support. George W. Bush's former chief political strategist, Karl Rove, not only played a key role in two presidential campaigns but is also widely credited with crafting the strategy that brought about a Republican victory in the 2002 national congressional races.

## Fund-Raising

Modern national political campaigns are fueled by enormous amounts of money. Together with their advisers, candidates must begin serious fund-raising efforts at an early stage in the campaign, usually by appealing both to the altruism of small donors and to the self-interest of large donors. To have a reasonable chance of winning a seat in the House of Representatives, a candidate may need to raise more than $500,000; in 2008, incumbent candidates in competitive House races typically spent close to $2 million to hold on to their seats. In 2008 Senate races, the average winner spent more than $4 million. In recent years, some Senate contests have cost $25 million or more, as have some races for governorships. In fact, 2010 California Republican gubernatorial candidate Meg Whitman spent more than $160 million, including $140 million of her own money, in an ultimately unsuccessful bid for office. Presidential candidates in particular must raise huge amounts of money. In 2012 fund-raising by presidential campaign shattered previous records.

*Candidates for national office hire professional campaign advisers to guide their campaigns and direct volunteers. Here, Mitt Romney talks with advisers Stuart Stevens and Eric Fehrnstrom in 2012.*

The Obama campaign, the Democratic Party, and the Priorities USA Action super PAC raised $934 million, while Mitt Romney's campaign, the Republican Party, and the Restore Our Future super PAC raised $881 million. These figures are unprecedented.

Candidates generally begin raising funds long before they face an election, and many politicians spend more time soliciting donations than engaging in any other campaign activity. Once in office, members of Congress find it much easier to raise campaign funds and are thus able to outspend their challengers (see Figure 10.2).[18] Members of the majority party in the House and Senate are particularly attractive to donors who want access to those in power.[19] In the "Money and Politics" section later in this chapter, we will discuss further the critical role that money plays in the electoral process.

## Polling

Virtually all contemporary campaigns for national and statewide office, and many local campaigns, make extensive use of opinion polling. To be competitive, a candidate must collect voting and poll data to assess the electorate's needs, hopes, fears, and past behavior. Polls, conducted throughout most political campaigns, provide the basic information that candidates and their staff use to craft campaign strategies—that is, to select issues, to assess the candidates' strengths and weaknesses and those of the opposition, to check voter response to the campaign, and to measure the degree to which various constituent groups may respond to campaign appeals. The themes, issues, and messages that candidates present during a campaign are generally based on polls and small face-to-face sessions with voters, called "focus groups." In recent years, pollsters have become central figures in most national campaigns, and some have continued as advisers to their clients after they've won the election.

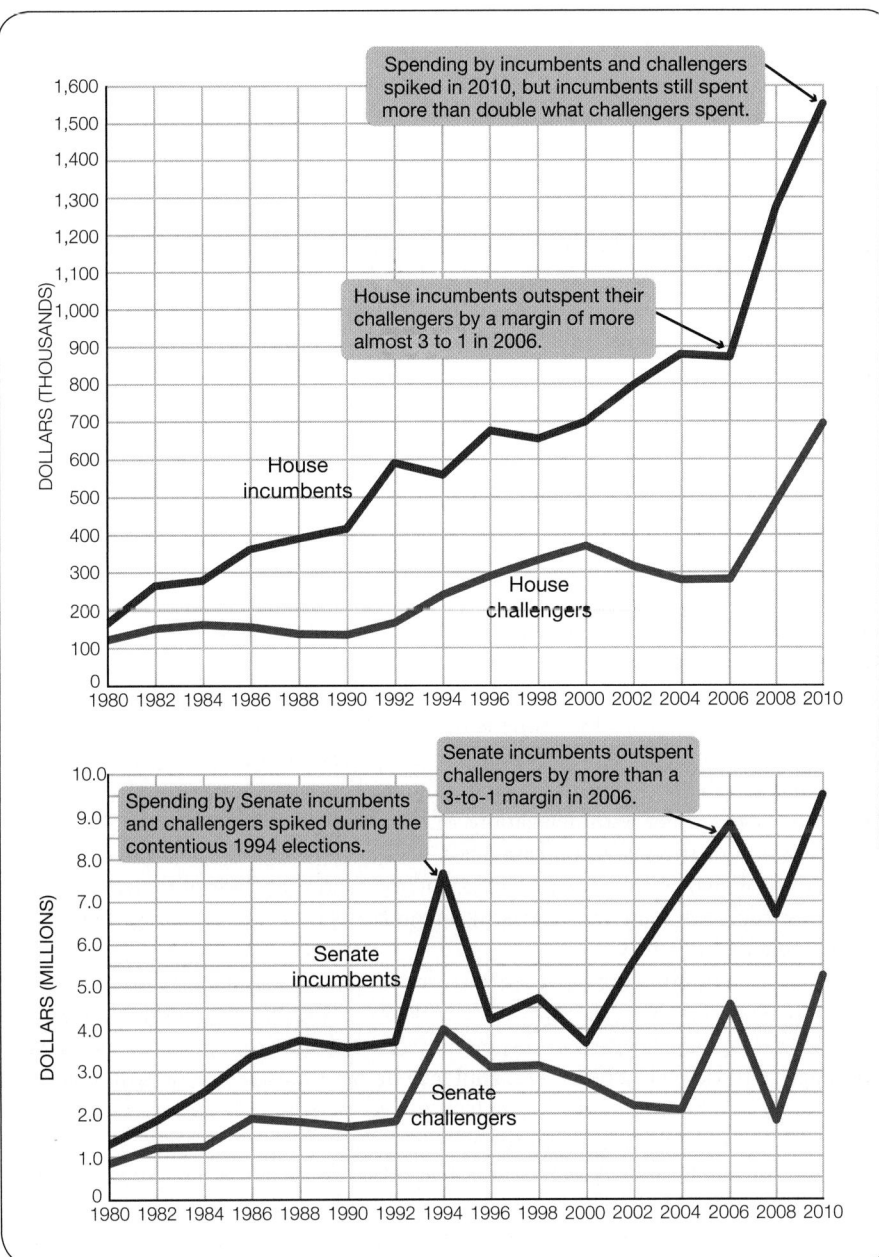

**FIGURE 10.2**

**Average House and Senate Campaign Expenditures, 1980–2010 (Net Dollars)**

The average amount spent by House and Senate incumbents to secure reelection has risen sharply in recent years, whereas spending by challengers has remained more stable. What would you expect to see as a consequence of this trend? Is legislation needed to level the playing field?

SOURCES: Norman J. Ornstein, Thomas E. Mann, and Michael J. Malbin. eds., *Vital Statistics on Congress, 2001–2002* (Washington, DC: American Enterprise Institute, 2002), 87, 93; and Campaign Finance Institute, www.cfinst.org (accessed 8/16/12).

Labels within figure:
- Spending by incumbents and challengers spiked in 2010, but incumbents still spent more than double what challengers spent.
- House incumbents outspent their challengers by a margin of more almost 3 to 1 in 2006.
- House incumbents
- House challengers
- Senate incumbents outspent challengers by more than a 3-to-1 margin in 2006.
- Spending by Senate incumbents and challengers spiked during the contentious 1994 elections.
- Senate incumbents
- Senate challengers

## Media Coverage and the Internet

For those candidates lucky enough to survive the nominating process, the last hurdle is the general election. There are essentially two types of general election in the United States today. The first type is the organizationally driven, labor-intensive election. Candidates campaign in local elections and many congressional elections by recruiting large numbers of volunteer workers to hand out leaflets and organize rallies. The candidates make appearances at receptions, community group meetings, local rallies, and even in shopping malls and on busy street corners. Generally, local and congressional campaigns depend less on issues and policy proposals

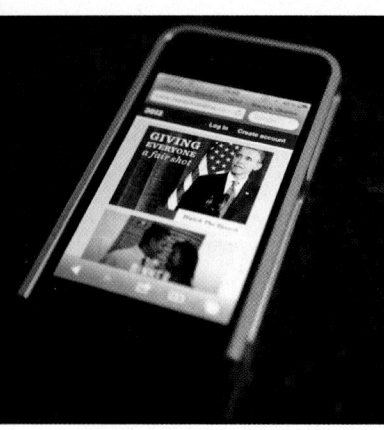

The Internet is an increasingly important tool in fundraising. Building on Obama's success in raising money online in 2008, his 2012 campaign introduced a new iPhone app and other new tools for soliciting donations.

and more on hard work designed to make the candidate more visible than his or her opponent. Statewide campaigns, some congressional races, and of course the national presidential election fall into the second category: the media-driven, capital-intensive electoral campaign.

In the nineteenth and early twentieth centuries, political campaigns were waged by the parties' enormous armies of patronage workers. Throughout the year, party workers cultivated the support of voters by assisting them with legal problems, helping them find jobs, and serving as liaisons with local, state, and federal agencies. On Election Day, throughout the nation, hundreds of thousands of party workers marched from house to house reminding their supporters to vote, helping the aged and infirm reach the polls, and calling in the favors they had accrued during the year. Campaigns resembled the maneuvers of huge infantries vying for victory. Historians have, in fact, referred to this traditional style of party campaigning as "militarist."

Contemporary political campaigns rely less on infantries and more on "air power" and the Internet. That is, rather than deploying huge armies of workers, contemporary campaigns make use of a number of communications tools to reach voters and bid for their support. Six tools are especially important: the media, debates, phone banks, direct mail, professional public relations, and the Internet.

**The Media** Extensive use of the broadcast media, television in particular, is the hallmark of the modern political campaign. Candidates endeavor to secure as much positive news and feature coverage as possible. This type of coverage is called *free media* because the cost of air time is borne by the media themselves. Candidates can secure free media coverage by participating in newsworthy events. Incumbents introduce legislation, sponsor hearings, undertake inspection tours of the sites of fires and floods, meet with delegations of foreign dignitaries, and so on, to capture the attention of the television cameras. Challengers announce new policy proposals, visit orphanages and senior centers, and demand that their opponents agree to a series of debates. Generally speaking, incumbents have the advantage in securing free media time.

In addition to pursuing free media coverage, candidates spend millions of dollars for *paid media* time, in the form of television and radio ads. Many of these ads consist of 15-, 30-, or 60-second **spots (advertisements)** that permit a candidate's message to be delivered to a target audience before uninterested or hostile viewers can tune it out. Examples of extremely effective spots include George H. W. Bush's 1988 "Willie Horton" ad, which implied that Bush's opponent, Michael Dukakis, coddled criminals, and Lyndon Johnson's 1964 "daisy" ad, which suggested that Johnson's opponent, Barry Goldwater, would lead the United States into nuclear war. Television spots are used to establish candidate name recognition, to create a favorable image of the candidate and a negative image of the opponent, to link the candidate with desirable groups in the community, and to communicate the candidate's stands on selected issues.

Often in the late stages of a campaign, candidates will "go negative," putting out ads attacking their opponents' character by exposing sordid incidents or unsavory associations. Though voters consistently say they reject so-called negative campaigning, attacks such as the 1988 "Willie Horton" ad can be devastatingly effective in the heat of a closely contested race, even when the ads are misleading or patently false. The targets of these attacks are forced to issue denials and use valuable campaign time defending themselves rather than promoting their ideas.

Journalists, voters, and scholars frequently complain that such ads undermine elections and even democratic government itself. The argument is that voters are

**Formation of an Exploratory Committee**
Formed 18 to 24 months before the election, this committee begins fund-raising and bringing the candidate's name to the attention of the media and influential groups.

**Fund-Raising**
Presidential candidated must develop fundraising strategies, hire expert fundraisers, and quickly build a subtantial "war chest" early on to show they are serious contenders.

**Campaigning**
Months before the primaries, candidates begin meetings with local leaders, public appearances, ad campaigns, and other strategies.

**Primaries and Caucuses**
Candidates need to do well in early contests such as Iowa and New Hampshire in order to build momentum and win their party's nomination. Party debates give candidates an opportunity to impress large television audiences.

**The Convention**
The Democratic and Republican parties hold national conventions in September prior to the November general election. The party's nominees for president and vice president are "officially" announced.

**The General Election Campaign**
In the months leading up to the November election, candidates focus on battleground or swing states as they aim to win at leat 270 votes in the electoral college. They run television ads and use new media to reach voters. They must continue to raise money throughout this process.

**The Debates**
In October, the major party candidates engage in several televised debates along with one vice presidential debate.

**The General Election**
On the Tuesday following the first Monday in November, voters in each state cast ballots. In most states, the candidate who wins the most votes in the state wins all of the state's votes in the electoral college.

**The Electoral College**
The electors meet in their state capitals in December, and their votes are officially counted in January.

**The Inauguration**
The president is officially inaugurated on January 20.

**FIGURE 10.3**

Electing the President: Steps in the Process

turned off by the negativity of politics and the media, and in turn are uninformed about politics and less likely to vote. Americans tend to see negative campaign ads as just that: negative. But political scientist John Geer has found that negative campaigns are more effective than positive campaigns in shaping voter decisions. He argues that when political candidates attack each other, raising doubts about each other's views and qualifications, voters benefit.[20] Negative ads are more likely to address important policy differences between candidates and provide supporting evidence. Positive ads tend to focus on candidates' personal characteristics rather than issues, and do not provide any supporting evidence regarding the candidates' claims. Thus voters may learn more from negative ads than positive ads.

In addition to ads sponsored by the candidates, numerous campaign ads are sponsored by the political parties and by political advocacy groups seeking to influence the outcome of the election. As discussed in Chapter 4, the 2003 Bipartisan Campaign Reform Act (BCRA) prohibited advocacy groups from running ads that mentioned a candidate's name within 30 days of a primary election and 60 days of a general election. The purpose of the ban was to prevent well-heeled groups from conducting ad blitzes just before an election, thus possibly distorting the results. In its 2007 decision in *Federal Election Commission v. Wisconsin Right to Life*, the Supreme Court struck down the ad ban as an unconstitutional restriction on speech.[21] Following the 2010 *Citizens United* decision, advocacy groups can form super PACs and run unlimited campaign ads for or against candidates, as long as the organizations are "independent" of the candidate's campaign. This decision prevented the spending limits in BCRA from playing a significant role in election campaigns.

The 1992 presidential campaign introduced two new media techniques that are still important today: the talk show interview and the "electronic town hall meeting." Candidates used interviews on television and radio talk shows to reach the large audiences drawn to this popular entertainment program format. The **town hall meeting** format allows candidates the opportunity to interact with ordinary citizens, thus showing the candidates' concern with the views and needs of the voters. Both talk show appearances and town hall meetings allow candidates to deliver their messages to millions of Americans without the input of journalists or commentators who might criticize or question the candidates' assertions.

**town hall meeting** an informal public meeting in which candidates meet with ordinary citizens. Allows candidates to deliver messages without the presence of journalists or commentators

**Debates** Public debates were a critical part of the democratic process of ancient Greece, where they were both a vital form of public entertainment and the principal means of what today would be called "voter education." Many successful American politicians, such as Abraham Lincoln, came to prominence largely because of their skill as debaters. Today, both presidential and vice-presidential candidates hold debates, as do candidates for statewide and even local offices. Debates give voters the opportunity to see how the candidates fare in direct, face-to-face exchanges outside the "campaign bubble" of stage-managed public appearances and carefully scripted speeches. Candidates who can "think on their feet" may be seen as demonstrating the kind of on-the-spot decision making that is more like actual governing than anything else they do in a campaign.

Televised presidential debates began with the famous 1960 Kennedy-Nixon clash. Kennedy's strong performance in the debate and the perception of many voters that the youthfully vigorous Kennedy "looked presidential" were major factors in bringing about his victory over the much better-known Richard Nixon. In 1980, Ronald Reagan was able to dispel misgivings that some voters had about his age with a well-timed joke about the "youth and inexperience" of his Democratic

# American Campaign Techniques Conquer the World

**Since the 1950s, American elec-**tion campaigns have been characterized by a reliance on technology in place of organization and personnel and by the rise of a new type of campaigner, the professional political consultant, in place of the old-time party boss. More and more, these campaign methods and even the consultants who wield them have spread to other parts of the world. American campaign consultants with their polls and phone banks and spot ads have directed campaigns in Europe, Latin America, and Asia. One American consultant recently said, "[We have] worked a lot in South America, Israel, [and the] Philippines and one of the things that I've discovered through that work is that the tools and techniques and strategies that we have developed here are applicable everywhere."[a]

This phenomenon, which is sometimes called the Americanization of politics, has important political implications. For the most part, the substitution of technology for organization in political campaigns works to the advantage of politicians and political forces repre-senting the upper ends of the social spectrum versus those representing the lower classes. Strong party organization was generally introduced by working-class parties as a way of maximizing their major political resource—the power of numbers. When politics is based mainly on organization and numbers, working-class parties can compete quite successfully. The growing use of technology in place of organization shifts the advantage to middle- and upper-class parties, which generally have better access to the financial resources needed to fuel the polls and television ads on which new-style campaigns depend.

In Britain and France, new techniques were introduced first by conservative parties and then copied by their opponents.

The development of the new technology in Europe and other parts of the world followed the American pattern.

This phenomenon is now becoming apparent in Africa. For example, in Kenya's 2008 presidential contest, President Mwai Kibaki made use of consultants, opinion polls, and media technology in his nation's presidential race. The linchpin of Kibaki's effort was the cell-phone campaign. Many Kenyan voters, especially in rural areas, lack Internet access or television service. Most, however, own cell phones. The president's ads, plastered on billboards throughout the nation, provided a cell-phone number and urged voters to call in their views. Voters were also likely to receive cell-phone calls and text messages from Kibaki supporters asking them to vote for the president. Not to be outdone, Kibaki's main rival, the populist Raila Odinga, hired Dick Morris, a former consultant to Bill Clinton, to offer advice to his campaign. Odinga used television ads designed by a media consultant and organized his own cell-phone campaign.[b]

Unfortunately, when Kibaki lost the election, he refused to cede power and a period of fighting ensued before a power-sharing agreement was reached. American consultants scurried for cover when the bullets flew.

[a]Paul Baines, Fritz Plasser, and Christian Scheucher, "Operationalising Political Marketing: A Comparison of US and Western European Consultants and Managers," Middlesex University Discussion Paper Series, No. 7, July 1999.
[b]Stephanie McCrummen, "Kenya Tests New Style of Politicking," *Washington Post,* December 22, 2007, p. A10.

## for critical analysis

1. Which foreign political parties were first to adopt American-style campaign techniques? Why?

2. What are the political implications and consequences of the shift from old-fashioned campaign styles to American-style, technology-intensive politics?

rival, Senator Walter Mondale. Indeed, candidates can make or break their campaigns with the strength of their debate performances, including even unconscious gestures and the nuances of their facial expressions. President George H. W. Bush was thought to have "lost" a 1992 debate when he was seen nervously glancing at his watch while his opponent, Bill Clinton, was speaking. In the 2012 presidential primaries, the Republicans held a dozen nationally televised debates, more than ever before, and the debates were spread out over the course of many months. In contrast with a process focusing on the state holding a primary or caucus that week, this series of debates before a nationwide audience had the effect of nationalizing the selection of the Republican presidential candidate. It also made or broke the presidential chances of a number of candidates. Before the debates, Texas governor Rick Perry was considered the ideal candidate to take the White House, given his policy positions and standing within the party. But a number of high-profile gaffes during the debates—including one in which he could not remember the name of one of the U.S. government departments he wished to eliminate if he were elected president—turned voters off. On the other hand, for former Speaker of the U.S. House Newt Gingrich, who has always been a natural orator, the televised debates allowed him to gain confidence. Throughout the series of debates, Gingrich was considered a front-runner at times, although he eventually lost to Mitt Romney. Candidates spend a great deal of time preparing for debate appearances, rehearsing their responses to likely questions and devising gambits to catch their opponents off guard. But because debates force candidates to react spontaneously, many voters believe that they provide the most important and revealing moments of a campaign.

**Phone Banks** Through the broadcast media, candidates communicate with voters en masse and impersonally. Phone banks, on the other hand, allow campaign workers to make personal contact with hundreds of thousands of voters. Personal contact of this sort is thought to be extremely effective. Again, polling data identify the groups that will be targeted for phone calls. Computers select phone numbers from areas in which members of these groups are concentrated. Staffs of paid or volunteer callers, using computer-assisted dialing systems and prepared scripts, then place calls to deliver their candidate's message. The targeted groups are generally those identified by polls as either uncommitted or weakly committed, and even strong supporters of the candidate who are contacted simply to be encouraged to vote. In 2008 and 2012 the presidential campaigns of both parties also placed hundreds of thousands of automated "robo calls" urging voters to support their candidates. In surveys of likely Iowa caucus attendees, as many respondents said they had been contacted by a robo call as by a live person. These types of campaign contacts are extremely effective and widespread.[22]

**Direct Mail** Direct mail is both a vehicle for communicating with voters and a mechanism for raising funds. The first step in a direct-mail campaign is the purchase or rental of a computerized mailing list of voters deemed to have some particular perspective or social characteristic. Often magazine subscription lists or lists of donors to various causes are employed. For example, a candidate interested in reaching conservative voters might rent subscription lists from the *National Review*, *Human Events*, or *Conservative Digest*; a candidate interested in appealing to liberals might rent subscription lists from the *New York Review of Books* or *The Nation*. Considerable fine-tuning is possible. After obtaining the appropriate mailing lists, candidates usually send pamphlets, letters, and brochures describing themselves and their views to voters believed to be sympathetic. Different types of mail appeals are made to different electoral subgroups. Often the letters sent to voters are personalized. The recipient is addressed by name in the text, and the letter appears actually to have been signed by the candidate. Of course, these "personal" letters and even the signatures are generated by a computer.

In addition to its use as a political advertising medium, direct mail has also become an important source of campaign funds. Computerized mailing lists permit campaign strategists to pinpoint individuals whose interests, background, and activities suggest that they may be potential donors to the campaign. Letters of solicitation are sent to these potential donors. Some of the money raised is then used to purchase additional mailing lists. Direct-mail solicitation can be enormously effective.

**Professional Public Relations** Modern campaigns are typically directed by professional public-relations consultants, who have expertise in contemporary communications strategies. Virtually all serious contenders for national and statewide office retain the services of professional campaign consultants. Increasingly, candidates for local office, too, have come to rely on professional campaign managers. Consultants offer candidates the expertise necessary to conduct accurate opinion polls, produce television commercials, organize direct-mail campaigns, and make use of sophisticated computer analyses.

**The Internet** The Internet has become a major weapon in modern political campaigns. The 2008 and 2012 campaigns made the Internet more central to their political strategies than ever before. Beginning with the primaries, every campaign developed an Internet strategy for fund-raising, generating interest in the candidate, mobilizing supporters, and getting out the vote. The Clinton primary campaign made extensive use of the Internet to mobilize potential supporters and to raise money. The innovative Obama campaign used the Internet to create events such as walkathons, community meet-ups, and fund-raisers all around the country. Both Obama and John McCain created social networking sites that allowed supporters to post information about themselves and chat with one another. (See Chapters 7 and 8 for more on this.) These sites help build enthusiasm and are potent fund-raising tools. Obama's website played a major role in the Illinois senator's ability to raise money and build strong ties to supporters.[23] The Digital Citizens box on the following page discusses the use of social media, such as Facebook, in recent campaigns.

# ● How Voters Decide

**Identify the major factors that influence voters' decisions**

Whatever the capacity of those with the money and power to influence the electoral process, it is the millions of individual decisions on Election Day that ultimately determine electoral outcomes. Sooner or later the choices of voters weigh more heavily than the schemes of campaign advisers or the leverage of interest groups.

Three factors influence voters' decisions at the polls: partisan loyalty, issues and policy preferences and candidate characteristics.

# DIGITAL CITIZENS

# Social Media, Crowdsourcing, and the 2012 Election

**While the Internet has created new** challenges for political parties and candidates in the realm of campaigns and elections, it has also provided many new opportunities for campaign outreach and organization. Social media are remaking the face of political campaigning—and that face might be yours!

Social media sites give candidates a free way to organize supporters across a district, a state, or the country. The ability to reach millions of people instantly with a message, a call for volunteers, money, or whatever else the campaign needs is revolutionary. By fall 2012, Barack Obama had 30 million "friends" on Facebook, and Mitt Romney had less than half as many.

Social media sites allow not only candidates to communicate directly with their supporters, but also supporters to *retransmit* that information instantly to all their friends. What used to take weeks can take a candidate less than a day. This is critical, as only a small percentage of social media users (an estimated 7 percent of Facebook users, for example) actually "friend" political campaigns,

but the messages they retransmit reach all their friends, and often friends of their friends—eventually reaching thousands of people the campaign would not otherwise have reached. Research shows that we trust information more when we hear it from a trusted friend or someone who is like us. Thus, social media and the retransmission of information by supporters expose candidates to a wide audience that trusts the source of the information.

The ability of candidates to promote their campaign by extending their network through friends of friends on Facebook or other social media sites leverages the power of crowdsourcing. *Wired* magazine writer Jeff Howe coined the term *crowdsourcing* to describe how the Internet has enabled large, widely distributed teams of citizens to do work that was previously the domain of isolated experts or corporations. Linux and Wikipedia are only two of hundreds of examples of this phenomenon. While originally applied to business, crowdsourcing may increasingly be a driving force in political campaigns.

The 2008 elections showed how social media's unique ability to transfer

information quickly was indispensable to campaigns, and social media played an even larger role in the 2012 election. More than 3 in 4 Americans went online for election news in 2012. In the run-up to the election, Facebook abounded with memes about the candidates and debates, which were shared by millions. Citizens' social media habits, browser histories, and mobile applications became new goldmines for the campaigns. New in 2012 was a flurry of online advertising, as Obama and Romney campaign ads popped up everywhere, from YouTube to Google. The 2012 election was dominated by data, election forecasts, live-streaming debates, Facebook memes, and tweets of horserace results, all side by side with traditional political journalism and political pundits. As the election unfolded, the story was shared by millions online via social media.

SOURCES: Jeffry Howe, *Crowdsourcing: Why the Power of the Crowd Is Driving the Future of Business.* New York: Crown Business, 2009. Lee Rainie, "Social Media and the 2012 U.S. Presidential Elections." Washington, DC: U.S. Department of State, 2012, http://fpc.state .gov/193458.htm (accessed 6/25/12).

facebook — Search for people, places and things — Lee Rider — Find

**Mitt Romney**
6,234,752 likes · 3,248,880 talking about this · 75 were here

Like — Message

Politician
To learn more visit my website:
http://www.mittromney.com/ or follow me on
Twitter http://twitter.com/mittromney or
About

Photos — Stand with Mitt — Donate — Romney Store App

## for critical analysis

1. What are some of the advantages and disadvantages of using social media for election campaigns?

2. *Crowdsourcing* is a term applied to communities of citizens doing work previously dominated by experts. Are citizens playing a larger role in political campaigns via social media? Why or why not?

## Partisan Loyalty

Partisan loyalty was considerably stronger during the 1940s and '50s than it is today, but even now most voters feel a certain sense of identification or kinship with the Democratic or Republican party. This sense of identification is often handed down from parents to children and is reinforced by social and cultural ties. Partisan identification predisposes voters in favor of their party's candidates and against those of the opposing party (see Figure 10.4). At the level of the presidential contest, issues and candidate personalities may become very important, although even here many Americans supported Mitt Romney or Barack Obama in the 2012 race only because of partisan loyalty. But partisanship is more likely to assert itself in the less visible races, where issues and the candidates are not as well known. State legislative races, for example, are often decided by voters' party ties. Once formed, voters' partisan loyalties seldom change. Voters tend to keep their party affiliations unless some crisis causes them to reexamine the bases of their loyalties and to conclude that they have not given their support to the appropriate party. During these relatively infrequent periods of electoral change, millions of voters can change their party ties. For example, at the beginning of the New Deal era, between 1932 and 1936, millions of former Republicans transferred their allegiance to Franklin Roosevelt and the Democrats.

## Issues and Policy Preferences

Policy preferences are a second factor influencing voters' choices at the polls. Voters may cast their ballots for the candidate whose position on economic issues they believe to be closest to their own, or the candidate who has what they believe to be the best record on foreign policy. Issues are more important in some races than others. If candidates articulate and publicize very different positions on important policy issues, voters are more likely to be able to identify and act on whatever policy preferences they may have.

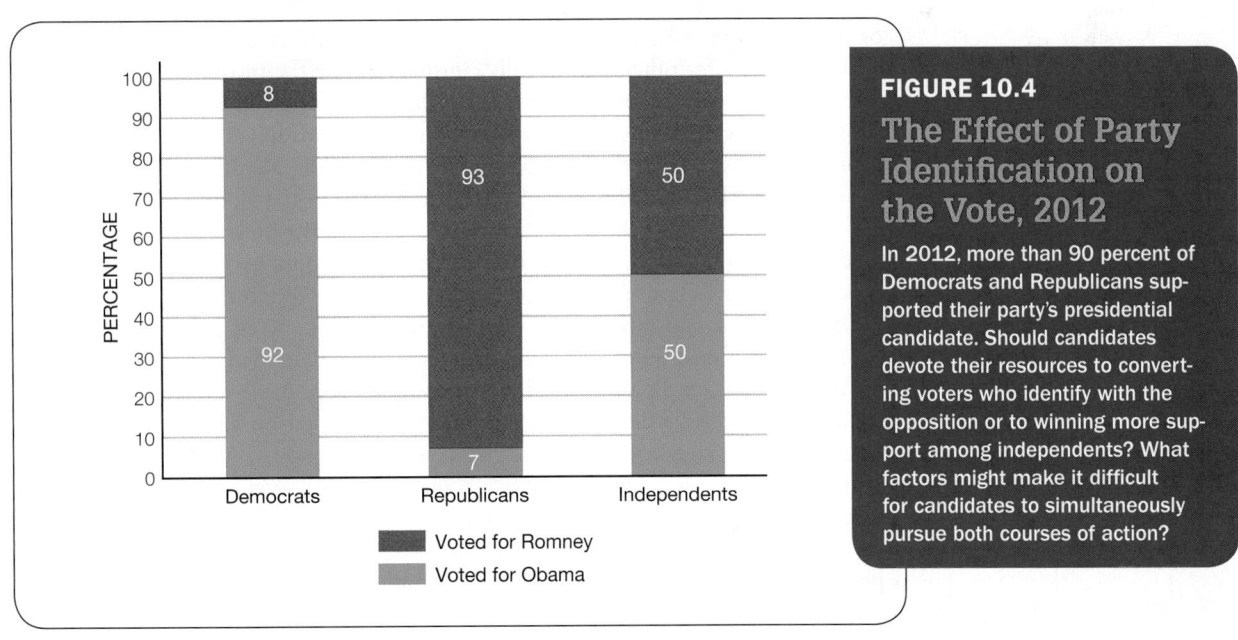

**FIGURE 10.4**

**The Effect of Party Identification on the Vote, 2012**

In 2012, more than 90 percent of Democrats and Republicans supported their party's presidential candidate. Should candidates devote their resources to converting voters who identify with the opposition or to winning more support among independents? What factors might make it difficult for candidates to simultaneously pursue both courses of action?

The ability of voters to make choices on the basis of policy preferences is diminished, however, if competing candidates do not differ substantially or do not focus their campaigns on policy matters. Very often, candidates deliberately take the safe course and emphasize positions that will not offend any voters. Thus, they often trumpet their opposition to corruption, crime, and inflation—things favored, presumably, by few voters. Such a strategy, though perfectly reasonable, makes it extremely difficult for voters to make their issue or policy preferences the basis for their choices at the polls.

Voters' issue choices usually involve a mix of their judgments about the past behavior of competing parties and candidates and their hopes and fears about candidates' future behavior. Political scientists call choices that focus on future behavior **prospective voting**, whereas those based on past performance are called **retrospective voting**. To some extent, whether prospective or retrospective evaluation is more important in a particular election depends on the strategies of competing candidates. Candidates always endeavor to define the issues of an election in terms that will serve their interests. Incumbents running during a period of prosperity will seek to take credit for the economy's happy state and will define the election as revolving around their record of success. This strategy encourages voters to make retrospective judgments. By contrast, an insurgent running during a period of economic uncertainty will tell voters it is time for a change and ask them to make prospective judgments. Thus, Bill Clinton focused on change in 1992 and prosperity in 1996, and through well-crafted media campaigns was able to define voters' agenda of choices.

The most important issue for voters in the 2012 election was the economy. Mitt Romney campaigned aggressively on his ability to turn around the deepest economic downturn since the Great Depression, and in exit polls was seen as the candidate better equipped to handle the economy. The Obama campaign touted the rebound of the auto industry after the president's bailout package in 2009, especially in Ohio, and his health care policy.

**The Economy** As we identify the strategies and tactics employed by opposing political candidates and parties, we should keep in mind that the best-laid plans of politicians often go awry. Election outcomes are affected by a variety of forces that candidates for office cannot fully control. Among the most important of these forces is the condition of the economy. If voters are satisfied with their economic prospects, they tend to support the party in power, while voter unease about the economy tends to favor the opposition. Thus, George H. W. Bush lost in 1992 during an economic downturn even though the American-led victory in the Gulf War had briefly given him a 90 percent favorable rating in the polls just one year earlier. And Bill Clinton won in 1996 during an economic boom even though voters had serious concerns about his moral fiber. As we shall see later in this chapter, the 2008 financial crisis gave Barack Obama and the Democrats a significant advantage. Over the past quarter-century, the Consumer Confidence Index, calculated by the Conference Board, a business research group, has been a fairly accurate predictor of presidential outcomes. The index is based on surveys asking voters how optimistic they are about the future of the economy. It would appear that a generally rosy view, indicated by a score over 100, augurs well for the party in power. An index score under 100, suggesting that voters are pessimistic about the economy's trend, suggests that incumbents should worry about their own job prospects (see Figure 10.5). The 2012 elections deviated from this pattern, with

**prospective voting** voting based on the imagined future performance of a candidate or political party

**retrospective voting** voting based on the past performance of a candidate or political party

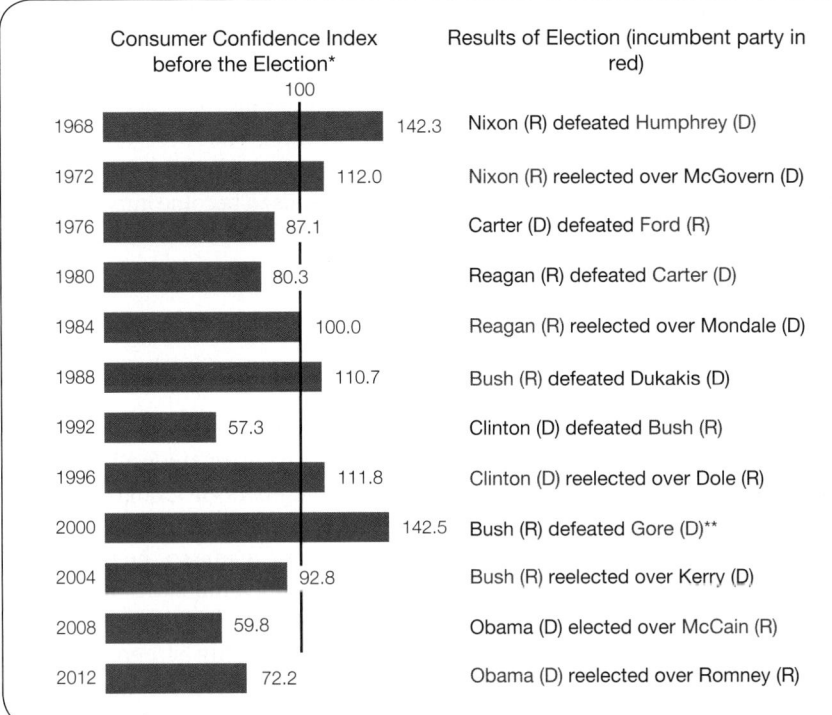

**Consumer Confidence Index before the Election\***

| Year | Index | Results of Election (incumbent party in red) |
|------|-------|-----------------------------------------------|
| 1968 | 142.3 | Nixon (R) defeated Humphrey (D) |
| 1972 | 112.0 | Nixon (R) reelected over McGovern (D) |
| 1976 | 87.1 | Carter (D) defeated Ford (R) |
| 1980 | 80.3 | Reagan (R) defeated Carter (D) |
| 1984 | 100.0 | Reagan (R) reelected over Mondale (D) |
| 1988 | 110.7 | Bush (R) defeated Dukakis (D) |
| 1992 | 57.3 | Clinton (D) defeated Bush (R) |
| 1996 | 111.8 | Clinton (D) reelected over Dole (R) |
| 2000 | 142.5 | Bush (R) defeated Gore (D)\*\* |
| 2004 | 92.8 | Bush (R) reelected over Kerry (D) |
| 2008 | 59.8 | Obama (D) elected over McCain (R) |
| 2012 | 72.2 | Obama (D) reelected over Romney (R) |

**FIGURE 10.5**

## Consumer Confidence and Presidential Elections

Since 1968, the Consumer Confidence Index has been a reliable predictor of incumbents' political fortunes. Was the result of the 2012 election consistent with this trend? What issues other than the economy influenced the 2012 election?

\*Survey was bimonthly prior to 1977 so figures for 1968, 1972, and 1976 are for October and they are for September from 1983 on.

\*\*Gore won the popular vote but Bush was elected by the Electoral College.

SOURCE: Bloomberg Financial Markets.

Obama re-elected despite a Consumer Confidence Index score of 72.2 before the election.

## Candidate Characteristics

Candidates' personal attributes always influence voters' decisions. Some analysts claim that voters prefer tall candidates to short ones, candidates with shorter names to candidates with longer names, and candidates with lighter hair to candidates with darker hair. Perhaps these rather frivolous criteria do play some role. But the more important candidate characteristics that affect voters' choices are race, ethnicity, religion, gender, geography, and social background. In general, voters may be proud to see someone of their ethnic, religious, or geographic background in a position of leadership, and they may presume that such candidates are likely to have views and perspectives close to their own. This is why, for many years, politicians sought to "balance the ticket," making certain that their party's ticket included members of as many important groups as possible.

Just as candidates' personal characteristics may attract some voters, they may repel others. Many voters are prejudiced against candidates from certain ethnic, racial, or religious groups. And for many years, voters were reluctant to support the candidacies of women, although this appears to be changing. Indeed, the fact that in 2008 the Democratic candidate was a black man and the Republican vice-presidential candidate a woman indicates the ongoing collapse of previously rigid political barriers.

Voters also pay attention to candidates' personality characteristics, such as "decisiveness," "honesty," and "vigor." In recent years, integrity has become a key election issue. In the 2012 election, Obama's opponents painted him as a weak leader, unable to turn the economy around, defend American industries from China's rising economic power, or defend the nation's interests globally. Romney's opponents said he only cared about the super rich, at the expense of the working class. He was also portrayed as anti-minority and, in particular, anti-Latino, as his rhetoric was harsh on illegal immigrants in terms of "self" deportation. However, voters seemed less concerned with these matters than with the ability of the candidates to deal with the nation's economic woes. In hard times, the electorate tends to become impatient with partisan mudslinging.

## ● The 2012 Elections

**Analyze the strategies, issues, and outcomes of the 2012 elections**

In the fall of 2012, more than 123 million Americans went to the polls to select a president, members of Congress, governors, and numerous other officials. Voters re-elected Barack Obama to the presidency and confirmed the Democratic Party's control of the Senate and the Republican Party's majority in the House of Representatives. Obama won more than 62 million votes, or roughly 51 percent, while his Republican challenger, Mitt Romney, had received about 59 million votes, or 48 percent. Though the president's margin of victory was about 5 percentage points less than in 2008, it was enough to give him 332 electoral votes, 62 more than the 270 needed to win the constitutionally mandated electoral college majority. The president's margin of victory was built on a coalition of women, working-class voters, and minority voters in several key battleground states. Despite the billions of dollars spent by candidates and the hoopla of the campaign, the 2012 election was decided more by demographic realities than political rhetoric.

Generally speaking, incumbent presidents have a substantial advantage when they seek re-election to a second term. During the course of American history, incumbent presidents standing for re-election have won about 70 percent of the time. Despite this advantage of incumbency, the re-election of President Barack Obama in 2012 was never a foregone conclusion. Obama had won handily in 2008 over his Republican rival, Senator John McCain. Obama had promised "Change we can believe in," and energized legions of young supporters who saw in the senator from Illinois a charismatic and energetic politician who would pursue a progressive social agenda and bring an end to America's wars in the Middle East. Many liberal voters had also been eager to elect America's first black president and thus make a break with the nation's long and unhappy history of racial oppression and discrimination.

Once in office, Obama was eager to make good on his promise of change. He worked to bring an end to the war in Iraq and to wind down the war in Afghanistan, partly in order to shift the nation's spending priorities from military to domestic social needs. In the realm of domestic policy, between 2008 and 2010, with the cooperation of a Congress controlled by the Democrats, the president succeeded in bringing about a massive overhaul of America's health care system. Under the terms of what came to be known as "Obamacare," tens of millions of previously uninsured Americans would be required to purchase federally subsidized health insurance policies through state insurance exchanges. Despite some

*Many winning candidates of the 2010 elections were supported by Tea Party groups. Here, Senator Rand Paul campaigns at a Tea Party event. The question was whether these trends would continue in 2012.*

initial doubt, the Supreme Court upheld the main provisions of Obamacare in 2012. The president also signed into law a major new program, the Dodd-Frank Wall Street Reform and Consumer Protection Act, aimed at protecting the nation's financial system from a future crisis like the one that nearly brought about a global financial catastrophe in 2008–09. The Dodd-Frank Act provided for tighter regulation of banks, prohibitions on some risky investment activities, and protections for consumers and borrowers. The president also signed a $700 billion economic stimulus bill to create jobs and spur investment and growth.

Despite the successes claimed by President Obama and his allies, Democrats lost control of the House of Representatives in the 2010 midterm elections. It is often the case that the president's party loses some seats in the midterm elections, but in 2010 the Democrats received a much larger drubbing than usual, losing 60 seats and ceding control of the House to the Republicans. In Senate races, the GOP failed to win enough seats to take control of the upper chamber but, with 46 seats, had enough votes to sustain filibusters if necessary. It seemed that what Obama and the Democrats had viewed as major accomplishments were seen by conservative Republican voters as a series of disasters. These voters saw Obamacare as a costly government takeover of a major industry and an unwarranted intrusion into the lives of all Americans. These same voters saw financial reform as a policy that would strangle America's financial services industry. With encouragement and momentum from the Tea Party movement, conservatives defeated numerous members of Congress who had supported Obama and left the president with a Republican House of Representatives that vowed to block any new presidential initiatives. Over the next two years, the president and Congress engaged in acrimonious battles over the federal budget and the federal government's borrowing power (the debt limit) that twice brought the U.S. government to the brink of financial ruin before last-minute compromises temporarily averted disaster.

All the while, the nation's economy, which had been battered by the 2007–08 recession, was showing only tepid signs of recovery. For much of the president's first term, unemployment remained in the uncomfortably high 8–9 percent range;

*The Romney campaign and other Republican groups attacked Obama's handling of the economy. As a sitting president presiding over a somewhat shaky economy, with unemployment uncomfortably high, Obama's re-election was not at all certain.*

OBAMA ISN'T WORKING .COM

Paid for by Romney for President, Inc.

the housing market was weak; a number of major financial institutions seemed tottering on the edge of failure; and job seekers, including hundreds of thousands of recent college graduates, found themselves unemployed or underemployed. Against this backdrop, President Obama's re-election hardly seemed assured. However, the Republicans needed to find a candidate who could defeat the president and appeal to the various factions of their party.

## Political Parties in 2012: Unity and Division

As recently as the 1950s, each of America's major political parties had been a coalition that included both liberal and conservative elements. The Democrats included the liberal forces of organized labor and the big cities and the more conservative groups in the states of the South. The Republicans, for their part, mobilized midwestern conservatives and the liberals of the northeastern Protestant establishment. Each party was said to be a "big tent."

As we saw in Chapter 9, the political upheavals of the 1960s and '70s, especially the civil rights revolution, triggered a national realignment of political forces. Angered by the national Democratic leadership's stances on civil rights issues, white Southerners largely shifted their allegiance to the GOP. At the same time, liberal Republicans on the East and West coasts shifted their support to the Democrats. Over time, the Democrats became a much more liberal party and the Republicans a much more conservative political force. This ideological realignment of the two parties is one reason that partisan struggles in Congress—and between Congress and the White House when party control of the two branches is divided—have become especially intense in recent years.

The growing ideological split between the two parties has not meant that each party is ideologically uniform. In fact, disputes among the various liberal groups within the Democratic Party and among the disparate conservative groups in the GOP have also been quite heated. Some liberal Democrats, for example, castigated President Obama as too moderate because he did not move quickly enough to end the wars in Iraq and Afghanistan and did not seek to create a fully nationalized health care system on the European or Canadian model. The GOP, for its part, is divided among fiscal conservatives, social conservatives, and other factions. For the fiscal conservatives, the major issues facing the nation today are excessive taxation and regulation. The social conservatives are more concerned with ending abortion, preventing same-sex marriage, and restoring the place of religion in American public life. The neoconservatives, a small group in the electorate but an influential element in the party's leadership, favor a robust military policy and an internationalist foreign policy. The paleoconservatives are suspicious of America's foreign involvements, favor restrictions on immigration, and generally have an isolationist bent. In 2012 divisions among the Democrats were relatively inconsequential for the simple reason that the party's presidential nominee was a given. Like it or not, all the party's factions had to accommodate themselves to President Obama. The Republican nomination, on the other hand, was sharply contested by several candidates representing different factions in the party. Former Massachusetts governor and successful financier Mitt Romney spoke for fiscal conservatives. Former Pennsylvania senator Rick Santorum and Minnesota congresswoman Michele Bachmann were the champions of the social conservatives. Libertarian Texas congressman Ron Paul spoke for the paleoconservatives, and former House Speaker Newt Gingrich represented neoconservatives. Several other candidates, who lacked significant bases of support, including business executive Herman Cain, Texas governor Rick Perry, former Utah governor and ambassador Jon Huntsman, former New Mexico governor Gary Johnson, and former Minnesota governor Tim Pawlenty, sought to stake out positions that might attract supporters if the front runners faltered.

Between May 2011 and February 2012, Republican hopefuls engaged in a series of televised debates where each argued that he or she would be best able to defeat the Democrats. The candidates were generally polite to one another and saved their criticisms for Obama and the Democrats. Gradually, candidates who found themselves unable to attract much support dropped out of the race, and by February 2012, only four remained: Gingrich, Paul, Romney, and Santorum. Over the next several months, these four candidates faced one another in a series of Republican primaries and caucuses, competing for the votes of 2,286 Republican convention delegates, with 1,144 needed to win the nomination.

From the beginning, Romney's superior organization and financial base made him the front-runner. The GOP's social and religious conservatives, though, were unenthusiastic about the former Massachusetts governor. Some saw him as a liberal in Republican clothing while others, particularly evangelical Protestants, were unhappy about the idea of a member of the Mormon faith leading the party. These groups gave their support to Rick Santorum, who eventually carried 11 states and more than 20 percent of the primary vote. By April 2012, though, Romney had clearly won the delegate votes needed for the nomination, and Santorum suspended his campaign. In the end, Romney carried 42 states and territories, and Santorum 11. Gingrich and Paul turned out to be nearly irrelevant, with the former Speaker carrying two states and the Texas congressman only one.

Having won the Republican nomination, Romney moved to reassure the party's social conservatives that he was worthy of their enthusiastic support in the general election. Conservatives would not jump to the Obama camp, but anything less than enthusiastic participation in the campaign on the part of social conservatives would doom the GOP's ticket to defeat. Accordingly, Romney endorsed a party platform that would appeal to this group. Its provisions included a constitutional amendment to ban abortion; elimination of government-funded family planning programs, with the exception of abstinence training; and a program of detention for "dangerous" aliens. Other provisions included partial privatization of the Medicare program, elimination of the federal income tax, and an end to various forms of federal regulation. As icing on the conservative cake, Romney chose as his vice-presidential running mate Congressman Paul Ryan of Wisconsin. Ryan had vigorously opposed Democratic fiscal and social policies and was enthusiastically supported by the GOP's social and fiscal conservatives. Yet, many conservatives remained unconvinced about Romney. Radio talk show hosts such as Glenn Beck and Michael Savage continued to attack the Massachusetts governor. But, particularly with Ryan on the ticket, most fell into line, and as the party became more united behind his candidacy, Romney was ready to face Obama and the Democrats.

## The General Election

In recent years, the bedrock base of GOP support has consisted of reasonably affluent, educated, middle-aged, middle-class white men living in suburban and rural areas. The Democrats, on the other hand, have been able to rely upon the votes of a majority of women, less affluent Americans, urban residents, younger voters, African Americans, and, increasingly, Hispanic voters. While there are certainly poor Republicans and affluent Democrats, this split approaches a classic division between the "have mores" and "have lesses." Romney alluded to this division when he said, in what he thought to be a closed-door meeting with Republican donors, that 47 percent of Americans paid few taxes, depended on government handouts, and would never vote for him. When news of Romney's comments leaked, Republicans sought to contain the damage but did not necessarily dispute the accuracy of Romney's analysis.

The division of the electorate into "have mores" and "have lesses" also dictated a major struggle in the campaign. In a number of states, Republican governors and legislatures enacted voter ID laws requiring prospective voters to present valid, government-issued photo identification cards at the polls. Republicans said such laws were needed to prevent fraudulent voting. The GOP's calculus, though, was that less-educated and minority voters (who tend to vote Democratic) were less likely to be able to produce valid ID at the polls and would thus be barred from voting. Two dozen states enacted voter ID laws, and though Democrats mounted court challenges, many of these laws were in effect on Election Day.

While America, of course, consists of 50 states, presidential elections are usually fought in only 9 or 10 states. This is so because some states are solidly Republican (sometimes called the red states) while others are solidly Democratic (known as the blue states). The states of the Deep South and mountain West, for example, are so securely in the Republican camp that Democratic presidential candidates hardly bother to campaign there. Most of the states of the Northeast and West Coast, on the other hand, are heavily committed to the Democrats and receive little attention from the GOP. In 2012 opinion polls indicated that only 8 of the 50 states were actually toss-ups. These were Colorado, Florida, Iowa, Nevada, New Hampshire, Ohio, Virginia, and Wisconsin. A handful of other states, including Michigan, Minnesota, New Mexico, and Pennsylvania were seen as leaning toward Obama, while Arizona, Indiana, and North Carolina were viewed as leaning toward Romney. The remaining 35 states seemed to be solidly in either the Democratic or Republican camp.

*Romney's remark—made at a private fundraiser—that 47 percent of Americans were dependent on government and not worth his campaign's time offended many Americans. The issue highlighted the division of the electorate into "have mores" and "have lesses."*

Thus, the 2012 presidential race was waged in 8 to 10 battleground states. Here the Obama and Romney campaigns and their various supporters spent hundreds of millions of dollars on television and online advertising, phone banks, voter registration drives, and rallies as well as numerous candidate visits. While voters in many states would hardly have reason to notice the presidential contest, voters in the battleground states could hardly turn on their television sets or answer their phones without being urged to support Obama or Romney.

## The Debates

Of course, while most campaigning was undertaken on a state-by-state basis, the candidates did face each other in one major set of national forums. These were the three nationally televised presidential debates along with the one vice-presidential debate. The first presidential debate, focusing on domestic policy, was held at the University of Colorado on October 3, 2012. The debate, which was watched by 67 million people, was more remarkable for style than substance. In terms of substance, the candidates discussed the economy, the federal deficit, Social Security, and the Affordable Care Act, with Romney criticizing Obama's record and the president defending his accomplishments. Though both candidates made mistakes and factual errors, both seemed to possess a thorough knowledge of the details of major American domestic policies. In terms of style, however, Obama and Romney differed sharply. Governor Romney seemed alert and aggressive, making points assertively and methodically as he accused the president of increasing the nation's debt, failing to bolster the economy, and undermining the private sector in favor of government-run programs. The president, for his part, appeared disengaged and listless. In the wake of the first debate, the national polls, which had constantly shown Obama with a slim lead over his Republican opponent, now suggested that the race was neck and neck. Republicans were elated and Democrats dismayed by the debate and its results.

The president improved his performance in the next two debates and was generally judged to have been the winner, as was Vice President Biden in his confrontation with Republican vice-presidential candidate Paul Ryan. As one commentator noted, however, Obama and Biden had won their victories on points while Romney had scored a knockout in the first debate. To add to the president's problem, in the 34 states that allowed early voting in 2012, hundreds of thousands of voters had cast their ballots after the first debate but before the other debates, introducing a wild card that would be discussed long after the election. At any rate, with the damage done, Obama had two weeks after the debates to slow his opponent's growing momentum.

Obama responded by redoubling his efforts in battleground states, with speeches and campaign commercials labeling Romney a multimillionaire who was out of touch with ordinary Americans and who sent American jobs overseas. The Obama campaign argued that Romney had favored allowing Detroit to go bankrupt, despite the potential loss of hundreds of thousands of jobs. Obama also coined the term *Romnesia*, to suggest that Romney continually changed positions for reasons of expedience and expected voters to forget what his previous positions had been. These efforts succeeded in shoring up Obama's

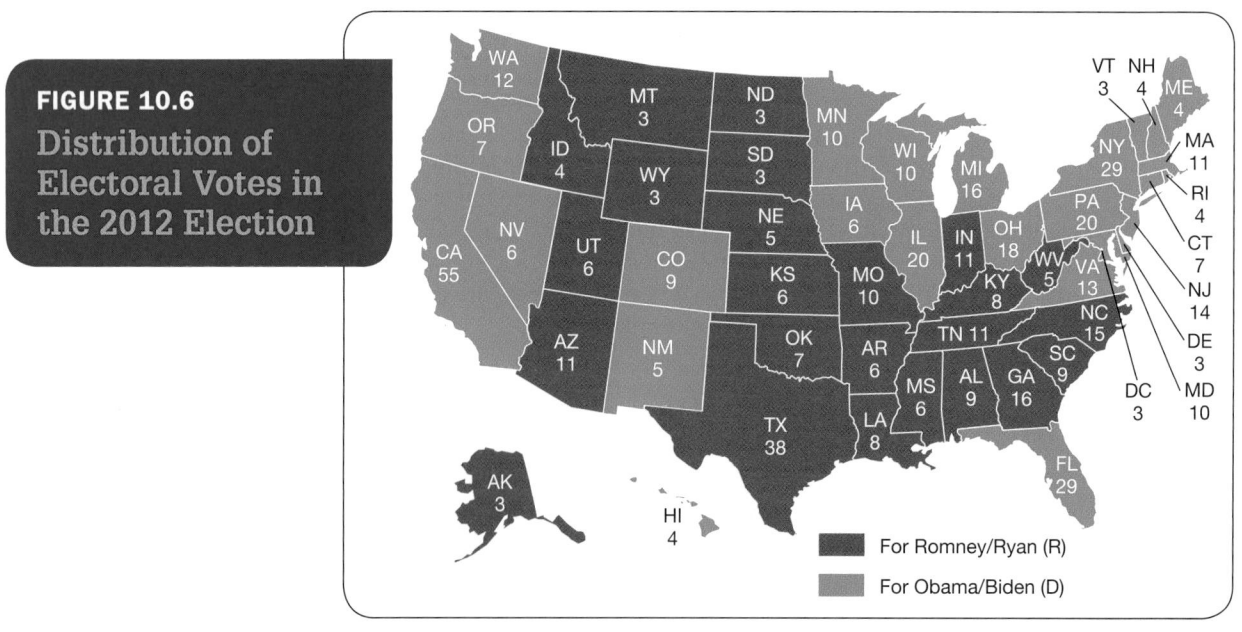

**FIGURE 10.6**

Distribution of Electoral Votes in the 2012 Election

# Who Supported Obama in 2012?

Barack Obama defeated Mitt Romney in the 2012 presidential election, winning 50 percent of the popular vote to Romney's 48 percent. The map in Figure 10.6, to the left, shows who won each state; there, red seems to dominate. However, if we adjust the map to show each state in proportion to its population, blue states—those won by Obama—clearly dominate.

## Election Results by State's Population

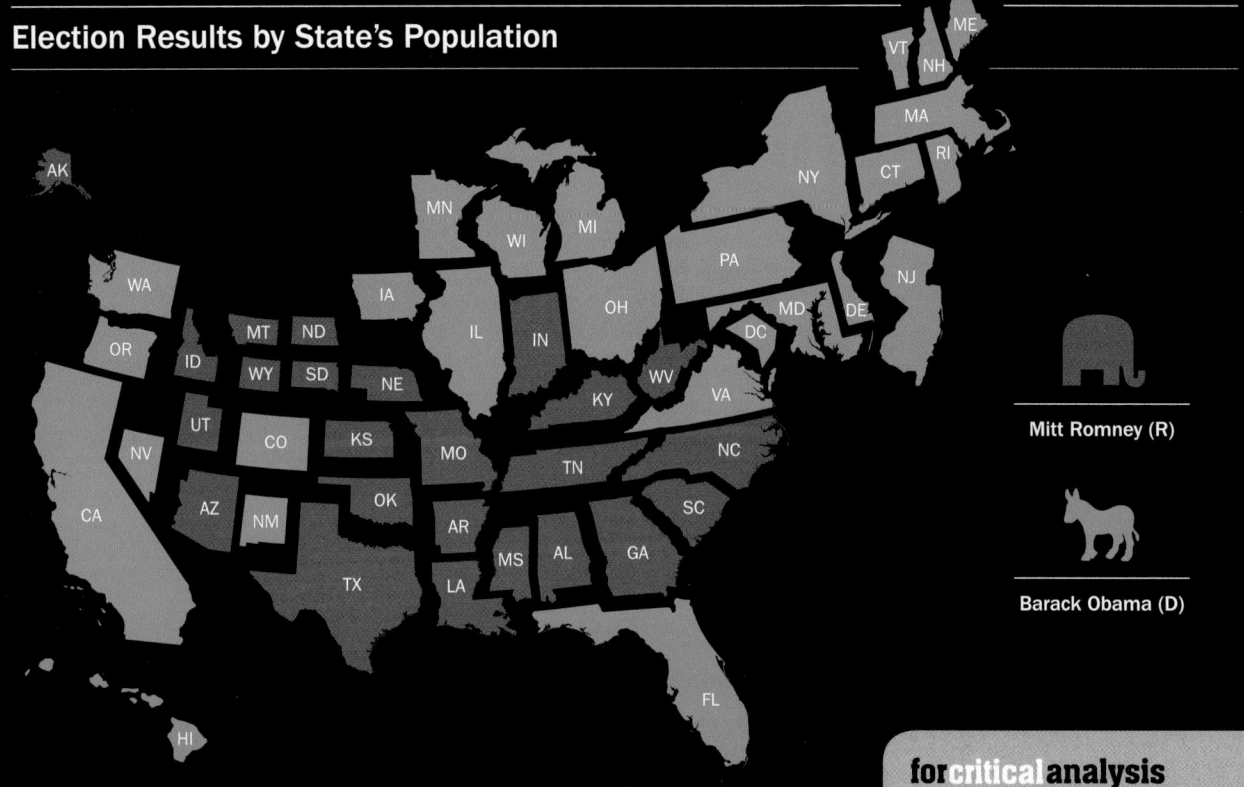

Mitt Romney (R)

Barack Obama (D)

## Votes in Electoral College

| | | | | | | | | |
|---|---|---|---|---|---|---|---|---|
| 55 | California | 10 | Maryland | 06 | Utah |
| 38 | Texas | 10 | Minnesota | 05 | New Mexico |
| 29 | Florida | 10 | Wisconsin | 05 | Nebraska |
| 29 | New York | 10 | Missouri | 05 | West Virginia |
| 20 | Illinois | 09 | Colorado | 04 | Hawaii |
| 20 | Pennsylvania | 09 | Alabama | 04 | Maine |
| 18 | Ohio | 09 | South Carolina | 04 | New Hampshire |
| 16 | Michigan | 08 | Louisiana | 04 | Rhode Island |
| 16 | Georgia | 08 | Kentucky | 04 | Idaho |
| 15 | North Carolina | 07 | Connecticut | 03 | Delaware |
| 14 | New Jersey | 07 | Oregon | 03 | District Of Columbia |
| 13 | Virginia | 07 | Oklahoma | 03 | Vermont |
| 12 | Washington | 06 | Iowa | 03 | Alaska |
| 11 | Massachusetts | 06 | Nevada | 03 | Montana |
| 11 | Indiana | 06 | Arkansas | 03 | North Dakota |
| 11 | Arizona | 06 | Kansas | 03 | South Dakota |
| 11 | Tennessee | 06 | Mississippi | 03 | Wyoming |

## for critical analysis

1. With the exception of Texas, Obama won the states with the largest populations—California, New York, Florida, and Illinois. How are these states different from those that Romney won? What do these differences tell us about the political differences between more densely populated areas (urban areas) and those with lower populations (rural areas)?

2. What do you think causes the differences between urban and rural America? Do you think these differences will continue long into the future?

*In 2012, as in past elections, both campaigns focused on a few battleground states. Romney and Obama campaigned extensively in Ohio, Florida, Virginia, Wisconsin, Colorado, Nevada, Iowa, and New Hampshire, and voters in these states saw thousands of campaign ads.*

support among working-class Americans. According to exit polls, the president won 63 percent of the votes of those whose family incomes were less than $30,000 per year and 57 percent of those who earned between $30,000 and $49,000 per year. Among more affluent voters, by contrast, Romney was the winner, taking 52 percent of the votes of those who earned between $50,000 and $100,000 per year and about 54 percent of the votes of those whose annual family incomes exceeded $100,000.

The Obama campaign also redoubled its efforts among women voters. In recent years, women have tended to give a majority of their votes to the Democrats, producing a so-called gender gap in the electoral arena. Democratic ads reminded women that it was the Democratic Party that supported such issues as equal pay. Foolish remarks on rape and abortion by GOP senatorial candidates in Indiana and Missouri were highlighted by the Democrats to underscore Republican insensitivity to women's concerns. On Election Day, 55 percent of women voters supported Obama, while Romney received the votes of 52 percent of America's men.

Finally, Obama campaign workers were determined to ensure high levels of turnout among minority voters, who potentially could be decisive in several battleground states. African American voters were a loyal Democratic constituency and could be counted upon to turn out for the president. But the Democrats had been making enormous efforts to bring Asian and, especially, Latino voters into their camp, too. Latinos are the most rapidly growing group in the American population and were responsible for about 10 percent of the votes cast in 2012. The Democratic Party had made a major effort to court Latinos on such issues as immigration and, in 2012, Democrats had pushed for ballot initiatives in a number of states that offered undocumented young Latinos who had been raised in the United States the opportunity to attend public colleges at the in-state tuition rate. These so-called "American Dream" referenda not only cemented the relationship between the Democratic Party and the Latino community, but also helped bring Latinos to the polls in large numbers. This strategy proved extremely successful. Not only did Obama capture 93 percent of the African American vote, but he also won approximately 70 percent of the Latino vote across the country. Among whites, by contrast, Romney received 58 percent of the vote.

Taken together, working-class voters, women, and minority constituents gave Obama the votes he needed for victory. This "one-two-three punch" was particularly important in the battleground states. Astonishingly, President Obama carried all the battleground states, and in each one, exit polls suggested that the critical margin was provided by low-income groups, minorities, and women.

## Digital Media in the 2012 Elections

The 2012 elections also reflected an ongoing change in how campaigns and elections are conducted since the rise of the Internet. Even more so than in 2008, both parties and candidates at all levels had to take account of the growing importance of online videos, mobile applications, social media, and digital fundraising.

According to reports released by the Pew Research Center soon after the election, in 2012 fully 55 percent of registered voters watched political videos online, including news reports about the election, debates, humorous and parody videos, and political ads. One in two registered voters had received recommendations for political videos to watch. Mobile phone politics also hit new highs in the 2012 election. Twenty-seven percent of registered voters who own a cell phone used their phone in this election campaign to keep up with news related to the election or politics. One in five cell phone owners sent text messages related to the campaign to friends, family members, or others.

Political discussions frequently took place via social media, where people tried to convince their friends how to vote. In the last 30 days of the campaigns, 30 percent of registered voters heard from family and friends via Facebook or Twitter that they should vote for Obama or Romney. This compares to 48 percent who had similar face-to-face conversations. Perhaps most important, one in five registered voters was the mobilizer, encouraging friends and family to get out and vote by posting on these forums.

Campaign donations continued to go digital in 2012, following Obama's successful campaign in 2008. Thirteen percent of American adults donated to one of the presidential candidates in 2012, a higher than average percentage roughly matching 2008. While 67 percent of these contributors donated in person, over the telephone, or by mail, roughly half donated online or via e-mail in 2012. There are partisan differences: 57 percent of Democratic campaign donors gave online or via e-mail in 2012, compared with just 34 percent of Republican donors. In 2012 the Federal Election Commission allowed political campaigns to accept campaign contributions via text message, and again, Democrats were more likely to contribute using the new technology.

While many factors—especially demographic trends—contributed to Obama's victory in 2012, it is also notable that the Obama campaign pioneered online fundraising and organizing techniques in 2008 and built on these successful strategies in 2012. The Republicans made up some ground and introduced a few online strategies of their own in 2012, but the Democrats appeared to hold an advantage in the effective use of digital politics.

## Looking toward the Future

As they surveyed the results, Republicans consoled themselves that 2012 had not been a complete disaster. To be sure, in Senate races, Democrats increased their majority by a net gain of two, from 51 to 53 seats. Democrats won formerly Republican seats in Massachusetts and Indiana as well as the Connecticut seat previously held by Independent Joe Lieberman. Republicans, for their part, captured a formerly Democratic seat in Nebraska. A formerly Republican seat long held by retiring senator Olympia Snowe was won by Independent former governor Angus King, who refused to say whether he planned to caucus with the Democrats or Republicans. Nevertheless, the GOP had successfully defended its bastion in the House of Representatives. In House races, the Democrats added only seven seats to their total, falling fall short of the number needed to take control of the lower chamber. And it appeared that Republicans might add one gubernatorial slot, North Carolina, to their tally of state chief executives.

But while 2012 was not an unmitigated disaster for the GOP; many Republicans reviewing the results of the election believed that their party must change, that it must reach out to women, Latinos, and others. If the GOP remained merely the party of affluent white men, particularly as the U.S. population became less white, demographics would doom it to the status of a permanent minority. Thus, ironically, if it hoped to become a party capable of winning majorities, the GOP would have to become a party able to woo minorities.

*Senator Claire McCaskill was one of several Democratic incumbents who were considered vulnerable in the 2012 elections. However, McCaskill won re-election, in part because her opponent Todd Akin lost support after making remarks on rape that were widely criticized.*

# Money and Politics

**Describe how candidates raise the money they need to run**

During the nineteenth century, national political campaigns in the United States employed millions of people. Indeed, as many as 2.5 million individuals did political work during the 1880s.[24] Most of these workers, however, were volunteers, so the direct cost of campaigns was relatively low. For example, in 1860, Abraham Lincoln spent only $100,000—which was approximately twice the amount spent by his chief opponent, Stephen A. Douglas.

Campaign tasks that were once performed by masses of party workers with some cash now require fewer personnel but a great deal more money, for the new political style depends on surveys, computers, and other electronic communication methods. The modern political campaign is enormously expensive. A 60-second spot on prime-time network television costs hundreds of thousands of dollars each time it is aired. Polling expenses in a statewide race can easily reach or exceed the six-figure mark. Campaign consultants can charge substantial fees. A serious national direct mail campaign requires at least $1 million in "front-end cash" to pay for mailing lists, printing, envelopes, and postage.[25]

Certainly "people power" is not irrelevant to modern political campaigns. Candidates continue to use the political services of tens of thousands of volunteer workers, especially for grassroots get-out-the-vote drives. Still, even the recruitment of campaign workers has become a job for electronic technology. Employing a technique called "instant organization," paid staff use phone banks to contact potential campaign workers in areas targeted by a computer (which they also do when contacting potential voters, as discussed earlier). Volunteer workers are recruited from among those called.

In the nineteenth century, labor-intensive campaigns allowed parties whose chief support came from groups nearer the bottom of the social scale to use their

*One way candidates raise money is through fundraisers, like this Republican Party event in Pennsylvania where Mitt Romney spoke. Supporters typically donate a certain amount in order to attend.*

numerical superiority as a partial counterweight to the institutional and economic resources more readily available to the opposition. The capital-intensive campaign of the modern era, by contrast, has given a major boost to the political fortunes of candidates whose supporters are able to furnish the large sums now needed to compete effectively.[26] Candidates with the most campaign dollars usually win, and that was certainly the case with President Obama, who in 2008 out-fund-raised his Republican opponent, John McCain. It was also the case with Republican Mitt Romney, who out-fund-raised his Republican challengers in 2012, including Newt Gingrich and Rick Santorum. Dominated by expensive technology, therefore, electoral politics has become a contest in which the wealthy and powerful have a decided advantage. The use of the Internet for campaigns offers hope for more equality, with millions of dollars in small donations increasingly raised in online fund-raising, as was the case with Obama in the 2008 presidential elections (see Chapter 8). The 2012 presidential election shattered previous records for campaign spending. In the aftermath of the 2010 Supreme Court decision allowing unlimited political spending by unaffiliated groups, both majority party candidates opted out of the campaign financing system. Spending by candidates, political parties and interest groups on the congressional and presidential races was $6 billion combined in 2012, as compared with $5.3 billion in 2008 and $4.2 billion in 2004.

## Sources of Campaign Funds

According to the Center for Responsive Politics, about 10 percent of the $3 billion spent by candidates for federal offices in 2008 came from **political action committees (PACs)**, mainly in support of congressional races; the remainder came from individual donors. Several million individuals donated money to political campaigns in that year, some in contributions of as little as five or ten dollars. One of the sources of Barack Obama's fund-raising advantage in the 2008 campaign was his ability to generate more than 2 million small- and medium-size contributions to his campaign.[27] Another $500 million in 2008 was raised and spent by individuals and advocacy groups—the so-called 527 and 501c(4) groups operating outside the structure of the Democratic and Republican campaigns. According to early estimates, as much as $4 billion was spent by candidates and their supporters during the 2010 midterm elections in the wake of the Supreme Court's ruling in the *Citizens United* case and other federal court decisions which eliminated many of the previous limits on campaign spending.[28]

**Individual Donors** Politicians spend a great deal of time asking people for money. Money is solicited via direct mail, through the Internet, over the phone, and in numerous face-to-face meetings. Under federal law, individuals may donate as much as $2,300 per candidate per election, $5,000 per PAC per calendar year (to a maximum of $65,500), $28,500 per national party committee per calendar year, and $10,000 to state and local committees per calendar year. Federal rules also impose an overall limit on individual contributors of $108,200 per election cycle. Individuals may contribute freely—without limits—to 527 committees and to 501c(4) groups. Additionally, they may attempt to enhance their influence by "bundling" their contributions with those of friends and associates.

**Political Action Committees** PACs are organizations established by corporations, labor unions, or interest groups to channel the contributions of their members into political campaigns. Under the terms of the 1971 Federal Election Campaign Act, which governs campaign finance in the United States, PACs are permitted to make larger contributions to any given candidate than individuals are allowed to make (see Table 10.2). Moreover, allied or related PACs often coordinate their campaign contributions, greatly increasing the amount of money a candidate actually receives from the same interest group. More than 4,500 PACs are registered with the Federal Election Commission (FEC), which oversees campaign finance practices in the United States. Nearly two-thirds of all PACs represent corporations, trade associations, and other business and professional groups. Alliances of bankers, lawyers, doctors, and merchants all sponsor PACs. The National Beer Wholesalers Association PAC was known for many years as "SixPAC." Labor unions also sponsor PACs, as do ideological, public interest, and nonprofit groups. The National Rifle Association sponsors a PAC, as does the Sierra Club. Many congressional and party leaders have established PACs, known as leadership PACs, to provide funding for their political allies.

**Independent Spending: 527, 501c(4), and Super PAC Committees** Committees known as **527s** and **501c(4)s** are independent groups that are currently not covered by the campaign-spending restrictions imposed in 2002 by the BCRA. These groups, named for the sections of the tax code under which they are organized, can raise and spend unlimited amounts on political advocacy as long as their efforts are not coordinated with those of any candidate's campaign. A 527 is a group established specifically for the purpose of political advocacy, whereas a

**527 committees** nonprofit independent groups that receive and disburse funds to influence the nomination, election, or defeat of candidates. Named after Section 527 of the Internal Revenue Code, which defines and provides tax-exempt status for nonprofit advocacy groups

**501c(4) committees** nonprofit groups that also engage in issue advocacy. Under Section 501c(4) of the federal tax code such a group may spend up to half its revenue for political purposes

## TABLE 10.2

## The Rules for Campaign Contributions

| WHO | MAY CONTRIBUTE . . . | TO . . . | IF . . . |
|---|---|---|---|
| Individuals | up to $2,300 | a candidate | they are contributing to a single candidate in a single election. |
| Individuals | up to $28,500 | a national party committee. | |
| Individuals | up to $5,000 | a PAC. | |
| PACs | up to $5,000 | a candidate | they contribute to the campaigns of at least five candidates. |
| Individuals and PACs | unlimited funds | a 527 committee | the funds are used for Issue advocacy and the 527 committee's efforts are not coordinated with any political campaign. |
| Individuals and | up to $10,000 | a state party committee | the money is used for Voter registration and get-out-the-vote efforts. |

*During the 2004 presidential campaign, dozens of independent 527 committees spent hundreds of millions of dollars on television advertising. One of the most notorious of these ads was the "Swift Boat Veterans for Truth," which challenged John Kerry's military record and activism against the Vietnam War.*

501c(4) is a nonprofit group, such as an environmental or other public interest group, that also engages in advocacy. A 501c(4) may not spend more than half its revenue for political purposes. Yet, unlike a 527, a 501c(4) is not required to disclose where it gets its funds or exactly what it does with them. As a result, it has become a common practice for wealthy and corporate donors to route campaign contributions far in excess of the legal limits through 501c(4)s. A new form of independent group, the independent expenditure committee, or "super PAC," came about as a result of an FEC ruling that the Supreme Court's 2010 decision in *Citizens United v. FEC* permitted individuals and organizations to form committees that could raise unlimited amounts of money to run advertising for and against candidates so long as their efforts were not coordinated with those of the candidates.[29] Outside spending via 527s and 501c(4)s played an unprecedented role in the 2012 presidential race, as groups ran extensive television ads. Priorities USA Action super PAC raised $64 million to support Democrats, while the Restore Our Future super PAC raised $132 million to help Republicans. The top spending super PACs were primarily those advocating against Obama, including American Crossroads ($85 million), the Republican National Committee ($41 million), Americans for Prosperity ($34 million), and the National Rifle Association of America Political Victory Fund ($7.4 million). Super PACs on both sides relied on very large contributions. Table 10.3 lists the top super PAC donors in 2012.

**Political Parties** Before 2002, most campaign dollars took the form of "soft money," unregulated contributions to the national parties nominally to assist in party building or voter registration efforts rather than for particular campaigns. Federal campaign finance legislation crafted by Senators John McCain and Russell Feingold and enacted in 2002 sought to ban soft money by prohibiting the national parties from soliciting and receiving contributions from corporations, unions, or individuals and preventing them from directing such funds to their affiliated state parties. However, it did not reduce the overall importance of money in politics, and political parties continue to play a major role in financing political campaigns. Under federal rules, a national political party committee may make unlimited "independent expenditures" advocating support for its own presidential candidate or advocating the defeat of the opposing party's candidate as long as these expenditures are not coordinated with the candidate's own campaign. A national party committee may

## TABLE 10.3

## Top Donors to Super PACs, 2012

**DEMOCRATIC SUPER PAC DONORS**

| AMOUNT DONATED (IN MILLIONS) | DONOR |
|---|---|
| 3.5 | Fred Eychaner   An Obama bundler and Chicago media mogul. |
| 3.5 | James H. Simons   President of Euclidean Capital and Board Chair of Renaissance Technologies Corp., a hedge fund company. |
| 3.0 | Jeffrey Katzenberg   Chief executive of Dreamworks Animation. |
| 2.0 | United Association of Journeymen & Apprentices of the Pipe Fitting Industry   Trade union. |
| 2.0 | Irwin Jacobs   Founder of chipmaker Qualcomm and former M.I.T. professor. |
| 2.0 | Jon Stryker   Gay rights activist and founder of the Arcus Foundation. |
| 2.0 | Steve Mostyn   Texas trial lawyer. |
| 2.0 | Anne Cox Chambers   Part owner of Cox Enterprises, the media conglomerate. |
| 1.5 | Ann Wyckoff   Seattle philanthropist. |
| 1.2 | National Air Traffic Controllers Association PAC   PAC of the air traffic controllers union. |

**REPUBLICAN SUPER PAC DONORS**

| AMOUNT DONATED (IN MILLIONS) | DONOR |
|---|---|
| 10.0 | Sheldon Adelson   Billionaire casino owner and Newt Gingrich's longtime friend and patron. |
| 10.0 | Miriam Adelson   Physician; wife of Sheldon Adelson. |
| 10.0 | Bob J. Perry   Houston homebuilder who was a major financier of Swift Boat Veterans for Truth in 2004. |
| 2.8 | Oxbow Carbon LLC   An oil and gas company based in West Palm Beach, Florida. It was founded by William Koch, the brother of David H. and Charles Koch, wealthy conservative businessmen and founders of Americans for Prosperity. |
| 2.3 | Harold Simmons   Dallas billionaire who was among the top donors to Governor Rick Perry of Texas. |
| 2.2 | Julian Robertson   Founder of Tiger Management, a hedge fund. |
| 1.6 | Robert Reynolds   Chief executive of Putman Investments. |
| 1.6 | Kenneth C. Griffin   Founder and chief executive of Citadel LLC. |
| 1.5 | A. Jerrold Perenchio   Billionaire and former chairman of Univision. |
| 1.2 | Stanley Herzog   Chairman and chief executive of Herzog Contracting Corp., a highway and railroad construction firm. |

SOURCE: http://elections.nytimes.com/2012/campaign-finance (accessed 11/11/12).

also spend up to $19 million in coordination with its Presidential candidate's campaign even if its candidate has accepted public funding. Thus, for example, even though John McCain accepted full public funding for his 2008 presidential bid, the national Republican Party helped fund McCain's advertising up to the federal limit. Neither major party candidate accepted public financing in 2012. As a result, many observers believe that the 2008 race may be the last time that a major-party candidate will forgo his or her own fund-raising in favor of public funding. Candidates who accept public funding may not engage in fund-raising for their own campaigns.

*Rules governing campaign finance have been the object of intense debate in recent years. Many Americans worry that government policies favor groups—such as Wall Street financiers—who make large donations to campaigns.*

**Public Funding** The Federal Election Campaign Act also provides for public funding of presidential campaigns. As they seek a major-party presidential nomination, candidates become eligible for public funds by raising at least $5,000 in individual contributions of $250 or less in each of 20 states. Candidates who reach this threshold may apply for federal funds to match, on a dollar-for-dollar basis, all individual contributions of $250 or less they receive. Currently, candidates who accept matching funds may spend no more than $42 million, including the matching funds, in their presidential primary campaigns. The funds are drawn from the Presidential Election Campaign Fund. Taxpayers may contribute $3 to this fund, at no additional cost to themselves, by checking a box on the first page of their federal income tax returns. Major-party presidential candidates receive a lump sum (about $91 million in 2012) during the summer prior to the general election. They must meet all their general expenses from this money. Third-party candidates are eligible for public funding only if they received at least 5 percent of the vote in the previous presidential race. This stipulation effectively blocks pre-election funding for third-party or independent candidates, although a third party that wins more than 5 percent of the vote can receive public funding after the election. In 1980, John Anderson persuaded banks to lend him money for an independent candidacy on the strength of poll data showing that he would receive more than 5 percent of the vote and thus would obtain public funds with which to repay the loans.

Under current law, no candidate is required to accept public funding for either the nominating races or general presidential election. Candidates who do not accept public funding are not affected by any expenditure limits. In 2008, John McCain accepted public funding for the general election campaign, receiving $84 million, but Barack Obama declined, choosing to rely on his own fund-raising prowess. Obama was ultimately able to outspend McCain by a wide margin. Candidates who accept public funding may not engage in fund-raising for their own campaigns. In 2010 the U.S. Supreme Court ruled in *Citizens United v. Federal Election Commission* that the government could not restrict independent expenditures by corporations or unions to political campaigns.[30] The Court said such restrictions violated the First Amendment. The United States has entered a new era of campaign finance in which corporations and unions can spend unlimited sums. These independent expenditures, meaning there is no coordination with the official candidate campaign, run through super PACs, or super political action committees.

**The Candidates Themselves**  On the basis of the Supreme Court's 1976 decision in *Buckley v. Valeo*, the right of individuals to spend their *own* money to campaign for office is a constitutionally protected matter of free speech and is not subject to limitation.[31] Thus, extremely wealthy candidates often contribute millions of dollars to their own campaigns. The New Jersey Democrat Jon Corzine, for example, spent approximately $60 million of his own funds in a successful U.S. Senate bid in 2000 and another $40 million when he ran for governor of New Jersey in 2005. The only exception to the *Buckley* rule concerns presidential candidates who accept federal funding for their general election campaigns. Such individuals are limited to $50,000 in personal spending.

# ● Thinking Critically about Elections and Democracy

The important role played by private funds in American elections affects the balance of power among contending economic groups. Politicians need large amounts of money to campaign successfully for major offices. This fact inevitably ties their interests to the interests of the groups and forces that can provide this money: the affluent. In a nation as large and diverse as the United States, to be sure, campaign contributors represent many different groups and, often, clashing interests. Business groups, labor groups, environmental groups, and pro-choice and right-to-life forces all contribute millions of dollars to political campaigns. One set of trade associations may contribute millions to win politicians' support for telecommunications reform, whereas another set may contribute just as much to block the same reform efforts. Insurance companies may contribute millions of dollars to Democrats to win their support for changes in the health care system, whereas physicians may contribute equal amounts to prevent the same changes from becoming law.

Interests that donate large amounts of money to campaigns expect and often receive favorable treatment from elected officials in return for their contributions. For example, in 2000 a number of major interest groups with specific policy goals made substantial donations to the Bush presidential campaign. These included airlines, energy producers, banks, tobacco companies, and a number of others. After Bush's election, these interests pressed the new president to promote their legislative and regulatory agendas. For instance, MBNA America Bank was a major donor to the 2000 Bush campaign. The bank and its executives gave Bush $1.3 million. The bank's president helped raise millions more for Bush and personally gave an additional $100,000 to the president's inaugural committee after the election. All told, MBNA and other banking companies donated $26 million to the GOP in 2000. Within weeks of his election, President Bush signed legislation providing

MBNA and the others with something they had sought for years: bankruptcy laws making it more difficult for consumers to escape credit card debt.

Similarly, a coalition of manufacturers led by the U.S. Chamber of Commerce and the National Association of Manufacturers also provided considerable support for Bush's 2000 campaign. This coalition sought, among other things, the repeal of federal rules promulgated in 2000 by the federal Occupational Safety and Health Administration (OSHA) that were designed to protect workers from repetitive-motion injuries. Again, within weeks of his election, the president approved a resolution rejecting the rules. In the 2010 and 2012 elections a number of corporate interests and labor unions took advantage of the Supreme Court's lifting of restrictions on campaign spending to pour tens of millions of dollars into congressional races. Corporate America, for the most part, supported the GOP. Labor, particularly public-sector unions fearing job cuts under the Republicans, gave tens of millions of dollars to support Democrats.

Despite the diversity of contributors, not all interests play a role in financing political campaigns. Only those groups that have a good deal of money to spend can make their interests known in this way. The poor and the downtrodden also live in America and have a stake in the outcome of political campaigns. Who speaks for them? Who benefits from the American system of private funding of campaigns? The Internet and online campaigns offer promise for levelling the playing field in elections.

# Explore Issues in Campaigning

## Inform Yourself

**Consider how the electoral college system influences presidential campaign strategy.** Presidential campaigns don't try to win over every voter in every state; rather, they focus on winning enough states to get to 270 votes in the electoral college. Check out www.270towin.org to see the battleground states in the 2012 election, compared to the 2008 and 2004 elections. Which states have changed? Which have stayed the same?

**Consider alternatives to the electoral college.** One proposed electoral reform is called the National Popular Vote. View the video *Make Every State Purple* (www .youtube.com/watch?v=JhOZCKac6os). What are the advantages of a system based on the popular vote? What are the advantages of the electoral college system?

**Find out who pays for campaigns.** Visit the *New York Times* 2012 Money Race (http://elections.nytimes.com/2012/campaign-finance) to see how much was money was raised and spent during the election. How much was raised by the candidates, the parties, and Super PACs? Visit Open Secrets via its Facebook page to see who the big spenders were in 2012. Are you surprised?

## Express Yourself

**Share your thoughts on where presidential candidates should campaign.** View a map of state populations using the 2010 census (http://2010.census .gov/2010census/popmap/). About a third of the population lives in one of five states (Texas, California, Florida, New York, or Illinois), yet only one of these has recently been a battleground state. The average voter in a battleground state will view nearly 300 television ads during the campaign, compared to just a half dozen in a non-swing state. Campaign ads and other campaign events help educate voters about the candidates and their policy positions. Where do you think candidates should campaign?

**Follow the money in your area.** Go to Follow the Money (www.followthemoney .org) and look up how much money was spent on elections in your state in the last few years. Enter your address to find out about money spent in your legislative district, or click on the "Who represents me?" boxes to find out. Which groups or industries provide the most money to your lawmakers? With this information, consider e-mailing or calling your lawmaker to express your opinion about money in politics.

*Find links to the sites listed above as well as related activities on wwnorton.com/studyspace.*

# study guide

## Elections in America

■ **Describe the major rules and procedures of elections in the United States (pp. 381–94)**

There are four types of American elections: primary elections, general elections, runoff elections, and initiative and referendum elections. While each election operates under its own set of rules, most elections in the United States today use the Australian ballot and operate under plurality, rather than the majority or the proportional representation, system. Unlike members of the House of Representatives, who are elected through a direct vote from districts whose boundaries are usually redrawn every 10 years, presidents are elected indirectly by the electoral college.

### Key Terms

**midterm elections** (p. 381)

**primary elections** (p. 382)

**closed primary** (p. 382)

**open primary** (p. 382)

**general election** (p. 383)

**runoff election** (p. 383)

**majority system** (p. 383)

**plurality system** (p. 383)

**proportional representation** (p. 383)

**straight-ticket vote** (p. 383)

**coattail effect** (p. 384)

**redistricting** (p. 385)

**gerrymandering** (p. 385)

**majority-minority district** (p. 385)

**electoral college** (p. 386)

**caucus (political)** (p. 388)

**platform** (p. 391)

**delegate** (p. 391)

**superdelegate** (p. 392)

**ballot initiative** (p. 392)

**referendum** (p. 392)

**recall** (p. 393)

### Practice Quiz

1. A closed primary is a primary election in which *(p. 382)*
   a) one's vote is kept private.
   b) only registered members of the party may vote.
   c) only registered members of the party may run.
   d) only two candidates are allowed to run.
   e) voting is conducted by mail.

2. Beginning with the 1993 case *Shaw v. Reno*, the Supreme Court has *(p. 385)*
   a) generally rejected efforts to create majority-minority districts and asserted that districting based exclusively on race is unlawful.
   b) generally supported efforts to create majority-minority districts and asserted that districting based exclusively on race is lawful.
   c) generally rejected efforts to create majority-minority districts but asserted that districting based exclusively on race is lawful.
   d) generally supported efforts to reduce the amount of soft money in election campaigns.
   e) generally rejected efforts to reduce the amount of soft money in election campaigns.

3. When a voter casts a ballot for a party's presidential candidate and then "automatically" votes for the rest of that party's candidates, it is referred to as *(p. 383)*
   a) primary voting.
   b) one-way voting.
   c) proportional representation.
   d) straight-ticket voting.
   e) split-ticket voting.

4. If a state has 10 members in the U.S. House of Representatives, how many electoral votes does that state have? *(p. 386)*
   a) 2
   b) 10
   c) 12
   d) 20
   e) It cannot be determined from this information.

# Election Campaigns

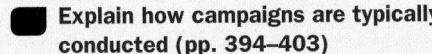

■ **Explain how campaigns are typically conducted (pp. 394–403)**

In order to successfully run for political office, candidates must organize exploratory committees and create formal campaign organizations that employ a campaign manager, a media consultant, a pollster, a financial advisor, a press spokesperson, and a staff director. Although local and congressional candidates campaign by recruiting large numbers of volunteer workers, most contemporary political campaigns rely less on labor-intensive mobilizations and more on "air power" and the Internet. These activities require enormous amounts of money, and many politicians spend more time soliciting donations than engaging in anything else.

## Key Terms

**campaign** (p. 394)

**incumbernt** (p. 394)

**spot (advertisement)** (p. 398)

**town hall meeting** (p. 400)

## Practice Quiz

5. The average amount of money spent by House incumbents to secure re-election has *(pp. 395–97)*
   a) been surpassed by the average amount of money spent by challengers since 1980.
   b) declined to zero after the passage of the Bipartisan Campaign Reform Act in 2003.
   c) remained the same as the average amount spent by challengers since 1980.
   d) increased at a greater rate than the average amount spent by challengers since 1980.
   e) decreased at a greater rate than the average amount spent by challengers since 1980.

 **Practice Online**
Interactive simulation: *Running a Successful Campaign*

# How Voters Decide

■ **Identify the major factors that influence voters' decisions (pp. 403–8)**

Three factors influence the decisions that voters make at the polls: partisan loyalty, issues and policy preferences, and candidate characteristics. Partisan attachments are usually handed down from parents to children and, once formed, tend to remain an important influence on which candidates a voter chooses to support. In addition, voters consider the past and future behavior of competing parties and candidates when casting a ballot. A candidate's race, ethnicity, religion, gender, and social background are also weighed by voters on election day.

## Key Terms

**prospective voting** (p. 406)

**retrospective voting** (p. 406)

## Practice Quiz

6. Partisan loyalty *(p. 405)*
   a) is often handed down from parents to children.
   b) changes frequently.
   c) is currently much stronger than it was in the 1940s and 1950s.
   d) is mandated in states with closed primaries.
   e) has little impact on voting in congressional and state-level elections.

7. When a voter decides which candidate to vote for based on past performance, the voter is engaged in *(p. 406)*
   a) prospective voting.
   b) retrospective voting.
   c) the coattail effect.
   d) candidate-centered voting.
   e) ticket splitting.

8. The Consumer Confidence Index *(p. 406)*
   a) measures how business leaders rate the federal government's regulation of the economy during election years.
   b) was a federal government program designed to increase economic growth during the Reagan administration.
   c) has been an inaccurate predictor of presidential outcomes.
   d) has been a fairly accurate predictor of presidential outcomes.
   e) is based on government reports of objective economic indicators.

 **Practice Online**
Video exercise: *Issue Ads*

# The 2012 Elections

**■ Analyze the strategies, issues, and outcomes of the 2012 elections (pp. 408–18)**

In the 2012, voters re-elected Barack Obama to the presidency, and Democrats retained control of the Senate while Republicans retained control of the House of Representatives. In the primaries, Mitt Romney competed with several other candidates to win the Republican nomination for the presidency. Throughout the campaigns both parties argued that they had a better plan for addressing the economic challenges facing the nation and other issues.

## Practice Quiz

9. The biggest issue in the 2012 national elections was *(pp. 408–10)*
   a) same-sex marriage.
   b) energy policy.
   c) abortion.
   d) the economy.
   e) Medicare.

10. During the Republican primaries, which faction within the party did Romney represent? *(p. 411)*

   a) social conservatives
   b) fiscal conservatives
   c) neoconservatives
   d) paleoconservatives
   e) extreme conservatives

11. In 2012, Romney and the Republicans received a majority of votes from *(pp. 416–17)*
   a) whites, Asian Americans, and young voters.
   b) whites, Latinos, and women.
   c) whites, men, and more affluent voters.
   d) African Americans, women, and more affluent voters.
   e) African Americans, Latinos, and young voters.

12. Which statement best characterizes the role of the Internet in the 2012 elections? *(pp. 417–18)*
   a) The Internet was less important than in previous elections.
   b) The Internet played a larger role than ever.
   c) The Internet was important mainly for the Democrats.
   d) The Internet was important mainly for the Republicans.
   e) Presidential candidates used the Internet as a campaign tool for the first time.

# Money and Politics

**■ Describe how candidates raise the money they need to run (pp. 419–25)**

Modern political campaigns in the United States are enormously expensive and candidates with the most money usually win. Candidates finance their campaigns with money from their own bank accounts, individual donors, political action committees, political parties, and independent 527 and 501c(4) groups. The Federal Elections Campaign Act also provides for public funding of presidential campaigns.

## Key Terms

**political action committee** (p. 420)

**527 committees** (p. 421)

**501c(4) committees** (p. 421)

## Practice Quiz

14. In 2002, federal campaign finance legislation crafted by John McCain and Russell Feingold sought to *(p. 422)*
   a) ban soft money by prohibiting national parties from soliciting and receiving contributions from corporations, unions, or individuals.
   b) increase the amount of soft money in elections by encouraging national parties to solicit and receive contributions from corporations, unions, and individuals.
   c) ban candidates from using their own personal resources in election campaigns.
   d) give corporations the power to contribute unlimited amounts of money to influence the outcome of election campaigns.
   e) create a system of publicly financed election campaigns.

15. In *Buckley v. Valeo*, the Supreme Court ruled that *(p. 425)*
   a) PAC donations to campaigns are constitutionally protected.
   b) candidates cannot spend any of their own money to run for office.
   c) the right of individuals to spend their own money to campaign is constitutionally protected.
   d) the political system is corrupt.
   e) the Federal Elections Campaign Act is unconstitutional.

 **Practice Online**
Video exercise: *Campaign Ads and PACs*

# For Further Reading

Abramson, Paul, John Aldrich, and David Rohde. *Change and Continuity in the 2008 Elections*. Washington, DC: Congressional Quarterly Press, 2009.

Ackerman, Bruce, and Ian Avres. *Voting with Dollars*. New Haven, CT: Yale University Press, 2004.

Browning, Graeme. *Electronic Democracy*. New York: Cyberage, 2002.

Ginsberg, Benjamin, and Martin Shefter. *Politics by Other Means: Institutional Conflict and the Declining Significance of Elections in America*. New York: Norton, 1999.

Heilemann, John, and Mark Halperin. *Game Change: Obama and the Clintons, McCain and Palin, and the Race of a Lifetime*. New York: Harper, 2010.

Maass, Matthias. *The World Views of the 2008 U.S. Presidential Election*. New York: Palgrave, 2009.

Nelson, Michael, ed. *The Elections of 2008*. Washington, DC: CQ Press, 2009.

Polsby, Nelson, Aaron Wildavsky, and David Hopkins. *Presidential Elections*. 12th ed. New York: Rowman and Littlefield, 2007.

Raymond, Allen, and Ian Spiegelman. *How to Rig an Election*. New York: Simon & Schuster, 2008.

Schier, Steven. *You Call This an Election?* Washington, DC: Georgetown University Press, 2003.

Wayne, Stephen. *Is This Any Way to Run a Democratic Election?* 3rd ed. Washington, DC: CQ Press, 2007.

# Recommended Websites

**Center for Voting and Democracy**
www.fairvote.org

The Center for Voting and Democracy is dedicated to open access to voting, equal representation, and a voice for all Americans. Read about some of their electoral reform proposals such as runoff elections, proportional representation, and alternatives to the electoral college.

**The Color of Money**
www.colorofmoney.org

Campaign funding affects the balance of power among contending social groups in America. Politicians are tied to groups that provide them with the large amounts of money needed to campaign for major office. This website examines federal campaign contributions with a focus on race and ethnicity to show how campaign money has the potential to skew government policy decisions.

**ElectionMail.com**
www.electionmail.com

Are you thinking about running for office? Whether you aspire to be student government president or president of the United States, here you can find links to affordable political printing, including political brochures, campaign literature, and campaign signs.

**Federal Election Commission**
www.fec.gov

The Federal Election Commission (FEC) is an independent government agency that was created in 1975 to administer and enforce the Federal Election Campaign Act (FECA). At the official FEC website you can read about the rules and regulations that govern the financing of federal elections and other topics of interest.

**JibJab.com**
www.jibjab.com

This website became famous for its political video clips during the 2004 presidential campaign. For a good laugh check out some of the political jokes or rummage through the video archives to find one of the original Bush or Kerry clips.

**MultiEducator.com**
www.multied.com/elections/

MultiEducator's History Central website features a major section on elections. Here you can find the history of every U.S. national election, including popular and electoral votes, turnout, and a map of the states carried by each competing candidate.

**National Archives and Records Administration**
www.archives.gov/federal-register/electoral-college/index.html

The U.S. National Archives and Records Administration's Electoral College page is a great resource on presidential elections. Find answers to frequently asked questions about our electoral system, read about how electors vote, or try predicting who will win the next presidential election with the electoral college calculator.

**OpenSecrets.org**
www.opensecrets.org

Campaign funds come from a variety of sources, including individual donors, political action committees (PACs), self-contributions, independent spending, parties, and public funding. At this site you can research funding for all federal officials, including your own members of Congress.

**Project Vote Smart**
www.votesmart.org

Project Vote Smart is a nonpartisan site dedicated to providing citizens with information on political candidates and elected officials. Here you can easily view a candidate's biographical information, position on issues, and voting record, so that you can make an informed choice on Election Day.

**Voter Information Services**
www.vis.org

Voter Information Services (VIS) is a nonpartisan, nonprofit organization dedicated to helping interested citizens learn about their elected members of Congress. Here you can obtain a Congressional Report Card for your members of Congress and find out where they stand on the issues.

The use of "fracking" to recover gas has brought environmental groups into conflict with the energy industry. Both sides have tried to influence government regulations related to fracking.

# Groups and Interests

**11**

**WHAT GOVERNMENT DOES AND WHY IT MATTERS** For the past several years, environmental groups and the nation's energy industry have been locked in a struggle over the issue of "hydraulic fracking." This is a method for recovering natural gas trapped in shale formations deep beneath the earth's surface. The energy industry, which stands to make enormous profits from extracting this gas, asserts that fracking is the key to achieving American energy independence. Environmental groups, on the other hand, argue that fracking produces greenhouse gas emissions, undermines air quality, and contaminates drinking water while discouraging investment in cleaner, renewable forms of energy.

Despite these environmental concerns, large sections of the United States, including tracts in New York, Pennsylvania, and Ohio, are being fracked for their natural gas. Environmental groups appear to be losing the battle. Why? The energy industry, organized in groups such as the Natural Gas Alliance, the Independent Petroleum Association of America, and the American Gas Association, has deployed an army of nearly 800 lobbyists, including former members of Congress and other former high-ranking government officials, to promote their cause on Capitol Hill and in the state capitals. The industry has also spent tens of millions of dollars on advertising and campaign contributions—filling the coffers of Democrats and Republicans alike. Even President Obama, a self-proclaimed environmentalist, was moved to declare in his 2011 State of the Union address that natural gas produced in America was an important part of America's energy future.

The case of fracking exemplifies the power of interest groups in action. Tens of thousands of organized groups have formed in the United States, ranging from civic associations to huge nationwide groups such as the National Rifle Association (NRA), whose chief cause is opposition to restrictions on gun ownership, and Common Cause, a public interest group that advocates a variety of liberal political reforms. Despite the array of interest groups in American politics, however, not all interests are represented equally, and the results of competition among various interests are not always consistent with the common good. In this chapter we will examine the nature and consequences of interest-group politics in the United States.

## chaptergoals

- Describe the major types of interest groups and whom they represent (pages 435–43)

- Analyze why the number of interest groups has grown in recent decades (pages 443–45)

- Explain how interest groups try to influence government (pages 445–60)

# The Character of Interest Groups

Describe the major types of interest groups and whom they represent

The framers of the U.S. Constitution feared the power that could be wielded by organized interests. Yet they believed that interest groups thrived because of liberty—the freedom that all Americans enjoy to organize and to express their views. If the government were given the power to regulate or in any way to forbid efforts by organized interests to interpose themselves in the political process, it would in effect have the power to suppress liberty. The solution to this dilemma was presented by James Madison:

> Take in a greater variety of parties and interests [and] you make it less probable that a majority of the whole will have a common motive to invade the rights of other citizens. . . . [Hence the advantage] enjoyed by a large over a small republic.[1]

According to Madison, a good constitution encourages multitudes of interests so that no single interest, which he called a "faction," can ever tyrannize the others. The basic assumption is that all the competing interests will regulate one another, producing balance.[2] Today, this Madisonian principle is called **pluralism**. According to pluralist theory, all interests are and should be free to compete for influence in the United States. Moreover, according to pluralist doctrine, the outcome of this competition is compromise and moderation, since no group is likely to be able to achieve any of its goals without accommodating itself to some of the views of its many competitors.[3]

An **interest group** is an organized group of people that makes policy-related appeals to government. This definition of interest groups includes membership organizations as well as businesses, corporations, universities, and other institutions that restrict membership to particular occupational groups or other categories of persons. Individuals form groups in order to increase the chance that their views

**pluralism** the theory that all interests are and should be free to compete for influence in the government. The outcome of this competition is compromise and moderation

**interest group** individuals who organize to influence the government's programs and policies

*As long as there is government, there will be interests trying to influence it. During the 1890s, for instance, business interests fought for protective tariffs from Congress and President McKinley. This 1897 cartoon satirizes their success in capturing Congress.*

*Public interest groups often advocate for interests that are not addressed by traditional lobbies. For example, in addition to many other activities, the Public Interest Research Group (PIRG) publishes an annual toy safety report to help protect consumers and to encourage policymakers to address problems in this area.*

will be heard and their interests treated favorably by the government. Interest groups are sometimes referred to as "lobbies." They are also sometimes confused with political action committees, which are actually groups that focus on influencing elections rather than trying to influence the elected (see Chapter 10). One final distinction is that interest groups are also different from political parties: interest groups tend to concern themselves with the *policies* of government; parties tend to concern themselves with the *personnel* of government.

The number of interest groups in the United States is enormous, and millions of Americans are members of one or more groups, at least to the extent of paying dues or attending an occasional meeting. By representing the interests of such large numbers of people and encouraging political participation, organized groups can and do enhance American democracy. Organized groups educate and mobilize their members for elections and grassroots lobbying efforts, thus encouraging participation. Groups lobby members of Congress and the executive, engage in litigation, and generally represent their members' interests in the political arena. Interest groups also monitor government programs to make certain that their members are not adversely affected by these programs. In all these ways, organized interests can be said to promote democratic politics. But because not all interests are represented equally, interest-group politics works to the advantage of some and the disadvantage of others.

It is also important to remember that not all organized interests are successful. Struggles among interest groups have winners and losers, and even large groups well represented in Washington are sometimes defeated in political struggle. In recent years, for example, despite relentless lobbying, physicians' groups such as the American Medical Association (AMA) have been unable to persuade Congress to increase Medicare funding for physicians' services. One reason for this failure is that physicians are forced to compete for funding with insurers, drug companies, and hospitals. The doctors have simply been overmatched.

## Common Types of Interest Groups

**Business and Agricultural Groups** Interest groups come in as many shapes and sizes as the interests they represent. The most obvious are groups with a direct economic interest in governmental actions. These groups are generally supported by groups of producers or manufacturers in a particular economic sector, such as the American Fuel and Petrochemical Manufacturers and the American Farm Bureau Federation. In addition to these broadly representative groups, specific companies, such as Exxon, IBM, and General Motors, may be active in Washington on certain issues that are of particular concern to them.

**Labor Groups** Labor organizations are equally active lobbyists. The AFL-CIO, the United Mine Workers, and the Teamsters all lobby on behalf of organized labor. In recent years, groups have arisen to further the interests of public employees, the most significant among these being the American Federation of State, County, and Municipal Employees (AFSCME).

**Professional Associations** Professional lobbies such as the American Bar Association and the AMA have been particularly successful at furthering their members' interests in state and federal legislatures. Financial institutions, represented by organizations such as the American Bankers Association and the National Savings and Loan League, although often less visible than other lobbies, also play an important role in shaping legislative policy.

**Public Interest Groups** Recent years have witnessed the growth of a powerful "public interest" lobby, purporting to represent the general good rather than its own selfish interests. **Public interest groups** have been most visible in the consumer protection and environmental policy areas, although public interest groups cover a broad range of issues. The Natural Resources Defense Council, the Sierra Club, the Union of Concerned Scientists, and Common Cause are all examples of public interest groups. Claims to represent *only* the public interest should be viewed with caution, however: it is not uncommon to find decidedly private interests seeking to hide behind the term *public interest*. For example, the benign-sounding Partnership to Protect Consumer Credit is a coalition of credit card companies fighting for less federal regulation of credit abuses, and Project Protect is a coalition of logging interests promoting increased timber cutting.[4]

**Ideological Groups** Closely related to and overlapping public interest groups are ideological groups, organized in support of a particular political or philosophical perspective. People for the American Way, for example, promotes liberal values, whereas the Christian Coalition focuses on conservative social goals, and the National Taxpayers Union campaigns to reduce the size of the federal government.

**Public-Sector Groups** The perceived need for representation on Capitol Hill has generated a public-sector lobby in the past several years, including the National League of Cities and the "research" lobby. The latter group comprises think tanks and universities that have an interest in obtaining government funds for research and support, and it includes such diverse institutions as Harvard University, the Brookings Institution, and the American Enterprise Institute. Indeed, universities have expanded their lobbying efforts even as they have reduced faculty positions and course offerings.[5]

**public interest groups** groups that claim they serve the general good rather than only their own particular interest

## What Interests Are Not Represented?

It is difficult to categorize unrepresented interests precisely because they are not organized and are not able to present to us (or governments) their identity and their demands. The political scientist David Truman referred to these interests as "potential interest groups."[6] And he is undoubtedly correct that at any time, as long as there is freedom, any interest shared by a lot of people can develop through "voluntary association" into a genuine interest group that can demand, usually successfully, to get some representation. But the fact remains that many interests—including some very widely shared interests—do not get organized and recognized. Such "potential interests" might include everything from the homeless through tall people.

## Organizational Components

Although interest groups are many and varied, most share certain key organizational components. These include leadership, money, an agency or office, and members.

# Do Foreign Interests Exert Influence in the United States?

**Discussions of interest groups** often focus on the efforts of competing domestic forces—business, labor, public interest groups, and so on—to influence the government. Often, however, foreign interests and foreign governments also lobby vigorously to influence U.S. policy. Much of this lobbying is undertaken by foreign firms hoping to do business in the United States or directly with the U.S. government on favorable terms. For example, every year, Americans purchase billions of dollars of goods manufactured in China. In some instances, these Chinese products fail to comply with American health and safety standards, leading to demands that the United States restrict Chinese imports. To protect their access to the U.S. market, Chinese firms, like those in many other countries, retain the services of international trade lobbyists. These lobbyists guide foreign firms through the intricacies of U.S. laws and customs and introduce foreign executives to American power brokers, movers, and shakers. Some see American citizens who work as international trade lobbyists as corporate traitors, but American lobbyists and their counterparts in other countries play an important role in promoting world trade and diminishing international rivalries.

Questions of loyalty are also often raised by the activities of another form of foreign lobby in the United States: the ethnic lobby. Many Americans retain a sense of identification with their family's country of origin or with those who share their religion in another country. Individuals with such ethnic or religious ties to another country are often willing to lobby vigorously on that country's behalf. The best-known case is that of the pro-Israel lobby. Through such organizations as AIPAC, the American Israel Public Affairs Committee, some Jewish Americans have worked to secure American

military, financial, and economic support for Israel since that nation's founding. Largely because of the pro-Israel lobby's activities, Israel is the largest recipient of American foreign aid and is usually supported by the United States in its conflicts with the Arab nations of the Middle East. Interestingly, Jewish Americans are not the only pro-Israel lobbyists. Israel is also strongly supported by so-called Christian Zionists, evangelical Protestants who see Israel's existence as the fulfillment of biblical prophecy.

In addition to the pro-Israel lobby, a number of other ethnic lobbies are active in Washington. Americans from the Indian subcontinent have lobbied effectively for the improvement of U.S.-Indian relations. Some Irish Americans have lobbied against British rule in Northern Ireland. Recently, despite a good deal of lobbying by Armenian Americans, Congress failed to pass a resolution condemning the murder of hundreds of thousands of Armenians by Turkish forces between 1914 and 1917. Turkey, an important U.S. military ally, was able to defeat the resolution with a lobbying campaign of its own.

Often, lobbying by foreign firms and governments is accompanied by extensive public-relations campaigns. One foreign government that lobbies vigorously in the United States and also spends tens of millions of dollars each year on public relations is the Kingdom of Saudi Arabia. For example, in a recent issue of *The New Republic*—a magazine read mainly by upper-middle-class professionals and intellectuals in New York, Washington,

and Boston—the Kingdom of Saudi Arabia sponsored a full-page ad promoting its efforts to combat terrorism.[a]

In point of fact, however, the Saudi government's long-standing practice has been to subsidize and support Islamic radicals as long as they do not make trouble within Saudi Arabia.[b] The Saudi ad campaign is designed to gloss over this rather embarrassing and politically inconvenient fact.

[a]*New Republic*, December 5, 2005, back cover.
[b]Craig Unger, *House of Bush, House of Saud* (New York: Scribner's, 2004).

## for critical analysis

1. Should foreign firms be allowed to lobby in the United States?
2. Is it un-American or disloyal for ethnic and religious groups to lobby on behalf of a foreign country with which they identify?

First, every group must have a leadership and decision-making structure. For some groups, this structure is very simple. For others, it can be quite elaborate and involve hundreds of local chapters that are melded into a national apparatus. Interest-group leadership is, in some respects, analogous to business leadership. Many interest groups are initially organized by political entrepreneurs with a strong commitment to a particular set of goals. Such entrepreneurs see the formation of a group as a means both for achieving those goals and for enhancing their own influence in the political process. And just as is true in the business world, successful groups often become bureaucratized; the initial entrepreneurial leadership is replaced by a paid professional staff. In the 1960s, for example, Ralph Nader led a ragtag band of consumer advocates (Nader's Raiders) in a crusade for product safety that resulted in the enactment of numerous laws and regulations, such as the requirement that all new cars be equipped with seat belts. Today, Nader remains active in the consumer movement, and his loosely organized band of raiders has been transformed into a well-organized and well-financed phalanx of interlocking groups led by professional staff.

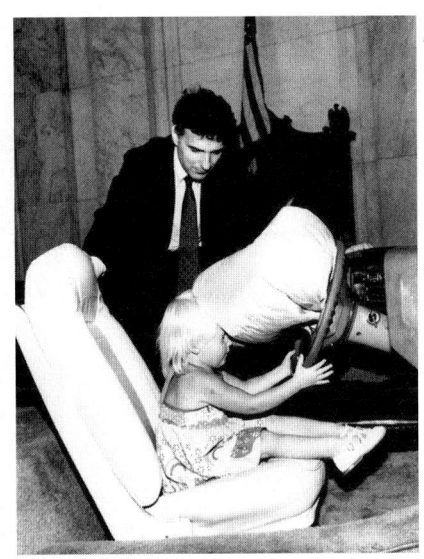

*Although there have always been groups trying to influence the government, since the 1960s the number of organized interests in Washington, D.C., has increased substantially. For instance, the consumer activist Ralph Nader, shown here at a demonstration in support of mandatory airbags in cars, founded a network of consumer advocacy groups.*

Second, every interest group must build a financial structure capable of sustaining an organization and funding the group's activities. Most interest groups rely on membership dues and voluntary contributions from sympathizers. Many also sell some ancillary services to members, such as insurance and vacation tours. Third, most groups establish an agency that actually carries out the group's tasks. This may be a research organization, a public relations office, or a lobbying office in Washington or a state capital.

Finally, almost all interest groups must attract and keep members. Somehow, groups must persuade individuals to invest the money, time, energy, or effort required to take part in the group's activities. Members play a larger role in some groups than in others. In **membership associations**, group members actually serve on committees and engage in projects. In the case of labor unions, members may march on picket lines; in the case of political or ideological groups, members may participate in demonstrations and protests. In another set of groups, **staff organizations**, a professional staff conducts most of the group's activities; members are called on only to pay dues and make other contributions. Among the well-known public interest groups, some, such as the National Organization for Women (NOW), are membership groups; others, such as Defenders of Wildlife and the Children's Defense Fund, are staff organizations.

**membership association**
an organized group in which members actually play a substantial role, sitting on committees and engaging in group projects

**staff organization** a type of membership group in which a professional staff conducts most of the group's activities

**The Characteristics of Members** Membership in interest groups is not randomly distributed in the population. People with higher incomes, higher levels of education, and management or professional occupations are much more likely to become members of groups than are those who occupy the lower rungs on the socioeconomic ladder.[7] Well-educated, upper-income business and professional people are more likely to have the time, money, concerns, and skills needed to play a role in a group or association. Moreover, for business and professional people, group membership may provide personal contacts and access to information that can help advance their careers. At the same time, of course, corporate entities—businesses and the like—usually have ample resources to form or participate in groups that seek to advance their interests.

The result is that interest-group politics in the United States tends to have a very pronounced upper-class bias. Certainly, many interest groups and political associations have a working-class or lower-class membership—labor organizations

*The NRA is a group that promotes the interests of gun owners. In addition to lobbying the government, the NRA offers members a wide range of services, from providing information about gun laws to organizing gun shows.*

or welfare-rights organizations, for example—but the great majority of interest groups and their members is drawn from the middle and upper-middle classes. In general, the "interests" served by interest groups are the interests of society's "haves." Even when interest groups take opposing positions on issues and policies, the conflicting positions they espouse usually reflect divisions among upper-income strata rather than conflicts between the upper and lower classes.

In general, to obtain adequate political representation, forces from the bottom rungs of the socioeconomic ladder must be organized on the massive scale associated with political parties. Parties can organize and mobilize the collective energies of large numbers of people who, as individuals, may have very limited resources. Interest groups, on the other hand, generally organize smaller numbers of the better-to-do. Thus, the relative importance of political parties and interest groups in American politics has far-ranging implications for the distribution of political power in the United States. In recent years, interest groups, as we shall see in the section "The Proliferation of Groups," have become much more numerous, more active, and more influential in American politics, with lobby groups and super PACs playing major roles in Congress and in electoral politics.

**The "Free Rider" Problem** Whether they need individuals to volunteer or merely to write checks, both types of groups need to recruit and retain members. Yet many groups find this task difficult, even when it comes to recruiting members who agree strongly with the group's goals. Why? As the economist Mancur Olson explains, the benefits of a group's success are often broadly available and cannot be denied to nonmembers.[8] Such benefits can be called **collective goods**. This term is usually associated with certain government benefits, but it can also be applied to beneficial outcomes of interest-group activity.

Olson offers this example: suppose a number of private property owners live near a mosquito-infested swamp. Each owner wants this swamp cleared. But if one or a few of the owners were to clear the swamp alone, their actions would benefit all the other owners as well, without any effort on the part of those other owners. Each of the inactive owners would be a **free rider** on the efforts of the ones who

**collective goods** benefits, sought by groups, that are broadly available and cannot be denied to nonmembers

**free riders** those who enjoy the benefits of collective goods but did not participate in acquiring them

cleared the swamp. Thus, there is a disincentive for any of the owners to undertake the job alone. Since the number of concerned owners is small in this particular case, they might eventually be able to organize themselves to share the costs as well as to enjoy the benefits of clearing the swamp.

But suppose the number of interested people is increased. Suppose the common concern is not the neighborhood swamp but polluted air or groundwater involving thousands of residents in a region, or in fact millions of residents in a whole nation. National defense is the most obvious collective good whose benefits are shared by all residents, regardless of the taxes they pay or the support they provide. As the number of involved persons increases, or as the size of the group increases, the free rider phenomenon becomes more of a problem. The group would no doubt be more influential if all concerned individuals were active members—if there were no free riders.

**Why Join?** Individuals do not have much incentive to become active members and supporters of a group that is already working more or less on their behalf. But groups do not reduce their efforts just because free riders get the same benefits as dues-paying activists. In fact, groups may try even harder precisely because there are free riders, with the hope that the free riders will be encouraged to join in, often by the lure of various "selective benefits" available only to group members. These benefits can be informational, material, solidary, or purposive. Of course, groups sometimes offer combinations of benefits. A community association, for example, can offer its members a sense of belonging (solidary benefit), involvement in community decision making (purposive benefit), and reduced rates on homeowners' insurance (material benefit). Table 11.1 gives some examples of the range of benefits in each of these categories.

**for critical analysis**

Could college students be organized as an interest group? What would such a group advocate? What might be some impediments to the creation of a National Organization of College Students?

**TABLE 11.1**

## Selective Benefits of Interest-Group Membership

| CATEGORY | BENEFITS |
| --- | --- |
| Informational benefits | Conferences |
| | Professional contacts |
| | Training programs |
| | Publications |
| | Coordination among organizations |
| | Research |
| | Legal help |
| | Professional codes |
| | Collective bargaining |
| Material benefits | Travel packages |
| | Insurance |
| | Discounts on consumer goods |
| Solidary benefits | Friendship |
| | Networking opportunities |
| Purposive benefits | Advocacy |
| | Representation before government |
| | Participation in public affairs |

SOURCE: Adapted from Jack Walker Jr., *Mobilizing Interest Groups in America: Patrons, Professions, and Social Movements* (Ann Arbor: University of Michigan Press, 1991), p. 86.

**informational benefits** special newsletters, periodicals, training programs, conferences, and other information provided to members of groups to entice others to join

**material benefits** special goods, services, or money provided to members of groups to entice others to join

**solidary benefits** selective benefits of group membership that emphasize friendship, networking, and consciousness raising

**purposive benefits** selective benefits of group membership that emphasize the purpose and accomplishments of the group

**Informational benefits** are the most widespread and important category of selective benefits offered to group members. Information is provided through conferences, training programs, and newsletters and other periodicals sent automatically to those who have paid membership dues. **Material benefits** include anything that can be measured monetarily, such as discount purchasing, shared advertising, and, perhaps most valuable of all, health and retirement insurance. **Solidary benefits** include the friendship and networking opportunities that membership provides. Extremely important to many of the newer nonprofit and citizen groups is "consciousness raising." One example of this can be seen in the claims of many women's organizations that active participation conveys to each member an enhanced sense of her own value and a stronger ability to advance individual as well as collective rights. Members of associations based on ethnicity, race, or religion also derive solidary benefits from interacting with individuals they perceive as sharing their own backgrounds, values, and perspectives.

A fourth type of benefit involves the appeal of the purpose of an interest group. An example of these **purposive benefits** is businesses' joining trade associations to further their economic interests. Similarly, individuals join consumer, environmental, or other civic groups to pursue goals important to them. Many of the most successful interest groups of the past 20 years have been citizen groups or public interest groups organized largely around shared ideological goals, including government reform, election and campaign reform, civil rights, economic equality, "family values," and even opposition to government itself.

**AARP and the Benefits of Membership** One group that has been extremely successful in recruiting members and mobilizing them for political action is AARP. The organization was founded as the American Association of Retired Persons in 1958 as a result of the efforts of a retired California high school principal, Ethel Percy Andrus, to find affordable health insurance for herself and the thousands of members of the National Retired Teachers Association (NRTA). In 1955 she found an insurer who was willing to give NRTA members a low group rate. In 1958, partly at the urging of the insurer (who found that insuring the elderly was quite profitable), Andrus founded AARP. For the insurer, it provided an expanded market; for Andrus, it was a way to serve the ever-growing elderly population, whose problems and needs were expanding along with their numbers and their life expectancy.

Today, AARP is a large and powerful organization with 38 million members and an annual income of $900 million. In addition, the organization receives $90 million in federal grants. Its national headquarters in Washington, D.C., staffed by nearly 3,000 full-time employees, is so large that it has its own zip code. Its monthly periodical, *AARP: The Magazine*, has a circulation larger than that of America's leading newsmagazines.[9]

How did this large organization overcome the free rider problem and recruit 38 million older people as members? First, no other organization on earth has ever more successfully provided the selective benefits necessary to overcome the free rider problem. It helps that AARP began as an organization to provide affordable health insurance for aging members rather than as an organization to influence public policy. But that fact only strengthens the argument that members need short-term individual benefits if they are to invest effort in a longer-term and less concrete set of benefits. As AARP evolved into a political interest group, its leadership added more selective benefits for individual members. It provided guidance against consumer fraud, offered low-interest credit cards, evaluated and endorsed products that were deemed valuable to members, and provided auto insurance and a discounted mail-order pharmacy.

In a group as large as AARP, members are bound to disagree on particular subjects, often creating serious factional disputes. But the resources of AARP are so extensive that its leadership has been able to mobilize itself for each issue of importance to the group. One of its most successful methods of mobilization for political action is the "telephone tree," with which AARP leaders can quickly mobilize thousands of members for and against proposals that affect Social Security, Medicare, and other questions of security for the aging. A "telephone tree" in each state enables the state AARP chair to phone all of the AARP district directors, who then can phone the presidents of the dozens of local chapters, who can call their local officers and individual members. Within 24 hours, thousands of individual AARP members can be contacting local, state, and national officials to express their opposition to proposed legislation. It is no wonder that AARP is respected and feared throughout Washington. In 2009, AARP's endorsement of the health care bill proposed by the House leadership convinced many wavering members of Congress to support the bill rather than risk offending such a powerful lobby group.

# ● The Proliferation of Groups

> **Analyze why the number of interest groups has grown in recent decades**

Interest groups and concerns about them are not new phenomena. As long as there is government, as long as government makes policies that add value or impose costs, and as long as there is liberty to organize, interest groups will abound; and if government expands, so will interest groups. There was, for example, a spurt of growth in the national government during the 1880s and '90s, arising largely from the first government efforts at economic intervention to fight large monopolies and to regulate some aspects of interstate commerce. In the latter decade, a parallel spurt of growth occurred in national interest groups, including the imposing National Association of Manufacturers (NAM) and numerous other trade associations. Many groups organized around specific agricultural commodities as well. This period also marked the beginning of the expansion of trade unions as interest groups. Later, in the 1930s, interest groups with headquarters and representation in Washington began to grow significantly, concurrent with that decade's historic and sustained expansion within the national government (see Chapter 3).

Over the past decades, there has been an even greater increase both in the number of interest groups seeking to play a role in the American political process and in the extent of their opportunity to influence that process. This explosion of interest-group activity has two basic origins: first, the expansion of the role of government during this period, and second, the coming-of-age of a new and dynamic set of political forces in the United States—forces that have relied heavily on "public interest" groups to advance their causes.

## The Expansion of Government

Modern governments' extensive economic and social programs have powerful politicizing effects, often sparking the organization of new groups and interests. The activities of organized groups are usually viewed in terms of their effects on governmental action. But interest-group activity is often as much a consequence as an antecedent of governmental programs. Even when national policies begin as responses to the appeals of pressure groups, government involvement in any area can be a powerful stimulus for political organization and action by those whose interests are affected. For example, during the 1970s, expanded federal regulation of the automobile, oil, gas, education, and health care industries impelled each of these interests to increase substantially its efforts to influence the government's behavior. These efforts, in turn, spurred the organization of other groups to augment or counter the activities of the first.[10] Similarly, federal social programs have occasionally sparked political organization and action on the part of clientele groups seeking to influence the distribution of benefits and, in turn, the organization of groups opposed to the programs or their cost. For example, federal programs and court decisions in such areas as abortion and school prayer sparked political organization and action by fundamentalist religious groups. Thus, the expansion of government in recent decades has also stimulated increased group activity and organization.

## The New Politics Movement and Public Interest Groups

The second factor accounting for the explosion of interest-group activity in recent years has been the emergence of a new set of forces in American politics that can collectively be called the New Politics movement.

The **New Politics movement** is made up of upper-middle-class professionals and intellectuals for whom the civil rights and antiwar movements were formative experiences, just as the Great Depression and World War II had been for their parents. The crusade against racial discrimination and the Vietnam War led these young men and women to see themselves as a political force, and in more recent years they have focused attention on issues such as environmental protection, women's rights, and nuclear disarmament.

**New Politics movement** a political movement that began in the 1960s and '70s, made up of professionals and intellectuals for whom the civil rights and antiwar movements were formative experiences. The New Politics movement strengthened public interest groups

*NOW (the National Organization for Women) emerged from the New Politics movement. Founded in 1966, the group continues to lobby government on issues such as abortion, gender discrimination, and economic rights. In 2012, NOW members held a vigil to mark the 39th anniversary of the* Roe v. Wade *decision.*

Members of the New Politics movement founded or strengthened public interest groups such as Common Cause, the Sierra Club, the Environmental Defense Fund, Physicians for Social Responsibility, and NOW. New Politics forces were able to influence the media, Congress, and even the judiciary, and enjoyed a remarkable degree of success during the late 1960s and early 1970s in securing the enactment of policies they favored. New Politics activists played a major role in securing the enactment of environmental, consumer, and occupational health and safety legislation.

Among the factors contributing to the rise and success of New Politics forces was technology. In the 1970s and '80s, computerized direct-mail campaigns allowed public interest groups to reach hundreds of thousands of potential sympathizers and contributors. Today, the Internet and e-mail serve the same function even more efficiently. Electronic communication allows relatively small groups to identify their adherents and mobilize them throughout the nation.

# ● Strategies: The Quest for Political Power

**Explain how interest groups try to influence government**

Interest groups work to improve the likelihood that they and their policy interests will be heard and treated favorably by all branches and levels of the government. The quest for political influence or power takes many forms. Insider strategies include access to key decision makers and use of the courts. Outsider strategies include going public and using electoral politics. These strategies do not exhaust all the possibilities, but they paint a broad picture of ways that groups use their resources in the fierce competition for power (see Figure 11.1).

Many groups employ a mix of insider and outsider strategies. For example, environmental groups such as the Sierra Club lobby members of Congress and key congressional staff members; participate in bureaucratic rule making by offering comments and suggestions to agencies on new environmental rules; and bring lawsuits under various environmental acts such as the Endangered Species Act, which authorizes groups and citizens to come to court if they believe the act is being violated. At the same time, the Sierra Club attempts to influence public opinion through media campaigns and to influence electoral politics by supporting candidates who it believes share its environmental views and by opposing candidates it views as foes of environmentalism.

## Direct Lobbying

**Lobbying** is an attempt by a group to influence the policy process through persuasion of government officials. Most Americans tend to believe that interest groups exert their influence through direct contact with members of Congress, but lobbying encompasses a broad range of activities that groups engage in with all sorts of government officials and the public as a whole.

The 1946 Federal Regulation of Lobbying Act defines a lobbyist as "any person who shall engage himself for pay or any consideration for the purpose of attempting to influence the passage or defeat of any legislation of the Congress of the United States." The 1995 Lobbying Disclosure Act requires all organizations employing

**lobbying** a strategy by which organized interests seek to influence the passage of legislation by exerting direct pressure on members of the legislature

FIGURE 11.1

## How Interest Groups Influence Congress

**FIGURE 11.1 How Interest Groups Influence Congress**

Media

Mobilizing public opinion—release of favorable research findings; news releases; public relations campaigns; tips to reporters

News stories and editorials favorable to interest group

Other members of Congress

Direct lobbying

Alliances and logrolls

PAC funds; endorsements; information campaigns; testimony

Interest group

Targeted members of Congress

Gaining access—information; development of personal contacts and ties; favors

Advice

Congressional staff

Activate constituents whose jobs or businesses are affected; provide them with information and arguments; help them organize, write letters, leaflets, etc.

Letters; e-mails; phone calls; letters to news editors; visits to Washington; work in elections

Constituents

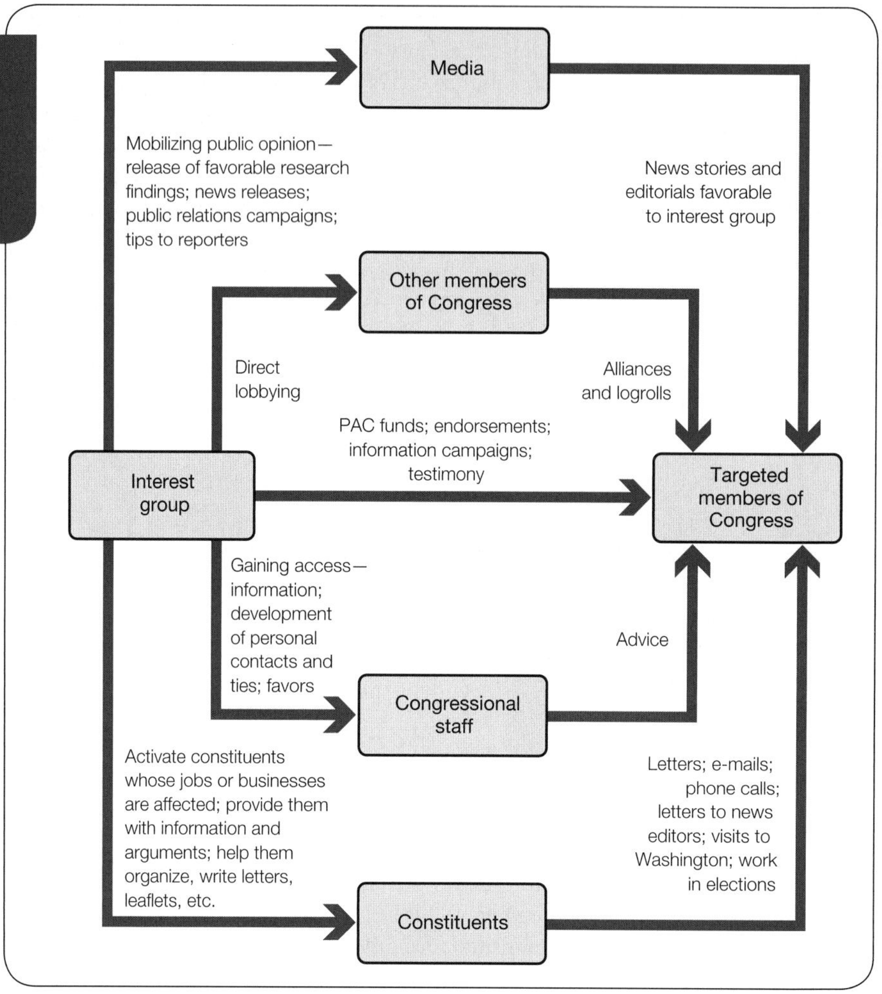

lobbyists to register with Congress and to disclose whom they represent, whom they lobby, what they are looking for, and how much they are paid. More than 12,000 lobbyists are currently registered.[11]

Lobbying involves a great deal of activity on the part of someone speaking for an interest, and lobbyists attempt to influence the policy process in a variety of ways.[12] Lobbyists badger and buttonhole legislators, administrators, and committee staff members with facts about pertinent issues and facts or claims about public support of certain issues or facts.[13] They often testify on behalf of their clients at congressional committee and agency hearings. Lobbyists talk to reporters, place ads in newspapers, and organize letter-writing and e-mail campaigns. They also play an important role in fund-raising, helping to direct clients' contributions to members of Congress and presidential candidates.

Further, sophisticated lobbyists win influence by providing information about policies to busy members of Congress. As one lobbyist noted, "You can't get access without knowledge. . . . I can go in to see [the former Energy and Commerce Committee chair] John Dingell, but if I have nothing to offer or nothing to say, he's not going to want to see me."[14] In 1978, during debate on a bill to expand the requirement for lobbying disclosures, the Democratic senators Edward Kennedy of Massachusetts and Dick Clark of Iowa joined with the Republican senator Robert Stafford of Vermont to issue the following statement: "Government without lobbying could not function. The flow of information to Congress and to every federal agency is a vital part of our democratic system."[15]

**Lobbying Congress** Traditionally, the term *lobbyist* referred mainly to individuals who sought to influence the passage of legislation in the Congress. The First Amendment to the Constitution provides for the right to "petition the Government for a redress of grievances." But as early as the 1870s, *lobbying* became the common term for petitioning. And since petitioning cannot take place on the floor of the House or Senate, petitioners must therefore confront members of Congress in the lobbies of the legislative chamber—hence the term *lobbying*.

The influence of lobbyists, in many instances, is based on personal relationships and the behind-the-scenes services they are able to perform for lawmakers. Many of Washington's top lobbyists have close ties to important members of Congress or were themselves important political figures, thus virtually guaranteeing that their clients will have direct access to congressional leaders. According to the Capitol Hill newspaper, *The Hill*, examples include Jim Blanchard of DLA Piper, who was a governor of Michigan; Chuck Brain of Capitol Hill Strategies, who worked in the White House Legislative Affairs office under President Clinton; Alfonse D'Amato of Park Strategies, who was a senator from New York; Mitchell Feuer of the Rich Feuer Group, who was counsel to the Senate Banking Committee; and Broderick Johnson of Bryan Cave, who was a senior aide in the Clinton White House. The list goes on.[16] Some important lobbyists have more than a business relationship to lawmakers: quite a few, in fact, are married to prominent political figures. For example, Linda Daschle of LHD and Associates is the wife of former Senate majority leader Tom Daschle, and Hadassah Lieberman, wife of Senator Joseph Lieberman, was for many years a lobbyist for the pharmaceutical industry.

Corporate interests endeavor to be strategic in their choice of lobbyists, often hiring lobbyists whom they know to be key fund-raisers for the politicians they hope to influence. In so doing, they are not making a campaign contribution that would have to be reported to the Federal Election Commission but are nevertheless seeking to ensure that the lobbyist promoting their interests will be seen by the targeted politician as an important source of campaign money. For example, a coalition of television networks seeking to loosen rules governing their ownership of local TV stations hired Gregg Hartley as their lobbyist. Hartley, formerly a top aide to former House Majority Whip Roy Blunt, whose support the coalition sought, was one of Blunt's top fund-raisers. Companies hiring Hartley to lobby for them were almost certain of receiving a positive reception from Blunt. Many members of Congress list lobbyists as treasurers of their re-election committees,[17] and, in turn, many of Washington's lobbyists also serve as campaign treasurers and major fund-raisers for political candidates.[18] Lobbyists such as Peter Hart, Tommy Boggs, Peter Knight, Ken Duberstein, and Vin Weber are influential, in part, because of their ability to raise money for politicians. Several members of the powerful House Appropriations Committee sponsor political action committees headed by lobbyists with business before the committee.[19]

POLITICAL MARKET.

*Concern about business having too much influence in Washington dates back to the early days of the country. Here, a mid-nineteenth-century cartoon lampoons the ease with which corporate executives could bribe politicians.*

*In 2008, the Senate Commerce and Labor Committee heard from lobbyists for the "payday loan" industry, which offers small loans at very high interest rates. Public advocacy groups complained that the payday lenders were taking advantage of consumers and should be regulated more closely by government. Lobbyists for the lenders argued that the industry provides a beneficial service to consumers and does not need stricter regulation.*

Through their lobbyists, interest groups also have substantial influence in setting the legislative agenda. They help to craft specific language in legislation and build broader coalitions and comprehensive campaigns around particular policy issues.[20] These coalitions do not rise from the grass roots but instead are put together by Washington lobbyists who launch comprehensive lobbying campaigns that combine simulated grassroots activity with information and campaign funding for members of Congress. In recent years, the Republican leadership worked so closely with lobbyists that critics charged that the boundaries between lobbyists and legislators had been erased and that lobbyists had become "adjunct staff to the Republican leadership."[21]

What happens to interests that do not engage in extensive lobbying? They often find themselves "Microsofted," that is, marginalized in the political process. In 1998 the software giant was facing antitrust action from the Justice Department and had few friends in Congress. One member of the House, Representative Billy Tauzin (R-La.), told Microsoft's chairman, Bill Gates, that without an extensive investment in lobbying, the corporation would continue to be "demonized." Gates responded by quadrupling Microsoft's lobbying expenditures and hiring a group of lobbyists with strong ties to Congress. The result was congressional pressure on the Justice Department resulting in a settlement of the Microsoft suit on terms favorable to the company.

Similarly, in 1999, members of Congress advised Wal-Mart that its efforts to win approval to operate savings and loans in its stores were doomed to failure if the retailer did not greatly increase its lobbying efforts. "They don't give money. They don't have congressional representation—so nobody here cares about them," said one influential member. Like Microsoft, Wal-Mart learned its lesson, hired more lobbyists, and got what it wanted.[22] By 2005, Wal-Mart had become a seasoned political player, creating a "war room" in its Arkansas headquarters. Staffed by a phalanx of veteran political operatives from both parties, the war room is the nerve center of the giant retailer's lobbying and public relations efforts.[23] Today, Wal-Mart spends about $5 million a year on its lobbying efforts.

**Lobbying the President** So many individuals and groups clamor for the president's time and attention that only the most skilled and best-connected members of the lobbying community can hope to influence presidential decisions. Typically, a president's key political advisers and fund-raisers will include individuals with ties to the lobbying industry who can help their friends gain access to the White House. For example, one of President George W. Bush's top fund-raisers was Tom Kuhn, a Washington lobbyist representing the electric power industry. Kuhn, also the president's personal friend and college classmate, was able to prevent the Environmental Protection Agency (EPA) from imposing new controls on electric power plant emissions of mercury, representing a savings of hundreds of millions of dollars for the industry.

During the 2008 presidential campaign, Barack Obama said, "Lobbyists won't find a job in my White House." Soon after his election, however, Obama appointed David Axelrod as his senior adviser. Before joining the Obama campaign and administration, Axelrod was a partner in ASK Public Strategies, a consulting group that had helped the giant Illinois utility Commonwealth Edison obtain a major

*Interest groups may also try to influence the president's decisions. In 2009, President Obama met with business leaders to discuss how a new health care policy would affect their employees' health insurance plans.*

rate hike. At least 30 other senior Obama administration officials have a lobbying background.[24] The lobbying industry is so much a part of Washington that it probably would have been impossible for the president to keep his campaign pledge.

**Lobbying the Executive Branch** Even when an interest group is very successful at getting its bill passed by Congress and signed by the president, the prospect of full and faithful implementation of that law is not guaranteed. Often a group and its allies do not pack up and go home as soon as the president turns their lobbied-for new law over to the appropriate agency. In some respects, interest-group access to the executive branch is promoted by federal law. The Administrative Procedure Act, first enacted in 1946 and frequently amended in subsequent years, requires most federal agencies to provide notice and an opportunity for comment before implementing proposed new rules and regulations. This "notice and comment rule-making" is designed to allow interests an opportunity to make their views known and to participate in the implementation of federal legislation that affects them. In 1990, Congress enacted the Negotiated Rulemaking Act to encourage administrative agencies to engage in direct and open negotiations with affected interests when developing new regulations. These two pieces of legislation—which have been strongly enforced by the federal courts—have played an important role in opening the bureaucratic process to interest-group influence. Today, few federal agencies would consider attempting to implement a new rule without consulting affected interests, known in Washington as "stakeholders."[25]

## Cultivating Access

*This photo from 2002 was introduced as evidence in the 2006 Abramoff case. It shows the lobbyist Jack Abramoff (left) with Senator Bob Ney (right) and the GSA chief of staff David Safavian (second from right) on a luxurious golf trip to Scotland that was arranged by Abramoff.*

In 2005 a prominent Washington lobbyist, Jack Abramoff, was indicted on numerous charges of fraud and violations of federal lobbying laws. During the investigation of his activities, it was revealed that Abramoff, along with his associate Michael Scanlon, had collected tens of millions of dollars from several American Indian tribes that operated lucrative gambling casinos. (Indian gambling is currently a $16 billion industry in the United States.) What Abramoff provided in exchange was access to key Republican members of Congress, who helped his clients shut down rival casino operators. Abramoff was closely associated with several House members, including the former House majority leader Tom DeLay as well as senators John Cornyn, Conrad Burns, and David Vitter. Millions of tribal dollars apparently found their way into the campaign war chests of Abramoff's friends in Congress. Thus, through a well-connected lobbyist, money had effectively purchased access and influence. Abramoff and several of his associates subsequently pleaded guilty to federal bribery and fraud charges, and Abramoff was sentenced to more than five years in prison.

In a similar vein, GOP representative Randy "Duke" Cunningham of California was found guilty of accepting $2.4 million in bribes from a defense contractor. Cunningham allegedly used his position on a defense appropriations subcommittee to funnel millions of dollars in contracts to the firm. In 2009, Democratic representative William Jefferson of Louisiana acquired considerable notoriety when FBI agents found $90,000 hidden in the congressman's freezer. He was later found guilty of accepting bribes.

For the most part, though, access to decision makers does not require bribes or other forms of illegal activity. In many areas, interest groups, government agencies, and congressional committees routinely work together for mutual benefit. The interest group provides campaign contributions for members of Congress, and it lobbies for larger budgets for the agency. The agency, in turn, provides government contracts for the interest group and constituency services for friendly members of Congress. The congressional committee or subcommittee, meanwhile, supports the agency's budgetary requests and the programs the interest group favors. This so-called **iron triangle** has one angle in an executive branch program, another angle in a Senate or House legislative committee or subcommittee, and a third angle in some highly stable and well-organized interest group. The angles in the triangular relationship are mutually supporting; they count as access only if they last over a long period of time. For example, access to a legislative committee or subcommittee requires that at least one committee member support the interest group in question. This member also must have built up considerable seniority in Congress. An interest cannot feel comfortable about its access to Congress until it has one or more of its "own" people with 10 or more years of continuous service on the relevant committee or subcommittee. Figure 11.2 illustrates one of the most important iron triangles in recent American political history: that of the defense industry.

A number of important policy domains, such as the environmental and welfare arenas, are controlled not by highly structured and unified iron triangles but by broader **issue networks**. These networks consist of like-minded politicians,

**iron triangle** the stable, cooperative relationship that often develops among a congressional committee, an administrative agency, and one or more supportive interest groups. Not all of these relationships are triangular, but the iron triangle is the most typical

**issue network** a loose network of elected leaders, public officials, activists, and interest groups drawn together by a specific policy issue

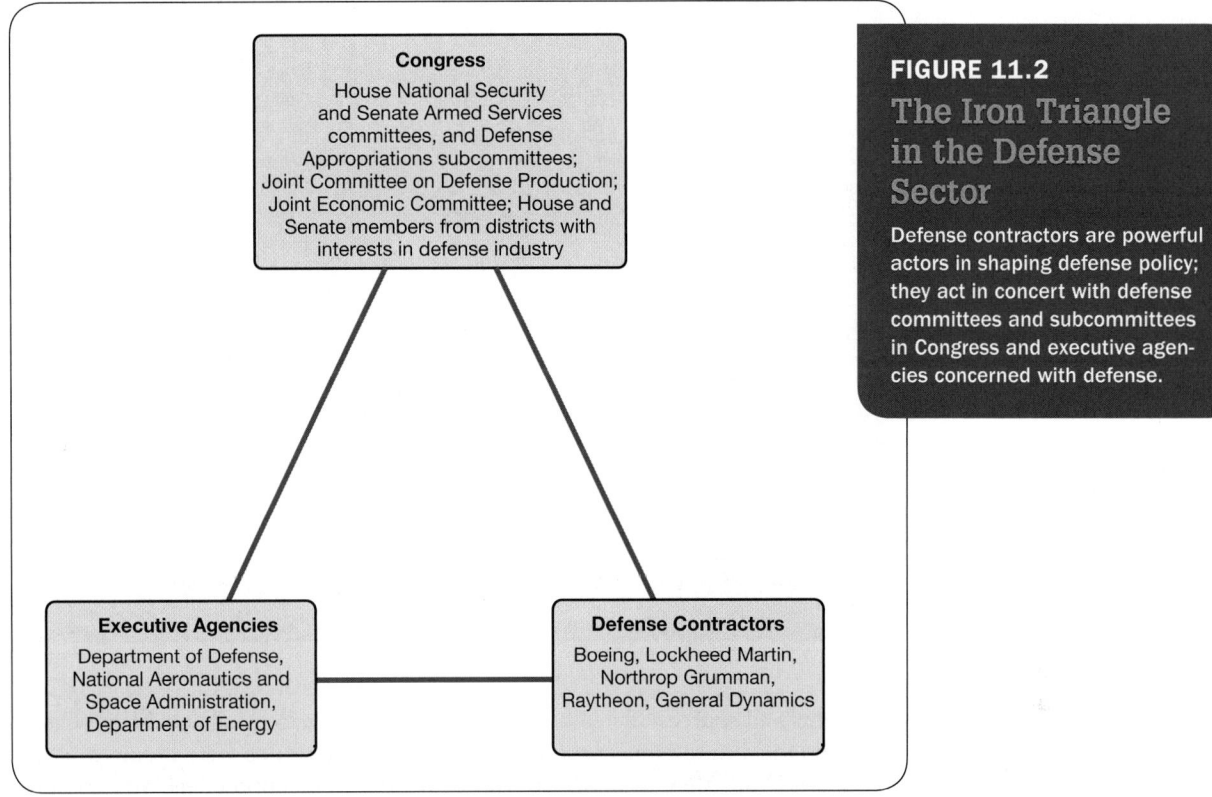

**FIGURE 11.2**

**The Iron Triangle in the Defense Sector**

Defense contractors are powerful actors in shaping defense policy; they act in concert with defense committees and subcommittees in Congress and executive agencies concerned with defense.

consultants, public officials, political activists, and interest groups having some concern with the issue in question. Activists and interest groups recognized as being involved in the area (the stakeholders) are customarily invited to testify before congressional committees or give their views to government agencies considering action in their domain.

**Attempts to Regulate Lobbying** To counter the growing influence of the lobbying industry, stricter guidelines regulating the actions of lobbyists have been adopted in the last decade. For example, as of 1993, businesses may no longer deduct lobbying costs as a business expense. Trade associations must report to members the proportion of their dues that goes toward lobbying, and that proportion of the dues may not be reported as a business expense. The most important attempt to limit the influence of lobbyists was the 1995 Lobbying Disclosure Act, which significantly broadened the definition of people and organizations that must register as lobbyists. This has led, as we saw earlier, to more than 12,000 registrations today.

In 1996, Congress passed legislation limiting the size of gifts to its own members: no gift could be worth more than $50, and no member could receive more than $100 from a single source. It also banned the practice of honoraria for giving speeches, which special interests had used to supplement congressional salaries. In 2007, congressional Democrats secured the enactment of a new package of ethics rules designed to fulfill their 2006 campaign promise to bring an end to lobbying abuses. The new rules prohibited lobbyists from paying for most meals, trips, parties, and gifts for members of Congress. Lobbyists were also required to disclose the

*After the Abramoff scandal, in which a prominent lobbyist pleaded guilty to conspiring to bribe members of Congress, both parties called for reform of the lobbying process. In 2007, Democrats in the House of Representatives passed new ethics rules designed to end lobbying abuses.*

amounts and sources of small campaign contributions they collected from clients and "bundled" into large contributions. And interest groups were required to disclose the funds they used to rally voters to support or oppose legislative proposals. According to the *Washington Post*, however, within a few weeks, lobbyists had learned how to circumvent many of the new rules, and lobbying firms were as busy as ever.[26]

## Using the Courts (Litigation)

Interest groups sometimes turn to litigation when they lack access or when they are dissatisfied with government in general or with a specific government program and feel they have insufficient influence to change the situation. Interest groups can use the courts to affect public policy in at least three ways: (1) by bringing suit directly on behalf of the group itself, (2) by financing suits brought by individuals, or (3) by filing a companion brief as an *amicus curiae* (literally "friend of the court") to an existing court case (see Chapter 15 for a discussion of *amicus curiae* briefs).

Among the best-known illustrations of using the courts for political influence is found in the history of the NAACP. The most important of these court cases was, of course, *Brown v. Board of Education of Topeka, Kansas*, in which the U.S. Supreme Court held that legal segregation of the schools was unconstitutional.[27] Later, extensive litigation accompanied the "sexual revolution" of the 1960s and the emergence of the movement for women's rights.

The 1973 Supreme Court case of *Roe v. Wade*, which took away a state's power to ban abortions, sparked a controversy that brought conservatives to the fore on a national level.[28] Since 1973, conservative groups have made extensive use of the courts to whittle away at the scope of the privacy doctrine initially defined by the Supreme Court in *Roe v. Wade*. They obtained rulings, for example, that prohibit the use of federal funds to pay for voluntary abortions. And in 1989, right-to-life groups were able to use the case of *Webster v. Reproductive Health Services* to restore the right of states to place restrictions on abortion, thus undermining the *Roe v.*

*Wade* decision (see Chapter 4).[29] The *Webster* case brought more than 300 interest groups on both sides of the abortion issue to the Supreme Court's door.

Litigation involving large businesses is especially mountainous in such areas as taxation, antitrust, interstate transportation, patents, and product quality and standardization. Often a business is brought to litigation against its will by virtue of initiatives taken against it by other businesses or by government agencies. But many individual businesses bring suit themselves to influence government policy, and business groups also frequently use the courts because of the number of government programs applied to them. Major corporations and their trade associations pay tremendous amounts of money each year in fees to the most prestigious Washington law firms. Some of this money is expended in gaining access. A great proportion of it, however, is used to keep the best and most experienced lawyers prepared to represent the corporations in court or before administrative agencies when necessary.

New Politics forces made significant use of the courts during the 1970s and '80s, and judicial decisions were instrumental in advancing their goals. Facilitated by changes in the rules governing access to the courts ("standing" is discussed in Chapter 15), the New Politics agenda was clearly visible in court decisions handed down in several key policy areas. In the environmental policy area, New Politics groups were able to force federal agencies to pay attention to environmental issues, even when an agency was not directly involved in activities related to environmental quality. For example, the Federal Trade Commission (FTC) became very responsive to the demands of New Politics activists during the 1970s and '80s. The FTC stepped up its activities considerably, litigating a series of claims arising under regulations prohibiting deceptive advertising in cases ranging from false claims for over-the-counter drugs to inflated claims about the nutritional value of children's cereal.

## Mobilizing Public Opinion

Going public is a strategy that attempts to mobilize the widest and most favorable climate of opinion. Many groups consider it imperative to maintain this climate at all times, even when they have no issue to fight about. An increased use of this kind of strategy is usually associated with modern advertising. As early as the 1930s, political analysts were distinguishing between the "old lobby" of direct group representation before Congress and the "new lobby" of public-relations professionals addressing the public at large to reach Congress.[30]

**Institutional Advertising** One of the best-known ways of going public is the use of **institutional advertising**. A casual scanning of important mass-circulation magazines and newspapers will provide numerous examples of expensive and well-designed ads by the major oil companies, automobile and steel companies, other large corporations, and trade associations. The ads show how much these organizations are doing for the country, for the protection of the environment, or for the defense of the American way of life. The purpose of the ads is to create and maintain a strongly positive association between an organization and the community at large in the hope of drawing on these favorable feelings as needed for specific political campaigns later on.

**institutional advertising**
advertising designed to create a positive image of an organization

**Protests and Demonstrations** Many groups resort to going public because they lack the resources, the contacts, or the experience to use other political strategies. The sponsorship of boycotts, sit-ins, mass rallies, and marches by Martin Luther King Jr.'s Southern Christian Leadership Conference (SCLC) and related organizations during the 1950s and '60s is one of the most significant and successful cases of going public to create a more favorable climate of opinion by calling attention to abuses. The success of these events inspired similar efforts by women's groups. Organizations such as NOW used public strategies in their drive for legislation and in their efforts to gain ratification of the Equal Rights Amendment. In 2004 and 2005, antiwar groups demonstrated near President Bush's ranch in Crawford, Texas, to demand an end to the American military presence in Iraq. The 2010 GOP takeover of the House of Representatives began with the spontaneous self-organization of the Tea Party movement in 2009 as an angry response to the Obama administration's health care initiatives. In 2011 the Occupy Wall Street movement sparked demonstrations across America and around the world, giving voice to those who are outraged by economic inequality.

**grassroots mobilization**
a lobbying campaign in which a group mobilizes its membership to contact government officials in support of the group's position

**Grassroots Mobilization**  Another form of going public is **grassroots mobilization**, in which a lobby group mobilizes its members and their families throughout the country to write to their elected representatives in support of the group's position. Among the most effective users of the grassroots effort in contemporary American politics is the religious right. Networks of evangelical churches have the capacity to generate hundreds of thousands of letters and phone calls to Congress and the White House. For example, the religious right was outraged when President Clinton announced soon after taking office that he planned to end the military's ban on gay and lesbian soldiers. The Reverend Jerry Falwell, an evangelical leader, called on viewers of his television program to dial a telephone number that would add their names to a petition urging Clinton to retain the ban on gays in the military. Within a few hours, 24,000 people had called to support the petition.[31]

Grassroots campaigns have been so effective in recent years that a number of Washington consulting firms have begun to specialize in this area. In 2007, for

*Many interest groups stage protests and demonstrations to draw attention to their cause and mobilize public opinion. This Sierra Club demonstration was intended to call attention to the problem of toxic pollution in Oregon's Willamette River.*

# Online Petitions and Group Mobilization

**You may have received e-mail or** social media notices about how you can take action by participating in an online petition. Websites like Change.org provide groups—from upstart community groups to national organizations—a way to mobilize and educate supporters by circulating and signing online petitions. Groups are increasingly turning to online petitions as a way to pressure elected officials. A petition with hundreds or thousands of signatures can become headline news in local and national newspapers, enhancing the legitimacy of the group's cause. Such petitions are also an important way for interest groups to overcome the challenge of getting individuals to contribute to a common cause even though they may not benefit personally. The ability to petition elected officials online—from local school boards to members of Congress—is a powerful new avenue that requires little effort on the part of citizens.

Online petitions are especially effective for communicating with members of Congress. A high-water mark for online petitions was January 11, 2011, when many major websites held an Internet blackout to protest proposed congressional legislation regulating the Internet (see Chapter 8 for more information on the SOPA/PIPA protests). Users of the online encyclopedia Wikipedia, for example, were redirected to a page providing information on the bills and links for users to click on to contact their members of Congress. In one day 4 million people accessed the information about contacting their member of Congress. In response to the online protests, Congress shelved the controversial legislation.

Groups can also organize grassroots e-mail campaigns using online petition forms. Groups provide pre-written messages that can be personalized simply by the user entering his or her name and address (or sometimes only the zip code). (The user's location is used to determine the appropriate representative.) From there the signed e-mail is routed automatically to the user's elected official. Before the advent of these easy petitions, individuals had to either call their elected representative or take the time to mail a letter. Often these mailed letters were simply form letters created by interest groups trying to mobilize their supporters, but the individual had to invest more time and effort than simply clicking a button.

A 2009 Pew survey showed that 20 percent of Internet users had signed an online petition in the previous year. Another survey found that among all adults 32 percent had signed a petition at some point (either online or offline). Among individuals who were active online, 61 percent had signed a petition; while among those who were not online, only 13 percent had signed a petition.

Interest groups wishing to bombard elected officials with requests from supporters are much more likely to use online petitions and e-mail campaigns than the old-fashioned paper petitions.

It saves them money, time, and effort, and the response is higher than with paper petitions. Since interest groups form to lobby for or against government legislation, the ability to send elected officials hundreds or thousands of e-mails in one day is an important form of grass-roots mobilization.

Research has found that petitions matter beyond their immediate effect on elected officials. Individuals who sign petitions are more likely to vote and participate in other ways. And individuals who use political information (including the information often included with online petitions) are more likely to initiate contact with government or elected officials.

Interest groups want the volume available through form petitions, but research has found that a well-written, personalized letter (or e-mail) holds vastly more weight with elected officials than 100 form letters (or form e-mails), as it shows the time and thought a person took in formulating his or her opinion. This is why on almost every petition there is a space for a personal message—the hope being that if enough people personalize the form e-mail, the elected official will take the petition more seriously.

SOURCES: J. Thomas and G. Streib, "The New Face of Government: Citizen-Initiated Contacts in the Era of E-Government," *Journal of Public Administration Theory and Research* 13, no. 1 (2003): 83–102.
Caroline Tolbert and Ramona McNeal, "Unraveling the Effects of the Internet on Political Participation." *Political Research Quarterly* 56, no. 2 (2003): 175–85.
Aaron Smith, Kay Lehman Schlozman, Sydney Verba, and Henry Brady, "The Internet and Civic Engagement," September 1, 2009, http://pewinternet.org/Reports/2009/15–The-Internet-and-Civic-Engagement.aspx (accessed 7/1/12).

## for critical analysis

1. Do you think online petitions are more or less effective than paper petitions for interest groups lobbying members of Congress? Why?

2. Do you think petitions are likely to be effective in shaping government policy, or do elected officials still respond primarily to well-established business interests, rather than citizen groups? Are online petitions more for show than for substance?

example, a grassroots firm called Grassfire.org led the drive to kill the immigration reform bill supported by President Bush and a number of congressional Democrats that would have legalized the status of many illegal immigrants. Grassfire.org used the Internet and talk radio programs to generate a campaign that yielded 700,000 signatures on petitions opposing the bill. The petitions, along with tens of thousands of phone calls, letters, and e-mails generated by Grassfire and several other groups, led to the bill's defeat in the U.S. Senate.[32]

Sometimes, unfortunately, such efforts are not genuine grassroots campaigns but instead represent "Astroturf lobbying" (a play on the name of the artificial grass used on many sports fields). Such campaigns, often using e-mail, have increased in frequency in recent years as members of Congress have grown more and more skeptical of Washington lobbyists and far more attentive to demonstrations of support for a particular issue by their actual constituents. Often Astroturf campaigns are carefully scripted efforts on behalf of corporate interests using names designed to disguise their true goals to help them gather public support for their efforts. For example, the Save Our Species Alliance is an industry group seeking to weaken the Endangered Species Act, and Citizens for Asbestos Reform seeks to limit the ability of individuals harmed by asbestos to seek redress in the courts. The Coalition to Protect America's Health Care is a group of for-profit hospitals that runs ads calling for increased federal funding for those entities. Citizens for Better Medicare actually represents the pharmaceutical industry. Voices for Choices was the alias used by a coalition of telecommunications companies that unsuccessfully advertised on behalf of continued regulation of local phone services. Both Americans for Balanced Energy Choices and the Coalition for Clean, Affordable, Reliable Energy sponsor ads promoting the virtues of coal as an energy source. "Some of us invest lots of time and money into making the world cleaner," announces the pitchman for Americans for Balanced Energy Choices. "And one thing that's helping is electricity from coal."

By the logic of these aliases, a coalition of strip-mining interests might call itself Citizens for a Cleaner Earth, while perhaps a coalition of health insurers—companies notorious for raising premiums but refusing to pay subscribers' claims—might operate under the alias Citizens against Costly Medical Services. A Senate bill proposed in 2006 would have required lobby groups using such aliases to disclose their true identities. Many groups treated this proposal as a vicious attack on their freedom of speech. Wayne LaPierre, president of the NRA, suggested that this sort of disclosure requirement would have thwarted the activities of the Revolutionary-era pamphleteer Tom Paine and perhaps undermined the American Revolution. The proposal ultimately failed.

## Using Electoral Politics

In addition to attempting to influence members of Congress and other government officials, interest groups also seek to use the electoral process to elect the right legislators in the first place and to ensure that those who are elected will owe them a debt of gratitude for their support. If we view matters in perspective, groups invest far more resources in lobbying than in electoral politics. Nevertheless, financial support and campaign activism can be important tools for organized interests.

**Political Action Committees** By far the most common electoral strategy employed by interest groups is that of giving financial support to the parties or to particular candidates. But such support can easily cross the threshold into outright

**for** critical **analysis**

Interest groups often use aliases in their advertising. For example, Americans for Balanced Energy Choices is an alias for a coal industry trade group. Should lobbying groups be required to disclose their actual identities?

bribery. Therefore, Congress has occasionally attempted to regulate this strategy. For example, the Federal Election Campaign Act of 1971 (amended in 1974) limits campaign contributions and requires that each candidate or campaign committee itemize the full name and address, occupation, and principal business of each person who contributes more than $100. These provisions have been effective up to a point, resulting in numerous embarrassments, indictments, resignations, and criminal convictions in the aftermath of the 1972 Watergate scandal.

The Watergate scandal was triggered by the illegal entry of a group of clandestine agents employed by the president's re-election committee into the office of the Democratic National Committee in the Watergate apartment and hotel complex. An investigation quickly revealed numerous violations of campaign finance laws, involving millions of dollars in unregistered cash from corporate executives to President Nixon's re-election committee. Reaction to Watergate produced further legislation on campaign finance in 1974 and 1976, but the effect was to restrict individual rather than interest-group campaign activity. Today, individuals may contribute no more than $2,300 to any candidate for federal office in any primary or general election. A **political action committee (PAC)**, however, can contribute $5,000, provided it contributes to at least five different federal candidates each year. (Campaign finance regulations are discussed in more detail in Chapter 10.) Beyond this, the laws permit corporations, unions, and other interest groups to form PACs and to pay the costs of soliciting funds from private citizens for the PACs. In other words, PACs are interest groups that operate in the electoral arena in addition to whatever they do within the interest-group system. The option to form a PAC was made available by law only in the early 1970s. Until then, it was difficult, if not downright illegal, for corporations, including unions, to get directly involved in elections by supporting parties and candidates.

The flurry of reform legislation of the 1970s attempted to reduce the influence that special interests have over elections, but the effect has been almost the exact opposite. Electoral spending by interest groups has been increasing steadily. The number of PACs has also increased significantly—from 480 in 1972 to more than 5,500 in 2012 (see Figure 11.3). Opportunities for legally influencing campaigns

**for critical analysis**

How do interest groups differ from political parties? In terms of America's core values of liberty and democracy, should we prefer a political process dominated by parties or one in which interest groups are more important?

**political action committee (PAC)**
a private group that raises and distributes funds for use in election campaigns

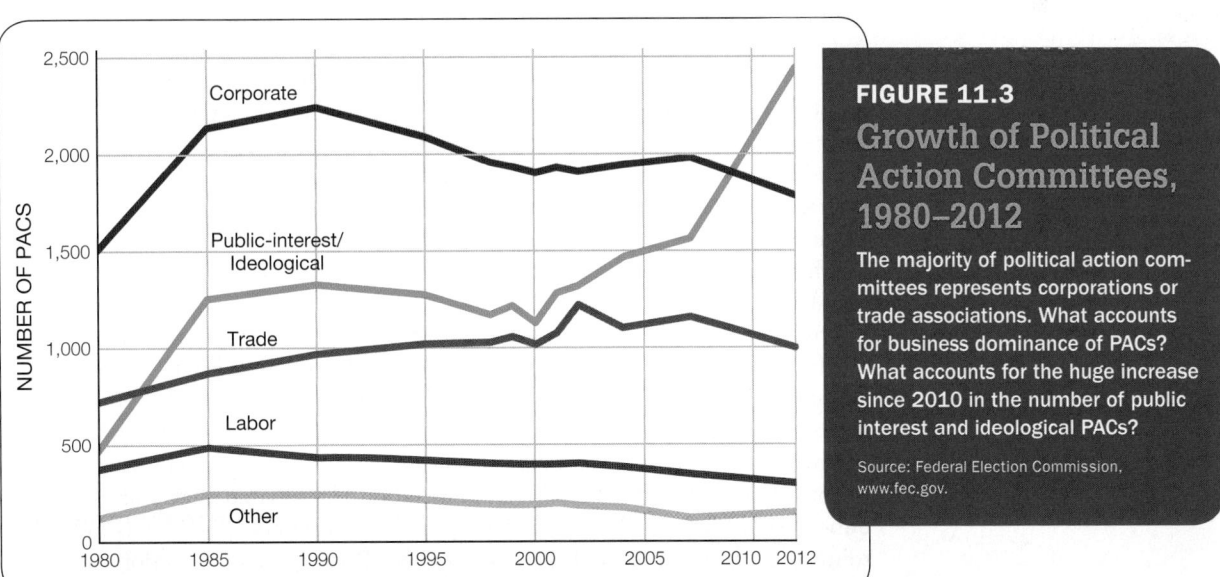

**FIGURE 11.3**

**Growth of Political Action Committees, 1980–2012**

The majority of political action committees represents corporations or trade associations. What accounts for business dominance of PACs? What accounts for the huge increase since 2010 in the number of public interest and ideological PACs?

Source: Federal Election Commission, www.fec.gov.

are now widespread. PACs contributed roughly 15 percent of the more than $5 billion spent on national, state, and local elections in 2012. As much as 50 percent was contributed or spent by 527s, 501c(4) groups, and super PACs, which can spend far more than is allowed under federal law for PACs.

Given the enormous costs of television commercials, polls, computers, and other elements of contemporary political technology, most politicians are eager to receive PAC contributions and are at least willing to give a friendly hearing to the needs and interests of contributors. Most politicians probably will not simply sell their services to the interests that fund their campaigns, but there is some evidence that interest groups' campaign contributions do influence the overall pattern of political behavior in Congress and in the state legislatures.

Concern about PACs grew through the 1980s and '90s, creating a constant drumbeat for reform of federal election laws. Proposals to abolish PACs were introduced in Congress on many occasions, with perhaps the most celebrated being the McCain-Feingold bill, which became the Bipartisan Campaign Reform Act (BCRA) of 2002. When originally proposed in 1996, McCain-Feingold was aimed at reducing or eliminating PACs. But in a stunning about-face, when campaign finance reform was adopted in 2002, it did not restrict PACs in any significant way. Rather, it eliminated unrestricted "soft money" donations to the national political parties. One consequence of this reform, as we saw in Chapters 9 and 10, was the creation of a host of new organizations, which include 527 committees, organizations created to promote particular ideas or candidates, and super PACs, formally called "independent expenditure-only committees," which were created for the purpose of promoting whatever candidacies their organizers wish. 527 committees and super PACs are nominally unaffiliated with the two parties but often directed by former party officials. This change has had the effect of strengthening interest groups and weakening parties.

Activist groups carefully keep their campaign spending separate from party and candidate organizations to avoid the restrictions of federal campaign finance laws. As long as a group's campaign expenditures are not coordinated with those of a candidate's campaign, the group is free to spend as much money as it wishes. Such expenditures are viewed as "issue advocacy" and are protected by the First Amendment. The Supreme Court's 2010 *Citizens United* decision increased the flow of money into 527s and super PACs by removing restrictions on corporate political spending, freeing business to back whatever politicians it chose.[33]

One powerful but little-known campaign finance tactic is the formation of strategic alliances between corporate interest groups and ideological or not-for-profit groups. Politicians are reluctant to accept money directly from what might have seemed to be unsavory sources, and corporate interests may find it useful to hide campaign contributions by laundering them through a not-for-profit. In the case of the former Washington super-lobbyist Jack Abramoff, discussed earlier in this chapter, gambling interests made contributions to religious groups led by Ralph Reed, the former executive director of the Christian Coalition, and Reverend Louis P. Sheldon, founder of the Traditional Values Coalition, and to tax-reform groups headed by Grover Norquist. In turn, these groups lobbied against the Internet gambling ban, providing laundered campaign funds for prominent members of Congress. This tactic, called "money swapping," is fairly common. The Clinton administration allegedly engaged in extensive money swapping with such organizations as the International Brotherhood of Teamsters. In one case, a foreign national hoping to influence the administration was advised that a direct contribution would be illegal. Instead, Democratic fund-raisers advised this individual to make a contribution to Teamster president Ron Carey's re-election campaign.

# Who Is Represented by PACs?

Following recent Supreme Court decisions that ended many restrictions on campaign spending and issue advocacy, the number of "nonconnected," or ideological, PACs has increased dramatically, making this the largest PAC category in terms of the number of groups. These groups are not connected to a specific corporation, labor organization, or membership association, and they work to elect candidates who support their ideals or agenda. However, in terms of contributions to candidates, spending by ideological groups is dwarfed by the combined contributions of PACs from various business sectors.

## PAC Contributions to Federal Candidates in 2010

By sector

Corporate
Nonconnected/ideological
Labor
Other

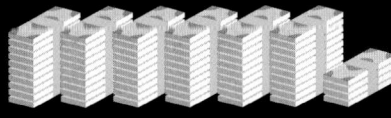

**Labor**
**$63,665,882**

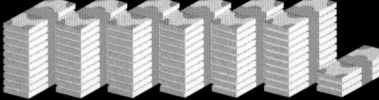

**Finance, insurance & real estate**
**$62,909,712**

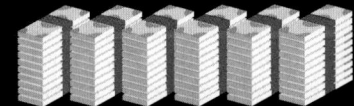

**Ideological**
**$60,279,974**

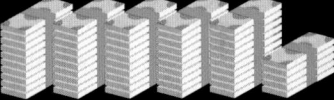

**Health**
**$54,641,685**

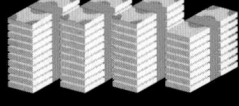

**Misc. business**
**$37,791,850**

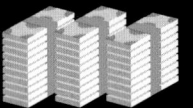

**Energy & natural resources**
**$28,858,057**

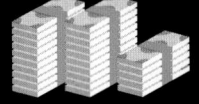

**Communications/electronics**
**$24,972,482**

**Agribusiness**
**$22,950,208**

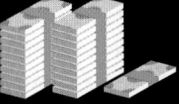

**Transportation**
**$21,118,906**

**Lawyers & lobbyists**
**$15,916,526**

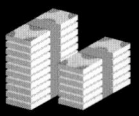

**Construction**
**$15,534,354**

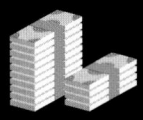

**Defense**
**$14,263,964**

Other
**$1,344,461**

## Registered PACs in 2011–12

By category

Nonconnected/Ideological **2,442**

Other **153**

Labor **297**

Trade/Membership/Health **989**

Corporate **1,786**

## for critical analysis

1. Business PACs are the biggest spenders. What effect might this have on which candidates get elected and what policies they pass?

2. If ideological PACs are now the most numerous type, what effects might this have on American politics and government?

SOURCES: www.fec.gov; www.opensecrets.org (accessed 9/26/12).

The Teamsters, in turn, made a legal contribution to the Clinton campaign. Such money swapping is illegal but almost impossible to prove.

**Campaign Activism** Financial support is not the only way that organized groups seek influence through electoral politics. Sometimes activism can be even more important than campaign contributions. Campaign activism on the part of conservative groups played a very important role in bringing about the Republican capture of both houses of Congress in 1994. For example, Christian Coalition activists played a role in many races, including those in which Republican candidates were not strongly identified with the religious right. One postelection study suggested that more than 60 percent of the more than 600 candidates supported by the Christian right were successful in state, local, and congressional races in 1994, especially in the South.[34] In many congressional districts, Christian Coalition efforts were augmented by grassroots campaigns launched by the NRA, which had been outraged by Democratic support for gun-control legislation, and the National Federation of Independent Business (NFIB), which had been energized by its campaign against employer mandates in the failed Clinton health care reform initiative. Both groups are well-organized at the local level and were able to mobilize their members across the country to participate in congressional races.

**Initiatives** Another political tactic that interest groups sometimes use is sponsorship of ballot initiatives at the state level. The initiative, a device adopted by a number of states around 1900, allows proposed laws to be placed on the general election ballot and submitted directly to the state's voters, bypassing the state legislature and the governor. The initiative was originally promoted by late-nineteenth-century Populists as a mechanism that would allow the people to govern directly—an antidote to interest-group influence in the legislative process.

Many studies have suggested that, ironically, most initiative campaigns today are actually sponsored by interest groups seeking to circumvent legislative opposition to their goals. In recent years, for example, initiative campaigns have been sponsored by the insurance industry, trial lawyers' associations, and tobacco companies.[35] The success of business groups promoting antitax initiatives and conservative activists seeking to ban same-sex marriage has led liberal activists to develop their own initiative campaigns to promote issues such as same-sex marriage, clean energy, and abortion rights. In 1998, liberal activists established the Ballot Initiative Strategy Center (BISC) to provide national coordination for these efforts, which led to successes such as the 2010 Oregon campaign for Propositions 66 and 67, which increased taxes for corporations and high-income wage earners. The role of interest groups in initiative campaigns should come as no surprise, since such campaigns can cost millions of dollars.

## ● Thinking Critically about Groups and Interests: The Dilemmas of Reform

We would like to think that policies are products of legislators representing the public interest. The truth of the matter is that few programs and policies ever reach the public agenda without the vigorous efforts of important national interest groups. In the realm of economic policy, social policy, international trade policy, and even such seemingly interest-free areas as criminal justice policy—where, in fact, private prison corporations lobby for longer sentences for lawbreakers—the activity of interest groups is a central feature.

*Some citizens worry that well-funded narrow interests, such as business groups, are better able to organize and lobby the government, while ordinary citizens have less influence in politics.*

James Madison wrote that "liberty is to faction as air is to fire."[36] By this he meant that the organization and proliferation of interests were inevitable in a free society. To seek to place limits on the organization of interests, in Madison's view, would be to limit liberty itself. Madison believed that interests should be permitted to regulate themselves by competing with one another. As long as competition among different interests were free, open, and vigorous—that is, as long as pluralism thrived—there would be some balance of power among them, and no one interest would be able to dominate the political or governmental process.

Indeed, there is considerable competition among organized groups in the United States. Pro-choice and antiabortion forces, for example, continue to be locked in a bitter struggle. Nevertheless, interest-group politics is not as balanced as Madisonian theory might suggest. Although the weak and poor do occasionally become organized to assert their rights, interest-group politics is generally a form of political competition best suited to the wealthy and powerful. In the realm of group politics, liberty seems inconsistent with equality.

Moreover, although groups sometimes organize to promote broad public concerns, they more often represent relatively narrow, selfish interests. Small, self-interested groups can be organized much more easily than large and more diffuse collectives. For one thing, the members of a relatively small group—say, bankers or hunting enthusiasts—are usually able to recognize their shared interests and the need to pursue them in the political arena. Members of large and more diffuse groups—say, consumers or potential victims of firearms—often find it difficult to recognize their shared interests or the need to engage in collective action to achieve them.[37]

To make matters still more complicated, group politics seems to go hand in hand with government. As we saw earlier, government programs often lead to a proliferation of interest groups as competing forces mobilize to support, oppose, or take advantage of the government's actions. Often the government explicitly encourages the formation of interest groups. Agencies such as the Department of Veterans' Affairs, the Social Security Administration, and the Department of Agriculture devote a great deal of energy to the organization and mobilization of groups of "stakeholders" to support the agencies and their efforts. One reason the Social Security program has endured despite its fiscal shortcomings is that it is so strongly supported by a powerful group: AARP. Significantly, the Social Security Administration played an important early role in the formation of AARP, precisely because agency executives realized that this group could become a useful ally.

The responsiveness of government agencies to interest groups is a challenge to democracy. Groups sometimes seem to have a greater impact than voters on the government's policies and programs. Yet, before we decide that we should do away with interest groups, we should think carefully: If there were no organized interests, would the government pay more attention to ordinary voters? Or would the government simply pay less attention to everyone? In his work *Democracy in America*, Alexis de Tocqueville argued that the proliferation of groups promoted democracy by encouraging governmental responsiveness. Does group politics foster democracy or impede democracy? It does both.

# Learn about Lobbying

## Inform Yourself

 **What counts as an interest group?** The number of interest groups and lobbyists has grown dramatically over the last 50 years. There is no central database of all these groups, but a relatively complete list is available at http://pag.vancouver.wsu.edu/. Click on a few of the categories and see what groups are listed there. Does any of them surprise you as being classified as an interest group?

 **Consider the example of professional sports interest groups.** The groups that lobby government are diverse. In professional sports, there are unions representing players, staff, and referees; there are corporations that run the teams; there are leagues themselves—each of these entities also lobbies the government for favorable policies. Check out the report at http://firststreetresearch.cqpress .com/2012/05/16/sports-lobby-is-a-multi-million-dollar-enterprise/.

## Express Yourself

 **Watch a video on the pros and cons of lobbying.** The American League of Lobbyists has created a video arguing that lobbying is beneficial to American politics. Watch it at: www.alldc.org/video.cfm. Compare what the first video argues with the factual information from the video available at www.youtube.com/ watch?v=R2DUM6jVasw. Consider sharing your opinion on what you learn.

 **Are current regulations on lobbying strong enough?** Explore how heavily regulated lobbyists are in Washington, D.C., today at www.voanews.com/content/lobbying -regulated-to-prevent-abuse-in-us-101407789/174277.html. Do you think lobbyists are regulated enough, or should we take further action against their influence? Contact your members of Congress to let them know your views.

## Connect with Others

 **Connect with interest groups.** A small sample of the groups on Facebook include AARP, MADD, the NRA, NOW, and the National Chamber of Commerce. Visit the Facebook pages of these groups (they all have Twitter pages as well) or find others that interest you. Find a post by one of the groups and join in the discussion. You can also join a membership group if you find one whose goals you share.

*Find links to the sites listed above as well as related activities on wwnorton.com/studyspace.*

## The Character of Interest Groups

■ **Describe the major types of interest groups and whom they represent (pp. 435–43)**

An interest group is an organized group of people that makes policy-related appeals to government. Although organized groups form around many different political interests, almost all interest groups share a similar set of organizational components, including leadership, money, an office and members. In order to overcome the free rider problem, interest groups attempt to provide their potential members with informational, material, solidary and purposive benefits.

### Key Terms

**pluralism** (p. 435)

**interest group** (p. 435)

**public interest groups** (p. 437)

**membership association** (p. 439)

**staff organization** (p. 439)

**collective goods** (p. 440)

**free riders** (p. 440)

**informational benefits** (p. 442)

**material benefits** (p. 442)

**solidary benefits** (p. 442)

**purposive benefits** (p. 442)

### Practice Quiz

1. The theory that competition among organized interests will produce balance, with all the interests regulating one another is *(p. 435)*
   a) pluralism.
   b) elite power politics.
   c) democracy.
   d) socialism.
   e) libertarianism.

2. Groups that have an interest in obtaining government funds for research, such as Harvard University, the Brookings Institution, and the American Enterprise Institute, are referred to as *(p. 437)*
   a) membership associations.
   b) public interest groups.
   c) professional associations.
   d) ideological groups.
   e) public-sector groups.

3. To overcome the free rider problem, groups *(p. 441)*
   a) provide general benefits.
   b) litigate.
   c) provide selective benefits.
   d) provide collective goods.
   e) go public.

4. Friendship and networking are examples of _____, while discount purchasing and health insurance are examples of _____. *(p. 442)*
   a) purposive benefits; material benefits
   b) purposive benefits; solidary benefits
   c) solidary benefits; purposive benefits
   d) material benefits; solidary benefits
   e) solidary benefits; material benefits

5. Which of the following best describes the reputation of AARP in the Washington, D.C., community? *(p. 443)*
   a) It is respected and feared.
   b) It is believed to be ineffective.
   c) It always wins the political battles it fights.
   d) It is corrupt and unrepresentative of most Americans.
   e) It is supported and well liked by all political forces.

**⑤ Practice Online**
"Who Are Americans?" exercise: *Who Is Represented by PACs?*

# The Proliferation of Groups

■ **Analyze why the number of interest groups has grown in recent decades (pp. 443–45)**

In recent decades there has been a significant growth in the number of interest groups seeking to influence the American political process. One reason for this change has been the dramatic expansion of the role of American government over the last four decades. Another reason for this change has been the emergence of a new set of political forces in the United States called the "New Politics" movement.

## Key Term

**New Politics movement** (p. 444)

## Practice Quiz

6. Which of the following is an important reason for the enormous increase in the number of groups seeking to influence the American political system? *(p. 443)*

a) the decrease in the size and activity of government during the last few decades
b) the increase in the size and activity of government during the last few decades
c) the increase in the amount of soft money in election campaigns in recent decades
d) the increase in legal protection provided to interest groups as a result of the Supreme Court's evolving interpretation of the First Amendment
e) the increase in the number of people identifying themselves as an independent in recent decades

7. Which types of interest groups are most often associated with the New Politics movement? *(p. 445)*

a) political action committees
b) professional associations
c) government groups
d) labor groups
e) public interest groups

# Strategies: The Quest for Political Power

■ **Explain how interest groups try to influence government (pp. 445–60)**

Interest groups take action to improve the probability that their policy interests will be treated favorably by all branches and all levels of government. These actions often take many different forms. Insider strategies include direct lobbying, cultivating access to decision makers and using the court system. Outsider strategies include mobilizing public opinion and using electoral politics.

## Key Terms

**lobbying** (p. 445)

**iron triangle** (p. 450)

**issue network** (p. 450)

**institutional advertising** (p. 453)

**grassroots mobilization** (p. 454)

**political action committee (PAC)** (p. 457)

## Practice Quiz

8. Which of the following best describes the federal government's laws regarding lobbying? *(pp. 445–46)*

a) Federal law allows lobbying but only on issues related to taxation.
b) Federal law allows lobbying but only if the lobbyists receive no monetary compensation for their lobbying.
c) Federal law strictly prohibits any form of lobbying.
d) Federal law requires all organizations employing lobbyists to register with Congress and to disclose whom they represent, whom they lobby, what they are looking for, and how much they are paid.
e) There are no laws regulating lobbying because the federal government has never passed any legislation on the legality of the activity.

9. A loose network of elected leaders, public officials, activists, and interest groups drawn together by a public policy issue is referred to as *(p. 450)*

a) an issue network.
b) a public interest group.
c) a political action committee.
d) pluralism.
e) an iron triangle.

10. Which of the following is a way that interest groups use the courts to influence public policy? *(p. 452)*

a) supplying judges with solidary benefits
b) joining an issue network
c) creating an iron triangle
d) forming a political action committee
e) filing *amicus* briefs

11. Which of the following are examples of the "going public" strategy? *(pp. 453–56)*

a) free riding, pluralism, and issue networking
b) donating money to political parties, endorsing candidates, and sponsoring ballot initiatives

c) institutional advertising, grassroots advertising, and protests and demonstrations

d) providing informational benefits, providing solidary benefits, and providing material benefits

e) filing an amicus brief, bringing a lawsuit, and financing those who are filing a lawsuit

12. According to this text, what is the limit a PAC can contribute to a candidate in a primary or general election campaign? *(p. 457)*
   a) $1,000
   b) $5,000
   c) $10,000
   d) $50,000
   e) $100,000

13. Which of the following is *not* an activity in which interest groups frequently engage? *(pp. 456–60)*
   a) starting their own political party
   b) litigation
   c) sponsoring ballot initiatives at the state level
   d) lobbying
   e) contributing to campaigns

14. "Money swapping" occurs when *(p. 458)*
   a) a member of a congressional committee trades his or her vote for a cash payment from an interest group.
   b) a candidate who is running in a competitive race convinces interest groups to contribute to a candidate who is running in a competitive race.
   c) an interest group combines its campaign spending with that of a political party or candidate organization.
   d) a lobbyist is paid to testify before a congressional committee.
   e) a corporate interest group attempts to hide its campaign contributions by laundering them through a not-for-profit group.

 **Practice Online**
Interactive simulation: *Legislative Affairs Director*

# For Further Reading

Abramoff, Jack. *Capitol Punishment: The Hard Truth about Washington Corruption from America's Most Notorious Lobbyist*. New York: WIND Books, 2011.

Ainsworth, Scott. *Analyzing Interest Groups*. New York: W.W. Norton, 2002.

Alexander, Robert, ed. *The Classics of Interest Group Behavior*. New York: Wadsworth, 2005.

Baumgartner, Frank, Jeffrey M. Berry, Beth L. Leech, David C. Kimball, and Marie Hojnacki. *Lobbying and Policy Change: Who Wins, Who Loses and Why*. Chicago: University of Chicago Press, 2009.

Berry, Jeffrey. *Interest Group Society*. 5th ed. New York: Longman, 2008.

Cigler, Allan J., and Burdett A. Loomis, eds. *Interest Group Politics*. 7th ed. Washington, DC: CQ Press, 2006.

Esterling, Kevin. *The Political Economy of Expertise*. Ann Arbor: University of Michigan Press, 2004.

Goldstein, Kenneth. *Interest Groups, Lobbying, and Participation in America*. New York: Cambridge University Press, 2008.

Kaiser, Robert. *So Damn Much Money: The Triumph of Lobbying and the Corrosion of American Government*. New York: Vintage, 2010.

Lessig, Lawrence. *Republic, Lost: How Money Corrupts Congress—and a Plan to Stop It*. New York: Twelve/Hachette Book Group, 2011.

Lowi, Theodore J. *The End of Liberalism: The Second Republic of the United States*. 2nd ed. New York: W.W. Norton, 1979.

Moe, Terry M. *The Organization of Interests: Incentives and the Internal Dynamics of Political Interest Groups*. Chicago: University of Chicago Press, 1980.

Nownes, Anthony. *Total Lobbying: What Lobbyists Want and How They Try to Get It*. New York: Cambridge University Press, 2006.

Olson, Mancur, Jr. *The Logic of Collective Action: Public Goods and the Theory of Groups*. Cambridge, MA: Harvard University Press, 1965.

Rozell, Mark, Clyde Wilcox, and David Madland. *Interest Groups in American Campaigns*. Washington, DC: CQ Press, 2005.

Sheingate, Adam. *The Rise of the Agricultural Welfare State: Institutions and Interest Group Power in the United States, France, and Japan*. Princeton, NJ: Princeton University Press, 2003.

Strolovitch, Dara. *Affirmative Advocacy: Race, Class, and Gender in Interest Group Politics*. Chicago: University of Chicago Press, 2007.

Truman, David B. *The Governmental Process: Political Interests and Public Opinion*. New York: Knopf, 1951.

# Recommended Websites

## AARP
www.aarp.org

AARP (formerly the American Association of Retired Persons) is one of the largest and most significant interest groups in the United States. Read about the history of this organization, its group benefits, and how it is affecting political issues and elections.

## AFL-CIO Legislative Alert Center
www.aflcio.org/issues/legislativealert/

Created in 1955, the AFL-CIO represents more than 10 million working men and women. See how this influential labor group is active and involved in political issues.

## American Civil Liberties Union
www.aclu.org
## American Conservative Union
www.conservative.org

The American Civil Liberties Union and the American Conservative Union are two of the nation's largest and most influential ideological interest groups. See what these opposing groups have to say about our government and current political issues.

## American Israel Public Affairs Committee (AIPAC)
www.aipac.org

Due to globalization, interest groups cannot limit their activities to one country. Decisions made in Washington, D.C., can affect countries around the world. The American Israel Public Affairs Committee (AIPAC) works with Republicans and Democrats to maintain a strong relationship between the United States and Israel.

## MoveOn
www.moveon.org

This progressive interest group is dedicated to bringing ordinary citizens back into the political process and electing liberal members of government. See how this group uses electoral politics, via political action committees and campaign activism, to achieve its agenda.

## National Rifle Association (NRA)
www.nra.org
## Coalition to Stop Gun Violence
www.csgv.org
## Brady Campaign to Prevent Gun Violence
www.bradycampaign.org

Lobbying is an attempt by a group to influence the policy process by persuading government officials. These three groups employ a variety of lobbying techniques on the issue of gun control.

## U.S. PIRG (United States Public Interest Research Group)
www.uspirg.org

This public interest group stands up for ordinary citizens. Its special emphasis is on consumer rights and the environment. U.S. PIRG mobilizes public opinion via institutional advertising, social movements, and grassroots efforts. PIRG chapters can be found in most states and at many colleges and universities.

## World Wildlife Fund
www.wwf.org

The World Wildlife Fund is dedicated to protecting nature. They provide information to policy makers about conservation and advocate policies to help preserve the natural environment.

In addition to its lawmaking powers, Congress plays a critical role in American democracy as a representative institution. The members of Congress—100 senators and 435 representatives—represent the voices of the people across America. Yet some observers worry that Congress does not represent all voices equally.

IN GOD WE TRUST

# 12

# Congress

**WHAT GOVERNMENT DOES AND WHY IT MATTERS** Early in 2012, Wikipedia went dark for a day. Visitors to the popular free online encyclopedia saw a black screen and an ominous warning: "Imagine a World without Free Knowledge." The day before, Wikipedia's cofounder Jimmy Wales sent out a tweet advising students, "Do your homework early."[1] Professors, of course, normally recommend that students not rely on Wikipedia's public-sourced format for their homework assignments. Still, the website made a point that day, with the help of other big names on the Internet, including Google. By organizing online petitions and e-mails, the sites succeeded in preventing Congress from enacting the Stop Online Piracy Act (SOPA) and the Protect Intellectual Property Act (PIPA). These regulatory measures would have given the Justice Department power to order websites to remove links suspected of copyright violation. To supporters in the film and recording industries, the proposed laws offered vital protection to writers, filmmakers, and recording artists, ensuring that they would receive appropriate compensation for their intellectual property. To opponents of SOPA and PIPA, the measures amounted to censorship, the heavy hand of the government stifling the free flow of information and the creativity that the Internet makes possible.

The conflict over the proposed laws highlighted how power works in Congress. For years, leaders in the entertainment industry, the key supporters of the restrictive legislation, had showered funds on members of Congress through campaign contributions. They also lobbied intensely, relying on expensive Washington-based lobbying firms to represent them. By contrast, Internet companies had paid much less attention to Congress, and most had only recently begun to build a presence in Washington.[2] Congress's initial support for SOPA and PIPA reflected the workings of power behind closed doors "inside the Beltway," as politics in Washington is sometimes called. But the success of the online mobilization in leading Congress to postpone its decision reflected the impact that broad-based mobilization of millions of citizens can have on Congress. It also revealed the power of the Internet as a way to mobilize people whose voices are often not heard in Washington.

Congress has vast authority over most aspects of American life. Laws related to federal spending, taxing, and regulation all pass through Congress. While the debates over these laws may seem hard to follow because they are complex and technical or because heated, partisan struggles distract from the substance of the issue, it is important for the American people to learn about what Congress is doing. As the example of SOPA and PIPA indicates, actions taken—or not taken—in Congress affect the everyday experiences we take for granted. With its power to spend and tax, Congress also affects the choices that people face and the opportunities they can expect in life. With so much information about Congress available on the Internet, it is not hard to get beyond the heated rhetoric and simplistic headlines and ask your own questions about a proposed law. How will it affect my life and the lives of people I care about? What is the impact on my country? Making laws is often compared to making sausage, because it is such a complex and often messy process. Even so, it is vital for citizens to monitor what Congress does because the laws it passes are so central to their lives.

## chaptergoals

- Describe who serves in Congress and how they represent their constituents (pages 471–84)

- Explain how party leadership, the committee system, the staff system, and caucuses help structure congressional business (pages 484–91)

- Outline the steps in the process of passing a law (pages 491–96)

- Analyze the factors that influence which laws Congress decides to pass (pages 496–504)

- Describe the oversight, "advice and consent," and impeachment powers of Congress (pages 504–7)

# ● Congress: Representing the American People

**Describe who serves in Congress and how they represent their constituents**

Congress is the most important representative institution in American government. Each member's primary responsibility is to the district, to his or her **constituency**, not to the congressional leadership, a party, or even Congress itself. Yet the task of representation is not a simple one. Views about what constitutes fair and effective representation differ, and constituents may have very different expectations of their representatives. Members of Congress must consider these diverse views and expectations as they represent their districts.

**constituency** the residents in the area from which an official is elected

## House and Senate: Differences in Representation

The framers of the Constitution provided for a **bicameral** legislature—that is, a legislative body consisting of two chambers. As we saw in Chapter 2, the framers intended each of these chambers, the House of Representatives and the Senate, to serve a different constituency. Members of the Senate, appointed by state legislatures for six-year terms, were to represent society's elite. Today, members of both House and Senate are elected directly by the people. The 435 members of the House are elected from districts apportioned according to population; the 100 members of the Senate are elected by their states, with two senators from each. Senators continue to have much longer terms in office and usually represent much larger and more diverse constituencies than do their counterparts in the House (see Table 12.1).

**bicameral** characterized as having a legislative assembly composed of two chambers or houses; distinguished from *unicameral*

The House and Senate play different roles in the legislative process. In essence, the Senate is the more deliberative of the two bodies—the forum in which any and all ideas that senators raise can receive a thorough public airing. The House is the more centralized and organized of the two bodies—better equipped to play a routine role in the governmental process. In part, this difference stems from the different rules governing the two bodies. These rules give House leaders more control over the legislative process and allow House members to specialize in certain

---

**TABLE 12.1**

### Differences between the House and the Senate

|  | HOUSE | SENATE |
| --- | --- | --- |
| Minimum age of member | 25 years | 30 years |
| U.S. citizenship | At least 7 years | At least 9 years |
| Length of term | 2 years | 6 years |
| Number representing each state | 1–53 per state (depends on population) | 2 per state |
| Constituency | Local | Local and state-wide |

*For its first 128 years, Congress was a decidedly masculine world. In 1917, three years before the ratification of the Nineteenth Amendment, Jeanette Rankin (R-Mont.) (pictured back row, far right) became the first woman to serve in Congress.*

legislative areas. The rules of the much smaller Senate give its leadership relatively little power and discourage specialization.

Both formal and informal factors contribute to differences between the two chambers of Congress. Differences in the length of terms and requirements for holding office, specified by the Constitution, generate differences in how members of each body develop their constituencies and exercise their powers of office. The result is that members of the House most effectively and frequently serve as the agents of well-organized local interests with specific legislative agendas—for instance, used-car dealers seeking relief from regulation, labor unions seeking more favorable legislation, or farmers looking for higher subsidies. The small size and relative homogeneity of their constituencies and the frequency with which they must seek re-election make House members more attuned to the legislative needs of local interest groups.

Senators, on the other hand, serve larger and more heterogeneous constituencies. As a result, they are somewhat better able than members of the House to act as the agents for groups and interests organized on a statewide or national basis. Moreover, with longer terms in office, senators have more time to consider "new ideas" or to bring together new coalitions of interests rather than simply serving existing ones.

## Sociological versus Agency Representation

We have become so accustomed to the idea of representative government that we tend to forget what a peculiar concept representation really is. A representative claims to act or speak for some other person or group. But how can one person be trusted to speak for another? How do we know that those who call themselves our representatives are actually speaking on our behalf, rather than simply pursuing their own interests?

There are two circumstances under which one person reasonably might be trusted to speak for another. The first occurs if the two individuals are so similar in background, character, interests, and perspectives that anything said by one would very likely reflect the views of the other as well. This principle is at the heart of what is sometimes called **sociological representation**—the sort of representation that takes place when representatives have the same racial, gender, ethnic, religious, or educational backgrounds as their constituents. The assumption is that sociological similarity helps to promote good representation; thus the composition of a properly constituted representative assembly should mirror the composition of society.

The second circumstance under which one person might be trusted to speak for another occurs if the two are formally bound together so that the representative is in some way accountable to those he or she is supposed to represent. If representatives can somehow be punished for failing to speak properly for their constituents, then we know they have an incentive to provide good representation even if their own personal backgrounds, views, and interests differ from the backgrounds of those they represent. This principle is called **agency representation**—the sort of representation that takes place when constituents have the power to hire and fire their representatives.

**sociological representation** a type of representation in which representatives have the same racial, gender, ethnic, religious, or educational backgrounds as their constituents. It is based on the principle that if two individuals are similar in background, character, interests, and perspectives, then one could correctly represent the other's views

**agency representation** the type of representation in which a representative is held accountable to a constituency if he or she fails to represent that constituency properly. This is incentive for good representation when the personal backgrounds, views, and interests of the representative differ from those of his or her constituency

Both sociological and agency representation play a role in the relationship between members of Congress and their constituencies.

**The Social Composition of the U.S. Congress** The extent to which the U.S. Congress is representative of the American people in a sociological sense can be seen by examining social characteristics of the House and Senate today. For example, the religious affiliations of members of both the House and Senate are overwhelmingly Protestant—the distribution is very close to the proportion in the population at large—although the Protestant category comprises more than 15 denominations. Catholics are the second-largest category of religious affiliation, and Jews a much smaller, third category.[3] Religious affiliations directly affect congressional debate on a limited range of issues where different moral views are at stake, such as abortion.

African Americans, women, Latinos, and Asian Americans have increased their congressional representation in the past two decades (see Figure 12.1), but the representation of minorities in Congress is still not comparable to their proportions in the general population. After the Democrats won a majority in the House in November 2006, Nancy Pelosi (D-Calif.) became the first female Speaker of the House and held that position through 2010. Following the 2012 elections, the 113th Congress (2013–14) included at least 77 women in the House of Representatives and 20 women in the Senate, an all-time high. Since many important contemporary national issues cut along racial and gender lines, pressure for reform in the representative process is likely to continue until all groups are fully represented.

The occupational backgrounds of members of Congress have always been a matter of interest because so many issues split along economic lines that are

**for critical analysis**

Why is sociological representation important? If congressional representatives have racial, religious, or educational backgrounds similar to those of their constituents, are they better representatives? Why or why not?

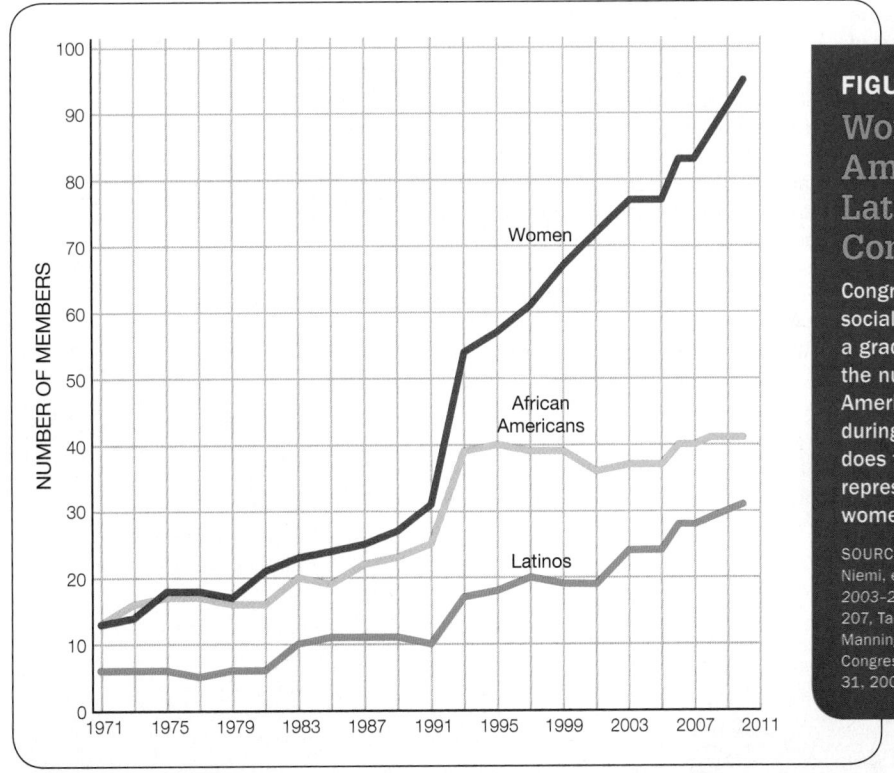

**FIGURE 12.1**

**Women, African Americans, and Latinos in the U.S. Congress, 1971–2010**

Congress has become much more socially diverse since the 1970s. After a gradual increase from 1971 to 1990, the number of women and African American members grew quickly during the first half of the 1990s. How does the pattern of growth for Latino representatives compare with that of women and African Americans?

SOURCES: Harold W. Stanley and Richard G. Niemi, eds., *Vital Statistics on American Politics 2003–2004* (Washington, DC: CQ Press, 2003), 207, Table 5–2; and Mildred Amer and Jennifer E. Manning, *Membership of the 11th Congress: A Profile*, Congressional Research Service 7-5700, December 31, 2008, assets.opencrs.com (accessed 1/31/10).

# New Media and Women Candidates for Congress

**Congress has entered the digital age.** As of 2009, 186 members of the House used Twitter, and 291 had Facebook pages. Every member of Congress had a website. Additionally, almost half of House members had a dedicated blog. However, there are differences in who is using these online avenues for constituent communication.

The 113th Congress (2013–14) includes 20 women serving in the 100-person Senate and at least 77 women serving in the House of Representatives (out of 435 members). These figures represent an all-time high. Yet women account for over 50 percent of the U.S. population but just 18 percent of the members of Congress. Are new media and digital communication helping or hurting women political candidates?

Members of Congress use blogs to claim credit and to raise awareness of issues. It is not uncommon for lawmakers to "leak" information to other bloggers to mobilize support for policy positions they favor. Members also use their own blogs because it allows unfiltered messages to reach constituents and the news media. Traditional media may report a 20-second clip of an interview, but a blog or website allows the member to get the full message to the public. Winning Senate candidate Elizabeth Warren (D-Mass.) became an overnight sensation when her campaign speech went viral on YouTube; in the video Warren talks about the need to raise taxes so all Americans, including large corporations, pay their fair share.

Members of the House are more likely to be on Twitter than Senators; however, use of Facebook is about the same in the two chambers. Republican officeholders are more likely than Democratic officeholders to be on either of these sites; in 2009, 69 percent of Republican lawmakers used Facebook, compared to only 45 percent of Democrats.

When broken down by gender, the posts reveal differences in format and content. Congresswomen are more likely than Congressmen to be on Facebook and are more likely to stress advertising and position taking. Women politicians try to downplay personal and procedural issues online, compared to men. Surveys show that women constituents also prefer Facebook to other forms of new media.

If women lawmakers are taking advantage of online media more often than men, does this translate into more support for women in elections? The answer is unclear. While new media such as Facebook, Twitter, blogs, and YouTube can offer female legislators an easier way to reach supporters and raise campaign funds, the Internet can also have a negative impact on women candidates.

Women running for Congress are often faced with a barrage of negative advertising, and online messages can be especially harsh and inaccurate. Bloggers can invert stories about a candidate, and by the time the message is corrected the damage to her legitimacy has been done. Of course male candidates face the same danger, but because women candidates face more criticism based on gender, negative press can be more damaging, reinforcing existing gender stereotypes.

Another reason the new media world can be problematic for women politicians is because individuals self-select information, thus only seeing "facts" that support their pre-existing opinions. People who believe in gender stereotypes and think women candidates are inferior to men may only be exposed to information online that supports their view. In contrast, mainstream media outlets tend to offer more balanced news coverage and avoid gender stereotypes. Research by political scientist Jennifer Lawless on the effects of new media on support for women candidates shows that individuals who rely primarily on blogs for political information are less likely to believe women candidates are competent, and are less likely to vote for women candidates, holding all else even.

SOURCES: Richard Davis, *Typing Politics: The Role of Blogs in American Politics* (New York: Oxford University Press, 2009). Jennifer L. Lawless, "Twitter and Facebook: New Ways for Members of Congress to Send the Same Old Messages?" in *iPolitics: Citizens, Elections, and Governing in the New Media Era*, ed. Richard L. Fox and Jennifer M. Ramos (Cambridge, UK: Cambridge University Press, 2012), pp. 206–32.

## for critical analysis

1. From a constituent's perspective, is it more helpful to receive information directly from your members of Congress via the Internet or through the news media? Why?

2. Do you think the use of online media will ultimately help or hurt women running for Congress and other political offices? Why?

*The increasing racial and ethnic diversity Congress is shown in the membership of the Congressional Hispanic Caucus, Black Caucus, and Asian Pacific American Caucus. Here, members of those three groups hold a press conference on the federal budget and debt.*

relevant to occupations and industries. The legal profession is the dominant career of most members of Congress prior to their election. Public service or politics is also a significant background, with many members coming from positions in state and local government. In addition, many members of Congress have important ties to business and industry.[4] Moreover, members of Congress are much more highly educated than most Americans. More than 9 in 10 members hold university degrees, and close to half of them have law degrees.[5] This is not a portrait of the U.S. population. Congress is not a sociological microcosm of American society.

Can Congress still legislate fairly or take account of a diversity of views and interests if it is not a sociologically representative assembly? The task is certainly much more difficult. Yet there is reason to believe it can. Representatives, as we shall see shortly, can serve as the agents of their constituents even if they do not precisely mirror their sociological attributes. Yet sociological representation is a matter of some importance, even if it is not an absolute prerequisite for fair legislation by members of the House and Senate. At the least, the social composition of a representative assembly is important for symbolic purposes: to demonstrate to groups in the population that the government takes them seriously. If Congress is not representative symbolically, then its own authority, and indeed that of the entire government, is reduced.[6]

**Representatives as Agents** A good deal of evidence indicates that whether or not members of Congress share their constituents' sociological characteristics, they *do* work very hard to speak for their constituents' views and to serve their constituents' interests. The idea of representative as agent is similar to the relationship of lawyer and client. True, the relationship between the member of Congress and an average of 710,767 "clients" in the district, or the senator and millions of "clients" in the state, is very different from that of the lawyer and client. But the criteria of performance are comparable. One expects at the very least that each representative will constantly seek to discover the interests of the constituency and take those interests into account as he or she governs. Whether members of Congress always represent the interests of their constituents is another matter, as we will see later in this chapter.[7]

There is constant communication between constituents and congressional offices, and the volume of e-mail from constituents and advocacy groups has grown so large so quickly that congressional offices have struggled to find effective ways to respond in a timely manner.[8] At the same time, members of Congress have found new ways to communicate with constituents. They have created websites describing their achievements, established a presence on social networking sites, and issued e-newsletters that alert constituents to current issues. Many also have set up blogs and used Twitter accounts to establish a more informal style of communication with constituents.

The seriousness with which members of the House attempt to behave as representatives can be seen in the amount of time they spend on behalf of their constituents. One way to measure the amount of time members of Congress devote to constituency service (called "casework") is to look at the percentage of personal House and Senate staff (personal staff being non-committee member staff) assigned to district and state offices. In 1972, 22.5 percent of House members' personal staff were located in district offices; by 2005 the number had grown to 50.7 percent.[9] For the Senate, the staff in state offices grew from 12.5 percent in 1972 to 39 percent in 2005. The service that these offices provide is not merely a matter of handling correspondence. It includes talking to constituents, providing them with minor services, presenting special bills for them, and attempting to influence decisions by regulatory commissions on their behalf.

Although no members of Congress are above constituency pressures (and they would not want to be), on many issues, constituents do not have very strong views, and representatives are free to act as they think best. Foreign policy issues often fall into this category. But in many districts, there are two or three issues on which constituents have such pronounced opinions that representatives feel they have little freedom of choice. For example, representatives from districts that grow wheat, cotton, or tobacco probably will not want to exercise a great deal of independence on relevant agricultural legislation. In oil-rich states such as Oklahoma and Texas, senators and members of the House are likely to be leading advocates of oil interests. For one thing, representatives are probably fearful of voting against their district interests; for another, the districts are unlikely to have elected representatives who would *want* to vote against them.

The influence of constituencies is so pervasive that both parties have strongly embraced the informal rule that nothing should be done to endanger the re-election chances of any member. Party leaders obey this rule fairly consistently by not asking any member to vote in a way that might conflict with a district interest.

## The Electoral Connection

The sociological composition of Congress and the activities of representatives once they are in office are very much influenced by electoral considerations. Three factors related to the U.S. electoral system affect who gets elected and what they do once in office. The first factor concerns who decides to run for office and which candidates have an edge over others. The second issue is that of incumbency advantage. Finally, the way congressional district lines are drawn can greatly affect

# Who Are the Members of Congress?

## Gender

| | U.S. Pop. | House | Senate |
|---|---|---|---|
| ● Female | 51% | 17% | 17% |
| ● Male | 49% | 83% | 83% |

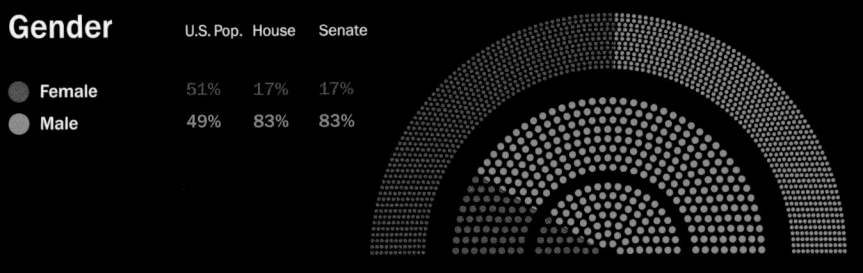

## Key

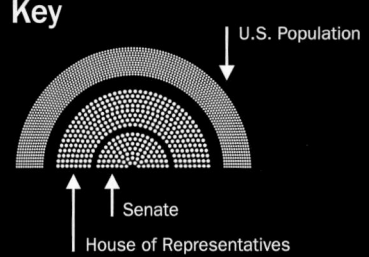

U.S. Population

Senate

House of Representatives

## Race

| | U.S. Pop. | House | Senate |
|---|---|---|---|
| ● White | 64% | 82% | 96% |
| ● Black | 13% | 10% | 0% |
| ● Hispanic | 16% | 7% | 2% |
| ● Asian | 5% | 3% | 2% |
| ● Native American | 1% | .002% | 0% |

Although the number of women, African Americans, and Latinos in Congress has increased in recent decades, Congress is still much less diverse than the American population. Members of Congress are predominantly male, white, Protestant Christian, and most commonly come from a professional and educational background as lawyers. These data compare the 112th Congress, which took office in 2011, with the U.S. population as a whole.

## Religion

| | U.S. Pop. | House | Senate |
|---|---|---|---|
| ● Protestant | 51% | 57% | 56% |
| ● Catholic | 24% | 30% | 24% |
| ● Mormon | 2% | 2% | 5% |
| ● Jewish | 2% | 6% | 12% |
| ● All Others | 21% | 4% | 4% |

## for critical analysis

1. Does it matter if the backgrounds of members of Congress reflect the population as a whole? Can members still represent their constituents effectively if they do not come from similar backgrounds?

2. Visit www.house.gov and www.senate.gov to identify your representatives in Congress and visit their Web pages. How similar are their backgrounds to yours? How closely do their policy positions, as expressed on their web pages, match your own?

## Education

Highest level attained:

| | U.S. Pop. | House | Senate |
|---|---|---|---|
| ● < High school | 15% | 0 | 0 |
| ● High school grad. | 58% | 8% | 1% |
| ● Bachelor's degree | 18% | 26% | 24% |
| ● Professional/ law degree | 2% | 38% | 55% |
| ● Other advanced degree | 8% | 28% | 20% |

## Average Age

| U.S. Pop. 37 | House 57 | Senate 62 |
|---|---|---|

SOURCE: Jennifer E. Manning, "Membership of the 112th Congress: A Profile," CRS Report R41647, March 1, 2011, www.senate.gov (accessed 8/15/12).

the outcome of an election. Let us examine more closely the impact that these considerations have on representation.

**Who Runs for Congress** Voters' choices are restricted from the start by who decides to run for office. In the past, decisions about who would run for a particular elected office were made by local party officials. A person who had a record of service to the party, or who was owed a favor, or whose "turn" had come up, might be nominated by party leaders. Today, few party organizations have the power to slate candidates in this way. Instead, parties try to ensure that well-qualified candidates run for Congress. During the 1990s, the Republican Party developed "farm teams" of local officials who were groomed to run for Congress. Their success led Democrats to attempt a similar strategy. Even so, the decision to run for Congress is a personal choice, and one of the most important factors determining who runs for office is an individual candidate's ambition.[10] A potential candidate may also assess whether he or she can attract enough money to mount a credible campaign. The ability to raise money depends on connections with other politicians, interest groups, and national party organizations. In the past, the difficulty of raising campaign funds posed a disadvantage to female candidates. Since the 1980s, however, a number of powerful political action committees (PACs) have emerged to recruit women and fund their campaigns. The largest of them, EMILY's List (an acronym for "Early Money Is Like Yeast," which raises dough), has become a powerful fundraiser. Research shows that money is no longer the barrier it once was to women running for office.[11] Even so, women candidates tend to face more competition in their primary elections.

Features distinctive to each congressional district also affect the field of candidates. For example, the way the congressional district overlaps with state legislative boundaries may affect a candidate's decision to run. A state-level legislator who is considering running for the U.S. Congress is more likely to assess her prospects favorably if her state district coincides with the congressional district (because the voters will already know her). And for any candidate, decisions about running must be made early, because once money has been committed to already declared candidates, it is harder for new candidates to break into a race. Thus, the outcome of a November election is partially determined many months earlier, when decisions to run are finalized.

**Incumbency** Incumbency plays a very important role in the American electoral system and in the kind of representation citizens get in Washington. Once in office, members of Congress gain access to an array of tools they can use to stack the deck in favor of their re-election. The most important of these is constituency service: taking care of the problems and requests of individual voters. Through such services and through regular newsletter mailings, incumbents seek to establish a "personal" relationship with their constituents. The success of this strategy is evident in the high rates of re-election for congressional incumbents: as high as 98 percent for House members and

**incumbency** holding a political office for which one is running

*One reason women have not increased their numbers more quickly in Congress is the incumbency advantage. Incumbents are more likely to win elections and most incumbents are men. In 2012, Senator Orrin Hatch (R-Utah) won re-election to his seventh term.*

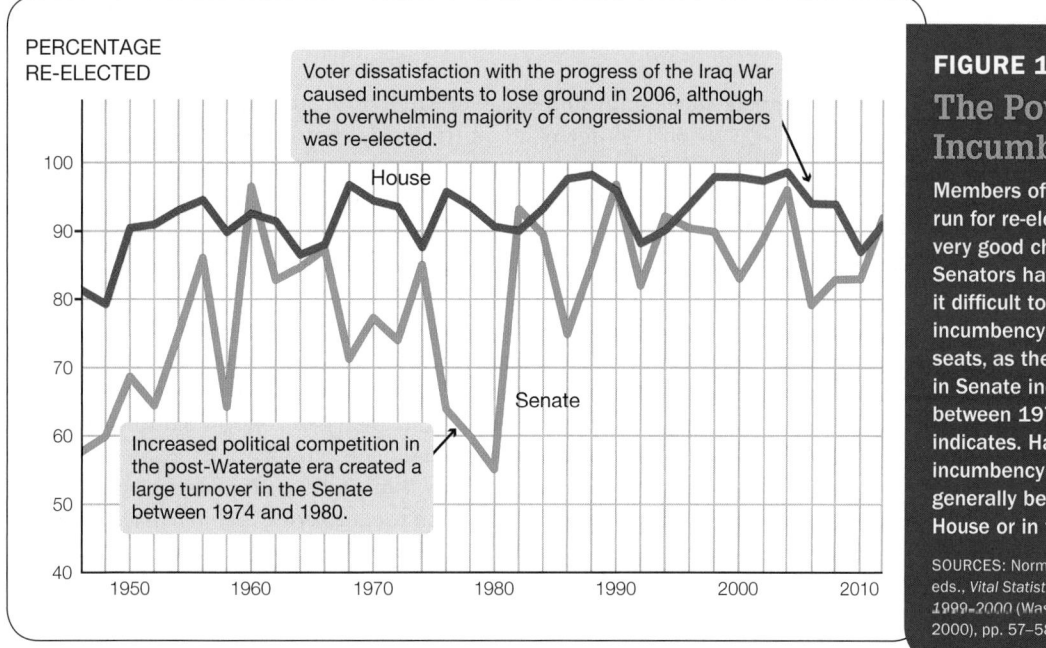

PERCENTAGE RE-ELECTED

Voter dissatisfaction with the progress of the Iraq War caused incumbents to lose ground in 2006, although the overwhelming majority of congressional members was re-elected.

House

Senate

Increased political competition in the post-Watergate era created a large turnover in the Senate between 1974 and 1980.

1950   1960   1970   1980   1990   2000   2010

**FIGURE 12.2**

## The Power of Incumbency

Members of Congress who run for re-election have a very good chance of winning. Senators have at times found it difficult to use the power of incumbency to protect their seats, as the sharp decline in Senate incumbency rates between 1974 and 1980 indicates. Has the incumbency advantage generally been greater in the House or in the Senate?

SOURCES: Norman J. Ornstein et al., eds., *Vital Statistics on Congress, 1999–2000* (Washington, DC: AEI Press, 2000), pp. 57–58; and authors' update.

90 percent for members of the Senate in recent years (see Figure 12.2). It is also evident in what is called "sophomore surge"—the tendency for candidates to win a higher percentage of the vote when seeking subsequent terms in office. Based on early estimates of the 2012 elections, approximately 92 percent of incumbents were re-elected in the House and roughly 93 percent in the Senate.

Incumbency can help a candidate by scaring off potential challengers. In many races, potential candidates may decide not to run because they fear that the incumbent simply has too much money or is too well liked or too well known, or that a district's partisan leanings are too unfavorable. The efforts of incumbents to raise funds to ward off potential challengers start early. A Connecticut Democrat, Joe Courtney, who earned the nickname "Landslide Joe" with his 91-vote margin of victory in 2006, began fund-raising for the 2008 election even before he was sworn in for his first term. In addition, the Democratic Congressional Campaign Committee placed him on its "Frontline team," a group of the 29 most vulnerable Democrats. The Democratic leadership took special efforts to raise the profile of these members of Congress. For example, Courtney and others in the Frontline team received high-profile speaking assignments on the floor of Congress and were appointed to key congressional committees. In 2008, Courtney won his seat by a comfortable margin, and he was easily re-elected in 2010 and again in 2012.[12]

The advantage of incumbency thus tends to preserve the status quo in Congress. This fact has implications for the social composition of Congress. For example, incumbency advantage makes it harder for women to increase their numbers in Congress because most incumbents are men. Women who run for open seats—that is, seats for which there are no incumbents—are just as likely to win as male candidates.[13] Supporters of **term limits** argue that such limits are the only way to get new faces into Congress. They believe that incumbency advantage and the tendency

**term limits** legally prescribed limits on the number of terms an elected official can serve

of many legislators to view politics as a career mean that very little turnover will occur in Congress unless limits are imposed on the number of terms a legislator may serve.

Yet the percentage of incumbents who are returned to Congress after each election also depends on how many members decide to run again. Because, each year, some members decide to retire, turnover in Congress is greater than the re-election rates of incumbents suggest. On average, 10 percent of the House and Senate decide to retire each election. In some years, the number of retirements is higher, as in 1992, when 20 percent of House members decided to retire; thus the 90 percent of incumbents who were re-elected that year was a subset of all the eligible incumbents (80 percent). The precarious economy and the backlash against the party in power made 2008 and 2010 difficult election years for some incumbents. Democrats felt particularly vulnerable in 2010, given that their party controlled the presidency and both houses of Congress in a year when economic woes contributed to strong anti-incumbent sentiment.[14] Even with these retirements during primaries, 54 incumbent Democratic members of the House and two incumbent Democratic senators lost their seats in 2010, including two who lost in the primaries. Incumbents fared better in the 2012 elections. In the House, 13 incumbents lost primary races and preliminary results showed that 22 incumbents lost their seats in the general election; while one incumbent Senator lost in the primaries and one lost the general election.

**Apportionment and Redistricting** The final factor affecting who wins a seat in Congress is the way congressional districts are drawn. Every ten years, state legislatures must redraw congressional districts to reflect population changes. Because the number of congressional seats has been fixed at 435 since 1929, redistricting is a zero-sum process; in order for one state to gain a seat, another must lose one. The process of allocating congressional seats among the 50 states is called **apportionment**. States with population growth gain additional seats; states with a population decline or with less population growth lose seats. Over the past several decades, the shift of the American population to the South and the West has greatly increased the size of the congressional delegations from those regions (see Figures 12.3 and 12.4). This trend continued after the 2010 census. Texas emerged as the biggest winner, with a gain of four additional seats, while Florida added two seats and Arizona, Georgia, Nevada, South Carolina, Utah, and Washington all added one extra seat.[15]

Not surprisingly, **redistricting** is a highly political process: districts are shaped to create an advantage for the party with a majority in the state legislature, which controls the redistricting process. In this complex process, those charged with drawing districts use sophisticated computer technologies to come up with the most favorable district boundaries. Redistricting can create open seats and may pit incumbents of the same party against one another, ensuring that one of them will lose. Redistricting can also give an advantage to one party by clustering voters with some ideological or sociological characteristics in a single district, or by separating those voters into two or more districts. The manipulation of electoral districts to serve the interests of a particular group is known as **gerrymandering** (see Chapter 10).

Redistricting attracts close political attention because the way districts are drawn always benefits one party over the other. In the redistricting following the 2000 census, the close balance of power in the House—with party control hinging on only six seats—made the process especially charged. Both Republicans and Democrats went to court to challenge remaps they viewed as unfair. In 2003, Texas Republicans took the unprecedented step of redrawing the lines set in 2001 rather than waiting for the next census. Even after Texas Democrats fled to Oklahoma

**apportionment** the process, occurring after every decennial census, that allocates congressional seats among the 50 states

**redistricting** the process of redrawing election districts and redistributing legislative representatives. This happens every 10 years to reflect shifts in population or in response to legal challenges to existing districts

**gerrymandering** the apportionment of voters in districts in such a way as to give unfair advantage to one racial or ethnic group or political party

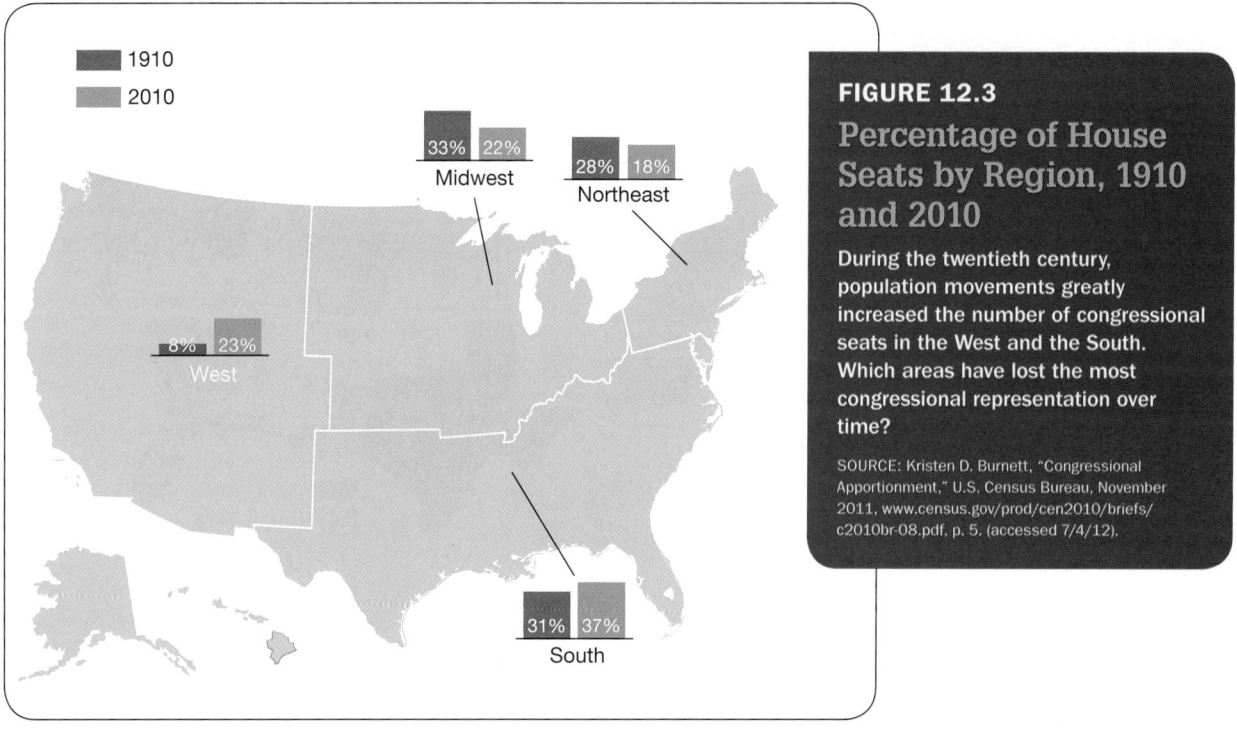

**FIGURE 12.3**

Percentage of House Seats by Region, 1910 and 2010

During the twentieth century, population movements greatly increased the number of congressional seats in the West and the South. Which areas have lost the most congressional representation over time?

SOURCE: Kristen D. Burnett, "Congressional Apportionment," U.S. Census Bureau, November 2011, www.census.gov/prod/cen2010/briefs/c2010br-08.pdf, p. 5. (accessed 7/4/12).

and New Mexico to prevent passage of the plan, the state legislature eventually approved the new map. Republicans benefited from the post-2010 redistricting, in part as a result of the population gains in states that have tended to vote Republican in the past. But they also benefited because Republicans control the state legislatures in the majority of the states in line to gain additional seats, which allowed them to redraw the districts in ways that consolidated Republican gains in 2010 and maximized the Republicans' future advantage.[16] As we saw in Chapter 10, since the passage of the 1982 amendments to the Voting Rights Act of 1965, race has become a major, and controversial, consideration in drawing voting districts. These amendments, which encouraged the creation of districts in which members of racial minorities have decisive majorities, have greatly increased the number of minority representatives in Congress. After the 1991–92 redistricting, the number of predominantly minority districts doubled, rising from 26 to 52. Among the most fervent supporters of the new minority districts were white Republicans, who used the opportunity to create more districts dominated by white Republican voters. These developments raise thorny questions about representation. Some analysts argue that the system may grant minorities greater sociological representation but has made it more difficult for minorities to win substantive policy goals. Others dispute this argument, noting that the strong surge of Republican voters was a more significant factor in Republican congressional victories than any Democratic losses due to racial redistricting.[17]

In the case of *Miller v. Johnson* (1995), the Supreme Court limited racial redistricting by ruling that race could not be the predominant factor in creating electoral districts.[18] The distinction between race being the "predominant" factor and its being one factor among many is very hazy. As a result, concerns about

**for critical analysis**

How does redistricting alter the balance of power in Congress? Why do political parties care so much about the redistricting process?

**FIGURE 12.4**

**Results of Congressional Reapportionment, 2010**

States in the South and the West were the big winners in the reapportionment of House seats following the 2010 census. The old manufacturing states in the Midwest and Mid-Atlantic regions were the biggest losers. Which states have the greatest number of House seats?

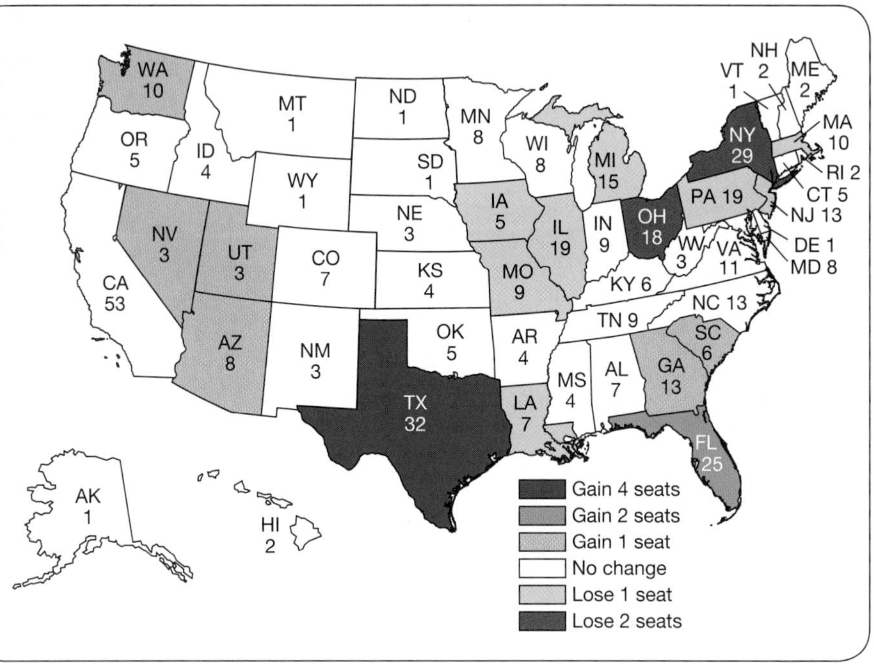

Map legend:
- Gain 4 seats
- Gain 2 seats
- Gain 1 seat
- No change
- Lose 1 seat
- Lose 2 seats

State seat counts shown on map: WA 10, OR 5, ID 4, MT 1, WY 1, ND 1, SD 1, NE 3, MN 8, WI 8, MI 15, NY 29, VT 1, NH 2, ME 2, MA 10, RI 2, CT 5, NJ 13, PA 19, OH 18, IN 9, IL 19, IA 5, NV 3, UT 3, CO 7, KS 4, MO 9, KY 6, WV 3, VA 11, DE 1, MD 8, CA 53, AZ 8, NM 3, OK 5, AR 4, TN 9, NC 13, SC 6, GA 13, MS 4, AL 7, LA 7, TX 32, FL 25, AK 1, HI 2

redistricting and representation have not disappeared.[19] Questions about minority representation emerged in 2011 in Texas, which gained four new seats as a result of reapportionment. The Republican legislature drew a map that advantaged Republicans in three of those districts. But the plan drew a legal challenge on the grounds that it underrepresented Hispanic voters, who accounted for most of the state's population growth. Although federal judges drew a map more favorable to minorities (and Democrats), the Supreme Court ruled that the state did not have to use the map drawn by judges. The state ultimately agreed to a map that added two Latino-dominated districts. However, federal courts ruled that this map also weakened Latino and African American political power. Because the drawing of district boundaries affects incumbents as well as the field of candidates who decide to run for office, it continues to be a key battleground on which political parties fight about the meaning of representation.

## Direct Patronage

As agents of their constituents, members of Congress have numerous opportunities to provide direct benefits, or **patronage**, for their districts. The most important such opportunity for direct patronage is in so-called **pork-barrel** legislation, which specifies a project to be funded within a particular district. Many observers of Congress argue that pork-barrel bills are the only ones that some members are serious about moving toward actual passage, because they are seen as so important to members' re-election bids.

A common form of pork-barreling is the "earmark," by which members of Congress insert into bills language that provides special benefits for their own constituents. When the Democrats took over Congress in 2007, they vowed to limit the use of earmarks, which had grown from 1,439 per year in 1995 to 15,268 in 2006. More troubling, earmarks were connected to congressional scandals. For example, the Republican House member Randy "Duke" Cunningham (R-Calif.)

**patronage** the resources available to higher officials, usually opportunities to make partisan appointments to offices and to confer grants, licenses, or special favors to supporters

**pork barrel (or pork)** appropriations made by legislative bodies for local projects that are often not needed but that are created so that local representatives can win re-election in their home districts

was sent to jail in 2005 for accepting bribes by companies hoping to receive earmarks in return.[20] The House passed a new rule requiring that those representatives supporting each earmark identify themselves and guarantee that they have no personal financial stake in the requested project. A new ethics law applied similar provisions to the Senate. The new requirements appear to have had some impact: the 2007 military bill, for example, cut in half the value of earmarks contained in the military bill passed in 2006. But in the midst of the sharp economic downturn in 2009, Congress passed an economic stimulus bill that contained more than 8,000 earmarks. In many cases, Republicans and some Democrats who voted against the bill were later happy to take credit from their constituents for the earmarks they had placed in it. In his 2010 State of the Union address, President Obama called for Congress to publish a list of all earmark requests on a single website. Congress not only failed to enact such legislation, but in 2010 it set a new record by passing 11,320 earmarks worth $32 billion. Still, in 2011 the House and the Senate agreed to a two-year moratorium on earmarks in spending bills. Despite the moratorium, some members of Congress charged that special provisions were creeping back into legislation, and few members of Congress supported making the moratorium permanent.[21]

Highway bills are a favorite vehicle for congressional pork-barrel spending. A 2005 highway bill was full of such items, containing more than 6,000 projects earmarked for specific congressional districts. These measures often have little to do with transportation needs, instead serving as evidence for constituents that congressional members can bring federal dollars back home. Perhaps the most extravagant item in the 2005 bill—and the one least needed for transportation—was a bridge in Alaska designed to connect a barely populated island to the town of Ketchikan, population just under 8,000. At a cost that could soar to $2 billion, the bridge would have replaced an existing five-minute ferry ride. Alaska's representative, Don Young (R), proudly claimed credit. After Hurricane Katrina, "the bridge to nowhere" became a symbol of wasteful congressional spending. Sensitive to this criticism, Congress removed the earmarks for the bridge from the final legislation. Even so, it allowed Alaska to keep the funds for other unspecified transportation projects. In 2007 the state quietly dropped the project.

There are a few other types of direct patronage (see Figure 12.5). One important form of constituency service is intervention with federal administrative agencies on behalf of constituents. Members of the House and Senate and their staff spend a great deal of time on the telephone and in administrative offices seeking to secure favorable treatment for constituents and supporters. For example, members of Congress can assist senior citizens who are having Social Security or Medicare benefit eligibility problems. Most members of Congress have a "constituent services" section on their websites, providing information about what they can and cannot do to assist their constituents. For example, Representative Tom Petri's (R-Wisc.) website puts it this way: "If you can't get an answer from a federal agency in a timely fashion, or if you feel you have been treated unfairly, my office may be able to help resolve a problem or get you the information you need. While we cannot guarantee you a favorable outcome, we will do our best to help you receive a fair and timely response to your problem."[22] A small but related form of patronage is securing an appointment to one of the military academies for the child of a constituent. Traditionally, these appointments are allocated one to a district.

A different form of patronage is the **private bill**. Unlike a public bill, which is supposed to deal with general rules and categories of behavior, people, and institutions, a private bill proposes to grant some kind of relief, special privilege, or exemption to the person named in the bill. As many as 75 percent of all private

**for** critical **analysis**
Why are earmarks so difficult to eliminate?

**private bill** a proposal in Congress to provide a specific person with some kind of relief, such as a special exemption from immigration quotas

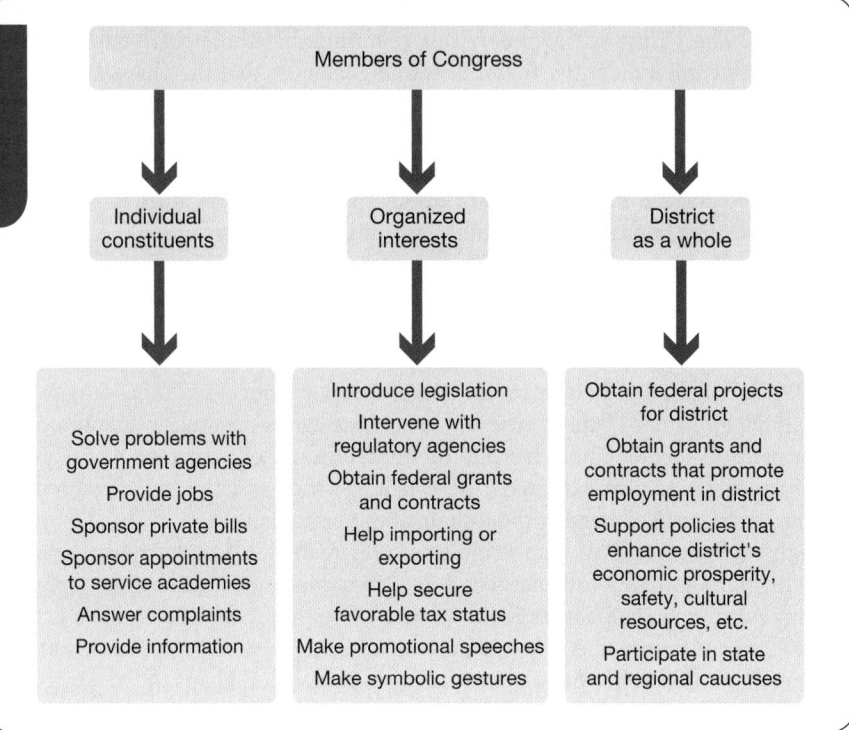

**Members of Congress**

| Individual constituents | Organized interests | District as a whole |
|---|---|---|
| Solve problems with government agencies<br>Provide jobs<br>Sponsor private bills<br>Sponsor appointments to service academies<br>Answer complaints<br>Provide information | Introduce legislation<br>Intervene with regulatory agencies<br>Obtain federal grants and contracts<br>Help importing or exporting<br>Help secure favorable tax status<br>Make promotional speeches<br>Make symbolic gestures | Obtain federal projects for district<br>Obtain grants and contracts that promote employment in district<br>Support policies that enhance district's economic prosperity, safety, cultural resources, etc.<br>Participate in state and regional caucuses |

bills introduced (and one-third of those that pass) are concerned with obtaining citizenship for foreign nationals who do not have resident status in the United States. For example, in 2010 a private bill granted legal immigrant status to the widow of a U.S. Marine from Tennessee who gave birth to their son after the marine was killed in Iraq in 2008.[23] Private legislation is a congressional privilege that could be abused, but it is impossible to imagine members of Congress completely giving up one of the easiest, cheapest, and most effective forms of patronage available to them. It can be defended as an indispensable part of the process by which members of Congress seek to fulfill their role as representatives. And obviously they like the privilege because it helps them win re-election.

## ● The Organization of Congress

**Explain how party leadership, the committee system, the staff system, and caucuses help structure congressional business**

The U.S. Congress is not only a representative assembly; it is also a legislative body. For Americans, representation and legislation go hand in hand, but many parliamentary bodies in other countries are representative without the power to make laws. It is no small achievement that the U.S. Congress both represents and governs.

To exercise its power to make laws, Congress must first bring about something close to an organizational miracle. The building blocks of congressional organization include the political parties, the committee system, congressional staff, the caucuses, and the parliamentary

**conference** a gathering of House Republicans every two years to elect their House leaders. Democrats call their gathering the caucus

**caucus (political)** a normally closed meeting of a political or legislative group to select candidates, plan strategy, or make decisions regarding legislative matters

rules of the House and Senate. Each of these factors plays a key role in the organization of Congress and in the process through which Congress formulates and enacts laws.

## Party Leadership in the House

Every two years, at the beginning of a new Congress, the members of each party gather to elect their House leaders. House Republicans call their gathering the **conference**. House Democrats call theirs the **caucus**. The elected leader of the majority party is later proposed to the whole House and is automatically elected to the position of **Speaker of the House**, with voting along straight party lines. The House majority conference or caucus then also elects a **majority leader**. The minority party goes through the same process and selects a **minority leader**. Each party also elects a **whip** to line up party members on important votes and to relay voting information to the leaders.

Next in order of importance for each party after the Speaker and majority or minority leader is what Democrats call the Steering and Policy Committee—Republicans have a separate steering committee and a separate policy committee—whose tasks are to assign new legislators to committees and to deal with the requests of incumbent members for transfers from one committee to another. At one time, party leaders strictly controlled committee assignments, using them to enforce party discipline. Today, in principle, representatives receive the assignments they want. But often several individuals seek assignments to the most important committees, which gives the leadership an opportunity to cement alliances when it resolves conflicting requests.

Generally, representatives seek assignments that will allow them to influence decisions of special importance to their districts. Representatives from farm districts, for example, may request seats on the Agriculture Committee.[24] Seats on powerful committees such as Ways and Means, which is responsible for tax legislation, and Appropriations are especially popular.

## Party Leadership in the Senate

Within the Senate, the majority party usually designates a member with the greatest seniority to serve as president pro tempore, a position of primarily ceremonial leadership. Real power is in the hands of the majority leader and minority leader, each elected by party conference. Together they control the Senate's calendar, or agenda for legislation.

Each party also elects a policy committee, which advises the leadership on legislative priorities. The structure of majority party leadership in the House and the Senate is shown in Figures 12.6 and 12.7.

## The Committee System

The committee system is central to the operation of Congress. At each stage of the legislative process, Congress relies on committees and subcommittees to do the hard work of sorting through alternatives and writing legislation. There are several different kinds of congressional committees: standing committees, select committees, joint committees, and conference committees.

**Standing Committees** The most important arenas of congressional policy making are **standing committees**. These committees remain in existence from

*As Speaker of the House, John Boehner attempted to keep his party unified, despite disagreements between the Tea Party members and other Republicans. Especially during the 2011 debate over the national debt, Boehner worked hard to persuade House Republicans to fall into line.*

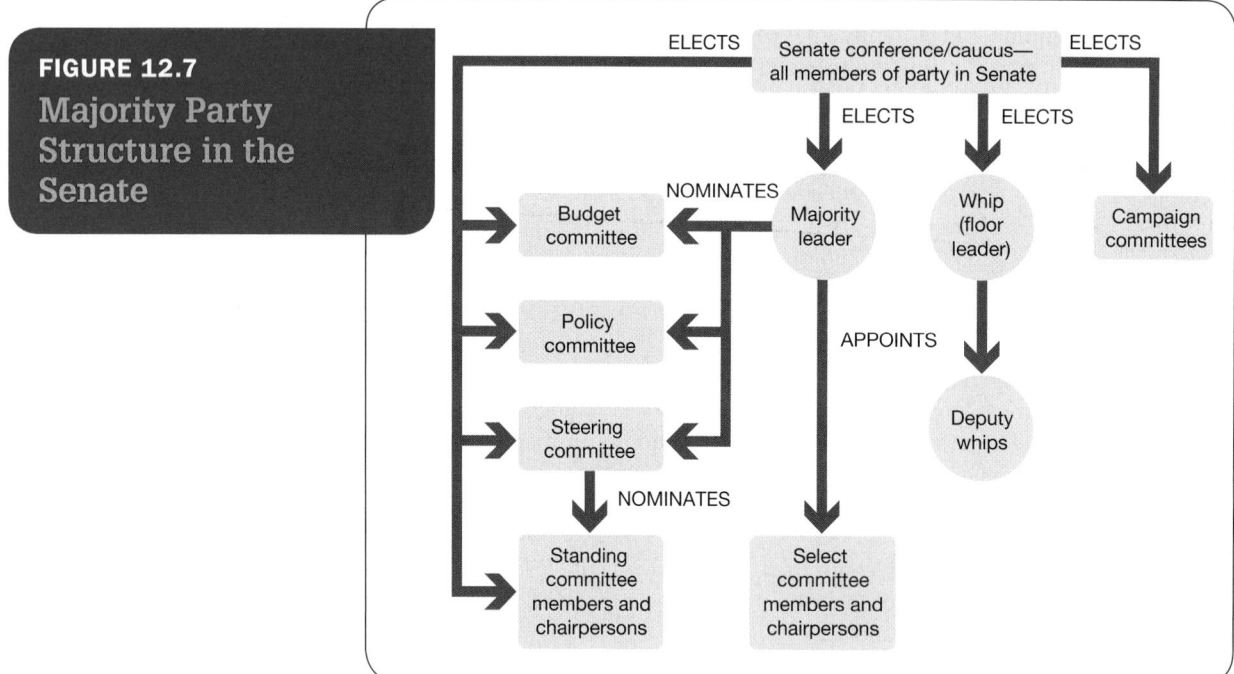

**FIGURE 12.6**
**Majority Party Structure in the House of Representatives**

*Includes Speaker, majority leader, chief and deputy whips, caucus chair, chairs of five major committees, members elected by regional caucuses, members elected by recently elected representatives, and at-large members appointed by the Speaker.

ELECTS
House conference/caucus—all members of party in House
ELECTS

ELECTS  ELECTS  ELECTS  ELECTS

NOMINATES
Rules committee
Speaker
Majority leader
Whip
Budget committee

NOMINATES
Committee members and chairpersons
Policy committee*
APPOINTS
Campaign committee

**FIGURE 12.7**
**Majority Party Structure in the Senate**

ELECTS
Senate conference/caucus—all members of party in Senate
ELECTS

ELECTS  ELECTS

NOMINATES
Budget committee
Majority leader
Whip (floor leader)
Campaign committees

Policy committee
APPOINTS
Deputy whips

Steering committee

NOMINATES
Standing committee members and chairpersons
Select committee members and chairpersons

one session of Congress to the next; they have the power to propose and write legislation. The jurisdiction of each standing committee covers a particular subject matter, which in most cases parallels a major department or agency in the executive branch (see Table 12.2). Among the most important standing committees are those in charge of finances. The House Ways and Means Committee and the Senate Finance Committee are powerful because of their jurisdiction over taxes, trade, and expensive entitlement programs such as Social Security and

## TABLE 12.2

## Permanent Committees of Congress

### HOUSE COMMITTEES

| | |
|---|---|
| Agriculture | Judiciary |
| Appropriations | Natural Resources |
| Armed Services | Oversight and Government Reform |
| Budget | Rules |
| Education and Labor | Science and Technology |
| Energy and Commerce | Small Business |
| Financial Services | Standards of Official Conduct |
| Foreign Affairs | Transportation and Infrastructure |
| Homeland Security | Veterans' Affairs |
| House Administration | Ways and Means |

### SENATE COMMITTEES

| | |
|---|---|
| Agriculture, Nutrition, and Forestry | Foreign Relations |
| Appropriations | Health, Education, Labor, and Pensions |
| Armed Services | Homeland Security and Governmental Affairs |
| Banking, Housing, and Urban Affairs | Judiciary |
| Budget | Rules and Administration |
| Commerce, Science, and Transportation | Select Intelligence |
| Energy and Natural Resources | Small Business and Entrepreneurship |
| Environment and Public Works | Veterans' Affairs |
| Finance | |

Medicare. The Senate and House Appropriations committees also play important ongoing roles because they decide how much funding various programs will actually receive; they also determine exactly how the money will be spent. A seat on an appropriations committee allows a member the opportunity to direct funds to a favored program—perhaps one in his or her home district.

Except for the House Rules Committee, all standing committees receive proposals for legislation and process them into official bills. The House Rules Committee decides the order in which bills come up for a vote on the House floor and determines the specific rules that govern the length of debate and opportunity for amendments. The Senate, which has less formal organization and fewer rules, does not have a rules committee.

**Select Committees** **Select committees** are usually not permanent and usually do not have the power to present legislation to the full Congress. (The House and Senate Select Intelligence committees are permanent, however, and do have the power to report legislation, which means they can send legislation to the full House or

**select committees** (usually) temporary legislative committees set up to highlight or investigate a particular issue or address an issue not within the jurisdiction of existing committees

Senate for consideration. These committees hold hearings and serve as focal points for the issues they are charged with considering. Congressional leaders form select committees when they want to take up issues that fall outside the jurisdictions of existing committees, to highlight an issue, or to investigate a particular problem. Examples of select committees investigating political scandals include the Senate Watergate Committee of 1973, the committees set up in 1987 to investigate the Iran-Contra affair, and the Whitewater Committee of 1995–96. Select committees set up to highlight ongoing issues have included the House Select Committee on Hunger, established in 1984, and the House Select Committee on Energy Independence and Global Warming, created in 2007 but abolished in 2011, when Republicans assumed control of the House. A few select committees have remained in existence for many years, such as the select committees on aging; hunger; children, youth, and families; and narcotics abuse and control. In 1995, however, congressional Republicans abolished most of these select committees, both to streamline operations and to remove a forum used primarily by Democratic representatives and their allies. In 2003 an important select committee, the House Select Committee on Homeland Security, was created to oversee the new Department of Homeland Security. Unlike most select committees, this one had the ability to present legislation. Initially the committee had only temporary status. It was made a regular permanent committee in 2005.

**joint committees** legislative committees formed of members of both the House and Senate

**Joint Committees** Joint committees involve members from both the Senate and the House. There are four such committees: economic, taxation, library, and printing. These joint committees are permanent, but they do not have the power to present legislation. The Joint Economic Committee and the Joint Taxation Committee have often played important roles in collecting information and holding hearings on economic and financial issues. In 2011, Congress created the Joint Select Committee on Deficit Reduction and, in an unusual move, gave the committee the power to write and report legislation. Informally known as "the supercommittee," the committee was charged with coming up with $1.2 trillion in debt reduction. Formed after a contentious debate about raising the debt limit (usually a routine matter), the supercommittee proved unable to come to an agreement and disbanded less than four months after it was created.

**conference committees** joint committees created to work out a compromise on House and Senate versions of a piece of legislation

**Conference Committees** Finally, **conference committees** are temporary committees whose members are appointed by the Speaker of the House and the presiding officer of the Senate. These committees are charged with reaching a compromise on legislation once it has been passed by the House and the Senate. Conference committees play an extremely important role in determining the laws that are actually passed, because they must reconcile any differences in the legislation passed by the House and Senate.

When control of Congress is divided between two parties, each is guaranteed significant representation in conference committees. When a single party controls both houses, the majority party is not obligated to offer such representation to the minority party. In 2003, Democrats complained that Republicans took this power to the extreme by excluding them and adding new provisions to legislation at the conference committee stage. Democrats even prevented several conference committees from convening in order to protest their near exclusion from conference committees on major energy, health care, and transportation laws. After they returned to power in 2007, the Democrats also largely bypassed the conference committees; when their early efforts to reach compromises in committee were derailed by partisan differences, the Democrats began making closed-door agreements between top leaders in the House and the Senate. Although the process facilitated compromises across the two chambers, it meant that important changes to bills were made in private, without the transparency that would have been part of the conference committee process. After 2010, Congress continued to avoid conference committees. Instead, the Republican House and Democratic Senate exchanged amendments as they sought to reach agreement on the final version of a bill, a practice known informally as "ping pong."[25]

**Politics and the Organization of Committees** Within each committee, hierarchy has usually been based on **seniority** determined by years of continuous service on that particular committee. In general, each committee is chaired by the most senior member of the majority party. But the principle of seniority is not absolute. When the Republicans took over the House in 1995, they violated the principle of seniority in the selection of key committee chairs. House Speaker Newt Gingrich defended the new practice, saying, "You've got to carry the moral responsibility of fielding the team that can win or you cheat the whole conference."[26] Since then, Republicans have continued to depart from the seniority principle, often choosing committee chairs on the basis of loyalty or fund-raising abilities rather than seniority. In 2007, Democrats returned to the seniority principle for choosing committee chairs but altered traditional practices in other ways by offering freshman Democrats choice committee assignments in order to increase their chances of re-election.[27]

Over the years, Congress has reformed its organizational structure and operating procedures. Most changes have been made to improve efficiency, but some reforms have also been a response to political considerations. In the 1970s, for example, Congress increased the number of subcommittees and gave greater autonomy to subcommittee chairs. (Subcommittees are responsible for considering a specific subset of issues under a committee's jurisdiction.) In the past, committee chairs had exercised considerable power; they determined hearing schedules, selected subcommittee members, appointed committee staff, and sometimes used their power to block consideration of bills they opposed. By enhancing subcommittee power and allowing more members to chair subcommittees and appoint subcommittee staff, the reforms undercut the power of committee chairs. Yet the reforms of the 1970s created new problems for Congress: power became more fragmented, making it harder to reach agreement on legislation. The Republican leadership of the 104th Congress (1995–97), seeking to reverse this fragmentation of congressional power and concentrate more authority in the party leadership, reduced the number of subcommittees and limited the time committee chairs could serve to three terms. They made good on this in 2001, when they replaced 13 committee chairs.

As a consequence of these changes, committees no longer have the central role they once held in policy making. When the Democrats took control of Congress in 2007, they repealed the term limits on committee chairs, but Republicans reinstated the practice when they reassumed control of the House in 2010. Still, sharp partisan divisions have made it difficult for committees to deliberate and bring bipartisan expertise to bear on policy making as in the past. With committees less able to engage in effective decision making, they typically do not deliberate for very long or call witnesses, and it has become more common in recent years for party-driven legislation to go directly to the floor, bypassing committees altogether.[28] Nonetheless, committees continue to play an important role in the legislative process, especially on issues that are not sharply partisan.[29]

**seniority** the ranking given to an individual on the basis of length of continuous service on a committee in Congress

# The Staff System: Staffers and Agencies

The congressional institution second in importance only to the committee system is the staff system. Every member of Congress employs many staff members whose tasks include handling constituent requests and, to a large extent, dealing with legislative details and the activities of administrative agencies. Staffers often bear the primary responsibility for formulating and drafting proposals, organizing hearings, dealing with administrative agencies, and negotiating with lobbyists. Indeed, legislators typically deal with one another through staff, rather than through direct personal contact. Staffers even develop policy ideas, draft legislation, and, in some instances, have a good deal of influence over the legislative process. Representatives and senators together employ 11,500 staffers in their Washington and home offices. In addition, Congress also employs roughly 2,000 committee staffers. These individuals make up the permanent staff that stays attached to every House and Senate committee regardless of turnover in Congress and that is responsible for organizing and administering the committee's work, including doing research, scheduling, organizing hearings, and drafting legislation. Committee staffers can play key roles in the legislative process.

One example of the importance that members of Congress attach to committee staffers was the conflict over hiring a new staff director for the House Ethics Committee in 2005. The Ethics Committee (officially known as the Committee on Standards of Official Conduct) has the power to investigate members for unethical practices and can issue reprimands or censures when it finds that members have violated House rules. The staff director is critical in determining how energetically and effectively the committee pursues its investigations. With allegations of ethics violations swirling around the congressional leadership, and criminal investigations of congressional lobbyist Jack Abramoff under way, the Ethics Committee was in a pivotal position. But for the first half of 2005, the committee was at a standstill as Republicans and Democrats fought over who would have the job of staff director. Despite House rules calling for the committee staff director to be nonpartisan, the committee chair, Doc Hastings (R-Wash.), initially sought to appoint a partisan Republican to the job. After nearly half a year of wrangling, Hastings agreed to appoint a staff director acceptable to both parties.

Not only does Congress employ personal and committee staff, but it has also established **staff agencies** designed to provide the legislative branch with resources and expertise independent of the executive branch. These agencies enhance Congress's capacity to oversee administrative agencies and to evaluate presidential programs and proposals. They include the Congressional Research Service, which performs research for legislators who wish to know the facts and competing arguments relevant to policy proposals or other legislative business; the Government Accountability Office, through which Congress can investigate the financial and administrative affairs of any government agency or program; and the Congressional Budget Office, which assesses the economic implications and likely costs of proposed federal programs. A fourth agency, the Office of Technology Assessment, which provided Congress with analyses of scientific or technical issues, was abolished by the Republican-dominated Congress in 1995.

**staff agencies** legislative support agencies responsible for policy analysis

*Members of Congress rely heavily on their personal staffs and on committee staffs, who often play an important role in the legislative process.*

## Informal Organization: The Caucuses

In addition to the official organization of Congress, an unofficial organizational structure also exists: the caucuses. **Caucuses** are groups of senators or representatives who share certain opinions, interests, or social characteristics. A large number of caucuses are composed of legislators representing particular economic or policy interests, such as the Travel and Tourism Caucus, the Steel Caucus, the Mushroom Caucus, and Concerned Senators for the Arts. Legislators who share common backgrounds have organized caucuses such as the Congressional Black Caucus, the Congressional Caucus for Women's Issues, and the Hispanic Caucus. All these caucuses seek to advance the interests of the groups they represent by promoting legislation, encouraging Congress to hold hearings, and pressing administrative agencies for favorable treatment. In recent years, some caucuses have evolved into powerful lobbying organizations, well funded by interest groups. For example, the Sportsmen's Caucus receives funds from a nonprofit foundation that itself benefits from donations from the National Rifle Association, sports equipment manufacturers, and firearms manufacturers. In 2010 conservative Republicans in the House and Senate formed the Tea Party Caucus to advance anti-spending policies.

**caucuses (congressional)** associations of members of Congress based on party, interest, or social group, such as gender or race

## ● Rules of Lawmaking: How a Bill Becomes a Law

**Outline the steps in the process of passing a law**

The institutional structure of Congress is a key factor in shaping the legislative process. A second and equally important set of factors is the rules of congressional procedure. These rules govern everything from the introduction of a **bill** through its submission to the president for signing (see Figure 12.8). Not only do these regulations influence the fate of every bill, but they also help determine the distribution of power in the Congress.

**bill** a proposed law that has been sponsored by a member of Congress and submitted to the clerk of the House or Senate

### Committee Deliberation

The first step in getting a law passed is drafting legislation. Members of Congress, the White House, and federal agencies all take roles in developing and drafting initial legislation. The bill is then officially submitted by a senator or representative to the clerk of the House or Senate and referred to the appropriate committee for deliberation. During the course of its deliberations, the committee typically refers the bill to one of its subcommittees, which may hold hearings, listen to expert testimony, and amend the proposed legislation before referring it to the full committee for consideration. The full committee may then accept the recommendation of the subcommittee or hold its own hearings and prepare its own amendments.

The next steps in the process are the **committee markup** sessions, in which committees rewrite bills to reflect changes discussed during the hearings. In the partisan fighting that has characterized Congress in recent years, the minority party has charged that its members are often not given enough time to study proposed legislation before markup. In 2003 conflict over this issue drew the Capitol police to

**committee markup** the session in which a congressional committee rewrites legislation to incorporate changes discussed during hearings on the bill

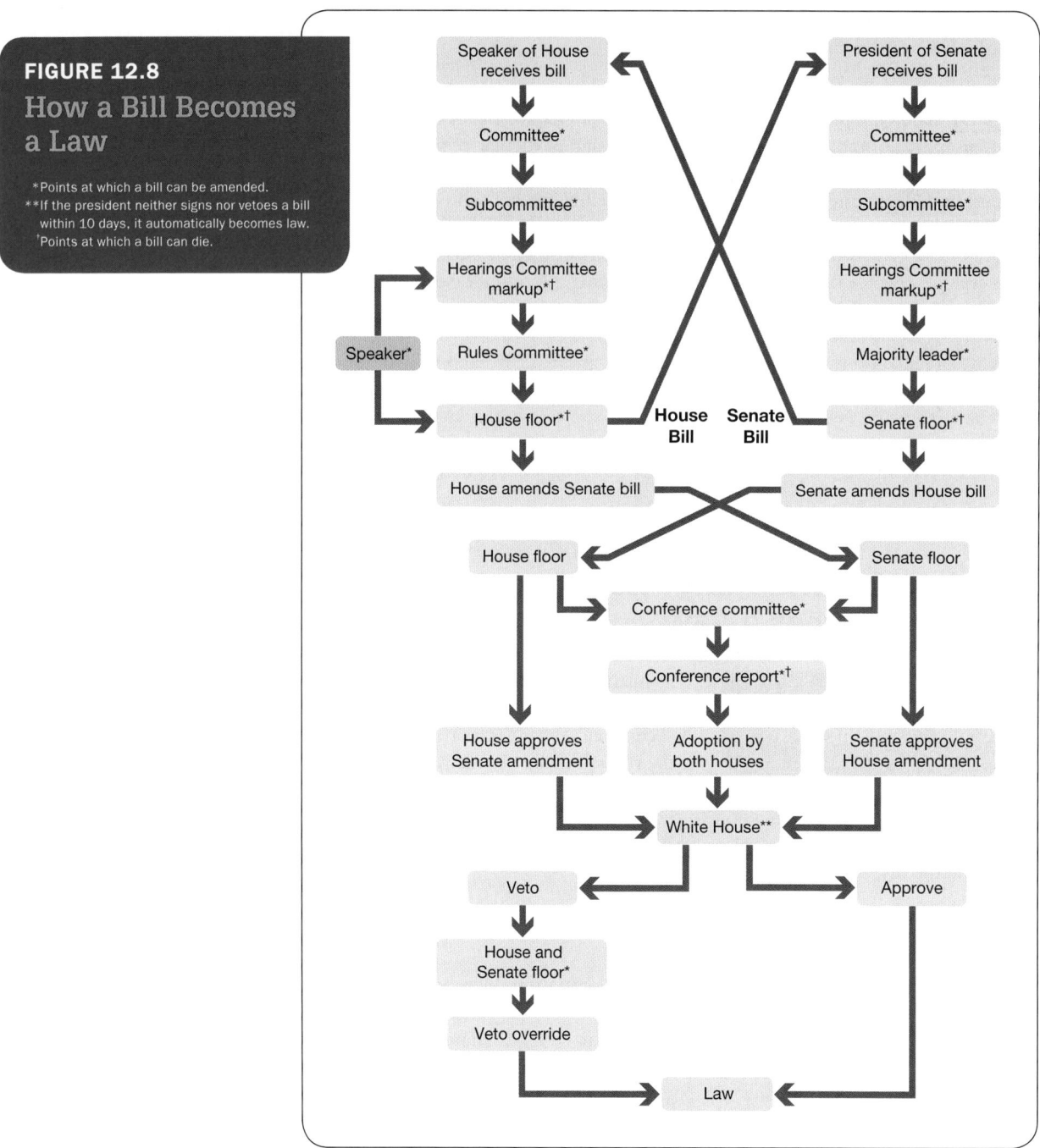

**FIGURE 12.8**

**How a Bill Becomes a Law**

*Points at which a bill can be amended.
**If the president neither signs nor vetoes a bill within 10 days, it automatically becomes law.
†Points at which a bill can die.

Speaker of House receives bill → Committee* → Subcommittee* → Hearings Committee markup*† → Rules Committee* → House floor*†

Speaker*

President of Senate receives bill → Committee* → Subcommittee* → Hearings Committee markup*† → Majority leader* → Senate floor*†

House Bill    Senate Bill

House amends Senate bill    Senate amends House bill

House floor    Senate floor

Conference committee*

Conference report*†

House approves Senate amendment    Adoption by both houses    Senate approves House amendment

White House**

Veto    Approve

House and Senate floor*

Veto override

Law

the House and almost resulted in a fistfight among representatives when Democrats protested their treatment by the House Ways and Means Committee. Charging that they had been given a complex pension bill only 10 hours before markup, House Democrats walked out. The ensuing commotion, with Republicans calling the police and a Democratic congressman threatening a Republican, presented a sorry spectacle for the evening news. Although Democrats lost a resolution to censure the committee for its actions, the committee chair, Bill Thomas (R-Calif.), later broke down in tears as he apologized on the House floor.

Frequently, the committee and subcommittee do little or nothing with a bill that has been submitted to them. Many bills are simply allowed to "die in committee" without serious consideration. Often, members of Congress introduce legislation that they neither expect nor even desire to see enacted into law but present merely to please a constituency group. These bills die a quick and painless death. Other pieces of legislation have ardent supporters and die in committee only after a long battle. But in either case, most bills are never reported out of the committees to which they are assigned. In a typical congressional session, 95 percent of the roughly 8,000 bills introduced die in committee.

In the House, the relative handful of bills that are presented out of committee must pass one last hurdle within the committee system—the Rules Committee, which determines the rules that will govern action on the bill on the House floor. In particular, the Rules Committee allots the time for debate and decides to what extent amendments to the bill can be proposed from the floor. A bill's supporters generally prefer a **closed rule**, which puts severe limits on floor debate and amendments. Opponents of a bill usually prefer an **open rule**, which permits potentially damaging floor debate and makes it easier to add amendments that may cripple the bill or weaken its chances for passage. Thus, the outcome of the Rules Committee's deliberations can be extremely important, and the committee's hearings can be an occasion for sharp conflict. In recent years, the Rules Committee has become less powerful because the House leadership exercises so much influence over its decisions.

**closed rule** a provision by the House Rules Committee limiting or prohibiting the introduction of amendments during debate

**open rule** a provision by the House Rules Committee that permits floor debate and the addition of new amendments to a bill

## Debate

The next step in getting a law passed is debate on the floor of the House and Senate. Party control of the agenda is reinforced by the rule giving the Speaker of the House and the president of the Senate the power of recognition during debate on a bill. Usually the chair knows the purpose for which a member intends to speak well in advance of the occasion. Spontaneous efforts to gain recognition are often foiled. For example, the Speaker may ask, "For what purpose does the member rise?" before deciding whether to grant recognition.

In the House, virtually all the time allotted by the Rules Committee for debate on a given bill is controlled by the bill's sponsor and by its leading opponent. In almost every case, these two people are the committee chair and the ranking minority member of the committee that processed the bill—or those they designate. These two participants are, by rule and tradition, granted the power to allocate most of the debate time in small amounts to members who are seeking to speak for or against the measure. Preference in the allocation of time goes to the members of the committee whose jurisdiction covers the bill.

In the Senate, the leadership has much less control over floor debate. Indeed, the Senate is unique among the world's legislative bodies for its commitment to unlimited debate. Once given the floor, a senator may speak as long as he or she wishes. On a number of memorable occasions, senators have used this opportunity to prevent action on legislation that they opposed. Through this tactic, called the **filibuster**, small minorities or even one individual in the Senate can force the majority to give in. Filibusters can be ended by a Senate vote to cut off debate, called **cloture**. From 1917 to 1975, it took two-thirds of the Senate or 67 votes to end a filibuster. In 1975 the Senate changed the rules to three-fifths of the Senate or 60 votes

**filibuster** a tactic used by members of the Senate to prevent action on legislation they oppose by continuously holding the floor and speaking until the majority backs down. Once given the floor, senators have unlimited time to speak, and it requires a vote of three-fifths of the Senate to end a filibuster

**cloture** a rule allowing a majority of two-thirds or three-fifths of the members of a legislative body to set a time limit on debate over a given bill. In the U.S. Senate, 60 senators (three-fifths) must agree in order to impose such a limit

needed for cloture. The threat of a filibuster ensures that, in crafting legislation and proposing judicial appointments, the majority takes into account the viewpoint of the political minority. For much of American history, senators only rarely used the filibuster, though during the 1950s and '60s, opponents of civil rights legislation often used filibusters to block its passage. In the last 20 years, the filibuster has become so common that observers routinely note that it takes 60 votes to get anything passed in the Senate. The 111th Congress (2009–10) holds the record, with 137 cloture votes; with 109 cloture votes, the 112th Congress (2011–12) had the third highest in history. Frustrated at the difficulty of moving his agenda through the Senate, President Obama noted in his 2010 State of the Union Address, "You had to cast more votes to break filibusters last year than in the entire 1950s and '60s combined."[30] Yet the filibuster is a tool that both parties have used, and with a 67-vote majority required to eliminate it, the filibuster is likely to remain a feature of American politics for the foreseeable future.

The filibuster is not the only technique used to block Senate debate. Under Senate rules, members have virtually unlimited ability to propose amendments to a pending bill. Each amendment must be voted on before the bill can come to a final vote. The introduction of new amendments can be stopped only by unanimous consent. This, in effect, can permit a determined minority to filibuster by amendment, indefinitely delaying the passage of a bill. Senators can also place "holds," or stalling devices, on bills to delay debate. Senators place holds on bills when they fear that openly opposing them will be unpopular. Because holds are kept secret, the senators placing the holds do not have to take public responsibility for their actions. There have been several efforts to eliminate holds. In 1997, opponents of this practice introduced an amendment that would have required publicizing the identity of the senator putting a bill on hold. But when the Senate voted on the measure, the proposal to end the practice of anonymous holds had "mysteriously disappeared."[31] Although no one took credit for killing the measure, it was evident that the majority of senators wanted to maintain the practice. In 2007, reformers succeeded in passing the Honest Leadership and Open Government Act. Although the new law did not eliminate holds, it contained provisions requiring senators who imposed a hold to identify themselves in the *Congressional Record* after six days and state the reasons for the hold.[32] Even with this provision,

In 2010, Senator Bernard Sanders of Vermont held the Senate floor for over eight hours, to draw attention to concerns about a tax plan. Sanders's long speech wasn't technically a filibuster (because it did not stop any Senate business), but it provides an example of the rule that a senator can speak as long he or she wants once given the floor.

senators have continued to impose holds on legislation and especially on presidential appointees. Senator Richard Shelby (R-Ala.) aroused the ire of the White House in 2010 for placing a "blanket hold" on more than 70 presidential nominees. Unusual in its sweeping nature, Shelby's hold aimed to force the White House to support several defense-related contracts that would benefit the state of Alabama.[33]

Once a bill is debated on the floor of the House and the Senate, the leaders schedule it for a vote on the floor of each chamber. By this time, congressional leaders know what the vote will be; leaders do not bring legislation to the floor unless they are fairly certain it is going to pass. As a consequence, it is unusual for the leadership to lose a bill on the floor. On rare occasions, the last moments of the floor vote can be very dramatic, as each party's leadership puts its whip organization into action to make sure that wavering members vote with the party. In September 2008 the House of Representatives surprisingly rejected a $700 billion bank rescue plan, which led the Dow Jones Industrial Index to decline nearly 7 percent in a single day—one of the biggest drops in recent history. As the *New York Times* reported, lawmakers were "almost speechless" on hearing that the bill had not passed; not only did the White House and the congressional leadership of both parties expect the bill to prevail, albeit narrowly, but so did even its most ardent opponents. As the end of the voting period drew close, it was clear that the bill was going down to defeat, with 205 votes for the bill and 228 against. Since members of the House can change their votes during the voting period, the Speaker decided to extend the period to forty minutes in order to corral votes. Despite the efforts of both Democratic and Republican leaders, they could not persuade enough members to switch their votes. A few days later, the House passed a revised version of the bill by 263 to 171 votes.[34]

## Conference Committee: Reconciling House and Senate Versions of Legislation

Getting a bill out of committee and through both houses of Congress is no guarantee that the bill will be enacted into law; it must be considered by a conference committee. Frequently, bills that begin with similar provisions in both chambers emerge with little resemblance to each other. Alternatively, a bill may be passed by one chamber but undergo substantial revision in the other chamber. In such cases, a conference committee composed of the senior members of the committees or subcommittees that initiated the bill may be required to iron out differences between the two now-dissimilar pieces of legislation. Sometimes members or leaders will let objectionable provisions pass on the floor, knowing that they will get the chance to make changes in conference. Usually, conference committees meet behind closed doors. Agreement requires a majority of each of the two delegations. Legislation that emerges successfully from a conference committee is more often a compromise than a clear victory of one set of forces over another. In recent years, as we have seen, polarization in Congress has led to much less reliance on conference committees. Instead, leaders exchange amendments in the hope of reaching agreement.

When a bill comes out of conference, it faces one more hurdle. Before it can be sent to the president for signing, the House-Senate conference committee's version of the bill must be approved on the floor of each chamber. Usually such approval is given quickly. Occasionally, however, a bill's opponents use this round of approval as one last opportunity to defeat a piece of legislation.

## Presidential Action

The final step in passing a law is presidential approval. Once adopted by the House and Senate, a bill goes to the president, who may choose to sign the bill into law or veto it. If the president does not sign the bill or veto it within 10 days, and Congress is in session, the bill automatically becomes law. The **veto** is the president's constitutional power to reject a piece of legislation. To veto a bill, the president returns it unsigned within 10 days to the house of Congress in which it originated. If Congress adjourns during the 10-day period, and the president has taken no action, the bill is also considered to be vetoed. This latter method is known as the **pocket veto**. The possibility of a presidential veto affects how willing members of Congress are to push for different pieces of legislation at different times. If they think a proposal is likely to be vetoed they might shelve it until a later time.

A presidential veto may be overridden by a two-thirds vote in both the House and Senate. A veto override says much about the support that a president can expect from Congress, and it can deliver a stinging blow to the executive branch. Presidents will often back down from a veto threat if they believe that Congress will override the veto.

**veto** the president's constitutional power to turn down acts of Congress. A presidential veto may be overridden by a two-thirds vote of each house of Congress

**pocket veto** a presidential veto that is automatically triggered if the president does not act on a given piece of legislation passed during the final 10 days of a legislative session

## ● How Congress Decides

> **Analyze the factors that influence which laws Congress decides to pass**

What determines the kinds of legislation that Congress ultimately produces? According to the simplest theories of representation, members of Congress respond to the views of their constituents. In fact, the process of creating a legislative agenda, drawing up a list of possible measures, and deciding among them is a very complex one, in which a variety of influences from inside and outside government play important roles. External influences include a legislator's constituency and various interest groups. Influences from inside government include party leadership, congressional colleagues, and the president. Let us examine each of these influences individually and then consider how they interact to produce congressional policy decisions.

## Constituency

Because members of Congress, for the most part, want to be re-elected, we would expect the views of their constituents to be a primary influence on the decisions that legislators make. Yet constituency influence is not so straightforward. In fact, most constituents pay little attention to politics and often do not even know what policies their representatives support. Nonetheless, members of Congress spend a lot of time worrying about what their constituents think, because they realize that the choices they make may be scrutinized in a future election and used as ammunition by an opposing candidate. Because of this possibility, members of Congress do try to anticipate their constituents' policy views, especially if they think that voters will take them into account during elections.[35] In this way, constituents may affect congressional policy choices even when there is little direct evidence of their influence. In October 1998, for example, 31 House Democrats broke party ranks and voted in favor of an impeachment inquiry against President Clinton because they believed a "no" vote could cost them re-election that November. In 2002 the White House successfully pressed to schedule the vote authorizing the use of force in Iraq right before the midterm elections in order to pressure members to vote for it.

## Interest Groups

Interest groups are another important external influence on congressional policies. When members of Congress are making voting decisions, those interest groups that have some connection to constituents in particular members' districts are most likely to be influential, and those groups with the ability to mobilize followers in many congressional districts may be especially influential. In recent years, Washington-based interest groups with little grassroots strength have recognized the importance of locally generated activity. Accordingly, they have sought to simulate grassroots pressure with so-called Astroturf lobbying (see Chapter 11). Such campaigns encourage constituents to sign form letters, postcards, or e-mails, which are then sent to congressional representatives. Campaigns set up toll-free telephone numbers for a system in which simply reporting your name and address to the listening computer will generate a letter to your congressional representative. One Senate office estimated that such organized campaigns to demonstrate "grassroots" support account for two-thirds of the mail the office received. As such campaigns increase, however, they become less influential, because members of Congress are aware of how rare real constituent interest actually is.[36]

Many interest groups now also use legislative "scorecards" that rate how members of Congress vote on issues of importance to that group. A high or low rating by an important interest group may provide a potent weapon in the next election. Interest groups can increase their influence over a particular piece of legislation by signaling their intention to include it in their scoring. Among the most influential groups that use scorecards, often posting them on their websites for members and the public to see, are the National Federation of Independent Business, the AFL-CIO, National Right to Life, the League of Conservation Voters, and the National Rifle Association.

Interest groups also have substantial influence in setting the legislative agenda and in helping to craft specific language in legislation. Today, sophisticated lobbyists win influence by providing information about policies to busy members of Congress. In the 2009–10 health reform effort, the biotechnology firm Genentech ghostwrote statements that more than a dozen members of Congress placed into the *Congressional Record*. Genentech's role came to light when it became evident that some members had used the exact same language in their entries.[37] In recent years, interest groups have also begun to build broader coalitions and comprehensive campaigns around particular policy issues. These coalitions do not rise from the grass roots but instead are put together by Washington lobbyists, who launch comprehensive lobbying campaigns that combine simulated grassroots activity with information and campaign funding for members of Congress.

Close financial ties between members of Congress and interest-group lobbyists often raise eyebrows because they

*Members of Congress often spend a great deal of time in their electoral districts meeting with constituents. Representative Elijah E. Cummings of Maryland is shown here greeting constituents at an event in Baltimore.*

suggest that interest groups get special treatment in exchange for political donations. Concerns about the influence of lobbyists in Congress mounted in the early 2000s when Republicans launched the K Street Project, named after the street in Washington where many high-powered lobbyists have offices. The K Street Project placed former Republican staffers in key lobbying positions and ensured a large and steady flow of corporate cash into Republican coffers. Congressional relationships to lobbyists came under close scrutiny when the lobbyist Jack Abramoff, a self-proclaimed big supporter of the K Street Project, pled guilty in early 2006 to charges of conspiracy, mail fraud, and tax evasion.

Concern over such corruption led Congress to enact new ethics legislation in 2007. The new law sets new restrictions on the gifts lobbyists can bestow on lawmakers and limits privately funded travel. The law also prohibits members of Congress from lobbying for two years after they retire and requires lawmakers to identify the earmarks they insert in legislation. Further, it aims to shine light on the practice of "bundling," whereby lobbyists assemble money from a number of clients to make a single political donation. Now lobbyists are required to disclose the names of the individual contributors to these political donations. Although the new law provides additional transparency, revealing more about the relationship between lobbyists and members of Congress, it is widely viewed as lacking sufficient authority to go after those who are suspected of ethics violations.[38] Moreover, the large sums of cash raised by "super PACs"—discussed in Chapter 10—have introduced a whole new set of questions about the role of special interests in politics, especially because donors to super PACs can remain anonymous. Although they cannot openly coordinate with candidates, super PACs can endorse candidates by name and are often run by people close to the candidates they support. In 2012 super PACs poured unprecedented sums of money into the race for president, but they also targeted key congressional contests in an effort to affect the balance of power between the parties in Congress.[39]

## Party

In both the House and Senate, party leaders have a good deal of influence over the behavior of their party members. This influence, sometimes called "party discipline," was once so powerful that it dominated the lawmaking process. In the late 1800s, party leaders could often command the allegiance of more than 90 percent of their members. A vote in which half or more of the members of one party take one position while at least half of the members of the other party take the opposing position is called a **party unity vote**. At the beginning of the twentieth century, nearly half of all **roll-call votes** in the House of Representatives were party votes. For much of the twentieth century, the number of party votes declined as bipartisan legislation became more common. The 1990s witnessed a return to strong party discipline as partisan polarization drew sharper lines between Democrats and Republicans, and congressional party leaders aggressively used their powers to promote party discipline. In 2005 party discipline was close to its all-time high.

Typically, party unity is greater in the House than in the Senate. House rules grant greater procedural control of business to the majority party leaders, which gives them more influence over House members. In the Senate, however, the leadership has few sanctions over its members. The former Senate minority leader Tom Daschle once observed that a Senate leader seeking to influence other senators has as incentives "a bushel full of carrots and a few twigs."[40]

**party unity vote** a roll-call vote in the House or Senate in which at least 50 percent of the members of one party take a particular position and are opposed by at least 50 percent of the members of the other party

**roll-call vote** a vote in which each legislator's yes or no vote is recorded as the clerk calls the names of the members alphabetically

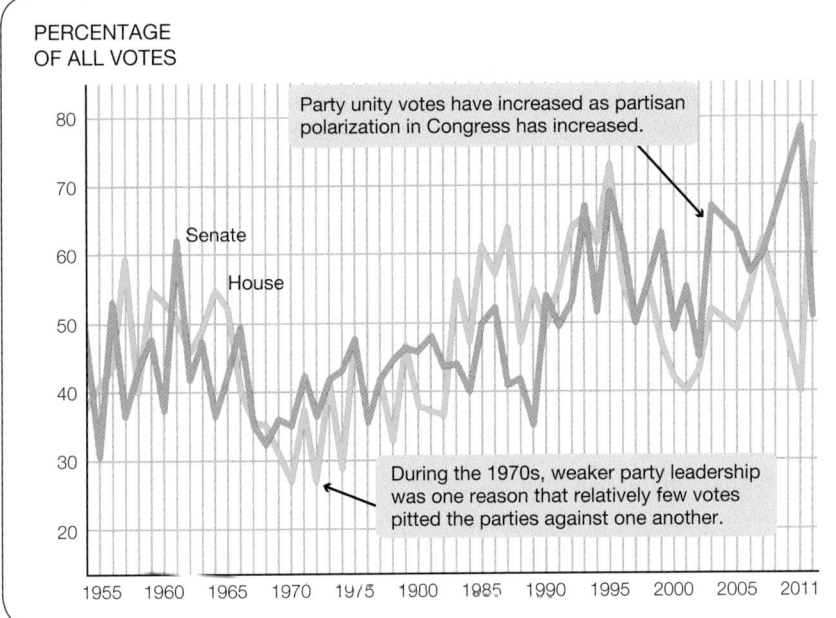

PERCENTAGE OF ALL VOTES

Party unity votes have increased as partisan polarization in Congress has increased.

Senate

House

During the 1970s, weaker party leadership was one reason that relatively few votes pitted the parties against one another.

1955 1960 1965 1970 1975 1900 1985 1990 1995 2000 2005 2011

**FIGURE 12.9**

**Party Unity Votes by Chamber**

Party unity votes are roll-call votes in which a majority of one party lines up against a majority of the other party. Party unity votes increase when the parties are polarized and when the party leadership can enforce discipline. Why did the percentage of party unity votes decline in the 1970s? Why has it risen in recent years?

SOURCES: Shawn Zeller, "2010 Vote Studies: Party Unity," *CQ Weekly*, January 3, 2012, p. 37; Emily Ethridge, "2011 Vote Studies: Party Unity," *CQ Weekly*, January 16, 2012, p. 111.

Though it has not reached nineteenth-century levels, party unity has been on the rise in recent years because the divisions between the parties have deepened on many high-profile issues such as abortion, health care, and financial reform (see Figure 12.9). Party unity scores rise when congressional leaders try to put a partisan stamp on legislation. For example, in 1995, then-Speaker Newt Gingrich sought to enact a Republican "Contract with America" that few Democrats supported. The result was more party unity in the House than in any year since 1954. Since then, the polarization of political parties has resulted in very high party unity scores. In 2011, House Democrats voted with the majority 87 percent of the time, slightly short of their all-time high of 92 percent in 2007 and 2008. In 2011, Senate Democrats set a record for party unity by voting with their caucus 92 percent of the time. In 2011, House Republicans voted with their party 91 percent of the time, matching their all-time high; Senate Republicans voted with their party 86 percent of the time.[41]

To some extent, party unity is based on ideology and background. Republican members of the House are more likely than Democrats to have been elected by rural or suburban districts. Democrats are likely to be more liberal on economic and social questions than their Republican colleagues in both houses. These differences certainly help to explain roll-call divisions between the two parties. Ideology and background, however, are only part of the explanation for party unity. The other part has to do with party organization and leadership. Among the resources that party leaders have at their disposal are (1) leadership PACs, (2) committee assignments, (3) access to the floor, (4) the whip system, (5) logrolling, and (6) the presidency.

**Leadership PACs** Leaders have increased their influence over members in recent years with aggressive use of leadership political action committees. Leadership PACs are organizations that members of Congress use to raise funds that they then distribute to other members of their party running for election. Republican congressional leaders pioneered the aggressive use of leadership PACs to win their congressional majority in 1995, and the practice has spread widely since that time. The former House majority leader Tom DeLay was especially aggressive in raising funds, creating several important PACs, including Americans for a Republican Majority (ARMPAC), Retain Our Majority Program (ROMP), and the Republican Majority Issues Committee. In recent years, Democrats have also formed well-funded leadership PACs. Money from leadership PACs can be directed to the most vulnerable candidates or to candidates who are having trouble raising money. It can also be used to influence primary elections. In 2010 and 2012, conservatives in the House and Senate used leadership PACs to support conservative candidates in Republican primaries. For example, Senator Jim DeMint's (R-S.C.) Senate Conservatives Fund was an early supporter of three conservative candidates who won in 2010: Marco Rubio (R-Fla.), Rand Paul (R-Ky.), and Pat Toomey (R-Pa.). Although leadership PACs have traditionally enhanced the power of the party and created a bond between the leaders and the members who receive their help, the aggressive use of PACs by Republican conservatives highlights their use for wings of the party who want to increase their power.[42]

**Committee Assignments** Leaders can create debts among members by helping them get favorable committee assignments. These assignments are made early in the congressional careers of most members and cannot be taken from them if they later balk at party discipline. Nevertheless, if the leadership goes out of its way to get the right assignment for a member, this effort is likely to create a bond of obligation that can be called on without any other payments or favors. This is one reason the Republican leadership gave freshmen favorable assignments when the Republicans took over Congress in 1995. When Nancy Pelosi assumed the position of Speaker in 2007, she sought to spread power more widely by limiting the number of committees that any one member could chair. She also gave freshmen representatives access to key committees that would raise their political stature.[43] By offering attractive committee assignments to members in competitive races, especially to new members, she sought to boost her party's chances in the next elections.

*Floor time—the opportunity to speak on the floor of Congress—gives members to argue their point of view and to show their constituents that they are actively working on their behalf. In 2011, Senator Roy Blunt (R-Mo.), spoke on the floor about the need for disaster relief funding for Missourians.*

**Access to the Floor** The most important everyday resource available to the parties is control over access to the floor. With thousands of bills awaiting passage and most members clamoring for access in order to influence a bill or publicize themselves, floor time is precious. In the Senate, the leadership allows ranking committee members to influence the allocation of floor time—who will speak for how long; in the House, the Speaker, as head of the majority party (in consultation with the minority leader), allocates large blocks of floor time. Thus, floor time is allocated in both houses of Congress by the majority and minority leaders. More important, the Speaker of the House and the majority leader in the Senate possess the power of recognition. This seemingly insubstantial authority is, in fact, quite formidable and can be used to stymie a piece of legislation completely or frustrate a member's attempts to speak on a particular issue. Because the power is significant, members of Congress usually attempt to stay on good terms with the Speaker and the majority leader to ensure they will continue to be recognized.

As House Speaker, Nancy Pelosi was particularly generous in offering freshmen Democrats and other especially vulnerable Democrats an opportunity to speak on the floor. When Republicans assumed control of the House in 2010, they likewise ensured that the voices of freshmen Republicans were heard on the House floor.[44]

**The Whip System** Some influence accrues to party leaders through the whip system, which is primarily a communications network for conveying the leaders' wishes and plans to the members. Between 12 and 20 assistant and regional whips are selected to operate at the direction of the majority or minority leader and the whip. They poll all the members in order to learn their intentions on specific bills, enabling the leaders to know if they have enough support to allow a vote as well as whether the vote is so close that they will need to put pressure on undecided members. In those instances, the Speaker or a lieutenant will go to a few party members who have indicated they will switch if their vote is essential—an expedient that the leaders try to limit to a few times per session.

The whip system helps maintain party unity in both houses of Congress, but it is particularly critical in the House of Representatives because of the large number of legislators whose positions and votes must be accounted for. The majority and minority whips and their assistants must be adept at inducing compromise among legislators who hold widely differing viewpoints. The whips' personal styles and their perception of their function significantly affect the development of legislative coalitions and the compromises that emerge. As Republican House whip from 1995 to 2002, Tom DeLay established a reputation as an effective vote counter and a tough leader, earning the nickname the Hammer. DeLay also expanded the reach of the whip, building alliances with Republicans outside Congress, particularly those in ideological and business-oriented groups. Since Republicans retook control of the House following the 2010 elections, the whip operation has been faced with significant challenges from the large number of freshmen members of Congress. An unusually high number of members (87) were freshmen, 40 percent of whom had never held elected office before, calling themselves "citizen politicians." More important, many of these new members identified themselves as members of the Tea Party movement. Given the divisions between more experienced and moderate members in leadership and the new influx of conservative freshmen, Speaker John Boehner adopted an unusually loose approach to party discipline, as typified by his statement "Let the House work its will."[45] This approach created problems for the leadership, forcing the Speaker to end his "grand bargain" negotiations with President Obama surrounding deficit reduction and a raise in the debt ceiling in summer 2011. It also led to the rejection by the Republican conference of a payroll tax cut extension that had previously been passed by a large bipartisan majority in the Senate in late 2011, although a two-month extension did eventually pass.

**Logrolling** An agreement between two or more members of Congress who have nothing in common except the need for support is called **logrolling**. The agreement states, in effect, "You support me on bill X, and I'll support you on another bill of your choice." Since party leaders are the center of the communications networks

**logrolling** a legislative practice whereby agreements are made between legislators in voting for or against a bill; vote trading

in the two chambers, they can help members create large logrolling coalitions. Hundreds of logrolling deals are made each year, and although there are no official record-keeping books, it would be a poor party leader whose whips did not know who owed what to whom. In some instances, logrolling produces strange alliances. A most unlikely alliance emerged in Congress in October 1991, an alliance that one commentator dubbed "the corn for porn plot."[46] The alliance joined Senate supporters of the National Endowment for the Arts (NEA) with senators seeking limits on the cost of grazing rights on federal lands. The NEA, which provides federal funding to the arts, had been under fire from the conservative senator Jesse Helms (R-N.C.) for funding some controversial artists whose work Helms believed to be indecent. In an effort to block federal support for such works, Helms attached a provision to the NEA's funding that would have prohibited the agency from awarding grants to any work that in a "patently offensive way" depicted "sexual or excretory activities or organs." Supporters of the NEA condemned such restrictions as a violation of free speech and pointed out that many famous works of art could not have been funded under such restrictions. When it appeared that the amendment would pass, NEA supporters offered western senators a deal. In exchange for voting down the Helms amendment, they would eliminate a planned hike in grazing fees. Republican senators from 16 western states switched their votes and defeated the Helms amendment. Although Helms called his defeat the product of "back-room deals and parliamentary flimflam," his amendment was simply the victim of the time-honored congressional practice of logrolling.[47] This type of logrolling has become much less common in recent years, as sharp partisan differences have limited the possibilities for compromise.

**The Presidency** Of all the influences that maintain the clarity of party lines in Congress, the influence of the presidency is probably the most important. Indeed, the office is a touchstone of party discipline in Congress. Since the late 1940s, under President Harry Truman, presidents each year have identified a number of bills that they want to be considered part of their administration's program. By the mid-1950s, both parties in Congress began to look to the president for these proposals, which became the most significant part of Congress's agenda. The president's support is a criterion for party loyalty, and party leaders are able to use it to rally some members. Since 2011, with the presidency in Democratic hands and the House of Representatives controlled by Republicans, party polarization has limited the president's agenda-setting powers. Instead, his proposals have become targets for congressional opponents.

## When Congress Can't Decide

We've considered the major factors that influence congressional decisions, but what happens if Congress as a whole can't decide and fails to act? In February 2012, Congress received the lowest levels of approval ever recorded in public opinion polls. Just 10 percent of those questioned approved of the job Congress was doing, while 86 percent expressed disapproval.[48] Two concerns lay behind the public's dissatisfaction with Congress. The first was the inability of the Republican House and the Democratic Senate to make decisions on numerous issues. The second was the pervasive belief that members of Congress listen more to special interests than to the American public.

By the end of 2011, 50 percent of Americans, a record high, said that the current Congress "had accomplished less than recent congresses."[49] Indeed partisan divisions

*Congress has been polarized in recent years. For example, Democrats and Republicans were sharply divided over the Affordable Care Act passed in 2010 to reform the health care system. Representative Michele Bachmann joined Tea Party supporters and other Republicans in calling for the repeal of the act.*

mired the 112th Congress in contentious arguments and prevented it from making many decisions. As we have seen, many of the usual procedures through which Congress enacted laws in the past—congressional committees to consider legislation, conference committees to reconcile House and Senate versions of legislation, a whip system to support leaders in the House of Representatives, logrolling, and presidential agenda setting—no longer functioned in the divided Congress. Even extraordinary efforts, such as the joint "supercommittee" appointed to reduce the deficit in 2011, failed to prompt Congress to reach agreement. Unable to decide the big issues, Congress resorted to passing short-term extensions of existing legislation.

The partisan divisions that prevented Congress from making decisions were especially acute because the unusually large class of freshman Republicans, many associated with the Tea Party movement, believed they had been sent to Congress to put an end to business as usual. Dedicated to reducing government spending, they used their power to hold up routine decisions, such as extension of the debt limit, as a way to extract concessions on government spending. Even when Republican leader John Boehner attempted to make a "grand bargain" with President Obama over taxes and spending—one very favorable to Republicans—conservative Republicans in the House rejected it as not going far enough. The political standoffs, which included regular threats of a government shutdown and resulted in the decision by rating agency Moody's to downgrade the U.S. credit rating, tarnished Congress's reputation with the public.

The public's disapproval of Congress was intensified by the belief that members of Congress pay attention to special interests. Much of the dissatisfaction with Congress appeared to be directed at members of Congress, not at the institution itself. In fact, a 2011 poll found that nearly half of those responding believed that most members of Congress are corrupt.[50] Both Occupy Wall Street on the left and the Tea Party movement on the right charged that Congress has been captured by special interests. This sense was intensified by the rise of super PACS after 2010, when several court decisions, including *Citizens United v. Federal Election Commission*, allowed outside groups and individuals to spend unlimited amounts of money on elections.[51]

Congressional gridlock is here to stay so long as voters elect representatives with sharply different views about what government should and shouldn't do. Until there is more agreement about the role of government and the best way to manage the budgetary challenges that face the country, congressional stand-offs on major legislation will remain a regular feature of American politics.

## ● Beyond Legislation: Other Congressional Powers

> **Describe the oversight, "advice and consent," and impeachment powers of Congress**

In addition to the power to make the law, Congress has at its disposal an array of other instruments through which to influence the process of government. The Constitution gives the Senate the power to approve treaties and appointments. And Congress has a number of other powers through which it can share with the other branches the capacity to administer the laws.

**oversight** the effort by Congress, through hearings, investigations, and other techniques, to exercise control over the activities of executive agencies

**appropriations** the amounts of money approved by Congress in statutes (bills) that each unit or agency of government can spend

### Oversight

**Oversight**, as applied to Congress, refers to the effort to oversee or to supervise how the executive branch carries out legislation. Oversight is carried out by committees or subcommittees of the Senate or the House, which conduct hearings and investigations in order to analyze and evaluate bureaucratic agencies and the effectiveness of their programs. Their purpose may be to locate inefficiencies or abuses of power, to explore the relationship between what an agency does and what a law intends, or to change or abolish a program. Most programs and agencies are subject to some oversight every year during the course of hearings on **appropriations**, the funding of agencies and government programs.

Committees or subcommittees have the power to subpoena witnesses, administer oaths, cross-examine, compel testimony, and bring criminal charges for contempt (refusing to cooperate) and perjury (lying under oath). Hearings and investigations are similar in many ways, but they differ on one fundamental point. A hearing is usually held on a specific bill, and the questions asked are usually intended to build a record with regard to that bill. In an investigation, the committee or subcommittee does not begin with a particular bill, but examines a broad area or problem and then concludes its investigation with one or more proposed bills.

In recent years, congressional oversight power has increasingly been used as a tool of partisan politics. The Republican Congress aggressively investigated President Clinton, racking up 140 hours of sworn testimony on whether the president had used the White House Christmas card list for partisan purposes. By contrast, the Republican-controlled Congress failed to scrutinize seriously the actions of the Bush administration during Bush's first six years in office. The investigation into the abuse of prisoners in Iraq's Abu Ghraib prison, for example, entailed only 12 hours of sworn testimony. Moreover, the few oversight hearings that the Republican Congress held sought mainly to support the leadership's policy goals—during a hearing on Arctic oil drilling, for example, much testimony was devoted

*Congress may call on members of the executive branch and others to testify at hearings. Here, Sandra Thompson of the FDIC testifies at a hearing on bank stability and the TARP program in 2011.*

to the benefits of such drilling. Congress also convened oversight hearings on issues that had nothing to do with the executive branch, such as the high-profile hearings on steroid use in Major League Baseball in 2005 and 2008.[52]

When the Democrats took control of Congress in 2007, congressional oversight increased dramatically. To highlight the importance of oversight, Democrats renamed the House Government Reform Committee, calling it the Committee on Oversight and Government Reform, and added four new subcommittees dedicated to oversight. They also hired more than 200 new investigative staffers.[53] Armed with these resources, Congress stepped up the number of oversight hearings: during its first six months in power, the Democratic Congress held 942 oversight hearings, compared with 579 for the same period when Republicans controlled Congress in 2005.[54] Congressional leaders are quite aware of oversight hearings as political tools. In 2012, with the presidential race looming, Republican House Speaker John Boehner urged Republicans to use their oversight powers aggressively, telling them, "Our obligation is to use our majority to shine a spotlight on the places where the president's failed policies are getting in the way of American job creation. And that means stepped-up oversight of the Obama administration's policies."[55]

## Advice and Consent: Special Senate Powers

The Constitution has given the Senate another special power, one that is not based on lawmaking. The president has the power to make treaties and to appoint top executive officers, ambassadors, and federal judges—but only "with the Advice and Consent of the Senate" (Article II, Section 2). For treaties, two-thirds of those present must concur; for appointments, a simple majority is required.

The power to approve or reject presidential requests includes the power to set conditions: In fact, the Senate only occasionally exercises its power to reject treaties and appointments, and despite recent debate surrounding judicial nominees, only a handful of judicial nominees have been rejected by the Senate during the past century, whereas hundreds have been approved.

Most presidents make every effort to take potential Senate opposition into account in treaty negotiations with foreign powers. Instead of treaties, presidents frequently resort to **executive agreements** that do not need Senate approval. The Supreme Court has held that such agreements are equivalent to treaties.[56] In the past, presidents sometimes concluded secret agreements without informing Congress of the agreements' contents, or even their existence. For example, American involvement in the Vietnam War grew in part out of a series of secret arrangements made between American presidents and the South Vietnamese during the 1950s and '60s. Congress did not even learn of the existence of these agreements until 1969. In 1972, Congress passed the Case Act, which requires that the president inform Congress of any executive agreement within 60 days of its having been reached. This provides Congress with the opportunity to cancel agreements it opposes. In addition, Congress can limit the president's ability to conduct foreign policy through executive agreement by refusing to appropriate the funds needed to implement an agreement. In this way, for example, Congress can modify or even cancel executive agreements to provide American economic or military assistance to foreign governments.

**executive agreement** an agreement, made between the president and another country, that has the force of a treaty but does not require the Senate's "advice and consent"

## Impeachment

The Constitution also grants Congress the power of **impeachment** over the president, vice president, and other executive officials. Impeachment means to charge a government official (president or otherwise) with "Treason, Bribery, or

**impeachment** the formal charge by the House of Representatives that a government official has committed "Treason, Bribery, or other high Crimes and Misdemeanors"

# What Is Congress's Role in Foreign Policy?

**During World War II, national** security dominated the congressional agenda. With the massive mobilization of American troops and economic production geared to support the war effort, domestic policy commanded only modest attention in Congress. Congress focused on supporting the president as the nation faced total mobilization for war. During other periods, Congress has been much less supportive of the president's foreign policy. For example, in the late 1960s, as widespread doubts about the wisdom of the Vietnam War began to grow, Congress convened hearings that questioned administration assumptions and priorities.

Americans disagree about Congress's proper role in foreign policy. Such disagreements become especially salient in times of war. Should Congress primarily support the president as commander in chief of the armed forces? Or should Congress play the role of watchdog, delving into the details of foreign policy to ensure that the president's policies best serve the public interest?

Intensive congressional scrutiny of the president's foreign policy is counterproductive, say those who believe Congress should unite behind the president. Some believe that congressional objec-

tions to the president's priorities only strengthen the nation's enemies by weakening our American resolve to take the measures needed to ensure the country's defense. Congress is more likely than the president to adopt a short-term, politicized perspective. Congress is also more likely to put domestic concerns ahead of foreign-policy priorities. These tensions grew more pronounced after public disenchantment with the war in Iraq gave control of Congress to the Democrats in the 2006 midterm election. House and Senate leaders pressed the president to announce a new strategy for reducing American forces in Iraq. The president insisted, however, that U.S. troops needed to stay in Iraq to end sectarian violence. In the end, some feel presidents are better equipped than Congress to know what needs to be done to

conduct a successful foreign policy. They have a large national security apparatus with extensive expertise, and they are able to keep the big picture in mind.

Critics disagree, arguing that Congress has a vital role to play in foreign policy. The absence of ongoing congressional scrutiny can lead to poor policy, detached from democratic accountability. The continuing violence in Iraq and the lack of progress toward political stability provided only one example where congressional leaders claimed the Bush administration had lost touch with the electorate. From this viewpoint, democratic checks and balances must extend to foreign policy. If the executive branch refuses to adjust its foreign policies in response to public opinion, then Congress may have to exercise its power of the purse by cutting off funds. Ultimately, Congress must closely monitor the executive to ensure that the arguments and evidence for U.S. foreign policy are sound.

Former president Bush's handling of the war in Iraq and the threat of terrorism brought tensions between Congress and the White House to a level not seen since the Vietnam War. President Obama, however, found he was not immune to these tensions. Although Obama succeeded in winning congressional approval for additional troops in Afghanistan, many members of Congress did not support his request. The president's reputation rests far more heavily on success or failure in foreign policy than do the reputations of members of Congress. Meanwhile, Congress is more responsive to popular pressures that also have a place in foreign policy.

## for critical analysis

1. Why is the president better equipped than Congress to conduct foreign policy, especially in matters such as terrorism?
2. Why is congressional oversight essential to good foreign policy? How does the experience of the war in Iraq point to the importance of strong congressional involvement in foreign policy?

other high Crimes and Misdemeanors" and bring him or her before Congress to determine guilt. Impeachment is thus like a criminal indictment in which the House of Representatives acts like a grand jury, voting (by simple majority) on whether the accused ought to be impeached. If a majority of the House votes to impeach, the impeachment trial moves to the Senate, which acts like a trial jury by voting whether to convict and forcibly remove the person from office (which requires a two-thirds majority of the Senate). The impeachment power is a considerable one; its very existence in the hands of Congress is a highly effective safeguard against the executive tyranny so greatly feared by the framers of the Constitution.

Controversy over Congress's impeachment power has arisen over the grounds for impeachment, especially the meaning of "high Crimes and Misdemeanors." A strict reading of the Constitution suggests that the only impeachable offense is an actual crime. But a more common working definition is that "an impeachable offense is whatever the majority of the House of Representatives considers it to be at a given moment in history."[57] In other words, impeachment, especially impeachment of a president, is a political decision.

The Senate possesses the power to impeach federal officials. In American history, 16 federal officials have been impeached, including two presidents. In 1998 the House impeached President Bill Clinton for lying under oath about his affair with the intern Monica Lewinsky.

The political nature of impeachment was very clear in the two instances of impeachment that have occurred in American history. In the first, in 1867, President Andrew Johnson, a southern Democrat who had battled a congressional Republican majority over Reconstruction, was impeached by the House but saved from conviction by one vote in the Senate. In 1998 the House impeached President Bill Clinton on two counts, for lying under oath and obstructing justice during the investigation into his sexual affair with the White House intern Monica Lewinsky. The vote was highly partisan, with only five Democrats voting for impeachment on each charge. In the Senate, where a two-thirds majority was needed to convict the president, only 45 senators voted to convict on the first count of lying and 50 voted to convict on the second charge of obstructing justice. As in the House, the vote for impeachment was highly partisan, with all Democrats and only five Republicans supporting the president's ultimate acquittal.

## ● Thinking Critically about Congress and Democracy

Much of this chapter has described the major institutional components of Congress and has shown how they work as Congress makes policy. But what do these institutional features mean for how Congress represents the American public? Does the organization of Congress promote the equal representation of all Americans? Or are there institutional features of Congress that allow some interests more access and influence than others?

As we noted at the beginning of this chapter, Congress instituted a number of reforms in the 1970s to make itself more accessible and to distribute power more

## forcriticalanalysis

Two of Congress's chief responsibilities are representation and lawmaking. How do these responsibilities support and reinforce each other? How might they also conflict with each other?

**delegate** a representative who votes according to the preferences of his or her constituency

**trustee** a representative who votes based on what he or she thinks is best for his or her constituency

## forcriticalanalysis

Why is it so hard to make the voice of the public heard in Congress over that of the special interests? What reforms can enhance the public's influence in congressional deliberations?

widely within the institution. These reforms sought to respond to public views that Congress had become a stodgy institution ruled by a powerful elite that made decisions in private. We have seen that these reforms increased the number of subcommittees, prohibited most secret hearings, and increased the staff support for Congress. These reforms spread power more evenly throughout the institution and opened new avenues for the public to contact and influence Congress.

But the opening of Congress ultimately did not benefit the broad American public, as reformers had envisioned. In fact the congressional reforms enacted during the 1970s actually made Congress less effective and, ironically, more permeable to special interests. Open committee meetings made it possible for sophisticated interest groups to monitor and influence every aspect of developing legislation. The unanticipated, negative consequences of these reforms highlighted the trade-off between representation and effectiveness in Congress.[58] Efforts to improve representation by opening Congress up made it difficult for Congress to be effective.

For the Founders, Congress was the national institution that best embodied the ideals of representative democracy. Throughout U.S. history, Congress has symbolized the American commitment to democratic values. Members of Congress, working to represent their constituents, bring these democratic values to life. A member of Congress can interpret his or her job as representative in two different ways: as a **delegate**, acting on the express preferences of his constituents; or as a **trustee**, more loosely tied to constituents and empowered to make the decisions he or she thinks best. The delegate role appears to be the more democratic because it forces representatives to heed the desires of their constituents. But this requires the representative to be in constant touch with constituents; it also requires constituents to follow each policy issue very closely. The problem with this form of representation is that most people do not follow every issue so carefully; instead they focus only on the issue or issues of particular interest to them. Many people are too busy to get the information necessary to make informed judgments even on issues they care about. Thus, adhering to the delegate form of representation runs the risk that the voices of only a few active and informed constituents get heard. Although it seems more democratic at first glance, the delegate form of representation may actually open Congress up to even more influence by special interests.

When congressional members act as trustees, on the other hand, they may not pay sufficient attention to the wishes of their constituents. In this scenario, the only way the public can exercise influence is by voting every two years for representatives or every six years for senators. In fact, most members of Congress take this electoral check very seriously. They try to anticipate the wishes of their constituents even when they don't know exactly what those wishes are, because they know that unpopular decisions can be used against them in the coming election. What the public dislikes most about Congress stems from suspicions that Congress acts as neither a trustee nor a delegate of the broad public interest, but instead is swayed by narrow special interests with lots of money.[59] Ideally, representative democracy grants all citizens equal opportunity to select their leaders and to communicate their preferences to these elected representatives. Yet, in reality, some citizens have more wealth, are more politically savvy, or belong to more effective organizations. Despite past efforts to reform Congress, these advantages provide special access for some interests even as they mute the voices of much of the American public. The dilemma that congressional reformers confront is how to devise safeguards that reduce the influence of special interests while allowing Congress to remain open to the wishes of the voting public.

# Know Your Members of Congress

## Inform Yourself

 **Know your members of Congress.** Find out who represents your college or hometown in the House of Representatives and the Senate by using the "Find your senators/representative" tool at www.house.gov and www.senate.gov.

 **Check your representatives' records.** After you've identified your senators and representative, go to www.rollcall.com and complete the Legislator Profiles report. Who gives them money and how long have they been in office? What was the last bill they sponsored and does it benefit you or a friend or family member? How well do their policy positions align with your own?

## Express Yourself

 **Let your members of Congress know how you feel** about issues that are important to you by sending them an e-mail. Members' e-mail addresses are given on their Web pages. Your message may be especially effective if Congress is expected to consider and vote on the issue in the near future.

## Connect with Others

 **Connect with Congress and other constituents.** Most members of Congress have Facebook pages (often linked through their websites) where you can learn about campaign events and policies and connect with other constituents the House district or state. What has your member of Congress posted in the past month? Which posts were the most popular in terms of "likes" or shares? Does visiting the Facebook page of your member of Congress change your evaluation of your representative?

 **Consider how congressional districting affects who represents you** and other Americans. Play the "Redistricting Game" at www.redistrictinggame.org (all five steps, including creating a partisan gerrymander and ending with a nonpartisan redistricting). After drawing the districts yourself, do you think legislative districts should be drawn using the partisan composition of the district or other criteria? Why are legislative districts so important to members of Congress?

*Find links to the sites listed above as well as related activities on wwnorton.com/studyspace.*

# study guide

## Congress: Representing the American People

■ **Describe who serves in Congress and how they represent their constituents (pp. 471-84)**

A member of Congress's primary responsibility is to his or her district and to his or her constituency. The House and Senate operate according to a very different set of rules and play very different roles in the legislative process. Although members of Congress do not share their constituents' sociological characteristics, they do work hard to speak for their constituents' views and to serve their constituents' interests. Generally speaking, there are three factors related to the U.S. electoral system that affect who gets elected and what they do once in office: who decides to run for Congress, the incumbency advantage, and the way congressional districts are drawn.

### Key Terms

**constituency** (p. 471)

**bicameral** (p. 471)

**sociological representation** (p. 472)

**agency representation** (p. 472)

**incumbency** (p. 478)

**term limits** (p. 479)

**apportionment** (p. 480)

**redistricting** (p. 480)

**gerrymandering** (p. 480)

**patronage** (p. 482)

**pork-barrel (or pork)** (p. 482)

**private bill** (p. 483)

### Practice Quiz

1. Because they have larger and more heterogeneous constituencies, senators *(pp. 471–72)*
   a) have less freedom to consider "new ideas" or to bring together new coalitions of interests.
   b) are more attuned to the needs of localized interest groups.
   c) care more about re-election than House members.
   d) can better represent the national interest.
   e) face less competition in elections than House members.

2. What type of representation is described when constituents have the power to hire and fire their representative? *(p. 472)*
   a) agency representation
   b) sociological representation
   c) democratic representation
   d) trustee representation
   e) economic representation

3. Sociological representation is important in understanding the U.S. Congress because *(p. 475)*
   a) members often vote on the basis of their religion.
   b) Congress is a microcosm of American society.
   c) most people vote for people who are just like them.
   d) the symbolic composition of Congress is important for the authority of the government.
   e) there is a distinct "congressional sociology."

4. Some have argued that the creation of minority congressional districts has *(p. 481)*
   a) made it easier to draw districts.
   b) lessened the sociological representation of minorities in Congress.
   c) made it more difficult for minorities to win substantive policy goals.
   d) been a result of the media's impact on state legislative politics.
   e) lessened the problem of "pork-barrel" politics.

5. One way members of Congress can work as agents of their constituents is by *(p. 482)*
   a) providing direct patronage.
   b) taking part in a party vote.
   c) joining a caucus.
   d) supporting term limits.
   e) spending time on fund-raising for their re-election campaign.

 **Practice Online**
"Get Involved" exercise: *Know Your Members of Congress*

# The Organization of Congress

**■ Explain how party leadership, the committee system, the staff system, and caucuses help structure congressional business (pp. 484–91)**

Congress is a representative body and lawmaking institution. The political parties, the committee system, congressional staff, the caucuses, and the parliamentary rules of the House and Senate play key roles in the process through which Congress formulates and enacts law. the committee system is particularly important to the legislative process because Congress relies on committees and subcommittees to do the difficult work of sorting through alternatives and writing bills.

## Key Terms

**conference** (p. 485)

**caucus (political)** (p. 485)

**Speaker of the House** (p. 485)

**majority leader** (p. 485)

**minority leader** (p. 485)

**whip** (p. 485)

**standing committee** (p. 485)

**select committees** (p. 487)

**joint committees** (p. 488)

**conference committees** (p. 488)

**seniority** (p. 489)

**staff agencies** (p. 490)

**caucus (congressional)** (p. 491)

## Practice Quiz

6. Which of the following types of committees does not include members of both the House and the Senate? *(pp. 485–89)*
   a) conference committee
   b) joint committee
   c) 527 committees
   d) No committees include both House members and senators.

7. A series of reforms instituted by Congress in the 1970s, including an increase in the number of sub-committees and greater autonomy for subcommittee chairs, was intended to *(p. 489)*
   a) reduce the power of committee chairs.
   b) increase the power of committee chairs.
   c) secure re-election for all committee chairs.
   d) ending the filibuster.
   e) guarantee the electoral defeat of all committee chairs.

 **Practice Online**
Video exercise: *What will It Take to Close the Partisan Rift in Congress?*

# Rules of Lawmaking: How a Bill Becomes a Law

**■ Outline the steps in the process of passing a law (pp. 491–96)**

The rules of congressional procedure influence the fate of every bill and determine the distribution of power in Congress. Debate over bills is much less restricted in the Senate than in the House, and the filibuster gives tremendous power to individual senators. The president's veto power also exerts an important influence on Congress's lawmaking because the possibility of a presidential veto affects how willing members of Congress are to push for different pieces of legislation.

## Key Terms

**bill** (p. 491)

**committee markup** (p. 491)

**closed rule** (p. 493)

**open rule** (p. 493)

**filibuster** (p. 493)

**cloture** (p. 493)

**veto** (p. 496)

**pocket veto** (p. 496)

## Practice Quiz

8. The difference between a closed rule and an open rule in the House is *(p. 493)*
   a) a closed rule puts severe limits on floor debate and amendments, whereas an open rule permits floor debate and makes amendments easier.
   b) an open rule puts severe limits on floor debate and amendments, whereas a closed rule permits floor debate and makes amendments easier.
   c) a closed rule allows journalists and members of the public to listen to debates about a bill, whereas an open rule prevents journalists and members of the public from listening to debates about the bill.
   d) an open rule allows journalists and members of the public to listen to debates about a bill, whereas a closed rule prevents journalists and members of the public from listening to debates about the bill.
   e) a closed rule prevents the federal judiciary from declaring a bill unconstitutional once passed, whereas an open rule allows the federal judiciary to declare a bill unconstitutional.

9. Which of the following is *not* a technique that can be used to block debate about a bill in the Senate? *(pp. 493–94)*
   a) filibuster
   b) caucus
   c) the introduction of new amendments
   d) cloture
   e) placing holds on bills

# How Congress Decides

■ **Analyze the factors that influence which laws Congress decides to pass (pp. 496–504)**

A variety of influences from inside and outside government play a role in congressional decision making. External influences include the policy preferences of the legislator's constituency and the lobbying of various interest groups. Party leaders within Congress use committee assignments, access to the floor, the whip system, logrolling and the president's support to influence how representatives behave.

## Key Terms

**party unity vote** (p. 498)

**roll-call vote** (p. 498)

**logrolling** (p. 501)

## Practice Quiz

10. Which of the following is *not* an important influence on how members of Congress vote on legislation? *(p. 496)*
    a) the media
    b) constituency
    c) the president
    d) interest groups
    e) party leaders

11. Which of the following is *not* a resource that party leaders in Congress use to create party discipline? *(pp. 498–502)*
    a) leadership PACs
    b) committee assignments
    c) access to the floor
    d) the whip system
    e) roll-call votes

12. An agreement between members of Congress to trade support for each other's bills is known as *(p. 501)*
    a) oversight.
    b) filibuster.
    c) logrolling.
    d) patronage.
    e) cloture.

 **Practice Online**
Video exercise: *Clay Shirky on the Influence of Interest Groups and the People*

# Beyond Legislation: Other Congressional Powers

■ **Describe the oversight, "advice and consent," and impeachment powers of Congress (pp. 504-7)**

Congress has many other powers than simply lawmaking. Using hearings, investigations and other techniques, Congress exercises control over the agencies of the executive branch. Under the Constitution, the president can only make treaties and appoint top executive officers, ambassadors, and federal judges "with the Advice and Consent of the Senate." The Constitution also grants Congress the power of impeachment over the president, vice president, and other executive officials.

## Key Terms

**oversight** (p. 504)

**appropriations** (p. 504)

**executive agreement** (p. 505)

**impeachment** (p. 505)

**delegate** (p. 508)

**trustee** (p. 508)

## Practice Quiz

13. When Congress conducts an investigation to explore the relationship between what a law intended and what an executive agency has done, it is engaged in *(p. 504)*
    a) oversight.
    b) advice and consent.
    c) appropriations.
    d) executive agreement.
    e) direct patronage.

14. Which of the following statements about impeachment is *not* true? *(pp. 505–7)*
    a) The president is the only official who can be impeached by Congress.

b) Impeachment means to charge a government official with "Treason, Bribery, or other high Crimes and Misdemeanors."

c) The House of Representatives decides by simple majority vote whether the accused ought to be impeached.

d) The Senate decides whether to convict and remove the person from office.

e) There have only been two instances of impeachment in American history.

# For Further Reading

Adler, E. Scott. *Why Congressional Reforms Fail.* Chicago: University of Chicago Press, 2002.

Dodd, Lawrence C., and Bruce I. Oppenheimer, eds. *Congress Reconsidered.* 9th ed. Washington, DC: CQ Press, 2008.

Dodson, Debra L. *The Impact of Women in Congress.* New York: Oxford University Press, 2006.

Fenno, Richard F. *Homestyle: House Members in Their Districts.* Boston: Little, Brown, 1978.

Fiorina, Morris. *Congress: Keystone of the Washington Establishment.* 2nd ed. New Haven, CT: Yale University Press, 1989.

Fowler, Linda, and Robert McClure. *Political Ambition: Who Decides to Run for Congress?* New Haven, CT: Yale University Press, 1989.

Hamilton, Lee. *How Congress Works.* Bloomington: Indiana University Press, 2004.

Koger, Gregory. *Filibustering: A Political History of Obstruction in the House and Senate.* Chicago: University of Chicago Press, 2010.

Mann, Thomas E., and Norman J. Ornstein. *The Broken Branch: How Congress Is Failing America and How to Get It Back on Track.* New York: Oxford University Press, 2006.

Mayhew, David R. *Congress: The Electoral Connection.* New Haven, CT: Yale University Press, 1974.

Palmer, Barbara, and Denise Simon. *Breaking the Political Glass Ceiling: Women and Congressional Elections.* 2nd ed. New York: Routledge, 2008.

Redman, Eric. *The Dance of Legislation.* Seattle: University of Washington Press, 2001.

# Recommended Websites

**Cook Political Report**
www.cookpolitical.com
The Cook Political Report, by Charlie Cook, is a nonpartisan analysis of electoral politics. Check out current House and Senate races for an in-depth analysis of past elections and previews of future congressional elections.

**Library of Congress: Thomas**
http://thomas.loc.gov
The Library of Congress's "Thomas" website is a superb place to find information about the U.S. Congress. Roll-call votes, current legislation, the full text of the *Congressional Record*, and committee reports are just a few of the archives you will find.

**National Committee for an Effective Congress**
www.ourcampaigns.com
Congressional redistricting is the process of redrawing House districts every 10 years to account for shifts in population. For information about redistricting in your state, log on to the Redistricting Resource Center, provided by the National Committee for an Effective Congress.

*Roll Call*
www.rollcall.com
*Roll Call*, the newspaper of Capitol Hill, provides daily coverage on the members, legislation, and events taking place in and around the U.S. legislature.

**The Sunlight Foundation and Taxpayers for Common Sense**
http://earmarkwatch.org
Earmarks are language that members of Congress insert in legislation that dedicates funds for specific uses, many whose broad benefits can be questioned. The Sunlight Foundation and Taxpayers for Common Sense are two watchdog groups that have joined forces to publish a database of congressional earmarks. Earmarks can be searched by state, congressional sponsor, recipient, and description of the project.

**U.S. House of Representatives**
www.house.gov

**U.S. Senate**
www.senate.gov
These are the official websites for the U.S. House of Representatives and the U.S. Senate. Here you can find information on your members of Congress, key congressional leaders, bills currently under consideration, and legislative committees.

In 2012, Americans re-elected Barack Obama to the presidency. During the campaign, Obama made promises about how he would use the powers of the office to address the challenges facing the nation.

# The Presidency

**WHAT GOVERNMENT DOES AND WHY IT MATTERS** As President Barack Obama began his second term, his administration confronted a number of problems. While the U.S. economy—which had been in recession since 2007—had gradually begun to recover, the unemployment rate was still high and new job creation lagged. Obama had accused his Republican challenger, Mitt Romney, of sending American jobs overseas when Romney was a business manager. Bringing those jobs back, though, might not be so easy for the president. The economy was also threatened by budget deficits, as government spending outpaced income from taxes, and no consensus existed on how to solve that problem. On the international front, Obama had brought an end to the long and costly wars in Iraq and Afghanistan. However, the nation was still threatened by shadowy terrorist groups, while Iran seemed to be working to build a nuclear weapon, despite American pressures and economic sanctions. The president also faced an economic crisis in Europe, unrest in the Arab world, challenges from China, and a host of other problems, large and small. Obama's campaign slogan in 2012 had been "Forward!" but just how to go forward was not entirely obvious.

The president also inherited a presidency considerably more powerful than the institution imagined by the framers of the U.S. Constitution. Ironically, the same wars that presented such an enormous challenge to the new administration also had the potential to enhance its power.

Presidential power generally increases during times of war. For example, President Abraham Lincoln's 1862 declaration of martial law and Congress's 1863 legislation giving the president the power to make arrests and use military tribunals to try suspects amounted to a "constitutional dictatorship" that lasted through the Civil War and Lincoln's re-election in 1864. During World War II, Franklin Delano Roosevelt, like Lincoln, did not bother to wait for Congress but took executive action first and expected Congress to follow. One dissenter on the Supreme Court called the president's assumption of emergency powers "a loaded weapon ready for the hand of any authority that can bring forward a plausible claim of an urgent need."

On the domestic side, however, presidents often wish they had more power. During the budget and deficit crises of 2011, President Obama seemed unable to persuade House Republicans to follow his lead and was forced to accept compromises not at all to his liking. With their control of the House of Representatives, Republicans threatened to bring about a default on federal debt unless the president accepted their proposals, and there was little Obama could do besides agree.

In this chapter, we examine the foundations of the American presidency and assess the origins and character of presidential power in the twenty-first century. National emergencies are one source of presidential power, but presidents are also empowered by democratic political processes and, increasingly, by their ability to control and expand the institutional resources of the office.

# chaptergoals

- Explain the role of the president in the American political system (pages 517–19)

- Outline the powers the Constitution gives the president (pages 519–32)

- Identify the institutional resources presidents have to help them exercise their powers (pages 532–37)

- Explain how modern presidents have become even more powerful (pages 538–47)

# ● Establishing the Presidency

The presidency was established by Article II of the Constitution, which begins by asserting, "The executive power shall be vested in a President of the United States of America." Article II describes the manner in which the president is to be chosen and defines the basic powers of the presidency. By vesting the executive power in a single president, the framers were emphatically rejecting proposals for various forms of collective leadership. Some delegates to the Constitutional Convention had argued in favor of a multiheaded executive or an "executive council" in order to avoid undue concentration of power in the hands of one individual. Most of the framers, however, wanted to provide for "energy" in the executive, and they thought that a unitary executive would be more energetic than some form of collective leadership. They believed that a powerful executive would help protect the nation's interests vis-à-vis other nations and promote the federal government's interests relative to the states.

The presidential selection process defined by Article II resulted from a struggle between those delegates who wanted the president to be selected by, and thus be responsible to, Congress and those delegates who preferred that the president be elected directly by the people. Direct popular election would create a more independent and more powerful presidency. With the adoption of a scheme of indirect election through an electoral college, with electors to be selected by the state legislatures (and close elections to be resolved in the House of Representatives), the framers hoped to achieve a "republican" solution: a strong president responsible to state and national legislators rather than directly to the electorate. This indirect method of electing the president probably did dampen the power of most presidents in the nineteenth century.

*The framers of the Constitution wanted an "energetic" presidency, capable of quick, decisive action. However, when George Washington was sworn in as the first president, in 1789, the presidency was a less powerful office than it is today.*

*As the method of selecting presidents became more democratic, the president came to be seen as the direct representative of the American people, increasing the power of the office. Here, President Ronald Reagan attends a memorial service for American soldiers killed in the 1983 bombing of the American embassy in Beirut, Lebanon.*

**caucus (political)** a normally closed political party business meeting of citizens or law makers to select candidates, elect officers, plan strategy, or make decisions regarding legislative matters

The presidency was strengthened somewhat in the 1830s with the introduction of the national convention system of nominating presidential candidates. Until then, presidential candidates had been nominated by their party's congressional delegates through a **caucus** system, derisively called "King Caucus" because any candidate for president was beholden to the party's leaders in Congress both for the party's nomination and for their support in the presidential election. The national nominating convention arose outside Congress in order to provide some representation for a party's voters who lived in districts where they were in the minority. The political party in each state made its own provisions for selecting delegates to attend the presidential nominating convention, and in virtually all states, the selection was dominated by the party leaders. (Only in recent decades have state laws intervened to regularize the selection process and to provide, in all but a few instances, for open election of delegates.) The convention system quickly became the most popular method of nominating candidates for all elective offices and remained so until well into the twentieth century, when it succumbed to the criticism that it was undemocratic and dominated by a few leaders in a "smoke-filled room." But during the nineteenth century, the convention system was seen as a victory for democracy against the congressional elite. Furthermore, the national convention gave the presidency a base of power independent of Congress.

This additional independence did not immediately transform the presidency into the office familiar to us today, but the national convention did begin to open the presidency to larger social forces and newly organized interests in society. In other words, it gave the presidency a broad popular base that would eventually demand and support increased presidential power. Improvements in the telegraph, the telephone, and other forms of mass communication enabled individuals to share their complaints and allowed national leaders (especially presidents and presidential candidates) to reach out directly to the people. Eventually, though more slowly, the presidential selection process began to be further democratized with the adoption of primary elections through which millions of ordinary citizens were given an opportunity to take part in the presidential nominating process by popular selection of convention delegates.

But despite political and social conditions favoring the enhancement of the presidency, the development of presidential government as we know it today did not mature until the middle of the twentieth century. For a long period, even as the national government began to grow, Congress was careful to keep a tight rein on the president's power. The real turning point in the history of American national government came during the administration of Franklin Delano Roosevelt. Since FDR and his "New Deal" of the 1930s, every president has been strong whether or not he was committed to the goal of a strong presidency.

# ● The Constitutional Powers of the Presidency

**Outline the powers the Constitution gives the president**

Whereas Section 1 of Article II of the Constitution explains how the president is to be chosen, Sections 2 and 3 outline the powers and duties of the president. These two sections identify two sources of presidential authority. Some presidential powers, called the **expressed powers** of the office, are specifically established by the language of the Constitution. For example, the president is authorized to make treaties, grant pardons, and nominate judges and other public officials. These specifically defined powers cannot be revoked by Congress or any other agency without an amendment to the Constitution. Other expressed powers include the authority to receive ambassadors and the command of the military forces of the United States.

In addition to the president's expressed powers, Article II declares that the president "shall take Care that the Laws be faithfully executed." Since the laws are enacted by Congress, this language implies that Congress is to delegate to the president the power to implement or execute its will. Powers given to the president by Congress are called **delegated powers**. In principle, Congress delegates to the president only the power to identify or develop the means through which to carry out its decisions. So, for example, if Congress determines that air quality should be improved, it might delegate to a bureaucratic agency in the executive branch the power to identify the best means of bringing about such an improvement as well as the power to implement the actual cleanup process. In practice, of course, decisions about how to clean the air are likely to have an enormous impact on businesses, organizations, and individuals throughout the nation. By delegating power to the executive branch, Congress substantially enhances the importance of the presidency. In most cases, Congress delegates power to bureaucratic agencies in the executive branch rather than to the president, but as we shall see, contemporary presidents have found ways to capture a good deal of this delegated power for themselves.

Presidents have claimed a third source of power beyond expressed and delegated powers. These are powers not specified in the Constitution or the law but said to stem from "the rights, duties and obligations of the presidency."[1] Referred to as the **inherent powers** of the presidency, they are most often asserted by presidents in times of war or national emergency. For example, after the fall of Fort Sumter and the outbreak of the Civil War, President Abraham Lincoln issued a series of executive orders for which he had no clear legal authority. Without even calling Congress into session, Lincoln combined the state militias into a 90-day national volunteer force, called for 40,000 new volunteers, enlarged the regular

**expressed powers** specific powers granted by the Constitution to Congress (Article I, Section 8) and to the president (Article II)

**delegated powers** constitutional powers that are assigned to one governmental agency but that are exercised by another agency with the express permission of the first

**inherent powers** powers claimed by a president that are not expressed in the Constitution but are inferred from it

army and navy, diverted $2 million in unspent appropriations to military needs, instituted censorship of the U.S. mail, ordered a blockade of southern ports, suspended the writ of habeas corpus in the border states, and ordered the arrest by military police of individuals whom he deemed to be guilty of engaging in or even merely contemplating treasonous actions.[2] Lincoln asserted that these extraordinary measures were justified by the president's inherent power to protect the nation.[3] Subsequent presidents, including Franklin Delano Roosevelt and George W. Bush, have made similar claims.

## Expressed Powers

The president's expressed powers, as defined by Sections 2 and 3 of Article II, fall into several categories:

1. *Military*. Article II, Section 2, provides for the power as "Commander in Chief of the Army and Navy of the United States, and of the Militia of the several States, when called in to the actual Service of the United States."

2. *Judicial*. Article II, Section 2, also provides the power to "grant Reprieves and Pardons for Offences against the United States, except in Cases of Impeachment."

3. *Diplomatic*. Article II, Section 2, further provides the power "by and with the Advice and Consent of the Senate to make Treaties." Article II, Section 3, provides the power to "receive Ambassadors and other public Ministers."

4. *Executive*. Article II, Section 3, also authorizes the president to see to it that all the laws are faithfully executed; Section 2 gives the chief executive power to appoint, remove, and supervise all executive officers and to appoint all federal judges.

5. *Legislative*. Article I, Section 7, and Article II, Section 3, give the president the power to participate authoritatively in the legislative process.

**commander in chief** the role of the president as commander of the national military and the state National Guard units (when called into service)

**Military Power**   The president's military powers are among the most important exercised by the chief executive. The position of **commander in chief** makes the president the highest military authority in the United States, with control of the entire defense establishment. The president is also head of the nation's intelligence network, which includes not only the Central Intelligence Agency (CIA) but also the National Security Council (NSC), the National Security Agency (NSA), the Federal Bureau of Investigation (FBI), and a host of less well known but very powerful international and domestic security agencies.

**War and Inherent Presidential Power**   The Constitution gives Congress the power to declare war. Presidents, however, have gone a long way toward capturing this power for themselves. Congress has not declared war since December 1941, but since then, American military forces have engaged in numerous campaigns throughout the world under the orders of the president. When North Korean forces invaded South Korea in June 1950, Congress was actually prepared to declare war, but President Harry S. Truman asserted that the president and not Congress could decide when and where to deploy America's military might. Truman dispatched American forces to Korea without a congressional declaration, and in the face of the emergency, Congress felt it had to acquiesce, and so passed a resolution approving the president's actions. This became the pattern for future

*In 2010, President Obama visited American troops in Afghanistan. A few months earlier, Obama ordered a "surge" of 30,000 reinforcements to be sent to Afghanistan. Although the strategy was controversial, even among Obama's own party, Congress approved funding for the increase in troops.*

congressional-executive relations in the military realm: the wars in Vietnam, Bosnia, Afghanistan, and Iraq, and a host of lesser conflicts, were all fought without declarations of war.

In 1973, Congress responded to presidential unilateralism by passing the **War Powers Resolution** over President Richard M. Nixon's veto. This resolution reasserted the principle of congressional war power, required the president to inform Congress of any planned military campaign, and stipulated that forces must be withdrawn within 60 days if there is no specific congressional authorization for their continued deployment. Presidents, however, have generally ignored the War Powers Resolution, claiming inherent executive power to defend the nation. Thus, President George W. Bush responded to the September 2001 attacks by Islamic terrorists by organizing a major military campaign to overthrow the Taliban regime in Afghanistan, which had sheltered the terrorists. In 2003, Bush ordered the invasion of Iraq, which he accused of posing a threat to the United States. U.S. forces overthrew the government of the Iraqi dictator, Saddam Hussein, and occupied the country. In both instances, Congress passed resolutions approving the president's actions, but the president was careful to assert that he did not need congressional authorization. The War Powers Resolution was barely mentioned on Capitol Hill and was ignored by the White House.

**Military Sources of Domestic Power**   The president's military powers extend into the domestic sphere. Article IV, Section 4, provides that the "United States shall [protect] every State . . . against Invasion . . . and . . . domestic Violence." Congress has made this an explicit presidential power through statutes directing the president as commander in chief to discharge these obligations.[4] The Constitution restrains the president's use of domestic force by providing that a state legislature (or governor when the legislature is not in session) must request federal troops before the president can send them into the state to provide public order. Yet this proviso is not absolute. First, presidents are not obligated to deploy national troops merely because the state legislature or governor makes such a request. More

**War Powers Resolution** a resolution of Congress that the president can send troops into action abroad only by authorization of Congress, or if American troops are already under attack or serious threat

# The President versus the World: How Presidents Seized Control of the War Power

**The 1973 War Powers Resolution** provided that presidents could not deploy military forces for more than 60 days without securing congressional authorization. Many in Congress saw this time limit as a restraint on presidential action, though it gave the president more discretion than the framers of the Constitution had provided. President Gerald Ford had carefully followed the letter of the law when organizing a military effort to rescue American sailors held by North Korea. But this was the first and last time that the War Powers Act was fully observed. Between 1982 and 1986, President Reagan presented Congress with a set of military faits accomplis that undermined the War Powers Act and, in effect, asserted a doctrine of sole presidential authority in the security realm.

In October 1983, while American forces were still in Lebanon, President Reagan ordered an invasion of the Caribbean island of Grenada after a coup had led to the installation of a pro-Cuban government on the island. Congress threatened to invoke the War Powers Act, but Reagan withdrew American troops before the Senate acted. In 1986, Reagan ordered the bombing of Libya in response to a terrorist attack in Berlin that the administration blamed on Libyan agents. In both cases, Reagan acted without consulting Congress and claimed that his authority had come directly from the Constitution.

Reagan's successor, George H. W. Bush, ordered an invasion of Panama designed to oust the Panamanian strongman General Manuel Noriega. Congress made no official response to the invasion. In 1990–91, the Bush administration sent a huge American military force into the Persian Gulf in response to Iraq's invasion and occupation of Kuwait. Both houses of Congress voted to authorize military action against Iraq, but Bush made it clear that he did not feel bound by any congressional declaration. Indeed, the president later pointed out that he had specifically avoided asking Capitol Hill for "authorization" since such a request might improperly imply that Congress "had the final say in . . . an executive decision."[a]

In 1994, President Clinton planned an invasion of Haiti under the cover of a UN Security Council resolution. Congress expressed strong opposition to Clinton's plans, but he pressed forward nonetheless, claiming that he did not need congressional approval. In a similar vein, between 1994 and 1998, the administration undertook a variety of military actions in the former Yugoslavia without formal congressional authorization.

In 2001, President George W. Bush ordered an attack that soon toppled Afghanistan's Taliban regime. In 2003, he sent American forces to oust Saddam Hussein's government in Iraq. Bush had congressional support for his actions but, like his predecessors, asserted that he did not need Congress's permission to undertake military action. In 2011, President Obama ordered American forces to assist in the ultimately successful NATO campaign to oust Libya's leader, Mu'ammar Qaddafi. Like his predecessors, Obama claimed Congress had no authority in this matter. It is no longer clear what war powers, if any, remain in the hands of Congress.

[a] George H. W. Bush and Brent Scowcroft, *A World Transformed* (New York: Knopf, 1998), p. 441.

## for critical analysis

1. Article I of the Constitution gives Congress the power to declare war. Why have modern presidents consistently refrained from asking Congress for such a declaration?

2. The scholar Edward Corwin said that the Constitution invited the president and Congress to struggle over war powers. What advantages have allowed presidents gradually to prevail in this struggle over the past century?

important, the president may deploy troops in a state or city without a specific request from the state legislature or governor if the president considers it necessary to maintain an essential national service during an emergency, to enforce a federal judicial order, or to protect federally guaranteed civil rights.[5]

One historic example of the unilateral use of presidential emergency power, even when the states don't request it, is the decision by President Dwight D. Eisenhower in 1957 to send troops into Little Rock, Arkansas, against the wishes of the state of Arkansas, to enforce court orders to integrate Little Rock's Central High School. The governor of Arkansas, Orval Faubus, had posted the Arkansas National Guard at the entrance to Central High School to prevent the court-ordered admission of nine black students. After an effort to negotiate with Governor Faubus failed, President Eisenhower reluctantly sent 1,000 paratroopers to Little Rock; they stood watch while the black students took their places in the all-white classrooms.

In most instances of domestic disorder, whether from human or from natural causes, presidents tend to exercise unilateral power by declaring a "state of emergency," thereby making available federal grants, insurance, and direct assistance. In 1992, in the aftermath of devastating riots in Los Angeles and hurricanes in Florida, American troops, sent in by the president, were very much in evidence, more in the role of Good Samaritans than of military police. In 2005, President Bush declared a state of emergency to allow the Federal Emergency Management Agency (FEMA) to coordinate the government's response to Hurricane Katrina, an immense storm that devastated the city of New Orleans. Bush sent federal troops to bolster local efforts.

Military emergencies have typically also led to expansion of the domestic powers of the executive branch. This was true during the First and Second World Wars and has been true in the wake of the "war on terror" as well. Within a month of the September 11, 2001, attacks, the White House had drafted and Congress had enacted the USA PATRIOT Act, expanding the power of government agencies to engage in domestic surveillance activities, including electronic surveillance, and restricting judicial review of such efforts. The act also gave the attorney general greater authority to detain and deport aliens suspected of having terrorist affiliations. The following year, Congress created the Department of Homeland Security, combining offices from 22 federal agencies into one huge new cabinet department that would be responsible for protecting the nation from attack and responding to natural disasters. The new agency includes the U.S. Coast Guard, Transportation

**TABLE 13.1**

## The Roles of the President

Chief of State (acting on behalf of all Americans)

Commander in Chief (in charge of the military)

Chief Jurist (judicial responsibilities)

Chief Diplomat (managing U.S. relations with other nations)

Chief Executive (as "boss" of the executive branch)

Chief Legislator (legislative powers)

Chief Politician (party leadership)

Security Administration, FEMA, Immigration and Customs Enforcement (ICE), and offices from the departments of Agriculture, Energy, Transportation, Justice, Health and Human Services, Commerce, and the General Services Administration, as well as other agencies. The actual reorganization plan was drafted by the White House, but Congress weighed in to make certain that the new agency's workers had civil service and union protections.

**Judicial Power**   The presidential power to grant reprieves, pardons, and amnesty involves power over all individuals who may be a threat to the security of the United States. Presidents may use this power on behalf of a particular individual, as did Gerald Ford when he pardoned Richard Nixon in 1974 "for all offenses against the United States which he . . . has committed or may have committed." Or they may use it on a large scale, as did President Andrew Johnson in 1868, when he gave full amnesty to all southerners who had participated in the "Late Rebellion," and President Carter in 1977, when he declared an amnesty for all the draft evaders of the Vietnam War. This power of life and death over others helped elevate American presidents to the level of earlier conquerors and kings, before whom supplicants might come to make their pleas for mercy.

**Diplomatic Power**   The president is America's "head of state," its chief representative in dealings with other nations, having the power to make treaties for the United States (with the advice and consent of the Senate). When President George Washington received Edmond Genêt ("Citizen Genêt") as the formal emissary of the revolutionary government of France in 1793 and had his cabinet officers and Congress back his decision, he established a greatly expanded interpretation of the power to "receive Ambassadors and other public Ministers," extending it to the power to "recognize" other countries. That power gives the president the almost unconditional authority to review the claims of any new ruling groups in order to determine whether they indeed control the territory and population of their country, so that they can commit it to treaties and other agreements.

*As head of state, the president is America's chief representative in dealings with other countries. At an official state dinner in 2011, President Obama and Michelle Obama welcomed Chinese president Hu Jintao to the White House.*

In recent years, presidents have expanded the practice of using executive agreements instead of treaties to establish relations with other countries.[6] An **executive agreement** is exactly like a treaty because it is a contract between two countries, but it does not require Senate approval. There are actually two types of executive agreements. One is the executive-congressional agreement. For this type of agreement, the president will submit the proposed arrangement to Congress for a simple majority vote in both houses, usually easier for presidents to win than the two-thirds approval of the Senate that is required for a treaty. The other type of executive agreement is the sole executive agreement, which is simply an understanding between the president and a foreign state and is not submitted to Congress for approval. In the past, sole executive agreements were used to flesh out commitments already made in treaties or to arrange for matters well below the level of policy. Since the 1930s, however, presidents have entered into sole executive agreements on important issues when they were uncertain about their prospects for securing congressional approval. For example, the General Agreement on Tariffs and Trade (GATT), one of the cornerstones of U.S. international economic policy in the post–World War II era, was based on an executive agreement. The courts have held that executive agreements have the force of law, as though they were formal treaties.

During the 1960s, Congress discovered that several presidents had entered into agreements with foreign governments and not informed Congress. This discovery led to the enactment of the 1972 Case-Zablocki Act, requiring the president to provide Congress each year with a complete list of all executive agreements signed during the course of that year. Presidents have not fully complied with this law. If they wish to keep an agreement secret, they call it by another name, such as "national security memorandum," and claim that it is not covered by the Case-Zablocki Act.

**Executive Power**   The Constitution focuses executive power and legal responsibility on the president. The famous sign on President Truman's desk, "The Buck Stops Here," was not merely an assertion of Truman's personal sense of responsibility but also his recognition of the legal and constitutional responsibility of the president. The most important basis of the president's power as chief executive is to be found in Article II, Section 3, of the Constitution, which stipulates that the president must see that all the laws are faithfully executed, and Section 2, which provides that the president will appoint, remove, and supervise all executive officers, and appoint all federal judges (with Senate approval). The power to appoint the principal executive officers and to require each of them to report to the president on subjects relating to the duties of their departments makes the president the true chief executive officer (CEO) of the nation. The president is subject to some limitations, because the appointment of all such officers, including ambassadors, ministers, and federal judges, is subject to a majority approval by the Senate. But these appointments are at the discretion of the president, and the loyalty and the responsibility of each appointee are presumed to be directed toward the president.

Another component of the president's power as chief executive is **executive privilege**, the claim that confidential communications between a president and close advisers should not be revealed without presidential consent. Presidents have made this claim ever since George Washington refused a request from the House of Representatives to deliver documents concerning negotiations of an important treaty. Washington refused (successfully) on the grounds that, first, the House was not constitutionally part of the treaty-making process, and second, diplomatic negotiations required secrecy.

**executive agreement** an agreement, made between the president and another country, that has the force of a treaty but does not require the Senate's "advice and consent"

**executive privilege** the claim that confidential communications between a president and close advisers should not be revealed without the consent of the president

Although many presidents have claimed executive privilege, the concept was not tested in the courts until the 1971 "Watergate" affair. President Richard Nixon refused congressional demands that he turn over secret White House tapes that congressional investigators suspected would establish his complicity in illegal activities. In *United States v. Nixon* (1974), the Supreme Court ordered Nixon to turn over the tapes.[7] The president complied with the order and was forced to resign from office. The *United States v. Nixon* case is often seen as a blow to presidential power, but in actuality, the Court's ruling recognized for the first time the legal validity of executive privilege, though holding that it did not apply in this particular instance. Subsequent presidents have cited *United States v. Nixon* in support of their claims of executive privilege. For example, the George W. Bush administration successfully invoked executive privilege when it refused congressional demands for records of Vice President Dick Cheney's 2001 energy task force meetings.

**Legislative Power**   The president plays a role not only in the administration of government but also in the legislative process. Two constitutional provisions are the primary sources of the president's power in the legislative arena. The first of these is the portion of Article II, Section 3, providing that the president "shall from time to time give to the Congress Information of the State of the Union, and recommend to their Consideration such Measures as he shall judge necessary and expedient." Delivering a "State of the Union" address may at first appear to be little more than the president's obligation to make recommendations for Congress's consideration. But as political and social conditions began to favor an increasingly prominent presidential role, each president, especially since Franklin Delano Roosevelt, began to rely on this provision in order to become the primary initiator of proposals for legislative action in Congress and the most important single participant in legislative decision making, as well as the principal source for public awareness of national issues.[8]

The second of the president's legislative powers is the veto power assigned by Article I, Section 7.[9] The **veto** is the president's constitutional power to reject acts of Congress (see Figure 13.1), making the president the most important single legislative leader.[10] No bill vetoed by the president can become law unless both the House and Senate override the veto by a two-thirds vote. In the case of a **pocket veto**, Congress does not have the option of overriding the veto, but must reintroduce the bill in the next session. Usually, if a president is presented with a bill and does not sign it within 10 days, it automatically becomes law. But this is true only while Congress is in session. If a president chooses not to sign a bill presented within the last 10 days of a legislative session, and Congress is out of session when the 10-day limit expires, instead of becoming law, the bill is vetoed.

Use of the veto varies according to the political situation each president confronts. George W. Bush did not find it necessary to use his veto power until 2007, when the Democrats took control of both houses of Congress. During his last two years in office, Bush vetoed 10 bills, including legislation designed to prohibit the use of harsh interrogation tactics, saying it "would take away one of the most valuable tools in the war on terror."[11] President Obama, who during his first two years in office initially enjoyed solid Democratic majorities in both houses of Congress, used his veto power only once during his

**veto** the president's constitutional power to turn down acts of Congress. A presidential veto may be overridden by a two-thirds vote of each house of Congress

**pocket veto** a presidential veto that is automatically triggered if the president does not act on a given piece of legislation passed during the final 10 days of a legislative session

*The Supreme Court's decision in* United States v. Nixon *is often seen as a blow to presidential power because Nixon was required to turn over secret tapes related to the Watergate scandal, despite his claim of executive privilege.*

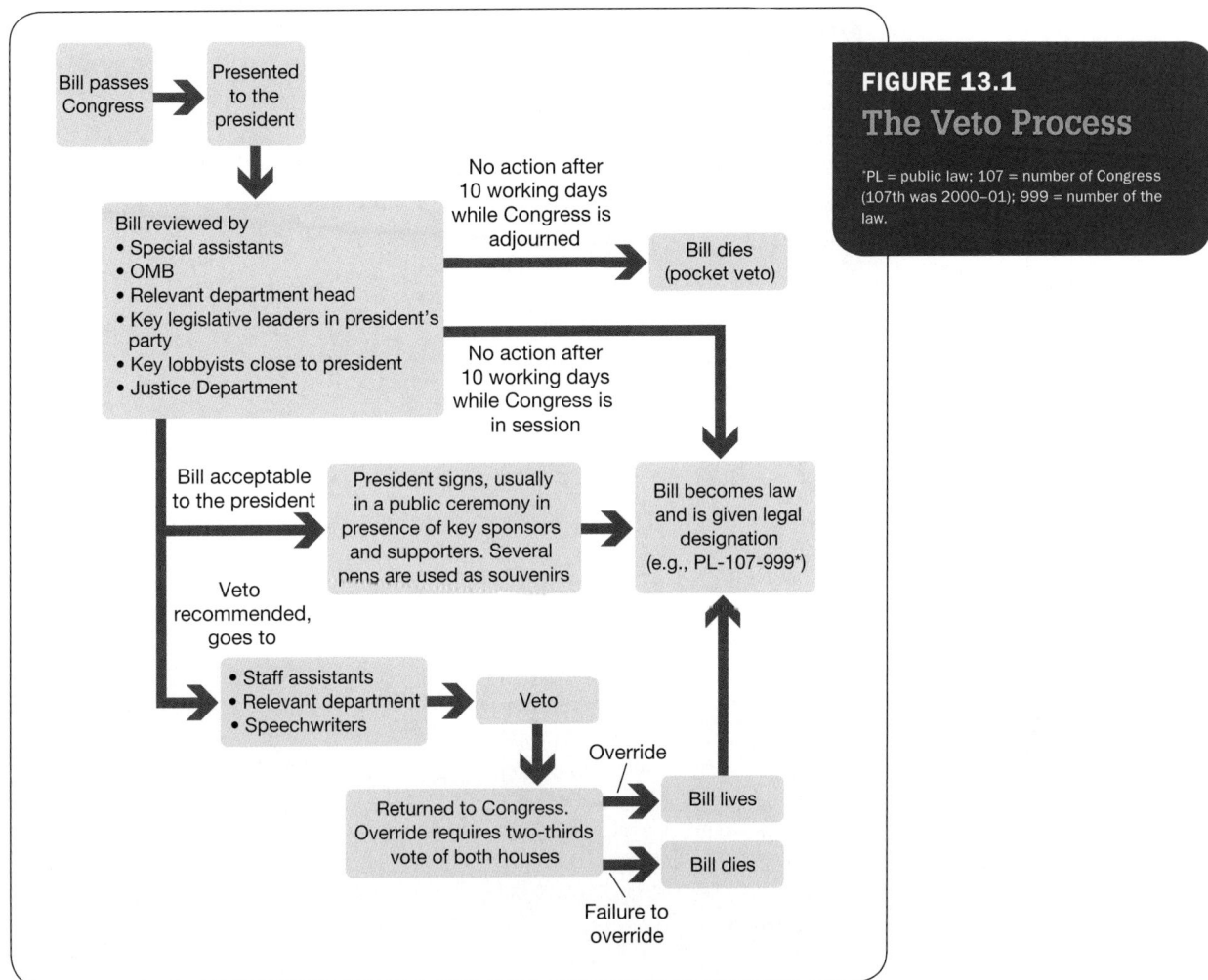

**FIGURE 13.1**
## The Veto Process

*PL = public law; 107 = number of Congress (107th was 2000–01); 999 = number of the law.

Bill passes Congress → Presented to the president → Bill reviewed by
- Special assistants
- OMB
- Relevant department head
- Key legislative leaders in president's party
- Key lobbyists close to president
- Justice Department

No action after 10 working days while Congress is adjourned → Bill dies (pocket veto)

No action after 10 working days while Congress is in session → Bill becomes law and is given legal designation (e.g., PL-107-999*)

Bill acceptable to the president → President signs, usually in a public ceremony in presence of key sponsors and supporters. Several pens are used as souvenirs → Bill becomes law and is given legal designation (e.g., PL-107-999*)

Veto recommended, goes to →
- Staff assistants
- Relevant department
- Speechwriters
→ Veto → Returned to Congress. Override requires two-thirds vote of both houses

Override → Bill lives

Failure to override → Bill dies

first year. As shown by Table 13.2, presidential vetoes are seldom overridden. Since the time of George Washington, presidents have used their veto power 2,560 times, and on only 109 occasions has Congress overridden them.

Though not explicitly, the Constitution also provides the president with the power of **legislative initiative**. The framers of the Constitution clearly saw legislative initiative as one of the keys to executive power. "Initiative" implies the ability to formulate proposals for important policies, and the president, as an individual with a great deal of staff assistance, is able to initiate decisive action more frequently than Congress, with its large assemblies that have to deliberate and debate before taking action. With some important exceptions, Congress depends on the president to set the agenda of public policy. And quite clearly, initiative confers the power of being able to set the terms of discourse in the making of public policy.

For example, during the weeks immediately following September 11, George W. Bush took many presidential initiatives to Congress, and each was given almost unanimous support—from commitments to pursue Al Qaeda, remove the Taliban, and reconstitute the Afghanistan regime, all the way to almost unlimited approval

**legislative initiative** the president's inherent power to bring a legislative agenda before Congress

## TABLE 13.2

## Presidential Vetoes, 1789–2012

| PRESIDENT | CONGRESSES | TOTAL VETOES | VETOES OVERRIDDEN |
|---|---|---|---|
| Washington | 1st–4th | 2 | ..... |
| Adams | 5th–6th | ..... | ..... |
| Jefferson | 7th–10th | ..... | ..... |
| Madison | 11th–14th | 7 | ..... |
| Monroe | 15th–18th | 1 | ..... |
| John Quincy Adams | 19th–20th | ..... | ..... |
| Jackson | 21st–24th | 12 | ..... |
| Van Buren | 25th–26th | 1 | ..... |
| Harrison | 27th | ..... | ..... |
| Tyler | 27th–28th | 10 | 1 |
| Polk | 29th–30th | 3 | ..... |
| Taylor | 31st | ..... | ..... |
| Fillmore | 31st–32nd | ..... | ..... |
| Pierce | 33rd–34th | 9 | 5 |
| Buchanan | 35th–36th | 7 | ..... |
| Lincoln | 37th–39th | 7 | ..... |
| Johnson | 39th–40th | 29 | 15 |
| Grant | 41st–44th | 93 | 4 |
| Hayes | 45th–46th | 13 | 1 |
| Garfield | 47th | ..... | ..... |
| Arthur | 47th–48th | 12 | 1 |
| Cleveland | 49th–50th | 414 | 2 |
| Harrison | 51st–52nd | 44 | 1 |
| Cleveland | 53rd–54th | 170 | 5 |
| McKinley | 55th–57th | 42 | ..... |
| Theodore Roosevelt | 57th–60th | 82 | 1 |
| Taft | 61st–62nd | 39 | 1 |
| Wilson | 63rd–66th | 44 | 6 |
| Harding | 67th | 6 | ..... |
| Coolidge | 68th–70th | 50 | 4 |
| Hoover | 71st–72nd | 37 | 3 |
| Franklin Delano Roosevelt | 73rd–79th | 635 | 9 |
| Truman | 79th–82nd | 250 | 12 |
| Eisenhower | 83rd–86th | 181 | 2 |
| Kennedy | 87th–88th | 21 | ..... |
| Johnson | 88th–90th | 30 | ..... |
| Nixon | 91st–93rd | 43 | 7 |
| Ford | 93rd–94th | 66 | 12 |
| Carter | 95th–96th | 31 | 2 |
| Reagan | 97th–100th | 78 | 9 |
| George H. W. Bush | 101st–102nd | 44 | 1 |
| Clinton | 103rd–106th | 37 | 2 |
| George W. Bush | 107th–110th | 10 | 3 |
| Barack Obama | 111th–112th | 2 | .... |
| **Total** | ............ | **2562** | **109** |

for mobilization of both military force and the power to regulate American civil liberties.

The president's initiative does not end with congressional policy making and the making of laws in the ordinary sense of the term. The president has still another legislative role (in all but name) within the executive branch. This is designated as the power to issue **executive orders**. The executive order is first and foremost simply a normal tool of management, a power that virtually any CEO has to make "company policy"—rules-setting procedures, etiquette, chains of command, functional responsibilities, and so on. But evolving out of this normal management practice is a recognized presidential power to promulgate rules that have the effect and the formal status of legislation. Most presidential executive orders provide for the reorganization of structures and procedures or otherwise direct the affairs of the executive branch—to be applied either across the board to all agencies or to a single agency or department. One of the most important examples is Executive Order No. 8248, September 8, 1939, establishing the divisions of the Executive Office of the President. Another one of equal importance is President Nixon's executive order in 1970–71 establishing the Environmental Protection Agency (EPA), which included establishment of the Environmental Impact Statement.

This legislative or policy leadership role of the presidency is an institutionalized feature of the office that exists independent of the occupant of the office. That is to say, anyone duly elected president would possess these powers regardless of his or her individual energy or leadership characteristics.[12]

**executive order** a rule or regulation issued by the president that has the effect and formal status of legislation

## Delegated Powers

Many of the powers exercised by the president and the executive branch are not found in the Constitution but are the products of congressional statutes and resolutions. Over the past century, Congress has voluntarily delegated a great deal of its own legislative authority to the executive branch. To some extent, this delegation of power has been an almost inescapable consequence of the expansion of government activity in the United States since the New Deal. Given the vast range of the federal government's responsibilities, Congress cannot execute and administer all the programs it creates and the laws it enacts. Inevitably, Congress must turn to the hundreds of departments and agencies in the executive branch or, when necessary, create new agencies to implement its goals. Thus, for example, in 2002, when Congress sought to protect America from terrorist attacks, it established a Department of Homeland Security with broad powers in the realms of law enforcement, public health, and immigration. Similarly, in 1970, when Congress enacted legislation designed to improve the nation's air and water quality, it assigned the task of implementing its goals to the new EPA, created by President Nixon's executive order and empowered by Congress to set and enforce air- and water-quality standards.

As they implement congressional legislation, federal agencies collectively develop thousands of rules and regulations and issue thousands of orders and findings every year. Agencies interpret Congress's intent, promulgate rules aimed at implementing that intent, and issue orders to individuals, firms, and organizations to impel them to conform to the law. When it establishes an agency, Congress sometimes grants it only limited discretionary authority, providing very specific guidelines and standards that must be followed by the administrators charged with the program's implementation. Take the Internal Revenue Service (IRS), for

**for critical analysis**

Presidents have expressed, delegated, and inherent sources of power. Which of the three do you think most accounts for the powers of the presidency?

*In 2011 the Obama administration instructed the Justice Department to stop enforcing the Defense of Marriage Act, a federal law that defines marriage as the union of one man and one woman. Although Congress makes the laws, the president (as head of the executive branch) oversees the agencies that implement the laws.*

example. Most Americans view the IRS as a powerful agency whose dictates can have an immediate and sometimes unpleasant impact on their lives. In fact, congressional tax legislation is very specific and detailed, leaving little to the discretion of IRS administrators.[13] The agency certainly develops numerous rules and procedures to enhance tax collection. It is Congress, however, that establishes the structure of the tax liabilities, tax exemptions, and tax deductions that determine each taxpayer's burdens and responsibilities.

In most instances, though, congressional legislation is not very detailed. Often, Congress defines a broad goal or objective and delegates enormous discretionary power to administrators to determine how that goal is to be achieved. For example, the 1970 act creating the Occupational Safety and Health Administration (OSHA) states as Congress's purpose "to assure so far as is possible every working man and woman in the nation safe and healthful working conditions." The act, however, neither defines such conditions nor suggests how they might be achieved.[14] The result is that agency administrators have enormous discretionary power to draft rules and regulations that have the effect of law. Indeed, the courts treat these administrative rules like congressional statutes. For all intents and purposes, when Congress creates an agency such as OSHA or the Department of Homeland Security, giving it a broad mandate to achieve some desirable outcome, it transfers its own legislative power to the executive branch.

During the nineteenth and early twentieth centuries, Congress typically wrote laws that provided fairly clear principles and standards to guide executive implementation. For example, the 1923 tariff act empowered the president to increase or decrease duties on certain manufactured goods in order to reduce the difference in costs between domestically produced products and those manufactured abroad. The act authorized the president to make the final determination, but his discretionary authority was quite constrained. The statute listed the criteria the president was to consider, fixed the permissible range of tariff changes, and outlined the procedures to be used to calculate the cost differences between foreign and domestic goods. When an importer challenged a particular executive decision as an abuse of

# Who Are America's Presidents?

American presidents have all been men and have all been Christians. Until the election of Barack Obama in 2008, they had all been white. As the data show, a majority of presidents have come from the southeastern United States, with Virginia producing the most American presidents, especially in the nation's first decades.

## U.S. Presidents, 1789–2013

| PRESIDENT | PARTY | RACE | RELIGION | STATE |
|-----------|-------|------|----------|-------|
| Washington | ■ | ● | ✚ | VA |
| Adams | ■ | ● | ✚ | MA |
| Jefferson | ▨ | ● | ✚ | VA |
| Madison | ▨ | ● | ✚ | VA |
| Monroe | ▨ | ● | ✚ | VA |
| Quincy Adams | ■ ▨ ▨ | ● | ✚ | MA |
| Jackson | ■ | ● | ✚ | * |
| Van Buren | ■ | ● | ✚ | NY |
| W. Harrison | ▨ | ● | ✚ | VA |
| Tyler | ▨ ■ | ● | ✚ | VA |
| Polk | ■ | ● | ✚ | NC |
| Taylor | ▨ | ● | ✚ | VA |
| Fillmore | ▨ | ● | ✚ | NY |
| Pierce | ■ | ● | ✚ | NH |
| Buchanan | ■ | ● | ✚ | PA |
| Lincoln | ▨ ■ | ● | ✚ | KY |
| A. Johnson | ■ ■ | ● | ✚ | NC |
| Grant | ▨ | ● | ✚ | OH |
| Hayes | ▨ | ● | ✚ | OH |
| Garfield | ▨ | ● | ✚ | OH |
| Arthur | ▨ | ● | ✚ | VT |
| Cleveland | ■ | ● | ✚ | NJ |

| PRESIDENT | PARTY | RACE | RELIGION | STATE |
|-----------|-------|------|----------|-------|
| B. Harrison | ▨ | ● | ✚ | OH |
| McKinley | ▨ | ● | ✚ | OH |
| T. Roosevelt | ▨ | ● | ✚ | NY |
| Taft | ▨ | ● | ✚ | OH |
| Wilson | ■ | ● | ✚ | VA |
| Harding | ▨ | ● | ✚ | OH |
| Coolidge | ▨ | ● | ✚ | VT |
| Hoover | ▨ | ● | ✚ | IA |
| F. Roosevelt | ■ | ● | ✚ | NY |
| Truman | ■ | ● | ✚ | MO |
| Eisenhower | ▨ | ● | ✚ | TX |
| Kennedy | ■ | ● | ✚ | MA |
| L. Johnson | ■ | ● | ✚ | TX |
| Nixon | ▨ | ● | ✚ | CA |
| Ford | ▨ | ● | ✚ | NE |
| Carter | ■ | ● | ✚ | GA |
| Reagan | ▨ | ● | ✚ | IL |
| G.H.W. Bush | ▨ | ● | ✚ | MA |
| Clinton | ■ | ● | ✚ | AR |
| G.W. Bush | ▨ | ● | ✚ | CT |
| Obama | ■ | ◐ | ✚ | HI |

**Key**

**PARTY**
- ▨ Federalist
- ▨ Democratic-Republican
- ▨ Whig
- ▨ Unionist
- ■ Democrat
- ▨ Republican

**RACE**
- ● White
- ◐ African American

**RELIGION**
- ✚ Christian: Protestant
- ✚ Christian: Catholic

*Waxhaw area, on North Carolina–South Carolina border

## U.S. Presidents, by Region

**Presidents**
- ○ 0
- ● 1
- ● 2
- ● 4
- ● 7
- ● 8

SOURCE: The Miller Center, "American President: A Reference Resource," millercenter.org (accessed 10/15/12).

## for critical analysis

1. Why do you think all presidents have been Christian men and all but one have been white? Do you think this is likely to change in coming years?

2. Why do you think so many presidents have come from the South and the East? What electoral or historical factors may have produced this trend?

delegated power, the Supreme Court had no difficulty finding that the president was merely acting in accordance with Congress's directives.[15]

At least since the New Deal, however, Congress has tended to give executive agencies broad mandates and to draft legislation that offers few clear standards or guidelines for implementation by the executive. For example, the 1933 National Industrial Recovery Act gave the president the authority to set rules to bring about fair competition in key sectors of the economy without ever defining what the term meant or how it was to be achieved.[16] Similarly, the 1938 Agricultural Adjustment Act, which led to a system of commodity price supports and agricultural production restrictions, authorized the secretary of agriculture to make agricultural marketing "orderly" but offered no guidance regarding the commodities to be affected, how markets were to be organized, or how prices should be determined. All these decisions were left to the discretion of the secretary and his agents.[17] This pattern of broad delegation became typical in the ensuing decades. The 1972 Consumer Product Safety Act, for example, authorizes the Consumer Product Safety Commission to reduce unreasonable risk of injury from household products but offers no suggestions to guide the commission's determination of what constitutes reasonable and unreasonable risks or how these are to be reduced.[18]

This shift from the nineteenth-century pattern of relatively well-defined congressional guidelines for administrators to the more contemporary pattern of broad delegations of congressional power to the executive branch is, to be sure, partially a consequence of the great scope and complexity of the tasks that America's contemporary government has undertaken. During much of the nineteenth century, the federal government had relatively few domestic responsibilities, and Congress could pay close attention to details. Today, the operation of an enormous executive establishment and literally thousands of programs under varied and changing circumstances requires that administrators be allowed some considerable measure of discretion to carry out their jobs. Nevertheless, the end result is to shift power from Congress to the executive branch.

## ● The Presidency as an Institution

> Identify the institutional resources presidents have to help them exercise their powers

The framers of the Constitution, as we saw, created a unitary executive because they thought this would make the presidency a more energetic institution. Nevertheless, since the ratification of the Constitution, the president has been joined by thousands of officials and staffers who work for, assist, or advise the chief executive (see Figure 13.2). Collectively, these individuals could be said to make up the institutional presidency and to give the president a capacity for action that no single individual, however energetic, could duplicate. The first component of the institutional presidency is the president's Cabinet.

### The Cabinet

In the American system of government, the **Cabinet** is the traditional but informal designation for the heads of all the major federal government departments. The

**Cabinet** the secretaries, or chief administrators, of the major departments of the federal government. Cabinet secretaries are appointed by the president with the consent of the Senate

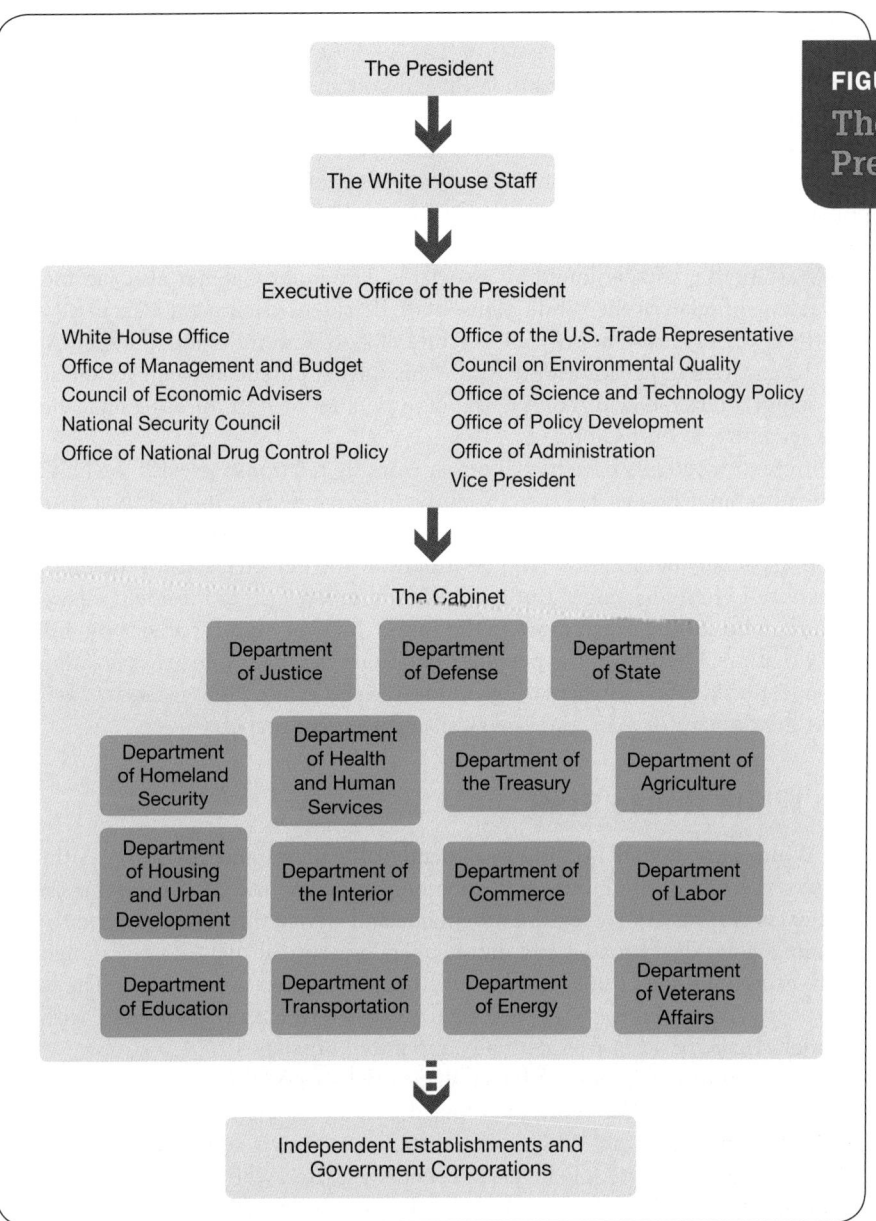

FIGURE 13.2
The Institutional
Presidency

The President

The White House Staff

Executive Office of the President

White House Office
Office of Management and Budget
Council of Economic Advisers
National Security Council
Office of National Drug Control Policy

Office of the U.S. Trade Representative
Council on Environmental Quality
Office of Science and Technology Policy
Office of Policy Development
Office of Administration
Vice President

The Cabinet

Department of Justice

Department of Defense

Department of State

Department of Homeland Security

Department of Health and Human Services

Department of the Treasury

Department of Agriculture

Department of Housing and Urban Development

Department of the Interior

Department of Commerce

Department of Labor

Department of Education

Department of Transportation

Department of Energy

Department of Veterans Affairs

Independent Establishments and Government Corporations

Cabinet has no constitutional status. Unlike in Great Britain and many other parliamentary countries, where the cabinet is the government, the American Cabinet is not a collective body. It meets but makes no decisions as a group. Each appointment must be approved by the Senate, but cabinet members are not responsible to the Senate or to Congress at large.

Since cabinet appointees generally have not shared political careers with the president or with one another, and since they may meet literally for the first time only after their selection, this motley collection of appointees is unlikely to form an effective governing group. Although President Clinton's insistence on a cabinet diverse enough "to look like America" could be considered an act of political wisdom, it virtually guaranteed that few of his appointees had ever spent much time working together or even knew the policy positions or beliefs of the other appointees.[19]

Some presidents have relied more heavily on an "inner cabinet." This includes the **National Security Council (NSC)**. The NSC, established by law in 1947, is composed of the president, the vice president, the secretary of state, the secretary of defense, and other officials invited by the president. It has its own staff of foreign policy specialists run by the special assistant to the president for national security affairs. For these highest appointments, presidents often turn to people from outside Washington, usually longtime associates. The inner Cabinet also can include the ranking officials of the White House staff. President Obama (at least in his early months in office) relied heavily on his chief of staff, Rahm Emanuel, who resigned in 2010 and was replaced by Pete Rouse; his former chief campaign strategist and now senior adviser, David Axelrod; the deputy chief of staff, Jim Messina; and the press secretary, Robert Gibbs.

Different presidents have had different working relationships with the NSC and other subcabinet bodies, because executive management is inherently a personal matter. For example, the NSC staff was of immense importance under President Nixon, especially because it served essentially as the personal staff of the presidential assistant Henry Kissinger. But it was of less importance to President George H. W. Bush, who turned much more to the Joint Chiefs of Staff for advice on military policy matters. Despite all the personal variations, however, one generalization can be made: presidents have increasingly preferred the White House staff to the Cabinet as their means of managing the gigantic executive branch.

## The White House Staff

The **White House staff** is composed mainly of analysts and advisers.[20] Although many of the top White House staff members are given the title "special assistant" for a particular task or sector, the judgments and advice they are supposed to provide are a good deal broader and more generally political than those coming from the Executive Office of the President or from the cabinet departments. The members of the White House staff also tend to be more closely associated with the president than are other presidentially appointed officials.

From an informal group of fewer than a dozen people (popularly called the **Kitchen Cabinet**) and no more than four dozen at its height during the Roosevelt presidency in 1937, the White House staff has grown substantially.[21] Richard Nixon employed 550 people in 1972. President Carter, who found so many of the trappings of presidential power distasteful, and who publicly vowed to keep his staff small and decentralized, built an even larger and more centralized staff. President Clinton reduced the White House staff by 20 percent, but a large White House staff is still essential.

## The Executive Office of the President

Created in 1939, the **Executive Office of the President (EOP)** is a major part of what is often called the "institutional presidency"—the permanent agencies that perform defined management tasks for the president. Somewhere between 1,500 and 2,000 highly specialized people work for EOP agencies.[22] The importance of each agency in the EOP varies according to the personal orientation of each president. The most important and the largest EOP agency is the Office of Management and Budget (OMB). Its roles in preparing the national budget, designing the president's program, reporting on agency activities, and overseeing regulatory proposals connect the OMB to every conceivable presidential responsibility. The status and power of the OMB have grown in importance with each successive president, and the director of the OMB is now one of the most powerful officials in Washington. At one time the process of budgeting was a "bottom-up" procedure, with expenditure and program requests passing from the lowest bureaus through the departments to "clearance" in the OMB and thence to Congress, where each agency could be called in to explain what its "original request" was before the OMB revised it. Now the budgeting process is "top-down": the OMB sets the terms of discourse for agencies as well as for Congress.

The staff of the Council of Economic Advisers (CEA) constantly analyzes the economy and economic trends in order to help the president anticipate events, rather than waiting and reacting to them. The Council on Environmental Quality was designed to do for environmental issues what the CEA does for economic issues. The NSC—the "inner Cabinet" mentioned earlier—is composed of designated cabinet officials who meet regularly with the president to give advice on the large national security picture. The staff of the NSC assimilates and analyzes data from all intelligence-gathering agencies (CIA, etc.). Other EOP agencies perform more specialized tasks.

## The Vice Presidency

The vice presidency is a constitutional anomaly even though the office was created along with the presidency by the Constitution. The vice president exists for two purposes only: to succeed the president in case of death, resignation, or incapacity and to preside over the Senate, casting a tie-breaking vote when necessary.[23]

The main value of the vice president as a political resource for the president is electoral. Traditionally, presidential candidates choose running mates who can win the support of at least one state (preferably a large one) that may not otherwise support the ticket. It is very doubtful that John Kennedy would have won in 1960 without his vice-presidential candidate, Lyndon Johnson, and the contribution Johnson made to winning in Texas. Another traditional guideline holds that the vice-presidential nominee should provide some regional balance and, wherever possible, ideological or ethnic balance as well. In 2008, Barack Obama chose Senator Joseph Biden of Delaware to be his running mate for a number of reasons. To begin with, Biden is Catholic and has blue-collar origins. Obama believed correctly

*Vice President Joseph Biden had 35 years' experience in the Senate before Barack Obama picked him as his running mate. In particular, Biden's foreign policy experience was seen as an important strength in the campaign and the Obama administration. Here, Biden meets with Jordan's King Abdullah II.*

that Biden would appeal to these important groups in such must-win states as Pennsylvania and Ohio. Perhaps even more important, Biden possesses enormous foreign policy experience and chaired the Senate Foreign Relations Committee. The Republicans had often pointed to Obama's lack of experience in the international realm as indicating that he was not ready to be president; Democrats hoped that Biden's presence on the ticket would put the "experience" issue to rest.

As the institutional presidency has grown in size and complexity, most presidents of the past 25 years have sought to use their vice presidents as a management resource after the election. President Clinton, for example, relied greatly on his vice president, Al Gore, to oversee the National Performance Review (NPR), an ambitious program to "reinvent" the way the federal government conducts its affairs. President George W. Bush granted unprecedented power and responsibility to his vice president, Dick Cheney, who helped shape the "war on terror." In the Obama White House, Vice President Biden is said to be regarded as the "skeptic-in-chief."[24] Biden's role is to question and criticize policy recommendations made to the president—until, of course, the president makes a decision, at which point the vice president falls loyally into step.

The vice president is also important because, in the event of the death or incapacity of the president, he or she will succeed to the nation's highest office. During the course of American history, six vice presidents have had to replace presidents who died in office. One vice president, Gerald Ford, found himself at the head of the nation when President Richard Nixon was forced to resign as a result of the Watergate scandal. During the 2004 vice-presidential debates, Dick Cheney sought to distinguish himself from the Democratic vice-presidential nominee, John Edwards, by averring that he, unlike the less-experienced Edwards, had been chosen for his ability to serve as president if that became necessary.

Until the ratification of the Twenty-Fifth Amendment in 1965, the succession of the vice president to the presidency was a tradition, launched by John Tyler when he assumed the presidency after William Henry Harrison's death, rather than a constitutional or statutory requirement. The Twenty-Fifth Amendment codified this tradition by providing that the vice president would assume the presidency in the event of the chief executive's death or incapacity and setting forth the procedures that would be followed. In the event that both the president and vice president are killed, the Presidential Succession Act of 1947 establishes an order of succession, beginning with the Speaker of the House and continuing with the president of the Senate and the Cabinet secretaries. This piece of legislation, adopted during the Cold War and prompted by fear of a nuclear attack, has taken on new importance in an age of global terrorism.

*During the 2008 and 2012 presidential campaigns, Michelle Obama campaigned for her husband, speaking at rallies and appearing on talk shows. As first lady, she has worked on numerous issues, including childhood obesity.*

## The First Spouse

The president serves as both chief executive and chief of state—the equivalent of Great Britain's prime minister and monarch rolled into one, simultaneously leading the government and representing the nation at official ceremonies and functions.

Because they are generally associated exclusively with the head-of-state aspect of America's presidency, presidential spouses are usually not subject to the same sort of media scrutiny or partisan attack as that aimed at the president. Traditionally, most first ladies have limited their activities to the ceremonial portion of the presidency: greeting foreign dignitaries, visiting other countries, and attending important national ceremonies.

Some first spouses, however, have had considerable influence over policy. Franklin Roosevelt's wife, Eleanor, was widely popular, but also widely criticized, for her active role in many elements of her husband's presidency. During the 1992 campaign, Bill Clinton often implied that his wife would be active in the administration; he joked that voters would get "two for the price of one." And indeed, after the election, Hillary Clinton took a leading role in many policy areas, most notably heading the administration's health care reform effort. She also became the first first lady to seek public office on her own, winning a seat in the U.S. Senate in 2000 and then running for president in 2008. Later, President Obama named Clinton secretary of state. Barack Obama's wife, Michelle, is a lawyer and served for a number of years as a senior administrator at the University of Chicago's Pritzker School of Medicine. Given her legal and policy background, Michelle Obama seemed likely to become a visible and activist first lady on the Hillary Clinton model, but generally she has played a mainly behind-the-scenes role.

## The President and Policy

The president's powers and institutional resources, taken together, give the chief executive a substantial voice in the nation's policy-making processes. Strictly speaking, presidents cannot introduce legislation—only members of Congress can formally propose new programs and policies. Nevertheless, a great many of the major bills acted on by the Congress are crafted by the president and his aides and then introduced by friendly legislators. Congress has come to expect the president to propose the government's budget, and the nation has come to expect presidential initiatives to deal with major problems. Some of these initiatives have come in the form of huge packages of programs—Franklin Delano Roosevelt's "New Deal" and Lyndon Johnson's "Great Society." Sometimes presidents craft a single program they hope will have a significant impact on the nation and on their political fortunes. For example, Bill Clinton developed a major health care reform initiative whose political defeat marked a significant setback for his presidency. George W. Bush made the "war on terror" the centerpiece of his administration and brought about the creation of a new cabinet department, the Department of Homeland Security, and the enactment of legislation such as the USA PATRIOT Act to give the executive branch more power to confront the terrorist threat. Bush also presided over a huge expansion of the Medicare program to provide prescription drug benefits for senior citizens. Bush may have lacked a strong claim of popular support in the wake of the controversial 2000 election, but the expressed and delegated powers of the office gave him the resources through which to achieve significant goals. President Barack Obama emphasized health care for all Americans by making the Affordable Care Act the centerpiece of his presidency.

At one time, historians and journalists liked to debate the question of strong versus weak presidents. Some presidents, such as Abraham Lincoln and FDR, were called "strong" for their leadership and their ability to guide the nation's political agenda. Others, such as James Buchanan and Calvin Coolidge, were seen as "weak" for failing to develop significant legislative programs and seeming to observe rather than shape political events. Today, the strong-versus-weak categorization has become moot. Every president is strong, not so much as a function of personal charisma or political savvy but as a reflection of the increasing power of the presidency. Let us see how this came about.

# The Contemporary Bases of Presidential Power

Explain how modern presidents have become even more powerful

During the nineteenth century, Congress was America's dominant institution of government, and members of Congress sometimes treated the president with disdain. Today, however, no one would assert that the presidency is unimportant. Presidents seek to dominate the policy-making process and claim the power to lead the nation in time of war. The expansion of presidential power over the course of the past century has come about not by accident but as the result of an ongoing effort by successive presidents to enlarge the powers of the office.

Generally, presidents can expand their power in three ways: through the party, through popular mobilization, and through the administration. In the first instance, presidents may create or strengthen partisan institutions that can exert influence in the legislative process and can help implement their programs. In addition, presidents may use popular appeals to create a mass base of support that will allow them to dominate their political foes, a tactic called "going public."[25] Third, presidents may seek to bolster their control of established executive agencies or to create new administrative institutions and procedures that will reduce their dependence on Congress and give them a more independent governing and policy-making capability. Perhaps the most obvious example of this is the use of executive orders to achieve policy goals in lieu of seeking to persuade Congress to enact legislation.

## Party as a Source of Power

Each president has relied on his own party to implement his legislative agendas. President George W. Bush, for example, worked closely with congressional GOP leaders on such matters as energy policy and Medicare reform. But the president does not control his party; party members have considerable autonomy. Moreover, in America's system of separated powers, the president's party may be in the minority in Congress and unable to do much for the chief executive's programs (see Figure 13.3). Consequently, although their party is valuable to chief executives, it has not been a fully reliable presidential tool. As a result, contemporary presidents are more likely to use the two other methods, popular mobilization and executive administration, to achieve their political goals.

## Going Public

In the nineteenth century, it was considered inappropriate for presidents to engage in personal campaigning on their own behalf or in support of programs and policies. When Andrew Johnson broke this unwritten rule and made a series of speeches vehemently seeking public support for his Reconstruction program, even some of his supporters were shocked at what they saw as his lack of decorum and dignity. The president's opponents cited his "inflammatory" speeches in one of the articles of impeachment drafted by the Congress.[26]

In the twentieth century, though, popular mobilization became a favored weapon in the political arsenals of most presidents. The first to make systematic

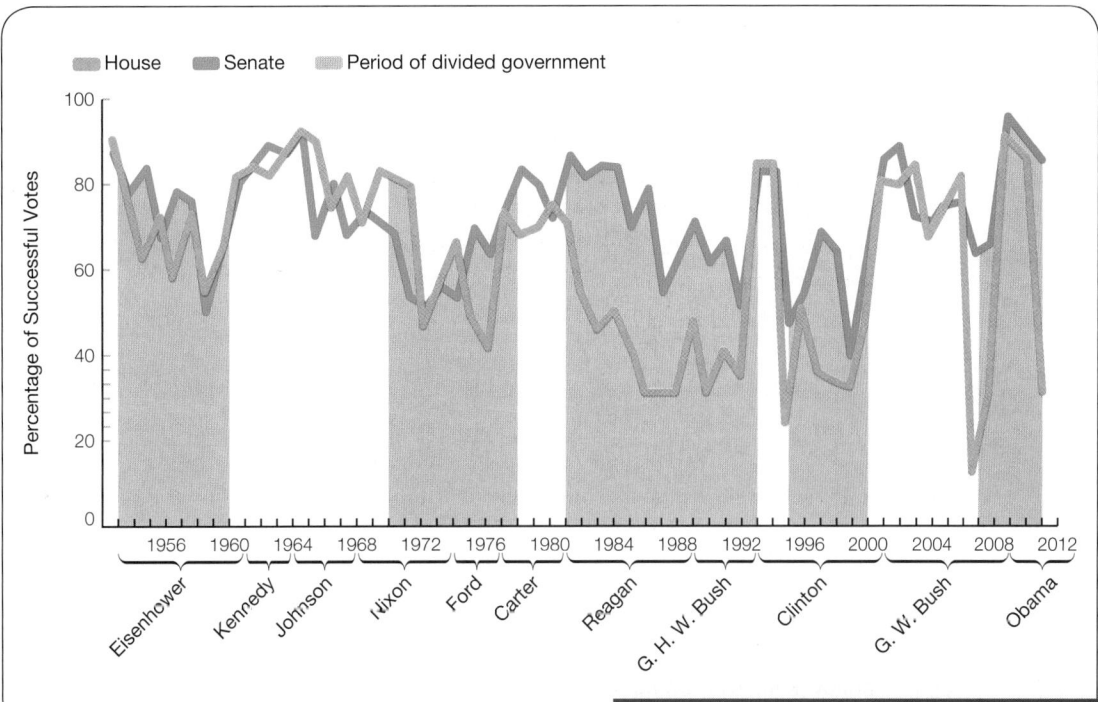

**FIGURE 13.3**

**Presidential Success on Congressional Votes, 1953–2011\***

Presidents have more success in Congress when their party is in the majority. Can you identify the periods when presidents had majority support in Congress and when they did not?

\*Percentages based on votes on which presidents took a position.
SOURCE: *Congressional Quarterly*
CREDIT: *Nelson HSU/NPR*

use of appeals to the public were Theodore Roosevelt and Woodrow Wilson, but the president who used public appeals most effectively was Franklin Delano Roosevelt. FDR was "firmly persuaded of the need to form a direct link between the executive office and the public."[27] Roosevelt developed a number of tactics for forging such a link. He often embarked on speaking trips around the nation to promote his programs. On one such tour, he told a crowd, "I regain strength just by meeting the American people."[28] In addition, FDR made effective use of a new electronic medium, the radio, to reach millions of Americans. In his famous "fireside chats," the president's voice could be heard in every living room in the country, discussing programs and policies and generally assuring Americans that Franklin Delano Roosevelt was aware of their difficulties and working diligently toward solutions.

Roosevelt was also an innovator in the realm of what now might be called press relations. When he entered the White House, FDR faced a mainly hostile press, typically controlled by conservative members of the business establishment. As the president wrote, "All the fat-cat newspapers—85 percent of the whole—have been utterly opposed to everything the Administration is seeking."[29] Roosevelt hoped to be able to use the press to mold public opinion, but to do so he needed to circumvent the editors and publishers who were generally unsympathetic to his goals. To this end, the president worked to cultivate the reporters who covered the White House. Roosevelt made himself available for biweekly press conferences where he offered candid answers to reporters' questions and made certain to make important policy announcements that would provide the reporters with significant stories

*President Franklin Delano Roosevelt's direct appeals to the American people allowed him to "reach over the heads" of congressional opponents and force them to follow his lead because their constituents demanded it.*

for their papers.[30] Roosevelt was the first president to designate a press secretary, Stephen Early, who was charged with organizing the press conferences and making certain that reporters observed the informal rules distinguishing those presidential comments that could be attributed directly to the president from those that were off the record.

Every president since FDR has sought to craft a public-relations strategy that would emphasize the incumbent's strengths and maximize his popular appeal. For John F. Kennedy, handsome and quick-witted, the televised press conference was an excellent public-relations vehicle. Johnson and Nixon lacked Kennedy's charisma, but both were effective television speakers, usually reading from a prepared text. Bill Clinton made extensive use of televised town meetings—carefully staged events that gave the president an opportunity to appear to consult with rank-and-file citizens about his goals and policies without having to face the sorts of pointed questions preferred by reporters.

One Clinton innovation was to make the White House Communications Office an important institution within the EOP. The Communications Office became responsible not only for responding to reporters' queries but also for developing and implementing a coordinated communications strategy—promoting the president's policy goals, developing responses to adverse news stories, and making certain that a favorable image of the president would, insofar as possible, dominate the news. George W. Bush relied heavily on material crafted by the Communications Office, whereas Barack Obama often relies on his own formidable speaking abilities.

**The Limits of Going Public**   Some presidents have been able to make effective use of popular appeals to overcome congressional opposition. Popular support, though, has not been a firm foundation for presidential power: the public is notoriously fickle. During his first two years in office, Ronald Reagan's approval rating ranged from a high of 59 percent in 1981 to a low of 37 percent in early 1983.[31] As Reagan's poll standing fell, his ability to overawe Democratic opponents and retain the support of wavering Republicans diminished sharply. After America's triumph in the 1990 Persian Gulf War, President George H. W. Bush scored a remarkable 90 percent approval rating in the polls. Two years later, however, after the 1991 budget crisis, Bush's support plummeted, and the president was defeated in his bid for re-election. His son, President George W. Bush, maintained an approval rating of over 70 percent for more than a year following the September 11 terrorist attacks. By the end of 2005, however, President Bush's approval rating had dropped to 39 percent as a result of the growing unpopularity of the Iraq War, the administration's inept handling of hurricane relief, and a number of White House scandals, including the conviction of Vice President Cheney's chief of staff on charges of lying to a federal grand jury. Such declines in popular approval during a president's term in office are nearly inevitable and follow a predictable pattern.[32] Both before and after they are elected, presidents generate popular support by promising to undertake important programs that will contribute directly to the well-being of large numbers of Americans. Almost without exception, presidential performance falls short of promises and popular expectations, leading to a decline in public support and the ensuing weakening of presidential influence.[33] It is a rare American president, such as Bill Clinton, who exits the White House more popular than when he went in.

# The Digital President

**As the only elected official** accountable to all Americans, the president has to make communication between him or herself and the people a priority. Communication with the people is also a key tool presidents can use to pressure Congress to enact their policy agendas. FDR's fireside chats were broadcast on the radio and brought the words of the president into citizens' homes during the crises of the Great Depression and World War II. In the early 1960s, President John F. Kennedy was the first to use television to communicate with the mass public.

President Barack Obama has also been the first to make full use of a new communication medium—in this case, the Internet. Some political commentators argue that without the Internet, Barack Obama would not have been elected president in 2008. Drawing on the interactive tools of the Web, Obama's campaign changed the way politicians organize supporters, advertise to voters, defend against attacks, and communicate with their constituents. His website, www.barackobama.com, was also the centerpiece of his 2012 campaign.

One reason the Internet is such an effective means of organizing presidential campaigns is because of cost. Obama's campaign organized supporters online, a feat that in the past would have required an army of volunteers and paid organizers on the ground. The Internet allows the organization of volunteers at a fraction of the cost of traditional campaigns. Obama's campaigns took advantage of free

advertising on YouTube rather than relying exclusive on television ads. Online political videos may be more effective than television ads because viewers make a conscious choice to watch them, instead of having their television program interrupted by an unwanted ad. Obama's YouTube video ads in the 2008 election were watched for 14.5 million hours. By comparison, purchasing 14.5 million hours on broadcast TV would have cost an estimated $47 million. President Obama's 37-minute speech on race ("A More Perfect Union") was watched online by 7 million people. The efficient use of the Internet allowed the Obama campaign to spend the vast funds raised from supporters more efficiently.

The Internet has not only changed the way modern presidents campaign but also how they govern. The Whitehouse .gov website keeps the president's constituents abreast of his policy agenda with a weekly streaming video address by the president, press briefings, speeches and remarks, a daily blog, photos of the president, the White House schedule, and other information. Virtually everything the president does is recorded online. YouTube airs Obama's press conferences and public appearances on a daily basis. Every presidential address is now streamed live online. Circumventing television and other traditional media, the Internet allows the president to broadcast his policy ideas directly to the citizens. In March 2012, Obama broke new media ground

again, appearing on Bill Simmons's "B.S. Report" (a regular series of podcasts on ESPN's website) in the first-ever podcast with a sitting U.S. president.

Obama's Facebook page personalizes the president's connection with his constituents and the causes they care about. As of July 2012, Barack Obama's Facebook page had more than 27 million "likes." In June 2012, Obama had 16.5 million Twitter followers.

A social media analysis firm found that social media users appear to be less influenced by negative advertising, which dominates campaign communications on television. Facebook users were more interested in positive posts focusing on successes, accomplishments, and the candidates' private lives than in standard campaign rhetoric. This suggests that new media hold promise for creating a positive forum for political discussion and increasing confidence in presidential leadership.

Websites, podcasts, Facebook, and other new media forums facilitate direct communication between the president and the people, creating a virtual network of constituents. Like FDR in the 1930s and '40s, and Kennedy in the 1960s, Obama may have changed how presidents govern for some time to come.

SOURCES: Juliana Gruenwald, "New Data Show Obama ahead in Social-Media Race." *National Journal*, June 14, 2012. Claire Cain Miller, "How Obama's Internet Campaign Changed Politics." *New York Times*, November 7, 2008. David Plouffe, *The Audacity to Win: The Inside Story and Lessons of Barack Obama's Historic Victory* (New York: Penguin Group Publishers, 2009).

## for critical analysis

1. Will the Internet and social media become more important to modern presidents than television, just as television replaced FDR's radio addresses?

2. What are the advantages and disadvantages of presidents governing via digital media?

*President Obama has held town hall meetings on issues such as health care reform and the economy, as a way to consult (or appear to consult) ordinary Americans about goals and policies.*

## The Administrative State

Contemporary presidents have increased the administrative capabilities of their office in three ways. First, they have enhanced the reach and power of the EOP. Second, they have sought to increase White House control over the federal bureaucracy. Third, they have expanded the role of executive orders and other instruments of direct presidential governance. Taken together, these three components of what might be called the White House "administrative strategy" have given presidents a capacity to achieve their programmatic and policy goals even when they are unable to secure congressional approval. Indeed, some recent presidents have been able to accomplish a great deal with remarkably little congressional, partisan, or even public support.

**The Growth of the EOP** The EOP has grown from six administrative assistants in 1939 to today's 400 employees working directly for the president in the White House office, along with some 1,400 individuals staffing the several (currently eight) divisions of the Executive Office.[34] The creation and growth of the White House staff gives the president an enormously enhanced capacity to gather information, plan programs and strategies, communicate with constituencies, and exercise supervision over the executive branch. The staff multiplies the president's eyes, ears, and arms, becoming a critical instrument of presidential power.[35]

In particular, the OMB serves as a potential instrument of presidential control over federal spending and hence a mechanism through which the White House has greatly expanded its power. The OMB has the capacity to analyze and approve all legislative proposals, not only budgetary requests, emanating from all federal agencies before being submitted to Congress. This procedure, now a matter of routine, greatly enhances the president's control over the entire executive branch. All legislation originating in the White House as well as all executive orders also go through the OMB.[36]

Thus, through one White House agency, the president has the means to exert major influence over the flow of money and the shape and content of national legislation.

**Regulatory Review**   A second tactic that presidents have used to increase their power and reach is the process of regulatory review, through which presidents have sought to seize control of rule making by the agencies of the executive branch (see also Chapter 14). Whenever Congress enacts a statute, its actual implementation requires the promulgation of hundreds of rules by the agency charged with administering the law and effecting the will of Congress. Some congressional statutes are quite detailed and leave agencies with relatively little discretion. Typically, however, Congress enacts a relatively broad statement of legislative intent and then delegates to the appropriate administrative agency the power to fill in many important details.[37] In other words, Congress typically says to an administrative agency, "Here is the problem: deal with it."[38]

The discretion that Congress delegates to administrative agencies has provided recent presidents with an important avenue for expanding their own power. For example, President Clinton believed the president had full authority to order agencies of the executive branch to adopt such rules as the president thought appropriate.

During the course of his presidency, Clinton issued 107 directives to administrators ordering them to propose specific rules and regulations. In some instances, the language of the rule to be proposed was drafted by the White House staff; in other cases, the president asserted a priority but left it to the agency to draft the precise language of the proposal. Republicans, of course, denounced Clinton's actions as a usurpation of power.[39] However, after President George W. Bush took office, he made no move to surrender the powers Clinton had claimed—quite the contrary. Bush vigorously continued the Clinton-era practice of issuing presidential directives to agencies, spurring them to issue new rules and regulations. Obama's first regulatory director, Cass Sunstein, not only issued a number of major regulatory directives to federal agencies but also launched a "look back" program. Under this program, the administration sought to eliminate several hundred existing federal rules it deemed obsolete.[40]

**Governing by Decree: Executive Orders**   A fourth mechanism through which contemporary presidents have sought to enhance their power to govern unilaterally is through the use of executive orders and other forms of presidential decrees, including executive agreements, national security findings and directives, proclamations, reorganization plans, signing statements, and a host of others.[41] Executive orders have a long history in the United States and have been the vehicles for a number of important government policies, including the purchase of Louisiana, the annexation of Texas, the emancipation of the slaves, the internment of Japanese Americans, the desegregation of the military, the initiation of affirmative action, and the creation of important federal agencies, among them the EPA, the FDA, and the Peace Corps.[42]

Although wars and national emergencies produce the highest volume of executive orders, such presidential actions also occur frequently in peacetime (see Figure 13.4). In the realm of foreign policy, unilateral presidential actions in the form of executive agreements have virtually replaced treaties as the nation's chief foreign policy instruments.[43] Presidential decrees, however, are often used for purely domestic purposes.

Presidents may not use executive orders to issue whatever commands they please. The use of such decrees is bound by law. If a president issues an executive order, proclamation, directive, or the like, in principle he does so pursuant to the powers granted to him by the Constitution or delegated to him by Congress, usually through

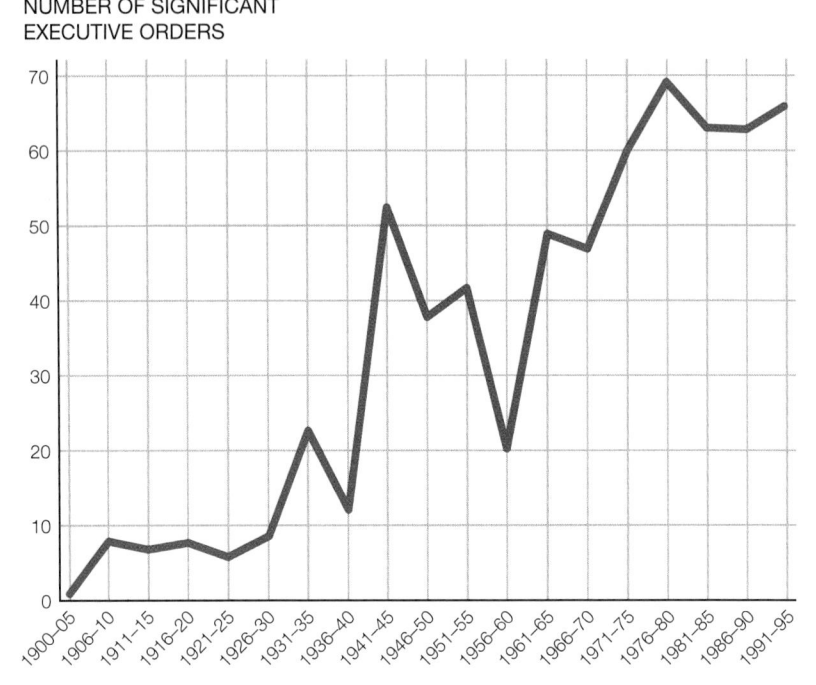

**FIGURE 13.4**

## Significant Executive Orders, 1900–95

Over the twentieth century, presidents made increasingly frequent use of executive orders to accomplish their policy goals. What factors explain this development? How has Congress responded to increased presidential assertiveness? What might explain the large number of executive orders issued during the 1940s?

SOURCE: William Howell, "The President's Powers of Unilateral Action: The Strategic Advantages of Acting Alone" (Ph.D. diss., Stanford University, 1999).

NUMBER OF SIGNIFICANT EXECUTIVE ORDERS

a statute. When presidents issue such orders, they generally state the constitutional or statutory basis for their actions. For example, when President Truman ordered the desegregation of the armed services, he did so pursuant to his constitutional powers as commander in chief. In a similar vein, when President Lyndon Johnson issued Executive Order No. 11246, he asserted that the order was designed to implement the 1964 Civil Rights Act, which prohibited employment discrimination. Where an executive order has no statutory or constitutional basis, the courts have held it to be void. The most important such is *Youngstown Co. v. Sawyer* (1952).[44] Here, the Supreme Court ruled that President Truman's seizure of the nation's steel mills during the Korean War had no statutory or constitutional basis and was thus invalid.

A number of court decisions, though, have established broad boundaries that leave considerable room for presidential action. For example, the courts have held that Congress might approve presidential action after the fact or, in effect, ratify presidential action through "acquiescence" by not objecting for long periods of time or by continuing to provide funding for programs established by executive orders. Further, the courts have indicated that some areas, most notably the realm of military policy, are presidential in character, allowing presidents wide latitude to make policy by executive decree. Thus, within the very broad limits established by the courts, presidential orders can be important policy tools.

President Clinton issued numerous orders designed to promote a coherent set of policy goals: protecting the environment, strengthening federal regulatory power, shifting America's foreign policy from a unilateral to a multilateral focus, expanding affirmative action programs, and helping organized labor.[45] President George W. Bush also did not hesitate to use executive orders, issuing more than 300 between his inauguration and the end of 2008. During his first months in office, Bush issued

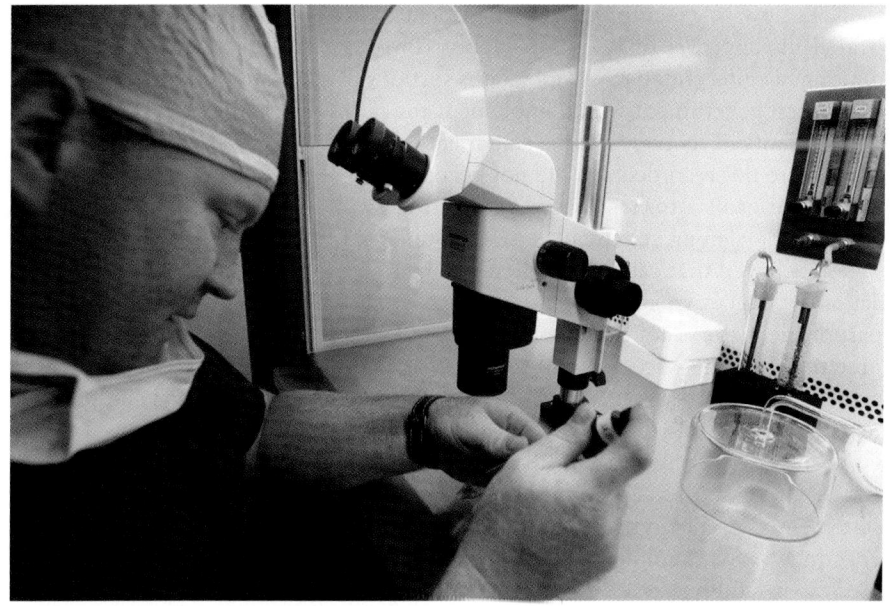

*In 2001, President Bush issued an executive order limiting the use of stem cells in federally funded research. In 2009, President Obama issued an executive order overturning Bush's order and allowing federal science programs more freedom.*

orders prohibiting the use of federal funds to support international family-planning groups that provided abortion counseling services, and limiting the use of embryonic stem cells in federally funded research projects. Throughout his administration, Bush made very aggressive use of executive orders in response to the threat of terrorism. In November 2001, for example, he issued a directive authorizing the creation of military tribunals to try noncitizens accused of involvement in acts of terrorism against the United States. In May 2007 he issued controversial national security directives that gave the president sole responsibility for determining when and how constitutional government could be reestablished in the event of a catastrophic attack on the United States.

During his first year in office, President Obama also issued a number of executive orders, many of which rescinded Bush-era orders. Thus, Obama ordered the closing of the Guantánamo prison and ordered an end to what were deemed unlawful methods of interrogation of terror suspects. In February 2010, with many elements of his legislative agenda stalled in Congress, Obama indicated that he might make increased use of executive orders to advance energy, environmental, fiscal, and other domestic priorities.[46] In June 2012, Obama issued an order designed to halt the deportation of undocumented immigrants who had come to the United States as children. These individuals would become eligible for work permits. Immigrant rights groups hailed the order while Republicans criticized the president for circumventing Congress.

**Signing Statements**   To negate congressional actions to which they objected, recent presidents have made frequent and calculated use of presidential **signing statements** when signing bills into law.[47] The signing statement is an announcement made by the president, at the time of signing a congressional enactment into law, that offers the president's interpretation of the law and usually innocuous remarks predicting the many benefits the new law will bring to the nation. Occasionally, presidents have used signing statements to point to sections of the law they have deemed improper or even unconstitutional, and to instruct executive branch

**signing statements**
announcements made by the president when signing bills into law, often presenting the president's interpretation of the law

agencies how to execute the law.[48] President Harry Truman, for example, accompanied his approval of the 1946 Hobbs Anti-Racketeering Act with a message offering his interpretation of ambiguous sections of the statute and indicating how the federal government would implement the new law.[49]

Presidents have made signing statements throughout American history, though many were not recorded and did not become part of the official legislative record. Ronald Reagan's attorney general, Edwin Meese, is generally credited with transforming the signing statement into a routine tool of presidential direct action.[50] Meese believed that carefully crafted signing statements would provide a basis for action by executive agencies and, perhaps even more important, would become part of the history and context of a piece of legislation if and when judicial interpretation became necessary. Indeed, to make certain of this, Meese reached an agreement with the West Publishing Company to include them in its authoritative texts of federal legislation.[51]

With the way thus paved, Reagan, followed by George H. W. Bush, Clinton, and George W. Bush, proceeded to use detailed and artfully designed signing statements—prepared by the Department of Justice—to reinterpret congressional enactments. For example, when signing the 1986 amendments to the Safe Drinking Water Act, President Reagan issued a statement that interpreted sections of the act to allow discretionary enforcement even though Congress seemed to call for mandatory enforcement.[52] Reagan hoped the courts would accept his version of the statute when examining subsequent enforcement decisions. In other cases, Reagan used his signing statements to attempt to nullify portions of statutes. George W. Bush issued more than 161 signing statements and used them to rewrite the law on numerous occasions. As a candidate, President Obama criticized Bush for excessive use of signing statements. As president, Obama has issued signing statements, but in far smaller numbers.[53]

**for critical analysis**

In recent years, presidents have expanded their power through increased use of executive orders, executive agreements, and other unilateral instruments. Is the United States becoming a "presidential republic"? Is this a development to be feared or welcomed?

**The Advantages of the Administrative Strategy**   Through the course of American history, party leadership and popular appeals have played important roles in presidential efforts to overcome political opposition, and both continue to be instruments of presidential power. Reagan's tax cuts and Clinton's budget victories were achieved with strong partisan support. George W. Bush, lacking the oratorical skills of Reagan or Roosevelt, nevertheless made effective use of sophisticated communications strategies to promote his agenda. Yet, as we have seen, in the modern era parties have waned in institutional strength, and the effects of popular appeals have often proven evanescent. The limitations of the alternatives have increasingly impelled presidents to try to expand the administrative capabilities of the office and their own capacity for unilateral action as means of achieving their policy goals. And in recent decades, the expansion of the Executive Office, the development of regulatory review, and the use of executive orders and signing statements have given presidents a substantial capacity to achieve significant policy results despite congressional opposition to their legislative agendas.

In principle, perhaps, Congress could respond more vigorously to unilateral policy making by the president than it has. Certainly, a Congress willing to impeach a president should have the mettle to overturn his or her administrative directives. But the president has significant advantages in such struggles with Congress. In battles over presidential directives and orders, Congress is on the defensive, reacting to presidential initiatives. The framers of the Constitution saw "energy," or the ability to take the initiative, as a key feature of executive power.[54] When the president takes action by issuing an order or an administrative directive, Congress must respond through the cumbersome and time-consuming lawmaking process, overcome internal divisions, and enact legislation that the president may ultimately veto. Moreover, as the political scientist Terry Moe has argued, in such battles Congress faces a significant collective action problem: members are likely to be more sensitive to the substance of a president's actions and its short-term effects on their constituents than to the more general long-term implications of presidential power for the vitality of their institution.[55]

*Presidents are not all-powerful. President Obama succeeded in getting health care legislation passed in his first term, but not without making major concessions to Congress regarding the type and scope of the reforms. Here, Obama signs the Affordable Care Act into law in 2010.*

## ● Thinking Critically about Presidential Power and Democracy

The framers of the Constitution created a system of government in which the Congress and the executive branch were to share power. At least since the New Deal, however, the powers of Congress have waned, whereas those of the presidency have expanded dramatically. An instance of congressional retreat in the face of presidential assertiveness occurred in October 2002, when both houses of Congress, pressed by President George W. Bush, voted overwhelmingly to authorize the White House to use military force against Iraq. The resolution adopted by Congress expressly allowed the president complete discretion to determine whether, when, and how to attack Iraq. The president had rejected language that might have implied even the slightest limitations on his prerogatives. Indeed, Bush's legal advisers had pointedly declared that the president did not actually need specific congressional authorization to attack Iraq if he deemed such action to be in America's interest. "We don't want to be in the legal position of asking Congress to authorize the use of force when the president already has that full authority," said one senior administration official. Few members of Congress even bothered to object to this apparent rewriting of the U.S. Constitution.

There is no doubt that Congress continues to be able to confront presidents and even, on occasion, hand the White House a sharp rebuff. During the 2011 debt crisis, President Obama was unable to force House Republicans to accept his plan for dealing with the nation's deficits and was compelled to accede to many of the GOP's demands in order to prevent a potentially disastrous default on government debt.

In the larger view, however, presidents' occasional defeats, however dramatic, have to be seen as temporary setbacks in a gradual but decisive shift toward increased presidential power. Louis Fisher, a leading authority on the separation of powers, recently observed that in what are arguably the two most important policy arenas, national defense and the federal budget, the powers of Congress have been in decline for at least the past 50 years. The last time Congress exercised its constitutional power to declare war was December 8, 1941, and yet, since that time, American forces have been committed to numerous conflicts around the world by order of the president. The much-hailed 1973 War Powers Resolution, far from limiting presidential power, actually allowed the president considerably more discretionary authority than what was granted by the Constitution, which seems to require congressional authorization before troops can be deployed for even one day. The War Powers Resolution gave the president the authority to deploy forces abroad for 60 days without congressional authority. And presidents have ignored even this stipulation.

As to spending powers, the framers of the Constitution conceived the "power of the purse" to be Congress's most fundamental prerogative. For more than a century this power was jealously guarded by powerful congressional leaders such as Taft-era House speaker "Uncle" Joe Cannon, who saw congressional control of the budget as a fundamental safeguard against "Prussian-style" militarism and autocracy. Since the New Deal, however, successive Congresses have yielded to steadily increasing presidential influence over the budget process. In 1939, Congress allowed Franklin Delano Roosevelt to take a giant step toward presidential control of the nation's purse strings when it permitted him to bring the Bureau of the Budget (BoB) into the newly created EOP. Roosevelt and his successors used the BoB (now called the OMB) effectively to seize the nation's legislative and budgetary agenda. In 1974, Congress attempted to respond to Richard Nixon's efforts to further enhance presidential control of spending when it enacted the Budget and Impoundment Control Act, legislation centralizing Congress's own budgetary process and apparently reinforcing congressional power. Yet, less than 10 years later, Congress watched as President Ronald Reagan essentially seized control of the congressional budget process. Subsequently, Congress has surrendered more and more power to the president.

Representative assemblies such as the U.S. Congress derive their influence from the support of groups and forces in civil society that believe these institutions serve their interests. A chief executive, such as the president of the United States, on the other hand, fundamentally derives power from the command of bureaucracies, armies, and the general machinery of the state. Presidents can certainly benefit from popular support. If we imagine, however, a fully demobilized polity in which neither institution could count on much support from forces in civil society, the president would still command the institutions of the state, whereas Congress would be without significant resources. In a fully mobilized polity, on the other hand, Congress might have a chance to counterbalance the president's institutional powers with the support of significant social forces.

A powerful presidency, a weak Congress, and a partially demobilized electorate make for a dangerous mix. Presidents have increasingly asserted the right to govern unilaterally and now appear able to overcome most institutional and political constraints. Presidential power, to be sure, can be a force for good. To cite one example from the not-so-distant past, it was President Lyndon Johnson, more than Congress or the judiciary, who faced up to the task of smashing America's racial apartheid system. Yet, as the framers knew, unchecked power is always dangerous. Americans of the founding generation feared that unchecked presidential power would lead to *monocracy*, a republican form of monarchy without a king. Inevitably, we will pay a price for our undemocratic politics.

**for critical analysis**

The presidency and Congress are both democratic institutions. Which is the more democratic? Why?

# Connect with the Presidency

## Inform Yourself

 **Who are America's presidents?** To learn about American presidents past and present, visit the University of Virginia's Miller Center (http://millercenter.org/president), which provides a one-stop reference for American presidents. See photos of each president, learn how long he served, his religion, home state, and much more. You can also visit the White House website www.whitehouse.gov/about/presidents, which counts down the presidencies from the first to the most recent.

 **Understand the president's role as head of the executive branch.** Freedom Project has created a 10-minute video that focuses on the powers and limitations of the executive branch (www.youtube.com/watch?v=mQGp4acvBs0&feature=related). The White House also has a section on how the modern executive branch is organized. Visit www.whitehouse.gov/our-government/executive-branch to understand the power of the modern executive branch.

 **Evaluate America's presidents.** Presidents in the United States are ranked by a multitude of factors. However, there is always disagreement about what should be considered in the rankings. After considering the many different types of rankings available at http://en.wikipedia.org/wiki/Historical_rankings_of_Presidents_of_the_United_States, consider the conservative blog's argument at www.theamericanconservative.com/articles/ranking-the-presidents/. What do you think should be considered when ranking the "best" and "worst" presidents? Whom would you list as the five best and five worst presidents?

## Express Yourself

 **Respond to the White House blog.** The White House website has a constantly updated blog on key issues and events involving the executive branch. Go to www.whitehouse.gov/blog and see the current events of the day. After reading a blog post, consider making a comment online.

 **Send an e-mail to the president.** Use the Whitehouse website to send a letter to the President (and his staffers) about what you would like to see changed in how the executive branch operates. This form will allow you send "questions, comments, concerns, or well-wishes to the President or his staff": www.whitehouse.gov/contact/submit-questions-and-comments.

*Find links to the sites listed above as well as related activities on wwnorton.com/studyspace.*

# study guide

## Establishing the Presidency

▪ **Explain the role of the president in the American political system (pp. 517–19)**

During the writing of the Constitution, the framers debated whether executive authority should be concentrated in the hands of one individual and whether this individual should be directly by the people. Once the idea of an "executive council" was rejected in favor of a creating "energy" in the executive branch, the framers chose to design an indirect system of selecting the president that would make the president responsible to state and national legislators rather than to the public. It was not until the emergence of the national convention system in the 1830s that the presidency obtained the broad popular base needed to increase presidential power.

### Key Term

**caucus (political)** (p. 518)

### Practice Quiz

1. Which article of the Constitution establishes the presidency? *(p. 517)*
   a) Article I
   b) Article II
   c) Article III
   d) Article IV
   e) Article V

2. The Founders chose to select the president through an indirect election in order to *(p. 517)*
   a) increase the strength and influence of political parties.
   b) build an imperial presidency that would overwhelm the power of Congress.
   c) force the president to be responsive to the will of the people.
   d) make the president responsible to the state and national legislatures.
   e) create a more independent chief executive.

>  **Practice Online**
> Video exercises: "*My Job*" on The Daily Show with Jon Stewart

## The Constitutional Powers of the Presidency

▪ **Outline the powers the Constitution gives the president (pages 519–32)**

Presidents have three kinds of powers: expressed, delegated and inherent. The president's expressed powers, as defined by Article II of the Constitution, fall into several broad categories: military, judicial, diplomatic, executive, and legislative. The president's delegated powers are not found in the Constitution but are, instead, the product of congressional statutes and resolutions that voluntarily transfer authority from the legislative to the executive branch. The president's inherent powers grow from "the rights, duties and obligations of the presidency" that presidents often assert during times of war and national crisis.

### Key Terms

**expressed powers** (p. 519)
**delegated powers** (p. 519)
**inherent powers** (p. 519)
**commander in chief** (p. 520)
**War Powers Resolution** (p. 521)
**executive agreement** (p. 525)

**executive privilege** (p. 525)
**veto** (p. 526)
**pocket veto** (p. 526)
**legislative initiative** (p. 527)
**executive order** (p. 529)

### Practice Quiz

3. Which of the following war powers does the Constitution *not* assign to the president? *(p. 520)*
   a) command of the army and navy of the United States
   b) the power to declare war
   c) command of the state militias
   d) the power to make treaties
   e) The Constitution assigns all of the powers above to the president.

4. The War Powers Resolution of 1973 was an act passed by Congress that *(p. 521)*
   a) required the CIA to collect inteligence on all Americans born in a foreign country.
   b) outlawed presidential use of executive agreements.
   c) created the National Security Council.

d) granted the president the authority to declare war.

e) stipulated military forces must be withdrawn within 60 days in the absence of a specific congressional authorization for their continued deployment.

5. Which of the following does *not* require the advice and consent of the Senate? *(p. 525)*
a) an executive agreement
b) a treaty
c) appointment of ambassadors
d) Supreme Court nominations
e) All of the above require the advice and consent of the Senate.

6. What did the Supreme Court rule in *United States v. Nixon*? *(p. 526)*
a) Nixon had to turn his secret White House tapes over to congressional investigators because presidents do not have the power of executive privilege.
b) Nixon did not have to turn his secret White House tapes over to congressional investigators because, in general, presidents have the power of executive privilege.
c) Nixon had to turn his secret White House tapes over to congressional investigators but, in general, presidents have the power of executive privilege.
d) Nixon did not have to turn his secret White House tapes over to congressional investigators but, in

general, presidents do not have the power of executive privilege.
e) All presidents are immune from criminal investigations and cannot, therefore, be tried in any court of law.

7. What are the requirements for overriding a presidential veto? *(p. 526)*
a) 50 percent plus one vote in both houses of Congress
b) two-thirds vote in both houses of Congress
c) two-thirds vote in the Senate only
d) three-fourths vote in both houses of Congress.
e) A presidential veto cannot be overridden by Congress.

8. When the president issues a rule or regulation that reorganizes or otherwise directs the affairs of the executive branch, such as the directives that established the Executive Office of the President and the Environmental Protection Agency, it is called *(p. 529)*
a) an executive agreement.
b) an executive order.
c) an executive mandate.
d) administrative oversight.
e) legislative initiative.

 **Practice Online**
Video exercise: *The Word—The Defining Moment*

# The Presidency as an Institution

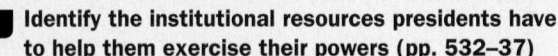 **Identify the institutional resources presidents have to help them exercise their powers (pp. 532–37)**

The institutionalized presidency is made up of the Cabinet, White House staff, Executive Office of the President, the Vice Presidency, and the First Spouse. Through their advice and assistance. these thousands of individuals give the president a capacity for action that he could never have by himself. When coupled with the president's formal powers, the institutionalized presidency makes the chief executive an important player in the country's policy-making process.

## Key Terms
**Cabinet** (p. 532)

**National Security Council (NSC)** (p. 534)

**White House staff** (p. 534)

**Kitchen Cabinet** (p. 534)

**Executive Office of the President (EOP)** (p. 534)

## Practice Quiz

9. Which of the following statements about vice presidents is *not* true? *(pp. 535–36)*
a) The vice president succeeds the president in case of death, resignation, or incapacitation.
b) The vice president casts the tie-breaking vote in the Senate when necessary.

c) The vice president also serves as an honorary member of the Supreme Court.
d) Six vice presidents have had to replace presidents who died in office during American history.
e) Presidential candidates typically select a vice presidential candidate who is likely to bring the support of a state that would not otherwise support the ticket.

10. The Office of Management and Budget is part of *(p. 533)*
a) the Executive Office of the President.
b) the White House staff.
c) the Kitchen Cabinet.
d) the Congressional Budget Office.
e) the Bureau of Economic Analysis.

11. How many people work for agencies within the Executive Office of the President? *(p. 534)*
a) 25 to 50
b) 700 to 1,000
c) 1,500 to 2,000
d) 4,500 to 5,000
e) 25,000 to 30,000

 **Practice Online**
Interactive simulation exercise: *Special Assistant to the President*

# The Contemporary Bases of Presidential Power

■ **Explain how modern presidents have become even more powerful (pages 538–47)**

Although Congress was the dominant institution in the American political system throughout the nineteenth century, recent presidents have expanded the policy-making power of their office in number of ways. While some presidents have relied primarily on the support of party members to advance their legislative goals, contemporary, presidents more commonly turn to popular mobilization and executive administration in pursuing policy change.

## Key Term

**signing statements** (p. 545)

## Practice Quiz

12. What are the three ways that presidents can expand their power? *(p. 538)*
    a) weakening national partisan institutions, avoiding popular appeals, and loosening their control of executive agencies
    b) strengthening national partisan institutions, using popular appeals, and bolstering their control of executive agencies
    c) weakening national partisan institutions, using popular appeals, and loosening their control of executive agencies

    d) strengthening national partisan institutions, avoiding popular appeals, and bolstering their control of executive agencies
    e) weakening national partisan institutions, avoiding popular appeals, and bolstering their control of executive agencies

13. The Supreme Court case *Youngstown Co. v. Sawyer* was significant because *(pp. 543–544)*
    a) it showed that the courts would never invalidate an executive order.
    b) it showed that the courts would invalidate executive orders that have no statutory or constitutional basis.
    c) it asserted that pocket vetoes were unconstitutional.
    d) it upheld the notion of executive privilege.
    e) it struck down the Budget and Impoundment Control Act.

14. When the president makes an announcement about his interpretation of a congressional enactment that he is signing into law, it is called *(p. 545)*
    a) a signing statement.
    b) a line item veto.
    c) an executive order.
    d) legislative initiative.
    e) executive privilege.

 **Practice Online**
"You Decide" exercise: *Presidential Power and Warrantless Wiretapping*

# For Further Reading

Barber, James David. *The Presidential Character.* Englewood Cliffs, NJ: Prentice-Hall, 1992.

Crenson, Matthew, and Benjamin Ginsberg. *Presidential Power: Unchecked and Unbalanced.* New York: W.W. Norton, 2007.

Draper, Robert. *Dead Certain: The Presidency of George Bush.* New York: Free Press, 2007.

Edwards, George. *Why the Electoral College Is Bad for America.* New Haven, CT: Yale University Press, 2004.

Edwards, George, and Stephen Wayne. *Presidential Leadership: Politics and Policy Making.* New York: Wadsworth, 2009.

Goldsmith, Jack. *The American Presidency: Power and Constraint.* New York: W.W. Norton, 2012.

Hayes, Stephen F. *Cheney: The Untold Story of America's Most Powerful and Controversial Vice President.* New York: HarperCollins, 2007.

Lowi, Theodore J. *The Personal President: Power Invested, Promise Unfulfilled.* Ithaca, NY: Cornell University Press, 1985.

Milkis, Sidney. *The American Presidency: Origins and Development.* Washington, DC: CQ Press, 2011.

Neustadt, Richard E. *Presidential Power: The Politics of Leadership from Roosevelt to Reagan.* Rev. ed. New York: Free Press, 1990.

Pfiffner, James. *Understanding the Presidency.* 6th ed. New York: Longman, 2010.

Pika, Joseph, and John A. Maltese. *Politics of the Presidency.* Washington, DC: Congressional Quarterly Press, 2009.

Skowronek, Stephen. *The Politics Presidents Make: Leadership from John Adams to Bill Clinton.* Cambridge, MA: The Belknap Press of Harvard University Press, 1997.

Yoo, John. *The Powers of War and Peace.* Chicago: University of Chicago Press, 2005.

# Recommended Websites

**Almanac of Policy Issues: War Powers Resolution**
www.policyalmanac.org/world/archive/war_powers
_resolution.shtml

The War Powers Resolution was passed in 1973 to define and limit the president's power during times of war. Read the full text of the resolution on this website.

**Dave Leip's Atlas of U.S. Presidential Elections**
www.uselectionatlas.org

For information on upcoming and past presidential elections, refer to this website. Experiment with the electoral college calculator to see how your state could affect the electoral outcome.

**The American Presidency Project**
www.americanpresidency.org

Directed by Gerhard Peters and John T. Woolley at UC Santa Barbara, this site contains over 88,000 documents related to the study of the presidency, including party platforms, candidates' remarks, statements of administration policy, documents released by the Office of the Press Secretary, and election debates. This site is also an excellent resource for data related to the study of the presidency.

**The National Archives: Executive Branch**
www.archives.gov/executive/

Research official executive branch documents at the Executive Branch website, provided by the U.S. National Archives and Records Administration.

**Vicepresidents.com**
www.vicepresidents.com

This website is dedicated to providing lots of interesting facts and archives about vice presidents, along with some lively humor.

**The White House**
www.whitehouse.gov

This is the official website of the White House. Here you can read about current presidential news, the president's Cabinet, executive orders, and presidential appointments.

**White House Historical Association**
www.whitehousehistory.org

The White House Historical Association is dedicated to the understanding, appreciation, and preservation of the White House. At its website you can find historical facts and take a detailed online tour of the numerous rooms and the property.

**The White House: Past First Ladies**
www.whitehouse.gov/history/firstladies/

The first lady is an important resource for the president in his role as head of state. Read about the current and past first ladies on this website.

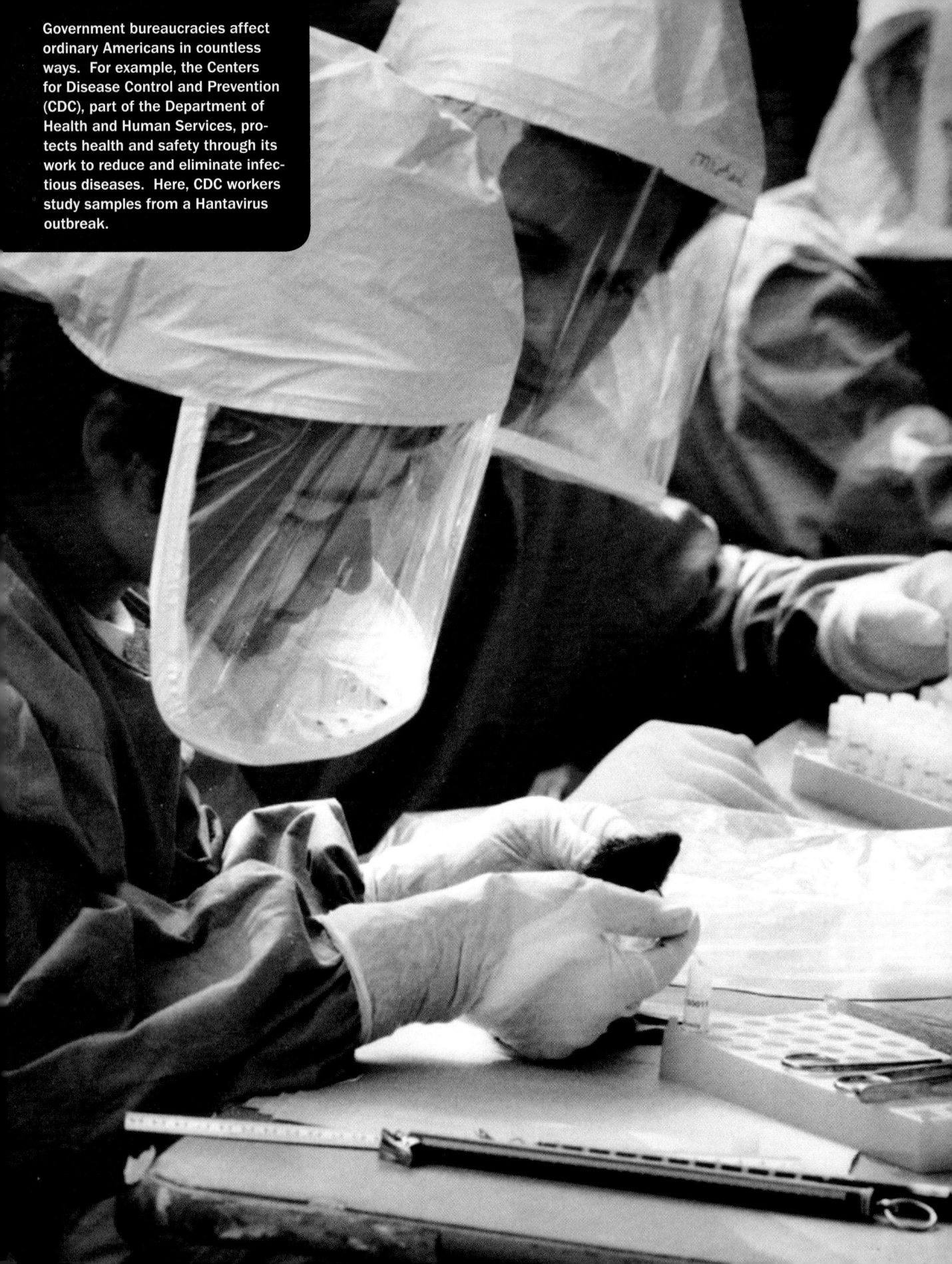

Government bureaucracies affect ordinary Americans in countless ways. For example, the Centers for Disease Control and Prevention (CDC), part of the Department of Health and Human Services, protects health and safety through its work to reduce and eliminate infectious diseases. Here, CDC workers study samples from a Hantavirus outbreak.

# Bureaucracy in a Democracy

**WHAT GOVERNMENT DOES AND WHY IT MATTERS** Americans depend on government bureaucracies to accomplish the most spectacular achievements as well as the most mundane. Yet they often do not realize that public bureaucracies are essential for providing the services they use every day and rely on in emergencies. On a typical day, a college student might check the weather forecast, drive on an interstate highway, mail the rent check, drink from a public water fountain, check the calories on the side of a yogurt container, attend a class, log on to the Internet, and meet a relative at the airport. Each of these activities is possible because of the work of a government bureaucracy: the U.S. Weather Service, the U.S. Department of Transportation, the U.S. Postal Service, the Environmental Protection Agency, the Food and Drug Administration, the student loan programs of the U.S. Department of Education, the Advanced Research Projects Agency (which developed the Internet in the 1960s), and the Federal Aviation Administration. Without the ongoing work of these agencies, many of these common activities would be impossible, unreliable, or more expensive. Even though bureaucracies provide essential services that all Americans rely on, they are often disparaged by politicians and the general public alike as "big government," and come into public view only when they are charged with fraud, waste, and abuse.

In emergencies, the national perspective on bureaucracy and, indeed, on "big government" shifts. After the September 11 terrorist attacks, all eyes turned to Washington. The federal government responded by strengthening and reorganizing the bureaucracy to undertake a whole new set of responsibilities designed to keep America safe. In the biggest government reorganization in over half a century, Congress created the Department of Homeland Security in 2002. The massive new department merged 22 existing agencies into a single department employing nearly 170,000 workers.

As we shall see in this chapter, Americans have a love-hate relationship with the federal bureaucracy. This ambivalence sometimes prompts politicians to promise that they will slash the federal bureaucracy or move government responsibilities to the private sector. Yet they rarely follow through on such promises. Because Americans rely on government in so many aspects of their lives, significant reductions in the federal bureaucracy would create disruptions that no one wishes to experience.

## chaptergoals

- Define bureaucracy and describe the basic features of the executive branch (pages 557–66)

- Describe the major goals we expect federal agencies to promote (pages 566–80)

- Evaluate some of the ways politicians have tried to make the bureaucracy more efficient (pages 580–88)

- Explain why it is often difficult to control the bureaucracy (pages 588–93)

# Bureaucracy and Bureaucrats

**Bureaucracy** is nothing more nor less than a form of organization, a complex structure of offices, tasks, and rules. *Bureau*, a French word, can mean either "office" or "desk." *Cracy* is from the Greek word for "rule" or "form of rule." Taken together, *bureau* and *cracy* produce an interesting definition: bureaucracy is rule by offices and desks. Each member of an organization has an office, meaning both a place and a set of responsibilities. That is, each "office" comprises a set of tasks that are specialized to the needs of the organization, and the person holding that office (or position) performs those specialized tasks. Specialization and repetition are essential to the efficiency of any organization. Therefore, when an organization is inefficient, it is often because it is not "bureaucratized" enough! But bureaucracies do not only perform specialized tasks that require routine action. As we shall see, they also undertake politically controversial tasks that require them to exercise a great deal of discretion and professional judgment. In many areas of policy, Congress writes laws that are very broad, and it is up to the bureaucracy to define what the policy will mean in practice. The decisions that bureaucrats make, often based on professional judgments, can themselves become politically contentious.

Both routine and exceptional tasks require the organization, specialization, and expertise found in bureaucracies. To provide services, government bureaucracies employ specialists such as meteorologists, doctors, and scientists. To do their jobs effectively, these specialists require resources and tools (ranging from paper to blood samples); they have to coordinate their work with others (for example, the traffic engineers must communicate with construction engineers); and there must be effective outreach to the public (for example, private doctors must be made aware of health warnings). Bureaucracy is a means of coordinating the many different parts that must work together for the government to provide useful services.

**bureaucracy** the complex structure of offices, tasks, rules, and principles of organization that are employed by all large-scale institutions to coordinate the work of their personnel

## The Size of the Federal Service

For decades, politicians from both parties have asserted that the federal government is too big. Ronald Reagan led the way in 1981 with his assertion that government was the problem, not the solution. Fifteen years later President Bill Clinton abandoned the traditional Democratic defense of government, declaring that "the era of big government is over." President George W. Bush voiced similar sentiments when he accepted his party's nomination for president in 2000, proclaiming, "Big government is not the answer!" President Obama struck a different tone. Addressing Congress on the topic of health care reform, he noted that while Americans had a "healthy skepticism about government," they also believed that "hard work and responsibility should be rewarded by some measure of security and fair

*After September 11, the federal government assumed a new role in airport security. With the passage of the Secure Aviation and Transportation Act, the federal government became involved with screening passengers and baggage.*

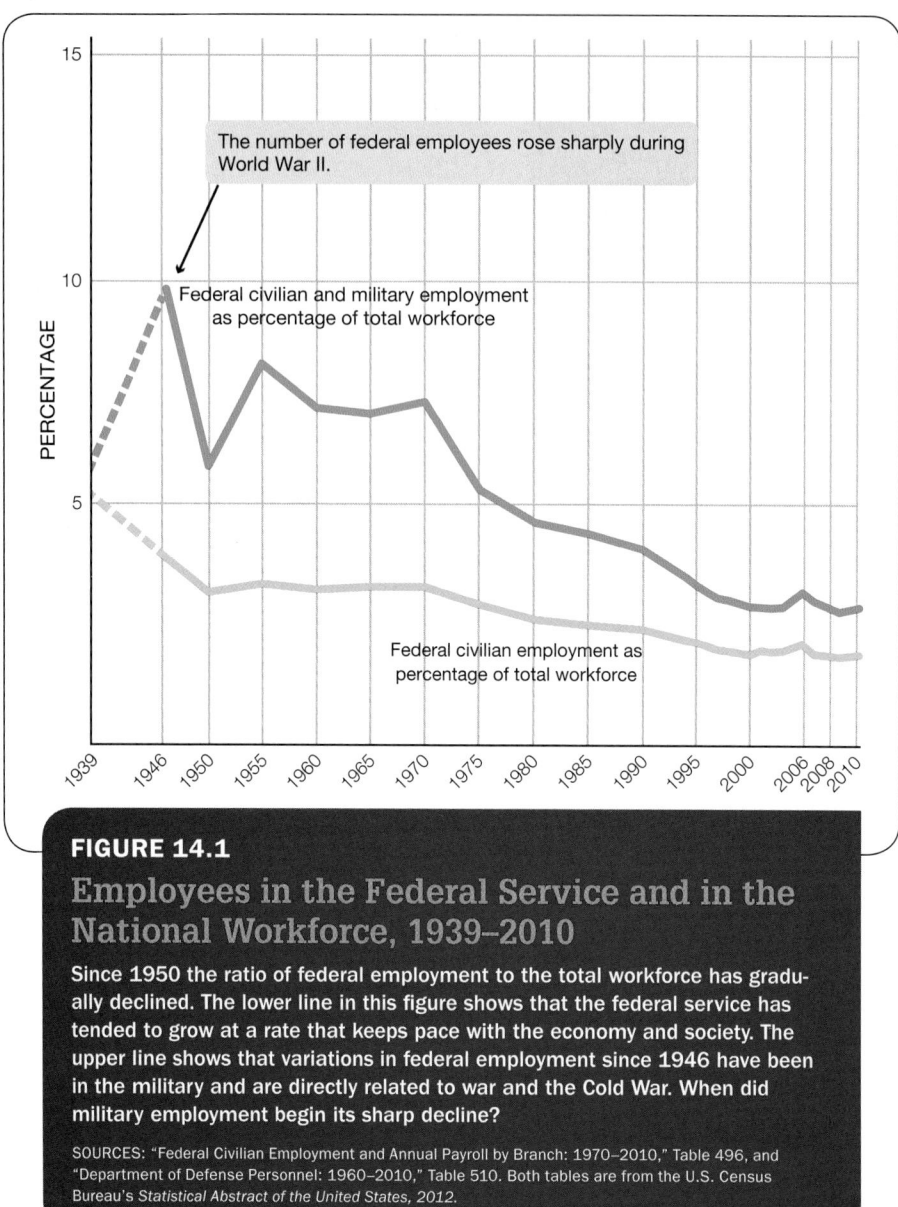

**FIGURE 14.1**

**Employees in the Federal Service and in the National Workforce, 1939–2010**

Since 1950 the ratio of federal employment to the total workforce has gradually declined. The lower line in this figure shows that the federal service has tended to grow at a rate that keeps pace with the economy and society. The upper line shows that variations in federal employment since 1946 have been in the military and are directly related to war and the Cold War. When did military employment begin its sharp decline?

SOURCES: "Federal Civilian Employment and Annual Payroll by Branch: 1970–2010," Table 496, and "Department of Defense Personnel: 1960–2010," Table 510. Both tables are from the U.S. Census Bureau's *Statistical Abstract of the United States, 2012.*

play" and recognized "that sometimes government has to step in to help deliver that promise."[1] Despite fears of bureaucratic growth getting out of hand, however, the federal service has hardly grown at all during the past 35 years; it reached its peak postwar level in 1968, with 3.0 million civilian employees plus an additional 3.6 million military personnel (a figure swollen by the war in Vietnam). The number of civilian federal employees has since fallen to approximately 2.8 million in 2010; the number of military personnel totals only 1.4 million.[2]

The growth of the federal service over the past 50 years is even less imposing when placed in the context of the total workforce and when compared with the size of state and local public employment. Figure 14.1 indicates that since 1950,

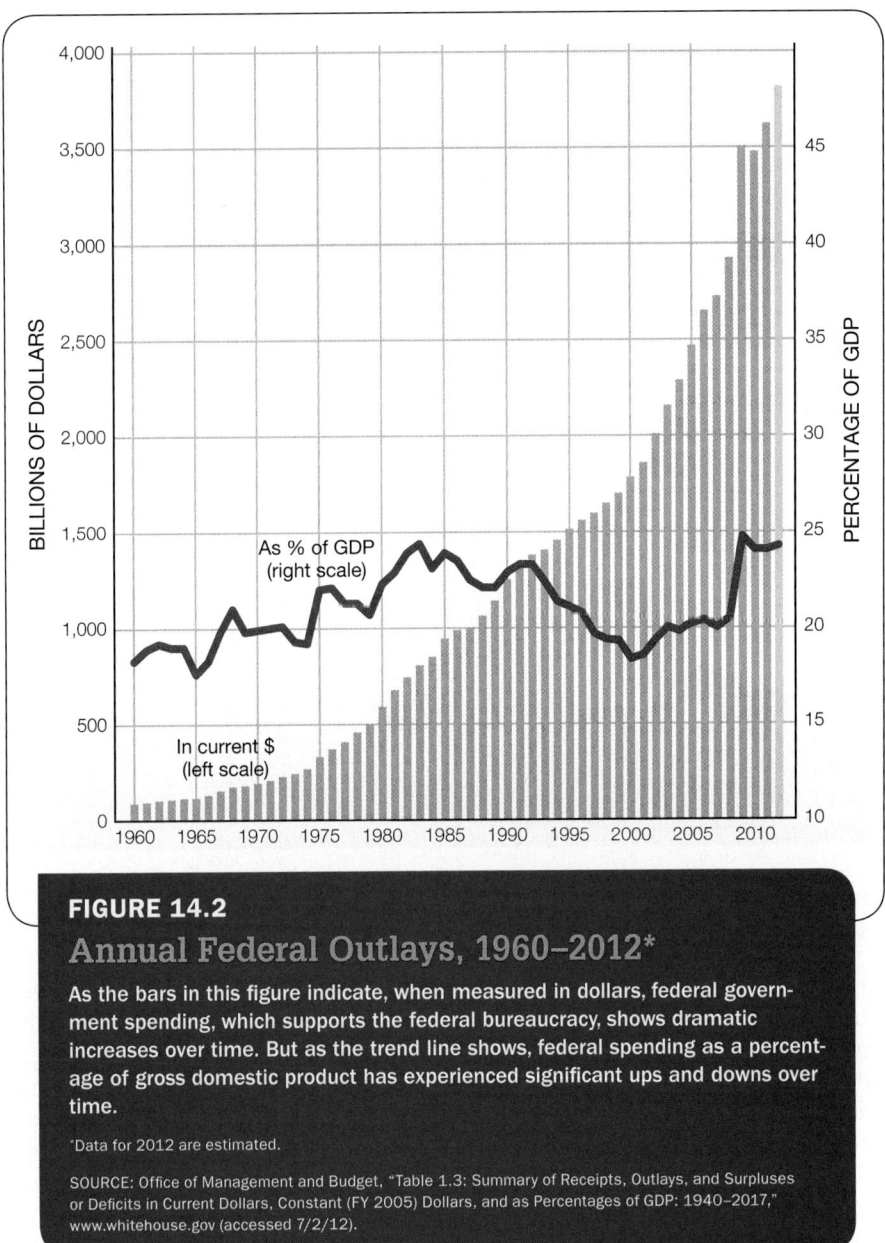

## FIGURE 14.2

### Annual Federal Outlays, 1960–2012*

As the bars in this figure indicate, when measured in dollars, federal government spending, which supports the federal bureaucracy, shows dramatic increases over time. But as the trend line shows, federal spending as a percentage of gross domestic product has experienced significant ups and downs over time.

*Data for 2012 are estimated.

SOURCE: Office of Management and Budget, "Table 1.3: Summary of Receipts, Outlays, and Surpluses or Deficits in Current Dollars, Constant (FY 2005) Dollars, and as Percentages of GDP: 1940–2017," www.whitehouse.gov (accessed 7/2/12).

the ratio of federal employment to the total workforce has been steady, and in fact has *declined* slightly in the past 30 years. In 1950 there were 4.3 million state and local civil service employees (about 6.5 percent of the country's workforce). In 2009 there were close to 20 million state and local employees (more than 14 percent of the nation's workforce).[3] Federal employment, in contrast, exceeded 5 percent of the workforce only during World War II, and almost all of that temporary growth was military.

Another useful comparison is to be found in Figure 14.2. Although the dollar increase in federal spending shown by the bars looks impressive, the trend line

*The Coast Guard, an agency within the federal bureaucracy, led the efforts to contain and clean up the* Deepwater Horizon *oil spill in 2010. These efforts included relocating endangered wildlife threatened by the spill. Here, pelicans rescued from the oil slick are loaded onto Coast Guard planes for release in a safer wildlife reserve.*

indicating the relation of federal spending to the gross domestic product (GDP) remained close to what it had been in 1960. This changed in 2009, when the recession pushed spending up dramatically, as the federal government sought to stimulate the economy, and spending rose on other recession-related programs, such as unemployment insurance. After 2009 the budget also reflected the costs of the wars in Iraq and Afghanistan, which had not been included in the Bush administration's budgets.

In sum, the national government is indeed "very large," but it has not been growing any faster than the economy or society. The same is roughly true of the growth pattern of state and local public personnel. Bureaucracy keeps pace with society, despite people's seeming dislike of it, because the control towers, the prisons, the Social Security system, and other essential elements of modern-day society cannot be operated without bureaucracy. Indeed, the recent growth of government spending does not reflect a growth in the federal bureaucracy but rather an increase in payments to individuals for valued social programs such as Social Security, and Medicare (which provides health care for people over 65), and a temporary boost in federal grants to the states to help them weather the recession.

Although the federal executive branch is large and complex, everything about it is commonplace because its many bureaucracies touch so many aspects of daily life. Government bureaucracies implement the decisions made through the political process. Bureaucracies are full of routine because that ensures the regular delivery of services and also the fulfillment of each agency's mandate. Public bureaucracies are powerful because legislatures and chief executives, and indeed the people, delegate vast power to them to make sure that society's collective needs are addressed, providing most citizens with the freedom to pursue their private ends.

## Bureaucrats

"Government by offices and desks" conveys to most people a picture of hundreds of office workers shuffling millions of pieces of paper. There is a lot of truth in that image, but we have to look more closely at what papers are being shuffled and why. More than 70 years ago, an astute observer defined bureaucracy as "continuous routine business."[4] As we saw at the beginning of this chapter, almost any organization succeeds by reducing its work to routine tasks performed by different specialists. But with specialization, one worker's output becomes another worker's input, making the timing of such relationships essential and therefore requiring these workers to stay in communication with each other. In fact, bureaucracy was the first information network.

**What Do Bureaucrats Do?** Congress is responsible for making the laws, but in most cases legislation only sets the broad parameters for government action. Bureaucracies are responsible for filling in the blanks by determining how the laws should be implemented. This requires bureaucracies to draw up detailed rules that guide the process of **implementation** and also to play a key role in enforcing the laws. Congress needs the bureaucracy to engage in rule making and implementation for several reasons. One is that bureaucracies employ people who have much more specialized expertise in specific policy areas than do members of Congress. Decisions about how to achieve many policy goals—from managing the national parks to regulating air quality to ensuring a sound economy—rest on the judgment of specialized experts. A second reason that Congress needs bureaucracy is that because updating legislation can take many years, bureaucratic flexibility can ensure that laws are administered in ways that take new conditions into account. Finally, members of Congress often prefer to delegate politically difficult decision making to bureaucrats.

One of the most important things that government agencies do is issue rules that provide more detailed and specific indications of what a given congressional policy will actually mean. For example, the Clean Air Act empowers the Environmental Protection Agency (EPA) to assess whether current or projected levels of air pollutants pose a threat to public health, to determine whether motor vehicle emissions are contributing to such pollution, and to create rules designed to regulate these emissions. Under the George W. Bush administration, the EPA claimed it did not have the authority to regulate a specific group of pollutants commonly referred to as "greenhouse gases" (for example, carbon dioxide). In 2007 the Supreme Court ruled that the EPA did have that authority and had to provide a justification for not regulating such emissions.[5] In the first year of the Obama administration, the agency ruled that greenhouse gases posed a threat to public health and that the emissions from new motor vehicles contributed to greenhouse gas pollution.[6] The agency then imposed new emission standards for automobiles, which would raise the average per-vehicle fuel economy for new vehicles to 35.5 miles per gallon starting in 2016, a standard later boosted to 54.4 miles per gallon by 2025.[7] Not only will this finding by the EPA have a significant effect on the automobile industry, but it could also lead to far-reaching regulations in the

**implementation** the efforts of departments and agencies to translate laws into specific bureaucratic rules and actions

future governing all industries that generate greenhouse gases. Not surprisingly, the agency's findings soon faced legal challenges by industries affected by the ruling.[8]

The rule-making process is thus a highly political one. Once a new law is passed, the relevant agency studies the legislation and proposes a set of rules to guide implementation. These proposed rules are then open to comment by anyone who wishes to weigh in. Representatives for the regulated industries and advocates of all sorts commonly submit comments. But anyone who wishes to can go to the website www.regulations.gov to read proposed rules, enter comments, and view the comments of others. Once rules are approved, they are published in the *Federal Register* and have the force of law.

In addition to rule making, bureaucracies play an essential role in enforcing the laws, thus exercising considerable power over private actors. For example, in 2011, Facebook reached a settlement with the Federal Trade Commission, which charged that the company had deceived consumers with unkept promises about privacy. Facebook agreed to change a number of its privacy practices and comply with the requirement that the company "obtain consumers' affirmative express consent before enacting changes that override their privacy preferences."[9] In 2010, to comply with federal regulations, the auto manufacturer Toyota was forced to recall several car models after identifying problems with their gas pedals and accelerators. The National Highway Traffic Safety Commission launched an investigation of Toyota and found that it had known of the defect but had installed the accelerators in cars anyway. The National Highway Traffic Safety Commission charged the company a fine of $16.4 million for failing to notify regulators of these problems. It also began to consider new rules designed to prevent such accidents in the future, such as new technical requirements for brake systems.[10]

Government bureaucrats do essentially the same things that bureaucrats in large private organizations do, and neither type deserves the disrespect often implied in the term *bureaucrat*. But because of the authoritative, coercive nature of government, far more constraints are imposed on public bureaucrats than on private bureaucrats, even when their jobs are the same. During the 1970s and '80s, the length of time required to develop an administrative rule from a proposal to actual publication in the *Federal Register* (when it takes on full legal status) grew from an average of 15 months to an average of 35 to 40 months. Inefficiency? No. Most of the increased time is attributable to new procedures requiring more public notice, more public hearings, more hearings held out in the field rather than in Washington, more cost-benefit analysis, and stronger legal obligations to prepare "environmental impact statements" demonstrating that the proposed rule or agency action will not have an unacceptably large negative impact on the human or physical environment.[11] Thus, a great deal of what is popularly decried as the lower efficiency of public agencies can be attributed to the political, judicial, legal, and public-opinion restraints and extraordinarily high expectations imposed on public bureaucrats. If a private company such as Microsoft were required to open up all its decision processes and management practices to full view by the media, its competitors, and all interested citizens, Microsoft—despite its profit motive and the pressure of competition—would likely appear far less efficient, perhaps no more efficient than public bureaucracies.

A good case study of the important role agencies can play is the story of how ordinary federal bureaucrats created the Internet. Yes, it's true: what became the Internet

*The rules established by regulatory agencies have the force of law. In 2010 the car company Toyota was forced by federal regulators to recall six million vehicles in the United States owing to safety defects with the gas pedal in some models.*

# Who Are "Bureaucrats"?

## Executive Branch Employees, 2010 (in thousands)

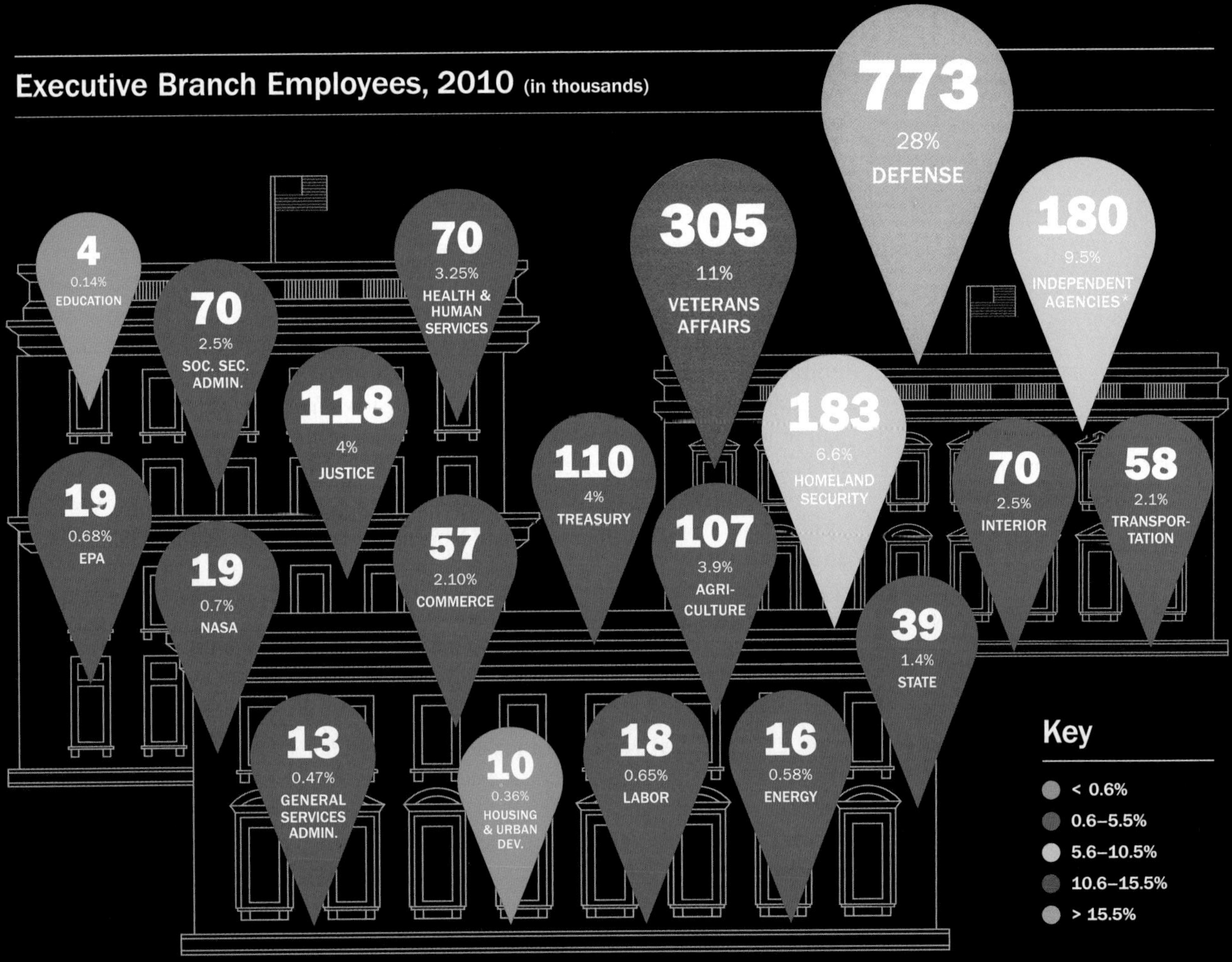

**773** 28% DEFENSE

**305** 11% VETERANS AFFAIRS

**180** 9.5% INDEPENDENT AGENCIES *

**183** 6.6% HOMELAND SECURITY

**4** 0.14% EDUCATION

**70** 2.5% SOC. SEC. ADMIN.

**70** 3.25% HEALTH & HUMAN SERVICES

**118** 4% JUSTICE

**19** 0.68% EPA

**19** 0.7% NASA

**57** 2.10% COMMERCE

**110** 4% TREASURY

**107** 3.9% AGRI-CULTURE

**70** 2.5% INTERIOR

**58** 2.1% TRANSPOR-TATION

**39** 1.4% STATE

**13** 0.47% GENERAL SERVICES ADMIN.

**10** 0.36% HOUSING & URBAN DEV.

**18** 0.65% LABOR

**16** 0.58% ENERGY

### Key
- < 0.6%
- 0.6–5.5%
- 5.6–10.5%
- 10.6–15.5%
- > 15.5%

## Location, 2008

**320** 17% WASHINGTON, D.C., AREA

**1,589** 83% — OTHER

* Independent agencies include NASA, the EPA, and the Social Security Administration (shown here), as well as other agencies.

SOURCES: U.S. Census Bureau 2012 Statistical Abstract; Bureau of Labor Statistics.

Contrary to popular notions of "paper pushers," the people who work in the federal bureaucracy perform a range of tasks essential to the functioning of American society. Nearly 2 million executive branch employees are involved in protecting the nation's security, managing the economy, and promoting public welfare through various means including environmental protection and health and safety regulations. Most federal employees work outside the Washington, D.C., area.

## for critical analysis

1. Which category of departments and agencies—security, economic, or public welfare—employs the most people? Why?

2. With 2 million people working for the executive branch, mostly outside of the Washington, D.C., area, how can Congress and the president be sure that they are serving the public's interests?

was developed largely by the U.S. Department of Defense, and defense considerations still shape the basic structure of the Internet. In 1957, immediately following the profound American embarrassment over the Soviet Union's launching of *Sputnik*, Congress authorized the establishment of the Advanced Research Projects Agency (ARPA) to develop, among other things, a means of maintaining communications in the event of a strategic attack on the existing telecommunications network (the telephone system). Since the telephone network was highly centralized and therefore could have been completely disabled by a single attack, ARPA developed a decentralized, highly redundant network with an improved probability of functioning after an attack. The full design, called by the acronym ARPANET, took almost a decade to create. By 1971 around 20 universities were connected to the ARPANET. The forerunner to the Internet was born.[12]

**The Merit System: How to Become a Bureaucrat** Although they face more inconveniences than their counterparts in the private sector, public bureaucrats are rewarded in part with greater job security than employees of most private organizations. More than a century ago the federal government attempted to imitate business by passing the Civil Service Act of 1883, which was followed by almost universal adoption of equivalent laws in state and local governments. These laws required that appointees to public office be qualified for the job to which they were appointed. This policy came to be called the **merit system**; its goal was not merely to put an end to political appointments under the "spoils system" but also to create a system of competitive examinations through which the very best candidates were to be hired for every job. At the higher levels of government agencies, including such posts as cabinet secretaries and assistant secretaries, many jobs are filled with political appointees and are not part of the merit system.

As a further safeguard against political interference (and to compensate for the lower-than-average pay given to public employees), merit-system employees (genuine civil servants) were given legal protection against being fired without a show of cause. Reasonable people may disagree about the value of such job security and how far it should extend in the civil service, but the justifiable objective of this job protection, cleansing bureaucracy of political interference while upgrading performance, cannot be disputed.

## The Organization of the Executive Branch

Cabinet departments, agencies, and bureaus are the operating parts of the bureaucratic whole. Figure 14.3 is an organizational chart of one of the largest and most important of the 15 **departments**, the Department of Agriculture. At the top is the head of the department, who in the United States is called the "secretary" of the department.[13] Below the secretary and the deputy secretary is a second tier of "undersecretaries," who have management responsibilities for one or more operating agencies, shown in the smaller print directly below each undersecretary's title. Those operating agencies are the third tier of the department, yet they are the highest level of responsibility for the actual programs around which the entire department is organized. This third tier is generally called the "bureau level." Each bureau-level agency usually operates under a statute, enacted by Congress, that set up the agency and gave it its authority and jurisdiction. The names of these bureau-level agencies are often quite well known to the public—the Forest

**merit system** a product of civil service reform, in which appointees to positions in public bureaucracies must objectively be deemed qualified for those positions

**department** the largest subunit of the executive branch. The secretaries of the 15 departments form the Cabinet.

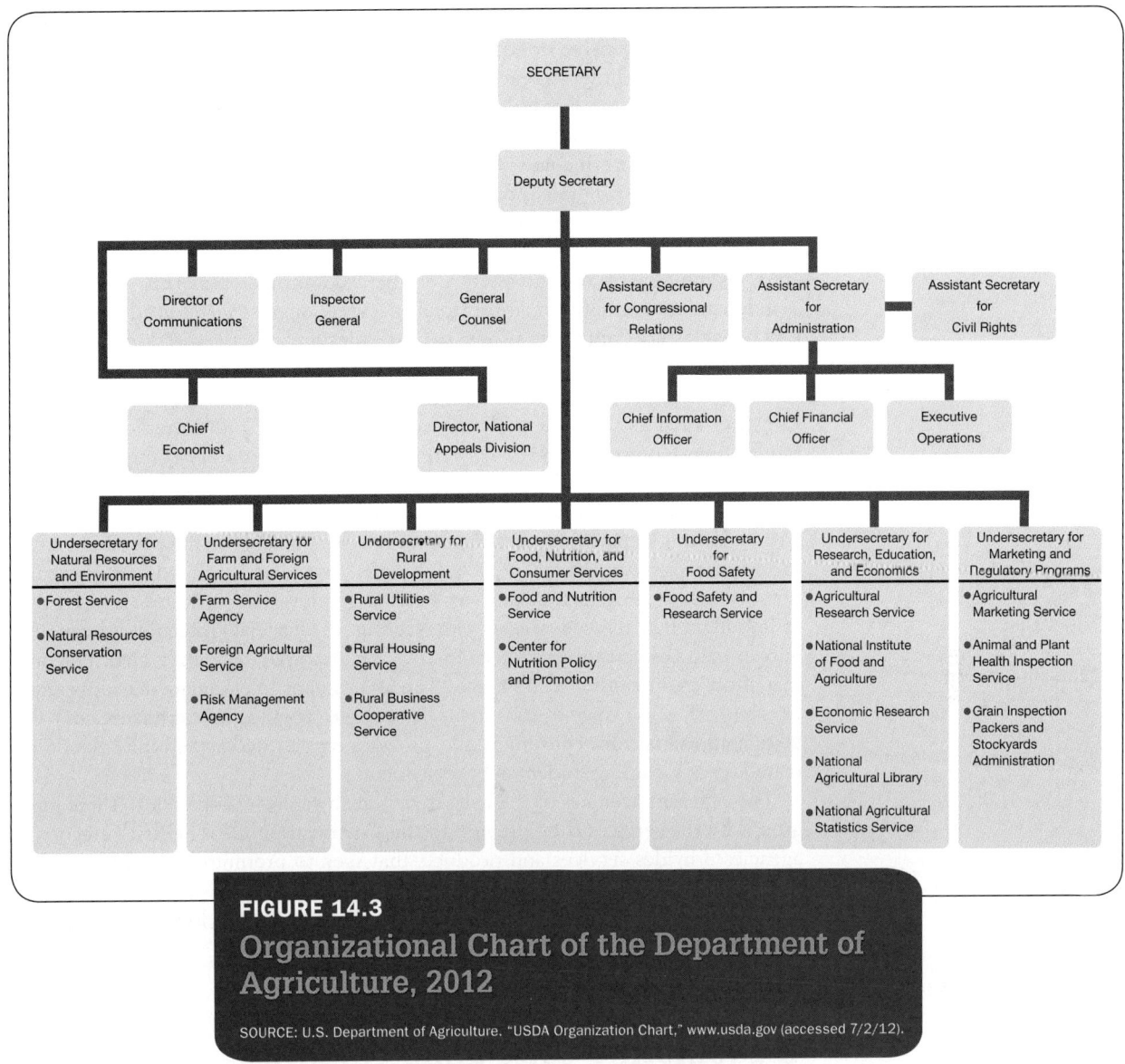

**FIGURE 14.3**

**Organizational Chart of the Department of Agriculture, 2012**

SOURCE: U.S. Department of Agriculture. "USDA Organization Chart," www.usda.gov (accessed 7/2/12).

Service and the Food Safety and Inspection Service, for example. These are the so-called line agencies, those that deal directly with the public. Sometimes these agencies are officially called "bureaus," such as the Federal Bureau of Investigation (FBI), which is part of the third tier of the Department of Justice. But "bureau" is also the conventional term for this level of administrative agency, even though many agencies or their supporters have preferred over the years to adopt a more politically palatable designation, such as "service" or "administration." Each bureau is, of course, even further subdivided into divisions, offices, or units—all are parts of the bureaucratic hierarchy.

Not all government agencies are part of cabinet departments. Some **independent agencies** are set up by Congress outside the departmental structure altogether, even though the president appoints and directs the heads of these agencies.

**independent agency** agency that is not part of a cabinet department

Independent agencies usually have broad powers to provide public services that are either too expensive or too important to be left to private initiatives. Some examples of independent agencies are the National Aeronautics and Space Administration (NASA), the Central Intelligence Agency (CIA), and the EPA. **Government corporations** are a third type of government agency but are more like private businesses in performing and charging for a market service, such as delivering the mail (the U.S. Postal Service) or transporting railroad passengers (Amtrak).

Yet a fourth type of agency is the independent regulatory commission, given broad discretion to make rules. The first regulatory agencies established by Congress, beginning with the Interstate Commerce Commission in 1887, were set up as independent regulatory commissions because Congress recognized that regulatory agencies are "minilegislatures," whose rules are exactly the same as legislation but require the kind of expertise and full-time attention that is beyond the capacity of Congress. Until the 1960s most of the regulatory agencies set up by Congress, such as the Federal Trade Commission (1914) and the Federal Communications Commission (1934), were independent regulatory commissions. But beginning in the late 1960s and the early 1970s, all new regulatory programs, with two or three exceptions (such as the Federal Election Commission), were placed within existing departments and made directly responsible to the president. After the financial crisis that began in 2008, Congress passed legislation to improve regulation of banks and other nonbank financial institutions. The legislation also created an important new regulatory agency, the Consumer Financial Protection Bureau. The bureau enforces consumer protection laws; for example, regulating bank practices that affect credit cards and mortgages. The agency aims to eliminate deceptive practices and act as the voice of consumers. Its website (www.consumerfinance.gov) also takes complaints from consumers and provides easy to understand information on many topics, including student debt repayment.

The different agencies of the executive branch can be classified into three main groups by the services they provide to the American public. The first category of agencies provides services and products that seek to promote the public welfare. The second group of agencies works to promote national security. The third group provides services that help maintain a strong economy. Let us look more closely at what each set of agencies offers to the American public.

# Promoting the Public Welfare

**Describe the major goals we expect federal agencies to promote**

One of the most important activities of the federal bureaucracy is to promote the public welfare. Americans often think of government welfare as a single program that goes only to the very poor; but a number of federal agencies provide services, build infrastructure, and enforce regulations designed to enhance the well-being of the vast majority of citizens. Departments that have important responsibilities for promoting the public welfare in this sense include the Department of Housing and Urban Development, the Department of Health and Human Services, the Department of Veterans Affairs, the Department of the Interior, the Department of Education, and the Department of Labor. Ensuring the public welfare is also the main activity of agencies in other departments, such as the Department of Agriculture's Food and Nutrition Service, which administers the federal school lunch program and the

Supplemental Nutrition Assistance Program (formerly known as food stamps). In addition, multiple independent regulatory agencies enforce regulations that aim to safeguard the public health and welfare.

**How Do Federal Bureaucracies Promote the Public Welfare?** Federal bureaucracies promote the public welfare with a diverse set of services, products, and regulations. The Department of Health and Human Services (HHS), for example, administers the program that comes closest to the popular understanding of welfare: Temporary Assistance for Needy Families (TANF). Yet this program is one of the smallest activities of the department. HHS also oversees the National Institutes of Health (NIH), which is responsible for cutting-edge biomedical research and for two major health programs of the federal government: Medicaid, which provides health care for low-income families and for many elderly and disabled people; and Medicare, which is the health insurance available to all elderly people in the United States.

A different notion of the public welfare but one highly valued by most Americans is provided by the National Park Service, under the Department of the Interior. First created in 1916, the National Park Service is responsible for the care and upkeep of national parks. Since the nineteenth century, Americans have seen protection of the natural environment as an important public goal and have looked to federal agencies to implement laws and administer programs that preserve natural areas and keep them open to the public.

The United States has no "Department of Regulation" but has many **regulatory agencies**. Some of these are bureaus within departments, such as the Food and Drug Administration (FDA), within the Department of Health and Human Services, and the Occupational Safety and Health Administration (OSHA), in the Department of Labor. As we saw earlier, other regulatory agencies are independent regulatory commissions, such as the Consumer Product Safety Commission, the FCC, and the EPA. But whether departmental or independent, an agency or commission is regulatory if Congress delegates to it relatively broad powers over a sector of the economy or a type of commercial activity and authorizes it to make rules within that jurisdiction. Rules made by regulatory agencies have the force and effect of law.

Often working behind the scenes, these agencies seek to promote the welfare of all Americans. The FDA, for example, works to protect public health by setting standards for food quality and inspecting plants to ensure that those standards are met. The EPA sets standards to limit polluting emissions from automobiles,

**regulatory agency** a department, bureau, or independent agency whose primary mission is to impose limits, restrictions, or other obligations on the conduct of individuals or companies in the private sector

*The agencies of the federal bueaucracy provide a range of services. The EPA creates and enforces regulations related to the environment, for example by testing for pollution (left). Amtrak, a government corporation, offers rail service throughout much of the United States.*

among other functions. On numerous occasions, EPA regulations have required automobile manufacturers to change the way they designed cars. The result has been cleaner air in many metropolitan areas.

**Bureaucracies, Clienteles, and the Public** Some of the public agencies that provide services are tied to a specific group or segment of American society that is often thought of as the main clientele of that agency. For example, the Department of Agriculture was established in 1862 to promote the interests of farmers. Likewise, the Department of Veterans Affairs has strong links to veterans' organizations such as the American Legion and the Veterans of Foreign Wars. The Department of Education relies on teachers' organizations for support. Figure 14.4 is a representation of this type of politics. This configuration is known as an **iron triangle**, a pattern of stable relationships among an agency in the executive branch, a congressional committee or subcommittee, and one or more organized groups of agency clientele. (Iron triangles were discussed in detail in Chapter 11.)

These relationships with particular clienteles are often important in preserving agencies from political attack. During his 1980 campaign, Ronald Reagan promised to dismantle the Department of Education as part of his commitment to get government "off people's backs." After his election, Reagan even appointed a secretary of the department who was publicly committed to eliminating it. Yet by the end

**iron triangle** the stable, cooperative relationship that often develops among a congressional committee, an administrative agency, and one or more supportive interest groups. Not all of these relationships are triangular, but the iron triangle is the most typical.

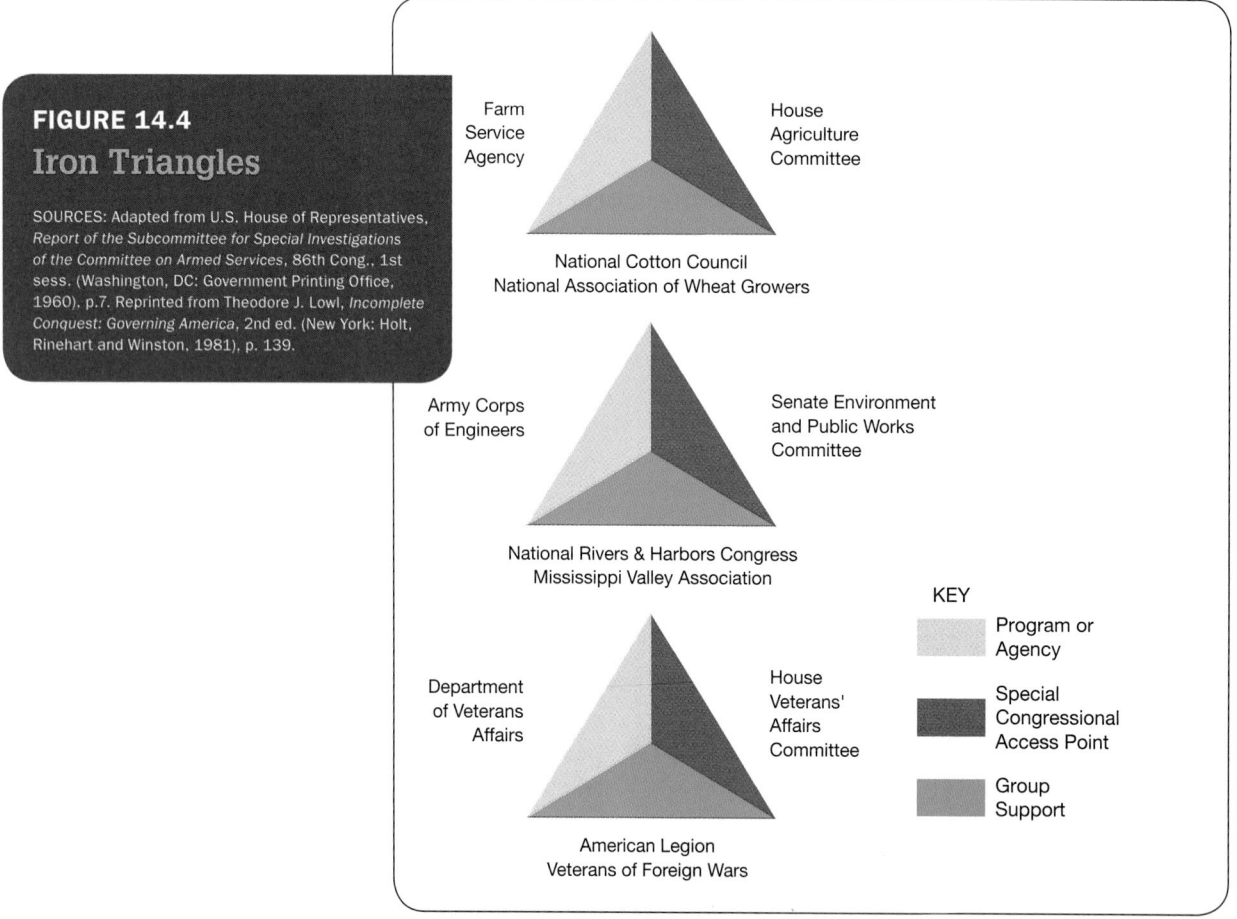

**FIGURE 14.4**
**Iron Triangles**

SOURCES: Adapted from U.S. House of Representatives, *Report of the Subcommittee for Special Investigations of the Committee on Armed Services*, 86th Cong., 1st sess. (Washington, DC: Government Printing Office, 1960), p.7. Reprinted from Theodore J. Lowi, *Incomplete Conquest: Governing America*, 2nd ed. (New York: Holt, Rinehart and Winston, 1981), p. 139.

Farm Service Agency

House Agriculture Committee

National Cotton Council
National Association of Wheat Growers

Army Corps of Engineers

Senate Environment and Public Works Committee

National Rivers & Harbors Congress
Mississippi Valley Association

Department of Veterans Affairs

House Veterans' Affairs Committee

American Legion
Veterans of Foreign Wars

KEY

Program or Agency

Special Congressional Access Point

Group Support

of his administration, the Department of Education was still standing and barely touched. In 1995 the Republican Congress vowed to eliminate the Department of Education, along with two other departments, but it, too, failed. The educational constituency of the department (its clientele) mobilized to save it each time.

Nevertheless, the ability of clientele groups to get their way is not automatic, as agencies have to balance limited resources, competing interests, and political pressures. For example, the Department of Veterans Affairs long resisted the efforts of Vietnam veterans to be compensated for exposure to Agent Orange, a chemical defoliant used extensively during the Vietnam War. Veterans charged that exposure to Agent Orange had left them with a variety of diseases ranging from cancer to severe birth defects in their children. Only after decades of lobbying, lawsuits, and federally sponsored studies did the Department of Veterans Affairs provide assistance to affected veterans.

Moreover, federal agencies increasingly seek public support outside their direct clients for their activities. In some cases, key clientele groups will work to build more widespread support for agency activities. For example, the American Federation of Labor and Congress of Industrial Organizations (AFL-CIO), which represents organized labor, built a broad coalition of student organizations, church groups, consumer groups, and civil rights activists opposed to sweatshops in the United States. These groups helped support the Department of Labor's campaign to uncover and eliminate such manufacturing practices in the United States. Agency failure to consider public opinion can result in embarrassment, which bureaucrats prefer to avoid. The Department of Homeland Security's color-coded system for warning about terrorism failed to command public respect and came in for ridicule by late-night television comedians. The public gradually began to ignore the alerts, especially as suspicions mounted that the system was being politically manipulated. Eventually, the federal government stopped issuing new alerts.

Attentiveness to the public often means making them aware of services and improving the way services are delivered. The Social Security Administration is an independent agency that administers old-age and disability insurance, the federal government's most important and expensive welfare program. Old-age insurance, or Social Security, is supported by AARP, an interest group representing people over 50, generally considered to be the most powerful interest group operating in the United States today. But worried that younger workers are losing confidence in Social Security, the agency began to issue annual statements to each worker, outlining the benefits that they can count on from Social Security when they retire and indicating what benefits are available if they become disabled before retirement.

## Providing National Security

One of the remarkable features of American federalism is that the most vital agencies for providing security for the American people (namely, the police) are located in state and local governments. But some agencies vital to maintaining national security are located in the national government, and they can be grouped into two categories: (1) agencies to confront threats to internal national security and (2) agencies to defend American security from external threats. The departments of greatest influence in these two areas are Homeland Security, Justice, Defense, and State.

**Agencies for Internal Security** The task of maintaining domestic security changed dramatically after the terrorist attacks of September 11, 2001. The creation of the Department of Homeland Security in late 2002 signaled the high priority that domestic security would now have. The orientation of domestic agencies shifted as well, as agencies geared up to prevent terrorism, a very different task from their former charge of investigating crime. With this shift in responsibility came broad new powers, many of them controversial, including the power to detain terrorist suspects and to engage in extensive domestic intelligence-gathering about possible terrorists.

Before September 11, most of the effort put into maintaining internal national security took the form of legal work related to prosecuting federal crimes. The largest and most important unit of the Justice Department is the Criminal Division. Lawyers in the Criminal Division represent the U.S. government when it is the plaintiff enforcing federal criminal laws, except for those cases (about 25 percent) specifically assigned to other divisions or agencies. Criminal litigation is handled by U.S. attorneys, who are appointed by the president. There is one U.S. attorney in each of the 94 federal judicial districts; he or she supervises the work of a number of assistant U.S. attorneys.

The Civil Division of the Justice Department deals with litigation in which the United States is the defendant being sued for injury and damages allegedly inflicted by a government official or agency. The missions of the other divisions of the Justice Department—Antitrust, Civil Rights, Environment and Natural Resources, and Tax—are described by their names.

When the prevention of terrorism took center stage, the Justice Department reoriented its activities accordingly. The Patriot Act, enacted by Congress soon after September 11, gave the Justice Department broad new powers, allowing the attorney general to detain any foreigner suspected of posing a threat to internal security. The Patriot Act also expanded the government's ability to use wiretaps and to issue search warrants without notifying suspects immediately. It required public libraries to keep lists of the public's book and Internet use for federal inspection. Although initially popular with most Americans, these measures created concern about civil liberties. In 2007, high-profile congressional hearings revealed extensive conflicts between the Justice Department and the White House over the use of warrantless wiretapping in the United States. Both publicly and behind the scenes, since 2001 the Justice Department has played a central role in setting the balance between national security and civil liberties.

In 2002 the new Department of Homeland Security joined the Justice Department as the major bureaucracy charged with domestic security. The department took over some of the security-oriented agencies previously controlled by other departments (see Table 14.1). For example, the Immigration and Naturalization Service (INS) was moved from Justice to Homeland Security. Once inside the new department, the INS was abolished; immigration services were consolidated into the newly created U.S. Citizenship and Immigration Services, and the enforcement functions of the old INS were combined with the U.S. Customs Services (formerly part of the Treasury Department) to create a new Bureau of Immigration and Customs Enforcement, known as ICE. ICE has extensive investigative capacities, with field offices around the United States and bureaus in more than 30 countries. Other agencies that were transferred to the Department of Homeland Security include the Coast Guard, the Secret Service, and the Federal Emergency Management Agency (FEMA).

Growing pains were evident in Homeland Security's first years. Different bureaucratic cultures, now part of a single operation, quickly became embroiled in turf battles with one another and with the FBI (which remained in the Justice

## TABLE 14.1

## The Shape of a Domestic Security Department

| DEPARTMENT OF HOMELAND SECURITY | AGENCIES AND DEPARTMENTS THAT WERE MOVED TO THE DEPARTMENT OF HOMELAND SECURITY | DEPARTMENT OR AGENCY THEY WERE PREVIOUSLY UNDER | FROM THE 2012 BUDGET REQUEST | |
|---|---|---|---|---|
| | | | BUDGET REQUEST, IN MILLION $ | ESTIMATED NUMBER OF EMPLOYEES |
| Border and Transportation Security | U.S. Customs and Border Protection | Treasury Department | 11,845 | 61,354 |
| | Immigration and Customs Enforcement | Justice Department | 5,823 | 20,546 |
| | U.S. Citizenship and Immigration Services | Justice Department | 2,907 | 11,633 |
| | National Protection and Program Directorate (includes domestic preparedness) | General Services Administration | 2,555 | 3,167 |
| | Transportation Security Administration | Transportation Department | 8,115 | 58,401 |
| | Federal Law Enforcement Training Center | Treasury Department | 276 | 1,103 |
| Emergency Preparedness and Response | Federal Emergency Management Agency | Independent agency | 10,063 | 10,255 |
| Domestic Nuclear Detection Office | (new) | (new) | 332 | 142 |
| Science and Technology | (multiple programs) | Department of Energy | 1,176 | 505 |
| Secret Service | Secret Service (includes presidential protection units) | Treasury Department | 1,943 | 7,054 |
| Coast Guard | Coast Guard | Transportation Department | 10,339 | 50,682 |
| Office of Health Affairs | (new) | (new) | 160.9 | 118 |
| Total DHS | | | 56,983 | 220,601 |

SOURCE: U.S. Department of Homeland Security, "Budget-in-Brief, Fiscal Year 2012," www.dhs.gov (accessed 7/4/12).

Department) as the two departments attempted to sort out their respective responsibilities. The department's most public failure was its terrible performance during Hurricane Katrina in 2005. Not only did Homeland Security, through FEMA, fail to move quickly to assist stranded residents of New Orleans, it mismanaged contracts and grants associated with the recovery efforts, which led to massive cost overruns and poor performance. Alarm bells went off again in 2007 when the Coast Guard, the largest agency under Homeland Security, renewed a $24 billion

*The Federal Bueau of Investigation (FBI) investigates crime and gathers intelligence within the United States. In 2010, FBI agents searched the apartment of Faisal Shazad, who had attempted to detonate a bomb in Times Square, New York City.*

contract for fleet modernization only 11 days after department officials testified about major flaws in the program.[14] Since 2009 the Department of Homeland Security has become embroiled in conflicts over immigration. In its Secure Communities program, the department, through ICE, works with the FBI and local police to detain suspected criminals who may be undocumented immigrants. In addition to provoking claims of civil rights violations, the program has attracted opposition from state and local politicians and some local police departments. These critics charge that the program undermines effective policing by reducing Latinos' and immigrants' trust in the government.[15]

**Agencies for External National Security** Two departments occupy center stage in maintaining external national security: the departments of State and Defense.

The State Department's primary mission is diplomacy. As the most visible public representative of American diplomacy, the Secretary of State works to promote American perspectives and interests in the world. For example, in 2011 Secretary of State Hillary Clinton made a widely publicized trip to Myanmar (also known as Burma) to underscore American support for democracy in that country and to pressure Myanmar's leaders to adopt more far-reaching democratic reforms. Although diplomacy is the primary task of the State Department, diplomatic missions are only one of its organizational dimensions. As of 2012 the State Department comprised 35 bureau-level units, each under the direction of an assistant secretary.[16]

These bureaus support the responsibilities of the elite foreign-service officers (FSOs), who staff U.S. embassies around the world and who hold almost all the most powerful positions in the department below the rank of ambassador.[17] The ambassadorial positions, especially the plum positions in the major capitals of the world, are filled by presidential appointees, many of whom get their posts by having been important donors to victorious political campaigns.

Despite the importance of the State Department in foreign affairs, fewer than 20 percent of all U.S. government employees working abroad are directly under its authority. By far the largest number of career government professionals working abroad are under the authority of the Defense Department.

The creation of the Department of Defense by legislation between 1947 and 1949 was an effort to unify the two historic military departments, the War Department and the Navy Department, and to integrate them with a new branch of the military, the U.S. Air Force. Real unification, however, did not occur. The Defense Department simply added another layer to an already pluralistic national security establishment. That establishment became more complex in 1952, with the creation of the National Security Agency, charged with electronic surveillance and intelligence gathering.

The American military, following worldwide military tradition, is organized according to a "chain of command," a tight hierarchy of clear responsibility and rank, made clearer by uniforms, special insignia, and detailed organizational charts and rules of order and etiquette. At the top of the chain of command of each branch of the military are, respectively, the chief of staff of the army, the chief of naval operations, the commandant of the marines, and the chief of staff of the air force. These officers also constitute the membership of the Joint Chiefs of Staff, the center of military policy and management.

In 2002 the Defense Department created the U.S. Northern Command, a regional command charged with ensuring homeland defense, directing military operations inside the nation's borders and providing emergency backup to state and local governments, which are the first responders to any security disaster. The creation of a regional command within the United States was an unprecedented move, breaching a long-standing line between domestic law enforcement and foreign military operations.

As the creation of a military capacity within the United States suggests, addressing the threat of terrorism calls for greater coordination of internal and external security. In 2004 the National Commission on Terrorist Attacks upon the United States (the 9/11 Commission) issued a widely read report that called for a major reorganization of bureaucratic responsibilities for internal and external security.[18] The report revealed that different departments of the American government had information that, if handled properly, might have prevented the attacks of September 11, 2001. To correct this, the commission made major recommendations designed to promote unity of effort across the bureaucracy.

The 9/11 Commission's work prompted a major reorganization of the fragmented intelligence community. In 2005 a new office, the Office of the Director of National Intelligence, took over responsibility for coordinating the efforts of the 16 different agencies that gather intelligence. The DNI reports directly to the president each morning.

**National Security and Democracy** Of all the agencies in the federal bureaucracy, those charged with providing national security most often come into conflict with the norms and expectations of American democracy. Two issues in particular arise as these agencies work to ensure the national security: (1) the trade-offs between respecting the personal rights of individuals versus protecting the general public, and (2) the need for secrecy in matters of national security versus the public's right to know what the government is doing. Standards for acceptable trade-offs vary depending on the nature of the threats facing national security and whether the country is at war or peace. Needless to say, Americans often disagree about what activities the government should be able to pursue to defend U.S. national security.

AMERICA IN THE WORLD

# Leading through Civilian Power

**During the opening years of the** twenty-first century, the military dominated America's presence in the world. The wars in Iraq and Afghanistan mobilized hundreds of thousands of troops and military contractors to engage in conflicts where decisive victories proved hard to win. Aiming to provide an alternative vision for America's international engagement, in 2010 the Department of State and the U.S. Agency for International Development (USAID) issued a blueprint for "leading through civilian power."[a]

The new plan called for the Department of State and USAID to play a more prominent role in preventing and resolving international conflicts. It highlighted the unique capacities of both organizations to offer distinct perspectives on conflict and alternative approaches to addressing international problems. For example, housed in missions across the world, State Department employees possess deep knowledge of the types of ethnic conflicts that bedeviled the military efforts in Iraq and Afghanistan. USAID, an independent agency of the U.S. government, has long experience in supporting successful economic development, which may help prevent conflict. By making use of civilian power, the State

Department aimed not only to pursue America's global interests more effectively but also to reflect more fully American values of democracy and human rights. In announcing its new approach, State Department officials emphasized that "civilian power has to be the first face of American power."[b]

As part of this new vision, the Department of State developed a reorganization plan that proposed several new bureaus. One of these, the Bureau of Conflict and Stabilization Operations, was established in late 2011. Responsible for promoting effective civilian engagement in states that are vulnerable to instability and conflict, the bureau is designed to coordinate the activities of different federal departments and nongovernmental agencies (NGOs). The new bureau builds on the work of the Office of the Coordinator for Reconstruction and

Stabilization (S/CRS), which was created in 2004 to promote civilian engagement in the reconstruction of Iraq and Afghanistan. One major lesson from these wars was that stabilizing insecure nations requires much more than military expertise. It involves mobilizing experts in areas including municipal administration; reconstruction of water supply, electricity, and telecommunications; humanitarian relief; housing; education; banking; and agriculture, to name just a few. Long-range stability entails strengthening political institutions and, where necessary, planting the seeds of entirely new institutions such as political parties, legislative assemblies, courts, and local governments. By coordinating the activities of diverse civilian experts, the Bureau of Conflict and Stabilization Operations will aim to address the root causes of instability and conflict.

The State Department's ambitious plan charts a new direction for advancing American interests in the world, one that relies much less on military capabilities than in the past. But building "civilian power" is a complex bureaucratic task. Whether the State Department can mobilize the resources and build the interdepartmental cooperation needed to carry out this new mission remains to be seen.

[a]U.S. Department of State and U.S. Agency for International Development, *Leading Through Civilian Power: The First Quadrennial Diplomacy and Development Review* (Washington, DC: 2010), www.state.gov/documents/organization/153142.pdf (accessed 1/4/12).
[b]Charles S. Clark, "State Department Review Promises Transparency, Civilian 'Face,'" *Government Executive*, December 20, 2010, www.govexec.com/dailyfed/1210/122010cc1.htm.

## for critical analysis

1. Why does the United States need so many different kinds of expertise to prevent and resolve conflicts abroad?
2. What are the pros and cons of assigning more responsibility for conflict prevention and resolution to the State Department instead of the Department of Defense?

When national security is at stake, federal agencies have taken actions that are normally considered incompatible with individual rights. For example, during World War II thousands of American citizens of Japanese descent were interned in camps due to national security concerns. Although the Supreme Court approved this action, the federal government has since acknowledged that it constituted unjustified discrimination and has offered reparations to those who were interned. In the 1960s, FBI director J. Edgar Hoover authorized extensive wiretaps to eavesdrop on telephone calls of the civil rights leader Martin Luther King Jr.; most people today would regard this as an illegal invasion of his personal privacy.

With the advent of the war on terrorism, the government gained unprecedented powers to detain foreign suspects, carry out wiretaps and searches, conduct secret military tribunals, and build an integrated law enforcement and intelligence system. Congress hastily enacted many of these sweeping provisions of the Patriot Act several weeks after the terrorist attacks, with little debate. Since then, extensive doubts about the broad powers of the Patriot Act have spread from civil libertarians on the left to libertarians on the right and even to librarians and city governments, who objected to its surveillance provisions. When Congress debated renewing the Patriot Act in 2005–06, these concerns about individual liberties threatened to block renewal. The act that was finally approved in 2006 did include modest revisions, such as exempting most libraries from having to turn over users' records to the government. Nonetheless, many in Congress felt the safeguards to individual liberties did not go far enough.

Protecting national security often requires the government to conduct its activities in secret. Yet, as Americans have come to expect a more open government in the past three decades, many believe that federal agencies charged with national security keep too many secrets from the American public. As one critic put it, "the United States government must rest, in the words of the Declaration of Independence, on 'the consent of the governed.' And there can be no meaningful consent where those who are governed do not know to what they are consenting."[19] The effort to make information related to national security more available to the public began in 1966 with the passage of the Freedom of Information Act (FOIA). Strengthened in 1974 after Watergate, the act allows any person to request classified information from any federal agency. The information obtained through the Freedom of Information Act often reveals unflattering or unsuccessful aspects of national security activities. One private organization, the National Security Archive, makes extensive use of FOIA to obtain information about the activities of national security agencies. The National Security Archive has published many of these documents on its website and maintains an archive in Washington, D.C., that is open to the public. For example, the organization's website contains "The Torture Archive," a searchable database of documents related to the detention of individuals in the Global War on Terror and the authorized use of torture by the American government.

The tension between secrecy and democracy sharpened dramatically with the threat of terrorism. FOIA was curtailed, and the range of information deemed sensitive has greatly expanded. President George W. Bush defended the new secrecy, declaring, "We're an open society, but we're at war. Foreign terrorists and agents must never again be allowed to use our freedoms against us." Although most Americans agreed that enhanced secrecy was needed to ensure domestic security, concerns about excessive secrecy mounted. Some analysts worried that secrecy would prevent Congress from carrying out its basic oversight responsibilities. They also claimed that much of the secrecy had nothing to do with

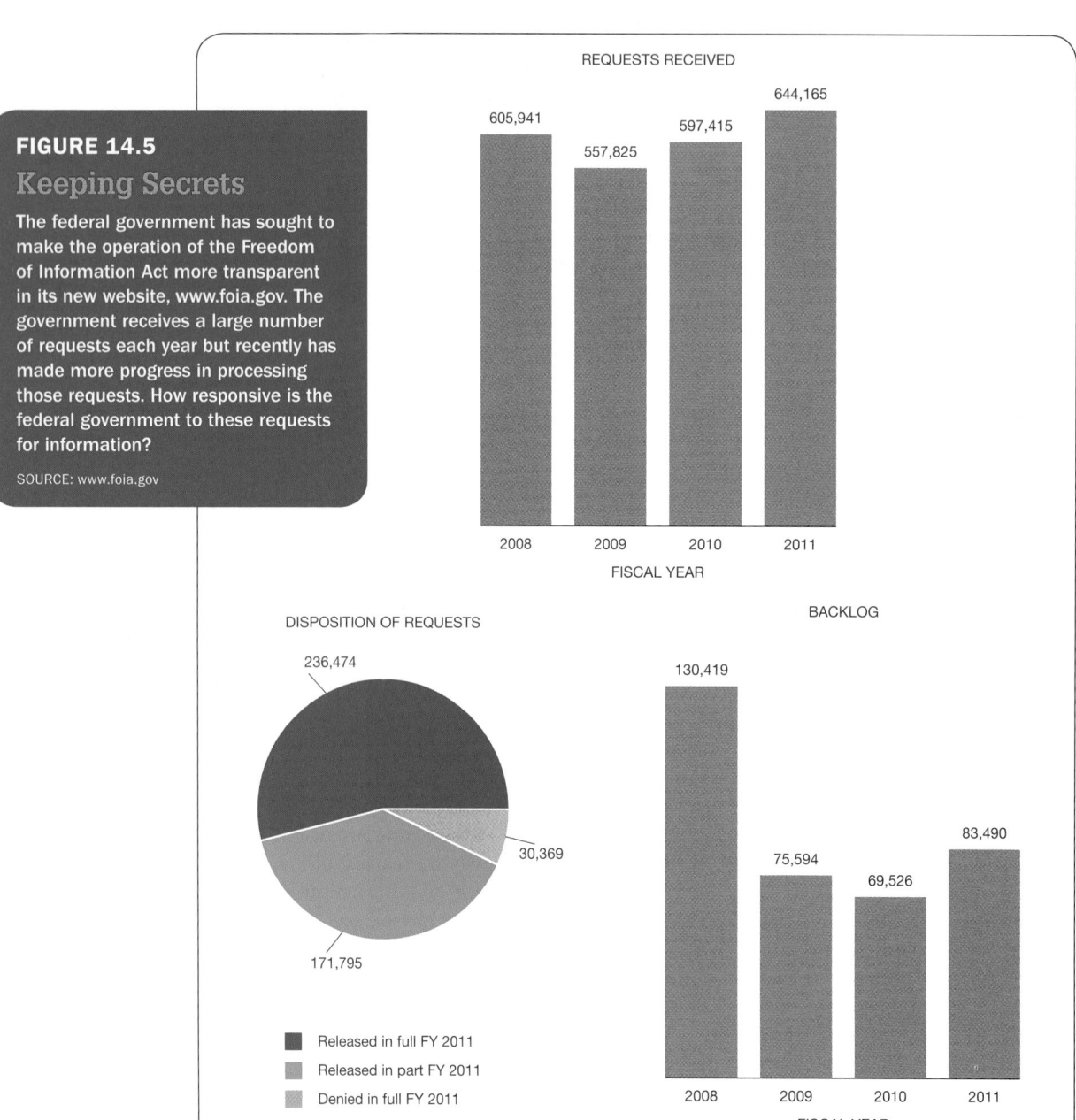

REQUESTS RECEIVED

605,941 557,825 597,415 644,165

2008 2009 2010 2011

FISCAL YEAR

DISPOSITION OF REQUESTS

236,474

30,369

171,795

Released in full FY 2011
Released in part FY 2011
Denied in full FY 2011

BACKLOG

130,419 75,594 69,526 83,490

2008 2009 2010 2011

FISCAL YEAR

national security. As a candidate, President Obama promised to reduce government secrecy. The day after his election, he launched a process that would culminate in an Open Government Directive. He also instructed federal agencies that they should administer the FOIA law liberally: when in doubt, err on the side of openness. In 2011 the Department of Justice created the website www .foia.gov so that the public could learn more about the FOIA process. The site presents data about the number of FOIA requests by agency and the size of the backlog in processing those requests (see Figure 14.5). And in the most substantive change, at the end of his first year in office, Obama issued an executive order designed to promote more rapid declassification of secret documents. However, the Obama administration also continued some of the secrecy practices initiated in the Bush years. Most notably, it invoked the state secrets privilege to prevent lawsuits related to warrantless wiretapping and torture from going to trial.[20] The cost of government secrecy has risen dramatically since 2001. In 2011 the federal government spent an estimated $13 billion protecting its secrets, up from $4.7 billion in 2000, as much as the entire budget of the Environmental Protection Agency.[21] Even so, secrecy is increasingly difficult to preserve. In 2010–11 the Australian anti-secrecy activist Julian Assange shocked the world by releasing hundreds of thousands of U.S. government classified documents online through WikiLeaks. The incident, which made secret State Department cables and other documents available online, underscored the vulnerability of government secrets in the Internet age. In an era when national security is foremost in the public's mind, conflicts between democracy and secrecy are sure to increase.

## Maintaining a Strong Economy

In our capitalist economic system, the government does not directly run the economy. Yet many federal government activities are critical to maintaining a strong economy. Foremost among these are the agencies responsible for fiscal and monetary policy. Other agencies, such as the Internal Revenue Service (IRS), transform private resources into use for public purposes. Tax policy may also strengthen the economy through decisions about whom to tax, how much, and when. Finally, the federal government, through such agencies as the Department of Transportation, the Commerce Department, and the Energy Department, may directly provide services or goods that bolster the economy.

**Fiscal and Monetary Agencies** Fiscal policy can refer to any government policy having to do with public finance. However, Americans often reserve *fiscal* for taxing and spending policies and use *monetary* for policies having to do with banks, credit, and currency.

While the responsibility for making fiscal policy lies with Congress, the administration of fiscal policy occurs primarily in the Treasury Department. In addition to collecting income, corporate, and other taxes, the Treasury also manages the enormous national debt: $16 trillion in 2012.[22] The Treasury Department is also responsible for printing U.S. currency, but currency is only a tiny proportion of the entire money economy. Most of the trillions of dollars used in the transactions of the private and public sectors of the U.S. economy exist virtually—in computerized accounts rather than actual currency.

A key monetary agency is the **Federal Reserve System**, which is headed by the Federal Reserve Board. The Federal Reserve System (called simply the Fed) has authority over the interest rates and lending activities of the nation's most important banks. Congress established the Fed in 1913 as a clearinghouse responsible for adjusting the supply of money and credit to the needs of commerce and industry in different regions of the country. The Fed is also responsible for ensuring that banks do not overextend themselves, a policy that guards against a chain of bank failures during a sudden economic scare, such as occurred in 1929 and again in 2008. The Federal Reserve Board directs the operations of the 12 district Federal Reserve Banks, which are essentially "bankers' banks," serving the monetary needs of the hundreds of member banks in the national banking system.[23] The Treasury and the Federal Reserve took center stage when a string of bank failures threatened

**fiscal policy** the government's use of taxing, monetary, and spending powers to manipulate the economy

**Federal Reserve System** a system of 12 Federal Reserve Banks that facilitates exchanges of cash, checks, and credit; regulates member banks; and uses monetary policies to fight inflation and deflation

*The Treasury Department helps maintain the economy in various ways. Here, Treasury Secretary Timothy Geithner meets with economic experts and business leaders to discuss oversight of the Troubled Asset Relief Program, which was designed to address the financial crisis that began in 2008.*

economic catastrophe in 2008. These agencies designed a $700 billion bailout package and convinced Congress that a rapid response was needed to avert a worldwide depression. Although the Treasury and the Federal Reserve sprang into action when economic calamity loomed, critics charged that the crisis could have been prevented if these agencies had exercised more regulatory oversight over the financial sector during the previous decade. In 2010 the Congress and the president created the Financial Stability Oversight Council, headed by the treasury secretary, with the Federal Reserve chairman also playing a key role. This body is responsible for identifying systemwide risks to the financial sector. The council initiated rule-writing processes designed to set up its operations and to implement new regulations related to financial stability. Most significant among the issues it has considered is whether to make nonbank financial institutions, such as hedge funds, subject to greater regulatory oversight, comparable to that which banks now receive.[24] The financial industry kept a close eye on these developments, aiming to limit the regulatory reach of the new council.[25]

**Revenue Agencies** One of the first actions Congress took under President George Washington was to create the Department of the Treasury, and probably its oldest function is the collection of taxes on imports, called tariffs. Now part of the Department of Homeland Security, federal customs agents are located at every U.S. seaport and international airport to oversee the collection of tariffs. But far and away the most important of the **revenue agencies** is the IRS. The U.S. Customs and Border Protection is one bureau of seven within the Department of Homeland Security, while the IRS is a bureau within the Treasury Department.

The IRS is the government agency that Americans love to hate. As one expert put it, "probably no organization in the country, public or private, creates as much clientele *dis*favor as the Internal Revenue Service. The very nature of its work brings it into an adversarial relationship with vast numbers of Americans every year [emphasis added]."[26] Taxpayers complain about the IRS's needless complexity, its lack of sensitivity and responsiveness to individual taxpayers, and its overall lack of

**revenue agency** an agency responsible for collecting taxes. Examples include the Internal Revenue Service for income taxes, the U.S. Customs Service for tariffs and other taxes on imported goods, and the Bureau of Alcohol, Tobacco, Firearms and Explosives for collection of taxes on the sale of those particular products.

efficiency. Such complaints led Congress to pass the IRS Restructuring and Reform Act of 1998, which instituted a number of new protections for taxpayers. By 2005, however, concern was shifting toward the problem of tax dodgers. When a 2005 report indicated that the gap between true income and income reported to the IRS was at an all-time high, the IRS vowed to step up enforcement activities, focusing especially on foreign tax shelters favored by the wealthy. The Obama administration has put an emphasis on shutting down overseas tax "havens." Aided by a 13 percent increase in funding for enforcement, the IRS has become more aggressive about pursuing wealthy individuals suspected of avoiding U.S. tax by illegally sheltering their income abroad. After the U.S. government reached deals with the Swiss and Maltese governments to turn over details of U.S. citizens with holdings in banks in those countries, more than 14,000 U.S. taxpayers came forward as part of an amnesty program, with some accounts amounting to as much as $100 million.[27] The Department of Justice continued to pursue the matter and, in 2012, charged employees of a Swiss bank with helping to shield $1.2 billion in American taxpayer assets from the IRS. The results of these efforts are limited, however, because many overseas tax shelters are legal. Despite several efforts, Congress has failed to enact legislation limiting such shelters.[28]

The politics of the IRS is most interesting because, although thousands upon thousands of corporations and wealthy individuals have a strong and active interest in American tax policy, key taxation decisions are set by agreements among the president, the Treasury Department, and the leading members of the two tax committees in Congress, the House Ways and Means Committee and the Senate Finance Committee. External influence is not spread throughout the 50 states but is much more centralized in the majority political party, a few key figures in Congress, and a handful of professional lobbyists. Suspicions of unfair exemptions and favoritism are widespread, and they do exist, but these exemptions come largely from Congress, *not* from the IRS itself.

**Economic Development Agencies** Federal agencies also conduct programs designed to strengthen particular segments of the economy or to provide specific services aimed at strengthening the entire economy. Created in 1889, the Department of Agriculture is the fourth-oldest cabinet department. Its initial mission, to strengthen American agriculture by providing information about effective farming practices, reflected the enormous importance of farming in the American economy. Through its Agricultural Extension Service, the Department of Agriculture established an important presence in rural areas throughout the country. It also built strong support for its activities among the nation's farmers and at the many land-grant colleges, where agricultural research has been conducted for over 100 years.

At first glance, the Department of Transportation, which oversees the nation's highway and air traffic systems, may seem to have little to do with economic development. But effective transportation is the backbone of a strong economy. The interstate highway system, for example, is widely acknowledged as a key factor in promoting economic growth in the decades after World War II. The departments of Commerce and Energy also oversee programs designed to ensure a strong economy. The Small Business Administration, in the Department of Commerce, provides loans and technical assistance to small businesses across the country.

In recent decades, dissatisfaction with government has led to calls to keep government out of the economy. Yet if the federal government were to disappear, the economy would almost certainly fall into chaos. There is widespread agreement that the federal government should set the basic rules for economic activity and should intervene—through such measures as setting interest rates—to keep the economy strong. Some analysts argue that the government's role should go beyond rule setting to include more active measures such as investment in infrastructure. Advocates of government action point to the economic benefits of government investments in the interstate highway system and of the government research in the 1960s that led to the creation of the Internet.

## ● Can the Bureaucracy Be Reformed?

When citizens complain that government is too bureaucratic, what they often mean is that government bureaucracies seem inefficient and waste money. The epitome of such bureaucratic inefficiency in the late 1980s was the Department of Defense, which was revealed to have spent $640 apiece for toilet seats and $435 apiece for hammers—although erroneous reports of $16 muffins bought by the Justice Department captured headlines in 2011.[29] Many citizens also had negative personal experience with the federal government: mountains of forms to fill out, lengthy waits, and unsympathetic service. Why can't government do better? many citizens asked. The application of new technologies and innovative management strategies in the private sector during the 1980s made government agencies look even more lumbering and inefficient by comparison. People were coming to expect faster service and more customer-friendly interactions in the private sector. But how can public-sector bureaucracies become more effective?

The government has sought to find various ways to make the federal bureaucracy more efficient. The key strategies used to promote reform include reinventing bureaucratic procedures, termination, devolution, and privatization. In general,

*In recent years there have been several attempts to "reinvent" government. In 1993, President Bill Clinton and Vice President Al Gore established the National Performance Review to reinvent government. Gore promoted this on David Letterman's show, where he railed against the government's procurement requirements, which even specified the number of pieces into which a government ashtray may shatter.*

*NASA's space shuttle program was terminated in 2011. In July of that year* Atlantis *flew its last mission.*

Democratic administrations have aimed to make the existing bureaucracy work more effectively, whereas Republican administrations have sought to sideline the bureaucracy, especially by contracting out government work to private companies.

## Reinventing the Bureaucracy

In 1993, President Clinton launched the National Performance Review (NPR)—part of his promise to "reinvent government"—to make the federal bureaucracy more efficient, accountable, and effective. The NPR sought to prod federal agencies into adopting flexible, goal-driven practices. Clinton promised that the result would be a government that would "work better and cost less." Virtually all observers agreed that the NPR made substantial progress. Its original goal was to save more than $100 billion over five years, in large part by cutting the federal workforce by 12 percent (more than 270,000 jobs) by the end of 1999. In fact, by 2000, $136 billion in savings were already assured through legislative or administrative action, and the federal workforce had been cut by 426,200.[30] The streamlining of government business procedures did help make government work more effectively, but it did not institute the more sweeping approach to reform demanded by some political leaders. These leaders have instead pursued efforts to terminate, devolve, or contract out government functions.

## Termination

The only *certain* way to reduce the size of the bureaucracy is to eliminate programs. Variations in the levels of federal personnel and expenditures (as were shown in Figures 14.1 and 14.2) demonstrate the futility of trying to make permanent cuts in existing agencies. Furthermore, most agencies have a supportive constituency that will fight to reinstate any cuts that are made. Termination (a rare occurrence) is the only way to ensure an agency's reduction. Even in the 12 years of the Reagan and George H. W. Bush administrations, both of which proclaimed a strong commitment to the reduction of the national government, not a single national government agency or program was terminated. In the 1990s, Republicans did succeed in eliminating two small agencies.

The overall difficulty in terminating bureaucracy is a reflection of Americans' love-hate relationship with the national government. As antagonistic as Americans may be toward bureaucracy in general, they benefit from the services being rendered and the protections being offered by particular bureaucratic agencies. They fiercely defend their favorite agencies while perceiving no inconsistency in their hostility toward the bureaucracy in general. A good case in point is the agonizing problem of closing military bases in the wake of the end of the Cold War with the former Soviet Union, when the United States no longer needed so many bases. Since every base was in some congressional member's district, it proved impossible for Congress to decide to close any of them. Consequently, beginning in 1988, Congress established the Defense Base Closure and Realignment Commission (BRAC) to decide on base closings, allowing Congress only an up or down vote on the commission's proposals.[31] Five different BRAC reports, the most recent in 2005, have formed the basis for closing bases and modifying the operations in the remaining bases.

Elected leaders have come to rely on a more incremental approach to downsizing the bureaucracy. Much has been done by budgetary means, reducing the budgets of all agencies across the board by small percentages and cutting some less-supported agencies by larger amounts. Yet these changes are still incremental, leaving the existence of agencies unaddressed.

## Devolution

**devolution** a policy to remove a program from one level of government by delegating it or passing it down to a lower level of government, such as from the national government to the state and local governments

The next most effective approach to genuinely reducing the size of the federal bureaucracy is **devolution**, downsizing the federal bureaucracy by delegating the implementation of programs to state and local governments. Devolution often alters the pattern of who benefits most from government programs. Opponents of devolution in social policy, for example, charge that it reduces the ability of the government to remedy inequality. They argue that state governments, which cannot run deficits, as the federal government does, and which have more limited taxing capabilities, will inevitably cut spending on programs that serve low-income residents. They point to the State Children's Health Insurance Program (SCHIP), which was created in 1997 to extend health insurance to low-income children. When the economy was booming, states added children to the rolls and some states even extended benefits to the children's parents. But by 2002, as states faced significant budget crises, many cut back on SCHIP. Although the federal government was initially able to compensate for state funding problems, states have found it difficult to keep pace with the rising number of children without health insurance. Moreover, because state revenues can fluctuate widely from year to year, states are often forced to cut back on expensive health coverage programs. By 2010, many states faced their worst budget crises since the Great Depression. Even though the federal government provided substantial assistance to states through a massive stimulus program, as those funds dried up in 2011, a number of states began to cut health benefits for children. Many of these children will now receive insurance through state health exchanges and insurance subsidies, both established by the Affordable Care Act. Others will be covered through the expansions of Medicaid mandated in the act. However, if states take advantage of the Supreme Court ruling on the act that allows them to opt out of expanded coverage, many low-income people may remain without health insurance.[32] Immediately after the court decision, the governors of Florida and South Carolina announced their intention to opt out, citing the burden of Medicaid on state budgets. Other states expressed doubts about whether they would accept the expansion. While some saw this as the beginning of a trend that would leave millions uninsured, others predicted that in the end, the favorable terms of the Medicaid expansion—the federal government pays for all the expanded coverage until 2016 and 90 percent thereafter—would lead states to participate in the program.[33]

Often the central aim of devolution is to provide more efficient and flexible government services. Yet by its very nature, devolution entails variation across the states. In some states, government services may improve as a consequence of devolution. In other states, services may deteriorate as the states use devolution as an opportunity to cut spending and reduce services. This has been the pattern in the implementation of the welfare reform passed in 1996, the most significant devolution of federal government social programs in many decades. Some states, such as Wisconsin, have used the flexibility of the reform to design innovative programs that respond to clients' needs; other states, such as Idaho, have virtually dismantled their welfare programs. The recession that began in 2008 provided the first real evidence about what increased state flexibility meant for low-income Americans. Studies showed that the number of people on public assistance rose by 14 percent even as the unemployment rate increased by 88 percent between 2007 and 2010.[34] Moreover, states varied widely in how they responded: for example, although unemployment rose by 146 percent in Arizona, public assistance rolls actually fell by 48 percent. In Oregon, by contrast, public assistance cases rose by 70 percent although unemployment grew by only 41 percent. The overall lack of growth and state variation in welfare contrasts sharply with the rise in the rise of food stamp recipients during 2008–09. Food stamp recipients grew by 45 percent between 2009 and 2010 and pulled an estimated 9 percent of Americans out of poverty in 2009.[35] Critics argued that devolution gave the states too much flexibility to design their own welfare programs and that the result has been a program unable to assist the poor when they need it most.

This is the dilemma that devolution poses. Up to a point, variation can be considered one of the virtues of federalism. But in a democracy, it is inherently dangerous to have large variations in the provisions of services and benefits.

## Privatization

Most of what is called privatization is the provision of government goods and services by private contractors under direct government supervision. Except for top-secret strategic materials, virtually all military hardware, from boats to bullets, is produced on a privatized basis by private contractors. Research services worth billions of dollars are bought under contract by governments from universities and from ordinary industrial corporations and private "think tanks." **Privatization** simply means that a formerly public activity is picked up under contract by a private company or companies. But such programs are still very much government programs—paid for by government and supervised by government. Privatization

**privatization** the transfer of all or part of a program from the public sector to the private sector

downsizes the government only in that the workers providing the service are no longer counted as part of the government bureaucracy.

President George W. Bush made privatization a central component of his effort to reform the federal bureaucracy. He introduced new procedures that would subject more than 800,000 federal jobs, nearly half the federal civilian workforce, to competitive outsourcing. If it were determined that a company could do the job more efficiently, the work would be contracted out. Under Bush, government outsourcing grew dramatically as the government sought to staff the new Department of Homeland Security and pursue wars in Afghanistan and Iraq without increasing the numbers of federal employees. One estimate of the growth of contracting showed that at the end of the Cold War in 1990, there were three and a half contractors and grantees for every civil servant; by 2005 the buildup connected with national security had altered the ratio to five and a half contractors and grantees for every civil servant.[36] Payments for federal contracts grew from $209 billion in 2000 to $528 billion in 2008.[37] Although military contracts account for much of the growth, contracting is common throughout the federal bureaucracy. In fact, contracting is now so widespread that it has been called a "virtual fourth branch of government."[38]

The central aim of privatization is to reduce the cost of government. Depending on how it is conducted, competitive outsourcing may not lead to extensive privatization; instead, competition may improve government performance by forcing federal agencies to reexamine how they can do their work more efficiently. When private contractors can perform a task as well as government can, but for less money, taxpayers win. But private firms are not necessarily more efficient or less costly than government, especially when there is little competition among private firms and when public bureaucracies are not granted a fair chance to bid in the contracting competition. In 2005 only 34 percent of existing contracts were subject to competition, whereas 45 percent were open to competition in 2000 (Figure 14.6).[39] When private firms have a monopoly on service provision, they may

One strategy to carry out the tasks of government is privatization. The United States' military operations have increasingly been privatized, with private contractors providing security services in Iraq and Afghanistan.

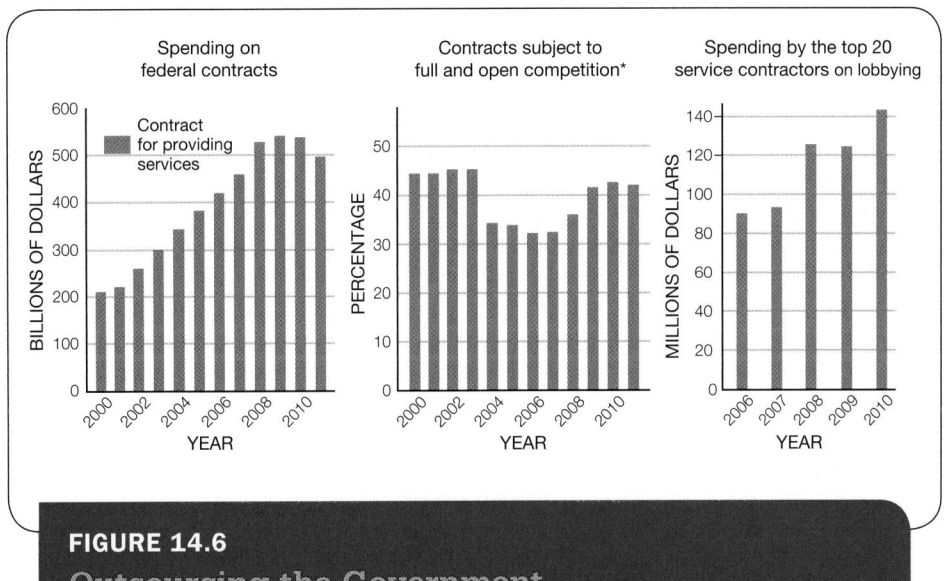

## FIGURE 14.6

## Outsourcing the Government

As spending on federal contracts has grown, the number of contracts subject to open competition has declined substantially. At the same time, the rise in spending by private contractors on lobbying and campaign contributions raises questions about improper political influence on government contracting decisions.

*Includes both new contracts and payments against existing contracts.

SOURCES: Fedspending.org, "Summary of Federal Spending: Financial Assistance and Procurement," www .fedspending.org (accessed 7/4/12); Fedspending.org, "Federal Contract Awards by Extent of Competition," www .fedspending.org (accessed 7/4/12); Government Executive, "Top 200 Federal Contractors," August 15, 2010, www.govexec.com (accessed 7/4/12); Center for Responsive Politics, "Lobbying Database," www.opensecrets.org (accessed 7/4/12).

be less efficient than government and more expensive. In fact, there is no good evidence that privatization saves the government money.

Concerns about adequate government oversight and accountability escalated as the scale of contracting has dramatically increased. Consider the use of private contractors in Iraq and Afghanistan. Congressional hearings revealed massive cost overruns by KBR (formerly a subsidiary of Halliburton, the firm that former vice president Dick Cheney headed), which held $9 billion in no-bid contracts to provide services ranging from supplying fuel for the military to preparing cafeteria meals in Iraq. Army auditors have challenged $1.9 billion of KBR's bills as improper, citing violations ranging from unserved meals to inflated gas prices.[40]

Private security firms pose even more serious oversight issues. The Department of Defense has made heavy use of such firms to provide services in Iraq and Afghanistan that were previously provided by the military directly. In 2011 a congressional commission reported that more than 260,000 private workers operated in Iraq and Afghanistan in 2010. Private workers outnumbered the federal military and federal civilian workforce in these countries.[41] High-profile congressional hearings into the role of Blackwater, a private security firm, in civilian killings in Iraq illustrated the difficulties of relying on private contractors to conduct a war. With a billion dollars of government contracts, Blackwater played an essential role in providing security in Iraq. But because they are not bound by the same rules of conduct as the military, private security forces were accused of being more likely than the regular military to kill civilians who posed little threat. And because the private security forces are not subject to the military code of justice, illegal behavior is difficult to sanction.

The private military is also costlier. Noting that "sergeants in the military generally cost the Government between $50,000 to $70,000 per year" and that "a comparable position at Blackwater costs the Federal Government over $400,000, six times as much," congressional critics have questioned whether the private military is cost effective.[42] Disparities in pay not only are demoralizing to the troops, but they also lure trained troops away from the military to the private contractors. Even more troubling is the possibility that private contractors undermined the mission in Iraq by creating hostility among the Iraqi people as reports of unprovoked civilian killings came to light.[43]

In most aspects of government activity, contract employees work side by side with government employees in what has been called a "blended workforce."[44] Many agencies that rely on technical expertise, such as the National Oceanographic and Atmospheric Administration, routinely rely on contractors. But although federal regulations forbid the outsourcing of "inherently governmental work," no clear line separates governmental and nongovernmental work. For example, in 2006 the General Services Administration hired a private firm, CACI International, to help it examine cases of fraud by other private contractors. Not only did the private contract workers hired by the GSA in this case cost double their public counterparts, but they were engaged in oversight of other private contractors, a clear conflict of interest.[45]

As alarm over the activities of contractors has grown, there have been several efforts to increase accountability. In 2002 the federal government created a centralized database to record how well contractors have performed. The aim of the database is to provide a resource for agencies as they offer new contracts. However, research by the Government Accountability Office (GAO) showed that after seven years, the database was poorly documented and was seldom used in agency decision making.[46] As part of the 2009 National Defense Authorization Act, Congress called for the creation of an additional database that will keep track of contractors who commit legal or contractual violations.[47] In 2008, Congress also responded to the concerns about contractors by creating a "Commission on Wartime Contracting." The commission, modeled on the 1941 Truman Commission set up to investigate wartime profiteering in World War II, had a two-year charge to investigate contracting abuse and waste in Afghanistan and Iraq. Its final report sharply criticized the use of private contractors, estimating that the practice had wasted between $31 billion and $60 billion during the two wars. It made numerous recommendations for reform but noted that successful reforms would require congressional action and funding for new oversight capabilities.[48]

Some members of Congress have sought far-reaching regulations on contractors. For example, Senator Chuck Schumer (D-N.Y.) and Representative Chris Van Hollen (D-Md.) proposed legislation in 2010 that would prohibit government contractors from making political contributions.[49] Members of Congress have also proposed forbidding contractors from performing sensitive functions in war settings, including interrogations, security, and intelligence functions. In 2011 the Obama administration considered issuing an executive order requiring federal contractors to disclose their contributions to groups that engage in politics. Proposals for such

## for critical analysis

Private security firms played a significant role in the Iraq War and its aftermath. What are the advantages and disadvantages of relying on private firms in wartime? Can government provide adequate oversight of these private companies?

# E-Government

**E-government refers to the delivery** of government information and services online via the Internet or other digital means. E-government holds promise for improved delivery of many types of public services, including online transactions such as filing taxes, applying for financial aid or licenses, reserving a campsite in a national or state park, or paying parking tickets. It also makes it easier to get information about the operation of government (for example, snow plow routes, evacuation routes, traffic delays, real-time rail and bus routes, and community events). E-government can improve communication between citizens and government. Perhaps most importantly, it can save money.

Before digital government, interacting with government was often slow and time-consuming. A typical transaction required travel to a government office, waiting in line, requesting a form, calling the office if there were questions about how to fill out the form, mailing it in, and so on. The Department of Motor Vehicles (DMV) is an example of a government office that still requires in-person visits, and usually waiting in long lines, to obtain a driver's license.

E-government is one of the fastest-growing online activities, and 2012 survey data show that more than three in four Internet users report using a federal, state, or local government website. The federal government has a central portal for all federal services (www.usa.gov), all 50 states have sophisticated websites, and most local governments maintain websites.

Trust in government has been declining for more than half a century, as the federal bureaucracy in particular has been seen as slow, inefficient, and unresponsive. E-government has been proposed as a way to improve citizen evaluations of government. Why might this occur?

By making available the information and services that citizens want, and by improving the speed and ease of interactions, e-government may enhance government responsiveness. Government websites, e-mail, and social media create convenient new opportunities for interaction with officials. Single, integrated portals and links to other sites have the potential to make information and services from a number of agencies available through a single website. Searchable databases can improve the accessibility of information, as does access to information seven days a week, 24 hours a day. E-government may improve participation in government by providing for citizen input via online town meetings, online forums, and deliberative processes for e-rulemaking. It may also improve government transparency through the posting of data, policies, laws, meeting schedules and minutes, and contact information.

A recent study drawing on Pew survey data found that people who use e-government tend to have more positive attitudes about government. Specifically, use of a local government website appears to be related to trust in local governments, and to other positive assessments of federal, state, and local governments in terms of responsiveness, accessibility, communication, and transparency.

Perhaps most important, e-government improves efficiency through use of the latest technology to automate processes, improve service delivery, produce budget savings, and save time. Online transactions and downloadable forms are examples of more efficient processes through e-government. More generally, however, automation emulates the convenience and efficiency of e-commerce, and suggests that government is adopting state-of-the-art private-sector practices. The political scientist Darrell West found that receiving information about e-government was associated with positive attitudes about government efficiency.

Darrell West argues that new technology requires organizational change, and this type of change is necessary for government innovation. The private sector has quickly adapted to a world of commerce online, using technology for organizational change, including "flattening" organizations so that there is less hierarchy. Government bureaucracies are typically hierarchical; to take full advantage of the new technology, they may need to decentralize. But can they?

SOURCES: Darrell West, *The Next Wave: Using Digital Technology to Further Social and Political Innovation* (Washington, DC: Brookings Institution Press, 2011). Darrell West, *Digital Government: Technology and Public-Sector Performance* (Princeton, NJ: Princeton University Press, 2005). Caroline Tolbert, Karen Mossberger, and Ramona McNeal, "Institutions, Policy Innovation and E-Government in the American States, *Public Administration Review* 68, no. 3 (2008): 549–63.

## for critical analysis

1. Beyond cost savings, what are the benefits of digital government or e-government? What are the disadvantages?

2. Can government bureaucracies update their organizational structure to take advantage of advances in information technology as private-sector organizations have done? Or is there a limit to the efficiency gains from new technology?

major reforms, however, are difficult to enact given the political connections of many federal contractors.

The Obama administration has sought to address the concerns about contracting in several ways. In July 2009 the White House Office of Management and Budget (OMB) took steps to reduce the government's reliance on outside contractors. Departments and agencies were told to cut contract spending by 7 percent over the next two years.[50] By 2011 the administration announced that for the first time in 13 years, spending on outside contractors had declined.[51]

# ⬤ Managing the Bureaucracy

> **Explain why it is often difficult to control the bureaucracy**

By their very nature, bureaucracies pose challenges to democratic governance. Although bureaucracies provide the expertise needed to implement the public will, they can also become entrenched organizations that serve their own interests. The public's task is neither to retreat from bureaucracy nor to attack it, but to take advantage of its strengths while making it more accountable to the demands of democratic politics and representative government.

We must return to James Madison's observation "You must first enable the government to control the governed; and in the next place oblige it to control itself."[52] Today, after more than 200 years, millions of employees, and trillions of dollars since the Founding, the problem is the same. Now, though, the process has a name, administrative accountability, which implies that some higher authority will guide and judge the actions of the bureaucracy. The highest authority in a democracy is *demos* ("the people"), and the guidance for bureaucratic action is the popular will. But that ideal of accountability must be translated into practical terms by the president and Congress.

## The President as Chief Executive

In 1937, President Franklin Roosevelt's Committee on Administrative Management officially addressed a plea that had been growing increasingly urgent: "The president needs help." The national government had grown rapidly during the preceding 25 years, but the structures and procedures necessary to manage the burgeoning executive branch had not yet been established. The response to the call for "help" for the president initially took the form of three management policies: (1) All communications and decisions that related to executive policy decisions must pass through the White House. (2) In order to cope with such a flow, the White House must have adequate staff of specialists in research, analysis, legislative and legal writing, and public affairs. (3) The White House must have additional staff to ensure that presidential decisions are made, communicated to Congress, and carried out by the appropriate agency.

**Making the Managerial Presidency** The story of the modern presidency can be told largely as a series of responses to the plea for managerial help. Indeed, each expansion of the national government into new policies and programs in the twentieth century was accompanied by a parallel expansion of the president's management authority. This pattern began even before FDR's presidency, with the policy innovations of President Woodrow Wilson between 1913 and 1920. Congress responded to Wilson's policies with the 1921 Budget and Accounting Act, which turned over the prime legislative power of budgeting to the White House. Each successive president has continued this pattern, creating what we now know as the "managerial presidency."[53]

President Jimmy Carter, in particular, was probably more preoccupied with administrative reform and reorganization than any other twentieth-century president. His reorganization of the civil service will long be recognized as one of the most significant contributions of his presidency. The Civil Service Reform Act of 1978 was the first major revamping of the federal civil service since its creation in 1883. The 1978 act abolished the century-old Civil Service Commission (CSC) and replaced it with three agencies, each designed to handle one of the CSC's functions on the theory that the competing demands of these functions had given the CSC an "identity crisis." The Merit Systems Protection Board (MSPB) was created to defend competitive merit recruitment and promotion from political encroachment. A separate Federal Labor Relations Authority (FLRA) was set up to administer collective bargaining and to address individual personnel grievances. The third new agency, the Office of Personnel Management (OPM), was created to manage recruiting, testing, training, and the retirement system. The Senior Executive Service—a top management rank for civil servants—was also created to recognize and foster "public management" as a profession and to facilitate the movement of "supergrade" career officials across agencies and departments.[54]

Carter also tried to impose a stringent budgetary process on all executive agencies. Called "zero-based budgeting," it was a method of budgeting from the bottom up whereby each agency was required to rejustify its entire mission rather than merely its next year's increase. Zero-based budgeting did not succeed, but the effort was not lost on President Reagan. Although Reagan gave the impression of being a hands-off president, he actually centralized management to an unprecedented degree. From Carter's "bottom-up" approach, Reagan went to a "top-down" approach, whereby the initial budgetary decisions would be made in the White

*Following the government's slow and inadequate response to Hurricane Katrina in 2005, some questioned President Bush's management of executive agencies. When Hurricane Rita threatened the Gulf states a month later, Bush worked closely with FEMA to make sure the error was not repeated.*

House and the agencies would be required to abide by those decisions. This process converted the OMB into an agency of policy determination and presidential management.[55] President George H. W. Bush took Reagan's centralization strategy even further in using the White House staff instead of cabinet secretaries for managing the executive branch.[56]

President Clinton was often criticized for the way he managed his administration. His loose approach to administration even included all-night "bull sessions," complete with pizza. Yet, as we have seen, Clinton also inaugurated one of the most systematic efforts "to change the way government does business" in his NPR. Heavily influenced by the theories of management consultants who prized decentralization, customer responsiveness, and employee initiative, Clinton sought to infuse these new practices into government.[57]

George W. Bush was the first president with a degree in business. His management strategy followed a standard business school dictum: select skilled subordinates and delegate responsibility to them. Bush followed this model closely in his appointment of highly experienced officials to cabinet positions and in his selection of Dick Cheney for vice president. But critics contended that the Bush administration's distrust of the bureaucracy led the administration to exercise inappropriate political control. Political appointees occupied high agency positions that allowed them to suppress the work of agency experts when they threatened to undercut the administration's political goals.

The Obama administration has sought to reinvigorate federal agencies, which reflects the Democrats' greater support for strong government institutions. Obama's approach to the managerial presidency features a deep belief in the importance of scientific expertise in government service. The president's appointments to head key regulatory agencies, including the EPA, OSHA, and the FDA, reflected this conviction. Some of the new agency leaders were well-known academic experts; others had won recognition for their achievements in state or local administrative settings.

*Congress holds hearings to determine whether federal agencies are successfully performing their jobs. In 2009, Attorney General Eric Holder testified at a congressional hearing on oversight of the Justice Department. Members of Congress were concerned about a recent Justice Department decision to try the suspects in the September 11 terrorist attacks in New York.*

Decades of reform have increased the managerial capacity of the presidency, but such reforms themselves do not ensure democratic accountability—presidents must put their managerial powers to use. Although Ronald Reagan was an enormously popular president, he was faulted for his disengaged management style. During his administration, the National Security Council staff was not prevented from running its own policies toward Iran and Nicaragua for at least two years (1985–86) after Congress had explicitly restricted activities toward Nicaragua and the president had forbidden negotiations with Iran. The Tower Commission, appointed to investigate the Iran-Contra affair, concluded that although there was nothing fundamentally wrong with the institutions involved in foreign-policy making, there had been a "flawed process," "a failure of responsibility," and a thinness of the president's personal engagement in the issues. The Tower Commission found that "at no time did [President Reagan] insist upon accountability and performance review."[58] In 2008, Congress held hearings to investigate the financial crisis. Members grilled banking and insurance executives and the former chairman of the Federal Reserve, Alan Greenspan. Greenspan, once hailed as a financial wizard, memorably admitted that inadequate regulation of lending practices had played a role in causing the crisis.

Presidents may also use their managerial capacities to limit democratic accountability if they believe it is a hindrance to effective government. Even in the unusual circumstances of the war on terrorism, critics question whether the Bush administration was too quick to assert **executive privilege** and shield its actions from public scrutiny. In such circumstances, the separation of powers among the branches of government may be the best way to ensure democratic accountability.

## Congressional Oversight

Congress is constitutionally essential to responsible bureaucracy because ultimately the key to bureaucratic responsibility is legislation. When a law is passed and its intent is clear, the accountability for implementation of that law is also clear. Then the president knows what to "faithfully execute," and the responsible agency understands what is expected of it. But when Congress enacts vague legislation, agencies must resort to their own interpretations. The president and the federal courts often step in to tell agencies what the legislation intended. And so do the most intensely interested groups. Yet when everybody, from president to courts to interest groups, gets involved in the actual interpretation of legislative intent, to whom and to what is the agency accountable?

Congress's answer is **oversight**. The more power Congress has delegated to the executive, the more it has sought to re-involve itself in directing the interpretation of laws through committee and subcommittee oversight of each agency. The standing committee system in Congress is well suited to oversight, inasmuch as most of the congressional committees and subcommittees have jurisdictions roughly parallel to one or more departments and agencies, and members of Congress who sit on these committees can develop expertise equal to that of the bureaucrats. The exception is the Department of Homeland Security, whose activities are now overseen by more than 20 committees. One of the central recommendations of the 9/11 Commission—as yet unimplemented—was to create a single committee with oversight of the Department of Homeland Security. Appropriations committees, as well as authorization committees, have oversight powers—as do their

**executive privilege** the claim that confidential communications between a president and close advisers should not be revealed without the consent of the president

**oversight** the effort by Congress, through hearings, investigations, and other techniques, to exercise control over the activities of executive agencies

**for** critical **analysis**

What are some of the important topics on which Congress has held oversight hearings? What was Congress trying to achieve by holding oversight hearings?

respective subcommittees. In addition to these, the Committee on Oversight and Government Reform (in the House) and the Homeland Security and Governmental Affairs Committee (in the Senate) have oversight powers not limited by departmental jurisdiction.

The most visible indication of Congress's oversight efforts is the use of public hearings, before which bureaucrats and other witnesses are summoned to discuss and defend agency budgets and past decisions. In 2011 and 2012, for example, Congress held high-profile hearings on topics as diverse as programs of the Bureau of Alcohol, Tobacco, Firearms and Explosives that inadvertently put guns into the hands of Mexican drug cartels; and VIP loans provided to prominent politicians by the defunct mortgage company Countrywide Financial Corporation.

The data drawn from systematic studies of congressional committee and subcommittee hearings and meetings show quite dramatically that Congress has tried through oversight to keep pace with the expansion of the executive branch. The annual number of oversight hearings has grown over time as the bureaucracy has expanded. Oversight hearings in both the Senate and the House increased dramatically in the 1970s in the aftermath of the Watergate scandal. In recent years, oversight has become a topic of substantial political concern. After the Republicans took over Congress in 1995, they concentrated their oversight power on investigating scandal. When George W. Bush became president in 2001, congressional oversight virtually disappeared. In the words of the congressional scholars Thomas Mann and Norman Ornstein, Republican members of Congress saw "themselves as field lieutenants in the president's army far more than they [did] as members of a separate and independent branch of government."[59] In Mann and Ornstein's view, Congress's failure to exercise its oversight role led to poor government performance and bureaucracies that were not accountable to the American people. After winning back Congress in 2006, the Democrats revived the oversight role, holding hearings on such issues as the use of government contractors in the Iraq and Afghanistan wars and the Troubled Asset Relief Program (TARP), which was instituted to help bail out the banks in 2008. When Republicans took control of the House in 2010, oversight hearings focused on the Democratic administration's programs, such as the Consumer Financial Protection Bureau.

Individual members of Congress can also carry out oversight inquiries. Such standard congressional "casework" can address significant questions of public responsibility even when they are motivated only by the demands of an individual constituent. Oversight also encompasses the communications between congressional staff and agency staff. In addition, Congress has created for itself three large agencies whose obligations are to engage in constant research on matters related to the executive branch. These are the GAO, the Congressional Research Service (CRS), and the Congressional Budget Office (CBO), each designed to give Congress information independent of the information it can get directly from the executive branch through hearings and other communications.[60] Another source of information for oversight is directly from citizens through the FOIA, which, as we have seen, gives ordinary citizens the right to gain access to agency files and agency data. Nevertheless, the information citizens gain through FOIA can be made effective only through the institutionalized channels of congressional committees and, though rarely, through public interest litigation in the federal courts.

*Most Americans dislike the idea of "big government," but they want the bueaucracy to be responsive when they need government services. Americans are increasingly likely to use the Internet to get information and help from bureaucratic agencies—a trend that may improve perceptions of government efficiency.*

The increasing use of federal contractors raises new questions about democratic accountability. When government work is outsourced, federal monitoring is essential to ensure that funds are spent in accordance with the public will and to confirm that the costs are fair. Yet government contracting is now so extensive that such monitoring has become extremely difficult. Even with monitoring, accountability may be hard to achieve; many of the mechanisms of democratic accountability do not apply to private firms that contract to perform public work. For example, private corporations can resist FOIA requests, and they are not constrained by the same ethics rules as public employees. Moreover, because private firms do not have to disclose information about their operations in the same way that public bureaucracies do, Congress has much more limited oversight. The move to privatization clearly presents major challenges to democratic accountability.

One of the most troubling aspects of outsourcing is that private contractors donate millions of dollars each year to political campaigns and lobbying. As Figure 14.6 shows, the top 20 federal contractors have substantially increased their spending on lobbying since 2000. These expenditures raise troubling questions about how assertive members of Congress are likely to be in scrutinizing the business practices of important political donors or in moving activities from the private to the public sector.

**for critical analysis**

Through elected officials (that is, the president and the Congress) the public can achieve some control over the bureaucracy. What are the relative advantages and disadvantages of presidential and congressional control of the bureaucracy?

## ● Thinking Critically about Responsible Bureaucracy in a Democracy

Americans' views about the federal government bureaucracy present something of a paradox. On the one hand, the public expresses dislike for "big government," exemplified by bureaucracy. From this perspective, the federal government is too large, inherently wasteful, and at odds with individual freedom. On the other hand, Americans support many government programs and have high expectations for government. Indeed, high expectations lead many Americans to blame bureaucrats when the country faces problems, such as the prolonged economic downturn of recent years. One consequence of these divergent views is that public discussion about bureaucracy is often high on emotion and short on facts.

Arguments contending that the federal government is too large ignore the fact that the number of government employees has not grown disproportionately large when compared with the size of the American workforce. Charges that government wastes the taxpayers' money must also be put into perspective. As we have seen in this chapter, outsourcing government activities to private contractors does not offer a remedy for wasteful spending. In fact, private firms may be more wasteful than the public sector unless there is strong government oversight of private activities. Finally, it is true that bureaucratic rules often limit the freedom of individuals and corporations. But the laws that bureaucracies implement were enacted by our elected representatives in Congress. They are, in fact, the product of our democratic political system. As these considerations suggest, building a bureaucracy that reflects American values is not a simple task. Adequate congressional oversight is one important part of the solution because a bureaucracy that is shielded from the public eye may wind up pursuing its own interests rather than those of the public. Even so, an administration whose every move is subject to intense public scrutiny may be hamstrung in its efforts to carry out the public interest. Finding the right balance between bureaucratic autonomy and public scrutiny is a central task of creating an effective government; it requires both presidential and congressional vigilance to build an effective and responsive bureaucracy.

# Untangling Bureaucratic Red Tape?

## Inform Yourself

**Explore federal agencies.** Go to the FirstGov A–Z Department and Agency Index (www.usa.gov/directory/federal/index.shtml) and select one of the federal agencies listed. What does it do? Under whose jurisdiction does it fall? Are you surprised by how many government agencies there are? Are you surprised that, in addition to well-known agencies such as the Postal Service and NASA, the list includes more obscure agencies such as Radio Free Asia and the Committee for the Implementation of Textile Agreements?

**See how the bureaucracy has grown.** The federal bureaucracy did not always exist in the large form it does today. The specialization and growth of the bureaucracy of the federal government occurred over the course of the country's 200-year history. Read about the development of the bureaucracy at www.ushistory.org/gov/8a.asp.

**Watch a *Futurama* clip portraying bureaucrats.** The modern-day perception of the bureaucracy has been portrayed in thousands of television episodes and movies. Watch the clip from Futurama at www.comedycentral.com/video-clips/fqqyi0/futurama-bureaucrat-s-song. Consider whether this is a fair description of federal bureaucrats.

## Connect with Others

**Find government agencies on Facebook.** Search for and visit at least one federal department's Facebook page and see what information members of the bureaucracy are posting. What are the responses to these posts? Consider whether you are affected by the regulations/rules discussed in the postings and what your response to them would be. Post a response if you feel strongly enough about the issue. Federal departments on Facebook include (but are not limited to) the Department of the Treasury, the Department of State, the Department of the Interior, and the U.S. Department of Commerce.

*Find links to the sites listed above as well as related activities on wwnorton.com/studyspace.*

## Bureaucracy and Bureaucrats

■ **Define bureaucracy and describe the basic features of the executive branch (pp. 557–66)**

Bureaucracy is defined as the complex structure of offices, tasks, and rules that private and public organizations use to coordinate the work of their personnel. The federal executive branch is composed of cabinet departments, independent agencies, government corporations, and independent regulatory commissions. Although many people express concerns that the national government is too large, the federal service has actually grown very little over the last 35 years. Through their rule making and enforcement decisions, the federal service touches on many important aspects of daily life.

### Key Terms

**bureaucracy** (p. 557)

**implementation** (p. 561)

**merit system** (p. 564)

**department** (p. 564)

**independent agency** (p. 565)

**government corporation** (p. 566)

### Practice Quiz

1. Which of the following best describes the growth of the federal service in the past 35 years? *(p. 558)*
   a) rampant, exponential growth
   b) little growth at all
   c) decrease in the total number of federal employees
   d) vast, compared to the growth of the economy and the society
   e) the federal service has been eliminated in favor of more state government employees

2. What task must bureaucrats perform if Congress charges them with enforcing a law through explicit directions? *(p. 561)*
   a) constitutional revisions
   b) implementation
   c) interpretation
   d) lawmaking
   e) quasi-judicial decision making

3. State and local laws similar to the Civil Service Act of 1883 require that appointees to public office *(p. 564)*
   a) pledge an oath of loyalty to the United States.
   b) be qualified for the job to which they are appointed.
   c) not belong to any political party.
   d) cannot be fired for any reason.
   e) cannot serve more than four years.

4. Which of the following are *not* part of the executive branch? *(pp. 564–66)*
   a) Cabinet departments
   b) government corporations
   c) independent regulatory commissions
   d) agencies
   e) All of the above are parts of the executive branch.

5. Which of the following is an example of a government corporation? *(p. 566)*
   a) National Aeronautics and Space Administration
   b) United States Postal Service
   c) Social Security Administration
   d) National Science Foundation
   e) Federal Express

> **Ⓢ Practice Online**
> "Who Are Americans?" exercise: *Who Are Bureaucrats?*

## Promoting the Public Welfare

■ **Describe the major goals we expect federal agencies to promote (pp. 566–80)**

The federal bureaucracy promotes the public's welfare through a diverse set of services, products, and regulations. Some federal agencies, such as the Federal Reserve System and the Internal Revenue Service, promote the public's welfare by helping maintain a strong economy. Other federal agencies, such as the Department of Defense, the Department of Justice, and the Department of Homeland Security, promote the public's welfare by protecting the country against internal and external security threats.

## Key Terms

**regulatory agency** (p. 567)

**iron triangle** (p. 568)

**fiscal policy** (p. 577)

**Federal Reserve System** (p. 577)

**revenue agency** (p. 578)

## Practice Quiz

6. A stable relationship between a bureaucratic agency, a clientele group, and a legislative committee is called *(p. 568)*
   a) a standing committee.
   b) a conference committee.
   c) a cabinet.
   d) an issue network.
   e) an iron triangle.

7. Americans refer to government policy about banks, credit and currency as *(p. 577)*
   a) interstate commerce policy.
   b) deficit policy.
   c) fiscal policy.
   d) monetary policy.
   e) regulatory policy.

 **Practice Online**
Interactive simulation: *Director of an Executive Agency*

# Can Bureaucracy Be Reformed?

■ **Evaluate some of the ways politicians have tried to make the bureaucracy more efficient (pp. 580–88)**

Many Americans express frustration with the performance of the federal bureaucracy. As a result, politicians have frequently explored various methods of making the federal bureaucracy more efficient. In general, politicians have attempted four strategies to promote bureaucratic reform: "reinventing" government, termination of programs, devolution, and privatization.

## Key Terms

**devolution** (p. 582)

**privatization** (p. 583)

## Practice Quiz

8. Which president instituted the bureaucratic reform of the National Performance Review? *(p. 581)*
   a) Richard Nixon
   b) Lyndon Johnson
   c) Jimmy Carter
   d) Bill Clinton
   e) George W. Bush

9. Devolution refers to *(p. 582)*
   a) the gradual decline in efficiency that always comes when government begins to implement a new program.
   b) removing all or part of a program from the public sector to the private sector.
   c) a policy of reducing or eliminating regulatory restraints on the conduct of individuals or private institutions.
   d) a policy to remove a program from one level of government by passing it down to a lower level of government.
   e) reducing the overall number of regulatory agencies in the federal bureaucracy.

10. Which of the following is *not* a way in which the bureaucracy might be reduced? *(pp. 581–88)*
    a) devolution
    b) termination
    c) privatization
    d) eminent domain
    e) all of the above

11. Which of the following best describes the changes in government contracting since 2000? *(p. 584)*
    a) Spending on government contracts has decreased while the number of government contracts subject to open competition has increased.
    b) Spending on government contracts has decreased while the number of government contracts subject to competition has decreased.
    c) Government contracting ended in 2000 as a result of the Supreme Court's decision in *Immigration and Naturalization Service v. Chadha*.
    d) Spending on government contracts has increased while the number of government contracts subject to open competition has decreased.
    e) Spending on government contracts has increased while the number of government contracts subject to open competition has increased.

 **Practice Online**
Video exercise: *World News Tonight—Wasteful Government Spending*

# Managing the Bureaucracy

■ **Explain why it is often difficult to control the bureaucracy (pp. 588–93)**

The federal bureaucracy provides the expertise that is needed to implement the law but they can also become entrenched organizations that serve their own interests rather than the public will. While the emergence of the "managerial presidency" during the twentieth century has given the president more authority over the bureaucracy, presidents have sometimes used their managerial capacities to limit rather than promote democratic accountability. Congress can exert control over the federal bureaucracy by enacting specific legislation and engaging in vigorous oversight.

## Key Terms

**executive privilege** (p. 591)

**oversight** (p. 591)

## Practice Quiz

12. Which of the following is a power sometimes invoked by presidents to shield their administration's actions from public scrutiny? *(p. 591)*
    a) executive oversight
    b) executive privilege
    c) executive protection
    d) congressional oversight
    e) administrative adjudication

13. The concept of *oversight* refers to the effort made by *(p. 591)*
    a) Congress to make executive agencies accountable for their actions.
    b) the president to make executive agencies accountable for their actions.
    c) the president to make Congress accountable for its actions.
    d) the courts to make executive agencies responsible for their actions.
    e) the states to make the executive branch accountable for its actions.

14. Which of the following agencies were created by Congress to engage in research on problems taking place in or confronted by the executive branch? *(p. 592)*
    a) Government Accountability Office, Congressional Research Service, Congressional Budget Office
    b) Department of Justice, Department of the Interior, Department of the Treasury
    c) Congressional Oversight Organization, Bureau of Government Performance, National Performance Review Association
    d) Office of Management and Budget, Council of Economic Advisors, Oversight and Government Reform Agency
    e) Congressional Oversight Organization, Council of Economic Advisors, Department of Justice

# For Further Reading

Aberbach, Joel D., and Mark A. Peterson, eds. *Institutions of American Democracy: The Executive Branch* (Institutions of American Democracy Series). New York: Oxford University Press, 2006.

Arnold, Peri E. *Making the Managerial Presidency: Comprehensive Organization Planning.* Princeton, NJ: Princeton University Press, 1986.

Gormley, William, and Stephen Balla. *Bureaucracy and Democracy: Accountability and Performance.* 3rd ed. Washington, DC: CQ Press, 2012.

Kettl, Donald F., and James W. Fesler. *The Politics of the Administrative Process.* 4th ed. Washington, DC: CQ Press, 2008.

Light, Paul C. *A Government Ill Executed: The Decline of the Federal Service and How to Reverse It.* Cambridge, MA: Harvard University Press, 2008.

Verkuil, Paul. *Outsourcing Sovereignty: Why Privatization of Government Functions Threatens Democracy and What We Can Do about It.* New York: Cambridge University Press, 2007.

Weiner, Tom. *Legacy of Ashes: The History of the CIA.* New York: Doubleday, 2007.

Wildavsky, Aaron. *The New Politics of the Budget Process.* 2nd ed. New York: HarperCollins, 1992.

Wilson, James Q. *Bureaucracy: What Government Agencies Do and Why They Do It.* New York: Basic Books, 1989.

# Recommended Websites

**Central Intelligence Agency**
www.cia.gov

The Central Intelligence Agency (CIA) is one of several bureaucracies responsible for providing national security. A major problem facing this clandestine agency is how to provide security and meet the public's right to know what the government is doing. At the official website for the CIA, see what questions are often asked.

**Department of Homeland Security**
www.dhs.gov

The Department of Homeland Security was created after 9/11 to promote bureaucratic communication and domestic security. See what the department is doing to protect America from foreign threats.

**Federal Emergency Management Agency**
www.fema.org

In the aftermath of Hurricane Katrina, the Federal Emergency Management Agency (FEMA) became infamous for its role in the disaster relief efforts. View the disaster history of your state and see what FEMA is currently doing to prevent disasters and assist Americans in need.

**Official U.S. Executive Branch Websites**
www.loc.gov

This resource page at the Library of Congress website provides links to every federal department, independent agency, and regulatory commission in the federal bureaucracy.

**Reason Foundation**
reason.org/areas/topic/privatization

The Reason Foundation is dedicated to promoting libertarian principles and limited government. Their website includes studies and opinion pieces on a range of policy issues, including many related to the size and effectiveness of the federal bureaucracy.

**Project on Government Oversight**
www.pogo.org

The Project on Government Oversight is an independent, nonprofit organization that seeks to make government more accountable by investigating corruption and misconduct. Originally set up to focus on the military, this organization now examines all types of government bureaucracies.

**U.S. Agency for International Development**
www.usaid.gov

In 1961 Congress created the U.S. Agency for International Development (USAID) to provide economic and social development assistance to foreign countries. Often criticized for promoting American values and foreign policy objectives, USAID is currently involved in numerous global issues.

The Supreme Court may seem like a distant and mysterious institution but its decisions affect ordinary Americans in countless ways. From health care to immigration to free speech on campus, the Court's rulings have a direct impact on everyday life.

# The Federal Courts

**WHAT GOVERNMENT DOES AND WHY IT MATTERS** Many Americans may think of the Supreme Court as a distant and mysterious institution whose decisions affect only giant corporations, wealthy individuals, and powerful politicians. They may see no direct relationship between the black-robed justices and the everyday lives of ordinary people. Occasionally, however, the Supreme Court is asked to hear questions that touch students' lives in a very direct way. One recent example, from 2007, is the case of *Morse v. Frederick*.[1] This case dealt with the policies of Juneau-Douglas High School in Juneau, Alaska. In 2002 the Olympic torch relay passed through Juneau on its way to Salt Lake City for the opening of the Winter Olympics. As the torch passed Juneau-Douglas High, a senior, Joseph Frederick, unfurled a banner that read, "Bong Hits 4 Jesus." The school's principal promptly suspended Frederick, who then brought suit for reinstatement, alleging that his right to freedom of speech had been violated.[2]

Like most of America's public schools, Juneau-Douglas High prohibits on school grounds any assemblies or expressions that advocate illegal drug use. Schools say that some federal aid is contingent on this policy. Civil libertarians see such policies as restricting students' right to free speech—a right that has been recognized by the Supreme Court since a 1969 case in which it ruled that an Iowa public school could not prohibit students from wearing antiwar armbands. Unfortunately for Joseph Frederick, today's Supreme Court has a more conservative cast than it did in 1969. Speaking for the Court's majority, Chief Justice John G. Roberts said that the First Amendment did not require schools to permit students to advocate illegal drug use. This decision affected not only Joseph Frederick, but also millions of other students whose views might be seen as inappropriate by school administrators. Far from being a remote institution, the Supreme Court turns out to have reached into every public school in America. The same could be said for a 2012 decision involving a religious school in Michigan that fired a teacher for actions that, in the school's view, violated church doctrine. The teacher brought a federal employment discrimination suit against the school, claiming that she had been fired in retaliation for filing an employment discrimination claim against the school. In a unanimous decision, the Supreme Court asserted what it called a "ministerial exception," allowing religious institutions wide latitude in their personnel decisions.[3]

Every year, nearly 25 million cases are tried in American courts, and one American in every nine is directly involved in litigation. Cases can arise from disputes between citizens, from efforts by government agencies to punish wrongdoing, or from citizens' efforts to prove that their rights have been infringed on as a result of government action—or inaction. Many critics of the U.S. legal system assert that Americans have become too litigious (ready to use the courts for all purposes). But the heavy use that Americans make of the courts is also an indication of the extent of conflict in American society. And given the existence of social conflict, it is far better that Americans seek to settle their differences through the courts than resort to violence or otherwise take matters into their own hands. The framers of the American Constitution called the Supreme Court the "least dangerous branch" of American government. Today, though, it is not unusual to hear the Court described as an all-powerful "imperial judiciary." Before we can understand this transformation and its consequences, we must look in some detail at America's judicial process.

## chaptergoals

- Identify the general types of cases and types of courts in our legal system (pages 603–8)

- Describe the different levels of federal courts and their functions (pages 608–14)

- Explain how the Supreme Court exercises the power of judicial review (pages 614–31)

- Consider the political influences on the courts (pages 632–34)

# The Legal System

Identify the general types of cases and types of courts in our legal system

Originally, a "court" was the place where a sovereign ruled—where the king or queen governed. Settling disputes between citizens was part of governing. In modern democracies, courts and judges have taken over the power to settle conflicts by hearing the facts on both sides and deciding which side possesses the greater merit. But since judges are not kings, they must have a basis for their authority. That basis in the United States is the Constitution and the law. Courts decide cases by hearing the facts on both sides of a quarrel and applying the relevant law or principle to the facts. This can be a sensitive matter because courts have been given the authority to settle disputes between not only citizens but also citizens and the government itself, where the courts are obliged to maintain the same neutrality and impartiality as they do in disputes involving two citizens. This is the essence of the "rule of law": that "the state" and its officials must be judged by the same laws as the citizenry.

## Cases and the Law

Court cases in the United States proceed under two broad categories of law: criminal law and civil law, each with myriad subdivisions.

Cases of **criminal law** are those in which the government charges an individual with violating a statute that has been enacted to protect public health, safety, morals, or welfare. In criminal cases, the government is always the **plaintiff** (the party that brings charges) and alleges that a criminal violation has been committed by a named **defendant**. Most criminal cases arise in state and municipal courts and involve matters ranging from traffic offenses to robbery and murder. Although the great bulk of criminal law is still a state matter, a large and growing body of federal criminal law deals with matters ranging from tax evasion and mail fraud to acts of

**criminal law** the branch of law that regulates the conduct of individuals, defines crimes, and specifies punishment for criminal acts

**plaintiff** the individual or organization that brings a complaint in court

**defendant** the one against whom a complaint is brought in a criminal or civil case

*In criminal cases, the government charges an individual with violating a statute protecting health, safety, morals, or welfare. Most such cases arise in state and municipal courts. Here, an Illinois county court hears testimony in a murder case.*

terrorism and the sale of narcotics. Defendants found guilty of criminal violations may be fined or sent to prison.

**civil law** the branch of law that deals with disputes that do not involve criminal penalties

Cases of **civil law** involve disputes among individuals, groups, corporations, and other private entities, or between such litigants and the government in which no criminal violation is charged. Unlike in criminal cases, the losers in civil cases cannot be fined or sent to prison, although they may be required to pay monetary damages for their actions. In a civil case, the one who brings a complaint is the plaintiff and the one against whom the complaint is brought is the defendant. The two most common types of civil cases involve contracts and torts. In a typical contract case, an individual or corporation charges that it has suffered because of another's violation of a specific agreement between the two. For example, the Smith Manufacturing Corporation may charge that Jones Distributors failed to honor an agreement to deliver raw materials at a specified time, causing Smith to lose business. Smith asks the court to order Jones to compensate it for the damage it allegedly suffered. In a typical tort case, one individual charges that he or she has been injured by another's negligence or malfeasance. Medical malpractice suits are one example of tort cases. Another important area of civil law is administrative law, which involves disputes over the jurisdiction, procedures, or authority of administrative agencies. A plaintiff may assert, for example, that an agency did not follow proper procedures when issuing new rules and regulations. A court will then examine the agency's conduct in light of the Administrative Procedure Act, the legislation that governs agency rule making.

**precedent** prior case whose principles are used by judges as the basis for their decision in a present case

In deciding cases, courts apply statutes (laws) and legal **precedents** (prior decisions). State and federal statutes, for example, often govern the conditions under which contracts are and are not legally binding. Jones Distributors might argue that it was not obliged to fulfill its contract with the Smith Manufacturing Corporation because actions by Smith, such as the failure to make promised payments, constituted fraud under state law. Precedents established in previous cases also guide courts' decisions in new cases. Attorneys for a physician being sued for malpractice might search for prior instances in which courts ruled that actions similar to those of their client did not constitute negligence. Such precedents are applied under the doctrine of *stare decisis*, a Latin phrase meaning "let the decision stand."

**stare decisis** literally, "let the decision stand." The doctrine that a previous decision by a court applies as a precedent in similar cases until that decision is overruled

If a case involves the actions of the federal government or a state government, a court may also be asked to examine whether the government's conduct was consistent with the Constitution. In a criminal case, for example, defendants might assert that their constitutional rights were violated when the police searched their property. Similarly, in a civil case involving federal or state restrictions on land development, plaintiffs might assert that government actions violated the Fifth Amendment's prohibition against taking private property without just compensation. Thus, both civil and criminal cases may raise questions of constitutional law.

## Types of Courts

In the United States, systems of courts have been established both by the federal government and by the governments of the individual states. Both systems have several levels, as shown in Figure 15.1. More than 99 percent of all court cases in the United States are heard in state courts. The overwhelming majority of criminal cases, for example, involve violations of state laws prohibiting such actions as murder, robbery, fraud, theft, and assault. If such a case is brought to trial, it will be heard in a state **trial court**, in front of a judge and sometimes a jury, who will determine whether the defendant violated state law. If the defendant is convicted, he or

**trial court** the first court to hear a criminal or civil case

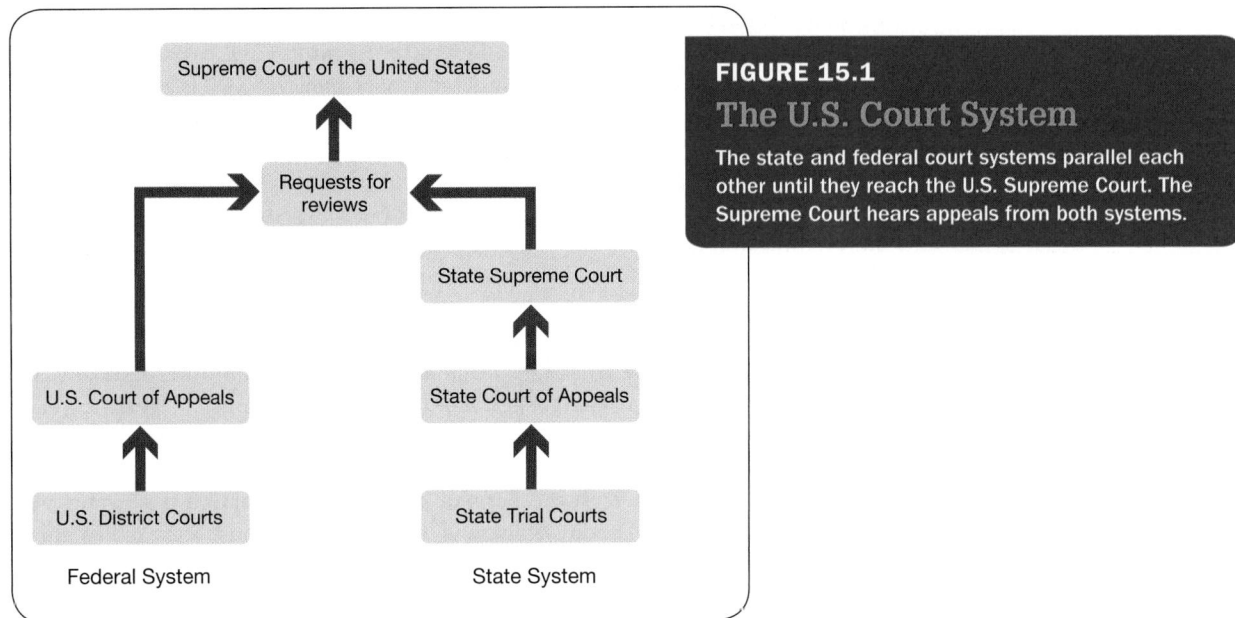

**FIGURE 15.1**

**The U.S. Court System**

The state and federal court systems parallel each other until they reach the U.S. Supreme Court. The Supreme Court hears appeals from both systems.

she may appeal the conviction to a higher court, such as a state **court of appeals**, and from there to a court of last resort, usually called the state's **supreme court**.

Similarly, in civil cases, most litigation is brought in the courts established by the state in which the activity in question took place. For example, a patient bringing suit against a physician for malpractice would file the suit in the appropriate court in the state where the alleged malpractice occurred. The judge hearing the case would apply state law and state precedent to the matter at hand. There is some variation in court structure among the 50 states. Several states lack an intermediate appellate level, and the court of last resort is the only appellate court. Two states, Oklahoma and Texas, have established two state courts of last resort, one for civil appeals and the other for criminal appeals. It should be noted that in both criminal and civil matters, most cases are settled before trial through negotiated agreements between the parties. In criminal cases these agreements are called **plea bargains**.

Although each state has its own set of laws, these laws have much in common from state to state. Murder and robbery, of course, are illegal in all states, although the range of possible punishments varies from state to state. Some states, for example, provide for capital punishment (the death penalty) for murder and other serious offenses; other states do not. However, some acts that are criminal offenses in one state may be legal in another state. Prostitution, for example, is legal in some Nevada counties, although it is outlawed in all other states. Considerable similarity among the states is also found in the realm of civil law. In the case of contract law, most states have adopted the Uniform Commercial Code in order to reduce interstate differences. In areas such as family law, however, which covers such matters as divorce and child custody arrangements, state laws vary greatly.

Cases are heard in the federal courts if they involve federal laws, treaties with other nations, or the U.S. Constitution; these areas are the official **jurisdiction** of the federal courts. In addition, any case in which the U.S. government is a party is heard in the federal courts. If, for example, an individual is charged with violating

**court of appeals** a court that hears appeals of trial court decisions

**supreme court** the highest court in a particular state or in the United States. This court primarily serves an appellate function

**plea bargain** a negotiated agreement in a criminal case in which a defendant agrees to plead guilty in return for the state's agreement to reduce the severity of the criminal charge or prison sentence the defendant is facing

**jurisdiction** the sphere of a court's power and authority

a federal criminal statute, such as evading the payment of income taxes, charges are brought before a federal judge by a federal prosecutor. Civil cases involving the citizens of more than one state and in which more than $75,000 is at stake may be heard in either the federal or the state courts, usually depending on the preference of the plaintiff.

But even if a matter belongs in federal court, how do we know which federal court should exercise jurisdiction over the case? The answer to this seemingly simple question is somewhat complex. The jurisdiction of each federal court is derived from the U.S. Constitution and federal statutes. Article III of the Constitution gives the Supreme Court appellate jurisdiction in all federal cases and original jurisdiction in cases involving foreign ambassadors and issues in which a state is a party. Article III assigns original jurisdiction in all other federal cases to the lower courts that Congress was authorized to establish. Over the years, as Congress enacted statutes creating the federal judicial system, it specified the jurisdiction of each type of court it established. For the most part, Congress has assigned jurisdictions on the basis of geography. The nation is currently, by statute, divided into 94 judicial districts, including one court for each of three U.S. territories. Each of the 94 U.S. district courts exercises jurisdiction over federal cases arising within its territorial domain. The judicial districts are, in turn, organized into 11 regional circuits and the D.C. circuit (see Figure 15.2). Each circuit court exercises appellate jurisdiction over cases heard by the district courts within its region.

Geography, however, is not the only basis for federal court jurisdiction. Congress has also established several specialized courts that have nationwide original jurisdiction in certain types of cases. These include the U.S. Court of International Trade, created to deal with trade and customs issues, and the U.S. Court of Federal Claims, which handles damage suits against the United States. Congress has also established a court with nationwide appellate jurisdiction, the U.S. Court of Appeals for the Federal Circuit, which hears appeals involving patent law and those arising from the decisions of the trade and claims courts. Other federal courts assigned specialized jurisdictions by Congress include the U.S. Court of Appeals for Veterans Claims, which exercises exclusive jurisdiction over cases involving veterans' claims, and the U.S. Court of Military Appeals, which deals with questions of law arising from trials by court-martial.

With the exception of the claims court and the Court of Appeals for the Federal Circuit, these specialized courts were created by Congress on the basis of the powers the legislature exercises under Article I, rather than Article III, of the Constitution. Article III is designed to protect judges from political pressure by granting them life tenure and prohibiting reduction of their salaries while they serve. The judges of Article I courts, by contrast, are appointed by the president for fixed terms of 15 years and are not protected by the Constitution from salary reduction. As a result, these "legislative courts" are generally viewed as less independent than the courts established under Article III of the Constitution. The three territorial courts (for Guam, the U.S. Virgin Islands, and Northern Mariana Islands) were also established under the provisions in Article I, and their judges are appointed for 10-year terms.

The appellate jurisdiction of the federal courts also extends to cases originating in the state courts. In both civil and criminal cases, a decision of the highest state court can be appealed to the U.S. Supreme Court by raising a federal issue. A defendant who appeals a lower-court decision in federal court might assert, for example, that they were denied the right to counsel or were otherwise deprived of

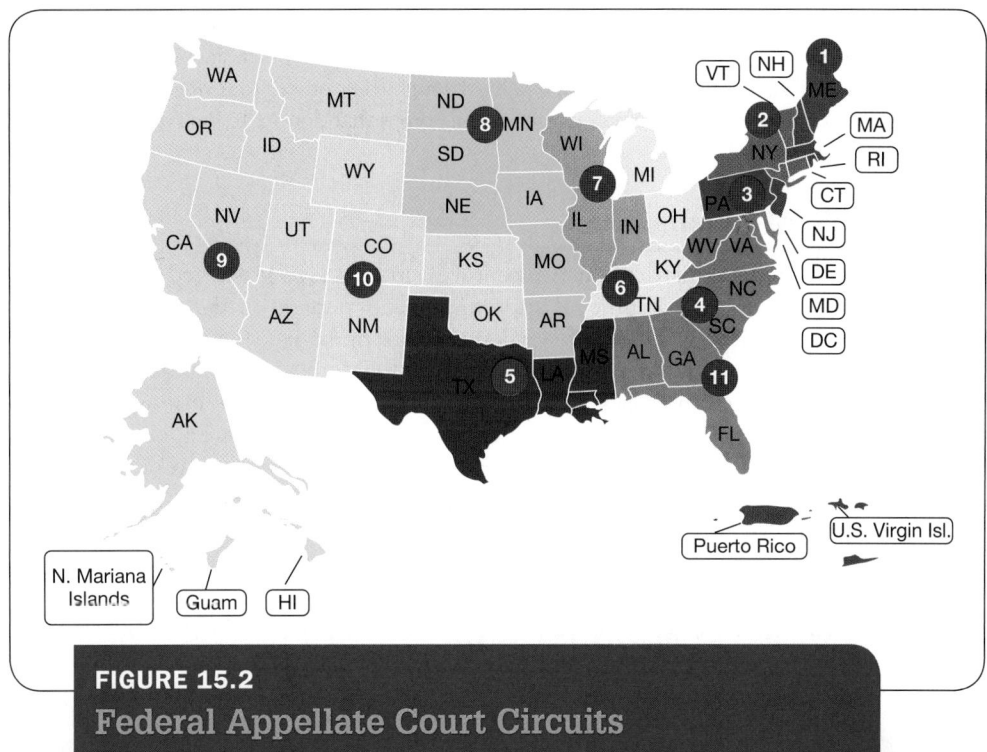

**FIGURE 15.2**

**Federal Appellate Court Circuits**

Federal district courts are organized into 12 regional circuits: the 11 shown here, plus the District of Columbia, which has its own circuit. Each circuit court hears appeals from lower federal courts within the circuit. A 13th federal circuit court, the U.S. Court of Appeals for the Federal Circuit, hears appeals from a number of specialized courts such as the U.S. Court of Federal Claims.

SOURCE: www.uscourts.gov/court_locator.aspx (accessed 7/27/10).

the **due process of law** guaranteed by the federal Constitution, or they might assert that important issues of federal law were at stake in the case. The U.S. Supreme Court is not obligated to accept such appeals, and will do so only if it believes that the matter has considerable national significance. In addition, in criminal cases, defendants who have been convicted in a state court may request a **writ of *habeas corpus*** from a federal district court. Sometimes known as the "Great Writ," *habeas corpus* is a court order to the authorities to release a prisoner deemed to be held in violation of his or her legal rights. In 1867 its distrust of southern courts led Congress to authorize federal district judges to issue such writs to prisoners who they believed had been deprived of constitutional rights in state court. Generally speaking, state defendants seeking a federal writ of *habeas corpus* must show that they have exhausted all available state remedies and must raise issues not previously raised in their state appeals. Federal courts of appeals and, ultimately, the U.S. Supreme Court have appellate jurisdiction for federal district court *habeas* decisions.

Although the federal courts hear only a small fraction of all the civil and criminal cases decided each year in the United States, their decisions are extremely important. It is in the federal courts that the Constitution and federal laws that govern all

**due process of law** the right of every citizen against arbitrary action by national or state governments

**writ of *habeas corpus*** a court order that the individual in custody be brought into court and shown the cause for detention. *Habeas corpus* is guaranteed by the Constitution and can be suspended only in cases of rebellion or invasion

Americans are interpreted and their meaning and significance established. Moreover, it is in the federal courts that the powers and limitations of the increasingly powerful national government are tested. Finally, through their power to review the decisions of the state courts, it is ultimately the federal courts that dominate the American judicial system.

## Federal Jurisdiction

In 2010 federal district courts (the lowest federal level) received 363,428 cases. Though large, this number is approximately 1 percent of the number of cases heard by state courts. The federal courts of appeal listened to 56,097 cases in 2010, and about 15 percent of the verdicts were appealed to the U.S. Supreme Court. Most of the cases filed with the Supreme Court are dismissed without a ruling on their merits. The Court has broad latitude to decide what cases it will hear, and generally listens to only those cases it deems to raise the most important issues. Only 76 cases were given full-dress Supreme Court review in 2010–11.[4]

# ● Federal Trial Courts

**Describe the different levels of federal courts and their functions**

**original jurisdiction** the authority to initially consider a case. Distinguished from appellate jurisdiction, which is the authority to hear appeals from a lower court's decision.

Most of the cases of original federal jurisdiction are handled by the federal district courts. Courts of **original jurisdiction** are the courts that are responsible for discovering the facts in a controversy and creating the record on which a judgment is based. Although the Constitution gives the Supreme Court original jurisdiction in several types of cases, such as those affecting ambassadors and those in which a state is one of the parties, most original jurisdiction goes to the lowest courts— the trial courts. (In courts that have appellate jurisdiction, judges receive cases after the factual record is established by the trial court. Ordinarily, new facts cannot be presented before appellate courts.)

There are 89 district courts in the 50 states, plus one in the District of Columbia and one in Puerto Rico, and three territorial courts. These courts are staffed by 679 federal district judges. District judges are assigned to district courts according to the workload; the busiest of these courts may have as many as 28 judges. Only one judge is assigned to each case, except where statutes provide for three-judge courts to deal with special issues. The routines and procedures of the federal district courts are essentially the same as those of the lower state courts, except that federal procedural requirements tend to be stricter. States, for example, do not have to provide a grand jury, a 12-member trial jury, or a unanimous jury verdict. Federal courts must provide all these things.

## Federal Appellate Courts

Roughly 20 percent of all lower-court cases, along with appeals from some federal agency decisions, are subsequently reviewed by federal appeals courts. As

*President George W. Bush nominated John Roberts (left photo, center) first as a Supreme Court justice and then as chief justice after the death of former chief justice William Rehnquist. Although Roberts's nomination was approved fairly easily in the Senate, President Bush's next nominee, Samuel Alito (right), was subjected to harsher questioning before being confirmed. Democratic senators were worried that Alito, who was replacing a more moderate justice, would shift the overall balance of the Court toward the right.*

noted, the country is divided geographically into 11 regional circuits and the D.C. circuit, each of which has a U.S. Court of Appeals. Every state, the District of Columbia, and each of the territories is assigned to the circuit in the continental United States that is closest to it. A 13th appellate court, the U.S. Court of Appeals for the Federal Circuit, has a subject matter, rather than a geographical, jurisdiction.

Except for cases selected for review by the Supreme Court, decisions made by the appeals courts are final. Because of this finality, certain safeguards have been built into the system. The most important is the provision of more than one judge for every appeals case. Each court of appeals has from 6 to 28 permanent judgeships, depending on the workload of the circuit. Although normally three judges hear appealed cases, in some instances a larger number of judges sits together en banc.

Another safeguard is provided by the assignment of a Supreme Court justice as the circuit justice for each of the 12 circuits. The circuit justice deals with requests for special action by the Supreme Court. The most frequent and best-known action of circuit justices is that of reviewing requests for stays of execution when the full Court is unable to do so—primarily during the summer, when the Court is in recess.

## The Supreme Court

The Supreme Court is America's highest court. Article III of the Constitution vests "the judicial power of the United States" in the Supreme Court, and this court is supreme in fact as well as form. The Supreme Court is the only federal court established by the Constitution. The lower federal courts are created by statute and can be restructured or, presumably, even abolished by the Congress. The Supreme Court is made up of the chief justice of the United States and eight associate justices. The **chief justice** presides over the Court's public sessions and

**chief justice** justice on the Supreme Court who presides over the Court's public sessions and whose official title is chief justice of the United States

conferences. In the Court's actual deliberations and decisions, however, the chief justice has no more authority than his or her colleagues. Each justice casts one vote. The chief justice, though, is always the first to speak and the last to vote when the justices deliberate. In addition, if the chief justice has voted with the majority, he or she decides which of the justices will write the formal opinion for the court. The character of the opinion can be an important means of influencing the evolution of the law beyond the mere affirmation or denial of the appeal on hand. To some extent, the influence of the chief justice is a function of his or her own leadership ability. Some chief justices, such as the late Earl Warren, have been able to lead the court in a new direction. In other instances, forceful associate justices, such as the late Felix Frankfurter, are the dominant figures on the Court.

The Constitution does not specify the number of justices who should sit on the Supreme Court; Congress has the authority to change the Court's size. In the early nineteenth century, there were six Supreme Court justices; later there were seven. Congress set the number of justices at nine in 1869, and the Court has remained that size ever since. In 1937, President Franklin Delano Roosevelt, infuriated by several Supreme Court decisions that struck down New Deal programs, asked Congress to enlarge the Court so that he could add a few sympathetic justices to the bench. Although Congress balked at Roosevelt's "court packing" plan, the Court gave in to FDR's pressure and began to take a more favorable view of his policy initiatives. The president, in turn, dropped his efforts to enlarge the Court.

## How Judges Are Appointed

Federal judges are appointed by the president and confirmed by the Senate. They are generally selected from among the more prominent or politically active members of the legal profession. Many federal judges previously served as state court judges or state or local prosecutors. Before the president makes a formal nomination, however, the senators from the candidate's own state must indicate that they

*In 2010, Barack Obama nominated former solicitor general Elena Kagan to the Supreme Court, bringing the number of women justices to three. Kagan's nomination was approved by the Senate, and she was sworn in by Chief Justice John Roberts (right) in August 2010.*

# Who Are Federal Judges?

One factor among many that presidents may take into account when selecting judicial nominees is diversity. The number of Supreme Court justices is relatively small, so it is easy to count the number of African Americans who have served as Supreme Court justices (2), female justices (4), and Hispanic justices (1). How diverse is the rest of the federal judiciary? The first section below shows the racial, ethnic, and gender composition of the lower federal courts.

---

## Federal Judges in 2009, by Race and Gender

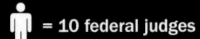 = 10 federal judges

White men  860

African American men  84

Hispanic men  58

White women  225

African American **women**  40

Hispanic women  26

---

## Appointments to Federal Courts, by Administration

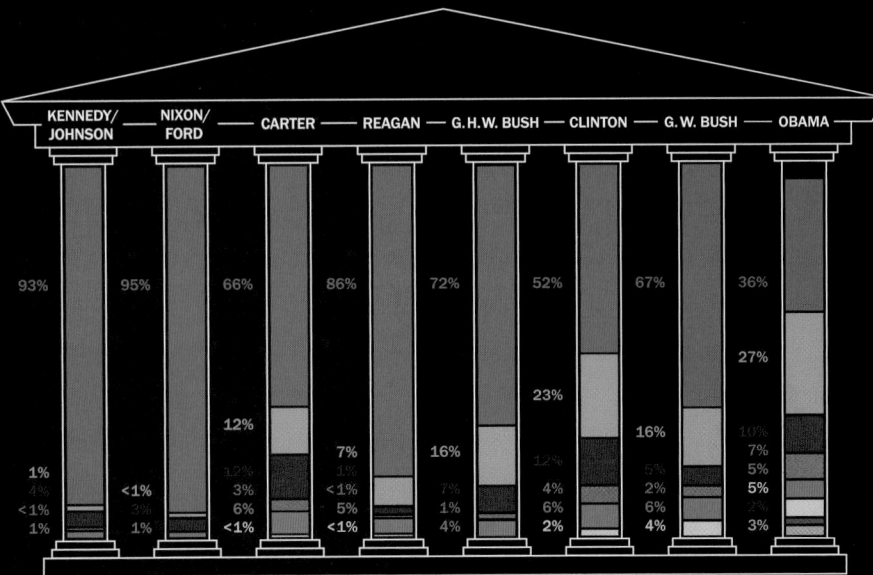

Legend:
- White men
- White women
- African American men
- African American women
- Hispanic men
- Hispanic women
- Asian American men
- Asian American women

| | KENNEDY/ JOHNSON | NIXON/ FORD | CARTER | REAGAN | G.H.W. BUSH | CLINTON | G.W. BUSH | OBAMA |
|---|---|---|---|---|---|---|---|---|
| | 93% | 95% | 66% | 86% | 72% | 52% | 67% | 36% |
| | | | | | | 23% | | 27% |
| | | | 12% | | 16% | | 16% | 10% |
| | 1% | | 12% | 7% | | 12% | | 7% |
| | 4% | <1% | 3% | 1% | 7% | 5% | 5% | 5% |
| | <1% | 3% | 6% | 5% | 1% | 6% | 6% | 5% |
| | 1% | 1% | <1% | <1% | 4% | 2% | 4% | 3% |

## for critical analysis

1. Would you describe the federal judiciary as diverse? Does racial, ethnic, and gender diversity of federal judges matter? Why or why not?

2. What similarities and differences do you notice among the judicial appointments of the presidents shown? What might account for the differences in terms of the diversity of their appointees?

SOURCE: Russell Wheeler, "The Changing Face of the Federal Judiciary" (Washington, DC: Brookings Institution, 2009). Data in first section above are from August 2009.

support the nominee. This is an informal but seldom violated practice called **senatorial courtesy**. If one or both senators from a prospective nominee's home state belong to the president's political party, the president will almost invariably consult them and secure their blessing for the nomination. Because the president's party in the Senate will rarely support a nominee opposed by a home-state senator from its ranks, this arrangement gives these senators virtual veto power over appointments to the federal bench in their own states. Senators also see nominations to the judiciary as a way to reward important allies and contributors in their states. If the state has no senator from the president's party, the governor or members of the state's House delegation may make suggestions. The practice of "courtesy" generally does not apply to Supreme Court appointments, only to district and circuit court nominations.

Federal appeals court nominations follow much the same pattern. Since appeals court judges preside over jurisdictions that include several states, however, senators do not have so strong a role in proposing potential candidates. Instead, potential appeals court candidates are generally suggested to the president by the Justice Department or by important members of the administration. The senators from the nominee's own state are still consulted before the president will formally act.

There are no formal qualifications for service as a federal judge. In general, presidents endeavor to appoint judges who possess legal experience and good character and whose partisan and ideological views are similar to their own. Once the president has formally nominated an individual, the nominee must be considered by the Senate Judiciary Committee and confirmed by a majority vote in the full Senate. In recent years, a good deal of partisan conflict has surrounded judicial appointments. Senate Democrats have sought to prevent Republican presidents from appointing conservative judges while Senate Republicans have worked to prevent Democratic presidents from appointing liberal judges. During the early months of the Obama administration, Republicans were able to slow the judicial appointment process through various procedural maneuvers so that only three of the president's 23 nominations for federal judgeships were confirmed by the Senate.[5] Some of Obama's allies urged the president to take a more aggressive stance, or risk allowing Republicans to block what had been considered a key Democratic priority, and by the beginning of his fourth year in office, the president had secured the appointment of 97 new district court judges and 25 new appeals court judges.[6]

If political factors play an important role in the selection of district and appellate court judges, they are decisive when it comes to Supreme Court appointments.

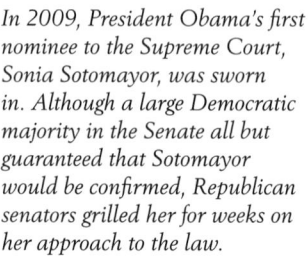

*In 2009, President Obama's first nominee to the Supreme Court, Sonia Sotomayor, was sworn in. Although a large Democratic majority in the Senate all but guaranteed that Sotomayor would be confirmed, Republican senators grilled her for weeks on her approach to the law.*

## TABLE 15.1

## Supreme Court Justices, 2012 (in Order of Seniority)

| NAME | YEAR OF BIRTH | PRIOR EXPERIENCE | APPOINTED BY | YEAR OF APPOINTMENT |
|------|---------------|------------------|--------------|---------------------|
| Antonin Scalia | 1936 | Law professor, federal judge | Reagan | 1986 |
| Anthony Kennedy | 1936 | Federal judge | Reagan | 1988 |
| Clarence Thomas | 1948 | Federal judge | G. H. W. Bush | 1991 |
| Ruth Bader Ginsburg | 1933 | Federal judge | Clinton | 1993 |
| Stephen Breyer | 1938 | Federal judge | Clinton | 1994 |
| John Roberts Jr. (*Chief Justice*) | 1955 | Federal judge | G. W. Bush | 2005 |
| Samuel Alito | 1950 | Federal judge | G. W. Bush | 2006 |
| Sonia Sotomayor | 1954 | Federal judge | Obama | 2009 |
| Elena Kagan | 1960 | Solicitor general | Obama | 2010 |

Because the high court has so much influence over American law and politics, virtually all presidents have made an effort to select justices who share their political philosophies.

It is important to note that five of the nine current justices as of 2012 were appointed by Republican presidents (Table 15.1). This conservative majority, consisting of Chief Justice Roberts and Justices Alito, Kennedy, Scalia, and Thomas, has propelled the Court in a more conservative direction in a variety of areas. In 2009 and 2010, for example, in a series of 5–4 decisions, the Court overturned limits on corporate campaign spending, ruled that the Federal Communications Commission was justified in penalizing the use of expletives on the airwaves, and blocked a suit against former attorney general John Ashcroft by a terrorist suspect alleging that the suspect had been mistreated in prison. In 2011 and 2012, however, Chief Justice Roberts responded to charges that the Court's decisions were political rather than judicial by joining the liberal bloc in two important cases. The first was the Court's decision to invalidate portions of an Arizona law designed to identify and apprehend illegal aliens.[7] The second was the Court's 5–4 decision to uphold the Affordable Care Act, President Obama's major legislative achievement. Critics had charged that the Act's requirement that all Americans purchase health insurance was unconstitutional. Roberts wrote that this requirement was just another federal tax.[8]

In recent decades, Supreme Court nominations have come to involve intense partisan struggle. Typically, after the president has named a nominee, interest groups opposed to the nomination mobilize opposition in the media, among the public, and in the Senate. When President George H. W. Bush proposed the conservative judge Clarence Thomas for the Court, for example, liberal groups launched a campaign to discredit Thomas. After extensive research into his background, opponents of the nomination were able to produce evidence suggesting that Thomas had sexually harassed a former subordinate, Anita Hill. Thomas denied the charge.

After contentious Senate Judiciary Committee hearings, highlighted by testimony from both Thomas and Hill, Thomas narrowly won confirmation.

Likewise, conservative interest groups carefully scrutinized Bill Clinton's somewhat more liberal nominees, hoping to find information about them that would sabotage their appointments. During his two opportunities to name Supreme Court justices, Clinton was compelled to drop several potential appointees because of information unearthed by political opponents.

In 2009, when President Obama nominated federal Judge Sonia Sotomayor to replace retiring justice David Souter, conservatives denounced Sotomayor as a "reverse racist" because of her support for affirmative action. Many Republican senators, however, were reluctant to oppose a Hispanic nominee. For several years the GOP has made efforts to attract America's rapidly growing Hispanic population. Republicans feared that opposing Sotomayor would undermine these efforts.[9] In 2010, Republicans severely criticized Obama's nomination of Elena Kagan, solicitor general and former Harvard law dean, to replace retiring justice John Paul Stevens. Kagan was, nevertheless, confirmed by the Senate.

# ● The Power of the Supreme Court: Judicial Review

**judicial review** the power of the courts to review and, if necessary, declare actions of the legislative and executive branches invalid or unconstitutional. The Supreme Court asserted this power in *Marbury v. Madison*.

> **Explain how the Supreme Court exercises the power of judicial review**

The term **judicial review** refers to the power of the judiciary to examine and, if necessary, invalidate actions undertaken by the legislative and executive branches if it finds them unconstitutional. The term is sometimes used also to describe the scrutiny that appellate courts give to the actions of trial courts, but, strictly speaking, this is an improper use. A higher court's examination of a lower court's decisions might be called "appellate review," but it is not judicial review.

## Judicial Review of Acts of Congress

*In* Marbury v. Madison *(1803), Chief Justice John Marshall established the Supreme Court's power to rule on the constitutionality of federal and state laws. This power makes the Court a lawmaking body.*

Because the Constitution does not give the Supreme Court the power of judicial review over congressional enactments, the Court's exercise of it is something of a usurpation. It is not known whether the framers of the Constitution opposed judicial review, but "if they intended to provide for it in the Constitution, they did so in a most obscure fashion."[10] Disputes over the intentions of the framers were settled in 1803 in the case of *Marbury v. Madison*.[11] This case arose after Thomas Jefferson replaced John Adams in the White House. Jefferson's secretary of state, James Madison, refused to deliver an official commission to William Marbury, who had been appointed to a minor office by Adams just before he left the presidency. Marbury petitioned the Supreme Court to order Madison to deliver the commission. Jefferson and his followers did not believe that the Court had the power to undertake such an action and might have resisted the order. Chief Justice John Marshall was determined to assert the power of the judiciary but knew he must avoid a direct confrontation with the president. Accordingly, Marshall turned down Marbury's petition but gave as his reason the unconstitutionality of the legislation upon which Marbury had based his claim. Thus, Marshall asserted the power of judicial review but did so in a way that would not provoke a battle with Jefferson.

The Supreme Court's decision in this case established the power of judicial review. The Court said:

> It is emphatically the province and duty of the Judicial Department [the judicial branch] to say what the law is. Those who apply the rule to particular cases must, of necessity, expound and interpret that rule. If two laws conflict with each other, the Courts must decide on the operation of each. . . . So, if a law [e.g., a statute or treaty] be in opposition to the Constitution, if both the law and the Constitution apply to a particular case, so that the Court must either decide that case conformably to the law, disregarding the Constitution, or conformably to the Constitution, disregarding the law, the Court must determine which of these conflicting rules governs the case. This is of the very essence of judicial duty.

Although Congress and the president have often been at odds with the Court, the Court's legal power to review acts of Congress has not been seriously questioned since 1803. One reason for this is that the Supreme Court makes a self-conscious effort to give acts of Congress an interpretation that will make them constitutional. In more than two centuries, the Court has concluded that only some 160 acts of Congress directly violate the Constitution. For example, in 2007 and 2010 the high court struck down key portions of the Bipartisan Campaign Reform Act, through which Congress had sought to regulate spending in political campaigns.[12] The Court found that provisions of the act limiting political advertising violated the First Amendment.

**supremacy clause** Article VI of the Constitution, which states that laws passed by the national government and all treaties are the supreme law of the land and superior to all laws adopted by any state or any subdivision

## Judicial Review of State Actions

The power of the Supreme Court to review state legislation or other state action and to determine its constitutionality is neither granted by the Constitution nor inherent in the federal system. But the logic of the **supremacy clause** of Article VI of the Constitution, which declares the Constitution itself and laws made under its

*In 2011 the Supreme Court struck down a California law that regulated the sale of violent video games to children, saying it violated the First Amendment. California state senator Leland Yee, who proposed the ban, held up some of the games the law would have regulated.*

authority to be the supreme law of the land, is very strong. Furthermore, in the Judiciary Act of 1789, Congress conferred on the Supreme Court the power to reverse state constitutions and laws whenever they are clearly in conflict with the U.S. Constitution, federal laws, or treaties.[13] This power gives the Supreme Court appellate jurisdiction over all the millions of cases that American courts handle each year.

The supremacy clause of the Constitution not only established the federal Constitution, statutes, and treaties as the "supreme Law of the Land," but also provided that "the Judges in every State shall be bound thereby, any Thing in the Constitution or Laws of the State to the Contrary notwithstanding." Under this authority, the Supreme Court has frequently overturned state constitutional provisions or statutes and state court decisions it deems to contravene rights or privileges guaranteed under the federal Constitution or federal statutes.

The civil rights arena abounds with examples of state laws that the Supreme Court has overturned because the statutes violated guarantees of due process and equal protection contained in the Fourteenth Amendment to the Constitution. For example, in the 1954 case of *Brown v. Board of Education*, the Court overturned statutes from Kansas, South Carolina, Virginia, and Delaware that either required or permitted segregated public schools, ruling that such statutes denied black schoolchildren equal protection under the law.[14] In 1967 the Court's ruling in *Loving v. Virginia* invalidated a Virginia statute prohibiting interracial marriages.[15]

State statutes in other areas of law are equally subject to challenge. In *Griswold v. Connecticut*, the Court invalidated a Connecticut statute prohibiting the general distribution of contraceptives to married couples on the basis that the statute violated the couples' rights to marital privacy.[16] In *Brandenburg v. Ohio*, the Court overturned an Ohio statute forbidding any person to urge criminal acts as a means of inducing political reform or to join any association that advocated such activities. The Court found that the statute punished "mere advocacy" and therefore violated the free speech provisions of the Constitution.[17]

One realm in which the Court constantly monitors state conduct is the area of law enforcement. As we saw in Chapter 4, over the years, the Supreme Court has developed a number of principles regulating police conduct to ensure that the police do not violate constitutional liberties. These principles, however, must often be updated to keep pace with changes in technology. In a 2012 decision, the Supreme Court found that police use of a GPS tracker—a device invented more than two centuries after the adoption of the Bill of Rights—constituted a "search" as defined by the Fourth Amendment. In the case of *United States v. Jones*, the Court ruled that the police were prohibited from attaching a global-positioning device to a car belonging to a suspected drug dealer without first obtaining a valid warrant.[18]

## Judicial Review of Federal Agency Actions

Although Congress makes the law, as we saw in Chapters 12 and 14, it can hardly administer the thousands of programs it has enacted and must therefore delegate power to the president and to a huge bureaucracy to achieve its purposes. For example, if Congress wishes to improve air quality, it cannot possibly anticipate all the conditions and circumstances that may arise with respect to that general goal. Inevitably, Congress must delegate to the executive substantial discretionary power to make judgments about the best ways to bring about improved air quality in the face of changing circumstances. Thus, over the years, almost any congressional program will result in thousands upon thousands of pages of administrative regulations developed by executive agencies nominally seeking to implement the will of the Congress.

Delegation of power to the executive poses a number of problems for Congress and the federal courts. If Congress delegates broad authority to the president, it risks seeing its goals subordinated to and subverted by those of the executive branch.[19] If Congress attempts to limit executive discretion by enacting precise rules and standards to govern the conduct of the president and the executive branch, it risks writing laws that do not conform to real-world conditions and that are too rigid to be adapted to changing circumstances.[20]

Over the past two centuries, the issue of delegation of power has led to a number of court decisions regarding the scope of the delegation. Courts have also been called on to decide whether the regulations adopted by federal agencies are consistent with Congress's express or implied intent.

As presidential power expanded during the New Deal era, one indication of increased congressional subordination to the executive was the enactment of laws that contained few, if any, principles limiting executive discretion. Congress enacted legislation, often at the president's behest, that gave the executive virtually unfettered authority to address a particular concern. For example, the Emergency Price Control Act of 1942 authorized the executive to set "fair and equitable" prices without spelling out what those terms might mean.[21] Although the Court initially challenged these delegations of power to the president during the New Deal, it retreated from its position when faced with a confrontation with President Franklin Delano Roosevelt. Perhaps as a result, no congressional delegation of power to the president since then has been struck down as impermissibly broad. Particularly in recent years, the Supreme Court has found that so long as federal agencies developed rules and regulations "based upon a permissible construction" or "reasonable interpretation" of Congress's statute, the judiciary would accept the views of the executive branch. Generally, the courts give considerable deference to administrative agencies as long as those agencies engage in a formal rule-making process as prescribed by the various statutes governing agency rule making.

## Judicial Review and Presidential Power

The federal courts are also called on to review the actions of the president. On many occasions, members of Congress as well as individuals and groups have challenged presidential orders and actions in the federal courts. In recent years, the federal bench

*The courts have the authority to settle disputes between not only individuals and other private entities but also individuals and the government. In recent "enemy combatant" cases, the Supreme Court has ruled on the rights of prisoners being held in the U.S. base in Guantánamo, Cuba. In 2008, demonstrators dressed as Guantánamo detainees protested outside the Court.*

has, more often than not, upheld assertions of presidential power in such realms as foreign policy, war and emergency powers, legislative power, and administrative authority. In June 2004, however, the Supreme Court ruled on three cases involving President George W. Bush's antiterrorism initiatives and claims of executive power, and in two of the three cases appeared to place some limits on presidential authority.

One important case was *Hamdi v. Rumsfeld*.[22] Yaser Esam Hamdi, apparently a Taliban soldier, was captured by American forces in Afghanistan and brought to the United States, where he was incarcerated at the Norfolk Naval Station. Hamdi was classified as an enemy combatant and denied civil rights, including the right to counsel, despite the fact that he had been born in Louisiana and held American citizenship. In June 2004 the Supreme Court ruled that Hamdi was entitled to a lawyer and "a fair opportunity to rebut the government's factual assertions." Thus the Supreme Court did assert that presidential actions were subject to judicial scrutiny and that the Court could place some constraints on the president's power. But at the same time, the Court affirmed the president's single most important claim: the unilateral power to declare individuals, including U.S. citizens, "enemy combatants," who could be detained by federal authorities under adverse legal circumstances. Several of the justices intimated that once designated an enemy combatant, a U.S. citizen might be tried before a military tribunal, without the normal presumption of innocence.

In the 2006 case of *Hamdan v. Rumsfeld*, Salim Hamdan, a Taliban fighter, was captured in Afghanistan and held at the Guantánamo Bay naval base. The Bush administration planned to try Hamdan before a military commission authorized by a 2002 presidential order. The Supreme Court ruled that the commissions created by the president planned to use procedures that would violate federal law and U.S. treaty obligations.[23] President Bush responded by demanding that Congress rewrite the law. Congress quickly obliged and enacted the Military Commissions Act, which gave the president statutory authority for his actions. In Section 7 of the act, Congress declared that Guantánamo prisoners could not bring *habeas corpus* petitions to federal courts to seek their release. In the 2008 case of *Boumediene v. Bush*, however, the Supreme Court struck down Section 7 and declared *habeas corpus* to be a fundamental right.[24]

## Judicial Review and Lawmaking

Much of the work of the courts involves the application of statutes to the particular case at hand. Over the centuries, judges have also developed a body of rules and principles of interpretation that are not grounded in specific statutes. This body of judge-made law is called **common law**.

**common law** law made through court precedent rather than legislative enactments

The appellate courts, however, are in another realm. Their rulings can be considered laws, but they govern the behavior only of the judiciary. The written opinion of an appellate court is about halfway between common law and statutory law. As in common law, the opinion is judge-made and draws heavily on the precedents of previous cases. But, as in statutory law, it tries to articulate the rule of law controlling the case in question and future cases like it. It differs from a statute in that a statute addresses itself to the future conduct of citizens, whereas a written opinion addresses itself mainly to the future willingness or ability of courts to take cases and render favorable opinions. Decisions by appellate courts affect citizens by opening or closing access to the courts.

A specific case illustrates the distinction. Before the Second World War, one of the most insidious forms of racial discrimination was the "restrictive covenant," a clause in a contract whereby the purchasers of a house agreed that if they later decided to sell the home, they would sell only to a Caucasian. When a test case finally reached the Supreme Court in 1948, the Court ruled unanimously that citizens had a right to discriminate with restrictive covenants in their sales contracts but that the courts could not enforce those contracts. Its argument was that enforcement would constitute violation of the Fourteenth Amendment provision that no state shall "deny to any person within its jurisdiction equal protection under the law."[25] The Court was thereby predicting what it would and would not do in future cases of this sort. Most states have now enacted statutes that forbid homeowners from placing such covenants in sales contracts.

Many areas of civil law have been constructed in the same way: by judicial messages to other judges, some of which are eventually codified into legislative enactments. An example of great concern to employees and employers is that of liability for injuries sustained at work. Courts have sided with employees so often that it has become virtually useless for employers to fight injury cases. It has become "the law" that employers are liable for such injuries, without regard to claims of negligence. But the law in this instance is simply a series of messages to lawyers that they should advise their corporate clients not to appeal injury decisions. In recent years, the Supreme Court has also been developing law in the realm of sexual harassment in the workplace. In a 2006 case, for example, the Court said that a victim of sexual harassment who was transferred from her job could sue her employer even though the company disciplined the perpetrator when the harassment was reported.[26]

The appellate courts cannot decide what types of behavior will henceforth be a crime. They cannot directly prevent the police from forcing confessions from suspects or intimidating witnesses. In other words, they cannot directly change the behavior of citizens or eliminate abuses of government power. What they can do, however, is make it easier for mistreated persons to gain redress.

In redressing wrongs, the appellate courts—and even the Supreme Court itself—often call for a radical change in legal principle. Changes in race relations, for example, would probably have taken a great deal longer if the Supreme Court had not rendered the 1954 decision *Brown v. Board of Education*, which redefined the rights of African Americans.

Similarly, the Supreme Court interpreted the doctrine of the separation of church and state so as to alter significantly the practice of religion in public institutions. For example, in a 1962 case, *Engel v. Vitale*, the Court declared that a once widely observed ritual—the recitation of a prayer by students in a public school—was unconstitutional under the establishment clause of the First Amendment.[27] Almost all the dramatic changes in the treatment of criminals and of persons accused of crimes have been made by the appellate courts, especially the Supreme Court. The Supreme Court brought about a veritable revolution in the criminal process with three cases over less than five years: *Gideon v. Wainwright*, in 1963, established the obligation of state courts to provide legal counsel to defendants who could not afford their own attorneys.[28] *Escobedo v. Illinois*, in 1964, gave suspects the right to remain silent and the right to have counsel present during questioning. But the *Escobedo* decision left confusions that allowed differing decisions to be made by lower courts.[29] In *Miranda v. Arizona*, in 1966, the Supreme

*Due process of law is an area in which federal courts have been critical in "making law" since the 1960s. In 2009 the Court heard the case of Savana Redding, who was strip-searched by school officials who suspected she was hiding prescription pills. The Court ruled that the search was illegal.*

Court cleared up these confusions by setting forth what is known as the Miranda rule: arrested people have the right to remain silent, the right to be informed that anything they say can be held against them, and the right to counsel before and during police interrogation (see Chapter 4).[30] In 2000 the Supreme Court considered overruling *Miranda* in *Dickerson v. United States*, but it decided that the wide acceptance of Miranda rights in the legal culture was "adequate reason not to overrule" it.[31]

One of the most significant changes brought about by the Supreme Court was the revolution in legislative representation unleashed by the 1962 case of *Baker v. Carr*.[32] In this landmark case, the Supreme Court held that it could no longer avoid reviewing complaints about the apportionment of seats in state legislatures. Following that decision, the federal courts went on to force reapportionment of all state, county, and local legislatures in the country.

## The Supreme Court in Action

Given the millions of disputes that arise every year, the job of the Supreme Court would be impossible if it were not able to control the flow of cases and its own caseload. The Supreme Court has original jurisdiction in a limited variety of cases defined by the Constitution. The original jurisdiction includes (1) cases between the United States and one of the 50 states, (2) cases between two or more states, (3) cases involving foreign ambassadors or other ministers, and (4) cases brought by one state against citizens of another state or against a foreign country. The most important of these cases are disputes between states over land, water, or old debts. Generally, the Supreme Court deals with these cases by appointing a "special master," usually a retired judge, to hear the case and present a report. The Supreme Court then allows the states involved in the dispute to present arguments for or against the master's opinion.[33] The fact that a matter falls within the Supreme Court's jurisdiction does not mean that the Court will necessarily hear the case.

**Rules of Access** Over the years, the courts have developed specific rules that govern which cases within their jurisdiction they will and will not hear. In order to be heard by the courts, cases must meet certain criteria that are initially applied by the trial court but may be reconsidered by appellate courts. These rules of access can be broken down into three major categories: case or controversy, standing, and mootness.

Article III of the Constitution and Supreme Court decisions define judicial power as extending only to "cases and controversies." This means that the case before a court must be an actual controversy, not a hypothetical one, with two truly adversarial parties. The courts have interpreted this language to mean that they do not have the power to render advisory opinions to legislatures or agencies about the constitutionality of proposed laws or regulations. Furthermore, even after a law is enacted, the courts will generally refuse to consider its constitutionality until it is actually applied.

**standing** the right of an individual or organization to initiate a court case, on the basis of their having a substantial stake in the outcome

Parties to a case must also have **standing**—that is, they must show that they have a substantial stake in the outcome of the case. The traditional requirement for standing has been to show injury to oneself; that injury can be personal, economic, or even aesthetic, such as a neighbor's building a high fence that blocks one's view of the ocean. In order for a group or class of people to have standing (as in class-action suits), each member must show specific injury. This means that a general interest in the environment, for instance, does not provide a group with sufficient basis for standing.

The Supreme Court also uses a third criterion in determining whether it will hear a case: that of **mootness**. In theory, this requirement disqualifies cases that are brought too late—after the relevant facts have changed or the problem has been resolved by other means. The criterion of mootness, however, is subject to the discretion of the courts, which have begun to relax the rules of mootness, particularly in cases where a situation that has been resolved is likely to come up again. In the abortion case *Roe v. Wade*, for example, the Supreme Court rejected the lower court's argument that because the pregnancy in question had already come to term, the case was moot. The Court agreed to hear the case because no pregnancy was likely to outlast the lengthy appeals process.[34]

**mootness** a criterion used by courts to screen cases that no longer require resolution

Putting aside the formal criteria, the Supreme Court is most likely to accept cases that involve conflicting decisions by the federal circuit courts, cases that present important questions of civil rights or civil liberties, and cases in which the federal government is the appellant. Ultimately, however, the question of which cases to accept can come down to the preferences and priorities of the justices. If a group of justices believes that the Court should intervene in a particular area of policy or politics, they are likely to look for a case or cases that will serve as vehicles for judicial intervention. For many years, the Court was not interested in considering challenges to affirmative action or other programs designed to provide particular benefits to minorities. In recent years, however, several of the Court's more conservative justices have been eager to push back the limits of affirmative action and racial preference, and have therefore accepted a number of cases that would allow them to do so. In the 2009 case of *Ricci v. DeStefano*, for example, the Court ruled that officials in New Haven, Connecticut, had discriminated against white firefighters when they threw out the results of a test in which whites had outscored minority candidates for promotion. The Court said employers must have a "strong basis in evidence" that a test is defective, rather than simply relying on disparate outcomes.[35] The case is also notable because it was an appeal following a decision by Judge Sonia Sotomayor, who, a few months later, joined the Supreme Court. In 2012 the Court was poised to rule on the constitutionality of "race-conscious" college admissions.

*The justices' preferences and priorities influence which cases are heard by the Supreme Court. Recently, the Court's conservative justices have been interested in cases involving challenges to affirmative action. In 2009 the Court found that officials in New Haven, Connecticut, including Mayor John DeStefano (pictured here), had discriminated against white firefighters in an effort to protect the rights of minority firefighters.*

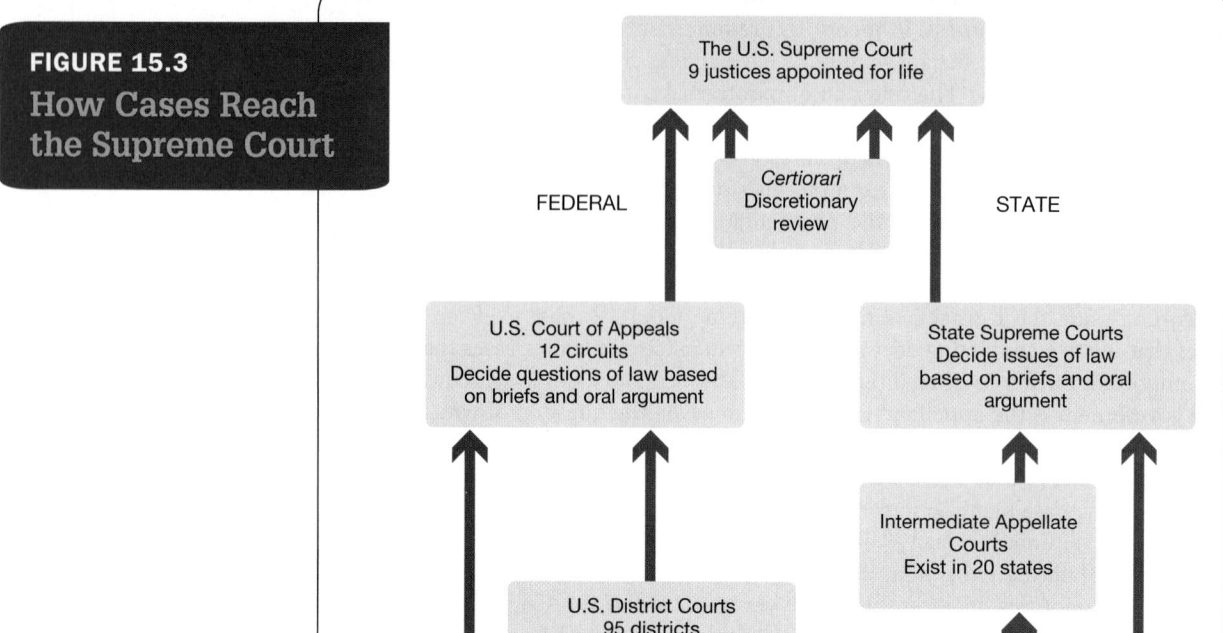

**FIGURE 15.3**
**How Cases Reach the Supreme Court**

The U.S. Supreme Court
9 justices appointed for life

FEDERAL

*Certiorari*
Discretionary review

STATE

U.S. Court of Appeals
12 circuits
Decide questions of law based on briefs and oral argument

State Supreme Courts
Decide issues of law based on briefs and oral argument

Intermediate Appellate Courts
Exist in 20 states

U.S. District Courts
95 districts
Decide issues of law and fact, with and without jury

State Trial Courts
Often known as Superior Court or Circuit Court. Try questions of law and fact, with and without a jury

Federal agencies

Inferior trial courts

**writ of *certiorari*** a decision of at least four of the nine Supreme Court justices to review a decision of a lower court; *certiorari* is Latin, meaning "to make more certain"

**Writs** Most cases reach the Supreme Court through a **writ of *certiorari*** (see Figure 15.3). *Certiorari* is an order to a lower court to deliver the records of a particular case to be reviewed for legal errors. The term *certiorari* is sometimes shortened to *cert*, and cases deemed to merit *certiorari* are referred to as "certworthy." An individual who loses in a lower federal court or state court and wants the Supreme Court to review the decision has 90 days to file a petition for a writ of *certiorari* with the clerk of the U.S. Supreme Court. There are two types of petitions: paid petitions and petitions *in forma pauperis* ("in the form of a pauper"). The former requires payment of filing fees, submission of a certain number of copies, and compliance with a variety of other rules. For *in forma pauperis* petitions, usually filed by prison inmates, the Court waives the fees and most other requirements. Petitions for thousands of cases are filed with the Court every year (see Figure 15.4).

Since 1972, most of the justices have participated in a "*certiorari* pool" in which their law clerks work together to evaluate the petitions. Each petition is reviewed by one clerk, who writes a memo for all the justices participating in the pool, summarizing the facts and issues and making a recommendation. Clerks for the other justices add their comments to the memo. After the justices have reviewed the memos, any one of them may place any case on the "discuss list," which is circulated by the chief justice. If a case is not placed on the discuss list, it

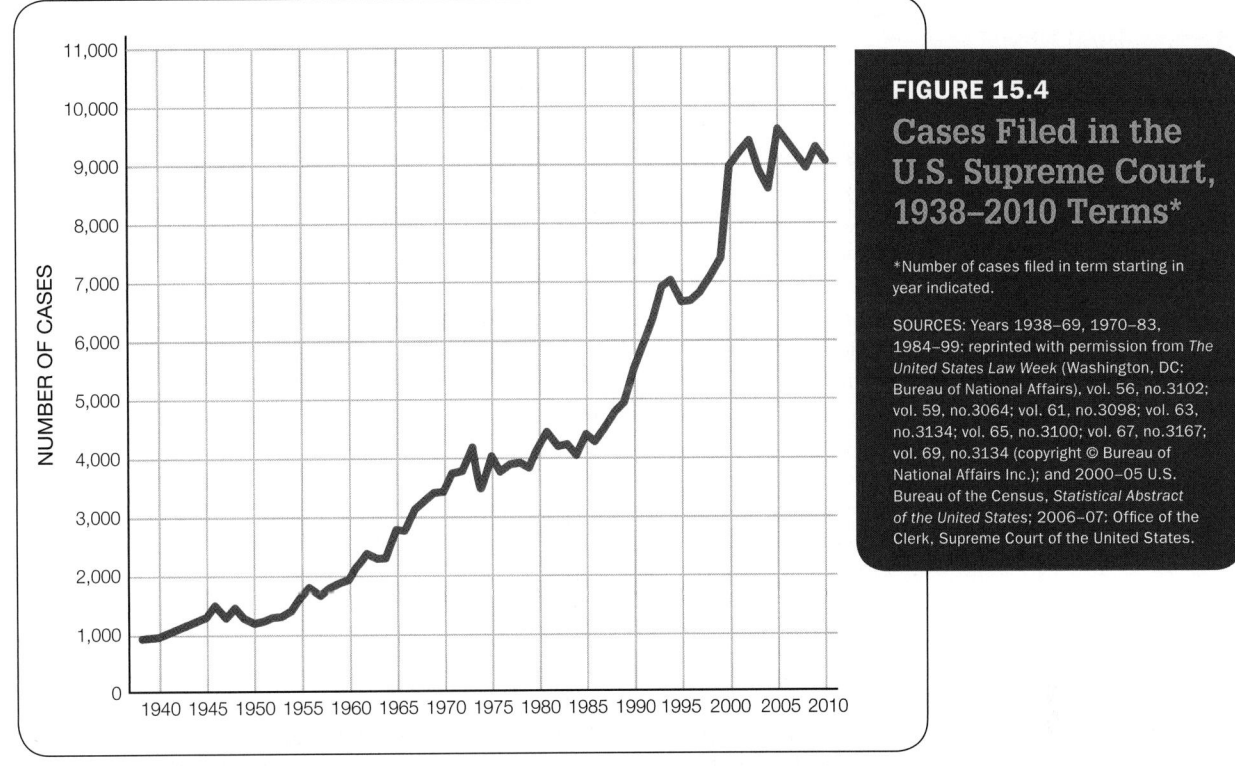

**FIGURE 15.4**

**Cases Filed in the U.S. Supreme Court, 1938–2010 Terms***

*Number of cases filed in term starting in year indicated.

SOURCES: Years 1938–69, 1970–83, 1984–99: reprinted with permission from *The United States Law Week* (Washington, DC: Bureau of National Affairs), vol. 56, no.3102; vol. 59, no.3064; vol. 61, no.3098; vol. 63, no.3134; vol. 65, no.3100; vol. 67, no.3167; vol. 69, no.3134 (copyright © Bureau of National Affairs Inc.); and 2000–05 U.S. Bureau of the Census, *Statistical Abstract of the United States*; 2006–07: Office of the Clerk, Supreme Court of the United States.

is automatically denied *certiorari*. Cases placed on the discuss list are considered and voted on during the justices' closed-door conference.

For *certiorari* to be granted, four justices must be convinced that the case satisfies Rule 10 of the Rules of the U.S. Supreme Court. Rule 10 states that *certiorari* is not a matter of right but is to be granted only when there are special and compelling reasons. These include conflicting decisions by two or more circuit courts, conflicts between circuit courts and state courts of last resort, conflicting decisions by two or more state courts of last resort, decisions by circuit courts on matters of federal law that should be settled by the Supreme Court, and a circuit court decision on an important question that conflicts with Supreme Court decisions. It should be clear from this list that the Court will usually take action under only the most compelling circumstances—when there are conflicts among the lower courts about what the law should be, when an important legal question has been raised in the lower courts but not definitively answered, or when a lower court deviates from the principles and precedents established by the high court. Few cases are able to gain the support of four justices needed for *certiorari*. In recent sessions, although thousands of petitions were filed, the Court has granted *certiorari* to barely more than 80 petitioners each year—about 1 percent of those seeking a Supreme Court review.

A handful of cases reach the Supreme Court through avenues other than *certiorari*. One of these is the writ of certification, which can be used when a U.S. court of appeals asks the Supreme Court for instructions on a point of law that has never been decided. A second alternative avenue is the writ of appeal, which is used to appeal the decision of a three-judge district court.

## Controlling the Flow of Cases

In addition to the judges, other actors play important roles in shaping the flow of cases through the federal courts: the solicitor general and federal law clerks.

**The Solicitor General** If any single person has greater influence than individual judges over the federal courts, it is the **solicitor general** of the United States. The solicitor general is the third-ranking official in the Justice Department (below the attorney general and the deputy attorney general) but the top government lawyer in virtually all cases before the Supreme Court in which the government is a party. The solicitor general has the greatest control over the flow of cases; his or her actions are not reviewed by any higher authority in the executive branch. More than half the Supreme Court's total workload consists of cases under the direct charge of the solicitor general.

**solicitor general** the top government lawyer in all cases before the Supreme Court where the government is a party

The solicitor general exercises especially strong influence by screening cases before any agency of the federal government can appeal them to the Supreme Court; indeed, the justices rely on the solicitor general to "screen out undeserving litigation and furnish them with an agenda to government cases that deserve serious consideration."[36] Typically, more requests for appeals are rejected than are accepted by the solicitor general. Agency heads may lobby the president or otherwise try to circumvent the solicitor general, and a few of the independent agencies have a statutory right to make direct appeals, but without the solicitor general's support, these requests are seldom reviewed by the Court. At best, they are doomed to ***per curiam*** ("by the court") rejection—rejection through a brief, unsigned opinion by the whole Court. Congress has given only a few agencies, including the Federal Communications Commission, the Federal Maritime Commission, and in some cases the Department of Agriculture (even though it is not an independent agency), the right to appeal directly to the Supreme Court without going through the solicitor general.

***per curiam*** a brief, unsigned decision by an appellate court, usually rejecting a petition to review the decision of a lower court

The solicitor general can enter a case even when the federal government is not a direct litigant by writing an ***amicus curiae*** ("friend of the court") brief. A friend of the court is not a direct party to a case but has a vital interest in its outcome. Thus, when the government has such an interest, the solicitor general can file an *amicus* brief or a federal court can invite such a brief because it wants an opinion in writing. Other interested parties may file briefs as well.

***amicus curiae*** literally, "friend of the court"; individuals or groups who are not parties to a lawsuit but who seek to assist the Supreme Court in reaching a decision by presenting additional briefs

In addition to exercising substantial control over the flow of cases, the solicitor general can shape the arguments used before the federal courts. Indeed, the Supreme Court tends to give special attention to the way the solicitor general characterizes the issues. The solicitor general is the person who appears most frequently before the Court and, theoretically at least, is the most disinterested. The credibility of the solicitor general is not hurt when several times each year he or she comes to the Court to withdraw a case with the admission that the government has made an error.

The solicitor general's sway over the flow of cases does not, however, entirely overshadow the influence of the other agencies and divisions in the Department of Justice. The solicitor general is counsel for the major divisions in the department, including the Antitrust, Tax, Civil Rights, and Criminal divisions. Their activities generate a great part of the solicitor general's agenda. This is particularly true of the Criminal Division, whose cases are appealed every day. These cases are generated by initiatives taken by the U.S. attorneys and the district judges before whom they practice.

**Law Clerks** Every federal judge employs law clerks to research legal issues and assist with the preparation of opinions. Each Supreme Court justice is assigned four clerks, almost always honors graduates of the nation's most prestigious law schools. A clerkship with a Supreme Court justice is a great honor and generally indicates that the fortunate individual is likely to reach the very top of the legal profession. The work of the Supreme Court clerks is a closely guarded secret, but it is likely that some justices rely heavily on their clerks for advice in writing opinions and in deciding whether the Court should hear specific cases. In a recent book, a former law clerk to the late justice Harry Blackmun charged that Supreme Court justices yielded "excessive power to immature, ideologically driven clerks, who in turn use that power to manipulate their bosses."[37]

## Lobbying for Access: Interests and the Court

At the same time that the Court exercises discretion over which cases it will review, groups and forces in society often seek to persuade the justices to listen to their problems. Lawyers representing interest groups try to choose the proper client and the proper case, so that the issues in question are most dramatically and appropriately portrayed. They also have to pick the right district or jurisdiction in which to bring the case. Sometimes they even have to wait for an appropriate political climate. Group litigants have to plan carefully when to make use of and when to avoid publicity. They must also attempt to develop a proper record at the trial court level, one that includes some constitutional arguments and even, when possible, errors on the part of the trial court. One of the most effective strategies that litigants use in getting cases accepted for review by the appellate courts is to bring the same type of suit in more than one circuit (that is, to develop a "pattern of cases"), in the hope that inconsistent treatment by two different courts will improve the chance of a Supreme Court review.

The two most notable users of the pattern-of-cases strategy in recent years have been the National Association for the Advancement of Colored People (NAACP) and the American Civil Liberties Union (ACLU). For many years, the NAACP (and its Defense Fund—now a separate group) has worked through local chapters and with many individuals to encourage litigation on issues of racial discrimination and segregation. Sometimes it distributes petitions to be signed by parents and filed with local school boards and courts, deliberately sowing the seeds of future litigation. The NAACP and the ACLU often encourage private parties to bring suit and then join the suit as *amici curiae*.

In many states, it is considered unethical and illegal for attorneys to engage in "fomenting and soliciting legal business in which they are not parties and have no pecuniary right or liability." The NAACP was sued by the state of Virginia in the late 1950s in an attempt to restrict or eliminate its efforts to influence the pattern of cases. The Supreme Court reviewed the case in 1963, recognized that the strategy was being used, and held that the NAACP strategy was protected by the First and Fourteenth amendments, just as other forms of speech and petition are protected.[38]

Thus, many pathbreaking cases are eventually granted *certiorari* because repeated refusal to review one or more of them would amount to a rule of law just as much as if the courts had handed down a written opinion. In this sense, the flow of cases, especially the pattern of significant cases, influences the behavior of the appellate judiciary.

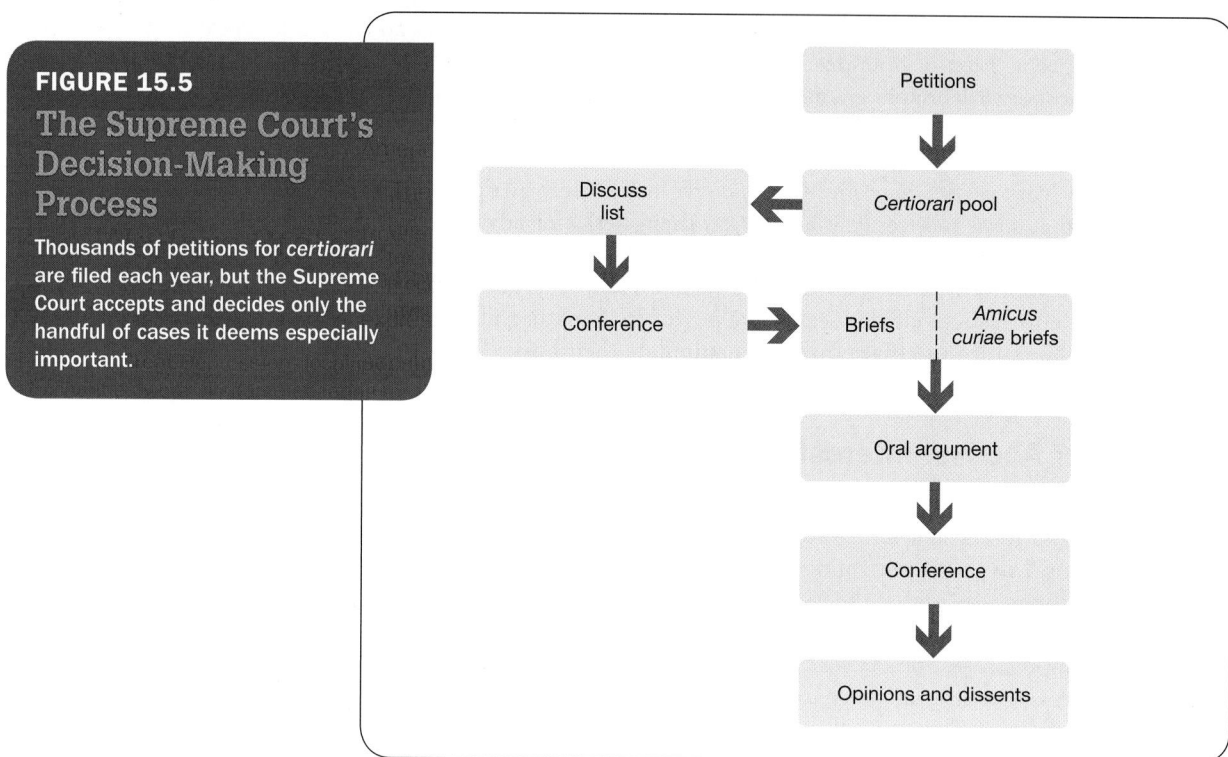

**FIGURE 15.5**

**The Supreme Court's Decision-Making Process**

Thousands of petitions for *certiorari* are filed each year, but the Supreme Court accepts and decides only the handful of cases it deems especially important.

Petitions

Discuss list ← Certiorari pool

Conference → Briefs | Amicus curiae briefs

Oral argument

Conference

Opinions and dissents

## The Supreme Court's Procedures

The Supreme Court's decision to accept a case is the beginning of what can be a lengthy and complex process (see Figure 15.5). After a petition is filed and *certiorari* is granted, the Court considers the reasoning on both sides as presented in briefs and oral argument, the justices discuss the case in conference, and opinions are carefully drafted.

**briefs** written documents in which attorneys explain, using case precedents, why the court should find in favor of their client

**The Preparation** First, the attorneys on both sides must prepare **briefs**, written documents in which the attorneys explain why the Court should rule in favor of their client. Briefs are filled with referrals to precedents specifically chosen to show that other courts have frequently ruled in the same way the attorneys are requesting that the Supreme Court rule. The attorneys for both sides muster the most compelling precedents they can in support of their arguments.

As the attorneys prepare their briefs, they often ask sympathetic interest groups for their help. These groups are asked to file *amicus curiae* briefs that support the claims of one or the other litigant. In a case involving separation of church and state, for example, liberal groups such as the ACLU and People for the American Way are likely to be asked to file *amicus* briefs in support of strict separation, whereas conservative religious groups are likely to file *amicus* briefs advocating increased public accommodation of religious ideas. Often dozens of briefs will be filed on each side of a major case. *Amicus* filings are one of the primary methods used by interest groups to lobby the Court. By filing these briefs, groups indicate to the Court where they stand and signal to the justices that they believe the case to be an important one.

**Oral Argument** The next stage of a case is **oral argument**, in which attorneys for both sides appear before the Court to present their positions and answer the justices' questions. Each attorney has only a half hour to present his or her case, and this time includes interruptions for questions. Certain members of the Court, such as Justice Antonin Scalia, are known to interrupt attorneys dozens of times. Others, such as Justice Clarence Thomas, seldom ask questions. For an attorney, the opportunity to argue a case before the Supreme Court is a singular honor and a mark of professional distinction. It can also be a harrowing experience, as when justices interrupt a carefully prepared presentation. Nevertheless, oral argument can be very important to the outcome of a case. It allows justices to understand better the heart of the case and to raise questions that might not have been addressed in the opposing sides' briefs. It is not uncommon for justices to go beyond the strictly legal issues and ask opposing counsel to discuss the implications of the case for the Court and the nation at large.

**The Conference** Following oral argument, the Court discusses the case in its Wednesday or Friday conference, a strictly private meeting that no outsiders are permitted to attend. The chief justice presides over the conference and speaks first; the other justices follow in order of seniority. The justices discuss the case and eventually reach a decision on the basis of a majority vote. If the Court is divided, a number of votes may be taken before a final decision is reached. As the case is discussed, justices may try to influence or change one another's opinions. At times, this may result in compromise decisions.

**Opinion Writing** After a decision has been reached, one of the members of the majority is assigned to write the **opinion**. This assignment is made by the chief justice or by the most senior justice in the majority if the chief justice is on the losing side. The assignment of the opinion can make a significant difference to the interpretation of a decision. Every opinion of the Supreme Court sets a major precedent for future cases throughout the judicial system. Lawyers and judges in the lower courts will examine the opinion carefully to ascertain the Supreme Court's intent. Differences in wording and emphasis can have important implications for future litigation. Thus, in assigning an opinion, the justices must give serious thought to the impression the case will make on lawyers and on the public, and to the probability that one justice's opinion will be more widely accepted than another's.

One of the more dramatic instances of this tactical consideration occurred in 1944, when Chief Justice Harlan F. Stone chose Justice Felix Frankfurter to write the opinion in the "white primary" case *Smith v. Allwright.* The chief justice believed that this sensitive case, which overturned the southern practice of prohibiting black participation in nominating primaries, required the efforts of the most brilliant and scholarly jurist on the Court. But the day after Stone made the assignment, Justice Robert H. Jackson wrote a letter to Stone urging a change of assignment and arguing that Frankfurter, a foreign-born Jew from New England, would not win the South with his opinion, regardless of its brilliance. Stone accepted the advice and substituted Justice Stanley Reed, an American-born Protestant from Kentucky and a southern Democrat in good standing.[39]

Once the majority opinion is drafted, it is circulated to the other justices. Some members of the majority may agree with both the outcome and the rationale but wish to emphasize or highlight a particular point. For that purpose, they draft a concurring opinion, called a *regular concurrence.* In other instances, one or more justices may agree with the majority but disagree with the rationale presented in

**oral argument** the stage in Supreme Court procedure in which attorneys for both sides appear before the Court to present their positions and answer questions posed by justices

**opinion** the written explanation of the Supreme Court's decision in a particular case

# Is Everyone on Facebook Now a "Constitutional Scholar"?

**The Supreme Court is used to** working in relative anonymity until a major case is decided, at which point the Court's decision attracts substantial public attention. This trend existed since before the 1954 *Brown v. Board of Education* decision to integrate the public schools, and was in full view immediately after the 1973 *Roe v. Wade* ruling allowing women the right to an abortion. But the aftermath of the Court's 2012 decision on the Patient Protection and Affordable Care Act, public interest reached a new level, as political discussion online exploded. In one day, Chief Justice John Roberts became a household name.

Googling "Supreme Court Affordable Care Act" in June 2012 immediately following the announcement of the decision resulted in more than 214 million stories. In Google News alone, the same search term found more than 150,000 results. The 2010 Affordable Care Act included an individual mandate that virtually all Americans buy health insurance. Five of the nine justices agreed that the penalty someone must pay if he or she refuses to buy health insurance is a kind of tax that Congress can impose using its taxing power. The

Court's decision meant that the controversial mandate was constitutional, and President's Obama universal health care bill would become law.

With the decision, the Supreme Court was shoved to the forefront of a political divide in the United States. The individual justices were simultaneously heroes and villains, depending on whether one supported or opposed the act. A Gallup poll taken immediately after the ruling found **Americans evenly divided over the Supreme Court decision, with 46 percent agreeing and 46 percent disagreeing with the Court's ruling that the law is constitutional. Opinion largely followed party lines, with Republicans opposing and Democrats favoring.** While there were millions of posts, blogs, articles, and tweets about the decision, only a small percentage reflected a deep understanding and analysis of the decision's significance.

While the justices were all in the spotlight in the aftermath of this decision, Chief Justice Roberts took the brunt of the blame from those opposed to the health care act, and he became a champion to supporters. Roberts is usually a member of the conservative bloc of justices, so his vote to uphold the individual mandate shocked the nation. Hundreds of people gathered around the Supreme Court building in Washington, D.C., the day the decision was released, including many Tea Party supporters who had organized online to have a protest rally if the act was upheld.

A clever picture caption (or "meme") with more than 30,000 "shares" on the social networking site Facebook became popular in blogs and other online media surrounding the Court's decision. It read, "Brace Yourselves: Everyone on Facebook Is About to Become a Constitutional Scholar." While making fun of the hoopla surrounding the decision and the strident arguments being made on both sides following the Court's ruling, the underlying mes-

sage referred to the educative effects of social media on citizens' political knowledge about the Court. Research has found that individuals who get political information online have higher levels of general political knowledge and are more likely to discuss politics with friends and family. While supporters of the Patient Protection and Affordable Care Act celebrated the Court's decision, and opponents ranted and railed against the Court and promised to overturn the act, the average American became one notch more informed about constitutional law.

SOURCES: "The Health Care Decision, Explained in 1 Paragraph on SCOTUSblog." *The Atlantic*, June 28, 2012. Karen Mossberger, Caroline Tolbert, and Ramona McNeal. *Digital Citizenship: The Internet, Society and Participation* (Cambridge, MA: MIT Press, 2008). Lydia Saad, "Americans Issue Split Decision on Healthcare Ruling," Gallup Organization, June 29, 2012.

## for critical analysis

1. Will the Internet and social media make the Supreme Court more responsive to public opinion, or will the Court continue to operate as it has for the past two centuries?

2. Does discussing politics on social networking sites make the public more informed about the court system and legal issues? Or do citizens merely gain a surface understanding of the issues, without substantive political knowledge?

the majority opinion. These justices may draft *special concurrences*, explaining their disagreements with the majority.

**Dissent** Justices who disagree with the majority decision of the Court may choose to publicize the character of their disagreement in the form of a **dissenting opinion**. The dissenting opinion is generally assigned by the senior justice among the dissenters. Dissents can be used to express irritation with an outcome or to signal to defeated political forces in the nation that their position is supported by at least some members of the Court. Ironically, the most dependable way an individual justice can exercise a direct and clear influence on the Court is to write a dissent. Because there is no need to please a majority, dissenting opinions can be more eloquent and less guarded than majority opinions. The current Supreme Court often produces 5–4 decisions, with dissenters writing long and detailed opinions that, they hope, will help them persuade a swing justice to join their side on the next round of cases dealing with a similar topic. During the Court's 2006–07 term, Justice Ruth Bader Ginsburg was so unhappy about the majority's decisions in a number of cases that she twice violated her own long-standing practice and read forceful dissents from the bench, thus underscoring her disagreement with current legal trends and pointing the way toward other possibilities.

Dissent plays a special role in the work and impact of the Court because it amounts to an appeal to lawyers all over the country to keep bringing similar cases. Therefore, an effective dissent influences the flow of cases through the Court and the arguments that lawyers will use in later cases. Even more important, dissent points out that although the Court speaks with a single opinion, it is the opinion only of the majority—and one day the majority might go the other way.

*On several occasions, Justice Ruth Bader Ginsburg has read her dissenting opinions aloud from the bench, to emphasize her strong disagreement with the majority. Dissenting opinions can encourage lawyers to bring similar cases in the future by letting the public know that not all the justices support the majority decision.*

**dissenting opinion** a decision written by a justice in the minority in a particular case in which the justice wishes to express his or her reasoning in the case

## Explaining Supreme Court Decisions

The Supreme Court explains its decisions in terms of law and precedent. But it is the Court itself that decides what the laws actually mean and what importance the precedent will actually have. Throughout its history, the Court has shaped and reshaped the law. In the late nineteenth and early twentieth centuries, for example, the Supreme Court held that the Constitution, law, and precedent permitted racial segregation in the United States. Beginning in the late 1950s, however, the Court found that the Constitution prohibited segregation on the basis of race and indicated that the use of racial categories in legislation was always suspect. By the 1970s and '80s, the Court once again held that the Constitution permitted the use of racial categories—when such categories were needed to help members of minority groups achieve full participation in American society. Since the 1990s, the Court has retreated from this position, too, indicating that governmental efforts to provide extra help to racial minorities could represent an unconstitutional infringement on the rights of the majority.

**Activism and Restraint** One element of judicial philosophy is the issue of activism versus restraint. Over the years, some justices have believed that courts should interpret the Constitution according to the stated intentions of its framers and defer to the views of Congress when interpreting federal statutes. Justice Felix Frankfurter, for example, advocated judicial deference to legislative bodies and avoidance of the "political thicket" in which the Court would entangle itself by deciding questions that were essentially political rather than legal in character. Advocates of

**judicial restraint** judicial philosophy whose adherents refuse to go beyond the clear words of the Constitution in interpreting the document's meaning

**judicial activism** judicial philosophy that posits that the Court should go beyond the words of the Constitution or a statute to consider the broader societal implications of its decisions

## for critical analysis

In its 2008 decision in the case of *District of Columbia v. Heller,* the Supreme Court struck down a District of Columbia law that prohibited most private citizens from keeping handguns in their homes. How does the *Heller* decision affect gun laws outside the District of Columbia?

**judicial restraint** are sometimes called "strict constructionists," because they look strictly to the words of the Constitution in interpreting its meaning.

The alternative to restraint is **judicial activism**. Activist judges such as Chief Justice Earl Warren believed that the Court should go beyond the words of the Constitution or a statute to consider the broader societal implications of its decisions. Activist judges sometimes strike out in new directions, promulgating new interpretations or inventing new legal and constitutional concepts when they believe these to be socially desirable. For example, Justice Harry Blackmun's opinion in *Roe v. Wade* was based on a constitutional right to privacy that is not found in the words of the Constitution but was, rather, from the Court's prior decision in *Griswold v. Connecticut*.[40] Blackmun and the other members of the majority in the *Roe* case argued that the right to privacy was implied by other constitutional provisions. In this instance of judicial activism, the Court knew the result it wanted to achieve and was not afraid to make the law conform to the desired outcome.

Activism and restraint are sometimes confused with liberalism and conservatism. For example, conservative politicians often castigate "liberal activist" judges and call for the appointment of conservative jurists who will refrain from reinterpreting the law. To be sure, some liberal jurists are activists and some conservatives have been advocates of restraint, but the relationships are by no means synonymous. Indeed, the Rehnquist court, dominated by conservatives, was among the most activist courts in American history, particularly in such areas as federalism and election law. The Roberts court is continuing along the same route. As the examples of these conservative courts illustrate, a judge may be philosophically conservative and believe in strict construction of the Constitution but also be jurisprudentially activist and believe that the courts must play an active and energetic role in policy making, if necessary striking down acts of Congress to ensure that the intent of the framers is fulfilled.

**Political Ideology** The philosophy of activism versus restraint is sometimes a smokescreen for political ideology, and indeed, the liberal or conservative attitudes of justices play an important role in their decisions.[41] In the past, liberal judges have often been activists, willing to use the law to achieve social and political change, whereas conservatives have been associated with judicial restraint. Interestingly, however, in recent years some conservative justices who have long called for restraint have actually become activists in seeking to undo some of the work of liberal jurists.

From the 1950s to the 1980s, the Supreme Court took an activist role in such areas as civil rights, civil liberties, abortion, voting rights, and police procedures. For example, the Supreme Court was more responsible than any other governmental institution for breaking down America's system of racial segregation. Since that time, however, the conservative justices appointed by presidents Ronald Reagan, George H. W. Bush, and George W. Bush have become the dominant bloc on the Court and, as we saw earlier, have moved the Court to the right on a number of issues, including affirmative action and abortion.

The political struggles of recent years amply illustrate the importance of judicial ideology. Is abortion a fundamental right or a criminal activity? How much separation must there be between church and state? Does application of the Voting Rights Act to increase minority representation constitute a violation of the rights of whites? The answers to these and many other questions cannot be found in the words of the Constitution. They must be located, instead, in the hearts and minds of the judges who interpret that text.

# The Supreme Court and International Law

**For most of its history the American** judiciary has been a particularly domestic institution. But in this epoch of globalization, the Court has had to give up what Justice Ruth Bader Ginsburg in 2003 called "our 'island' or 'lone ranger' mentality." Ginsburg went on to note that increasingly the justices were considering the perspectives of comparative and international law. Despite Ginsburg's comment, one of the most important Supreme Court decisions in this realm, *Medellin v. Texas*, decided in March 2008, seemed to uphold our "island" mentality.[a] In that case the Court said that an international treaty is not binding domestic law unless Congress enacts statutes implementing it. Lacking such statutory authority, the president has no power to enforce a treaty or decision of an international tribunal. In the Medellin case, the defendant, a Mexican national, had been convicted of rape and murder in Texas and sentenced to death. Medellin said, however, that when he was arrested he had not been notified of his right to contact the Mexican consulate as required by international treaty. Medellin received a favorable ruling from the International Court of Justice, a UN entity recognized by the United States, which declared that Medellin was entitled to a review and reconsideration of his conviction. The U.S. Supreme Court, however, declared that U.S. courts were not bound by the rulings of an international tribunal unless Congress had enacted legislation to that effect. Medellin was executed.

Despite the Medellin case, America's relationship to international law is changing. Along One numerous cases involves such things as interpreting the terms of an international treaty that regular "cross-border transactions" in which international law not only is relevant but could be the governing law. U.S. courts had a difficult time with these because they required research on international law and decisions by foreign courts. And our various courts continually disagree over the weight to put on the rulings of foreign tribunals: Are these foreign decisions to be taken as precedents in our courts? Or do U.S. courts apply U.S. law to such transnational cases?

A second path of change is the extent to which our courts should be influenced by international opinion and by the decisions by foreign legislators and courts in their domestic disputes. One of the most striking was the 2003 decision that a Texas statute making it a crime for two persons of the same sex to engage in consensual sexual conduct violated the due process clause.[b] More controversial than the ruling itself was part of its argument: that other nations, including Great Britain, had repealed such laws 10 years earlier. Another decision of equal import was the 2002 decision in which the majority opinion noted that "within the world community the imposition of the death penalty for crimes committed by mentally retarded offenders is overwhelmingly disapproved." Chief Justice Rehnquist and Justice Scalia vigorously dissented on this point.

Another international influence is the UN treaty to establish an International Criminal Court (ICC), to be given jurisdiction over the conduct of military personnel in any international campaign. Since the ICC's creation in 1998, 130 countries have signed the treaty. Although President Clinton signed for the United States, he continued to bargain over terms, and the U.S. Senate has never had to confront a vote on ratification. However, Clinton's signature committed the United States to avoid acting in any way that would undermine the treaty. Consequently, fears persist that U.S. military personnel could be subject to prosecution if one of the ratifying UN member states comes forward with an allegation that a "war crime" has been committed. The Bush administration was generally hostile to the ICC, asserting that its actions infringed on American sovereignty. The Obama administration, on the other hand, indicated a desire to cooperate with the ICC and suggested that it might be time to renegotiate and revise the treaty establishing the court to deal with American concerns and potentially secure U.S. ratification.

[a]*Medellin v. Texas*, 552 U.S. 491 (2008).
[b]*Lawrence v. Texas*, 539 U.S. 558 (2003).
[c]*Atkins v. Virginia*, 536 U.S. 304 (2002).

## for critical analysis

1. Who should have jurisdiction if American soldiers are charged by the Iraqi government with war crimes for having mistreated Iraqi prisoners and civilians during the conflict there? Iraqi courts? American courts? The ICC?

2. Who should have jurisdiction if an American soldier is arrested by Afghan police and charged with molesting an Afghan woman?

# Judicial Power and Politics

**Consider the political influences on the courts**

One of the most important institutional changes to occur in the United States during the past half-century has been the striking transformation of the role and power of the federal courts, and of the Supreme Court in particular. Understanding how this transformation came about is the key to understanding the contemporary role of the courts in America.

## Traditional Limitations on the Federal Courts

For much of American history, the power of the federal courts was subject to a number of limitations.[42] To begin with, unlike other governmental institutions, courts cannot exercise power on their own initiative. Judges must wait until a case is brought to them before they can make authoritative decisions. Traditionally, moreover, courts were constrained by judicial rules of standing that limited access to the bench. Claimants who simply disagreed with governmental action or inaction could not obtain access to the courts, which was limited to individuals who could show that they were particularly affected by the government's behavior in some area. This limitation on access diminished the judiciary's capacity to forge links with important political and social forces.

Second, courts were traditionally limited in the character of the relief they could provide. In general, courts acted only to offer relief or assistance to individuals and not to broad social classes, again inhibiting the formation of alliances between the courts and important social forces.

Third, courts lacked enforcement powers of their own and were compelled to rely on executive or state agencies to ensure compliance with their edicts. If the executive or state agencies were unwilling to assist the courts, judicial enactments could go unheeded, as when President Andrew Jackson declined to enforce Chief Justice John Marshall's 1832 order to the state of Georgia to release two missionaries it had arrested on Cherokee lands. Marshall asserted that the state had no right to enter the lands without the Cherokees' assent.[43] Jackson is reputed to have said, "John Marshall has made his decision, now let him enforce it."

Fourth, federal judges are, of course, appointed by the president (with the consent of the Senate). As a result, the president and Congress can shape the composition of the federal courts and ultimately, perhaps, the character of judicial decisions. Finally, Congress has the power to change both the size and jurisdiction of the Supreme Court and other federal courts. In many areas, federal courts obtain their jurisdiction not from the Constitution but from congressional statutes. On a number of occasions, Congress has threatened to take matters out of the Court's hands when it was unhappy with the Court's policies.[44] For example, in 1996, Congress enacted several pieces of legislation designed to curb the jurisdiction of the federal courts. One of these laws was the Prison Litigation Reform Act, which limits the ability of federal judges to issue "consent decrees," under which the judges could take control of state prison systems. As to the size of the Court, on one memorable occasion that we mentioned earlier, presidential and congressional threats to expand the size of the Supreme Court—Franklin Delano Roosevelt's "court packing" plan—encouraged the justices to drop their opposition to New Deal programs.

**for critical analysis**

Are the federal courts "imperial," or are they subordinate to the elected branches of government? In what respect does the federal judiciary still play a "checks and balances" role?

As a result of these limitations on judicial power, through much of their history the chief function of the federal courts was to provide judicial support for executive agencies and to legitimize acts of Congress by declaring them to be consistent with constitutional principles. Only on rare occasions have the federal courts dared to challenge Congress or the executive branch.[45]

## Two Judicial Revolutions

Since the Second World War, however, the role of the federal judiciary has been strengthened and expanded. There have been two judicial revolutions in the United States since then. The first and more visible of these was the substantive revolution in judicial policy. As we saw earlier in this chapter and in Chapters 4 and 5, in many policy areas, including school desegregation, legislative apportionment, and criminal procedure, and in obscenity, abortion, and voting rights, the Supreme Court was at the forefront of a series of sweeping changes in the role of the U.S. government and, ultimately, the character of American society.[46] But at the same time that the courts were introducing important policy innovations, they were also bringing about a second, less visible revolution. During the 1960s and '70s, the Supreme Court and other federal courts instituted a series of changes in judicial procedures that fundamentally expanded the power of the courts in the United States.

First, the federal courts liberalized the concept of standing to permit almost any group that seeks to challenge the actions of an administrative agency to bring its case before the federal bench. In 1971, for example, the Supreme Court ruled that public interest groups could use the National Environmental Policy Act to challenge the actions of federal agencies by claiming that the agencies' activities might have adverse environmental consequences.[47]

Congress helped to make it even easier for groups dissatisfied with government policies to bring their cases to the courts by adopting Section 1983 of the U.S. Code, which permits the practice of "fee shifting"—that is, allowing citizens who successfully bring a suit against a public official for violating their constitutional rights to collect their attorneys' fees and costs from the government. Thus, Section 1983 encourages individuals and groups to bring their problems to the courts rather than to Congress or the executive branch. These changes have given the courts a far greater role in the administrative process than ever before. Many federal judges are concerned that federal legislation in areas such as health care reform will create new rights and entitlements that give rise to a deluge of court cases. "Any time you create a new right, you create a host of disputes and claims," warned Barbara Rothstein, chief judge of the federal district court in Seattle, Washington.[48]

Second, the federal courts broadened the scope of relief to permit themselves to act on behalf of broad categories or classes of persons in "class action" cases, rather than just on behalf of individuals.[49] A **class-action suit** is a procedural device that permits large numbers of persons with common interests to join together under a representative party to bring or defend a lawsuit. One example of a class-action suit is the case of *In re Agent Orange Product Liability Litigation,* in which a federal judge in New York certified Vietnam War veterans as a class with standing to sue a manufacturer of herbicides for damages allegedly incurred from exposure

**class-action suit** a legal action by which a group or class of individuals with common interests can file a suit on behalf of everyone who shares that interest

*Today, the Supreme Court is frequently at the center of major political issues. In 2012 it decided a case related to the state versus federal power in immigration policy. In the past, the power of the courts was generally more limited than it is today.*

to the defendant's product while in Vietnam.[50] The class potentially numbered in the tens of thousands.

Third, the federal courts began to employ so-called structural remedies, in effect retaining jurisdiction of cases until the court's mandate had actually been implemented to its satisfaction.[51] The best known of these instances was federal judge W. Arthur Garrity Jr.'s effort to operate the Boston school system from his bench in order to ensure its desegregation. Between 1974 and 1985, Judge Garrity issued 14 decisions relating to different aspects of the Boston school desegregation plan that had been developed under his authority and put into effect under his supervision.[52] In 1985, as a result of a suit brought by the NAACP five years earlier, federal judge Leonard B. Sand imposed fines that would have forced the city of Yonkers, New York, into bankruptcy if it had refused to accept his plan to build public housing in white neighborhoods. Twenty-two years and $1.6 million in fines later, in 2007, the city finally gave in to the judge's ruling.

Through these three judicial mechanisms, the federal courts paved the way for an unprecedented expansion of national judicial power. In essence, liberalization of the rules of standing and expansion of the scope of judicial relief drew the federal courts into linkages with important social interests and classes, while the introduction of structural remedies enhanced the courts' ability to serve these constituencies. Thus, during the 1960s and '70s, the power of the federal courts expanded in the same way the power of the executive expanded during the 1930s: through links with constituencies, such as civil rights, consumer, environmental, and feminist groups, that staunchly defended the Supreme Court in its battles with Congress, the executive, and other interest groups.

**for critical analysis**

In what ways are courts, judges, and justices shielded from politics and political pressure? In what ways are they vulnerable to political pressure? Are the courts an appropriate place for politics?

## ● Thinking Critically about the Judiciary, Liberty, and Democracy

In the original conception of the framers, the judiciary was to be the institution that would protect individual liberty from the government. As we saw in Chapter 2, the framers believed that in a democracy the great danger was what they termed "tyranny of the majority"—the possibility that a popular majority, "united or actuated by some common impulse or passion," would "trample on the rules of justice."[53] The framers hoped that the courts would protect liberty from the potential excesses of democracy. And for most of American history, the federal courts' most important decisions were those that protected the freedoms—to speak, worship, publish, vote, and attend school—of groups and individuals whose political views, religious beliefs, or racial or ethnic backgrounds made them unpopular.

Today, Americans of all political persuasions seem to view the courts as useful instruments through which to pursue their goals rather than protectors of individual rights. Conservatives want to ban abortion and help business maintain its profitability, whereas liberals want to promote school integration and help enhance the power of workers in the workplace. These may all be noble goals, but they present a basic dilemma for students of American government. If the courts are simply one more set of policy-making institutions, who is left to protect the liberty of individuals?

# get involved/go online

# Explore the Court System

## Inform Yourself

 **Watch a video on the power of the courts.** The perception and power of the federal court system have changed over the course of the nation's history. Even at the Constitutional Convention, held in 1787, there were disagreements over what exactly the court system should look like. Watch the Standard Deviants' introduction to the judicial branch at www.youtube.com/watch?v=YdCkCRLyfpk and consider what was included in the Constitution versus the Judiciary Act.

 **Compare the jurisdictions of federal and state courts.** The federal courts are not the only courts in the United States. Which cases are heard by state courts? The cases that are deemed federal or state fall into specific categories, listed at www .uscourts.gov/EducationalResources/FederalCourtBasics/CourtStructure/ JurisdictionOfStateAndFederalCourts.aspx. Do any of these classifications surprise you?

## Express Yourself

 **Take a stand on free speech and technology.** The American Civil Liberties Union (ACLU) often files *amicus curiae* briefs on cases that involve civil rights or civil liberties infringements. A recent case originating in Virginia argues that "liking" something on Facebook is equivalent to protected speech and that employers should not be able to fire employees for this action. Read the ACLU post at www .aclu.org/blog/free-speech-technology-and-liberty/aclu-facebook-tell-appeals- court-free-speech. Consider whether you would rule for the plaintiff or the defendant in this case. Share your opinion by posting a comment to the ACLU blog or Facebook page.

 **Weigh in on judicial elections.** Are judicial elections held in your state? View the map of the United States and see whether members of your home state's supreme court are elected or appointed (www.justiceatstake.org/state//index .cfm). If they are elected, are they elected in partisan or non-partisan elections? If they are appointed, is it using the merit plan or another system?

After viewing this information on the appointment versus the election of judges, what is your opinion? What is the fairest method of selecting judges? Follow the "Justice at Stake" Twitter feed (http://twitter.com/justicestake) and consider sharing your opinion online. If your state holds judicial elections, how will you choose between judicial candidates in the next race?

*Find links to the sites listed above as well as related activities on wwnorton.com/studyspace.*

# study guide

## The Legal System

**Identify the general types of cases and types of courts in our legal system (pp. 603–8)**

American court cases proceed under two broad categories of law: criminal law and civil law. There are court systems at both the federal and state level in the United States. While state courts hear only cases involving questions of state law, the federal courts decide cases addressing federal laws, treaties with other nations and the Constitution.

### Key Terms

**criminal law** (p. 603)

**plaintiff** (p. 603)

**defendant** (p. 603)

**civil law** (p. 604)

**precedent** (p. 604)

***stare decisis*** (p. 604)

**trial courts** (p. 604)

**court of appeals** (p. 605)

**supreme court** (p. 605)

**plea bargain** (p. 605)

**jurisdiction** (p. 605)

**due process of law** (p. 607)

**writ of *habeas corpus*** (p. 607)

### Practice Quiz

1. What is the name for the body of law that involves disputes between private parties? *(p. 604)*
   a) civil law
   b) privacy law
   c) plea bargains
   d) household law
   e) common law

2. By what term is the practice of the courts to uphold precedent known? *(p. 604)*
   a) *habeas corpus*
   b) *certiorari*
   c) *stare decisis*
   d) rule of four
   e) senatorial courtesy

3. Where do most trials in America take place? *(p. 604)*
   a) state and local courts
   b) appellate courts
   c) federal courts
   d) federal circuit courts
   e) the Supreme Court

4. The term "writ of *habeas corpus*" refers to *(p. 607)*
   a) a court order that an individual in custody be brought into court and shown the cause for his or her detention.
   b) a criterion used by courts to screen cases that no longer require resolution.
   c) a decision of at least four of the nine Supreme Court justices to review a decision of a lower court.
   d) a short, unsigned decision by an appellate court, usually rejecting a petition to review the decision of a lower court.
   e) a brief filed by the solicitor general when the federal government is not a direct litigant in a Supreme Court case.

## Federal Trial Courts

**Describe the different levels of federal courts and their functions (pp. 608–14)**

The federal courts hear a very small percentage of the cases decided in the United States each year. Presidents typically nominate judges for the federal judiciary who are prominent members of the legal profession and who share their partisan and ideological views. The importance of appointments to the federal judiciary has made the confirmation process in the Senate increasingly contentious in recent years.

### Key Terms

**original jurisdiction** (p. 608)

**chief justice** (p. 609)

**senatorial courtesy** (p. 612)

## Practice Quiz

5. Under what authority is the number of Supreme Court justices decided? *(p. 610)*
   a) the president
   b) the chief justice
   c) the Department of Justice
   d) Congress
   e) the Constitution

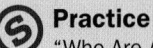

# The Power of the Supreme Court: Judicial Review

■ **Explain how the Supreme Court exercises the power of judicial review (pp. 614–31)**

Although the Supreme Court reviews a small number of cases each year under its original jurisdiction, most cases arrive at the Supreme Court by a writ of *certiorari*. The Supreme Court is most likely to grant a writ of *certiorari* to cases that involve conflicting decisions by the federal circuit courts, cases that present important questions of civil rights or civil liberties, and cases in which the federal government is the appellant. Much of the Supreme Court's power in the American political system comes from its power to invalidate actions taken by the legislative and executive branches of government if they violate Constitution.

## Key Terms

**judicial review** (p. 614)

**supremacy clause** (p. 615)

**common law** (p. 618)

**standing** (p. 620)

**mootness** (p. 621)

**writ of *certiorari*** (p. 622)

**solicitor general** (p. 624)

**per curiam** (p. 624)

**amicus curiae** (p. 624)

**briefs** (p. 626)

**oral argument** (p. 627)

**opinion** (p. 627)

**dissenting opinion** (p. 629)

**judicial restraint** (p. 630)

**judicial activism** (p. 630)

## Practice Quiz

6. The Supreme Court's decision in *Marbury v. Madison* was important because *(pp. 614–15)*
   a) it invalidated state laws prohibiting interracial marriage.
   b) it ruled that the recitation of prayers in public schools are unconstitutional under the establishment clause of the First Amendment.
   c) it established that arrested people have the right to remain silent, the right to be informed that

anything they say can be held against them, and the right to counsel before and during police interrogation.
   d) if provided an expansive definition of "commerce" under the interstate commerce clause.
   e) it established the power of judicial review.

7. Which of the following cases involved the "right to privacy"? *(p. 616)*
   a) *Griswold v. Connecticut*
   b) *Brown v. Board of Education*
   c) *Schneckloth v. Bustamante*
   d) *Marbury v. Madison*
   e) *Texas v. Johnson*

8. Which of the following Supreme Court cases did not involve the rights of criminal suspects? *(p. 620)*
   a) *Gideon v. Wainright*
   b) *Miranda v. Arizona*
   c) *Escobedo v. Illinois*
   d) *Baker v. Carr*
   e) *Dickerson v. United States*

9. Which of the following is *not* included in the original jurisdiction of the Supreme Court? *(p. 620)*
   a) cases between the United States and one of the 50 states
   b) cases brought by one state against citizens of another state or against a foreign country
   c) cases involving challenges to the constitutionality of state laws
   d) cases between two or more states
   e) cases involving foreign ambassadors or other ministers

10. Which of the following influences the flow of cases heard by the Supreme Court? *(p. 624)*
    a) the attorney general and the Secretary of State
    b) the solicitor general and law clerks
    c) the president and Congress
    d) state legislatures
    e) the federal district and circuit courts

11. Which government official is responsible for arguing the federal government's position in cases before the Supreme Court? *(p. 624)*
    a) the vice president
    b) the attorney general
    c) the chief justice
    d) the U.S. district attorney
    e) the solicitor general

12. Which of the following is a brief submitted to the Supreme Court by someone other than one of the parties in the case? *(p. 624)*
    a) *amicus curiae*
    b) *habeas corpus*
    c) solicitor general
    d) *ex post* brief
    e) *de jure* brief

13. Justices who favored going beyond the words of the Constitution to consider the broader societal implications of the Supreme Court's decisions would be considered advocates of which judicial philosophy? *(p. 630)*
    a) original intent
    b) judicial restraint
    c) judicial activism
    d) judicial constitutionalism
    e) *stare decisis*

 **Practice Online**
Video exercise: *Interviews with Supreme Court Justices*

# Judicial Power and Politics

■ **Consider the political influences on the courts (pp. 632–34)**

Throughout most of American history, the federal courts avoided confrontations with the other branches of government and worked primarily to provide support for executive actions and congressional laws by declaring them to be consistent with constitutional principles. During the 1960s and '70s, the federal courts liberalized the concept of standing, broadened the scope of relief courts could provide, and began to employ structural remedies. As a result of these changes, the power of the federal court system expanded dramatically.

## Key Term

**class-action suit** (p. 633)

## Practice Quiz

14. Which of the following would *not* be accurately characterized as a traditional limitation on the power of the federal courts? *(p. 632)*
    a) The president can dissolve the Supreme Court if it oversteps its powers.
    b) Courts lack enforcement powers of their own and are compelled to rely on executive or state agencies to ensure compliance with their rulings.
    c) Congress has the power to change both the size and jurisdiction of the federal courts.
    d) Courts can act to offer relief or assistance to broad social classes but not to specific individuals.
    e) Courts cannot exercise power on their own initiative and must wait for cases to be brought to them.

15. How have changes in judicial policy areas and judicial procedure affected the power of the federal judiciary since World War II? *(p. 633)*
    a) Strong involvement in sweeping policy change has expanded the courts' power, but changes in procedure have sought to limit judicial power.
    b) Changes in procedure have expanded the courts' power, but the courts have played only minor roles in policy change.
    c) Both policy and procedure changes have expanded judicial power.
    d) Both policy and procedure changes have lessened judicial power.
    e) Judicial policy and judicial procedure have remained largely unchanged since World War II.

 **Practice Online**
"Video exercise: *The End of Choice?*

# For Further Reading

Baum, Lawrence. *The Supreme Court.* Washington, DC: CQ Press, 2009.

Cross, Frank. *Decision Making in the U.S. Courts of Appeals.* Stanford, CA: Stanford University Press, 2007.

Dorsen, David. *Henry Friendly, Greatest Judge of His Era.* Cambridge, MA: Harvard University Press, 2012.

Epstein, Lee. *Constitutional Law for a Changing America.* Washington, DC: CQ Press, 2007.

Greenberg, Jan Crawford. *Supreme Conflict: The Inside Story of the United States Supreme Court.* New York: Penguin, 2008.

Hall, Kermit L., James W. Ely Jr., and Joel B. Grossman. *The Oxford Companion to the Supreme Court of the United States.* 2nd ed. New York: Oxford University Press, 2005.

Irons, Peter. *A People's History of the Supreme Court.* New York: Penguin, 2006.

McClosky, Robert, and Sanford Levinson. *The American Supreme Court.* Chicago: University of Chicago Press, 2004.

O'Brien, David M. *Storm Center: The Supreme Court in American Politics.* 8th ed. New York: W.W. Norton, 2008.

Peppers, Todd, and Artemus Ward. *In Chambers: Stories of Supreme Court Law Clerks and Their Justices,* Charlottesville, VA: University of Virginia Press, 2012.

Raskin, Jamin B. *We the Students: Supreme Court Decisions for and about Students.* Washington, DC: Congressional Quarterly Press, 2003.

Rehnquist, William H. *The Supreme Court.* New York: Vintage, 2002.

Rosen, Jeffrey. *The Supreme Court: The Personalities and Rivalries That Defined America.* New York: Henry Holt, 2007.

Rosenberg, Gerald. *The Hollow Hope: Can Courts Bring about Social Change?* Chicago: University of Chicago Press, 1991.

Rossum, Ralph. *Antonin Scalia's Jurisprudence.* Lawrence: University Press of Kansas, 2006.

Stevens, John Paul. *Five Chiefs: A Supreme Court Memoir.* Boston: Little, Brown, 2011.

Sunstein, Cass. *Are Judges Political?* Washington, DC: Brookings Institution Press, 2006.

Toobin, Jeffrey. *The Nine: Inside the Secret World of the Supreme Court.* New York. Anchor Books 2008.

Whittington, Keith. *Political Foundations of Judicial Supremacy: The President, the Supreme Court, and Constitutional Leadership in U.S. History.* Princeton, NJ: Princeton University Press, 2008.

# Recommended Websites

**Concourts**
**www.concourts.net**
The U.S. Supreme Court has the responsibility for examining and interpreting the Constitution. The Concourts website assumes a comparative perspective and looks at systems of constitutional review in over 150 countries.

**FindLaw**
**www.findlaw.com**
FindLaw's website provides answers to most legal questions and helps individuals find legal counsel.

**Justice Talking**
**www.justicetalking.org**
*Justice Talking* is a public radio program that examines current legal issues and important court cases.

**Legal Information Institute**
**www.law.cornell.edu**
The Legal Information Institute at Cornell University is a wonderful website for conducting legal research.

**Office of the Solicitor General**
**www.usdoj.gov/osg**
The solicitor general conducts litigation on behalf of the U.S. Supreme Court and has a tremendous amount of control over the cases that it hears. See what cases are currently being considered by this powerful official of the Justice Department.

**U.S. Courts**
**www.uscourts.gov**
The U.S. court system consists of trial, appellate, and supreme courts. The U.S. Courts website provides a look at the different types of courts in the federal judiciary.

**U.S. Supreme Court**
**www.supremecourtus.gov**
The website for the U.S. Supreme Court provides information on recent decisions. Take a moment to read some oral arguments, briefs, or court opinions.

**U.S. Supreme Court Media**
**www.oyez.com**
The website for U.S. Supreme Court Media has a great search engine for finding information on such landmark cases as *Marbury v. Madison, Miranda v. Arizona,* and *Roe v. Wade.*

The federal government spent nearly a trillion dollars in response to the economic crisis that began in 2008, but unemployment remained a problem in the years that followed. At this hiring fair in New York, long lines of job seekers awaited the opportunity to find work.

# Government and the Economy

**WHAT GOVERNMENT DOES AND WHY IT MATTERS** Many of the students reading this book, and the members of their families, were affected by the global economic crisis that began in 2008. Families lost homes and jobs. Students have been financially pressed, with many unable to afford college tuition. Recent graduates have been unable to find full-time employment. For many, the American dream of prosperity suddenly seemed beyond reach.

Since the 1930s, Americans have counted on the federal government to ensure a prosperous economy. Political leaders have a wide variety of tools they can use to improve economic performance. Among the most widely used are public spending, tax cuts, and interest rate changes, all of which aim to stimulate economic activity or reduce inflation, and regulations that influence competition among firms. Political leaders' choice of economic tools depends on their perceptions about what the most pressing economic problem is, beliefs about which tools are most likely to be effective, and considerations about who is likely to benefit from a particular economic policy and who is likely to be hurt. Although economic policy is a highly technical field, the choice of policy tools is fundamentally a political decision.

In 2008, with the financial sector seemingly on the brink of collapse, the federal government launched a series of major interventions designed to prop up failing banks and insurance companies. It was not just financial institutions that faced collapse. As the economic instability spread, Washington bailed out other distressed industries, ending up as a major stakeholder in both the financial sector and the auto industry. The federal government also passed a sweeping package in 2009 to help stimulate the economy, save jobs, and make longer-term investments to help build future prosperity.

As the economic crisis began to ebb, however, Congress struggled to implement enduring reforms to the financial regulatory system. Worries about the nation's ballooning debt mounted, and conflicts erupted over whether government had now gotten too big.

These developments raised fundamental questions about the role of the government in the economy. On one side of the spectrum are those who believe that the government should have a minimal role in the economy. Government's main purpose should be to set and enforce rules that ensure economic stability. In this perspective, the government is sometimes called the "night watchman state."[1] At the other end of the spectrum are those who want to see the state actively engaged in shaping economic outcomes. Not only should the government promote economic growth, according to this perspective, but it should also step in to protect individuals from economic harm. The government's role in the economy should be active, to shape the kind of society we want.

American economic policy has historically reflected the belief that individual liberty is the key to a thriving economy. In this view, the government's role is to set the basic rules that govern economic transactions and then stand back and let individuals engage in the market. However, periodically Americans have demanded restrictions on market freedoms to protect the public. An array of laws governing competition and protecting consumers and the environment is the consequence of these democratic demands. Although American economic policy has not traditionally sought to reduce inequality, the growth in inequality over the past three decades has spurred new interest in understanding the impact of government policy on economic inequality.

## chaptergoals

- Identify the broad reasons government gets involved in the economy (pages 643–54)

- Describe how the government uses monetary, fiscal, and regulatory policies to influence the economy (pages 654–66)

- Explain why the government tries to balance economic prosperity with policies that protect the environment (pages 666–72)

- Explore why economic policy is often controversial (pages 672–78)

# ● The Goals of Economic Policy

**Identify the broad reasons government gets involved in the economy**

The job of this and the next chapter is to step beyond the politics and the institutions to look at the goals of government: the public policies. **Public policy** can be defined simply as an officially expressed purpose or goal backed by a sanction (a reward or a punishment). Public policy can be embodied in a law, a rule, a regulation, or an order. This chapter will focus on policies aimed at the economy.

**public policy** a law, rule, statute, or edict that expresses the government's goals and provides for rewards and punishments to promote those goals' attainment

At the most basic level, government makes it possible for the economy to function efficiently by setting the rules for economic exchange and punishing those who violate those rules. Among the most important rules for the economy are those that define property rights, contracts, and standards for goods. This kind of government rule making allows markets to expand by making it easier for people who do not know each other to engage in economic transactions: they no longer have to rely only on personal trust to do business. Likewise, government helps markets expand by creating money and standing behind its value. Money allows diverse goods to be traded and greatly simplifies economic transactions. The importance of government to basic market transactions is evident in periods when government authority is very weak. Governments that are on the losing side of wars, for example, are often so weak that they cannot enforce the basic rules needed for markets to function. In these settings, markets often break down, money loses its value, and economies contract as the basic conditions for doing business disappear.

Government involvement in the economy now extends far beyond these basic market-creating functions. As we shall see in this section, government has become involved in many aspects of the economy in order to promote the public well-being. Of course, there is often vigorous disagreement about the extent

*President Obama urged Congress to pass new financial and banking regulations. For example in 2012, he asked for new legislation to bring more stability to commodities markets, especially the oil market. Treasury secretary Timothy Geithner and Gary Gensler of the Commodity Futures Trading Commission appeared with Obama.*

to which government should intervene in the economy. Further, beliefs about which forms of government intervention in the economy are most necessary and most effective have changed over time. Although the policies have changed, government intervention in the economy has, for nearly a century, sought to achieve four fundamental goals: (1) to promote economic stability, (2) to stimulate economic growth, (3) to promote business development, and (4) to protect employees and consumers.

## Promoting Stable Markets

One of the central reasons for government involvement in the economy is to protect the welfare and property of individuals and businesses.

Maintaining law and order is one of the most important ways government can protect welfare and property. The federal government has also enacted laws designed to protect individuals and businesses in economic transactions. Federal racketeering laws, for example, aim to end criminal efforts to control businesses through such illegal means as extortion and kickbacks.

Another way in which the government promotes economic stability is by regulating competition. Beginning in the nineteenth century, as many sectors of the national economy flourished, certain companies began to exert monopolistic control over those sectors. Decreased competition threatened the efficiency of the market and the equitable distribution of its benefits. As a result, the national government stepped in to "level the playing field."

Another major reason that Congress began to adopt national business regulatory policies was that companies felt burdened by the inconsistent regulations across the various states. Companies often preferred a single, national regulatory authority, no matter how burdensome, because it would ensure consistency throughout the United States; the companies could thereby treat the nation as a single market.[2]

The government also promotes economic stability by providing **public goods**. This term refers to facilities the state provides because no single participant can afford to provide those facilities. The provision of public goods may entail supplying the physical marketplace itself—such as the commons in New England towns or the provision of an interstate highway system to stimulate the trucking industry. The provision of public goods is essential to market operation, and the manner in which the government provides those goods will affect the market's character.

In the United States, public goods related to transportation have been particularly important in promoting economic development. From the first canal systems that spread commerce into the interior of the country to the contemporary public role in supporting and regulating air transportation, government has created the conditions for reliable and efficient business activity. In some cases, government will supply a public good to stimulate the economy and then allow private companies to take over. The federal government brought electricity to rural areas in the 1930s to promote economic development, but over time the provision of electricity has been taken up by private companies. Government often supplies public goods that are too big or too risky for private actors to tackle. Major dams and hydroelectric projects are an example. By bring-

**public goods** goods or services that are provided by the government because they either are not supplied by the market or are not supplied in sufficient quantities

*One way that the government promotes economic stability is by regulating competition and preventing monopolies. Monopolistic "trusts" became a particular concern in the late 1800s, and in 1904, President Teddy Roosevelt was depicted taking a swing at the railroad trust, the oil trust, and others that he believed were stifling competition.*

NO MOLLY-CODDLING HERE

ing water and energy to new areas, such public projects transformed the American West. More recently, government-supplied public goods have enhanced public security through such measures as the federal takeover of airport security, the creation of a pharmaceutical stockpile to protect against bioterrorism, and the support for research to develop vaccines to counter bioterrorism agents. The 2009 American Recovery and Reinvestment Act (ARRA) offered funding for several future-oriented infrastructure investments, including high-speed rail, high-speed Internet access for rural areas, and promotion and development of "green" energy.

## Promoting Economic Prosperity

In addition to setting the basic conditions that allow markets to function, governments may actively intervene in the economy to promote economic growth. Although the idea that government should stimulate economic growth can be traced back to Alexander Hamilton's views about promoting industry, it was not until the twentieth century that the federal government assumed such a role.

**Measuring Economic Growth** Since the 1930s the federal government has carefully tracked national economic growth by measuring it in several different ways. The two most important measures are the gross national product (GNP), which is the market value of the goods and services produced in the economy, and the **gross domestic product (GDP)**, the same measure but excluding income from foreign investments. In the late 1990s the American economy grew at a rate of over 4 percent a year, considered high by modern standards (see Figure 16.1). Growth was slower during the 2000s, averaging 1.9 percent annually. This was largely the result of two recessions: one in the early 2000s and the recession that began in 2008. In the middle part of the decade (2003–07), the economy grew at a strong 2.8 percent annually.[3]

**gross domestic product (GDP)** the total value of goods and services produced within a country

The engine of American economic growth has shifted over the centuries. In the 1800s, the nation's rich endowment of natural resources was especially important in propelling growth. Manufacturing industries became the driving force of economic growth during the late nineteenth century as mass production made it possible to manufacture goods at a pace that was once unimaginable. In more recent times, the high-technology boom fostered unanticipated and vigorous economic growth that made the United States the envy of the world. Despite these very different economic engines, the basic prerequisites of growth were similar in each case: strong investment, technological innovation, and a productive workforce. Throughout the nation's history, the federal government has adopted policies to promote each of these conditions needed to sustain economic growth.

The most fundamental way that government affects investment is by promoting business, investor, and consumer confidence. When businesses fear political instability, unpredictable government action, or widespread disregard of the law, they are unlikely to invest. When consumers are insecure about the future, they are unlikely to spend.

The federal government also promotes investment through its regulation of financial markets. The most important federal agency in this regard is the Securities and Exchange Commission (SEC), created after the stock market crash of

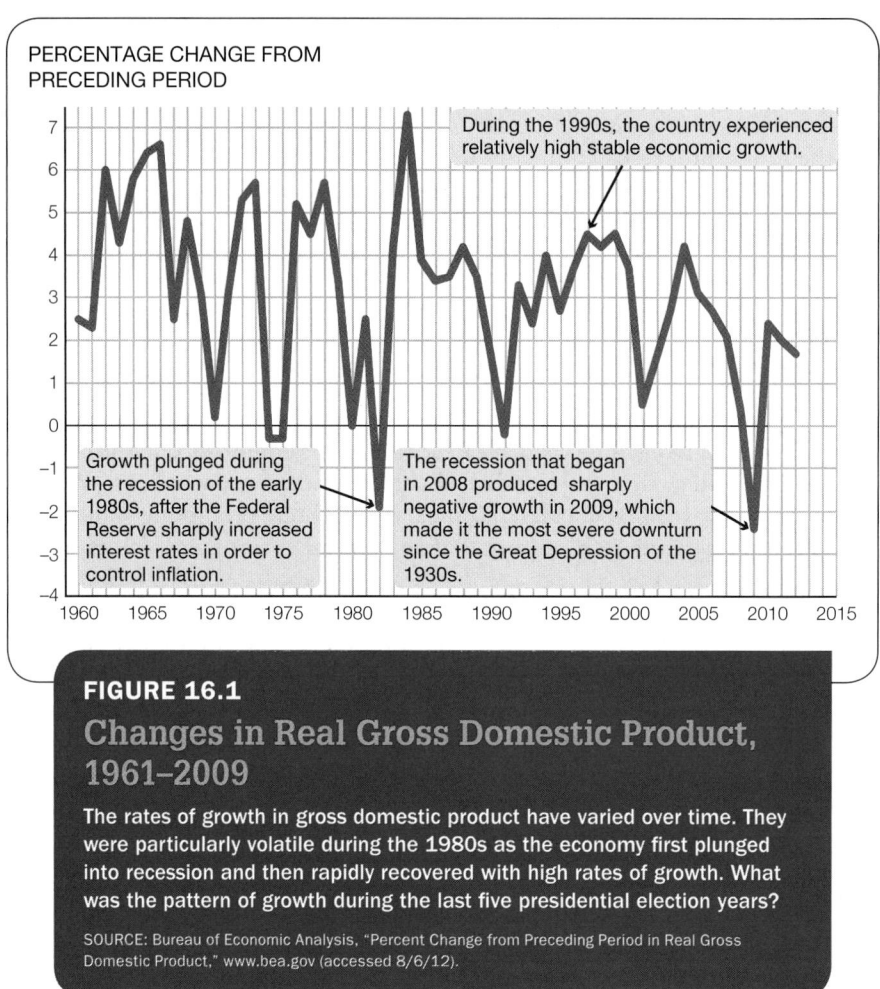

PERCENTAGE CHANGE FROM PRECEDING PERIOD

During the 1990s, the country experienced relatively high stable economic growth.

Growth plunged during the recession of the early 1980s, after the Federal Reserve sharply increased interest rates in order to control inflation.

The recession that began in 2008 produced sharply negative growth in 2009, which made it the most severe downturn since the Great Depression of the 1930s.

**FIGURE 16.1**

## Changes in Real Gross Domestic Product, 1961–2009

The rates of growth in gross domestic product have varied over time. They were particularly volatile during the 1980s as the economy first plunged into recession and then rapidly recovered with high rates of growth. What was the pattern of growth during the last five presidential election years?

SOURCE: Bureau of Economic Analysis, "Percent Change from Preceding Period in Real Gross Domestic Product," www.bea.gov (accessed 8/6/12).

1929. The SEC requires companies to disclose information about the stocks and bonds they are selling, inform buyers of the investment risks, and protect investors against fraud. In this way the SEC helps maintain investor confidence and a strong supply of capital for American business. The SEC came in for harsh criticism during the financial crisis in 2008. Analysts pointed to weak SEC oversight and regulation as an important factor in the near-collapse of the financial sector. Major financial reforms enacted in 2010 substantially beefed up the SEC's enforcement capabilities and require the agency to take the lead in implementing many of the key regulations.[4]

Public investment is another important source of growth in the American economy. In the 1930s and again in the late 1970s the federal government promoted public investment as a means to spark economic growth. Some kinds of public investment promote growth as a by-product of other, more central objectives. One of the most important of these is spending on the nation's defense. Many analysts credited the rise in military spending associated with the war in Iraq with helping to spur economic growth in 2003.

The second important condition for economic growth is innovation. The federal government has sought to support innovation in a variety of ways. One of the most important is through the National Science Foundation. Created in 1950, the National Science Foundation supports basic research across a range of scientific fields in order to advance fundamental knowledge that may be broadly useful.[5] Federal government sponsorship of health research began in the late 1800s. Today, the National Institutes of Health (NIH) conducts basic and applied research in biomedicine. The Human Genome Project—the effort to map the basic genetic structure of human life—was initiated by government researchers and only later taken up by private corporations. Recently, the NIH has taken the lead in basic research to counter bioterrorism. Its efforts to understand the biology of various infectious agents and to develop vaccines are expected to produce important new knowledge about the human immune system. Research sponsored by the military has long been an important source of innovation for the American economy. Such key twentieth-century innovations as radar and nuclear power stemmed from military research. And as we saw in Chapter 14, military research also created the technology for the twenty-first century with ARPANET, the precursor to the Internet.

A third fundamental condition for economic growth is a sufficient and productive workforce. Federal immigration policy has played a key role in ensuring an adequate supply of labor throughout American history. Immigration laws routinely give special priority to workers who have skills that are in demand among American employers. Immigrants with nursing degrees, for example, have long received special priority.

Today, a productive workforce is a highly educated workforce. Education, as we will see in Chapter 17, is primarily the responsibility of state and local governments. The federal government, however, supports the development of a productive workforce with a variety of programs to promote higher education, such as educational grants, tax breaks, and loans. The federal government also

*When the government fails to enforce financial regulations, investors lose confidence and the economy suffers. When Bernard Madoff defrauded investors of billions of dollars, many people blamed lax oversight by the Securities and Exchange Commission.*

sponsors a limited array of job-training programs that focus primarily on low-skilled workers. Some analysts argue that the federal government must do much more to support the development of a highly skilled workforce if the United States is to sustain economic growth in the future.

**Full Employment** Before the 1930s, neither the federal nor the state governments sought to promote full employment. Unemployment was widely viewed as an unfortunate occurrence that government could do little to alter. The New Deal response to the prolonged and massive unemployment of the Great Depression changed that view. The federal government put millions of people back to work on public projects sponsored by such programs as the Works Progress Administration (WPA). The bridges, parks, and buildings they constructed can still be seen across the United States today. The federal government viewed these programs as temporary measures, however. As the buildup for World War II boosted the economy and unemployment melted away, the employment programs were dismantled.

The New Deal and government wartime spending, however, showed that government could help ensure full employment. Public expectations changed as well: after the war, Americans looked to the federal government to reduce unemployment.

**inflation** a consistent increase in the general level of prices

*One reason unemployment rose after 2008 was that numerous companies went out of business. The Circuit City chain, which had already begun layoffs before the economic crisis, closed all 500 of its stores by early 2009.*

Moreover, economic theory now supported their expectations. John Maynard Keynes's theories that government could boost employment by stimulating demand had become very influential.

Federal policy placed the most emphasis on achieving full employment during the 1960s. Keynesian economists in the Council of Economic Advisers persuaded President Kennedy to enact the first tax cut designed to stimulate the economy and promote full employment.[6] The policy was widely seen as a success, and unemployment declined to a low of 3.4 percent in 1968.

Favorable economic conditions in the 1990s reduced unemployment to record lows once again. Many analysts contended that the economy had changed so much that the old trade-offs between inflation and unemployment had ceased to exist.

The worldwide economic recession of 2008 led to the loss of an estimated 8 million American jobs. The Obama administration and Congress responded by passing a sweeping stimulus package called the American Recovery and Reinvestment Act in 2009, to help encourage economic growth, save existing jobs, and make longer-term investments that would encourage job creation, such as in weatherization projects and clean-technology construction.

**Low Inflation** During the 1970s and early 1980s, **inflation**, a consistent increase in the general level of prices, was one of America's most vexing problems. There was much disagreement over what to do about it. The first effort, beginning in 1971, was the adoption of strict controls over wages, prices, dividends, and rents—that is, authorizing an agency in the executive branch to place limits on what wages people could be paid for their work, what rents their real estate could bring, and what interest they could get on their money. After two years of effort, these particular policies were fairly well discredited. Since oil prices had so clearly become a major source of inflation in the late 1970s, President Carter experimented with the licensing of imports of oil from the Middle East, with tariffs and excise taxes on unusually large oil profits made by producers, and with sales taxes on gasoline at the pump to discourage the casual consumption of gasoline. Carter also attempted to reduce consumer spending in general by raising income taxes.

President Reagan continued the battle against inflation by raising Social Security taxes. This fought inflation by discouraging consumption. Inflation is caused by too many dollars chasing too few goods, bidding up prices. Any tax will take dollars out of consumption, but since the Social Security tax hits middle- and lower-middle-income people the heaviest, and since those in the middle-income category account for the largest share of consumption in the United States, such a tax reduces consumer dollars. Another policy supported by the Reagan administration was restraining the amount of credit in the economy by pushing up interest rates.

Inflation was finally reduced from its historic highs of nearly 20 percent down toward 2 and 3 percent each year. Noting that the inflation of the 1970s was America's only "peacetime inflation," the economist Bradford DeLong contends that it wasn't until inflation had risen to dizzying heights late in the decade that the Federal Reserve truly had a mandate to reduce inflation.[7] Once it had full political support for reducing inflation in 1979, the Federal Reserve raised interest rates sharply and brought inflation rates down at the same time that it provoked a sharp recession.

## Promoting Business Development

During the nineteenth century, the national government was a promoter of markets. National roads and canals were built to tie states and regions together. National tariff policies promoted domestic markets by restricting imported goods; a tax on an import raised its price and weakened its ability to compete with similar domestic products. The national government also heavily subsidized the railroad system. Until the 1840s, railroads were thought to be of limited commercial value. But between 1850 and 1872, Congress granted more than 100 million acres of public-domain land to railroad interests, and state and local governments pitched in an estimated $280 million in cash and credit. Before the end of the century, 35,000 miles of track existed, almost half the world's total at the time.

Railroads were not the only clients of federal support for the private markets. Many sectors of agriculture began receiving federal subsidies during the nineteenth century. Agriculture remains highly subsidized to this day. In 2005, 40 percent of farms in the United States received subsidies; by 2006 the total subsidy was estimated at more than $20 billion. One of the many criticisms of the farm subsidy program is that it disproportionately supports large-scale farmers rather than small family farmers. The list of farm subsidy recipients includes many large corporations.

**categorical grants** congressional grants given to states and localities on the condition that expenditures be limited to a problem or group specified by the law

The national government also promotes business development indirectly through **categorical grants** (see Chapter 3), whereby the federal government offers grants to states on condition that the state (or local) government undertake a particular activity. Thus, in order to use motor transportation to improve national markets, a 900,000-mile national highway system was built during the 1930s, based on a formula whereby the national government would pay 50 percent of the cost if the state provided the other 50 percent. Over 20 years, beginning in the late 1950s, the federal government constructed an additional 45,000 miles of interstate highways. In this program, the national government agreed to pay 90 percent of the construction costs on the condition that each state provide 10 percent of the costs of any portion of a highway built within its boundaries.[8] The tremendous growth of highways was a major boon to the automobile and trucking industries.

The federal government supports specific business sectors with direct subsidies, loans, and tax breaks. In 1953 the Small Business Administration (SBA) was created to offer loans, loan guarantees, and disaster assistance to small businesses. Recognizing that such businesses often find it harder to obtain financing and to recover from unexpected events such as fires, the federal government has provided assistance where the market would not. Today, the SBA provides more than $45 billion in such assistance to small businesses.

Among the many contemporary examples of policies promoting private industry, Sematech may be the most instructive. Sematech is a nonprofit research and development (R&D) consortium of major U.S. computer microchip manufacturers, set up in 1987 to work with government and academic institutions to reestablish U.S. leadership in semiconductor manufacturing. (The United States appeared to be in danger of losing out to the Japanese in this area during the 1980s.) The results of its research were distributed among the 14 consortium members.[9] For nine years, industry and government together spent $1.7 billion to make the American microchip industry the leader in the world. The government contributed about half of the total expenditures. In 1997, federal funding was phased out. Industry leaders, convinced they no longer needed federal support,

*The nation's infrastructure has always been important for commerce. Today, the national government's programs to expand broadband Internet access support a new form of infrastructure, with important implications for businesses.*

themselves initiated the break with government. At a critical moment, the federal government had stepped in to save the chip industry; it stepped out once that goal had been achieved.

Since September 11, 2001, the federal government has taken on a major role in promoting technological innovation related to national security. Even before the September 11 terrorist attacks, the CIA had set up its own venture capital firm, In-Q-Tel (the Q stands for a character in the James Bond movies), to invest in high-tech start-ups whose work could enhance intelligence efforts. With defense and homeland security at the top of the national agenda, military spending increased by 20 percent during the first two years of the George W. Bush administration. A new emphasis on technological innovation accompanied the increase in spending. As a way to promote its access to the latest technology, the Department of Defense runs a $1 billion program that funds the early stages of research and development for innovative small firms.[10]

## Protecting Employees and Consumers

Stable relations between business and labor are important elements of a productive economy. During the latter half of the nineteenth century, strikes over low wages or working conditions became a standard feature of American economic life. In fact, the United States has one of the most violent histories of labor relations in the world. Yet for most of American history, the federal government did little to regulate relations between business and labor. Local governments and courts often weighed in on the side of business by prohibiting strikes and arresting strikers.

As the economic depression enveloped the United States in the 1930s, plummeting wages and massive strikes for union recognition prompted Congress to pass the 1935 National Labor Relations Act, which set up a new framework for industrial relations. The new law created a permanent agency, the National Labor Relations Board (NLRB), charged with overseeing union elections and collective bargaining between labor and industry. The federal government weighed in further on the side of organized labor in 1938, when it passed the Fair Labor Standards Act, which created the minimum wage. Because it is not indexed to inflation, the

# The Digital Economy

**While e-mail and information** searches remain the most common activities online—6 in 10 adults engage in these activities daily in the United States—some core economic activities are also becoming prevalent online. Today a majority of Americans uses the Internet for shopping and online banking. Americans also use the Internet on the job. As a result, government policy, including fraud protection and rights for identity theft victims, is racing to catch up.

Since 1995, websites such as Amazon .com have revolutionized the marketplace by making millions of products available to purchase online, many at significant cost savings over local retail stores. Craigslist and eBay transformed neighborhood garage sales into worldwide marketplaces.

A 2011 Pew survey found that seven in 10 American adults had purchased a product online (up from 50 percent in March 2003), with women slightly more likely to do so than men. But there are significant disparities in who shops online. Individuals 65 years and older are considerably less likely to engage in online commerce than younger people. Income matters as well. More than 90 percent of families who earn $75,000 a year or more have purchased products online, compared with just half of families with incomes of $30,000 or less. Latinos are less likely to shop online than are non-Hispanic whites and African Americans. Education matters because it provides literacy and technology skills. Of individuals without a high school degree, only 33 percent purchase products online, compared with almost 90 percent of college graduates.

We also find differences in who uses online banking. As of May 2011, 6 in 10 American adults used online banking, with slightly lower rates among Latinos than whites and African Americans. While 75 percent of college graduates bank online, only half of people with only a high school degree do. The poor are half as likely to bank online than the affluent. Individuals over 65 years of age are less likely to bank online as people in younger age groups.

Not only has the Internet transformed core economic activities, but the future of money and currency may change with the move online. Just as credit cards slowly reduced the need to carry cash, within the next decade, mobile payments could largely replace cash and credit cards for online and in-store purchases. This technology involves payment by smartphone or tablet. Some analysts believe the security and convenience of "mobile wallet" systems will lead to widespread adoption of mobile purchases by 2020. One step in this direction is the use of PayPal payments on mobile phones to purchase everything from concert tickets to vacation home rentals. However, privacy concerns, the demand for anonymous payments that cannot be tracked, a lack of infrastructure, and, most important, resistance from credit card companies that collect fees from retailers may slow the speed of change.

Government policy is necessary to promote broadband infrastructure, protect consumers, and encourage Internet adoption and online markets. As the activities online become more sophisticated—along with the requirements for passwords!—and the nation's economic growth is tied ever more closely to the technology sector, government policy will determine how well the United States manages the new digital economy.

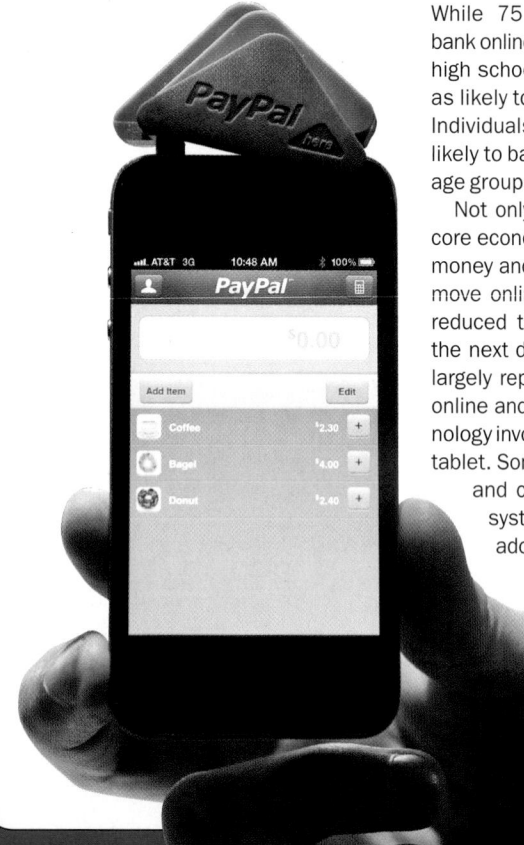

SOURCES: "Digital Differences," Pew Internet and American Life Project, April 2012. P. DiMaggio and B. Bonikowski, "Make Money Surfing the Web? The Impact of Internet Use on the Earnings of U.S. Workers," *American Sociological Review* 73, no. 2 (2008): 227–50. Karen Mossberger, Caroline Tolbert, and Ramona McNeal, *Digital Citizenship: The Internet, Society and Participation* (Cambridge, MA: MIT Press, 2008). Karen Mossberger, Caroline Tolbert, and William Franko, *Digital Cities: The Internet and the Geography of Opportunity* (New York: Oxford University Press, 2012). Aaron Smith, Janna Anderson, and Lee Rainie, "The Future of Money in a Mobile Age," Pew Internet and American Life Project, April 17, 2012.

## for critical analysis

1. With one in five Americans completely offline, how will this segment of the population participate in the new digital economy? What should be done to address the digital divide in terms of economic participation and opportunity?

2. Is government involvement necessary to reap the full benefits of the digital economic revolution? Why or why not?

value of the minimum wage declines if it is not raised periodically. Since 1938, conflicts over increasing the minimum wage have been a regular feature of American politics.

During the 1950s and '60s, the federal government played an active role in industrial relations. The Department of Labor and occasionally even the president directly intervened in labor-management disputes to ensure peaceful industrial relations. Although Democrats were generally seen as more supportive of labor, both parties sought to achieve a balance between business and labor that would promote a strong, stable economy.

President Reagan made a decisive break with this tradition of compromise in 1981, when he fired striking air traffic controllers (who were federal employees) and hired permanent replacements to take their jobs. Politicians are now much less likely to intervene in labor relations.

Economic policies also protect consumers. The idea that the federal government should protect consumers emerged in the first decade of the 1900s. Upton Sinclair's graphic exposé of the meatpacking industry, *The Jungle* (1906), galvanized public concern about unsanitary food processing. These concerns prompted the U.S. Department of Agriculture to inspect packing plants and the meat they produced, stamping approved meats with the now-familiar "USDA" certification. Similar concern about the safety of food, drugs, and cosmetics led to the creation of the Food and Drug Administration in 1927.

The movement for consumer protection took off again in the 1960s. The consumer advocate Ralph Nader's 1965 book *Unsafe at Any Speed* helped spark new demands for federal action. Nader's book showed that design flaws in the Corvair, a popular car model, had caused deaths that could have been prevented. Nader's book not only led to the demise of the Corvair, but also mobilized calls for more federal action to protect consumers. The first response was the 1966 National Traffic and Motor Vehicle Safety Act, which gave the Department of Transportation responsibility for ensuring vehicle safety. Federal responsibility for consumer safety expanded in 1972, when Congress created the Consumer Product Safety Commission, an independent agency that informs consumers about hazards associated with products and works with industry to set product standards. In cases where safety concerns are severe, the commission will see that such products are recalled. Through the Consumer Product Safety Commission, the Department of Transportation, and the Food and Drug Administration, the federal government continues to play an active role in protecting the public from unsafe products.

In 2007 the Consumer Product Safety Commission became the target of vigorous criticism for failing to fulfill its mission. Recalls of popular children's toys, reports of injuries to children from magnetic toys, dogs and cats dying from tainted pet food, and reported dangers from imported toothpaste all raised questions about the agency's effectiveness. Congressional hearings probed the capacity

*Protecting consumers has been a central goal of economic policy since the early twentieth century. For example, the FDA tests food and drugs to make sure they are safe. Here, an FDA worker collects samples of imported food for analysis in a lab.*

## for critical analysis

What does the American government do to ensure that the products Americans buy are safe? What challenges does it face in making certain that products are safe?

of the agency to monitor consumer safety, given that its staff had declined from more than 800 in 1980 to 420 in 2007. At the same time, the growth of consumer products manufactured in China made the agency's job tougher. In 2008, 43 percent of imported consumer goods had been manufactured in China or Hong Kong; 85 percent of all product recalls came from imported products, and the vast bulk of those were manufactured in China, where rapid economic expansion and fewer consumer protections contributed to the problem.[11] Concern about the Consumer Product Safety Commission's ability to protect Americans led to a significant reform in 2008, which provided new resources to the agency and established new requirements governing toy safety.

# ● The Tools of Economic Policy

**Describe how the government uses monetary, fiscal, and regulatory policies to influence the economy**

The U.S. economy is no accident; it is the result of specific policies that have expanded American markets and sustained massive economic growth. The Constitution provides that Congress shall have the power

> To lay and collect Taxes, . . . to pay the Debts and provide for the common Defence and general Welfare; . . . To borrow Money; . . . To coin Money [and] regulate the Value thereof.

These clauses of Article I, Section 8, are the constitutional sources of the fiscal and monetary policies of the national government. The Constitution says nothing, however, about *how* these powers can be used, although the way they are used shapes the economy. As it works to meet the multiple goals of economic policy just outlined, the federal government relies on a broad set of tools that has evolved over time. Let us now turn to the actual tools designed to accomplish the goals of economic policy.

## Monetary Policies

**monetary policies** efforts to regulate the economy through the manipulation of the supply of money and credit. America's most powerful institution in this area of monetary policy is the Federal Reserve Board

**Monetary policies** manipulate the growth of the entire economy by controlling the availability of money to banks. With a very few exceptions, banks in the United States are privately owned and locally operated. Until well into the twentieth century, banks were regulated, if at all, by state legislatures. Each bank was granted a charter, which gave it permission to make loans, hold deposits, and make investments within that state. Although more than 25,000 banks continue to be chartered by the states, they are less important in the overall financial picture than they used to be, as the most important banks now are members of the federal banking system.

But banks did not become the core of American capitalism without intense political controversy. The Federalist majority in Congress, led by Alexander Hamilton, did in fact establish a Bank of the United States, in 1791, but it was vigorously opposed by agrarian interests, led by Thomas Jefferson, who feared that the interests of urban, industrial capitalism would dominate such a bank. The Bank of the

United States was terminated during the administration of Andrew Jackson, but the fear of a central, public bank lingered eight decades later, when, in 1913, Congress established an institution, the **Federal Reserve System**, to integrate private banks into a single national system. The Federal Reserve System did not become a central bank in the European tradition but rather is composed of 12 Federal Reserve banks, each located in a major commercial city. The Federal Reserve banks are not ordinary banks; they are banker's banks that make loans to other banks, clear checks, and supply the economy with currency and coins. They also play a regulatory role over the member banks. Every national bank must be a member of the Federal Reserve System and must follow national banking rules. State banks and savings and loan associations may also join if they accept national rules. At the top of the system is the Federal Reserve Board—"the Fed"—comprising seven members appointed by the president (with Senate confirmation) for 14-year terms. The chairman of the Fed is selected by the president from among the seven members of the board for a four-year term. In all other concerns, however, the Fed is an independent agency (see Chapter 14) inasmuch as its members cannot be removed during their terms except "for cause," and the president's executive power does not extend to them or their policies. Nonetheless, observers charged the longtime Federal Reserve chairman, Alan Greenspan, with being attentive to politics, for example, in his endorsement of President George W. Bush's tax cuts. In his 2005 confirmation hearings to head the Fed, the economist Ben Bernanke promised Congress that he would be "strictly independent of all political influences."[12]

The major advantage that a bank gains from being in the Federal Reserve System is that it can borrow from the system. This enables banks to expand their loan operations continually, as long as there is demand for loans in the economy. On the other hand, it is this very access of member banks to the Federal Reserve System that gives the Fed its power: the ability to expand and contract the *amount of credit* available in the United States.

The Fed can affect the total amount of credit through the interest (called the federal funds rate) that member banks charge one another for loans. If the Fed significantly decreases the federal funds rate, this can give a boost to a sagging

**Federal Reserve System** a system of 12 Federal Reserve banks that facilitates exchanges of cash, checks, and credit; regulates member banks; and uses monetary policies to fight inflation and deflation

**for critical analysis**
Why is the Federal Reserve so important to economic policy?

*Ben Bernanke, appointed by President George W. Bush to chair the Federal Reserve Board in 2005, and whose reappointment by President Obama was confirmed by the Senate in 2010, promised Congress that he would not be influenced by politics. The Fed seeks to regulate the U.S. economy by manipulating the supply of money and credit.*

economy. During 2001 the Fed cut interest rates 11 times to combat the combined effects of recession and the terrorist attacks. In the steep recession that began in 2008, the Fed acted aggressively. By December 2008 it had cut rates 9 times from a high in September 2007 of 4.75 percent to a historically low zero percentage rate. Moreover, the Federal Reserve kept interest rates at that same level well into 2010, in an attempt to encourage lending again and thus economic growth.[13] If the Fed raises the federal funds rate, it can put a brake on the economy, because the higher discount rate also increases the general interest rates that leading private banks charge to their customers. Although the Federal Reserve is responsible for ensuring high employment as well as price stability, it has been particularly important in fighting inflation. During the late 1970s and early 1980s, with inflation at record high levels, Federal Reserve chairman Paul Volcker aggressively raised interest rates in order to dampen inflation. Although his actions provoked a sharp recession, they raised the stature of the Fed, demonstrating its ability to manage the economy. Because the Fed is so closely associated with inflation fighting, Senate Democrats pressed Ben Bernanke, President George W. Bush's nominee to head the Fed, to indicate at his nomination hearings that he would view maximum employment as a goal of equal importance to that of fighting inflation.

**reserve requirement** the amount of liquid assets and ready cash that banks are required to hold to meet depositors' demands for their money

A second power of the Fed is control over the **reserve requirement**—the amount of cash and negotiable securities every bank must hold readily available to cover withdrawals and checks written by its depositors. When the Fed decides to increase the reserve requirement, it can decrease significantly the amount of money banks have to lend; conversely, if the Fed lowers the reserve requirement, banks can be more liberal in extending loans.[14]

**open-market operations** methods by which the Open Market Committee of the Federal Reserve System buys and sells government securities and other investment instruments to help finance government operations and to reduce or increase the total amount of money circulating in the economy

A third power of the Fed is called **open-market operations**, whereby the Fed buys and sells government securities. When the Fed buys government securities in the open market, it is pumping money into the economy and stimulating economic activity; when it sells securities, it is applying brakes to the economy.

Finally, a fourth power is derived from one of the important services the Federal Reserve System renders, which is the opportunity for member banks to borrow from one another. One of the original reasons for creating a Federal Reserve System was to balance regions of the country that might be vigorously expanding with other areas that might be fairly dormant: the national system would enable the banks in a growing region, facing great demand for credit, to borrow money from banks in regions of the country where the demand for credit was much lower. This exchange is called the "federal funds market," and as we saw earlier, the interest rate charged by one bank to another, the **federal funds rate**, can be manipulated to expand or contract credit.[15]

**federal funds rate** the interest rate on loans between banks that the Federal Reserve Board influences by affecting the supply of money available

The federal government also provides insurance to foster credit and encourage private capital investment. The Federal Deposit Insurance Corporation (FDIC) insures bank deposits up to $250,000. Another important promoter of investment is the federal insurance of home mortgages through the Department of Housing and Urban Development (HUD). By guaranteeing mortgages, the government can reduce the risks that banks run in making such loans, thus allowing banks to lower their interest rates and making such loans more affordable to middle- and lower-income families. Such programs have enabled millions of families who could not otherwise have afforded it to finance the purchase of a home.

This system began to unravel in the first decade of the 2000s, with the growth of the subprime market for lending. This market made home loans available to people who could not otherwise have afforded to buy a home. At the same time, however, it created new instabilities in the market by offering risky loans that would become more costly due to adjustable interest rates. The slowing housing market in 2007 set off a wave of foreclosures as many homeowners discovered that they could not pay back their loans. After the recession hit in 2008, many more Americans lost their homes to foreclosures: by 2012, nearly 3 million homes had been lost. Estimates showed that another 3 million homes could be foreclosed over the next three years.[16]

The foreclosure crisis in turn sent shock waves through the financial system, as investment banks found themselves holding worthless loans. One casualty of the home loan meltdown was the Wall Street investment bank Bear Stearns, which faced bankruptcy early in March 2008. Seeking to limit the harm to the broader economy that such a bankruptcy would cause, Fed chairman Bernanke arranged for Bear Stearns to be bought, at bargain-basement prices, by JPMorgan Chase, another investment bank. In making this move, Bernanke was exercising powers of the Federal Reserve Act that had not been used since the 1930s.[17] After the firm Lehman Brothers collapsed in 2008 and several other investment banks and insurance companies moved closer to insolvency, the Federal Reserve also provided billions of dollars to banks so that they could continue to lend money for student loans, auto loans, and residential mortgages. In all, the Fed gave nearly $400 billion in emergency loans to financial institutions.[18] Although many were impressed by the swift action undertaken by the Fed, critics charged that its supervision of the banking system prior to the crisis had been too lax. This led to an unusually contentious set of Senate confirmation hearings for Chairman Bernanke, whom President Obama had renominated in 2009.

## Fiscal Policies

**Fiscal policy** includes the government's taxing and spending powers. Personal and corporate income taxes, which raise most of the U.S. government's revenues, are the most prominent examples. Although the direct purpose of an income tax is to raise revenue, each tax has a different impact on the economy, and government can attempt to plan for that impact.

**fiscal policy** the government's use of taxing, monetary, and spending powers to manipulate the economy

**Taxation** During the nineteenth century, the federal government received most of its revenue from a single tax, the **tariff**. It also relied on excise taxes, which are taxes levied on specific products, such as tobacco and alcohol. As federal activities expanded in the 1900s, the federal government added new sources of tax revenue. The most important was the income tax, proposed by Congress in 1909, ratified by the states, and added to the Constitution in 1913 as the Sixteenth Amendment. The income tax is levied on individuals and corporations. With the creation of the Social Security system in 1935, social insurance taxes became an additional source of federal revenue.

**tariff** a tax on imported goods

Before World War II, individual income taxes accounted for only 14 percent of federal revenues.[19] The need to raise revenue for World War II made the income tax much more important. Congress expanded the base of the income tax so that most Americans paid income taxes after World War II. Table 16.1 shows several notable shifts that have occurred in taxes since 1960. Social insurance taxes now compose a much greater share of federal revenues, rising from 15.9 percent of revenues in 1960 to an estimated 40.4 percent in 2010. Receipts from corporate income taxes declined over the same period, dropping from 23.2 percent of receipts in 1960 to 7.2 in 2010. The share of the federal individual income tax has remained fairly stable; it was 44.0 percent in 1960 and estimated at 43.2 percent in 2010. One of the most important features of the American income tax is that it is a "progressive," or "graduated," tax, with the heaviest burden carried by those most able to pay. A tax is called **progressive** if the rate of taxation goes up with each higher income bracket. A tax is called **regressive** if people in lower income brackets pay a higher

**progressive taxation** taxation that hits upper income brackets more heavily

**regressive taxation** taxation that hits lower income brackets more heavily

## TABLE 16.1

## Federal Revenues by Type of Tax as Percentage of Total Receipts, 1960–2010

The federal government collects revenue from a variety of different taxes. Most important is the individual income tax. Since 1960, revenues from the corporate income tax have fallen significantly. At the same time, taxes for social insurance and retirement programs have grown substantially. Does the federal government draw more of its revenue from progressive taxes or from regressive taxes?

| YEAR | INDIVIDUAL INCOME TAXES | CORPORATE INCOME TAXES | SOCIAL INSURANCE AND RETIREMENT RECEIPTS | EXCISE TAXES | OTHER |
|------|------|------|------|------|------|
| 1960 | 44.0 | 23.2 | 15.9 | 12.6 | 4.2 |
| 1970 | 46.9 | 17.0 | 23.0 | 8.1 | 4.9 |
| 1980 | 47.2 | 12.5 | 30.5 | 4.7 | 5.1 |
| 1990 | 45.2 | 9.1 | 36.8 | 3.4 | 5.4 |
| 2000 | 49.6 | 10.2 | 32.2 | 3.4 | 4.5 |
| 2001 | 49.9 | 7.6 | 34.9 | 3.3 | 4.3 |
| 2002 | 46.3 | 8.0 | 37.8 | 3.6 | 4.3 |
| 2003 | 44.5 | 7.4 | 40.0 | 3.8 | 4.3 |
| 2004 | 43.0 | 10.1 | 39.0 | 3.7 | 4.2 |
| 2005 | 43.1 | 12.9 | 36.9 | 3.4 | 3.8 |
| 2006 | 43.4 | 14.7 | 34.8 | 3.1 | 4.0 |
| 2007 | 45.3 | 14.4 | 33.9 | 2.5 | 3.9 |
| 2008 | 45.4 | 12.1 | 35.7 | 2.7 | 4.2 |
| 2009 | 43.5 | 6.6 | 42.3 | 3.0 | 4.7 |
| 2010 | 41.5 | 8.9 | 40.0 | 3.1 | 6.5 |
| 2011 | 47.4 | 7.9 | 36.8 | 3.1 | 6.1 |
| 2012 | 47.2 | 9.6 | 34.1 | 3.2 | 6.0 |

SOURCE: Office of Management and Budget, "Percentage Composition of Receipts by Source: 1934–2015," *The Budget for Fiscal Year 2011, Historical Tables*, www.whitehouse.gov (accessed 8/6/12).

proportion of their income toward the tax than people in higher income brackets. For example, a sales tax is deemed regressive because everybody pays at the same rate, so that people who make less money end up paying a greater share of their income in sales taxes than do people who make more money. The Social Security tax is another example of a regressive tax. In 2010, Social Security law applied a tax of 6.2 percent on the first $106,800 of income for the retirement program and an additional 1.45 percent on all income (without limit) for Medicare benefits, for a total of 7.65 percent in Social Security taxes. This means that a person earning an income of $106,800 pays $8,170 in Social Security taxes, a rate of 7.65 percent. But someone earning twice that income, $213,600, pays a total of $11,267 in

Social Security taxes, a rate of 5.3 percent. As one's income continues to rise, the amount of Social Security taxes also rises (until the cap is reached), but the rate, or the percentage of one's income that goes to taxes, declines.

Although the primary purpose of the graduated income tax is, of course, to raise revenue, an important second objective is to collect revenue in such a way as to reduce the disparities of wealth between the lowest and the highest income brackets. We call this a policy of **redistribution**. Another policy objective of the income tax is the encouragement of the capitalist economy by rewarding investment. The tax laws allow individuals or companies to deduct from their taxable income any money they can justify as an investment or a "business expense"; this gives an incentive to individuals and companies to spend money to expand their production, their advertising, or their staff, and reduces the income taxes that businesses have to pay. These kinds of deductions are called incentives or "equity" by those who support them; others call them **loopholes**. The tax reforms of the 1980s actually closed a number of important loopholes in U.S. tax laws. But others still exist—on home mortgages and on business expenses, for example—and others will likely return, because there is a strong consensus among members of Congress, both Democrats and Republicans, that businesses often need such incentives. The differences between the two parties focus largely on which incentives are justifiable.[20]

The tax reform laws of 1981 and 1986 significantly reduced the progressiveness of the federal income tax. Drastic rate reductions were instituted in 1986. Before George W. Bush's 2001 reform, there were five tax brackets, ranging from a 15 percent tax on those in the lowest income bracket to 39.6 percent on those in the highest income bracket. Prior to the 1980s, the highest tax brackets sometimes were taxed at a rate of 90 percent on the last $1 million of taxable income earned in a given year. Meanwhile, Social Security taxes, the most regressive taxes of all, remain high and are likely to be increased.[21]

Taxes became a controversial issue during the George W. Bush administration. After passing major cuts in income tax rates in 2001, President Bush proposed, and Congress passed, a sweeping new round of cuts in 2003. Bush's plan was intended to promote investment by reducing taxes on most stock dividends, to spur business activity by offering tax breaks to small businesses, and to stimulate the economy by reducing the tax rates for all taxpayers. In 2006, Congress extended the rate reductions on dividends and capital gains, a move that estimates showed would cost the treasury $70 billion over five years. The argument for the tax cuts was largely a supply-side argument: the cuts would make for a prosperous economy. Opponents charge that it made no sense to cut taxes since the benefits of the tax cuts went primarily to the wealthy. Critics also charge that the tax cuts caused the federal budget, which was in surplus when Bush took office, to fall into deficit.[22]

President Obama and the Democratic leadership proposed extending the tax cuts for everyone with annual incomes under $250,000; those making more would have their income taxes revert back to the rates in the 1990s. Republicans preferred to extend the tax cuts for everyone. In late 2010, Congress agreed to a two-year extension of the cuts until December 2012. As the new deadline loomed in 2012, many analysts warned that the pending expiration of the tax cuts, which might amount to as much as $500 billion in additional taxes, coupled with $100 billion in federal spending cuts to which Congress and the president had previously agreed, could push the still-faltering U.S. economy over a "fiscal cliff" if they came to pass. It seemed that further negotiations between Congress and the White House would be needed.

**redistribution** a policy whose objective is to tax or spend in such a way as to reduce the disparities of wealth between the lowest and the highest income brackets

**loophole** incentive to individuals and businesses to reduce their tax liabilities by investing their money in areas the government designates

**for critical analysis**

What are the multiple goals of tax policy in America? How else might some of these goals be achieved? In what ways is the tax system in the United States progressive? In what ways is it regressive?

**Spending and Budgeting** The federal government's power to spend is one of the most important tools of economic policy. Decisions about how much to spend affect the overall health of the economy. They also affect every aspect of American life, from the distribution of income to the availability of different modes of transportation to the level of education in society. Not surprisingly, the fight for control over spending is one of the most contentious in Washington, as interest groups and politicians strive to determine the priorities and appropriate levels of spending. Decisions about spending are made as part of the annual budget process. During the 1990s, when the federal budget deficit first became a major political issue and when parties were deeply split on spending, the budget process became the focal point of the entire policy-making process. Even though the **budget deficit** disappeared in the late 1990s, the budget continued to dominate the attention of policy makers (Figure 16.2). With the rapid swing from budget surpluses in 2000 to record deficits by 2003, deficits once again emerged as a political issue. This time, however, Republican leaders, who had made deficits the focal point of politics in the mid-1990s, largely dismissed their importance. As House majority leader Tom DeLay put it, "The Soviet Union had a balanced budget. Well, you can raise taxes until you balance it, but the economy will go into the toilet."[23] Nonetheless, with deficits identified as causing future reductions in Social Security and other programs, they are likely to remain on the political agenda.

**budget deficit** amount by which government spending exceeds government revenue in a fiscal year

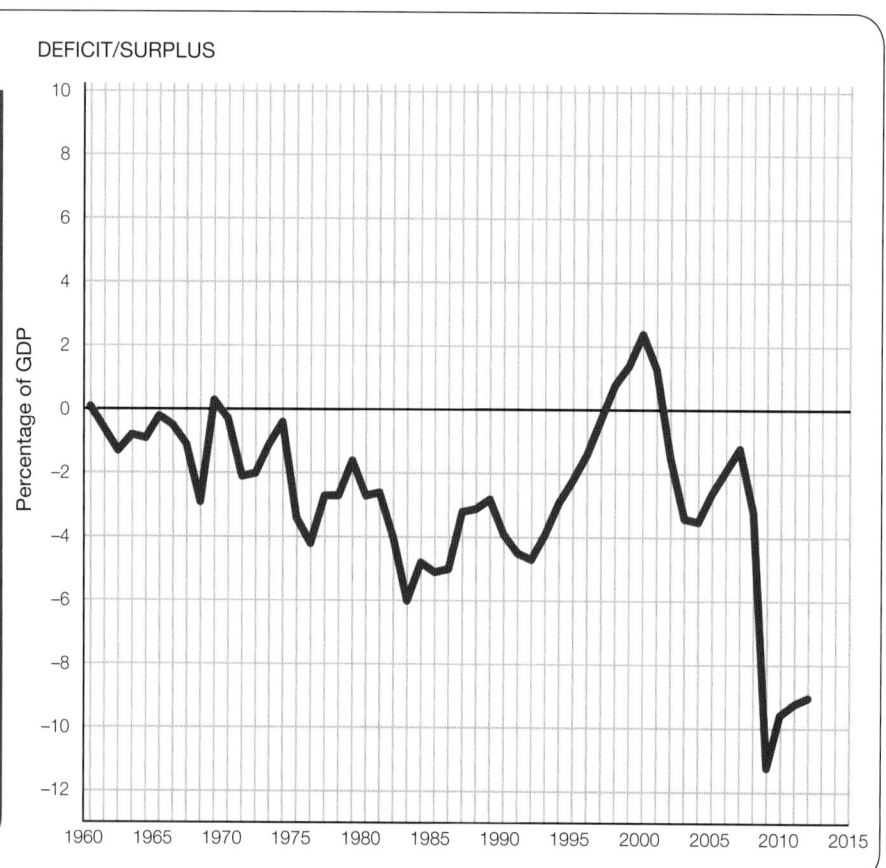

**FIGURE 16.2**

**U.S. Budget Deficits and Surpluses, 1960–2012\***

The federal deficit grew substantially during the 1980s under President Reagan. During the 1990s, the budget deficit declined significantly but then grew dramatically after 2001. When was the last time that the federal budget showed a surplus? Why did the budget deficit grow so much after 2001?

\*Data for 2012 are estimated.

SOURCE: Office of Management and Budget, "Summary of Receipts, Outlays, and Surpluses or Deficits (–) as Percentages of GDP: 1930–2015," *The Budget for Fiscal Year 2011, Historical Tables,* www.whitehouse .gov (accessed 8/6/12).

The president and Congress have each created institutions to assert control over the budget process. The Office of Management and Budget (OMB) in the Executive Office of the President is responsible for preparing the president's budget. This budget contains the president's spending priorities and the estimated costs of the president's policy proposals. It is viewed as the starting point for the annual debate over the budget. When different parties control the presidency and Congress, the president's budget may have little influence on the budget that is ultimately adopted. Members of the president's own party also may have different priorities. In 2009, President Obama made clear that he wanted to strip $1.75 billion in funding for new F-22 fighter jets from the defense budget, arguing that funding for the Cold War–era jets was wasteful. The Democratic-controlled Senate committee responsible for defense appropriations resisted that pressure and included the funding in the budget. In the end, the president won the battle, and the measure was removed from the final bill.[24]

Congress has its own budget institutions. Congress created the Congressional Budget Office (CBO) in 1974 so that it could have reliable information about the costs and economic impact of the policies it considers. At the same time, it set up a budget process designed to establish spending priorities and to consider individual expenditures in light of the entire budget. A key element of the process is the annual budget resolution, which designates broad targets for spending. By estimating the costs of policy proposals, Congress hoped to control spending and reduce deficits. When the congressional budget process proved unable to hold down deficits in the 1980s, Congress established stricter measures to control spending, including "spending caps" that limit spending on some types of programs.

A very large and growing proportion of the annual federal budget is **mandatory spending**, expenditures that are, in the words of the OMB, "relatively uncontrollable." Interest payments on the national debt, for example, are determined by the actual size of the national debt. Legislation has mandated payment rates for such programs as retirement under Social Security, retirement for federal employees, unemployment assistance, Medicare, and farm price supports (see Figures 16.3 and 16.4). These payments increase with the cost of living; they increase as the average age of the population goes up; they increase as national and world agricultural surpluses go up. In 1970, 38.5 percent of the total federal budget was made up of these **uncontrollables**; in 1975, 52.5 percent fell into that category; and by 2012, around 65 percent was in the uncontrollable category. This means that the national government now can do very little **discretionary spending** that will allow it to counteract fluctuations in the business cycle.

Government spending as a fiscal policy works fairly well when deliberate deficit spending is used to stop a recession and to speed up the recovery period, but it does not work very well in fighting inflation, because elected politicians are often politically unable to make the drastic expenditure cuts and tax hikes necessary to balance the budget, much less to produce a budgetary surplus.

## Regulation and Antitrust Policy

Americans have long been suspicious of concentrations of economic power. Federal economic regulation aims to protect the public against potential abuses by concentrated economic power in two ways. First, the federal government can establish

**mandatory spending** federal spending that is made up of "uncontrollables," budget items that cannot be controlled through the regular budget process

**uncontrollables** budgetary items that are beyond the control of budgetary committees and can be controlled only by substantive legislative action in Congress. Some uncontrollables, such as interest on the debt, are beyond the power of Congress, because the terms of payments are set in contracts

**discretionary spending** federal spending on programs that are controlled through the regular budget process

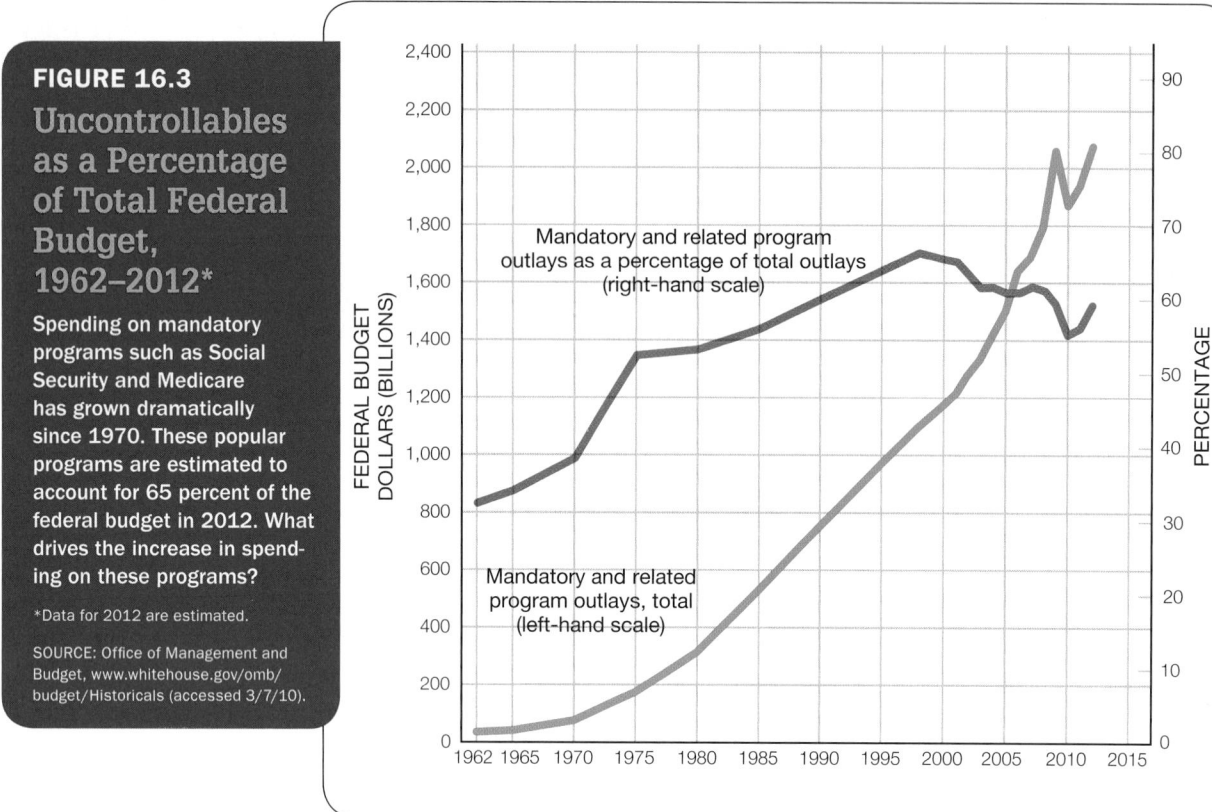

**monopoly** a single firm in a market that controls all the goods and services of that market; absence of competition

**antitrust policy** government regulation of large businesses that have established monopolies

conditions that govern the operation of big businesses to ensure fair competition. For example, it can require a business to make information about its activities and account books available to the public. Second, the federal government can force a large business to break up into smaller companies if it finds that the business has established a **monopoly**. This is called **antitrust policy**. In addition to economic regulation, the federal government engages in social regulation. Social regulation establishes conditions on businesses in order to protect workers, the environment, and consumers.

Federal regulatory policy has evolved, in part, as a reaction to public demands. As the American economy prospered throughout the nineteenth century, some companies grew so large that they were recognized as possessing "market power." This meant that they were powerful enough to eliminate competitors and to impose conditions on consumers rather than catering to consumer demand. The growth of billion-dollar corporations led to collusion among companies to control prices, much to the dismay of smaller businesses and ordinary consumers. Small businesses, laborers, farmers, and consumers all began to clamor for protective regulation. Although the states had been regulating businesses in one way or another all along, interest groups turned to Washington as economic problems appeared to be beyond the reach of the individual state governments. If markets were national, there would have to be national regulation.[25]

The first national regulatory policy was the Interstate Commerce Act of 1887, which created the first national independent regulatory commission, the Interstate

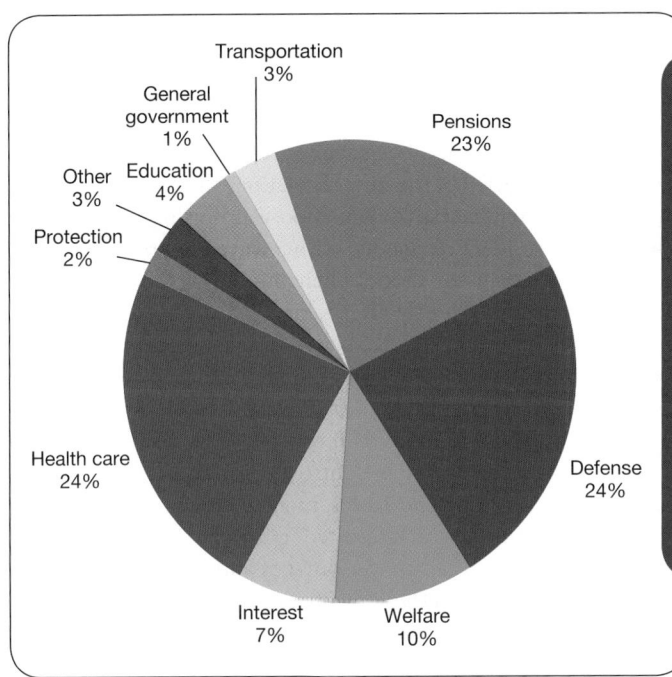

**FIGURE 16.4**

## Discretionary Spending by the Federal Government, 2013*

The biggest items in the federal budget are mandatory programs, including Social Security and Medicare. These programs are supported by contributory taxes and enjoy broad support. It is easier to cut discretionary spending, because appropriations must be approved each year. With rising budget deficits and congressional unwillingness to raise taxes, discretionary spending—including defense, but especially domestic programs—are the easiest programs to cut.

*Data are estimated. Percentages sum to more than 100 because of rounding.

SOURCE: www.usgovernmentspending.com (accessed 8/6/12).

Commerce Commission (ICC), designed to control the monopolistic practices of the railroads. Three years later, the Sherman Antitrust Act extended regulatory power to cover all monopolistic practices, which are designed to eliminate competition. The ICC and the Sherman Antitrust Act were strengthened in 1914 with the enactment of the Federal Trade Commission Act (creating the Federal Trade Commission, or FTC) and the Clayton Antitrust Act. The only significant addition of economic regulatory policy beyond regulation of interstate trade, however, was the establishment in 1913 of the Federal Reserve System, which was given powers to regulate the banking industry along with its general monetary powers. At the same time, public demands to protect consumers led the federal government to enact a more limited number of social regulations. As we have seen, Upton Sinclair's best-seller about the meatpacking industry, *The Jungle*, led to the Federal Meat Inspection Act of 1906. Two decades later, the Food and Drug Administration was given broad powers to test and regulate products viewed as essential to public health.

The modern era of comprehensive national regulation began in the 1930s. Most of the regulatory programs of the 1930s were established to regulate the conduct of companies within specifically designated sectors of American industry. For example, the jurisdiction of one agency was the securities industry; the jurisdiction of another was the radio (and eventually television) industry. Others included banking, coal mining, and agriculture. At this time, Congress also set the basic framework of American labor regulation, including the rules for collective bargaining and the minimum wage.

When Congress turned once again to regulatory policies in the 1970s, it became still bolder, moving beyond the effort to regulate specific industrial sectors and toward regulating aspects of the entire economy. The scope or jurisdiction of such agencies as the Occupational Safety and Health Administration

(OSHA), the Consumer Product Safety Commission (CPSC), and the Environmental Protection Agency (EPA) is as broad as the entire economy, indeed the entire society.

Despite occasional high-profile regulatory cases such as the one against Microsoft in the 1990s, the trend since the late 1970s has been against regulation. Over the years, businesses complained about the burden of the new regulations they confronted, and many economists began to argue that excessive regulation was hurting the economy. In the 1980s, Congress and the president responded with a wave of **deregulation**. For example, President Reagan went about the task of changing the direction of regulation by way of "presidential oversight." Shortly after taking office, he gave the OMB authority to review all executive branch proposals for new regulations. By this means, Reagan reduced the total number of regulations issued by federal agencies, dropping the number of pages in the *Federal Register* from 74,000 in 1980 to 49,600 in 1987.[26] By 2009 the *Federal Register* had grown to more than 69,000 pages. Nonetheless, the movement for deregulation became steadily more controversial during the presidency of George W. Bush. In the late 1980s and the 1990s, many states had opened their electrical power markets to competition, which resulted in lower prices. But in 2001, severe energy shortages in California caused power outages and skyrocketing prices. California officials charged that Enron and other out-of-state suppliers had used their market power to drive up the price of energy and then employed their political clout to dissuade federal regulators from intervening.

The financial crisis that began in 2008 put regulation on the agenda once again. As the economic emergency subsided, Congress began to consider long-term reform of the financial industry. A central question was how to create regulations that would prevent excessive risk-taking by investors, seen as the principal cause of the recession. The complex reform that Congress enacted in 2010 (the Dodd-Frank Wall Street Reform and Consumer Protection Act) included a range of new regulations on the financial industry. It created a Consumer Financial Protection Bureau, placed under the auspices of the Federal Reserve but independent of it. The new agency has a broad mandate to regulate consumer financial products, such as mortgages and credit cards, to ensure that they are fair and competitive. The reform also created a new Financial Stability Oversight Council, headed by the Treasury secretary, with responsibility for identifying risks to the economy before they spread.

## Subsidies and Contracting

Subsidies and contracting are the carrots of economic policy. Their purpose is to encourage people to do something they might otherwise not do or to get people to do more of what they are already doing. Sometimes the purpose is merely to compensate people for something done in the past.

**Subsidies** Subsidies are simply government grants of cash or other valuable commodities, such as land. Although subsidies are often denounced as "giveaways," they have played a fundamental role in the history of government in the United States. Subsidies were the dominant form of public policy of the national government and the state and local governments throughout the nineteenth century. They continue to be an important category of public policy at all levels of government. The first planning document ever written for the national government, Alexander Hamilton's *Report on Manufactures*, was based almost entirely on Hamilton's assumption that American industry could be encouraged by federal subsidies and that these were not only desirable but constitutional.

**deregulation** a policy of reducing or eliminating regulatory restraints on the conduct of individuals or private institutions

**subsidies** government grants of cash or other valuable commodities, such as land, to an individual or an organization; used to promote activities desired by the government, to reward political support, or to buy off political opposition

The thrust of Hamilton's plan was not lost on later policy makers. Subsidies in the form of land grants were given to farmers and to railroad companies to encourage western settlement. Substantial cash subsidies have traditionally been given to shipbuilders to help build the commercial fleet and to guarantee the use of the ships as military personnel carriers in times of war. Policies using the subsidy technique continued to be plentiful in the twentieth century and into the twenty-first, even after the 1990s, when there was widespread public and official hostility toward subsidies. For example, in 2007 the annual value of corporate subsidies, not including agriculture, was estimated at more than $92 billion.[27]

Politicians have always favored subsidies because subsidies can be treated as "benefits" that can be spread widely in response to many demands that might otherwise produce profound political conflict. Subsidies can, in other words, be used to buy off the opposition.

Another secret to the popularity of subsidies is that those who receive the benefits do not perceive the controls inherent in them. In the first place, most of the resources available for subsidies come from taxation. (During the nineteenth century, there was a lot of public land to distribute, but that is no longer the case.) Second, the effect of any subsidy has to be measured somewhat indirectly in terms of what people *would be doing* if the subsidy were not available. For example, many thousands of people settled in lands west of the Mississippi only because land subsidies were available. Similarly, hundreds of research laboratories exist in universities and corporations only because certain types of research subsidies from the government are available to fund them.

**Contracting** Like any corporation, a government agency must purchase goods and services by contract. The law requires open bidding for a substantial proportion of these contracts because government contracts are extremely valuable to businesses in the private sector and because the opportunities and incentives for abuse surrounding contracting are very great. But contracting is more than a method of buying goods and services. It is also an important technique of policy, because government agencies are often authorized to use their **contracting power** as a means of encouraging corporations to improve themselves, helping to build up whole sectors of the economy, and encouraging certain desirable goals or behavior, such as equal employment opportunity. For example, the infant airline industry of the 1930s was nurtured by the national government's lucrative contracts to carry airmail. A more recent example is the use of government contracting to encourage industries, universities, and other organizations to engage in research and development on a wide range of issues in basic and applied science.

Military contracting has long been a major element in government spending. So tight was the connection between defense contractors and the federal government during the Cold War that as he was leaving office, President Eisenhower warned the nation to beware of the powerful "military-industrial complex." After the Cold War, as military spending and production declined, major defense contractors began to look for alternative business activities to supplement the reduced demand for weapons. For example, Lockheed Mar-

**contracting power** the power of government to set conditions on companies seeking to sell goods or services to government agencies

*The Obama administration has supported subsidies for green technology. For example, buyers of hybrid cars like the Chevy Volt are eligible for a $7,500 tax break.*

tin, the nation's largest defense contractor, began to bid on contracts related to welfare reform. Since the terrorist attacks of 2001, however, the military budget has been awash in new funds, and military contractors are flooded with business. President Bush increased the Pentagon budget by more than 7 percent a year, requesting so many weapons systems that one observer called the budget a "weapons smorgasbord."[28] Military contractors geared up to produce not only weapons for foreign warfare but also surveillance systems to enhance domestic security.

# ● The Environment and the Economy

> Explain why the government tries to balance economic prosperity with policies that protect the environment

One of the most important reasons that the government intervenes in the economy is to protect the environment. Although federal interest in environmental conservation stretches back to the 1900s, federal regulation of industry grew more extensive with the rise of the modern environmental movement in the 1970s. By then the consequences of economic growth that paid little attention to environmental impact were evident all over America. Cleveland's Cuyahoga River, long a dumping ground for industrial waste, had caught fire in 1969, and the burning river became an especially vivid symbol of environmental neglect. The first "Earth Day," in 1970, highlighted the new ecological concerns, which became a major feature of American politics in subsequent decades.[29]

A wave of new laws wrote environmental goals into policy. The 1969 National Environmental Policy Act (NEPA), the Clean Air Act amendments of 1970, the 1972 Clean Water Act, and the 1974 Safe Drinking Water Act together established a new set of goals and procedures for protecting the environment. These acts are properly considered part of economic policy because they affect virtually every aspect of the economy. NEPA, for example, requires federal agencies to prepare an environmental impact statement for every major development project they propose. In this way, environmental impacts routinely become factored into considerations about whether a particular project is feasible or desirable.

Environmental disasters have often drawn attention to new environmental hazards and have prompted greater federal regulation. For example, during the mid-1970s the residents of the Love Canal neighborhood in Buffalo, New York, discovered that their neighborhood had been built on a toxic waste dump. Many of the chemicals in the soil were suspected carcinogens. At federal and state cost, residents were moved to new homes. Partly as a result of this highly publicized incident, Congress passed legislation to facilitate cleanup of hazardous waste sites.

Yet government action and corporate liability are often bitterly contested issues in this area. Protecting the environment presents policy makers with difficult trade-offs. Compliance with environmental regulations can be very costly. Moreover, critics maintain that federal standards are sometimes too high. How clean should the air be? What is the difference between pure drinking water and safe drinking water? Who should bear the costs of protecting the environment? Not only do citizens, consumers, and businesses take different perspectives on these questions but the goals themselves often present a moving target. As new scientific evidence shows (or fails to find evidence for) new or suspected environmental hazards, conflicts emerge over the proper role of government.

## The Debate on Climate Change

Nowhere have these conflicts been more acute than in the debate over climate change. A large and growing body of scientific evidence suggests that greenhouse gas emissions from cars, power plants, and other human-made sources are causing temperatures on earth to rise.[30] The projected environmental consequences are dire: melting polar ice caps, extreme weather, droughts, fire, rising sea levels, and disease. All would have profound economic consequences. Yet these projections come with considerable uncertainty. How likely are most catastrophic scenarios? Should we prepare for the most damaging outcomes or only the most likely outcomes of climate change?[31] These questions are important because the costs of transforming the world's carbon-based technologies through lower energy use and newer green technologies are enormous. These questions are especially salient for the United States, which has the world's largest economy and is responsible for 25 percent of the world's greenhouse gas emissions but has only 10 percent of the world's population.[32] And because the United States relies so heavily on fossil fuels for its energy sources, the effort to reduce carbon emission requires a major shift in how we obtain and use energy.

As scientists have learned more about the effects of human activity on the climate, the issue of climate change has risen on the national agenda. For example, in 2007, 84 percent of Americans reported believing that human activity was at least a contributing factor in climate change.[33] However, the economic recession and political controversy over climate change seemed to shift public perceptions about the existence and importance of climate change. In 2010, only 57 percent of America reported believing that global climate change was happening at all,

*Former vice president Al Gore's 2006 film,* An Inconvenient Truth, *attracted broad attention to the issue of climate change. The film won an Academy Award, and Gore was a co-recipient of the Nobel Peace Prize for his efforts to raise public awareness.*

What are some of the policies that can be used to address climate change? Which policies have the best chance of being enacted?

with just 50 percent of respondents "very" or "somewhat" worried about climate change. In another survey, respondents ranked climate change last in importance in a list of 21 top public policy issues.[34] In the same survey, just over half of the public said they would support protecting the environment over stimulating the economy, while 36 percent chose the economy.[35] The Obama administration has made climate change an important focus of attention and encouraged federal agencies to move aggressively on this issue. In 2009 the EPA began to set standards so that it could, for the first time ever, regulate greenhouse gas emissions under the Clean Air Act. The administration also proposed creating a new Climate Service that would centralize the collection and analysis of data on climate change across the world. The new attitude was epitomized by Commerce Secretary Gary Locke, who noted in his announcement of the planned Climate Service that "whether we like it or not, climate change represents a real threat."[36]

## Environmental Policies

Policy makers charged with devising approaches to climate change have identified three basic policy approaches. The first is mitigation, or reduction, of greenhouse gas emissions. The second is large-scale research and development to promote alternative technologies. The third consists of measures that allow us to adapt to a warmer climate. Each of these strategies entails potentially gargantuan costs in the form of higher energy prices, subsidies to industry, infrastructure projects, and relocation decisions. When specific policy proposals are discussed and these costs become apparent, the consensus for addressing climate change breaks down.

**Mitigation: Reducing Emissions** The mitigation approach, which seeks to reduce greenhouse gas emissions, has garnered the most attention from policy makers. Two proposed policies that aim to achieve this goal, both controversial,

*One approach to addressing climate change is reducing emissions—from factories, power plants, and cars. Capping emissions can be controversial if it imposes costs on businesses and ultimately on consumers, but recent cap-and-trade proposals may offer a more efficient way to reduce pollution.*

are tougher standards for auto fuel mileage and higher taxes on gasoline. Although the public strongly supports higher gas-mileage standards, auto companies resisted such standards for nearly 30 years after they were first put in place in the early 1970s. In 2009 the EPA announced that it would set standards for greenhouse gas emissions for automobiles under the Clean Air Act, raising the fuel economy standards for new vehicles to 35.5 miles per gallon beginning in 2016.[37] As for proposals to increase gasoline taxes, public opinion polls routinely show that a majority of Americans oppose a tax on gasoline as a way to reduce emissions, and few politicians want to sponsor such an unpopular policy.[38]

International agreements on climate change, such as the Kyoto Protocol, seek to reduce carbon emissions by establishing mandatory caps on the total amount of emissions that developed countries can emit. Although the United States signed the protocol in 1998, congressional and presidential opposition prevented any effort to implement its provisions. Policy makers have since considered several ways to reduce carbon emissions. A "carbon tax" would tax the producers of energy, who would then pass the higher costs on to consumers. Carbon taxes could substantially raise the costs of all sorts of consumer products, and only a handful of politicians have expressed interest in supporting them.

Proponents of reducing carbon emissions pinned their hopes on a "cap-and-trade" system as the most politically feasible strategy to achieve their goal. This approach sets a target for carbon emissions for each industry but allows companies to trade "carbon credits" with one another. This market-based system is attractive to political leaders because it achieves its goals by creating incentives for private actors and allows them flexibility as they seek to reduce emissions. More than 23 large firms, including leading automakers, have joined environmentalists in a coalition called the U.S. Climate Action Partnership (USCAP) to press for a cap-and-trade system to reduce carbon emissions.[39] In 2009 the House of Representatives passed a landmark cap-and-trade bill aimed at reducing greenhouse gas emissions. However, opposition from some Democrats and most Republicans in the Senate made further movement toward final passage of cap-and-trade legislation unlikely. New signs of progress emerged, however, in early 2010, with three senators of both parties—Senators John Kerry (D-Mass.), Joseph Lieberman (I-Conn.), and Lindsey Graham (R-S.C.)—proposing legislation that would apply carbon controls to specific sectors of the economy rather than setting the overall national target envisioned by the cap-and-trade scheme.[40] One of the central elements of the proposal was a requirement that power plants limit their emissions, with the cap becoming more stringent over the next decade. Another key provision was the imposition of a carbon tax on gasoline, with the money raised being used to fund alternative fuel vehicle technologies such as electric cars.[41] Though this proposal was not enacted, its central ideas continue to be the focus of congressional discussion.

**Promoting Alternative Technologies** Many analysts and politicians prefer a second strategy for addressing the problems associated with fossil fuels, one that centers on increased research and development to promote alternative technologies. President Obama came out strongly in favor of a comprehensive energy and climate change bill that would, among other things, provide funding and large tax incentives for the production and adoption of clean-energy technologies. He also warned that the United States was falling behind other countries, including China, in the production of clean-energy products, arguing that this industry would be a vital source of millions of new jobs over the next few decades.[42] The 2009 Recovery

# The United States and Global Climate Change

**Concerns about climate change** began to surface more than two decades ago. The international scope of the question became apparent when more than 150 countries, including the United States, signed the United Nations Framework Convention on Climate Change (UNFCCC) in 1992 at the so-called Earth Summit in Rio de Janeiro. By 1997 the signatory parties had agreed on the Kyoto Protocol for reducing the level of heat-trapping gases in the earth's atmosphere. To achieve this goal, the Kyoto Protocol set binding targets for greenhouse gas emissions to be met by each country by the year 2012 at levels 5.2 percent lower than their 1990 levels.

Since the Kyoto Protocol, the United States has been a hesitant participant in international climate negotiations. It signed the protocol during the Clinton presidency, but disagreement quickly erupted over the economic costs that industry would incur if forced to lower greenhouse emissions. As a result, President Clinton never submitted the protocol to the Senate for ratification. On taking office in 2001, President Bush then announced he would not submit the Kyoto agreement to the Senate because it exempted China and other developing countries from binding limits while imposing excessive costs on the U.S. economy.

Even as the scientific basis for climate change gained wider acceptance, the politics of implementing binding limits produced a growing split between wealthy industrialized countries and the developing world. China and Brazil argued that the industrialized countries and especially the United States had contributed far more to climate change over time than had the developing countries. The indus-

trialized leaders, especially the United States, should therefore shoulder the burden of limiting worldwide emissions while giving poorer countries a chance to develop their economies.

In the ensuing debates, many other Kyoto signatories also came to see the United States as a laggard in international efforts to control climate change. With only 10 percent of the world's population, the United States emitted approximately 25 percent of greenhouse gases, more than any other single country.

It was hoped that the 2009 Copenhagen Summit would produce a new legally binding international agreement with specific emission-reduction targets for both developed and developing nations. Ultimately, however, the agreement fell well short of this goal: the meeting ended with no legally binding agreement and no deadline set to reach one. Wealthy nations agreed to provide funds to developing nations to help them integrate clean technology, though the sum of $10 billion a year was considered too low to be effective. The agreement did mark the first time the developing world, including major polluters such as China, India, and Brazil, committed to reducing their carbon output. This is particularly important as these countries will produce nearly all the growth in emissions over the coming decades.[a]

[a]Juliet Eilperin and Anthony Faiola, "Climate Deal Falls Short of Key Goals," *Washington Post*, December 19, 2009, www.washingtonpost.com (accessed 3/8/10).

## for critical analysis

1. Why did many countries that signed the Kyoto Protocol come to see the United States as a laggard in efforts to control climate change?

2. Why was it so important to U.S. negotiators that mandatory limits on greenhouse gas emissions be applied to China as well as to the developed countries?

Act allocated nearly $30 billion to support alternative energy technology investment and to improve energy efficiency.

Green technologies may prove to be a boon for the American economy. Because highly skilled labor is required to produce most such technologies, America has a competitive advantage over many other countries. Furthermore, a move toward green technologies could significantly improve American national security. Indeed, some argue that reducing the use of fossil fuels and adopting more fuel-efficient technologies would take money away from regimes that support terrorism against the United States.

Part of the attraction of green technologies is that they appear to entail fewer politically difficult costs. A closer look, however, reveals that this is not entirely true. For example, the search for cleaner technologies has renewed interest in nuclear power. But nuclear power has long suffered from NIMBY ("Not in My Backyard") problems: few people want a nuclear power plant close by. The question of how to dispose of nuclear waste poses similar problems. And even less dangerous technologies, such as wind farms, attract opposition, as an effort to establish a large wind farm off Cape Cod demonstrated. Resistance to some of the new technologies and the time required to develop these alternatives mean that they are not the magic bullet that many proponents wish they were.

**Adaptation Policies** A final approach to climate change is adaptation to a warmer climate. Adaptation would entail a diverse set of policies, including establishment of green corridors, pest and disease control, water conservation to deal with drought, and new infrastructure such as seawalls to cope with rising sea levels.[42] Many scientists believe that deliberate adaptation has to be part of any approach to climate change because even if we take major steps to mitigate carbon emissions and pour resources into developing new technologies, climate change has already arrived.

Many aspects of a deliberate adaptation strategy would be difficult to implement in the market-oriented, decentralized context of the United States. Although some European countries, such as the low-lying Netherlands, are relocating people as part of their adaptation strategy, American politicians have little stomach for initiating such controversial measures. Moreover, the combination of conservation and new infrastructure requires considerable public resources and broad coordination across multiple public agencies. Both are hard to achieve in the context of American politics. For example, the environmentally sensitive Sacramento Delta is extremely vulnerable to rising sea levels. The delta, a swath of land that lies below sea level, is economically important because it supplies much of Northern California, including California agribusiness, with water. Yet decisions about what happens in the delta involve more than 200 government agencies.[44]

Global climate change poses a difficult economic challenge for the United States. It presents the opportunity for American industry to take the lead in developing green technologies, placing the nation's economic prosperity on a fundamentally new base. Yet it also calls for government to enforce the reduction of carbon emissions and adapt current practices to a changing world. Many industries have expressed support for action to address climate change, but such a major economic transformation creates winners and losers. Firms, such as the auto companies, whose profits are jeopardized and workers whose jobs are threatened by change have successfully blocked bold action in the past. The diffuse long-term harms that climate change poses are hard to pit against the specific concentrated costs that industries face today. Nonetheless, growing recognition that climate change is real and poses potentially catastrophic consequences ensures that economic policy and environmental policy will be ever more closely intertwined in the future.

# ● The Politics of Economic Policy Making

**Explore why economic policy is often controversial**

Addressing economic challenges and maintaining a healthy economy are extremely important to political leaders. As presidents from Herbert Hoover (who presided over the beginning of the Great Depression of the 1930s) to Jimmy Carter (who faced double-digit inflation) discovered, voters will punish politicians for poor economic performance. Yet even though all politicians want a healthy economy, they often differ in their views about how to attain it. Moreover, politicians disagree about what the priorities of economic policy should be. Democrats and Republicans alike want to promote economic growth, but Democrats are generally more concerned about inequality and unemployment than are Republicans. Republicans stress the importance of economic freedom for maintaining a healthy economy, whereas Democrats are often more willing to support economic regulation to attain social objectives. Such differences along party lines are not hard and fast ones, however. The politics of economic policy making are also greatly influenced by economic ideas.

## Four Schools of Economic Thought

As politicians, interest groups, and the public debate which goals are most important and appropriate for economic policy to achieve, their views are informed by underlying theories. Different theories about how the economy works present quite distinct roles for government.

The idea that government should have only a minimal role in the economy is often called **laissez-faire capitalism**. Proponents of laissez-faire (literally, "let do") argue that the economy will flourish if the government leaves it alone. The argument for laissez-faire was first elaborated in the late 1700s by the great Scottish economist Adam Smith. Smith believed that most government involvement in the economy (such as the government-authorized monopolies that dominated trade in his day) suppressed economic growth. Instead, he argued that competition among free enterprises would unleash economic energy, fostering growth and innovation. In his view, the self-seeking behavior of individuals, when subject to the discipline of market competition, would create products that consumers wanted at the best possible price. Smith praised "the invisible hand" of the market, by which he meant that millions of individual economic transactions together create a greater good—far better than the government could create. Smith believed that the government role should be restricted to national defense, establishing law and order

**laissez-faire capitalism** an economic system in which the means of production and distribution are privately owned and operated for profit with minimal or no government interference

(including the protection of private property), and providing basic public goods (such as roads) that facilitate commerce.

In the 1930s, the ideas of the British economist John Maynard Keynes laid the foundation for a revolution in thinking about the role of the government in the economy. **Keynesians** argue that by pumping money into the economy, particularly by running deficits during periods of recession, government can stimulate demand and create a cycle of increased production and jobs that will pull the economy out of recession. Governments can do this in several ways. For one, they can increase public spending through such measures as public works or public employment. Alternatively, governments can stimulate demand through temporary tax cuts. Tax cuts will allow workers to keep more of their earnings; their increased spending power will boost consumption and increase demand.[45] On the other hand, when inflation threatens, governments can then cut back on spending or increase taxes.

After World War II, Keynesian ideas guided economic policy making across the industrialized world. By the 1960s, Keynesians believed they could ensure ongoing prosperity by "fine-tuning" the economy. Even President Richard Nixon, a Republican, reflected the strong consensus behind Keynesian ideas when he remarked, "I am now a Keynesian." Yet by the time Keynesian ideas became the accepted wisdom, new economic conditions threatened their effectiveness. Many observers argued that increased international trade made Keynesian remedies less useful. Confidence that the government can fine-tune the economy diminished, and Keynesians lost the great influence they once had in economic policy.

In contrast to Keynesians, **monetarists** believe that the role of the government in managing the economy should be limited to regulating the supply of money. More active government management of the economy, monetarists argue, either has little effect or actually makes the economy worse. Monetarists do not believe that government can act quickly enough to fine-tune the economy. Instead, they maintain that government should promote economic stability by regulating the money supply. The most prominent monetarist in the United States, the late economist Milton Friedman, recommended a strict version of monetarism that envisions a hands-off approach for the government; the theory calls for little exercise of discretion on the part of government officials. Instead, they must follow a simple rule: the federal government should let the growth in the money supply match the rate of economic growth. In this way, inflation can be kept low even as economic growth continues.

In the late 1970s, when high levels of inflation plagued the American economy, monetarists became especially influential in economic policy making. However, today, monetarism has few followers. Instead, most economic policy makers favor manipulating interest rates to ensure a healthy and stable economy.

Proponents of **supply-side economics** believe that reducing the role of government in the economy will promote investment and spur economic growth. Reducing tax rates is the centerpiece of the supply-side economic strategy. Supply-siders maintain that lower tax rates create

**Keynesians** followers of the economic theories of John Maynard Keynes, who argued that the government can stimulate the economy by increasing public spending or by cutting taxes

**monetarists** followers of economic theories that contend that the role of the government in the economy should be limited to regulating the supply of money

**supply-side economics** a social science that posits that reducing the marginal rate of taxation will create a productive economy by promoting levels of work and investment that would otherwise be discouraged by higher taxes

*"Supply-siders" argue that reducing tax rates will spur economic growth, as people are able to spend and invest more of their money. In the 1980s, President Ronald Reagan—shown here holding an oversize tax form— sought to simplify the tax laws and reduce taxes.*

incentives for more productive and efficient use of resources. When individuals know they can keep more of their earnings, they are more likely to be productive workers and creative investors. In this perspective, decreasing taxes could yield more tax revenue by spurring economic activity. This view marked a shift for conservatives by placing more emphasis on tax cuts and less on budget deficits.

The ideas behind supply-side economics emerged in the 1970s, when Keynesian solutions appeared to have little impact on the high rates of inflation and a sluggish economy. Supply-side ideas were very influential in the administrations of the Republican presidents Ronald Reagan and George W. Bush, both of whom pointed to supply-side ideas as a sound reason for enacting significant tax cuts.

## The Changing Federal Role in the Economy

Until 1929, most Americans believed that government had little to do with actively managing the economy. The world was guided by the theory that the economy, if left to its own devices, would produce full employment and maximum production. This traditional view of the relationship between government and the economy crumbled in 1929 before the stark reality of the Great Depression of 1929–33. Some misfortune befell nearly everyone. Around 20 percent of the workforce became unemployed, and few of these individuals had any monetary resources or the old family farm to fall back on. Banks failed, wiping out the savings of millions who had been prudent enough or fortunate enough to have any. Thousands of businesses closed, throwing middle-class Americans onto the bread lines alongside unemployed laborers and dispossessed farmers. The Great Depression proved to Americans that the economic system was not, in fact, perfectly self-regulating, as had been generally believed.

Demands grew for the federal government to act. In Congress, some Democrats proposed that the federal government finance public works to aid the economy and put people back to work. Other members introduced legislation to provide federal grants to the states to assist their relief efforts.

When President Franklin Delano Roosevelt took office in 1933, he energetically threw the federal government into the business of fighting the Depression. He proposed a variety of temporary measures to provide federal relief and work programs. Most of the programs he proposed were to be financed by the federal government but administered by the states. In addition to these temporary measures, Roosevelt presided over the creation of several important federal programs designed to provide future economic security for Americans. Since that time, the public has held the government, and the president in particular, responsible for ensuring a healthy economy.

The experience of the 1930s transformed public expectations about federal government involvement in the economy. As we have seen, Keynesian ideas, which used spending and tax policy to promote growth and low unemployment, dominated economic policy during the 1960s and the first half of the 1970s. The Council of Economic Advisers (CEA) played a central role in economic policy during that time because the president relied on its advice about whether to stimulate or depress the economy. As Keynesian prescriptions became less effective, however, the CEA began to lose its central role. Since the late 1970s, when President Carter began to emphasize monetary policy, the chairman of the Federal Reserve has occupied the pivotal position in economic policy making. The long run of economic prosperity in the 1990s made the former Fed chairman Alan Greenspan into something of a cult figure. Universally praised by Democrats and Republicans alike for his management of the economy, Greenspan served four four-year terms as head of the Federal Reserve. As the economy fell into recession in the early 2000s, critics complained that Greenspan had lost his touch and had helped create the conditions for recession.

Presidents who preside over periods of economic downturn are generally punished by the electorate. In 1992, economic recession and relatively high levels of unemployment imperiled the presidency of George H. W. Bush and helped lead to the election of the challenger, Bill Clinton. Clinton's campaign took as a central theme the unofficial slogan "It's the economy, stupid." The uncertain direction of the economy made it an issue in the 2004 presidential campaign. Anxious not to repeat his father's experience in 1992, President George W. Bush claimed in 2004 that his policies were creating new jobs, and he touted the benefits of his tax cuts for middle-income families. Democrats countered that Bush's policies benefited the wealthy but left most Americans economically worse off. In 2012, Republican candidate Mitt Romney charged that President Obama had failed to lead the nation to prosperity and, instead, had worsened budget deficits and America's long-term economic prospects. Many voters, however, continued to blame Bush for the recession and thought Obama had worked to improve the economy.

## Politics and the Great Recession of 2008

As the near-collapse of the financial sector in 2008 reverberated throughout the U.S. (and world) economy, thousands of Americans lost their homes, banks refused to lend, and unemployment rose. The federal government, first under George W. Bush and then under Barack Obama, initiated large-scale government interventions in the hope of staving off the downward economic spiral. These included emergency measures to bail out failing companies, short-term stimulus to get the economy moving again, and proposals for regulations that would prevent similar financial meltdowns in the future. However, support for these measures wavered as fear of rising deficits, exploding long-term debt, and, more abstractly, "big government" grew.

As we have seen, propping up the financial sector presented an economic challenge for federal officials. Having made a number of ad hoc loans to a variety of financial institutions in early to mid-2008, the Treasury and Federal Reserve realized that they needed a more comprehensive approach as the financial crisis escalated after the collapse of investment bank Lehman Brothers and the rescue of the insurance company American International Group (AIG). Congress ultimately approved a $700 billion emergency "bailout" of financial institutions in October 2008 (known as the Troubled Asset Relief Program, or TARP), which the Treasury Department drew on to infuse major financial institutions with capital.

It was not just major banking institutions that faced ruin. Auto companies, too, teetered on the edge of bankruptcy. Wishing to avoid the loss of hundreds of thousands of jobs in the automobile industry, the outgoing Bush administration controversially made emergency bridging loans to General Motors (GM), GM's car financing business (called GMAC), and Chrysler in December 2008, using funds from the financial rescue plan package approved by Congress two months

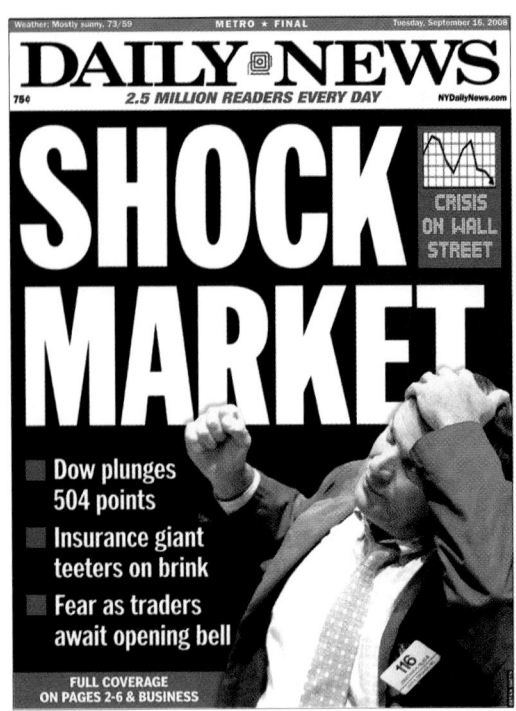

*After the Lehman Brothers investment bank collapsed and the giant insurance company AIG announced it was near collapse in September 2008, the stock market plummeted and Americans looked to the government to address the crisis. However, Democrats and Republicans disagreed about the best response.*

earlier. In return, GM and Chrysler agreed to restructure their operations to cut costs and become more competitive. However, only a few months later, the companies returned to the federal government to ask for further assistance; by June 2009, GM and Chrysler had received a total of $82 billion in government assistance.[46] The federal government also effectively subsidized the earnings of auto manufacturers by approving $3 billion in subsidies over the course of 2009 for people willing to trade in their old cars for more fuel-efficient vehicles, a program commonly known as "cash for clunkers."[47] As a condition of receiving these subsidies, the bailed-out companies had to comply with the decisions of a federal "pay czar" responsible for ensuring that the subsidized industries did not provide excessive executive compensation.

By late 2010, the economy had stabilized sufficiently that many of the financial institutions that had received funds under TARP were able to pay the federal government back. The CBO estimated that TARP would end up costing taxpayers $34 billion, far less than the initial $700 billion.[48] This $34 billion did not include the hundreds of billions of dollars spent by the Federal Reserve in buying up mortgage-related debts held by banks.

Congress also passed a sweeping package in 2009 to help stimulate the economy, save jobs (particularly in the public sector), and make longer-term investments that would help stimulate economic growth. The $789 billion American Recovery and Reinvestment Act (more commonly known as the "stimulus" bill of 2009) contained a number of measures to stimulate growth in the short term and prevent drastic cuts to public services. Among the most important measures in the act were reductions in individual and business taxes by $288 billion in order to generate more spending and job hiring. The measure also spent $195.5 billion on aid, health insurance subsidies, and job training for low-income and unemployed workers, and $44.5 billion designed to limit teacher layoffs and cutbacks in local school districts. The rest of the investments not only aimed to create new jobs in the short term, but also sought to be long-term investments in infrastructure and education that would help future growth.

Although only some Republicans and Democrats had balked at supporting the financial bailout package in 2008, by early 2009 a sharp partisan rift had become evident. No Republicans in the House and only three in the Senate voted to support the 2009 stimulus package. Republicans denounced the House measure as overly tilted toward spending rather than tax cuts. But even when Senate Democrats added significant new tax cuts to the bill, most Republicans still opposed it. While Democrats defended the measure as an infusion of funds needed to prevent a depression, Republicans denounced it as wasteful spending and made their opposition a defining stance toward the Obama administration. Mounting unemployment complicated the political judgments about the stimulus; despite the injection of public funds into the economy, national unemployment rose to a seasonally adjusted rate of 9.6 by September 2010, with rates much higher in some states.[49] While those defending the stimulus measure argued that unemployment would have been still higher without it, the inability of the stimulus to bring unemployment rates down led opponents to brand it a failure. The nonpartisan

CBO estimated that ARRA increased the number of full-time jobs by as many as 2 million.[50] Yet because unemployment remained high, ARRA did not get much credit from the public for helping the economy, and it attracted considerable criticism for contributing to the budget deficit. When President Obama proposed additional measures to stimulate the economy, he was unable to win sufficient support in Congress. When Congress considered a second stimulus bill focused on job creation, it succeeded in enacting a relatively small job creation package worth $15 billion, most of which consisted of tax credits for businesses that hired new employees.[51]

Although economists largely agree that the bailouts and recovery spending prevented a depression and saved millions of jobs, there is significant controversy over the long-term effect of this historically high level of government spending. Opposition to the Recovery Act, for example, partly reflected a growing concern over the long-term sustainability of such large increases in government spending, particularly their effect on the growing national debt. Over the past decade, large annual budget deficits have become common, requiring more borrowing by the government. **Deficit** refers to a shortfall in government revenue versus expenditures in a given year. The **national debt** is the total amount the government owes to its creditors. The national debt increased from 40 percent of annual GDP in 2008 to 62 percent in 2010. The OMB estimates that the national debt is equivalent to the entire GDP of the U.S. economy though some of this is "intra-governmental borrowing," that is, money owed by agencies to one another.[52] As the national debt has risen, so has the annual amount the government must pay to service the debt; in 2011, interest payments on the debt will were $454 billion, which is roughly equivalent to annual spending on domestic programs.[53] Economists suggest that without broad tax increases and spending cuts, the deficit and debt will ultimately rise to unsustainable levels, leading foreign investors to demand higher interest rates or, perhaps, to stop lending money to the U.S. government altogether. Yet there is little political will in either party to take these steps, in large part because of deep public opposition to both tax increases and spending cuts. For example, polls show that Americans favor spending cuts in the abstract but oppose cuts in both health and military spending—the most costly federal programs.[54]

Partisan divisions also arose over what longer-term actions the federal government should take to prevent a future economic collapse like that of 2008. While a majority of Democrats favored strict regulations to limit the kinds of risky financial transactions that caused the recession, most Republicans and some Democrats resisted stronger economic regulation.

President Obama came to office vowing to pursue bipartisanship as he sought to revive the economy. Both tasks proved difficult to achieve. Rather than cementing a new consensus on the role of government in the economy, Obama saw his first two years in office dogged by partisan rancor. Fueled by a combination of political maneuvering for partisan advantage and philosophical differences over the proper role of government and the economy, congressional Democrats and Republicans made partisan division the defining feature of national politics.

## Business and Labor in the Economy

The groups that influence decisions about economic policy are as wide-ranging as the objectives of policy. Consumer groups, environmentalists, businesses, and labor all attempt to shape economic policy. Of these groups, organized labor and business

**deficit** the total amount the government owes its creditors

**national debt** the amount that government spending exceeds the government's revenue in any year

are the most consistent actors who weigh in across the spectrum of policies. In the past, organized labor was much more important in influencing economic policy than it is today. At the height of their strength in the 1950s, unions represented some 35 percent of the labor force. Today, labor unions, representing 12.3 percent of the labor force, are much less powerful in influencing economic policy. Democratic presidents continue to court labor because unions control resources and votes important to Democratic politicians, but labor's overall power has waned. On particular issues, organized labor can still exercise significant influence. For example, labor played a key role in Congress's decision to increase the minimum wage in 1996. Labor has recently sought to boost its political profile and has particularly sought to influence trade policy.

Business organizations are the most consistently powerful actors in economic policy. Business groups are most united around the goal of reducing government regulation. Organizations such as the U.S. Chamber of Commerce, which represents small business, and the Business Roundtable and the National Association of Manufacturers, which represent big business, actively worked to roll back government regulation in the 1970s and '80s.

In addition to subsidies and tax breaks, business also relies on the federal government for protection against unfair foreign competition. For example, over the past several years, the film production industry has lobbied Washington to help it compete with film industries in countries where films can be made more cheaply than in the United States. This country loses an estimated $10 billion in annual revenues to these foreign competitors. Television shows and films with American locales are routinely filmed in Canada, where tax incentives and lower costs make production considerably cheaper. Industry representatives, fearing that Los Angeles could turn into a "rust belt" for film production, have sought legislation to secure wage credits.[55] The Screen Actors Guild went so far as to ask the federal government to investigate Canada for unfair trade practices.

## ● Thinking Critically about Economic Policy

Historically, Americans have been more concerned with ensuring economic liberty than with promoting economic equality. The widespread perception of openness and opportunity in American society has made Americans more tolerant than Europeans of economic inequality. American economic policy has rarely aimed to promote economic equality. Instead, economic policy has sought to ensure fairness in the marketplace and to protect against the worst side effects of the free market. One of the central ways to ensure fair markets is to guard against the emergence of businesses so large that they can control markets. As we have seen, antitrust policy aims to break up such concentrations of power in the name of free and fair competition. The laws designed to strengthen labor in the 1930s likewise aimed to limit the power of big business by creating a countervailing power; they did not attempt directly to create equality. Consumer and environmental regulations are key economic policy protections against the worst side effects of the free market. Over time, as Americans have grown more concerned about the quality of life,

# Who Are the 1 Percent?

Starting in 2011, the Occupy movement drew Americans' attention to income inequality, arguing that current economic policies help Wall Street firms and the richest 1 percent of Americans, rather than the other 99 percent. These data show that the incomes of the top 1 percent have indeed increased much more rapidly than the rest of the population, but also that "the 1 percent" aren't all Wall Street financiers.

## U.S. Real Average After-Tax Income, 1979–2007

1979 = 100%

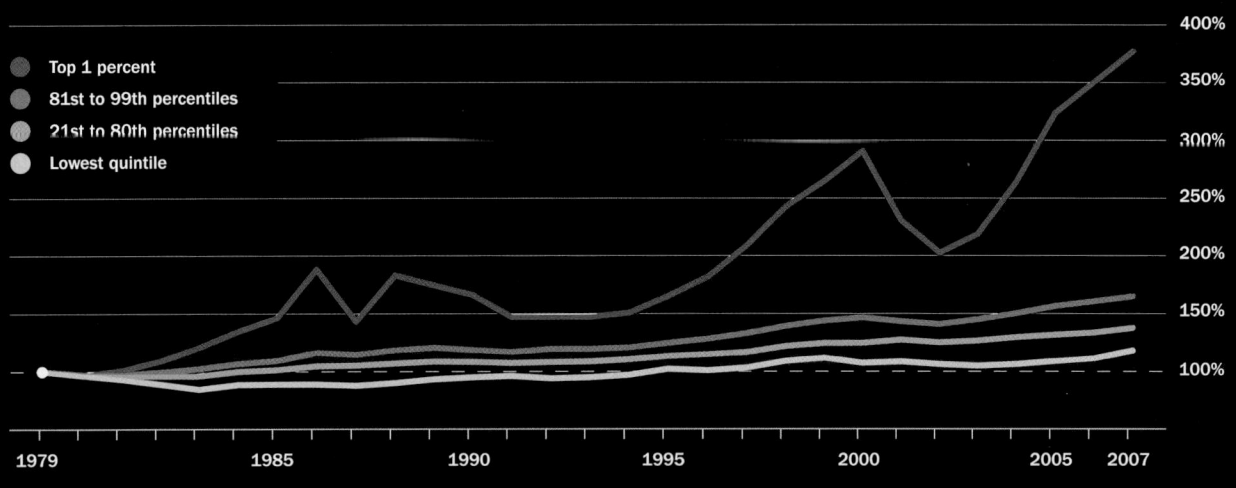

Top 1 percent
81st to 99th percentiles
21st to 80th percentiles
Lowest quintile

## Occupations of the Top 1 Percent

> 30%   5–10%
10–30%   < 5%

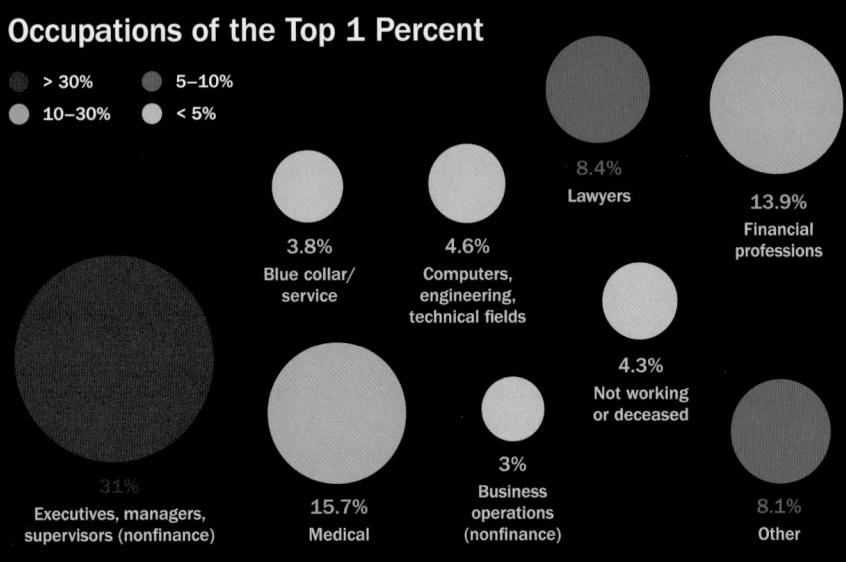

31%
Executives, managers, supervisors (nonfinance)

3.8%
Blue collar/ service

4.6%
Computers, engineering, technical fields

8.4%
Lawyers

13.9%
Financial professions

15.7%
Medical

3%
Business operations (nonfinance)

4.3%
Not working or deceased

8.1%
Other

3.2%
Real estate

4.2%
Skilled sales

### for critical analysis

1. What are some of the policies that the government can use to address inequality? What are some of the arguments against policies that redistribute wealth toward poorer Americans?

2. "The 99 percent" is a diverse group, including over 300 million Americans. Can it really be said to have a common interest when it comes to economic policy?

SOURCES: Congressional Budget Office, "Trends in the Distribution of Household Income between 1979 and 2007," October 25, 2011, www.cbo.gov/publication/42729; Jon Bajika, et al., "Jobs and Income Growth of Top Earners and the Causes of Changing Income Inequality," 2012, http://web.williams.edu/Economics/wp/BakijaColeHeimJobs IncomeGrowthTopEarners.pdf (both accessed 5/23/12).

policies in these areas have placed greater restrictions on the market. In a sense, economic prosperity and market success laid the foundation for such restrictions. As Americans felt more economically secure, they could afford to worry about how the economy affected the nonfinancial aspects of their lives, such as the environment. It is no accident that social regulation of the economy took off after the unprecedented prosperity of the 1960s.

The growth in economic inequality over the past three decades raises new questions about economic policy. Increased global competition, computerization, and the decline of unions and worker skills have all been identified as sources of growing inequality.[56] Taxes are another policy area that affects inequality. Depending on how they are designed, tax policies put relatively more money in the pockets of people with either lower or higher incomes. For example, tax cuts on investment income and reductions in the estate tax are more likely to increase the after-tax income of the wealthy because this group derives more of its income from investments and inheritances than do people with lower incomes.[57] Likewise, income tax rates can be reduced for all groups, but depending on the proportion of tax cuts for each group, some income brackets may benefit more than others. One of the major criticisms of the tax cuts of 2001, 2003, and 2006 (known collectively as the Bush-era tax cuts) is that they increased the gap between rich and poor. They did so by allowing the rich to retain a greater proportion of their after-tax income than did middle- and lower-income taxpayers. The liberal Center on Budget and Policy Priorities analyzed the impact of these tax cuts. As Figure 16.5 shows, the tax cuts allowed households in the bottom fifth of the income range to keep an additional 0.5 percent of their pretax income. For the middle-income group, after-tax income grew by 2.3 percent, while the top 20 percent gained 4.6 percent in after-tax income. The gains for the top 1 percent of households were much larger: an increase of 6.8 percent of after-tax income each year.[58] These differences matter because long-term trends in growth are widening the gap between rich and poor, as the Who Are Americans infographic shows. Because after-tax incomes are *more unequal* as a consequence of the tax changes, liberals identify those tax changes as regressive.

Conservatives take a different view. They argue that even with these changes, the rich paid by far the greatest share of federal taxes. In fact, as the second half of Figure 16.5 shows, in 2005, the top fifth of households paid 68.7 percent of all taxes, whereas the bottom fifth paid less than 1 percent. Most crucial in judging the impact of the tax cuts, the rich paid a *larger share* of the total federal tax bill after the tax cuts than before. As Figure 16.5 shows, the share of the total tax bill fell for households in the lowest- and middle-income categories, but it increased for the top categories. Therefore, although the lowest group paid .09 percent *less* as a share of total taxes, the top 20 percent of earners paid 2.1 percent *more*.

What is fair? As long as the rich are still taxed at higher rates, should we worry that the tax cuts are making after-tax income distribution more unequal? After all, as the rich have gotten richer, they have paid an ever higher share of the total federal tax bill. The answer to this question depends on different views about the consequences of income inequality. Those who believe that the growth of income inequality harms the middle class by increasing prices or undermines democracy believe that tax policy should be designed to lessen these inequalities. Those who think that inequality is not a major problem believe that tax cuts give individuals incentives to be productive and thus promote economic growth. In this view, tax

**for critical analysis**

How does economic policy affect inequality among Americans? Should economic policy makers take equality into account as they decide among different economic tools?

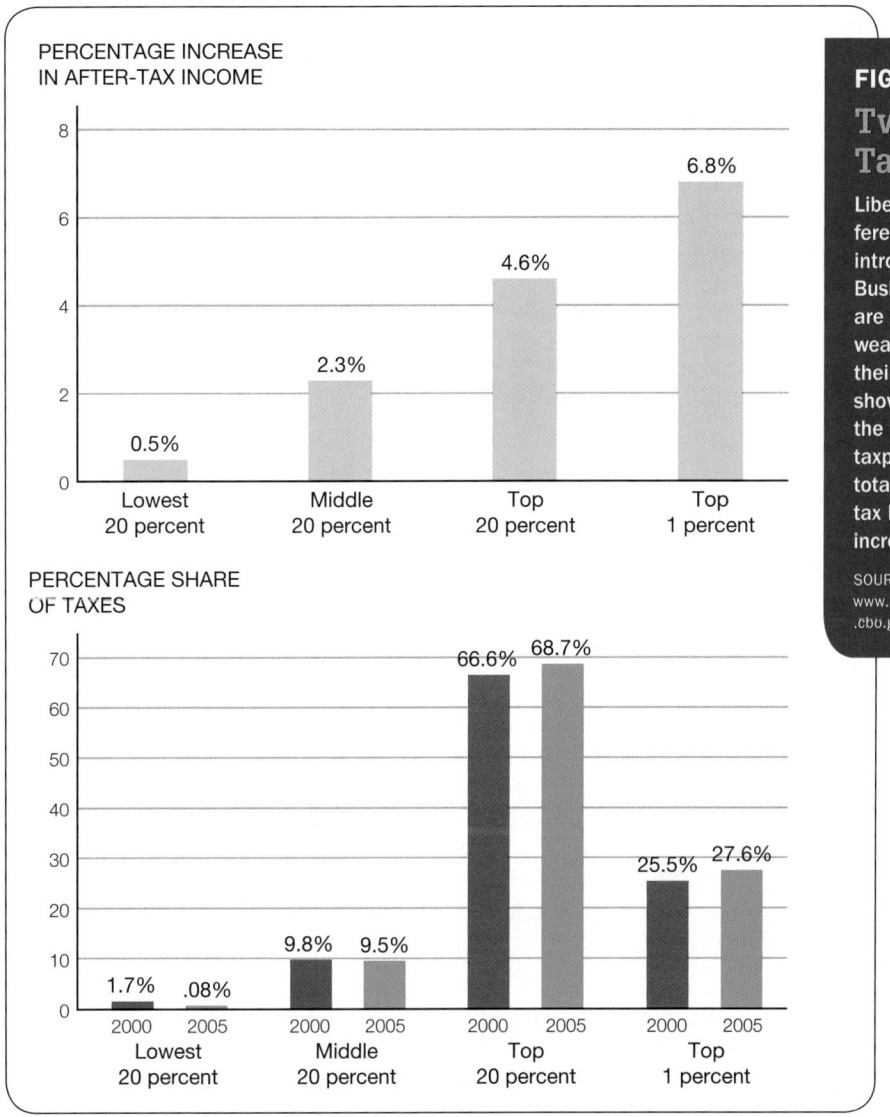

PERCENTAGE INCREASE
IN AFTER-TAX INCOME

- Lowest 20 percent: 0.5%
- Middle 20 percent: 2.3%
- Top 20 percent: 4.6%
- Top 1 percent: 6.8%

PERCENTAGE SHARE
OF TAXES

- Lowest 20 percent: 2000: 1.7%, 2005: .08%
- Middle 20 percent: 2000: 9.8%, 2005: 9.5%
- Top 20 percent: 2000: 66.6%, 2005: 68.7%
- Top 1 percent: 2000: 25.5%, 2005: 27.6%

**FIGURE 16.5**

## Two Perspectives on Tax Cuts

Liberals and conservatives take different perspectives on the tax cuts introduced by President George W. Bush. Liberals charge that the cuts are regressive because they allow wealthy people to keep much more of their pretax income, as the top chart shows. Conservatives contend that the tax cuts benefited less-wealthy taxpayers because their share of the total tax burden declined while the tax burden of the richest taxpayers increased, as the bottom chart shows.

SOURCES: Center on Budget and Policy Priorities, www.cbpp.org; Congressional Budget Office, www.cbo.gov (accessed 3/22/08).

policies designed to reduce after-tax income inequalities would be harmful to the society and the economy.[59]

Are Americans concerned about inequality? Do they want economic policy to reduce inequality? A 2003 study by the Princeton political scientist Larry Bartels showed that the public is indeed aware of rising inequality and that a majority think it is a bad thing.[60] Nonetheless, his research showed that people "fail to connect inequality and public policy." Part of the reason is that many people do not understand where they fit in the tax system. One survey showed that half of the respondents thought that "most families" have to pay the estate tax, when in fact only 2 percent of estates had to pay the tax. Americans' aversion to taxes can make it difficult to have a national debate about raising taxes on higher-income earners. This became evident in the waning days of the 2008 campaign. Questioned about his tax plan, Barack Obama defended his proposal to increase taxes for high earners and to allow many Bush-era tax cuts to expire, as scheduled, in 2010. Obama's casual remark that it made sense to "spread the wealth around" ignited a firestorm of criticism from his opponent, John McCain, who had pledged not to raise taxes at all. The rancor that ensued highlighted the difficulties in conducting a public debate about taxes and inequality.

If widespread concern about inequality is to drive changes in economic policy, the American public needs a better understanding of the relation between economic policy and inequality.

# The Digital Economy

## Inform Yourself

**Read an article about the Internet and the U.S. economy.** While the Internet has changed commerce, business practices, and how individuals communicate, it has also helped grow the U.S. economy. Read an article on this topic at http://money.cnn.com/2012/03/19/news/economy/internet_economy/index.htm. Why do you think the United States lags behind other advanced industrialized countries in the percentage of GDP coming from Internet-related sources?

**Consider whether paper money and credit cards will be replaced by new payment technologies.** Read the "Future of Money" report by the Pew Internet and American Life at http://pewinternet.org/Reports/2012/Future-of-Money.aspx. What do you think? Will the dollar go the way of the dinosaur, or will change to our currency come about more slowly? What are the major barriers to mobile money?

**Watch a video on government Internet policy.** Consider the news report on a program intended to provide Internet to residents of Tampa, Florida, at www.youtube.com/watch?v=RaBOVgMpUCA. What are the pros and cons to government and private-sector programs to provide Internet to more Americans? Should other cities implement such programs? Should the federal government have a role in providing Internet access in the United States? What about state governments?

## Express Yourself

**Weigh in on the future of Internet policy.** The United States is one of 34 countries with market-based economies that are members of the Organisation for Economic Co-operation and Development (OECD). Recently the OECD began to create a standard Internet policy for all the member countries. This report is available at: http://usoecd.usmission.gov/mission/internet.html. Do you support adopting these policies? Contact your members of Congress to let them know. (See Chapter 12 to learn how to identify and contact your representatives.)

*Find links to the sites listed above as well as related activities on wwnorton.com/studyspace.*

## The Goals of Economic Policy

◼ **Identify the broad reasons government gets involved in the economy (pp. 643–54)**

Public policies, which are officially expressed purposes backed by sanctions, can be embodied in laws, rules, regulations, or orders. In contemporary societies, government makes it possible for the economy to function efficiently by setting the rules for economic exchange and punishing those who violate the rules. Through a variety of different policies, the U.S. government has pursued four economic goals over the last century: to promote economic stability, to stimulate economic growth, to promote business development, and to protect employees and consumers.

### Key Terms

**public policy** (p. 643)

**public goods** (p. 644)

**gross domestic product (GDP)** (p. 645)

**inflation** (p. 648)

**categorical grants** (p. 650)

### Practice Quiz

1. Which of the following is *not* one of the reasons that government is involved in the economy? *(pp. 643–54)*

a) to guarantee economic equality
b) to promote economic stability
c) to stimulate economic growth
d) to promote business development
e) to protect employees and consumers

2. The total value of goods and services produced within a country is referred to as *(p. 645)*
a) the Gross National Product.
b) the Gross Domestic Product.
c) the Dow Jones Industrial Average.
d) the federal funds rate.
e) the Gini coefficient.

3. Inflation refers to *(p. 648)*
a) a lack of change in the general level of prices.
b) a tax on imported goods.
c) a consistent increase in the general level of prices.
d) a consistent decrease in the general level of prices.
e) an increase in the interest rate on loans between banks.

 **Practice Online**
Interactive simulation: *Local Planning Commission*

## The Tools of Economic Policy

◼ **Describe how the government uses monetary, fiscal, and regulatory policies to influence the economy (pp. 654–66)**

The sustained growth of the American economy is the result of specific policies enacted by the U.S. government. The Constitution gives the federal government the power to set monetary and fiscal policies. Monetary policy in the United States is determined primarily by the Federal Reserve Board. Most of the U.S. government's revenues come from personal and corporate income taxes, and most of the federal government's budget is now made up of mandatory, rather than discretionary, spending.

### Key Terms

**monetary policies** (p. 654)

**Federal Reserve System** (p. 655)

**reserve requirement** (p. 656)

**open-market operations** (p. 656)

**federal funds rate** (p. 656)

**fiscal policy** (p. 657)

**tariff** (p. 657)

**progressive taxation** (p. 657)

**regressive taxation** (p. 657)

**redistribution** (p. 659)

**loophole** (p. 659)

**budget deficit** (p. 660)

**mandatory spending** (p. 661)

**uncontrollables** (p. 661)

**discretionary spending** (p. 661)

**monopoly** (p. 662)

**antitrust policy** (p. 662)

**deregulation** (p. 664)

**subsidies** (p. 664)

**contracting power** (p. 665)

## Practice Quiz

4. Monetary policy seeks to influence the economy through *(p. 654)*
   a) taxing and spending.
   b) privatizing and nationalizing selected industries.
   c) the availability of credit and money.
   d) foreign exchange of currency.
   e) administrative regulation.

5. Monetary policy is handled largely by *(p. 655)*
   a) Congress.
   b) the Department of the Treasury.
   c) the federal judiciary.
   d) the Federal Reserve System.
   e) the president.

6. A situation in which the government attempts to affect the economy through taxing and spending is an example of *(p. 657)*
   a) a reserve requirement.
   b) an expropriation policy.
   c) a monetary policy.
   d) a fiscal policy.
   e) eminent domain.

7. A tax that places a greater burden on those who are better able to afford it is called *(p. 657)*

a) regressive.
b) progressive.
c) inflationary.
d) a flat tax.
e) voodoo economics.

8. A policy whose objective is to tax or spend in such a way as to reduce the disparities of wealth between the highest and lowest income brackets is called *(p. 659)*
   a) antitrust policy.
   b) deregulation.
   c) discretionary spending.
   d) equalization.
   e) redistribution.

9. Which of the following statements best describes the U.S. budget deficit? *(pp. 660–61)*
   a) The budget deficit grew substantially in the 1980s and declined substantially in the 1990s before rising sharply again in the 2000s.
   b) The budget deficit declined substantially in the 1980s and grew substantially in the late 1990s into the new 2000s.
   c) The budget deficit grew consistently between 1980 and the present.
   d) The budget deficit declined consistently between 1980 and the present.
   e) The budget deficit has remained exactly the same since 1980.

10. Which of the following statements best describes spending in the federal budget? *(p. 661)*
    a) Mandatory and discretionary spending now make up approximately equal parts of the total budget.
    b) Mandatory spending has been outlawed and the total budget is now made up of discretionary spending.
    c) Mandatory spending is now a much larger percentage of the total budget than discretionary spending.
    d) Discretionary spending has been outlawed, and the total budget is now made up of mandatory spending.
    e) Discretionary spending is now a much larger percentage of the total budget than mandatory spending.

# The Environment and the Economy

◼ **Explain why the government tries to balance economic prosperity with policies that protect the environment (pp. 666–72)**

The federal government frequently regulates industry in order to protect the environment. One of the most important environmental issues currently facing the U.S. government is climate change. Policy makers charged with devising approaches to the problem of climate change have identified three basic approaches: mitigation of greenhouse emissions, promotion of alternative energy technologies, and adaptation to a warmer climate.

## Practice Quiz

11. A cap-and-trade system is an example of which kind of policy approach to global warming? *(p. 669)*
    a) adaptation to a warmer climate
    b) Not in My Backyard (NIMBY)
    c) "drill, baby, drill"
    d) mitigation
    e) promoting alternative technologies

# The Politics of Economic Policy Making

■ **Explore why economic policy is often controversial (pp. 672–78)**

Although all politicians want a healthy economy, they often have different views about how to attain it and what the priorities of economic policy should be. The four schools of economic thought that have been most influential with American policy makers, interest groups, and members of the public are laissez-faire capitalism, Keynesianism, monetarism, and supply-side economics. Business organizations are most united around the goal of reducing government regulation and they are the most consistently powerful actors in determining national economic policy.

## Key Terms

**laissez-faire capitalism** (p. 672)

**Keynesians** (p. 673)

**monetarists** (p. 673)

**supply-side economics** (p. 673)

**deficit** (p. 677)

**national debt** (p. 677)

## Practice Quiz

12. The argument for laissez-faire was first elaborated by *(p. 672)*
    a) Ben Bernake.
    b) Milton Friedman.
    c) Alan Greenspan.
    d) James Madison.
    e) Adam Smith.

13. Which of the following economic perspectives argues for an ongoing role for government in the economy? *(p. 673)*
    a) Keynesianism
    b) laissez-faire
    c) libertarianism
    d) monetarism
    e) rational expectations

14. The theories of which economist were used to help justify the increase in government spending during the New Deal? *(p. 674)*
    a) Milton Friedman
    b) Alan Greenspan
    c) John Maynard Keynes
    d) Robert Lucas
    e) Karl Marx

15. Which groups currently have the most political influence in economic policy making? *(p. 678)*
    a) consumer groups
    b) labor unions
    c) business groups
    d) religious organizations
    e) environmental groups

 **Practice Online**
"Video Exercise" *Bush and the Bailout*

# For Further Reading

Auerbach, Alan J., David Card, and John M. Quigley, eds. *Public Policy and the Income Distribution*. New York: Russell Sage Foundation, 2006.

Baldwin, Robert, Martin Cave, and Martin Lodge. *Understanding Regulation*. New York: Oxford University Press, 2012.

Blanchard, Olivier, Paul Romer, Michael Spence, and Joseph Stiglitz. *In the Wake of the Crisis: Leading Economists Reassess Economic Policy*. Cambridge, MA: MIT Press, 2012.

Frank, Robert H. *Falling Behind: How Rising Inequality Harms the Middle Class*. Berkeley: University of California Press, 2007.

Friedman, Milton, and Walter Heller. *Monetary versus Fiscal Policy*. New York: W.W. Norton, 1969.

Hacker, Jacob S., and Paul Pierson. *Winner-Take-All Politics: How Washington Made the Rich Richer—and Turned Its Back on the Middle Class* (New York: Simon and Schuster, 2010).

Harris, Richard A., and Sidney M. Milkis. *The Politics of Regulatory Change*. 2nd ed. New York: Oxford University Press, 1996.

Jacobs, Lawrence, and Theda Skocpol, eds. *Inequality and American Democracy: What We Know and What We Need to Learn*. New York: Russell Sage Foundation, 2005.

Page, Benjamin I., and Lawrence R. Jacobs. *Class War: What Americans Really Think about Economic Inequality*. Chicago: University of Chicago Press, 2009.

Schick, Allen. *The Federal Budget: Politics, Policy, Process.* 3rd ed. Washington, DC: Brookings Institution Press, 2007.

Stein, Robert M., and Kenneth N. Bickers. *Perpetuating the Pork Barrel: Policy Subsystems and American Democracy.* New York: Cambridge University Press, 1995.

Stiglitz, Joseph E. *Globalization and Its Discontents.* New York: W.W. Norton, 2003.

Weir, Margaret. *Politics and Jobs: The Boundaries of Employment Policy in the United States.* Princeton, NJ: Princeton University Press, 1992.

Wells, David. *The Federal Reserve System.* Jefferson, NC: McFarland, 2004.

# Recommended Websites

**Board of Governors of the Federal Reserve System**
www.federalreserve.gov
   The Federal Reserve System consists of 12 banks that use monetary policy to fight inflation and deflation. Visit the Fed's official website to see how it is working to maintain a strong economy.

**Citizens for Tax Justice**
www.ctj.org
   Review federal, state, and local tax laws at the website of Citizens for Tax Justice. This nonprofit organization is dedicated to educating ordinary citizens about tax laws and reducing the tax burden on low- and middle-income Americans.

**National Bureau of Economic Research**
www.nber.org
   The National Bureau of Economic Research is a nonprofit, nonpartisan organization dedicated to creating a better understanding of the economy. Take a minute to review some of its free research publications.

**Tax Foundation**
www.taxfoundation.org/research/topic/9.html
   The Tax Foundation is a respected organization that has been providing Americans with information about tax policy for more than 50 years. Click on your state to learn about current tax and spending policies.

**Treasury Direct**
www.treasurydirect.gov/govt/govt.htm
   Treasury Direct, part of the U.S. Department of the Treasury, provides a statistical look at federal, state, and public debt.

**U.S. Census Bureau: The 2010 Statistical Abstract**
www.census.gov/compendia/statab/brief.html
   The Annual Statistical Abstract, provided by the U.S. Census Bureau, makes available an abundance of statistics on education, welfare, housing, employment, and agriculture.

**U.S. Department of Commerce**
www.commerce.gov
   The U.S. Department of Commerce promotes domestic and international commerce to foster economic progress. Review the initiatives and programs designed to encourage economic development.

Health care is an area of social policy that has been controversial. Although most Americans support universal access to health care, they disagree about the best way to ensure high-quality health care. As Congress considered various proposals in 2009 and 2010, the debate heated up.

# Social Policy

**WHAT GOVERNMENT DOES AND WHY IT MATTERS** Social policies promote a range of public goals. The first is to protect against the risks and insecurities that most people face over the course of their lives. These include illness, disability, temporary unemployment, and the reduced earning capability that comes with old age. Most spending on social welfare in the United States goes to programs that serve these purposes, such as Social Security and medical insurance for the elderly. These programs are widely regarded as successful and popular. Although large projected deficits in both programs have generated conflict, they are the least controversial areas of social spending.

Comprehensive health care reform is more controversial. Most Americans support universal access to health care, but when it comes to specific proposals, they often express doubts. Democrats experienced the public ambivalence about health care reform after they enacted major changes to the system in 2010. The Affordable Care Act is complex legislation that many people find hard to understand. Some parts of it are clearly popular, such as the provision that allows young people to remain on their parents' insurance until they reach the age of 26. Other features, such as the requirement that everyone purchase insurance, with federal assistance, remain unpopular. When the Supreme Court ruled that most of the act, including the individual mandate, was constitutional, the public remained divided. One poll taken right after the Court's ruling showed that 47 percent of Americans approved while 43 percent opposed the decision. Ten percent remained unsure. Nearly two years after its enactment, Americans could not agree about the role government should play in ensuring health care for all.[1]

Two other goals of social policy have also been controversial: promoting equality of opportunity and assisting the poor. Although Americans admire the ideal of equal opportunity, there is no general agreement about what government should do to address inequalities of results: groups that have suffered from past inequality generally support much more extensive government action to promote equality of opportunity than do others. Yet most Americans support some government action, especially in the area of education.

The third goal of social policy, to alleviate poverty, has long generated controversy in the United States. Americans take pride in their strong work ethic and prize the value of self-sufficiency. As a result, the majority of Americans express suspicion that the able-bodied poor will not try hard enough to support themselves if they are offered too much assistance or if they receive the wrong kind of assistance. Yet Americans also recognize that poverty may be the product of past inequality of opportunity. Since the 1960s, a variety of educational programs and income-assistance policies have sought to end poverty and promote equal opportunity. Much progress has been made toward these goals. However, the disproportionate rates of poverty among minorities suggest that our policies have not solved the problem of unequal opportunity. Likewise, the high rates of child poverty challenge us to find new ways to assist the poor.

American social policy reflects the nation's views about which risks should be borne by the individual and which should be shared by society as a whole. As such, social policy reflects public wishes, as would be expected in a democracy. However, Americans often have quite different views about how social policy should advance the value of equality. A majority now believes that America has grown too unequal, and there is broad consensus that equality of opportunity is not only desirable but also an essential part of American culture. There is much less agreement about which social policies are needed to reduce the gulf between the rich and the poor and to promote equality of opportunity. Americans also have different views about how social policy affects liberty. Some argue that it entails no significant curtailment of liberty, whereas others believe that social policy reduces liberty by increasing the size of government and raising taxes.

## chaptergoals

- Trace the history of government programs designed to help the poor (pages 691–703)

- Describe how education, health, and housing policies try to enable people to reach their potential (pages 703–14)

- Explain how contributory and noncontributory programs benefit different groups of Americans (pages 714–20)

# The Welfare State

**Trace the history of government programs designed to help the poor**

For much of American history, local governments and private charities were in charge of caring for the poor. During the 1930s, when this largely private system of charity collapsed in the face of widespread economic destitution, the federal government created the beginnings of an American welfare state. The idea of the welfare state was new; it meant that the national government would oversee programs designed to promote economic security for all Americans—not just for the poor. The American system of social welfare comprises many different policies enacted over the years since the Great Depression. Because each program is governed by distinct rules, the kind and level of assistance available vary widely.

## The History of the Social Welfare System

America has always had a welfare system, but until 1935 it was almost entirely private, composed of an extensive system of voluntary donations through churches and other religious groups, ethnic and fraternal societies, communities and neighborhoods, and philanthropically inclined wealthy individuals. Most often it was called "charity," and although it was private and voluntary, it was thought of as a public obligation.

There were great variations in the generosity of charity from town to town, but one thing seems to have been universal—the tradition of distinguishing between two classes of poor: the "deserving poor" and the "undeserving poor." The deserving poor were widows and orphans and others rendered dependent by some misfortune, such as the death or serious injury of the family's breadwinner in the course

*The creation of the modern social welfare system in the 1930s shifted responsibility for alleviating poverty from private charities, such as settlement houses, to the government. Here, young girls at Minneapolis's Pillsbury Settlement House are taught cooking and other basic housekeeping skills.*

of war or honest labor. The undeserving poor were able-bodied persons unwilling to work, transients new to the community, and others of whom, for various reasons, the community did not approve. This private charity was a very subjective matter: the givers and their agents spent a great deal of time and resources examining the qualifications, both economic and moral, of the seekers of charity.

Before the Great Depression, much of the private charity was given in cash, called "outdoor relief." But because of fears that outdoor relief spawned poverty rather than relieving or preventing it, many communities set up settlement houses and other "indoor relief" institutions. Some of America's most dedicated and unselfish citizens worked in the settlement houses, and their efforts made a significant contribution to the development of the field of social work.

A still-larger institution of indoor relief was the police station, where many of America's poor sought temporary shelter. But even in the severest weather, the homeless could not stay in police stations for many nights without being jailed as vagrants.[2] Indeed, the settlement houses and the police departments were not all that different in their approaches, since social workers in those days tended to consider "all social case work [to be] mental hygiene."[3] And even though not all social workers were budding psychiatrists, "it was true that they focused on counseling and other preventive techniques, obscuring and even ignoring larger structural problems."[4]

The severe limitations on financing faced by private charitable organizations and settlement houses slowly produced a movement by many groups toward public responsibility for some of these charitable or welfare functions. Workers' compensation laws were enacted in a few states, for example, but the effect of such laws was limited because they benefited only workers injured on the job, and of them, only those who worked for certain types of companies. A more important effort, one that led more directly to the modern welfare state, was public aid to mothers with dependent children. Beginning in Illinois in 1911, the movement for mothers' pensions spread to include 40 states by 1926. Initially such aid was viewed as simply an inexpensive alternative to providing "indoor relief" to mothers and their children. Moreover, applicants not only had to pass a rigorous means test but also had to prove they were deserving, because the laws provided that assistance would be given only to individuals who were deemed "physically, mentally, and morally fit." In most states, a mother was deemed unfit if her children were illegitimate.[5]

In effect, these criteria proved to be racially discriminatory. Many African Americans in the South and ethnic immigrants in the North were denied benefits on the grounds of "moral unfitness." Furthermore, local governments were allowed to decide whether to establish such pension programs. In the South, many counties with large numbers of African American women refused to implement assistance programs.

Despite the spread of state government programs to assume some of the obligation to relieve the poor, the private sector remained dominant until the 1930s. Even as late as 1928 only 11.6 percent of all relief granted in 15 of the largest cities came from public funds.[6] Nevertheless, the various state and local public experiences provided guidance and precedents for the national government's welfare system.

The traditional approach, dominated by the private sector, with its severe distinction between deserving and undeserving poor, crumbled in the face of the stark reality of the Great Depression in 1929. During the depression, misfortune became so widespread and private wealth shrank so drastically that private charity was out of the question, and the distinction between deserving and undeserving became

*During the Depression, the government took a more active role in helping poor and struggling Americans. Here, people line up to receive free bread.*

impossible to draw. Around 20 percent of the workforce immediately became unemployed; this figure grew as the depression stretched into years. Moreover, few of these individuals had any monetary resources or any family farm on which to fall back. Banks failed, wiping out the savings of millions who had been fortunate enough to have any savings at all. Thousands of businesses failed as well, throwing middle-class Americans onto the bread lines along with unemployed laborers, dispossessed farmers, and those who had never worked in any capacity whatsoever. The Great Depression proved to Americans that poverty could be a result of imperfections in the economic system as well as of individual irresponsibility. It also forced Americans to drastically alter their standards regarding who was deserving and who was not.

Once poverty and dependency were accepted as problems inherent in the economic system, a large-scale public policy approach was not far away. By the time the Roosevelt administration took office in 1933, the question was not whether there was to be a public welfare system but how generous or restrictive that system would be.

## Foundations of the Welfare State

If the welfare state were truly a state, its founding would be the Social Security Act of 1935. This act created two separate categories of welfare: contributory and noncontributory. The Who Are Americans? page lists some of the key areas in which the government provides assistance and presents recent data on the numbers of beneficiaries and the money spent on these programs.

**Contributory Programs** The category of welfare programs financed by taxation can justifiably be called "forced savings"; these programs force working Americans to contribute a portion of their earnings to provide income and benefits for present-day retirees, with the understanding that younger workers will one

**contributory programs** social programs financed in whole or in part by taxation or other mandatory contributions by their present or future recipients

**Social Security** a contributory welfare program into which working Americans contribute a percentage of their wages and from which they receive cash benefits after retirement

**Medicare** a form of national health insurance for the elderly and the disabled

**indexing** periodic process of adjusting social benefits or wages to account for increases in the cost of living

**cost-of-living adjustments (COLAs)** changes made to the level of benefits of a government program based on the rate of inflation

**noncontributory programs** social programs that provide assistance to people on the basis of demonstrated need rather than any contribution they have made

**means testing** a procedure by which potential beneficiaries of a public-assistance program establish their eligibility by demonstrating a genuine need for the assistance

day provide for them in the same way. These **contributory programs** are what most people have in mind when they refer to **Social Security** or social insurance. Under the original contributory program, old-age insurance, the employer and the employee were each required to pay equal amounts, which in 1937 were set at 1 percent of the first $3,000 in wages, to be deducted from the paycheck of each employee and matched by the same amount from the employer. This percentage has increased over the years; the contribution in 2012 was 7.65 percent subdivided as follows: 6.2 percent on the first $110,100 of income for Social Security benefits, plus 1.45 percent on all earnings for Medicare.[7]

Social Security may seem to be a rather conservative approach to welfare. In effect, the Social Security tax, as a forced saving, sends a message that people cannot be trusted to save voluntarily to take care of their own needs. But in another sense, it is quite radical. Social Security is not real insurance; workers' contributions do not accumulate in a personal account, as they would in an annuity. Consequently, contributors do not receive benefits in proportion to their contributions, and this means that a redistribution of wealth is occurring. In brief, Social Security mildly redistributes wealth from higher- to lower-income people, and it quite significantly redistributes wealth from younger workers to older retirees.

Congress increased Social Security benefits every two or three years during the 1950s and '60s. The biggest single expansion in contributory programs since 1935 was the establishment in 1965 of **Medicare**, which provides substantial medical services to elderly persons who are already eligible to receive old-age, survivors', and disability insurance under the original Social Security system. In 1972, Congress decided to end the grind of biennial legislation to increase benefits by establishing **indexing**, whereby benefits paid out under contributory programs would be modified annually by **cost-of-living adjustments (COLAs)** designed to increase benefits to keep up with the rate of inflation. But of course Social Security taxes (contributions) also increased after almost every benefit increase. This made Social Security, in the words of one observer, "a politically ideal program. It bridged partisan conflict by providing liberal benefits under conservative financial auspices."[8] In other words, conservatives could more readily yield to the demands of the well-organized and ever-growing constituency of elderly voters if benefit increases were automatic; liberals could cement conservative support by agreeing to finance the increased benefits through increases in the regressive Social Security tax, paid into a special Social Security fund, rather than out of the general revenues coming from the more progressive income tax, which are paid into the Treasury. (See Chapter 16 for a discussion of regressive and progressive taxes.)

**Noncontributory Programs** Programs to which beneficiaries do not have to contribute—**noncontributory programs**—are also known as "public assistance programs," or, more commonly, as "welfare." Until 1996 the most important noncontributory program was Aid to Families with Dependent Children (AFDC)—originally called Aid to Dependent Children, or ADC—which was founded in 1935 by the original Social Security Act. In 1996, Congress abolished AFDC and replaced it with the Temporary Assistance for Needy Families (TANF) block grant. Eligibility for public assistance is determined by **means testing**, a procedure that requires applicants to show a financial need for assistance. Between 1935 and 1965, the government created programs to provide housing assistance, school lunches, and food stamps to other needy Americans.

Like contributory programs, the noncontributory public assistance programs also made their most significant advances during the 1960s and '70s. The largest single

# Who Benefits from Social Programs?

Almost all Americans benefit from public welfare programs at some point in their lives. The biggest public welfare programs are contributory programs like Social Security (retirement and old-age benefits) and Medicare. Programs that offer income maintenance benefits—including the TANF benefits that people sometimes refer to when they talk about "being on welfare"—are generally smaller and less expensive.

## Number of Recipients, 2009 (in millions)

52.5 million **Old-Age, Survivors, and Disability Insurance**

46.6 million **Medicare**

12.96 million **Unemployment compensation**

*CONTRIBUTORY PROGRAMS*

61.825 million **Medicaid**

31.3 million **School Lunch Program**

33.5 million **SNAP (Food Stamps)**

7.7 million **State Children's Health Insurance Program***

7.7 million **Supplementary Security Income**
**(for aged, blind, disabled)**

4.193 million **Temporary Assistance to Needy Families (TANF)**

3.9 million **Veterans Benefits Payments**

*NONCONTRIBUTORY PROGRAMS*

## Public Welfare Programs, 2011 (in billions)

$913.038 billion **Medical payments**

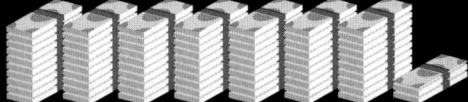

$724.174 billion **Retirement and disability insurance benefits**

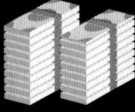

$188.405 billion
**Income maintenance benefits**

$118.607 billion
**Unemployment insurance benefits**

$107.776 billion
**Veterans benefits**

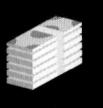

$58.565 billion
**Federal education and training assistance**

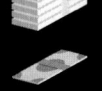

$2.8 billion **Other**

\* 2010 data.

SOURCES:
U.S. Census Bureau,
2012 Statistical Abstract;
Office of Management and
Budget, Fiscal Year 2013
Historical Tables.

## for critical analysis

1. Which group does the government spend more money on—the elderly or poor families with children?

2. If contributory programs are paid for by contributions from the future recipients, why are they sometimes controversial?

*After 1935 the federal government created new programs to help poor families. For example, the federally funded school lunch program provides nutritious meals for needy children.*

**Medicaid** a federally and state-financed, state-operated program providing medical services to low-income people

**Supplemental Nutrition Assistance Program (SNAP)** the largest anti-poverty program, which provides recipients with a debit card for food at most grocery stores; formerly known as *food stamps*

**in-kind benefits** noncash goods and services provided to needy individuals and families by the federal government

category of expansion was the establishment in 1965 of **Medicaid**, a program that provides extended medical services to all low-income persons who have already established eligibility through means testing under AFDC or TANF. Noncontributory programs underwent another major transformation during the 1970s in the level of benefits they provide. Besides being means tested, noncontributory programs are federal rather than state-based; grants-in-aid are provided by the federal government to the states as incentives to establish the programs (see Chapter 3). Thus, from the beginning there were considerable disparities in benefits from state to state. The national government sought to rectify the disparities in levels of old-age benefits in 1974 by creating the Supplemental Security Income (SSI) program to augment benefits for the aged, the blind, and the disabled. SSI provides uniform minimum benefits across the entire nation and includes mandatory COLAs. States are allowed to be more generous if they wish, but no state is permitted to provide benefits below the minimum level set by the national government. As a result, 25 states increased their SSI benefits to the mandated level.

The TANF program is also administered by the states and, as with the old-age benefits just discussed, benefit levels vary widely from state to state (see Figure 17.1). For example, in 2008, the states' monthly TANF benefits for a family of three varied from $170 in Mississippi to $923 in Alaska.[9] Even the most generous TANF payments are well below the federal poverty line. In 2011 the poverty level for a family of three included those earning less than $18,123 a year or $1,51 a month.[10]

The number of people receiving AFDC benefits expanded in the 1970s, in part because new welfare programs had been established during the mid-1960s: Medicaid (discussed earlier) and the **Supplemental Nutrition Assistance Program (SNAP)**, which is still sometimes called by its old name, food stamps. These programs provide what are called **in-kind benefits**—noncash goods and services that would otherwise have to be paid for in cash by the beneficiary. Because AFDC recipients automatically received Medicaid and food stamps, these new programs created an incentive for poor Americans to establish their eligibility for AFDC.

Another, more complex reason for the growth of AFDC in the 1970s was that it became more difficult for the government to terminate people's AFDC benefits

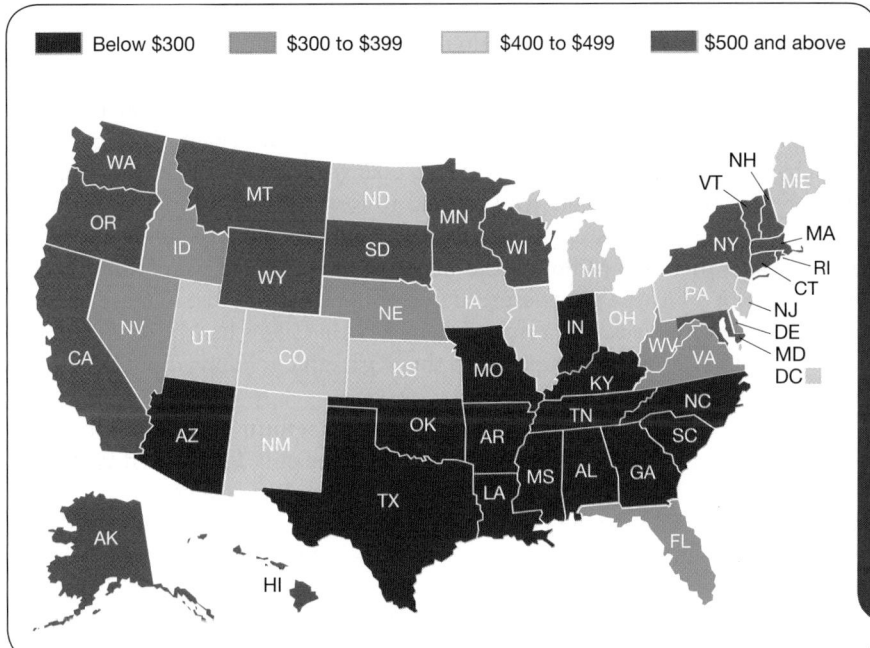

| Below $300 | $300 to $399 | $400 to $499 | $500 and above |

**FIGURE 17.1**

## Monthly Spending on TANF Benefits

Spending on TANF benefits varies widely across the country. In 14 states, monthly benefits for a family of three are below $300; in 17 states, they are above $500 a month. In which regions does spending on TANF benefits tend to be higher? In which regions is it generally lower?

SOURCE: Gene Falk, "The Temporary Assistance for Needy Families Block Grant, Congressional Research Service," October 11, 2011, www.nationalaglawcenter.org/assets/crs/RL32760.pdf (accessed 7/6/12).

for lack of eligibility. In the 1970 case of *Goldberg v. Kelly*, the Supreme Court held that the financial benefits of AFDC could not be revoked without due process—that is, a hearing at which evidence is presented.[11] This ruling inaugurated the concept of **entitlement**, a class of government benefits with a status similar to that of property (which, according to the Fourteenth Amendment, cannot be taken from people "without due process of law"). *Goldberg v. Kelly* did not provide that the beneficiary had a "right" to government benefits; it provided that once a person's eligibility for AFDC was established, and as long as the program was still in effect, that person could not be denied benefits without due process. The decision left open the possibility that Congress could terminate the program and its benefits by way of legislation. If the welfare benefit were truly a property right, Congress would have no authority to deny it.

**entitlement** a legal obligation of the federal government to provide payments to individuals, or groups of individuals, according to eligibility criteria or benefit rules

Thus the establishment of in-kind benefit programs and the legal obstacles involved in terminating benefits contributed to the growth of the welfare state. But it is important to note that real federal spending (that is, spending adjusted for inflation) on AFDC itself did not rise after the mid-1970s. Unlike Social Security, AFDC was not indexed to inflation; without cost-of-living adjustments, the value of AFDC benefits fell by more than one-third. Moreover, the largest noncontributory welfare program, Medicaid, actually devotes less than one-third of its expenditures to poor families; the rest goes to the disabled and the elderly in nursing homes.[12]

## Welfare Reform

From the 1960s to the 1990s, opinion polls consistently showed that the public viewed welfare beneficiaries as "undeserving."[13] Underlying that judgment was the belief that welfare recipients did not want to work. The Progressive-era reformers who first designed AFDC wanted single mothers to stay at home with their children. Motivated by horror stories of children killed in accidents while their mothers were off working or of children tied up at home all day in order to be kept safe, these reformers believed that it was better for the child if the mother did not work. By the 1960s, as more women entered the labor force and as welfare rolls rose, welfare recipients appeared in a more unfavorable light. Common criticisms charged that welfare recipients were taking advantage of the system, that they were irresponsible people who refused to work. These negative assessments were amplified by racial stereotypes. By 1973, 46 percent of welfare recipients were African American. Although the majority of recipients were white, media portrayals helped create the widespread perception that the vast majority of welfare recipients were black. A careful study by Martin Gilens has shown how racial stereotypes of blacks as uncommitted to the work ethic reinforced public opposition to welfare.[14]

Despite public opposition, it proved difficult to reform welfare. While many reformers wanted to require work in exchange for benefits, few wished to be seen as harming children by eliminating benefits. Yet providing services, such as child care, that would enable single mothers to work would require spending substantially more on welfare. And most reformers wished to spend less, not more, on the program. Congress added modest work requirements in 1967, but little changed in the administration of welfare. A more significant reform in 1988 imposed stricter work requirements but also provided additional support services, such as child care and transportation assistance. This compromise legislation reflected a growing consensus that effective reform entailed a combination of sticks (work requirements) and carrots (extra services to make work possible). The 1988 reform also created a new system to identify the absent parent (usually the father) and enforce child-support payments.

These reforms were barely implemented when welfare rolls rose again with the recession of the early 1990s, reaching an all-time high in 1994. Sensing continuing public frustration with welfare, when Bill Clinton was a presidential candidate he vowed "to end welfare as we know it," an unusual promise for a Democrat. Once in office, Clinton found it difficult to design a plan that would provide an adequate safety net for recipients unable to find work. One possibility, to provide government jobs as a last resort, was rejected as too expensive. Clinton's major achievement in the welfare field was to increase the Earned Income Tax Credit. This credit now allows working parents whose annual income falls below $49,078 (for a family of three or more) to file through their income tax return for an income supplement of up to $5,751, depending on their income and family size. It was a first step toward realizing Clinton's campaign promise to ensure that "if you work, you shouldn't be poor."

Congressional Republicans proposed a much more dramatic reform of welfare, which Clinton, facing a campaign for re-election in 1996, signed. The Personal Responsibility and Work Opportunity Reconciliation Act (PRWORA) repealed AFDC. In place of the individual entitlement to assistance, the new law created block grants to the states and allowed states much more discretion in designing their cash-assistance programs to needy families. The new law also established time limits, restricting recipients to two years of assistance and creating a lifetime limit of five years. It imposed new work requirements on those receiving welfare, and it restricted most legal immigrants from receiving benefits. The aim of the new law was to reduce welfare caseloads, promote work, and reduce out-of-wedlock births. Notably, reducing poverty was not one of its stated objectives.

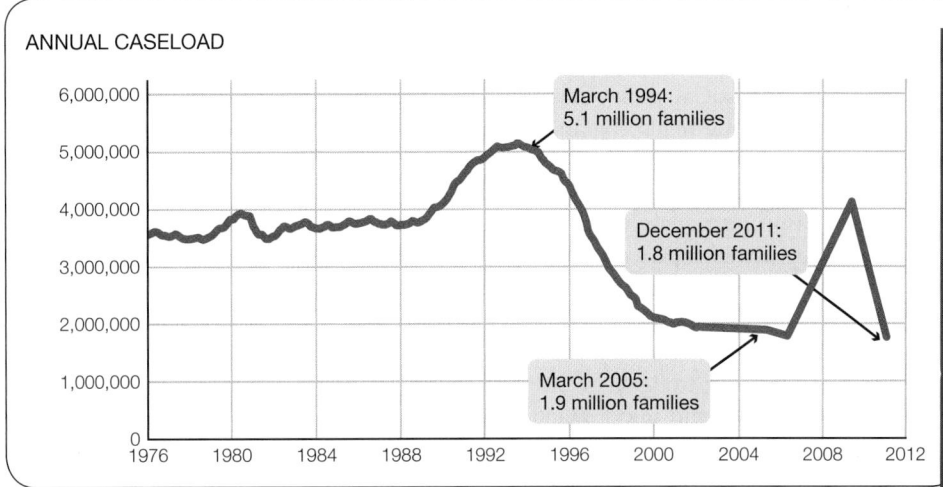

ANNUAL CASELOAD

March 1994:
5.1 million families

December 2011:
1.8 million families

March 2005:
1.9 million families

FIGURE 17.2

Welfare Caseload, 1976–2011

Welfare caseloads began to decline even before the 1996 reform. They have continued to plummet in the years since welfare reform. Welfare caseloads remained low even during the recession of the that began in 2008. Does the decline in the welfare caseload show that the 1996 reform was successful?

SOURCE: U.S. Department of Health and Human Services, Administration for Children and Families, Data and Reports, www .acf.hhs.gov/programs/ ofa/data-reports/index.htm (accessed 7/6/12).

After this law was enacted, the number of families receiving assistance dropped by 60 percent nationwide (see Figure 17.2). The sharp decline in the number of recipients was widely hailed as a sign that the welfare reform was working. Indeed, former welfare recipients have been more successful at finding and keeping jobs than many critics of the law predicted. One important indicator of how welfare has changed is the proportion of funds it provides in cash assistance. Before the 1996 reform, assistance was provided largely in the form of a cash grant. By 2008, 70 percent of welfare funds were allocated for noncash assistance and 30 percent for cash assistance. This means that an increasing proportion of welfare funds is spent on such costs as assistance with transportation to work, temporary shelter, or one-time payments for emergencies so that people do not go on the welfare rolls. The orientation of assistance has shifted away from subsidizing people who are not in the labor force and toward addressing temporary problems that low-income people face and providing assistance that facilitates work.[15] The law has been less successful in other respects: researchers have found no clear evidence that it has helped reduce out-of-wedlock births. And critics point out that most former welfare recipients are not paid enough to pull their families out of poverty. The law has helped reduce welfare caseloads, but it has done little to reduce poverty.[16]

As the economy soured in 2009 and 2010, the number of people on welfare rolls began to move upward, but at a very slow rate. The American Recovery and Reinvestment Act of 2009 included a TANF Emergency Fund that provided monies for states to create subsidized jobs for low-income parents and young adults. Despite these measures, many advocates for the poor worried that the state TANF programs were not assisting enough poor families. After the Emergency Fund expired in 2011, advocates for the poor charged that, with states making deep cuts to their budgets, TANF was not keeping pace with the growth of poverty caused by the recession.[17] They contrasted it to the growth of the supplemental nutrition program (SNAP, or food stamps), whose growth closely tracked the rise in unemployment and poverty during the recession. In 2007, before the recession took hold, approximately 26.3 million individuals received SNAP benefits. By 2012, that number had risen to more than 46 million people a month, close to 15 percent of all Americans.[18]

for critical analysis

Why was AFDC such an unpopular program? How did the creation of TANF alter welfare and what has it meant for TANF as an anti-poverty program? Should TANF be reformed again?

## How Do We Pay for the Welfare State?

Since the 1930s, when the main elements of the welfare state were first created, spending on social policy has grown dramatically. Most striking has been the growth of entitlement programs, the largest of which are Social Security and Medicare. The costs of entitlement programs grew from 26 percent of the total federal budget in 1962 to 61 percent by 2012. Funds to pay for these social programs have come disproportionately from increases in payroll taxes. In 1970, social insurance taxes accounted for 23 percent of all federal revenues; in 2012 they had grown to 34.1 percent of all federal revenues. Revenue from social insurance taxes dropped between 2010 and 2012 because Congress enacted a temporary payroll tax cut to help stimulate the sagging economy.[19] Since 1970, corporate taxes have fallen from 17 percent to 9.6 percent of all federal revenues. Because the payroll tax is regressive, low- and middle-income families have carried the burden for funding increased social spending.

Although much public attention has centered on welfare and other social spending programs for the poor, such as food stamps, these programs account for only a small proportion of social spending. For example, even at its height, AFDC made up only 1 percent of the federal budget. In recent years, Congress has tightly controlled spending on most means-tested programs, and lawmakers and government officials currently express little concern that spending on such programs is out of control. The biggest spending increases have come in social insurance programs that provide benefits to a broad spectrum of the population. Such expenditures are hard to control because these programs are entitlements, and the government has promised to cover all people who fit the category of beneficiary. So, for example, the burgeoning elderly population will require that spending on Social Security automatically increase in the future. Furthermore, because Social Security benefits are indexed to inflation, there is no easy way to reduce benefits. Spending on medical programs (Medicare and Medicaid) has also proved difficult to control, in part because of the growing numbers of people eligible for the programs but also because of rising health care costs. Health care expenditures have risen much more steeply than inflation in recent years (Figure 17.3).

*Recent reports have estimated that by 2033 the Social Security system will be unable to pay full benefits. President Bush advocated creating private retirement accounts as a way of reforming Social Security, but opponents of the plan successfully argued that it was too risky.*

Concern about social spending has centered on Social Security because the aging of the baby-boom generation will force spending up sharply in the coming decades. Indeed, under current law, the Social Security Trust Fund, the special government account from which Social Security payments are made, is projected to experience a shortfall beginning in 2033. Critics also contend that Americans are not getting their money's worth from Social Security and that workers would be better off if they could take at least part of the payroll tax that currently pays for Social Security and invest it in individual accounts. They highlight unfavorable rates of return in the current system, noting, for example, that a male worker born in 2000 who is single can expect to see a return of only 0.86 percent on his Social Security contributions. This is well below what an insured bank account would pay and far below stock market returns over the past decades.[20] These arguments have received less attention since the economic recession, which started in 2008, and the stock market volatility that accompanied it. President George W. Bush came to office supporting Social Security reforms, including the creation of private retirement accounts. Soon after taking office, the president appointed a Social Security Commission, whose final report

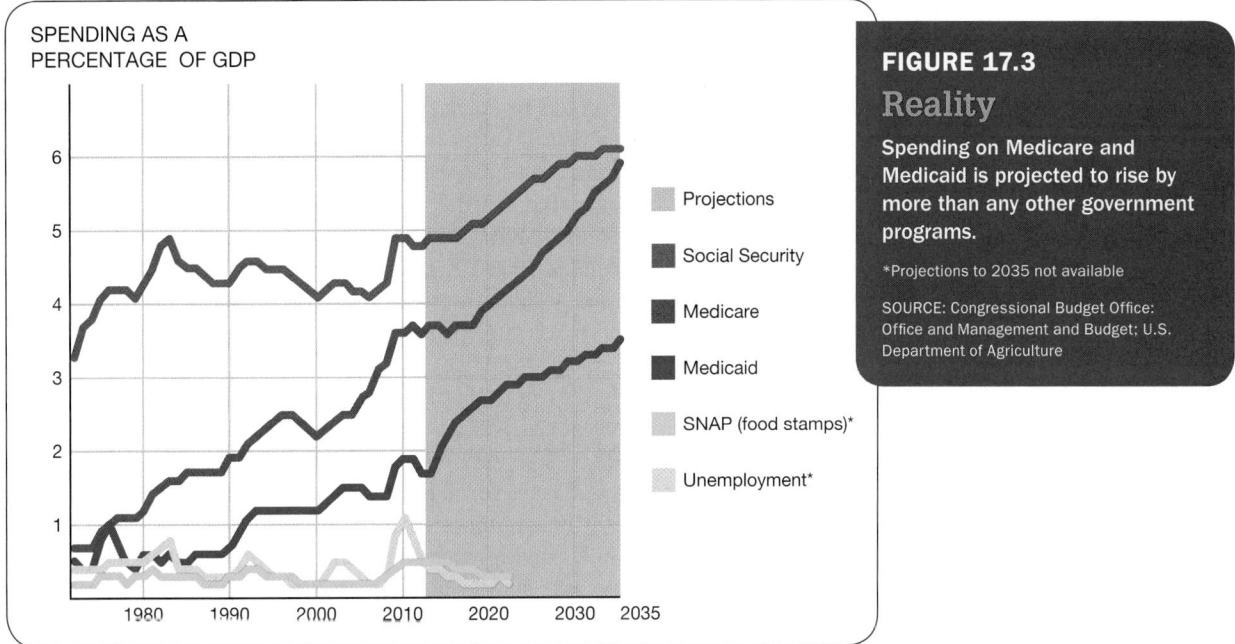

SPENDING AS A PERCENTAGE OF GDP

**FIGURE 17.3**
Reality

Spending on Medicare and Medicaid is projected to rise by more than any other government programs.

*Projections to 2035 not available

SOURCE: Congressional Budget Office; Office and Management and Budget; U.S. Department of Agriculture

Legend:
- Projections
- Social Security
- Medicare
- Medicaid
- SNAP (food stamps)*
- Unemployment*

prominently featured individual accounts as a reform strategy. The commission recommended three reform plans, each of which offered workers the choice of contributing a portion (ranging from 2 to 4 percent) of the payroll tax to an individual account. The worker's traditional benefits would be reduced by the amount diverted to the individual account. According to the commission, individual plans would create a better system because they would allow workers to accumulate assets and build wealth that could be passed on to their children.[21]

Because Social Security is such a popular program, proposed changes that might weaken it are generally greeted with suspicion. Given the politically volatile character of debates about Social Security, the president backed off from proposing any changes in the program during his first term. Nonetheless, in 2004, immediately after his reelection, Bush announced that he would make Social Security reform a centerpiece of his next administration. Although the president did not put forth a precise plan, private accounts were at the heart of his approach to reform. During the first half of 2005, the president toured the country attempting to win support for his ideas. But he immediately faced huge opposition as unions and AARP mobilized to oppose him. AARP launched a national advertising campaign against private accounts, with slogans designed to highlight the risks and radical nature of the president's proposal: "If we feel like gambling, we'll play the slots," and "If you have a problem with the sink, you don't tear down the entire house." Senate Democrats, displaying unusual unity, closed ranks against the president's ideas. By October 2005 the president had to admit that Social Security reform was dead. When Republicans gained control of the House of Representatives in 2011, they remembered Bush's experience and refrained from proposing changes to Social Security.

Supporters of the current Social Security system contend that the system's financial troubles are exaggerated. They dispute arguments that deficits require cuts in Social Security. They point out that Social Security taxes were raised in 1983 and that the program's trust funds were officially placed "off budget," in a so-called lockbox, so that the program would be prepared to serve the aging baby-boom generation.[22]

**for critical analysis**

Is Social Security a policy "in crisis"? What changes are policy makers discussing to alter Social Security so that future generations can have a secure retirement?

They argue that instead of saving that money, however, the federal government cut taxes on the wealthy and used Social Security taxes to finance the deficit in the federal operating budget. Advocates of the current system believe that many of Social Security's troubles could be solved by raising income taxes on the wealthy and eliminating the cap on payroll taxes. In 2012 only the first $110,100 in income was subject to the payroll tax. If this cap were lifted, these critics argue, the resulting revenues would cut the expected shortfall in the Social Security Trust Fund in half.

Supporters of the current system are also deeply skeptical about the benefits of individual accounts. They charged that President Bush presented a rosy scenario that overestimated likely gains through the stock market. When more realistic assumptions are adopted and the costs of the private accounts are considered, the critics argue, individual accounts would not provide higher benefits than the current system. Moreover, they note that individual accounts would do nothing to solve the budget crisis that Social Security will face.[23]

Finally, supporters of the present system emphasize that Social Security is not just a retirement account but also a social insurance program that provides "income protection to workers and their families if the wage earner retires, becomes disabled, or dies."[24] Because it provides this social insurance protection, supporters argue, Social Security's returns should not be compared with those of a private retirement account.

In 2010, President Obama appointed a bipartisan commission on reducing the national debt, which recommended reforms to Social Security. The commission recommended increasing Social Security taxes on the wealthy, increasing the age for receiving benefits, and gradually reducing future benefits. But in a charged political context, neither party wanted to take the initiative on reforms that would ensure that Social Security remain solvent.

Although much of the public debate has focused on the costs of Social Security, most experts agree that Medicare and Medicaid pose the biggest budget challenge. The rapidly rising cost of health care—often at twice the rate of inflation—makes it much harder to control how much the government spends. Moreover, as more of the large baby-boom generation reaches 65, the costs of Medicare are expected to skyrocket. While payroll taxes are sufficient to cover Social Security payments fully until 2036, and small changes in benefits and taxes would see the program through the baby-boom retirement years, the cost challenges to Medicare are much more significant. In 2010, payroll taxes accounted for only 37 percent of all Medicare revenues; 43 percent came from general revenues.[25] In 2011, Medicare accounted for 15 percent of the federal budget, and Medicare costs present an ongoing challenge in the effort to reduce the deficit.

A sweeping plan for reforming Medicare and Medicaid came from Paul Ryan (R-Wisc.), who in 2011 proposed replacing the current program with payments—called "premium support"—that could be used to help pay for private insurance. The plan called for converting Medicaid from an entitlement program, where costs are shared between the federal government and the states, to a block grant. The block grant would provide federal funds to the state but would not guarantee eligibility to some groups as does an entitlement.

An analysis of the Ryan Plan by the Congressional Budget Office showed that while the plan might reduce the deficit, it would require elderly beneficiaries to pay substantially more for health care and would likely leave current Medicaid beneficiaries without health care coverage.[26] These proposals met with intense opposition from Democrats. Public opposition to the proposed Medicare changes played a significant role in Republican defeat in a 2011 special election for a normally

Republican New York state district. After that defeat, Republicans backed off on their proposals to redesign Medicare and Medicaid. Even so, rising health care expenditures and budget deficits meant that the issue of controlling costs in Medicare and Medicaid will remain on the national agenda.

# ● Opening Opportunity

**Describe how education, health, and housing policies try to enable people to reach their potential**

The welfare state not only supplies a measure of economic security, but also provides opportunity. The American belief in **equality of opportunity** makes such programs particularly important. Programs that provide opportunity keep people from falling into poverty and offer a hand up to those who are poor. At their best, opportunity policies allow all individuals to rise as high as their talents will take them. Three types of policies are most significant in opening opportunity: education policies, health policies, and housing policies.

**equality of opportunity** a widely shared American ideal that all people should have the freedom to use whatever talents and wealth they have to reach their fullest potential

## Education Policies

Those who understand American federalism from Chapter 3 already are aware that most of the education of the American people is provided by the public policies of state and local governments. What may be less obvious is that these education policies—especially the policy of universal compulsory public education—are the most important single force in the distribution and redistribution of opportunity in America.

For most of American history, the federal government has played only a minor role in education. In the early years of the nation, the government assisted schools through the Land Ordinance of 1785 and the Northwest Ordinance of 1787, both of which ensured that lands were set aside for public schools and their maintenance. In 1862, Congress established land-grant colleges with the Morrill Act. After World War II the federal government stepped up its role in education policy with the enactment of the GI Bill of Rights of 1944, the National Defense Education Act (NDEA) of 1958, the Elementary and Secondary Education Act of 1965 (ESEA), and various youth and adult vocational training acts since 1958. Note, however, that since the GI Bill was aimed almost entirely at postsecondary schooling, the national government did not truly enter the field of elementary education until after 1957.[27]

What finally brought the national government into elementary education was embarrassment that the Soviet Union had beaten the United States into space with the launching of *Sputnik*. The national policy under NDEA was aimed specifically at improving education in science and mathematics. General federal aid for education did not come until ESEA, in 1965, which allocated funds to school districts with substantial numbers of children from families who were unemployed or earning less than $2,000 a year. By the early 1970s, federal expenditures for elementary and secondary education were running over $4 billion per year, and rose to a peak in 1980 at $4.8 billion.[28]

Ronald Reagan's administration signaled a new focus for federal education policy: the pursuit of higher standards. In 1983 the Department of Education issued

**for critical analysis**
What factors led to the expansion of governmental power (both state and national) over social policy? What factors might lead to a decrease in governmental activity in social policy? How do you think social policy in the United States will change in the future?

*A Nation at Risk*, an influential report that identified low educational standards as the cause of America's declining international economic competitiveness. The report did not suggest any changes in federal policy, but it urged states to make excellence in education their primary goal. This theme was picked up again by President George H. W. Bush. Because Republicans have historically opposed a strong federal role in education, the initiatives of Reagan and Bush remained primarily advisory, but they were very influential in focusing educational reform on standards and testing, now widely practiced across the states.

The federal role was substantially increased by President George W. Bush's signature education act, the No Child Left Behind Act of 2001. This act created stronger federal requirements for testing and school accountability. It requires that every child in grades three through eight be tested yearly for proficiency in math and reading. For a school to be judged a success, it has to show positive test results for all subcategories of children—minority race and ethnicity, English learners, and disability—not just overall averages. Parents whose child is in a failing school have the right to transfer the child to a better school. Because of strong congressional opposition to creating a national test, the states were made responsible for setting standards and devising appropriate tests.

As we saw in Chapter 3, No Child Left Behind initially attracted broad bipartisan support, but it quickly generated considerable controversy. Many states branded it an unfunded mandate, noting that the law placed expensive new obligations on the schools to improve their performance but provided woefully inadequate resources. Teachers objected that "teaching to the test" undermined critical thinking. In some states, up to half the schools failed to meet the new standards, presenting a costly remedial challenge. Under the federal law, they were required to improve student performance by providing such new services as supplemental tutoring, longer school days, and additional summer school.

Faced with these conflicts, the Obama administration sought a major overhaul of No Child Left Behind. But by 2011, with Congress unable to agree on new legislation, the administration initiated its own reform. The president announced that states could apply for waivers that would exempt them from some of the

**for critical analysis**

Why is the No Child Left Behind Act, initially passed with bipartisan support, so controversial today? Should the federal government be involved in setting standards for educational progress? Or is this a job better left to the states?

*Education policy is the most important means of providing equal opportunity for all Americans. President Obama sought to overhaul some problematic aspects of the No Child Left Behind Act, but Congress struggled to agree on the new provisions.*

requirements of No Child Left Behind. Waivers would be granted if states could show that they had their own plans for improving student achievement. One requirement that had become especially troublesome was the mandate that all students be proficient in reading and math by 2014. As that date drew closer, it became apparent that few, if any, schools would meet that standard. In 2012 the administration made good on its promise and granted 26 states waivers from key requirements of No Child Left Behind.[29] As other states prepared to request waivers, it became apparent that a rebalancing of federal and state responsibilities was taking place, with a return to more state control over educational standards and student achievement. Even so, the Obama administration had put its own imprint on schools with its strong support for charter schools—publicly funded schools that are free from the bureaucratic rules and regulations of the school district in which they are located and free to design specialized curricula and to use resources in ways they think most effective. Since the creation of the first charter schools in Minnesota in 1990, states across the country have passed legislation to authorize them. Many states, however, proceeded slowly, establishing caps on the number of new charter schools that could be created each year. The Obama administration put its weight behind charter schools in one of its first pieces of legislation, the American Reinvestment and Recovery Act, sometimes called the stimulus bill. The act included a new $4.3 billion program called Race to the Top, which offered competitive grants to state education systems. To be eligible for the grants, states had to agree to lift the caps on the number of charter schools that could be created each year. In the end, the administration awarded sizeable grants to 11 states and Washington, D.C., praising the states for proposing bold new programs for assessing teachers and overhauling failing schools.[30]

## Health Policies

Until recent decades, no government in the United States (national, state, or local) concerned itself directly with individual health. But public responsibility was always accepted for *public* health. After New York City's newly created Board of Health was credited with holding down a cholera epidemic in 1867, most states created statewide public health agencies. Within a decade, the results were obvious. Between 1884 and 1894, for example, Massachusetts's rate of infant mortality dropped from 161.3 per 1,000 to 141.4 per 1,000.[31]

The U.S. Public Health Service (USPHS) has been in existence since 1798 but was a small part of public health policy until after World War II. Established in 1937 but little noticed for 20 years was the National Institutes of Health (NIH), an agency within the USPHS that was created to do biomedical research. Between 1950 and 2012, NIH expenditures by the national government increased from $160.0 million to $30.9 billion. NIH research on the link between smoking and disease led to one of the most visible public-health campaigns in American history. The Centers for Disease Control and Prevention (CDC), which monitors outbreaks of disease and implements prevention measures, coordinates such public-health campaigns. Subsequently, NIH's focus turned to cancer and acquired immunodeficiency syndrome (AIDS). As with smoking, this work on AIDS resulted in massive public-health education as well as new products and regulations.

Other recent commitments to the improvement of public health are the numerous laws aimed at cleaning up and defending the environment (including the creation in 1970 of the Environmental Protection Agency) and laws attempting to improve the health and safety of consumer products (regulated by the Consumer Product Safety Commission, created in 1972). Health policies aimed directly at the poor include Medicaid and nutritional programs, particularly food stamps and the school lunch program.

In 2010, federal grants to states for Medicaid totaled $255 billion, up from $41 billion in 1990. Federal programs for HIV/AIDS research, treatment, prevention, and income support had a budget of $3.2 billion in 2010, a major increase from the $2.9 billion spent in 1990.[32] President Clinton put greater emphasis on HIV/AIDS by appointing an "AIDS czar" to coordinate federal HIV/AIDS policy, and by giving this position cabinet status. Under Presidents Bush and Obama, the coordinator for national HIV/AIDS policy directed the Office of National AIDS Policy as part of the White House Domestic Council. Although this federal attention to HIV/AIDS has contributed to new treatments that have saved many lives, the rates of infection have remained unchanged for the past decade. The Obama administration made AIDS prevention its highest priority.[33]

## Health Care Reform

Until the passage of the Patient Protection and Affordable Care Act in March 2010, the United States was the only advanced industrial nation without universal access to health care. Opposition from the American Medical Association, the main lobbying organization of doctors, prevented President Roosevelt from proposing national health insurance during the 1930s, when other elements of the welfare state became law. As a result, the United States developed a patchwork system: in early 2010, approximately 60 percent of the nonelderly population received health insurance through their employers, older Americans were covered through Medicare, and the poor and disabled were assisted with Medicaid. However, the growing costs of employer-provided insurance means that increasing numbers of workers cannot afford it. Many small employers cannot even afford to offer benefits because they are so expensive. And both Medicaid and Medicare face severe fiscal strain due to rising costs.

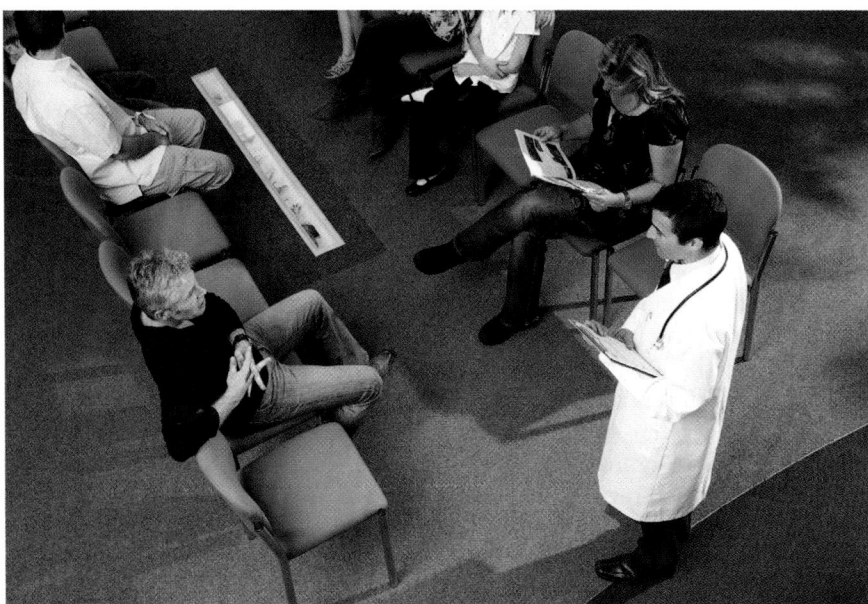

*While almost everyone agrees that rising health care costs are a problem, there is disagreement over how to make the health care system more efficient while also ensuring that all Americans have access to health care.*

# The American Health Care System in Comparison

**When compared with other** advanced democracies, the United States is unique: it is the only one that does not provide universal access to health care. The American approach to health care is a patchwork of different programs. About 60 percent of Americans under the age of 65 receive health care from their employers, who contract with private insurance companies to provide care. There is also a large federal role (accounting for half of all medical expenditures) composed of three different programs: Medicare, which provides health insurance for people over 65; Medicaid, which covers low-income people, the disabled, and elderly people who need long-term care; and the State Children's Health Insurance Plan (SCHIP), a federal-state program for uninsured children.

The trouble with the American approach is twofold: it leaves some people without coverage, and it is expensive. Not all employers provide health insurance for their workers, and not all workers opt to purchase the health plans that employers offer. The number of uninsured in 2010 was 49.1 million, or around 16 percent of the population. Moreover, the American system is the world's most expensive. The costs of health care in the United States have made it increasingly difficult for indi-

viduals to pay for care, even with employer help. And employers complain that the costs of providing health care are making them uncompetitive in world markets.

The health systems in Europe and Canada rely on two different models to offer universal coverage at much lower cost than in the United States. The first model is the single-payer approach; the second is the compulsory insurance model.

In single-payer systems, the government plays the central role in collecting revenues to fund health care, and it pays for the care that is supplied. The fact that the government is the "single payer" allows it to bargain for the lowest prices from providers. The British National Health Service is a truly socialized system in which the government both pays for and provides health care. The French system is similar to the American Medicare program because the government pays (using contributions

from employers and employees), but care is delivered by private providers, and individuals are free to choose their care providers. It has been called the best in the world because of the broad coverage it provides at low costs, along with provisions that allow those who want to pay more for extra services to do so.[a]

The compulsory insurance model is used in Germany, the Netherlands, and Switzerland. In these countries, individuals make contributions to "sickness funds," which are public-private organizations that pay for and provide health care. Many of the funds are attached to work settings, similar to employer-provided health insurance in the United States. What is different in these systems is that the sickness funds are highly regulated by the government: funds are required to provide specific basic services and are not allowed to expel individuals if they lose their jobs.

The health care legislation passed by the U.S. Congress in 2010 is a step toward providing broader coverage, but ongoing opposition to the Affordable Care Act (ACA) may create new challenges for its implementation. Moreover, the Supreme Court's decision to let states opt out of the act's expansions to Medicaid may reduce number of uninsured people who receive coverage as a result of the reform. Even if the ACA is implemented with few problems, the high cost of the American health care system will be an ongoing problem.

[a]Victor G. Rodwin, "The Health Care System under French National Health Insurance: Lessons for Health Reform in the United States," *American Journal of Public Health* 93, no. 1 (2003): 31–37.

## for critical analysis

1. What is a single-payer system of health care? How does it differ from that of the United States? What are some of the political obstacles to creating a single-payer system in the United States?

2. How do compulsory health insurance systems work? Do you think such a system could work in the United States? Why or why not?

President Clinton's major attempt to reshape federal health policy, and the boldest policy initiative of his administration, was his effort to reform America's health care system. In September 1993, Clinton announced a plan with two key objectives: to limit the rising costs of the American health care system and to provide universal health insurance coverage for all Americans. (More than 41 million Americans lacked health insurance.) Clinton's plan, spearheaded by the first lady, Hillary Rodham Clinton, at first garnered enormous public support and seemed likely to win congressional approval in some form. But the plan, which entailed a major expansion of federal administration of the health care system, gradually lost momentum as resistance to it took root among those who feared changes in a system that worked well for them. Although Clinton had pledged to make health care the centerpiece of his 1994 legislative agenda, no health care bill even came up for a full congressional vote that year. Following the failure of President Clinton's health care initiative, Congress passed a much smaller program expanding health insurance coverage for low-income children not already receiving Medicaid, called the State Children's Health Insurance Program.

**Medicare Reform** In 2003, Congress enacted a major reform of the Medicare program, which has provided health care to seniors since 1965. Most notably, Congress added a prescription drug benefit to the package of health benefits for the elderly. The high cost of prescription drugs had been an issue of growing concern to millions of older Americans. Yet the bill proved very controversial. Critics charged that the bill included a sweetheart deal with drug companies, because the legislation contained a provision prohibiting the federal government from using its purchasing power to reduce drug prices. Many Democrats also objected to the legislation because it opened the door for private health plans to play a significant role in health care provision for the elderly. They feared that the entry of such plans would significantly weaken Medicare, which has been one of the most strongly supported federal social programs. Fiscal conservatives worried about the costs of the prescription drug package. This concern escalated several months after the bill's passage, when the administration issued new, much higher cost estimates for the prescription drug benefit than the estimates presented when the bill was being debated. Adding fuel to the growing controversy over drug prices was the disclosure that the former Medicare administrator had prevented his chief actuary from releasing the higher cost estimates to Congress as it was considering the Medicare bill.

The conflict over Medicare reform highlights the problems surrounding health care more generally. A majority of Americans believe that government should ensure that all people receive adequate health care. Yet how to deliver such benefits and how to pay for them are extremely contentious issues.[34]

**Health Care Legislation in 2010** After the 2008 election, the Obama administration and the Democratic Congress pressed forward with comprehensive health reform. Seeking to avoid the conflicts that broke out in Congress over the Clintons' fully formed and highly complex health reform proposal, Obama offered Congress broad principles for reform, not a detailed proposal. The administration aimed at covering most Americans who lacked health insurance with a reform strategy that built on the existing system. The plan that ultimately passed had three key features: the first was the creation of new state-based insurance exchanges where individuals could buy health insurance, along with insurance regulation that would prohibit insurers from denying benefits for a variety of reasons such as preexisting conditions; the second was a provision, known as "the individual mandate," that required uninsured individuals to purchase health insurance; and the third was a set of subsidies to help the uninsured and small businesses purchase insurance as well as an expansion of the public programs Medicaid and the SCHIP. One controversial provision considered was a "public option" that would allow individuals to purchase government-provided insurance from the insurance exchange. Aware that this idea had become a flashpoint for opponents, Democratic congressional leaders ultimately dropped it from consideration in their final negotiations.

Even so, opponents branded the reform proposals as "big government" and sometimes as "socialism," a charge that has been levied against health reform initiatives since the 1940s. Republicans closed ranks against the proposal, meaning that all the credit—or blame—for the act would fall on the Democrats.

The Democrats did ultimately enact comprehensive health care reform in 2010, through a set of complex parliamentary maneuvers, but the politics of health care reform remained a focus of partisan contention. All the new Republican house members elected in 2010 favored repeal of the measure, and in 2012 Republican congressional candidates vowed to repeal the measure. Republican presidential candidate Mitt Romney likewise pledged to roll back the measure.

As noted in the chapter introduction, a sizeable minority of Americans opposed the act, and nearly two years after its passage many remained confused about exactly what the act would do. For example, although the law's provision eliminating co-pays for preventive care had been in effect for over a year by the end of 2011, one poll showed that only 36 percent of those questioned were aware of this benefit.[35] Some misconceptions fell along partisan lines: 48 percent of Republicans (a majority of those questioned) believed that the law authorized a government panel—a so-called death panel—to make end-of-life decisions, while only 28 percent of Democrats thought the law created such panels. The law contains no such provision. Seniors (those aged over 65) were among the strongest opponents of the law and remained split even after the law had been in effect for over a year, with 41 percent saying they were worse off under the law and 31 percent reporting that they were better off.[36] Seniors were concerned that they would not see any new benefit from the law, since most already receive generous health coverage through the Medicare plan, with nearly half of seniors worried that they would have a harder time getting benefits under the new law. In fact, the law offers a mixture of new benefits to seniors, such as lower drug costs for some, along with higher premiums for higher-income Medicare recipients. Tea Party activists, fearful that the law involved too much government control, also mobilized against it. These activists were angered by the Supreme Court decision declaring most of the

Some Americans opposed the 2010 Affordable Care Act because they were concerned that decisions previously left to patients and their doctors would be made by the government.

# Government Social Services and "Telehealth"

**The Internet has changed how** individuals learn about health and access to medical advice, and how governments provide social services. While doctors, nurses, and other health professionals continue to be the first source of advice for most people with health concerns, online resources are a significant source of health information in the United States. When people have health questions, they are increasingly likely to go online. Websites including WebMD, Mayo Clinic, MedicineNet, eMedicine, Cleveland Clinic, and Wikipedia, may provide answers. When faced with a medical concern, many people search for information from others who have similar health concerns. Among Internet users, 34 percent have read someone else's commentary or experience concering health or medical issues online, and one in four has consulted online reviews of particular drugs or medical treatments.

According to a 2010 Pew survey, 80 percent of Internet users (59 percent of American adults) look online for health information. Of cell phone owners with Internet access, 17 percent have used their phone to look up health or medical information. The most common health-related searches are for specific diseases or conditions (including symptoms), treatments, or procedures, and for doctors or other health professionals.

Women are much more likely than men to search for information about a disease

or medical problem (74 versus 57 percent). Similarly, college graduates are 20 percent more likely to search for such information than those with only a high school degree. Among white Internet users, 70 percent have searched for disease or medical condition information, compared with 54 percent of blacks and 58 percent of Latinos. These gaps reflect the digital divide between those who use the Internet regularly and those who do not.

Health care providers are also turning to digital communication to deliver services more efficiently. Health care professionals are reaching patients directly through computers and other mobile devices, including remote monitoring and video-conferencing. Telemedicine is the use of information technologies to provide clinical care at a distance, which can be particularly valuable in rural communities and for emergency care. Imaging and radiology, for example, can be conducted at rural clinics and the results evaluated by physicians in urban areas or even in other countries.

Also, governments are turning to the Internet to save money in delivering health care services, from local counties and cities to the federal government. The Medicare.gov website, for example, provides valuable information to its 48 million American clients (40 million elderly aged 65 and older and 8 million younger people with disabilities). This information includes what Medi-

care covers; how to sign up for the program; how to get drug coverage; how to find doctors, hospitals, and supplemental insurance programs; how to appeal claims; and how to log into mymedicare.gov. Individuals serving themselves online help the government save tax dollars that would otherwise be used for staffing phone lines and other expenses.

A recent study found that the people most need of Medicare and Medicaid information online, the elderly and the poor, are accessing it more frequently. Some disparities are narrowing as the elderly and poor in need of access to public health insurance are searching for it online. However, individuals without Internet access or experience (perhaps the oldest and poorest) remain disadvantaged with respect to accessing critical information that can link them to needed health care services.

SOURCES: Susannah Fox, "Pew Internet: Health," March 2012. Pew Internet and American Life. Susannah Fox, and Joanna Brenner, "Family Caregivers Online." July 2012. Pew Internet and American Life. Mary Schmeida, and Ramona McNeal, "The Telehealth Divide: Disparities in Searching Public Health Information Online," *Journal of Health Care Poor Underserved* 18, no. 3 (2007): 637–47.

## for critical analysis

1. How does inequality in Internet use, otherwise known as the "digital divide," affect access to health care information online? Should all Americans have access to health and insurance information online?

2. How can telemedicine and public health announcements be used to save governments money in providing social services such as health care?

Affordable Care Act constitutional. One poll found that 82 percent of Tea Party activists wanted to continue their efforts to block the law.[37]

Throughout the 2012 presidential campaign, the Affordable Care Act remained a target for Republicans. When the administration announced a provision requiring all employers to provide contraceptive services at no cost as part of their insurance plans, it ignited a firestorm of partisan contention. Republicans charged that the administration was interfering with religious freedom; Democrats countered that Republicans were trying to take the country back to the 1950s. In fact, polls showed significant partisan division on the issue: while 62 percent of all Americans approved of the measure, and 83 percent of Democrats approved, only 42 percent of Republicans did.[38] The president's compromise proposal, which required the insurance companies, not the religious institutions, to provide contraception, did little to quell the controversy.

The new health reform law faced challenges from state governments soon after it was enacted. Twenty-one state attorneys general filed lawsuits against the legislation on the grounds that the provision requiring individuals to purchase health insurance expanded the Commerce Clause beyond its constitutional limits. The states also objected to provisions that required them to expand their Medicaid programs to cover more poor people or lose the all the Medicaid funds that they received from the federal government. Even though the federal government will initially pay for 100 percent of the expansion and after 2016 will cover 90 percent of new costs, the states argued that the federal government had overstepped its powers in withdrawing all federal Medicaid funds if states did not comply with new coverage requirements.

The Supreme Court decided these suits in 2012, ruling that most of the act was constitutional.[39] Chief Justice John Roberts, regarded as a conservative, surprised many observers by personally writing the decision that declared the individual mandate constitutional. However, the decision found that the mandate could not be justified as constitutional under the commerce clause, which the administration relied on in its arguments before the Court. Because the mandate regulated economic *inactivity* (i.e., failure the purchase health insurance) Roberts argue that it could not be justified under the commerce clause, which regulates economic *activity*. Instead the Court ruled that the requirement to purchase insurance was legal under Congress's taxing powers (since, under the law, failure to purchase insurance will result in a penalty). The decision on Medicaid, the second contested feature of the act, also came as a surprise. The Court ruled that Congress did not have the power to take existing Medicaid funds away from states if they did not comply with the expansion requirements. The governors of several states including Florida and South Carolina immediately announced their intention to opt out of the expansion. The ruling left the effectiveness of the new law in some doubt because Medicaid expansion was estimated to cover 17 million of the uninsured. The Court's decision put an end to legal conflict over the law, but the political fight showed little sign of stopping.

## Housing Policies

The United States has one of the highest rates of home ownership in the world, and the central thrust of federal housing policy has been to promote home ownership. The federal government has traditionally done much less to provide housing for low-income Americans who cannot afford to buy homes. Federal housing programs were first created during the Great Depression of the 1930s, when many Americans found themselves unable to afford housing.

Through public housing for low-income families, which originated in 1937 with the Wagner-Steagall National Housing Act and subsidized private housing after 1950, the percentage of American families living in overcrowded conditions was reduced from 20 percent in 1940 to 9 percent in 1970. Federal policies made an even greater contribution to reducing "substandard" housing, defined by the U.S. Census Bureau as dilapidated houses without hot running water and without some other plumbing. In 1940 almost 50 percent of American households lived in substandard housing. By 1950 this had been reduced to 35 percent; by 1975, to 8 percent.[40] Despite these improvements in housing standards, federal housing policy until the 1970s was largely seen as a failure. Restricted to the poorest of the poor and marked by racial segregation and inadequate spending, public housing contributed to the problems of the poor by isolating them from shopping, jobs, and urban amenities. Dilapidated high-rise housing projects stood as a symbol of the failed American policy of "warehousing the poor." By the 1980s the orientation of housing policy had changed: most federal housing policy for low-income Americans came in the form of housing vouchers (called Section 8 vouchers and now called housing choice vouchers) that provided recipients with support to rent in the private market. Although this program did not promote the same kind of isolation of the poor, it was often useless in very active housing markets, where the vouchers provided too little money to cover rental costs. Most cities and suburbs have long waiting lists to receive vouchers, and many housing authorities have closed their lists for five to 10 years because they have so few vouchers to hand out. The demand for a small number of vouchers can lead to problems, as happened in the Atlanta area in 2010. When a small suburb opened its list for the first time in many years, 30,000 people showed up to get their names on a waiting list for 655 slots. Unprepared for such numbers, the police were unable to control the crowd, and 65 people ended up in the hospital.[41] The lack of affordable rental housing in the United States has become an increasingly pressing problem, made much worse by the recession that started in 2008. Neither the federal government nor the states have enacted policies that go far toward addressing this issue.

*Many cities have been replacing high-rise housing projects with new mixed-income units, such as these homes in New Haven, Connecticut.*

The Clinton administration at first showed a strong ideological commitment to encouraging housing policies and combating homelessness. But especially after 1994, the Clinton administration began to retreat. HUD secretary Henry Cisneros continually had to waive, virtually to the point of abandonment, a long-standing one-for-one HUD rule that provided that for every public housing unit destroyed, another would have to be built. This rule mattered because during the 1990s the main public housing program, called HOPE VI, allowed local public housing authorities to tear down the high-rise public housing that had been such a failure. In its place, city after city dismantled its old public housing projects and replaced them with new mixed-income units. The policy assumed that reducing concentrations of poverty would benefit the poor. Unfortunately, few of the original residents have been able to move into the new units.[42] The Bush administration placed less emphasis on housing policy. It proposed transforming the federal voucher program into a block grant to the states. The initiative, which never came to a vote in Congress, faced opposition from housing proponents who feared that it would greatly reduce assistance to low-income renters.

Beginning in 2007 and 2008, a home loan foreclosure crisis presented the government with a different kind of housing problem. During the housing boom of the early 2000s, many homeowners received loans that they later could not afford to repay. This was due in part to the deregulation of the mortgage industry in 1999. The deregulation allowed many new mortgage companies to form, offering loans that cost little at first but later required large payments from homeowners. This form of "predatory lending" targeted unsophisticated buyers and made it very hard for borrowers to understand the terms of the loans, which contained pages and pages of small print written in legalese. Lending standards were relaxed to the point that rising numbers of borrowers were offered "no-doc" loans, which required no documentation of the borrowers' income. As more and more Americans took out such loans, demand for housing rose, and housing prices skyrocketed. This was the housing bubble—a bubble that was bound to burst because so many borrowers would not be able to pay back their loans. As growing numbers of homeowners began to default on their loans in 2007, banks foreclosed on their houses and the value of housing began to drop. This downward spiral set off the major recession that began in 2007. As borrowers defaulted, banks holding that debt, including the biggest banks in America, teetered on the edge of failure and threatened to destabilize the entire economy. Many of the new mortgage companies, which had grown into huge businesses, went bankrupt. As unemployment rose, more families, unable to pay their mortgages, lost their homes. Many homeowners found that their homes were "underwater," meaning the homeowners owed more on their mortgages than the mortgaged properties were now worth.

By 2012, nearly 4 million homes had been lost to foreclosure.[43] The federal government responded with a plan that would slow the rising interest rates that were the cause of the problem for some homeowners. It also created several additional programs designed to help homeowners facing foreclosure. However, these programs did not experience much success. Many argued that a program reducing the amount of principal owed on a mortgage was the only way to stem the foreclosure crisis. But banks objected to such a program, as did a significant segment of the public. Some of the opposition to this kind of homeowner bailout stemmed from different perspectives on who was responsible for the mortgage crisis. While some people blamed predatory lenders, others blamed the borrowers themselves, who had taken out loans they couldn't afford, sometimes misrepresenting their ability to pay. In fact, the Tea Party movement got its start in 2009, when Rick Santelli, a cable television reporter, launched into a passionate rant against helping troubled homeowners, who, he claimed, had only themselves to blame.[44]

The federal government and the states continued to look for ways to stem the tide of foreclosures, which remained a major barrier to economic recovery. In 2012, states announced a legal settlement with banks that required the latter to pay $26 billion to homeowners who had received foreclosure notices without proper documentation. In the rush to foreclose on homes, banks had systematically violated the legal requirements, including by employing the practice of "robo-signing," in which documents were forged or never reviewed. However, given the size of the foreclosure crisis, this settlement was unlikely to make a major impact. By 2012, homeownership rates in the United States had dropped from 69.2 percent at their height in 2004 to 66.0 percent in 2012. In the West, where the foreclosure rates were among the highest in the country, homeownership had dropped to 60.1 percent.[45] As the millions of families who have lost their homes struggle to get back on their feet and neighborhoods across the country grapple with vacant homes, the effects of the housing bubble will be felt for many years to come.

# Who Gets What from Social Policy?

**Explain how contributory and noncontributory programs benefit different groups of Americans**

The two categories of social policy, contributory and noncontributory, generally serve different groups of people. We can understand much about the development of social policy by examining which constituencies benefit from different policies.

The strongest and most generous programs are those in which the beneficiaries are widely perceived as deserving of assistance and also are politically powerful. Because Americans prize work, constituencies that have "earned" their benefits in some way or those who cannot work because of a disability are usually seen as most deserving of government assistance. Politically powerful constituencies are those who vote as a group, lobby effectively, and mobilize to protect the programs from which they benefit.

When we study social policies from a group perspective, we can see that the elderly and the middle class receive the most benefits from the government's social policies and that children and the working poor receive the fewest. In addition, America's social policies do little to change the fact that minorities and women are more likely than white men to be poor.

## The Elderly

The elderly are the beneficiaries of the two strongest and most generous social policies: old-age pensions (what we call Social Security) and Medicare (medical care for the elderly). As these programs have grown, they have provided most elderly Americans with economic security and have dramatically reduced the poverty rate among the elderly. In 1959, before very many people over the age of 65 received social insurance, the poverty rate for the elderly was 35 percent; by 2010 it had dropped to 9 percent.[46] Because of this progress, many people call Social Security the most effective antipoverty program in the United States.[47] This does not mean that the elderly are rich, however; in 2010 the median income of elderly

In 1995 the Republican-led Congress proposed cuts in Medicare spending, prompting vigorous protests from senior citizens. Fearing negative political repercussions in the 1996 elections, Congressional Republicans retreated from their efforts to overhaul the Medicare system. In 2003 the support of senior groups such as AARP was critical to the passage of a new Medicare prescription drug plan.

households was $31,408, well below the national median income.[48] The aim of these programs is to provide security and prevent poverty rather than to assist people once they have become poor. And they have succeeded in preventing poverty among most of the aged.

One reason that Social Security and Medicare are politically strong is that the elderly are widely seen as a deserving population. They are not expected to work, because of their age. Moreover, both programs are contributory, and a work history is a requirement for receiving a Social Security pension. But these programs are also strong because they serve a constituency that has become quite powerful. The elderly are a very large group: in 2010 there were 38.6 million Americans over the age of 65. Because Social Security and Medicare are not means tested, they are available to nearly all people over the age of 65, whether they are poor or not. The size of this group is of great political importance because the rates of voter turnout are greater among the elderly than among the rest of the population.

In addition, the elderly have developed strong and sophisticated lobbying organizations that can influence policy making and mobilize elderly Americans to defend these programs against proposals to cut them. One important and influential such organization is AARP. Originally the American Association of Retired Persons, in 1999 the organization changed its name to its initials only because 44 percent of AARP members work full or part time. AARP had more than 40 million members in 2010, amounting to one-fifth of all voters. It also has a sophisticated lobbying organization in Washington, which employs 63 lobbyists and a staff of 165 policy analysts.[49] (See Chapter 11 for more discussion of AARP's lobbying efforts.) Although AARP is the largest and the strongest organization of the elderly, other groups, such as the Alliance for Retired Americans, to which many retired union members belong, also lobby Congress on behalf of the elderly.

When Congress considers changes in programs that affect the elderly, these lobbying groups pay close attention. They mobilize their supporters and work with legislators to block changes they believe will hurt the elderly.[50] As we saw in Chapters 11 and 16, the power of this lobby was apparent in 2003, and again in 2005, during the effort to reform Social Security. AARP had long opposed any reform that allowed private health care firms to provide Medicare benefits. But in 2003 it changed its position and supported the president's bill, which combined prescription drug benefits and an opening for private firms. AARP's vocal support, including its television advertisements in favor of the bill, was widely credited with making the legislative victory possible. In 2005, AARP switched sides and opposed the president's proposals to reform Social Security. AARP opposition was a key factor in the proposal's failure to attract political support. In 2009 and 2010, AARP came out in support of health reform, although it avoided endorsing any specific bill. Although thousands of members left AARP in protest, their actions had little impact given the size of the organization.

## The Middle Class

Americans don't usually think of the middle class as benefiting from social policies, but government action promotes the social welfare of the middle class in a variety of ways. First, medical care and pensions for the elderly help the middle class by relieving them of the burden of caring for elderly relatives. Before these programs existed, old people were more likely to live with and depend financially on their adult children. Many middle-class families whose parents and grandparents are in nursing homes rely on Medicaid to pay nursing home bills.

In addition, the middle class benefits from what some analysts call the shadow welfare state.[51] These are the social benefits that private employers offer to their workers: medical insurance and pensions, for example. The federal government subsidizes such benefits by not taxing the payments that employers and employees make for health insurance and pensions. These **tax expenditures**, as they are called, are an important way the federal government helps ensure the social welfare of the middle class. (Such programs are called "tax expenditures" because the federal government helps finance them through the tax system rather than by direct spending.) Another key tax expenditure that helps the middle class is the tax exemption on mortgage interest payments: taxpayers can deduct the amount they have paid in interest on a mortgage from the income they report on their tax return. By allowing these payments to be counted as deductions, the government makes home ownership less expensive.

People often don't think of these tax expenditures as part of social policy because they are not as visible as the programs that provide direct payments or services to beneficiaries. But tax expenditures represent a significant federal investment: they cost the national treasury some $1.26 trillion a year and make it easier and less expensive for working Americans to obtain health care, save for retirement, and buy homes.[52] These programs are very popular with the middle class, and Congress rarely considers reducing them. On the few occasions when public officials have tried to limit these programs—with proposals to limit the amount of mortgage interest that can be deducted, for example—they have quickly retreated. These programs are simply too popular among Americans, whose power comes from their numbers at the polling booth.

## The Working Poor

People who are working but are poor or just above the poverty line receive only limited assistance from government social programs. This is somewhat surprising, given that Americans value work so highly. But the working poor are typically employed in jobs that do not provide pensions or health care; often they are renters because they cannot afford to buy homes. This means they cannot benefit from the shadow

**tax expenditures** government subsidies provided to employers and employees through tax deductions for amounts spent on health insurance and other benefits

welfare state that subsidizes the social benefits enjoyed by most middle-class Americans. At the same time, however, they cannot get assistance through programs such as Medicaid and TANF, which are largely restricted to the nonworking poor.

Two government programs do assist the working poor: the Earned Income Tax Credit (EITC) and the Supplemental Nutrition Assistance Program (or SNAP, formerly known as food stamps). The EITC was implemented in 1976 to provide poor workers some relief from increases in the taxes that pay for Social Security. As it has expanded, the EITC has provided a modest wage supplement for the working poor, allowing them to catch up on utility bills or pay for children's clothing.

Poor workers can also receive benefits from SNAP. These two programs help supplement the income of poor workers, but they offer only modest support. Because the wages of less-educated workers have declined significantly over the past 15 years and minimum wages have not kept pace with inflation, the problems of the working poor remain acute.

Even though the working poor may be seen as deserving, they are not politically powerful because they are not organized. There is no equivalent to AARP for the poor. Nonetheless, because work is highly valued in American society, politicians find it difficult to cut the few social programs that help the working poor. In 1995, efforts to cut the EITC were defeated by coalitions of Democrats and moderate Republicans, although Congress did place new restrictions on food stamps and also reduced the level of spending on this type of aid.

## The Nonworking Poor

The only nonworking, able-bodied poor people who receive federal cash assistance are parents who are caring for children. The primary source of cash assistance for these families was AFDC and now is the state-run TANF program, but they also rely on SNAP and Medicaid. Able-bodied adults who are not caring for children are not eligible for federal assistance other than food stamps. Many states provide small amounts of cash assistance to such individuals through programs called "general assistance," but in the past decade, many states have abolished or greatly reduced their general assistance programs in an effort to encourage these adults to work. Americans don't like to subsidize adults who are not working, but they do not want to harm children.

AFDC was the most unpopular social spending program ever undertaken by the federal government; as a result, spending on it declined after 1980. Under TANF, states receive a fixed amount of federal funds, whether the welfare rolls rise or fall. Because the number of people on welfare has declined so dramatically since 1994 (by more than 50 percent) states have had generous levels of federal resources for the remaining welfare recipients. Many states, however, have used the windfall of federal dollars to cut taxes and indirectly support programs that benefit the middle class, not the poor.[53] Welfare recipients have little political power to resist cuts to their benefits. During the late 1960s and early 1970s, the short-lived National Welfare Rights Organization sought to represent the interests of welfare recipients. But keeping the organization in operation proved difficult because its members and its constituents had few resources and were difficult to organize.[54] Because welfare recipients are widely viewed as undeserving, and because they are not politically organized, they have played little part in recent debates about welfare.

The impact of the recession has meant that record numbers of Americans are receiving food assistance through SNAP. With unemployment well above 8 percent since early 2009 and the numbers of long-term unemployment very high, nutrition assistance has been the most responsive program. In 2012 more than 46 million people (15 percent of the population) received SNAP benefits.[55]

## Minorities, Women, and Children

Minorities, women, and children are disproportionately poor. Much of this poverty is the result of disadvantages that stem from the position of these groups in the labor market. In 2010 the poverty rate for African Americans was 27.4 percent, and for Latinos it was 26.6 percent. Both rates are more than double the poverty rate for non-Hispanic whites, which was 9.9 percent.[56] The median income for black households in 2010 was $32,068. For Hispanics it was $37,759, whereas for non-Hispanic white households the median household income was $54,620.[57] Much of this economic inequality occurs because minority workers tend to have low-wage jobs. Minorities are also more likely to become unemployed and to remain unemployed for longer periods of time than are white Americans. African Americans, for example, typically have experienced twice as much unemployment as have other Americans. The combination of low-wage jobs and unemployment often means that minorities are less likely to have jobs that give them access to the shadow welfare state. They are more likely to fall into the precarious categories of the working poor or the nonworking poor.

In the past several decades, policy analysts have begun to talk about the "feminization of poverty," or the fact that women are more likely than men to be poor. This problem is particularly acute for single mothers, who are more than twice as likely to fall below the poverty line as the average American (see Figure 17.4). When the Social Security Act was passed in 1935, the main programs for poor women were Aid to Dependent Children (ADC) and survivors' insurance for widows. The framers of the act believed that ADC would gradually disappear as more women

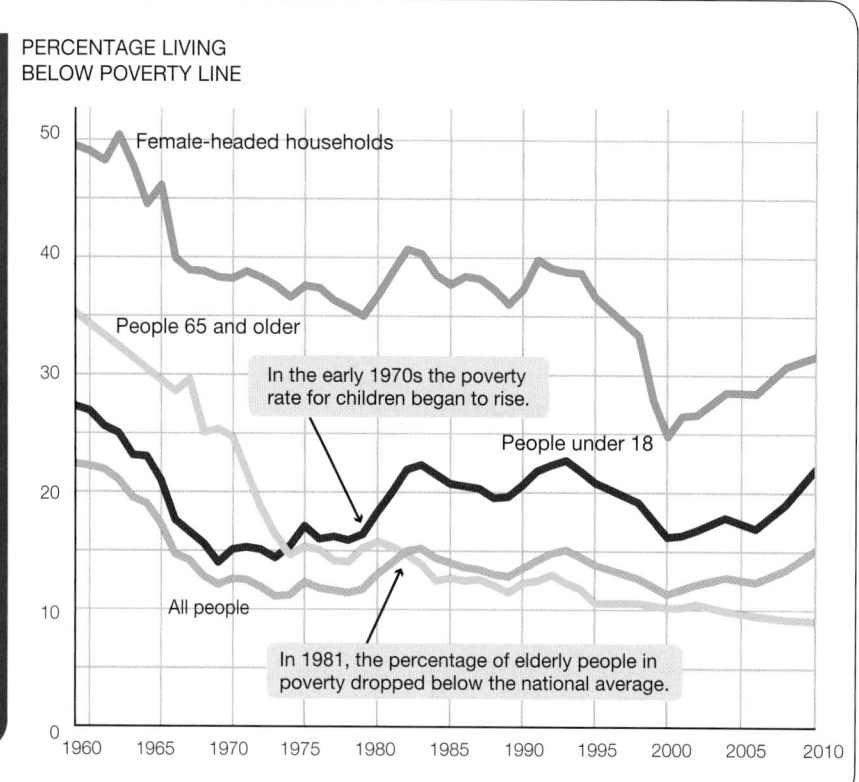

### FIGURE 17.4

## Poverty Level in the United States, 1960–2010

Poverty among all Americans has declined markedly since 1960. However, the rate of progress has varied significantly across groups. Female-headed households have very high poverty rates. Although poverty rates for this group dropped sharply after 1994, they have increased since 2000. Which group has seen the greatest reduction in its poverty level since 1960?

Source: Carmen DeNavas-Walt, Bernadette D. Proctor, and Jessica C. Smith, "Income Poverty and Health Insurance Coverage in the United States," U.S. Census Bureau, September 2011, www.census.gov/prod/2011pubs/p60-239.pdf, p.16 (accessed 7/7/12).

PERCENTAGE LIVING BELOW POVERTY LINE

Female-headed households

People 65 and older

In the early 1970s the poverty rate for children began to rise.

People under 18

All people

In 1981, the percentage of elderly people in poverty dropped below the national average.

became eligible for survivors' insurance. The social model behind the Social Security Act was that of a male breadwinner with a wife and children. Women were not expected to work, and if a woman's husband died, ADC or survivors' insurance would help her stay at home and raise her children. The framers of Social Security did not envision today's large number of single women heading families. At the same time, they did not envision that so many women with children would also be working. This combination of changes helped make AFDC (the successor program to ADC) more controversial. Many people asked why welfare recipients shouldn't work, if the majority of women who were not on welfare worked. Such questions led to the welfare reform of 1996, which created TANF.

The need to combine work and child care was understood as a challenging problem for most single parents. This problem is more acute for single mothers than for single fathers, because on average, women still earn less than men and because working creates new expenses such as child care and transportation costs. Many women working in low-wage jobs do not receive health insurance as a benefit of their jobs; they must pay the cost of such insurance themselves. As a result, many poor women found that once they were working, the expenses of child care, transportation, insurance, and other needs left them with less cash per month than they would have received if they had not worked and had instead collected AFDC and Medicaid benefits. These women concluded that it was not "worth it" for them to leave AFDC and go to work. Some states are now experimenting with programs to encourage women to work by allowing them to keep some of their welfare benefits even when they are working. Although Americans want individuals to be self-sufficient, research suggests that single mothers with low-wage jobs are likely to need continuing assistance to make ends meet.[58]

One of the most troubling issues related to American social policy is the number of American children who live in poverty. The rate of child poverty in 2010 was 22 percent—6.9 percent higher than that of the population as a whole. These high rates of poverty stem in part from the design of American social policies. Because

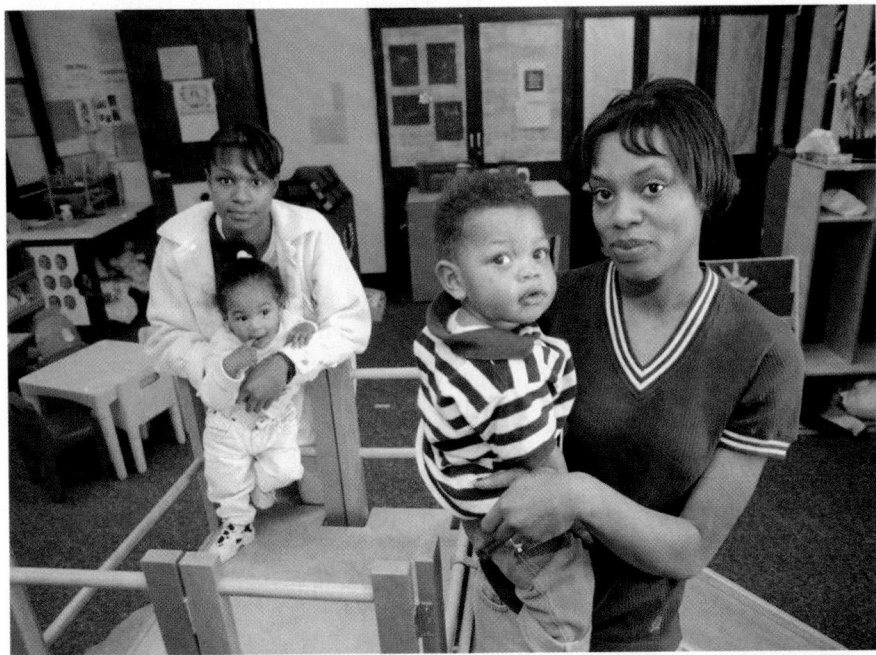

*The poor and working poor (including many single mothers with children) have little influence on government. Although organized protests representing their interests occasionally do occur, they fail to have the impact of similar protests by other groups, such as senior citizens.*

these policies do not generously assist able-bodied adults who aren't working, and because these policies offer little help to the working poor, the children of these adults are likely to be poor as well.

As child poverty has grown, several lobbying groups have emerged to represent children's interests; the best known of these is the Children's Defense Fund. But even with a sophisticated lobbying operation, and although their numbers are large, poor children do not vote and therefore cannot wield much political power.[59]

## ● Thinking Critically about Social Policy and Equality

The development of social policy in the United States reflects shifts in our views about how government can best help accomplish fundamental national goals. Until the 1930s the federal government did very little in the domain of social policy. The country's major social policy was free public education, which was established by the states and administered locally. Americans placed especially strong emphasis on education because an educated citizenry was seen as an essential component of a strong democracy.[60] Given the strength of these beliefs, it is not surprising that free public education was available in the United States well before European nations established public education systems.

Other public social policies, established from the 1930s on, have stirred up much more controversy. Liberals often argue that more generous social policies are needed if America is truly to ensure equality of opportunity. Some liberals have argued that the government needs to go beyond simply providing opportunity and should ensure more equal conditions, especially where children are concerned. Conservative critics, on the other hand, often argue that social policies that offer income support take the ideal of equality too far and, in the process, do for individuals what those individuals should be doing for themselves. From this perspective, social policies make the government too big, and big government is seen as a fundamental threat to Americans' liberties.

Where do average Americans fit in these debates? Americans are often said to be philosophical conservatives and operational liberals.[61] When asked about government social policy in the abstract, they say they disapprove of activist government—a decidedly conservative view. But when they must evaluate particular programs, Americans generally express support—a more liberal perspective. Some programs, of course, are preferred over others. Policies in which the recipients are regarded as deserving, such as programs for the elderly, receive more support than those that assist working-age people. Programs that have a reputation for effectiveness and those that require people to help themselves through work are also viewed favorably.[62]

In sum, most Americans take a pragmatic approach to social welfare policies: they favor programs that work and they want to reform those that seem not to work. By rejecting the policy extremes, Americans signal their awareness of the tensions that social policies generate among their most deeply held values. The most productive political debates prompt the public to consider which mix of social policies represents the appropriate balance among these three ideals: liberty, equality, and democracy.

# Weigh In on Social Policy

## Inform Yourself

 **Visit the main poverty page of the U.S. Census Bureau** (www.census.gov/hhes/ www/poverty/). There you will find the most recent statistics on poverty in the United States and data on those without health insurance. In 2011 more than 46 million people lived in poverty; that is, one in six Americans. Of children under the age of 18, 21 percent live in poverty. Poverty trends aren't constant. The number of people in poverty has risen steadily over the past decade (www.census .gov/hhes/www/poverty/data/incpovhlth/2011/figure4.pdf). What do think you drives these trends?

 **Watch a video on the government's role in social policy.** Why do we ultimately care about social policy? Why does our government provide services to low-income individuals and families? Watch a short video on the subject at www .youtube.com/watch?v=kQQcNkWyXms. Consider Professor Mary Jo Bane's answers versus what you have heard in the past. Given her argument, do you think the government should be providing these services?

## Express Yourself

 **Map social issues and share what you find.** Go to www.patchworknation.org and click on the "Latest Data" tab on the bottom right. Click on "Food Stamps," for example, and generate a map of the percentage of the population using food stamps. Some parts of America have nearly one in two Americans on food stamps. Put your cursor on the map to see which counties are high and low in food stamp use. Then look at the change in food stamp use from 2007 to 2009. Consider exporting the map and sharing what you find with your friends or class-mates, using Facebook or Twitter.

## Connect with Others

 **Connect with the Center for Law and Social Policy.** The Center for Law and Social Policy is a nonprofit organization that has been around since the 1960s. Its mission is "to improve the lives of low-income people [so that] children grow up safe, healthy, nurtured and prepared to succeed." Visit its Facebook page www .facebook.com/#!/CLASP.org and see what issues its posts address. Does this organization seem to have a political bias in what it posts and how it portrays the issues? Do you agree or disagree with its posts?

*Find links to the sites listed above as well as related activities on wwnorton.com/studyspace.*

# study guide

## The Welfare State

■ **Trace the history of government programs designed to help the poor (pp. 691–703)**

Prior to the Great Depression, local governments and private charities were in charge of caring for the poor and the federal government did very little. The Social Security Act of 1935 ended this system and created two separate categories of welfare: contributory and noncontributory. Spending on social policy, particularly entitlement programs, has grown dramatically ever since the 1930s, and the costs have been paid primarily through payroll taxes.

### Key Terms

**contributory programs** (p. 694)

**Social Security** (p. 694)

**Medicare** (p. 694)

**indexing** (p. 694)

**cost-of-living adjustments (COLAs)** (p. 694)

**noncontributory programs** (p. 694)

**means testing** (p. 694)

**Medicaid** (p. 696)

**Supplemental Nutritional Assistance Program (SNAP)** (p. 696)

**in-kind benefits** (p. 696)

**entitlement** (p. 697)

### Practice Quiz

1. Prior to 1935, the private welfare system in the United States made a distinction between *(p. 691)*
   a) contributory and noncontributory programs.
   b) citizens and recent immigrants.
   c) the deserving poor and the undeserving poor.
   d) mandatory and discretionary spending.
   e) religious and secular assistance.

2. America's welfare state was constructed initially in response to *(pp. 692–93)*
   a) the Civil War.
   b) World War II.
   c) political reforms of the Progressive era.
   d) the Great Depression.
   e) the growth of the military-industrial complex.

3. Which of the following is an example of a contributory program? *(p. 694)*
   a) Medicaid
   b) Medicare
   c) Temporary Assistance for Needy Families
   d) Supplemental Nutrition Assistance Program
   e) Aid to Families with Dependent Children

4. Means testing requires that applicants for welfare benefits show *(p. 694)*
   a) that they are capable of getting to and from their workplace.
   b) that they have the ability to store and prepare food.
   c) some definite need for assistance plus an inability to provide for it.
   d) that they have the time and resources to take full advantage of federal educational opportunities.
   e) that they are natural-born citizens who have never been convicted of a felony.

5. In 1996, as part of welfare reform, Aid to Families with Dependent Children was abolished and replaced by *(p. 694)*
   a) the Earned Income Tax Credit.
   b) Aid to Dependent Children.
   c) the Affordable Care Act.
   d) Supplemental Security Income.
   e) Temporary Assistance for Needy Families.

6. Which of the following are examples of in-kind benefits? *(p. 696)*
   a) Medicaid and SNAP
   b) Social Security payments and cost-of-living adjustments
   c) Medicare and unemployment compensation
   d) the GI Bill of Rights and the Equal Rights Amendment
   e) the Earned Income Tax Credit and No Child Left Behind

7. Government benefits to individuals that *cannot* be taken away without due process of the law are called *(p. 697)*
   a) cost-of-living adjustments.
   b) noncontributory programs.
   c) entitlement programs.
   d) indexing programs.
   e) tax expenditure programs.

# Opening Opportunity

■ **Describe how education, health, and housing policies try to enable people to reach their potential (pp. 703–14)**

The federal government enacts three types of policies in order to keep people from falling into poverty and to help those who are already poor: education policies, health policies, and housing policies. Although the federal government has played only a minor role in education throughout most of American history, it has become more active since the 1950s. Until the passage of the Patient Protection and Affordable Care Act in 2010, the United States was the only advanced industrial nation without universal access to health care. The federal government has concentrated most of its efforts on housing policy to promote home ownership rather than to provide housing for low-income Americans who cannot afford to buy homes.

## Key Term

**equality of opportunity** (p. 703)

## Practice Quiz

8. What event prompted the federal government to enter the field of elementary education? *(p. 703)*
   a) the Civil War
   b) the Great Depression
   c) World War II
   d) the Soviet Union's launching of *Sputnik*
   e) the Civil Rights movement

9. Which of the following was *not* part of the No Child Left Behind Act of 2001? *(p. 704)*
   a) a provision allowing parents whose child is attending a failing school to transfer the child to a better school

   b) a requirement that all students be proficient in reading and math by 2014
   c) a requirement that schools show positive results for all subcategories of students and not just positive overall averages
   d) a requirement that a national test be used to evaluate every student around the country
   e) a requirement that every child in grades 3 through 8 be tested yearly for proficiency in math and reading

10. A charter school is *(p. 705)*
    a) a publicly funded school that is free from the rules and regulations of local school districts.
    b) a privately funded school that is subject to the rules and regulations of local school districts.
    c) a privately funded school that is free from the rules and regulations of local school districts.
    d) a school that meets the requirements spelled out in the No Child Left Behind Act of 2001.
    e) a school created by the GI Bill of Rights of 1944.

11. Most nonelderly adults receive health insurance through *(p. 706)*
    a) Social Security.
    b) Medicare.
    c) Medicaid.
    d) their employers.
    e) local charitable organizations.

 **Practice Online**
Video exercise: *No Child Left Behind*

# Who Gets What from Social Policy?

■ **Explain how contributory and noncontributory programs benefit different groups of Americans (pp. 714–20)**

The federal government's social policies tend to provide the largest benefits to those groups that are politically organized and to those groups that the public perceives to be deserving of assistance. As a result, children and the working poor receive the fewest benefits from the federal government and the middle class and the elderly receive the most. Government policies do little to change the fact that minorities and women are more likely than white men to be poor.

## Key Term

**tax expenditures** (p. 716)

## Practice Quiz

12. In terms of receiving benefits of social policies, what distinguishes the elderly from the working poor? *(pp. 714–17)*
    a) The elderly are perceived as deserving, whereas the working poor are not.
    b) The elderly receive fewer benefits from the government's social policies.
    c) The elderly are more organized and more politically powerful than are the working poor.
    d) The elderly are less organized and less politically powerful than are the working poor.
    e) There is no significant difference between these two groups.

13. Who are the chief beneficiaries of the "shadow welfare state"? *(p. 716)*
    a) children
    b) the elderly
    c) the nonworking poor
    d) the working poor
    e) the middle class

14. Which two government programs provide direct assistance to the working poor? *(p. 717)*
    a) Medicaid and the Earned Income Tax Credit
    b) Temporary Assistance for Needy Families and SNAP
    c) Temporary Assistance for Needy Families and the Earned Income Tax Credit
    d) SNAP and the Earned Income Tax Credit
    e) Social Security and Medicare

15. Which of the following statements about the poverty in the United States is most accurate? *(p. 718)*
    a) African Americans have a lower poverty rate than whites.
    b) Hispanics have a lower poverty rate than whites.
    c) Hispanics have a higher poverty rate than whites.
    d) The rate of child poverty is less than the rate of adult poverty.
    e) Women are less likely than men to fall below the poverty line.

 **Practice Online**
"Who Are Americans?" exercise: *Who Benefits from Social Programs?*

# For Further Reading

Campbell, Andrea Louise. *How Policies Make Citizens: Senior Political Activism and the American Welfare State.* Princeton, NJ: Princeton University Press, 2005.

Hacker, Jacob S. *The Great Risk Shift: Why American Jobs, Families, Health Care, and Retirement Aren't Secure—and How We Can Fight Back.* New York: Oxford University Press, 2006.

Howard, Christopher. *The Welfare State Nobody Knows: Debunking Myths about U.S. Social Policy.* Princeton, NJ: Princeton University Press, 2007.

Katz, Michael. *In the Shadow of the Poorhouse: A Social History of Welfare in America.* New York: Basic Books, 1986.

Katznelson, Ira, and Margaret Weir. *Schooling for All: Race, Class, and the Democratic Ideal.* New York: Basic Books, 1985.

Light, Paul. *Artful Work: The Politics of Social Security Reform.* New York: Random House, 1985.

Mettler, Suzanne. *The Submerged State: How Invisible Government Policies Undermine American Democracy.* Chicago: University of Chicago Press, 2011.

Murray, Charles. *Losing Ground: American Social Policy, 1950–1980.* New York: Basic Books, 1984.

Patterson, James T. *America's Struggle against Poverty in the Twentieth Century.* Cambridge, MA: Harvard University Press, 2000.

Skocpol, Theda. *The Missing Middle: Working Families and the Future of American Social Policy.* New York: W.W. Norton, 2000.

Soss, Joe, Richard C. Fording, and Sanford F. Schramm, *Disciplining the Poor: Neoliberal Paternalism and the Persistent Power of Race.* Chicago: University of Chicago Press, 2011.

Weir, Margaret, Ann Orloff, and Theda Skocpol, eds. *The Politics of Social Policy in the United States.* Princeton, NJ: Princeton University Press, 1988.

# Recommended Websites

**Center for Retirement Research**
http://crr.bc.edu/index.php
Americans pay for their retirement with a mix of Social Security, employer-sponsored savings plans, and private savings. This website provides analyses of the challenges that face all aspects of the current arrangements and includes a downloadable "Social Security Fix-It Book."

**Center on Budget and Policy Priorities**
www.cbpp.org
The Center on Budget and Policy Priorities is a nonpartisan, liberal-leaning nonprofit organization that provides

timely data and analysis of social programs that serve low-income Americans. It also studies economic and social changes that affect the well-being of low-income people. Areas of research include the Earned Income Tax Credit, Food Assistance, Social Security, and climate change. The center focuses on state and local policies as well as national programs.

**Libertarian Party**
www.lp.org
Contrary to many other Americans, libertarians believe that social programs pose a threat to personal freedom

and should be eliminated. Go to the Libertarian Party's website to read the organization's opinions and positions on most current social policies.

**Medicare**
**www.medicare.gov**
Health care is one of the largest and most controversial social programs in the United States. At the Medicare website, find out what services the Department of Health and Human Services provides.

**Modern American Poetry: The Great Depression**
**www.english.uiuc.edu/maps/depression/depression.htm**
The Great Depression changed American opinion about the causes of and responsibility for poverty. This website, by Carey Norton at the University of Illinois at Urbana-Champaign, provides information, statistics, and photos of this historical period as well as analysis of poems by Depression-era writers.

**Poverty.com**
**www.poverty.com**
Poverty is a problem that exists in the United States and around the world. Read about how poverty, hunger, and related problems affect people in other areas of the globe.

**Public Agenda**
**www.publicagenda.com**
Public Agenda is a nonpartisan organization that tries to bridge the gap between American leaders and public opinion on current social, domestic, and foreign policy issues.

**U.S. Department of Education**
**www.ed.gov**
The U.S. Department of Education is dedicated to providing equal access to education and improving academic programs throughout America. At the department's website, you can learn about the No Child Left Behind Act and other policies.

While foreign policies—such as the ongoing American presence in Afghanistan—are often controversial, some Americans argue that it is important for the nation to put aside partisan differences in dealing with international issues.

# 18

# Foreign Policy and Democracy

**WHAT GOVERNMENT DOES AND WHY IT MATTERS** Ever since George Washington, in his Farewell Address, warned the American people "to have . . . as little political connection as possible" with foreign nations and to "steer clear of permanent alliances," Americans have been distrustful of foreign policy. But despite their distrust, the United States has been forced to pursue its national interests in the world through a variety of means, including diplomacy, economic policy, and precisely the sorts of entangling alliances with other nations and involvements with international organizations that would have troubled Washington.

To some college students, foreign policy may seem like a distant or abstract matter, but not too long ago tens of thousands of students were drafted and sent to serve in Korea and Vietnam. Even today, in the era of the all-volunteer military, thousands of recent college graduates (and numerous current college students) have served in America's military forces in Iraq and Afghanistan, and many others know someone who has been wounded or killed on distant battlefields.

War is only one aspect of American foreign policy, but America has fought a large number of wars. Though Americans like to regard themselves as a peaceful people, since our own Civil War, American forces have been deployed abroad on hundreds of occasions for major conflicts and minor skirmishes. Writing in 1989, historian Geoffrey Perret commented that no other nation "has had as much experience of war as the United States."[1] America has not become less warlike in the years since Perret published his observation. Between 1989 and the present, American forces have fought two wars in the Persian Gulf and a war in Afghanistan, while engaging in lesser military actions in

Panama, Kosovo, Somalia, and elsewhere. Every year, of course, America's military arsenal and defense budget dwarf those of other nations. America currently spends more than $700 billion per year on its military and weapons programs—a figure that represents nearly half of the world's total military expenditure and nearly six times the amount spent by the People's Republic of China, the nation that currently ranks second to the United States in overall military outlays. The debt we incur for these programs is likely to be paid by today's college students for their entire working lives.

Foreign policy, especially military policy, is often a major political issue in the United States. An old American adage asserts that "politics stops at the water's edge." The point of this saying is that unless we put our domestic political disunity aside and work together to protect our nation's political, economic, and security interests in the wider world, all Americans will suffer. In today's world, however, the water's edge does not neatly demarcate the difference in interests between "us" and "them." As the global economic crisis that began in 2008 revealed, "our" economic interests and "their" economic interests are intertwined. Environmental concerns are global, not national. And even in the realm of security interests, some risks and threats are shared and require international rather than national responses. Our national government, created to further our national interests, must find ways of acting internationally and striking the right balance between competition and cooperation in the international arena. Writing in the 1830s, Alexis de Tocqueville declared that democracies are not well suited to successfully pursuing foreign policy goals. "A democracy can only with great difficulty regulate the details of an important undertaking, persevere in a fixed design, and work out its execution in spite of serious obstacles. It cannot combine its measures with secrecy or await their consequences with patience."[2] Let us see if Tocqueville's assessment is still true today.

## chaptergoals

- **Explain how foreign policy is designed to promote security, prosperity, and humanitarian goals** (pages 729–38)

- **Identify the major players in foreign-policy making, and describe their roles** (pages 738–44)

- **Describe the means the United States uses to carry out foreign policy** (pages 745–52)

# The Goals of Foreign Policy

**Explain how foreign policy is designed to promote security, prosperity, and humanitarian goals**

The term *foreign policy* refers to the programs and policies that determine America's relations with other nations and foreign entities. Foreign policy includes diplomacy, military and security policy, international human rights policies, and various forms of economic policy, such as trade policy and international energy policy. Of course, foreign policy and domestic policy are not completely separate categories but are instead closely intertwined. Take security policy, for example. Defending the nation requires the design and manufacture of tens of billions of dollars' worth of military hardware. The manufacture and procurement of this military equipment involve a host of economic policies, and paying for it shapes America's fiscal policies.

Many of the basic contours of the foreign policy arena are similar to those of America's other policy domains. The nation's chief foreign-policy makers are the president, Congress, and the bureaucracy. Just as in economic and social policy, battles over foreign policy often erupt among and within these institutions as competing politicians and a variety of organized groups and rival political forces pursue their own versions of the national interest or their own narrower purposes that they seek to present as the national interest. In the foreign policy arena, the institutional powers of the presidency give presidents and their allies an advantage over political forces based in Congress, although Congress is not without resources of its own through which to influence the conduct of foreign policy. Moreover, like domestic policy matters, foreign policy issues often figure prominently in public debate and in national election campaigns as competing forces seek to mobilize popular support for their positions, or at least to castigate the opposition for the putative shortcomings of its policies.

In this section we will examine the goals of American foreign policy. Although U.S. foreign policy has a number of purposes, three main goals stand out. These are security, prosperity, and the creation of a better world. These goals are, of course, closely intertwined and can never be pursued fully in isolation from one another. Then, in the following sections, we will discuss the actors and institutions that shape foreign policy. Next, we will analyze the instruments that policy makers have at their disposal to implement foreign policy.

*In 2009, President Obama hosted a meeting between Israeli prime minister Benjamin Netanyahu and Palestinian president Mahmoud Abbas. As the dominant world power today, the United States is involved in issues all over the world.*

## Security

To many Americans, the chief goal of the nation's foreign policy is protection of America's security in an often hostile world. Traditionally, the United States has been concerned about threats that might emanate from other nations, such as Nazi Germany during the 1940s and then Soviet Russia until the Soviet Union's collapse in the late 1980s. Today, American security policy is concerned not only with the actions of other nations but also with the activities of terrorist groups and other hostile non-state actors.[3] To protect the nation's security from foreign threats, the United States has built an enormous military apparatus and a complex array of intelligence-gathering institutions, such as the Central Intelligence Agency (CIA), charged with evaluating and anticipating challenges from abroad.[4]

*Security* is, of course, a broad term. Policy makers must be concerned with Americans' physical security. The September 11 terrorist attacks killed and injured thousands of Americans, and the government constantly fears that new attacks could be even more catastrophic. Policy makers must also be concerned with such matters as the security of America's food supplies, transportation infrastructure, and energy supplies. Many of our efforts in the Middle East, for example, are aimed at ensuring continuing American access to vital oil fields. In recent years, cyber-space has become a new security concern. The nation's dependence on computers means that the government must be alert to efforts by hostile governments, groups, or even individual "hackers" to damage computer networks.

During the eighteenth and nineteenth centuries, American security was based mainly on the geographic isolation of the United States. We were separated by two oceans from European and Asian powers, and many Americans thought that our security would be best preserved by our remaining aloof from international power struggles. This policy was known as **isolationism**. In his 1796 Farewell Address, President George Washington warned Americans to avoid permanent alliances with foreign powers, and in 1823, President James Monroe warned foreign powers not to meddle in the Western Hemisphere. Washington's warning and what came to be called the Monroe Doctrine were the cornerstones of the U.S. foreign policy of isolationism until the end of the nineteenth century. The United States saw itself as the dominant power in the Western Hemisphere and, indeed, believed that its "manifest destiny" was to expand from sea to sea. The rest of the world, however, should remain at arm's length.

In the twentieth century, technology made oceans less of a barrier to foreign threats, and the world's growing economic interdependence meant that the United States could no longer ignore events abroad. At the beginning of the twentieth century, despite its isolationist sentiments, the United States entered World War I on the side of Great Britain and France when the Wilson administration concluded that America's economic and security interests would be adversely affected by a German victory. In 1941, America was drawn into World War II when Japan attacked the U.S. Pacific fleet anchored at Pearl Harbor, Hawaii. Even before the Japanese attack forced America to fight, the Roosevelt administration had already concluded that the United States must act to prevent a victory by the German-Japanese-Italian Axis alliance. Until the Japanese attack, however, President Roosevelt had not been able to overcome proponents of American isolationism, who declared that our security was best served by leaving foreigners to their own devices. With their attack, the Japanese proved that the Pacific Ocean could not protect the United States from foreign foes and effectively discredited isolationism as a security policy.

In the aftermath of World War II, the United States developed a new security policy known as **deterrence**, designed to "contain" the growing power of the Soviet Union. By the end of the 1940s, the Soviets had built a huge empire and enormous military forces. Most threatening of all, it had built nuclear weapons and intercontinental bombers capable of attacking the United States. Some Americans argued that we should attack the Soviets before it was too late—a policy known as **preventive war**. Others said that we should show our peaceful intentions and attempt to placate the Soviets. This policy is called **appeasement**.

The policies that the United States actually adopted, deterrence and containment, could be seen as midway between preventive war and appeasement. A nation pursuing a policy of deterrence, on the one hand, signals its peaceful intentions, but on the other hand indicates its willingness and ability to fight if attacked. Thus, during the era of confrontation with the Soviet Union, known as the **Cold War**, the United States frequently asserted that it had no intention of attacking the Soviet Union. At the same time, however, the United States built a huge military force, including a vast arsenal of nuclear weapons and intercontinental missiles, and frequently asserted that, in the event of a Soviet attack, it had the ability and will to respond with overwhelming force. The Soviet Union announced that its nuclear weapons were also intended for deterrent purposes. Eventually the two sides possessed such enormous arsenals of nuclear missiles that each potentially had the ability to destroy the other in the event of war. This heavily armed standoff came to be called a posture of mutually assured destruction. During the 1962 "Cuban missile crisis," the United States and the USSR came to the brink of war when President Kennedy declared that the Soviet Union must remove its nuclear missiles from Cuba and threatened to use force if the Soviets refused. After an extremely intense several weeks, the crisis was defused by a negotiated compromise in which the Soviets agreed to remove their missiles in exchange for a guarantee from the United States that it would not invade Cuba. The two superpowers had come so close to nuclear war that, afterward, the leaders of both nations sought ways of reducing tensions. This effort led to a period of "détente," in which a number of arms control agreements were signed and the threat of war was reduced.

*During the Cold War, the United States and the Soviet Union engaged in an arms race, each acquiring nuclear weapons to deter the other from attacking.*

**Cold War** the period of struggle between the United States and the former Soviet Union lasting from the late 1940s to about 1990

A policy of deterrence requires not only the possession of large military forces but also that the nation pursuing such a policy convince potential adversaries that it is willing to fight. France had a large army in the 1930s, but Nazi Germany was not deterred from pursuing its expansionist goals in Europe because the German chancellor, Adolf Hitler, did not believe that the French were actually willing to fight. Thus, as part of its policy of deterrence, the United States engaged in wars in Korea, Vietnam, and elsewhere in response to what it believed to be Soviet aggression. Though the United States had no particular interests in Korea or Vietnam, American policy makers believed that if the United States did not fight in these areas, the Soviets would be emboldened to pursue an expansionist policy elsewhere, thinking that the Americans would not respond. Interventions in Korea and Vietnam were also justified by the so-called Truman Doctrine, which called for American assistance to any nation threatened by the Soviet Union and its allies.

The dissolution of the Soviet Union began in 1985, and the final collapse occurred in 1991, partly because the USSR's huge military expenditures undermined its creaky and inefficient centrally planned economy. The new Russia, though still a formidable and sometimes unfriendly power, seemed to pose less of a threat to the United States. Americans celebrated the end of the Cold War and believed that the enormous expense of America's own military forces might be reduced. Within a few years of the Soviet collapse, however, a new set of security threats emerged, requiring new policy responses. The September 11 terrorist attacks demonstrated a threat against which some security scholars had long warned: that non-state actors and so-called rogue states might acquire significant military capabilities, including nuclear weapons, and would not be affected by America's deterrent capabilities.

A policy of deterrence assumes certainty and rationality. Certainty means that a potential adversary must know for sure that the United States will reply with force if attacked. Rationality means that, to be deterred, a potential adversary must be capable of rationally assessing the risks and costs of aggression against the United States. These two assumptions, which were valid when we sought to counter the Soviet Union, may not be valid in the context of contemporary security threats. Unlike **nation-states**, which are countries with governments and fixed borders, terrorist groups are non-state actors having no fixed geographic location that can be attacked. Terrorists may believe they can attack and melt away, leaving the United States with no one against whom to retaliate. Hence, the threat of massive retaliation does not deter them. Rogue states are nations with unstable and erratic leaders who seem to pursue policies driven by ideological or religious fervor rather than careful consideration of economic or human costs. The United States considers North Korea and Iran to be rogue states.

To counter these new security threats, the George W. Bush administration shifted from a policy of deterrence to one of **preemption**—another name for preventive war or willingness to strike first in order to prevent an enemy attack. The United States declared that it would not wait to be attacked but would, if necessary, take action to disable terrorist groups and rogue states before they could do it harm. The Bush administration's "Global War on Terror" is an expression of this notion of preemption, as was the U.S. invasion of Iraq. The United States has also refused to rule out the possibility that it would attack North Korea or Iran if it

**nation-states** political entities consisting of a people with some common cultural experience (nation) who also share a common political authority (state), recognized by other sovereignties (nation-states)

**preemption** the principle that allows the national government to override state or local actions in certain policy areas. In foreign policy, the willingness to strike first in order to prevent an enemy attack

*The U.S. invasion of Iraq was an example of preemptive war. The Bush administration argued that it had to strike Iraq first, before Iraq used weapons of mass destruction to attack American interests.*

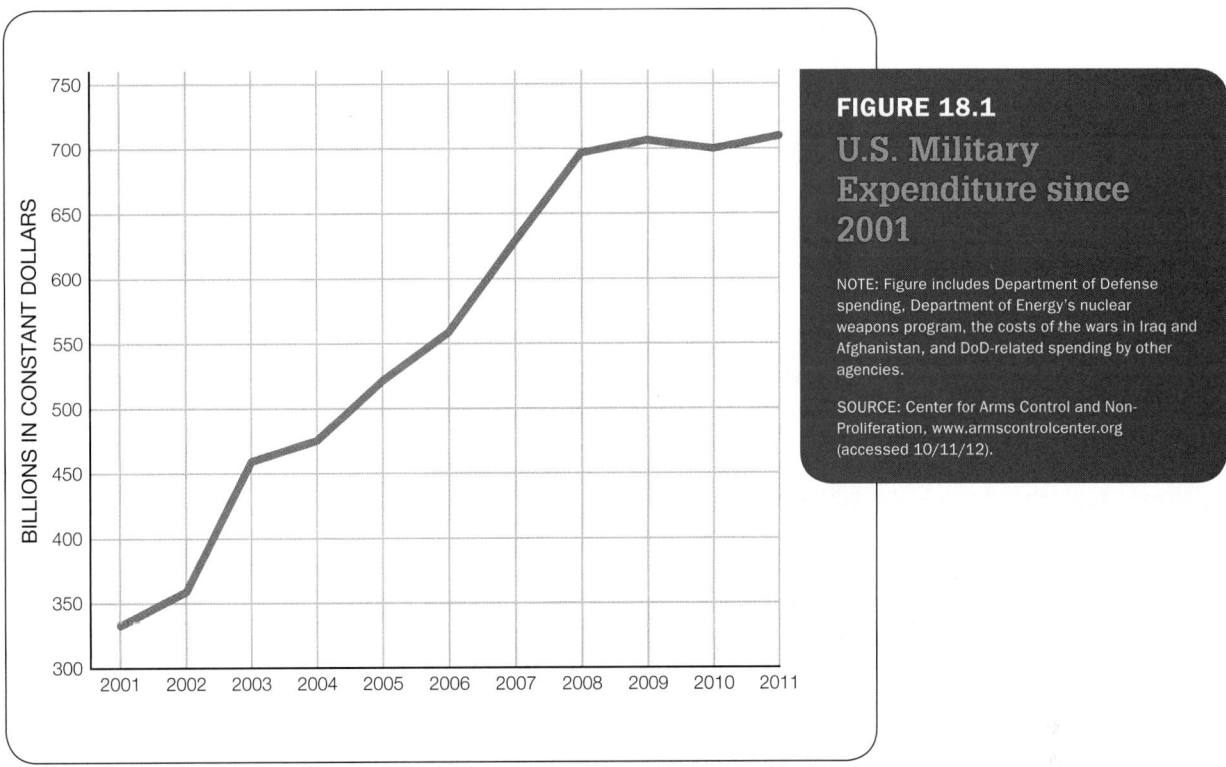

**FIGURE 18.1**

**U.S. Military Expenditure since 2001**

NOTE: Figure includes Department of Defense spending, Department of Energy's nuclear weapons program, the costs of the wars in Iraq and Afghanistan, and DoD-related spending by other agencies.

SOURCE: Center for Arms Control and Non-Proliferation, www.armscontrolcenter.org (accessed 10/11/12).

deemed those nations' nuclear programs to be an imminent threat to American security interests. Accompanying this shift in military doctrines has been an enormous increase in overall U.S. military spending (see Figure 18.1). It remains to be seen whether America's doctrine of preemption will successfully counter threats. The Obama administration declared that it would endeavor to establish constructive dialogues with North Korea, Iran, and other hostile states. However, Obama did not necessarily renounce the Bush Doctrine for those states that declined to become constructively engaged. In 2012 the administration continued pondering how to respond to Iranian plans to acquire nuclear weapons. Should Iran be appeased, deterred, or attacked? Many Republicans and some Democrats seemed to suggest the latter, while the Obama administration hoped the Iranians could be engaged via peaceful means.

## Economic Prosperity

A second major goal of U.S. foreign policy is promoting American prosperity. America's international economic policies are intended to expand employment opportunities in the United States, to maintain access to foreign energy supplies at a reasonable cost, to promote foreign investment in the United States, and to lower the prices Americans pay for goods and services.

Among the most visible and important elements of U.S. international economic policy is trade policy. The promotion and advertising of American goods and services abroad is a long-standing goal of U.S. trade policy, and it is one of the major obligations of the Department of Commerce. Yet modern trade policy involves a complex arrangement of treaties, tariffs, and other mechanisms of policy

# The United States and the World Trade Organization

**The United States has been the** strongest proponent of free trade on the world stage for more than half a century. The American government played a central role in creating international institutions designed to reduce barriers to trade, including the World Trade Organization. Formed in 1995, the WTO is a forum for enforcing international rules to promote free trade. Member countries can appeal to the WTO when they believe another nation is violating international rules by imposing excessive tariffs or protective subsidies. If the WTO decides in favor of the challengers, it allows them to retaliate by imposing their own tariffs on the offending country.

One of the most controversial areas of trade liberalization is agriculture. Since 2001, the WTO trade talks—called the Doha Round because they began in Doha, Qatar, in 2001—have especially focused on reducing trade barriers in agriculture. Since the formation of the WTO, the United States has pressured the developing world to reduce trade barriers. At the same time, however, the United States and Europe have offered heavy subsidies to their own agricultural industries. Such subsidies keep the prices of commodities high, helping to ensure that farmers make a profit. Developing countries have long imposed tariffs to limit the entry of these artificially cheap products, which would otherwise destroy their agricultural sector. During the Doha Round, the developing world charged the richer nations with hypocrisy for demanding that poor countries lower tariffs yet refusing to reduce their agricultural subsidies.

Both the United States and Europe have been reluctant to reduce subsidies and tariffs because farmers are important political constituencies. During the mid-1990s the United States began to cut agricultural subsidies, but in the leadup to the 2002 elections, President Bush signed a very generous farm bill that reinstated many of these subsidies. By 2006, American farm subsidies neared record highs. U.S. trade officials have sought to persuade American farmers that the costs of reduced subsidies will be far outweighed by the benefits gained from opening new markets for their products.

American farmers are not the only constituency blocking more liberalized trade in agricultural products. European nations also have highly subsidized agricultural industries. Despite years of trade talks on the issue, by 2005 the European Union (EU) continued to resist making substantial changes in its tariff levels.

In July 2006, the Doha Round of trade talks finally collapsed. The deep conflicts over liberalizing agricultural trade underscore the high stakes involved in promoting free trade. The United States and the rest of the developed world must be willing to bear the domestic economic and political costs of reducing trade barriers if world trade is to occur on a more level playing field.

## for critical analysis

1. What is the role of the World Trade Organization? What have been some of the obstacles to promoting open markets around the world?

2. Why do agricultural protections pose a particularly difficult problem for advocates of liberalizing world trade? Why have the richer countries, which espouse free trade, been so reluctant to reduce protections for their own agricultural sectors?

formation. For example, the United States has a long-standing policy of granting **most favored nation status** to certain countries—that is, the United States offers to another country the same tariff rate it already gives to its most favored trading partner, in return for trade (and sometimes other) concessions. In 1998, to avoid any suggestion that "most favored nation" implied some special relationship with an undemocratic country (China, for example), President Clinton changed the status label from "most favored nation" to "normal trade relations."[5]

The most important international organization for promoting trade is the **World Trade Organization (WTO)**, which officially came into being in 1995. The WTO grew out of the **General Agreement on Tariffs and Trade (GATT)**. Since World War II, GATT had brought together a wide range of nations for regular negotiations designed to reduce barriers to trade. Such barriers, many believed, had contributed to the breakdown of the world economy in the 1930s and had helped cause World War II. The WTO has 151 members worldwide, including the United States. Similar policy goals are pursued in regional arrangements, such as the **North American Free Trade Agreement (NAFTA)**, a trade treaty among the United States, Canada, and Mexico.

Working toward freer trade has been an important goal of each presidential administration since World War II. Yet as globalization has advanced, concerns about free trade, and about the operation of the WTO in particular, have grown. The WTO meetings held in Seattle in 1999 provoked unprecedented protests by groups that included environmentalists and labor unions. Tens of thousands of protesters denounced the undemocratic decision-making process of the WTO, which, they charged, was dominated by the concerns of business. These critics believe that the WTO does not pay sufficient attention to the concerns of developing nations or to such issues as environmental degradation, human rights, and labor practices, including the use of child labor in many countries. The Seattle meetings were adjourned with no agreement having been reached. Since those meetings, the major problem in WTO negotiations has been conflicts between poor, developing nations and rich, developed countries. Countries in the developing world accuse the United States and Europe of hypocrisy in preaching free trade but then using patents and subsidies to protect their markets. There have been some successes on these issues, notably new WTO guidelines that allow poor countries to override expensive patents. Such patents make desperately needed drugs unavailable to most of the developing world. It has been more difficult to reach agreement on agricultural subsidies. Both the United States and Europe provide massive subsidies to their own agricultural industries. The prospects for resolving this issue are dim. The developed world has been reluctant to confront the economic dislocations and political costs of reducing the subsidies.

For over a half century, the United States has led the world in supporting free trade as the best route to growth and prosperity. Yet the American government, too, has sought to protect domestic industry when it is politically necessary. Subsidies, as we have seen, have long boosted American agriculture, artificially lowering the price of American products on world markets. In 2002, President George W. Bush, a vocal advocate of free trade, angered the rest of the world when he imposed protective tariffs on imported steel. Accused of hypocrisy and faced with retaliation from trading partners, the administration defended its actions by pointing to the damage that imports were doing to the domestic steel industry. When the WTO ruled that the steel tariffs violated WTO rules, Bush faced an unhappy choice: he could allow the European Union to retaliate by imposing tariffs, many of them on goods produced in politically important states, or he could lift the tariffs, thus angering steel producers and workers. The president chose to lift the steel tariffs.

**most favored nation status** agreement to offer a trading partner the lowest tariff rate offered to other trading partners

**Word Trade Organization (WTO)** international organization promoting free trade that grew out of the General Agreement on Tariffs and Trade

**General Agreement on Tariffs and Trade (GATT)** international trade organization, in existence from 1947 to 1995, that set many of the rules governing international trade

**North American Free Trade Agreement (NAFTA)** trade treaty among the United States, Canada, and Mexico to lower and eliminate tariffs among the three countries

## for critical analysis

What are the arguments in favor of free trade (versus restrictions on trade)? Do the advocates of restrictions on trade always favor narrow special interests, or can they, too, be seen as favoring the public interest?

Trade was also an issue in the 2008 election. During their third debate, John McCain accused Barack Obama of promoting protectionist policies, while Obama said Republicans had exported American jobs abroad and allowed an enormous trade deficit to develop. The U.S. trade deficit (a negative trade balance) reached nearly $60 billion (see Figure 18.2), and jobs growth in the United States had been low for several years. Analysts predicted that many of the 2.8 million manufacturing jobs lost in the recession of the early 2000s would never return to the United States. Moreover, outsourcing, the practice of moving jobs to other countries, began to hit the white-collar workforce, as jobs for workers such as call center operators and computer programmers moved to India and other countries with cheaper labor forces. In 2010, the United States accused China of manipulating trade rules to its own advantage, and China, in return, accused the United States of mismanaging its own economy. In 2012, China announced that it would reduce its purchases of U.S. government securities in order to become less vulnerable to fluctuations in the value of the dollar. The United States pointed out that this might result in a reduction of its imports of Chinese goods. Trade creates both economic interdependence and political friction. The same has been true in the case of the 2012 European financial crisis in which several members of the European Union, including Greece, Spain, and Italy, have threatened to default on their loans. The United States favors a strong Europe as a market for American goods but is always concerned about a too-strong Europe whose manufactured products rival America's.

## International Humanitarian Policies

A third goal of American policy is to make the world a better place for all its inhabitants. The main forms of policy that address this goal are international environmental policy, international human rights policy, and international peacekeeping. The United States also contributes to international organizations that work for global health and against hunger, such as the World Health Organization. These

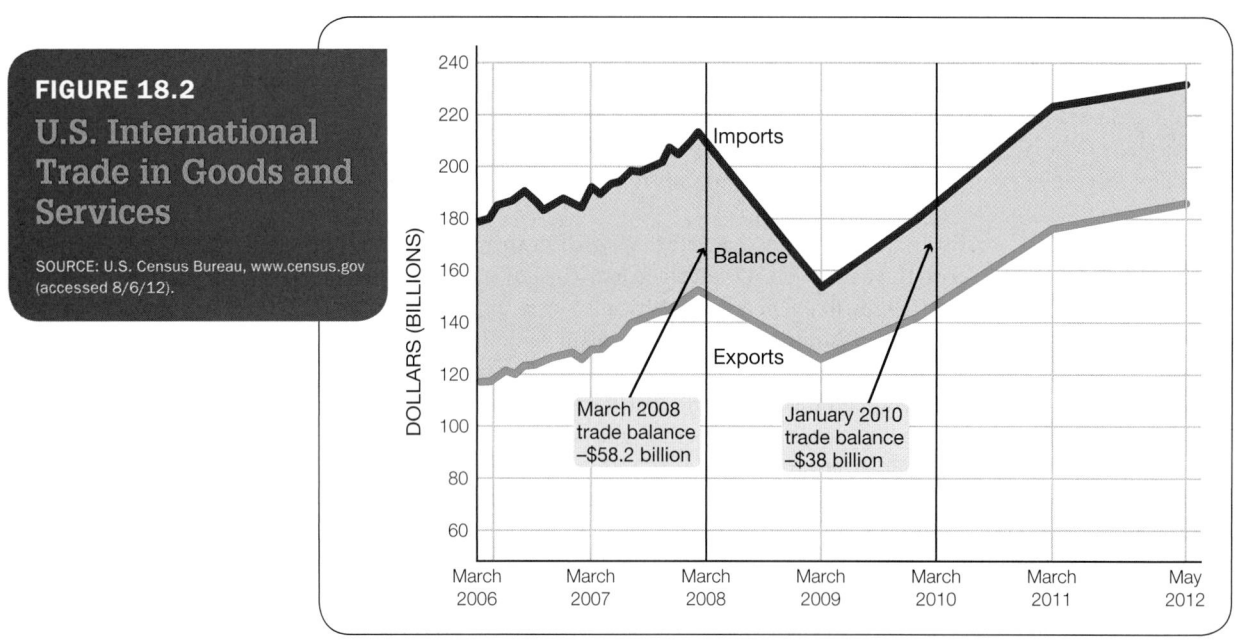

**FIGURE 18.2**

**U.S. International Trade in Goods and Services**

SOURCE: U.S. Census Bureau, www.census.gov (accessed 8/6/12).

policies are often seen as secondary to the other goals of American foreign policy, and are forced to give way if they interfere with security or foreign economic policy. Moreover, although the United States spends billions annually on security policy and hundreds of millions on trade policy, it spends relatively little on environmental, human rights, and peacekeeping efforts. Some critics charge that America has the wrong priorities, spending far more to make war than to protect human rights and the global environment. Nevertheless, a number of important American foreign policy efforts are, at least in part, designed to make the world a better place.

In the realm of international environmental policy, the United States supports a number of international efforts to protect the environment. These include the United Nations Framework Convention on Climate Change, an international agreement to study and ameliorate harmful changes in the global environment, and the Montreal Protocol, an agreement signed by more than 150 countries to limit the production of substances potentially harmful to the world's ozone layer. Other nations have severely criticized the United States for withdrawing from the 1997 Kyoto Protocol, an agreement setting limits on emissions of greenhouse gases from industrial countries. The United States has asserted that the Kyoto Protocol would be harmful to American economic interests. Although the United States is concerned with the global environment, national economic interests took precedence in this case. In preparation for the 2012 expiration of the Kyoto agreement, world leaders gathered in Copenhagen, Denmark, in 2009 to begin the process of negotiating a new climate treaty. The "Copenhagen Climate Summit," however, failed to produce a binding international agreement and ended with the United States, Europe, and China blaming one another for the lack of concrete results.

The same national priorities seem apparent in the area of human rights policy. The United States has a long-standing commitment to human rights and is a party to most major international human rights agreements. These include the International Covenant on Civil and Political Rights, the UN Convention against Torture, the International Convention on the Elimination of All Forms of Racial Discrimination, and various agreements to protect children. The State Department's Bureau of Democracy, Human Rights, and Labor works cooperatively with international organizations to investigate and focus attention on human rights abuses. In 1998 the United States enacted the International Religious Freedom Act, which calls on all governments to respect religious freedom. The act lists a number of sanctions that the United States and other signatories may employ to punish nations found to be in violation.

Although the United States is committed to promoting human rights, this commitment has a lower priority in American foreign policy than the nation's security concerns and economic interests. Thus, the United States is likely to overlook human rights violations by its major trading partners, such as China, and remain silent in the face of human rights violations by such allies as Saudi Arabia. Nevertheless, human rights concerns do play a role in American foreign policy. For example, beginning in 2007 the United States has annually made available several million dollars in small grants to pay medical and legal expenses incurred by individuals who have been the victims of retaliation in their own countries for working against their governments' repressive practices. In this small way, the United States is backing its often-asserted principles.

Another form of U.S. policy designed to improve the condition of the world is support for international peacekeeping efforts. At any point in time, a number

*Many Americans believe that protecting human rights around the world should be a goal of U.S. foreign policy. These protesters called for U.S. government action to stop human rights abuses by China in Tibet. However, humanitarian goals in foreign policy sometimes conflict with political and economic goals.*

of border wars, civil wars, and guerrilla conflicts flare somewhere in the world, usually in its poorer regions. These wars often generate humanitarian crises in the form of casualties, disease, and refugees. In cooperation with international agencies and other nations, the United States funds a number of efforts to keep the peace in volatile regions and to deal with the health care and refugee problems associated with conflict. In 2012 the United States provided more than $1 billion in funding for United Nations (UN) peacekeeping operations in Bosnia, the Democratic Republic of Congo, East Timor, Kosovo, Lebanon, and Sierra Leone.

Although the United States did not intervene directly, it supported NATO operations that helped oust Libya's strongman, Mu'ammar Qaddafi, in 2011 and has offered encouragement to Syrian rebels who sought to overthrow Bashar al-Assad in 2012. The United States was also pleased to see the emergence of democracy in Egypt but concerned when Egypt's 2012 election resulted in a government controlled by the Muslim Brotherhood, a group with which the United States has had difficult relations in the past. Because Americans were generally supportive of the "Arab Spring," many were shocked when the U.S. ambassador to Libya was murdered in an attack on the U.S. Consulate.

As the world's wealthiest nation, the United States also recognizes an obligation to render assistance to nations facing crises and emergencies. In 2010, for example, the United States sent medical aid, food relief, and rescue teams to Haiti when that impoverished island nation was struck by a devastating earthquake, and in 2011 the United States provided support to Japan when a tsunami devastated a portion of the Japanese coast and damaged a Japanese nuclear reactor.

America's humanitarian policies are important. Without American efforts and funding, many international humanitarian programs would be far less successful than they are today. In general, though, security and economic interests take precedence in the eyes of U.S. policy makers over humanitarian concerns.

## ● Who Makes American Foreign Policy?

**Identify the major players in foreign-policy making, and describe their roles**

As we have seen, domestic policies are made by governmental institutions and influenced by a variety of interest groups, political movements, and even the mass media. The same is true in the realm of foreign policy. The president and his chief advisers are the principal architects of U.S. foreign policy. However, Congress, the bureaucracy, the courts, political parties, interest groups, and trade associations also play important roles in this realm. Often the president and Congress are at odds over foreign policy. When the Democrats took control of Congress in 2006, they vowed to force President Bush to end the war in Iraq. The president vowed, in turn, to resist the Democrats' efforts, and generally prevailed. Ethnic lobbies such as the pro-Israel lobby and the Armenian lobby also seek to affect foreign policy. In 2007 the Armenian lobby persuaded Congress to condemn Turkey's actions in 1915 that led to the deaths of more than a million Armenians. The president, fearing that Turkey, an important U.S. ally, would be offended, blocked the effort. Let us examine the major institutions and forces shaping American foreign policy.

## The President

Most American presidents have been domestic politicians who set out to make their place in history through achievements in domestic policy. A standard joke during Bill Clinton's 1992 campaign, extending well into his first year, was that he had learned his foreign policy at the International House of Pancakes. Thus, it was not unusual that Clinton's successor, George W. Bush, had virtually no foreign policy preparation prior to taking office. He had traveled very little outside the United States, and he had had virtually no foreign experience as governor of Texas.

Nonetheless, Bush was decisive in the initiatives he took to define America's national interest for his administration. Examples include revival of the controversial program to develop a nuclear missile shield ("Star Wars"); his abandonment of the Anti-Ballistic Missile (ABM) treaty, which alienated Russia; changes in policy priorities away from humanitarian and environmental goals and toward goals more specifically within the realm of national security; and turning America's concerns (by degree or emphasis) away from Europe and toward an "Asia-first" policy.

September 11 and its aftermath immensely accentuated the president's role and his place in foreign policy.[6] By 2002, foreign policy was the centerpiece of the Bush administration's agenda. In a June 1 speech at West Point, the **"Bush Doctrine"** of preemptive war was announced. Bush argued that "our security will require all Americans ... to be ready for preemptive action when necessary to defend our liberty and to defend our lives." Bush's statement was clearly intended to justify his administration's plans to invade Iraq, but it had much wider implications for international relations and for the central role of the American president in guiding foreign policy.

**Bush Doctrine** foreign policy based on the idea that the United States should take preemptive action against threats to its national security

In 2008, John McCain, the Republican presidential candidate, was an exception to the usual rule emphasizing domestic priorities. McCain had specialized in foreign policy matters in the Senate. During the presidential race, McCain emphasized his foreign policy expertise. Obama countered by naming Senator Joseph Biden, chairman of the Senate Foreign Relations Committee, as the vice-presidential candidate. After his election, President Obama surrounded himself with experienced foreign policy advisers, such as General James Jones, appointed to serve as national security adviser, and Robert Gates, asked to stay on as defense secretary. In October 2010, Jones announced his resignation and was replaced by his deputy, Thomas E. Donilon. In 2011 only one of the candidates for the Republican presidential nomination, former ambassador Jon Huntsman, had extensive foreign policy experience. The other aspirants emphasized their domestic economic and social credentials.

By 2010, President Obama had put his own stamp on American foreign policy, altering the conduct of America's war in Afghanistan and seeking to compel the Israelis and Palestinians to accept a Middle East peace deal. Obama also sought to engage more fully America's allies, who had been miffed by the previous administration's tendency to engage in unilateral action. Thus, as mentioned above, the United States worked closely with its NATO allies in 2011 to bring an end to the Libyan dictatorship of Mu'ammar Qaddafi.

During the course of his first year in office, Obama also concluded direct U.S. military involvement in Iraq and began to withdraw American forces from Afghanistan.

One of Obama's triumphs was the military raid that resulted in the killing of Osama bin Laden, who had long been sought by the United States for his role in the September 11 terrorist attacks. At the end of his first term, however, President Obama faced a number of challenges, including continuing unrest throughout the Middle East and the question of what to do about Iran's evident plan to build nuclear weapons. While presidents have more leeway in the realm of foreign policy than in the domestic sphere, the problems they face in the world sometimes seem intractable.

## The Bureaucracy

The major foreign policy actors in the bureaucracy are the secretaries of the departments of State, Defense, and the Treasury; the Joint Chiefs of Staff (JCS), especially the chair of the JCS; and the director of the CIA. Since 1947 a separate unit in the White House has overseen the vast foreign policy establishment for the purpose of synthesizing all the messages arising out of the bureaucracy and helping the president make his own foreign policy. This is the National Security Council (NSC). It is a "subcabinet" made up of the president, the vice president, the secretary of defense, and the secretary of state, plus others each president appoints. Since the profound shake-up of September 11, two additional key players have been added. The first of these was the secretary of the new Department of Homeland Security (DHS), composed of 22 existing agencies relocated from all over the executive branch on the theory that their expertise could be better coordinated, more rational, and more efficient in a single organization designed to fight international terrorism and domestic natural disasters. The second key player was imposed at the top as the war in Iraq was becoming a quagmire: a director of national intelligence, to collate and coordinate intelligence coming in from multiple sources and to report a synthesis of all this intelligence to the president, on a daily basis.

*Military leaders may play a role in making foreign policy, as they often advise Congress and the president. In 2012, U.S. Marine general John Allen—the chief U.S. and NATO commander in Afghanistan—testified before the House Armed Services Committee.*

Since the creation of the CIA in 1947 and the Department of Defense in 1949 (replacing the Department of War), the secretary of defense and the director of the CIA have often been rivals engaged in power struggles for control of the intelligence community.[7] For the most part, secretaries of defense have prevailed in these battles, and the Defense Department today controls more than 80 percent of the nation's intelligence capabilities and funds. The creation of the position of director of national intelligence in 2005 to coordinate all intelligence activities set off new Washington power struggles as the "intelligence czar" faced opposition from both the CIA and the Department of Defense. As of 2010, the Defense Department has continued to resist cooperating with civilian intelligence agencies and has moved to expand its own intelligence capabilities at the other agencies' expense.

In addition to these top cabinet-level officials, key lower-level staff members have policy-making influence as strong as that of the cabinet secretaries, and occasionally even stronger. These include the two or three specialized national security advisers in the White House, the staff of the NSC (headed by the national security adviser), and a few other career bureaucrats in the departments of State and Defense, whose influence varies according to their specialty and to the foreign policy issue at hand. A few civilian intelligence agencies are also involved in foreign policy and national security, the most important of which are the Federal Bureau of Investigation (FBI), the U.S. Citizenship and Immigration Services, and the Internal Revenue Service (IRS).

In the wake of September 11, military and law enforcement agencies increased their role in America's foreign policy making.[8] To a significant extent, American foreign policy is driven by military and antiterrorism concerns, and the agencies deemed capable of addressing these concerns are coming to play a larger and larger role in American foreign policy. In recent years, American ambassadors have complained that they have been relegated to secondary status as the White House has looked to military commanders for information, advice, and policy implementation. For every region of the world, the U.S. military has assigned a "combatant commander," usually a senior general or admiral, to take charge of operations in that area. In many instances, these combatant commanders, who control troops, equipment, and intelligence capabilities, have become the real eyes, ears, and voices for American foreign policy in their designated regions.

## Congress

Although the Constitution gives Congress the power to declare war (see Table 18.1), Congress has exercised this power on only five occasions: the War of 1812, the Mexican War (1846), the Spanish-American War (1898), World War I (1917), and World War II (1941). For the first 150 years of American history, Congress's foreign policy role was limited because the United States' role in world affairs was limited. During this time, the Senate was the only important congressional foreign policy player because of its constitutional role in reviewing and approving treaties. The treaty power is still the primary entrée of the Senate into foreign-policy making. But since World War II and the continual involvement of the United States in international security and foreign aid, Congress as a whole has become a major foreign-policy maker because most modern foreign policies require financing, which requires action by both the House of Representatives and the Senate. For example, Congress's

| TABLE 18.1 | | |
|---|---|---|
| **Principal Foreign Policy Provisions of the Constitution** | | |
| | **POWERS GRANTED** | |
| | PRESIDENT | CONGRESS |
| War power | Commander in chief of armed forces | Provide for the common defense; declare war |
| Treaties | Negotiate treaties | Ratification of treaties by two-thirds majority (Senate) |
| Appointments | Nominate high-level government officials | Confirm president's appointments (Senate) |
| Foreign commerce | No explicit powers, but treaty negotiation and appointment powers pertain | Explicit power "to regulate foreign commerce" |
| General powers | Executive power; veto | Legislative power; power of the purse; oversight and investigation |

first act after September 11, 2001, was to authorize the president to use "all necessary and appropriate force," coupled with a $40 billion emergency appropriations bill for homeland defense. And although President Bush believed he possessed the constitutional authority to invade Iraq, he still sought congressional approval, which he received in October 2002. After the Democrats took control of Congress in 2007, the Democratic leadership proposed a new resolution opposing President Bush's policies in Iraq. The president asserted that he would not be bound by such a vote.

Not only does the president need Congress to provide funding for foreign and military policy initiatives, but under the Constitution, many presidential agreements with foreign nations also have to be approved by Congress. Article II, Section 2, of the Constitution declares that proposed treaties with other nations must be submitted by the president to the Senate and approved by a two-thirds vote. Because this "supermajority" is usually difficult to achieve, presidents generally prefer a different type of agreement with other nations, called an **executive agreement**. An executive agreement is similar to a treaty and has the force of law but usually requires only a plurality vote (that is, 50 percent plus one) in both houses of Congress for approval.

Another aspect of Congress's role in foreign policy is the Senate's power to confirm the president's nominations of cabinet members, ambassadors, and other high-ranking officials (such as the director of the CIA, but not the director of the NSC). A final constitutional power of Congress is the regulation of "commerce with foreign nations."

Other congressional players are the foreign policy, military policy, and intelligence committees: in the Senate, these are the Foreign Relations Committee, the Armed Services Committee, and the Homeland Security and Governmental Affairs Committee; in the House, these are the Foreign Affairs and Homeland Security Committees and the Armed Services Committee. Usually a few members of these committees who have spent years specializing in foreign affairs become trusted members of the foreign policy establishment and are influential makers of foreign policy. In fact, several members of Congress have left the legislature to become key foreign affairs cabinet members. After September 11, 2001, congressional committees conducted hearings on the failure of the intelligence agencies, but at the time, most members of Congress were reluctant to take on these agencies or a popular president. In 2007, though, with Congress under Democratic control and the president's popularity fading, a number of congressional committees launched inquiries into the conduct of the war in Iraq and the more general operations of the intelligence and defense communities. Within weeks, congressional testimony revealed flaws in military procurement procedures, military planning, and other aspects of the administration's programs and policies. Congressional investigations and the publicity they generate are weapons Congress frequently uses to blunt presidential power.

## Interest Groups

Although the president, the executive branch "bureaucracy," and Congress are the true makers of foreign policy, the "foreign policy establishment" is a much larger arena, including what can properly be called the shapers of foreign policy: a host of unofficial, informal players who possess varying degrees of influence depending on their prestige, reputation, socioeconomic standing, and, most important, the party and ideology that are dominant at a given moment.

By far the most important category of nonofficial player is the interest group—that is, the interest group to which one or more foreign policy issues are of longstanding and vital relevance. Economic interest groups are reputed to wield the

**executive agreement** an agreement, made between the U.S. president and another country, that has the force of a treaty but does not require the Senate's "advice and consent"

most influence, but the myths about their influence far outnumber and outweigh the realities. In fact, the influence of organized economic interest groups in foreign policy varies enormously from issue to issue and year to year. Most of these groups are "single-issue" groups and are therefore most active when their particular issue is on the agenda. On many of the broader and more sustained policy issues—such as NAFTA or the general question of American involvement in international trade—the larger interest groups, sometimes called peak associations, find it difficult to maintain tight enough control of their many members to speak with a single voice. The most systematic study of international trade policies and their interest groups concluded that the leaders of these large economic interest groups spend more time maintaining consensus among their members than they do lobbying Congress or pressuring major players in the executive branch.[9] The more successful economic interest groups, in terms of influencing foreign policy, are the narrower, single-issue groups such as the tobacco industry, which over the years has successfully kept American foreign policy from putting heavy restrictions on international trade in and advertising of tobacco products; and the computer hardware and software industries, which have successfully hardened the American attitude toward Chinese piracy of intellectual property rights.

Another type of interest group with a well-founded reputation for influence in foreign policy is made up of people with strong attachments to and identification with their country of national origin. The interest group with the reputation for the greatest influence is Jewish Americans, whose family and emotional ties to Israel make them one of the most alert and active interest groups in the whole field of foreign policy. In 2010 a dispute between Israel and the Obama administration over Israel's construction of new Jewish housing in Jerusalem led to an intense effort by American Jews to generate congressional support for Israel's position. Similarly, Americans of Irish heritage, despite having lived in the United States for two, three, or four generations, still maintain vigilance about American policies toward Ireland and Northern Ireland. Many other ethnic and national interest groups wield similar influence over American foreign policy.

These ethnic or national-origin interest groups, exhibiting a kind of dual loyalty that Americans generally welcome as a worthy sentiment, are more influential than their counterparts in other democratic countries. But there are limits, especially when national origin is coupled with or tied to countries in which a single religion is dominant. For example, Jews with strong ties to Israel and Catholics with connections to Ireland have on occasion been blocked from group influence on foreign policy because "dual loyalty" can be taken by other groups as "doubtful loyalty."[10] Nevertheless, Irish and Jewish groups, and a variety of other ethnic American interest groups, are vigorously involved in salient aspects of foreign policy, and it is an irrational or nonrational elected politician who disregards their signals. It is quite possible that the "electoral connection"[11] and the politics of representation in Congress (and the White House) are at their most intense when national origin is linked to a foreign policy issue. Many will argue that the rationality principle "need not . . . be equated with such narrowly self-serving actions."[12] However, the nationality interest is often the strongest electoral connection.

A third type of interest group, one with a reputation that has been growing in the past two decades, is devoted to human rights. Such groups are made up of people who, instead of having self-serving economic or ethnic interests in foreign policy,

*Members of Amnesty International asked the U.S. government to take action to end the violence in the Darfur region of Sudan. Interest groups such as Amnesty International may influence foreign policy by lobbying the government directly and by raising public awareness of certain issues.*

are genuinely concerned about the welfare and treatment of people throughout the world—particularly those who suffer under harsh political regimes. A relatively small but often quite influential example is Amnesty International, whose exposés of human rights abuses have altered the practices of many regimes around the world. In recent years, the Christian right has been a vocal advocate for the human rights of Christians who are persecuted in other parts of the world for their religious beliefs, most notably in China. For example, in the 1990s, the Christian Coalition joined groups such as Amnesty International in lobbying Congress to restrict trade with countries that permitted attacks against religious believers.

A related type of group with rapidly growing influence is the ecological or environmental group, sometimes collectively called "greens." Groups of this nature often depend more on demonstrations than on the usual forms and strategies of influence in Washington, such as lobbying and using electoral politics, for example. Environmental activists staged major protests at the 2009 London and 2010 Toronto international economic summits.

## Putting It Together

What can we say about who actually makes American foreign policy? First, except for the president, the influence of players and shapers varies from case to case—this is a good reason to look with some care at each example of foreign policy in this chapter. Second, because the one constant influence is the centrality of the president in foreign-policy making, it is best to evaluate other actors and factors as they interact with the president.[13] Third, the reason influence varies from case to case is that each case arises under different conditions and with vastly different time constraints: for issues that arise and are resolved quickly, the opportunity for influence is limited. Fourth, foreign policy experts will usually disagree about the level of influence any player or type of player has on policy making.

Let's make a few tentative generalizations to frame the remainder of this chapter. First, when an important foreign policy decision has to be made under conditions of crisis, when time is of the essence, the influence of the presidency is at its strongest. Second, within these time constraints, access to the decision-making process is limited almost exclusively to the narrowest definition of the foreign policy establishment. The arena for participation is tiny; any discussion at all is limited to the officially and constitutionally designated players. To put this another way, in a crisis, the foreign policy establishment works as it is supposed to.[14] As time becomes less restricted, even when the decision to be made is of great importance, the arena of participation expands to include more government players and more nonofficial, informal players—the most concerned interest groups and the most important journalists. In other words, the arena becomes more pluralistic and, therefore, less distinguishable from the politics of domestic-policy making. Third, because there are so many other countries with power and interests on any given issue, there are severe limits on the choices the United States can make. That is, in sharp contrast to domestic politics, U.S. policy makers in the foreign policy realm are engaged not only in infighting but also in strategic interaction with policy makers in other nations; their choices are made both in reaction to and in anticipation of these strategic interactions. As one author concludes, in foreign affairs, "policy takes precedence over politics."[15] Thus, even though foreign-policy making in noncrisis situations may closely resemble the pluralistic politics of domestic-policy making, foreign-policy making is still a narrower arena with fewer participants.

# The Instruments of Modern American Foreign Policy

Any government has at hand certain instruments, or tools, to use in implementing its foreign policy. An instrument is neutral, capable of serving many goals. There have been many instruments of American foreign policy, and we can deal here only with those instruments we deem most important in the modern epoch: diplomacy, the United Nations, the international monetary structure, economic aid and sanctions, collective security, military force, and arbitration. Each of these instruments will be evaluated in this section for its utility in the conduct of American foreign policy, and each will be assessed in light of the history and development of American values.

## Diplomacy

We begin this treatment of instruments with diplomacy. **Diplomacy** is the representation of a government to other foreign governments. Its purpose is to promote national values or interests by peaceful means. According to Hans Morgenthau, "a diplomacy that ends in war has failed in its primary objective."[16]

**diplomacy** the representation of a government to other governments

The first effort to create a modern diplomatic service in the United States was made through the Rogers Act of 1924, which established the initial framework for a professional foreign service staff. But it took World War II and the Foreign Service Act of 1946 to forge the foreign service into a fully professional diplomatic corps.

Diplomacy, by its very nature, is overshadowed by spectacular international events, dramatic initiatives, and meetings among heads of state or their direct personal representatives. The traditional American distrust of diplomacy continues today, albeit in a weaker form. Impatience with or downright distrust of diplomacy has been built into not only all the other instruments of foreign policy but also the modern presidential system itself.[17] So much personal responsibility has been heaped on the presidency that presidents are reluctant to entrust any of their authority or responsibility in foreign policy to professional diplomats in the State Department and other bureaucracies.

In 2008 both parties' presidential candidates criticized the Bush administration for having failed to use diplomacy to secure greater international support for the Iraq War. Both promised to revitalize American diplomacy. President Obama appointed Hillary Clinton secretary of state in part to underline the importance he attached to diplomacy by choosing such a prominent figure as America's chief diplomat.

The significance of diplomacy and its vulnerability to politics may be better appreciated as we proceed to the other instruments. While Americans have traditionally distrusted diplomacy, it was an instrument more or less imposed on them as the prevailing means of bargaining among nation-states in the nineteenth century. The other

*The secretary of state is America's chief diplomat. In 2012, Secretary of State Hillary Clinton met with the leaders of numerous other countries, including King Abdullah of Saudi Arabia.*

instruments to be identified and assessed here are instruments that Americans self-consciously crafted for themselves to take care of their own chosen place in the world affairs of the second half of the twentieth century and beyond. The instruments therefore better reflect American culture and values than diplomacy does.

## The United Nations

**United Nations (UN)** an organization of nations founded in 1945 to be a channel for negotiation and a means of settling international disputes peaceably. The UN has had frequent successes in providing a forum for negotiation and, on some occasions, a means of preventing international conflicts from spreading. On a number of occasions, the UN has been a convenient cover for U.S. foreign policy goals

The utility of the **United Nations (UN)** to the United States as an instrument of foreign policy can be too easily underestimated because the UN is a very large and unwieldy institution with few powers and no armed forces to implement its rules and resolutions. Its supreme body is the UN General Assembly, comprising one representative of each of the 192 member states; each member representative has one vote, regardless of the size of the country. Important issues require a two-thirds-majority vote, and the annual session of the General Assembly runs only from September to December (although it can call extra sessions). It has little organization that can make it an effective decision-making body, with only six standing committees, few tight rules of procedure, and no political parties to provide priorities and discipline. Its defenders are quick to add that although it lacks armed forces, it relies on the power of world opinion—and this is not to be taken lightly. The powers of the UN devolve mainly to the organization's "executive committee," the UN Security Council, which alone has the real power to make decisions and rulings that member states are obligated by the UN Charter to implement. The Security Council may be called into session at any time, and each member (or a designated alternate) must be present at UN headquarters in New York at all times. The council is composed of 15 members: 5 are permanent (the victors of World War II), and 10 are elected by the General Assembly for unrepeatable two-year terms. The 5 permanent members are China, France, Russia, the United Kingdom, and the United States. Each of the 15 members has only one vote, and a 9-vote majority of the 15 is required on all substantive matters. But each of the five permanent members also has a negative vote, a "veto," and one veto is sufficient to reject any substantive proposal.

The UN can serve as a useful forum for international discussions and an instrument for multilateral action. Most peacekeeping efforts to which the United States contributes, for example, are undertaken under UN auspices.

*The United Nations is not always but can be an important instrument of American foreign policy. In trying to build international support for the U.S. case against Iraq, President Bush went before the General Assembly and urged the United Nations to compel Iraq to disarm. Two months later, the UN Security Council gave its qualified support to Bush's position.*

## The International Monetary Structure

Fear of a repeat of the economic devastation that followed World War I brought the United States together with its allies (except the USSR) to Bretton Woods, New Hampshire, in 1944 to create a new international economic structure for the postwar world. The result was two institutions: the International Bank for Reconstruction and Development (commonly called the World Bank) and the International Monetary Fund.

The World Bank was set up to finance long-term capital. Leading nations took on the obligation of contributing funds to enable the World Bank to make loans to capital-hungry countries. (The U.S. quota has been about one-third of the total.)

The **International Monetary Fund (IMF)** was set up to provide for the short-term flow of money. After the war, the U.S. dollar replaced gold as the chief means by which the currencies of one country would be "changed into" currencies of another country for purposes of making international transactions. To permit debtor countries with no international balances to make purchases and investments, the IMF was set up to lend dollars or other appropriate currencies to such needy member countries to help them overcome temporary trade deficits.

During the 1990s the importance of the IMF increased through its efforts to reform some of the largest debtor nations and formerly Communist countries, to bring them more fully into the global capitalist economy. For example, in the early 1990s, Russia and 13 other former Soviet republics were invited to join the IMF and the World Bank, with the expectation that they would receive $10.5 billion from these two agencies, primarily for a currency stabilization fund. Each republic was to get a permanent IMF representative, and the IMF increased its staff by at least 10 percent to provide the expertise necessary to cope with the problems of these emerging capitalist economies.[18]

The IMF, with tens of billions of dollars contributed by its members, has more money to lend poor countries than does the United States, Europe, or Japan (the three leading IMF shareholders) individually. It makes its policy decisions in ways that are generally consonant with the interests of the leading shareholders.[19] Two weeks after September 11, 2001, the IMF approved a $135 million loan to economically troubled Pakistan, a key player in the war against the Taliban government of Afghanistan because of its strategic location. Turkey, also because of its strategic location in the Middle East, was likewise put back in the IMF pipeline.[20] The future of the IMF, the World Bank, and all other private sources of international investment will depend in part on extension of more credit to developing countries, because credit means investment and productivity. But the future may depend even more on reducing the debt that is already there from previous extensions of credit.

**International Monetary Fund (IMF)** an institution established in 1944 that provides loans and facilitates international monetary exchange

## Economic Aid and Sanctions

Every year, the United States provides nearly $30 billion in economic assistance to other nations. Some aid has a humanitarian purpose, such as helping to provide health care, shelter for refugees, or famine relief. A good deal of American aid, however, is designed to promote American security interests or economic concerns. For example, the United States provides military assistance to a number of its allies in the form of advanced weapons or loans to help them purchase such weapons. These loans generally stipulate that the recipient must purchase the designated weapons from American firms. In this way, the United States hopes to bolster its security and economic interests with one grant. The two largest recipients

**for critical analysis**

There has been a good deal of debate about whether economic sanctions can convince North Korea or Iran to halt its nuclear weapons programs. What factors might help to determine the effectiveness of economic sanctions?

*The United States has imposed economic sanctions in an effort to discourage North Korea from further developing its nuclear weapons program. In talks with the leader Kim Jong-Un in 2012, the United States also offered to renew food aid to North Korea as an incentive.*

of American military assistance are Israel and Egypt, American allies that fought two wars against each other. The United States believes that its military assistance allows both countries to feel sufficiently secure to remain at peace with each other.

Aid is an economic carrot. Sanctions are an economic stick. Economic sanctions that the United States employs against other nations include trade embargoes, bans on investment, and efforts to prevent the World Bank or other international institutions from extending credit to a nation against which the United States has a grievance. Sanctions are most often employed when the United States seeks to weaken what it considers a hostile regime or when it is attempting to compel some particular action by another regime. Thus, for example, in order to weaken the Castro government, the United States has long prohibited American firms from doing business with Cuba. In recent years, the United States has maintained economic sanctions against Iran and North Korea in an effort to prevent those nations from pursuing nuclear weapons programs.

As the Iranian example shows, unilateral sanctions by the United States usually have little effect, since the target can usually trade elsewhere, sometimes even with foreign affiliates of U.S. firms. If, however, the United States is able to persuade its allies to cooperate, sanctions have a better chance of success. International sanctions against Libya, for example, were decisive in compelling that nation to enter into negotiations with the United States over Libyan responsibility for the 1988 bombing of an airliner over Lockerbie, Scotland, that killed more than 100 Americans. The Libyans ultimately agreed to accept responsibility and pay compensation to the victims' families.

## Collective Security

In 1947 most Americans hoped that the United States could meet its world obligations through the UN and economic structures alone. But most foreign-policy makers recognized that was a vain hope, even as they were permitting and encouraging Americans to believe it. These policy makers had anticipated the need for military entanglements at the time of drafting the original UN Charter by insisting on language that recognized the right of all nations to provide for their mutual defense independent of the UN. And almost immediately after enactment of the Marshall Plan, designed to promote European economic recovery, the White House and a parade of State and Defense Department officials followed up with an urgent request to the Senate to ratify, and to both houses of Congress to finance, mutual defense alliances.

The Senate, at first quite reluctant to approve treaties providing for national security alliances, ultimately agreed with the executive branch. The first collective security agreement was the Rio Treaty (ratified by the Senate in September 1947), which created the Organization of American States (OAS). This was the model treaty, anticipating all succeeding collective security treaties by providing that an armed attack against any of its members "shall be considered as an attack against all the American States," including the United States. A more significant break with U.S. tradition against peacetime entanglements came with the North Atlantic Treaty (signed in April 1949), which created the **North Atlantic Treaty Organization (NATO)**. The Australian, New Zealand, United States Security (ANZUS) Treaty, which tied Australia and New Zealand to the United States, was signed in

**North Atlantic Treaty Organization (NATO)** an organization, comprising the United States, Canada, and most of Western Europe, formed in 1948 to counter the perceived threat from the Soviet Union

September 1951. Three years later, the Southeast Asia Treaty created the Southeast Asia Treaty Organization (SEATO).

In addition to these multilateral treaties, the United States entered into a number of **bilateral treaties** (treaties between two countries), such as the treaty with Vietnam that resulted in ultimately unsuccessful American military action to protect that nation's government. As one author has observed, the United States has been a *producer* of security, whereas most of its allies have been *consumers* of security.[21]

This pattern has continued in the post–Cold War era, and its best illustration is in the Persian Gulf War, where the United States provided the initiative, the leadership, and most of the armed forces, even though its allies were obliged to reimburse over 90 percent of the cost.

It is difficult to evaluate collective security and its treaties, because the purpose of collective security as an instrument of foreign policy is prevention, and success of this kind has to be measured in terms of what did *not* happen. Critics have argued that U.S. collective security treaties posed a threat of encirclement to the Soviet Union, forcing it to produce its own collective security, particularly the Warsaw Pact.[22] Nevertheless, no one can deny the counterargument that more than 60 years have passed without a world war.

In 1998 the expansion of NATO took its first steps toward including former Warsaw Pact members, extending membership to the Czech Republic, Hungary, and Poland. Most of Washington embraced this expansion as the true and fitting end of the Cold War, and the U.S. Senate echoed this with a resounding 80-to-19 vote to induct these three former Soviet satellites into NATO. The expansion was also welcomed among European member nations, who quickly approved the move, hailing it as the final closing of the book on Yalta, the 1945 treaty that divided Europe into Western and Soviet spheres of influence after the defeat of Germany. Expanded membership seems to have made NATO less threatening and more acceptable to Russia. Russia became a partner when the NATO-Russia Council was formed in 2002. Finally, although the expanded NATO membership (28 countries in 2012) reduces the threat to Russia, it also reduces the utility of NATO as a military alliance. The September 11, 2001, attack on the United States was the first time in its more than 50-year history that Article 5 of the North Atlantic Treaty had to be invoked; it provides that an attack on one country is an attack on all the member countries. In fighting "the war on terror," the Bush administration recognized that no matter how preponderant American power was, some aspects of U.S. foreign policy could not be achieved without multilateral cooperation.

On the other hand, the United States did not want to be constrained by its alliances. The global coalition initially forged after September 11, 2001, numbered more than 170 countries. Not all joined the war effort in Afghanistan, but most if not all provided some form of support for some aspect of "the war on terror," such as economic sanctions and intelligence.

Two years later, however, the war in Iraq put this coalition to the test. The Bush administration was determined not to make its decision to go to war subject to the UN, NATO, or any other international organization. The breadth of the United States' coalition was deemed secondary to the coalition's being nonconstraining. As a result, other than the British government, no major power supported the United States' actions.

*Military force is the most visible instrument of foreign policy. The use of such force, however, almost always engenders unanticipated consequences and problems, as America's experience in Iraq has shown.*

## Military Force

The most visible instrument of foreign policy is, of course, military force. The United States has built the world's most imposing military, with army, navy, marine, and air force units stationed in virtually every corner of the globe. The United States spends nearly as much on military might as the rest of the world combined (Figure 18.3). The Prussian military strategist Carl von Clausewitz famously called war "politics by other means." By this he meant that nations used force not simply to demonstrate their capacity for violence. Rather, force or the threat of force is a tool nations must sometimes use to achieve their foreign policy goals. Military force may be needed to protect a nation's security interests and economic concerns. Ironically, force may also be needed to achieve humanitarian goals. For example, without international military protection, the refugees in Darfur camps would be completely at the mercy of the violent Sudanese regime.

Though force is sometimes necessary, military force is generally seen as a last resort and avoided if possible because of a number of problems commonly associated with its use. First, the use of military force is extremely costly in both human and financial terms. In the past 50 years, tens of thousands of Americans have been killed and hundreds of billions of dollars spent in America's military operations. Before they employ military force to achieve national goals, policy makers must be certain that achieving those goals is essential and that other means are unlikely to succeed.

Second, the use of military force is inherently fraught with risk. However carefully policy makers and generals plan for military operations, results can seldom be fully anticipated. Variables ranging from the weather to unexpected weapons and tactics deployed by opponents may upset the most careful calculations and turn military operations into costly disasters or convert maneuvers that were expected to be quick and decisive into long, drawn-out, expensive struggles. For example, American policy makers expected to defeat the Iraqi army quickly and easily in 2003—and they did. Policy makers did not anticipate, however, that American forces would still be struggling years later to defeat the insurgency that arose in the war's aftermath.

**FIGURE 18.3**

Military Spending, 2011

SOURCE: Stockholm International Peace Research Institute, www.sipri.org (accessed 8/6/12).

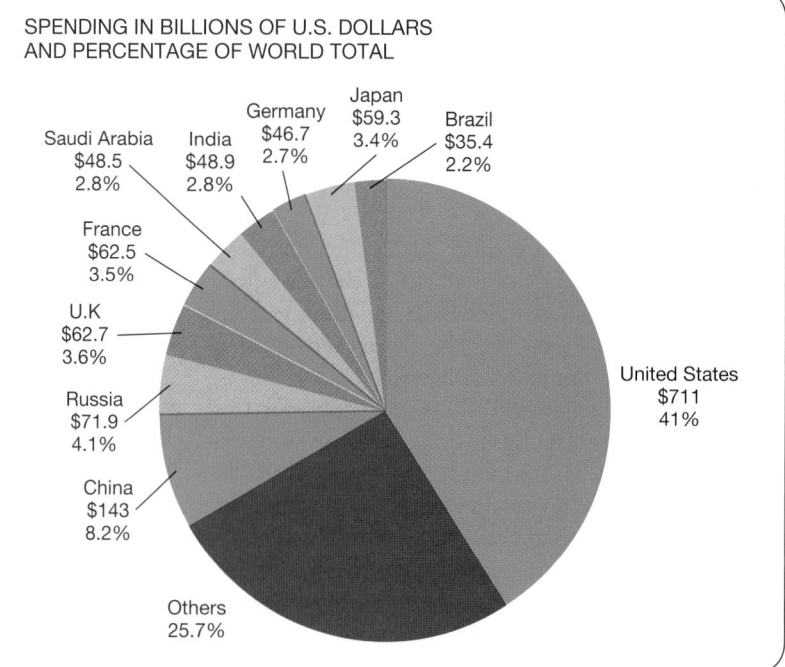

SPENDING IN BILLIONS OF U.S. DOLLARS AND PERCENTAGE OF WORLD TOTAL

- Germany $46.7 2.7%
- Japan $59.3 3.4%
- Brazil $35.4 2.2%
- Saudi Arabia $48.5 2.8%
- India $48.9 2.8%
- France $62.5 3.5%
- U.K $62.7 3.6%
- Russia $71.9 4.1%
- China $143 8.2%
- United States $711 41%
- Others 25.7%

# Who Serves in the U.S. Military?

## Gender

**U.S. Military**
14% Female
86% Male

86%

**U.S. Population**

51% Female
49% Male

49%

## Race/Ethnicity

**U.S. Military**
66% White       3% Asian
16% Black       5% Other
10% Hispanic

66%

**U.S. Population**

64% White
13% Black
16% Hispanic
5% Asian
3% Other

64%

## Education

New enlistees, 2010

**U.S. Military**
98% High school
graduates

98%

**U.S. Population**

86% High school
graduates

86%

The Department of Defense and the military are often responsible for implementing foreign policy that relates to security. Who are the men and women in the armed forces? The military has a far greater proportion of men to women than the general population, but in terms of race and ethnicity, the military is fairly similar to the United States as a whole. Residents of southern states are significantly more likely to enlist than those from other regions.

SOURCES: Department of Defense, "Population Representation in the Military Services, 2010." U.S. Census, 2010.

## Geographic Origin

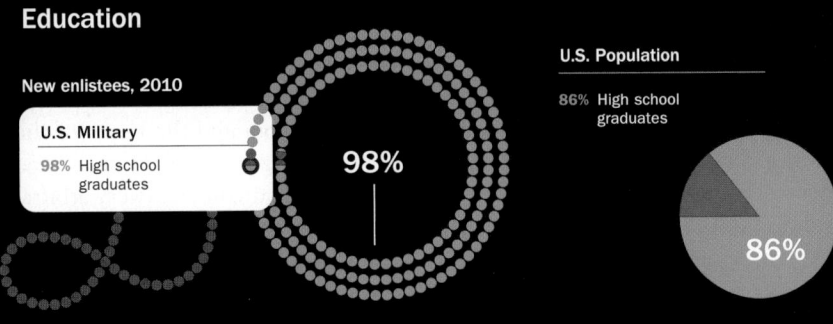

U.S. military new enlistees, 2012

12.4%
19.7%
23%
42.2%

| Northeast | 12.4% | Midwest | 19.7% |
| South | 42.2% | West | 23% |

U.S. population

18%
22%
23%
37%

| Northeast | 18% | Midwest | 22% |
| South | 37% | West | 23% |

### for critical analysis

1. The move to an all-volunteer military in the United States in 1973 resulted in a more educated and professionalized force. However, the United States has used the draft in the past, and some countries require military service of all citizens. Can you think of some arguments for and against each approach?

2. Does it matter if some groups are more heavily represented in the armed forces than others?

Finally, in a democracy, any government that chooses to address policy problems through military means is almost certain to encounter political difficulties. Generally speaking, the American public will support relatively short and decisive military engagements. If, however, a conflict drags on, producing casualties and expenses with no clear outcome, the public loses patience and opposition politicians point to the government's lies and ineptitude. The wars in Korea, Vietnam, and Iraq are all examples of protracted conflicts whose domestic political repercussions became serious liabilities for the governments that initially decided to make use of military force.

Thus, military force remains a major foreign policy tool, and the United States currently possesses a more powerful and effective set of military forces than any other nation. Nevertheless, even for the United States, the use of military force is fraught with risk and is not to be undertaken lightly.

## Arbitration

The final foreign policy tool we shall consider is dispute arbitration. Arbitration means referring an international disagreement to a neutral third party for resolution. Arbitration, like diplomacy, is sometimes seen as a form of "soft power" as distinguished from military force, economic sanctions, and other coercive foreign policy instruments. The United States will occasionally turn to international tribunals to resolve disputes with other countries. For example, in February 2008 the U.S. government asked the International Court of Justice to resolve a long-standing dispute with Italy over American property confiscated by the Italian government more than 40 years ago. To take another example, in 1981 the United States and Iran established an arbitral tribunal to deal with claims arising from Iran's seizure of the U.S. embassy in Tehran in 1979; the tribunal resulted in a settlement.

More important, the United States relies heavily on the work of arbitral panels to maintain the flow of international trade on which America's economy depends. U.S. firms would be reluctant to do business abroad if they could not be certain that their property and contractual rights would be honored by other nations. Arbitration helps produce that certainty. Almost every international contract contains an arbitration clause requiring that disputes between the parties will be resolved not by foreign governments but by impartial arbitral panels accepted by both sides. By the terms of the New York Convention, virtually every nation in the world has agreed to accept and enforce arbitral verdicts. The United States has incorporated the terms of the New York Convention into federal law, and U.S. courts vigorously enforce arbitral judgments. The United States may not be happy with the outcome of every arbitral proceeding, but the arbitral system is essential to America's economic interests.

## ● Thinking Critically about America's Role in the World Today

The nineteenth-century British statesman Lord Palmerston famously said, "Nations have no permanent friends or allies; they only have permanent interests." Palmerston's comment illustrates what is sometimes known as the "realist" view of foreign policy. The realist school holds that foreign policies should be guided by the national interest (mainly security and economic interest) and that policy makers should steel themselves to the necessity of making decisions that might be viewed from the outside as cold and ruthless if they serve the nation's interests. Although many public officials have denounced such views in public—especially if they were running for

# DIGITAL CITIZENS

# Using Technology to Topple a Government: The Case of Egypt

**The mass protests that raged** against the Egyptian government in early 2011 were part of a broader movement across many North African and Middle Eastern countries with nondemocratic governments. The movement started in Tunisia in late 2010, and by mid-January 2011, it had resulted in a new Tunisian government and protests in other countries across the region. As in the other nations, the Egyptian protests focused on the lack of free elections or freedom of speech, and on political corruption, state-of-emergency laws, police brutality, and economic hardships, including unemployment, low wages, and high food prices.

The first documented use of the Internet to organize the Egyptian protesters occurred on January 20, with a Facebook group organizing street protests for January 25. The plan focused on nonviolent protest, including demonstrations, marches, and civil disobedience. The group originally formed to organize a silent protest in response to the beating death of a boy by police. The boy had supposedly been in possession of video of police selling illegal drugs.

Estimates suggest that, at the time of the protests, one in five Egyptians had Internet access, and the young and educated—who were among those most likely to have access—used social media to spread the word of the revolution. In response to the January 25 street protests, Egypt's security forces sought to monitor Internet activities by block-ing social media sites, disconnecting cell phone services, and ultimately disabling Internet access for the country.

By Friday, January 29, millions of protesters had taken to the streets. Shutting off Internet access was an attempt to stop the organizing. However, the government-controlled blackout of Internet and mobile phone service was not enough to stop the protesters. Organizers turned to fax machines and other forms of communication. On this same day, supporters of the protesters in Egypt organized and protested outside the Egyptian embassy in Washington, D.C. In response to the Internet blackout, the United Nations declared access to the Internet a human right.

Reports of beatings, rampant abuse, and arrests of foreign journalists emerged as military tanks rolled down the streets of Egyptians cities, and the protests became headline news worldwide. By January 31, the U.S. State Department had entered the fray to free journalists and evacuate Americans in Egypt. By February 2, more than 400 people had been killed in clashes between protesters and the police, the military, and supporters of the Egyptian government.

A Google executive who helped ignite the protests in Egypt was detained by the government for 12 days before a release was negotiated. When the executive, Wael Ghonim, was interviewed after Egyptian president Hosni Mubarak finally stepped down on February 11, Ghonim credited the Internet and Facebook with the success of the revolution: "This revolution started online. This revolution started on Facebook . . . I've always said that if you want to liberate a society just give them the Internet." Scholarly research backs this claim. Work by communications scholar Philip Howard indicates that digital communication is effective at instigating democratic protests in authoritarian countries, despite government censorship.

One of the other founders of the Facebook page that started the Egyptian revolution learned about the protest via a Twitter feed. His response was "Who does a Facebook event for a revolution, you know?"

SOURCES: Anne Alexander, "Internet Role in Egypt's Protests," BBC News, February 9, 2011, www.bbc.co.uk/news/world-middle-east-12400319 (accessed 10/11/12). Kenneth Chamberlain, "Timeline: Revolt in the Middle East and North Africa," *National Journal*, February 11, 2011, www.nationaljournal.com/timeline-revolt-in-the-middle-east-and-north-africa-20110128 (accessed 10/11/12). Wael, Ghonim, interviewed on CNN, February 11, 2011, http://cnnpressroom.blogs.cnn.com/2011/02/11/cnn-interviews-wael-ghonim-following-mubarak-resignation/ (accessed 00/00/00). Philip N. Howard, *The Digital Origins of Dictatorship and Democracy* (New York: Oxford University Press, 2010). John D. Sutter, "The Faces of Egypt's 'Revolution 2.0,'" CNN, February 21, 2011, www.cnn.com/2011/TECH/innovation/02/21/egypt.internet.revolution/index.html (accessed 10/11/12).

## for critical analysis

1. Does shutting off the Internet for an entire country violate the rights of citizens? Should the international community support this right along with other human rights?

2. Will the availability of political information online spur revolutions and demands for free elections and free speech in authoritarian countries worldwide? Or was what happened in Egypt unique?

753

office—many became realists once in power. Every one of America's post–World War II presidents, liberals and conservatives, Democrats and Republicans alike, has been willing to order young Americans into battle and to visit death and destruction on the citizens of foreign states if he believed the national interest required it.

The harsh rationality of foreign policy often clashes with America's history and ideals. U.S. democratic and liberal traditions lead Americans to hope for a world in which ideals rather than naked interests govern foreign policy and in which U.S. leaders pay heed to ideals. The ideals that Americans historically have espoused (though not always lived by) assert that U.S. foreign policies should have a higher purpose than the pursuit of self-interest and that America is to use force only as a last resort. Since the realities of U.S. foreign policy often clash with these historic ideals, American policy makers often struggle to explain their actions and avoid admitting to motivations that don't embody those ideals.

"I have previously stated and I repeat now that the United States plans no military intervention in Cuba," said President John F. Kennedy in 1961 as he planned military intervention in Cuba. "As president, it is my duty to the American people to report that renewed hostile actions against United States ships on the high seas in the Gulf of Tonkin have today required me to order the military forces of the United States to take action in reply," said President Lyndon Johnson in 1964, referring to a fabricated incident used to justify expansion of American involvement in Vietnam. "We did not, I repeat, did not trade weapons or anything else [to Iran] for hostages, nor will we," said President Ronald Reagan in November 1986, four months before admitting that U.S. arms had been traded to Iran in exchange for Americans being held hostage there. "Simply stated, there is no doubt that Saddam Hussein now has weapons of mass destruction," said Vice President Dick Cheney in 2002. When it turned out that these weapons did not exist, Assistant Defense Secretary Paul Wolfowitz explained, "For bureaucratic reasons, we settled on one issue, weapons of mass destruction [as justification for invading Iraq], because it was the one reason everyone could agree on."[23] Falsehoods may hide discrepancies between historic ideals and rationality, but they do not resolve them.

The ever-present conflicts between ideals and harsh realities manifested themselves again in 2009. As a candidate for the presidency, Barack Obama was praised for denouncing the Bush administration's treatment of enemy combatants. Obama was especially critical of the Guantánamo detention facility, where some alleged enemy combatants were incarcerated, and of the creation of military tribunals, which are outside the regular court system, to hear their cases. Once in office, however, Obama did not rush to close the Guantánamo facility—though he continued to plan for its eventual closure. As for the tribunals, President Obama ordered a resumption of their use in terrorist cases at the end of 2011. Ideals seemed to have given way to interests yet again.

Must America always choose between its ideals and its interests? The founders of the Republic believed that America would be different from other nations. They believed that its ideals would be its source of power; that its ideals would allow it to inspire and lead others as a "shining beacon." If, in the pursuit of national power and security, our political leaders always choose narrow interests over transcendent ideals, might they be robbing America of its true source of international power and global security?

*In 2011 the United States succeeded in killing Osama bin-Laden, the Al Qaeda leader responsible for the September 11, 2001, terrorist attacks. Here, bin-Laden's supporters protest his death. Even some of America's allies questioned the use of "assassination" on Pakistani soil without the prior knowledge of the Pakistani government.*

# Explore Perspectives
# on Foreign Policy

## Inform Yourself

 **How do Americans see the world?** The Pew Research Center and Carnegie Foundation have an interactive graphic on U.S. foreign policy attitudes at http://carnegieendowment.org/publications/interactive/how-do-americans-view. Use the site to explore U.S. public opinion on different countries and foreign policy issues.

 **How do people around the world see the United States and other nations?** The Pew Research Center Global Attitudes Project (www.pewglobal.org/database/) shows public opinion data from countries around the world. Click on the "Questions by Topic" tab at the top menu, and then "Rating Countries and Organizations." Click on China. How does public opinion about China vary around the world? Compare what you find about China to global opinions about the United States. How have these opinions changed since 2000?

 **Watch a video on U.S. foreign policy toward Iran.** A current question in foreign policy concerns tensions between the United States and Iran over Iran's nuclear program. This issue raises the question of what Americans actually know about Iran. In this video (www.youtube.com/watch?v=J3KVOecnJUc), former diplomat Professor Nicholas Burns provides a short overview of why U.S. relations with Iran have become so difficult.

## Connect with Others

 **Share news stories from the international media.** Considering an outside perspective can help you develop a deeper understanding of foreign policy. *The Guardian* is a well-respected British newspaper. What are the top stories on its U.S. foreign policy page (www.guardian.co.uk/world/usforeignpolicy) and how are they different from what you've heard about in U.S. media? A reputable foreign website that covers U.S. foreign policy is Al Jazeera (www.aljazeera.com). Which of its top stories involve U.S. foreign policy? Consider sharing an international news story with others using social media.

*Find links to the sites listed above as well as related activities on wwnorton.com/studyspace.*

## The Goals of Foreign Policy

■ **Explain how foreign policy is designed to promote security, prosperity, and humanitarian goals (pp. 729–38)**

The programs and policies that determine U.S. relations with other nations and foreign entities are referred to as *American foreign policy*. The three main goals of American foreign policy are security, prosperity, and the creation of a better world. Although each of these goals is important in understanding the contours of American foreign policy, most policy makers usually give precedence to security and economic interests over humanitarian concerns.

### Key Terms

**non-state actors** (p. 730)

**isolationism** (p. 730)

**deterrence** (p. 730)

**preventive war** (p. 730)

**appeasement** (p. 730)

**Cold War** (p. 731)

**nation-states** (p. 732)

**preemption** (p. 732)

**most favored nation status** (p. 735)

**World Trade Organization (WTO)** (p. 735)

**General Agreement on Tariffs and Trade (GATT)** (p. 735)

**North American Free Trade Agreement (NAFTA)** (p. 735)

### Practice Quiz

1. Which of the following terms best describes the American posture toward the world prior to the middle of the twentieth century? *(p. 730)*
   a) interventionist
   b) isolationist
   c) appeasement
   d) humanitarian
   e) internationalist

2. The "Cold War" refers to the *(p. 731)*
   a) competition between the United States and Canada over Alaska.
   b) the years between World War I and World War II when the United States and Germany were hostile to one another.
   c) the long-standing conflict over which nation controls Antarctica.
   d) the period of struggle between the United States and the Soviet Union between the late 1940s and the late 1980s.
   e) the economic competition between the United States and Japan today.

3. Which of the following terms describes the idea that the development and maintenance of military strength discourages attack? *(p. 730)*
   a) appeasement
   b) détente
   c) deterrence
   d) containment
   e) "Minuteman" theory of defense

4. If the United States has granted most favored nation status to a country it means that *(p. 735)*
   a) the United States has offered that country the lowest tariff rate it already offers to other countries.
   b) the United States has agreed to give foreign aid to that country.
   c) the United States has signed a bilateral treaty with that country.
   d) the United States has offered to eliminate tariffs for that country.
   e) the United States has promised never to invade that country.

5. Which of the following statements about the General Agreement on Tariffs and Trade is *not* true? *(p. 735)*
   a) It set many of the rules governing international trade.
   b) It has 151 members worldwide, including the United States.
   c) It was the precursor to the World Trade Organization.
   d) It was designed to reduce barriers to trade.
   e) It was in existence from 1791 to 1947.

**⑤ Practice Online**
Video exercise: *Blueprint for Change*

# Who Makes American Foreign Policy?

■ **Identify the major players in foreign-policy making and describe their roles (pp. 738–44)**

While the president and his chief advisers are the principal architects U.S. foreign policy, many other actors in the American political system play an important role in determining how the United States interacts with other nations. Specifically, Congress, the bureaucracy, the courts, political parties, interest groups, and trade associations all exert some influence over American foreign policy. With the exception of the president, the precise influence of each of these actors varies from case to case.

## Key Terms

**Bush Doctrine** (p. 739)

**executive agreement** (p. 742)

## Practice Quiz

6. The Bush Doctrine refers to *(p. 739)*
   a) the idea that the United States should not allow foreign powers to meddle in the Western Hemisphere.
   b) the idea that the United States should avoid future wars by giving in to the demands of hostile foreign powers.
   c) the idea that the United States should take preemptive action against threats to its national security.
   d) the idea that the United States should never take preemptive action against threats to its national security.
   e) the idea that the United States should always secure international approval before taking any military action.

7. The Constitution assigns the power to declare war to *(p. 741)*
   a) the National Security Council.
   b) the president.
   c) Congress.
   d) the secretary of defense.
   e) the chief justice of the United States.

8. An agreement made between the president and another country that has the force of a treaty but requires only a plurality vote in both houses of Congress for approval is called *(p. 742)*
   a) an executive order.
   b) an executive privilege.
   c) an executive agreement.
   d) a diplomatic decree.
   e) arbitration.

9. The making of American foreign policy during noncrisis moments is *(p. 744)*
   a) dominated entirely by the president.
   b) dominated entirely by Congress.
   c) dominated entirely by interest groups.
   d) dominated entirely by the Department of Defense.
   e) highly pluralistic, involving a large mix of both official and unofficial players.

 **Practice Online**
Interactive simulation: *National Security Advisor to the President*

# The Instruments of Modern American Foreign Policy

■ **Describe the means the United States uses to carry out foreign policy (pp. 745–52)**

The most important tools for the United States in implementing its foreign policy in the modern epoch have been diplomacy, the United Nations, the international monetary structure, economic aid and sanctions, collective security, military force, and arbitration. Many of the international organizations that influence contemporary American foreign policy, such as the United Nations, the International Monetary Fund, the World Bank, NATO, and the International Court of Justice, were formed in the years immediately following World War II. As a result of the fact that that the United States possesses a more powerful and effective military than any other nation, military force is a particularly important tool for American foreign policy.

## Key Terms

**diplomacy** (p. 745)

**United Nations (UN)** (p. 746)

**International Monetary Fund (IMF)** (p. 747)

**North Atlantic Treaty Organization (NATO)** (p. 748)

**bilateral treaties** (p. 749)

## Practice Quiz

10. Which of the following are important international economic institutions created in the 1940s? *(p. 747)*
    a) the Federal Reserve System and the Council of Economic Advisors
    b) the North Atlantic Treaty Organization and the Southeast Asia Treaty Organization

c) the International Monetary Fund and the World Bank
d) the International Court of Justice and the Warsaw Pact
e) the Office of Management and Budget and the General Agreement on Tariffs and Trade

11. Which of the following was dedicated to the relief, reconstruction, and economic recovery of Western Europe? *(p. 748)*
   a) the Marshall Plan
   b) the Lend-Lease Act
   c) the General Agreement on Tariffs and Trade
   d) the North American Free Trade Agreement
   e) the International Monetary Fund

12. The North Atlantic Treaty Organization was formed in 1949 by the United States, *(p. 748)*
   a) Canada, and most of Eastern Europe.
   b) Canada, and the Soviet Union.
   c) Canada, and Mexico.
   d) Canada, and most of Western Europe.
   e) Canada, and the United Kingdom.

13. Which statement best describes the United States' military spending compared to other countries? *(p. 750)*
   a) The United States spends about the same as most other countries in the world.

   b) The United States spends significantly more than any other country in the world.
   c) The United States spends significantly more than any other country in the world except for China.
   d) The United States spends significantly less than any other country in the world.
   e) The United States spends slightly less than most other countries in the world.

14. Which of the following statements about the United Nations is *not* true? *(p. 746)*
   a) It gives every country one vote in the General Assembly.
   b) It has a powerful army to implement its decisions.
   c) The five permanent members of the UN Security Council are China, France, Russia, the United Kingdom, and the United States.
   d) It was designed to be a channel for negotiation and a means of settling international disputes peaceably.
   e) Important issues require a two-thirds majority vote.

 **Practice Online**
Video exercise: *NGOs and Nonprofit Groups*

# For Further Reading

Art, Robert. *The Use of Force: Military Power and International Politics*. New York: Rowman and Littlefield, 2009.

Bacevich, Andrew. *The New American Militarism: How Americans Are Seduced by War*. New York: Oxford University Press, 2006.

————. *The Limits of Power: The End of American Exceptionalism*. New York: Metropolitan Books, 2008.

Drezner, Daniel. "The Realist Tradition in American Public Opinion." *Perspectives on Politics* (March 2008): 51–70.

Fisk, Robert. *The Great War for Civilization: The Conquest of the Middle East*. New York: Knopf, 2005.

Gaddis, John L. *The Cold War: A New History*. New York: Penguin Press, 2005.

Herring, George C. *From Colony to Superpower: U.S. Foreign Relations since 1776*. New York: Oxford University Press, 2011.

Hook, Steven. *U.S. Foreign Policy: The Paradox of World Power*. Washington, DC: CQ Press, 2010.

Ikenberry, John. *American Foreign Policy*. New York: Wadsworth, 2010.

Jentleson, Bruce W. *American Foreign Policy—The Dynamics of Choice in the 21st Century*. 4th ed. New York: W.W. Norton, 2010.

Kagan, Robert. *Dangerous Nation*. New York: Knopf, 2006.

Kaufman, Joyce. *A Concise History of U.S. Foreign Policy*. New York: Rowman and Littlefield, 2010.

Kennan, George F. *Around the Cragged Hill: A Personal and Political Philosophy*. New York: W.W. Norton, 1993.

Mandelbaum, Michael. *The Case for Goliath: How America Acts as the World's Government in the 21st Century*. Washington, DC: Public Affairs Press, 2005.

Pillar, Paul. *Intelligence and U.S. Foreign Policy*. New York: Columbia University Press, 2011.

Renshon, Stanley. *National Security in the Obama Administration*. New York: Routledge, 2009.

Snow, Donald. *National Security for a New Era*, 4th ed. Englewood Cliffs, NJ: Prentice Hall, 2010.

# Recommended Websites

**American Israel Public Affairs Committee**
www.aipac.org

Interest groups are some of the main shapers of foreign policy. One of the top lobbies in the nation, the American Israel Public Affairs Committee (AIPAC) works to strengthen the U.S.-Israel relationship.

**Foreign Policy Association**
www.fpa.org

This nonprofit organization tries to generate interest in and draw attention to global issues and policies.

**International Monetary Fund**
www.imf.org
**World Trade Organization**
www.wto.org

The International Monetary Fund (IMF) and the World Trade Organization (WTO) have been considered instruments of modern American foreign policy. Read about how these organizations are trying to promote capitalism, free trade, and economic development.

**National Security Council**
www.whitehouse.gov/nsc/

The National Security Council was formed in 1947 and consists of senior advisers and cabinet officials who keep the president informed on all matters of national security and foreign policy.

**Peterson Institute for International Economics**
www.iie.com

The Peterson Institute for International Economics is dedicated to analyzing international economic policy. Take a minute to review some of the studies that have influenced the policies of such international organizations as NAFTA, the WTO, and the IMF.

**United Nations**
www.un.org

Founded in 1945, the United Nations promotes international peace and security. Visit the UN website for information on the General Assembly, the Security Council, economic and social development, and humanitarian issues.

**U.S. Department of State**
www.state.gov

The U.S. Department of State is the primary bureaucratic department for American diplomacy and national security.

**U.S. Senate: Treaties**
http://senate.gov/pagelayout/legislative/d_three_sections_with_teasers/treaties.htm

The most important foreign policy task of the Senate is reviewing and approving treaties. Learn more about the Senate's treaty-making powers and find information about treaty action at this U.S. Senate website.

In some ways, state-level politics in Texas resembles national politics, but in other ways Texas's political culture is quite distinctive.

# The Political Culture, People, and Economy of Texas

**WHAT GOVERNMENT DOES AND WHY IT MATTERS** Certain myths define Texas—and Texans—in the popular imagination. The cowboy who challenges both Native American and Mexican rule, the rancher and farmer who cherish their economic independence, the wildcatter who is willing to risk everything for one more roll of the dice, and the independent entrepreneur who fears the needless intrusion of government into his life—such are the myths about Texans. But the reality of the people of Texas is a far cry from the myths.

Texas today is not only the second-largest state in the Union, comprising more than 261,000 square miles; it is also the second most populous state. Texas has a rapidly expanding population of more than 25 million people that is becoming more and more diverse. Anglos constitute a little more than 45 percent of the population, while people of Hispanic descent constititue more than 37 percent. Just fewer than 12 percent of the population are African American, and 3.8 percent are of Asian descent. Eighty-eight percent live in urban areas, with many of them involved in an economy that is driven by the twin engines of high-tech industry and globalization. More than a quarter of the population have a bachelor's degree. On the whole, Texans are young, with 27.3 percent under the age of 18 and 10.3 percent over the age of 65.

Texas today is a political community that is dominated by the Republican Party. The Democratic Party of Vice President John Nance Garner (1868–1967), Speaker of the House Sam Rayburn (1882–1961), President Lyndon Johnson (1908–73), and Lieutenant Governor Bob Bullock (1929–99) no longer controls the key political offices in the state. Texas politics and government are largely controlled by a Republican Party led by such individuals as President George W. Bush (b. 1946), Governor Rick Perry (b. 1950), and Texas Speaker of the House Joe Straus (b. 1959). In recent years, the Texas Republican Party has advocated increasingly conservative political positions on a variety of social and economic issues, including abortion, birth control, gay marriage, immigration, and lower taxes. Conservatives in the Republican Party in Texas have been revitalized at the grassroots level by the Tea Party movement. Tea Party supporters have pushed Texas Republicans further to the right by melding a cultural conservatism on issues like abortion and gay rights to an anti-Washington rhetoric that calls for lower taxes, less government spending and regulation, and a balanced budget.

A new myth has emerged about the people of Texas: that they are business-savvy conservatives who reject government interference in the economy but want a government that protects "traditional" values such as the family and marriage. As with many myths, there is some truth to this one. But the reality of Texas, its people, and its politics is much more complex. Republicans may control the short- and near-term political agenda of the state, but their long-term dominance in politics and government is by no means certain. Long-term demographic pressures appear to favor the Democrats. The future of the state and its people will be determined in large part by the struggle between an assertive Republican majority and a resurgent Democratic minority as both try to address the various political, economic, and demographic challenges facing the state.

## chaptergoals

- Describe the defining characteristics of political culture in Texas (pages 763–65)
- Identify the major geographic regions in Texas (pages 765–67)
- Trace the evolution of Texas's economy (pages 767–77)
- Explain how the population of Texas has changed over time (pages 777–84)
- Describe the shift from a rural society to an urban one in Texas (pages 784–90)

# Texas Political Culture

**Describe the defining characteristics of political culture in Texas**

Studies of Texas politics often begin with a discussion of the **political culture** of the state. Though the concept is somewhat open ended, states do often exhibit a distinctive culture that is the "product of their entire history." Presumably the political culture of a state has an effect on how people participate in politics and how individuals and institutions interact.[1] Daniel Elazar has created a classification scheme for state political cultures that is used widely. He uses the concepts of moralistic, individualistic, and traditionalistic to describe such cultures. These three state political cultures are contemporary manifestations of the ethnic, socioreligious, and socioeconomic differences that existed among the original thirteen colonies.[2]

According to Elazar, **moralistic political cultures** were rooted in New England, where Puritans and other religious groups sought to create the Good Society. In such a culture, politics is the concern of everyone and government is expected to be interventionist in promoting the public good and in advancing the public welfare. Citizen participation in politics is viewed as positive; people are encouraged to pursue the public good in civic activities.

**Individualistic political cultures**, on the other hand, originated in the middle states, where Americans sought material wealth and personal freedom through commercial activities. A state with an individualistic political culture generally places a low value on citizen participation in politics. Politics is a matter for professionals rather than for citizens, and the role of government is strictly limited. Government's role is to ensure stability so that individuals can pursue their own interests.

**Traditionalistic political culture** developed initially in the South, reflecting the values of the slave plantation economy and its successor, the Jim Crow era. Rooted in preindustrial values that emphasize social hierarchy and close interpersonal, often familial, relations among people, traditional culture is concerned with the preservation of tradition and the existing social order. In such states, public participation is limited and government is run by an established **elite**. Public policies disproportionately benefit the interests of those elites.

States can, of course, have cultures that combine these concepts. One book classified Colorado, for example, as having a "moralistic" political culture. California was classified as having a "moralistic individualistic" political culture and New York an "individualistic moralistic" culture. New Jersey was classified as "individualistic" and Georgia "traditionalistic." Florida and Kentucky were seen as "traditionalistic individualistic."

Often Texas is categorized as having a "traditionalistic individualistic" political culture.[3] Taxes are kept low, and social services are minimized. Political elites, such as business leaders, have a major voice in how the state is run. In spite of the difficulty in measuring the concept of political culture in any empirical way, it is a concept widely regarded as useful in explaining fundamental beliefs about the state and the role of state government.

Yet, the political culture of a state can change over time. Texas is undergoing dramatic changes, including some change in its political culture. It is also difficult to classify the political culture of a state as large and as diverse as Texas in any one category. In fact, Texas has many different political cultures or subcultures within its borders.[4] These people of Texas reside in a state that is larger in area than the

**political culture** broadly shared values, beliefs, and attitudes about how the government should function and politics should operate. American political culture emphasizes the values of liberty, equality, and democracy

**moralistic political culture** the belief that government should be active in promoting the public good and that citizens should participate in politics and civic activities to ensure that good

**individualistic political culture** the belief that government should limit its role to providing order in society, so that citizens can pursue their economic self-interests

**traditionalistic political culture** the belief that government should be dominated by political elites and guided by tradition

**elite** a small group of people that dominates the political process

*The Lone Star is the symbol of Texas and reflects its individualistic political culture.*

**for critical analysis**

How would one describe Texas political culture? What patterns of Texas politics reflect its political culture?

combined area of the 15 smallest states. Texarkana, in the far northeastern corner of the state, is actually closer to Chicago than it is to El Paso. El Paso is closer to the Pacific Ocean than it is to the eastern boundary of Texas, and the eastern boundary is closer to the Atlantic Ocean than it is to El Paso. One can drive in a straight line for over 800 miles without leaving Texas—almost the same distance as from New York City to St. Louis.

Three long-lasting patterns in Texas politics seem to indicate a "traditionalistic individualistic" state political culture. These patterns relate to a domination of the state by political elites interested in limited government with low taxes and few social services. It is also the case that at least some of these characteristics of state politics are undergoing rapid change. These three patterns of state politics are described below.

## The One-Party State

For over 100 years, Texas was dominated by the Democratic Party. Winning the Democratic Party primary was tantamount to winning the general election. As we will see in later chapters, this pattern no longer holds. During the 1990s, substantial competition emerged between the parties for control of the state legislature. Following redistricting in 2002, the Republicans secured a 7-vote majority in the state Senate and a 24-vote majority in the state House. Between 2002 and 2012, all major statewide elected offices were controlled by Republicans. The question today is not whether the political culture of Texas will continue to be defined by a powerful Democratic Party, but how that culture will be redefined by two forces: a powerful Republican Party in most suburban and rural areas and a resurgent Democratic Party in Texas's most urban counties.

## Provincialism

**provincialism** a narrow, limited, and self-interested view of the world

A second pattern that once defined Texas political culture is **provincialism**, a narrow view of the world that is often associated with rural values and Jeffersonian notions of limited government. The result often was an intolerance of diversity and a notion of the public interest that dismissed social services and expenditures for education. Some of the more popular politicians in Texas have stressed corn pone, intolerance, and a narrow worldview rather than policies that might offer advantages to the state as it competes with other states and with other nations. Like the one-party Democratic state, Texas provincialism has faded as a defining feature of the political culture. The growing influence of minorities, women, and gays in state politics and the ongoing urbanization of the state have undercut provincialism.

## Business Dominance

A third, continuing pattern that has helped define Texas's political culture is its longtime dominance by business. Labor unions are rare in Texas except in the oil-refinery areas around Beaumont–Port Arthur. Other groups that might offer an alternative to a business perspective, such as consumer interests, are poorly organized and poorly funded. Business groups are major players in Texas politics, in terms of campaign contributions, organized interest groups, and lobbyists.

This chapter will investigate the economic, social, and demographic changes that transformed Texas's political culture during the twentieth century. These changes shook Texas government and politics in the 1990s and have continued to shape them in the second decade of the twenty-first century.

*Ties between business and political leaders in Texas have always been strong. Here, Governor Rick Perry appears with Ralph Babb, the chief executive of Comerica Bank, to announce that Comerica would move its corporate headquarters to Dallas.*

## ● The Land

> **Identify the major geographic regions in Texas**

Much of Texas's history has been shaped by the relationship forged between its people and the land. Texas is the second-largest state in size, next to Alaska, comprising 267,000 square miles. The longest straight-line distance across the state from north to south is 801 miles; the longest east–west distance is 773 miles. To put this into perspective, the east–west distance from New York City to Chicago is 821 miles, cutting across five different states. The north–south distance between New York City and Charleston, South Carolina, is 763 miles, cutting across six different states.

Distances alone do not tell the whole story of the diverse geography found in Texas. There are four distinct physical regions in Texas: the Gulf Coastal Plains, the Interior Lowlands, the Great Plains, and the Basin and Range Province (Figure 19.1).[5]

### The Gulf Coastal Plains

The Gulf Coastal Plains extend from the Louisiana border and the Gulf of Mexico, along the Rio Grande up to Del Rio, and northward to the line of the Balcones Fault and Escarpment. As one moves westward, the climate becomes increasingly arid. Forests become less frequent as post oak trees dominate the landscape until they too are replaced by the prairies and brushlands of central Texas.

The eastern portion of the Gulf Coastal Plains—so-called east Texas—is characterized by hilly surfaces covered by forests of pine and hardwoods. Almost all of

FIGURE 19.1

## The Physical Regions of Texas

SOURCE: Dallas Morning News, *Texas Almanac 2000–2001* (Dallas: Dallas Morning News, 1999), p. 55.

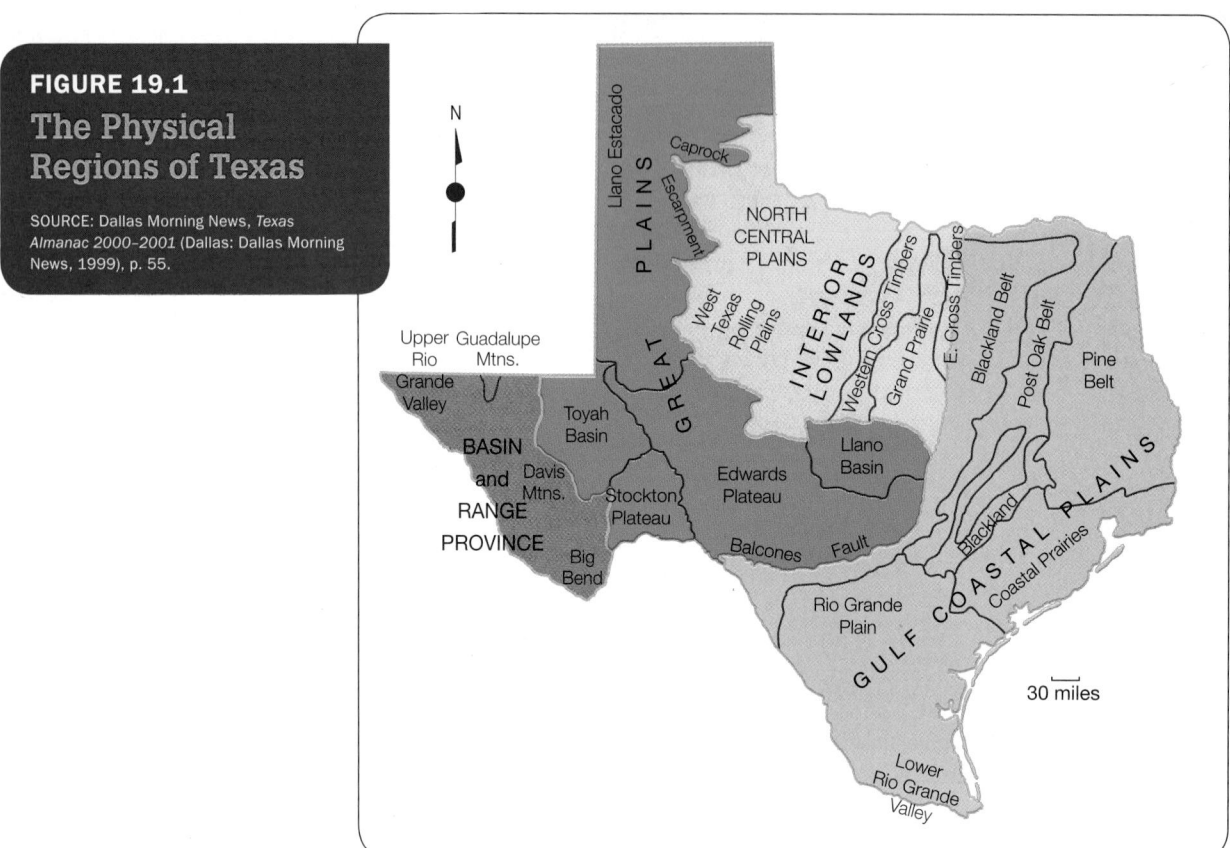

Texas's timber production takes place here. It is also the home of some of Texas's most famous oilfields. To the west is the Blackland Belt. A rolling prairie soil made the Blackland Belt a prime farming area during the late nineteenth and early twentieth centuries. It was a major center of cotton production in Texas. Today it is the most densely populated area of the state and has a diversified manufacturing base.

The Coastal Prairies around Houston and Beaumont were the center for the post–World War II industrial boom, particularly in the petrochemical industry. Winter-vegetable and fruit production plays a major role in the Lower Rio Grande Valley, while livestock is important in the Rio Grande Plain, an area that receives less than 24 inches of rainfall on average every year and during the summer months experiences rapid evaporation.

## The Interior Lowlands

The Interior Lowlands are an extension of the interior lowlands that run down from Canada. They are bordered by the Balcones Escarpment on the east and south and the Caprock Escarpment on the west. Beginning to the west of Fort Worth, the eastern edge of the Interior Lowlands has predominantly an agricultural economy and a rural population. The western portion, meanwhile, rises from 750 to 2,000 feet in elevation. The West Texas Rolling Plains contain much level, cultivable land and are home to a large cattle-raising industry. Many of the state's largest ranches are located here.

## The Great Plains

Pushing down into northwest Texas from the Rocky Mountains to the Balcones Fault, the Great Plains define the terrain in much of western Texas, rising from 2,700 feet in the east to more than 4,000 feet along the New Mexico border. The major city on the northern plains is Amarillo. Ranching and petroleum production dominate the economy. The southern plains economy centers on agriculture and cotton production, with Lubbock as the major city. Large-scale irrigation from underwater reservoirs, particularly the Ogallala Aquifer, has played a major role in the economic development of this region. A major concern of policy makers is that pumping out of the aquifer exceeds replenishment, raising questions of the viability of basing future growth on the irrigation practices of the past.[6]

**forcriticalanalysis**

How has the diverse geography of Texas affected its development?

## The Basin and Range Province

The fourth geographic region in Texas is the Basin and Range Province. Here one finds Texas's true mountains in the Guadalupe Range along the border with New Mexico, which includes Guadalupe Peak (8,749 feet) and El Capitan (8,085 feet). To the southeast is Big Bend country, so named because the Rio Grande River surrounds it on three sides as the river makes its southward swing. Rainfall and population are sparse in this region.

## ● Economic Change in Texas

**Trace the evolution of Texas's economy**

The famous twentieth-century economist Joseph Schumpeter characterized the capitalist economic system as being a process of "creative destruction."[7] By this he meant that capitalism was an economic system that underwent periodic waves of transformation fueled by technological innovations in production and distribution. These waves of technological transformation were put into place by entrepreneurs who had visions of new ways to produce and distribute goods and services and who were willing to act on those visions. The capitalist process of creative destruction not only creates a new economic and social world; it destroys old ones. The world of railroads, steam, and steel transformed American economic and social life by nationalizing the market and making new opportunities available to businesses and individuals during the late nineteenth century. It also destroyed the local markets that had defined rural American communities since the Founding. Similarly, the technological innovation tied to gasoline combustion engines, electricity, and radio restructured the American economy again in the 1920s, leaving in its wake a society and economy that would never be the same.

Schumpeter's theory of creative destruction provides a useful way to think about the economic changes that have shaped and reshaped the Texas economy since the days of the Republic. Three great waves of technological change have helped define and redefine the Texas political economy over the last 150 years. The first centered on the production of cotton and cattle and their distribution by an extensive railroad system. The second grew out of the oil industry. The third and most recent is tied to the development of the high-tech digital economy.

## Cotton

Cotton is one of the oldest crops grown in Texas.[8] Missions in San Antonio in the eighteenth century are reported to have produced several thousand pounds of cotton annually, which were spun and woven by local artisans. Serious cultivation of cotton began in 1821 with the arrival of Anglo Americans. Political independence, statehood, and the ongoing removal of the Native American "threat" in the years before the Civil War promoted the development of the cotton industry. By the mid-nineteenth century, cotton production in Texas soared, placing Texas eighth among the top cotton-producing states in the Union. Although production fell in the years following the Civil War, by 1869 it had begun to pick up again. By 1880, Texas led all states in the production of cotton in most years.

A number of technological breakthroughs further stimulated the cotton industry in Texas. In the 1870s, barbed wire was introduced, enabling farmers to cordon off their lands and protect their cash crop from grazing cattle. Second, the building of railroads brought Texas farmers into a national market. Finally, a newly designed plow made it easier to dig up the prairie soil and significantly increase farm productivity.

Throughout the 1870s, immigrants from the Deep South and Europe flooded the prairies of Texas to farm cotton. Most of these newly arrived Texans became tenant farmers or sharecroppers. Tenants lived on farms owned by landowners, providing their own animals, tools, and seed. They generally received two-thirds of the final value of the cotton grown on the farm, while the landlords received the other third. Sharecroppers furnished only their labor but received only one-half of the value of the final product. Almost half of the state farmers were tenants by the turn of the century.[9]

Two important consequences resulted from the tenant and sharecropping system. First, it condemned many rural Texans to lives of social and economic dependency. The notorious "crop-lien" system was developed to extend credit to farmers in exchange for liens on their crops. The result often was to trap farmers in a debt

*During the late nineteenth century, in most years Texas produced more cotton than any other state. But although one-quarter of the cotton produced in the United States still comes from Texas, the importance of the cotton industry to the state's economy has declined since the 1920s. This photo shows land and machinery used to farm cotton.*

cycle from which they could not escape. Second, the tenant and sharecropping system helped fuel radical political discontent in rural areas, sparking both the Grange and Populist movements. These movements played a major role in defining the style of Texas politics throughout much of the late nineteenth and early twentieth centuries.

Cotton production cycled up and down as farmers experienced a series of crises and opportunities during the late nineteenth and early twentieth centuries, ranging from destructive boll weevils to an increased demand brought on by World War I to a collapse in prices following the war. Although some sharecroppers returned to the farm during the Great Depression in the 1930s, the general decline of the cotton culture continued after World War II. The production of cotton also shifted from east and central Texas to the High Plains and Rio Grande Valley.[10]

## Cattle Ranching

The history of ranching and the cattle industry parallels that of cotton in many ways.[11] The origins of ranching and the cattle industry extend back to the late seventeenth century, when the Spanish brought livestock to the region to feed their missionaries, soldiers, and civilians. Ranching offered immigrants an attractive alternative to farming during the periods of Mexican and Republican rule. In the 1830s, traffic in cattle was limited to local areas. This began to change as cattle drives and railroads began opening up new markets in the East.

Following the Civil War, the cattle industry took off, expanding throughout the state. As with cotton, the invention of barbed wire helped close off the lands used for grazing. By the end of the nineteenth century, ranch lands had been transformed from open range to fenced pasturing. As a result, conflicts over land often broke out between large and small ranchers, as well as between ranchers and farmers. As cattle raising became a more specialized and efficient business, periodic conflicts broke out between employers and employees. Throughout the twentieth century, ranching remained a cyclical industry, struggling when national and international prices collapsed and thriving during upturns in the economy.

*Cattle ranching is another of Texas's dominant industries. The most famous ranch in Texas is the King Ranch, shown here in 1950. Currently covering almost 1,300 square miles, it is larger than the state of Rhode Island.*

Ranching and cotton production remain important industries in the state, although increasingly dominated by big agribusiness companies. As in the past, in 2010 Texas continued to lead the nation in livestock production. Similarly, it leads all other states in cotton production. Approximately one-quarter of the total cotton production in the United States comes from Texas. In 2008, the annual cotton crop was 4.6 million bales, down from a peak in 2005 of 8.4 million bales. The decline was in large part caused by a severe drought. However, after two years of low production, cotton production dramatically increased to 8.05 million bales in 2010.[12]

Neither cotton production nor ranching drives the Texas political economy as in the past. The number of people making a living from agriculture has dropped significantly over the last 50 years as agribusiness has pushed out the family farm and ranch. In 1940, 23 percent of the population worked on farms and ranches. Another 17 percent were suppliers to farms and ranches or helped assemble, process, or distribute agricultural products. Currently, fewer than 2 percent of the population live on farms and ranches, with an additional 15 percent of the population providing support, processing, or distribution services to agriculture in Texas.

A new set of technological breakthroughs challenged the nineteenth-century dominance of cotton and cattle in the early twentieth century. These breakthroughs focused not on what grew on the land, but on what lay beneath it.

## Oil in the Texas Economy

Oil was first sighted in the mid-seventeenth century by Spanish explorers.[13] There was no market or demand for the product, and nothing was done to develop this natural resource. Over a century later, encouraged by a growing demand for petroleum products following the Civil War, a scattering of entrepreneurs dug wells, although they were not commercially viable. The first economically significant oil discovery in Texas was in 1894 in Navarro County near Corsicana. By 1898, the state's first oil refinery was operating at the site. Although production peaked in 1900, the economic viability of oil production had been proven.

What catapulted Texas into the era of oil and gas was the discovery at Spindletop on January 10, 1901. Located three miles south of Beaumont along the Gulf Coast, the Spindletop discovery produced Texas's first oil boom. The success of Spindletop encouraged large numbers of speculators and entrepreneurs to try their luck in the new business. Within three years, three major oilfields had been discovered within 150 miles of Spindletop.

Oil fever spread throughout Texas over the next decade. In north central Texas, major discoveries took place at Brownwood, Petrolia, and Wichita Falls. In the teens, major discoveries were made in Wichita County, Limestone County near Mexia, and once again in Navarro County. In 1921, oil was found in the Panhandle, and by the end of the decade major oilfields were being developed all across the state. The biggest oilfield in the state was found in October 1930 in east Texas. As Mary G. Ramos notes, "By the time the East Texas field was developed, Texas's economy was powered not by agriculture, but by petroleum."[14]

The oil and gas industry transformed the social and economic fabric of Texas in a number of important ways. By providing cheap oil and gas, the industry made possible a new industrial revolution in twentieth-century America that was fueled by hydrocarbons. Cheap oil provided a new fuel for transportation and manufacturing. Railroads and steamships were able to convert from coal to oil. Manufacturing plants and farms were able to operate more efficiently with a new, cheap source of energy, encouraging individuals to migrate to cities away from farms. Automobile production was encouraged, as was the building of roads. The Interstate Highway System that was built during the 1950s and 1960s changed fundamentally the transportation patterns that shaped the movements of people and goods in Texas. The triangle formed by I-35 from San Antonio to Dallas–Fort Worth, I-45 from Dallas–Fort Worth to Houston, and I-10 from Houston to San Antonio became the heartland of the Texas economy and the location of an increasing percentage of the state's population (see Figure 19.2).

The oil and gas industry also sparked a rapid industrialization of the Gulf Coast region. Among the companies developing the Gulf Coast oilfields were Gulf Oil, Sun Oil, Magnolia Petroleum, the Texas Company (later Texaco), and Humble Oil (which later became Esso, then Exxon, and finally ExxonMobil). The refineries, pipelines, and export facilities laid the foundations for the large-scale industrialization that would take place along the Gulf Coast in the Houston–Beaumont–Port Arthur region. By 1929 in Harris County, for example, 27 percent of all manufacturing employees worked in refineries. By 1940, the capacity of all the refineries had increased fourfold.[15] The petrochemical industry continued to flourish throughout the 1960s when demand for its products grew at the rate of 10 percent a year.

One important effect of the oil and gas boom in Texas was the development of a new rhythm to economic life in the state. There had been a natural pace to the economy when it was tied to the production of cotton and cattle. Prices of products could rise and fall, bringing prosperity or gloom to local economies. But there was

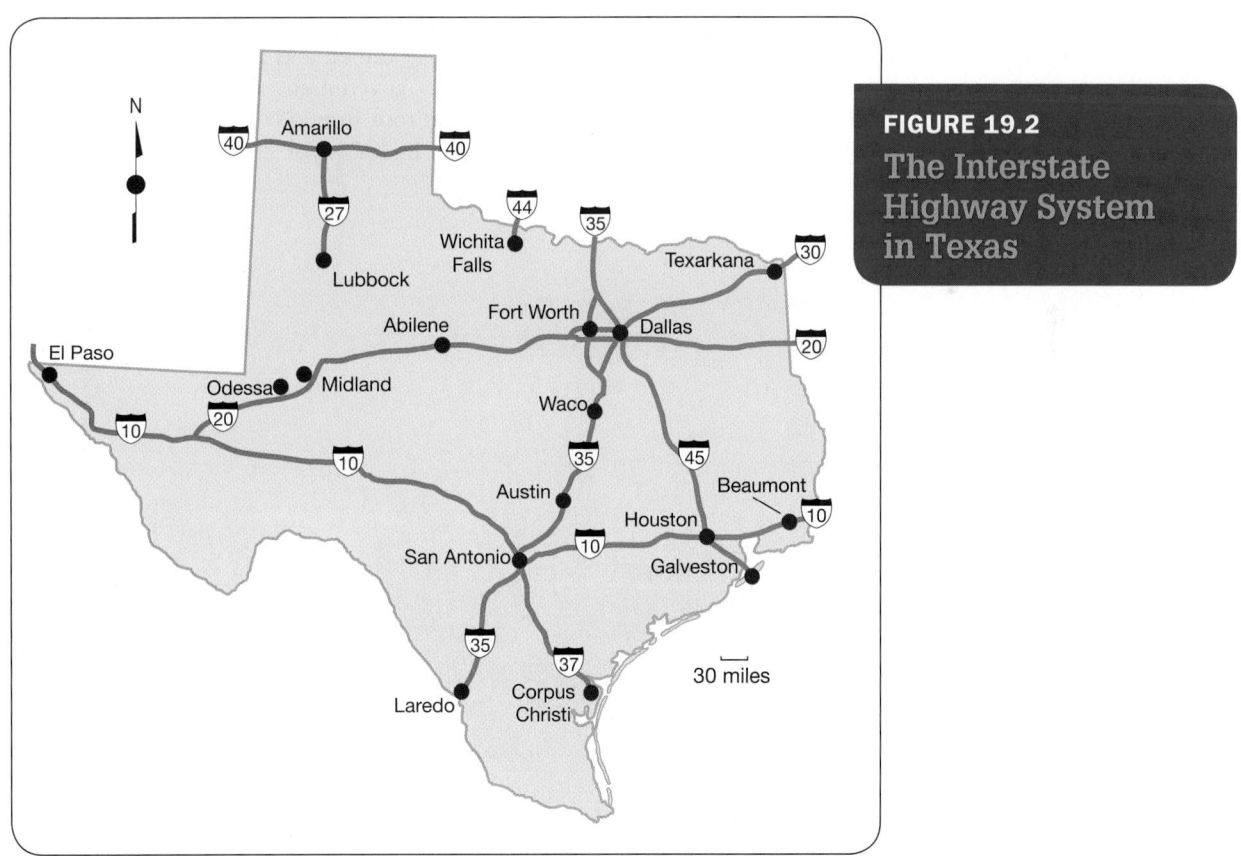

**FIGURE 19.2**

The Interstate Highway System in Texas

a bond between the land and the people and the communities that formed around them. Oil and gas, on the other hand, introduced a boom-and-bust mentality that carried over into the communities that sprang up around oil and gas discoveries. Rural areas were often unprepared for the population explosion that followed an oil or gas strike. Housing was often inadequate or nonexistent. Schools quickly became overcrowded. General living conditions were poor as people sought to "make it big." The irony of the oil and gas business was that a major discovery that brought large amounts of new oil and gas to market could lead to a sudden collapse in prices. Prosperous economic times could quickly turn into local depressions. And when particular fields were tapped out, boom towns could quickly become ghost towns.

The oil and gas industry also transformed government and the role that it played in the economy. Following the Civil War, a series of attempts to regulate the railroads had largely failed. In 1890, after considerable controversy fueled by Populist anti-railroad sentiment, a constitutional amendment was passed to create an agency to regulate the railroads, the Texas Railroad Commission. This regulatory agency was extended in 1917 to regulate energy. The Railroad Commission was empowered to see that petroleum pipelines were "common carriers" (that they transported all producers' oil and gas) and to promote well-spacing rules. In an attempt to bring stability to world oil prices brought on by the glut of oil on world markets in the 1930s, the commission won the authority to prorate oil and determine how much every oil well in Texas might produce. Through the late 1960s, the Texas Railroad Commission was one of the most important regulatory bodies in the nation. It was also one of the few democratically elected agencies.

Helping to expand the power of state government in the economy through the Railroad Commission was only one effect of the oil and gas industry in Texas. It also had an important fiscal effect on state government. Beginning in 1905, the state collected oil-production taxes. These rose from $101,403 in 1906 to over $1 million in 1919 and almost $6 million in 1929. For 2010–11, oil production

*The oil industry transformed the social and economic fabric of Texas, leading to, among other things, the creation of boom towns—hastily constructed communities built around the oilfields in rural areas such as the Permian Basin.*

taxes, or severance taxes, contributed $1.8 billion to the state budget. Natural gas production taxes added another $2 billion to the state budget.[16]

Much like the state coffers, higher education in Texas has benefited from the oil and gas industry. What many thought was worthless land at the time had been set aside by the state constitution of 1876 and the state legislature in 1883 to support higher education (the Permanent University Fund). As luck would have it, oil was discovered in the West Texas Permian Basin in 1923 on university lands. Soon 17 wells were producing oil on university lands, sparking a building boom at the University of Texas. In 1931, the income of the Permanent University Fund was split between the University of Texas at Austin and Texas A&M University, with the former receiving two-thirds and the latter one-third. In 1984, the income was opened up to all University of Texas and Texas A&M schools. Along with the royalties from other natural resources on university land, oil and gas royalties created one of the largest university endowments in the world. In August 2010, the net asset value of the Permanent University Fund was calculated to be $10.725 billion.[17]

The oil and gas industry had one other effect on life in Texas that is worth noting. Fortunes were made in the industry that paved the way for an expansion of private philanthropy that would have a major influence in shaping Texas's culture. Among the most famous of these were the Meadows Foundations, established in 1948 to promote programs in health, education, visual arts, social services, and historical preservation. The Sid W. Richardson Foundation was founded in 1947 and supported health and education programs, as well as the development of the arts in Fort Worth. The Bass Performance Hall, which opened in May 1998, was funded by the Bass brothers, grandnephews of the independent oilman Sid Richardson.

One can trace the rise and decline of the oil and gas industry in Texas through production figures (see Table 19.1). In the early decades of the twenty-first century,

**for critical analysis**

During the 1980s, the price of oil fell from almost $35 a barrel to $10 a barrel, bringing Texas's economy close to collapse. To what extent has the economy of Texas changed so that devastation in one industry will not have the catastrophic effect that the failure of the oil industry did in the 1980s?

**TABLE 19.1**

## Oil Production in Texas

| YEAR | CRUDE OIL PRODUCTION IN THOUSANDS OF BARRELS | AVERAGE PRICE PER BARREL |
|---|---|---|
| 1915 | 24,943 | $0.52 |
| 1945 | 751,045 | 1.21 |
| 1955 | 1,002,480 | 2.93 |
| 1965 | 932,810 | 3.01 |
| 1975 | 1,185,683 | 12.21 |
| 1980 | 931,078 | 37.42 |
| 1985 | 830,597 | 26.92 |
| 1990 | 645,941 | 23.19 |
| 1995 | 511,962 | 16.75 |
| 2000 | 398,678 | 27.39 |
| 2005 | 344,226 | 50.04 |
| 2010 | 356,911 | 71.21 |
| 2011 | 393,880 | 87.04 |

SOURCE: Texas Railroad Commission and "Historical Crude Oil Prices," InflationData.com.

oil and gas remained significant industries in the Texas economy. New technologies such as horizontal drilling and fracking raise the possibility of a new boom era of oil and gas production in Texas. Nevertheless, new industries and technologies have come to assume significant roles in plotting the state's economic future. Among the most important of these was the burgeoning high-tech industry.

## The Emergence of the High-Tech Digital Economy

The movement out of the era of oil and gas and into that of high tech was not an easy one.[18] World oil prices rose in 1981 to almost $35 per barrel. At the time, oil-related businesses accounted for 26 percent of the gross state product. From 1971 to 1981, the average rate of economic growth was 4.4 percent. Fueled by a booming oil-based economy and a rapidly increasing population, real estate prices shot up in urban areas such as Houston and Dallas. Projections were made that as oil prices rose, perhaps to $70 or $80 per barrel on the world market, future prosperity was inevitable. Indeed, there was some talk that Texas's oil-driven economy had become recession-proof. Such talk proved to be premature, to say the least.

World oil prices began to collapse in 1982, bottoming out on March 31, 1986, at $10 per barrel. Other sectors of the economy began to suffer as the price of oil fell. Real estate deals fell through, and construction projects slowed and then shut down. Speculators defaulted on their loans, and banks began to fail. Throughout the 1980s, 370 banks went under in Texas. At the same time, the state went through two major recessions, one in 1982 and another in 1986–87. The average annual economic growth slowed to 1.7 percent, the worst since World War II.

Texas emerged from the economic malaise of the 1980s with a transformed state economy. Though remaining an important sector in the economy, the oil and gas business was no longer the primary driving force. By 1992, the production of oil had fallen to 642 million barrels worth only $11.8 billion. Production continued to fall until 2000 to just under 349 million barrels worth a little over

*In the 1990s, Texas emerged as a leader in high-tech industries. Here, a Texas Instruments employee oversees the production of silicon wafers in the company's Dallas semiconductor plant.*

$10 billion. Over 146,000 jobs had been lost in the oil industry throughout the 1980s. By the early 1990s, oil accounted for only about 12 percent of the gross state product.

In contrast to the 1980s, the 1990s were a period of rapid growth. Unlike early periods of speculative booms, such as the 1970s, the economy's growth was grounded in a rapidly diversifying economy. At the heart of this boom was a fast-growing manufacturing sector tied to high tech. In the 1990s, Texas went from seventh in the nation in total manufacturing employment to second. By 2008, 13 percent of the $160.8 billion gross state product came from manufacturing.[19]

Two metropolitan areas stand out as national centers for the rapidly evolving high-tech industry. The Austin–San Marcos metropolitan area has become a production center for computer chips, personal computers, and other related computer hardware. Seven of the area's largest employers are part of the computer or semiconductor industry. The Dallas metropolitan area, particularly north of the city, is the home of a number of important electronic and electronic-equipment companies.

## NAFTA

Texas's place in national and international markets has been shaped by its central location, its border with Mexico, and its sophisticated transportation infrastructure. There are 306,404 miles of highways in Texas (the most in the nation) along with 45 railroads operating on 10,405 rail miles (the most in the nation). There are 12 deep-water ports in Texas, including the Port of Houston, which was ranked second nationally for total trade and thirteenth globally for total cargo volume. The Dallas–Fort Worth International Airport and the George Bush Intercontinental in Houston ranked high on the list of the world's busiest airports and were major hubs for both national and international travel. Over 3.2 million trucks, 31.5 million personal vehicles, and 17.1 million people crossed the Texas-Mexico border in 2010.[20]

One defining feature of the Texas economy in the 1990s and 2000s was the **North American Free Trade Agreement (NAFTA)**. Signed on December 17, 1992, by Prime Minister Brian Mulroney of Canada, President Carlos Salinas de Gortari of Mexico, and President George H. W. Bush of the United States, NAFTA sought to create a free-trade zone in North America that was the largest of its kind in the world. Considerable controversy surrounded the passage of NAFTA, with many groups arguing that free trade would hurt U.S. workers and companies because of the cheap labor available in Mexico. An important milestone in the agreement was reached on October 19, 2001, when Mexican trucks were finally allowed to cross over into the United States with goods for U.S. markets. Despite NAFTA provisions, Mexican trucks had been banned in the United States for almost 20 years because of strong labor union opposition and concerns over safety.

After 20 years, it appears that the trade agreement has had both negative and positive impacts on Texas. A 2011study by the Economic Policy Institute calculated that almost 683,000 jobs had been lost in the United States because of NAFTA. The study estimated that three-fifths of these jobs were in the manufacturing sector. Over 55,000 of these displaced jobs came from Texas.[21] U.S. workers generally lost their jobs because of the stiffer competition from low-wage businesses in Mexico or because plants had been relocated to Mexico. (Under federal law such workers are entitled to additional unemployment compensation.)

**North American Free Trade Agreement (NAFTA)** trade treaty among the United States, Canada, and Mexico to lower and eliminate tariffs among the three countries

*The signing of NAFTA in 1992 created a free-trade zone in North America. Although many Texas workers were adversely affected by the availability of cheaper labor in Mexico, NAFTA appears to have had a beneficial effect on the state's economy as a whole. Here, President George H. W. Bush stands between President Carlos Salinas de Gortari of Mexico and Prime Minister Brian Mulroney of Canada at the signing ceremony.*

Although there were some losers in the movement toward free trade with Mexico and Canada, there were also big winners. According to a Texas Public Policy Foundation report, conservative estimates are that Texas increased exports to Canada and Mexico by over $10 billion in the first five years of NAFTA. Of the 32 industries in Texas that export to Mexico, 24 had double-digit gains. Meanwhile, 27 of the 31 industries that exported to Canada showed gains as well. Studies by the Department of Commerce and the Council of the Americas put the total number of jobs added to Texas's economy by NAFTA at 190,000 or higher. The following statistics from 2010 put the importance of Texas's international trade, particularly with Mexico and Canada, into perspective:[22]

- Texas exports totaled $207 billion, a $38.7 billion increase from 2007, with 16.2 percent of all U.S. exports originating in Texas.
- The North American market (Mexico and Canada) was the destination for 44.2 percent of these exports.
- Mexico was the top importer of Texas exports at almost $79.0 billion.
- Canada's imports from Texas totaled $13.0 billion.

For the past 20 years, the information age and the global economy have transformed the Texas economic landscape. It is impossible to say exactly how these forces will continue to change Texas over the next 20 years, or which companies will become the Texacos or ExxonMobils of the information age. We can say, however, that it will be an economy as different from that of the oil and gas era as the oil and gas era was from the era of cotton and cattle.

## Texas in the Great Recession

In December 2007, the nation entered what some have called "the Great Recession," a time of chronic economic problems that drew analogies to the Great Depression of the 1930s. A speculative bubble in the housing market fueled by cheap credit and poor business practices culminated in a credit crisis that brought some of America's largest banks and investment houses to their knees. Only the massive intrusion of the Federal Reserve System into credit markets in the fall of 2008 prevented the banking system from melting down. The Federal Reserve reported that between November 2007 and March 2009, 86 percent of American industries cut back production. The GNP dropped 1.7 percent and household net worth fell $11 trillion or 18 percent during the recession.[23]

Compared with the rest of the nation, Texas weathered the Great Recession relatively well. The housing market declined much less severely in Texas than in the rest of the nation. Most of Texas did not experience the surge in real estate values found in other states like California, Nevada, Florida, and Arizona. While foreclosure rates throughout the country increased sixfold between 2005 and 2009, in Texas they rose only marginally. Texas's banking industry also appeared to have weathered the storm better than its counterparts in other states. Article XVI of the Texas Constitution, as amended in 1997, forbids consumers from using home-equity loans for credit that exceeds 80 percent of the mortgage, and this probably provided a cushion against the credit crunch.[24]

Texas was not hit as hard as other states by the recession that started in 2007 and deepened in 2008. However, some Texans—including these Tea Party protesters—were alarmed by the massive spending involved in the national government's stimulus efforts.

Texas was one of the last states to enter the Great Recession and seems likely to be one of the first to exit. In 2010, Texas led the nation with 209,800 jobs added to the state's economy, and unemployment in Texas stood well below the national rate. Housing starts and exports were also up, as were other leading economic indicators in the state. However, Texas faces huge budget shortfalls that have no easy solution. A diversified economy has helped Texas weather the economic storm to a considerable degree, but there are no guarantees that the Great Recession is over.[25]

## ● The People: Texas Demography

> **Explain how the population of Texas has changed over time**

The population in Texas has grown rapidly since the early days of the Republic. In 1850, the population stood at a little more than 210,000 people, more than one-quarter of whom were African American slaves. Texas in 1850 also was an overwhelmingly rural state. Only 4 percent of the population lived in urban areas. By 1900 the population had increased to more than 3 million people, with 83 percent continuing to live in rural areas. The 1980s began as boom years for population growth, with increases running between 2.9 percent and 1.6 percent per year from 1980 through 1986. With the collapse of oil prices, however, population growth slowed significantly between 1987 and 1989 to less than 1 percent.[26]

With a recovering economy, however, population growth surged forward in the 1990s (see Table 19.2). In 1990, 17 million people resided in the state. By 2010, the number of people was estimated to be 25.1 million. Forty-five percent of the population were non-Hispanic white in 2009, down from 61 percent in 1990.

**TABLE 19.2**

## The Changing Face of Texas, 1850–2010

|  | 1850 | 1900 | 1950 | 1990 | 2010 |
|---|---|---|---|---|---|
| Population | 213,000 | 3,050,000 | 7,710,000 | 17,000,000 | 25,146,000 |
| Anglo | 72% | 80% | 87% | 61% | 47% |
| African American | 28% | 20% | 13% | 12% | 11% |
| Hispanic | NA | NA | NA | 25% | 37% |
| Other | NA | NA | NA | 2% | 5% |

NA=not available

SOURCES: *Statistical Abstract of the United States:* 1994 (Washington, DC: U.S. Department of Commerce, Bureau of the Census, 1994); Dallas Morning News, *Texas Almanac 2004–2005* (Dallas: Dallas Morning News, 2004), p. 10; 2010 U.S. Census.

Eleven percent were African American. Thirty-eight percent were Hispanic, up from 25 percent in 1990.

Three factors account for the population growth in Texas: natural increase due to the difference between births and deaths; international immigration, particularly from Mexico; and domestic immigration from other states. The makeup of the growth in population shifted in significant ways over the course of the decade. In 1991, almost two-thirds of population growth was accounted for by natural increases. A little more than 20 percent was due to international immigration, while less than 14 percent was due to domestic immigration. By 2009, natural increases accounted for only 54 percent of population growth, while international immigration accounted for about 20 percent and domestic immigration for about 30 percent.[27] In the early decades of the twenty-first century, Texas was being redefined not by native-born Texans but by individuals coming to Texas to share in and contribute to the state's high-tech economic boom.

## Anglos

For most of the nineteenth and twentieth centuries, the dominant ethnic group was non-Hispanic white, or Anglo. Anglos in Texas comprise a wide range of European ethnic groups, including English, Germans, Scots, Irish, Czechs, and European Jews. The first wave of Anglos came to Texas before the break with Mexico. Encouraged by impresarios such as Moses Austin and his son Stephen F. Austin, who were authorized by the Spanish and later the Mexican leaders to bring people to Texas, these Anglos sought inexpensive land. But they brought along a new set of individualistic attitudes and values about democratic government that paved the way for the Texas Revolution. Following the revolution, a new surge of Anglo immigrants came from the Deep South. Like their predecessors, they sought cheap land. But they brought with them new cultural baggage: slavery. By the time of the American Civil War, this group had come to dominate the political culture of the state. Although most Texas farmers did not own slaves themselves, the vast majority supported the institution as well as secession from the Union.

*Prior to statehood, many of Texas's Anglos were European immigrants. For instance, in 1844 close to 5,000 Germans arrived and soon thereafter established the towns of New Braunfels and Fredericksburg. This painting from the 1850s shows a German American family from Fredericksburg "going visiting."*

Defeat in the Civil War shattered the dominance of the traditional Anglo power structure in the state. By the end of Reconstruction, however, it had reasserted itself, establishing the three patterns that defined Texas politics for the next hundred years: the one-party Democratic state, provincialism, and business dominance. Anglos continued to dominate and define Texas's political culture throughout much of the twentieth century, but by the end of that century much had changed. As a percentage of the population, Anglo influence peaked in 1950, when 74 percent of the population was officially categorized as Anglo. This percentage began to fall, reaching 45 percent in 2010, and will likely continue to fall (see Figure 19.3).

Numbers alone do not tell the whole story. Anglos living in Texas at the end of the twentieth century were not cut from the same cloth as those who had preceded them. A new wave of Anglo immigration into Texas over the past 40 years has redefined what it means to be an Anglo in Texas. No longer can one say that an Anglo lives on a farm, holds culturally conservative values, and is firmly tied to the Democratic Party. On the contrary, he or she may be an urbanite or suburbanite who wasn't born in Texas and who votes Republican.

## Latinos

Most Hispanics in Texas are people of Mexican descent.[28] Prior to independence from Spain, this included people born of Iberian (Spanish) parents as well as mestizos (people of mixed Spanish and Native American ancestry). In the early nineteenth century, approximately 5,000 people of Mexican descent were living in Texas. Although this number fluctuated considerably over the years, by 1850 it was estimated that 14,000 Texans were of Mexican origin. Texas became for many a refuge from the political and economic instability that troubled Mexico from the late 1850s to the 1920s. Despite periodic attempts to curtail the growth of the Mexican American population in Texas, it grew from an estimated 700,000 in 1930 to 1,400,000 in 1960. The 2000 census counted 5.1 million Mexican Americans living in Texas. In 2010, there were 9.5 million Hispanics residing in Texas. Texas Hispanics constituted 19 percent of all Hispanics in the United States.[29]

**FIGURE 19.3**

Anglo Population in Texas Counties, 2010

SOURCE: Data are drawn from the 2010 census. Texas State Data Center, www .texastribune.org/library/data/census-2010/ (accessed 5/2/12).

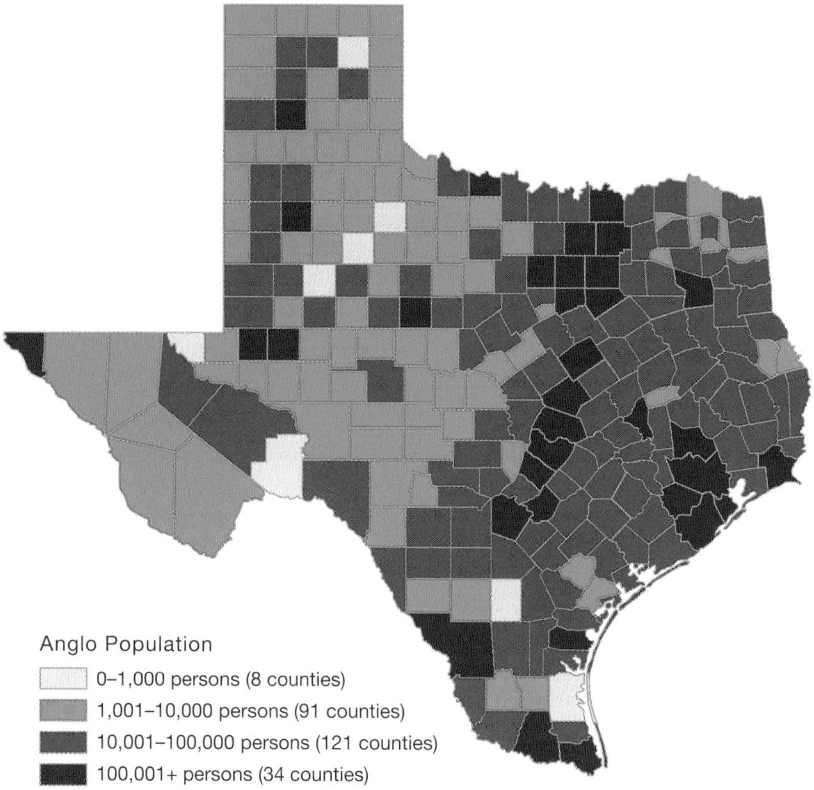

Anglo Population

☐ 0–1,000 persons (8 counties)

☐ 1,001–10,000 persons (91 counties)

■ 10,001–100,000 persons (121 counties)

■ 100,001+ persons (34 counties)

*Most Latinos in Texas are Mexican American. During the first half of the twentieth century, Mexicans immigrated to Texas to work in the emerging cotton industry. This 1939 photo shows cotton pickers laboring in the sun over rows of white cotton.*

Until 1900, Hispanics constituted a majority in south Texas along the border with Mexico and in certain border counties of west Texas. During the first few decades of the twentieth century, Hispanics migrated to northwest Texas and the Panhandle to work as laborers in the newly emergent cotton economy. Labor segregation limited the opportunities available to many Hispanics before World War II. After World War II, however, many Hispanics left agricultural work and took jobs in the rapidly growing urban areas of Texas. By the end of the century, Hispanics constituted majorities in the cities of San Antonio and El Paso and sizable minorities in Houston, Dallas, Austin, and Fort Worth (see Figure 19.4).

The political status of Latinos in Texas has changed considerably over the past hundred years. In the nineteenth century, numerous obstacles limited their participation in the political life of the state. Voting, particularly among the lower economic classes, was discouraged or tightly controlled. The white-only primary and the poll tax actively discouraged voting by Latinos. Only after World War II were Latinos politicians able to escape some of the strictures that had been imposed on them by the dominant Anglo political culture of the time. A more tolerant atmosphere in the growing urban areas enabled Latino politicians to assume positions of importance in the local political community. In 1956, Henry B. Gonzalez became the first Mexican American to be elected to the Texas Senate in modern times. In the mid-1960s a political movement emerged in the Raza Unida Party, which sought to confront many of the discriminatory practices that isolated Texas Latinos from the political and economic mainstream. By the 1980s, Latino political leaders were playing a growing role in state politics, and Latino voters were courted

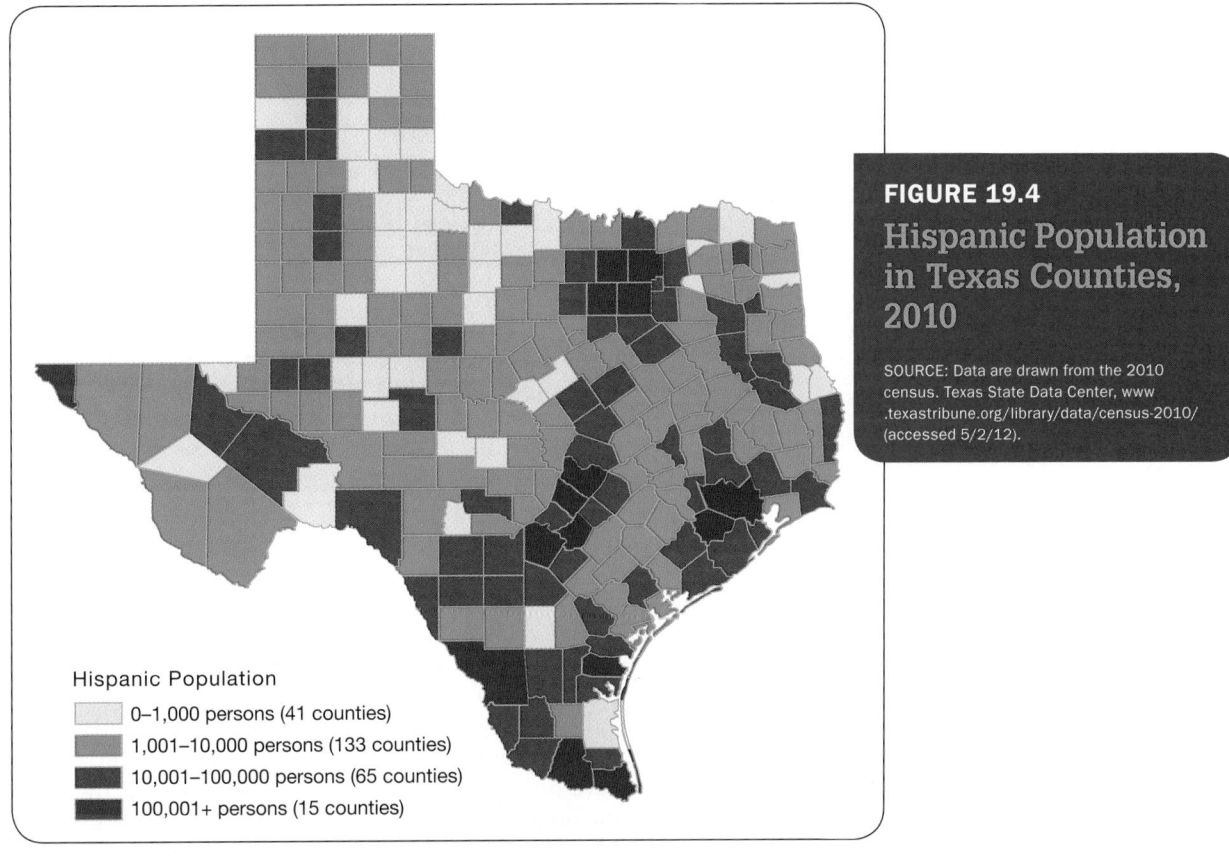

**FIGURE 19.4**

**Hispanic Population in Texas Counties, 2010**

SOURCE: Data are drawn from the 2010 census. Texas State Data Center, www .texastribune.org/library/data/census-2010/ (accessed 5/2/12).

Hispanic Population

- 0–1,000 persons (41 counties)
- 1,001–10,000 persons (133 counties)
- 10,001–100,000 persons (65 counties)
- 100,001+ persons (15 counties)

heavily by both political parties. The number of Latinos elected to public office rose from 1,466 in 1986 to 2,521 in 2011. After the 2010 elections, the National Association of Latino Elected and Appointed Officials Education Fund reported that 6 Latinos represented Texas in the U.S. House of Representatives, 7 Latinos were in the Texas State Senate, and 31 Latinos were elected to the Texas House of Representatives.[30] The use of the terms *Hispanic* and *Latino* can be confusing. We often use the words interchangeably to refer to people of "Spanish" descent or people from Latin America. Many statistical databases use the term *Hispanic*, as will we when presenting data from these databases.

## African Americans

People of African descent were among the earliest explorers of Texas.[31] Most African Americans, however, entered Texas as slaves. Anglo Americans from the upper and lower South brought slaves with them to Texas. At first, antislavery attitudes among Spanish and Mexican authorities kept the slave population down. However, independence from Mexico lifted the restrictions on slavery, creating an incentive for southerners to expand the system of slavery westward. The number of slaves in Texas rose from 5,000 in 1830 to 11,000 in 1840 to 58,000 in 1850. By the Civil War, over 182,000 slaves lived in Texas, approximately one-third of the state's entire population.

Emancipation for African Americans living in Texas came on June 19, 1865. Emancipation, however, did not bring anything approaching equality. Between 1865 and 1868, a series of Black Codes were passed by the state legislature and

*As in most former slave states, there was initial resistance to the civil rights movement in Texas. These signs appeared in Fort Worth's Riverside section in September 1956 during a protest over a black family's moving into a previously all-white block of homes.*

various cities that sought to restrict the rights of former slaves. Military occupation and congressional reconstruction opened up new opportunities for former slaves, who supported the radical wing of the Republican Party. Ten African American delegates helped write the Texas Constitution of 1869. Forty-three served as members of the state legislature between 1868 and 1900. The end of Reconstruction and the return to power of the Democratic Party in the mid-1870s reversed much of the progress made by former slaves in the state. In 1900, over 100,000 African Americans voted in Texas elections. By 1903, the number had fallen to under 5,000, largely because of the imposition of the poll tax in 1902 and the passage of an early version of the white-primary law in 1903. In 1923, the legislature explicitly banned blacks from voting in the Democratic primary. Segregation of the races became a guiding principle of public policy, backed by the police power of the state and reinforced by lynchings and race riots against African Americans. For all intents and purposes, African Americans had become second-class citizens, disenfranchised by the political system and marginalized by the political culture.

Federal court cases in the 1940s and 1950s offered some hope of relief to African Americans living in Texas. The white primary was outlawed in 1944 in the Supreme Court decision in *Smith v. Allwright*. In 1950, African Americans were guaranteed admission to Texas's graduate and professional schools in *Sweatt v. Painter*. Finally, the segregation of public schools was outlawed by the Supreme Court in *Brown v. Board of Education* in 1954.

Political progress was much slower. The Civil Rights Act of 1964 and the Voting Rights Act of 1965 helped to open up the political system in Texas to African Americans. In 1966, a small number of African American candidates actually began to win political office in the state. In 1972, Barbara Jordan became the first African American woman to be elected to the United States House of Representatives from Texas.

Today the African American population is concentrated in east Texas, where the southern plantation and sharecropping systems were dominant during the nineteenth century. Large numbers of African Americans had also migrated to form sizable minorities in the urban and suburban areas of Houston and Dallas

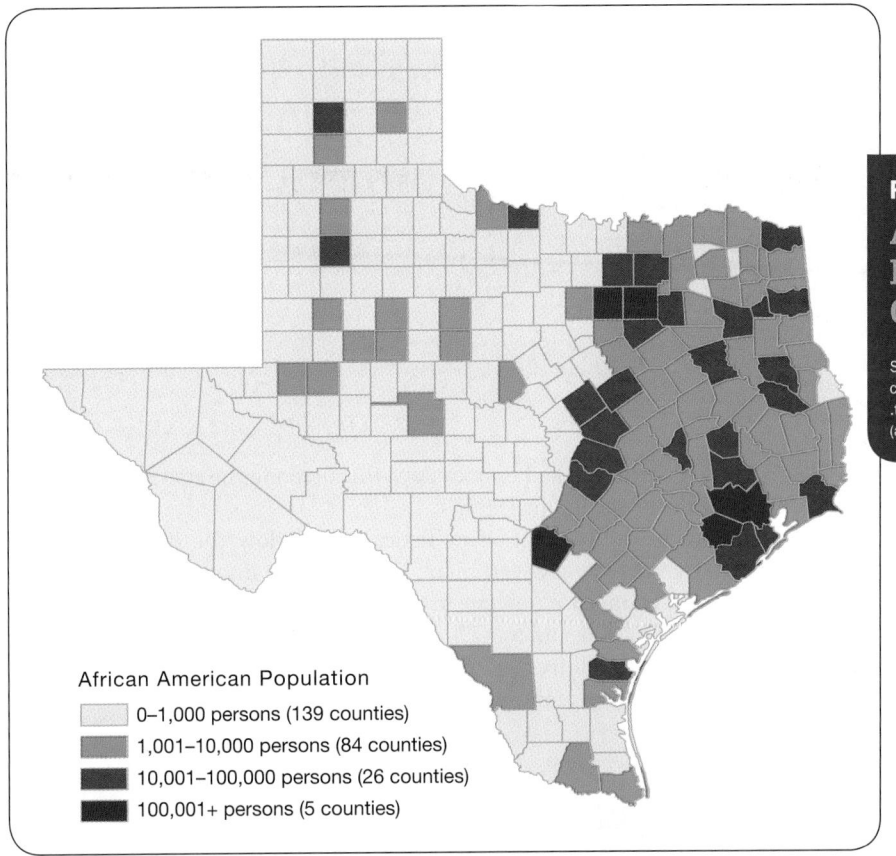

FIGURE 19.5

African American Population in Texas Counties, 2010

SOURCE: Data are drawn from the 2010 census. Texas State Data Center, www .texastribune.org/library/data/census-2010/ (accessed 5/2/12).

**African American Population**

- 0–1,000 persons (139 counties)
- 1,001–10,000 persons (84 counties)
- 10,001–100,000 persons (26 counties)
- 100,001+ persons (5 counties)

(see Figure 19.5). African American political leaders have come to play major roles in these areas as members of Congress, the state legislature, and city councils. African Americans were also elected mayors of Houston and Dallas in the late 1990s. The political influence of African Americans in Texas has not been extended to west Texas, where few African Americans live.

## Age

When compared with the rest of the nation, the population of Texas is relatively young. In 2010, 27.8 percent of the population were under 18 years old, compared with 24.3 percent nationally. In addition, only 10.2 percent of the population in Texas were 65 years of age or older, compared with 12.9 percent nationally.[32] Having a relatively young population compared with those of other states presents Texas with a variety of problems and opportunities, as we shall see in later chapters.

## Poverty and Wealth

Younger populations tend to be poorer, as income and poverty statistics bear out. As noted above, the 1990s were a period of rapid economic growth in Texas. Despite this growth, however, Texas continued to lag behind the nation as a whole (see Table 19.3). Per capita income in Texas, however, rose from $17,421 in 1990

**for critical analysis**

How did the population of Texas change during the 1990s? What is its racial and ethnic composition? How do these changes complicate the idea of the "typical" Texan?

**TABLE 19.3**

## Per Capita Income in Texas and the United States, 1990–2010 (in Nominal Nonadjusted Dollars)

|       | 1990     | 1995     | 2006     | 2010     |
|-------|----------|----------|----------|----------|
| USA   | $19,477  | $23,076  | $36,276  | $40,584  |
| Texas | $17,421  | $21,033  | $34,257  | $39,493  |

SOURCE: U.S. Department of Commerce, Bureau of Economic Analysis.

to $39,493 in 2010. Texas ranked only twenty-third among the states in per capita income, up from thirty-second in 1990.

The percentage of the population in Texas living below the poverty level—a level established by the federal government, which will be discussed in more detail in Chapter 27—fell from 15.7 percent to 14.9 percent between 1990 and 2004, rose to 16.9 percent in 2006, and to 17.1 percent in 2009. During the same period, the national poverty rate fell from 13.5 percent to 11.7 percent, rose to 13.3 percent in 2006, and to 14.3 percent in 2009.[33]

## ● Urbanization

**urbanization** the process by which people move from rural areas to cities

> **Describe the shift from a rural society to an urban one in Texas**

**Urbanization** is the process by which people move from rural to urban areas. Suburbanization is the process by which people move out of central city areas to surrounding suburban areas. Much of Texas's history is linked to ongoing urbanization. By the end of the twentieth century, this process was largely complete, as 88 percent of the population now reside in urban areas (see Table 19.4). Suburbanization, however, continues as city populations spill over into surrounding suburban areas.

Most Texas cities are the result of Anglo settlement and culture.[34] The Spanish influence on urban life in Texas grew out of efforts to extend territorial control northward out of Mexico through a series of presidios (garrisons), missions (churches), and pueblos (towns). The physical organization and planning of the towns reflected this imperial mission. For example, the largest Spanish settlement was San Antonio. It was initially established as a supply depot to missions in east Texas. Later it expanded as missions were established to convert local Native Americans to Christianity and farms were cultivated to feed the local population. By the early nineteenth century, San Antonio's population had reached 2,500. Other smaller settlements were located in east Texas, along the border with French and, later, American territory.

Anglo American influence began with the arrival of Moses Austin in 1820 in San Antonio. Soon his son Stephen F. Austin followed. The Spanish offered the Austins and other impresarios grants of land to encourage the inflow of Americans into underpopulated regions of Texas. Small towns emerged as administrative units

# How Is the Texas Population Changing?

The face of Texas is changing rapidly and will continue to change well into the future. The figures below show projections of how the Texas population will change over the next 30 years. The state's population will continue to grow quickly, especially as the number of Hispanic Texans increases. Further, most of the population growth in the state will happen in metropolitan areas—Dallas-Fort Worth, Houston, San Antonio, and Austin.

## Race and Total Population

| | 1980 | | | | 2010 | | | | 2040 | | |
|---|---|---|---|---|---|---|---|---|---|---|---|
| = 250,000 people | White | 66% | Hispanic | 21% | White | 47% | Hispanic | 37% | White | 32% | Hispanic | 53% |
| | Black | 12% | Other | 1% | Black | 11% | Other | 4% | Black | 10% | Other | 6% |

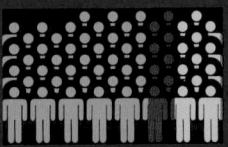 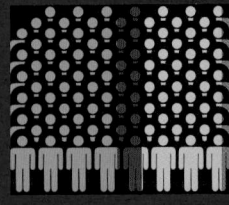 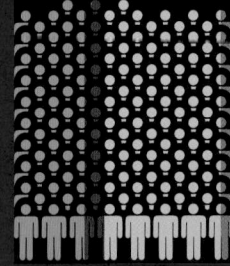

| TOTAL POPULATION = | 14,229,191 | 24,330,646 | 35,761,165 |
|---|---|---|---|

## Geography    Projected Population Growth from the year 2000, by Metropolitan Area

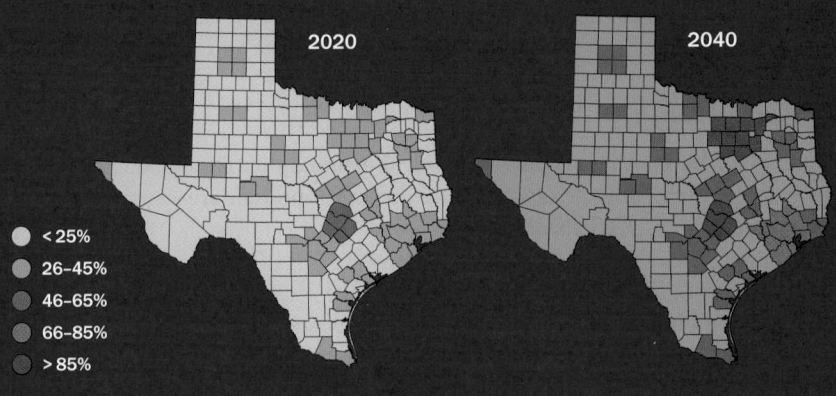

2020          2040

● < 25%
● 26–45%
● 46–65%
● 66–85%
● > 85%

| | 2000 | 2020 | | 2040 | |
|---|---|---|---|---|---|
| Rural Areas | 2,907,272 | 3,452,327 | +19% | 3,825,783 | +32% |
| Other Metropolitan Areas | 5,106,131 | 6,689,146 | +31% | 8,254,026 | +62% |
| San Antonio Area | 1,711,703 | 2,179,553 | +27% | 2,514,097 | +49% |
| Houston Area | 4,715,407 | 6,443,005 | +37% | 8,398,069 | +78% |
| Dallas-Ft. Worth Area | 5,161,544 | 7,340,276 | +42% | 10,107,348 | +96% |
| Austin Area | 1,249,763 | 1,901,433 | +52% | 2,661,842 | +113% |

SOURCES: Texas State Data Center; Office of State Demographer.

### for critical analysis

1. How do you think the increase in the Hispanic portion will change the nature of Texas politics? Will it change the issues that the state government focuses on? Will it have an impact on what party wins elections in Texas?

2. Texas is traditionally associated with images of farming, ranching, and other elements of rural life. How do you think the growth of the urban population will change the image of Texas?

**TABLE 19.4**

## Urbanization in Texas, 1850–2010

|       | 1850 | 1900 | 1950 | 2010 |
| ----- | ---- | ---- | ---- | ---- |
| Urban | 4%   | 17%  | 63%  | 88%  |
| Rural | 96%  | 83%  | 37%  | 12%  |

SOURCES: *Statistical Abstracts of the United States: 1994* (Washington, DC: U.S. Department of Commerce, Bureau of the Census, 1994); Dallas Morning News, *Texas Almanac 2001–2002* (Dallas: Dallas Morning News, 2001); U.S. Department of Agriculture, Economic Research Service.

for impresario grants. There were considerably more freedom and dynamism in Anglo American urban areas than in Spanish ones. Americans brought with them a host of new interests and ideas that would transform urban life in Texas, including a new language, slavery, Protestantism, and a commitment to free enterprise and democracy. The courthouse became a central feature of many Anglo American towns, often located in the center of the town surrounded by shops.

The expansion of Anglo American urban life initially began along the Gulf Coast and gradually expanded east to west, particularly along rivers. New technologies transformed the urban landscape of Texas. Dredging technologies helped to stimulate the growth of port cities such as Houston, Galveston, Corpus Christi, and Brownsville. Railroad construction in the second half of the nineteenth century opened up new lands, which had been difficult for populations to reach, to urban development. In 1880, there were only 11 towns of 4,000 or more people in all of Texas. Following the rapid expansion of the railroads in the 1880s and 1890s, the number rose to 36. By 1910, when the railroad network of 13,110 miles was completed, Texas had 49 towns with a population of 4,000 or more. By 1920, 5 cities—Dallas, El Paso, Fort Worth, Houston, and San Antonio—had populations of more than 50,000. Later technological breakthroughs in transportation, such as cars and air travel, would reinforce the population grid laid out by the railroads.

## The Urban Political Economy

**political economy** the complex interrelations between politics and the economy, as well as their effect on one another

Understanding the complexity of the **political economy** of Texas today demands having some sense of how Texas's three major metropolitan areas compare with each other (see Tables 19.5 and 19.6).

**Houston** Houston, located in Harris County, is the largest city in Texas and the fourth-largest city in the United States—with a population of 2.1 million—behind New York, Los Angeles, and Chicago. Its consolidated metropolitan area encompasses eight counties, with an estimated population of 6.1 million in 2011. Houston grew by 7.5 percent during the first decade of the twenty-first century.

The city originated in 1836 out of the entrepreneurial dreams of two brothers, Augustus Chapman Allen and John Kirby Allen, who sought to create a "great interior commercial emporium of Texas."[35] The town was named after Sam Houston, the leader of Texas's army during its war of independence from Mexico. Early settlers came from the South, bringing with them the institution of slavery. As a

## TABLE 19.5

### Populations of the Largest Cities in Texas (2010)

| | |
|---|---|
| Houston (Harris County) | 2,099,451 |
| San Antonio (Bexar County) | 1,327,407 |
| Dallas (Dallas County) | 1,197,816 |
| Austin (Travis County) | 790,390 |
| Ft. Worth (Tarrant County) | 741,206 |
| El Paso (El Paso County) | 649,121 |

SOURCE: 2010 Census.

## TABLE 19.6

### Race and Ethnic Breakdown of Texas and Its Largest Counties (2010)

| | WHITE | OTHER | BLACK | ASIAN | MULTIPLE RACE | HIS-PANIC* | TOTAL |
|---|---|---|---|---|---|---|---|
| Texas | 70% | 11% | 12% | 4% | 3% | 38% | 25,145,561 |
| Harris | 57% | 15% | 19% | 6% | 3% | 41% | 4,092,459 |
| Dallas | 54% | 16% | 22% | 5% | 3% | 38% | 2,368,139 |
| Tarrant | 67% | 11% | 15% | 5% | 3% | 27% | 1,809,034 |
| Bexar | 73% | 14% | 8% | 2% | 4% | 59% | 1,714,773 |
| Travis | 69% | 13% | 9% | 6% | 4% | 34% | 1,024,266 |
| El Paso | 82% | 11% | 3% | 1% | 3% | 82% | 800,647 |
| Collin | 72% | 6% | 9% | 11% | 3% | 15% | 782,341 |

*Hispanic in this classification can be any race. Numbers are rounded.
SOURCE: 2010 U.S. Census.

consequence, segregation was built into the social structure from the outset. For the first half of the twentieth century, African Americans were either denied or given limited access to a variety of public services such as parks, schools, buses, restrooms, and restaurants. Although not enforced legally, residential segregation divided the city into a number of distinct racially divided neighborhoods for much of the twentieth century.

In the late nineteenth century, Houston's economic well-being depended on cotton and commerce. Railroads played an integral role in placing Houston at the hub of the Texas economy. The opening of the Houston Ship Channel further enhanced Houston's place in the state economy by helping to turn it into the second or third (depending on whose ranking is used) deep-water port in the United States. But

In some areas of Texas, Asian immigrants are a growing force. The signs at this shopping center in Houston attest to the changing demographic landscape of Texas.

it was oil that fundamentally transformed the Houston area in the twentieth century. Oil refineries opened along the ship channel and a petrochemical industry emerged, making Houston one of the leading energy centers in the world. Today it continues to rank first in the nation in the manufacture of petroleum equipment.

By 1930, Houston had become the largest city in Texas, with a population of around 292,000 people. The population continued to expand throughout the 1940s, 1950s, and 1960s, assisted by a liberal annexation policy that enabled the city to incorporate into itself many of the outlying suburban areas. Although the oil bust in the mid-1980s slowed the city's growth, that growth continued in the 1990s, extending into suburban areas such as Clear Lake City and other urban areas such as Galveston.

Of the 2.1 million people living in Houston at the time of the 2010 census, 28.3 percent of the population were non-Hispanic white, 22.2 percent were black, and Hispanics counted for 42.4 percent of the overall population.

**Dallas–Fort Worth** The Metroplex is an economic region encompassing the cities of Dallas and Fort Worth, as well as a number of other suburban cities, including Arlington (population 365,438), Mesquite (139,824), Garland (226,876), Richardson (99,223), Irving (216,290), Plano (259,841), Carrollton (119,097), Grand Prairie (175,396), Denton (113,383), and Frisco (116,989).[36] The major counties in the area are Dallas, Tarrant, and Collin. The Metroplex is joined together by a number of interlocking highways running north–south and east–west, and a major international airport that is strategically located in the national air system.

Dallas was founded as a trading post in 1841, near where two roads were to be built by the Republic.[37] By the 1850s, it had become a retail center servicing the rural areas. By 1870, the population had reached 3,000 people. The coming of the Houston and Texas Central Railroad in 1871 and the Texas and Pacific Railroad in 1873 made Dallas the first rail crossroads in Texas and transformed forever its place in the state's economy. Markets now beckoned east and north, encouraging entrepreneurs and merchants to set up shop. Cotton became a major cash crop, and the population expanded over threefold to more than 10,000 people in 1880. By the turn of the twentieth century, the city had grown to more than 42,000 people.

As with Houston, the oil economy changed the direction and scope of the city's economic life. With the discovery of oil in east Texas in 1830, Dallas became a major center for petroleum financing. By the end of World War II, the economy had diversified, making Dallas a minor manufacturing center in the nation. In the 1950s and 1960s, technology companies such as Ling-Temco-Vought (LTV) and Texas Instruments were added to the industrial mix, transforming Dallas into the third-largest technology center in the nation. The high-tech boom of the 1990s was built from the corporate infrastructure laid down in the 1950s and 1960s.

Dallas grew from 844,401 people in 1970 to 904,078 in 1980 to 1,197,816 in 2010. In 2010, 29 percent of the population were non-Hispanic white, 25 percent were black, and 42 percent were Hispanic.

Although they are locked together in important ways economically, Dallas and Fort Worth are as different as night and day. Whereas Dallas looks to the East and embodies a more corporate white-collar business culture, Fort Worth looks to the West. It is where the West begins in Texas.

Fort Worth originated as an army post in 1849.[38] By 1853, the post had been abandoned as new forts were located to the west. Although settlers took the fort over, population growth was slow through the early 1870s. The spark that enabled the town to begin to prosper was the rise of the cattle industry. Fort Worth was a convenient place for cowboys to rest on their cattle drives to Kansas. Cattle buyers established headquarters in the city. Gradually other businesses grew up around these key businesses. Transportation and communication links improved with the establishment of stage lines to the west and railroad lines to the north and east.

By 1900, Fort Worth was served by eight different railroad companies, many of them transporting cattle and cattle-related products to national markets. The two world wars encouraged further economic development in Fort Worth. Over 100,000 troops were trained at Camp Bowie during World War I. World War II brought an important air force base and, along with it, the aviation industry. The Consolidated Vultee Aircraft Corporation, which was later bought by General Dynamics, became the largest manufacturing concern in the city. Between 1900 and 1950, the population grew from 26,668 to 277,047. In 2010, Fort Worth's population was 741,206. The overall metropolitan area of Dallas–Fort Worth included 6.7 million people in 2011.

**San Antonio**  San Antonio is located in Bexar County, the fourth-largest county in Texas today. San Antonio grew out of the Spanish presidio San Antonio de Bexar, which was founded in 1718.39 In 1773, it became the capital of Spanish Texas, with a population of around 2,100 people. Because of the threats posed by Native Americans and Mexicans after the Texas Revolution, the population declined to about 800 people by 1846. On Texas's entry into the Union, however, the population took off, reaching 3,488 in 1850 and 8,235 in 1860. By the Civil War, San Antonio was the largest city in Texas.

Following the Civil War, San Antonio grew rapidly, stimulated by the building of the San Antonio Railroad in 1877. By 1880, the population had reached more than 20,000 people, mostly Anglo Americans from southern states. The population continued to grow through the first two decades of the twentieth century, reaching 161,000 by 1920. Mexican immigration increased significantly following the Mexican Revolution of 1910 and the building of a city infrastructure that provided paved roads, utilities, water, telephones, and hospitals. By midcentury, San Antonio had become a unique blend of Hispanic, German, and southern Anglo American cultures. Population growth slowed down in the 1930s but picked up again during World War II, reaching over 408,000 in 1950. Major military bases came to dot the landscape around San Antonio. By 1960, the population topped 587,000 people.

Today, San Antonio is Texas's second-largest city. The population of the city was 1,327,407 in 2010, and the San Antonio metropolitan area as a whole had a population of 2,150,918, making it the twenty-seventh-largest metropolitan area in the country. San Antonio's population has become increasingly Hispanic. Approximately 62 percent of the people are Hispanic, 29 percent are Anglo American, and 6 percent are African American.[40]

Unlike Houston or Dallas, San Antonio lacks high-paying manufacturing jobs, and average metropolitan income is lower than in Houston and Dallas.

The economy rests on four legs: national military bases, educational institutions, tourism, and a large medical research complex.

# ● Thinking Critically about Texas's Political Culture

In this chapter, we have studied the political culture of Texas and seen how the state has been transformed by economic and demographic shifts over the past hundred years. Three great technological revolutions have reshaped the economic life of the state. The first—based on the production of agricultural products such as cotton and cattle and on the newly built railroad system—defined economic life in the latter decades of the nineteenth and early twentieth centuries. The second—based on the production of oil and the industries that cheap oil made possible—dominated the economy well into the second half of the twentieth century. The third—the era of high tech—has transformed the state by diversifying its economy and tying it closely to the growing international economy. Accompanying and fueling these economic revolutions have been ongoing demographic changes, which have redefined who the "typical" Texan is and where this person lives. No longer can it be said that a "typical" Texan is simply an extension of an Anglo American culture rooted in southern tradition. No longer does this person reside in a small town, living life close to the land much as his or her ancestors did. Like the economy, the people of Texas have been diversified. Increasing numbers of Hispanics from Mexico and Anglo Americans from other parts of the United States have created a new melting pot of cultures and concerns throughout the state. These cultures have come together in the big metropolitan areas across Texas.

The chapters that follow will analyze the way specific aspects of Texas politics and government work. In the process, we will explore the meaning of liberty, equality, and democracy in Texas and how these ideas are influencing Texas politics and government today. One of our central concerns will be to see how the ideas of liberty, equality, and democracy often play out very differently in Texas than they do in the nation as a whole.

As we have seen in this chapter, the majority of Texans today continue to view liberty through the lens of a political culture dominated by both traditionalistic and individualistic values. There is a tendency in the political culture to defer to leaders in positions of authority. But this deferential politics is checked by a healthy suspicion of giving too much power to those in authority. As a result, in Texas, government is often perceived as something that gets in the way of our individual liberty rather than something through which we accomplish collective objectives.

Two notions of equality also play important roles in Texas political life. First, there is the idea of equality of opportunity. This aspect of equality is deeply rooted in Texas's traditional individualistic political culture. The job of government is to treat individuals fairly and to ensure them a fair chance to make it on their own through their own skills and initiative. Few Texans believe that it is the task of state government to redistribute resources from the rich to the poor, ensuring some equality of result.

In addition to equality of opportunity, political equality has been an issue in Texas politics, with the growing importance of African American and Hispanic minorities in the state. Much of the history of Texas from 1950 to the present

*In 2006 an estimated half million people marched in Dallas to demand fairer treatment for immigrants. As immigration has changed the demographic profile of Texas, it has also given rise to numerous political debates.*

represents an effort to expand the political rights of these groups. Additionally, debates over the meaning of equal participation and representation at all levels of state government have reshaped the broad contours of political life in Texas and given rise to one of the bitterest and most controversial issues to face the state legislature in recent decades: congressional and legislative redistricting.

Like liberty and equality, the ideals of democratic self-government are enshrined in various constitutions under which Texas has operated since the days of the Republic. The people are formally given a number of important roles to play in the political process, including choosing the members of all three branches of government and approving constitutional amendments. As we will see, however, the actual operations of state government and politics tend to work in seemingly undemocratic ways. Arcane rules in the legislative and executive branches allow power to concentrate in the hands of a few individuals. Elections of judges politicize their selection in a way unimaginable in national politics. Well-funded special-interest groups have been able to exert their influence on elections in Texas and to penetrate the legislative process. The rise to power of the Republican Party in the state may be best understood as the triumph of a new set of interests that have successfully displaced those attached to the traditional Democratic Party.

**for critical analysis**

In Texas political culture, governmental power is often seen as a threat to individual liberty. However, Texans also tend to value equality of opportunity and political equality for all citizens. To what extent should the Texas state government use its power to ensure equality?

Texans in general and Texas political leaders in particular may be committed to the idea of democracy. The Texas Constitution may enshrine the values of democratic self-government. As we will see, however, the actual operations of Texas politics and government raise serious questions about what kind of democracy the state really is. The tension between the ideal and reality of democracy in Texas may come to play an important role in restructuring the political system as it responds to ongoing economic and demographic change in the state.

# study guide

(S) **Practice online with:** Chapter 19 Diagnostic Quiz ▪ Chapter 19 Key Term Flashcards

## Texas Political Culture

■ **Describe the defining characteristics of political culture in Texas (pp. 763–65)**

Texas political culture can best be characterized as individualistic and traditional. Texans have great pride in their state and have adopted a famous phrase "Don't mess with Texas" for those external forces wishing to change the state's way of doing things. Texas is a low tax state with distrust for large government programs. Business plays a major role in defining the political culture of the state.

### Key Terms

**political culture** (p. 763)

**moralistic political culture** (p. 763)

**individualistic political culture** (p. 763)

**traditionalistic political culture** (p. 763)

**elite** (p. 763)

**provincialism** (p. 764)

### Practice Quiz

1. In terms of area, how does Texas rank among the 50 states? *(p. 761)*
   a) first
   b) second
   c) third
   d) fifth
   e) seventh

2. *Provincialism* refers to *(p. 764)*
   a) a narrow view of the world.
   b) a progressive view of the value of diversity.
   c) a pro-business political culture.
   d) an urban society.
   e) a group of counties.

 **Practice Online**
Video exercise: *The Handbook of Texas Online*

## The Land

■ **Identify the major geographic regions in Texas (pp. 765–67)**

Because of Texas's immense size, the state's topography is diverse, with East Texas's flat lands, West Texas's arid climate, and Central Texas's hill country all representing diverse ecosystems and land patterns.

### Practice Quiz

3. Which of Texas's physical regions is characterized by the presence of many of the state's largest ranches? *(p. 766)*

   a) Gulf Coastal Plains
   b) Great Plains
   c) Interior Lowlands
   d) Basin and Range Province
   e) Rio Grande Valley

4. Which of Texas's physical regions is found in West Texas? *(p. 767)*
   a) Gulf Coastal Plains
   b) Great Plains
   c) Interior Lowlands
   d) Basin and Range Province
   e) Pine Belt

## Economic Change in Texas

■ **Trace the evolution of Texas's economy (pp. 767–77)**

The Texas economy has undergone a series of technological transformations over the past 100 years. Once the Texas economy was grounded in cotton and ranching. Oil production came to play an important role in the twentieth century. Today, high technology and international trade play important roles in the state's economy. Texas appears to have weathered the Great Recession better than most other states.

## Key Term

**North American Free Trade Agreement (NAFTA)** (p. 775)

## Practice Quiz

5. Creative destruction *(p. 767)*
   a) destroys both old and new economies.
   b) creates new economies and destroys old ones.
   c) maintains old economies and creates new ones.
   d) creates and maintains old and new economies.
   e) does not affect economies.

6. Which industry controlled the politics and economy of Texas for most of the twentieth century? *(p. 770–73)*
   a) cotton
   b) cattle
   c) railroad
   d) oil
   e) technology

7. Which of the following statements is true? *(p. 773)*
   a) Oil production in Texas is greater today than it was 50 years ago.
   b) Oil production no longer plays an important role in the state's economy.
   c) Oil production declined in Texas in the early twenty-first century.
   d) The DFW region has become a major producer of oil in the early twenty-first century.
   e) None of the above

8. Unlike earlier eras, the Texas economy of the twenty-first century features *(p. 775)*
   a) computers, electronics, and other high-tech products.
   b) transportation, oil and natural gas, and banking.
   c) insurance, construction, and banking.
   d) ranching, oil, and tourism
   e) education, the military, and agriculture.

9. NAFTA refers to *(p. 775)*
   a) an oil company.
   b) an independent regulatory commission.
   c) an interstate road network.
   d) an interest group.
   e) an international trade agreement.

10. What is meant by the "Great Recession"? *(p. 776)*
    a) the post–Vietnam War era in the mid 1970s when housing prices rose
    b) the period of high inflation during the early 1980s
    c) a time of chronic economic problems beginning in late 2007 that drew analogies to the Great Depression of the 1930s
    d) the time when Democrats lost control of the Texas House for the first time since Reconstruction
    e) a period of high unemployment in the early 1990s

# The People: Texas Demography

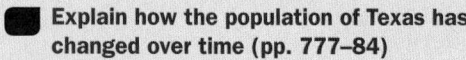 **Explain how the population of Texas has changed over time (pp. 777–84)**

Texas demography has changed over the last century. Once dominated by Anglos, Texas now has a large Latino population that, when coupled with the African American population and other minorities, now makes Texas a majority-minority state. Despite considerable wealth on average, Texans are younger and poorer than the average American.

## Practice Quiz

11. Which of the following accounts for most of Texas's population growth? *(p. 778)*
    a) immigration
    b) natural increases due to the difference between births and deaths
    c) domestic immigration
    d) NAFTA
    e) movement from rural to urban areas

12. Which of the following is not true? *(p. 780)*
    a) Hispanics are increasing as a percentage of the population in Dallas.
    b) More African Americans live in East Texas than West Texas.
    c) San Antonio has a larger Anglo population than Hispanic.
    d) Houston's largest minority population is Hispanic.
    e) The Hispanic population in Texas has grown rapidly in recent decades.

 **Practice Online**
"Exploring Texas Politics" exercise: *Texas Demographics*

# Urbanization

■ **Describe the shift from a rural society to an urban one in Texas (pp. 784–90)**

Initially a rural state, Texas has urbanized, with Houston, San Antonio, and Dallas–Fort Worth representing the largest metropolitan areas in the state. This process of urbanization has changed the state's economy from an agricultural powerhouse to a high tech and innovative economy.

## Key Terms

**urbanization** (p. 784)

**political economy** (p. 786)

## Practice Quiz

13. *Urbanization* refers to a process in which *(p. 784)*
    a) people move from rural to urban areas.
    b) people from the north and west move to Texas.
    c) people move out of urban centers to the suburbs.
    d) people move out of urban centers to rural areas.
    e) minorities assume political control of a city.

14. The three major metropolitan areas in Texas are *(pp. 786–89)*
    a) Houston, Dallas–Fort Worth, and San Antonio.
    b) Houston, Dallas–Fort Worth, and El Paso.
    c) El Paso, Houston, and Austin.
    d) San Antonio, El Paso, and Brownsville-Harlingen-McAllen.
    e) San Antonio, El Paso, and Houston.

# Recommended Websites

**Business QuickFacts**
http://quickfacts.census.gov/qfd/states/48000.html

**Federal Reserve Bank of Texas**
http://dallasfed.org/index.cfm

**Handbook of Texas**
www.tshaonline.org/handbook/online/

**Office of the Governor, Economic Development and Tourism, Business and Industry Data Center**
www.governor.state.tx.us/ecodev/divisions/bidc/

**Texas Almanac**
www.texasalmanac.com

**Texas State Data Center and Office of the State Demographer**
www.txsdc.utsa.edu

The Texas Constitution has been amended hundreds of times. In 2011, Texans voted on and approved the Texas Permanent School Fund Amendment. The measure amended the constitution to make additional funding available to public school districts.

# 20

# The Texas Constitution

**WHAT GOVERNMENT DOES AND WHY IT MATTERS** Every few years, the Texas legislature presents to the voters a list of proposed amendments to the state constitution. Voter approval is necessary for the amendments to take effect. In 2011, 10 amendments were proposed. Among these amendments was one that would allow the Texas Water Development Board to issue bonds so loans could be given for local governments for water projects and a proposed amendment that would give El Paso more borrowing authority. In 2009, 11 amendments were proposed, among them an amendment protecting private property from some property takings involving eminent domain, an amendment establishing a National Research University Fund, and an amendment allowing members of emergency services districts to serve for four years. In 2007, 16 amendments were put forward spanning a wide range of matters. Some amendments grappled with essential problems of constitutional government and public policy. Others were more technical, reflecting efforts to clean up specific language in the state constitution. Some had an air of whimsy about them that belied a serious critique: that the current state constitution is a clumsy document and is, in many respects, out of date. Such is the case with Proposition 10, an amendment proposed in 2007 to abolish the constitutional authority of the county Office of the Inspector of Hides and Animals.[1]

In 1871 the state legislature established the office for the inspection of the brands on all hides and animals that were shipped out of a county.[2] Over time, the need for inspectors declined. By 1945, only about one-third of Texas counties still had an inspector of hides and animals. Nonetheless, under constitutional amendments passed in 1954 and 1958, the office acquired constitutional status. By the 1990s, few counties still had an inspector of hides and animals, and in those that did, the office was not taken all that seriously.

In Fort Bend County, Jeff McMeans served as the inspector for 17 years, after running for the position initially as a joke in 1986. "It was the perfect office," McMeans told a *Dallas Morning News* reporter. "No pay, no office, no responsibility, no nothing." In Travis County, Glenn Maxey was elected inspector of hides and animals in 1986. Before he could file as a candidate, he had to convince the county clerk in Travis County that there really was such an office. Running unopposed, Maxey was elected, but he refused to take the oath of office, noting that his objective in running was not to win but to abolish a useless county office.

The demise of the office of inspector of hides and animals eventually took place in 2003 when the legislature changed the Agricultural Code. But the language in the constitution remained unchanged. Finally, during the 2007 session, the legislature passed a proposed amendment to the constitution (Proposition 10) that would delete any reference to the office in the constitution itself. Although there was no serious opposition to Proposition 10, some used it to draw attention to the fact that the amendment process and the state constitution itself were seriously flawed. A group of Austin Community College students rallied against Proposition 10, to show that the constitution was woefully out of date and that piecemeal amendments such as Proposition 10 only made matters worse. Not surprisingly, the proposition passed.

Efforts have been made in the past to rethink the constitutional foundations of political life in Texas. In spite of reform efforts, the Texas Constitution remains a document much disparaged and not well understood by the population as a whole. However, the Texas Constitution probably has a greater immediate impact on the lives of Texans than does the U.S. Constitution.

## chaptergoals

- Identify the main functions of state constitutions (pages 799–800)
- Describe the five Texas constitutions that preceded the current constitution (pages 800–809)
- Explain the circumstances that led to the Texas Constitution that is still in use today (pages 809–11)
- Analyze the major provisions of the Texas Constitution today (pages 811–17)
- Describe modern efforts to change the Texas Constitution (pages 817–24)

# The Role of a State Constitution

Identify the main functions of state constitutions

State **constitutions** perform a number of important functions. They legitimate state political institutions by clearly explaining the source of their power and authority. State constitutions also delegate power, explaining which powers are granted to particular institutions and individuals and how those powers are to be used. They prevent the concentration of political power by providing political mechanisms that check and balance the powers of one political institution or individual officeholder against another. Finally, they define the limits of political power. Through declarations of rights, state constitutions explicitly forbid the intrusion of certain kinds of governmental activities into the lives of individuals.

The idea of constitutional government in Texas since its first constitution has been heavily indebted to the larger American experience (see Chapter 2). Five ideas unite the U.S. and Texas constitutional experiences. First, political power in both the United States and Texas is ultimately derived from the people. Political power is something that is artificially created through the constitution by a conscious act of the people. Second, political power is divided into three separate parts and placed in separate branches of government. The legislative, executive, and judicial branches of government have their own unique powers and corresponding duties and obligations. Third, the U.S. and Texas constitutions structure political power in such a way that the power of one branch is checked and balanced by the power of the other two branches. The idea of checks and balances reflects a common concern among the framers of the U.S. Constitution and the authors of Texas's various constitutions that the intent of writing a constitution was not just to establish effective governing institutions. Its purpose was also to create political institutions that would not tyrannize the very people who established them. The concern for preventing the emergence of tyranny is also found in a fourth idea that underlies the U.S. and Texas constitutions: the idea of individual rights. Government is explicitly forbidden to violate a number of particular rights that the people possess.

The final idea embodied in both the U.S. and Texas constitutions is that of **federalism**. Federalism is the division of government into a central government and a series of regional governments (see Chapter 3). Both kinds of government exercise direct authority over individual citizens of the United States and of each particular state. Article IV, Section 4, of the U.S. Constitution guarantees that every state in the Union will have a "Republican Form of Government." Curiously, no attempt is made to explain what exactly a "Republican Form of Government" entails. The Tenth Amendment to the U.S. Constitution also recognizes the importance of the idea of federalism to the American political system. It reads: "The powers not delegated to the United States by the Constitution, nor prohibited by it to the States, are reserved to the States respectively, or to the people." According to the U.S. Constitution, enormous reservoirs of political power are thus derived from the people who reside in the states themselves.

However, some important differences distinguish the constitutional experience of Texas from that of the United States. Most important is the subordinate role that Texas has in the federal system. Article VI of the U.S. Constitution contains the **supremacy clause**, declaring the Constitution and the laws of the United States to be "the supreme Law of the Land." The supremacy clause requires all judges in every state to be bound by the U.S. Constitution, notwithstanding the laws or

**constitution** the legal structure of a government, which establishes its power and authority as well as the limits on that power

**federalism** a system of government in which power is divided, by a constitution, between a central government and regional governments

**supremacy clause** Article VI of the U.S. Constitution, which states that the Constitution and laws passed by the national government and all treaties are the supreme law of the land and superior to all laws adopted by any state or any subdivision

constitution of their particular state. In matters of disagreement, the U.S. Constitution thus takes precedence over the Texas Constitution.

One of the major issues of the Civil War was how the federal system was to be understood. Was the United States a confederation of autonomous sovereign states that were ultimately independent political entities capable of secession (much like the current European Union)? Was the United States a perpetual union of states that were ultimately in a subordinate relationship to the central government? The results of the war and the ratification of the Fourteenth Amendment in 1868 ultimately resolved this question in terms of the latter. The idea that the United States was a perpetual union composed of subordinate states would have profound implications for constitutional government in Texas throughout the late nineteenth and twentieth centuries. The incorporation of the Bill of Rights through the Fourteenth Amendment, which made much of the Bill of Rights apply to the states, became a dominant theme of constitutional law in the twentieth century. The Fourteenth Amendment effectively placed restrictions on Texas government and public policy that went far beyond those laid out in Texas's own constitution.

Another major difference between the U.S. and Texas constitutions lies in the **necessary and proper clause** of Article I, Section 8. Section 8 begins by listing in detail the specific powers granted to Congress by the Constitution. The Founders apparently wanted to limit the scope of national government activities. But Section 8 concludes by granting Congress the power necessary to accomplish its constitutional tasks. The net effect of this clause was to provide a constitutional basis for an enormous expansion of central government activities over the next 200 plus years.

Drafters of Texas's various constitutions generally have been unwilling to grant such an enormous loophole in the exercise of governmental power. Although granting state government the power to accomplish certain tasks, Texas constitutions have generally denied officeholders broad grants of discretionary power to accomplish their goals.

## ● The First Texas Constitutions

> **Describe the five Texas constitutions that preceded the current constitution**

Since declaring independence from Mexico, Texas has had six constitutions. Each was shaped by historical developments of its time and, following the first constitution, attempted to address the shortcomings of each previous constitution. In this section, we look at the five Texas constitutions that preceded the current constitution. First, though, we consider the constitution that governed Texas when it was part of Mexico.

**The Constitution of Coahuila y Tejas, 1827**  Despite the growing fears of American expansionism following the Louisiana Purchase, in 1803 Spanish Texas was still sparsely populated. In 1804, the population of Spanish Texas was estimated to be 3,605. In 1811, Juan Bautista de las Casas launched the first revolt against Spanish rule in San Antonio. The so-called Casas Revolt was successfully put down by the summer of 1811. The next year, a second challenge to Spanish rule took place along the border between Texas and the United States. After capturing Nacogdoches, La Bahia, and San Antonio, rebel forces under José Bernardo Gutiérrez de Lara issued a declaration of independence from New Spain and drafted a constitution. By 1813, however, this revolt had also been put down, and bloody reprisals

**necessary and proper clause**
Article I, Section 8, of the U.S. Constitution; it provides Congress with the authority to make all laws "necessary and proper" to carry out its powers

In the image, handwritten speech bubbles read:

"...lundered as she is let him that is without sin, cast the first stone at her!"

"Welcome, sister, Your Valor has won you liberty and independence, and you have fairly won the right to be identified with 'the land of the brave, and the home of the free.'"

"Shall the slanders that have been urged against your sister, sever those whose blood flows from the same fountain?"

"Stand back, Madam Texas! for we are more holy than thou! Do you think we will have anything to do with gamblers, horse-racers, and licentious profligates?"

"Softly, Softly friend Harry. Thou hast mentioned the very reason that we cannot Vote for thee!"

Labels below figures: DALLAS. POLK. TEXAS. CLAY. QUAKER.

This 1844 cartoon satirized congressional opposition to the annexation of Texas. Personified as a beautiful young woman, Texas is holding a cornucopia filled with flowers. Though James K. Polk, elected to the presidency in 1844, welcomes Texas, the Whig Party leader Senator Henry Clay, with arms folded, warns, "Stand back, Madam Texas! For we are more holy than thou! Do you think we will have anything to do with gamblers, horse-racers, and licentious profligates?"

had depopulated the state. Texas remained part of New Spain until the Mexican War of Independence.[3]

The Mexican War of Independence grew out of a series of revolts against Spanish rule during the Napoleonic Wars. Burdened by debts brought on by a crippling war with France, Spain sought to extract more wealth from its colonies. The forced abdication of Ferdinand VII in favor of Napoleon's brother Joseph in 1808 and an intensifying economic crisis in New Spain in 1809 and 1810 undermined the legitimacy of Spanish rule. Revolts broke out in Guanajuato and spread throughout Mexico and its Texas province. Although these rebellions were initially put down by royalist forces loyal to Spain, by 1820 local revolts and guerrilla actions had helped to weaken continued royal rule from Spain. On August 24, 1821, Mexico was formally granted independence by Spain.

Because Texas was part of Mexico, the first federal constitution that it operated under was the Mexican Constitution. At the national level, there were two houses of Congress. The lower house was composed of deputies serving two-year terms. In the upper house, senators served four-year terms and were selected by state legislatures. The president and vice president were elected for four-year terms by the legislative bodies of the states. There was a supreme court, composed of 11 judges, and an attorney general. Although the Mexican Constitution mandated separate legislative, executive, and judicial branches, no attempt was made to define the scope of states rights in the Mexican confederation. Local affairs remained independent of the central government. Although the Mexican Constitution embodied many of the ideas found in the U.S. Constitution, there was one important difference: Catholicism was established as the state religion and was supported financially by the state.[4]

Under the Mexican Constitution, the state of Coahuila and the sparsely populated province of Texas were combined together into the state of Coahuila and Texas. Saltillo, Mexico, was the capital. More than two years were spent drafting a constitution for the new state. It was finally published on March 11, 1827.

The state was formally divided into three separate districts, with Texas composing the District of Bexar. Legislative power for the state was placed in a **unicameral**

**unicameral** comprising one body or house, as in a one-house legislature

legislature composed of 12 deputies elected by the people. The people of the District of Bexar (Texas) elected 2 of these. Along with wide-ranging legislative powers, the legislature was also empowered to elect state officials when no majority emerged from the popular vote, to serve as a grand jury in political and military matters, and to regulate the army and militia. Executive power was vested in a governor and a vice governor, each elected by the people for a four-year term. Judicial power was placed in state courts. The Constitution of 1827 formally guaranteed citizens the right to liberty, security, property, and equality. Language in the Constitution of 1827 also supported efforts to curtail the spread of slavery, an institution of vital importance to planters who were immigrating from the American South. The legislature was ordered to promote education and freedom of the press. As in the Mexican federal constitution, Catholicism was the established state religion.[5]

## The Constitution of the Republic of Texas, 1836

Texas's break with Mexico was in large part a constitutional crisis that culminated in separation. Political conventions held in San Felipe de Austin in 1832 and 1833 reflected a growing discontent among Texans over their place in the Mexican federal system. Along with demands for a more liberal immigration policy for people from the United States and for the establishment of English- and Spanish-speaking primary schools, calls for separate statehood for Texas emerged from the conventions. The 1833 convention actually drafted a constitution for this newly proposed state modeled on the Massachusetts Constitution of 1780. Stephen F. Austin's attempt to bring the proposed constitution to the attention of the central government in Mexico City led to his imprisonment, which, in turn, pushed Texas closer to open rebellion against the central Mexican government.

On November 7, 1835, a declaration was adopted by a meeting of state political leaders at San Felipe, which stated the reasons Texans were beginning to take up arms against the Mexican government. The declaration proclaimed that Texas was rising up in defense of its rights and liberties as well as the republican principles articulated in the Mexican Constitution of 1824. This declaration was but a prelude to the formal Texas Declaration of Independence that emerged out of the convention of 1836 held at Washington-on-the-Brazos.

Of the 59 delegates attending the Convention of 1836, only 10 had lived in Texas prior to 1830. Two had arrived as late as 1836. Thirty-nine of the delegates were from southern slave states, 6 were from the border state of Kentucky, 7 were from northern states, 3 were from Mexico (including 2 born in Texas), and 4 were from other English-speaking lands.[6] The final products of the convention—the Texas Declaration of Independence and the Constitution of 1836—reflected the interests and values of these participants.

In their own Declaration of Independence, delegates to the convention proclaimed that the federal constitutional regime they had been invited to live under by the rulers of Mexico had been replaced by a military tyranny that combined a "despotism of the sword and the priesthood." Echoing the American Declaration of Independence, they presented a long list of grievances against the central government, including the failure to provide freedom of religion, a system of public education, and trial by jury.

**The Texas Declaration of Independence** Like the Founders during the American Revolution, leaders of the Texas Revolution felt they needed to justify their actions in print. Written by George C. Childress and adopted by the general convention at Washington-on-the-Brazos on March 2, 1836, the Texas Declaration of Independence stated why it was necessary to separate from Mexico and create an

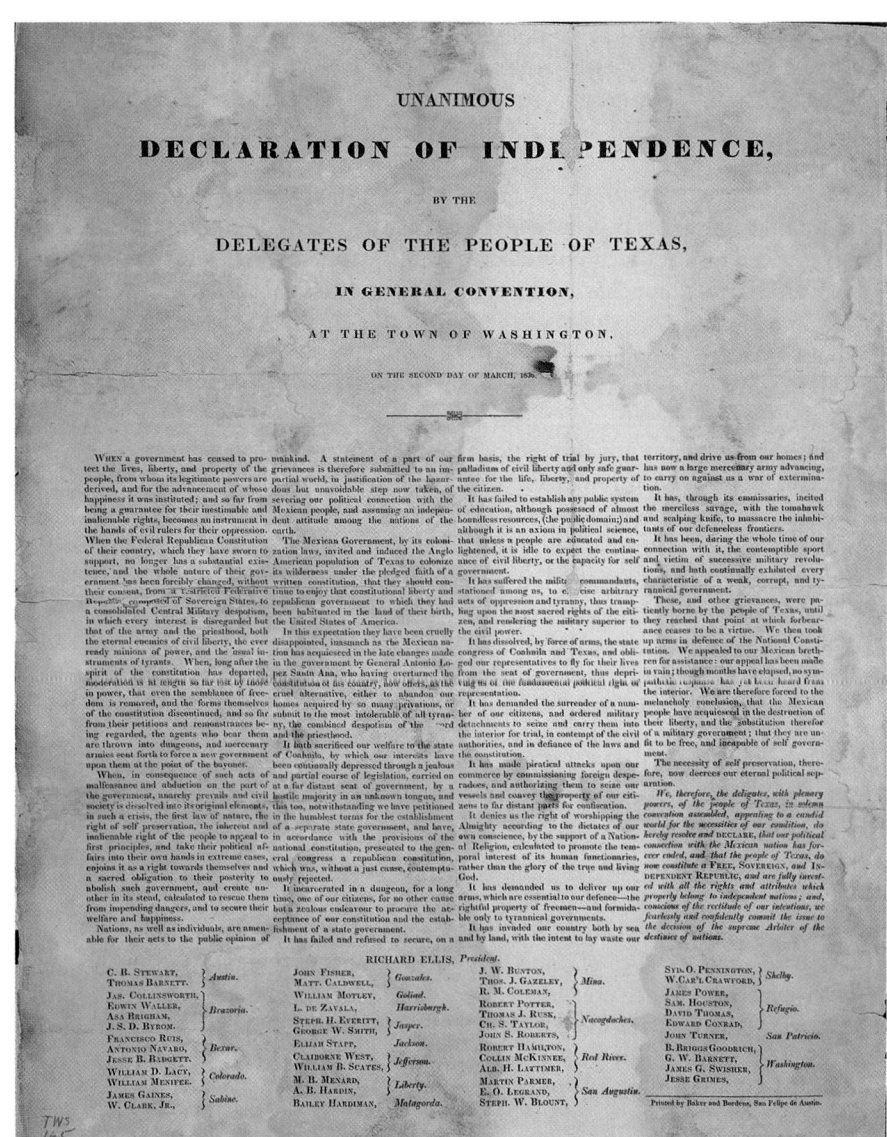

*The Texas Declaration of Independence was written by George C. Childress and adopted at the Convention of 1836. Childress modeled the document on the American Declaration of Independence.*

independent republic. Not surprisingly, the document draws heavily on the ideas of John Locke and Thomas Jefferson for inspiration. The description of the role of the government, "to protect the lives, liberty, and property of the people," repeated verbatim Locke's litany of the primary reasons for establishing government. Like Jefferson's Declaration, Texas's declaration catalogues a list of grievances against the Mexican regime. According to Texas's declaration, the existing government had abdicated its duties to protect the governed and had broken the trustee relationship that binds a people to those in authority. By dissolving civil society into its original elements, the government had forced the people to assert their inalienable right of self-preservation and to take political affairs into their own hands again. The "melancholy conclusion" of Texas's declaration echoed ideas that Locke and Jefferson would have understood well: any government that stripped a people of their liberty was unacceptable to those raised on principles of self-government. Self-preservation demanded "eternal political separation" from the very state (Mexico) that had invited them to settle in Texas.

After declaring Texas a separate republic independent from Mexico, the convention proceeded to draft and pass a new constitution reflecting these republican sentiments. Resembling the U.S. Constitution in being brief and flexible (fewer than 6,500 words), the 1836 Constitution established an elected chief executive with considerable powers, a **bicameral** legislature, and a four-tiered judicial system composed of justice, county, district, and supreme courts.[7] Power was divided among these three branches, and a system of checks and balances was put into place. Complicated procedures were included for amending the constitution, and a bill of rights was elaborated.

A number of important provisions from Spanish-Mexican law were adapted for the Texas Republic in the constitution, including the idea of community property, homestead exemptions and protections, and debtor relief. The values of American democracy percolated through the document. White male suffrage was guaranteed. Ministers and priests were ineligible for public office. But one of the most important aspects of the Constitution of 1836, at least from the perspective of newly immigrated Americans from the South, may have been the defense of slavery as an institution.

The Constitution of Coahuila y Tejas of 1827 had challenged, albeit unsuccessfully, the existence of slavery as an institution. Although the 1836 Constitution of the Republic of Texas outlawed the importation of slaves from Africa, it guaranteed that slaveholders could keep their property and that new slaveholding immigrants could bring their slaves into Texas with them. The results of this constitutional protection were monumental. In 1836, Texas had a population of 38,470, including 5,000 slaves. By 1850, the slave population had grown to 58,161, over one-quarter of the state's population. By 1860, there were more than 182,566 slaves, accounting for more than 30 percent of the state's population.[8] To all intents and purposes, the Constitution of 1836 not only saved slavery as an institution in Texas but also provided the protections needed for it to flourish.

It was one thing to declare independence from Mexico, but quite another to win independence. Only after the Battle of San Jacinto, where on April 21 Sam Houston's force of 900 men overran the 1,300-man force of Santa Anna and captured Santa Anna himself, did Texas become an independent state.[9]

## The Texas State Constitution of 1845

Although the 1836 Constitution called for annexation by the United States, Texas remained an independent republic for nine years. There were concerns in the United States that if Texas were admitted to the Union, it would be as a slave state. Texas's admission to the Union could alter the delicate balance between slave and free states and further divide the nation over the sensitive subject of slavery. Additionally, it was feared that annexation by the United States would lead to war with Mexico. The defeated Mexican general and dictator Santa Anna had repudiated the Treaty of Velasco, which had ended the war between Texas and Mexico. Still claiming Texas as part of its own territory, Mexico undoubtedly would have gone to war to protect what it felt to be rightfully its own.

Hesitation over admitting Texas to the Union was overcome by the mid-1840s. On March 1, 1845, the U.S. Congress approved a resolution that brought Texas into the Union as a state. The annexation resolution had a number of interesting provisions. First, the Republic of Texas ceded to the United States all military

*The lowering of the Republic flag marked Texas's annexation to the Union on March 1, 1845. A state constitution was drafted shortly thereafter to reflect Texas's new role.*

armaments, bases, and facilities pertaining to public defense. Second, Texas retained a right to all "its vacant and unappropriated lands" as well as to its public debts. This was no small matter, because Texas claimed an enormous amount of land that extended far beyond its present state boundaries. The boundary issues were not resolved until Congress passed the Compromise of 1850 which, among other things, established Texas's boundaries in exchange for a payment from the federal government where some of the funds were used to pay Texas's debts. Finally, Texas was given permission to break up into four additional states when population proved adequate.

On July 4, 1845, Anson Jones, fourth and final president of the Republic of Texas, called a convention in Austin to draft a state constitution. Drafters of the constitution relied heavily on the Constitution of 1836, although the final document ended up being almost twice as long. The familiar doctrines of separation of powers, checks and balances, and individual rights defined the basic design of government.

Under the Constitution of 1845, the legislature would be composed of two houses. The House of Representatives would have between 45 and 90 members, elected for two-year terms. Members were required to be at least 21 years of age. The Senate would be composed of between 19 and 33 members, elected for four-year terms. Half of the Senate would be elected every two years. As in the U.S. Constitution, revenue bills would originate in the House. Executive vetoes could be overturned by a two-thirds vote of each house. In a separate article on education, the legislature was ordered to establish a public school system and to set aside lands to support a Permanent School Fund. Another interesting power granted to the legislature was the power to select the treasurer and comptroller in a joint session.

This constitution provided for an elected governor and lieutenant governor. The governor's term was set at two years. He could serve only four years as governor in any six-year period. Among the executive powers granted to the governor were the powers to convene and adjourn the legislature, to veto legislation, to grant pardons and reprieves, and to command the state militia. The governor also had the power to appoint the attorney general, secretary of state, and district and supreme court judges, subject to the approval of the Senate.

The Constitution of 1845 established a judicial branch consisting of a supreme court composed of three judges, district courts, and lower courts deemed necessary by the legislature. Judges on the higher courts were to be appointed to six-year terms and could be removed from office subject to a two-thirds vote of both houses of the legislature.

Amending the Constitution of 1845 was difficult. After being proposed by a two-thirds vote of each house, amendments had to be approved by a majority of the voters. In the next legislature, another two-thirds vote of each house was necessary for ratification. Only one amendment was ever made to the Constitution of 1845. In 1850, an amendment was added to provide for the election of state officials who were originally appointed by the governor or by the legislature.[10]

This constitution retained some of the unusual provisions from the annexation resolution. Texas could divide itself into as many as five states and was responsible for paying its own foreign debt. It would retain title to its public lands, which could be sold to pay its debt. There was even a provision allowing Texas to fly its flag at the same height as the U.S. flag.

## The Constitution of 1861: Texas Joins the Confederacy

The issue of slavery had delayed Texas's admission into the United States for nine years, until 1845. It drove Texas from the Union in 1861. By 1860, slavery had become a vital institution to the Texas economy. Concentrated in east Texas and along the Gulf Coast, slaves had come to constitute 30 percent of the population. However, in large sections of the state, particularly in the north and west, the economy was based on ranching or corn and wheat production rather than cotton. There slavery was virtually nonexistent. The question of whether Texas should secede was a controversial one that divided the state along regional and ethnic as well as party lines.

Pressure to secede mounted following the presidential election of Abraham Lincoln in November 1860. A staunch Unionist, Governor Sam Houston refused to convene a special session of the legislature to discuss secession. Seeking to bypass Houston, a number of influential political leaders in the state, including the chief justice of the Texas Supreme Court, called for a special convention in January 1861 to consider secession. Giving in to the pressure, Houston called a special session of the legislature in the hopes of undercutting the upcoming secession convention. The legislature, however, had other ideas, validating the call for the convention and turning its chambers over to the convention.

Lawyers and slaveholders dominated the secession convention. Lawyers composed 40 percent of the delegates; slaveholders composed 70 percent. The Texas Ordinance of Secession, produced by the convention on February 2, 1861, reflected this proslavery membership. In striking language, it proclaimed that the northern states had broken faith with Texas, particularly regarding the institution of slavery. Northerners had violated the very laws and constitution of the federal Union by appealing to a "higher law" that trampled on the rights of Texans. In language that people living in the twenty-first century find hard to understand, the Ordinance of Secession proclaimed,

> We hold as undeniable truths that the governments of the various States, and of the confederacy itself, were established exclusively by the white race, for themselves and their posterity; that the African race had no agency in their establishment; that they were rightfully held and regarded as an inferior and dependent race, and in that condition only could their existence in this country be rendered beneficial and tolerable.[11]

*Prior to the Civil War, Governor Sam Houston opposed secession from the Union and attempted to block efforts by those wishing to secede.*

Texas voters approved secession from the Union on February 23, 1861. The secession convention reconvened to enact a new constitution to guide the state as it entered the **Confederacy**. There were surprisingly few changes in the final document. This constitution was similar to the Constitution of 1845 except that references to the United States of America were replaced with references to the Confederate States of America. Public officials had to declare allegiance to the Confederacy, and slavery and states' rights were defended. A clause in the 1845 Constitution that provided for the emancipation of slaves was eliminated, and freeing slaves was declared illegal. But for the most part, the document accepted the existing constitutional framework. Controversial proposals, such as resuming the African slave trade, were rejected. The move out of the Union into the Confederacy may have been a radical one, but the new constitution was conservative insofar as it reaffirmed the existing constitutional order in the state.[12]

**Confederacy** the Confederate States of America, those southern states that seceded from the United States in late 1860 and 1861 and argued that the power of the states was more important than the power of the central government

## The Constitution of 1866: Texas Rejoins the Union

Defeat in the Civil War led to the institution of another state constitution in 1866. The provisional governor, Andrew Jackson Hamilton, called a constitutional convention on November 15, 1865, a little over six months after the surrender of Lee's army in Virginia. Delegates were elected on January 8, 1866, and the convention was held February 7. Few former secessionists were excluded from voting, with the result that there were strong Unionist and secessionist factions at the convention.

A number of actions were taken to bring the state into compliance with President Andrew Johnson's policy of Reconstruction, including the rejection of the right to secession, a repudiation of the war debt incurred by the state, and an acceptance of the abolition of slavery. The convention granted freedmen fundamental rights to their persons and property and gave them the right to sue and be sued as well as the right to contract with others. However, there was little support for extending suffrage to blacks, and they were banned from holding public office. The convention also made a few changes to the existing constitutional system in Texas. These changes came to be known as the Constitution of 1866.

As in the two previous constitutions, the size of the House was set between 45 and 90, and that of the Senate between 19 and 33. Terms of office remained the same as under the 1845 and 1861 constitutions, although salaries were increased. Reapportionment was to be based on the number of white male citizens, who would be counted in a census every 10 years.

The governor's salary was also increased, and the term was extended to 4 years, with a limit of 8 years in any 12-year period. The governor was also granted, for the first time, a line-item veto on appropriations. The comptroller and the treasurer were to be elected by the voters for 4-year terms.

Under the new constitution, the state supreme court was expanded from three to five judges and terms were increased to 10 years. Their salaries also were increased. The chief justice was to be selected from the five judges on the supreme court. District court judges were to be elected for 8-year terms, and the attorney general for a 4-year term.

Voters ratified the Constitution of 1866 in June in a relatively close referendum, 28,119 to 23,400. The close vote was attributed to a widespread unhappiness with the increase in salaries of the various state officers.[13]

## The Reconstruction Constitution of 1869

**Radical Republicans** a bloc of Republicans in the U.S. Congress who pushed through the adoption of black suffrage as well as an extended period of military occupation of the South following the Civil War

In 1869, Texas wrote still another constitution to meet the requirements of the Congressional Reconstruction Acts of 1867. A vote calling for a constitutional convention was ordered by General Winfield Scott Hancock, the commander of the Texas and Louisiana military district, in early 1868. Against Democratic opposition, **Radical Republicans** easily won the vote for a convention by 44,689 to 11,440. Of the 90 delegates to the convention, only 6 had served in the previous constitutional convention. Ten were blacks. The vast majority represented the interests of various wings in the Republican Party. The convention was a rancorous affair as delegates argued over a wide range of issues, including railroad charters, lawlessness in the state, and whether laws passed during the war years were legal. In the final days of the convention, delegates finally got down to the constitutional matters and the problems of accepting the Thirteenth and Fourteenth Amendments. Although delegates never completed their task of reworking the Constitution of 1866, their efforts were published under orders by military officials and became the Constitution of 1869.

A number of features of the Constitution of 1869 stand out.[14] The U.S. Constitution was declared to be the supreme law of the land. Slavery was forbidden, and blacks were given the right to vote. Fourteenth Amendment guarantees of equality before the law were recognized. Additionally, the constitution altered the relationship among the three branches of government.

The House of Representatives was set at 90 and the Senate at 30 members. Senatorial terms were extended to six years, with one-third of the seats to be elected every biennium. Legislative sessions were to be held annually.

The most critical changes were in the executive branch and the courts. The powers of the governor were vastly expanded. Among other things, the governor was given wide-ranging appointment powers that included the power to appoint judges. The state supreme court was reduced from five to three judges. The term

*This image shows what the Texas State House looked like in the 1850s. Texas's first constitution after joining the Union as a state was ratified in 1845. It lasted until 1861 when Texas seceded from the Union along with other southern states.*

of supreme court judges was also lowered to nine years, with one new judge to be appointed every three years. Salaries for state officials were increased.

A Republican affiliated with the Radical faction of the party and a former Union general, Edmund Davis, governed under this constitution. Davis had vast authority, since the constitution had centralized power in the executive while reducing local governmental control. Varying interpretations exist of the government provided by Davis, though the popular perception at the time was that Davis presided over a corrupt, extravagant administration that eventually turned to the state police and the militia to attempt to maintain its regime.

In 1872 the Democrats regained control of the state government, and in 1873 the Democrat Richard Coke was elected governor. Davis attempted to maintain control over the governor's office by having his handpicked supreme court invalidate Coke's election. Davis refused to give up his office and surrounded himself with state police in the capitol building. However, when Democrats slipped past guards and gathered upstairs in the capitol building to organize a government, Davis was unable to obtain federal troops to retain him in office. Democrats were able to form a government, and Davis left office.

# ● The Constitution of 1876

**Explain the circumstances that led to the Texas Constitution that is still in use today**

To prevent another government such as Davis's, efforts were made to write a new constitution. In 1874 a constitution was proposed and later rejected by a sitting legislature.[15] Finally, in 1875 a constitutional convention was called. Three delegates were selected by popular vote from each of the 30 senatorial districts. The final composition of the convention included 75 white Democrats and 15 Republicans, 6 of whom were black. Not one of the elected delegates had participated in the constitutional convention of 1868–69. Forty of the delegates were farmers, and 40 were members of the **Grange**, a militant farming organization that had emerged to improve the plight of farmers.

The document that emerged from this convention, the Constitution of 1876, is still the basis for Texas government today. In an era of agriculture when prices and incomes were low and when little was demanded or expected from government, much in the 1876 Constitution made sense. However, one might question whether a constitution designed primarily by white males for whites in a rural agrarian society—and for the purpose of keeping the likes of Edmund Davis from ever controlling the state again—is the best foundation for government in the modern era.

The framers were committed to a constitution with four major themes. First, they wanted strong popular control of state government. Second, they believed that a constitution should seriously limit the power of state government. Third, they sought economy in government. Fourth, the framers sought to promote agrarian interests, particularly those of small farmers, who formed the basis of support for the Grange movement.

Popular control of state government meant that the governor's vast appointment powers were limited by making judges and other public officials subject to election. But popular control of the government did not mean that all the

**Grange** a militant farmers' movement of the late nineteenth century that fought for improved conditions for farmers

Constitution of the State of Texas

Preamble

Humbly invoking the blessings of Almighty God, the people of the State of Texas, do ordain and establish this Constitution

Article I

Bill of Rights

*The example of Davis's reign motivated the revision of executive branch power in the Constitution of 1876. The framers of that constitution sought popular control of state government in order to limit the appointment powers of the governor as provided by the Constitution of 1869.*

### for critical analysis

Consider the characteristics of the constitutions adopted prior to 1876. What were the major provisions of each? Which were incorporated into the present Texas Constitution? Why does the state constitution place so many limits on state government? What changes could be made to the constitution to increase its effectiveness?

electorate voted. When the framers of the 1876 Constitution thought of popular control of state government, they thought of control by white males.

In the effort to limit the powers of state government, the constitution placed great restrictions on the actions of government, restrictions that could be modified only through a complex constitutional amendment process. Executive authority was diffused among numerous officeholders, rather than concentrated in the hands of the governor. Although subsequently changed by constitutional amendment, an initial provision further limited gubernatorial power by setting a two-year term limit for the office. The legislature was part-time, ordinarily sitting for a proscribed time period every other year. This was in contrast to the 1869 Constitution, which provided that the legislature meet in annual sessions.

Economy in government was accomplished in several ways. The constitution restricted the extent of government debt and of government's power to tax. In addition, there were limits on the salaries of state officials, especially those of legislators. A major economic depression had begun in 1873, and many Texans were experiencing economic hardship. One way money was saved was by decentralizing public education. Schools were segregated, and compulsory education laws were eliminated. By having local control over education, white landowners could avoid paying taxes for the education of black students.

Texas at that time was an agricultural state. Wishing to protect agrarian interests, the framers wrote provisions protecting homesteads and restricting institutions that at that time were perceived to be harmful to farmers, such as banks and railroads. Greater responsibility was placed on local instead of state officials. There were also detailed regulations on railroad competition, freight and passenger rates, and railroad construction incentives.

Even in its earliest stages, the Texas Constitution of 1876 was a lengthy, rigid, and detailed document, and purposely so. Regulations curtailing government power were placed not in statutes where they could easily be reversed, but in the body of the constitution. The goal of this design was to ensure that the Radical Republicans and Edmund Davis would never again be able to reign and spend in Texas. They, of course, never did, although over the years the constitution became an increasingly unwieldy document.

# The Constitution of Texas Today

**Analyze the major provisions of the Texas Constitution today**

The U.S. Constitution has two great virtues: brevity and flexibility. Neither of these virtues can be said to characterize the Texas Constitution. The U.S. Constitution is limited to 7 short articles and 27 amendments, and takes up only 8 pages of the *World Almanac*. Much in the federal document is left unsaid, allowing lawmaking to be accomplished by statute. In contrast, in 2012 the Texas Constitution contained 16 articles (Table 20.1, another article that concerned Spanish and Mexican land titles has been deleted from the constitution) and had been amended 474 times (Table 20.2).

**TABLE 20.1**

## The Texas Constitution: An Overview

Article I: The Bill of Rights

Article II: Separation of Powers in State Government

Article III: The State Legislature

Article IV: The Plural Executive

Article V: The Judicial Department

Article VI: Suffrage in Texas

Article VII: Public Education in Texas

Article VIII: Taxation and State Revenues

Articles IX and XI: Concerning Local Government, including Counties and Municipal Corporations

Article X: Empowering the State to Regulate Railroads and to Create the Texas Railroad Commission

Article XII: Empowering the State to Create General Laws for Corporations

Article XIII: Concerning Spanish and Mexican Land Titles, Now Deleted from the Constitution

Article XIV: Creates the General Land Office to Deal with Registering Land Titles

Article XV: Impeachment Provisions

Article XVI: General Provisions Covering a Wide Range of Topics

Article XVII: Amendment Procedures

Many of the articles are lengthy, complex affairs, taking up over 67 pages of text in one edition of the *Texas Almanac*. But it is not just the length that differentiates the two constitutions. There is a difference in tone. The Texas Constitution reflects the writers' fears of what government could do if the principle of **limited government** was not clearly established.

In addition to its severe limits on executive power, the Texas Constitution also addresses a number of specific policy problems directly in the text, turning what might appear to be matters of public policy into issues of constitutional authority. By granting a variety of boards and districts a special place in the constitution, the framers set out additional checks and balances that make it difficult for governors to exercise power effectively. Quite unintentionally, the Texas Constitution became a place where special interests could seek to promote and protect their own agendas, even in the face of considerable political opposition.

The contrasts in character between the federal and Texas constitutions are a direct reflection of the differences in their framers' underlying goals. The U.S. Constitution was written to overcome the liabilities of the Articles of Confederation and create a government that could act effectively in the public welfare in a variety of policy areas. The Texas Constitution was written to prevent the expansion of governmental authority and the return of a system of political power that was perceived as acting against the interests of the people.

## The Preamble

The preamble to the Texas Constitution is surprisingly short: "Humbly invoking the blessings of Almighty God, the people of the State of Texas do ordain and establish this Constitution." This brevity is more than made up for in what follows.

## Article I: Bill of Rights

Article I of the U.S. Constitution establishes and delegates power to the legislative branch of government. One of the overriding concerns of the Founders was to create a legislature that could act effectively in public affairs. What came to be known as the Bill of Rights—the first 10 amendments to the Constitution—was added after the original Constitution was drafted and approved.

In contrast, the Texas Constitution puts its Bill of Rights up front as Article I, well before any discussion of the legislature, the executive, or the courts. From the beginning, the purpose of the Texas Constitution was not simply to create a set of institutions that could wield political power. It was to limit the way political power is used and to prevent it from being abused.

The Texas Bill of Rights embodies certain ideas captured in the U.S. Bill of Rights. All "free men" are declared to have free and equal rights that cannot be denied or abridged because of sex, race, color, creed, or national origin. Freedom of religious worship is guaranteed, and there will be no religious test for office. Liberty of speech and press are guaranteed. Individuals are protected from unreasonable search and seizure, from excessive bail, from bills of attainder or ex post facto laws, and from double jeopardy. Article I also guarantees an individual a right to trial by jury and the right to bear arms "in the lawful defense of himself or the State; but the Legislature shall have the power, by law, to regulate the wearing of arms, with a view to prevent crime" (Article I, Section 23).

Article I also contains some ideas that move beyond those guaranteed by the first 10 amendments to the U.S. Constitution. The right to **republican government**,

**limited government** a principle of constitutional government; a government whose powers are defined and limited by a constitution

**republican government** a representative democracy, a system of government in which power is derived from the people

something clearly stated in the main body of the U.S. Constitution but not in the U.S. Bill of Rights, is powerfully articulated in the first two sections of Article I. According to Article I of the Texas Constitution, all political power is inherent in the people, and the people of Texas have at all times the "inalienable right to alter, reform or abolish their government in such manner as they may think expedient" (Article I, Section 2).

The differences between the Texas Bill of Rights and the U.S. Bill of Rights are not simply matters of where best to articulate a philosophy of republican government. They also involve very concrete matters of public policy. Section 26, for example, forbids monopolies that are contrary to the public interest, and states that the law of primogeniture and entail (a law designed to keep large landed properties together by restricting inheritance to the firstborn) will never be in effect in the state. Although monopolies remain a public concern today, primogeniture and entail do not. Section 11 grapples with the complicated issue of bail and under what specific circumstances an individual can be denied bail. Significantly, Section 11 has been the subject of three major constitutional revisions: in 1955, 1977, and 1993. Section 30, adopted in 1989, provides a long list of the "rights of crime victims," including the right to be treated fairly and with dignity, the right to be protected from the accused, and the right to restitution. Although these are important matters of public policy for Texas today, they could hardly be considered proper material for the U.S. Constitution.

## Article II: The Powers of Government

Like the U.S. Constitution, Article II divides the power of government in Texas into three distinct branches: the legislative, the executive, and the judicial (see Figure 20.1). It also stipulates that no one in any one branch shall be attached to either of the other branches, except where explicitly permitted (as in the case of the lieutenant governor's role in the Senate). The article—one short paragraph of text—assures that a version of the **separation of powers** doctrine found in the U.S. Constitution will be embodied in Texas institutions.

**separation of powers** the division of governmental power among several institutions that must cooperate in decision making

## Article III: Legislative Department

Article II is one of the shortest articles in the Texas Constitution. Article III is the longest, comprising almost one-third of the text. Like Article I of the U.S. Constitution, Article III of the Texas Constitution vests legislative power in two houses: a Senate of 31 members and a House of Representatives of no more than 150 members. It stipulates the terms of office and qualifications. House members serve two-year terms, whereas senators serve four-year terms, half being elected every two years. House members must be citizens of the United States, must be at least 21 years of age, and must have resided in the state for two years and in their district for one year. Senators must be citizens of the United States, must be at least 26 years old, and must have resided in the state for five years and in their districts for one year. In addition, Article III provides for the selection of officers in both houses of the legislature, states when and for how long the legislature shall meet (Section 5), and explains how the legislative proceedings will be conducted (Sections 29–41) and how representative districts will be apportioned (Sections 25, 26, and 28).

Like Article I, Texas's Bill of Rights, Article III moves well beyond the U.S. Constitution, putting limits on what the legislature can do. For example, it puts limits on legislators' salaries and makes it difficult to increase those salaries. Article III

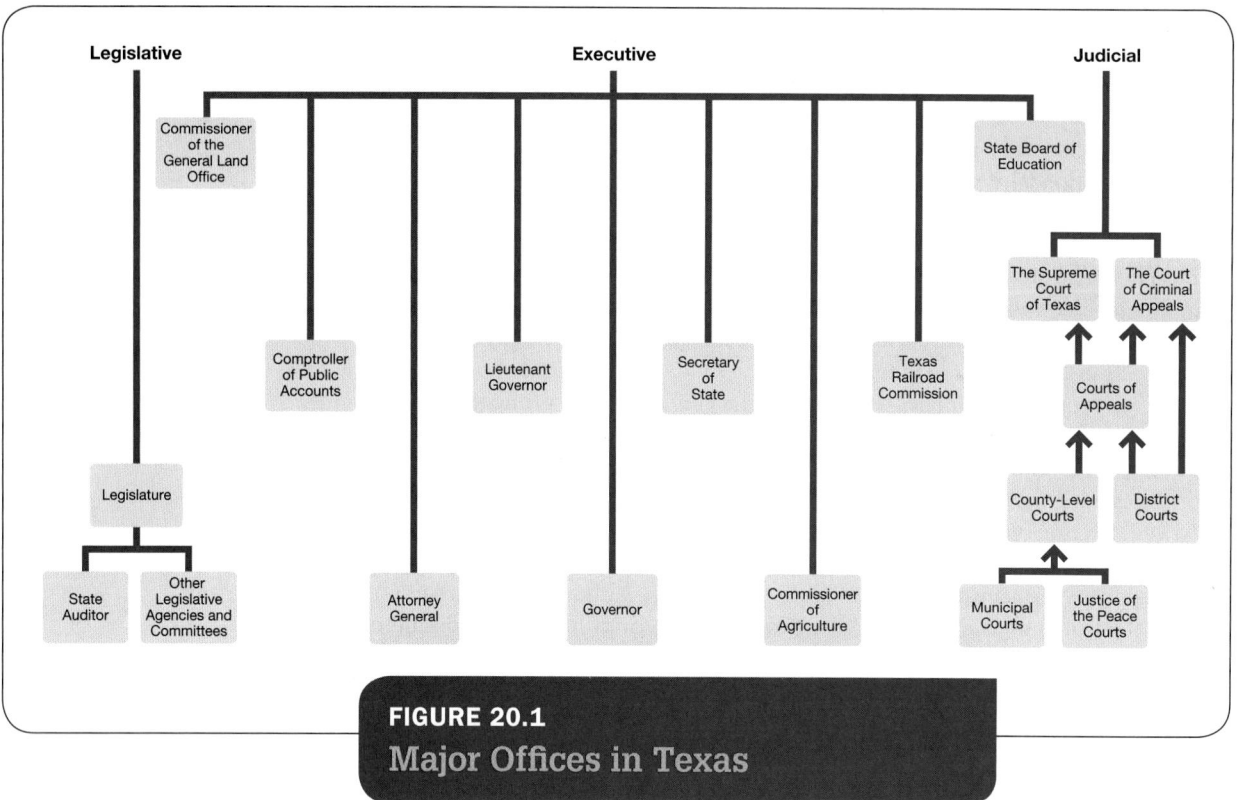

**FIGURE 20.1**

**Major Offices in Texas**

also creates a bipartisan Texas Ethics Commission whose job, among other things, is to recommend salary increases for members of the legislature and to set per diem rates for legislators and the lieutenant governor. Article III, Section 49(a), also subjects the legislature to the actions of the comptroller of public accounts, whose duty is to prepare a report prior to the legislative session on the financial condition of the state treasury and to provide estimates of future expenditures by the state. This provision of the Texas Constitution effectively limits the state legislature to the financial calculations and endorsements of the comptroller, a check on the legislature all but unimaginable to the writers of the U.S. Constitution.

Putting constraints on certain legislative actions is only part of the story. The largest portion of Article III (Sections 47–64) is dedicated to addressing a variety of policy problems, including lotteries, emergency service districts, the problem of debt creation, problems surrounding the Veterans' Land Board and the Texas Water Development Board, Texas park development, the creation of a state medical education board, and even the establishment of an economic development fund in support of the now defunct superconducting supercollider.

## Article IV: Executive Department

Article II of the U.S. Constitution concentrates executive power in the presidency. The desire was to create a more effective and more responsible executive than had been possible under the Articles of Confederation. In contrast, Article IV of the Texas Constitution states that the executive shall consist of six distinct offices: the governor, who serves as the chief executive; the lieutenant governor, who serves as the president of the Senate; the secretary of state, who keeps the official seals of the state; the comptroller of public accounts; the commissioner of the General Land Office; and the attorney general, who acts as the state's chief legal officer. With the exception of the secretary of state, who is appointed by the governor and approved by the Senate, offices are elected by qualified voters every four years. Besides creating a **plural executive**, Article IV guarantees its members will have independent political bases in the electorate. This provides an additional check against any concentration of powers in the hands of any one person. Interestingly, other elective executive offices, such as the Commissioner of Agriculture, Texas Railroad Commission, and the State Board of Education, do not derive their authority from Article IV but from other articles or statutory provisions.

**plural executive** an executive branch in which power is fragmented because the election of statewide officeholders is independent of the election of the governor

## Article V: Judicial Department

Article III of the U.S. Constitution succinctly provides for a Supreme Court and empowers Congress to create any necessary lower courts. Nothing could be further from the detailed discussion of the state courts found in Article V of the Texas Constitution. Besides creating one supreme court to hear civil cases and one court of criminal appeals to hear criminal cases, Article V provides for such lesser courts as courts of appeal, district courts, commissioner's courts, and justice of the peace courts, and empowers the legislature to establish other courts as deemed necessary. It also goes into such details as the retirement and compensation of judges, the jurisdictions of the various courts, and the duties of judges; it states what to do in the case of court vacancies, and includes a series of discussions on particular issues involving the lower courts.

An even greater difference between the federal Constitution and the Texas Constitution is the crucial role the latter gives to elections. Federal judges are appointed by the executive and approved by the Senate. In Texas, the people elect state judges. Nine supreme court and nine court of criminal appeals judges are elected at large in the state. Lower court positions are elected by voters in their relevant geographic locations. Much like the U.S. Constitution, the Texas Constitution seeks to create an independent judiciary that can check and balance the other two branches of government. But it seeks an additional check as well. It wants the people to watch over the courts.

## Article VI: Suffrage

Article VI contains a short but detailed discussion about who may vote in Texas. It also empowers the legislature to enact laws regulating voter registration and the selection of electors for president and vice president.

## Article VII: Education

The concerns found in the Texas Declaration of Independence over the need for public schools to promote a republican form of government are directly addressed in Article VII. Section 1 makes it a duty of the state legislature to support and maintain "an efficient system of public free schools." The Texas Supreme Court's interpretation of this provision as applying to school funding in the state has led to the current political battles over school finance. Sections 2–8 provide for their funding and the creation of a State Board of Education to oversee the operations of elementary and secondary education in the state. State universities are the subject of over half of Article VII, where detailed discussions of the funding and operations of particular state institutions are put directly into the text.

## Article VIII: Taxation and Revenue

The complex issue of taxation is the subject of Article VIII. Once again we find a highly detailed account of several important policy issues built directly into the text of the constitution. One of the most controversial sections of the Texas Constitution centers on the issue of the income tax. Section 1 enables the legislature to tax the income of individuals and businesses. This power, however, is subject to Section 24, which was passed by the 73rd legislature in 1993. Section 24 requires that the registered voters in the state approve a personal income tax and that the proceeds from this tax be dedicated to education and tax relief. As with other portions of the constitution, the net effect of these provisions is to curtail severely what the state legislature can do and how it is to do it. If Section 24 of Article VIII is any indication, the public fear of unresponsive and potentially tyrannical government was as alive during the 1990s as it was in 1876.

## Articles IX and XI: Local Government

These articles provide highly detailed discussions of the creation, organization, and operation of counties and municipal corporations.

## Articles X, XII, XIII, and XIV

These heavily revised articles deal with a series of specific topics: the railroads (X), private corporations (XII), Spanish and Mexican land titles (XIII), and public lands (XIV). Article X empowers the state to regulate railroads and to establish the Railroad Commission. Article XII empowers the state to create general laws creating private corporations and protecting the public and individual stockholders. Article XIII, now entirely deleted from the constitution, dealt with the nineteenth-century issue of Spanish and Mexican land titles. Article XIV created a General Land Office to deal with the registration of land titles.

## Article XV: Impeachment

**impeachment** Under the Texas Constitution, the formal charge by the House of Representatives that leads to trial in the Senate and possible removal of a state official

**Impeachment** is, in the U.S. Constitution, one of the major checks Congress holds against both the executive and judicial branches of government. The House of Representatives holds the power to impeach an individual; the Senate is responsible for conducting trials. A two-thirds vote in the Senate following impeachment by the House leads to the removal of an individual from office.

A similar process is provided for in Article XV of the Texas Constitution. The House has the power to impeach. The Senate has the power to try the governor, lieutenant governor, attorney general, land-office commissioner, and comptroller, as well as judges of the supreme court, the courts of appeal, and district courts. Conviction requires a two-thirds vote of the senators present. In contrast to the U.S. Constitution, the Texas Constitution rules that all officers against whom articles of impeachment are proffered are suspended from their office. The governor is empowered to appoint a person to fill the vacancy until the decision on impeachment is reached.

Despite these similarities to the impeachment procedures in the U.S. Constitution, the Texas Constitution has its own caveats. Most notably, the Texas Constitution does not explicitly define impeachable offenses in terms of "Treason, Bribery, or other high Crimes and Misdemeanors," as the U.S. Constitution does. The House and Senate (and the courts) decide what constitutes an impeachable offense.[16] In addition, the supreme court has original jurisdiction to hear and determine whether district court judges are competent to discharge their judicial duties. The governor may also remove judges of the supreme court, courts of appeal, and district courts when requested by the two-thirds vote of each legislature. Significantly, the reasons for removing a judge in this case need not rise to the level of an impeachable offense, but need only involve a "willful neglect of duty, incompetence, habitual drunkenness, oppression in office, or other reasonable cause" (Article XV, Section 8). The barriers to removing a judge by political means are thus, at least on paper, much lower in Texas than in national government.

In 1980, Section 9 was added to Article XV, providing a new way to remove officials appointed by the governor. With the advice and consent of two-thirds of the members of the senate present, a governor may remove an appointed public official. If the legislature is not in session, the governor is empowered to call a special two-day session to consider the proposed removal.

## Article XVI: General Provisions

Article XVI is one of the lengthiest in the Texas Constitution and has no parallel in the U.S. Constitution. It is literally a catchall article tackling a variety of issues ranging from official oaths of office to community property to banking corporations and stock laws to the election of the Texas Railroad Commission to the state retirement systems. Here, perhaps more than anywhere else, we see the complexity and confusion of the philosophy reflected in Texas's Constitution.

## Article XVII: Amending the Constitution

Like the U.S. Constitution, the Texas Constitution explicitly delineates how it can be amended. Essentially, amendments undergo a four-stage process: First, the legislature must meet in either regular or special session and propose amendments. Second, these amendments must be approved by a two-thirds vote of all the members elected to each house. Third, a brief statement explaining the amendments must be published twice in each recognized newspaper in the state that meets the publication requirements for official state notices. Finally, the amendments must be approved by a majority of the state voters.

# ● Recent Attempts to Rewrite the Texas Constitution

> **Describe modern efforts to change the Texas Constitution**

Given the difficulty of amending the state constitution, a surprising number of amendments have been proposed since 1876. A considerable number of these have been turned down in the popular vote. As Table 20.2 shows, demands for amending the Constitution have intensified in recent years, as legislators have dealt with the problem of making changes in public policy while being constrained by an unwieldy constitutional document.

## Sharpstown and the Failed Constitutional Reforms of 1974

A drive to rewrite the Texas Constitution grew out of a major stock fraud that broke in the early 1970s, involving the Sharpstown State Bank and the National

## TABLE 20.2

## Amending the Texas Constitution

The Constitution of Texas has been amended 474 times since its inception in 1876.

| YEARS | NUMBER PROPOSED | NUMBER ADOPTED |
|---|---|---|
| 1876–1900 | 31 | 17 |
| 1901–20 | 56 | 21 |
| 1921–40 | 71 | 47 |
| 1941–60 | 78 | 59 |
| 1961–80 | 151 | 98 |
| 1981–2000 | 180 | 148 |
| 2001–10 | 79 | 77 |
| 2011 | 10 | 7 |
| Totals | 656 | 474 |

SOURCE: Texas Legislative Council and Texas Secretary of State.

Bankers Life Insurance Corporation. Following the 1970 elections, which had been dominated, as generally was the case, by the conservative wing of the Democratic Party, a suit was filed in Dallas federal court. Attorneys for the Securities and Exchange Commission alleged that a number of influential Democrats, including Governor Preston Smith, the state Democratic chairman and state banking board member Elmer Baum, Speaker of the House Gus Mutscher, and others, had been bribed. By the fall of 1971, Mutscher and two of his associates had been indicted. On March 15, 1972, they were convicted and sentenced to five years' probation.

The convictions fueled a firestorm in the state to "throw the rascals out." During the 1972 elections, "reform" candidates dominated the Democratic primary and the general election. The conservative rancher-banker Dolph Briscoe became governor, but only by a plurality, making him the first governor in the history of the state not to receive a majority of the popular vote. Other reform-minded candidates such as William P. Hobby Jr. and John Hill were successful. Hobby won the lieutenant governor's race, while Hill became attorney general, defeating the three-term Democratic incumbent Crawford C. Martin. When the smoke cleared, half of the House seats were occupied by new members, and the Senate had witnessed a higher-than-normal rate of turnover. The elections had one other outcome: an amendment was passed empowering the legislature to sit as a constitutional convention whose task would be to rewrite the Constitution.[17]

The constitutional convention met on January 8, 1974, in Austin. The idea was for the convention to draft a new constitution that would then be presented to state voters for ratification. Originally scheduled to last 90 days, the convention was extended to 150 days. Even so, it did not have enough time. Bitter politics, coupled with the intense demands of highly mobilized special interests, made it impossible to reach the necessary agreement. In the end, proponents of a new constitution failed to achieve a two-thirds majority by three votes (118 to 62, with 1 abstention).

# Why Is the Texas Constitution So Long?

## State Constitution Length (estimated)

- ● < 19,999 words
- ● 20,000–39,999 words
- ● 40,000–59,999 words
- ● 60,000–79,999 words
- ● > 79,999 words

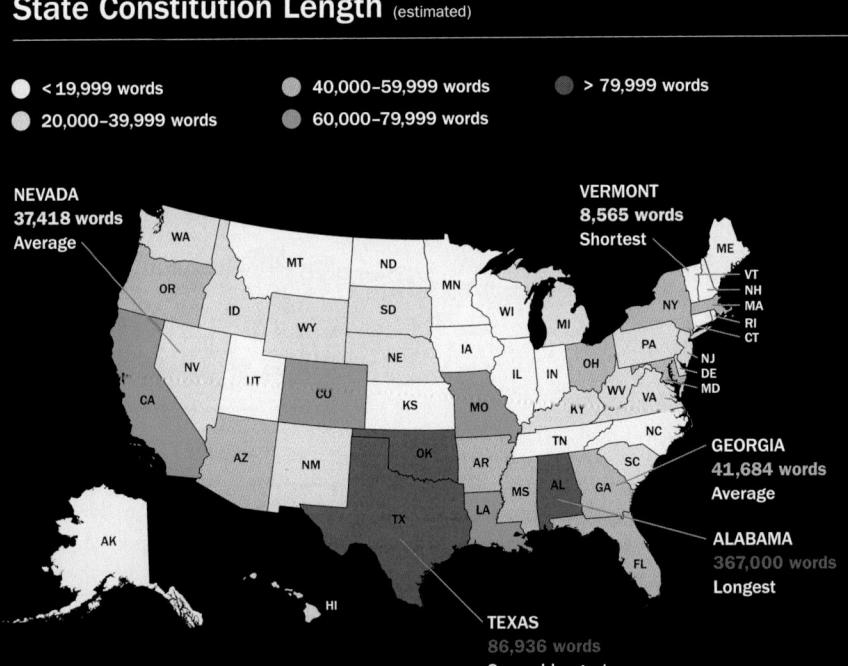

**NEVADA**
37,418 words
Average

**VERMONT**
8,565 words
Shortest

**GEORGIA**
41,684 words
Average

**ALABAMA**
367,000 words
Longest

**TEXAS**
86,936 words
Second longest

The Texas Constitution is the second longest state constitution in the United States. The framers of the Texas Constitution gave the state government very specific powers so that the government could not use ambiguity to expand its powers. As a result, the Texas Constitution requires frequent amendments to address situations not covered specifically in the original constitution. The Texas Constitution has been amended 467 times as of 2010, fourth most of any state.

## Amendments Added to Constitution

- ● < 75 amendments
- ● 75–149 amendments
- ● 150–224 amendments
- ● 225–300 amendments
- ● > 300 amendments

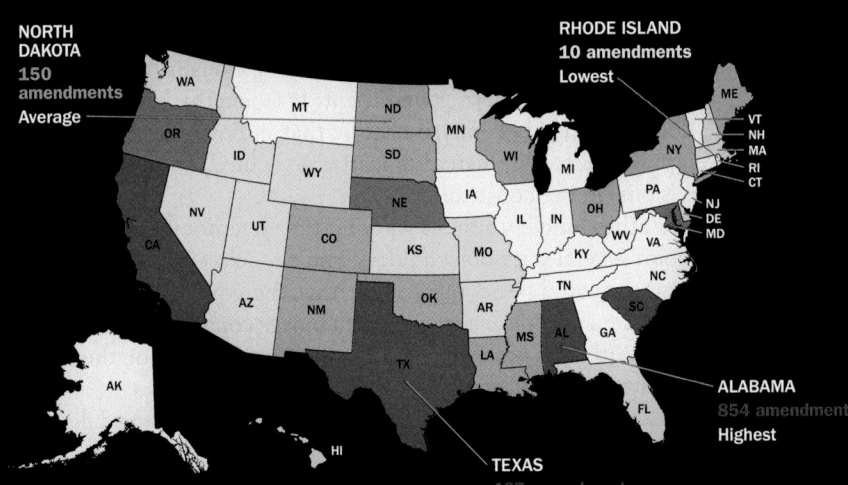

**NORTH DAKOTA**
150 amendments
Average

**RHODE ISLAND**
10 amendments
Lowest

**ALABAMA**
854 amendments
Highest

**TEXAS**
467 amendments
Fourth highest

### for critical analysis

1. How would such a long and detailed state constitution achieve the framers' goal of limiting the scope and power of government in Texas?

2. The U.S. Constitution is a much shorter document than the Texas Constitution and has only 27 amendments. Why would a shorter constitution lead to fewer amendments?

—By BOB TAYLOR, Times Herald Staff Cartoonist

"This baby has a wart...off with his head!"

*The Sharpstown State Bank scandal led to a demand for a new constitution to replace the outmoded 1876 document. This cartoon, which shows Governor Dolph Briscoe regally proclaiming, "This baby has a wart . . . off with his head!" satirizes Briscoe's stance against the new constitution.*

## for critical analysis

What was the rationale for attempting to rewrite the constitution in 1974 and 1999? What changes were proposed? Why did these attempts fail?

The movement to rewrite the constitution did not die at the convention. During the next session of the legislature, eight constitutional amendments were passed that effectively would have rewritten the constitution through the normal amendment process. Each proposal, however, was turned down by the electorate in a special election on November 4, 1975. The Constitution of 1876 remained alive, if not well.

## The 1999 Ratliff-Junell Proposal

For the first time since the unsuccessful effort to revise the constitution in the mid-1970s, state senator Bill Ratliff and state representative Rob Junell, both powerhouses in the state legislature, proposed a new constitution for Texas in 1999. Ratliff argued, "It's time for Texas to have a constitution that's appropriate for the twenty-first century." They were concerned that the 1876 Constitution was too restrictive and cumbersome for modern government. It is lengthy, cluttered, and disorganized. The document had become so chaotic that in both 1999 and 2001, amendments were approved "to eliminate duplicative, executed, obsolete, archaic, and ineffective provisions" in the constitution.

Among the major Ratliff-Junell proposals was that the governor would be given the authority to appoint several state officeholders who are now elected. Additionally, the executive branch would be reorganized so that the governor would have an appointed cabinet of department heads, subject to senate confirmation, much as the U.S. president does. With that proposal, only the lieutenant governor, the attorney general, and the state comptroller would be elected.

The governor would also be given the power to appoint all appellate and district judges. Afterward, the judges would be subject to voter approval in retention elections—where they have no opponent on the ballot but where voters are asked if they wish to retain the appointed judge in office for a specified time period. Ratliff argued that the changes would make the governor more accountable for how state government works.

The legislature would remain part-time and would continue to meet in regular session every other year. It would also convene in a special 15-day "veto session," in order to consider overriding any gubernatorial vetoes from previous sessions. State senators now serve four-year terms and state representatives two-year terms. Under the proposed constitution, these terms would be increased to six years for state senators and four years for state representatives. For the first time, there would also be term limits so that representatives' service would be limited to eight regular sessions in the House or 16 years in office, and senators' service could not exceed nine regular sessions in the Senate or 18 years in office.

Although county government would remain as it is today, local voters would be given the authority to abolish their own county's obsolete offices without state-wide approval through constitutional amendments.

Even as it was proposed, its sponsors realized that the revamped constitution would be tough to pass. And they were right—it did not pass, but suffered the fate of earlier efforts to change the 1876 Constitution.

## Recent Amendments

In the 2011 constitutional amendment elections, voters were asked to consider 10 proposed amendments. Seven of the amendments passed, although only approximately 5.2 percent of registered voters bothered to vote. One thing that is clear about elections that deal with constitutional amendments is that voting participation is invariably low. Table 20.3 compares the percentage turnout of registered voters in November special elections on constitutional amendments with the percentage turnout in presidential elections (which tend to produce the highest turnout). There are two likely reasons for the low voter turnout in constitutional amendment elections: (1) Constitutional amendment elections are held in "off" years when there are no elections with candidates on the ballot. Because of this, the political parties take a less active role in getting out the vote, and there are no candidates to generate voter turnout. As a result, advertising campaigns to get out the vote are frequently limited only to the activities of interest groups that support or oppose the issues on the ballot. (2) Many of the amendments are relatively insignificant to most voters.

Most of the 2011 proposed constitutional amendments listed in Table 20.4 were uncontroversial. The controversial ones were those that the Tea Party and other antitax groups saw as increasing the financial burden upon Texans. For example, Proposition 4 was defeated because it would have expanded the ability of counties to issue bonds to finance the development of unproductive areas where those bonds were to be repaid with property tax revenues. Critics of the proposal argued that it would clear the way for new toll roads. Proposition 7 was defeated because it would have given El Paso new borrowing authority. Proposition 8 passed the legislature with bipartisan support. It would have given property owners the opportunity to opt out of agricultural or wildlife conservation property tax exemptions in favor of water conservation property tax exemptions. The Tea Party successfully opposed the proposition on the grounds that it would shift the tax burden to others.[18]

*In 2005 social conservatives urged Texans to vote in favor of Proposition 2, which defined marriage in Texas as the union of one man and one woman. This appeal to traditional values contributed to relatively high turnout, and Proposition 2 passed by more than a 3-to-1 margin.*

## TABLE 20.3

### Voter Turnout in Texas Constitutional Amendment Elections Compared with Texas Turnout for Presidential Elections

| ELECTION | % TURNOUT OF REGISTERED VOTERS |
|---|---|
| 2011 constitutional amendment | 5.2 |
| 2009 constitutional amendment | 8.2 |
| 2008 presidential | 59.5 |
| 2007 constitutional amendment (November) | 8.4 |
| 2007 constitutional amendment (May) | 7.1 |
| 2005 constitutional amendment | 17.97 |
| 2004 presidential | 56.6 |
| 2003 constitutional amendment | 12.2 |
| 2001 constitutional amendment | 6.9 |
| 2000 presidential | 51.8 |
| 1999 constitutional amendment | 8.38 |
| 1997 constitutional amendment (August) | 6.94 |
| 1997 constitutional amendment (November) | 10.6 |
| 1996 presidential | 52.24 |
| 1995 constitutional amendment | 7.86 |
| 1993 constitutional amendment | 12.59 |
| 1992 presidential | 72.92 |
| 1991 constitutional amendment | 26.25 |

SOURCE: Texas Secretary of State.

While the Tea Party and other antitax groups could not defeat all of the propositions they opposed, low voter turnout enabled them to exert a significant influence. Indeed, their defeat of three proposals broke the modern pattern in which amendments are routinely approved. For example, between 2001 and 2010, 77 of 79 proposed amendments were approved.

Highly visible, controversial propositions can lead to higher turnout. For example, in 2003, voter participation rose to 12.2 percent, well over twice the turnout in 2011. That was because in 2003, Proposition 12 authorized the legislature to limit noneconomic damages assessed against a provider of medical or health care. After January 1, 2005, the legislature could place limits on awards in other types of cases as well. A major change in the state's tort law, Proposition 12 prompted a voter turnout in the 2003 constitutional amendment election that was the highest for such an election since 1993.[19]

Approved with only about 51 percent support of the voters, Proposition 12 inspired the costliest battle ever waged in Texas over a proposed state constitutional amendment. Donations to support the amendment came largely from doc-

## TABLE 20.4

## Passed Constitutional Amendments, November 8, 2011

Proposition 1 (S.J.R. 14).The constitutional amendment authorizing the legislature to provide for an exemption from ad valorem taxation of all or part of the market value of the residence homestead of the surviving spouse of a 100 percent or totally disabled veteran.

Proposition 2 (S.J.R. 4). The constitutional amendment providing for the issuance of additional general obligation bonds by the Texas Water Development Board in an amount not to exceed $6 billion at any time outstanding.

Proposition 3 (S.J.R. 50). The constitutional amendment providing for the issuance of general obligation bonds of the State of Texas to finance educational loans to students.

Proposition 5 (S.J.R. 26). The constitutional amendment authorizing the legislature to allow cities or counties to enter into interlocal contracts with other cities or counties without the imposition of a tax or the provision of a sinking fund.

Proposition 6 (H.J.R. 109). The constitutional amendment clarifying references to the permanent school fund, allowing the General Land Office to distribute revenue from permanent school fund land or other properties to the available school fund to provide additional funding for public education and providing for an increase in the market value of the permanent school fund for the purpose of allowing increased distributions from the available school fund.

Proposition 9 (S.J.R. 9). The constitutional amendment authorizing the governor to grant a pardon to a person who successfully completes a term of deferred adjudication community supervision.

Proposition 10 (S.J.R. 37). The constitutional amendment to change the length of the unexpired term that causes the automatic resignation of certain elected county or district officeholders if they become candidates for another office.

SOURCE: Texas Legislative Council.

tors, hospitals, medical groups, insurance companies, and businesses. Amendment supporters spent $7.8 million in the campaign to get the amendment approved. Opponents of the amendment spent $9.3 million, with most of the money coming from lawyers and law firms.[20] Much of the campaign focused on the caps of noneconomic damages for medical malpractice awards. Supporters argued that huge medical malpractice awards were driving doctors from medical practice and reducing the availability of medical care for Texans. Opponents, on the other hand, claimed that the proposal reduced access to the courts for Texans and provided no control over the underlying problem of medical malpractice. And although the immediate consequence of the battle was a reduction in the amount of noneconomic damages that could be awarded in medical malpractice cases, the language of the amendment allows for reduction of damage awards in other types of cases in the future. It was a close vote, but a victory for the new Republican-controlled Texas government, which was sympathetic to tort reform efforts. At the same time, it was a defeat for Democrats who had been unsympathetic toward tort reform, and it was a real blow for trial lawyers—once a mighty interest group in Texas politics but now left with only a fraction of their former political influence.[21]

Most of the 2005 proposed constitutional amendments were, like the previously discussed propositions, of significance only to a narrow group of people.

*Amendments to the state constitution affect many areas of Texans' lives. The amendments passed in 2011 included one intended to help address drought in Texas by making additional funds available to local governments for water projects.*

For example, one of the nine proposed amendments provided for clearing land titles in Upshur and Smith Counties. Another authorized the legislature to provide for a six-year term for a board member of a regional mobility authority. Yet the turnout in this election was much higher than is typically seen in constitutional amendment elections. The reason was Proposition 2, which defined marriage in Texas as the union of one man and one woman. The proposition also prohibited the state or any political subdivision of the state from creating or recognizing any legal status identical to or similar to marriage. The proposition generated a strongly favorable vote—1,723,782 in favor versus 536,913 against. Unlike Proposition 12 in 2003, this was not an economic battle involving interests concerned with tort law; rather, this was an issue pitting social conservatives against those more sympathetic to gay rights. The strength of the social conservative vote in the state was, of course, remarkable, since the amendment carried by more than a 3-to-1 margin. Many churches and religious organizations strongly supported the proposed amendment. Their activities probably generated the relatively high voter turnout. The proposition was unusual in that people felt it was important to their lives because it affected their value systems. Although it is doubtful the amendment was necessary to support the traditional concept of marriage and although the ambiguity of the provision rejecting any legal status similar to marriage is disturbing, a significant part of the voting population apparently believed that it was important to vote their moral values, even if the proposal was largely symbolic.

Although most constitutional amendments are not of great importance, there are some notable exceptions. Table 20.5 identifies some of those amendments that, like Proposition 12 in 2003 or Proposition 2 in 2005, have had great significance in the public policy of the state.

## ● Thinking Critically about the Texas Constitution

In this chapter, we explored the history of constitutional government in Texas. We analyzed the seven constitutions under which Texas has been governed and explained the similarities and differences between the U.S. Constitution and Texas's current constitution (the Constitution of 1876). We also discussed attempts over the past 30 years to replace this constitution with a new one. The ideas of liberty and equality are enshrined in the Texas Constitution as they are in the U.S. Constitution. In some ways, the Texas Constitution does a better job of protecting liberty and providing for equality than does the U.S. Constitution. Where the Texas Constitution most fundamentally differs from the U.S. Constitution is in its view of

## TABLE 20.5

## Some Important Constitutional Amendments

In 1894, Texans strongly supported an amendment providing for the election of railroad commissioners. In later years, when Texas became a major oil producer, the railroad commission gained the authority to regulate oil production and became the most powerful elected regulatory agency in the country.

In 1902, Texans by a huge majority backed an amendment "requiring all persons subject to a poll tax to have paid a poll tax and to hold a receipt for same before they offer to vote at any election in this state, and fixing the time of payment of said tax." The poll tax required a payment of money prior to voting. The effect was to reduce the size of the electorate, limiting the opportunity of those with lower incomes to vote.

In 1919, the same year the national prohibition amendment was ratified, Texas ratified a state prohibition amendment.

In 1935, Texans repealed statewide prohibition. In its place was a local option whereby local communities chose whether alcohol would be sold in those communities. This was two years after repeal of national prohibition.

In 1954, Texans passed an amendment requiring women to serve on juries. Previous to that, women were exempt on the grounds that they were needed at home as the center of home life.

In 1966, Texans repealed the poll tax as a voting requirement in the face of pressures from the U.S. Supreme Court and from a national constitutional amendment that eliminated the poll tax in national elections.

In 1972, Texans overwhelmingly passed a constitutional amendment "to provide that equality under the law shall not be denied or abridged because of sex, race, color, creed or national origin." This amendment was primarily seen as an equal rights amendment banning sex discrimination, since federal civil rights statutes largely dealt with discrimination on other grounds. It was the state version of a proposed sexual equal rights amendment that was never ratified and made part of the U.S. Constitution.

In 2003, a constitutional amendment promoting the tort reform agenda passed that placed limitations on lawsuits. In "civil lawsuits against doctors and health care providers, and other actions," the legislature was authorized "to determine limitations on non-economic damages."

In 2005 a constitutional amendment was passed "providing that marriage in this state consists only of the union of one man and one woman and prohibiting this state or a political subdivision of this state from creating or recognizing any legal status identical or similar to marriage." The amendment was passed in response to the movement toward the recognition of civil unions and same-sex marriage in some states.

In 2009, Texans supported an amendment establishing "the national research university fund to enable emerging research universities in this state to achieve national prominence as major research universities." The amendment was a recognition that the Texas economy would benefit by the development of nationally recognized research universities in the state.

In 2009, in reaction to a U.S. Supreme Court decision involving eminent domain—the taking of private property for public use—that was seen as unsympathetic to property rights, Texans passed an amendment "to prohibit the taking, damaging, or destroying of private property for public use unless the action is for the ownership, use, and enjoyment of the property by the State, a political subdivision of the State, the public at large, or entities granted the power of eminent domain under law or for the elimination of urban blight on a particular parcel of property, but not for certain economic development or enhancements of tax revenue purpose."

democracy. Although championing democratic forms of government, the writers of the Texas Constitution were even more suspicious of centralized institutions of power than were the Founders of the United States. The Texas Constitution places serious constraints on the Texas legislature's ability to act as an independent body. It creates a weak plural executive, in which executive power is limited and decentralized. Finally, the Texas Constitution subjects the courts to periodic elections. In Texas, the institutions of democracy were never meant to be too far removed from the guiding hand of the people.

A number of additional themes were emphasized in this chapter. First, Texas's current constitution is far more complex than its predecessors or the U.S. Constitution. Matters that are considered public policy in most other states often must be addressed as constitutional issues in Texas. Second, the Texas Constitution is based on a general distrust of politicians and political power. It was originally written to prevent the expansion of political power that had taken place during Reconstruction and to make sure that political power could not be centralized in a way that might hurt the liberties and civil rights of the people. By limiting and decentralizing power, the Texas Constitution makes it hard to implement and successfully administer public policies. Third, the Texas Constitution has been a difficult document to replace. Although amended 474 times, it has not been replaced by a new constitution to date and will probably not be replaced in the future. One reason for this is that mobilizing support for a wholesale reworking of the constitution has proven to be difficult. Another is that the general distrust of government and political power that gave birth to the Constitution of 1876 continues to hold sway among the citizenry.

Many people see some desirable features in the Texas Constitution. Like many state constitutions, the Texas Constitution has a Bill of Rights. Nor are all the rights in the Texas Bill of Rights merely a duplication of those in the U.S. Constitution. To some extent, the Texas Bill of Rights provides more constitutional protections than does the U.S. Constitution. State constitutions may do this under the doctrine of independent state grounds. That is, although a state constitution may provide more rights than the U.S. Constitution, it may not take away rights granted by the U.S. Constitution. One may think of the U.S. Constitution as a baseline to which states can add but not subtract protections. One of the most interesting Texas rights is an amendment adopted in 1972. It states, "Equality under the law shall not be denied or abridged because of sex, race, color, creed, or national origin. This amendment is self-operative." Although the amendment is not the subject of much litigation, note that it provides explicit protection from sex discrimination, something that is not mentioned in the U.S. Constitution. It is, in fact, a state version of the federal Equal Rights Amendment, which was almost ratified in the 1970s but which never quite received sufficient support from the states to become a part of the U.S. Constitution.

Still, in spite of its positive aspects, the Texas Constitution is a lengthy, confusing, and highly restrictive document. Yet efforts to drastically change the document seem doomed to failure. There is little public outcry over the large numbers of amendments on which voters regularly must cast ballots. Additionally, the Texas Constitution provides protections for the interests of key groups in Texas society, groups that are reluctant to give up those protections in exchange for a more flexible document.

**for critical analysis**

How does the supremacy clause of the U.S. Constitution affect Texas government?

# study guide

## The Role of a State Constitution

■ **Identify the main functions of state constitutions (pp. 799–800)**

The state constitution is the governing document of the state much in the same way the U.S. Constitution sets up the framework for the nation as a whole. Many of the ideas found in the U.S. Constitution are also found in Texas's constitutions, including republican government, separation of powers, checks and balances, and individual rights.

### Key Terms

**constitution** (p. 799)

**federalism** (p. 799)

**supremacy clause** (p. 799)

**necessary and proper clause** (p. 800)

### Practice Quiz

1. Which idea is contained in both the U.S. and Texas Constitutions? *(p. 799)*
   a) separation of powers
   b) Keynesianism
   c) laissez-faire economics
   d) *Rebus sic stantibus*
   e) none of the above

2. Which of the following is *not* an important function of a state constitution? *(p. 799)*
   a) prevents the concentration of political power
   b) delegates power to individuals and institutions
   c) allows government to intrude in the lives of businesses and individuals
   d) legitimizes political institutions
   e) limits application of U.S. Constitution

3. Which part of the U.S. Constitution reserves power to the states? *(p. 799)*
   a) Article I
   b) Article VI
   c) First Amendment
   d) Tenth Amendment
   e) Nineteenth Amendment

4. Under the U.S. Constitution, the government of Texas is most limited by *(p. 800)*
   a) Article IV of the U.S. Constitution.
   b) the implied powers clause and the Tenth Amendment of the U.S. Constitution.
   c) the Fourteenth Amendment of the U.S. Constitution.
   d) all matter equally
   e) none matter

 **Practice Online**
Video exercise: *Governor Mark White on the Separation of Powers*

## The First Texas Constitutions

■ **Describe the five Texas constitutions that preceded the current constitution. (pp. 800–809)**

Texas has had six constitutions reflecting the concerns of the historical periods in which they were written. The Civil War and Reconstruction played a major role in shaping Texans' attitudes toward the dangers of strong state government.

### Key Terms

**unicameral** (p. 801)

**bicameral** (p. 804)

**Confederacy** (p. 807)

**Radical Republicans** (p. 808)

### Practice Quiz

5. The Constitution of 1861 *(pp. 806–7)*
   a) generally accepted the existing constitutional framework.
   b) guided Texas's entry into the Confederate States of America.
   c) supported slavery.
   d) defended states' rights.
   e) all of the above

6. A unique feature of the Constitution of 1869 was that *(p. 808)*
   a) explicitly rejected the power of the federal government in Texas.
   b) fewer than 1 percent of voters opposed it.
   c) it was less than four pages long.
   d) it was never submitted to the voters.
   e) it is considered the best of Texas's constitutions.

# The Constitution of 1876

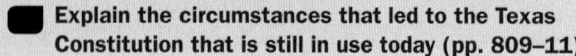

■ **Explain the circumstances that led to the Texas Constitution that is still in use today (pp. 809–11)**

The Constitution of 1876 sought to limit the powers that had been wielded under the previous constitution by Republican governor Edmund Davis. It remains, though much amended, the existing state constitution of Texas.

## Key Term

**Grange** (p. 809)

## Practice Quiz

7. The Constitution of 1876 was a reaction to the Reconstruction Constitution of 1869 because *(p. 809)*
   a) the 1869 Constitution was too short.
   b) the 1869 Constitution forbade slavery.
   c) the 1869 Constitution increased state officials' salaries.
   d) the 1869 Constitution was seen as giving the governor too much power.
   e) none of the above

8. A new Texas constitution was written *(pp. 809–11)*
   a) when Reconstruction ended.
   b) when the Compromise of 1850 was adopted.

c) at the start of World War I.
d) in 1999.
e) none of the above

9. The present Texas constitution *(pp. 809–10)*
   a) is well organized and well written.
   b) is considered to be one of the best of the 50 state constitutions.
   c) delegates a great deal of power to the governor.
   d) severely limits the power of the governor and other state officials.
   e) has 226 amendments.

10. Those who wrote the Constitution of 1876 wanted to return control of government to the people. By "the people" they meant *(pp. 809–10)*
    a) all adult citizens of Texas.
    b) all adult male citizens of Texas.
    c) all adult white male citizens of Texas.
    d) all citizens except carpetbaggers and scalawags.
    e) none of the above

 **Practice Online**
"Exploring Texas Politics" exercise: *The Texas Constitution*

# The Constitution of Texas Today

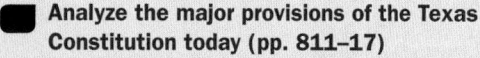

■ **Analyze the major provisions of the Texas Constitution today (pp. 811–17)**

Today's Texas constitution is lengthy and includes numerous amendments. It limits the power of state government and tries to prevent the concentration of power in the hands of one person.

## Key Terms

**limited government** (p. 812)

**republican government** (p. 812)

**separation of powers** (p. 813)

**plural executive** (p. 815)

**impeachment** (p. 816)

## Practice Quiz

11. Article I of the Texas Constitution *(p. 812)*
    a) contains the Texas Bill of Rights.
    b) renounces the use of the death penalty.
    c) rejects the U.S. Constitution's Bill of Rights.
    d) recognizes the supremacy of the national government.
    e) accepts the principle of rapprochement.

12. The Texas Bill of Rights *(pp. 812–13)*
    a) guarantees some rights not found in the U.S. Bill of Rights.
    b) duplicates the U.S. Bill of Rights.
    c) is unusual, since state constitutions generally do not have Bills of Rights.
    d) guarantees gay marriage.
    e) outlaws abortion.

13. The Texas Constitution requires that Texas judges *(p. 815)*
    a) be appointed by the governor.
    b) be a member of the Republican Party.
    c) be senior lawyers.
    d) be elected by the people.
    e) cannot receive campaign contributions.

 **Practice Online**
"Who Are Texans?" interactive exercise: *Why Is the Texas Constitution So Long?*

# Recent Attempts to Rewrite the Texas Constitution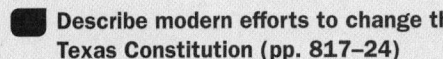

**■ Describe modern efforts to change the Texas Constitution (pp. 817–24)**

Recent attempts to rewrite the Texas constitution have been unsuccessful. Amendments continue to be the easiest way to modify the document.

## Practice Quiz

14. A new constitution for Texas *(pp. 817–24)*
    a) is unlikely to be ratified before 2015.
    b) is scheduled for a vote in 2014.
    c) has a 50–50 chance of being ratified.
    d) has a very small chance of being written and ratified.
    e) none of the above

15. Voter turnout for constitutional amendment elections could be improved if *(p. 821)*
    a) they were held at the same time as presidential elections.
    b) there were more voter awareness of the proposed amendments.
    c) the amendments involved significant issues for voters.
    d) all of the above
    e) none of the above

**ⓢ Practice Online**

Interactive simulation: *Re-writing the Texas Constitution*

# Recommended Websites

**Handbook of the State of Texas**
www.tshaonline.org/handbook/online/

**Texas Constitution**
www.constitution.legis.state.tx.us/

**Texas Constitutions 1824–76**
http://tarlton.law.utexas.edu/constitutions/

In 2012, Ted Cruz won the U.S. Senate race in Texas after defeating Lieutenant Governor David Dewhurst in the Republican primary. During the primary race, Cruz argued that Dewhurst was not a true conservative.

# Parties and Elections in Texas

**WHAT GOVERNMENT DOES AND WHY IT MATTERS** On the surface, the 2012 general election appeared to confirm the place of the Republican Party as the dominant political party in Texas. Republican presidential candidate Mitt Romney may have lost the popular vote and the electoral college vote nationally by sizeable margins, but in Texas, Romney secured over 57 percent of the vote. Other Republican candidates were equally successful in Texas. Republicans won the race for the U.S. Senate as well as all statewide races for the Texas Railroad Commission, the Texas Supreme Court, and the Texas Court of Criminal Appeals by significant margins. Republicans won 10 of the 15 spots on the State Board of Education. Texas Republicans also won 24 of the 36 U.S. House seats allocated to Texas. Although their majority in the Texas House fell by 7 seats, the Republican Party still dominated the legislature with a 95-to-55 majority in the House and a 19-to-12 majority in the Senate.

But recent elections have also revealed divisions in the Republican Party in Texas. In 2010, U.S. Senator Kay Bailey Hutchison's unsuccessful challenge to Governor Perry in the Republican primary may have been an opening salvo in the battle between moderate and conservative Republicans for control of the state party. But after winning the governorship handily in 2010, Perry was unable to take his increasingly strident conservative message outside the state. His national campaign for the 2012 Republican presidential nomination collapsed almost before it began, undermining many Texans' beliefs that Perry was the future of the national or even the state Republican Party. Perry's image was further tarnished in 2012 when his choice to replace Hutchison in the U.S. Senate, Lieutenant Governor David Dewhurst, lost in a run-off in the Republican primary to the Tea Party candidate, Ted Cruz.

Cruz is the son of Cuban immigrants and a former solicitor general of Texas. He launched his campaign for the U.S. Senate with a conference call to conservative bloggers and tied his message to the Tea Party movement, calling for limited government, tax cuts, and strict immigration controls along the U.S.–Mexico border. Although Dewhurst was initially favored to win, Cruz weathered a vitriolic campaign and soundly defeated Dewhurst in the primary election runoff by winning 57 percent of the Republican Party vote. Cruz's defeat of Democratic candidate Jerry Sadler in the general election confirmed the political strength of his conservative message.

Cruz's victory may be a mixed blessing for the Republican Party over the long run. Moving the leadership of the Republican Party in Texas toward the principles of the insurgent Tea Party movement may isolate the party from national political and demographic trends. Nationwide, Cruz was probably the most successful Tea Party candidate to win a high profile senatorial race in 2012. Some commentators argued that identification with the Tea Party movement in the last two election cycles may have actually cost the Republican Party up to four or five seats in the U.S. Senate, the difference between being the majority and the minority party. Moreover, other commentators began to question whether Cruz and his stridently conservative message—especially his opposition to more lenient immigration policies—would help the party appeal to the growing Latino population in the state.

## chaptergoals

- **Describe how parties organize elections and the electorate in Texas** (pages 833–35)

- **Explain what it means to be a "one-party state"** (pages 835–39)

- **Analyze why it is difficult to be elected as an independent** (pages 839–44)

- **Identify the types of elections held in Texas** (pages 844–46)

- **Assess voting patterns and the reasons so few Texans vote** (pages 846–54)

- **Explain why political campaigns are so expensive in Texas** (pages 854–57)

# The Role of Political Parties in Texas Politics

**Describe how parties organize elections and the electorate in Texas**

Elections are the most important vehicles by which the people express themselves in the democratic process in Texas. Political parties help candidates win elections and assist voters in making their electoral choices. At the national level, elections are limited to the selection of the president and vice president and members of Congress. In Texas, however, voters select candidates for various offices in all three branches of government. In theory, such elections are meant to enable the people to exercise some direct control over each branch. In practice, however, one-party dominance and low levels of voter participation have often told a different story, leaving the government exposed to special interests and big money.

Perhaps the most important function of parties in Texas is that they provide a label under which candidates can run and with which voters can identify. Because Texas elects very large numbers of officeholders, it is unlikely that voters will be familiar with the views or the qualifications of every candidate. However, Texas voters overwhelmingly identify with or lean toward either the Republican Party or the Democratic Party.[1] Those voters use the party affiliation of the candidates as a way to decide for whom to vote. Thus, for many voters, without other information, the party label becomes the standard they apply in casting a ballot for a candidate. Voters often use the party label as a cue to the ideology of candidates. A voter may assume that, for example, a Republican candidate is a "conservative" and may vote for or against that candidate because of the ideology that a party affiliation implies.[2]

Parties to some extent help in raising money for candidates' campaigns and in assisting candidates with legal requirements and training for a campaign. They sometimes recruit candidates for political races, although in Texas any candidate may run in a party primary, and, if victorious in the primary, will become the party nominee. Parties also assist in "getting out the vote" for candidates through phone banks, door-to-door contacts, and other efforts.

Once a candidate is elected to office, party affiliation helps in organizing the government. Governors will usually appoint people who are members of their own party. Increasingly, the Texas legislature is divided by party. Public officials may also feel a greater sense of loyalty and cooperation toward other public officials of their party. After all, they often campaign together and make appearances at the same political events, and their fortunes often rise and fall together based on the popularity of the party. In that sense, the banding together of officeholders with the same party affiliation provides voters an opportunity to hold the party accountable for its policies or its failures.

## Party Organization

Although it is common for Texans to proclaim that they are "registered Republicans" or "registered Democrats," Texas does not have a system of party registration. Registered voters may vote in either the Democratic or Republican primary. When they do vote in a primary, their voter registration card will be stamped "Democrat" or "Republican" to prevent them from voting in the other primary as well.

In 2012 the Democratic Party of Texas officially announced their candidates for the general election at their state convention in Houston. One of the most important functions of political parties is to select candidates to run for office under the party label.

**precinct** a local voting district

**precinct chair** the local party official, elected in the party's primary election, who heads the precinct convention and serves on the party's county executive committee

**county executive committee** the party group, made up of a party's county chair and precinct chairs, that is responsible for running a county's primary elections and planning county conventions

**county chair** the county party official, who heads the county executive committee

**state executive committee** the committee responsible for governing a party's activities throughout the state

**state chair** and **vice chair** the top two state-level leaders in the party

**precinct convention** a meeting held by a political party to select delegates for the county convention and to submit resolutions to the party's state platform; precinct conventions are held on the day of the party's primary election and are open to anyone who voted in that election

One of the most important functions of political parties is to select candidates to run for office under the party label. Today that is done through primary elections. If several candidates are running for the party nomination in a primary election, it may be that none receives a majority vote. In that case, the party will hold a runoff election to determine who will be nominated. Primaries were not always used to select the party nominee. During the nineteenth century, candidates were nominated at party conventions, but early in the twentieth century the state moved to the primary as a way to select candidates.

To understand how the parties are organized, think first in terms of the permanent organization of the party and then in terms of the temporary (campaign) organization (see Figure 21.1). In each election **precinct**, a **precinct chair** will be elected in the party primary. The precinct chair will head the precinct convention and will serve on the party's **county executive committee**. In the primary, the **county chair** will also be elected. The county chair will head the county executive committee, which is composed of the chair and the precinct chairs. The main responsibility of the county executive committee is to run the county primary and plan the county conventions. There may be other district committees as well for political divisions that do not correspond to the county lines.

At the state level, there is a **state executive committee**, which includes a **state chair** and **vice chair**. These officers are selected every two years at the state party conventions. The state executive committee accepts filings by candidates for statewide office. It helps raise funds for the party, and it helps establish party policy. Both the Democratic and Republican parties also employ professional staff to run day-to-day operations and to assist with special problems that affect the party.

The temporary organization of the party includes the **precinct conventions**. The main role of the precinct conventions is to select delegates to the **county convention** and possibly to submit resolutions that may eventually become part of the party platform.

Delegates chosen by the precinct convention then go to the county conventions (or in urban areas, district conventions). These conventions will elect delegates

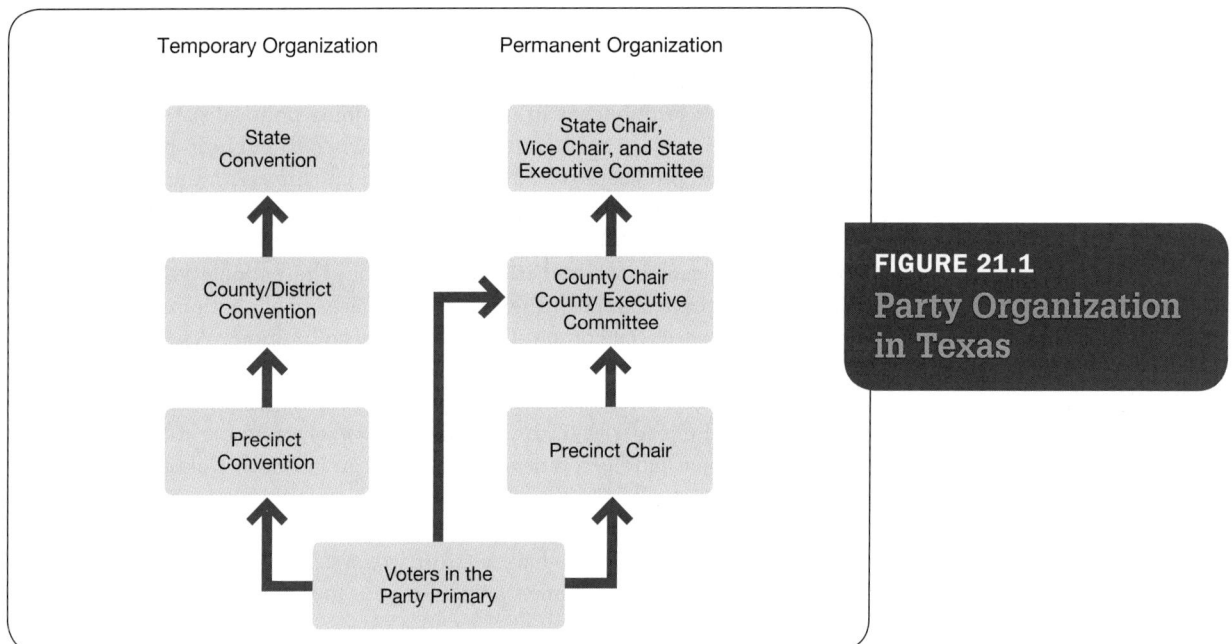

**FIGURE 21.1**
**Party Organization in Texas**

Temporary Organization

- State Convention
- County/District Convention
- Precinct Convention

Permanent Organization

- State Chair, Vice Chair, and State Executive Committee
- County Chair County Executive Committee
- Precinct Chair

Voters in the Party Primary

to the **state convention**. Both the Democratic and Republican parties hold state conventions every other year. These conventions certify the nominees of the party for statewide office; adopt a platform; and elect a chair, a vice chair, and a state executive committee. In presidential election years, the state conventions select delegates for the national party conventions; elect delegates for the national party committee; and choose presidential electors, who, if the party's choice for president carries the state in the election, will formally cast the state's electoral votes for the president in the electoral college.

Battles for control of a state party have often been fought in Texas politics, where rival ideological and other interest groups have struggled to control precinct, county, and state conventions and to elect their candidates for precinct chair, county chair, and state executive committee. In the 1950s, struggles for control of the Democratic Party between liberals and conservatives were fierce. There have also been calmer times in Texas politics, where involvement in the parties has been minimal and battles have been few. Sometimes, apathy has been so great that precinct conventions have been sparsely attended and offices such as precinct chair have gone unfilled.

**county convention** a meeting held by a political party following its precinct conventions, for the purpose of electing delegates to its state convention

**state convention** a party meeting held every two years for the purpose of nominating candidates for statewide office, adopting a platform, electing the party's leadership, and in presidential election years selecting delegates for the national convention and choosing presidential electors

## ● Texas's History as a One-Party State

> **Explain what it means to be a "one-party state"**

With the defeat of the Republican governor Edmund J. Davis in 1873, Texas entered a period of Democratic dominance that would last for over a century. Often the Republican Party would not contest major state offices, and other parties—such as the Populist or People's Party—though having some influence for brief periods, did not have staying power. In general elections, it was a foregone conclusion that the Democratic nominee would win. If there was a meaningful election contest, it was in the Democratic Party primary.

Republicans tended to have a limited role in Texas politics. Most commonly, people remained Republicans in the hope of gaining political patronage (usually local postmaster or rural mail carrier positions) when Republican presidents were in office. Some Republicans were businesspeople unhappy with the liberal policies of Democratic presidents such as Franklin D. Roosevelt or Harry Truman. However, the Republican Party was not a threat to Democratic dominance in the state. Indeed, Republicans interested in patronage from the national government may have had an incentive to keep the Republican Party small, because the fewer the Republicans, the less the competition for patronage positions. When the father of the late senator Lloyd Bentsen first moved to the Rio Grande Valley, he visited with R. B. Creager, who was then state chairman of the Republican Party. Lloyd Bentsen Sr. told Creager that he wanted to get involved in the Republican Party because his father had been a devoted Republican in South Dakota. Rather than welcoming Bentsen into the Republican Party, Creager told Bentsen, "You go back to Mission [Texas] and join the Democratic Party, because what's best for Texas is for every state in the union to have a two-party system and for Texas to be a one-party state. When you have a one-party state, your men stay in Congress longer and build up seniority."[3]

In 1952 and 1956, however, the Democratic governor Allan Shivers led a movement often known as the **Shivercrat movement**, which presaged a dramatic change in party alignments a quarter-century later. Governor Shivers was a conservative Democrat and widely regarded as one of the most able Texas governors of the twentieth century. He supported the candidacy of the Republican Dwight Eisenhower for the presidency against the Democratic nominee, Adlai Stevenson. Stevenson opposed the Texas position on the Tidelands, offshore lands claimed by both Texas and the national government, which were believed to contain oil. Additionally, Stevenson was much more liberal than Shivers, and Eisenhower was a famous and popular hero of World War II. Governor Shivers not only supported Eisenhower for the presidency, he and all statewide officeholders except the agriculture commissioner, John White, ran on the ballot as Democrats *and* Republicans. It was an act of party disloyalty condemned by loyal Democrats such as Speaker of the U.S. House of Representatives Sam Rayburn, and it led to much tension in the Democratic Party between liberal and conservative Democrats as well as between party loyalists and the Shivercrats.

The Shivercrat movement sent a strong message that many conservative Democrats were philosophically opposed to the national Democratic Party and, although they were unwilling to embrace the Republican Party fully, they found the Republican Party more compatible with their views. A pattern in voting known as **presidential Republicanism** was strengthening, whereby conservative Texas voters would vote Democratic for state offices, but vote Republican for presidential candidates. With the Shivercrat movement, those conservatives were more numerous and more closely aligned with the Republican Party.

Still, in state elections, the Democratic Party was overwhelmingly the dominant party. There might be pockets of the state where Republicans showed strength. Traditionally, in the post–Civil War era, the "German counties" in the Texas Hill Country, which were settled by German immigrants, showed Republican leanings. Dallas County, whose voters were influenced by a powerful group of conservative businesspeople and a conservative newspaper, the *Dallas News*, showed early Republican strength, electing a very conservative Republican congressman in the

**Shivercrat movement** a movement led by the Texas governor Allan Shivers during the 1950s in which conservative Democrats in Texas supported the Republican presidential ticket of Eisenhower and Nixon in 1952 and 1956; they believed that the national Democratic Party had become too liberal

**presidential Republicanism** a voting pattern in which conservatives vote Democratic for state offices, but Republican for presidential candidates

*Although the Democratic Party dominated state politics for much of the twentieth century, by the 1950s it faced internal divisions between liberal and conservative Democrats. Governor Allan Shivers (third from left) was a conservative Democrat who encouraged his supporters to vote for Republican Dwight Eisenhower in the 1952 and 1956 presidential races.*

1950s. However, for the most part, the Democratic Party was so dominant in state elections that the Republican Party did not field opponents to the Democratic nominees.

During this era, the Democratic Party was an umbrella party that held a variety of groups and interests. Liberals and conservatives belonged to the party, as did members of labor unions and businesspeople, farmers and city dwellers. Often liberals and conservatives within the party battled for control of the party and its offices. But when liberals and conservatives were not engaged in periodic intraparty battles, battles that occurred with considerable regularity, what political organization existed tended to be based on personal ties and personal popularity of individual candidates.

With the imposition of the poll tax and the white primary at the beginning of the twentieth century (discussed later in this chapter), stable factions ceased to exist in the Democratic Party. Earlier factions in Texas politics reflected "have" and "have-not" economic interests. Until about the 1940s, Texas politics was often chaotic and confused. By about the mid-1940s, however, a split between liberals and conservatives developed in the Democratic Party that focused on New Deal economic policies and civil rights measures. This liberal-conservative split became a characteristic division within the Democratic Party, and liberals and conservatives battled in the party primaries. Between the mid-1940s and the mid-1970s, the victor in these primary squabbles would then go on to win the general election. However, by the late 1970s, the winner of the Democratic primary had to face a significant conservative challenge from Republicans in the general election.[4]

## The Growth of the Republican Party

One of the most important developments in Texas politics has been the growth of the Republican Party. In the 1950s, more than 60 percent of Texans identified with the Democratic Party and fewer than 10 percent identified themselves as Republicans. The remainder considered themselves independents. In the 1960s, Republican identification in Texas rose above 10 percent; Democratic identification remained above 60 percent; and identification with independents dropped slightly. The 1970s saw a decline in Democratic affiliation and an increase in Republican affiliation. That pattern of increase of Texans who identified themselves as Republicans and decline among those who identified themselves as Democrats accelerated during the 1980s.[5] In 2008, Texans who identified themselves as Republicans saw a drop from 37 percent in 2004 to 33 percent, whereas Democratic Party affiliation remained steady at 30 percent.[6] A 2009 Gallup poll study identified Texas as being a competitive state with Republican leanings.[7] However, there is a difference between potential voters who respond to surveys and actual voters. Among actual voters, Texas is strongly Republican in statewide elections.

In the first quarter of the twentieth century, the Republican Party was only a token party. In the state legislature, for example, Republicans never held more than one seat in the Texas Senate and never more than two seats in the Texas House from 1903 to 1927. From 1927 to 1951, there were no Republicans in the Texas legislature, and then a lone Republican was elected from Dallas to serve only one term in the Texas House. It was another decade before Republicans were again elected to the legislature, when two served in the Texas House. Then in 1962, six Republicans were elected to the House from Dallas County and one from Midland County. By 1963, there were 10 Republicans in the Texas House and none in the Texas Senate.[8]

As Table 21.1 shows, as late as 1974, there were not many more than 75 Republican officeholders in the entire state of Texas. One of those officeholders was U.S. Senator John Tower, and there were 2 Texas Republicans in the U.S. House of Representatives. No Republicans were elected to state office in statewide elections. There were only 3 Republicans in the Texas Senate and only 16 Republicans in the Texas House of Representatives. By contrast, in 2012 both U.S. senators from Texas were Republican and 24 Texas members of the U.S. House of Representatives were Republican. A majority of the Texas Senate, 19 of the 31 members, and of the Texas House of Representatives, 95 of the 150 members, was Republican.

It was a record of remarkable Republican growth and Democratic decline. By 1998, every statewide elected official was Republican. (This remained true in 2012 as well.) That included the governor, lieutenant governor, attorney general, comptroller, land commissioner, agriculture commissioner, all three members of the Texas Railroad Commission, and all nine members of both the Texas Supreme Court and

**for critical analysis**

Consider how electoral decisions could be made if candidates were not identified by party membership. Would it be more or less difficult for individuals to discover the candidates' views on the issues? Would fund-raising be more or less difficult?

## TABLE 21.1

## Growth of the Republican Party in Texas

| YEAR | U.S. SENATE | OTHER STATEWIDE | U.S. HOUSE | TEXAS SENATE | TEXAS HOUSE | COUNTY OFFICE | DISTRICT OFFICE | SCHOOL BOARD | TOTAL |
|---|---|---|---|---|---|---|---|---|---|
| 1974 | 1 | 0 | 2 | 3 | 16 | 53 | NA | NA | 75+ |
| 1980 | 1 | 1 | 5 | 7 | 35 | 166 | NA | NA | 215+ |
| 1990 | 1 | 6 | 8 | 8 | 57 | 547 | 170 | 5 | 802 |
| 2000 | 2 | 27 | 13 | 16 | 72 | 1,233 | 336 | 10 | 1,709 |
| 2010 | 2 | 27 | 23 | 19 | 101 | 1,500 | 386 | 11 | 2,069 |
| 2012 | 2 | 27 | 24 | 19 | 95 | NA | NA | NA | NA |

SOURCE: Republican Party of Texas.

the Texas Court of Criminal Appeals. Only 20 years earlier, William Clements was the first statewide official elected as a Republican since Reconstruction.

## Issues in Texas Party Politics

**Analyze why it is difficult to be elected as an independent**

Political parties are among the most important features in Texas politics. Most ideological battles are fought within the two parties and a party affiliation seems necessary to be elected to office in Texas.

### Running as an Independent

It is unusual for a candidate to run for office in Texas as an independent. One reason is that there are substantial requirements for getting one's name on the ballot. Additionally, an independent candidate lacks the political support of party organizations and the advantage of having a party label on the ballot. In 2006, however, Texas had two independent candidates for governor. One was the musician and humorist Kinky Friedman. The other was Carole Keeton Strayhorn, the state comptroller, who had been elected to that office as a Republican

Both candidates were obviously hoping that an independent candidacy would attract the votes of Democrats who believed that a Democratic candidate for governor could not win in such a strongly Republican state. They also were hoping to get substantial votes from Republicans disaffected with the policies and performance of the Republican governor, Rick Perry. Strayhorn, in particular, seemed to have strong appeal to Democrats who usually contributed large sums to Democratic nominees. One study of Strayhorn's contributions from July through December of 2005, for

*Independent candidates face considerable challenges in elections. Although the musician and writer Kinky Friedman's 2006 candidacy for governor attracted major media attention, Friedman received only 12.4 percent of the vote.*

example, found that 52 percent of her campaign funds were from people who had given exclusively or almost exclusively to Democrats over the previous five years.[9]

In general, however, independents have a hard time getting on the ballot in Texas. For Friedman and Strayhorn to get on the ballot, for example, they had to meet the following requirements:

1. The candidates must obtain signatures on a petition from registered voters. The signatures must equal 1 percent of the total votes in the last governor's race. This meant that Friedman and Strayhorn each had to obtain 45,540 signatures.

2. The signatures must come from registered voters who did not participate in any political party primary election.

3. Signature collection cannot begin until the day after the last primary election. In 2006, this was March 8.

4. Voters may sign only one candidate's petition. If they sign both, only the first signature provided will count.[10]

Making it difficult for independents to get their names on the ballot helps to ensure that the two major political parties will continue to dominate politics in the state well into the future. Elections may be open in Texas, but they work through the dominant political parties, helping to solidify their control over the political process and the major political offices in the state. The electoral performances of Friedman and Strayhorn also point to the difficulties of independent candidacies. Friedman received only 12.4 percent of the vote and Strayhorn got only 18.1 percent.

## Party Unity and Disunity

All groups have factions within them, and political parties are no exception. When a party becomes dominant in a state, however, these factional battles become particularly important because the stakes are higher for the factions of the dominant party.

When the Democratic Party was the dominant party in Texas, factional battles were common between liberals and conservatives in the party. These conflicts in the Democratic Party were especially notable during the 1950s in the struggles between the pro-Eisenhower conservative Democrats, led by Allan Shivers, and the pro-Stevenson liberal and loyalist Democrats, led by Sam Rayburn, Lyndon Johnson, and Ralph Yarborough. Now that the Republican Party is the dominant party in Texas, major factional battles have occurred for control of that party. One faction is the religious right. This group includes religious conservatives who are especially concerned with social issues such as abortion, prayer in public schools and at school events, the teaching of evolution in public schools, and the perceived decline in family values. The other major segment of the party is composed of economic conservatives. This group is primarily concerned with reduced government spending, lower taxes, and greater emphasis on free enterprise.

In the 2006 primary, some Republicans, including two of the party's largest contributors in Texas, believed that Republicans in the Texas House were too moderate and spent money to try to defeat them.[11] At least six Republican incumbents were aided by a political action committee that poured about $300,000 into their campaigns to help protect them from Republican challengers. Nevertheless, two of the six incumbents were defeated and one was thrown into a runoff.[12] The 2010 primary battle between Kay Bailey Hutchison and Rick Perry highlighted the ideological tensions in the Republican Party between what are essentially a conservative faction and an even more conservative faction. As we discussed in the chapter introduction, the latter faction has been identified with the Tea Party movement,

The Republican Party of Texas has faced internal conflicts between traditional Republicans and the more conservative faction associated with the Tea Party movement.

a loosely knit alliance of conservative groups that is suspicious of the national government, opposes tax increases, and calls for a reduction in the national debt.

To maintain their political strength, the Republican Party has to keep these factional disputes within the party. For years, the Democratic Party battles between its liberal and conservative wings were kept inside the party because there was no rival party where one of the factions could go. Eventually, however, the Republican Party emerged as a home where many conservative Democrats felt comfortable. Conceivably, the factional disputes in the Republican Party could lead one of the factions—most likely the more moderate Republicans—to move to the Democratic Party.

## Latinos and the Future of Party Politics in Texas

In the media coverage of the 2000 presidential election, one little judicial race in Dallas County was almost overlooked. Only one puzzled article on the race's results appeared in the *Dallas Morning News*.[13] A three-time Republican judge, Bill Rhea, won re-election against a first-time Democratic candidate, Mary Ann Huey. That should have been no surprise. By the late 1980s, the only Democrat who could win a judicial race in Dallas County was Ron Chapman, a Democratic judge who happened to share the name of the most popular disk jockey in the county.[14] In the early 1980s, there had been a wholesale rush of incumbent Democratic judges to the Republican Party. Although varying explanations were given by the party switchers, perhaps the most honest and straightforward was by Judge Richard Mays: "My political philosophy about general things has nothing to do with me [*sic*] being a judge. . . . That's not the reason I'm switching parties. The reason I'm switching is that to be a judge in Dallas County you need to be a Republican." With Mays's switch in August 1985, 32 of the 36 district judges in Dallas County were Republicans, though none were Republicans before 1978.[15] It would not take long, of course, until all judges in Dallas County were Republican.[16]

**for critical analysis**

What is the significance of Hispanic population growth to parties and elections in Texas?

So what was remarkable about that one district court race between a Democratic challenger and a longtime Republican incumbent, other than the fact that a Democrat had the temerity to challenge an incumbent in a Republican bastion such as Dallas County? Out of 560,558 votes cast, only 4,150 votes separated the two candidates. In other words, a three-term Republican judge with no scandal or other controversy surrounding his name won with only 50.3 percent of the vote. It is no wonder that the judge commented, "I'm thrilled to be serving again and duly humbled by the vote count."[17] Even more astounding, Judge Rhea's Democratic opponent, Mary Ann Huey, had run with no money, no political experience, and no support from the legal community. She ran in the same year that George W. Bush was the presidential nominee, with no other Democratic judicial candidates on the ballot at the county level, and with little more than audacity on her side.

Judge Rhea's humbling experience, of course, was not caused by his judicial performance but rather by demographic changes. The Republican base in Dallas County has moved to places such as Collin, Denton, and Rockwall counties. That suburban growth has changed those traditionally Democratic counties into Republican counties, but has left the old Republican base—Dallas—with a larger African American population and an even larger Hispanic population and has returned to the Democratic column that it left a little over 20 years ago.

In the 2004 elections, President George W. Bush carried Dallas County by fewer than 10,000 votes (50.72 percent), and Dallas County elected Democrats as sheriff and four countywide elected judges. The 2006 elections in Dallas County were truly a watershed in the county's politics. A Democrat was elected county judge, a Democrat was elected district attorney, and all 42 Democrats who ran for Dallas County judgeships were elected. Democrats continued their sweep of countywide elections in 2008, 2010, and 2012.

How will the growing number of Latino voters affect Texas politics? In recent elections, both parties have tried to appeal to Latinos, but to date, most Latino voters have favored the Democrats.

In 2008, Harris County also dramatically shifted to the Democratic column, electing a large number of Democrats to county office. It seemed to be following in Dallas County's footsteps. However, the 2010 elections moved Harris County back into the Republican column, and in 2012, it was a virtual tied between Obama and Romney.

The 2002 elections, raised questions about how soon the Latino vote would transform politics in Texas. In an attempt to break the lock that the Republicans had on statewide offices, the Democratic Party put forward a "Dream Team" with Tony Sanchez, a wealthy Latino businessman, running for governor alongside Ron Kirk (a former mayor of Dallas who is African American) running for the U.S. Senate, and John Sharp (a former state comptroller and white conservative Democrat) running for lieutenant governor. The idea was to mobilize minority voters to vote for the Democratic ticket while holding traditional white voters. The strategy failed as Sanchez lost to the Republican candidate Perry (40 percent to 58 percent), Kirk lost to the Republican Cornyn (43 percent to 55 percent), and Sharp lost to the Republican Dewhurst (46 percent to 52 percent). Especially disappointing because Sanchez was the first Latino major party nominee for governor, Latino voter turnout was only 32.8 percent. Sanchez had money and spent it with abandon, but he was a poor campaigner who could not even mobilize the Latino vote.

Additionally, Democrats didn't anticipate the grassroots get-out-the-vote effort put forth by the Republicans. Republican straight-ticket voting in key urban and suburban counties across the state appeared to have outdistanced Democratic straight-ticket voting. Further, it appeared that the negative campaigning, particularly that directed at Tony Sanchez, may have undercut support for the Democratic ticket among traditional white conservative voters. Bob Stein, a political science professor at Rice University, estimates that 15 percent of Democrats abandoned Sanchez because of questions raised by his involvement in a failed savings and loan bank that was accused of laundering money for Mexican drug kingpins.

The 2010 election has been described as a Republican tsunami running throughout the nation. Texas experienced this wave in three important ways. First, three Democratic incumbent U.S. House members were defeated. Second, Republicans maintained their monopoly over statewide elected offices. Third, Republicans gained 22 seats in the Texas House. A conservative majority reasserted itself in Texas politics and remained dominant in 2012.

Despite the final results of the 2008, 2010, and 2012 elections, few commentators were willing to dismiss the growing importance of the Latino vote in the state. One indication of that importance is that in 2010, it was estimated that Latinos make up about 20 percent of the registered voters in Texas.[18]

However, Latinos have not fully realized their potential voting strength. Table 21.2 shows Latino voting in comparison to voting by other racial and ethnic groups, comparing the group's share of the population with its share of voters in the 2008 election. It does seem likely that Latinos will at some point significantly increase their share of the vote in

**TABLE 21.2**

## Racial/Ethnic Groups' Share of Texas's Population and the State's 2008 Vote

| GROUP | % SHARE OF POPULATION | % SHARE OF ELIGIBLE VOTERS |
|---|---|---|
| White | 50.5 | 61.5 |
| Hispanic | 37.4 | 25.5 |
| African American | 12 | 13 |

SOURCE: Pew Hispanic Center, "Hispanics in the 2008 Election: Texas," February 20, 2008.

Texas, although one obstacle may be that large numbers of Latinos are not citizens and are ineligible to vote.[19] When Latino voting does increase, the key question will be whether Republicans can make inroads into the Latino vote to the extent necessary to keep the Democratic Party from emerging as a dominant party in Texas once again. Currently, Hispanics constitute 37 percent of the Texas population and 25 percent of the eligible voters, yet they are only 20 percent of registered voters and only 12 to 14 percent of actual voters.[20]

# ● Elections in Texas

**Identify the types of elections held in Texas**

Elections are the mechanisms people use to select leaders, authorize actions by government, and borrow money on behalf of government. In Texas, there are a multitude of elections: primary elections, general elections, city elections, school board elections, special elections, elections for community college boards of regents and the boards of directors for many special districts, and bond elections for city, county, and state governments.

## Primary Elections

**primary elections** election held to select a party's candidate for the general election

**Primary elections** are the first elections held. In Texas, they are held on the second Tuesday in March of even-numbered years. Primary elections determine the party's nominees for the general election. They are conducted by the political party and funded jointly by the party and the state. Essentially, parties collect filing fees from those seeking nomination and use these funds to pay for their share of holding the primary election.

Both parties conduct primaries in all of Texas's 254 counties. Within each county, voters cast ballots in precincts. The number of voting precincts varies depending on the population of the county. Less-populated counties such as Loving and Kenedy have as few as 6 precincts, whereas Harris County contains more than 1,000 voting precincts.[21]

**runoff primary** where no candidate received a majority, a second primary election is held between the two candidates who received the most votes in the first primary election

**open primary** a primary election in which the voter does not have to declare a party affiliation prior to voting in the party primary

Republicans seeking their party's nomination file papers and pay a filing fee to the Republican Party. Likewise, Democrats file papers and pay a filing fee to the Democratic Party. If several Republicans (or Democrats) seek the office of governor, they will campaign against each other and one will be chosen to run in the general election. Winning the primary election requires an absolute majority. The party's nominees must have more votes than all opponents combined. If no candidate receives an absolute majority, there is a **runoff primary** held the second Tuesday in April between the two candidates receiving the most votes. Voters who participate in the Republican Party primary cannot vote in a Democratic runoff; likewise, anyone who voted in the Democratic Party primary cannot vote in a Republican runoff. However, those who vote in neither the Democratic nor Republican primary can vote in either the Republican or Democratic runoff primary.

An **open primary** allows any registered voter to cast a ballot in either primary but not both primaries. There are no party restrictions. One can consider oneself a Republican and vote in the Democratic primary or can leave home intending to vote in the Democratic primary, change one's mind, and vote in the Republican primary.

*Some blame the relatively low voter turnout for Texas elections on the frequency of elections and the large number of candidates. Also, state officials are not elected in presidential election years, when voter participation tends to be highest.*

The Texas Constitution and election laws call the Texas system a **closed primary** because one must declare one's party affiliation before voting, but in practice it is an open primary. Before receiving a primary ballot, the voter signs a roll sheet indicating eligibility to vote and pledging to support the party's candidates. By signing the roll sheet, the voter makes a declaration of party affiliation prior to voting. However, because the voter declares a party affiliation only a few moments prior to voting in the primary, the primary is closed only in the narrowest sense of the term.

**closed primary** a primary election in which voters can participate in the nomination of candidates, but only of the party in which they are enrolled for a period of time prior to the primary day

## General Election

The **general election** is held the first Tuesday following the first Monday in November of even-numbered years. The Democratic Party's nominee runs against the nominee of the Republican Party. It is possible that independent and minor party candidates will also appear on the general election ballot.

**general election** a decisive election that determines who is elected to office

Major state officials (governor, lieutenant governor, comptroller of public accounts, attorney general, and so on) are elected in nonpresidential election years. This is intended to prevent popular presidential candidates from influencing the outcomes of Texas races. For example, it is possible that a popular Republican presidential candidate might draw more than the usual number of Republican votes, and an unusually large Republican presidential vote might swing the election for statewide candidates running under the Republican banner. Likewise, it prevents an uncommonly popular statewide candidate from influencing the presidential election. If statewide elections were held in presidential election years, a Democratic candidate for governor might influence Texas's presidential voting by increasing the number of votes for Democratic candidates in general.

General elections are held in November to select national and state officeholders. Members of city councils, school boards, and other local government entities are also selected by general elections; however, these elections usually take place outside the traditional early November time period.

## Special Elections

**special election** an election that is not held on a regularly scheduled basis; in Texas, a special election is called to fill a vacancy in office, to give approval for the state government to borrow money, or to ratify amendments to the Texas Constitution

In Texas, **special elections** are used to fill vacancies in office, to give approval to borrow money, or to ratify amendments to the Texas Constitution. The dates for special elections are specified by the Texas legislature. If a Texas senator resigns, for example, the governor will call a special election to fill the vacancy.

Laws require voter approval before any governmental agency can borrow money and undertake long-term debt. If the local school district wants to borrow money to build a new high school and repair three elementary schools, a special election must be held. During the election, voters decide whether they will allow the school board to borrow the money.

The legislature proposes amendments to the Texas Constitution, and they are ratified by the voters in a special election.

## ● Participation in Texas Elections

> **Assess voting patterns and the reasons so few Texans vote**

We will now focus on voting in Texas. Issues include who can vote, how easy it is to register to vote, and why few Texans vote.

### Earlier Restrictions on the Franchise

For much of the period of one-party Democratic control that began in the late nineteenth century, there were restrictions on the franchise.

**Women**  Women were allowed to vote in primaries and party conventions in Texas in 1918 and obtained the right to vote in all elections as a result of the Nineteenth Amendment to the U.S. Constitution in 1920. However, some of the most influential politicians in the state opposed the franchise for women. Joseph Weldon Bailey, for example, who had been Democratic leader in the U.S. House of Representatives and later the informal Democratic leader in the U.S. Senate, was an eloquent opponent of women's suffrage, arguing that women could not vote because they could not perform the three basic duties of citizenship: jury service, *posse comitatus* service (citizens who are deputized to deal with an emergency), and military service. He believed that women's morals dictated their beliefs and that women would force their beliefs on men. The result, he felt, would be prohibition.[22] Tinie Wells, the wife of Jim Wells, perhaps the most influential south Texas political leader of his day, was also an important and influential spokesperson for the anti–women's suffrage movement.[23] Governor "Farmer Jim" Ferguson was another opponent of women's suffrage, but when he was impeached, his successor, William P. Hobby, proved a key supporter of women's right to vote. It was Governor Hobby who called the legislature into special session in 1919 to consider the Nineteenth Amendment. Thus Texas became the ninth state and the first state in the South to ratify the women's suffrage amendment.[24]

**The Poll Tax**  Minorities had an even tougher time gaining access to the ballot in Texas. In the early part of the twentieth century, powerful political bosses such as Jim Wells and Archer Parr had economic power and personal influence over

# When Did Texas Become Republican?

The Republican Party is the dominant party in Texas. However, this is a fairly recent development. Before the 1970s, Texans were less likely than the rest of the nation to support Republican presidential candidates. And it was only in the 1990s and the early 2000s that Republicans came to hold a majority of seats in the Texas delegation to the U.S. House and in the Texas legislature.

## Republican Share of the Presidential Vote

■ Texas  ■ National

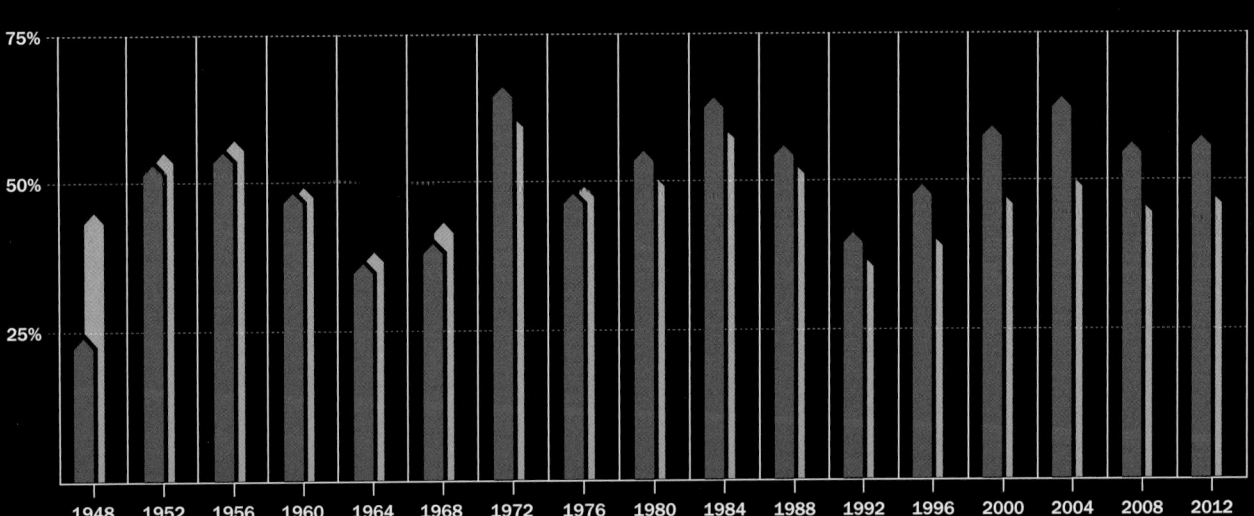

SOURCES: First figure: 1948–2004 data from the CQ Elections and Voting Collection. 2008 data from the Associated Press. Second figure: 1974–2002 data from Republican Party of Texas. 2004–10 data calculated by author from election results archived at the Texas Secretary of State.

## Republican Share of Offices Held

**Texas statewide offices**
0%                                                                100%

**Texas House**
10.7%                                                              66%

**Texas Senate**
9.7%                                                              61.3%

**Texas delegation to U.S. House**
8.3%                                                              71.9%

1974   1978   1982   1986   1990   1994   1998   2002   2006   2010

## for critical analysis

1. Consider the timing of the shift toward the Republican Party in Texas. What factors contributed to this shift?

2. The figures show that in the last few elections, the growth of the Texas Republican Party has leveled out somewhat. Do you think the growth of the Texas Republican Party has stalled, or will the party's strength continue to grow in Texas?

Hispanic voters. They used this power to support national politicians such as John Nance Garner. Garner represented a huge part of south Texas, which stretched from Laredo to Corpus Christi and then north almost to San Antonio. A lifelong Democrat, he began his service in the House of Representatives in 1903 and served until 1933. From 1931 to 1933, he was Speaker of the U.S. House of Representatives, and from 1933 to 1941, he was vice president of the United States. Garner was the first speaker from Texas and the first vice president from Texas. His south Texas political base was secured by votes that were controlled by the south Texas political bosses.[25]

One restriction on voting that affected poor people in general was the **poll tax**. Enacted in 1902, it required voters to pay a tax, presumably to cover the costs of elections. That tax was usually between $1.50 and $1.75. It was a small sum, but it had to be paid in advance of the election, and in the first third of the century, the tax could be one, two, or even more days' wages for a farm worker. Thus, it tended to disenfranchise poorer people.

The south Texas political bosses used the poll tax, however, to great advantage. They would purchase large numbers of poll tax receipts and provide those receipts to their supporters, who often depended on the bosses for jobs and other economic, legal, and political assistance and who therefore would vote as the bosses wanted.

Although the poll tax was made illegal in federal elections in 1964 by the passage of the Twenty-Fourth Amendment to the U.S. Constitution, it remained legal in state elections in Texas until 1966, when it was held unconstitutional.[26] After the elimination of the poll tax, Texas continued to require **early registration** for voting—registration more than nine months before the general election. Early reg-

**poll tax** a state-imposed tax on voters as a prerequisite for voting. Poll taxes were rendered unconstitutional in national elections by the Twenty-Fourth Amendment, and in state elections by the Supreme Court in 1966

**early registration** the requirement that a voter register long before the general election; in effect in Texas until 1971

*Participation in elections in Texas is low relative to that in other states. In the past, there were restrictions on the franchise. One such restriction that discouraged poor people from voting was the poll tax, which remained legal in Texas until 1966. Here, voters are being asked to "buy" or pay the poll tax and then promise to vote against Pappy O'Daniel.*

istration was required on a yearly basis. This requirement effectively prevented migrant workers from voting. These provisions lasted until 1971, when they were voided by the federal courts.[27] Texas even prohibited anyone who was not a property owner from voting in revenue bond and tax elections until the practice was stopped by federal courts.[28] Texas also required an unusually long period of residency. Voters had to have lived in the state for at least one year and to have lived in the county for at least six months prior to voting. This was another restriction on the franchise that was struck down by the federal courts.[29]

**White Primary** The most oppressive restriction on the franchise, however, was designed to minimize the political strength of African American voters. It was the **white primary**. In 1923, the Texas legislature flatly prohibited African Americans from voting in the Democratic primary. Because Texas was a one-party state at that time the effect, of course, was to prevent African Americans from participating in the only "real" election contests. Texas was able to do this because of a 1921 U.S. Supreme Court decision, *Newberry v. United States*, which dealt with a federal campaign-expenditures law. In interpreting the law, the Court stated that the primary election was "in no real sense part of the manner of holding the election."[30] This cleared the way for southern states, including Texas, to discriminate against African Americans in the primaries.

In 1927, however, the Supreme Court struck down the Texas white primary law, claiming that the legal ban on black participation was a violation of the equal protection clause of the Constitution.[31] In response, the Texas legislature passed another law that authorized the political parties, through their state executive committees, to determine the qualifications for voting in the primaries. That law, of course, allowed the parties to create white primaries. The theory was that what a state could not do directly because of the Fourteenth Amendment, it could authorize political parties to do. However, in *Nixon v. Condon*, the U.S. Supreme Court held that the state executive committees were acting as agents of the state and were discriminating in violation of the Fourteenth Amendment.[32] As a result, the Texas Democratic Party convention, acting on its own authority and without any state law, passed a resolution that confined party membership to white citizens. That case was also appealed to the U.S. Supreme Court and, in *Grovey v. Townsend*, the Court held there was no violation of the Fourteenth Amendment. It is "state action" that violates the "equal protection of the laws" that the Fourteenth Amendment protects against. Because there was no state law authorizing the white primary, the Court believed there was no "state action," only discrimination by a private organization, the Democratic Party, which is not banned by the Fourteenth Amendment.[33] Thus, the Court upheld the white primary until 1944, when, in *Smith v. Allwright*, it decided that the operation of primary elections involved so much state action and so much public responsibility that the white primary did involve unconstitutional state action.[34]

Even with the *Smith* decision, at least one Texas county held unofficial primaries by the Jaybird Party. This was a Democratic political organization that excluded African Americans. The winners in the Jaybird primary then entered the regular Democratic Party primary, in which they were never defeated for county office and where they seldom had opposition. In *Terry v. Adams*, the U.S. Supreme Court finally ruled that the Jaybird primary was an integral, and the only effective, part of the elective process in the county. Thus, the Fifteenth Amendment (which deals with the right to vote) was applicable, and the white "preprimary" primary of the Jaybird Party was ruled unconstitutional.[35]

**white primary** primary election in which only white voters are eligible to participate

What made the white primary restriction work for Democrats during this era was the fact that Texas was a one-party state, where elections were decided in the Democratic Party primary. If Texas had had a competitive two-party system during this era, the state might have had a more difficult time imposing and maintaining these restrictions on the franchise. In a competitive two-party system, to obtain and retain power, both parties would have to search for ways to build and increase their base of support in order to be the victorious party. In a one-party system, there is a greater incentive to restrict participation in the party in order to retain control over it. Losers in a battle for control of a one-party system essentially have no place to go. If they cannot maintain a place in the dominant party's councils, then they have no other avenue for expressing their political views.

**Expanding the Franchise** At least since the 1940s, there has been a gradual expansion of the franchise in Texas. Much of that expansion was brought about by litigation in the federal courts, often by African American and Hispanic civil rights organizations. Federal laws also played an important role in the expansion of the franchise. The most important of these laws was the 1965 Voting Rights Act, which applied to Texas as a result of congressional amendments after 1975.

**Contracting the Franchise?** Highly partisan legislation passed in 2011 may make it more difficult for some people to vote. Over Democratic opposition, the Texas legislature passed a voter identification law that requires a photo identification in order to vote. Republicans claimed that the photo identification requirement is necessary in order to prevent voter fraud. Democrats, in contrast, have argued that evidence of voter fraud is minimal and that the law will make it harder for low-income persons, students, and the elderly (all of whom typically support Democrats) to vote.[36] Acceptable forms of photo identification are a driver's license, an election identification certificate, a Department of Public Safety personal ID card, a U.S. military ID, a U.S. citizenship certificate, a U.S. passport, and a Department of Public Safety–issued concealed handgun license.[37] It is intriguing that university-issued photo ID cards are not acceptable. It remains to be seen whether the voter identification law is in violation of the 1965 Voting Rights Act as this legislation remains in litigation.

## Qualifications to Vote

Today, meeting the qualifications to register to vote in Texas is relatively easy. A voter must be

1. 18 years of age
2. a U.S. citizen
3. a resident of Texas for 30 days
4. a resident of the county for 30 days

To be eligible to vote, one must be a registered voter for 30 days preceding the election and a resident of the voting precinct on the day of the election. Two groups of people cannot vote even if they meet all the above qualifications: felons (who have not completed the sentence or period of state supervision) and those judged by a court to be mentally incompetent.

About 69.3 percent of the state's voting-age population are registered to vote.[38] The **motor voter law**, which allows individuals to register to vote when apply-

**motor voter law** a national act, passed in 1993, that requires states to allow people to register to vote when applying for a driver's license

ing for or renewing driver's licenses, is one factor in increased registration. Public schools distribute voter registration cards as students turn 18. Cooperative efforts between the secretary of state's office and corporations such as Diamond Shamrock, Stop 'n' Go, and the Southland Corporation (which operates 7-Eleven stores) also increase the number of registered voters. In 2010, Texas had about 13 million registered voters out of a voting-age population of more than 18.8 million.[39]

## Low Voter Turnout

In most elections, fewer than 50 percent of U.S. citizens vote.[40] Even fewer Texans exercise their right to vote. Historically, Texans rank in the bottom third in terms of voter participation. Table 21.3 provides data on the abysmal turnout of registered voters in the various types of recent Texas elections. Considering the ease of registration and the ability to vote early, voter participation should be higher. Why do so few Texans vote?

A more detailed analysis reveals several factors that may contribute to low participation rates:

1. low levels of educational attainment
2. low per capita income
3. high rate of poverty
4. location in the South
5. young population
6. traditionalistic and individualistic political culture
7. large numbers of undocumented residents and felons

Education and income appear to be the two most important factors in determining whether someone votes. In Texas, low levels of education and high levels of poverty are both predictors of low voter participation.

In the southern states that composed the Confederacy, individuals participate in smaller numbers than in other parts of the United States. Texas was part of the Confederacy, and its level of participation is consistent with lower levels of voting in the South. Young people vote in smaller numbers as well; the average age of Texans is less than the national average.

According to the political scientist Daniel Elazar (see Chapter 19), Texas's political culture is traditionalistic and individualistic. Low levels of voting characterize these cultures. In a traditionalistic political culture, the political and economic elite discourage voting. People choose not to vote in individualistic cultures because of real or perceived corruption in government.

Interestingly, there are still other possible explanations for low voter participation in Texas. In keeping with the Texas tradition of decentralized government, there are so many elections in Texas and so many candidates for office that voters are simply overloaded with elections and candidates. Note that as shown in Table 21.3, voter participation was much higher in the general election than in the special constitutional election. If there were fewer elections, the ballot might be longer, but voter turnout would likely be higher, because more voters would be attracted to at least some races or issues on the ballot. Additionally, the practice of having elections in nonpresidential election years decreases voter turnout because the highest voter participation tends to occur for presidential elections. A third problem is that most elections in Texas involve very low-visibility offices.

**for critical analysis**

Voter participation in Texas is among the lowest in the nation. What accounts for the state's low levels of participation? What can be done to increase voter participation in the short term? In the long term?

## TABLE 21.3

## Turnout by Registered Voters in Texas Elections

| ELECTION | PERCENTAGE OF VOTING TURNOUT TO REGISTERED VOTERS |
|---|---|
| 2000 Democratic Primary (Presidential) | 6.8 |
| 2000 Republican Primary (Presidential) | 9.7 |
| 2000 Democratic Runoff Primary | 2.1 |
| 2000 Republican Runoff Primary | 1.9 |
| 2000 General Election (Presidential) | 51.8 |
| 2001 Special Election (Constitutional Amendments) | 6.9 |
| 2002 Democratic Primary (Gubernatorial) | 8.4 |
| 2002 Republican Primary (Gubernatorial) | 5.1 |
| 2002 General Election (Gubernatorial) | 36.2 |
| 2003 Special Election (Constitutional) | 12.2 |
| 2004 Democratic Primary (Presidential) | 6.8 |
| 2004 Republican Primary (Presidential) | 5.6 |
| 2004 General Election (Presidential) | 56.6 |
| 2005 Special Election (Constitutional Amendments) | 18.0 |
| 2006 Democratic Primary (Gubernatorial) | 4.0 |
| 2006 Republican Primary (Gubernatorial) | 5.2 |
| 2006 General Election (Gubernatorial) | 33.6 |
| 2007 Special Election (Constitutional Amendments) | 8.7 |
| 2008 Republican Primary (Presidential) | 10.7 |
| 2008 Democratic Primary (Presidential) | 22.54 |
| 2008 General Election (Presidential) | 59.5 |
| 2009 Special Election (Constitutional Amendments) | 8.2 |
| 2010 Democratic Primary (Gubernatorial) | 5.2 |
| 2010 Republican Primary (Gubernatorial) | 11.4 |
| 2010 General Election (Gubernatorial) | 38.0 |
| 2011 Special Election (Constitutional Amendments) | 5.0 |
| 2012 Republican Primary (Presidential) | 11.3 |
| 2012 Democratic Primary (Presidential) | 5.0 |

SOURCE: Texas Secretary of State.

Voters likely know little about the candidates for these positions or the offices themselves, and such a lack of knowledge would naturally discourage voter participation. Efforts have been made in a number of states, most notably Washington, to increase voter knowledge by having the state provide biographical information about the candidates to voters, but Texas makes little effort to enhance voter knowledge of candidates. Finally, it may be that the new voter identification law will reduce voter turnout even more.

## Early Voting

**Early voting** is a procedure that increases the polling period from 12 hours on Election Day to an additional two weeks prior to the election. The legislature has allowed early voting in an effort to increase participation. Early voting is designed for those who have trouble getting to the polls between 7 A.M. and 7 P.M. on Election Day. For most elections, early voting commences on the seventeenth day before the elections and ends four days prior to Election Day.

Voting early is basically the same as voting on Election Day. An individual appears at one of the designated polling places, presents appropriate identification, and receives and casts a ballot. Each general election has seen an increase in early voting, but overall turnout has increased only modestly. Those who normally vote on the official Election Day simply cast their ballots early.

Predictions that Democrats would benefit from early voting did not hold true after Texas moved strongly into the Republican column. Republican candidates for the highest office on the ballot get a much larger proportion of early votes than do the Democratic candidates. In 2004, for example, 63 percent of the early votes for president in Texas were cast for George W. Bush, compared with 37 percent of the early votes for John Kerry. In seven of the nine elections examined, however, Republicans got a slightly smaller proportion of overall votes (votes cast in early voting plus Election Day voting) than early votes. And in five of the nine elections, Democrats got a slightly larger proportion of overall votes than early votes. This suggests that early voting has been a bit more beneficial to Republicans than to Democrats, although the advantage has been very slight (see Table 21.4).

**early voting** a procedure that allows voters to cast ballots during the two-week period before the regularly scheduled election date

*In 2010 only 38 percent of registered voters cast ballots in the Texas gubernatorial election. Turnout is higher in presidential elections in Texas but still below the national average.*

## TABLE 21.4

### Early Voting and Overall Voting by Party in Texas

| YEAR | OFFICE | EARLY/OVERALL VOTES FOR REPUBLICANS (% OF TOTAL) | EARLY/OVERALL VOTES FOR DEMOCRATS (% OF TOTAL) |
|---|---|---|---|
| 1994 | Senate | 62/61 | 37/38 |
| 1996 | President | 52/49 | 45/44 |
| 1998 | Governor | 68/69 | 32/31 |
| 2000 | President | 63/59 | 35/38 |
| 2002 | Senator | 57/55 | 42/43 |
| 2004 | President | 63/61 | 37/38 |
| 2006 | Senator | 56/56 | 44/44 |
| 2008 | President | 54/55 | 45/44 |
| 2010 | Governor | 56/55 | 41/42 |

SOURCE: Texas Secretary of State.

# Campaigns

**Explain why political campaigns are so expensive in Texas**

Political campaigns are efforts of candidates to win support of the voters. The goal of the campaign is to attain sufficient support to win the primary election in March and the general election in November. Some campaigns last a year or more; however, the more accepted practice is to limit the campaign to a few weeks before the election. In Texas, campaigns to win the party primary begin in January and continue to the second Tuesday in March. Labor Day is the traditional start of the general election campaign, which lasts from early September to the first Tuesday following the first Monday in November. However, in recent elections, statewide campaigns began even earlier than September.

In 2010 and 2012, interestingly, the distinguishing feature of the campaigns was the lack of emphasis on state issues, including the pressing issue of the state budget. Instead, Republicans ran against the national Democratic administration, whereas Democrats tried to distance themselves from President Obama and his policies.

Campaigns involve attempts to reach the voters through print and electronic media, the mail, door-to-door campaigning, speeches to large and small groups, coffee hours, and telephone solicitation. Costs are enormous. During the 1980s and 1990s, individual candidates for statewide races spent as much as $30 million. A new record up to that point for campaign spending was set in the 2002 gubernatorial race, when the Democrat Tony Sanchez and the Republican Rick Perry spent a total of $88 million. In 2006, the amount raised in the gubernatorial race fell to $53.4 million, 28.7 percent of which went to the two independent candidates, Carole Keeton Strayhorn and Kinky Friedman. In 2010 total campaign contributions by Democrats seeking the governorship came to nearly $37 million and total contributions by Republicans came to nearly $55 million—an amount far larger than the $30 million raised by Republicans in 2006 because of the primary challenge to Rick Perry by Kay Bailey Hutchison. For all statewide offices, Republican campaign contributions overwhelmed Democratic campaign contributions. Total contributions in state house and state senate races were also far greater for Republicans than for Democrats (see Table 21.5 and Table 21.6).

In some places in the United States, the parties have a major role in the running of political campaigns. That is not the case in Texas. Here the candidates have the major responsibility for campaign strategy, for running their campaigns, and for raising money. At times, party leaders will try to recruit individuals to run for office, especially if no candidates volunteer to seek an office or if the candidates appear to be weak ones. For the most part, the benefit of the party to a candidate in Texas is that the party provides the party label under which the candidate runs. That "Democratic" or "Republican" label is, of course, important to candidates because many voters use the party label in casting their votes, especially for low-visibility races. The party also contains numerous activists whom the candidate can tap for campaign tasks such as manning phone banks, preparing mailings, and posting campaign ads. Additionally, the party does provide some support for the candidate, most commonly through campaigns to get out the vote for the party's candidates. Campaigning in Texas, however, is generally left up to the candidate, and in that effort, the parties take a secondary role.

Name recognition is essential for candidates. Incumbents hold a distinct advantage in this regard. Officeholders have many ways to achieve name visibility. They can mail out news releases, send newsletters to their constituents, appear on radio talk shows, and give speeches to civic clubs. Challengers have a more difficult time getting this crucial name visibility.

In 1978, William R. Clements was a political unknown. He spent thousands of dollars of his own fortune to gain name recognition. He leased hundreds of billboards throughout the state. Each had a blue background with white letters proclaiming "CLEMENTS." In the print media, early ads bore the simple message, "ELECT CLEMENTS." The unprecedented scale of this advertising effort made Clements's name better known among the voters in Texas. This, in turn, stimulated

**TABLE 21.5**

## Amount Raised by All Candidates in Texas, 2010, Listed by Political Party*

| OFFICE | DEMOCRATIC | REPUBLICAN | THIRD-PARTY |
| --- | --- | --- | --- |
| Governor | $36,994,646 | $54,682,462 | $0 |
| Judicial | 401,025 | 2,592,108 | 110 |
| Other Statewide | 3,150,119 | 21,387,407 | 1,547 |
| House | 28,780,507 | 48,634,984 | 26,552 |
| Senate | 3,979,924 | 6,991,616 | 23,007 |

*Excludes contributions to candidates not up for election in 2010 and one candidate for state senate who withdrew.
SOURCE: Calculated from Institute on Money in State Politics.

**TABLE 21.6**

## Campaign Contributions in Statewide Executive Offices: Texas General Elections, 2010

| OFFICE | CANDIDATE | $ CONTRIBUTED | % VOTE* |
|---|---|---|---|
| Governor | R. Perry (R) | $39,328,540 | 54.97% |
| | B. White (D) | 26,291,535 | 42.29 |
| Lt. Governor | D. Dewhurst (R) | 9,240,480 | 61.78 |
| | L. Chavez-Thompson | 958,040 | 34.83 |
| Agriculture Commissioner | Todd Staples (R) | 1,742,941 | 60.82 |
| | Hank Gilbert (D) | 336,363 | 35.79 |
| Attorney General | Greg Abbott (R) | 5,828,370 | 64.05 |
| | Barbara Radnafsky(D) | 1,135,031 | 33.66 |
| Comptroller | Susan Combs (R) | 2,744,001 | 83.16 |
| | None | | |
| Land Commissioner | Jerry Patterson (R) | 864,688 | 61.66 |
| | Hector Uribe (D) | 102,487 | 35.28 |
| Railroad Commissioner | David Porter (R) | 564,488 | 59.40 |
| | Jeff Weems (D) | 287,248 | 36.23 |

*Numbers do not add to 100 percent because of the presence of third-party candidates.
SOURCES: Institute on Money in State Politics and Texas Secretary of State.

interest in his campaign's message. Clements won the race for governor, becoming the first Republican to hold that office in Texas since the end of Reconstruction.

Running for statewide office is significantly different from seeking the office of state representative from an urban area. One obvious difference is the amount of money needed for the campaign, but there are others. Traveling tens of thousands of miles, the statewide candidate flies from city to city, gives a speech, shakes a few hands, and climbs back into the plane for another campaign stop 200 miles away. In a more localized race, candidates also spend much time traveling, but on a smaller, more personal scale. Typically a local candidate walks from house to apartment to condominium complex, knocking on doors and visiting with potential voters.

Media account for the greatest expense in most campaigns. In metropolitan areas, television, radio, and print advertising are very costly. Full-page ads in metropolitan newspapers can be as much as $40,000. Candidates for metropolitan districts in the Texas House of Representatives and Texas Senate need to reach only a small portion of the population, but they are forced to purchase ads in media sources that go to hundreds of thousands of people not represented. In rural areas, any individual ad is relatively inexpensive. However, candidates must advertise in dozens of small newspapers and radio stations, and costs mount.

Even more important, the campaigns must be well designed. A slipup in a well-funded campaign can do great harm, as David Dewhurst discovered in the early stages of his 2002 campaign for lieutenant governor. Dewhurst's personal wealth and his willingness to spend it had already pushed Bill Ratliff, the state senator elected by his colleagues to succeed Rick Perry as lieutenant governor, out of the race for the office. And Dewhurst was not remiss in spending money. He purchased a very expensive four-page ad in *Texas Monthly* that was intended to advertise his appointment by Governor Perry as the state's new chairman of the Governor's Task Force on Homeland Security. In the wake of the September 11 terrorist attacks, such an appointment might be turned into an important political asset. Indeed, Dewhurst listed "protecting the physical safety of all Texans" as the top issue in his campaign. In the ad, a military officer appears in dress uniform against a background of the American flag. Unfortunately for Dewhurst, the officer is not wearing an American military uniform, but the uniform of the German Luftwaffe with German military insignia and a name tag bearing a German flag. Alongside the picture is a plea from Dewhurst to support "the brave men and women of our armed forces." Such an ad can be a candidate's worst nightmare. Dewhurst had spent a substantial sum to show in a widely circulated, full-color magazine on glossy paper that the person in charge of homeland security for the state did not know the difference between an American officer and a German officer![41]

Some impressive but limited evidence indicates that television can be a very valuable tool for a Texas political candidate. On four occasions in the 1990s, Republican supreme court candidates were challenged in the primary by candidates with little, if any, organized support and minimal funding. Yet the insurgent candidates all showed great strength in areas where the established candidates did not run television ads. Of course, there may be additional explanations for the strength of established candidates in areas where ads were shown. Perhaps the candidates worked harder in those areas or were better organized. And in some areas, candidates may have had stronger name recognition than their opponents.[42]

None of the insurgent candidates had the resources to run television ads; only the established candidates did, and only in some media markets. It was the support the established candidates received in the areas where they ran television ads that led to their victories. It is important to note that because the data all relate to the Republican primary, the effect of the political party label is controlled. If we compare the percentage difference in votes for established candidates in areas where television ads were run with votes in areas where no ads were run, the difference is remarkable: established candidates received between 12 percent and 18.5 percent more votes in media markets where they bought television time.[43]

Given the myriad factors that may explain electoral success, we should beware of imputing victory in these judicial races solely to television ads. On the other hand, the general pattern of high margins of victory in areas where television was used is so powerful that it cannot be ignored.

## ● Thinking Critically about Political Parties and Elections

Political parties provide a structure through which candidates strive to win office. Moving through that structure, however, is a massive undertaking. The candidate must first run in a party primary; then, if the candidate does not receive a majority of the votes, he or she must run in a runoff primary. Ideally, the battles of primaries and runoff primaries will be forgotten and the party will come together in support of the nominee in order to win the election. However, what often happens is that the primaries and runoffs create enormous conflicts and divisions in the party that are not healed. The opposition then exploits those party divisions so that their candidate can win the election.

Texas is so large and diverse, and has so many media markets, that campaigns—especially statewide campaigns—are very expensive. For the most part, the candidates themselves must raise the money necessary to win an election. Gubernatorial campaigns can cost $40 million or more. One effect of the high cost of campaigns in Texas is that candidates are often very wealthy individuals willing to use their own money in their campaigns.

Although Texas once tried to narrow the franchise, primarily by limiting the right to vote through poll taxes and white primaries, in recent years it has tried to expand the franchise through the motor voter law and through early voting. Yet voter participation in Texas is quite low. That is probably because of the demographics of Texas voters, but it may also be because of the scheduling of elections in Texas, the vast number of elections, and the large number of low-visibility candidates for office. And it is likely the new voter identification law will further reduce voter participation.

One of the most striking developments in Texas politics over the past 20 to 25 years is that one-party Democratic dominance is gone from the Texas political scene. That decline in Democratic dominance corresponds to the rise of the Republican Party in Texas. In 2012 every statewide elected officeholder in Texas was a Republican.

Currently, the most significant division in the Republican Party is the split between religious conservatives who have a social agenda and economic conservatives who have a low-taxing, low-spending agenda. This split was strikingly revealed in the primary battle between Perry and Hutchison. Perry's victory in the primary may signal the triumph of the social conservatives and their increasingly powerful role in the state's politics. Republicans are not necessarily secure as the dominant party. It is important that they grow and expand their base of support. One of the Republican Party's great weaknesses is its lack of support among Latinos, the fastest-growing ethnic group in Texas. If the Republicans are to continue their remarkable successes in Texas politics, they will have to make greater inroads with Hispanic voters.

Democrats still have a significant base of support in urban counties with large minority populations, and with older Texans, with native Texans, and with liberals. For Texas to be a competitive two-party state, the Democrats need to win some statewide elections. The party needs to regroup and redirect its appeal to Texans. Most important, if the Democratic Party is to do more than lose elections, it must do what parties have traditionally done in states that have political machines. That is, it must get out the vote. The key to success in future Texas elections is a party's ability to mobilize the Hispanic vote in the state.

## The Role of Political Parties in Texas Politics

■ **Describe how parties organize elections and the electorate in Texas (pp. 833–35)**

In Texas, political parties serve as brand labels for voters to determine who to vote for in elections with little public visibility. Texas political parties also have conventions and committees that help their members organize and mobilize in elections.

### Key Terms

**precinct** (p. 834)

**precinct chair** (p. 834)

**county executive committee** (p. 834)

**county chair** (p. 834)

**state executive committee** (p. 834)

**state chair** and **vice chair** (p. 834)

**precinct convention** (p. 834)

**county convention** (p. 835)

**state convention** (p. 835)

### Practice Quiz

1. Providing a label that helps voters identify those seeking office is an important function of *(p. 833)*
   a) the state.
   b) political parties.
   c) interest groups.
   d) regional and subregional governments.
   e) the governor.

2. In the state of Texas, the highest level of temporary party organization is the *(p. 835)*
   a) precinct convention.
   b) state convention.
   c) state executive committee.
   d) governor's convention.
   e) civil executive committee.

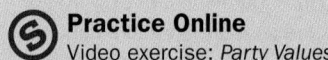 **Practice Online**
Video exercise: *Party Values*

## Texas's History as a One-Party State

■ **Explain what it means to be a "one-party state" (pp. 835–39)**

Texas has traditionally been a one-party state, meaning that one party has been in control of state politics for a lengthy period of time. From the fall of Governor Edmund Davis in the late 1800s, the Democrats held power in the state, but since 1994, the Republicans have won every statewide election and consequently dominate state politics.

### Key Terms

**Shivercrat movement** (p. 836)

**presidential Republicanism** (p. 836)

### Practice Quiz

3. The Shivercrat movement *(p. 836)*
   a) was a group of conservative Democrats in Texas who supported Republicans.
   b) was a group of liberal Democrats who supported equal rights for all Americans.
   c) was a group of conservative Republicans who rejected the Obama administration.
   d) was a movement to form a third political party in the 1950s.
   e) was a movement to elect Democratic presidents but Republican state legislators.

4. In Texas, the Republican Party became the dominant party in the *(p. 838)*
   a) 1960s.
   b) 1970s.
   c) 1980s.
   d) 1990s.
   e) 2000s.

 **Practice Online**
"Exploring Texas Politics" exercise: *Party in Texas*

# Issues in Texas Party Politics

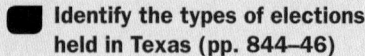 **Analyze why it is difficult to be elected as an independent (pp. 839–44)**

Rarely do candidates run for office as independents. Political parties play a major role in getting elected to office. Texas is a diverse state with divisions between north and south and east and west. Latinos currently make up over 35 percent of the state's population and currently favor the Democratic Party, although their registration and turnout rates are lower than the other major demographic groups.

## Practice Quiz

5. How does an independent candidate get on the ballot? *(p. 840)*
   a) affirm they are not a Republican or Democrat.
   b) win a party primary.
   c) get approval from the Texas Supreme Court.
   d) declare membership in a third party.
   e) obtain signatures from a certain number of registered voters.

6. Which demographic group has the largest percentage share of voters in Texas? *(p. 843)*
   a) white/Anglo.
   b) Asian.
   c) Hispanic.
   d) African American.
   e) Native American.

# Elections in Texas

**Identify the types of elections held in Texas (pp. 844–46)**

Texas allows all registered voters the choice to vote in one party primary during an election season. Should a candidate not receive a majority of votes in a primary, a runoff is held to determine who the party nominee will be. The general election ultimately decides who is elected to office.

## Key Terms

**primary election** (p. 844)

**runoff primary** (p. 844)

**open primary** (p. 844)

**closed primary** (p. 845)

**general election** (p. 845)

**special election** (p. 846)

## Practice Quiz

7. In a primary election, *(p. 844)*
   a) voters choose all local officials who will hold office in the following year.
   b) voters select representatives to the state convention.
   c) voters select party leaders.
   d) voters select a party's candidate for a general election.
   e) voters choose independent candidates for a general election.

8. Which of the following is *not* a type of election found in Texas? *(pp. 844–46)*
   a) general.
   b) primary.
   c) distinguished.
   d) special.
   e) runoff primary.

9. Officially, Texas has a(n) *(p. 845)*
   a) joint primary.
   b) extended primary.
   c) open primary.
   d) closed primary.
   e) early primary.

10. The first Tuesday following the first Monday in November of even-numbered years is the day for which election? *(p. 845)*
    a) primary election
    b) runoff primary
    c) general election
    d) runoff for the general election
    e) special election

# Participation in Texas Election

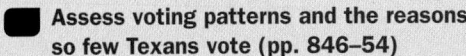 **Assess voting patterns and the reasons so few Texans vote (pp. 846–54)**

Voter participation in Texas elections has expanded over the twentieth century with the expansion of the franchise to women and minorities and the elimination of the poll tax. A variety of factors explain low voter turnout in elections, including low levels of education, low per capita income, and ethnicity. Early voting has become increasingly popular. Turnout is lowest in party primaries, constitutional amendment elections, and then elections when a presidential candidate is not on the ballot. Latinos and those of lower socioeconomic status are also less likely to vote in state elections.

## Key Terms

**poll tax** (p. 848)

**early registration** (p. 848)

**white primary** (p. 849)

**motor voter law** (p. 850)

**early voting** (p. 853)

## Practice Quiz

11. Which of the following is *true*? (p. 848)
    a) Women acquired the right to vote in the original 1876 Texas Constitution.
    b) The poll tax restricted the participation of poor people in the general election.
    c) Texas has the highest voter turnout rate in the country.
    d) You do not have to be a resident of Texas to vote in Texas.
    e) You do not have to be a resident of the county to vote in that county.

12. In which of the following elections is voter turnout the highest? (p. 851)
    a) presidential elections
    b) gubernatorial general elections
    c) off-year congressional elections
    d) special elections
    e) primary elections

13. The two most important factors in determining whether someone will vote are (p. 851)
    a) income and education.
    b) education and family history of voting.
    c) income and gender.
    d) party membership and gender.
    e) age and geographic region.

14. Who has benefited the most from early voting? (p. 853)
    a) Republicans
    b) Democrats
    c) Third-party candidates
    d) All parties have benefited equally.
    e) Independents

# Campaigns

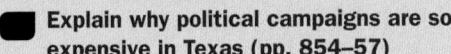 **Explain why political campaigns are so expensive in Texas (pp. 854–57)**

Because of Texas's size, state-wide campaigns can be expensive. There are several major media markets which make television advertising very expensive. Grassroots efforts to mobilize voters are also costly because of the large territory. These means wealthy candidates are often on the ballot.

## Practice Quiz

15. The most costly item for most political campaigns is (p. 856)
    a) travel.
    b) security.
    c) in-person events.
    d) signage.
    e) media.

 **Practice Online**
Interactive simulation: *Being a Campaign Director*

# Recommended Websites

**Libertarian Party of Texas**
www.tx.lp.org

**Republican Party of Texas**
www.texasgop.org

**Texas Democrats**
www.txdemocrats.org

**Texas Secretary of State**
www.sos.state.tx.us/

The highway construction industry had a strong interest in the Trans-Texas Corridor project and attempted to forward that interest through lobbying and campaign contributions. Here, construction company executives appear with Governor Perry and transportation officials after signing a contract related to the proposed project.

# 22

# Interest Groups and Lobbying

**WHAT GOVERNMENT DOES AND WHY IT MATTERS** In 2002, Governor Rick Perry proposed the Trans-Texas Corridor. It was to be the largest privatized tollway in the United States, consisting of 4,000 miles of state roads at a cost of $175 billion. The idea of privatized roads was nothing new. Indiana, for example, has a 157-mile toll road that has been leased to a private entity since 2006, and Chicago has leased its 8-mile Skyway since 2004. It was the massive size of the Trans-Texas Corridor, however, that made Governor Perry's proposal so extraordinary.

In June 2003, Governor Perry signed legislation that authorized the Trans-Texas Corridor and expanded the powers of the Texas Department of Transportation to include road privatization. The creation of such a vast new highway system would be an enormous boon to the highway construction industry. Accordingly, the industry tried to promote its interests in the highway system through campaign contributions to key politicians. Prior to Governor Perry's announcement of his highway plan, three major construction industry companies (Zachry Construction, Pate Engineers, and Othon) had made political contributions totaling $113,280 from 1999 to 2000. In the 2002 election cycle after Governor Perry announced his construction plans, these three companies tripled their contributions. The same occurred with the construction companies Williams Brothers, Ballenger Construction, Parsons Corporation, and Klotz Associates. Contractors were particularly interested in contributing to Lt. Governor David Dewhurst, who possesses significant power in the Texas Senate. Governor Perry also received large contributions, as did state senators who sit on the Senate Transportation Committee. The Trans-Texas Corridor contractors also spent somewhere between $2,770,000 and $6,130,000 (exact amounts are unknown because Texas reporting laws provide for huge ranges in lobbying contracts) on 163 different contracts with lobbyists.

As the size of the project sank into the public consciousness, opposition emerged, most notably from the landowners who became aware of the massive acreage that would be condemned for the Corridor. In 2005 property owners were angered by the U.S. Supreme Court decision in *Kelo v. City of New London*,[1] which upheld the condemnation of private property in order to enhance city revenues. That led to public outcry in Texas (and to a considerable degree nationwide) favoring private property rights over the taking of property for questionable public uses. The public outcry increased when estimates were made that these privatized roads could still cost Texans billions of dollars. Interest group discontent soon spread to the political arena. During the 2006 primary and election seasons, all Governor Perry's opponents came out against the Trans-Texas Corridor, as did both political parties in their official platforms.

Responding to this overwhelming opposition, the Department of Transportation in 2009 decided to abandon the idea of a Trans-Texas Corridor, replacing it with a series of more traditional right-of-way improvements in the state's transportation and utility infrastructure. In 2010 the Federal Highway Administration formally ended the project by issuing a "no action" ruling on the proposal. This had the effect of canceling the agreement between the Texas Department of Transportation and the private construction companies. The final nail in the coffin came at the end of the 2011 legislative session when a bill ending the proposal passed both houses and was signed by the governor. The controversy over the Trans-Texas Corridor continued to haunt Perry throughout the Republican presidential primary debates.

The case of the Trans-Texas Corridor is a classic example of interest group politics where powerful economic and political interests are mobilized both for and against controversial pieces of legislation. We will explore interest group politics in Texas in more detail in this chapter.

## chaptergoals

- **Define interest groups and describe the major ways they try to influence Texas government** (pages 865–72)

- **Describe the role of PACs in Texas elections** (pages 872–76)

- **Explain how ordinary individuals can influence Texas government** (pages 876–77)

# Interest Groups in the Political Process

It is probably true that all of us have political interests, goals, or objectives that can be achieved with governmental intervention. Many of us, however, will never act to achieve those goals. A few of us may speak privately to a legislator or other official. However, some of us will join with others to try to convince the government to help us achieve our interests. When we do that, we have formed an **interest group**.

**interest group** an organization established to influence the government's programs and policies

It has often been claimed that business-oriented interest groups dominate the Texas legislature. Using campaign contributions, political pressure, and sometimes corruption, "The Lobby," as pro-business groups were called, was once purported to run Texas government. Some of the most influential business leaders of the state belonged to the "8F Crowd." 8F was the number on a suite of rooms at the Lamar Hotel in Houston, where George R. Brown held court. Brown was a founder of Brown & Root, one of the world's largest construction firms and until April 2007 part of the even larger Halliburton Company. He met regularly with other fabulously wealthy Texans such as Jesse Jones of Texas Commerce Bank and Tenneco, Gus Wortham of American General Insurance, and James Elkins of the Vinson & Elkins law firm. These men socialized together and worked together to promote their political interests. For 40 years they were considered the kingmakers in Texas politics who determined much of the important policy of state government.[2]

*Lobbying, derided by some as "Austin's oldest profession," is big business in Texas. When the legislature is in session, many lobbyists can be spotted around the capitol waiting to meet with legislators. When the legislature is not in session, lobbyists are often busy with campaign activities.*

The "8F Crowd" was, of course, an interest group—an elite, wealthy, powerful, pro-business interest group. Although the "8F Crowd" is long gone from the Texas political scene, much of what they did is still done in Texas politics by other interest groups, though no modern-day group is ascribed the influence that was allegedly held by the "8F Crowd."

Nevertheless, Texas is known as a state that has long had powerful interest groups. During the Texas Constitutional Convention of 1875, an interest group played an important role. That was the Grange, a powerful farmers' organization, of which many of the framers were members. As Chapter 20 indicated, the Constitution of 1876 reflected many of the values of Grange members. It was a document for rural Texas that was pro–small farmer and opposed to a powerful state government.

With the development of a strong oil and gas industry in Texas in the first half of the twentieth century, the oil industry began playing an important role in state politics. In one-party states, interest groups often become powerful political actors, perhaps because one-party states tend to have a small number of important sectors in their economies and limited economic development. However, as Chapter 21 showed, Texas has in the past 20 years moved from a Democratic one-party system to a competitive two-party system to a Republican-dominated system. And with an expanding Hispanic vote, it may soon become a more competitive two-party system again. It also now has a strong and diversified economy. Yet interest groups maintain great influence.[3]

## Interest Groups and Policy Makers

Interest groups want something from policy makers: they want policy that is beneficial for their groups. On the other hand, policy makers benefit from developing relationships with interest groups. From those groups, the policy maker gains information, since the interest groups can provide substantial expertise in areas that are their special concern. Additionally, interest groups can provide campaign funds to the policy maker. In a state as large as Texas, with numerous media markets and with some party competition, considerable campaign funds are necessary to run and win elections. An interest group can help raise money from its membership for a candidate sympathetic to the interest group's goals. Also, interest groups can supply votes to the policy maker. They can assist in mobilizing their own groups, and they can supply campaign workers to distribute campaign leaflets and to operate phone banks to get out the vote. Interest groups can also publicize issues through press conferences, press releases, publications, conferences, and hearings and even by filing lawsuits. Finally, interest groups can engage in research and education programs. It has become increasingly common for interest groups to engage in public education programs by running advertisements in the Texas media explaining why their particular approaches to a public policy problem would be more beneficial to Texans in general.

Unlike a private citizen interested in and involved in politics, larger or better-funded interest groups have several advantages: (1) time; (2) money; (3) expertise; and (4) continuity.

Although concerned citizens do have an impact on public policy in Texas, organized and well-funded interest groups have an advantage in affecting the policy process. It is difficult for a concerned citizen from Houston to spend time in Austin developing relationships with policy makers and trying to convince those policy makers to support public policies that are compatible with the individual's goals. On the other hand, if that individual joins with like-minded people to create an organized interest group, the group may have a greater likelihood of achieving policy goals. It might be possible to fund an office in Austin with a staff that could monitor events in state government on a daily basis and develop relationships with key policy makers. Additionally, although some individuals in Texas do have the money to provide substantial campaign support to policy makers, even those individuals can get more "bang for the buck" if they join with others in **bundling** their funds into a larger contribution from the interest group. The creation of an organized interest group also allows for the development of a staff. The staff can gain in-depth knowledge of an area of policy far greater than could be gained by most individuals working alone. Also, an individual may be intensely concerned with an issue in one legislative session, but may find it difficult to sustain that interest over a period of many legislative sessions. The larger, better-funded, more successful organized interest groups have continuity. They are in Austin, developing relationships with policy makers and presenting the views of the organization day in and day out, year in and year out. The result is that legislators and other policy makers can develop long-standing relationships with the interest groups and the groups' representatives in Austin.

On September 15, 2010, Governor Perry received a briefing on tort reform at the Austin airport. He then flew to Houston and was taken to the Petroleum Club, where he dined with the tort reform political action committee (PAC) of an interest group, Texans for Lawsuit Reform. He was then driven to Mach Industrial Group in Houston, where he held a press conference about his endorsement by the PAC.[4] It was an important day for Perry—though not surprising—he had gotten the official support of a group described as "arguably the most powerful interest group in Texas politics, in large part because of the massive amounts of money it raises from the state's business community."[5] Texans for Lawsuit Reform helped reshape the Texas Supreme Court into a more pro-business court, and it has reshaped the legislature into a more pro-business body. With Texans for Lawsuit Reform on Perry's side, he had an incredibly powerful and wealthy interest group backing him in the 2010 election. And Texans for Lawsuit Reform knew it could help re-elect a pro-business candidate to the governorship.

## Types of Interest Groups and Lobbyists

Interest groups strive to influence public opinion, to make their views known to policy makers, and to elect and support policy makers who are friendly to their points of view. To accomplish these goals, interest groups usually maintain **lobbyists** in Austin who try to gain access to policy makers and communicate their objectives to them. There are several different types of lobbyists. Some interest groups have full-time staffs in Austin whose members work as lobbyists. One form of interest group is, of course, a corporation, and companies often have government relations departments that lobby for the companies' interests. Lobbyists may be employed by an interest group to deal with one issue, or they may be employed by an interest group on a regular basis. Some lobbyists represent only one client; others will represent large numbers of clients. All lobbyists, however, must be able to reach and communicate with policy makers. Corporate interest groups tend to use either government relations departments or law firms to represent their interests in Austin. Often industries have broad interests that need representation. For example, an insurance company may have one specific interest it wishes to have represented. However, the insurance industry as a whole also has a wide range of issues that need representation, and thus it will form an industry-wide interest group.

**bundling** the interest-group practice of combining campaign contributions from several sources into one larger contribution from the group, so as to increase the group's impact on the candidate

**lobbyist** an individual employed by an interest group who tries to influence governmental decisions on behalf of that group

Some interest groups focus on a single issue, such as abortion. When Texas passed a law requiring women to undergo a sonogram 24 hours before having an abortion, anti-abortion groups applauded the measure, but some women's groups protested against it.

Interest groups may also represent professional groups. One of the most influential professional groups in Austin is the Texas Medical Association, which represents the interests of doctors in state government. Other professional groups represent accountants, chiropractors, opticians, dentists, and teachers.

That teachers are an important interest group suggests still another type of interest group—public-employee interest groups. Public school teachers may be the largest and most effective of these groups, but firefighters, police officers, and even justices of the peace and constables all are represented in Austin.

Some interest groups are formed with a single issue in mind. For example, an interest group may be concerned about the regulation of abortion or school vouchers or tort reform or the environment. Other interest groups are concerned with multiple issues that affect the groups. Public school teachers, for example, are concerned about job security, qualifications of teachers, health insurance, pensions, salaries, and other matters that affect the lives of their members.

Civil rights groups such as the National Association for the Advancement of Colored People, the League of United Latin American Citizens, or the Mexican American Legal Defense Fund are concerned about civil rights issues affecting the lives primarily of African Americans and Latinos. Interestingly, not only do these groups often try to influence public opinion and the legislature, but they have had notable success in representing their groups' interests through litigation, especially in the federal courts.

Other public-interest groups try to promote consumer, environmental, and general public issues. Examples of these groups are Public Citizen, the Sierra Club, and Common Cause. Groups such as the Sierra Club work to promote environmental interests, whereas groups such as Public Citizen and Common Cause tend to have broader interests and work to promote more open government. These groups rarely have much funding, but they often can provide policy makers with information and expertise. In addition, they can mobilize their membership to support or oppose bills, and they can publicize matters that are important to their goals.

## Getting Access to Policy Makers

In order to communicate the goals of their interest groups to policy makers, lobbyists must first gain access to those policy makers. Gaining access to policy makers, of course, imposes on the time of legislators, so lobbyists will often spend significant sums entertaining them. That entertainment is one of the most criticized aspects of lobbying. But from the lobbyists' perspective, entertainment is an important tool for reaching policy makers and putting them in a congenial frame of mind. Entertainment by lobbyists can involve expensive dinners, golfing, and other activities. For example, lobbyists for Texas Utilities (TXU) bought a $300 saddle for one state representative and a $200 bench for another. TXU lobbyists also treated a state senator to a trip to the Masters golf tournament and picked up the dinner tab, as well. One House member received a gun as a gift, another received a jacket, and several got "deer-processing" costs paid for by these lobbyists.[6]

When Representative Lon Burnam proposed legislation to regulate consumer versions of "stun guns," the lobbyist for TASER International as a joke gave Burnam a gift of a pink "stun gun" valued at more than $150. The "stun gun" was, of course, a minor expenditure.[7] Others are much more lavish. When Governor Perry wanted to go to the Rose Bowl game, the trucking lobby picked up the costs of a private jet for $14,580. The former Texas Motor Transportation Association president who arranged the trip said, "Let's face it, if you have a way to help the sitting governor get somewhere he wants to be and to help our industry get where it needs to be, to me it becomes a no-brainer."[8] In the first two months of 2011, lobbyists spent more than $1.2 million, with much of that money going toward events, goods, and gifts for lawmakers and others in state government.[9]

Texas lawmakers receive only $600 per month plus $150 a day when on legislative business, but lawmakers are permitted to use campaign contributions for expenses associated with holding office. This allows interest groups to fund significant lavish benefits for lawmakers. Indeed, about one-third of the spending of North Texas lawmakers—about $3.4 million of roughly $10 million in 2007–09—has gone to fund things other than campaign expenditures. Senator Florence Shapiro, for example, has used her contributions to fund a car lease for a Mercedes Benz and to pay for conference stays at the Ritz-Carlton in Palm Beach, the Venetian in Las Vegas, and the Hay-Adams in Washington, D.C. Thirty-six North Texas lawmakers spent nearly $560,000 on travel and entertainment, $470,000 on Austin living expenses, and $290,000 on food.[10]

Sometimes lobbyists have long-standing personal ties to policy makers, and those bonds can be invaluable to the lobbyists' clients. Access to policy makers may also be gained by building support for an issue among their constituents. Constituents may be encouraged, for example, to write or call legislators about a bill and offer their opinions. Essentially, the interest group tries to mobilize interested voters to get involved in the political process on behalf of the groups' goals.

One important way of gaining access to those in government is to employ former officials as lobbyists. A lobbyist who is a former legislator often has friends in the legislature and can use that friendship to gain access. Additionally, a former legislator often is in an exceptionally good position to understand the personal relationships and informal power centers that must be contacted to accomplish a legislative objective. As a result, some of the best-paid lobbyists in Austin are former Texas state officials and often are former legislators.

In 2010, 65 registered lobbyists were former legislators. What they have in common is knowledge of "how to pass bills, to kill them, whom to talk to, which clerks are friendly, whose birthdays are coming up—all inside stuff that makes the government machine whir."[11] Other especially valuable lobbyists have been former committee clerks for major committees and chiefs of staff of members who were on major committees.[12] Ten recently retired lawmakers were lobbyists in the 2009 legislative session. The 10 had a total of 68 lobbying contracts allowing them to generate between $2,025,000 and $3,890,000 in fees. One gets a sense of the value of these ex-legislators-turned-lobbyists from the explanation Representative Jim Pitts gave for sponsoring an amendment that was pushed by an AT&T lobbyist and former legislator, Pat Heggerty. The amendment would have forced the state to pay for rerouting phone lines for road projects. Said Representative Pitts of the amendment, "I was just trying to help Pat out."[13] The amendment later failed to pass.

It is not only former legislators who can move on to successful lobbying careers. Forty Perry aides either have left the administration to become lobbyists or have joined the administration after having been lobbyists. Some have moved back and forth from administration to lobbying in a revolving door fashion. Five of Perry's closest campaign aides have been lobbyists. Two of his ex-aides are now lobbyists who are also heading pro-Perry PACs.[14]

One former-legislator-turned-lobbyist who reversed course and went back into the legislature is Todd Hunter. Hunter had served in the legislature from 1989 to 1997. An active lobbyist as late as 2007, he was elected to the Texas House in 2008.[15] Jerry Patterson, now Texas land commissioner, was a state senator, became a lobbyist, and was able to move to his current statewide office with little criticism of his role as a lobbyist. However, David Sibley, a state senator who became a lobbyist and then tried to regain his old position, caught tremendous political flak for this decision and, to a considerable degree, lost the Republican primary because of that career choice.[16] The issue of lobbying by former officials and their staffs is a significant one, as there is concern that policy decisions may be made with an eye toward future lucrative lobbying jobs.

Texas has only weak laws dealing with lobbying by former government officials. A former member of the governing body or a former executive head of a regulatory agency cannot lobby the agency for two years after leaving office. Senior employees or former officers of Texas regulatory agencies cannot ever lobby a government entity on matters they were involved in when employed by the government. However, there are no legal restrictions on lobbying by a former governor, former lieutenant governor, former legislator, or any former aides to these officials.[17]

In March 2012 there were 1,377 registered lobbyists in Texas.[18] This is a decrease over the 1,836 registered lobbyists in 2011, probably because more lobbying was needed in 2011 when the legislature was in session compared to 2012 when it was not in session. An analysis that was done of the lobbying reports in 2011 found these lobbyists had 2,908 clients.[19] Because of the loose nature of the Texas reporting laws, it is unclear what these lobbyists were paid, but it was as much as $345 million in 2011.[20] Over the past 10 years, lobbyists in Texas have been paid as much as $2.8 billion. Some Texas lobbyists make enormous sums. Thirty of them reported maximum lobbying incomes of at least $1.5 million.[21]

Once lobbyists obtain access to policy makers, they provide information that may be useful. For example, they may explain how a bill benefits a legislator's district, or how it benefits the state, or how it is perceived as being unfair. Since the staffs of Texas legislators are small, lobbyists perform useful functions by explaining what numerous bills are intended to do. They may even write bills to be introduced by friendly legislators or write amendments to bills. Almost certainly, if a bill affects the interests of a lobbyist's client and reaches a point in the process where hearings are held on the bill, the lobbyist will arrange for testimony to be given at the hearing explaining the interest group's viewpoint on the proposed legislation.

Lobbyists do not limit their activities to the legislative process, of course. Rules proposed by the bureaucracy or the courts can affect the interests of lobbyists' clients. Lobbyists will testify at hearings on rules and try to provide information to administrators in face-to-face meetings as well.

There is always a concern that lobbyists may corrupt policy makers by bribing them in order to accomplish the interest groups' policy objectives. Early in the twentieth century, Sam Rayburn, later a famed U.S. congressman and Speaker of the House, served in the Texas House of Representatives for six years. At that time, he was especially concerned with corruption and refused to accept free meals and entertainment from lobbyists. He called some of his fellow legislators "steak men." By that he meant that the legislators would sell their votes on a bill for a steak dinner at the Driskill Hotel in Austin. "Steak men" (and women) may still exist in Texas politics, but, for the most part, lobbyists provide information, campaign contributions, and political support (or opposition) rather than bribes.

Still, from time to time lobbying does stoop to very low levels. In 1989, "Bo" Pilgrim, a large poultry producer, distributed $10,000 checks to state senators in the capitol while he was lobbying them on workers' compensation reform. Perhaps even more troubling, some senators accepted the checks until media attention forced them to reconsider. Yet this practice of offering $10,000 while asking for a senator to vote on a specific bill was not illegal. A year later, the Speaker of the Texas House of Representatives, "Gib" Lewis, got in trouble for his close relationship with a law firm that specialized in collecting delinquent taxes for local governments. In 1991, Speaker Lewis was indicted for receipt of an illegal gift from the law firm. Ultimately, Lewis plea-bargained and received a minor penalty. The result of these scandals, however, was legislation that created a state ethics commission. The legislation imposed additional lobbying reporting requirements and restrictions on speaking fees that interest groups paid legislators and pleasure trips that lobbyists provided. By no means was the law a major regulation of or restriction on lobbying practices, but it did put some limits on lobbying behavior.

## Who Represents Ordinary Texans?

Another problem with lobbying was well described by the director of a public-interest lobby, Craig McDonald: "Legislators are rubbing shoulders with . . . lobbyists, almost all of whom hustle for business interests. While corporate interests dominate our legislative process, there is virtually no counterbalancing lobby to represent ordinary Texans. Nowhere on the list of Texas' biggest lobby spenders will you find a single group dedicated to the interests of consumers, the environment or human services. No wonder these citizen interests repeatedly get steamrolled in Austin."[22]

Figure 22.1 classifies the interests represented by the registered lobbyists and estimates the value of those lobbying expenditures. The Who Are Texans? box on p. 873 looks at campaign contributions to Texas legislators in 2010. Although the categories in both are very broad, it is clear that business interests dominate in

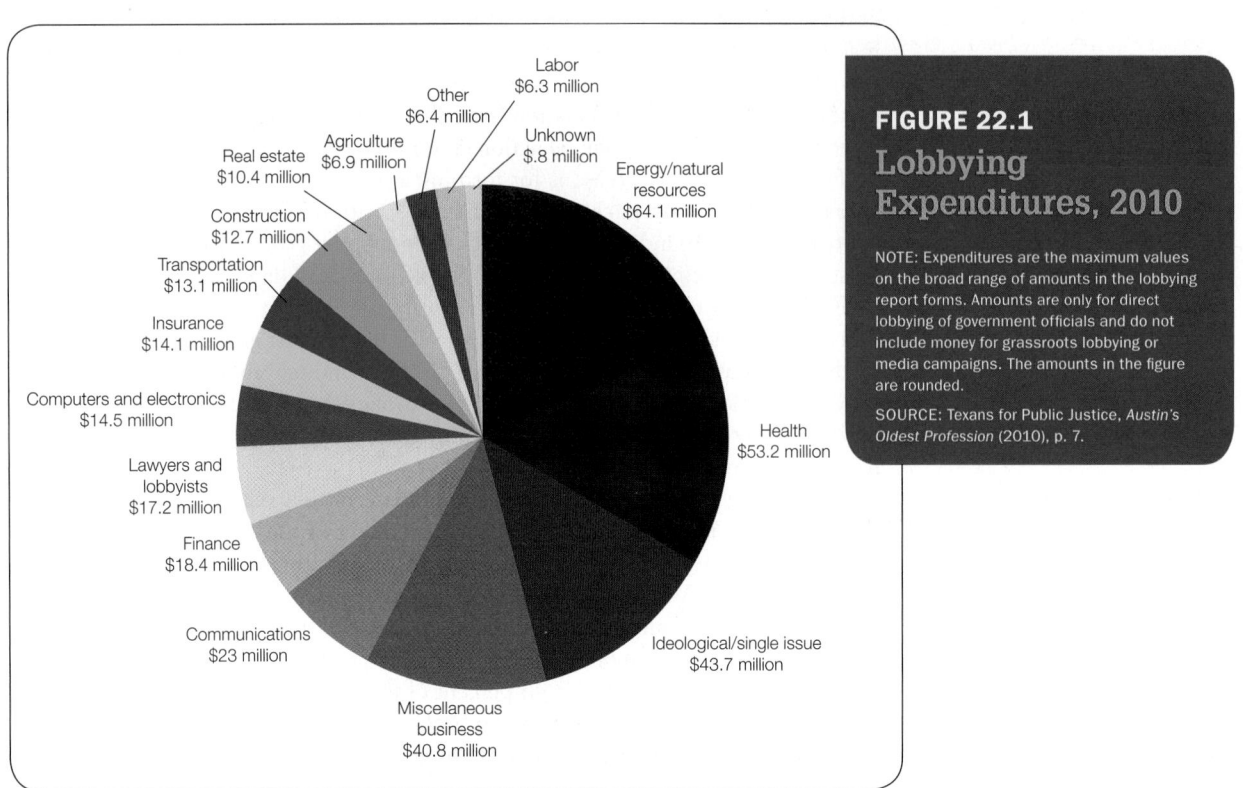

Labor
$6.3 million

Other
$6.4 million

Agriculture
$6.9 million

Real estate
$10.4 million

Unknown
$.8 million

Construction
$12.7 million

Energy/natural
resources
$64.1 million

Transportation
$13.1 million

Insurance
$14.1 million

Computers and electronics
$14.5 million

Lawyers and
lobbyists
$17.2 million

Health
$53.2 million

Finance
$18.4 million

Communications
$23 million

Ideological/single issue
$43.7 million

Miscellaneous
business
$40.8 million

**FIGURE 22.1**

Lobbying
Expenditures, 2010

NOTE: Expenditures are the maximum values on the broad range of amounts in the lobbying report forms. Amounts are only for direct lobbying of government officials and do not include money for grassroots lobbying or media campaigns. The amounts in the figure are rounded.

SOURCE: Texans for Public Justice, *Austin's Oldest Profession* (2010), p. 7.

Texas government. Of course, many issues considered by Texas government may pit one business interest against another, and sometimes a business or professional organization may find itself aligned with consumer interests. For example, the Texas Trial Lawyers Association, an organization of plaintiffs' lawyers in Texas, frequently allies with consumer interests. Many of the clients of these lawyers are consumers who sue large businesses. The interests of these lawyers and their clients are especially close, since the lawyers are paid on a contingent fee basis, which means they don't receive payment unless their clients receive payment. It is also the case that lobbying is not all there is to the representation of interests in Austin. Interest groups without money may still mobilize their members in order to accomplish their objectives, or they may influence public opinion.

Still, there is no question that money does help in politics. Figure 22.1 provides support for concern that in this battle of mostly business interests, there may not be an objective voice, or at the very least a voice, for the public interest that reaches the ears of legislators.

## ● Another Side to Lobbying

> **Describe the role of PACs in Texas elections**

Lobbyists in Texas represent mostly business interests, and they are active in trying to gain access to government officials and inform them of the legislative desires of their clients. But interest groups are not simply information channels between business and government. They also promote the political interests of elected officials who support their viewpoints and oppose the interests of those who do not. One major way that interest groups engage in this activity is by making campaign contributions. Interest groups may encourage individual members to make contributions to candidates, or they may collect funds from their members, bundling those funds as a donation from the interest group. When this is done, the interest group creates a **political action committee (PAC)** to make the contribution.

**political action committee (PAC)** a private group that raises and distributes funds for use in election campaigns

There are numerous reasons for forming a political action committee. A candidate is more likely to notice a substantial contribution from a PAC than many small contributions from individual members of an interest group. Additionally, the lobbyist who delivers a substantial PAC check to a candidate can more likely gain political access than can a lobbyist who simply asks interest group members to mail individual checks. The PAC becomes a way for the interest group to send a message to the candidate that its members care strongly enough about their agenda that they are prepared to back those goals with money. In some cases, a PAC can even serve as an intermediary to provide money to candidates that the PAC's members might not want to support publicly.

**issue advocacy** independent spending by individuals or interest groups on a campaign issue but not directly tied to a particular candidate

PACs may give money directly to the candidate, or they may engage in **issue advocacy** that supports the candidate but is independent of the candidate's control. The candidate does not report these independent expenditures on contribution disclosure statements. PACs may also spend money to support an issue rather than a specific candidate or to support such activities as "get-out-the-vote" campaigns. In 2008, about 55 percent of the money given to Democratic and Republican legislative candidates was given by PACs. About 45 percent of the money was given by individuals.[23]

Campaign contributions can be, to a considerable degree, divided in terms of the economic interests represented by the contributors. The Who Are Texans box

# Who Represents Me?

Interest groups try to achieve favorable policies not only by lobbying members of the Texas legislature directly but also by influencing who becomes members of the legislature in the first place by donating to the election campaigns of favored candidates. The chart below breaks down contributions from employees of different industries by party in 2010.

## Contributions to Texas Legislature Candidates in 2010

 = $100,000

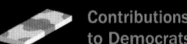 Contributions to Democrats

 Contributions to Republicans

70% (R)
30% (D)

**Finance, insurance, and real estate**
$10,776,573

72.3% (R)
27.7% (D)

**General business**
$10,686,103

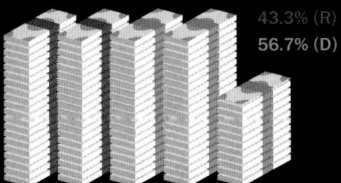

43.3% (R)
56.7% (D)

**Lawyers and lobbyists**
$9,112,629

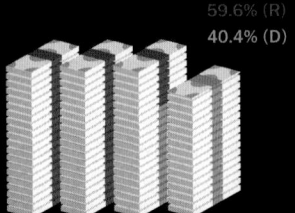

59.6% (R)
40.4% (D)

**Health**
$7,620,831

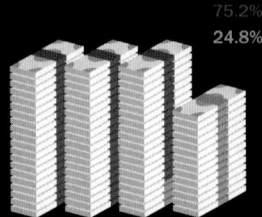

75.2% (R)
24.8% (D)

**Construction**
$7,390,407

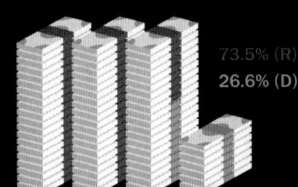

73.5% (R)
26.6% (D)

**Energy and natural resources**
$6,671,325

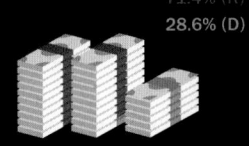

71.4% (R)
28.6% (D)

**Communications and electronics**
$2,503,293

26.1% (R)
73.9% (D)

**Labor**
$2,290,397

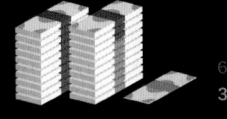

61.7% (R)
38.3% (D)

**Agriculture**
$2,114,058

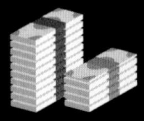

70% (R)
30% (D)

**Transportation**
$1,432,021

69% (R)
31% (D)

**Defense**
$70,947

## for critical analysis

1. What industries tend to donate more to Republicans? Why do you think they do so? What industries tend to donate more to Democrats? Why do you think they do so?

2. Why do interest groups want to donate to candidates before they reach office? What goals are they trying to achieve in doing so?

SOURCE: National Institution on State Money in Politics Industry Influence,
www.followthemoney.org/database/IndustryTotals.phtml?s=TX&y=2010 (accessed 1/3/13).

in this chapter shows that the largest contributor was the finance, insurance, and real estate sector. This sector is a major part of the Texas economy and is subject to significant state regulation. That is also true of general business, energy and natural resources, construction, and health. In contrast to business, political parties, agriculture, and even candidates providing funds to their own campaigns, labor represents a small amount of campaign spending.

## Getting Out the Vote

The Texas Medical Association constructed a grassroots campaign in 1988 to elect its slate of candidates to the Texas Supreme Court. Physicians were encouraged to give to TEXPAC, the medical association PAC. They were also encouraged to make individual contributions to certain candidates. Additionally, physicians were given slate cards with recommended candidates, literature endorsing candidates, and even expensively produced videotapes. They were asked not only to encourage families and friends to vote for the candidates endorsed by the medical association but also to encourage their patients to vote for them. The effort by the medical association was remarkable for its fund-raising success and for its reaching and mobilizing the grass roots.[24] It was probably the most successful get-out-the-vote campaign ever run by an interest group in Texas.

Most efforts by interest groups, however, are far less sophisticated. Generally, interest groups' PACs simply provide resources for the candidates to get out the vote. Unfortunately for the interest groups, sometimes they misjudge the political viability of the candidates they support. Backing an unsuccessful candidate results in a waste of the interest group's funds and the likely alienation of the winning candidate. In the 2010 primary campaign, Texans for Lawsuit Reform, the pro-business and pro–tort reform interest group that has had spectacular successes in forwarding its agenda over the past 15 years, suffered a remarkable failure. Although it had contributed $602,290 to 28 candidates, 53 percent of this money was spent on 4 incumbent candidates who lost their primaries, and another 28 percent of their money was spent on 3 candidates—2 of them incumbents— who were forced into a runoff election. Obviously, Texans for Lawsuit Reform thought these candidates were important for achieving its agenda, but it is questionable how desirable it is for an interest group to pump huge amounts of money into the campaigns of incumbent candidates who do not have the political strength even to win in their own party primary elections. And the high degree of financial support for candidates can be hurtful to the candidate. In one of these races, the winning candidate's main issue was that the defeated incumbent had received money from an organization known for giving huge sums to Republican candidates. This, contended the winner, was proof that the incumbent Democrat was not a real Democrat but a Republican with a Democratic label.[25]

Nevertheless, Texans for Lawsuit Reform scored impressive victories in the 2010 general election. It gave more than $550,000 to Republican Marva Beck to defeat Democratic representative Jim Dunnam and $300,000 to Republican Larry Gonzales to defeat Democrat Diana Maldonado.[26]

## Defeating Opponents

Generally, incumbents have a huge advantage over challengers in an election. Since they are officeholders, they usually have greater name recognition than challengers, and it is easy for incumbents to get publicity by holding town hall meetings, by announcing the relocation of new businesses to the district, or simply by attending community events. Additionally, they usually have an established network of supporters who helped them get into office at least once previously. There are two great exceptions to incumbency advantage: (1) scandal can destroy incumbency advantage, and (2) redistricting can ruin the political base of incumbents.

Except in cases of scandal or redistricting, however, it is far safer for interest groups to try to work with incumbents. Campaign money, for example, overwhelmingly goes to incumbents. In the 2010 campaign for the Texas House of Representatives, as Table 22.1 shows, incumbents raised two and one half times the amount raised by challengers, and in the Texas Senate incumbents raised 15 times the amount raised by challengers. Incumbents win elections to an overwhelming degree.[27]

Of course, sometimes an interest group does not want to help a candidate or even pressure a candidate; it wants to defeat that candidate. This can be a risky strategy because if the candidate wins, then the interest group will be faced with not only an unfriendly public official but also one displeased with the interest group for its opposition. When that happens, the interest group will often "get well" or "get on the late train." This means that the interest group will make a substantial political contribution to the winning candidate whom it formerly opposed. Often, winning candidates have significant campaign debts after a grueling election battle, and they appreciate the late contributions of former enemies, which are offered as a way of making amends.

Although "late-train" contributions may improve the relationship between officials and interest groups, usually candidates reserve a special loyalty for those supporters who backed them early. Without support at the very beginning of a campaign, it is hard for a candidate to build an organization and get the support necessary to make a decent campaign start. That is why early supporters are so valuable. The best lobbyists start early in trying to develop relationships with candidates and with new legislators. One national PAC, EMILY's List (EMILY stands for Early Money Is Like Yeast), is funded by women and provides early campaign contributions to female candidates. Legislators remember who was with them at the beginning of their political careers—and this can be immensely beneficial to the lobby that cultivated that early relationship.[28]

Sometimes PACs give to both candidates as a way to avoid alienating either one, though the possibility remains that such dual giving will wind up alienating both. At other times, interest groups simply don't care if they alienate a candidate. The 2010 Democratic primary election between State Representatives Tara Rios Ybarra and Jose Manuel Lozano highlighted the lines that can clearly separate interest groups during a campaign. Texans for Lawsuit Reform contributed $256,610 to Ybarra, which was 56 percent of her campaign funds. Ybarra lost to Lozano, who was backed by trial lawyers who were not the least bit sympathetic to the goals of Texans for Lawsuit Reform.[29]

An extraordinary battle occurred in the 2012 Republican primary where Texans for Lawsuit Reform backed Railroad Commissioner Elizabeth Ames Jones in her challenge to Republican state senator Jeff Wentworth. Wentworth served nearly five years in the Texas House before being elected to the state senate in 1992. He appeared to be well established and unbeatable. An early poll showed him with a

## TABLE 22.1

### Average Dollars Raised by Incumbents and Challengers for the Texas Legislature, 2010

| OFFICE | INCUMBENTS | CHALLENGERS |
| --- | --- | --- |
| House | $349,233 | $139,862 |
| Senate | $656,908 | $43,687 |

SOURCE: National Institute on Money in State Politics.

*Former governor Ann Richards received support from the PAC EMILY's List early in her career. EMILY's List is a national organization that provides campaign funding to female candidates.*

large lead. But although Wentworth supported 21 of 23 bills considered by Texans for Lawsuit Reform to be "major" legislation, he angered the interest group by criticizing a 2003 constitutional amendment that limited the amounts patients could receive in medical malpractice suits. He also voted against a bill that reduced the amount of money coastal homeowners could receive after hurricanes. While Wentworth was defeated, it was not by Jones, but by Donna Campbell who had Tea Party backing. Nevertheless, Wentworth blamed his defeat on the "mammoth $2 million-plus negative campaign launched against me by Texans for Lawsuit Reform."[30] The defeat no doubt sent a message to Republican lawmakers that they had better not cross Texans for Lawsuit Reform.

When an interest group is convinced that it cannot work with a public official, the interest group may undertake an all-out effort to defeat that official. But spending money by no means guarantees success. Dr. James Leininger is one of the biggest contributors to Republican candidates. In the 2006 election cycle, he gave over $5 million to Republican candidates in Texas, either through individual contributions or by giving to PACs that then made contributions. Leininger and some of the PACs he supports are strong supporters of school vouchers. Much of this money backed challengers to Republican incumbents who were unfavorable to vouchers. The effort was unsuccessful and the result, according to Texans for Public Justice, was a legislature "even less receptive to vouchers than its predecessor."[31]

## ● Individuals as Lobbyists

> **Explain how ordinary individuals can influence Texas government**

Sometimes ordinary individuals can have a remarkable impact on public policy, although interest groups clearly have an advantage in influencing the legislative process. Nevertheless, a persistent individual with a well-reasoned argument can make a difference. For example, Tyrus Burks lost his wife and two children in a late-night electrical fire in West Dallas. Burks did not awaken in time to save them because he is deaf and did not hear the audible smoke alarm. Texas's state property code required the installation of audible smoke alarms but not visual alarms. In 2009, Burks became an advocate for a bill that would require property managers to buy and install visual smoke alarms if hearing-impaired tenants requested them and to put the alarms in visible locations such as bedrooms. Supported by state senator Royce West, the Sephra Burks Law, named for Tyrus's wife, who was also deaf, went into effect at the start of 2010. Tyrus Burks was an active lobbyist for the bill and gave legislative testimony in support of it with the aid of a sign language interpreter.

Burks's efforts benefited from the support of the Texas Apartment Association, a major interest group representing apartment property interests, who backed the bill. Burks's story was tragic and his argument was compelling. It would have been difficult for opposition to emerge against such a proposal. Still, his efforts resulted in a major victory for the deaf, who are protected by such a law requiring visual smoke alarms in only three other states and the District of Columbia.[32] Burks's achievement demonstrates that individuals can, at least sometimes, be successful lobbyists.

*Occasionally, ordinary individuals can have a direct influence on policy. Barbara Brown, of Plano, lobbied local government and the state legislature to get better bicycle safety laws and programs passed. Brown's son was killed in an accident while riding his bicycle.*

## ● Thinking Critically about Interest Groups

Interest groups play an important role in Texas politics even though Texas is no longer a one-party state with limited economic development. Even with two major political parties and a diverse economy, Texas politics cannot be understood without also examining the role of interest groups. Interest groups in Texas have a notable pro-business flavor. Labor is weak in Texas, and its role in the political process is quite limited. Trial lawyers are an especially wealthy and important interest group that promotes liberal policies in Texas, but with the growth of the Republican Party and tort reform interest groups, the influence of the trial lawyers has waned.

Though no single interest group or coalition of interest groups dominates Texas politics, by far most lobbyists represent business interests, and the bulk of PAC money comes from business interests. Often, of course, businesses are pitted against one another in the political process. Also, public interest, civil rights, consumer, and environmental groups may still be successful by mobilizing public opinion and influencing the media. However, there are only a few interest groups that offer alternatives to business perspectives on policy issues. Less frequently, ordinary individuals are able to influence public policy. Although they tend to be at a disadvantage in terms of money and other resources, dedicated individuals with a compelling argument sometimes succeed in lobbying for specific legislation. This is especially true when they are pursuing goals that do not put them in conflict with well-organized and well-funded interest groups.

# study guide

## Interest Groups in the Political Process

■ **Define interest groups and describe the major ways they try to influence Texas government (pp. 865–72)**

Interest groups in Texas are organizations of interested citizens who band together to influence public policy. Lobbyists are hired to cultivate relationships with legislators and convince them of their clients' interests. The goal of lobbyists is to gain access to policy makers to persuade them to support the positions of the interest group.

### Key Terms

**interest group** (p. 865)

**bundling** (p. 867)

**lobbyist** (p. 867)

### Practice Quiz

1. The "8F Crowd" *(p. 865)*
   a) was a group of legislators who failed the eighth grade.
   b) was a group of extremely wealthy Texans who met in Suite 8F of the Lamar Hotel in Houston and controlled Texas politics for more than forty years.
   c) were 25 legislators who boycotted the eighth session of the legislature in order to prevent the legislators from taking any action because it lacked a quorum.
   d) was made up of eight lobbyists who were close friends of the governor.
   e) were the eight most powerful officials in the state who met in Suite F of the Austin State Office Building.

2. Interest groups provide public officials with all the following *except (p. 866)*
   a) information.
   b) money.
   c) media coverage.
   d) votes.
   e) committee assignments.

3. The goals of interest groups include all *except (p. 866–67)*
   a) electing people to office in order who support the groups' goals.
   b) influencing those who control government.
   c) educating the public and members about issues of importance to the group.

   d) providing campaign funds for favored candidates.
   e) maintaining a heterogeneous membership.

4. Interest groups have an advantage over individuals in influencing policy because interest groups usually have *(pp. 866–67)*
   a) more time to influence officials.
   b) greater expertise than individuals.
   c) more money to influence elections.
   d) more staff.
   e) all of the above.

5. The most important thing interest groups need to be effective is *(p. 868)*
   a) the support of a majority of Texans.
   b) office space in Austin.
   c) a variety of issues on which to lobby.
   d) a large, paid staff.
   e) access to politicians.

6. Trial lawyers are which type of interest group? *(p. 868)*
   a) professional group.
   b) public employee group.
   c) single-issue group.
   d) consumer group.
   e) business group.

7. Interest groups often hire former legislators as lobbyists to *(p. 869)*
   a) gain greater access to current legislators.
   b) benefit from the policy expertise of former legislators.
   c) benefit from the personal "insider" knowledge of the former legislator.
   d) all of the above.
   e) none of the above.

8. Lobbying takes place in the *(p. 870)*
   a) legislative branch only.
   b) legislative and executive branches only.
   c) executive and judicial branches.
   d) time immediately before an election.
   e) legislative, executive, and judicial branches.

 **Practice Online**
Interactive Simulation: *Interest Groups and Lobbying*

# Another Side to Lobbying

■ **Describe the role of PACs in Texas elections (pp. 872–76)**

Political action committees are private groups that raise and distribute funds for election campaigns. Interest groups play a major role in getting out the vote. Interest group money can play a major role in defeating as well as electing candidates.

## Key Terms

**political action committee (PAC)** (p. 872)

**issue advocacy** (p. 872)

## Practice Quiz

9. When PACs combine small contributions from many sources to form one large contribution it is called *(p. 872)*
   a) bundling.
   b) compacting.
   c) cracking.
   d) polling.
   e) packing.

10. Lobbyists are *(p. 872)*
    a) all corrupt.
    b) all unethical.
    c) important sources of information for legislators.
    d) harmful to the democratic process.
    e) never retired legislators.

11. In Texas, the most powerful interest groups represent which interests? *(p. 872)*
    a) consumer.
    b) civil rights.
    c) business.

d) owners of oil wells.
e) public employee.

12. PACs are used to *(pp. 872–74)*
    a) stir the public's interest in politics.
    b) raise money from individuals, which is then bundled and given to candidates.
    c) create media campaigns to influence the course of government.
    d) create grass-roots campaigns.
    e) all of the above.

13. One of the most important grassroots tactics of interest groups is *(p. 874)*
    a) gain support from all the mayors of town in a district.
    b) to get out the vote.
    c) to form political alliances with executive and legislative leaders.
    d) to lobby the judicial branch of national and state government.
    e) to interpret the needs of their members.

14. Interest groups have a hard time defeating incumbent legislators unless *(p. 875)*
    a) the legislator is involved in scandal.
    b) the legislator has been redistricted.
    c) the legislator's positions have generated overwhelming opposition in the district.
    d) all of the above.
    e) none of the above.

 **Practice Online**

Video exercise: *PACs and Lobbying Expenditures*

# Individuals as Lobbyists

■ **Explain how ordinary individuals can influence Texas government (pp. 876–77)**

Citizens can lobby their legislators by calling, writing, or visiting their offices. Industries and well-financed interests can afford professional lobbyists to try to influence legislation, but legislators will listen to individual citizens, especially if they join together in large numbers.

## Practice Quiz

15. Individuals have the best chance to influence public policy when they *(p. 876)*
    a) are not opposed by organized interest groups.
    b) are polite.
    c) entertain legislators.
    d) vote.
    e) live in Austin.

# Recommended Websites

**Texans for Public Justice**
www.tpj.org

**Texas Ethics Commission**
www.ethics.state.tx.us/

**Texas Medical Association**
www.texmed.org

**Texas Trial Lawyers Association**
www.ttla.com/TX/

**TEXPAC**
www.texpac.org

**Texans for Lawsuit Reform**
www.tortreform.com/

Like the U.S. Congress, the Texas Legislature is bicameral, with two chambers: a house of representatives and a senate. Here, members of the Texas House of Representatives take a break during the 2011 session.

# 23

# The Texas Legislature

**WHAT GOVERNMENT DOES AND WHY IT MATTERS** The Speaker is the most powerful member of the Texas House of Representatives. One might expect that the Speaker would be selected by a simple vote of the majority party in caucus as in the U.S. House of Representatives. In recent years, however, a different dynamic has led to the election of the Speaker, one that reflects the tensions that have broken out between moderates and conservatives in the majority Republican Party. The story of the speakership is also the story of the shifting sands of political life in Texas.

Following the 2002 election, Republicans seized control of the House for the first time in over 100 years with an 88-to-62 majority. They elected Tom Craddick, a conservative businessman from Midland, to lead them. A Republican stalwart since 1968 when he was first elected to the Texas House, Craddick had long promoted a partisan agenda. Assuming power in the midst of a fiscal crisis that gripped the state, Craddick began pushing a conservative Republican agenda that included lawsuit limitations, private school vouchers, pro-business legislation, and congressional redistricting. By the end of the term, bad blood had spilled across party lines as 50 Democratic members of the House fled the state for Oklahoma, seeking to deny the Speaker a quorum.

In 2008 the bad blood in the House spilled over into the Republican Party as a bitter fight broke out between the conservative Speaker and disgruntled moderate Republicans. Failing to defeat Craddick's re-election to a third term as Speaker at the beginning of the session, opponents tried to remove him from office at the end of the session by a motion on the House floor. Although this effort failed, a group of 11 moderate Republicans let it be known after the 2008 elections that they would not support the conservative Craddick for another term as Speaker. By January 2009, a makeshift coalition of 72 Democrats and disgruntled Republicans had come out in support of Representative Joe Straus, a moderate Republican from San Antonio, to replace Craddick as Speaker. Socially conservative Republicans tried to mobilize against Straus's candidacy, but their efforts failed as the coalition of Democrats and insurgent Republicans held fast, ushering in a new period of moderate Republican leadership in the House. The price that Democrats in the House extracted from Straus was steep: 16 chairmanships went to Democrats and 18 to Republicans, many of a moderate ideological stamp.

This alignment of political forces was only temporary as the 2010 election pushed the legislature back toward the right. The Republican majority increased as the party took control of 99 of the 150 seats in the House. Soon after the election, two Democratic members switched to the Republican Party, creating a supermajority for the Republicans. Another member switched in early 2012, bringing the Republican supermajority to 102. That Republican majority, however, dropped to 95 after the 2012 election. The 2011 session of the state legislature was dominated by conservative policies on issues such as spending cuts, immigration, abortion, and gay marriage. Speaker Joe Straus, facing conservative opposition in the aftermath of the 2010 election, had the votes necessary for re-election as Speaker. But throughout the session he was forced to move in a more conservative direction, abandoning many issues that concerned Democrats who supported him in his rise to the Speakership. One problem that he will face in the 2013 legislative session will be the loss of major leaders from both parties with whom he worked. This included the loss to retirement of such experienced and respected legislators as State Representatives Jerry Madden, Scott Hochberg, Pete Gallego, Will Harnett, and Burt Solomon. Straus may remain Speaker after the 2012 election cycle. But the political interests he will serve will likely be much more conservative than the moderate interests that initially put him into office.[1]

## chaptergoals

- Describe the bicameral organization of the legislature and the rules for membership (pages 883–87)

- Explain when the legislature meets (pages 887–88)

- Outline the legislative and nonlegislative powers of the legislature (pages 888–90)

- Trace the process through which law is made in Texas (pages 890–97)

- Describe the roles of other state officials in shaping legislation (pages 897–98)

- Analyze how party leadership and redistricting affect power in the legislature (pages 899–906)

# ● Structure of the Texas Legislature

**Describe the bicameral organization of the legislature and the rules for membership**

The Texas state legislature is the most important representative institution in the state. Members share many of the duties and responsibilities that are taken up at the national level by members of the U.S. Congress. Like members of the U.S. Congress, the members of the Texas House and Senate are responsible for bringing the interests and concerns of their constituencies directly into the democratic political processes. But the important constitutional and institutional differences between the U.S. Congress and the Texas state legislature must be taken into account if we are to understand the role that the state legislature plays in democracy in Texas.

**bicameral** having a legislative assembly composed of two chambers or houses

## Bicameralism

Like the U.S. Congress and all the states except Nebraska, Texas has a **bicameral** legislature, with two chambers: the Texas House of Representatives and the Texas Senate. Its 150 House members and 31 senators meet in regular session for 140 days every odd-numbered year. Senators serve four-year terms and House members serve for two years. Each represents a single-member district. Members of the Texas House represent approximately 168,000 people. Senators represent over 811,000 constituents. A state senator now represents more people than does a member of the U.S. House of Representatives. Elections are held in November of even-numbered years, and senators and House members take office in January of odd-numbered years.

Bicameralism creates interesting dynamics in a legislature. For one thing, it means that before a law is passed, it will be voted on by two deliberative bodies representing different constituencies. In 2009, for example, the Texas Senate passed legislation to allow college students and faculty with concealed handgun licenses to carry their firearms on campus. That legislation, however, was killed in the Texas House of Representatives.[2] In 2011, the Texas Senate again passed a bill with an amendment allowing guns on campus, and in the Texas House, the bill had support from a majority of members. However, the bill failed in the House because of a successful parliamentary objection that the gun amendment was not germane to the bill it amended, which dealt with scholarships.[3] If a bill cannot be killed in one house, it can be killed or modified in the other body.

One effect of bicameralism in Texas is that the author of a bill in one house whose bill has been amended in the other body has the option of accepting or rejecting the amendment. If the author accepts the amendment, the bill moves forward; if the author rejects the amendment, the bill is killed.

*Before becoming law in Texas, a bill must pass in both houses of the legislature. In 2009 and 2011, the Texas Senate passed bills to allow concealed firearms on college campuses, but the bill did not pass in the Texas House and thus failed to become law.*

Bicameralism allows a member of one legislative body can retaliate against a member of either body for not cooperating on desired legislation. A "local and consent" calendar in the House is usually reserved for uncontroversial bills or bills limited to a localized problem. In order for a bill to be passed from that calendar, it has to pass without the objection of any member of the House. That requirement provides a perfect opportunity for members to retaliate against other members for perceived slights.[4]

## Membership

The constitutional requirements for becoming a member of the Texas Legislature are minimal. A senator must be a U.S. citizen, a qualified voter, and a resident of the state for at least five years and of the district for at least one year. Additionally, the senator must be at least 26 years of age. Members of the House must be at least 21, U.S. citizens, qualified voters, and residents of the state for two years and of the district for one year. These requirements are in keeping with the political philosophy of those who wrote the Constitution of 1876. They believed holding public office required little or no formal training and should be open to most citizens.

In Texas, the typical legislator is white, male, Protestant, college educated, and affluent, and has a professional or business occupation. These characteristics do not mean that a poor high school dropout who is a day laborer cannot be elected to the state legislature, but they do indicate that individuals with most of these informal characteristics have a distinct advantage. Members of the legislature must have jobs that allow them the flexibility to campaign for office and to work in the legislature for 140 days every other year, as well as in special legislative sessions and meetings of committees when the legislature is not in session. Thus, about one-third of the members of the legislature are attorneys. The legal profession is one of the few careers that pays well and offers the necessary degree of time flexibility a legislator needs. Lawyers who serve in the legislature may even gain increased legal business either from interests with legislative concerns or because of the enhanced visibility of a lawyer-legislator.[5]

*Although the "typical" member of the Texas state legislature is white and male, women and minority groups have increased their representation in recent years. For example, state Senator Leticia Van de Putte has become a prominent figure in Texas politics.*

# Who Are the Members of the Texas Legislature?

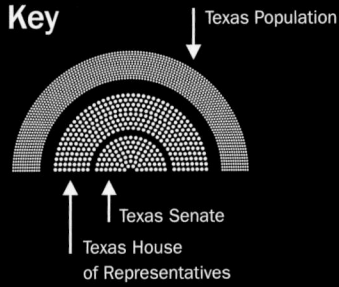

Texas Population
Texas Senate
Texas House
of Representatives

The Texas legislature is designed to be a representative body, which looks and sounds like the state as a whole. How well does the legislature represent Texas? In many ways, the legislature does not look like Texas. The data to the left are for the Texas legislature in 2011–12. The state is evenly split between men and women, while the legislature is four-fifths male. While the state has no ethnic majority in its population, more than two-thirds of Texas legislators are white. Perhaps the biggest differences, though, relate to socioeconomic status. Over half of the members of the legislature hold graduate degrees, while only 9 percent of the population does.

## Gender

| | Texas Pop. | Texas House | Texas Senate |
|---|---|---|---|
| Female | 50% | 21% | 19% |
| Male | 50% | 79% | 81% |

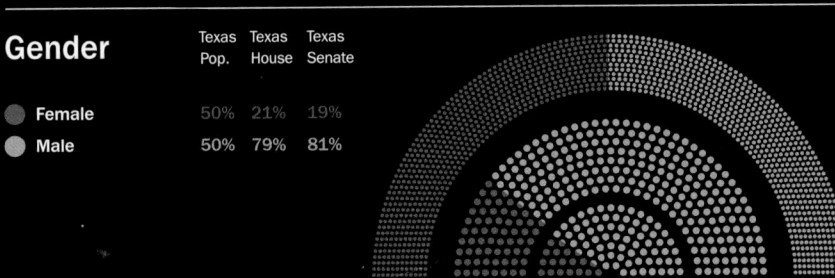

## Race

| | Texas Pop. | Texas House | Texas Senate |
|---|---|---|---|
| White | 45% | 68% | 71% |
| Black | 12% | 11% | 7% |
| Hispanic | 38% | 20% | 23% |
| Asian | 4% | 1% | 0 |

## Education

| | Texas Pop. | Texas House | Texas Senate |
|---|---|---|---|
| < HS diploma | 20% | 0 | 0 |
| High school grad. | 48% | 9% | 7% |
| Associate's degree | 6% | 2% | 0 |
| Bachelor's degree | 17% | 41% | 39% |
| Graduate degree | 9% | 51% | 55% |

## Occupation

- Business
- Attorney
- Community service
- Health care
- Education
- Other

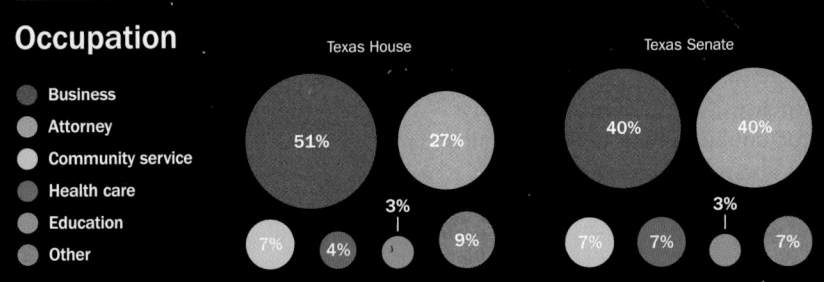

Texas House

51%   27%
7%  4%   3%   9%

Texas Senate

40%   40%
7%   7%   3%   7%

## for critical analysis

1. How much do you think the racial, gender, and socio-economic makeup of the Texas legislature matter to the type of laws that the legislature passes? If the legislature had more people of color, more women, or more middle class members, would it pass different policies?

2. Why do you think that members of the Texas legislature come from the more educated, higher socioeconomic groups? Does the structure of the Texas legislature encourage or discourage people from particular occupations to run?

SOURCES: For Texas House, numbers calculated by author based on data from the Directory of Elected Officials of the Texas Tribune: www.texastribune.org/directory/. State demographic data calculated from the US Census Bureau American Community Survey, www.census.gov.

## TABLE 23.1

### Gender and Minority Membership in the Texas Legislature

| | % OF TEXAS POPULATION | % OF 2011 TEXAS HOUSE MEMBERSHIP | % OF 2011 TEXAS SENATE MEMBERSHIP |
|---|---|---|---|
| Men | 50% | 78% | 81% |
| Women | 50 | 21 | 19 |
| African American | 12 | 11 | 6 |
| Anglo | 47 | 61 | 71 |
| Hispanic | 38 | 27 | 23 |
| Asian | 4 | 1 | 0 |

SOURCES: *Texas State Directory*; Texas House Legislative Black Caucus; National Association of Latino Elected and Appointed Officials. State demographic data calculated from the 2010 Census.

Legislators in Texas cannot expect to live on their legislative salaries. In keeping with the Texas constitutional tradition of a low-cost, part-time legislature, Texas representatives receive a salary of only $7,200 a year. Legislators also receive a payment of $150 a day when the legislature is in session. When the legislature is not in session, legislators may claim up to 12 days per month of **per diem** pay if they are in Austin on official business, or 16 days if they are committee chairs. The legislators themselves determine what qualifies as official business. It is common to pay expenses from officeholder expense accounts and to pocket the per diem so that it becomes a salary supplement. Legislative retirement pensions are very generous. The pension is tied to district judges' salaries, which are $125,000 a year. That salary is multiplied by the years of service of the legislator times 2.3 percent That amount would be the lawmaker's pension as long as the lawmaker served at least eight years. With 8 years of service, the lawmaker can start collecting a pension at age 60. With 10 years of service, a lawmaker can start collecting at age 50.[6]

Originally, per diem rates were set by the Texas Constitution, and a constitutional amendment was necessary to change this. In 1991, Texans adopted an amendment allowing the Texas Ethics Commission to propose changes in legislative salaries, which then require voter approval. To date, the commission has not recommended a salary increase. At the start of each regular session, the Ethics Commission sets the legislative per diem. In the 2011 session, with major belt-tightening throughout state government, the legislature asked the Texas Ethics Commission to reduce their scheduled per diem of $168 a day to $150.[7] One Texas legislator found a way to increase his income by billing both the state and his campaign funds for his travel expenses. Representative Joe Driver of Garland pled guilty to a third-degree felony for double billing thousands of dollars in expenses. His conviction raises questions about how closely legislators' expenses are monitored.[8]

Table 23.1 shows the proportions of minorities and women serving in the legislature. Although those numbers have increased over the years, they are not in proportion to their strength in the population of Texas. Civil rights laws have increased voting by minorities, and those laws provide protection for minority political districts. Thus, more minority officeholders have been elected and, as the Hispanic

**per diem** daily payment to a public official engaged in state business

population in Texas increases, additional Latino legislators will be elected. Women have also had an increased role in politics, especially since the 1970s, and as a result, it is likely that additional women will be elected to legislative office.

# ● Sessions of the Legislature

**Explain when the legislature meets**

Not all state legislatures meet for the same time periods. Some state legislatures meet every year like the U.S. Congress. Texas's legislature generally meets every other year unless they are called by the governor to meet between regular meetings.

**regular session** the 140-day period during which the Texas Legislature meets to consider and pass bills; occurs only in odd-numbered years

**biennial** occurring every two years

## Regular Sessions ●

The Texas Constitution specifies that **regular sessions** of the Texas Legislature be held for 140 days in odd-numbered years. The **biennial** legislative sessions have their origin in the nineteenth-century idea that legislative service is a part-time job and a belief that short, biennial sessions would limit the power of the legislature. For a few years, legislators were encouraged to end their work early by being paid for only 120 days of service.

Thousands of bills and resolutions are introduced into the legislature during a regular session, and the 140-day limitation places a considerable restriction on the legislature's ability to deal with this workload. Hundreds of bills pass in the last hours of a legislative session, most with little or no debate. More die in the end-of-session crush of business because there isn't time to consider them.

**for critical analysis**

Texas is the second largest state and the second most populous state. Can a legislature that meets only 140 days every other year meet the needs of this modern, urban state? Will changes in the economy make a full-time legislature necessary?

## Special Sessions

If the legislature does not complete its agenda before the end of the legislative session or if problems arise between regular sessions, the governor may call a **special session**. Special sessions last no more than 30 days, but there is no limit to the number of special sessions a governor can call and the governor sets their agenda. Texas has averaged one special session a year since 1876, although years may go by with no special session, whereas in some years there may be three or four sessions.

The ability to call and set the agenda of a special session provides the governor with control over which issues are discussed and what bills are passed. In many instances, the governor, the Speaker of the Texas House, the lieutenant governor, and various committee chairs will meet to decide what will be done to solve the problem at hand. Once the leaders address the issue and develop solutions, the governor calls the special session.

Once the session begins, the governor can open it to different issues. At times, the governor bargains for a legislator's vote in return for adding to the special session agenda an issue of importance to that legislator. In 2003, Governor Perry called three special sessions of the legislature to address congressional redistricting. In 2004, a fourth special session was called to address school finance. In 2005, in addition to the regular session, two special sessions addressed school finance. There was also a special session in 2006, 2009, and 2011.

Between legislative sessions, members serve on interim committees that may require a few days of their time each month. Legislators are also frequently called on to present programs to schools, colleges, and civic clubs. They supervise the staff

**special session** a legislative session called by the governor that addresses an agenda set by him or her and that lasts no longer than thirty days

of their district offices and address the needs of their constituents. Special sessions, interim committee meetings, speeches, and constituent services require long hours, with little remuneration. Many members devote more than 40 hours a week to legislative business in addition to maintaining their full-time jobs.

When Texas was a rural, predominantly agricultural state, biennial sessions worked well; however, Texas has moved beyond this description. In the twenty-first century, Texas is a modern state with more than 80 percent of its population living in metropolitan areas. Population growth continues at a rapid rate. Texas is home to many high-tech and biotech corporations. It is a center for medical research, and hosts the headquarters for NASA and the Lyndon Johnson Space Center. The state's gross domestic product exceeds that of many nations. Part-time legislators serving biennial 140-day sessions may not work well anymore in allowing the state to respond quickly and effectively to problems that arise.

# ● Powers of the Legislature

**Outline the legislative and nonlegislative powers of the legislature**

The Texas Legislature sets public policy by passing bills and resolutions, but it also supervises the state bureaucracy through the budgetary process and the Sunset Act, an act that provides for the review and, when deemed appropriate, the termination of state agencies. This supervision is achieved using legislative and nonlegislative powers. Legislative powers consist of passing bills and resolutions. Nonlegislative powers are those functions falling outside the lawmaking function.

## Legislative Powers

**bill** a proposed law that has been sponsored by a member of the legislature and submitted to the clerk of the House or Senate

**local bill** a bill affecting only units of local government, such as a city, county, or special district

**special bill** a bill that gives an individual or corporation a special exemption from state law

**general bill** a bill that applies to all people and/or property in the state

**resolution** an expression of opinion on an issue by a legislative body

**concurrent resolution** a resolution of interest to both chambers of the legislature and which must pass both the House and Senate and generally be signed by the governor

**Bills**   Revenue bills must begin in the House of Representatives. All other bills may start in either the House or the Senate. For decades, a **bill** would be introduced in either the House or the Senate and work its way through the legislative process in that chamber. A bill introduced in the Senate would be passed by the Senate prior to going to the House. Today, it is customary for a bill to be introduced into the House and the same bill, a companion bill, to be introduced into the Senate at the same time. This simultaneous consideration of bills saves time in the legislature.

There are three classifications of bills in the Texas Legislature: (1) local bills, (2) special bills, and (3) general bills. **Local bills** affect only units of local government such as a city, a county, special districts, or more than one city in a county. A local bill, for example, might allow a county to create a sports authority or to establish a community college. **Special bills** give individuals or corporations an exemption from state law. A special bill could grant compensation to an individual wrongly convicted and sentenced to prison. **General bills** apply to all people and/or property in the state. General bills define criminal behavior; establish standards for divorce, child custody, or bankruptcy; and address other matters affecting people and property throughout the state.

**Resolutions**   There are three types of **resolutions** in the Texas Legislature: (1) concurrent resolutions, (2) joint resolutions, and (3) simple resolutions. **Concurrent resolutions** must pass both the House and Senate, and except for resolutions setting the time of adjournment, they require the governor's signature. These resolutions involve issues of interest to both chambers. They may request information from a state agency or call on Congress for some action. Senate Concurrent Resolution 6 might, for example, call on Congress to propose an amendment requiring a balanced federal budget.

**Joint resolutions** require passage in both the House and Senate but do not require the governor's signature. The most common use of joint resolutions is to propose amendments to the Texas Constitution or to ratify amendments to the U.S. Constitution. Resolutions that propose amendments to the Texas Constitution require a two-thirds vote of the membership of both houses of the state legislature. Ratification of amendments to the U.S. Constitution requires a majority vote in both the Texas House and Senate.

**Simple resolutions** concern only the Texas House or the Senate, and they do not require the governor's signature. They are used to adopt rules, to request opinions from the attorney general, to appoint employees to office in the House or Senate, or to honor outstanding achievements by Texas residents. For example, SR 27 could recognize the achievements of a Nobel Prize winner or the San Jacinto College baseball program for accomplishments in the National Junior College Athletic Association.

Resolutions of honor or recognition are acted on without debate and without requiring members to read the resolution. Resolutions are mostly symbolic acts that are designed to promote goodwill with voters. However, at times these simple symbolic acts can go terribly wrong. A Fort Worth doctor was twice honored by the Texas House of Representatives as the "doctor of the day." It was then, to the embarrassment of the House and the legislators who introduced him to the House, reported that the doctor was a registered sex offender who had been convicted of having a sexual relationship with a seventeen-year-old female patient.[9]

**joint resolution** a resolution, commonly a proposed amendment to the Texas Constitution or ratification of an amendment to the U.S. Constitution, that must pass both the House and Senate but which does not require the governor's signature

**simple resolution** a resolution that concerns only the Texas House or Senate, such as the adoption of a rule or the appointment of an employee, and which does not require the governor's signature

## Nonlegislative Powers

Nonlegislative powers include the power to serve constituents, electoral powers, investigative powers, directive and supervisory powers, and judicial powers. The functions of these powers fall outside the scope of passing bills and resolutions; however, the passage of legislation may be necessary to exercise these powers.

Legislators have the power to get things done for or in the name of **constituents**. Efforts on behalf of constituents may involve legislative activity, such as introducing a bill or voting on a resolution. Often, however, working on behalf of constituents involves nonlegislative activity, such as arranging an appointment for a constituent with a government agency that regulates some aspect of the constituent's life, writing a letter of recommendation for a constituent, or giving a speech to a civic group in the legislator's district.

**Electoral powers** of the legislature consist of formally counting returns in the elections for governor and lieutenant governor. This is accomplished during a joint session of the legislature when it is organized for the regular session.

**Investigative powers** can be exercised by the House of Representatives, by the Senate, or jointly by both bodies. The legislature can undertake to investigate problems facing the state, the integrity of a state agency, or almost anything else it wishes. A special investigative committee is established by a simple resolution creating the committee, establishing the jurisdiction of the committee, and explaining the need for the investigation. If the special committee is formed in the House, the Speaker appoints the members of the committee. The lieutenant governor appoints members for special committees in the Senate. The Speaker and the lieutenant governor share appointments if it is a joint investigation.

**constituent** a person living in the district from which an official is elected

**electoral power** the legislature's mandated role in counting returns in the elections for governor and lieutenant governor

**investigative power** the power, exercised by the House, the Senate, or both chambers jointly, to investigate problems facing the state

**directive and supervisory power** the legislature's power over the executive branch; for example, the legislature determines the size of appropriations for state agencies

**judicial power** the power of the House to impeach and of the Senate to convict members of the executive and judicial branches of state government

**impeachment** according to the Texas Constitution, the formal charge by the House of Representatives that leads to a trial in the Senate and possibly to the removal of a state official

**Directive and supervisory powers** enable the legislature to have considerable control over the executive branch of government. The legislature determines the size of the appropriation each agency has to spend for the next two years. The amount of money an agency has determines how well it can carry out its goals and objectives. A review of each agency of state government takes place every 12 years.

**Judicial powers** include the ability of the House to impeach members of the executive and judicial branches of state government. On **impeachment**, a trial takes place in the Senate. A majority vote of the House is required to bring charges, and a two-thirds vote of senators attending is necessary to convict an individual of the impeachment charges. Unlike the U.S. Constitution, the Texas Constitution does not explicitly define what constitutes an impeachable offense. This will be determined by the House and Senate in the impeachment process itself.[10]

Each body can compel attendance at regular and special sessions. More than once, Texas Rangers have handcuffed absent members and brought them to the legislature. On rare occasions, a chamber will punish nonmembers who disrupt proceedings by imprisoning them for up to 48 hours. The House and Senate judge the qualifications of members and can expel a member for cause.

**introduction** the first step in the legislative process, during which a member of the legislature gets an idea for a bill and files a copy of it with the clerk of the House or secretary of the Senate

**referral** the second step in the legislative process, during which a bill is assigned to the appropriate standing committee by the Speaker (for House bills) or the lieutenant governor (for Senate bills)

**consideration by standing committee** the third step in the legislative process, during which a bill is killed, amended, or heard by a standing committee

**floor action** the fourth step in the legislative process, during which a bill referred by a standing committee is scheduled for floor debate by the Calendars Committee

**conference committee** a joint committee created to work out a compromise on House and Senate versions of a piece of legislation

**action by the governor** the final step in the legislative process, during which the governor signs, vetoes, or refuses to sign a bill

# How a Bill Becomes a Law in Texas

> **Trace the process through which law is made in Texas**

Anyone can write a bill, but only members of the legislature can introduce a bill. Bills may be written by members of the executive branch, by lobbyists, by constituents, or by local governmental entities. Legislators may also write bills, often with the help of a legislative staff expert in drafting legislation. There are, of course, innumerable reasons for drafting and introducing a bill.

Revenue bills must start in the House of Representatives. Other bills can start in either the House or Senate. During the 82nd Legislature regular session that met in 2011, a total of 5,796 bills were introduced in the legislature. Of those bills, 1,379 passed the legislature, and the governor vetoed 25 of them.[11]

Figure 23.1 shows the flow of a bill from the time it is introduced in the Texas House of Representatives to final passage and submission to the governor. A bill introduced in the Senate would follow the same procedure in reverse. Examining this figure suggests that the process of how a bill becomes law is long, detailed, and cumbersome. However, when the process is distilled to its basic parts, there are only six steps in how a bill becomes law. For a bill that starts in the House these steps are (1) **introduction**, (2) **referral**, (3) **consideration by standing committee**, and (4) **floor action**. Steps (1) through (4) are repeated in the Senate. Step (5) is action by a **conference committee** and approval by both houses, and finally, (6) is **action by the governor**.

## Introduction in the House

A legislator introduces a bill by placing copies of the bill with the clerk of the House. In the Senate, the secretary of the Senate receives the bill. The clerk or secretary numbers the bill and enrolls it by recording its number, title, caption, and sponsor in a ledger. Similar information is entered into a computer.

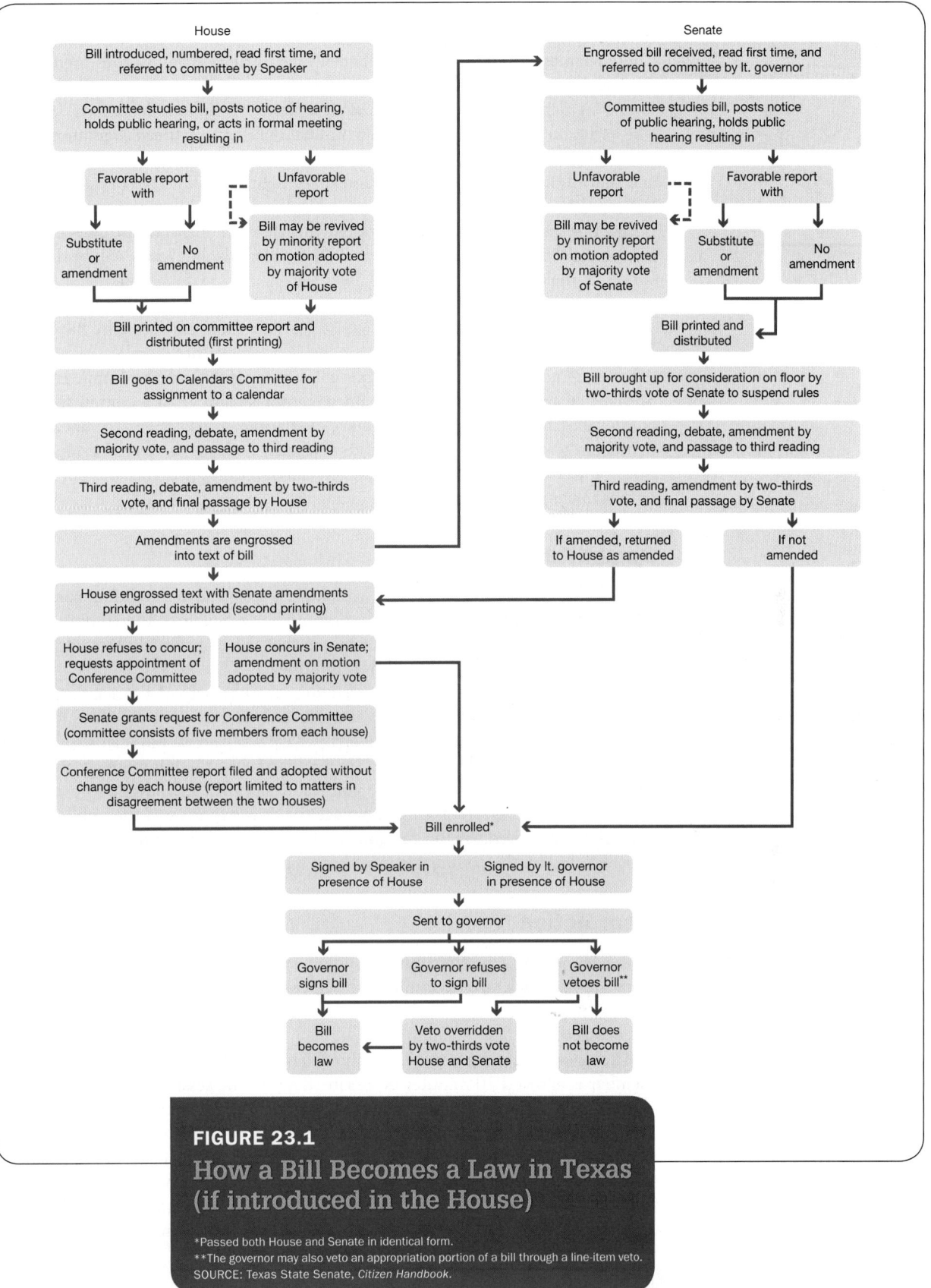

House

Bill introduced, numbered, read first time, and referred to committee by Speaker

↓

Committee studies bill, posts notice of hearing, holds public hearing, or acts in formal meeting resulting in

↓                                    ↓

Favorable report with          Unfavorable report

↓          ↓          ⌐ - - →  Bill may be revived by minority report on motion adopted by majority vote of House

Substitute or amendment      No amendment

↓          ↓

Bill printed on committee report and distributed (first printing)

↓

Bill goes to Calendars Committee for assignment to a calendar

↓

Second reading, debate, amendment by majority vote, and passage to third reading

↓

Third reading, debate, amendment by two-thirds vote, and final passage by House

↓

Amendments are engrossed into text of bill

↓

House engrossed text with Senate amendments printed and distributed (second printing)

↓                                    ↓

House refuses to concur; requests appointment of Conference Committee          House concurs in Senate; amendment on motion adopted by majority vote

↓

Senate grants request for Conference Committee (committee consists of five members from each house)

↓

Conference Committee report filed and adopted without change by each house (report limited to matters in disagreement between the two houses)

Senate

Engrossed bill received, read first time, and referred to committee by lt. governor

↓

Committee studies bill, posts notice of public hearing, holds public hearing resulting in

↓                                    ↓

Unfavorable report          Favorable report with

Bill may be revived by minority report on motion adopted by majority vote of Senate          Substitute or amendment      No amendment

↓

Bill printed and distributed

↓

Bill brought up for consideration on floor by two-thirds vote of Senate to suspend rules

↓

Second reading, debate, amendment by majority vote, and passage to third reading

↓

Third reading, amendment by two-thirds vote, and final passage by Senate

↓                                    ↓

If amended, returned to House as amended          If not amended

Bill enrolled*

↓

Signed by Speaker in presence of House          Signed by lt. governor in presence of House

↓

Sent to governor

↓                    ↓                    ↓

Governor signs bill      Governor refuses to sign bill      Governor vetoes bill**

↓                    ↓                    ↓

Bill becomes law      Veto overridden by two-thirds vote House and Senate      Bill does not become law

**FIGURE 23.1**

## How a Bill Becomes a Law in Texas (if introduced in the House)

*Passed both House and Senate in identical form.
**The governor may also veto an appropriation portion of a bill through a line-item veto.
SOURCE: Texas State Senate, *Citizen Handbook*.

Rules of the legislature require that the bill be read on three separate occasions. After enrollment, the bill is read for the first time by its number, title, and caption. There is great variation in the number of bills introduced by various members of the legislature. Senator John Whitmire of Houston, for example, introduced 5 bills in one legislative session; Senator Eliot Shapleigh of El Paso filed nearly 100 bills. The variation is related, in part, to the political philosophy of the legislators. Whitmire, for example, believes his constituents think there are already too many laws and that his job is to look at legislation that ought to be killed or opposed. Others believe that constituents judge them on the number of bills they introduce. Still others think it is important to represent the views of their constituents by introducing the bills their district wants. Still others file bills they know will be defeated, simply to make a point.[12]

## Referral

After undergoing first reading, the bill is assigned to a standing committee by the Speaker. In the Senate, the lieutenant governor assigns it to a committee. Since committees in the Texas Legislature have overlapping jurisdictions, the Speaker and lieutenant governor can assign a bill to a friendly committee or an unfriendly one. The committee to which a bill is assigned can determine whether the bill survives or dies in committee.

## Committee Action

**standing committee** a permanent committee with the power to propose and write legislation that covers a particular subject, such as finance or agriculture

**pigeonholing** a step in the legislative process during which a bill is killed by the chair of the standing committee to which it was referred, as a result of his or her setting the bill aside and not bringing it before the committee

Every bill introduced in the Texas Legislature is assigned to a **standing committee**, and the vast majority of bills die in committee. The chair of the committee kills most by pigeonholing. **Pigeonholing** means that the committee chair sets the bill aside and never brings it before the committee.

Standing committees are considered the "workhorses" of the legislature (see Table 23.2). If the bill does not die, it most likely is amended. Few bills leave the committee in the same form as they arrived. Parts of several bills can also be combined to form a single bill. Changes are made to make the bill more acceptable to the entire legislature or to meet the political desires of the leadership or members of the committee. Hearings can take place to allow experts and the public to educate committee members on the good and bad points of the bill. In the Senate, all bills reported by the committee must have a public hearing.

## Floor Action

**filibuster** a tactic used by members of the Senate to prevent action on legislation they oppose by continuously holding the floor and speaking until the majority backs down. Once given the floor, senators have unlimited time to speak, and it requires a vote of three-fifths of the Senate to end a filibuster

In the House, bills referred by a standing committee go next to the Calendars Committee, which, after consulting the Speaker, schedules bills for debate. In the Senate, the lieutenant governor controls the agenda and decides when a bill will be considered.

The Speaker determines the length of debate in the House. Customarily, each member is allowed 10 minutes of debate. Early in the session when the agenda is not crowded, debate may last longer. Later in the session when there is a crush of legislative business, debate will be more limited. Some bills will be voted on without debate; however, important or controversial bills are usually allocated adequate time. Debate in the Senate is unlimited, which means it is possible for a senator to **filibuster**. A filibuster occurs when a senator talks for a lengthy period of time in an effort to kill a bill or to obtain amendments or other compromises. There are

## TABLE 23.2

## Standing Committees of the Texas Senate and House (82nd Legislature)

### SENATE COMMITTEES

| | | |
|---|---|---|
| Administration | Finance | Jurisprudence |
| Agriculture & Rural Affairs | Government Organization | Natural Resources |
| Business & Commerce | Health & Human Services | Nominations |
| Criminal Justice | Higher Education | State Affairs |
| Economic Development | Intergovernmental Relations | Transportation & Homeland Security |
| Education | International Relations & Trade | Veteran Affairs & Military Installations |

### HOUSE COMMITTEES

| | | |
|---|---|---|
| Agriculture & Livestock | Environmental Regulation | Pensions, Investments & Financial Services |
| Appropriations | General Investigating & Ethics | Public Education |
| Border & Intergovernmental Affairs | Government Efficiency and Reform | Public Health |
| Business & Industry | Higher Education | Redistricting |
| Calendars | Homeland Security & Public Safety | Rules & Resolutions |
| Corrections | House Administration | State Affairs |
| County Affairs | Human Services | Technology |
| Criminal Jurisprudence | Insurance | Transportation |
| Culture, Recreation & Tourism | Judiciary & Civil Jurisprudence | Urban Affairs |
| Defense & Veterans' Affairs | Land & Resource Management | Ways & Means |
| Economic & Small Business Development | Licensing & Administrative Procedures | |
| Elections | Local & Consent Calendars | |
| Energy Resources | Natural Resources | |

certain rules that apply to the filibuster in the Texas Senate that are quite different from those in the U.S. Senate. There is no eating or drinking during a filibuster. Senators must stand at their desks and may not lean, sit, or use their desk or chair in any way. Remarks must be confined to the issue under consideration. Finally, one must speak in an audible voice.

In the past 72 years, there have been more than 100 filibusters. The longest filibuster was in 1977 by Senator Bill Meier, who spoke for 43 hours. Given the time constraints under which the Texas Legislature operates, even the threat of a filibuster may be sufficient to kill or force changes in a bill.

Another tactic used in both the House and the Senate to prevent or delay passage of a bill is called "chubbing." Here, one or more members debate bills at length to slow down the legislative process. Like the filibuster, this is a particularly effective tactic as the legislative session draws to a close.

Sponsors of a bill are expected to gather sufficient votes to pass the bill. In fact, before the Calendars Committee schedules the bill for floor debate, sponsors often assure the committee that they have enough votes to pass the bill.

The Texas Senate has a rule that bills shall be considered according to the "regular order of business." This means that bills and resolutions are considered on second reading and listed in the order in which the committee report was received by the Secretary of the Senate. Bills and resolutions are considered on the third reading in the order in which they were passed on the second reading. In order to conduct business, especially when dealing with legislation that is controversial, this "regular order" blocks consideration of legislation because it can be considered only if the Senate suspends this rule requiring consideration in order. A two-thirds vote is required to suspend the rules. Thus, for all practical purposes, legislation in the Senate must have two-thirds support to pass rather than a simple majority. In the 2011 legislative session, the highly partisan issue of requiring an identification document to vote was excluded from the two-thirds rule, which made it possible for Senate Republicans to pass the legislation.

*Before a law is passed in Texas, it is voted on by the two chambers of the legislature—the House and the Senate. Here, former state senator Jeff Wentworth casts a vote; raising one finger means "yes" and two fingers mean "no."*

When a bill passes both the House and Senate, it is examined. If there are differences between the bill passed by the House and that passed by the Senate, the two bills are sent to a conference committee.

## Conference Committee

Bills must pass the House and Senate in exactly the same form. If the bill is different in any way, it is sent to a conference committee. Conference committees have 10 members: 5 members from the House appointed by the Speaker, and 5 members from the Senate appointed by the lieutenant governor.

Under legislative rules, the conference committee consists of 5 members from the House and Senate. Senate rules require that 2 members of the standing committee that considered the bill must be appointed. Unless specifically instructed, the conference committee cannot change parts of the bill that are the same. Changes are made and compromises reached only on parts of the bill that differ.

Once a compromise is reached, the report of the conference committee goes to the House and Senate. It can be debated in each chamber, but the report cannot be changed. It must be either accepted or rejected as is. If either chamber fails to approve the report of the conference committee, the bill is dead. Although it is possible for the conference committee to try a second time to reach a compromise, it is unusual for conference committees to do so.

If the report is agreed to in both chambers of the legislature, a final copy of the bill is prepared. The Speaker of the House, the clerk of the House, the president of the Senate (lieutenant governor), and the secretary of the Senate sign the bill. The next stop is the governor's desk.

# The Governor

It is the governor's responsibility to sign or **veto** legislation. During the first 130 days of a regular session, the governor has 10 days from the time a bill arrives on his desk to sign or veto the legislation. If he neither signs nor vetoes the bill in the 10 days, it becomes law without his signature. In the last 10 days of a session, he has 20 days from the time the bill arrives on his desk to sign or veto the legislation. Again, if he does neither, it becomes law without his signature. Unlike the U.S. president, who may sometimes kill a bill without signing it through what is called a "pocket veto," the Texas governor does not have this power.

The governor's veto can be overridden by a two-thirds vote of both the House and Senate. Anytime the governor vetoes a bill, he attaches a message explaining why it was vetoed. It is then returned to the chamber that originated the bill. If the presiding officer elects to allow a vote to override the veto, a vote is scheduled. Only two vetoes have been overridden in more than 70 years.

Many bills arrive on the governor's desk in the last few days of a session. Almost all important or controversial bills reach the governor in the waning moments of a session. If the governor wants to veto a bill that comes to him from day 131 to day 140, he simply waits until the legislature adjourns to exercise the veto. His veto cannot be overridden because the legislature has adjourned. Vetoing legislation after legislative adjournment is called a **post adjournment veto**, or a strong veto, since the legislature has no opportunity to overturn the veto. The post-adjournment veto

**veto** according to the Texas Constitution, the governor's power to turn down legislation; can be overridden by a two-thirds vote of both the House and Senate

**post-adjournment veto** a veto of a bill that occurs after the legislature adjourns, thus preventing the legislature from overriding it

*The governor can influence legislation through the veto or the line-item veto. The threat of a veto can be powerful, as legislators often try to take the governor's preferences into account and avoid a veto.*

## TABLE 23.3

### Total Number of Vetoes by Texas Governors

| YEAR | GOVERNOR | TOTAL VETOES |
|------|----------|--------------|
| 2011 | Perry | 25 |
| 2009 | Perry | 38 |
| 2007 | Perry | 54 |
| 2005 | Perry | 19 |
| 2003 | Perry | 48 |
| 2001 | Perry | 82* |
| 1999 | Bush | 33 |
| 1997 | Bush | 37 |
| 1995 | Bush | 25 |
| 1993 | Richards | 26 |
| 1991 | Richards | 36 |

*Record number of vetoes by a Texas governor.
SOURCE: Texas Legislature, "Legislative Statistics," April 20, 2010; Legislative Reference Library of Texas, "Bill Statistics."

provides the governor with an excellent bargaining tool, since he can threaten a veto unless changes are made in a bill.

**line-item veto** the power of the executive to veto specific provisions (lines) of an appropriations bill passed by the legislature

The governor also has a **line-item veto** that allows him or her to sign a bill and draw lines through specific items, deleting them from the bill. Except for the items that the governor has deleted, the bill becomes law. In Texas, the line-item veto applies only to the state's omnibus appropriations bill. Governor Perry used the line-item veto in 2009 to reduce the state budget by $97.2 million in general revenue and $288.9 from all funding sources.[13] In 2011, it was expected that Governor Perry would veto the funding for the Texas Historical Commission, as he had earlier proposed the abolition of the commission. Surprisingly, he did not do so.[14] Table 23.3 provides the total number of vetoes by Texas governors since 1991.

**Other Ways in Which the Governor Influences Legislation**  Message power is the governor's ability to communicate with the legislature. Early in each session, the governor delivers a State of the State message that is similar to the president's State of the Union message. In this address, the governor puts forth a vision for Texas and what legislation will accomplish that vision. If the governor chooses to submit an executive budget, a letter stating why this budget should be adopted accompanies it.

Periodically, the governor will visit with legislators to gain their vote on a bill. A personal visit can be persuasive, but increasingly, it is members of the governor's paid staff who are sent on these legislative visits. Like lobbyists for corporations and interest groups, the governor's representatives use their skills to encourage passage of bills the governor favors and to kill bills the governor opposes. However, there is a problem with this practice. The Texas Constitution forbids use of tax dollars to influence the legislature, and the governor's staff is, of course, paid through tax dollars. The governor's representatives avoid this ban by claiming they are simply providing needed information to the legislators. One should not underestimate the informal power that the governor has to influence legislation.

# Additional Players in the Legislative Process

Describe the roles of other state officials in shaping legislation

In addition to the legislators and the governor, there are others involved in the lawmaking process during both regular and special sessions. One official, the comptroller, has direct involvement in the legislative process, while other players are involved indirectly.

## The Comptroller of Public Accounts

The comptroller of public accounts issues revenue estimates to inform the legislature of the amount of money it can spend in the next two years. Texas's operating budgets must balance The Texas Constitution forbids borrowing money to conduct the daily operations of government. The estimate provided by the comptroller sets the limit on state spending. If the legislature wants to spend more than the comptroller estimates, it must enhance revenue—that is, increase taxes and fees.

The comptroller's estimates can be political in nature. The comptroller can provide a low revenue estimate and tell the legislature that the estimate will remain low until it passes bills the comptroller wants. On passage of those bills, the comptroller can revise the estimate to increase the spending limit and allow the legislature to complete its business.

## The Media

Media can determine issues of importance by the selection of stories they cover. If the media cover more stories on crime, crime and criminal justice issues will move toward the top of the legislature's agenda. A media focus on corporate fraud, rising homeowners insurance rates, alcohol-related traffic deaths, or poor performance by Texas public school students will increase legislative attention to these issues.

The media inform the public about the issues the legislature is considering and about the job the legislature is doing during the session. Media coverage of the legislature provides the public with needed information on what is going on in Austin. Stories portraying the legislature as modern, efficient, and hardworking provide the public with a positive image of the legislature, whereas stories about legislators sleeping at their desks or killing legislation on technicalities provide a negative image.

## The Courts

Federal and state courts influence the legislative agenda. In recent years, the courts' scrutiny has included the prison system, the state's treatment of patients in state mental hospitals,

*The media can influence the legislative agenda through the stories that they cover. Accordingly, legislators try to attract media attention that will support their positions. Here, House Speaker Joe Straus speaks at a press conference.*

the funding of public education, and equality of funding for colleges and universities in South Texas. The ability to rule acts of the legislature and actions of state agencies unconstitutional gives courts significant power over issues the legislature addresses. To a remarkable degree, state and federal courts have issued decisions that have forced the Texas Legislature to act in areas that the legislature would have preferred to avoid—largely because action required a significant expenditure of money. For example, many recent legislative actions directed toward criminal justice and public education are responses to court rulings.

## Lobbyists

During a regular session, roughly 1,800 individuals register as lobbyists and attempt to influence the legislature. A lobbyist's responsibility is to convince legislators to support the interest the lobbyist represents. Lobbyists want legislators' votes on bills. At the least, they desire access to legislators.

## The Public

Individuals can influence legislators. Legislators are evaluated at each election. If the people believe their elected officials are representing them well, legislators are reelected. A legislator who fails to live up to expectations might not be re-elected.

The public can serve as lobbyists. Letters, e-mail, or telephone calls urging representatives or senators to vote a certain way constitute a lobbying effort. Members of the public can also write legislation, but must convince at least one legislator to sponsor it and introduce it for consideration by the legislature.

*The public and interest groups may also influence the legislature. During a special session in which the legislature dealt with tax reduction, these Houston-area realtors and others demonstrated in favor of property tax relief.*

# Power in the Legislature

**Analyze how party leadership and redistricting affect power in the legislature**

Among the most powerful political figures in Texas are the leaders of the House and Senate. They play a key role in structuring the committees of the legislature, setting the states political agenda, and passing (or defeating) bills.

## Leadership

The **Speaker** of the Texas House of Representatives and the lieutenant governor are two of the most powerful political figures in the state. Republican representative Joe Straus of San Antonio is currently the Speaker of the House. Republican David Dewhurst is the current lieutenant governor. The Texas House and Senate endow both officials with considerable control over the legislative process. It is fair to say that either of them can usually kill legislation they oppose, and often they have the power to pass legislation they support.

Members of the House elect the Speaker at the beginning of the regular session. Additionally, at the start of each regular session, members of the House adopt rules that give the Speaker institutional powers sufficient to control the work of the House. Speakers usually are the dominant figures in the Texas House and wield vast power.

One of the most interesting developments in modern times in the Texas Legislature was the turmoil surrounding the 2002–08 speakership of Republican Tom Craddick. Craddick first challenged the Democratic Speaker "Pete" Laney and ultimately displaced Laney when the Republicans gained control of the House. Craddick worked to redistrict Texas congressional districts so as to increase substantially the number of Republicans in the Texas congressional delegation. As Speaker, Craddick was accused of micro-managing the House, of taking discretion away from committee chairs, and of insisting that members support his views on key issues even when contrary to the desires of their constituents. Republicans also lost seats in the Texas House between 2004 and 2006—a loss blamed in part on Craddick's leadership. The result was an open rebellion against Craddick, who was able to retain his position in the 2007 session only by resorting to a questionable parliamentary maneuver: he refused to recognize a motion to "vacate the chair," which would have caused a vote on his fate as Speaker.[15] It is doubtful that such dissension over a Speaker has occurred since Ira Evans was removed as Speaker in 1871.[16] In 2009, Craddick lost his speakership to Joe Straus, a Republican from San Antonio, who was elected Speaker by a coalition of anti-Craddick Republicans and Democrats. Straus faced opposition in 2011 from conservatives who saw him as too moderate and as too favorable to Democrats, but Straus was able to retain his position as Speaker.

The lieutenant governor is elected statewide to a four-year term. His or her major responsibility is to serve as president of the Senate and to preside

> **Speaker** the chief presiding officer of the House of Representatives. The Speaker is the most important party and House leader, and can influence the legislative agenda, the fate of individual pieces of legislation, and members' positions within the House

*The Speaker of the House is one of the most powerful people in Texas politics. In 2009, Tom Craddick (left) was replaced as Speaker by Joe Straus (right).*

over the Senate. Unlike the Speaker, the lieutenant governor is not a member of the Senate, simply its presiding officer, who may vote only to break a tie.

At the start of each regular session, senators adopt rules that the Senate will follow for the next two years. These rules give the lieutenant governor enormous control of the work of the Senate.

## Centralizing Power: Sources of the Leadership's Power

The operation of the Texas Legislature is significantly different from that of the U.S. Congress. In the U.S. Congress, the leader of the president's party in the House and the Senate is the president's spokesperson in that house of Congress. Additionally, the level of partisanship is high. Committee appointments are made in such a way that the majority party controls every important committee, and chairs of those committees are always members of the majority party. Each house of Congress has majority party leadership and minority party leadership. Such divisions do not exist in the Texas Legislature. No member of the Texas Legislature is formally known as the governor's spokesperson.

Although there is partisanship in the Texas Legislature, it is not at the level found in the U.S. Congress. There is no majority and minority party leadership, for example. Committee assignments and committee chairmanship appointments cross party lines so that in the Texas House, for example, where the majority party is now Republican, a Democrat may chair an important committee and successfully sponsor important legislation.[17] This somewhat nonpartisan structure of the Texas Legislature is important from the perspective of leadership. If the governor has no leader in the legislature, and if the membership does not owe allegiance to party leaders in the legislature, then leadership and power are further centralized in the Speaker and lieutenant governor. The Speaker and lieutenant governor can make appointments with limited regard for party affiliation, thus ensuring that members will be loyal to them rather than to the party.

Nevertheless, the redistricting controversy in 2003 did result in a more partisan legislature in 2005. It is clear that since that time, the Texas Legislature has moved into a more partisan era. Other factors may also undermine the tradition of nonpartisan politics in the state legislature. Most of the powers of the Speaker and of the lieutenant governor are granted by the rules that each chamber's membership votes on at the beginning of the legislative session. The powers of the Speaker and of the lieutenant governor could potentially be greatly reduced if the members of the legislature so chose. One could, for example, imagine a future Republican Senate that would reduce the powers of the lieutenant governor over the Texas Senate if a Democrat were elected lieutenant governor. Of course, one of the first rules that would have to change is the requirement of a two-thirds vote for a bill in the Senate to be voted on out of order. Indeed, the two-thirds rule in the state Senate encourages some degree of bipartisanship, because Republicans do not quite control two-thirds of the Senate and so need Democratic votes.

The two-thirds rule came under attack in the 2009 special session of the legislature and it continued to be criticized in 2011, mainly because the requirement of such a large supermajority makes it difficult to pass bills that arouse partisan tensions. Democrats support the rule because with it, Democratic support is needed to pass any bill in the Senate. Some Republicans wanted to abandon the rule in order to allow their majority to pass legislation without Democratic support. Others want to weaken the requirement of a supermajority by having a three-fifths rule instead of a two-thirds rule. Still other Republicans are inclined to support the

*In 2011, Representative J. M. Lozano announced that he was leaving the Democrats and joining the House Republicans. This switch gave the Republicans a supermajority of 100 members in the House, enabling them to pass legislation without fear of Democratic interference.*

long precedent of a two-thirds requirement. At least for the time being, the two-thirds rule remains. However, it can be easily changed at some point, as the rules of the Senate are passed by majority vote.[18]

The Republican congressional redistricting bill in 2003 led to abandonment of the two-thirds rule for that bill so that redistricting that was beneficial to Republicans could be passed. That bill would have been impossible to pass without changes in the rules that allowed passage by majority vote. In the 2009 special session of the legislature, the Texas Senate passed a highly partisan bill that required voters to show identification solely because the two-thirds rule was abandoned for that bill.[19] It was not until 2011, when the Texas Senate again abandoned the two-thirds rule, that the voter identification bill became law.

As the Texas Senate becomes more partisan, it seems likely that there will be increased use of special rule changes to allow for the passage of controversial bills, a lowering of the two-thirds supermajority requirement for passing a bill, or a complete abandonment of the two-thirds rule in favor of majority rule.

The structure of the Texas Legislature and the lack of formal lines of gubernatorial authority in the legislature are very important in centralizing power in the hands of the Speaker and the lieutenant governor. However, these officials have other important sources of power as well. One of those powers—a power especially important in the Texas House—is the power of **recognition**. The Senate rule allowing unlimited debate decreases the lieutenant governor's power in this area. In the House, the Speaker controls legislative debate, including who speaks and how long debate will last. On occasion, the Speaker ignores or skips a member seeking recognition to speak. This is a signal to other members of the House that this individual has fallen from the Speaker's good graces. That ability to pick and choose among those desiring to speak on the House floor, however, allows the Speaker to structure the debate and to affect the outcome of legislation.

As mentioned earlier, the Senate has a rule that for bills to be voted on, they must be taken in order and, for a bill to be taken out of order, there must be a two-thirds vote. Given the vast powers of the lieutenant governor, on issues that

**recognition** the power to control floor debate by recognizing who can speak before the House and Senate

are important to him, he can usually control the votes of at least one-third of the membership. Thus, if a bill is opposed by the lieutenant governor, he can frequently prevent it from being taken out of order for consideration.

One of the most important sources of power for the Speaker and the lieutenant governor is the committee assignment power. The committees on which legislators serve are important to individual members and to the presiding officer. For members, assignments to powerful committees increase their prestige in the legislature. Committee assignment also affects how well constituents are represented. Assigning members to standing committees is one of the most important duties of the lieutenant governor and the Speaker.

The Speaker and the lieutenant governor have major roles in appointing the membership of committees, appointing chairs of committees, and setting the legislative agenda. Party affiliation and seniority are of only moderate importance in committee assignments. The most important factor in committee assignments is the members' relationships with the presiding officer. In order to maintain control over the legislature, the Speaker and lieutenant governor use their committee assignment powers to appoint members who are loyal to them and who support their legislative agendas. When chairs and vice chairs of important committees are appointed, usually only the most loyal friends and allies of the Speaker and lieutenant governor are chosen. In 2011, 6 of the 18 standing committee chairs in the Senate were Democrats. Eleven of the 36 standing committee chairs in the House were Democrats.

Not only do the Speaker and the lieutenant governor have vast committee assignment powers, but committees in the Texas Legislature also have overlapping jurisdiction. Although each bill must be assigned to a committee, it can be assigned to more than one committee. Since the Speaker and the lieutenant governor assign bills to committees in their respective chambers, they use the bill assignment power to influence the fate of the bill. They can, for example, assign bills they oppose to committees they believe hostile to the bill and those they support to committees they believe will favor the bill.

Since bills must pass the House and Senate in exactly the same form, the Speaker and the lieutenant governor can exercise still another important influence on policy through their power to appoint conference committees. As we have seen, if any differences exist in a bill passed by both the House and the Senate, the bill goes to a conference committee that works out the differences in the House and Senate versions. By appointing the conference committee members, the Speaker and lieutenant governor can affect the language and even the fate of the bill.

## Redistricting

**redistricting** the process of redrawing election districts and redistributing legislative representatives in the Texas House, Texas Senate and U.S. House. This usually happens every 10 years to reflect shifts in population or in response to legal challenges in existing districts

One of the most controversial and partisan issues is **redistricting**—the redrawing of district lines for the Texas House, the Texas Senate, and the U.S. House of Representatives, which must be done at least every 10 years, after the federal census.

There are 150 Texas House districts and 31 Texas Senate districts. One senator or one member of the House represents each district. This is called representation by **single-member districts**.

**single-member district** an electorate that is allowed to elect only one representative for each district

After each census, the legislature draws new boundaries for each Texas House and Senate district. Newly drawn districts for the Texas House and Senate must contain an almost equal number of people in order to ensure equal representation. That requirement guarantees that each person's vote counts the same whether the vote is cast in Houston, Big Lake, El Paso, Presidio, Brownsville, or Commerce.

For much of the first half of the twentieth century, Texas and other states failed to draw new boundaries, and even after U.S. Supreme Court decisions, Texas did not do so willingly. Not until the U.S. Supreme Court's decisions in *Baker v. Carr* (1962) and *Reynolds v. Sims* (1964), compelling the legislature to draw new districts, were boundaries drawn that represented the population fairly.[20] These and subsequent decisions meant that Texas had to draw legislative districts of roughly equal populations— a concept known as the **one-person, one-vote principle**.

Congressional redistricting is also a responsibility of the legislature. Once the U.S. Congress apportions itself, the Texas Legislature divides Texas into the appropriate number of congressional districts. According to the 1964 Supreme Court case *Wesberry v. Sanders*, each state's U.S. House districts must be equal in population.[21] Depending on how the districts are drawn, the representation of the two political parties in the U.S. House of Representatives can be significantly changed. Indeed, reapportionment can so change the division of the parties that control of the U.S. House of Representatives can be affected. Thus, maneuvering over redistricting is highly partisan.

If the legislature fails to redistrict at the first regular session after the census, the task falls to the Legislative Redistricting Board (LRB). The LRB has five ex officio members: the lieutenant governor, the Speaker of the House, the attorney general, the commissioner of the General Land Office, and the comptroller of public accounts.

When the legislature adjourns without redistricting the LRB convenes. The LRB must meet within 90 days of legislative adjournment and complete its responsibilities within another 60 days. Even here, the influence of the Speaker and the lieutenant governor is clearly visible.

Texas redistricting plans must comply with the federal Voting Rights Act which, among other things, protects minorities from being disadvantaged by a redistricting plan. A federal court can temporarily redraw district lines if a redistricting violates this law.

Partisan differences in the state legislature resulted in the failure to pass a redistricting plan in 2001 during its regular session, transferring the responsibility to the Republican-dominated LRB. On a split vote, the board developed redistricting plans that appeared to favor the Republican Party. The board's decision, in turn, was appealed to the federal courts. A three-judge panel, composed of two Democrats

**one-person, one-vote principle**
the principle that all districts should have roughly equal populations

*In 2006 the U.S. Supreme Court upheld most of the new boundaries drawn in the Republicans' controversial redistricting but found that some of the redrawn districts failed to protect minority voting rights. Here, Governor Perry displays the new redistricting map. The new map drawn by Republicans after the 2010 census again went to the federal courts.*

and one Republican, approved the lines drawn for the state Senate, noting that the U.S. Justice Department had determined that the plan did not violate the Voting Rights Act. However, the court modified the board's plan for the House, arguing that the Department of Justice had rejected the plan because it was seen as diluting Hispanic voting strength in three areas of the state. The court felt that its role in the entire redistricting process was constrained. In their decision, the judges commented that "federal courts have a limited role in considering challenges to precleared, legislatively adopted redistricting plans."[22]

The final plan approved by the court appeared to be a great victory for the Republican Party. Twenty-seven incumbent Democrats found themselves placed in districts with other Democratic incumbents. Four Democrats who chaired key committees announced that they would not seek reelection. Many observers felt that redistricting would make the Republicans the majority party in the House and would maintain their majority status in the Senate. And many doubted that the Speaker of the House, Democrat Pete Laney, would be able to mobilize the votes needed for reelection to the speakership in the next session. After the 2002 elections, these observers were proven correct.[23]

## Power and Partisanship in the Redistricting Battle

Republican control of the Texas House and Senate in 2002 heralded more than simply a shift in party control of the legislature. With Republican control came a significant decline in the harmonious, bipartisan spirit that had largely governed the Texas Legislature. The Republican leadership, especially House Speaker Tom Craddick, chose to govern in a more partisan fashion. Additionally, a number of Democrats in the House who saw their power slipping away chose a rebellious

*Although the Texas Legislature is not as susceptible to partisan squabbling as the U.S. Congress, flare-ups between the Democrats and Republicans do occur. For example, in this photo, Texas House Democrats celebrate their return to Texas in May 2003, after spending four days in Ardmore, Oklahoma, to kill a GOP-produced congressional redistricting plan.*

course. They worked to make Craddick's speakership a difficult one, obstructing Republican legislative efforts as much as possible.

This new partisan tension in the Texas Legislature rose to a fever pitch in 2003 when Republicans, with the support of the Republican majority leader Tom DeLay, sought to alter the Texas congressional districts for partisan advantage. The Republican goal was to increase Republican representation in the Texas congressional delegation and, in so doing, help ensure a continuing Republican majority in the U.S. House of Representatives. The Republican effort was unconventional in that it occurred in mid-cycle—that is, it was the second redistricting after the 2000 census. As a rule, redistricting occurs only once after each decennial census, although there is no legal requirement that this be the case.

After the 2000 census, the Texas Legislature could not agree on redistricting, and a federal court devised a plan. The 2000 congressional redistricting gave the Democrats an advantage. With control of the state legislature, however, Republicans argued that the existing redistricting plan was unsatisfactory because it reflected a Democratic majority that no longer existed. Republicans wanted a plan that more clearly reflected Republican voting in Texas.[24] In 2000, Democrats won 17 congressional seats and Republicans won 13, even though Republicans won 59 percent of votes in the state and Democrats received only 40 percent. In 2002, Democrats got only 41 percent of the statewide vote, but they won 17 seats to 15 for the Republicans. In fact, since 1996, Republicans had never received less than 55 percent of the statewide vote, and Democrats never won more than 44 percent, yet Republicans were a minority in the Texas congressional delegation. With the new redistricting plan in 2004, Republicans got 58 percent of the statewide vote and elected 21 members of Congress from Texas. Democrats got 41 percent of the statewide vote and elected 11 members of Congress from Texas.[25]

The Republican congressional redistricting plan was not enacted without political turmoil, however. At the end of 2003, 51 Democrats from the state legislature walked out and gathered in Ardmore, Oklahoma, where the Texas state police did not have jurisdiction to bring them back to the state capitol. The result was that a quorum could not be reached to pass the plan. The Democratic legislators did not return to Austin until redistricting was taken off the agenda. A special legislative session was called to deal with redistricting, but the two-thirds rule in the state Senate prevented the bill from being passed. In a second special session that was called to deal with redistricting, 11 of the 12 Democratic members of the Senate fled to Albuquerque in order to prevent a Senate vote. Finally, a third special session produced a plan that passed both houses of the legislature.[26]

Most notable about the 2004 redistricting was that seven incumbent congressional Democrats were targeted for defeat. A lawsuit that challenged the redistricting on the grounds that it diluted minority votes stressed that the Democrats had been elected with minority support. The lawsuit also pointed out that these seven Democrats had either been paired so that they had to run against another incumbent or had been given a more Republican district.[27] A case before the U.S. Supreme Court challenged the extremely partisan gerrymandering of the Texas redistricting, its reduction of the strength of minority voters, and its use of the now outdated 2000 census. The Court did find that there had been a reduction in the strength of minority voters. However, the extremely partisan gerrymander and the mid-decennial redistricting using the 2000 census were upheld. For the most part, Republicans were successful in reshaping the partisan composition of the Texas delegation to the U.S. House of Representatives. However, the 2006 election led to Democratic control of the U.S. House and to a Texas congressional delegation with vastly weakened power due to the loss of key Democrats in the redistricting.[28]

The 2010 census led to another round of redistricting for the Texas Legislature and the U.S. House of Representatives. The overwhelmingly Republican legislature designed a redistricting plan strongly favorable to Republicans, but the plan ran afoul of a federal court which held that minority voting rights were violated. The court ordered a redistricting plan that was more favorable to Democrats.

## ● Thinking Critically about the Texas Legislature

The Texas Legislature has undergone great changes and continues to do so. Perhaps the most significant change has been the increasing partisanship. The Texas Legislature is less partisan than the U.S. Congress, but the Texas party divide was especially notable under Speaker Tom Craddick, during the redistricting battles, and during the battles over a voter identification law in 2009 and 2011.

The two-thirds rule in the Texas Senate is under attack. That rule requires considerable consensus to pass legislation from that body. If the two-thirds rule is reduced to a three-fifths rule or even majority rule, there will be renewed partisanship and rancor in the Texas Senate.

The Texas Legislature seems in some ways like an archaic institution. Unless there are special sessions, it meets once every two years and is a part-time body with very limited compensation for its members. The structure of the legislature, however, has survived since the 1876 Constitution, and there seems little likelihood that the structure will soon change.

Especially notable regarding the legislature is the vast power held by the Speaker and the lieutenant governor. The 1876 Constitution showed its distrust of a powerful governor, and the result is that in Texas the governor must share political influence with two other major powers in Texas government—the Speaker and the lieutenant governor, over whom the governor exerts no formal control. Still, the revolt against Speaker Craddick does remind us that it is perilous for the Speaker to try to exert so much power that he becomes subject to rebuke from a constituency whose views he ultimately must reflect—the views of a majority of the members of the Texas House.

# study guide

⑤ **Practice online with:** Chapter 23 Diagnostic Quiz ▪ Chapter 23 Key Term Flashcards

## Structure of the Texas Legislature

■ **Describe the bicameral organization of the legislature and the rules for membership (pp. 883–87)**

The Texas Legislature is bicameral. The leader of the House is the Speaker, and the Lieutenant Governor presides over the Texas Senate. Although the typical member of the legislature is white and male, women and minorities have increased their representation in recent years.

### Key Terms

**bicameral** (p. 883)

**per diem** (p. 886)

### Practice Quiz

1. There are _____ members of the Texas Senate, and state senators serve a _____ year term. *(p. 883)*
   a) 31/4
   b) 100/6
   c) 150/2
   d) 300/6
   e) 435/2

2. Texas House members differ from Texas Senate members because *(p. 884)*
   a) House members represent smaller districts and are subject to more frequent elections.
   b) House members represent people and senators represent counties.
   c) House members are elected from single-member districts and senators from multimember districts.
   d) House members have term limits and senators do not have term limits.
   e) House members must live in the state for 10 years before standing for election.

⑤ **Practice Online**
"Who Are Texans?" interactive exercise: *Who Are the Members of the Texas Legislature?*

## Sessions of the Legislature

■ **Explain when the legislature meets (pp. 887–88)**

The Texas Legislature meets once every two years for 140 days and additionally as required in special sessions called by the governor. Special sessions must have a specific purpose, such as redistricting or school finance.

### Key Terms

**regular session** (p. 887)

**biennial** (p. 887)

**special session** (p. 887)

### Practice Quiz

3. The Texas Legislature meets in regular session *(p. 887)*
   a) 90 days every year.
   b) 180 days every year.
   c) 140 days each odd-numbered year and 60 days each even-numbered year.
   d) 140 days each odd-numbered year.
   e) 180 days each even-numbered year.

4. The agenda for a special session of the Texas Legislature is set by the *(p. 887)*
   a) lieutenant governor and the Speaker of the House.
   b) governor.
   c) Texas Supreme Court.
   d) chair of the Joint committee on Special Sessions.
   e) The agenda-setting committee.

## Powers of the Legislature

■ **Outline the legislative and nonlegislative powers of the legislature (pp. 888–90)**

The Texas Legislature passes bills and resolutions and supervises the state bureaucracy through the budgetary process and sunset legislation.

### Key Terms

**bill** (p. 888)

**local bill** (p. 888)

**special bill** (p. 888)

general bill (p. 888)

resolution (p. 888)

concurrent resolution (p. 888)

joint resolution (p. 889)

simple resolution (p. 889)

constituent (p. 889)

electoral power (p. 889)

investigative power (p. 889)

directive and supervisory power (p. 890)

judicial power (p. 890)

impeachment (p. 890)

 **Practice Online**

Video exercise: *Senator Eliot Shapleigh—A Day in the Life of a Texas Legislator*

# How a Bill Becomes a Law in Texas

■ **Trace the process through which law is made in Texas (pp. 890–97)**

The process of a how a bill becomes a law is similar to the federal level. A key difference is the governor's use of the line item veto by which he can eliminate individual appropriations or line itemsin the state budget. Additionally, the lieutenant governor and the Speaker of the Texas House have exceptionally strong powers. The committee system plays a major role in shaping the legislative process.

## Key Terms

**introduction** (p. 890)

**referral** (p. 890)

**consideration by standing committee** (p. 890)

**floor action** (p. 890)

**conference committee** (p. 890)

**action by the governor** (p. 890)

**standing committee** (p. 892)

**pigeonholing** (p. 892)

**filibuster** (p. 892)

**veto** (p. 895)

**post-adjournment veto** (p. 895)

**line-item veto** (p. 896)

## Practice Quiz

5. If a bill fails to pass the Texas House and Texas Senate in exactly the same form, the bill *(p. 894)*
   a) dies.
   b) is returned to the standing committee in the House or Senate that originally considered the bill.
   c) is sent to a conference committee.
   d) is sent to the governor, who decides which version of the bill will be signed.
   e) becomes a law

6. The _____ provides the governor with a powerful tool with which to bargain with the legislature. *(pp. 895–96)*
   a) ability to introduce five bills in a regular session
   b) post-adjournment veto
   c) pocket veto
   d) message power
   e) initiative

7. Which state official, in large part, determines the total amount of money the legislature may appropriate? *(p. 896)*
   a) governor
   b) lieutenant governor
   c) treasurer
   d) comptroller of public accounts
   e) attorney general

# Additional Players in the Legislative Process

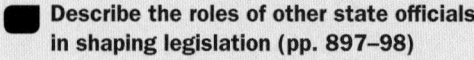

■ **Describe the roles of other state officials in shaping legislation (pp. 897–98)**

Other than the two leaders in the House and the Senate, committee chairs have enormous influence in crafting legislation in Texas. The Comptroller plays an important role in legislation by issuing revenue estimates to inform the legislation about the money available for the legislature to spend.

# Power in the Legislature

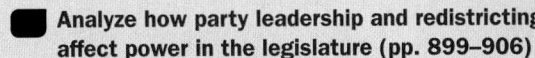 **Analyze how party leadership and redistricting affect power in the legislature (pp. 899–906)**

The Speaker of the House and the lieutenant governor are the most important actors in the legislature. Together they help to centralize power in the legislature, and they facilitate or prevent the passage of legislation. The legislature has become increasingly partisan with one of the most partisan issues involving redistricting.

## Key Terms

**Speaker** (p. 899)

**recognition** (p. 901)

**redistricting** (p. 902)

**single-member districts** (p. 902)

**one-person, one-vote principle** (p. 903)

## Practice Quiz

8. The lieutenant governor is the presiding officer of the (p. 899)
   a) Texas Senate.
   b) governor's cabinet.
   c) Texas Legislature.
   d) Legislative Conference committees.
   e) Treasury.

9. The two most powerful political figures in the Texas Legislature are the (p. 899)
   a) governor and the lieutenant governor.
   b) governor and the attorney general.
   c) Speaker of the House and the governor.
   d) Speaker of the House and the lieutenant governor.
   e) chairs of the finance committee in each house.

10. The Speaker of the Texas House is chosen (p. 899)
    a) in a statewide election.
    b) in a party-line vote by members of the Texas House.

    c) by of majority of the members of the House whether Democrat or Republican.
    d) by seniority in the House.
    e) by lot.

11. The chairs of the Texas House committees are (p. 900)
    a) of the same party as the Speaker.
    b) selected on the basis of seniority.
    c) chosen because of their experience.
    d) both Democrats and Republicans.
    e) independents.

12. The ability of the lieutenant governor and the Speaker of the House to control the final outcome of legislation comes from their power to (p. 902)
    a) appoint members of conference committees.
    b) refuse to approve the work of standing committees.
    c) exercise the legislative line-item veto.
    d) change up to three lines in any bill.
    e) control floor debate.

13. An important issue for the legislature at least every 10 years is (p. 902)
    a) adopting a budget.
    b) deciding the order of succession to the office of governor.
    c) impeaching the lieutenant governor.
    d) redistricting.
    e) electing the president.

14. In recent years, the Texas Legislature has (p. 903)
    a) become more partisan.
    b) become less partisan.
    c) become more experienced in lawmaking.
    d) been more inclined to let the governor make policy.
    e) been more respectful of county officials.

 **Practice Online**
Interactive simulation: *A Member of the Speaker's Team*

# Recommended Websites

**Speaker of the Texas House of Representatives**
www.house.state.tx.us/speaker/welcome.htm

**Texas Legislative Council**
www.tlc.state.tx.us

**Texas Legislature Online**
www.capitol.state.tx.us

**Texas Lieutenant Governor**
www.senate.state.tx.us/75r/LtGov/Ltgov.htm

Although the governor is the most visible leader in Texas politics, Texas governors have fewer powers than governors in other states. This is in keeping with Texans' mistrust of excessive governmental power. Like other Texas governors before him, Governor Rick Perry has frequently been checked by the legislature.

# 24

# The Texas Executive Branch

**WHAT GOVERNMENT DOES AND WHY IT MATTERS** Candidates for the governorship in Texas can pursue several electoral strategies when seeking office. For example, they can try to direct attention to state issues, emphasizing their special abilities to address the concerns and problems facing Texans today. Alternatively, an unpopular presidential administration can drive state and local candidates to focus on their differences with national leaders and why the state and local candidates are better able to address the needs of the state. Or candidates can embrace a popular presidential administration and try to identify themselves with its larger vision of where the state and nation must go. By nationalizing the election, candidates seek to move the electorate's attention away from state politics to national politics.

The Texas Constitution limits the intrusion of national politics into state elections by scheduling the election of its governor and other executive officers every four years in "off-presidential years." Holding elections in off-presidential years, however, is no guarantee that national politics does not intrude into statewide elections. Indeed, the 2010 election was a classic example of how gubernatorial elections can be nationalized.

Governor Rick Perry rode anti-Washington sentiment to victory in the 2010 Republican primary and carried these anti-Washington themes into the general election campaign. Perry portrayed himself as a leader who would protect Texas from the excesses of the Obama administration. Although Perry's legislative accomplishments in two and a half terms as governor were modest at best, his popularity rose as his anti-Washington, anti-Democrat, anti-Obama message intensified.

Perry refused to debate his Democratic opponent Bill White on television, citing his opponent's failure to release certain tax returns as a reason. Commentators from the press were highly critical of this decision, bemoaning the fact that the key issues facing the state would never be discussed in an open forum. Conversation about the issues that ensued was largely one-sided, either between the press and one candidate or across campaign ads. One of the most important consequences of this limited debate over the issues was that Perry was able to sidestep discussing the most difficult issue that was facing the state—a burgeoning budget deficit.

Perry's strategy of nationalizing the 2010 gubernatorial race was highly successful. The week following the election, he published his first book: *Fed Up! Our Fight to Save America from Washington*. The book reads less like a conclusion to a race for the governorship than it does a preface to a future campaign for national office. Its anti-Washington theme is typical of Perry's 2010 campaign, which focused not on state issues—even as pressing as a gargantuan budget deficit—but on the evils of Washington and national power.

After the 2011 legislative session, Perry launched a national campaign for the Republican presidential nomination. Following an initial surge in the polls, the Perry campaign sputtered along after a series of gaffes by the candidate and his supporters. Unlike his predecessor in the governorship, George W. Bush, Perry had considerable difficulty translating his popularity in Texas into a national political presence.

## chaptergoals

- Describe the powers of the Texas governor and the limits of the governor's power (pages 913–24)

- Identify the other elected officials who make up the plural executive (pages 924–31)

- Explain the roles played by boards, commissions, and regulatory agencies (pages 931–36)

# ● The Governor

**Describe the powers of the Texas governor and the limits of the governor's power**

At the national level, the president represents and is responsible to the people as a whole. The president is the spokesperson for the government and the people in national and international affairs. Throughout the twentieth century, various presidents parlayed the powers granted them by the U.S. Constitution into what some commentators call the "imperial presidency." The governorship in Texas is not an analogous imperial one. Compared with the president, the governor of Texas is weak. Executive power in Texas is divided among a number of separately elected officials, all of whom are elected by and responsible to the people as a whole. This plural executive has important implications for democratic life in the Lone Star State.

Although the governor of Texas is the most visible state official, Texas's governor has far less formal power than most governors. In 1983, a study of the appointment, budget, removal, and organizational powers of governors ranked Texas's governor forty-ninth in the nation, ahead only of the governor of South Carolina.[1] In 1990, a study of gubernatorial authority in the nation also ranked Texas's governor forty-ninth, ahead of the governor of Rhode Island.[2]

To understand the restrictions placed on the office, it is necessary to remember that the Constitution of 1876 was a reaction to the Reconstruction government that existed in Texas following the Civil War. During Reconstruction, the governor was very powerful, and many regarded state government as oppressive and corrupt. When a new constitution was drafted at the end of the Reconstruction era, Texans did their best to ensure that no state official had extensive power. The Texas Constitution of 1876 placed strict limits on the governor's ability to control the people appointed to office and almost eliminated the possibility that appointees to office could be removed. Power was further fragmented among other officeholders, who are collectively known as the plural executive. Each of these officeholders is elected and has separate and distinct responsibilities. Members of major state boards, such as the Railroad Commission and the State Board of Education, are also elected and are largely outside the control of the governor.

Governors who are successful in pushing their programs through the legislature and seeing them implemented by the bureaucracy are able to use the limited formal powers available to them, exercise their personal political power, exploit the prestige of the office of governor, and marshal various special interests to their cause. One political writer likens the office of governor to a bronco that breaks most who attempt to ride it and will be successfully handled by very few. In short, successful governors are successful politicians.[3]

Former state representative Brian McCall has written about the modern Texas governorship, arguing that Texas governors can be quite powerful in spite of the weaknesses of the office that are inherent in the Texas Constitution. He points out that governors who develop a collaborative relationship with the legislature can realize many of their goals if they are flexible, have a vision, are willing to motivate others to achieve that vision, and will work cooperatively with the legislature. McCall notes that when former governor Allan Shivers was asked about the weak governorship of Texas, he responded, "I never thought it was weak. I had all the power I needed." McCall, in stressing that the Texas governorship can be parlayed

**for critical analysis**

What can governors do to overcome the inherent weakness of the position? What are the implications for democratic government of a weak chief executive?

into a position of power by capable individuals, noted that the governor has the only power to call special sessions of the legislature. The governor can pardon criminals and can permit fugitives to be extradited to other states. The governor appoints people to state governing boards and commissions. Only the governor can declare martial law. Only the governor can veto acts of the legislature. Through the traditional State of the State address delivered at the beginning of every legislative session, the governor can outline state priorities and convince others of the importance of those priorities. The governor can be a major persuasive force in mobilizing interest groups, editorial boards of newspapers, and opinion leaders to support his or her agenda.

Not all governors have the personal skills to turn the office into a powerful one. Some have been unable to develop a collaborative relationship with the legislature. Others have not had the interest or the ability to develop their own vision and political agenda. Still others have been unable to accomplish their goals because of economic downturns that have limited their resources. However, McCall argues that modern governors such as John Connally, Ann Richards, and George Bush have had the persuasive skills that have enabled them to achieve major political objectives in spite of the constitutional limitations on the powers of the office.[4]

Still, even many successful governors have not acted as if the job is a demanding one. George W. Bush, according to McCall, would typically arrive at the office by eight in the morning, leave for a run and a workout at 11:40 A.M., return at 1:30 P.M., and play video golf or computer solitaire until 3 P.M.[5] Governor Perry was so detached from the operation of state government that he did not receive a full briefing on the raid on a polygamist cult that put 400 children in protective custody and involved a half-dozen state agencies and 1,000 state personnel until five days after the event. One review of Governor Perry's schedule during the first four months of the 2011 legislative session showed that he averaged only 21 hours per week on state business and took six three-day weekends.[6]

*George W. Bush was governor of Texas from 1995 until he was elected president of the United States in 2000. Here, Bush is seen campaigning for re-election as governor in 1998. Like Rick Perry, Bush was able to achieve a number of his political goals as governor, despite the limited powers of the office.*

## Qualifications

Only three formal constitutional qualifications are required to become governor of Texas. Article IV of the Texas Constitution requires the governor to (1) be at least 30 years of age; (2) be a U.S. citizen; and (3) live in Texas five years immediately before election. Texas governors have tended to be male, white, conservative, either personally wealthy or with access to wealth, Protestant, and middle-aged, and they have had considerable prior political experience.

Women compose more than 50 percent of the population of the United States and Texas, but only two women—Miriam Ferguson (1925–27, 1933–35) and Ann Richards (1991–95)—have served as governor of Texas.

William Clements's victory over John Hill in the gubernatorial campaign of 1978 was the first time since Reconstruction that a Republican had won the office. George W. Bush was the second Republican elected governor and the first individual elected for two consecutive four-year terms.

Access to money is important because running for governor is inordinately expensive. A campaign for the governorship can cost tens of millions of dollars, and few Texans have that kind of money. The 2010 gubernatorial campaign set a record, costing about $91 million when all primary and general election candidates are considered. Tony Sanchez, the Democratic nominee for governor in 2002, spent over $66 million in that campaign, a record for an individual candidate. About $60 million of those funds came from his family's fortune in a losing effort for the governor's mansion.

Sam Kinch, a former editor of *Texas Weekly*, suggests that prior political experience is an important consideration in selecting a governor. Kinch maintains that although experience may not mean that someone will be a better governor, it does mean he or she is more likely to know how to handle the pressures of the office.[7]

## Election and Term of Office

Before 1974, Texas governors served two-year terms, with most being elected to a maximum of two consecutive two-year terms. As Table 24.1 shows, there have been exceptions, such as Coke Stevenson, Price Daniel, and John Connally, who each served for six years, or Allan Shivers, who served for eight years. In 1972, Texas voters adopted a constitutional amendment changing the governor's term to four years. In 1974, Dolph Briscoe was the first governor elected to a four-year term of office. Rick Perry, who has served as governor since 2000, has been the longest serving Texas governor.

Gubernatorial elections are held in off-years (years in which a president is not elected) to minimize the effect of presidential elections on the selection of the Texas governor. The Texas Legislature, controlled at the time by Democrats, designed the off-year system to eliminate the possibility that a popular Republican presidential candidate would bring votes to a Republican candidate for governor. Likewise, party leaders wanted to negate the chances of an unpopular Democratic presidential candidate costing a Democratic gubernatorial candidate votes in the general election. Unfortunately, because of this timing, voter turnout in gubernatorial contests is relatively low.

## Campaigns

Campaigns for governor of Texas last at least 10 months. Candidates hit the campaign trail in January of an election year to win their party's primary election in March; then they continue campaigning until the November general election.

## TABLE 24.1

### Governors of Texas and Their Terms of Office since 1874

| | | | |
|---|---|---|---|
| Richard Coke | 1874–76 | Miriam Ferguson | 1933–35 |
| Richard B. Hubbard | 1876–79 | James V. Allred | 1935–39 |
| Oran M. Roberts | 1879–83 | W. Lee O'Daniel | 1939–41 |
| John Ireland | 1883–87 | Coke Stevenson | 1941–47 |
| Lawrence S. Ross | 1887–91 | Beauford H. Jester | 1947–49 |
| James S. Hogg | 1891–95 | Allan Shivers | 1949–57 |
| Charles A. Culberson | 1895–99 | Price Daniel | 1957–63 |
| Joseph D. Sayers | 1899–1903 | John Connally | 1963–69 |
| S. W. T. Lanham | 1903–07 | Preston Smith | 1969–73 |
| Thomas M. Campbell | 1907–11 | Dolph Briscoe | 1973–79* |
| Oscar B. Colquitt | 1911–15 | William Clements | 1979–83 |
| James E. Ferguson | 1915–17 | Mark White | 1983–87 |
| William P. Hobby | 1917–21 | William Clements | 1987–91 |
| Pat M. Neff | 1921–25 | Ann Richards | 1991–95 |
| Miriam Ferguson | 1925–27 | George W. Bush | 1995–2000** |
| Dan Moody | 1927–31 | Rick Perry | 2000– |
| Ross Sterling | 1931–33 | | |

*Term changed to four years with the 1974 general election.
**Resigned to become president of the United States.
SOURCE: Dallas Morning News, *Texas Almanac and State Industrial Guide 1998–99* (Dallas: A. H. Belo, 1999).

Successful candidates spend thousands of hours and millions of dollars campaigning. The money goes to pay staff salaries and for travel, opinion polls, telephone banks, direct mailings, and advertisements in print and broadcast media. Texas is so large that statewide candidates must purchase print and electronic advertisements in 19 media markets to reach every corner of the state.

In the 2010 Republican primary, Kay Bailey Hutchison spent over $14 million in her losing battle against Rick Perry. Perry spent nearly $13 million in the primary. Overall, Perry spent about $39 million and Bill White spent about $26 million in their campaigns. That is $14.37 for every vote Perry received and $12.48 for every vote White received. High-priced campaigns illustrate that successful candidates need personal wealth or access to wealth.

## Removal of a Governor

In Texas, the only constitutional method of removing a governor from office is by **impeachment** and conviction. "To impeach" means to accuse or to indict, and impeachment is similar to a true bill (indictment) by a grand jury. The Texas Constitution notes that the governor may be impeached but does not give any grounds for impeachment. Possible justifications for impeachment are failure to perform the duties of governor, gross incompetence, or official misconduct.

**impeachment** the formal charge by the House of Representatives that leads to a trial in the Senate and the possible removal of a state official

Impeachment begins in the Texas House of Representatives. A majority vote of the Texas House is required to impeach, or to bring charges. If the House votes for impeachment, the trial takes place in the Texas Senate. One or more members of the Texas House prosecute the case, and the chief justice of the Supreme Court of Texas presides over the impeachment proceedings. A two-thirds vote of the senators present and voting is necessary to convict. If convicted, the governor is removed from office and disqualified from holding any other state office.

Any member of the executive or judicial branch may be impeached. Once the House votes for impeachment charges against an official, that individual is suspended from office and cannot exercise any of his duties. Governor James Ferguson was the only Texas governor to be impeached and convicted.

## Succession

The Texas Constitution provides for the lieutenant governor to become governor if the office becomes vacant through impeachment and conviction, death, resignation, or the governor's absence from the state.

In December 2000, a succession occurred when Governor George W. Bush became president-elect of the United States and resigned as governor. Lieutenant Governor Rick Perry immediately took the oath to become governor of Texas. The *Houston Chronicle* has characterized Rick Perry as "a politician who so looks the part that it's been joked that he was ordered straight from central casting."[8] Perry, a former state legislator from Haskell, was a conservative Democrat who switched to the Republican Party in 1990 and ran successfully for commissioner of agriculture. His six years in the Texas House, eight years as head of a major state agency, and two years as lieutenant governor and president of the Texas Senate provided him with a great deal more experience than any other governor of the last three decades.[9]

Should the governor leave the bounds of the state, the lieutenant governor becomes acting governor. If the governor is impeached, the lieutenant governor serves as acting governor before and during the trial. While serving as acting governor, the lieutenant governor earns the governor's daily salary, which is far better than the $20 earned as lieutenant governor. (However, a governor who is absent from the state still earns the same daily salary.)

When out of the state, the governor is legally entitled to Department of Public Safety protection. George W. Bush spent part of 1999 and 2000 campaigning to be president of the United States. During fiscal year 1999, it cost Texans an additional $2,365,000 to provide protection for the governor while he was on the presidential campaign trail.[10] In 1992, Governor Ann Richards was often out of the state campaigning for Bill Clinton, and the Texas taxpayers picked up the cost of her security detail. Governor Perry was also out of the state a great deal during his campaign for the 2012 Republican presidential nomination.

Constitutionally, the governor's office is weak. Former lieutenant governor Bill Hobby noted that about the only way he knew when he was acting governor was by a note his secretary left on his daily calendar.[11] In the first three months of 2000, Rick Perry, then lieutenant governor, served as acting governor more days than George W. Bush was in the state to serve as governor. Perry's press secretary

*Governor Rick Perry spent millions of dollars on his 2010 campaign for re-election, as he first fended off a serious challenge from Kay Bailey Hutchison in the Republican primary election and then campaigned in the general election.*

commented that the added duties of being acting governor were not very notice-able and that those duties made little difference in Perry's schedule.[12] State govern-ment takes little notice of the governor's absences. Former Speaker of the Texas House Pete Laney has said that the governor's office is "holding court and cutting ribbons" and in 2000 commented on Governor Bush's out-of-state campaigning by saying, "I guess we've been doing pretty well without [a governor]."[13]

Legislation further defines succession from the governor to the lieutenant gov-ernor, to the president pro tempore of the Texas Senate, Speaker of the House, attorney general, and the chief judges of the Texas courts of appeal in descending order.

## Compensation

The governor's salary is set by the legislature. Texas pays its governor $150,000 annually. In addition to this salary, the governor receives use of an official man-sion near the capitol grounds, although fire damage prevented its use as an official residence from June 2008 to the summer of 2011. Governors and the legislature often squabble about the amount of money needed for upkeep of the mansion and its grounds. The governor also receives use of a limousine, a state-owned aircraft, and a personal staff.

## Staff

The governor's staff consists of nearly 250 individuals. This includes a chief of staff, a deputy chief of staff, a general counsel, and a press secretary. A scheduler coor-dinates the governor's appointments, personal appearances, and work schedule. Governor Perry has 35 staff members who focus solely on policy issues.[14]

The staff keeps the governor informed about issues and problems facing the state, and it may suggest courses of action. In addition, during a four-year term, a governor makes several thousand appointments to various state posts. It is impos-sible for a governor to be acquainted personally with each appointee. Some of the staff find qualified individuals for each post and recommend them to the governor. Other staff members track legislation. They talk with legislators, especially key people such as committee chairpersons. The staff lets the governor know when his or her personal touch might make a difference in the outcome of legislation. For each bill that passes the legislature, a staff member prepares a summary of the bill with a recommendation that the governor sign or veto the bill.

Recent governors have used their staffs to be more accessible to the public. Governor Perry, like his immediate predecessors, wants his staff to be no more than a phone call away from those who need assistance. In theory, individuals need only call a member of the governor's staff to receive help or find out where to go for help. The Office of the Governor has a Citizen's Assistance Hotline that handles thousands of calls each year from Texans needing assistance with their problems with state government.

## Executive Powers of the Governor

Texas has a board or agency form of government. Approximately 200 state boards, commissions, and agencies make up the executive branch of Texas government. Agencies may be as obscure as the Texas Funeral Commission or the State Preser-vation Board or as well-known as the Public Utilities Commission of Texas or the

# Who Re-Elected Governor Perry in 2010?

Rick Perry is from Paint Creek, Texas, a rural community in Haskell County. Bill White served as mayor of Houston, Texas's largest city. The results of the 2010 governor's election reflect this urban/rural divide between the two candidates. Perry did best in rural counties, especially in his native West Texas. Outside of the Rio Grande Valley, White did best in the urban counties.

## 2010 Election Results, by County

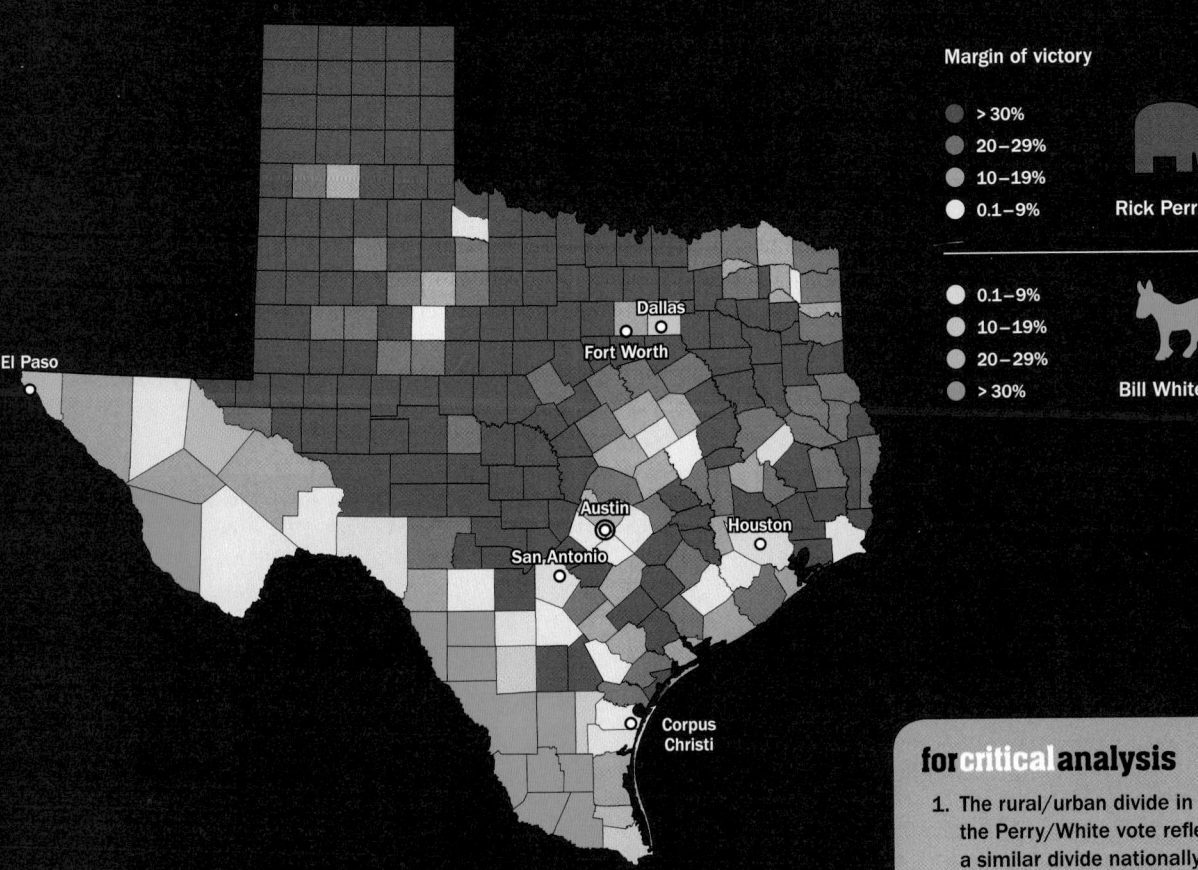

**Vote Share** = Rick Perry = Bill White

| | Perry | White |
|---|---|---|
| Urban | 46% | 52% |
| Suburban | 62% | 35% |
| Rural & small city | 63% | 34% |

SOURCE: Texas Secretary of State

**for critical analysis**

1. The rural/urban divide in the Perry/White vote reflects a similar divide nationally between Republicans and Democrats. What do you think prompts rural voters to vote differently from urban voters?

2. Having won the election, do you think Perry will tend to favor urban or rural areas in his actions as governor? What policies might he support that will be more favorable to rural areas?

Texas Department of Human Services, but each is important to its constituents. These multimember boards are the policy-making bodies for their agencies. They employ and oversee the people who operate the agencies on a daily basis.

**appointment** the power of the chief executive, whether the president of the United States or the governor of a state, to appoint persons to office

**Appointment Power** The governor's power of **appointment** is the most significant executive power. It allows a degree of control over about 200 state agencies. Governor Perry's long tenure has allowed him to appoint more than 4,000 people to these boards, and through these appointments he has been able to exert control throughout state government. One lobbyist described Perry's appointees as much different from Governor Bush's in that they "appear to be much more concerned with the larger political context and what sort of direction, either signaled or voiced, is coming from the governor's office."[15]

The power of appointment enables the governor to exercise the power of **patronage**. It permits the governor to reward supporters by appointing them to office. Most of the offices pay very little, but they do offer supporters some prestige. The governor can also use the appointment power to repay political favors by appointing friends and associates of legislators to office as well as to garner political IOUs from politicians. Most important, a governor can use the appointment power to influence agency policy. To a great degree, the effectiveness of a governor's use of the appointment power will determine the governor's success in office.

**patronage** the resources available to higher officials, usually opportunities to make partisan appointments to offices and to confer grants, licenses, or special favors to supporters

A governor, however, must exert some care in appointments. In 2007 there was a scandal within the Texas Youth Commission, which has authority over institutionalized juveniles. It became clear that not only was there a widespread pattern of physical and sexual abuse of juveniles in the facilities, but authorities tried to cover up the abuse. As a result, Governor Perry's appointees had to resign from the commission and it was necessary to reorganize the agency.

The governor appoints people to office, but the Texas Senate must also confirm them. However, because the Senate may not meet for almost two years, the

*The authority to appoint many state officials is an important executive power. In 2008, Rick Perry appointed Esperanza "Hope" Andrade as Texas secretary of state.*

appointee takes office immediately and does not wait for Senate confirmation. An important limitation on the power of the governor to appoint persons to office is the requirement that the individual's state senator must approve the appointment. This is known as **senatorial courtesy** and applies regardless of the party affiliation of the governor, senator, or appointee. Usually, if the appointee's senator concurs in the appointment, the remainder of the Senate will agree. However, if the appointee's senator opposes the appointment, the remainder of the Senate will also oppose the appointment.

The process for removing an appointee is also complicated. A governor cannot remove an appointee who refuses to resign unless the governor can show cause and get two-thirds of the Texas Senate to approve.[16] This complex procedure for the termination of members of boards and commissions, along with the practice of senatorial courtesy, can be a significant limitation on the governor's power to influence the policies of state agencies. Chairs of boards, however, serve at the pleasure of the governor and so can easily be removed if they do something that displeases the governor.

**Budgetary Power** Officially, the Texas governor is the state's chief budget officer. As such, governors submit an **executive budget** to the legislature. This budget suggests a plan for revenue and expenditure for Texas, but more important, it indicates the governor's priorities for the state in the next biennium.

In 1949, in an effort to gain more control over the state's budget, the legislature established the Legislative Budget Board (LBB), which is responsible for preparing a **legislative budget**. Thus, two budgets are prepared and submitted to the legislature: an executive budget by the governor and a legislative budget by the LBB. As a creation of the legislature, the LBB's budget proposal receives more consideration by the House and Senate than the governor's recommendations, and in recent years the governor's budget has fallen into disuse. Legend has it that the governor's budget has been used as a doorstop and a paperweight, and one diminutive legislator used two copies as a booster in his office chair. In 1989, Governor Clements recognized the futility of submitting an executive budget and simply endorsed the recommendations of the LBB. Ann Richards followed Clements's precedent, but Governor George Bush took a more active role in budget preparation and Governor Perry was very involved in dealing with the state's 2011 budgetary shortfall.

The governor has some control over the final appropriations bill through the use of the line-item veto; however, the governor cannot impound funds or transfer funds from one agency to another, even if circumstances change from the time the money was appropriated. Overall, the budgetary process does not provide the governor with an effective means of controlling state agencies.

**Military Power** The governor is commander in chief of the state's National Guard units when they are not under presidential orders. These units are headed by the adjutant general, who is appointed by the governor. The governor can declare martial law, which suspends most civil authority and imposes military rule over an area. Martial law can be declared in the event of a riot, flood, hurricane, tornado, or other disaster to protect lives and property.

**Police Power** In Texas, law enforcement and police power are primarily a local responsibility, and the governor has few responsibilities in this area. The governor appoints, with Senate approval, the three-member Public Safety Commission that directs the work of the Department of Public Safety (DPS). The DPS is responsible for highway traffic enforcement (highway patrol), drivers' licensing, motor vehicle

**senatorial courtesy** the practice whereby the president, before formally nominating a person for a federal judgeship, seeks the indication that senators from the candidate's own state support the nomination; in Texas, the practice whereby the governor seeks the indication that the senator from the candidate's home supports the nomination

**executive budget** the state budget prepared and submitted by the governor to the legislature, which indicates the governor's spending priorities. The executive budget is overshadowed in terms of importance by the legislative budget

**legislative budget** the state budget that is prepared and submitted by the Legislative Budget Board (LBB) and that is fully considered by the House and Senate

**for critical analysis**

What are the governor's formal powers? How does the governor exercise these powers?

*Deployment of the state's national guard in times of emergency is one aspect of the governor's military power. Here, Texas National Guard troops deliver relief supplies after Hurricane Ike in 2009.*

inspection, truck weighing stations, and the Texas Rangers. When circumstances warrant, the governor can assume command of the Rangers, an elite, highly trained force of about 100 officers. If there is evidence of ongoing violence or corruption, the governor can use informal powers, the prestige of the governor's office, and appeals to the media to compel appropriate action from local law enforcement officials.

## Legislative Powers of the Governor

As we saw earlier, the governor's legislative powers include message power, power of the veto, and the authority to call special sessions and set their agendas. If a governor uses these powers effectively, he or she can have considerable control over the state's legislative business, but they do not enhance his or her ability to control the executive branch of state government.

**Message Power** Any communication between the governor and the legislature is part of the message power. Early in each regular session, the governor delivers a State of the State message. In this speech to a joint session of the legislature, the governor explains his or her plan for the state in the coming two years. The governor may propose specific programs or simply set general goals for the state. The speech is covered by most news media, and it is often broadcast on public television and radio stations.

If the governor submits an executive budget, he or she may address the legislature on the important items in the proposed plan of spending and revenue. At the very least, the budget proposal is forwarded to the legislature with a letter briefly explaining the budget.

Lobbying by governors is part of the message power. Governors try to pass or defeat bills important to them. For example, early in 1991, Governor Ann Richards successfully lobbied for legislation that would expand higher educational opportunities in the Rio Grande Valley and that resulted in the creation of the University of Texas at Brownsville.

Although Governor Bill Clements personally lobbied the legislature, he preferred to use his five full-time paid lobbyists to influence the legislature. Although not exactly part of the governor's message power, the use of lobbyists is an effective way for a governor to communicate with and influence the legislature.

**Veto Power** Governors of Texas can sign or **veto** legislation—but in most cases they sign legislation. In the 82nd Legislature (2011), Governor Perry vetoed 25 bills. Since becoming governor in 2000, Perry has vetoed 273 bills.[17]

When the governor vetoes a bill after the legislature adjourns, it is called a **post-adjournment** or strong veto. This veto is absolute, because the legislature that passed the vetoed bills no longer exists. As a result, if the governor decides to veto a bill, it stays vetoed.

Texas governors possess the **line-item veto**, which is the ability to veto individual parts of an appropriations bill. The governor signs the bill but strikes out particular lines in the bill. Items struck from the bill do not become law, but the remainder of the appropriations bill does.

In 2007, Governor Perry used the line-item veto to cut $646.5 million from the total state budget. One of his most controversial vetoes was for group insurance contributions for community and junior colleges that came to $153 million. He cut another $36 million in special-item funding for higher education, such as $2 million for obesity research at the Texas Cooperative Extension and $5 million for public health programs at the University of Texas Health Science Center at Houston.[18]

This line-item veto allows Texas governors considerable control over appropriations to state agencies, and this power can be used by the governor to reduce state expenditures or to punish agencies or programs disfavored by the governor.[19] It is one important power of the governor that is greater than that of the president of the United States, who does not have the power to issue a line-item veto because the U.S. Supreme Court has held that such a power violates separation of powers in the U.S. Constitution.

**Special Sessions** Special sessions of the Texas Legislature are called by the governor, last for no more than 30 days, and may consider only those items placed on the agenda by the governor. **Special sessions** are called to address critical problems that have arisen since the last regular session. The nature of special sessions allows the legislature to focus attention on specific issues.

From 1989 through 2011, the legislature met in 19 special sessions. These sessions considered the complicated and divisive issues of reform of workers' compensation laws, public school finance, reapportionment, and voter identification. The sessions ranged from 30 days to 2 days, with six of the sessions occurring in 1989–90 and five occurring from 2005 through 2011.[20]

## Judicial Powers of the Governor

Texas elects each of its appellate and district court judges, but when vacancies occur because of the death, resignation, or retirement of the incumbent or as a result of creation of new courts, the governor is responsible for appointing individuals to fill these vacancies.

Once appointed to office, judges tend to remain in office. More than 95 percent of incumbents win re-election. Through this power to appoint judges, the governor has considerable influence over the Texas judicial system.

Clemency normally includes the power to issue pardons, grant paroles, and issue reprieves. The governor's power in this area is severely limited because of abuses of previous governors. Pardons can be granted only on the recommendation of the Board of Pardons and Paroles. Texas governors can neither grant nor deny

**veto** the governor's power to turn down legislation; can be overridden by a two-thirds vote of both the House and Senate

**post-adjournment veto** a veto of a bill that occurs after the legislature adjourns, thus preventing the legislature from overriding it

**line-item veto** the power of the executive to veto specific provisions (lines) of an appropriations bill passed by the legislature

**special session** a legislative session called by the governor that addresses an agenda set by him or her and that lasts no longer than 30 days

paroles. Governors have the ability to grant each person condemned to death one 30-day reprieve. Additional reprieves and any other act of clemency must be recommended by the Board of Pardons and Paroles.

## The Office and Its Occupants

People often expect governors to be able to do things they are not equipped to do. They are expected to be chief executives in more than name only despite being granted little in the way of formal power. Constitutionally and statutorily, the governor is ill-equipped to exert control and direction over the Texas bureaucracy.

John Connally was regarded as a strong governor, whereas Dolph Briscoe was regarded as weak. In part, the difference was that Connally actively sought to lead. As governor, he had a dynamic personality, whereas Briscoe was more retiring in his personal style and did not seek to have the impact Connally had. Allan Shivers was an imperial governor, as Richard Nixon was called an imperial president. Preston Smith was described as one of the most ordinary people ever to serve as governor. Smith is seldom given credit for doing anything as governor, yet he established the first actual planning organization in Texas government. Rick Perry has used his lengthy service and his appointment powers over state boards and commissions to exert unusually strong control over the operation of government.

In large part, the office of governor is what the person holding the position makes it. Whether the governor is viewed as strong or weak depends on how the governor conducts him- or herself in office, uses the position's formal power, and exercises political influence.

# ● The Plural Executive

**plural executive** an executive branch in which power is fragmented because the election of statewide officeholders is independent of the election of the governor

> **Identify the other elected officials who make up the plural executive**

When Texans drafted a constitution in 1876, they chose to limit executive power and disperse it through several elected officials called the **plural executive**. Texans elect six of the seven people who make up the plural executive: the governor, lieutenant governor, attorney general, comptroller of public accounts, commissioner of the General Land Office, and commissioner of agriculture (see Table 24.2 and Table 24.3). The governor appoints the seventh person, the secretary of state. Except for the lieutenant governor, who receives the same salary as a legislator, salaries of members of the plural executive are set by the legislature. Additionally, two major regulatory agencies, the Railroad Commission of Texas and the State Board of Education, are run by officials who are independently elected. The result is vast fragmentation of responsibility for public policy in the state.

Elections are partisan, and each member of the plural executive may choose to operate

## TABLE 24.2

### Elected Officials in Texas with Executive Responsibilities

| SINGLE-ELECTED EXECUTIVES | MULTI-ELECTED EXECUTIVES |
| --- | --- |
| Governor | Railroad Commission (3 members) |
| Lieutenant Governor | |
| Attorney General | |
| Land Commissioner | State Board of Education (15 members) |
| Agriculture Commissioner | |
| Comptroller | |

independently of the others. At times, members of the plural executive may be in competition with each other, often because of conflicting personal ambitions. That occurred when John Hill was attorney general and sought to take the governorship from Dolph Briscoe, and when Mark White was attorney general and sought the governorship from Bill Clements. Because of the difficulty of defeating incumbents, however, it is far more likely that members of the plural executive will wait for a vacancy in a more prestigious office before seeking that higher office. Champions of the plural executive believe that it limits the power of executive officials and makes these officers more accountable to the public. Opponents assert the plural executive is inefficient and does not promote good government. The governor is a member of the plural executive, but this multipart executive limits the governor's control of the executive branch because he or she has little authority over this group.

One can get a sense of the importance of the various positions in the plural executive simply by looking at the campaign contributions received by winning candidates for these offices in the 2010 elections. Table 24.4 shows the contributions received by both the Democratic and the Republican nominees in 2010. Governor Rick Perry, the incumbent Republican, received over $39 million in contributions. In contrast, his Democratic opponent, Bill White, received much less. The incumbent Republican lieutenant governor David Dewhurst had over $9 million in contributions, compared with only about $958,000 in contributions for his opponent. The winning candidate for attorney general had nearly $6 million in contributions, the winning candidate for comptroller more than $2.7 million in contributions even though she had no Democratic opponent. The agriculture commissioner had more than $1.7 million, and the land commissioner had more than $864,000. Two things are especially notable about these figures. One is the enormous amounts of money that are contributed to candidates for the plural executive offices. The other is how lopsided the contributions are in favor of the Republican candidates. It is a sign of the strength of the Republican Party and the weakness of the Democratic Party in Texas elections that Republican candidates raise so much more money for their campaigns than do Democratic candidates.

| TABLE 24.3 | |
|---|---|
| **State Executive Officeholders, 2013** | |
| Governor | Rick Perry (Republican) |
| Lieutenant Governor | David Dewhurst (Republican) |
| Attorney General | Greg Abbott (Republican) |
| Comptroller of Public Accounts | Susan Combs (Republican) |
| Commissioner of the General Land Office | Jerry Patterson (Republican) |
| Commissioner of Agriculture | Todd Staples (Republican) |
| Railroad Commissioners | Barry Smitherman (Republican) |
| | David Porter (Republican) |
| | Christi Craddick (Republican) |
| Secretary of State (appointed) | John Steen (Republican) |

**for critical analysis**

What are the effects of a plural executive on accountability in state government?

## Secretary of State

Strangely, given Texas's fragmentation of power, the governor does appoint the Texas **secretary of state**, even though this office is an elective one in 37 other states.[21] Though once considered a "glorified keeper of certain state records," the secretary of state is now an important officer.[22] The secretary of state has myriad responsibilities, and the appointment of a secretary of state is one of the governor's most important tasks.

As Texas's chief election official, the secretary of state conducts voter registration drives. His or her office works with organizations such as the League of Women Voters to increase the number of registered voters. The secretary of state's

**secretary of state** state official, appointed by the governor, whose primary responsibility is administering elections

## TABLE 24.4

## Campaign Contributions in 2010 and the Plural Executive

| OFFICE | LOSING CANDIDATE | CONTRIBUTIONS TO LOSER | WINNING CANDIDATE | CONTRIBUTIONS TO WINNER |
|---|---|---|---|---|
| Governor | B. White (Dem.) | $26,291,535 | R. Perry (Rep.) | $39,328,540 |
| Lieutenant Governor | L. Chavez-Thompson (Dem.) | 958,040 | D. Dewhurst (Rep.) | 9,240,480 |
| Attorney General | B. Radnotsky (Dem.) | 1,135,031 | G. Abbott (Rep.) | 5,828,370 |
| Comptroller | (No Dem. candidate) | 0 | S. Combs (Rep.) | 2,744,001 |
| Agriculture Commissioner | P. Gilbert (Dem.) | 336,363 | T. Staples (Rep.) | 1,742,941 |
| Land Commissioner | H. Uribe (Dem.) | 102,487 | J. Patterson (Rep.) | 864,688 |

SOURCE: National Institute on Money in State Politics.

office also collects election-night returns from county judges and county clerks and makes the results available to the media. This service provides media and voters with a convenient method of receiving the latest official election returns in Texas.

All debt and Uniform Commercial Code filings are placed with the secretary of state's office. When any individual borrows money from a financial institution, a copy of the loan agreement is placed in the secretary of state's office.

## Lieutenant Governor

**lieutenant governor** the second-highest elected official in the state and president of the state Senate

The **lieutenant governor** has executive responsibilities, such as serving as acting governor when the governor is out of state and succeeding a governor who resigns, is incapacitated, or is impeached. The real power of the office of lieutenant governor, however, is derived from its place in the legislative process.

According to the Texas Constitution, the lieutenant governor is the "Constitutional President of the Senate" and has the right to debate and vote on all issues when the Senate sits as a "Committee of the Whole." The Texas Constitution also grants the lieutenant governor the power to cast a deciding vote in the Senate when there is a tie. Like the Speaker of the House, the lieutenant governor signs all bills and resolutions. The constitution names the lieutenant governor to the Legislative Redistricting Board, a five-member committee that apportions the state into senatorial and House districts if the legislature fails to do so following a census. Other powers of the lieutenant governor are derived from various statutes passed by the legislature. For example, the lieutenant governor is chair of the LBB and is a member of a number of other boards and committees, including the Legislative Audit Committee, the Legislative Education Board, the Cash Management Committee, and the Bond Review Board.

The Texas Constitution grants the Senate the power to make its own rules, and lieutenant governors traditionally have been granted significant legislative power by the Senate itself. The Senate rules empower the lieutenant governor to decide all parliamentary questions and to use discretion in following Senate procedural rules. The lieutenant governor is also empowered to set up standing and special committees and to appoint committee members and chairs of the committees. The Senate rules, and not just the Texas Constitution, make the lieutenant governor one of the most powerful political leaders in the state. New Senate rules passed by a future Senate could, of course, substantially alter the power possessed by the lieutenant governor.

**Political Style of Lieutenant Governors** Bob Bullock served as lieutenant governor of Texas from 1991 to 1999. A force in Texas politics for over 40 years, he was one of the strongest and most effective lieutenant governors Texas politics had ever seen. He took a bluff, rough, tough, head-knocking approach to leadership. He was feared and respected by friends and foes alike.

His successor, Rick Perry, brought a very different style to the office. The first Republican elected lieutenant governor in over 100 years, Perry had served two terms as the Texas commissioner of agriculture from 1985 to 1991. Prior to that, he served in the Texas House of Representatives, representing a rural west Texas district as a Democrat. His switch to the Republican Party

*Republican David Dewhurst was re-elected as lieutenant governor of Texas in 2010. The lieutenant governor's most important powers derive from his or her role in the legislature.*

reflected the broader movement of rural conservatives in the 1980s and 1990s. Expectations for Perry were low when he assumed office. In contrast to Bullock, Perry had a low-key style. But his style was appreciated by senators long under the demanding eye of Bob Bullock. Perry compared himself with a football player following in the footsteps of the Heisman Trophy winner Ricky Williams from the University of Texas. Like a running back imagining himself scoring a touchdown, Perry actually practiced banging a gavel in the empty Senate chamber. Perry's situation was also made more difficult by the fact that then–incumbent governor George W. Bush was actively pursuing the presidency, leaving additional jobs and uncertainties on Perry's shoulders.

Democratic senator John Whitmire, whom Perry had removed as chairman of the Senate Criminal Justice Committee, may have offered the best evaluation of Perry's leadership ability when commenting on a newspaper article that claimed Perry had lost control of the Senate during a debate over hate-crime legislation. Whitmire said, "I don't know how in the hell you say he lost control of the Senate. Was it a major difference in the way Bullock would have done it? Yeah. Serious difference. But I think members kind of appreciated the fact he didn't use his position as lieutenant governor to strong-arm members into positions that were contrary to their districts. Do I agree with all his decisions or operations, philosophy? Of course not. Essentially he was a freshman. . . . I'm sure he would be the first to tell you he learned by doing. No one's ever tried to govern us while the governor's been running for president. He had a good session."[23]

When George W. Bush became president and Lieutenant Governor Rick Perry became governor, the Senate elected one of its members to serve as lieutenant governor. That person was Bill Ratliff, a Republican from Mount Pleasant who was chairman of the powerful Senate Finance Committee. Ratliff had been in the Senate since 1989. A civil engineer, Ratliff was a strong believer in bipartisanship and was fascinated by the policy-making process. Known for his candor and moderation, he quickly alienated conservatives in his party when he named the Democratic senator Rodney Ellis of Houston as his replacement as chairman of the Finance Committee. As the presiding officer of the Senate, Ratliff oversaw a legislative session that had considerable accomplishments, such as passage of a statewide teacher health plan and the extension of Medicaid coverage to hundreds of thousands of poor children.

**for critical analysis**

How does the power of the lieutenant governor differ from that of the governor?

One poll showed Ratliff the leader in a Republican primary for lieutenant governor, and so he announced he would seek the office in the next election. However, one of his opponents was Land Commissioner David Dewhurst, who claimed he would spend tens of millions of dollars of his own money in the race. Ratliff soon ran into trouble with Republican contributors whom he needed in order to compete with Dewhurst's money. Ratliff quickly discovered that his political moderation was not favored by many contributors and, with love for policy but distaste for politics, Ratliff concluded he should withdraw and not be a candidate for the office. One of his advisers suggested that Ratliff claim he was dropping out of the race because of a fatal disease. The fatal disease, noted Ratliff, was "independence and moderation."[24]

Dewhurst successfully ran for lieutenant governor in 2002 and was re-elected in 2006 and in 2010. As lieutenant governor, Dewhurst is in very different political circumstances from his two Republican predecessors, Perry and Ratliff. Republicans held a majority in the Senate throughout the Dewhurst years. Though Dewhurst pledged to work with state Democrats and appointed some as committee chairmen, partisanship became an increasingly divisive force in the state Senate under Dewhurst. Far more low-key than Bob Bullock and much less dominant a personality, Dewhurst has proven an effective lieutenant governor who unsuccessfully sought to replace Kay Bailey Hutchison as U.S. senator from Texas.

## Attorney General

**attorney general** elected state official who serves as the state's chief civil lawyer

The **attorney general** (AG) is elected to a four-year term and acts as the chief lawyer for the state of Texas. The AG is, in effect, head of Texas's civil law firm. Currently the Texas AG oversees the work of over 700 lawyers.

The AG's office is concerned primarily with civil matters. When a lawsuit is filed against the state or by the state, the AG manages the legal activities surrounding that lawsuit. Any time a state agency needs legal representation, the AG's office represents the agency. In any lawsuit to which Texas is a party, the AG's office has full responsibility to resolve the case and can litigate, compromise, settle, or choose not to pursue the suit.

One of the more important powers of the AG's office comes from the opinion process. Any agency of state or local government can ask the AG's office for an advisory opinion on the legality of an action. The AG's office will rule on the question, and the ruling has the force of law unless overturned by a court or the legislature.

Probably the most controversial and criticized aspect of the work of the AG's office is child support collection. Almost one-half of the AG's 4,000 employees are involved in collecting child support, and they have collected more than $21 billion since Greg Abbott became attorney general. However, this program is the subject of intense criticism because much child support remains uncollected.

The AG's office has little responsibility in criminal law but may appoint a special prosecutor if a local district attorney asks the AG for assistance. This can happen when there is a potential conflict of interest, as, for example, if the district attorney is a friend of or works with a local official who is under criminal investigation. In one recent case, lawyers from the AG's office prosecuted a state district judge in Collin County on bribery charges.

Generally, criminal cases in Texas are prosecuted by district or county attorneys elected in each county. The county is usually responsible for the costs of the trial and for all appeals in state court. If a criminal case is appealed to the federal courts, the AG's office assumes responsibility.[25]

## Commissioner of the General Land Office

The General Land Office (GLO) is the oldest state agency in Texas. Historically the **land commissioner** gave away land. Today, the GLO is the land manager for most publicly owned lands in Texas. Texas owns or has mineral interest in 13 million acres of land in the state, plus all submerged lands up to 10.35 miles into the Gulf of Mexico. All but 28 of Texas's 254 counties have some of these public lands.

The GLO also awards grazing and oil and gas exploration rights on this land. Thousands of producing oil and gas wells are found on state-owned land and are managed by the GLO. These responsibilities make the office of land commissioner quite influential. A significant portion of royalties on oil and natural gas produced by these wells goes to the Permanent School Fund and the Permanent University Fund.

The commissioner also manages the Veterans' Land Program, through which the state makes low-cost loans to Texas veterans. The program includes loans for land, housing, and home improvements. Recently, the GLO was given authority over some environmental matters. The land commissioner is responsible for environmental quality on public lands and waters, especially along the Texas coast. All of Texas's Gulf Coast beaches are publicly owned and under the jurisdiction of the GLO.

In recent years, the commissioner of the GLO, Jerry Patterson, was involved in considerable controversy over the disposition of 9,269 acres of state land in the Christmas Mountains just north of Big Bend National Park. The Christmas Mountains land was under the control of the GLO and Patterson offered to sell the land to either public or private entities. After a public outcry over the proposed sale, the National Park Service expressed interest in accepting a donation of the land. However, Patterson, who is staunchly pro-hunting and pro-handgun, rejected the proposed donation because at the time the National Park Service banned hunting and the carrying of handguns in national parks. Finally, in 2011, the land was transferred to the Texas State University System, where it will serve as an "outdoor classroom." To satisfy Patterson's concerns, it was agreed that the land will be open to those who are licensed to carry handguns and to hunting.[26]

*The General Land Office is influential in large part because it awards oil and gas exploration rights for publicly owned lands. Land Commissioner Jerry Patterson was re-elected in 2010.*

**land commissioner** elected state official who is the manager of most publicly owned lands

## Commissioner of Agriculture

The **agricultural commissioner** is primarily responsible for enforcing agricultural laws. These include administration of animal quarantine laws, inspection of food, and enforcement of disease- and pest-control programs. Enforcement of the state's laws helps to ensure that Texas's farm products are of high quality and are disease free.

The Department of Agriculture checks weights and measures. Each year a representative of the department checks each motor fuel pump to make sure that it dispenses the correct amount of fuel. Scales used by grocery stores and markets are checked to guarantee that they weigh products correctly.

Farming and ranching are big business in Texas. Although a large number of small family farms exist in the state, large corporate farms increasingly dominate Texas agriculture. These large agribusinesses are greatly affected by the decisions of the commissioner. Such decisions can increase or decrease the cost of production. Changes in production costs affect the profit margins of these agribusinesses and ultimately the price consumers pay for food products.

**agricultural commissioner** elected state official who is primarily responsible for enforcing agricultural laws

## Comptroller of Public Accounts

comptroller elected state official
who directs the collection of taxes
and other revenues

The **comptroller** is a powerful state official because he or she directs the collection of tax and nontax revenues and issues an evaluation and estimate of anticipated state revenues before each legislative session. Tax collection is the most visible function of the comptroller. The taxes collected by the comptroller include the general sales tax, severance tax on natural resources, motor fuel tax, inheritance tax, most occupational taxes, and many minor taxes.

Although collecting billions in revenue is important, estimating revenues provides the comptroller with more power. These estimates, issued monthly during legislative sessions, are vital to the appropriations process because the legislature is prohibited from spending more than the comptroller estimates will be available. Final passage of any appropriations bill is contingent on the comptroller's certifying that revenues will be available to cover the monies spent in the appropriation. Because most bills require the expenditure of monies, this certification function provides the comptroller with significant power over the legislative process. If the comptroller is unable to certify that monies are available to pay for the appropriation, the legislature must reduce the appropriation or increase revenues. More than just an auditor, accountant, and tax collector, the comptroller is a key figure in the appropriations process.

In 1996, the office of state treasurer was eliminated, and the comptroller of public accounts assumed the duties of that office. Since then, the comptroller of public accounts has been the official custodian of state funds and is responsible for the safety of the state's money and for investing that money.

To ensure the safety of Texas's money, funds are deposited only in financial institutions designated by the State Depository Board as eligible to receive state monies. Deposits are required to earn as much money as possible. The more money earned as interest on deposits, the fewer tax dollars are needed.

An interesting responsibility of the comptroller is returning abandoned money and property to their rightful owners. In October of each year, the comptroller publishes a list of individuals with unclaimed property. One list included $117,000 in a forgotten savings account, a certificate of deposit for $104,000, gold coins, diamond rings, family photos, and rare baseball trading cards. Money or property that remains unclaimed goes to the state.

## Accountability of the Plural Executive

### for critical analysis

The commissioner of agriculture, the land commissioner, the state comptroller, and the attorney general each head agencies that have significant responsibility for the operation of state government. To what extent is the public aware of these agencies and the major role they play in government?

Except for the secretary of state, each member of the plural executive is directly accountable to the people of Texas through elections. The plural executive is accountable to the legislature in three ways: the budgetary process, Sunset Review and the impeachment process.

The legislature can demonstrate its satisfaction, or lack thereof, with an agency of the plural executive by the amount of money it appropriates to that agency. A significant increase in appropriations indicates an agency in good standing with the legislature, whereas little or no increase in funds indicates legislative displeasure. Sunset Review can lead to reforms of an agency and even its elimination.

The Texas Constitution, not the legislature, creates most of the plural executive. Impeachment and conviction are the ultimate check on an elected official. The Texas House of Representatives can impeach an official for such things as criminal activity or gross malfeasance in office. The Texas Senate then tries the official. If convicted by the Senate, the official is removed from office.

## The Plural Executive and the Governor

The plural executive dilutes the ability of the governor to control state government. The governor appoints the secretary of state but has no control over other members of the plural executive. Officials are elected independently, and they do not run as a slate. They do not answer to the governor, and they do not serve as a cabinet. They tend to operate their offices as independent fiefdoms, and they jealously guard their turf. The plural executive can make state government appear as if it is going in several different directions at once. This is especially true when members of the plural executive are political rivals. For example, widely publicized tensions between Governor Rick Perry and Comptroller Carole Strayhorn led to Strayhorn's unsuccessful campaign as an independent against Perry in 2006.

With each member of the plural executive having separate and distinct responsibilities, state government and statewide planning lack cohesiveness. However, the plural executive is a product of Texas's history and environment. Like much of Texas government, it was a result of the public's negative reaction to Governor Edmund J. Davis at the close of Reconstruction.

## Boards, Commissions, and Regulatory Agencies

> **Explain the roles played by boards, commissions, and regulatory agencies**

The state **bureaucracy** in Texas has approximately 200 state boards and commissions as well as major agencies within the plural executive. In addition to the agencies under the direct control of the single executives who are part of the elected plural executive, there are also (1) agencies run by multimember boards appointed by the governor and confirmed by the Senate; (2) agencies with single executives appointed by the governor and confirmed by the Senate; and (3) agencies run by multimember boards elected by the people.

**bureaucracy** the complex structure of offices, tasks, rules, and principles of organization that are employed by all large-scale institutions to coordinate the work of their personnel

Governor Perry's lengthy service has given him enormous influence throughout state government, as he is the only Texas governor in modern history to have made every appointment in state government that a governor can make—and he has also made numerous appointments to vacancies in office such as the Texas appellate courts and scores of district judgeships. State law usually sets the terms of persons on state boards at four or six years. As a result, each new governor spends a great deal of time replacing holdover appointments from previous governors. With Perry's lengthy tenure as governor, however, those holdover appointments are long gone. The result, according to former state representative and author Brian McCall, is that "in this regard, [Perry] is by far the most powerful governor in Texas history. No governor has been able to do what he has done."

Perry has placed many of his closest advisers in key positions, which has spread not only his personal influence but also his personal political philosophy of a pro-business state government. To compare Perry's influence with previous governors, McCall noted that Governor Preston Smith in 1969 was able to appoint the entire board of regents at Texas Tech by getting an amendment inserted into a minor bill that changed the name of Texas Technological to Texas Tech University. When the name change took effect, the entire board of regents lost their positions

*The Department of Parks and Wildlife is an agency in the Texas executive branch and is led by a board appointed by the governor. The department manages natural resources and fishing, hunting, and outdoor recreation in the state. Here, an employee measures fish caught near Corpus Christi.*

and Smith was able to appoint the board. Perry has appointed the entire boards of 17 public colleges and universities and has had a voice in selecting the chancellors of those universities.[27]

Perry has also been willing to discipline board members who have displeased him. For example, in 2009, he refused to reappoint three members of the Texas Forensic Science Board two days before they were to examine a flawed arson investigation. Perry also appointed a new chair of the Forensic Science Board, who abruptly canceled its meeting, and the review of the arson case never took place.[28] In that same year, a Texas Tech regent who was a Perry appointee claimed that a former Perry staff member had told him to resign from the Board of Regents because the regent had endorsed Kay Bailey Hutchison in the Republican primary for governor.[29]

Not all of Perry's nominees have been approved by the overwhelmingly Republican state senate. His nominee for the Board of Pardons and Paroles, best known for her political activism and opposition to sex-toy parties in the Burleson, Texas, area, was turned down by the Senate with an overwhelming 27-to-4 vote against her confirmation. State senator John Whitmire, a Democrat and the chair of the Senate Criminal Justice Committee, argued that she was turned down not because the issue was a partisan one, but simply because she was not qualified for a position that considers "life and death matters."[30]

## Multimember Appointed Boards

Most boards and commissions in Texas are headed by members appointed by the governor and confirmed by the Senate. Multimember commissions with heads appointed by the governor include innocuous agencies, such as the Bandera County River Authority, the State Seed and Plant Board, the Caddo Lake Compact Commission, and the Texas Funeral Commission. There are also better-known agencies, such as the Texas Alcoholic Beverage Commission, the Department of Parks and Wildlife, the Texas Youth Commission, and the Texas Department of Corrections. Except in the case of a major controversy, such as the sexual abuse scandal that embroiled the Texas Youth Commission in 2007, these agencies work in anonymity, although several of them have a direct effect on the lives of Texans. One such example is the Public Utilities Commission.

**Public Utilities Commission (PUC)** More than any other agency, the Public Utilities Commission (PUC) has a direct effect on consumers' pocketbooks. Before 1975, cities in Texas set utility rates. The PUC was established in 1975, in part to protect consumers and to curb the rate at which utility costs were increasing. The commission is responsible for setting all local telephone and some electric rates.

Local telephone rates vary from one part of Texas to another, but all rates in a service area are the same. The commission also determines the maximum charge for pay telephones and approves additional services such as caller ID, call waiting, and call forwarding. A rule that took effect in September 1999 prohibits an individual's local service from being disconnected for nonpayment of long-distance bills. Another regulation by the PUC establishes a "no call" list for phone numbers of Texas residents who do not wish to receive telemarketing calls from companies that do not have a business relationship with the phone customer.

With the introduction of retail competition to the electric industry, the PUC has had a major role in providing information to consumers and in setting requirements for providers of electric services. The PUC maintains a website that allows electric customers to compare the costs of electricity from the various electric service providers.

## Appointed Single Executives

**The Texas Department of Insurance** Whereas the PUC is run by a multimember body appointed by the governor and confirmed by the Texas Senate, the Texas Department of Insurance is run by one commissioner appointed by the governor for a two-year term and confirmed by the Senate. This single-member appointive system has been in effect since 1993, when governance of the agency by a three-member appointed board was abandoned in favor of single-member governance. The purpose of the Department of Insurance is to regulate the insurance market in Texas, a complicated task that affects most Texans.[31]

In the early 2000s Texas was faced with huge increases in the cost of homeowners' insurance brought on at least in part by major increases in insurance claims, most notably for mold damage. From the first quarter of 2000 to the fourth quarter of 2001, the number of mold claims increased from 1,050 to 14,706. Additionally, the costs of these claims increased significantly to the point that insurance payments became greater than insurance premiums. And with a declining economy during this period, insurance companies were no longer making substantial profits on their investment of insurance premiums. Homeowner premiums increased rapidly. Between 2001 and 2002, homeowners' premiums rose 21.8 percent. Some companies chose not to write any new homeowners' policies; other companies simply pulled out of the Texas market. In 1997, 166 companies were writing homeowners' policies in Texas; by 2003, only 101 companies were writing such policies.

In response, the Texas Department of Insurance began to deregulate insurance coverage so that, for example, policies could be written that charged more for complete mold coverage, less for reduced mold coverage, and significantly less for no mold coverage.

The legislature also stepped into the homeowners' insurance cost issue, which by 2002–03 was reaching crisis proportions. One effect of the legislature's involvement was a "file and use" regulatory system that was implemented at the end of 2004. This system allowed insurers to institute new rates immediately after filing them with the Texas Department of Insurance. The commissioner of insurance can then disapprove of the new rates and may force the company to issue rebates to policyholders.[32] Thus, the commissioner of insurance appears to wield great power over insurance rates but only after those rates have gone into effect.

In 2007, Insurance Commissioner Mike Geeslin canceled Allstate's 5.9 percent rate hike, but Allstate got a court order allowing it to keep charging higher rates, at least temporarily. State Farm has been battling the Department of Insurance for years after ignoring an order from the commissioner to cut its rates by 12 percent.

State Farm's battle with the Texas Insurance Department has taken on the characteristics of a marathon. The company has shown no sign of compromising with the state in its legal battle over the state's claim that it overcharged homeowners. Additionally, in 2009–10 it twice filed to increase its insurance rates and ignored the insurance commissioner's claim that customers deserved a break from increases.

The result was a 35 percent boost in insurance rates for many customers in Dallas and nearby counties. It has also successfully sued the Texas Department of Insurance to keep the agency from publicizing documents related to its rate increases. State Farm's obstinacy in dealing with the Insurance Commission means that for a 10-year-old brick home in north Dallas with an insured value of $150,000, the premium would average about $1,679 per year compared with the average premium charged by other companies of $1,298 per year.[33] While the department's battles with Allstate and State Farm continue, insurance companies have been reducing coverage of homes on the Texas coast out of fear that a hurricane could cause the companies major losses.[34]

Although insurance companies advocate less regulation, consumer groups argue that the insurance commissioner has inadequate powers to deal with insurance companies. Indeed, it is doubtful that the commissioner has sufficient power to force an uncooperative insurer to comply with his or her decisions. The commissioner is also faced with the seemingly intractable problem of keeping rates low and coverage available in hurricane-prone areas to which more and more people are moving.

## Multimember Elected Boards

Members of two state agencies are elected by the voters: the Railroad Commission of Texas and the State Board of Education. The Railroad Commission has 3 members elected statewide to six-year terms of office. One of the 3 members is elected every two years. The Board of Education is a 15-member board elected to four-year terms from single-member districts.

**Railroad Commission of Texas (RRC)** At one time, the Railroad Commission of Texas (RRC) was one of the most powerful state agencies in the nation. It regulated intrastate railroads, trucks, and bus transportation and supervised the oil and natural gas industry in Texas. For most of the RRC's existence, regulation of the oil and gas industry was the RRC's primary focus.

Today, the RRC is a shadow of its former self. Court decisions, deregulation of the transportation industry, other state and federal legislation, and the decline in the nation's dependence on Texas's crude oil production have diminished the commission's power. In 2005 the RRC's limited authority over railroads was transferred to the Texas Department of Transportation, so the RRC now has no authority over what was once its major reason for existence. During the RRC's heyday when Texas was a major oil producer, the commission limited production to conserve oil and to maintain prices. Because it restricted oil production, the RRC was one of the most economically significant governmental bodies on the national and international stage. As oil production shifted to the Middle East, the RRC became the model for OPEC, the Organization of Petroleum Exporting Countries, which also seeks to limit oil production to maintain prices. At one time, members of the Texas RRC wielded such vast economic power that they were among the state's most influential politicians. As the power of the office has been weakened through declining oil production in the state and decreasing dependence on Texas oil, it has become increasingly difficult for railroad commissioners to move into higher offices, and their political visibility has waned.

**State Board of Education (SBOE)** The State Board of Education (SBOE) sets policy for public education (pre-kindergarten to twelfth-grade programs supported by the state government) in Texas. The education bureaucracy that enforces

*The State Board of Education sets policy for public education, from pre-kindergarten through 12th grade. In recent years, some of the board's decisions concerning curriculums and textbooks have generated controversy.*

the SBOE's rules and regulations is called the Texas Education Agency (TEA). Together these two bodies control public education in Texas by determining licensing requirements for public school teachers, setting minimum high school graduation criteria for recommended or advanced curriculums, establishing standards for accreditation of public schools, and selecting public school textbooks.

Texas spends millions of dollars each year purchasing textbooks, and the state furnishes these books without charge to students. Books must meet stringent criteria, and because the state buys so many textbooks, publishers print books especially for students in Texas. Often states that spend less money on textbooks than Texas must purchase those originally printed for Texas.

The commissioner of education is appointed by the governor from a list of candidates submitted by the SBOE. He or she is administrative head of the TEA and serves as adviser to the SBOE. The commissioner of education is at the apex of the public education bureaucracy in Texas.

In recent years, the Texas SBOE has become an ideological battleground. In 2009, that conflict led the board to review how evolution was taught. In what was a partial defeat for the social conservatives, no longer would teachers be required to teach "strengths and weaknesses" of evolution, although they would be encouraged to teach "all sides." Other battles have broken out over other aspects of educational policy. For example, one policy goal was that high school students were to learn how the cultural contributions of "people from various racial, ethnic, gender, and religious groups shape American culture." One of the leading social conservatives on the board proposed an unsuccessful amendment that would delete the words "from various racial, ethnic, gender, and religious groups." That suggested, of course, that teaching would not focus on the role of those specific groups in shaping American culture. Another amendment proposed that students be required to evaluate the contributions of significant Americans—Thurgood Marshall, Billy Graham, Newt Gingrich, William F. Buckley Jr., Hillary Rodham Clinton, and Edward Kennedy. All passed the board except for Edward Kennedy. Other issues involve whether César Chávez was significant enough to be in social studies textbooks and whether greater emphasis should be placed on Christianity in the founding of the nation.

Although many Texas voters may not be aware of them, the battles fought within the SBOE have wide-reaching effects. They affect not only the education of Texas schoolchildren, but also that of children across the nation. Because the state's textbook market is so large, the content of the textbooks used in Texas sets the tone for textbook content in other states that are less populous and therefore have smaller markets for texts.[35]

As a result of the 2010 elections, there was a power shift on the SBOE when the leader of the social conservatives who was the chair of the board was defeated. The 2012 elections created a new battle for control of the board. Because of changes in the single-member districts of the SBOE that were caused by redistricting, all members of the board were up for election.[36] The 2012 election reduced the social conservative bloc still further, continuing the anti–social conservative trend begun in the 2010 elections.

## Making Agencies Accountable

In a democracy, elected officials are ultimately responsible to the voters. Appointed officials are indirectly accountable to the people through the elected officials who appoint them. Both are responsible to legislatures that determine responsibilities and appropriate money to carry out those responsibilities. In Texas, the plural executive is responsible to the legislature for its biennial funding and to the voters for re-election. The myriad state agencies look to the legislature for funding, and once every 12 years they must justify their existence to the **Sunset Advisory Commission (SAC)**.

The 12-member SAC has 5 members from the Texas Senate and 1 public member appointed by the lieutenant governor. Five members from the Texas House and 1 public member are appointed by the Speaker of the Texas House.

The Sunset Review Act created the SAC in 1977. The act established specific criteria to be considered in evaluating the continuing need for an agency. One of several laws enacted in the mid-1970s to bring more openness and accountability to Texas government, the Sunset process establishes a date on which an agency is abolished unless the legislature passes a bill for the agency to continue in operation.

During its Sunset review, an agency must, among other things, document its efficiency, the extent to which it meets legislative mandates, and its promptness and effectiveness in handling complaints, and it must establish the continuing need for its services. The review process is lengthy, lasting almost two years.

After a thorough study of an agency, the SAC recommends one of three actions to the legislature: (1) the agency continues as is, with no change in its organization or functions; (2) the agency continues but with changes (reorganization, a new focus for the agency, or merger with other agencies); or (3) the agency is abolished.

If option 1 or 2 is recommended, specific action by the legislature is required before the date of the agency's abolition. Option 1 requires specific legislation to re-create the agency in its existing form. Option 2 requires the legislature to re-create the agency with some or all of the changes recommended by the SAC. If the legislature agrees the agency should be abolished, no action is necessary. It will expire at the Sunset deadline; the sun sets and the agency is no more.

Each state agency has been through the Sunset process. The legislature has allowed the sun to set on more than 58 agencies; 12 agencies have been merged with existing bodies. Since 1978, the legislature has accepted the majority of recommendations of the SAC.

**Sunset Advisory Commission (SAC)** a commission created in 1975 for the purpose of reviewing the effectiveness of state agencies

**for critical analysis**

What is the source of power of Texas bureaucratic agencies? How are these agencies held accountable to other elected public officials or the public?

# ● Thinking Critically about the Executive in Texas

At the national level, the president is elected, through the Electoral College, by the people as a whole. The president is the spokesperson for the nation in the world and is the commander in chief of the armed forces. When there is a national crisis, the people look to the president for leadership. As we saw earlier, throughout the twentieth century, the power and authority of the presidency increased significantly, often at the expense of Congress. American democracy has become an executive-led system, with a weak Congress and a partially demobilized electorate.

Such is not the case in Texas. The fear of a strong executive who could ignore the wishes of either the legislature or the people, as was the case during Reconstruction in Texas, led in 1876 to a constitution that created a plural executive. The governor is the chief executive officer in the state, elected directly by the popular vote of all the people of Texas. People turn to the governor for leadership and direction during times of crisis. But compared with that of the president, the power of the Texas governor is more limited. Many key executive officials, including the lieutenant governor, the attorney general, the comptroller, and the land commissioner, are elected—like the governor—directly by the people. These members of the plural executive, along with other popularly elected statewide boards and commissions, possess power and authority that under other constitutional arrangements the governor might possess. As has been noted throughout this chapter, Governor Perry's ability to accumulate power in the governor's office is unprecedented in recent history. That his successors will be able to wield the limited powers of the governor as efficiently is by no means certain.

The existence of an institutionally weak office of the governor and a plural executive has a number of important implications for democracy in Texas. First, because power and authority are divided among a number of distinct officers, no individual is fully responsible for executive initiatives in the state. Indeed, executive officials can struggle with each other for power as they seek to move the state government in different directions. Partisanship can exacerbate the natural conflict built into the executive branch in Texas. A Democratic lieutenant governor may or may not be willing to work closely with a Republican governor. But the worst clashes may be among executive officials of the same party. The fight between Governor Rick Perry and Comptroller Caroline Strayhorn, both Republicans, culminating in Strayhorn's running against the incumbent governor as an independent in 2006, is only the latest example of a fundamental truth in Texas politics: the executive does not have to speak with one voice or in harmony with itself.

A second consequence of the plural executive for democracy in Texas is that it has given rise to a powerful executive officer in the state legislature, outside the office of the governor. The lieutenant governor has become, along with the Speaker of the House, one of the two most important officials in the state legislature. The lieutenant governor, not the governor, runs the Senate. The lieutenant governor, not the governor, is the executive branch's chief legislative official.

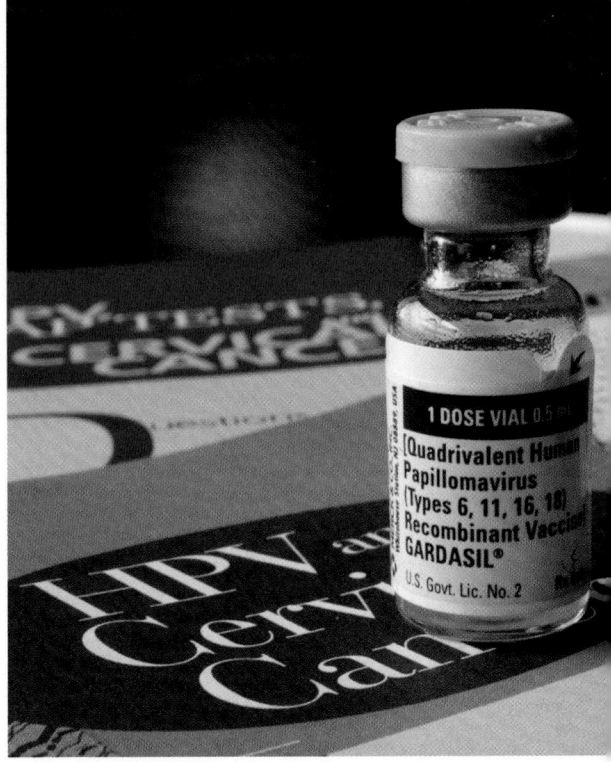

*Governor Perry experienced a significant check from the legislature in 2007 after he issued an executive order for girls in Texas to be vaccinated against HPV, a sexually transmitted disease linked to cervical cancer. The legislature passed a bill overturning the order.*

The dispersal of power and authority among a number of different executive offices in the state has a third consequence for democracy in the state. Additional points of access are created for interest groups seeking to influence government and public policy, making it easier for special interests to impose their will on the policy-making process. The 2012 elections have continued the Republican Party's firm hold over the plural executive and will have major consequences for policy and politics in Texas.

# study guide

**Practice online with:** Chapter 24 Diagnostic Quiz ▪ Chapter 24 Key Term Flashcards

## The Governor

■ **Describe the powers of the Texas governor and the limits of the governor's power (pp. 913–24)**

Although the Texas governor is considered weak compared to other states, the power of appointing members to boards has made Governor Rick Perry the most powerful governor in state history largely because of his long tenure. Among the executive powers the governor possesses are appointment, budgetary, military, and police powers. Among his legislative powers are message and veto powers and the ability to call special sessions of the legislature.

### Key Terms

**impeachment** (p. 916)

**appointment** (p. 920)

**patronage** (p. 920)

**senatorial courtesy** (p. 921)

**executive budget** (p. 921)

**legislative budget** (p. 921)

**veto** (p. 923)

**post-adjournment veto** (p. 923)

**line-item veto** (p. 923)

**special session** (p. 923)

### Practice Quiz

1. Which of the following is *not* necessary to become governor of Texas? *(p. 915)*
   a) A governor must be at least 30 years of age.
   b) A governor must have lived in Texas for at least five years.
   c) A governor must be a U.S. citizen.
   d) A governor must be a lawyer.
   e) A governor must have substantial campaign funding.

2. The election for governor of Texas is held in an off-year in order to *(p. 915)*
   a) increase voter participation in elections in odd-numbered years.

   b) influence the presidential vote in Texas.
   c) decrease the likelihood of voter fraud.
   d) give governors an opportunity to campaign for presidential candidates.
   e) prevent the presidential vote in Texas from influencing the election of state officials.

3. The only constitutional method of removing the governor is *(p. 916)*
   a) *quo warranto* proceedings.
   b) *ex post facto* removal.
   c) a vote of no confidence.
   d) impeachment.
   e) impeachment and conviction.

4. The governor's most effective power in controlling the executive branch of state government is the power *(p. 920)*
   a) of the veto.
   b) of appointment.
   c) of removal.
   d) of judicial review.
   e) to create a state budget.

5. The governor's veto is absolute when it is a *(p. 923)*
   a) line-item veto.
   b) special veto.
   c) budgetary veto.
   d) post-adjournment veto.
   e) select veto.

6. The governor can grant *(p. 923)*
   a) pardons.
   b) suspended sentences.
   c) probation.
   d) retrials.
   e) parole.

 **Practice Online**
Video exercise: *The 2010 Governor's Election*

## The Plural Executive

■ **Identify the other elected officials who make up the plural executive (pp. 924–31)**

Unlike the national level, the governor does not appoint a "cabinet." Voters in Texas elect the lieutenant governor and other major statewide offices in separate elections. This disperses power within the executive branch, which means that executive officers must compromise not only with the legislature, but within the executive branch.

## Key Terms

**plural executive** (p. 924)

**secretary of state** (p. 925)

**lieutenant governor** (p. 926)

**attorney general** (p. 928)

**land commissioner** (p. 929)

**agricultural commissioner** (p. 929)

**comptroller** (p. 930)

## Practice Quiz

7. Which member of the plural executive is appointed? *(p. 924)*
   a) secretary of state
   b) land commissioner
   c) lieutenant governor
   d) comptroller of public accounts
   e) attorney general

8. The attorney general is *(p. 928)*
   a) part of the governor's Cabinet.
   b) elected independently of the governor.
   c) appointed by the Texas Supreme Court.
   d) the governor's lawyer.
   e) chosen by the State Bar of Texas.

9. The land commissioner *(p. 929)*
   a) records all property deeds.
   b) administers state land.
   c) surveys property in Texas.
   d) is appointed by the state Senate.
   e) administers Big Bend National Park.

10. Members of the plural executive are accountable to the *(p. 930)*
    a) voters and the governor.
    b) legislature and voters.
    c) constitution.
    d) state supreme court.
    e) legislature.

 **Practice Online**
"Exploring Texas Politics" exercise: *The Role of Lieutenant Governor*

# Boards, Commissions, and Regulatory Agencies

■ **Explain the roles played by boards, commissions, and regulatory agencies (pp. 931–36)**

The governor's most important power is the ability to appoint people to boards, commissions, and regulatory agencies. Such institutions have important powers to interpret state regulations and make a difference in the lives of everyday Texans.

## Key Terms

**bureaucracy** (p. 931)

**Sunset Advisory Commission (SAC)** (p. 936)

## Practice Quiz

11. The Public Utilities Commission *(pp. 932–33)*
    a) regulates some electric rates.
    b) regulates local phone rates.
    C) maintains a website so consumers can compare electric rates.
    d) maintains a "do not call" registry.
    e) All of the above are features of the Public Utilities Commission.

12. The Texas Department of Insurance *(p. 933)*
    a) has limited power to regulate insurance rates.
    b) collects the penalties for not buying health insurance under Obamacare.
    c) sells insurance for mold coverage.
    d) is run by a five-member elected board.
    e) All of the above are features of the Texas Department of Insurance.

13. The Railroad Commission of Texas *(p. 934)*
    a) is responsible for the safety of the state's railroads.
    b) issues bonds to support the state's transportation needs.
    c) regulates oil and gas production in Texas.
    d) approves mergers of railroads.
    e) is the most powerful agency in the state.

14. The State Board of Education *(p. 935)*
    a) has a major role in determining the books used in Texas public schools.
    b) is appointed by the legislature.
    c) reviews applications to state colleges and universities.
    d) is responsible for school property tax rates.
    e) governs local boards of education.

15. Which agency investigates the performance of state agencies and recommends whether an agency should be abolished, continued as is, or continued with changes? *(p. 936)*
    a) Legislative Budget Board
    b) Legislative Research Bureau
    c) Texas Research League
    d) Public Utilities Commission
    e) Sunset Advisory Commission

# Recommended Websites

Attorney General of Texas
www.oag.state.tx.us/

Lieutenant Governor of Texas
www.ltgov.state.tx.us/

Office of the Governor
www.governor.state.tx.us/

Railroad Commission of Texas
www.rrc.state.tx.us/

Sunset Advisory Commission
www.sunset.state.tx.us/

Texas Department of Agriculture
www.agr.state.tx.us/

Texas General Land Office
www.glo.state.tx.us/

Texas Secretary of State
www.sos.state.tx.us/

Window on State Government (Comptroller's Office)
www.window.state.tx.us/

Some opponents of the death penalty argue that Texas's system of electing judges and prosecutors leads to more executions, as elected officials try to show voters that they are tough on crime. Texas executes more people than any other state.

# The Texas Judiciary

**WHAT GOVERNMENT DOES AND WHY IT MATTERS** The presiding judge of the Texas Court of Criminal Appeals, Sharon Keller, has cultivated a "tough on crime" image. Her campaign literature, for example, has shown a figure behind bars with the headline, "He Won't Be Voting for Judge Sharon Keller."

However, Keller may have crossed the line in terms of her harshness toward criminal defendants on September 25, 2007. That evening, Michael Richard was scheduled to die by lethal injection. Earlier that day, the Supreme Court of the United States had agreed to hear a challenge to the constitutionality of death by lethal injection. Ordinarily, that would lead to a petition to the Court of Criminal Appeals for a stay of execution, in order to wait for the decision of the U.S. Supreme Court.

Things went terribly wrong. The lawyers for Michael Richard were working against a tight deadline for their petition and they claimed they experienced computer problems that created a delay in preparing their documents. They called the Court of Criminal Appeals and asked that the court stay open an extra 20 minutes past the 5:00 P.M. closing time so that the stay of execution request could be filed. Judge Keller refused to keep the court open. In making this decision, she did not consult with other judges on the court, some of whom were working in the same building. Other judges on the court have stated that they would have stayed late to hear the appeal if they had known about it. Michael Richard was executed that evening.

Complaints were filed against Judge Keller with the State Commission on Judicial Conduct. The hearing officer, known as a special master, found plenty of blame to go around in this case. He found that the Texas Defender Service (TDS), which provided legal representation for Michael Richard, was unable to show that it actually had computer problems that made it unable to file the petition on time. In fact, the TDS did not even contemplate filing its petition until over two hours after the Supreme Court had agreed to hear the lethal injection case. Then the TDS assigned a junior attorney to prepare documents, the first of which was not ready until 4:45 P.M. and the rest of which were not completed until 5:56 P.M. that day.

Nor did the Court of Criminal Appeals escape criticism. And though Judge Keller's behavior did not, according to the special master, justify removal from office or reprimand, it "was not exemplary of a public servant." He stated, "Although [Judge Keller] says that if she could do it all over again she would not change any of her actions, this cannot be true. Any reasonable person, having gone through this ordeal, surely would realize that open communication, particularly during the hectic few hours before an execution, would benefit the interests of justice. Further, her judgment in not keeping the clerk's office open past 5:00 to allow the TDS to file was highly questionable. In sum, there is a valid reason why many in the legal community are not proud of Judge Keller's actions." In the fall of 2010, a special court of review dismissed the public warning against Keller on the grounds that a warning cannot be a penalty following a formal proceeding against a judge. Currently she is challenging in court a $100,000 fine by the Texas Ethics Commission—the largest fine the commission has imposed against a political figure—for failing to disclose about $3.8 million in assets in financial statements that are required to be filed with the commission. Keller claimed she was vindicated in the Michael Richard execution case and that the Ethics Commission fine is "excessive" and that her violation was unintentional.[1] She ran for re-election as presiding judge on the Court of Criminal Appeals in 2012. Keller won with about 55.5 percent of the vote.

This case highlights some notable characteristics of the Texas judiciary: (1) Texas judges are elected, which encourages judges and judicial candidates to behave in ways that may cultivate the favor of voters even as the judges seem to sidestep notions of justice; and (2) one reason that Texas is the death penalty capital of the nation may be that it has a partisan election system for selecting not only judges but also the district attorneys, who prosecute crimes.

## chaptergoals

● **Identify the types of courts in Texas and their jurisdictions** (pages 945–49)

● **Describe the types of cases heard in Texas courts** (pages 949–52)

● **Explain how judges are selected in Texas** (pages 952–62)

● **Analyze how courts impact the lives of Texans** (pages 962–71)

# Court Structure

Like the federal courts, the state and local courts in Texas are responsible for securing liberty and equality under the law. However, the democratic mechanisms put into place in Texas to select judges and to hold them accountable for their actions are quite different from those at the national level. Federal judges are appointed by the president and confirmed by the Senate. They have lifetime appointments. This means that federal judges, subject to good behavior in office, are largely free from the ebb and flow of politics. They do not have to cater to public opinion and are empowered to interpret the law as they see fit, without fear of reprisal at the polls. In Texas, however, judges are elected to office. Although they may initially be appointed to their offices, sooner or later they are responsible to the people for their decisions in office. Election of judges brings not only the people but also interest groups into the selection and retention of judges. The influence of special interest money in judicial campaigns raises important questions about the relationship between the rule of law and the nature of democratic politics.

Texas has a large and complex court structure consisting of a hodgepodge of courts with overlapping jurisdiction (see Figure 25.1). Additionally, some courts have specialized jurisdiction, whereas others have broad authority to handle a variety of cases. At the highest level for civil cases is the **Texas Supreme Court**, which consists of nine justices, including a chief justice. This court hears civil and juvenile cases only and, at the state level, it has final appellate jurisdiction. The only requirements for being a Texas Supreme Court justice are that one must be a citizen of the United States and a resident of Texas, be at least 35 years of age, and have been either a practicing lawyer or judge for at least 10 years. The term of a justice is six years, with at least three justices being elected every two years.

**Texas Supreme Court** the highest civil court in Texas; consists of nine justices and has final state appellate authority over civil cases

*The Texas Supreme Court is the highest civil court in Texas. The court consists of nine justices, who are pictured here (as of 2012).*

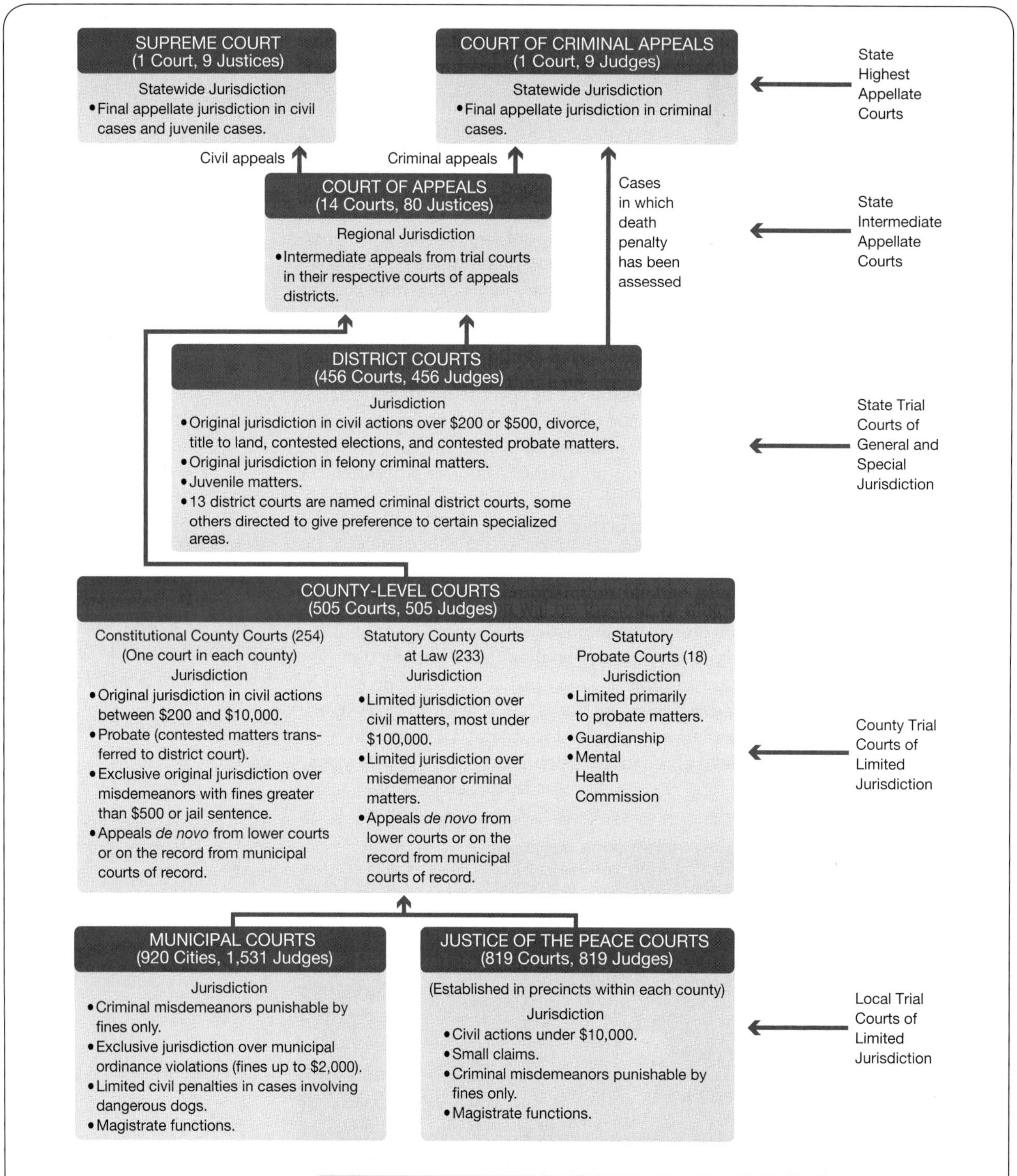

**FIGURE 25.1**

## The Structure of the Texas Court System

SOURCE: Texas Office of Court Administration.

The diagram contains the following elements:

**SUPREME COURT (1 Court, 9 Justices)**
Statewide Jurisdiction
- Final appellate jurisdiction in civil cases and juvenile cases.

**COURT OF CRIMINAL APPEALS (1 Court, 9 Judges)**
Statewide Jurisdiction
- Final appellate jurisdiction in criminal cases.

State Highest Appellate Courts

Civil appeals — Criminal appeals

Cases in which death penalty has been assessed

**COURT OF APPEALS (14 Courts, 80 Justices)**
Regional Jurisdiction
- Intermediate appeals from trial courts in their respective courts of appeals districts.

State Intermediate Appellate Courts

**DISTRICT COURTS (456 Courts, 456 Judges)**
Jurisdiction
- Original jurisdiction in civil actions over $200 or $500, divorce, title to land, contested elections, and contested probate matters.
- Original jurisdiction in felony criminal matters.
- Juvenile matters.
- 13 district courts are named criminal district courts, some others directed to give preference to certain specialized areas.

State Trial Courts of General and Special Jurisdiction

**COUNTY-LEVEL COURTS (505 Courts, 505 Judges)**

Constitutional County Courts (254) (One court in each county)
Jurisdiction
- Original jurisdiction in civil actions between $200 and $10,000.
- Probate (contested matters transferred to district court).
- Exclusive original jurisdiction over misdemeanors with fines greater than $500 or jail sentence.
- Appeals *de novo* from lower courts or on the record from municipal courts of record.

Statutory County Courts at Law (233)
Jurisdiction
- Limited jurisdiction over civil matters, most under $100,000.
- Limited jurisdiction over misdemeanor criminal matters.
- Appeals *de novo* from lower courts or on the record from municipal courts of record.

Statutory Probate Courts (18)
Jurisdiction
- Limited primarily to probate matters.
- Guardianship
- Mental Health Commission

County Trial Courts of Limited Jurisdiction

**MUNICIPAL COURTS (920 Cities, 1,531 Judges)**
Jurisdiction
- Criminal misdemeanors punishable by fines only.
- Exclusive jurisdiction over municipal ordinance violations (fines up to $2,000).
- Limited civil penalties in cases involving dangerous dogs.
- Magistrate functions.

**JUSTICE OF THE PEACE COURTS (819 Courts, 819 Judges)**
(Established in precincts within each county)
Jurisdiction
- Civil actions under $10,000.
- Small claims.
- Criminal misdemeanors punishable by fines only.
- Magistrate functions.

Local Trial Courts of Limited Jurisdiction

The **Texas Court of Criminal Appeals** is the highest appeals court in the state for criminal cases. This court also has nine judges, including a presiding judge. The pay, terms, and qualifications of Court of Criminal Appeals judges are the same as for Texas Supreme Court justices. Perhaps the most important task of the Court of Criminal Appeals is its jurisdiction over automatic appeals in death penalty cases.

Both the Supreme Court and the Court of Criminal Appeals have appellate jurisdiction. This means that they have the authority to review the decisions of lower courts to determine whether legal principles and court procedures were followed correctly. This authority also provides the power to order that a case be retried if mistakes were made. Texas has 14 other appellate courts, located in various parts of the state, which have both criminal and civil jurisdiction. These courts are intermediate appellate courts and hear appeals from the trial courts. Usually, before the Supreme Court or the Court of Criminal Appeals hears a case, the initial appeal has been heard by one of the **courts of appeal**. Presently, there are 80 judges who serve on the 14 courts of appeal, which range in size from 3 to 13 judges. Although there are occasions when every judge on a court of appeal will hear a case, mostly appeals at this level are heard by panels of three judges. The requirements for a court of appeals justice are the same as those for justices of the higher courts. Each of the 14 courts has one chief justice.

The major trial courts in Texas are the **district courts**. Each county has at least one district court, although rural parts of Texas may have several counties that are served by one district court. Urban counties have many district courts. Harris County (Houston), for example, has 59 district courts and Dallas County has 48. District courts usually have general jurisdiction, meaning that they hear a broad range of civil and criminal cases. However, in urban counties, some district courts with specialized jurisdiction hear only civil, criminal, juvenile, or family law matters. Those district courts having general jurisdiction would hear felonies, divorces, land disputes, election contests, and civil lawsuits. Currently, there are 456 district judges.

**Texas Court of Criminal Appeals** the highest criminal court in Texas; consists of nine justices and has final state appellate authority over criminal cases

**courts of appeal** the fourteen intermediate-level appellate courts that hear appeals from district and county courts to determine whether the decisions of these lower courts followed legal principles and court procedures

**district courts** the major trial courts in Texas, which usually have general jurisdiction over a broad range of civil and criminal cases

*The Texas Court of Criminal Appeals is the highest court in the state for criminal cases. Like the Texas Supreme Court, it has nine justice (pictured here as of 2012).*

**county judge** the person in each of Texas's 254 counties who presides over the constitutional county court and the county commissioners court, with responsibility for the administration of county government; only some county judges carry out judicial responsibilities

**constitutional county courts** the courts that exist in some counties that are presided over by county judges

**statutory county courts at law** courts that tend to hear less serious cases than those heard by district courts

**statutory probate courts** specialized courts whose jurisdiction is limited to probate and guardianship matters

**justice of the peace courts** local trial courts with limited jurisdiction over small claims and very minor criminal misdemeanors

Texas is unusual in having the office of **county judge** (also known as constitutional county court judge) in each of its 254 counties. Not only does the county judge preside over the county commissioners court and thus have responsibilities for administration of county government, but the county judge also presides over the county court. Often these **constitutional county courts** have jurisdiction over uncontested probate cases and over the more serious misdemeanor criminal offenses involving fines greater than $500 or a jail sentence as well as over civil cases where the amounts in dispute are relatively small generally in the $200 to $10,000 range. The county court may also hear appeals from municipal courts or from justice of the peace courts. Thus, the county judge combines political-administrative functions with some judicial functions. However, in the more populated counties, there are county courts at law and sometimes probate courts. As a result, in the larger counties most, and sometimes all, of the county judges' judicial duties are now performed by other courts.

In larger counties, there are **statutory county courts at law**. Since the county courts at law were created by statute, often at widely different times, the jurisdiction of these courts varies significantly. Usually, the county courts at law hear appeals from justices of the peace and from municipal courts. In civil cases, they usually hear cases involving sums greater than would be heard by a justice of the peace court, but less than would be heard by district courts. Typically, county courts at law hear civil cases involving less than $100,000. In comparison to the district courts, the county courts at law hear less serious criminal offenses.

Some of the county courts at law have specialized jurisdiction; most commonly these are in the most urban counties, where some of the courts will have only civil jurisdiction and others only criminal jurisdiction. Currently there are 233 county court at law judges.

In the most urban areas of the state, the legislature has created courts known as **statutory probate courts**. These courts are highly specialized, as their primary activity involves probate matters that relate to the disposition of property of deceased persons. They may also deal with matters relating to guardianship of people unable to handle their own affairs, and they may handle mental-health commitments. In other parts of the state, depending on the statute, probate matters may be heard by the county court, the county court at law, or the district court. Currently, there are 18 statutory probate court judges.

Each county in Texas has between one and eight justice of the peace precincts, depending on population, although large urban counties have more than one judge in each precinct. Harris County, for example, has two in each of eight precincts. Within each precinct are **justice of the peace courts**. There are 819 justice of the peace courts in Texas. These courts hear class C misdemeanors, which are less serious crimes. They also have jurisdiction over minor civil matters, and they function as small claims courts. Suits in small claims court must be for less than $10,000, but the suits can be handled more informally in small claims court than in a higher level court and they can be handled without a lawyer. Justices may issue search and arrest warrants. In counties without medical examiners, judges may fulfill the administrative functions of coroners.

Justices of the peace mostly handle traffic misdemeanors. Of the more than 2.45 million criminal cases disposed of by justice of the peace courts in the year ending August 31, 2010, over 1.9 million were traffic misdemeanors. In contrast, justice of the peace courts heard only about 546,000 civil cases.[2]

Justices of the peace have faced considerable criticism in recent years. In Dallas County, an auditor discovered 22,000 unprocessed traffic cases. The justice of the peace had failed to collect as much as $2 million in fines. Unlike any other judge in Texas except for the county judge (who is often an administrator rather than a

*The boxes of evidence that the State of Texas prepared for the trial against tobacco companies in 1997 occupied an entire gym in Texarkana. In a civil case, the plaintiff bears the burden of proof and must demonstrate that the defendant is more than not likely responsible for the harm suffered by the plaintiff.*

judge), 92 percent of the 819 justices of the peace in Texas are non-lawyers, and their lack of legal credentials has led to considerable debate in the state.[3] The office has its origins in medieval England and has existed in Texas since 1837, even before statehood. A justice of the peace was supposed to be a respected person in the community who was chosen for ability, judgment, and integrity. In the days of the frontier, they provided legal authority where no other existed. Indeed, the famed Judge Roy Bean was a justice of the peace. Today, as the former State Bar president Frank Newton has pointed out, "In almost every large metropolitan area, there are some JPs who do virtually nothing and sort of get lost in the shuffle. People don't tend to get all excited about JP elections. Most people don't know what a JP does. JP is not a very prestigious job."[4]

**Municipal courts** have been created by the legislature in each of the incorporated cities of the state. There are 920 cities and towns in Texas that have these courts; larger cities have multiple courts. There are 1,531 municipal court judges in the state. Municipal courts have jurisdiction over violations of city **ordinances** and, concurrent with justice of the peace courts, have jurisdiction over class C misdemeanors, for which the punishment for conviction is a fine. Municipal judges may issue search and arrest warrants, but they have only limited civil jurisdiction.[5] Municipal courts, like justice of the peace courts, function primarily as traffic courts. In the year ending August 31, 2010, municipal courts disposed of almost 7 million cases. About 5.1 million of these cases were non-parking traffic misdemeanors; another 663,091 were parking cases.[6]

**municipal courts** local trial courts with limited jurisdiction over violations of city ordinances and very minor criminal misdemeanors; municipal courts are located in each of Texas's incorporated cities and towns

**ordinance** a regulation enacted by a city government

# ● The Legal Process

> **Describe the types of cases heard in Texas courts**

Just as the Texas Supreme Court hears civil cases and the Texas Court of Criminal Appeals hears criminal cases, it is useful to think of the law as divided into these parts. **Civil law** involves a dispute, either between private individuals or between businesses,

**civil law** a branch of law that deals with disputes that do not involve criminal penalties over relationships, obligations, and responsibility. Though there are exceptions with a violation of the civil law, the remedy is often for the offending party to pay compensation to the injured party.

In contrast, **criminal law** involves the violation of concepts of right and wrong as defined by criminal statutes. In criminal law, the state accuses individuals of violations and, if found guilty, the violator is subject to punishment. In some cases, that punishment may involve loss of liberty or even loss of life.

In civil law, an aggrieved person will usually obtain a lawyer and file a petition that details the **complaint** against the person accused of causing the harm. The petition is filed with the clerk of court, who issues a citation against the defendant. The defendant will usually file an **answer** explaining why the allegations are not valid. Depending on the issue, the amounts of money that may be awarded as damages, and the probability of success, the aggrieved person may be able to obtain the services of a lawyer on a **contingent fee** basis. This means that the lawyer will not be paid if the case is lost but will obtain a portion of the damages awarded if the case is won. It is not unusual for such contingent fee arrangements to involve one-third or more of the damages award plus expenses. Lawyers who handle cases on contingent fee agreements often handle personal-injury cases and are known as trial lawyers. Traditionally, these lawyers will contribute money to judicial candidates who are sympathetic to plaintiffs. The reason is that they make money only if they win, so they have a strong economic interest in supporting the election efforts of judicial candidates who are sympathetic to plaintiffs and to the award of large damages.

The person being sued either will have to hire an attorney on his or her own or, if insured, will be represented by an attorney paid for by the insurance company. Fee arrangements vary for civil defense lawyers, but often they are paid by the hour. Their economic incentives to contribute money to judicial campaigns may be different from trial lawyers, but they do contribute large sums to judicial campaigns in order to elect judges who support their views in tort law.

The court to which a civil case is taken depends on the type of case and the amount of money involved. Most commonly, a civil case will be settled, meaning the dispute is resolved without going to court. Settlements may, however, occur during trial, sometimes immediately before a jury renders its decision. If a case is not settled and goes to trial, it may be heard either by a judge or, if requested by either side, by a jury. Although civil jury cases do not have to be unanimous in Texas, the burden of proof is on the plaintiff. The standard of proof that the plaintiff must meet is **preponderance of the evidence**. That means that the plaintiff must show that it is more likely than not that the defendant is the cause of the harm suffered by the plaintiff.

Civil cases may involve tiny amounts of damages or they may involve billions of dollars, which have the potential of breaking even huge corporations. Such was the case in the 1980s when Pennzoil successfully sued Texaco in a dispute over the takeover of the Getty Oil Company.[7]

Civil case verdicts may, of course, be appealed. Appeals are usually from the trial court to the intermediate court of appeal and perhaps further to the state supreme court. Given the cost of appeals and the delay that is involved, it is not unusual for a settlement to be reached after the verdict, but before the case goes through the appellate process. For example, a plaintiff might agree to settle for much less than the verdict in the case to avoid the expense, delay, and risk of losing in further appeals.

In criminal cases, the state alleges a violation of a criminal law and is usually represented in court by a prosecutor. Some prosecutors are career prosecutors with

**criminal law** the branch of law that regulates the conduct of individuals, defines crimes, and specifies punishment for criminal acts

**complaint** the presentation of a grievance by the plaintiff in a civil case

**answer** the presentation of a defendant's defense against an allegation in a civil case

**contingent fee** a fee paid to the lawyer in a civil case and which is contingent on winning the case

**preponderance of the evidence** the standard of proof in a civil jury case, by which the plaintiff must show that the defendant is more likely than not the cause of the harm suffered by the plaintiff

vast trial experience. These people will often prosecute the most difficult and complex cases, such as felonies and **capital cases.** However, because the pay of prosecutors is often much lower than that of private lawyers who do litigation in the private sector, it is common for most prosecutors to be quite young and inexperienced. Once they gain trial experience, prosecutors commonly move into the private sector.

Defendants may hire criminal defense attorneys, who usually charge a flat fee to handle the case. Criminal defense lawyers, of course, do not work on a contingent fee basis. Since most criminal defendants are found guilty, criminal defense lawyers often prefer to obtain as much of their fee as possible in advance of the verdict. For defendants who cannot afford their own attorney, free legal representation is provided in one of two ways, depending upon the location of the case.

Some parts of Texas have public defender offices where salaried lawyers provide criminal defense services for at least some indigent adult defendants in a county. Bexar County has established the first public defender office for indigent criminal appeals. Travis County has a public defender office representing only indigents with mental impairments.[8] A public defender office represents indigents in capital cases in west Texas.[9]

More commonly in Texas, indigent criminal defendants are represented by court-appointed lawyers. Usually, these lawyers receive government-paid fees that are less than what they would receive from defendants who pay privately. Thus, some lawyers are reluctant to fulfill court appointments; others may not put the time and energy into a court-appointed case that they would if they were privately paid; others take court appointments because they have a limited number of paying clients; and still others take court appointments to gain experience. Concern over the poor quality of legal representation provided indigent criminal defendants, especially in capital cases, led to legislation in 2001 to increase the pay and qualifications of court-appointed lawyers.

Serious crimes are **felonies.** In those cases, as well as many lesser offenses known as **misdemeanors,** prior to the trial there will be an indictment by a grand jury. In Texas, a **grand jury** consists of 12 persons who sit for two to six months. Depending on the county, a grand jury may meet only once or twice, or it may meet several times a week. Although sometimes grand juries are selected randomly from a pool of qualified citizens, mostly Texas grand jurors are chosen by a commissioner system. A district judge will appoint several grand jury commissioners, who will then select 15 to 20 citizens of the county. The first 12 who are qualified become the grand jury.[10]

Grand juries can inquire into any criminal matter but usually spend most of their time on felony crimes. They work in secret and rely heavily on the information provided by the prosecutor, though in some cases grand juries will work quite independently of the prosecutor. These grand juries are called "runaway grand juries" because the prosecutor has lost control of them, but such cases are very rare. If nine of the grand jurors decide a trial is warranted, they will indict a suspect. An **indictment** is also known as a "true bill." On the other hand, sometimes a grand jury does not believe a trial is warranted. In those cases, the grand jury issues a "no bill" decision.

Although a defendant has the right to trial by jury, he or she may waive that right and undergo a **bench trial** before the judge only. Most commonly, the defendant

*In 2008 members of the Fundamentalist Church of Jesus Christ of Latter-Day Saints appealed to the Texas courts after Child Protective Services took more than 400 children from the polygamist compound into custody.*

**capital case** a criminal case where the death penalty is a possible punishment

**felony** a serious criminal offense, punishable by a prison sentence or a fine. A capital felony is possibly punishable by death.

**misdemeanor** a minor criminal offense, usually punishable by a small fine or a short jail sentence

**grand jury** jury that determines whether sufficient evidence is available to justify a trial; grand juries do not rule on the accused's guilt or innocence

**indictment** a written statement issued by a grand jury that charges a suspect with a crime and states that a trial is warranted

**bench trial** a trial held without a jury and before only a judge

**plea bargain** negotiated agreement in a criminal case in which a defendant agrees to plead guilty in return for the state's agreement to reduce the severity of the criminal charge or prison sentence the defendant is facing

**beyond a reasonable doubt** the legal standard in criminal cases, which requires the prosecution to prove that a reasonable doubt of innocence does not exist

will engage in a **plea bargain**, which is an agreement to plead guilty in exchange for a lighter sentence than might be imposed if the defendant were found guilty at trial. Approximately 97 percent of criminal convictions in Texas are the result of plea bargains.[11] If the defendant does choose trial by jury, felony juries will have 12 members; misdemeanor juries will have 6 members. There must be a unanimous verdict of guilty or not guilty. If the jurors are not unanimous, the result is a hung jury and a mistrial is declared. The prosecutor may then choose to retry the case. In addition to the requirement of unanimity in jury decisions, another important difference between civil and criminal cases is the standard of proof. In criminal cases, rather than preponderance of the evidence, the standard is **beyond a reasonable doubt**. This means that the prosecutor must prove the charges against the defendant to such a high standard that no reasonable doubt of innocence exists in the minds of the jurors.

If a guilty verdict is returned, there will be a separate hearing on the sentence, which in Texas is sometimes also determined by the jury. At the sentencing hearing, factors such as prior conviction record and general background will be considered, even though it is likely these factors could not be considered during the trial.

Of course a defendant may also appeal a verdict. Usually the appeals are by a convicted defendant who alleges that an error in the trial may have affected the case's outcome. In rare cases, a prosecutor may also appeal. For the most part, however, criminal defendants will appeal their convictions to an intermediate appeals court and perhaps further to the Texas Court of Criminal Appeals. In capital cases, however, the appeal will be directly to the Texas Court of Criminal Appeals.

# ● Judicial Politics

**Explain how judges are selected in Texas**

Although there are still generalist lawyers who handle all sorts of cases, much of the practice of law is very specialized. Thus, in the process of selecting civil court judges, trial lawyers and civil defense lawyers tend to back opposing candidates for judgeships. It is not unusual for trial lawyers to support one candidate, often the Democrat, who is more likely to be the more liberal, or pro-plaintiff candidate, and for the civil defense lawyers to support the Republican, who is more likely to be the conservative, or pro-defendant, candidate. The civil defense lawyers will often align themselves with business groups and with professional groups, such as medical doctors, to support judges inclined to favor the civil defense side.

In the process of selecting criminal court judges, it is sometimes possible to see criminal defense lawyers backing one candidate and prosecutors backing the other. Some prosecutors' offices are quite political, and the prosecutors will publicly support pro-prosecution judicial candidates. They will often be aligned with victims' rights groups. Criminal defense lawyers, on the other hand, will often back one of their own in contested criminal court races.

One big difference in the campaigns of civil court judges versus criminal court judges is the amount of money involved. Enormous amounts can be at stake in civil cases, and so it is worth lots of money to trial lawyers and civil defense interests to elect candidates favorable to their points of view. On the other hand, with the exception of a relatively few highly paid criminal defense lawyers, the practice of criminal law is not very lucrative. Prosecutors are on salary, and usually the salaries are not large. Criminal defense lawyers often represent clients with little

# How Do Texans Choose Their Judges?

Texans elect many, many judges. Most voters know little about the individual judicial candidates, and use the party affiliations of the candidates to fill in the gaps about who the candidate is and what type of judge he or she will be. As a result, voters often vote "straight party," punching one place on the ballot to vote for all the nominees of their party.

The results of the 2010 election show how closely the results of district judge elections track straight ticket voting. The graphs below compare the percentage of the vote won by the average district court judicial candidate to the percentage of gubernatorial votes won in Texas's five largest counties.

## Vote Share of Gubernatorial Candidates and District Judges, 2010

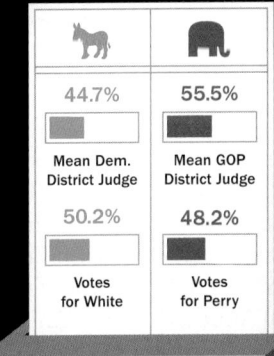

HARRIS COUNTY

| 44.7% | 55.5% |
|---|---|
| Mean Dem. District Judge | Mean GOP District Judge |
| 50.2% | 48.2% |
| Votes for White | Votes for Perry |

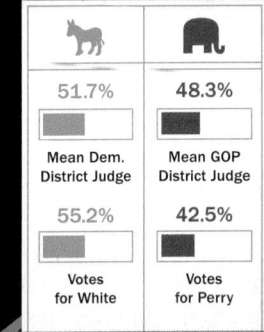

DALLAS COUNTY

| 51.7% | 48.3% |
|---|---|
| Mean Dem. District Judge | Mean GOP District Judge |
| 55.2% | 42.5% |
| Votes for White | Votes for Perry |

TARRANT COUNTY

| 37.4% | 62.6% |
|---|---|
| Mean Dem. District Judge | Mean GOP District Judge |
| 41.0% | 56.0% |
| Votes for White | Votes for Perry |

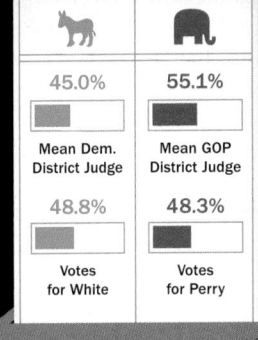

BEXAR COUNTY

| 45.0% | 55.1% |
|---|---|
| Mean Dem. District Judge | Mean GOP District Judge |
| 48.8% | 48.3% |
| Votes for White | Votes for Perry |

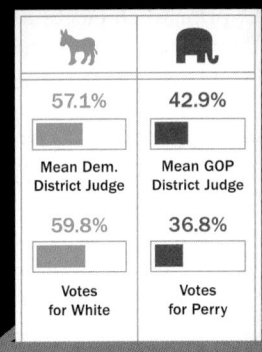

TRAVIS COUNTY

| 57.1% | 42.9% |
|---|---|
| Mean Dem. District Judge | Mean GOP District Judge |
| 59.8% | 36.8% |
| Votes for White | Votes for Perry |

## for critical analysis

1. Why do you think voters rely on party as a cue to tell them about what type of judge a candidate would be? What are the advantages of using party as a cue? What are the disadvantages?

2. How does holding partisan judicial elections affect what type of judges get elected? If Texas changed to a system of appointed judges like we have for federal courts, would a different type of judge be selected? If so, why?

SOURCE: Data are from the appropriate County Clerk office.

Note: Percentages are all two-party vote share. "Mean GOP (or Dem.) District Judge" is the mean vote share for all Republican (or Democrat) district judge candidates in that county.

*Is justice for sale in Texas? Because statewide judicial races have been increasingly expensive, candidates for judgeships have been forced to raise more money. This, in turn, has led to criticism that judicial decisions are, in effect, being bought.*

money. And most criminal cases are plea-bargained. The economic incentives to contribute large sums to criminal court races don't exist. The result is that a strong candidate for the Texas Supreme Court may raise in the neighborhood of $1 million for a campaign, whereas a strong candidate for the Texas Court of Criminal Appeals may raise $100,000. However, as Texas has become Republican at the statewide level, hard-fought contests between Democrats and Republicans for the Texas Supreme Court and the Texas Court of Criminal Appeals have become rare.

## Initial Appointment of Judges by the Governor

A notable aspect of the Texas judiciary is that with the exception of municipal judges, who tend to be appointed by local governments, all judges are elected in partisan elections. Still, because the governor appoints district and appellate judges to fill vacancies prior to an election or to fill judgeships on new courts, large percentages of judges initially get on the bench through appointment. Although there has been some controversy over the relatively small number of appointments of minorities made by some governors, gubernatorial appointment has generated little additional controversy.[12] Table 25.1 shows the percentage of district and appellate judges who have initially gained their seats through appointment by the governor. Currently, about 52 percent of appellate judges and 37 percent of the trial judges initially got on the bench through appointment.[13] Still, the controversial issue in Texas judicial politics deals with how the remaining judges obtained their seats and how all judges retain their seats if they wish to remain in office. That controversy involves the partisan election of judges in Texas.

## The Elections Become Highly Partisan

Until 1978, the selection of judges in partisan elections did not create much concern. Texas was overwhelmingly a Democratic state, and judges were elected as Democrats. The only real competition occurred in the Democratic primary, and

## Percentage of Judges Obtaining Their Position Initially through Appointment

| YEAR | TRIAL COURTS* (%) | APPELLATE COURTS** (%) |
|------|-------------------|------------------------|
| 1962 | 57 | 50 |
| 1984 | 67 | 51 |
| 1998 | 46 | 40 |
| 2001 | 34 | 38 |
| 2003 | 43 | 43 |
| 2006 | 43 | 50 |
| 2009 | 36 | 51 |
| 2011 | 37 | 52 |

* Trial courts are the district and criminal district courts.
** Appellate courts are the supreme court, the court of criminal appeals, and the courts of appeal.
SOURCES: Anthony Champagne, "The Selection and Retention of Judges in Texas," *Southwestern Law Journal* 40 (May 1986): 66; Texas Office of Court Administration, "Profile of Appellate and Trial Judges" as of September 1, 1998, 2001, 2003, 2006, and 2009 and March 1, 2011.

with the political advantage of incumbency, judges were rarely defeated even in the primary. The only real competition in judicial races occurred in those relatively rare cases where there was an open seat in which no incumbent sought office. Beginning in 1978, however, changes began to occur in Texas judicial politics. William Clements, the first Republican governor since Reconstruction, was elected. The governor has the power to appoint judges to the district and higher courts when new courts have been created or when a judicial vacancy occurs as a result of death, resignation, or retirement. Unlike the previous Democratic governors, who appointed members of the Democratic Party, Clements began appointing Republicans. With that advantage of incumbency and with the increasing popularity of the Republican party label, some of the Republican judges began to win re-election.

Helped by the popularity of Ronald Reagan in Texas, other Republicans began seeking judicial offices and winning. Thus, by the early 1980s, in statewide elections and in several counties in Texas, competition began to appear in judicial races. With that competition, incumbent judges began to be defeated. Sensing the growth of Republican strength, a number of Democratic judges switched to a Republican Party affiliation. From 1980 through July 24, 1985, 13 district and appellate judges changed from the Democratic to the Republican Party; 11 county court judges switched; and 5 justices of the peace changed parties. Judge Don Koons switched parties in early 1985 and explained his move to the Republican Party by saying: "I ran as a Democrat in 1982. It was a long, tough year, but we won. On the other hand, it cost a lot more money and time away from the bench to run as a Democrat. The work suffers some, and you've got to be always hustling money."[14] Koons apparently believed that with the emerging strength of the Republican Party, a switch in party affiliation would make his job more secure.

Judicial elections became more expensive because judicial candidates needed money to run meaningful campaigns. In particular, campaigns that used television advertising became very expensive because of high media costs.

Judicial candidates needed money because judicial races tend to have low-visibility campaigns in which voters are unaware of the candidates. The races tend to be overshadowed by higher-visibility races, such as the race for governor or U.S. senator. Money was needed to give judicial candidates some degree of name visibility by voters. However, in general, Texas voters do not give much money to judicial campaigns. Instead, it is lawyers, interest groups, and potential litigants who tend to be donors in judicial races.[15] That has raised concerns about the neutrality of Texas judges who are deciding cases that involve the financial interests of persons who have given them campaign funds. A Texas poll found that 83 percent of the public thought that judges were strongly or somewhat influenced by contributions in their decisions. Ninety-nine percent of lawyers believed that campaign contributions have at least some influence on judges. Perhaps even more striking, 86 percent of judges reported that they believed campaign contributions had at least some influence on judicial decisions.[16]

Contributions for judicial races in Texas can sometimes amount to several hundred thousand dollars, especially for hotly contested district court races or appellate races. In general, however, the most expensive races are for the Texas Supreme Court. When races are contested between Democratic and Republican candidates, a candidate can raise well over $1 million, though these hard-fought races are increasingly rare as statewide elections have moved into the Republican column. Table 25.2 shows the average contribution to Texas Supreme Court candidates for each election period from 1982 through 2010. The contribution data are reported for those races that were contested by both a Republican and a Democratic candidate. In the 2000 Texas Supreme Court elections, the Republicans were so strong that no Democrat even bothered to run for any position on the Texas Supreme Court.

In spite of judicial campaigns, however, voters often know little about judicial candidates. As a result, they vote not for the best-qualified or most experienced judicial candidate, but for the party label. As the Republican Party has become increasingly dominant in statewide races, it is the Republican label that has determined the outcome of judicial races. Related to the importance of party label in judicial races is the effect of top-of-the-ticket voting. In 1984, the popularity of Ronald

*In 2012, Democrat Keith Hampton ran against Sharon Keller for presiding judge of the Court of Criminal Appeals. Although he ran a fairly strong campaign, Hampton faced a major difficulty because Texas has more Republicans than Democrats, and voters tend to follow party labels in judicial races. Keller defeated Hampton 55.5 percent to 41.2 percent in the general election.*

**TABLE 25.2**

## Average Contributions to Texas Supreme Court Candidates*

| YEAR | AVERAGE FOR ALL CANDIDATES | AVERAGE FOR WINNING CANDIDATES |
|---|---|---|
| 1980 | $155,033 | $298,167 |
| 1982** | 173,174 | 332,998 |
| 1984** | 967,405 | 1,922,183 |
| 1986 | 519,309 | 1,024,817 |
| 1988 | 859,413 | 842,148 |
| 1990 | 970,154 | 1,544,939 |
| 1992 | 1,096,001 | 1,096,687 |
| 1994 | 1,499,577 | 1,627,285 |
| 1996 | 656,190 | 1,277,127 |
| 1998 | 521,519 | 829,794 |
| 2000 | NA† | 584,719†† |
| 2002† | 425,474 | 568,430 |
| 2004** | 394,906 | 548,685 |
| 2006** | 995,218 | 1,792,523 |
| 2008 | 654,819 | 910,973 |
| 2010 | 438,854 | 744,033 |

*Averages are reported for candidates from contested races featuring both a Republican and Democratic candidate.
**The 1982, 1984, 2004, and 2006 elections each featured only one contested race with both a Democratic and Republican candidate.
†No Democrats ran in the three Supreme Court elections in 2000.
††Average campaign contributions for the three victorious Republicans; none had a Democratic opponent.
*Chief Justice Tom Phillips ran for re-election and refused to accept any campaign contributions beyond his cash on hand, which amounted to $19,433. His Democratic opponent, however, raised almost no funds—$12,815. Phillips was the victor in this race, which lowers the average contributions for this year.
SOURCES: Kyle Cheek and Anthony Champagne, *Judicial Politics in Texas* (New York: Peter Lang, 2005), 38; Institute on Money in State Politics.

Reagan seemed to help Texas judicial candidacies as many voters cast straight or almost straight Republican ballots. In that year, Reagan received nearly 64 percent of the presidential vote in Texas. All four Republican incumbent district judges who were challenged by Democrats won. Sixteen Democratic incumbent district judges were challenged by Republicans. Only three of those Democrats won. In contrast, in 1982, U.S. senator Lloyd Bentsen ran for re-election. Bentsen was a very popular senator and a Democrat. His candidacy on the Democratic ballot seems to have encouraged voters to cast ballots for Democrats further down on the ticket. Bentsen received slightly more than 59 percent of the vote in Texas. In that year, 26 Republican incumbent district judges faced Democratic opposition; only 14 won. Yet 16 Democratic district judges faced opposition, and 14 of them won.[17]

Even voters who try to make a serious effort to learn about judicial candidates can have a hard time. In Houston, for example, voters are faced with ballots loaded with so many judicial candidates that it becomes nearly impossible to be an informed voter. In 1994, one of the most extreme examples of a long judicial ballot occurred in Harris County, where voters were faced with 45 judicial elections that were primary elections followed by 8 additional runoff primary elections. In the general election, there were 59 contested judicial elections and 16 more elections where the judicial candidate was unopposed. In 2010, Harris County voters cast ballots in 10 contested appellate court races and 36 contested district court races.

## The Name Game

**for**critical**analysis**

How does the selection process influence who becomes a judge in Texas?

In 1994, Cathy Herasimchuk ran for the Texas Court of Criminal Appeals. In a three-way Republican primary she won only 26 percent of the statewide vote. The candidates in the Democratic and Republican primaries who did make the runoff for that seat all had simple, easy-to-spell and easy-to-pronounce names. Herasimchuk was appointed to the Court of Criminal Appeals in 2001, but in running for election to the court in 2002, she realized she had a problem with her name. As she said, "Everybody told me you couldn't win city dog catcher with the name Herasimchuk, and they all turned out to be accurate." Herasimchuk's problems getting elected certainly had nothing to do with her credentials. She has been a Harris County prosecutor, a criminal defense lawyer, an adviser to then-governor Bush, and a law school lecturer. When she ran in 2002, she did so under the name Cathy Cochran.[18]

The name game continued in the 2008 elections for judges in Harris County. Most Republican judges in that county were swept out of office, but four Republicans survived. They had all been challenged by Democrats with unusual names. As a result, the incumbent Republican judge Sharon McCally was able to defeat the Democratic challenger Ashish Mahendru; Republican judge Mark Kent Ellis defeated Democrat Mekisha Murray; Judge Patricia Kerrigan, a Republican, defeated the Democrat, Andres Pereira; and Judge Joseph Halback defeated his Democratic challenger, Goodwille Pierre.[19]

## Minority Representation in the Texas Judiciary

**for**critical**analysis**

Few minorities hold judicial office in Texas. Although African Americans and Hispanics make up over 45 percent of the Texas population, relatively few Texas judges belong to these groups. Offer at least three suggestions, including alternative selection methods, to increase the number of minorities holding judicial office in Texas.

Minority groups have been concerned that countywide and larger partisan judicial races make it difficult for minorities to get elected to judgeships—and that Texas judges do not reflect the diversity of the state. Table 25.3 lists the ethnicity of Texas judges as of March 1, 2011.

Although women do not make up 50 percent of the judiciary as they do in the population, there is a higher proportion of women in the Texas judiciary than minorities. Women were at one time a great rarity on the bench. In 1970, only 1 percent of the nation's judiciary was female. As late as 1979, only 4 percent of the nation's judges were women.[20] In Texas, the first woman to serve as a state judge was Sarah Hughes, who was appointed in 1935 and who served as a district judge until 1961, when she was appointed to the federal bench. Famous for a number of her decisions, including one that forced Dallas County to build a new jail, she is probably best known as the judge who swore in Lyndon Johnson as president after the assassination of John F. Kennedy. In March 2011, however, 41 percent of appellate judges in Texas were women, and 28 percent of district judges were women. Thirty-five percent of county court-at-law judges were female, as were 33 percent of the probate judges. Sixteen percent of county judges, 35 percent of municipal judges, and 35 percent of justices of the peace were women.[21]

## TABLE 25.3

## Race and Ethnicity of Texas Judges, 2011

| RACE AND ETHNIC STATUS | APPEALS COURTS | DISTRICT COURTS | COUNTY COURTS AT LAW | PROBATE COURTS | COUNTY COURTS | MUNICIPAL COURTS | JP COURTS |
|---|---|---|---|---|---|---|---|
| % White | 85% | 77% | 72% | 78% | 91% | 78% | 77% |
| % Black | 3% | 5% | 4% | 0% | 1% | 5% | 3% |
| % Hispanic | 11% | 16% | 23% | 22% | 8% | 15% | 20% |
| % Other | 1% | 2% | 1% | 0% | 0% | 3% | 0% |
| Total number of responding judges | 93 | 373 | 164 | 9 | 176 | 1,069 | 555 |

SOURCE: Texas Office of Court Administration, "Profile of Appellate and Trial Judges," March 1, 2011.

Different interpretations have been offered for the low numbers of minorities on the bench. The lack of racial and ethnic diversity on the bench is a nationwide problem. Ninety-two percent of the state judges in the nation are white.[22] Civil rights groups in several states with elective judiciaries, including Texas, have argued that white voters dominate countywide and larger districts and will vote against minority judicial candidates. Civil rights organizations representing Latinos and African Americans have argued that for minorities to get elected to office, there must be smaller judicial districts where minority voters make up the majority.

An alternative argument is that minority candidates in Texas, like minority voters, tend to be Democrats at a time when Republicans increasingly are winning judicial races. Thus, minorities do not get elected to judicial office because they run as Democrats.[23] Still another argument is that there are few minority judges because there are few minority lawyers and, with the exception of constitutional county court judges and justices of the peace, judges in Texas must be lawyers.

The issue of minority representation on the bench has been the subject of major concern by minority and civil rights leaders in Texas. It was also the subject of prolonged federal litigation. In 1989, a case was tried in federal court in Midland. The case, *League of United Latin American Citizens v. Mattox*, was a suit against countywide election of judges in 10 of the larger counties in Texas.[24] The suit, filed by minority plaintiffs, argued that countywide election of judges diluted the strength of minority voters and violated the Voting Rights Act. The trial judge agreed with the plaintiffs and, after a political solution failed, ordered that judges be elected in nonpartisan elections from smaller judicial districts. The trial court order, however, was blocked by the Fifth Circuit, which is the federal court of appeals for the region that includes Texas.[25] The case was then appealed to the U.S. Supreme Court, and the Supreme Court held that the Voting Rights Act did apply to judicial elections.[26] The case was then returned to the Fifth Circuit to examine whether minority voting strength was diluted and to determine the state's interest in maintaining countywide elections. A three-judge panel decided in favor of the minority plaintiffs, resulting in an apparent settlement agreement that in the larger counties judges would be elected from smaller districts. However, in important cases, it is sometimes possible to appeal the decision of a panel to the entire court of appeals.

When this happens, the court is said to sit **en banc**. That happened when some of the defendants in the suit were unhappy with the settlement. On appeal, the entire Fifth Circuit ruled in 1993 that party affiliation of minority candidates explained the failure of minority judicial candidates to win election rather than the candidates' minority status. Thus, countywide election of judges was not illegal, and there was no legal need to reduce the size of districts from which judges were elected.[27]

Since that decision, minority leaders and minority groups have continued to express concerns about the small numbers of minority judges, but any solution that would involve smaller districts would have to result from an act of the legislature rather than the actions of a federal court. Judicial reform bills in the legislature since this decision have included provisions for smaller judicial districts, but those bills have not passed.

Perhaps the strongest judicial reform bill was one backed by then-Democratic lieutenant governor, Bob Bullock, who created a task force to try to develop an acceptable compromise on the judicial selection issue. The proposed constitutional amendment designed by the task force passed the Texas Senate in 1995 but failed to pass the Texas House. Under the plan, all appellate judges would be appointed by the governor. District judges, on the other hand, would be chosen from county commissioner precincts in nonpartisan elections. After serving for a time, they would run countywide in **retention elections**, in which there would be a "yes" or "no" vote on their retention in office and where they would face no opponent on the ballot.

On the surface, the compromise seemed to offer something for almost everyone. Because the governor appointed appellate judges, judges would have greater career security and no worries about campaign funding. The business community, recognizing that Texas tended to elect conservative governors and was increasingly likely to elect conservative Republican governors, got appointed appellate judges. Nonpartisan elections would protect trial judges from party sweeps in which judges are voted out of office solely because of their party affiliation. Minorities would get smaller judicial districts for the major trial courts. But what looked like a great compromise fell through.

Although African Americans supported the compromise, Latinos did not. The two largest counties in Texas—Harris and Dallas—elected a total of 96 of the 386 district judges then chosen in Texas. Under the compromise, one-fourth of Harris and Dallas county judges would be elected from each of the county commissioners' precincts in that county. Both Dallas and Harris counties had three white county commissioners and one African American. Latinos, on the other hand, elected no county commissioner and believed that the compromise would not promote the election of more Latino judges. They believed that to elect Latino judges, considerably smaller districts were needed. As a result, much Latino support was not forthcoming. The political parties also opposed the compromise. Nonpartisan elections might protect the interests of judges, but they weakened the political parties. Additionally, an appointive system for appellate judges reduced the number of elective offices, thereby reducing the role of the political parties. Further, the business community had concerns that smaller districts might create a narrower electorate, which in some areas might prove unduly sympathetic to plaintiffs who file suit against businesses. Finally, although his powers would have increased with an appointed appellate judiciary, Governor George W. Bush opposed the compromise, probably because he did not want to oppose the Republican Party. In the face of opposition from so many key players, the Bullock proposal was defeated.[28]

Whatever the cause of the low number of minority judges, the lack of diversity on the bench, the role of money in judicial races, the defeat of incumbents, the importance of party label, top-of-the-ticket voting, and the "name game" have all led to dissatisfaction with the practice of selecting judges by partisan election. Neither is selection by gubernatorial appointment an entirely satisfactory alternative. It is contrary to Texas's traditional distrust of a powerful chief executive, and at a time when Texas governors are Republicans, it also is not a system that Democrats tend to favor. All of these factors have created support for alternative judicial selection systems.

## Alternative Means of Selection

One alternative system for selecting judges is nonpartisan election. Such a system for selecting judges in Texas would eliminate much of the partisan politics, but, at the same time, it would make it more difficult for candidates to reach voters. This is because in a truly nonpartisan election, judicial candidates would have to run for office without the support of political parties. In some states that have ostensibly nonpartisan elections, such as Ohio, the parties continue to take an active role to the point that it is difficult to distinguish that type of nonpartisan system from a partisan election system. If Texas instituted a truly nonpartisan system, however, candidates would require even more campaign money to reach voters they could no longer reach through the mechanisms of the political parties.

Most commonly, however, judicial reformers argue for a system of judicial selection that is commonly called **merit selection** of judges. In this system, a blue-ribbon committee consisting of lawyers and lay people supplies to the governor the names of a small number of candidates for a judgeship. The governor makes the judicial appointment from this list, and after the judge serves for a brief time, he or she runs unopposed in a retention election. As might be expected in an election where one does not have an opponent, the incumbent usually wins. One study of retention elections found that only 1.6 percent of incumbent judges were defeated in retention elections.[29] Yet from time to time, interest groups will organize—and spend a great deal of money—to oppose a judge in a retention election, and sometimes these efforts have been successful. One of the chief concerns about merit selection is the nature of the merit selection commission, since those commissioners filter out all but a handful of prospective judges. Some are quite fearful of this centralized method of determining who should be judges, and although there is much support for merit selection in Texas, there is also much opposition.[30]

In recent years, one of the most popular reform proposals has been a system known as "appoint-elect-retain." Under this system, the governor would appoint a judge with confirmation by two-thirds of the state senate. The governor-appointed nominee would not assume office until confirmed by the senate, which would meet year-round for the purpose of dealing with judicial confirmations. In the first election thereafter, the judge would run in a contested nonpartisan election and subsequently in retention elections. This is, of course, a hybrid plan that encompasses aspects of gubernatorial appointment, nonpartisan election, and merit selection.

Another reform plan would have appellate vacancies filled by gubernatorial appointment with senatorial confirmation. The appellate judges would then run in nonpartisan elections followed by retention elections. In Dallas, Tarrant, and Bexar counties, district court judges would be elected from county commissioner precincts rather than from one district encompassing the entire county. Additionally, in Harris County, district judges would be elected from smaller geographic regions than county commissioner precincts. Supporters of this plan tend to believe that it would increase the number of minority judges, especially trial court judges in urban areas. Of course, this is also a hybrid plan designed to combine various reform proposals in order to gain sufficient support to become the new way Texas selects its judges.

*In 2009, Rick Perry appointed Eva Guzman—the first Latina woman to serve on the Texas Supreme Court—to fill a vacancy on the court. Guzman was elected to a full term in the 2010 election.*

**merit selection** a judicial reform under which judges would be nominated by a blue-ribbon committee, would be appointed by the governor, and, after a brief period in office, would run in a retention election

At least for the time being, however, it seems likely that not much will change in the way Texas selects its judges. Restructuring the system would be a major change, and these are always difficult to initiate. Changing might upset many voters, who like being able to vote for judges, and it would surely upset the political parties, which like having large numbers of judicial candidates running under their party label. It might also upset lawyers accustomed to the traditional ways of selecting judges and even judges who have benefited from the present system.

This resistance to change has led some to argue that judicial reform needs to be less drastic and more incremental. These reformers have suggested lengthening judicial terms of office on the grounds that longer terms mean fewer election contests and therefore less need for campaign money, less of a chance for defeat of incumbents, and less involvement of judges in politics. Another proposed incremental reform is to remove judges from the straight party vote. This means that a voter would actually have to cast a ballot for the judicial candidate rather than simply voting for every judge on the Republican or Democratic slate. Such a reform would remove judicial candidates from the effects of top-of-the-ticket voting. It would, of course, also reduce the votes that judges receive and lessen their dependence and reliance on the political parties. Still another suggested reform is to increase the levels of experience needed to serve on the bench. The idea is that even if judicial races are subject to the whims of voters, high qualifications for judges would mean that there would be experienced judges on the bench rather than novice judges who won simply because they were good campaigners or because they had the right party affiliation in that election year.

**Judicial Campaign Fairness Act**
a judicial reform under which campaign contributions are limited

Perhaps the most significant judicial reform in Texas is the **Judicial Campaign Fairness Act** of 1995. Texas is the only state with a campaign finance regulation of this type. Among the most important aspects of compliance with the act are campaign contribution limitations. For example, statewide judicial candidates limit themselves to contributions of no more than $5,000 from any individual in any election. Additionally, statewide candidates can receive no more than $30,000 per election from any law firm. Although the amounts of money that can be donated are still quite high, there has been a significant reduction from contribution amounts in the 1980s, when some donations exceeded $50,000. A recent strengthening of campaign contribution limits requires that if a judge receives campaign contributions from a party to a lawsuit, or if the party's lawyer had made contributions in excess of the limits in the Judicial Campaign Fairness Act, the judge must recuse him- or herself from the case.[31]

For many, the role of money in judicial campaigns is the most troubling issue in Texas judicial politics. As long as judges are elected, however, money will be necessary to run judicial campaigns, and where elections are competitive, a great deal of campaign money will be necessary.

# ● The Importance of the Texas Courts

**Analyze how courts impact the lives of Texans**

The Texas courts have an important impact on the lives of Texans in all sorts of ways, whether it involves the adjudication of a traffic accident, determination of child support, imposition of a jail sentence, or imposition of the most serious punishment of all, the death penalty. (Other aspects of criminal justice, especially sentencing and prison policy issues, are discussed in Chapter 27.)

## The Death Penalty

The most serious aspect of the judicial system in Texas, and one of the most controversial, is the death penalty. One study of the death penalty found that between 1973 and 1995, while 68 percent of death penalty appeals were successful nationwide, only 52 percent of appeals in Texas were successful. Another study found that after Texas created a new and faster system for handling death penalty appeals in 1995, only 8 of 278 cases were overturned by the Texas Court of Criminal Appeals.[32]

Another reason for defendants' lack of success in death penalty cases has to do with the quality of legal representation defendants receive if they have a court-appointed lawyer. One study found that more than 100 death-row inmates in Texas have been represented by court-appointed attorneys with troubled histories whose performance became an issue on appeal. In one case, for example, a lawyer with less than two years' experience practicing law, no permanent license to do so, and no background in capital murder cases was appointed to handle a death penalty appeal. And the Texas Court of Criminal Appeals let him stay on the case even when he asked the court to delay the appeal so that he could take an introductory course in death penalty defense. When the lawyer did get an extension to take his class, he still missed a filing deadline and filed his brief only after the court threatened him with jail for contempt. When it came time for him to argue the case before the court, he did not show. The court left him on the case and denied the appeal, noting that 6 of his 11 arguments were inadequately briefed and presented nothing for review. That lawyer was paid $8,647 by Smith County for his work on the case and subsequently lost his probationary law license when he

*Texas has made greater use of the death penalty than other states, but opponents argue that the legal system does not do enough to protect defendants in death penalty cases. In 2007, Johnny Ray Conner became the 400th person to be executed in Texas since 1982. In this photo, his family and death penalty opponents demonstrate against his execution.*

bounced checks for state bar dues and occupational taxes and failed to appear at a board hearing to defend himself. The board expressed concern that if he continued to practice law, there was a "likelihood that he would harm a client, obstruct the administration of justice, or violate [state bar rules]."[33]

Texas has led the nation in the number of executions since the death penalty was reinstated in 1976. Beginning in 1923, the state ordered that executions be carried out in Huntsville by electrocution. Prior to that time, each county was responsible for carrying out executions.[34] Since 1977, lethal injection has been the means for execution in Texas. The first execution by lethal injection was on December 7, 1982.

Between December 7, 1982, and July 21, 2011, Texas executed 472 people. As of July 2011, there were 311 people on death row.[35]

In Texas, one is subject to the death penalty for the murder of a public safety officer, fireman, or correctional employee; murder during commission of a kidnapping, burglary, robbery, aggravated rape, or arson; murder for hire; multiple murders; murder during a prison escape; murder by a prison inmate serving a life sentence; or murder of a child under the age of six.

A stay on death row can be a lengthy one, even in Texas. The average time spent on death row prior to execution is 10.6 years, although the time varies considerably. One inmate under a death sentence waived his appeals and spent only a little more than eight months on death row prior to execution. On the other hand, David Lee Powell spent 31 years on death row prior to being executed in 2010.[36] A death sentence carried out in February 1998, however, initiated the greatest controversy over the death penalty. The case of Karla Faye Tucker, a convicted ax murderer, generated national demands for clemency. Tucker was widely believed to have undergone a religious conversion after her 1983 conviction. She was also attractive and articulate and was the first woman in modern times condemned to be executed in Texas. Supporters of her execution argued that her gender, appearance, demeanor, and possible religious conversion were irrelevant to the fact that she was a convicted murderer who should be treated like others in similar situations.

One of the issues involving the death penalty is whether all offenders are treated in the same way. Racial/ethnic minorities, especially African Americans, are disproportionately represented on death row. On July 28, 2011, there were 122 African Americans on death row, 92 Hispanics, 93 whites, and 4 of "other" racial/ethnic classifications. Since 1982, 218 whites have been executed, 173 African Americans, 79 Hispanics, and 2 of "other" racial/ethnic groups. It may be that there is a bias in the criminal justice system that subjects minorities disproportionately to the death penalty. There has been considerable argument at the national level that minorities are unfairly sentenced to death more than are whites; however, the U.S. Supreme Court has refused to strike down the death penalty on the basis of statistical generalizations.[37]

The Texas Board of Pardons and Paroles votes on whether to recommend clemency for death-row inmates. Both a federal and a state judge have been highly critical of this process.[38] This board was originally considered to be a remedy for possible corruption in clemency granted by the governor. Prior to 1936, the governor essentially had unlimited power to grant clemency. This power was often abused, especially by Governor Miriam Ferguson, who granted 4,000 requests for commutations of sentences in 1922 alone. It was widely believed that payments were made for many of these acts of executive clemency. In reaction, a constitutional amendment was passed in 1936 that charged the board with giving the governor recommendations on clemency. Without such a recommendation, the governor can only grant a single 30-day reprieve. No other state so limits the powers of the governor.

In August 2007, the board recommended commutation of Kenneth Foster's sentence to be executed—only seven hours before Foster was scheduled to die. Governor Perry commuted Foster's sentence to life imprisonment about one hour later.[39] Foster's much-publicized case challenged two aspects of the death penalty in Texas: (1) Foster had been tried simultaneously with the other capital defendants rather than getting a separate trial; and (2) he was the getaway driver, not the actual shooter, in the robbery-murder.

Although Texas has been called the nation's "Death Penalty Capital," in recent years the number of death penalties imposed in the state has dropped. Comparing the periods 1992–96 and 2005–09, one study of the Texas death penalty found a 70 percent drop in death sentences in the latter period. One explanation offered for this finding was a decline in capital murder convictions over this time period. Another explanation was that, beginning in 2005, Texas juries could impose a sentence of life without parole. Additionally, U.S. Supreme Court decisions now prevent execution of juveniles or the mentally challenged. The study also noted that the cost of death penalty prosecutions has also greatly reduced the number of these cases in all but the 12 largest counties. Finally, it noted that a significant reduction occurred in Harris County, where most of the state's death sentences are imposed. Changes in its district attorney, scandal in the Houston crime lab, and improvements in the quality of capital defense work in Houston all contributed to the decrease in death penalties in Harris County.[40]

## Other Criminal Punishments

Although the death penalty is the most significant punishment that can be imposed, the Texas courts impose other deprivations of liberty as well.

Texas had 12.2 percent of the nation's total state prison population in January 1, 2010. Only the federal system had more prisoners under its jurisdiction.[41] Figure 25.2 shows the numbers of criminal cases disposed of by the courts of appeal and by the trial courts in 1990, 1998, 2000, 2003, 2006, and 2010. As can be seen from the figure, Texas judges dispose of large numbers of criminal cases, a caseload that is increasing over time.

## The Integrity of the Texas Criminal Justice System

In recent years, Texas has been more aggressive than any other state in imposing the death penalty. In 2000, Illinois suspended the death penalty after revelations of a number of wrongful convictions. New Jersey, North Carolina, and California are all considering moratoriums on the death penalty. Since 1989, 280 people wrongfully convicted of crimes in 34 states have been cleared as a result of DNA testing, including 17 people who served time on death row. Among those cleared of charges, the average prison time served was 13 years.[42] In the summer of 2005, Supreme Court Justice John Paul Stevens publicly noted that DNA evidence had shown that a number of death sentences had been erroneously imposed.[43]

This concern about the death penalty has even affected the internal dynamics of the Texas Court of Criminal Appeals, which is the state's court of last resort for death penalty appeals. Judge Tom Price challenged Presiding Judge Sharon Keller in the Republican primary in 2006 in part because he thought Judge Keller was too strict in her support of the decisions of trial courts in death penalty and

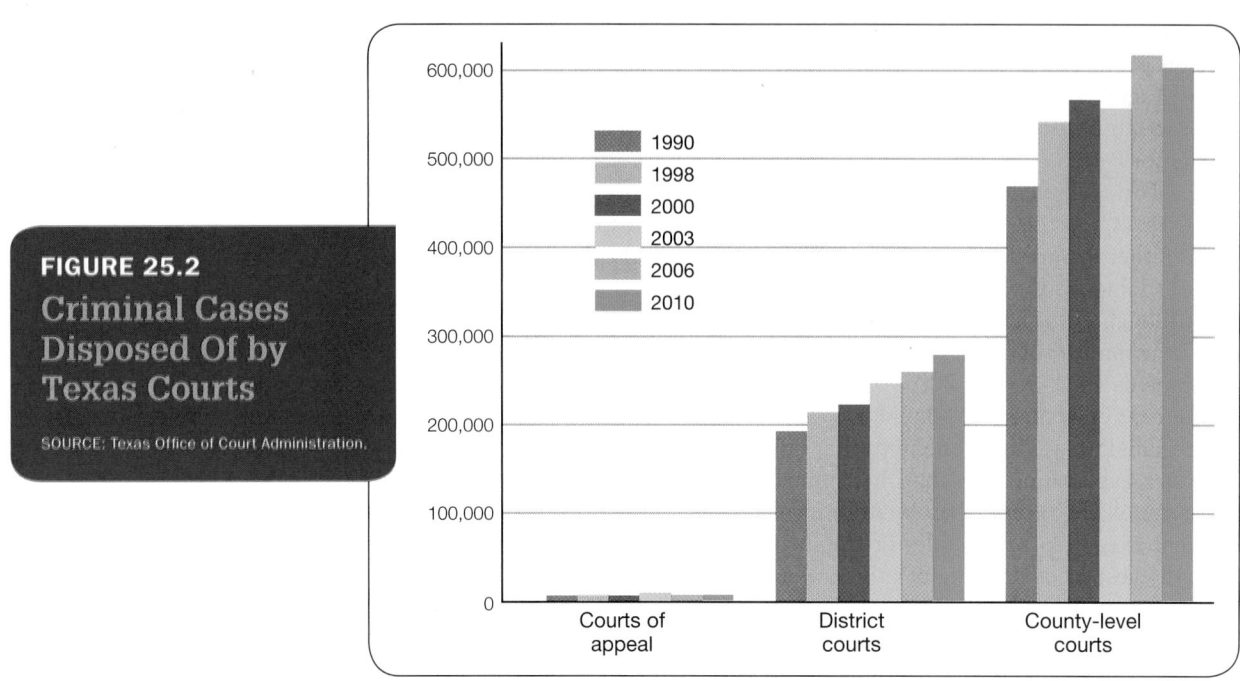

**FIGURE 25.2**

**Criminal Cases Disposed Of by Texas Courts**

SOURCE: Texas Office of Court Administration.

Legend:
- 1990
- 1998
- 2000
- 2003
- 2006
- 2010

Y-axis: 0, 100,000, 200,000, 300,000, 400,000, 500,000, 600,000

X-axis categories: Courts of appeal, District courts, County-level courts

## for critical analysis

During 1999 and 2000, Governor George W. Bush issued pardons to six prison inmates who were cleared by DNA testing. In June 2000, State Attorney General John Cornyn reported that at least six death-row inmates were sentenced to death on the basis of racially biased testimony. What can the state do to ensure that Texans receive equal treatment under the law? Can the judicial system ever ensure that only the guilty are convicted? Explain.

other criminal cases. The Price-Keller primary battle reflects an emerging concern in Texas that the state has been too free in its imposition of the death penalty and too unquestioning of the evidence that leads to the imposition of criminal punishments.

Other widely publicized matters, however, have also contributed to the questions raised about the adequacy of the Texas criminal justice system in protecting the innocent. One of those matters in particular became a national scandal—drug arrests in 1999 in Tulia, Texas. An undercover narcotics officer was responsible for the arrests of 47 persons in Tulia, 38 of whom were black and represented about 20 percent of the black adults in the town. The defendants were zealously prosecuted. Though they were charged with possessing only small amounts of cocaine, the defendants, including those with no prior records, received long sentences—including one as long as 361 years. The undercover officer was supported by local authorities even as questions about his veracity mounted, and he was even named Officer of the Year in Texas. Doubts about the arrests and convictions, however, did not die. The officer never wore a wire, never videotaped his alleged drug buys, and was never observed by another officer. Indeed, most of his alleged drug buys had no corroboration at all.

Two and a half years after the last trials of the Tulia defendants, the undercover officer had been fired from two other narcotics assignments. It became clear that he had no undercover narcotics experience prior to coming to Tulia and that he had left jobs as a deputy sheriff in two other towns, leaving behind significant unpaid debts. One of the sheriffs who had employed him had filed criminal charges against him for stealing from the county. Most importantly, his testimony in some of the cases involving the Tulia defendants was found to be false.

It eventually became clear that the Tulia drug busts were a massive miscarriage of justice. Thirty-five of the 47 defendants were pardoned by the governor; 9 had their charges dismissed prior to trial or were placed on deferred adjudication. One was a juvenile at the time of his alleged crime and so will not have an adult criminal record. The remaining two were sent to prison on probation violations. Most disturbing is that without the efforts of a small number of concerned citizens, lawyers, and the press, this gross abuse of the criminal justice process would have remained undetected and unresolved.[44]

Nor was the Tulia affair the only major problem with drug arrests. In 2001, the Dallas Police Department agreed to pay an informant $1,000 per kilogram of confiscated drugs. In order to avoid the dangers of implicating the actual drug dealers he knew, the informant instead planted drugs on law-abiding citizens—many of them Mexican immigrants and legal residents. Apparently the informant also realized he could make more money with less risk if he passed off gypsum, a mineral found in chalk, as cocaine. Convictions on dozens of drug cases were obtained without any testing to see if the seized material contained real drugs. The informant was the Dallas Police Department's highest paid in 2001, earning more than $210,000 for the seizure of nearly 1,000 pounds of cocaine and amphetamines that turned out to be fake drugs. Twenty fake drug cases were multi-kilo seizures, and two were the largest busts in the history of the Dallas police. Yet nothing seemed to arouse the suspicions of the police about the arrests.

This scandal reached deep into the police department, where there was a lack of supervision of undercover officers and an extreme push for numbers, both in terms of amounts of drugs seized and number of arrests. The implausibility of some of the arrests is amazing: a lone mechanic working under his car, with no guns or cash seized; a drug buy made on credit, according to the uncorroborated word of a confidential informant; and a seizure of 25 kilos of fake cocaine, for example. Nor did the district attorney's office escape blame: its policy was not to test seized drugs unless plea bargains failed and a case went to trial. When more than 80 of the drug cases were dismissed, Dallas district attorney Bill Hill appeared on television, insisting that many of those who were released were guilty. Were it not for the efforts of some criminal defense attorneys who were suspicious of the drug seizures, the Dallas Police Department might well still be seizing huge quantities of gypsum, paying top dollar for bogus information, and sending innocent men and women to prison.[45]

In 2002 the Houston Police Department Crime Laboratory was closed. An independent audit of the lab's DNA section had identified enormous problems. Analysts did not know how to do their jobs, and supervisors were incompetent. There were no quality control system and few standardized procedures. Other sections of the lab had problems as well, but the most serious were in the DNA section. Harris County sends more people to death row than any other county in the nation, and it had done thousands of other tests in non-death-penalty cases. All these tests were now placed in doubt. One of the first retests of the lab's work showed that a man who had been convicted of rape in 1998 at the age of 16 and had been given a 25-year sentence largely on the basis of DNA evidence was actually innocent.

Analysts in the lab received no training to help them keep pace with changes in DNA technology; they were overworked and were following procedures inconsistently. Additionally, the lab was never inspected by an outside agency and did not seek accreditation. Nor were judges, prosecutors, and defense attorneys able to spot the lab's sloppy work—they had not kept up with DNA technology either. The lab's facilities were not conducive to good forensic science. A leaky roof over the DNA section of the crime lab went unrepaired. In 2001, when Tropical Storm Allison hit Houston, water poured through the roof and DNA evidence in three dozen murder and rape cases was soaked. Bloody water was seen seeping out of evidence boxes.[46] DNA is often considered definitive proof of guilt or innocence in many serious crimes, but it is hardly definitive when the facilities are defective and the analysts are incompetent.

Texas is the home of more verified wrongful convictions than any other state. Forty-four exonerations have occurred in Texas as a result of DNA testing.[47] Dallas County, in particular, has emerged as the national leader in DNA exonerations; by late 2011, 22 men in Dallas County were exonerated by DNA evidence.[48] One reason for the large number of DNA exonerations is simply that Dallas County has a policy of preserving physical evidence for lengthy periods of time, but the findings also suggest a pattern of convictions based on eyewitness identification with little or questionable forensic evidence. Many of the wrongfully convicted were prosecuted during the administration of District Attorney Henry Wade, whose office was known for high conviction rates. Critics claimed his office prized those high conviction rates above all else.[49]

The case of Cameron Todd Willingham raises serious questions about whether an innocent man was executed for the arson murders of his three children. In 1991, Willingham's three girls were killed in a fire at their home shortly before Christmas. Willingham was convicted of starting the fire that killed them. Even though he was offered a plea bargain of a life sentence, he refused the plea, claiming that he was innocent. Willingham was executed in 2004. His conviction largely relied on expert testimony that the fire was arson. To a great extent, that testimony was based on the opinion that the fire had burned so hot that an accelerant must have been used to start the fire. Additionally, forensic tests had found evidence of an accelerant on the front porch of the house. However, before Willingham was executed, a noted arson expert examined the case and reported that the fire patterns could have occurred without the presence of an accelerant and that the prosecution's experts were relying on outdated information about the behavior of fire to reach their conclusions. The new report was submitted to the Board of Pardons and Paroles, but the board rejected the plea for clemency.

After Willingham's execution, reporters for the *Chicago Tribune* investigated the case and asked three fire experts to examine the evidence. They concluded that

*DNA evidence has been at the center of numerous recent legal controversies in Texas. In Dallas, new DNA technology led to the exonerations of 22 men who had been wrongfully convicted. Cornelius Dupree Jr. (center) served 30 years in prison before he was proven innocent by DNA testing and exonerated in 2011.*

the fire was not arson. Later, the Innocence Project, an organization dedicated to overturning wrongful convictions, asked four fire experts to review the Willingham case. They all agreed that the fire was not arson.

In 2005, Texas created a commission, the Texas Forensic Science Commission, to investigate claims of error or misconduct by forensic scientists. A fire scientist was hired by the commission to investigate the Willingham case and he, too, concluded there was no evidence the fire was arson.[50] In September 2009, 48 hours prior to the review of the report by the Texas Forensic Science Commission, Governor Perry replaced the head of the commission and two of its members. The meeting of the commission was canceled as a result. Earlier, Governor Perry had expressed confidence in Willingham's guilt, called the critics of the original arson investigation "supposed experts," and said that he had not "seen anything that would cause me to think that the decision [to execute Willingham] was not correct."[51] In July 2011, after a new commission chair showed greater interest in the case, Attorney General Greg Abbott issued a ruling that restricted any further investigation. Nevertheless, cases of persons currently in prison on arson charges will now be reviewed to determine if their imprisonment was due to bad arson science.[52]

Another area of concern is the use of dog scent evidence to convict persons accused of crimes. Some prosecutors have claimed this evidence is as powerful as DNA evidence in supporting a conviction. This technique does not involve following a scent or picking out a package of drugs by trained dogs. Instead, it involves distinguishing different odors among people, identifying one odor, and then matching that odor to evidence obtained from a crime scene. A dog is first introduced to a scent sample collected at a crime scene and then presented with a series of containers with similar scents—one taken from a suspect and others taken from other people matching the general description of the suspect. The dog indicates to its handler if the first scent matches one of the scents in the containers. The handler will then testify that the dog accurately picked out the scent of a particular person or suspect. Known as a "scent lineup," this procedure has become a prosecution tool in parts of Texas. The problem is that "scent lineups" are not reliable scientific evidence. Though prosecutors in Texas have used them since the mid-1990s, defense lawyers have only recently successfully challenged them. The Innocence Project of Texas is currently trying to identify prisoners who were convicted on the basis of "scent lineups" in the hope that they can be exonerated.[53]

The case of Anthony Graves is one of the most disturbing incidents in the Texas criminal justice system. Graves was wrongfully imprisoned in 1992 based on false testimony for a horrific murder of a family in Somerville, Texas. At the outset, Texas Rangers identified a suspect, Robert Carter, who falsely implicated Anthony Graves. Carter then recanted his implication and confessed to committing the murders on his own. The district attorney withheld that information about the recantation from the defense. At trial, the district attorney made a deal with Carter for his testimony against Graves. Carter implicated Graves at trial in spite of his earlier recantation and later recanted the trial testimony that implicated Graves. Graves got the death penalty.

It is a violation of the defendant's constitutional rights for a prosecutor to withhold such evidence from the defense. Years later, Graves was granted a new trial. This time the prosecution was handled by a special prosecutor from Harris County who was known as one of that county's most aggressive. She found no credible evidence implicating Graves. The special prosecutor squarely placed the blame for the miscarriage of justice on the former Burleson County district attorney, saying Graves's trial had been a "travesty." Graves was finally released in 2010.[54]

Perhaps the criminal justice system in Texas works well. Overall, the previous examples may be exceptions to the rule. However, the Tulia drug arrests, the Dallas fake-drugs scandal, the Houston DNA lab's failures, the Willingham case, the use of dog scent evidence, the Anthony Graves case, and the DNA exonerations do cast doubt on whether the criminal justice system in Texas is working as well as it should.

## Civil Cases

Figure 25.3 shows the numbers of civil cases disposed of by the courts of appeal and the trial courts in 1990, 1998, 2000, 2003, 2006, and 2010. The Texas court system is overloaded and would not be able to function adequately without the aid of visiting judges who are retired or defeated judges who continue hearing cases in order to assist with the growing caseloads.

The Texas Supreme Court sets the tone for civil cases throughout the state. Most important of those types of cases, because of the large amounts of money involved, is tort law. In the early to mid-1980s, the Democrat-dominated court tended to be sympathetic to the plaintiffs' positions in tort cases. That is, they tended to support the side in a case that was suing businesses, professionals, and insurance companies. However, in 1988, the tide turned with the election of more conservative justices who favored the defendants in civil lawsuits. Another explanation is that interest groups that were harmed by the pro-plaintiff tendencies of the older court began to organize, raise and spend money, and elect justices more sympathetic to their perspective.

In 1996–97, civil defendants won three-fourths of the time, and insurance companies won almost all their substantive cases. Physicians, hospitals, and pharmaceutical companies won all seven of their cases before the Texas Supreme Court. In 1997–98, civil defendants won 69 percent of the time.[55] However, by 1998–99, the court was not as strongly pro-defendant, perhaps because of

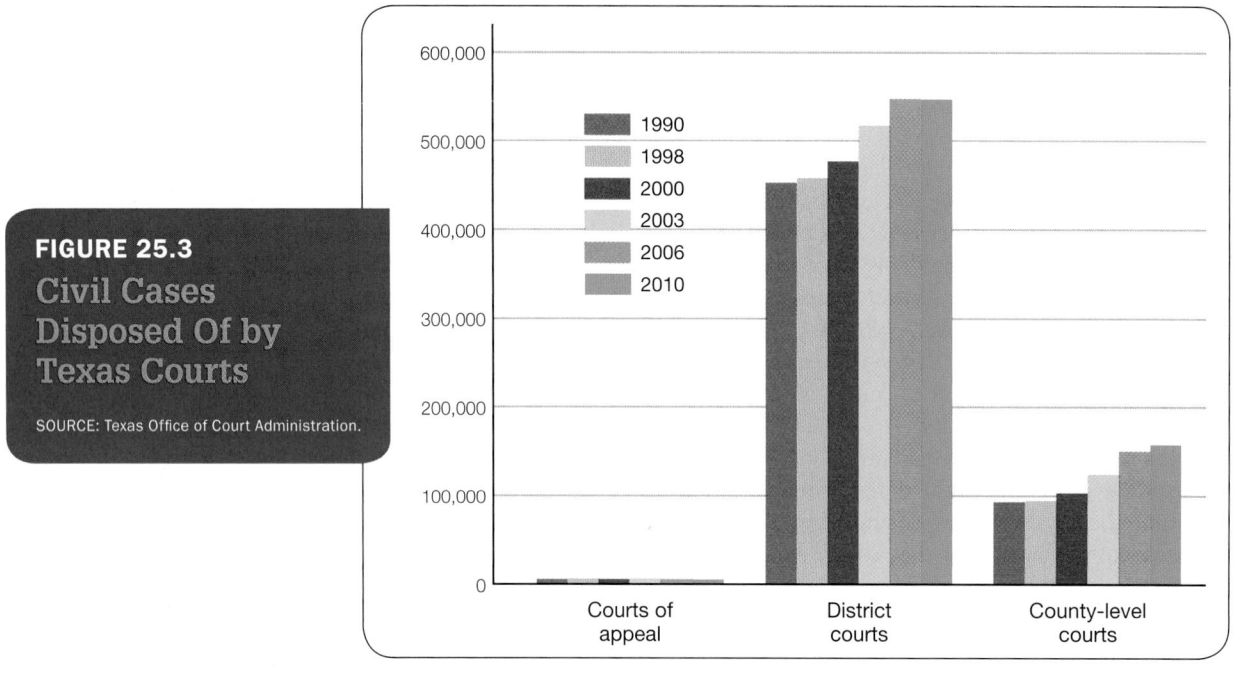

**FIGURE 25.3**

Civil Cases Disposed Of by Texas Courts

SOURCE: Texas Office of Court Administration.

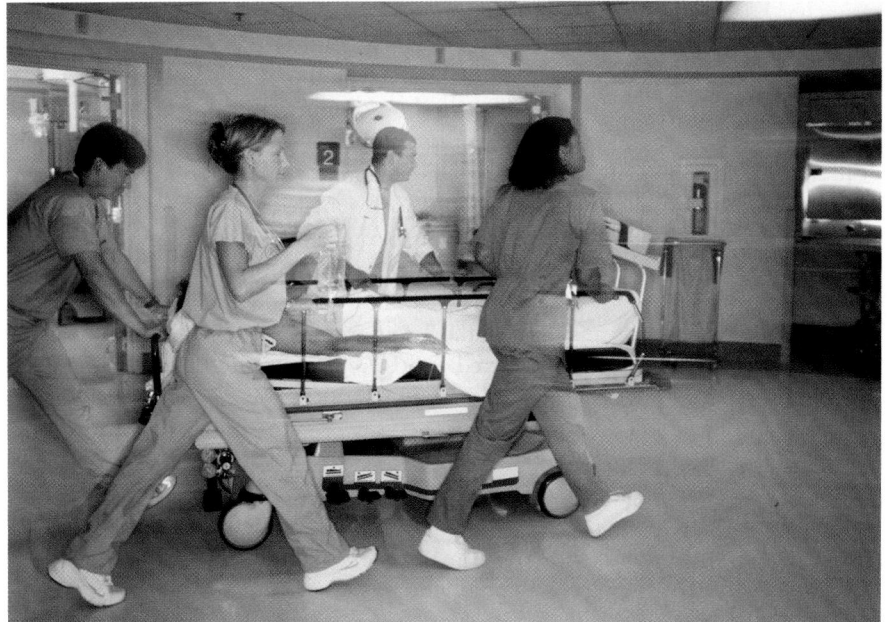

*Tort law reforms in Texas have made it more difficult for plaintiffs to sue doctors and hospitals for malpractice and have capped the damages defendants pay if they lose. Proponents of the reforms argued that they are necessary to keep medical costs down and hospitals open.*

several new justices on the court who were regarded as somewhat moderate in their judicial philosophy. In insurance cases, defendants won 40 percent of the time; plaintiffs won 40 percent of the time; and the decision of the court was a split decision 20 percent of the time. Defendants in medical cases, however, still won 100 percent of the time.[56] Most recently, the court seems to have shifted once again back to a position strongly in favor of civil defendants. A study of the decisions of the Texas Supreme Court in tort cases found that defendants won 87 percent of the time.[57] It is this power of the Texas Supreme Court to set the tone in civil cases that makes that court a political battleground, since millions—even billions—of dollars can be at stake as a result of the court's decisions.

## ● Thinking Critically about the Texas Judicial System

Texas elects its judges in partisan judicial elections. For many years, when the Democratic Party was dominant, Texas judicial elections were staid, low-budget, noncompetitive events. However, with the growth of the Republican Party, judicial elections became highly political, and large amounts of money have been raised for judicial candidates, especially in Texas Supreme Court races. Often these judicial races pitted business interests against candidates backed by the plaintiffs' bar because the Supreme Court sets the tone of tort law in the state. These elections have calmed down in recent years as the Democratic Party has weakened and, at least in statewide races, judicial elections have become less competitive.

There have been problems in Texas judicial races, in large part because voters often don't know much about judicial candidates. As a result, voters often decide on the basis of the candidate's party affiliation or the candidate's name appeal. The result has been the election of several judicial candidates who lacked significant qualifications for the job.

Numerous efforts have been proposed to change the way judges are selected in Texas. There have been efforts to change the system of selection to "merit selection" and to nonpartisan election. Minority groups have pushed to reduce the size of judicial districts in order to increase the election of minority judges. However, no change so far has been successful. No majority coalition can agree on appropriate changes in the judicial selection system, and significant opposition to change comes from groups such as the political parties and business interests. Additionally, Texans seem satisfied with the current system of selection and seem to prefer to elect their judges. Recent injustices in the Texas criminal system do raise questions about how the system can be improved. One might speculate that a criminal justice system where both judges and prosecutors are elected creates political pressures to gain convictions at all costs, and that this produces the kinds of problems discussed in this chapter.

Texas courts handle large caseloads of both civil and criminal cases. The highest civil court in the state is the Texas Supreme Court, currently an all-Republican court elected with strong support from business interests. The court has been severely criticized for being too sympathetic to those interests. The highest criminal court in the state is the Texas Court of Criminal Appeals. That court is also an all-Republican court, which was elected with strong support from prosecutors and victims' rights groups. Perhaps its most important function is as the appellate court for the death penalty in the state. It is a strongly pro-death-penalty court, and Texas ranks first in the nation in executions, although there has been a decline in Texas in the imposition of the death penalty.

Because the Texas court system affects the liberty and the pocketbooks of Texans, it will continue to be an area of concern and controversy. And the most controversial area of Texas justice will continue to be the process by which judges are selected.

# study guide

 **Practice online with:** Chapter 25 Diagnostic Quiz · Chapter 25 Key Term Flashcards

## Court Structure

■ **Identify the types of courts in Texas and their jurisdictions (pp. 945–49)**

The appellate court system in Texas is divided into civil and criminal tracks with the Texas Supreme Court being the highest state level court for civil cases and the Texas Criminal Court of Appeals being the highest for criminal cases. Texas has an intermediate appellate court system and trial courts that range from district courts for the most important criminal and civil cases, to county courts for less important criminal and civil cases, to justice of the peace and municipal courts for settling the lowest level of conflicts.

### Key Terms

**Texas Supreme Court** (p. 945)

**Texas Court of Criminal Appeals** (p. 947)

**courts of appeal** (p. 947)

**district courts** (p. 947)

**county judge** (p. 948)

**constitutional county courts** (p. 948)

**statutory county courts at law** (p. 948)

**statutory probate courts** (p. 948)

**justice of the peace courts** (p. 948)

**municipal courts** (p. 949)

**ordinances** (p. 949)

### Practice Quiz

1. The highest criminal court in the state of Texas is the *(p. 947)*
   a) Texas Supreme Court.
   b) Texas Court of Appeals.
   c) Texas Court of Criminal Appeals.
   d) district court.
   e) county court.

2. The major trial courts in Texas are the *(p. 947)*
   a) courts of appeals.
   b) justice of the peace courts.
   c) district courts.
   d) municipal courts.
   e) county courts.

3. Which of the following judges do not have to be lawyers? *(p. 949)*
   a) Texas Supreme Court justices
   b) district judges
   c) justices of the peace
   d) Texas Criminal Court of Appeals
   e) none of the above

 **Practice Online**
Interactive simulation: *Monday Morning in Travis County*

## The Legal Process

■ **Describe the types of cases heard in Texas courts (pp. 949–52)**

Civil and criminal law are dramatically different with the burden of proof relying on different standards. Plaintiffs are the initiators of legal actions in civil cases. Defendants in civil cases attempt to deflect plaintiff suits—sometimes in trial and often through settlements reached before trial. Criminal cases can involve fines or incarceration.

### Key Terms

**civil law** (p. 949)

**criminal law** (p. 950)

**complaint** (p. 950)

**answer** (p. 950)

**contingent fee** (p. 950)

**preponderance of the evidence** (p. 950)

**capital case** (p. 951)

**felony** (p. 951)

**misdemeanor** (p. 951)

**grand jury** (p. 951)

**indictment** (p. 951)

**bench trial** (p. 951)

**plea bargain** (p. 952)

**beyond a reasonable doubt** (p. 952)

## Practice Quiz

4. Grand juries *(p. 951)*
   a) determine the guilt of defendants.
   b) decide whether a trial of an accused is warranted.
   c) agree to plea bargains.
   d) recommend that defendants undergo bench trials.
   e) none of the above

5. On conviction, the criminal's punishment is determined *(p. 952)*
   a) by the Grand Jury.
   b) in a separate hearing by the jury or the judge that determined the person's guilt.

   c) by the prosecuting attorney.
   d) by the prosecuting and defense attorneys.
   e) none of the above

 **Practice Online**
"Exploring Texas Politics" exercise: *The Texas Judiciary*

# Judicial Politics

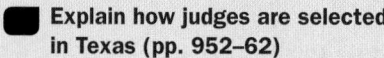 **Explain how judges are selected in Texas (pp. 952–62)**

Unlike federal judges, Texas judges are elected in partisan elections. Partisan elections make judges accountable to voters, but critics claim that unqualified judges are elected solely because of their party labels. These critics advocate alternatives for choosing judges such as merit selection. Minorities are not proportionately represented, possibly in part because most judges are elected from large Anglo-dominated districts.

## Key Terms

*en banc* (p. 960)

**retention elections** (p. 960)

**merit selection** (p. 961)

**Judicial Campaign Fairness Act** (p. 962)

## Practice Quiz

6. In civil cases, defense lawyers often align themselves with *(p. 952)*
   a) business and industry.
   b) labor groups.
   c) groups that support workers.
   d) judges supported by the Democratic Party.
   e) the grand jury.

7. In Texas, which event marked the rise of the Republican Party and partisan judicial elections? *(p. 955)*
   a) the election of President Ronald Reagan
   b) the impeachment of William Jefferson Clinton
   c) the appointment of Tom Phillips as Chief Justice of the United States
   d) the election of Bill Clements as governor of Texas
   e) none of the above

8. Texas's movement from being a Democratic to a Republican state led to *(pp. 955–56)*
   a) defeats of large numbers of incumbent judges.
   b) party switching by incumbent judges.

   c) large campaign contributions to judges.
   d) all of the above
   e) none of the above

9. Which of the following groups has the largest number of judges? *(p. 958)*
   a) African American
   b) Asian American
   c) Native American
   d) women
   e) Hispanic

10. Elections lost due to party membership rather than race or ethnicity do not violate *(pp. 959–60)*
    a) the Fifth Amendment to the U.S. Constitution.
    b) Article I of the Texas Constitution.
    c) *Clements v. Maddox.*
    d) the Voting Rights Act.
    e) Fair Elections Act.

11. How likely is Texas to change its method of selecting judicial candidates? *(p. 962)*
    a) Texas is scheduled to change to the Missouri Plan in January 2015.
    b) extremely likely in the next two decades
    c) likely in the next decade
    d) likely in 2013
    e) unlikely

12. Which of the following sets campaign contribution limits for judicial candidates in Texas? *(p. 962)*
    a) Judicial Campaign Fairness Act
    b) Judicial Campaign Act
    c) Voting Rights Act
    d) Civil Rights Act
    e) Voting Rights Act

# The Importance of the Texas Courts

■ **Analyze how courts impact the lives of Texans (pp. 962–71)**

Texas courts make decisions affecting Texans on a variety of issues, including the ultimate penalty of death. Recent evidence in a number of Texas locales suggest that there have been miscarriages of justice regarding wrongful convictions based on faulty evidence.

## Practice Quiz

13. In Texas, a person is subject to the death penalty for all except *(p. 964)*
    a) murder during commission of a robbery.
    b) murder of a fireman.
    c) murder for hire.
    d) murder of a child under the age of six.
    e) rape of a child.

14. Which of the following leads to questions about the integrity of the Texas criminal justice system? *(pp. 965–69)*
    a) the large number of exonerations of people imprisoned in Texas
    b) the drug scandal in Tulia, Texas

    c) the Dallas fake-drug scandal
    d) all of the above
    e) none of the above

15. Philosophically, in the past few years, Texas courts became *(p. 971)*
    a) more pro-defendant in civil cases.
    b) more liberal.
    c) more pro-defendant in criminal cases.
    d) more conservative.
    e) none of the above

 **Practice Online**
Video exercise: *Judicial Campaigns*

# Recommended Websites

**The Supreme Court of Texas**
www.supreme.courts.state.tx.us/

**Texans for Public Justice**
www.tpj.org

**Texas Court of Criminal Appeals**
www.cca.courts.state.tx.us/

**Texas Courts Online: Texas Court Structure**
www.courts.state.tx.us/

Recent scandals involving the Dallas County constables—including the high number of traffic tickets issued and the high number of cars impounded by constables—have raised questions about local government in Texas.

# Local Government in Texas

**WHAT GOVERNMENT DOES AND WHY IT MATTERS** Local government is generally praised for being closer to the people it serves and, therefore, being more responsive to those people than the state or national government can be. The problem is that sometimes local governmental officials work in relative obscurity, avoiding media and public scrutiny. This means that if they abuse their power, their behavior often takes longer to come to light. One example has been a recent scandal involving two of the five constables in Dallas County. Traditionally in Texas, the office of constable has been an elective office with limited duties. Constables have served civil court papers and have provided bailiffs for justices of the peace. However, some constables, such as those in Dallas County, transformed their offices into full-fledged police departments. Dallas County constables, for example, developed a traffic enforcement role. In Dallas County, in 1995, no deputy constable positions were devoted to traffic enforcement; in 2010, 76 deputy constables in that county handled traffic enforcement. Constables also formed heavily armed, tactical units. They patrolled high-crime areas, shut down drug houses, arrested parents who were behind on child support, and cracked down on drug dealers selling "cheese" heroin to students. County commissioners not only approved some of the expanded activities of constables, but also implemented new legal strategies to expand their law enforcement functions. Since constables are elected officials, they are not subject to much oversight and instead function as law enforcement fiefdoms in larger counties in Texas.

In two constables' precincts in Dallas County, there have been problems with vehicles being impounded. These constables have impounded thousands of vehicles without requiring that the towing companies account for what happened to the vehicles. Subsequent investigations of the two constables have also identified issues such as complaints that deputy constables have been forced to work on unpaid security details and to sell raffle tickets to raise money for constables' re-election campaigns.[1] These problems, going on for years, have only recently caused county commissioners to reconsider the expanded role of constables.

Sadly, it is not only the office of constable that shows problems at the local governmental level. Recent scandals in Dallas involving city council members show still other disturbing aspects of local government in Texas. Former mayor pro tem Don Hill and a number of associates were accused of taking bribes from low-income housing developers in exchange for political support for their projects. The corruption probe first became public in 2005, but did not result in convictions until toward the end of 2009. Hill was convicted of selling his votes in a bribery and extortion scheme that involved pressuring low-income housing developers for kickbacks.[2]

The cases of the constables and Don Hill show that while local government provides many of the services people depend on, the fact that few people pay close attention to local government means there is room for abuses of power and action that go against the interests of the public. In this chapter, we will take a closer look at the main features of local government in Texas.

## chaptergoals

- Explain the importance of county government in Texas (pages 979–86)

- Describe the major types of city government in Texas (pages 986–92)

- Examine the role of special districts in Texas government (pages 992–98)

# ● County Government in Texas

**Explain the importance of county government in Texas**

Local government institutions play a major role in Texas. There are roughly 4,835 general purpose local governments, an average of 19.1 per county. Of these, 254 were county governments and 1,221 were municipal governments. There were also 3,373 special purpose governments, including 1,082 public school systems and 2,291 special district governments.[3] Local government is everywhere in Texas, providing water, electricity, and sewer services, as well as police protection and public education.

All but two states have governmental units known as counties (or parishes), but Texas has 254 counties, more than any other state.[4] County government in Texas is primarily a way of governing rural areas. Because Texas is so vast, with huge areas that are sparsely populated, county government remains an important aspect of local government. As was discussed in previous chapters, the Texas Constitution places numerous restrictions on government, and numerous provisions of the constitution place restrictions on counties. Indeed, in Texas, counties have very constricted governmental powers. Unlike city governments, county governments usually do not have powers to legislate. Because they lack much of the power of self-government, they often function primarily as an administrative arm of the state government.

Texas counties have their origins in the "municipality," which was the local governmental unit under Spanish and Mexican rule. These municipalities were large and included settlements and surrounding rural territories. In 1835, Texas was divided into 3 departments and 23 municipalities. With the Republic of 1836, the 23 municipalities became counties. By the time Texas became a state in 1845, there were 36 counties, and when Texas entered the Confederacy in 1861, there were 122 counties. The number of counties increased steadily until 1921, when the 254th county was created. The underlying goal of the proliferation of counties was that any citizen could travel to the county seat—on horseback, of course—and return home in a day. Given the sparse population of west Texas, in particular, that initial plan for county organization was eventually rejected, but it does show that Texans believed that the local center of government, the county seat, should be accessible to the people.[5]

## Numerous County Offices: Checks and Balances or Built-In Problems?

As with the state government, one of the characteristics of county government in Texas is a multiplicity of elected governmental officials. Some argue that the large number of public officials at the county level is desirable because it creates a strong system of checks and balances, allowing no one official to dominate county government.[6] However, that system of checks and balances comes at a high price. There are problems of coordination of governmental activity, much as at the state level. One of the most important bodies of county elected officials is the **county commissioners court,** which is the main governing unit in the county. Although the commissioners court is not really a judicial court, it may have gotten its name from the Republic of Texas Constitution (1836–45), in which the county governing unit consisted of the chief justice of the county court and the justices of the peace within the county.[7]

**county commissioners court**
the main governing body of each county; has the authority to set the county tax rate and budget

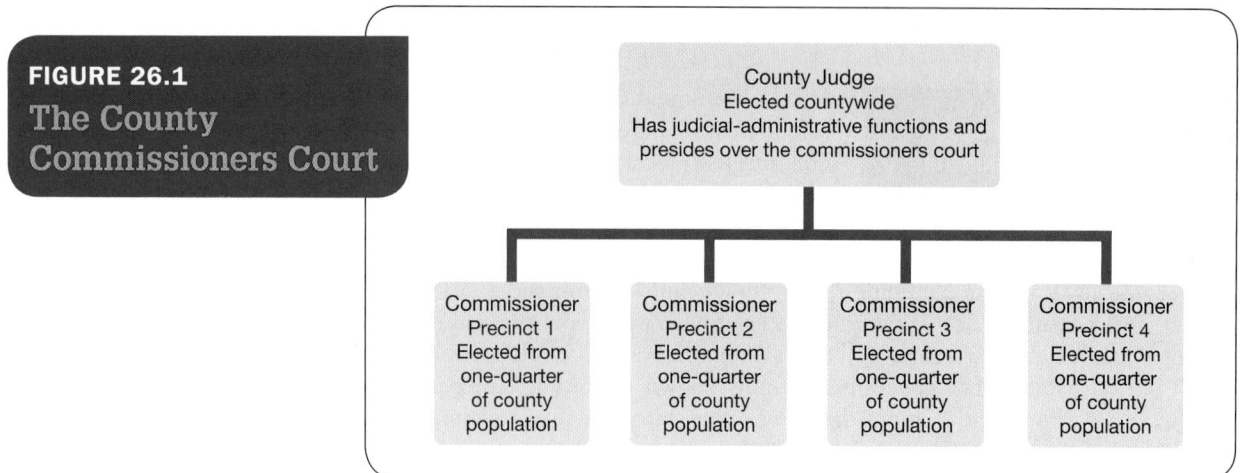

**FIGURE 26.1**
The County
Commissioners Court

County Judge
Elected countywide
Has judicial-administrative functions and
presides over the commissioners court

| Commissioner Precinct 1 Elected from one-quarter of county population | Commissioner Precinct 2 Elected from one-quarter of county population | Commissioner Precinct 3 Elected from one-quarter of county population | Commissioner Precinct 4 Elected from one-quarter of county population |

**county judge** the person in each of Texas's 254 counties who presides over the constitutional county court and county commissioners court, with responsibility for the administration of county government; some county judges carry out judicial responsibilities

**county commissioner** government official (four per county) on the county commissioners court whose main duty is the construction and maintenance of roads and bridges

The current structure of the county commissioners court, shown in Figure 26.1, consists of a **county judge** and four commissioners. The county judge is elected countywide and serves for four years. He or she presides over the meetings of the commissioners court and has administrative powers as well as judicial powers in rural counties. In those counties, the county judge hears minor criminal cases and handles some civil matters such as probate matters. In larger counties, the county judge is an administrator only, with the judicial duties of the office removed by the creation of judgeships, such as probate judgeships and county court-at-law judgeships.

Each commissioners court also has four **county commissioners**; each of these officials is elected from a precinct that encompasses roughly one-fourth the population of the county. In the late 1960s, one of the great issues in constitutional law involved the issue of malapportionment, the allegation that election districts did not represent equal population groupings. The malapportionment of Texas's county commissioners courts became an important case before the U.S. Supreme Court because those precincts tended to be drawn to represent fairly equal land areas rather than equal population groupings. In *Avery v. Midland County* (1968), the U.S. Supreme Court held that the principle of "one person, one vote" applies to commissioners courts just as it applies to legislative districts. The result was that commissioners precincts must now be drawn to reflect equal population groupings within counties.[8]

The main duty of county commissioners is the construction and maintenance of roads and bridges; usually each commissioner provides for roadwork within his or her precinct. That aspect of a commissioner's work is, of course, very important to rural residents; it can be politically controversial and has sometimes been tinged with corruption.[9]

The commissioners court also sets the county tax rate and the county budget. Related to its taxing and budgeting powers is its power to make contracts and pay bills. Perhaps the most important expenditure of most county commissioners courts, other than road and bridge expenditures, is the cost of building and maintaining county jails. Indigent health care can be a significant cost for counties as well, along with, in some cases, fire protection and sanitation. Some counties also have costs associated with the maintenance of libraries and hospitals and costs for

## TABLE 26.1

## Countywide and Precinct-Level Elected Officials

| COUNTYWIDE OFFICIALS | PRECINCT-LEVEL OFFICIALS |
|---|---|
| County judge | County commissioners |
| Possibly county court-at-law judges, possibly probate judges, and district judges | Justices of the peace |
| County and district attorney or criminal district attorney | Constables |
| Sheriff | |
| County and district clerk or district clerk | |
| Possibly county treasurer | |
| Tax assessor-collector | |
| Possibly county surveyor | |

emergency welfare expenditures, such as those brought on by natural disasters or fires. The commissioners court can appoint certain county officials, and it can hire personnel as well as fill vacancies in county offices. It also administers elections in the county.

However, as noted earlier, there are numerous elected officials in Texas counties, each with an independent power base. It seems nearly inevitable that tensions would develop between the budgetary powers of the commissioners courts and the needs and desires of other elected county officials.

As Table 26.1 shows, other officeholders are elected at the county level and still others at the precinct level of the county. There is some variation in the numbers of officeholders, depending on the county. For example, larger counties will have more justices of the peace and more **constables** than smaller ones. In some counties, constables serve legal papers, while in others, as discussed in the introduction to this chapter, constables also have a law-enforcement role with the authority to patrol, give tickets, and make arrests. Some counties use constables to check on truants from school, having found a niche area that others in law enforcement do not seem to want.

**constable** precinct-level county official involved with serving legal papers and, in some counties, enforcing the law

Larger counties may have probate judges, numerous district judges, and county court-at-law judges. Smaller counties may not have probate judges or even county court-at-law judges. Some of the smaller counties may share district judges and district attorneys with other counties. Laws setting up different offices often vary from county to county as well. As a result, some counties have county attorneys and district attorneys; others have criminal district attorneys that combine the county attorney and district attorney offices. Some counties have county clerks and district clerks; smaller counties may combine the offices in one person. Some counties have county treasurers; others do not have such an office.

## Are Some Counties Too Small?

The reason for the variation in offices is not simply that laws were passed at different times, thus sacrificing uniformity among counties. It is also the case that Texas is a large, diverse state with great variation among its counties. The result is

*The county commissioners court is the main governing unit at the county level, with control over the county budget and projects such as road construction. Here, Denton County Commissioner Andy Eads appears with Texas Motor Speedway president Eddie Gossage at the groundbreaking for a highway extension near the speedway.*

great variation in the numbers of government officials, the duties of officials, and the services provided by the different county governments. Brewster County has a population of only 9,232, but it covers a territory of 6,193 square miles, about the size of Connecticut and Rhode Island combined. Rockwall County, in contrast, has only 149 square miles and a population of 78,337. Although Harris County has a population of 4,092,059, Loving County has a population of only 82; yet Loving County covers a huge land area—nearly 677 square miles.[10] Most residents of Loving County work for the Loving County government. The fact that the county government is the major employer in the county may be the main justification for Loving County's continuing existence as a governmental unit—although people with taxable property may also prefer the Loving County tax structure to that of another governmental unit.[11]

A small population may create a sense of community and closeness to local government, but it can place a terrific strain on county resources when unusual events occur.

One of the medium-size Texas counties is Jasper County in east Texas, which has a population of 35,710. Jasper County had huge costs as a result of the capital murder trials of three men accused in the 1998 dragging death of James Byrd Jr. Two of the three men were sentenced to death; the third got life in prison. Costs associated with the trial came to over $1.02 million. The result was such a strain on the $10 million annual county budget that the county was forced to increase property taxes by 6.7 percent over two years to pay for the trial. Only a massive flood in the county in the late 1970s had come close to creating a financial burden similar to that of the trial.

Jasper County is not the only county struggling with a huge financial burden from capital murder trials. The basic cost of prosecuting a capital case averages $200,000 to $300,000, and that does not include the costs of indigent-defense lawyers, appeals, and trial transcripts.

The burden of the capital case on Jasper County convinced Texas lawmakers to expand a program to assist counties in paying the "extraordinary costs" of prosecuting capital murder cases. That aid program was motivated by a fear that underpopulated counties would pursue lesser charges than those carrying the death penalty to avoid incurring financial hardship. One of the sponsors of the legislation, for example, said that he had often heard concerns expressed over the cost pressures of capital trials from officials in the 17 rural counties he represented.

Polk County in east Texas (population about 45,413) estimated that it had unanticipated costs of $200,000 when the U.S. Supreme Court overturned the sentence of Johnny Paul Penry, who was convicted in the stabbing death of a woman in 1979, and sent the case back for another trial. Even with $100,000 in aid from the state to help pay the bill, the costs of one trial tremendously burdened Polk County.[12] An even more severe situation faced tiny Franklin County (population 10,605) in 2007, when it needed to come up with a minimum of $250,000 for a murder trial.[13] Since capital murder cases were so rare in the county, the commissioners had no money at all budgeted for such a purpose. For small counties such as Polk and Franklin, expenses like these require either major cuts in other budget items or tax increases.

*The county commissioners court is also responsible for constructing and maintaining bridges, such as this one near Houston.*

One hundred sixty Texas counties have populations of fewer than 30,000, and 137 of those counties have populations of fewer than 20,000. One recent study confirmed fears that Texas has wide variations in its counties' application of capital punishment, in part because of the costs of death penalty cases to smaller counties. Between 1976, when the U.S. Supreme Court reinstated capital punishment, and July 2011, Texas sent just over 1,060 inmates to death row. Only four of the state's most heavily populated counties—Harris, Bexar, Dallas, and Tarrant—accounted for 534 of these death sentences. By itself, Harris County, the county with the largest population, accounted for 280, or 28 percent, of the death sentences. In contrast, 135 Texas counties with relatively small populations have not sent an inmate to death row in the last three decades.[14]

Counties exist as they do for a variety of reasons. The original goal of making county seats easily accessible by horseback is, of course, no longer pertinent. Other reasons are political. For example, wealthy landowners may have urged the legislature to create counties so that they could control county government and hence the amount of property taxes they might pay. Still, we must wonder if so many small counties are needed. The Jasper County situation suggests that even moderate-size counties by Texas standards may be too small to function adequately in unusual situations.

## The Functions of County Government

What, then, are the main functions of Texas county government? Table 26.2 lists them. Like most other aspects of county government in Texas, these five primary functions are performed with great variation among the counties.

County road and bridge construction and maintenance have traditionally been such important functions of the commissioners court that often county commissioners are called "road commissioners." County commissioners maintain more than one-half of the roads in the state.[15] There are roughly 134,000 miles of rural roadways and 17,000 rural bridges in Texas. Maintenance of these roads and bridges is

**TABLE 26.2**

**Primary Functions of County Government**

- Construction and maintenance of roads and bridges
- Law enforcement
- Dispute resolution
- Record-keeping
- Social services

a major cost for county government.[16] For example, a twenty-foot asphalt road for lightweight traffic costs a county $45,000 per mile to resurface; a road for heavy trucks costs about $100,000 per mile.[17] Although a 1947 law allowed counties to place the road system under the authority of a county engineer, in most counties roads and bridges remain one of the most important responsibilities of the commissioners.

Law enforcement is another important responsibility of county government. This job is undertaken by constables and by the sheriff. The sheriff is the chief law-enforcement officer within county government. In rural counties with few city police departments, the sheriff may be the major law-enforcement official in the county. In addition to law enforcement and the provision of deputies for the district and county courts, sheriffs are responsible for the county jail. In many counties, operating a county jail is an expensive and major undertaking. On August 1, 2011, for example, Harris County was guarding and supervising 9,009 inmates in its county jail, Dallas County had 6,462 inmates in its jail, and Tarrant County had 3,519. On the other hand, 19 counties had no jails. Glasscock County had room for 12 inmates in its jail but had no inmates; Trinity County had room for 7 inmates but had only 1 inmate. Real County had a jail capacity of 3 and had no inmates, and Terrell County had a capacity of 8 and had no inmates.[18]

Although the law-enforcement budget is approved by the county commissioners court, sheriffs often have considerable influence in county government and develop their own law enforcement styles. The sheriff of Smith County, for example, has not only a SWAT team but also two armored personnel carriers, each of which weighs 13 tons, moves on tracks at up to 40 miles per hour, and is capable of climbing 60-degree grades and floating.[19]

**County attorneys** and **district attorneys** also perform a law-enforcement role by prosecuting criminal cases. Usually, the district attorneys prosecute the more serious criminal cases in the district courts, whereas the county attorneys prosecute

**county attorney** county official who prosecutes lesser criminal cases in the county court

**district attorney** public official who prosecutes the more serious criminal cases in the district court

*County governments are important for law enforcement. Here, a captain from the McLennan County sheriff's office discusses the procedures for a protest with Cindy Sheehan. After Sheehan's son died in Iraq, she and her supporters demonstrated against the Iraq War outside President Bush's Texas ranch.*

*In rural parts of Texas, county courts are where civil and criminal cases are heard. This photo shows the Jasper County Courthouse during the capital murder case of the men accused of the 1998 dragging death of James Byrd Jr.*

the lesser criminal cases in the county courts. In more urban counties, the offices of county attorney and district attorney may be combined into one office that is usually called the office of criminal district attorney.

Record-keeping is an important function of county government. **County clerks** keep vital statistics for the county and issue licenses; they maintain records for the commissioners court and the county courts. Most important, the county clerk is responsible for records relating to property transactions. Sometimes the county clerk maintains election and voting records. If there is a **district clerk**, he or she maintains records for the district courts, though in small counties this office is combined with the office of the county clerk. Tax records are maintained by the **county tax assessor-collector**, who also collects taxes, though in the smaller counties the sheriff often performs this job. Although constitutional amendments have eliminated the office of county treasurer in many counties, where the office does exist, the treasurer is responsible for receiving and expending county funds. The **county auditor** now does much of the work of the county treasurer. There are now about 200 county auditors in Texas. Auditors are not elected; they are appointed by the county's district judges. Not only do they audit the county's funds, but in large counties they will often prepare the county budget for the commissioners court.

Counties also have an important role in dispute resolution through their court system. Civil law is a way to resolve disputes between people, and the justice of the peace court and the county and district courts deal with large numbers of civil disputes as well as criminal matters. County and district attorneys may also represent the interests of the county or state in disputes that involve governmental interests.

Finally, counties may perform a social service function. The social services provided vary from county to county. However, the most important social services involve emergency welfare assistance to individuals. This may include the

**county clerk** public official who is the main record-keeper of the county

**district clerk** public official who is the main record-keeper of the district court

**county tax assessor-collector** public official who maintains the county tax records and collects the taxes owed to the county

**county auditor** public official, appointed by the district judges, who receives and disburses county funds; in large counties, this official also prepares the county budget

provision of food, housing, rental assistance, or shelter to needy individuals. Larger counties have health departments to work on the prevention and control of communicable diseases. Some counties operate mental health services. Some counties provide parks, airports, fire protection, and sanitation facilities. One of the most important social services provided by counties is indigent health care.

## County Government in Perspective

County government occupies an important role in Texas local government, although the powers of county government are greatly restricted by the Texas Legislature. One of the most notable features of Texas counties is their great variation in geographical size, population, and even in county offices, duties of county officials, and services provided by county government. Additionally, like state government, county government has a large number of elected county officials. Although this may limit the power of any one county official, it also produces disagreement, conflict, and difficulty in accomplishing objectives.

Many of Texas's counties are very small, possibly too small to meet the needs of Texans in the twenty-first century, although there is no serious effort to change the current structure of counties. Counties perform important and often expensive functions. Some of those functions of county government and the costs associated with them—for example, road and bridge construction and maintenance, jail construction and operation, and indigent health care—are likely to increase significantly in the future.

## TABLE 26.3

### Municipal Governments in Texas, 2010

| SIZE | NUMBER |
|---|---|
| 100,000 or more | 28 |
| 50,000–99,999 | 30 |
| 10,000–49,999 | 157 |
| 5,000–9,999 | 115 |
| Fewer than 5,000 | 891 |
| Total | 1,221 |

SOURCE: Calculated from www.texasalmanac.com/topics/government/government.

# ● City Government in Texas

> **Describe the major types of city government in Texas**

As of 2010, there were 1,221 municipal governments in Texas, ranging in size from 27 residents in Corral City to nearly 2.1 million in Houston (see Table 26.3). Like county governments, municipal governments are creations of the state of Texas. In the early years of the Republic of Texas, the Texas Congress was responsible for enacting laws that incorporated cities. The number of urban areas grew in the state in the late nineteenth and early twentieth centuries, making the management of local affairs a growing burden on the state legislature. In 1912, the legislature passed the Home-Rule Charter Amendments that enabled cities of more than 5,000 inhabitants to adopt home-rule charters with a majority vote of qualified voters.

**Home-rule charters** essentially lay down the rules under which a city will operate.[20] They provide for the form of government that operates in the city and specify the number of members serving on the city's governing body. They also may grant the governing body the power to annex land adjacent to the city as well as to set property tax rates up to $2.50 per $100 valuation. Home-rule cities are also constitutionally authorized to borrow money in ways not available to smaller municipal entities. Home-rule charters must be consistent with the state constitution and any other relevant statutory provisions. For example, the state has mandated that most city elections take place on a date provided by the Texas Election Code. City elections must be conducted under the general guidelines set by the state. Nevertheless, home rule in Texas has delegated enormous power to local city governments. According to a report by the Advisory Commission on Intergovernmental

**home-rule charter** the rules under which a city operates

## TABLE 26.4

### The Largest Home-Rule Cities, 2010

| NAME | POPULATION | FORM OF GOVERNMENT | FIRST CHARTER | PRESENT FORM ADOPTED |
|------|-----------|--------------------|--------------|----------------------|
| Houston | 2,099,451 | Mayor-council | 1905 | 1994 |
| San Antonio | 1,327,407 | Council-manager | 1914 | 1951 |
| Dallas | 1,197,816 | Council-manager | 1889 | 1907 |
| Austin | 790,390 | Council-manager | 1919 | 1994 |
| Fort Worth | 741,206 | Council-manager | 1924 | 1985 |
| El Paso | 649,121 | Mayor-council | 1873 | 1907 |
| Arlington | 365,438 | Council-manager | 1920 | 1990 |
| Corpus Christi | 305,215 | Council-manager | 1926 | 1993 |
| Plano | 259,841 | Council-manager | 1961 | 1993 |
| Laredo | 236,091 | Council-manager | 1848 | 1911 |

SOURCES: Compiled from *Texas Almanac 2006–2007* (Dallas: *Dallas Morning News*, 2006), 340–64; *Texas Almanac 2008–2009* (Dallas: *Dallas Morning News*, 2008), 8; Texas State Data Center; www.citypopulation.de/USA Texas .html; City Charter of the City of Laredo as Amended (2010).

Relations, the Texas Constitution leaves cities more "home rule" than does any other state. There are now 335 home-rule cities in Texas.[21] Table 26.4 lists the 10 largest of these.

Cities and towns of fewer than 5,000 people are chartered by general statute, as was the case for all cities and towns prior to the 1912 home-rule amendments. These "general-law" cities and towns may act or organize themselves only as explicitly permitted by statutory law passed by the state legislature. The constitution also limits what they can do. For example, general-law cities may levy, assess, and collect taxes as authorized by statute. But the constitution sets a maximum property tax rate of $1.50 per $100 valuation, compared with $2.50 per $100 valuation for home-rule cities.

Politics at the local level is often politics at its most basic. Unlike in presidential elections, in which the issues may well involve questions of war and peace, or state elections, which may involve issues such as whether a state should have an income tax, in local elections the most pressing issue may well be potholes in the city streets. Although pothole repair may not seem earthshaking in the hierarchy of political concerns, it is exactly such an issue that most directly and routinely affects most people's lives, and thus it becomes a prime issue for discussion among candidates. As mundane as such concerns are, these are the fundamental issues in most local elections because they reflect the needs and expectations that residents have of local government.

## Forms of Government in Texas Cities

Texas home-rule cities have had three major forms of city government: the mayor-council form, the commissioner form, and the council-manager form. The **mayor-council form of government** is the oldest. It consists of an elected mayor and city

**mayor-council form of government** a form of city government in which the mayor is the chief executive and the city council is the legislative body; in the *strong mayor-council* variation, the mayor's powers enable him or her to control executive departments and the agenda of the city council; in the *weak mayor-council* variation, the mayor's power is more limited

**at-large election** an election in which officials are selected by voters of the entire geographical area, rather than from smaller districts within that area

**single-member district** a district whose voters elect only one representative to represent that district

council. The mayor is elected from the city in an **at-large election**. The council may be elected either at-large or from a series of **single-member districts**, or a mixture of the two. In the mayor-council form of government, the mayor is the chief executive officer of the city. He or she presides over council meetings and has a variety of appointment powers. The city council, meanwhile, serves as the legislative body in the city, passing local laws and watching over the executive departments.

There have been both strong mayor–council systems and weak ones, depending on the powers given to the mayor by the city charter or state statute. In the *strong mayor-council* variation, various executive powers, such as appointive and removal powers to boards and departments or veto powers, are concentrated in the office of mayor. These powers enable the mayor to establish effective control over various executive departments in the city and to control the legislative agenda of the city council. In the *weak mayor-council* variation, these executive powers are much more limited, fragmenting power between the mayor and other elected or appointed officials.

In the 1990s, the mayor-council form of government was the dominant form of government in most of the incorporated cities in Texas, particularly among general-law cities. However, among home-rule cities the mayor-council government was not popular. According to a 1995 survey of 284 home-rule cities conducted by the *Texas Almanac*, only 31 had adopted the mayor-council form of government.

A second form of city government found in Texas is the **commissioner form of government**.[22] Under the commissioner system, the city is run by a small commission, composed of between five and seven members generally elected at-large. The commission acts in both a legislative and an executive capacity. As a group, commissioners enact laws for the city. Each commissioner is in charge of one of a variety of departments. One commissioner is also designated as the mayor to preside at meetings.

**commissioner form of government** a form of city government in which the city is run by a small group of elected commissioners who act in both legislative and executive capacities

The commission plan was developed as a response to the devastating hurricane that hit Galveston in 1900, claiming an estimated 6,000 lives. It reflected a desire to bring good business practices to city government that would somehow escape

*The commissioner form of government was developed as a response to the devastating hurricane that hit Galveston in 1900.*

the squabbles and inefficiency of traditional local government found in the mayor-council form. The commission plan was adopted by Houston in 1905 and by a number of other Texas cities in 1907, including Dallas, Fort Worth, and El Paso. Republicans and Democratic Progressives across the country supported the plan and other reform principles often integrated with it, including nonpartisan elections, merit selection of employees, and such direct democracy techniques as the initiative, referendum, and recall. At its peak in 1918, the commission form was used by approximately 500 cities across the country and 75 cities in Texas. Following World War I, the number of commission-form cities decreased. By 2000, no city in Texas had a pure commission form of government, although 26 still claimed to have some variation of a commission-manager form of government.[23] In practice, none of the "commissioners" in these cities exercised executive control over specific city departments as envisioned in the original commission system. Instead, they functioned more like council members under the council-manager form of city government.[24]

The third form of city government found in Texas is the **council-manager form of government**.[25] As originally envisioned, a city council elected in at-large elections was to be the policy-making body. Council members generally received little or no pay and were intended to be publicly motivated citizens interested in serving the public good, rather than professional politicians. A mayor was selected from among the council members. The city manager was to be a professional public manager who served as the chief executive and administrative official in the city. As in the commissioner form of government, the goal of the council-manager form of government was twofold: to free local government from the seamier side of politics and to bring administrative expertise to local government.

In 1913, Amarillo was the first city to abandon the commissioner form of government for the council-manager system. In 1914, Taylor and Denton followed suit. By 1947, there were 47 council-manager systems in Texas. By the mid-1990s, 251 of the home-rule cities had council-manager systems. Across the United States, it has become the most popular form of government for cities of over 10,000 residents.

Today, council-manager systems vary across the state in a number of ways. The desire for professional administration of local government remains high. Most city managers have graduate degrees and are paid high salaries like other executive officers in the private sector. But a desire for more political accountability through traditional democratic processes has introduced some changes. The growing ethnic and racial diversity of some Texas cities has forced many political leaders to question the wisdom of freeing local government too much from democratic controls. In most cities, mayors now are elected at large from the population as a whole, rather than only from the council. Many cities also elect council members from single-member districts rather than only from at-large districts. Many see at-large districts as undercutting minority representation by diluting minority votes. Only when Dallas moved from an at-large council to a council elected from single-member districts in 1991 did minorities come to play a major role in the decision-making processes of city government. But most cities and towns under the council-manager system continue to view local political offices as part-time jobs. Mayoral and council salaries remain low. A few cities, such as Austin, offer considerably higher salaries. The demand for more democratic accountability in local government will likely continue to lead to more changes in the council-manager system of government across Texas. Balancing an efficient city government run by professionals with democratic political processes will continue to be a problem as Texas's metropolitan areas grow and diversify in the early twenty-first century.

**council-manager form of government** a form of city government in which public policies are developed by the city council and executive and administrative functions are assigned to a professional city manager

# A Tale of Three Cities

Houston is the largest city in Texas, with nearly 2.1 million people. It has a strong mayor-council form of government. There are 16 elected officials in the city serving concurrent two-year terms, including a mayor, a controller, and 14 council members. The mayor serves as the chief executive official in the city and is the city's chief administrator and official representative. Much of the mayor's power stems from the authority to appoint department heads and people serving on advisory boards, subject to council approval. The mayor also presides over the city council with voting privileges. The 14-member council is a legislative body composed of five at-large seats and nine single-member district seats.

Unlike in most other cities, the city controller in Houston is an elected official.[26] The city controller, currently Ronald Green, is the city's chief financial officer. Besides investing city funds, conducting internal audits of city departments, and operating the city's financial management system, the controller is also responsible for certifying the availability of funds for city council initiatives. In the end, the office of the controller is both a professional position and a political position. Not surprisingly, the controller often comes into conflict with the mayor and the council over important policy issues.

Although local politics in Houston is nominally nonpartisan, in recent years it has taken on a partisan flavor. Houston's current mayor is Annise Parker, who serves as executive officer of the city. She is a well-known Democrat and is also a lesbian who supports gay marriage. Her call for legalizing gay marriage and her proclamation that Valentine's Day was Freedom to Marry Day have led to a political outcry among social conservatives including Republican leaders who claim that she is putting her personal political agenda ahead of the interests of Houston. Parker barely escaped a runoff in her election campaign in November 2011, and two incumbent city council members were defeated by opponents of gay marriage. Even after the election, the partisan furor over gay marriage has not died down in Houston.

Recently, San Antonio has overtaken Dallas as the second largest city in Texas. San Antonio has a council-manager form of government. The council is composed of members elected from 10 single-member districts on a nonpartisan basis. The mayor, currently Julián Castro, is the eleventh member of the council and is selected at large. All members of the council serve for two-year terms and receive largely honorific salaries. The mayor's salary is a paltry $3,000 per year in addition to payment as a council member; other council members are paid $20 per meeting, not to exceed $1,040 per year. Members are subject to recall if 10 percent of the qualified voters in a district sign a petition of recall and a recall election is successful. The city charter also provides for initiatives and referendums that emerge from the voters.

The city manager in San Antonio serves at the pleasure of the council as the chief executive and administrative official in the city. He or she has wide-ranging appointment and removal authority over officers and employees in the administrative service of the city. The current city manager is Sheryl Sculley. Prior to becoming city manager, she was assistant city manager of Phoenix. She supervises the activities of all city departments, a budget of $2 billion, and 12,000 employees.

*Annise Parker is the current mayor of Houston. She previously served as a member of the city council and as city controller.*

San Antonio mayor Julián Castro, elected in 2009, previously served as a member of the city council.

Dallas also operates under a council-manager form of government. For years, city politics had been dominated by the white business community. At-large non-partisan elections tended to elect a council that was relatively united in its understanding of the problems facing the city and its vision of where the city should go. A bitter struggle in the late 1980s and early 1990s over rewriting the city charter divided the city along racial lines. The new charter, which went into effect in 1991, called for a 14-member council elected from single-member districts and a mayor elected at large. Members are limited to serving four 2-year terms consecutively. Under the new charter, membership on the council was transformed as a significant number of African Americans and Hispanics were elected to the council.

As in other council-manager systems, the power of the mayor in Dallas is weak. The mayor—currently Mike Rawlings—presides over council meetings, creates council committees, and appoints members, chairs, and co-chairs. In many ways, however, the mayor is only first among equals on the council. The council as a whole is the legislative body for the city, approving budgets, determining the tax rate, and appointing key public

Mayor Mike Rawlings of Dallas was elected in 2011. He was previously the CEO of Pizza Hut.

officials, including the city manager, city attorney, city auditor, city secretary, municipal court judges, and various citizen boards and commissions. The city manager serves at the will of the council and is removable by a two-thirds vote of the council. As in San Antonio, the city manager's powers in Dallas are great. As the chief administrative officer, the city manager has the power to appoint and remove all heads of departments and subordinate officers and employees in the city, subject to civil service provisions. Despite the attempt to remove the city manager from the pressures of political life in Dallas, recent city managers have found themselves forced to accommodate the reality of an increasingly politicized city council. The political pressures emerging from Dallas's single-member district council may ultimately compel the city to reexamine the wisdom of retaining a council-manager system. As Dallas learned in the 1990s, efficient government and democratic governance are not as easy to balance as advocates of the council-manager system once thought.

One illustration of the push for change is that in 2001–02, each of the three major candidates for mayor suggested that the structure of city government needs reexamining. One of the mayoral candidates publicly commented on the need for more power to be in the hands of the mayor. A city council member argued that council members have so little power to set spending priorities or influence city staff that individual citizens do not see city government as a way to influence their lives. There has even been some discussion of the value of partisan elections in city races.

# ● Special Districts

**special district** a unit of local government that performs a single service, such as education or sanitation, within a limited geographical area

> **Examine the role of special districts in Texas government**

A **special district** is a unit of local government that performs a single service in a limited geographical area. These governments solve problems that cross borders of existing units of government. Special districts can be created to serve an entire county, part of a county, all of two or more counties, or parts of two or more counties. The number of special districts has increased dramatically in the last 50 years. In the United States, the number increased by 400 percent.[27] In Texas, the number increased by more than 600 percent.[28] By the year 2002, there were more special districts than any other form of local government.

Districts can be created to do almost anything that is legal. Some districts are formed to provide hospital care, others to furnish pure water to cities that, in turn, sell it to their residents. Mosquito control, navigation, flood control, sanitation, drainage, and law enforcement are a few more examples of services provided by special district government.

## Types of Special Districts

**school district** a specific type of special district that provides public education in a designated area

There are two types of special districts in Texas. The first is the **school district**, which consists of independent school districts in the state. These districts offer public education from pre-kindergarten through twelfth grade. Almost all school districts offer the full range of educational opportunities; however, some small, rural schools provide education only through the eighth grade. Others limit their programs to the sixth grade, and still others end with the fourth grade. Those with limited offerings contract with nearby districts to complete the education of their students.

**nonschool special district** any special district other than a school district; examples include municipal utility districts (MUDs) and hospital districts

The second classification of special districts is the **nonschool special district**. Everything except the school districts is included in this category. Municipal utility districts, economic development corporations, hospital districts, and fire-prevention districts are the most common examples.

## School Districts

Every inch of land in Texas is part of a school district, and the state contains slightly more than 1,000 school districts. Some districts in east and west Texas cover an entire county. In metropolitan counties, there may be a dozen or more districts.

# Who Represents Texans at the Local Level?

Texas has many local governments, and as a result Texans have many elected representatives in different local governments. The charts show all of the local elected officials for two places in the state—the West Campus neighborhood in Austin and the Woodcreek neighborhood in North Harris County. Between county, city, school district, and community college district officials, Texans have many, many people serving them in local government.

## AUSTIN—WEST CAMPUS AREA

### COUNTY

**County Judge,** Sam Biscoe
**County Commissioner, Precinct 2,** Sarah Eckhardt
**District Attorney,** Rosemary Lehmberg
**County Attorney,** David Escamilla
**County Sheriff,** Greg Hamilton
**County Tax Assessor-Collector,** Bruce Elfant
**District Clerk,** Amalia Rodriguez-Mendoza
**County Clerk,** Dana DeBeauvoir
**County Treasurer,** Dolores Ortega Carter
**County Constable, Precinct 5,** Carlos Lopez
**Justice of the Peace, Precinct 5,** Herb Evans

### CITY

**Mayor,** Lee Leffingwell
**Council, Place 1,** Chris Riley
**Council, Place 2,** Mike Martinez
**Council, Place 3,** Kathie Tovo

### CITY (continued)

**Council, Place 4,** Laura Morrison
**Council, Place 5,** Bill Spelman
**Council, Place 6,** Sheryl Cole

### SCHOOL DISTRICT: AUSTIN ISD

**District 5,** Mark Williams

### COMMUNITY COLLEGE DISTRICT: AUSTIN COMMUNITY COLLEGE

**Place 1,** Tim Mahoney
**Place 2,** John-Michael Cortez
**Place 3,** Nan McRaven
**Place 4,** Jeffrey Richard
**Place 5,** Victor Villareal
**Place 6,** Guadalupe Sosa
**Place 7,** Barbara Mink
**Place 8,** James McGuffie
**Place 9,** Allen Kaplan

## NORTH HARRIS COUNTY—WOODCREEK AREA

### COUNTY

**County Judge,** Ed Emmett
**County Commissioner, Precinct 4,** Jack Cagle
**District Attorney,** Patricia Lyons
**County Attorney,** Vince Ryan
**County Sheriff,** Adrian Garcia
**County Tax Assessor-Collector,** Mike Sullivan
**District Clerk,** Chris Daniel
**County Clerk,** Stan Stanart
**County Treasurer,** Orlando Sanchez
**County Constable, Precinct 4,** Ron Hickman
**Justice of the Peace, Precinct 4, Place 1,** J. Kent Adams
**Justice of the Peace, Precinct 4, Place 2,** Tom Lawrence
**School Trustee, Position 2,** Angie Chesnut
**School Trustee, At Large, Position 7,** Jim Henley
**School Trustee, Position 5,** Debra Kerner
**School Trustee, Position 3,** Michael Wolfe

### SCHOOL DISTRICT: ALDINE ISD

**Board, Position 1,** Rick Ogden
**Board, Position 2,** Marine Jones
**Board, Position 3,** Rose Avalos
**Board, Position 4,** Merlin Griffs
**Board, Position 5,** Steve Mead
**Board, Position 6,** Alton Smith
**Board, Position 7,** Violet Garcia

### COMMUNITY COLLEGE DISTRICT: LONE STAR COLLEGE SYSTEM

**Board, Position 1,** David Holsey
**Board, Position 2,** Thomas Forestier
**Board, Position 3,** Stephanie Marquard
**Board, Position 4,** Robert Adam
**Board, Position 5,** David Vogt
**Board, Position 6,** Bob Wolfe
**Board, Position 7,** Linda Good
**Board, Position 8,** Randy Bates
**Board, Position 9,** Priscilla Kelley

## for critical analysis

1. Why would there be so many local elected officials? What are the advantages of having many elected officials? How does this system promote democratic values?

2. Think of your own local school board. Do you know the elected officials who serve on it? How many people in your community do you think know all their local elected officials? If people do not know who is in office, can they evaluate the job their officials are doing at election time?

Each is governed by an elected board of trustees composed of five to nine members. The board employs a superintendent to oversee the daily operation of the district. On the recommendation of the superintendent, the trustees

- set overall policy for the school district
- adopt the budget for the district
- set the tax rate for the district (The maximum tax rate for a district is $1.04 for each $100 the property is worth. A rate higher than $1.04 requires voter approval.)
- select textbooks for classroom use
- hire principals, faculty, and support staff
- set the school calendar
- determine salaries and benefits for employees

Educating millions of students is a daunting task. By localizing public education, the state places much of the burden on the local school districts. This allows local residents to participate in governing the school districts. Unfortunately, few people vote in the elections to select members of the board of trustees. Even fewer individuals attend meetings of the school board.

## Nonschool Special Districts

**municipal utility district (MUD)**
a special district that offers services such as electricity, water, sewage, and sanitation outside the city limits

**Municipal Utility Districts** Municipal utility districts (MUDs) offer electricity, water, sewer, and sanitation services outside the city limits. These governments might offer all utility services or only one or two, depending on the needs of the special district. Though located throughout Texas, the vast majority are found in the Houston greater metropolitan area.

MUDs can be a financial blessing for developers. Entrepreneurs who build housing additions outside the city limits must furnish utilities to the homes they build, but few developers can afford to do this over a long period of time.

Banks and finance companies, legislators, and land developers maintain a warm and snug relationship with each other. Banks and finance companies willingly lend land developers millions of dollars to establish residential subdivisions, build new homes, and run water and sewer services to these houses. When a few houses are sold, the developer asks the residents to establish a MUD. The enabling legislation is seldom a problem because of the close relationship between developers and local legislators.

Once the MUD is up and running, the board of directors sets a tax rate and determines how much to charge residents for its services. One of its first activities is to borrow money by issuing bonds. The bond proceeds are used to purchase the utilities from the developer, often at a premium. Using the proceeds from the sale of the utilities, the developer is able to repay loans. By establishing the MUD, residents agree to pay a property tax to retire the bonded indebtedness. In addition to the property tax, residents pay a monthly fee for the water, sewer, and sanitation services.

**Flood-Control Districts** Flooding is seldom confined to a single county, and a flood-control district can be created to solve a multicounty flood-control problem.

**Community College Districts** Community college districts are classified as nonschool special districts because they do not offer public education from prekindergarten through grade twelve. Community colleges offer postsecondary academic and vocational programs. They are governed by an elected board of regents. Residents of the district pay a property tax to the district. In return, residents pay lower tuition. The board employs a president or chancellor, who operates the college on a daily basis. The regents set policy on the recommendation of the president or chancellor. Among the regents' responsibilities are to

- set overall policy for the district
- set the tax rate
- set the cost of tuition and fees
- build new buildings and repair older ones
- hire teachers, counselors, administrators, and nonprofessional staff
- set the school calendar
- determine salaries and benefits for employees

**Creating a Special District** Special districts are created by voters of the area to be served. Creating a special district requires

- a petition signed by the residents of the area to be served, requesting the legislature to authorize an election to create a special district
- enabling legislation in the form of a law that authorizes a special election to create the district
- a majority positive vote of those voting in the special election

**Governing a Special District** Most special districts are governed by boards elected by the voters of the district. The board of a school district is called the board of trustees, the governing board of a community college is often called the board of regents, and the governing boards of other special districts are known as boards of directors. Each board is the policy-making group for its district. The directors set the tax rate and establish rules and policy for the operation of the district. The district employs an individual who runs the district on a day-to-day basis.

**Revenues** **Property taxes** are the primary source of revenue for special districts. This was not always the case. In 1949, school districts received 80 percent of their income from the state, and the school district furnished 20 percent of necessary funds, primarily from property taxes. Today, property taxes comprise as much as 90 percent of revenues for some districts. The second largest source of income is **user fees**. State and federal aid furnish the remainder of special district funding.

Property tax rates and actual user fees are set by governing boards. User fees are raised from providing goods and services. Water districts, for example, sell water, sewer, and possibly sanitation services.

Hospital districts set fees for room occupancy, medicine dispensed, use of surgical suites, X-rays taken and evaluated, nursing and laboratory service, and myriad other charges. The board of trustees of a school district sets the local property rate for taxes, which fund pre-kindergarten through twelfth grade education. Tuition paid by in-district and out-of-district students, building fees, student fees, and technology and lab fees are determined by the board of regents of a community college district.

**Hidden Governments** Everyone in Texas lives in at least one special district, their school district. Most people live in several, have the opportunity to vote for people

**property tax** a tax based on an assessment of the value of one's property, which is used to fund the services provided by local governments, such as education

**user fee** a fee paid for public goods and services, such as water or sewage service

to represent them on the governing board of each district, and pay property taxes to these agencies of government. Yet few people are aware these agencies exist, thus their reputation as "**hidden governments**."

Special districts provide needed services in specific geographic areas. Existing governments may lack authority to provide the service or the necessary funds to finance the project. In theory, special districts are an example of democracy at work. Districts are created by a vote of the residents of the area to be served, and the districts' governing boards are elected by the voters. Board meetings, at which decisions on policy, taxing, and fees are made, are open for attendance by any interested residents. However, fewer than 10 percent of eligible voters cast ballots in special district elections and fewer than 1 percent of district residents ever attend a board meeting.

**Problems with Special Districts** There is a potential for abuse in the creation of special districts. Many special districts were originally authorized by the Texas Legislature to develop the economies of poor, rural counties. More recently, however, developers of large tracts of land began creating these districts to place the burden of developing the property's infrastructure on future owners of the property. In order to comply with the law, all the developers must do is create the district and hold an election where at least one short-term resident must vote. These short-term residents then approve bonds in the millions of dollars that must be paid for with the taxation of future homes and property owners. In the 1980s, this kind of special district creation in Harris County led to defaults on bond issues after a housing bust.

*The creation of special districts by developers has sometimes been controversial. Recent investigations have charged developers with abusing the process in order to circumvent inconvenient laws and to give the developers greater control over taxes and other government functions in the district.*

In 2001, a major investigation of special districts created by developers in Dallas found unusual and questionable practices. Some developers drew district boundaries to exclude existing residents of an area. The developers then moved people into rent-free mobile homes shortly before the special district election. These newly established "residents" were the only ones eligible to vote in the election. After the election, the voters for the new district would often move away after approving large bond sales for the construction of roads, water lines, and sewers. Future homeowners in the area were then expected to pay for the bonds with property taxes on their homes. The investigation found that sometimes a single voter—and always fewer than 10 voters—approved the bonded indebtedness that helped the developers create an infrastructure for their properties. In the Lantana subdivision near Flower Mound, for example, a family of three voted to authorize $277 million in bond sales by two water districts. That bond proposition rivals the biggest bond proposals by the city of Dallas.[29]

Similar schemes have been especially prevalent in Travis, Harris, and Denton counties. In 2006, developers in Denton County housed six people at below-market rents on property to be developed. These temporary residents were thus eligible to vote in a special tax-district election that would affect the taxation of thousands of future homeowners.[30]

In 2010, two voters in the Four Seasons Ranch Municipal Utility District No. 1 approved $292.5 million in bonds, including $138.5 million in bonds for water, sewer, and storm sewer systems and $154 million in roads. Recent special district elections near the Four Seasons Ranch district in Denton and Collin Counties have authorized close to $1 billion dollars in public debt.[31]

The pervasiveness of these government bodies is shown by one study of Texas special districts that address water issues. The study found that about 1,000 MUDs were engaged in supplying water; 48 special districts existed to deal with water drainage issues; 66 special districts existed solely to supply fresh water. Others had these purposes: 91 to conserve groundwater, 25 for irrigation, 46 to improve levees, 42 to manage municipal water, 26 to deal with navigation, 31 to deal with rivers. Fifty-five special utility districts dealt with general water issues; 221 were water control and improvement districts; and 18 were water improvement districts. Of course, this hodgepodge of special districts dealing with all aspects of water makes a coherent approach to statewide water policy virtually impossible.[32]

Special districts are among the least-studied areas of Texas politics, but their use as an instrument of private gain and their use by developers as a way to minimize their financial risks suggest the need for much greater scrutiny. Of course, developers may defend this system as a way to improve property and enhance the tax base of communities. On the other hand, the extent of enlistment of governmental taxing powers with little public scrutiny or accountability is disturbing. And if the huge bond issues floated by these entities default, thousands of people could suffer the financial consequences.

## Councils of Government (COGs)

One of the greatest problems facing local governments in Texas today is coordination across legal boundaries. The Regional Planning Act of 1965 initially provided for the creation of regional **councils of government (COGs)** to promote coordination and planning across all local governments in a particular region. There are 24 regional councils in Texas today, each with its own bylaws or articles of agreement. The governing body of a regional council must consist of at least two-thirds of

**council of government (COG)** a regional planning board composed of local elected officials and some private citizens from the same area

local elected officials of cities and counties, and may include citizen members and representatives of other groups.

The basic responsibilities of regional councils include planning for the economic development of an area, helping local governments carry out regional projects, contracting with local governments to provide certain services, and reviewing applications for state and federal financial assistance. Originally, COGs focused considerable attention on meeting federal mandates for water and sewer provision, open space, and housing planning. More recently, activities have focused on comprehensive planning and service delivery in such policy areas as aging, employment and training, criminal justice, economic development, environmental quality, and transportation.[33]

# ● Thinking Critically about Local Government

In this chapter, we have investigated the role of local government in Texas government and politics. In many ways, local government affects the average citizen's life much more than either the federal or the state government. Sadly, local government may not be functioning as well as we might hope. Part of the problem may lie in the conflicting demands we have come to place on it. On the one hand, Texans want local government of all kinds to provide an efficient delivery of services to all in a fair and equitable manner. On the other hand, Texans also want to keep local government under some sort of democratic control. But what sort of local controls are the best? The demands of efficiency and democracy are not easily balanced. The social, political, and economic changes of the last 20 years may spark a rethinking of local government in Texas for the first time since the early decades of the twentieth century.

**Practice online with:** Chapter 26 Diagnostic Quiz ▪ Chapter 26 Key Term Flashcards

## County Government in Texas

■ **Explain the importance of county government in Texas (pp. 979–86)**

There are more counties in Texas than in any other state. County governance in Texas affects the lives of everyday Texans in ways ranging from hospital care to trash pickup.

### Key Terms

**county commissioners court** (p. 979)

**county judge** (p. 980)

**county commissioner** (p. 980)

**constable** (p. 981)

**county attorney** (p. 984)

**district attorney** (p. 984)

**county clerk** (p. 985)

**district clerk** (p. 985)

**county tax assessor-collector** (p. 985)

**county auditor** (p. 985)

### Practice Quiz

1. Which of the following is *not* a type of local government found in Texas? *(p. 979)*
   a) city
   b) council of government
   c) county
   d) special district
   e) parish

2. The basic governing body of a county is known as *(p. 979)*
   a) a council of government.
   b) a county council.
   c) a city-manager governement.
   d) a county commissioners court.
   e) a county governing committee.

3. How many counties are there in Texas? *(p. 979)*
   a) 25
   b) 56
   c) 110
   d) 254
   e) 500

4. All county commissioner's precincts must be equal in population according to *(p. 980)*
   a) Article I of the Texas Constitution.
   b) the Civil Rights Act of 1964.
   c) the Voting Rights Act of 1975.
   d) *Avery v. Midland County.*
   e) *Marbury v. Madison.*

5. A county judge *(p. 980)*
   a) only hears appellate cases from JP courts.
   b) is an appointive position from the governor.
   c) presides over the constitutional county court and the county commissioner's court.
   d) implements all the decisions of the Supreme Court affecting the county.
   e) judges juvenile cases.

6. Which county officials are responsible for the jail and the safety of the prisoners? *(p. 984)*
   a) sheriff
   b) county council
   c) county commissioners court
   d) council of mayors
   e) city manager

 **Practice Online**
"Exploring Texas Politics" exercise: *County Tax Rates*

# City Government In Texas

■ **Describe the major types of city government in Texas (pp. 986–92)**

Municipalities in Texas vary in terms of how they are governed. Some cities have strong mayors who run the city, while other cities have weak mayors where the day-to-day running of the city is delegated to city managers. Mayors and city councils often decide issues which directly affect the lives of everyday people.

## Key Terms

**home-rule charter** (p. 986)

**mayor-council form of government** (p. 987)

**at-large election** (p. 988)

**single-member district** (p. 988)

**commissioner form of government** (p. 988)

**council-manager form of government** (p. 989)

## Practice Quiz

7. To adopt a home-rule charter, a city must have a minimum population of *(p. 986)*
   a) 201.
   b) 5,000.
   c) 10,000.
   d) 50,000.
   e) There is no minimum.

8. The two legal classifications of Texas cities are *(pp. 986–87)*
   a) local and regional.
   b) general law and home rule.
   c) tax and nontax.
   d) charter and noncharter.
   e) big and small.

9. The form of city government that allows the mayor to establish control over most of the city's government is called the *(p. 987)*
   a) commissioner form of city government.
   b) council-manager form of city government.
   c) council of government form of city government.
   d) strong mayor–council form of city government.
   e) none of the above.

10. A city controller *(p. 990)*
    a) works directly for the governor.
    b) controls and manages the election in a city.
    c) is a city's chief elected official who presides over the city council.
    d) is independent of all political control in a small statutory city.
    e) is a city's chief financial officer.

 **Practice Online**

Video exercise: *Texas Mayors and National Publicity—Castro and Parker in the Media*

# Special Districts

■ **Examine the role of special districts in Texas government (pp. 992–98)**

Special districts often span different cities and counties. They are tasked with operating such things as school districts or water utility districts. They have the authority to levy property taxes to fund the operation of services essential to the lives of many residents.

## Key Terms

**special district** (p. 992)

**school district** (p. 992)

**nonschool special district** (p. 992)

**municipal utility district (MUD)** (p. 994)

**property tax** (p. 995)

**user fee** (p. 995)

**"hidden government"** (p. 996)

**council of government (COG)** (p. 997)

## Practice Quiz

11. Which local government provides a single service not provided by any other local government? *(p. 992)*
    a) special district
    b) council of government
    c) police district
    d) city
    e) county

12. What are the two types of special districts found in Texas? *(p. 992)*
    a) school and nonschool
    b) home rule and general law
    c) tax and nontax
    d) statutory and constitutional
    e) none of the above.

13. A special district *(p. 992)*
    a) must be limited to under 150,000 people.
    b) covers the entire state to provide a particular service.

c) is a unit of local government that provides a special service to a limited geographic area.

d) temporarily combines two congressional districts.

e) none of the above

14. A MUD *(p. 994)*

a) serves the needs of developers.

b) is generally opposed by banks and real estate developers as being too expensive.

c) provides ambulance service inside a city's geographic limits.

d) delegates the setting of tax rates to the state legislature in a particular geographic area.

e) provides funding for special districts.

15. Comprehensive planning and service delivery in a specific geographic area is the function of a *(p. 997)*

a) special district.

b) council of government.

c) city.

d) county.

e) town.

## Recommended Websites

**Individual State Descriptions**
www.census.gov

**Texas Association of Counties**
www.county.org

**Texas Local Government Code**
www.statutes.legis.state.tx.us/

**U.S. Census Bureau, State and County QuickFacts**
http://quickfacts.census.gov/qfd/

The Religious Viewpoints Anti-discrimination Act required Texas school districts to protect religious speech on campus, allowing students to express their faith in public. These students at Grapevine High School sang along with a Christian band at an event organized by the Christian organization Students Standing Strong.

# 27

# Public Policy in Texas

**WHAT GOVERNMENT DOES AND WHY IT MATTERS** Like other states, Texas is involved in a broad range of public-policy initiatives. Some of these activities, such as crime prevention and corrections or public education, are largely state responsibilities. Although the national government may contribute some funds and regulate various aspects of these public-policy areas, they remain for the most part the duty and responsibility of the state of Texas. Other public-policy areas, however, have involved considerable intermingling of state and federal government responsibilities. The balance of power between the state and federal governments in these areas has shifted over time.

Throughout the first decade of the twenty-first century, state policy makers in Texas waded through a variety of policy problems, including tax reform, educational testing, and criminal incarceration. Republican domination of both houses of the state legislature and the executive offices in the state ensured that a new conservative agenda would dominate policy debates across a variety of issues. Perhaps nothing captured this ideological orientation in public policy better than a new law that was passed during the 2007 session of the state legislature: the Religious Viewpoints Antidiscrimination Act.[1]

The law, which many claimed simply codified existing constitutional rulings by the federal courts, required Texas school districts to adopt a number of policies that would protect religious speech on campus. School districts were ordered to develop a neutral method for choosing student speakers at school events and graduation ceremonies, to ensure that religious-oriented clubs had the same access to school facilities as secular-oriented clubs, and to protect students who wished to express their religious beliefs in classroom assignments. The legislation did more than just give students permission to express their religious views in public schools; it also mandated the creation of a "limited public forum" for student speakers at public events that wouldn't discriminate against expressions of faith.

Social conservatives were ecstatic about the Religious Viewpoints Antidiscrimination Act, claiming that, at last, individual religious expression would be protected in the schools. Professional educators were somewhat hesitant in their praise for the bill, citing concerns about how the bill would be implemented and what it might mean for members of religious minorities.[2]

The Religious Viewpoints Antidiscrimination Act brings out two important truths about public policy in Texas. First, what goes on in Austin matters. The state legislature plays a major role in defining how public policy is conducted in the state. Second, public policy involves more than just introducing a bill in the legislature, passing it, and getting it signed. Laws also must be implemented. Implementation of policy by state agencies such as school boards is where the rubber meets the road in political life.

## chaptergoals

- Explain why Texas is considered a "low-tax, low-service" state (pages 1005–16)

- Describe the major issues in corrections policy in Texas (pages 1016–21)

- Describe the major issues in education policy in Texas (pages 1021–28)

- Trace how welfare policy has evolved in Texas (pages 1028–34)

# ● Taxing and Spending in Texas

**Explain why Texas is considered a "low-tax, low-service" state**

Texas has a reputation of being a "low-tax, low-service" state that seeks to maintain a favorable environment for business. For the most part, this reputation is well earned. Texas is one of nine states that still do not have a personal income tax. There is a high sales tax in Texas of 6.25 percent, the tenth highest in the nation. Combined state and local sales taxes in the state are 8.25 percent.[3] State taxes per capita in 2007 were $1,704, ranking Texas forty-eighth among the 50 states.

Although Texas state taxes are low compared with other states' taxes, local taxes are a different story. In 2008, Texas ranked seventeenth among the states in terms of property taxes paid per capita at $1,393. When state and local taxes are taken together, however, Texas remains a low-tax state. Combined state and local taxes were $3,197 per capita in 2009, ranking Texas forty-fifth in the nation. A 2011 study conducted by the Tax Foundation concluded that Texas had the thirteenth most business-friendly tax system.[4]

The 1970s and early '80s were boom years for the Texas economy. Rising inflation coupled with high oil prices and rapid economic growth drove the economy forward.[5] Tax increases were unnecessary as tax revenues soared. The problem facing the legislature was not how to balance the budget, but how to spend revenue windfalls. There were no tax increases in Texas during this time.

The collapse of oil prices and a sputtering state economy in the mid-1980s, particularly severe in real estate and construction, brought on a budget crisis. As projected deficits mounted, tax increases became commonplace. Between 1985 and 1986, state tax collections fell. Income from the oil severance tax alone dropped 28 percent. Tax rates were increased and the tax base was broadened in almost every year between 1984 and 1991.

As the state's economy turned around in the early 1990s, the budgetary situation brightened considerably. However, renewed budget surpluses did not bring a return to the spending patterns of the pre–oil crash years. Business and political leaders from both parties expressed an ongoing concern that taxes were becoming burdensome, perhaps placing Texas at a disadvantage with other states in trying to create a favorable environment for business. Additionally, a growing concern that state government was expanding too fast sparked demands for making government more efficient. With the recession beginning in 2008, Texas has weathered the downturn far better than many other states, but declining state revenues and expanding demands for services pose a chronic problem for policy makers.

## The Constitution and the Budget

A number of constitutional factors affect the way the budget is made in Texas. First, the legislature is compelled to write a two-year, or **biennial**, budget because of the constitutional provision that the legislature may meet in regular session only once every two years. One of the effects of this restricted time frame is to force government agencies to project their budgetary needs well in advance of any clear understanding of the particular problems they may be facing during the biennium. Second, the legislature can meet for only 140 days in regular session. This seriously limits the amount of time that the legislature can spend analyzing the budget or developing innovative responses to pressing matters of public importance.

**biennial** occurring every two years

*After the legislature passes the biennial state budget, the state comptroller certifies the budget, confirming that it is within current revenue estimates for the period. Here, State Comptroller Susan Combs discusses the 2012–13 budget.*

**dedicated funds** a portion of the state budget that is dedicated to mandatory spending on programs such as health care for the poor

Third, a large portion of the biennial budget is dedicated for special purposes by federal law or by the Texas Constitution or state statute. These **dedicated funds** include federal monies earmarked for financing health care for the poor (Medicaid), as well as state funds for highways, education, teachers' retirement, and numerous other purposes. The purpose of dedicated funds is not difficult to understand. Supporters of particular programs want to create a stable revenue source for priority programs. But in protecting their own programs, supporters encourage other interests to do likewise, with the result that the legislature loses control of a large portion of the budget.

Fourth, a number of specific constitutional provisions constrain the legislature's control of the budget.[6]

**appropriations** the amounts of money approved by the state legislature in statutes that each unit or agency of government can spend

**pay-as-you-go limit** a requirement in the Texas Constitution that requires the state to balance its budget

**The Pay-as-You-Go Limit** Article III, Section 49a, requires the state to maintain a balanced budget. All bills that get as far as **appropriations** in the legislative process must be sent to the comptroller of public accounts so the comptroller can certify that they are within available budget limit projections. One of the most important consequences of the **pay-as-you-go limit** is to put the comptroller at the heart of the budget process.

**The Welfare Spending Limit** Article III, Section 51a, provides that the amount of money the state pays for assistance to or on behalf of needy dependent children and their caretakers shall not exceed 1 percent of the state budget in any biennium. This article sets a constitutional limit on the amount of money that the state may pay out to welfare beneficiaries under the Temporary Assistance for Needy Families program. This restriction has not been particularly important in recent years.

**The Limit on the Growth of Certain Appropriations** Article VIII, Section 22, limits the biennial rate of growth of appropriations from state revenue not dedicated by the Texas Constitution to the estimated growth of the state's economy.

The state of Texas collects a tax of 20 cents per gallon on motor fuels. The federal government collects an additional 18.4 cents per gallon, but Texans still pay less tax on gasoline than residents of some other states.

**Limitation on Debt Payable from the General Revenue Fund** Under a 1997 amendment to Article III of the Texas Constitution, the legislature is prohibited from authorizing additional state debt if the resulting **debt service** from the general revenue exceeds 5 percent of the average amount of the General Revenue Fund revenue for the three preceding fiscal years.

**debt service** the amount of a budget spent by a government on paying interest on its debt

## The Budgetary Process

In theory, Texas has a "dual-budget" system. This means that responsibility for preparing an initial draft of the budget is shared by the governor and the legislature. In practice, the budget is the responsibility of the legislature.

Before 1949, there was little coordination in public budgeting. Financial procedures varied, and state agencies were funded by individual appropriations. In 1949, a law was enacted to establish a 10-member Legislative Budget Board (LBB) whose primary job would be to recommend appropriations for all agencies of state government. The board is chaired by the lieutenant governor. The vice chair is the Speaker of the House. Other members include the chairs of the House Appropriations Committee, the House Committee on Ways and Means, the Senate Finance Committee, and the Senate State Affairs Committee. Two additional members from the Senate and the House are chosen by the lieutenant governor and the Speaker, respectively.

The LBB appoints a budget director, who brings together budgeting requests from the various state agencies and prepares appropriations bills for them. Since 1973, the LBB has also been responsible for evaluating agency programs and developing estimates of the costs of implementing legislation introduced in a legislative session. The LBB's draft budget, not the governor's, is the basis for final legislation.

The budgetary process involves two stages.[7] In the first stage, the LBB develops a draft budget based on requests supplied by state agencies. Hearings are conducted well before the legislature goes into session. Since 1992, each agency has been required to develop a five-year plan that includes goals, objectives, strategies, and performance measures. This information provides the basis for LBB funding recommendations for each agency.

While the draft budgets are being prepared, the comptroller's office prepares the Biennial Revenue Estimate (BRE). The BRE is a detailed forecast of the total revenue that the state is expected to take in over the next biennium. The comptroller effectively sets a ceiling on what the state legislature may spend. Although the legislature can override the comptroller's estimates with a four-fifths vote of each house, this has never happened. The BRE is updated when economic conditions change significantly and for special sessions of the legislature.

The second stage of the budget process involves the legislative process. Budgets are submitted to the House Appropriations Committee and the Senate Finance Committee. The budgets then work their way through the committee system and are subject to hearings, debates, and revisions. Final versions of the budget are prepared by the House Appropriations Committee and the Senate Finance Committee. Differences are reconciled in a conference committee.

The comptroller then formally certifies the budget. "Certification" means that the comptroller's office has analyzed the budget and concluded that it is within the current revenue estimates. After certification, the budget moves on to the governor, who decides whether to veto certain items.

## Revenue in Texas

Government and public policy in Texas are funded from a variety of sources, including sales tax, severance taxes on oil and natural gas produced in the state, licensing income, interest and dividends, and federal aid. In 2011, 41.2 percent of government revenues came from taxes of one sort or another. Many of these taxes are based on complex formulas. People often are unaware that they are paying them. But they are important sources of state revenue (see Table 27.1).

**TABLE 27.1**

### Texas Revenue by Source for Fiscal Year 2011

| | TAX COLLECTIONS BY MAJOR TAX | | |
|---|---|---|---|
| MAJOR TAXES | AMOUNT | PERCENT OF TOTAL | PERCENT CHANGE FROM 2010 |
| Sales tax | $21,478,982,942 | 22.8 | 9.4 |
| Motor vehicle sales/rental taxes | 2,977,664,128 | 3.2 | 13.2 |
| Motor fuels taxes | 3,104,200,331 | 3.3 | 2.0 |
| Franchise tax | 3,932,114,437 | 4.2 | 2.0 |
| Insurance taxes | 1,349,641,599 | 1.4 | 1.9 |
| Natural gas production tax | 1,109,718,098 | 1.2 | 53.0 |
| Cigarette and tobacco taxes | 1,559,505,630 | 1.7 | 12.3 |
| Alcoholic beverages taxes | 862,032,126 | 0.9 | 6.5 |
| Oil production tax | 1,472,846,659 | 1.6 | 46.0 |
| Inheritance tax | 1,806,641 | 0.0 | 2,117.9 |
| Utility taxes | 457,722,479 | 0.5 | (4.4) |
| Hotel tax | 348,796,113 | 0.4 | 5.4 |
| Other taxes | 201,144,550 | 0.2 | 40.6 |
| Total taxes | $38,856,175,733 | 41.2 | 9.9 |

SOURCE: Texas Comptroller of Public Accounts.

**Sales and Use Tax** The most important single tax financing Texas government is the sales tax. Today, the sales tax in Texas is 6.25 percent of the retail sales price of tangible personal property and selected services. Together county, city, and metropolitan transit authorities are authorized to impose an additional 2 percent sales and use tax. In 2011, the 6.25 percent sales and use tax accounted for 22.8 percent of state revenues.

**Oil Production and Regulation Taxes** The oil severance tax is 4.6 percent of the market value of oil produced in the state. As late as 1980, the state took in $786 million in oil production taxes, over 6 percent of total state revenues. By 1999, this once vital revenue source had fallen to $211 million, only .44 percent of state revenues. Although revenues produced by the oil severance tax increased to $1,472,846,659 (1.6% of total state revenues) in 2011, there is little likelihood that this revenue source will ever become as important as it once was.

**for critical analysis**
Is Texas's reputation as a low-tax state deserved?

**Natural Gas Production Tax** There is a 7.5 percent tax on the market value of all natural gas produced in the state. As in the case of the oil production tax, revenues fell significantly from $734 million, or 6.9 percent of state revenues, in 1980 to $489 million, or a little more than 1 percent of state revenues in 1997. In 2011, it accounted for $1,109,718,098, or 1.2 percent of the total revenue flowing to the state.

**Motor Fuels Tax** The motor fuels tax in Texas is 20 cents per gallon of gasoline and diesel fuel. There is a 15-cents-per-gallon tax on liquefied gas. In 2011, the motor fuels tax took in approximately $3,104,200,331, or 3.3 percent of all state revenues.

**Motor Vehicle Sales and Rentals and Manufactured Home Sales Tax** There is a 6.25 percent tax on the sales price of all motor vehicles in the state. There is also a 10 percent tax on all rental vehicles up to 35 days and 6.25 percent thereafter. Newly manufactured homes are also taxed at 5 percent of 65 percent of the sales price. In 2011, these taxes took in $2,977,664,128, or 3.2 percent of total state revenues.

**Corporate Franchise Tax** The franchise tax is imposed on all corporations in Texas. Corporations pay a tax based on net taxable capital or net taxable earned surplus (the net assets of a corporation minus its stated capital). In 2011, the corporate franchise tax took in $2,977,664,128, or 4.2 percent of total state revenues.

**Tobacco Taxes** Texas imposes a variety of taxes on cigarettes and other tobacco products. For example, every pack of 20 cigarettes has a $1.41 tax included in the purchase price. In 2011, $1,559,505,630 came to the state in the form of taxes on tobacco products.

**Alcoholic Beverage Taxes** As with tobacco, a variety of taxes are imposed on alcoholic beverages. For example, beer is taxed at the rate of $6.00 per 31-gallon barrel. Liquor is taxed at the rate of $2.40 per gallon. Mixed drinks are taxed at 14 percent of gross receipts. This tax took in $862,032,126 in 2011 and accounted for .9 percent of state revenues.

**Insurance Occupation Taxes** A complex schedule of tax rates is applied to insurance premiums. For example, life, health, and accident insurance are taxed at the rate of 1.75 percent on gross premium receipts. For life insurance premiums, a half-rate is applied to the first $450,000 in premiums. In 2011, insurance premium taxes came to $1,349,641,599, or 1.4 percent of state revenue.

**Utility Taxes** There is a tax of one-sixth of 1 percent on the gross receipts of public utilities. For gas, electric, and water utilities there is a tax on gross receipts ranging from .581 percent in towns of fewer than 2,500 people to 1.07 percent in cities of between 2,500 and 9,999 people to 1.997 percent in cities of 10,000 or more. There is also a tax on gas utility administration of one-half of 1 percent of the gross income of gas utilities. In 2011, $457,722,479 came into the state through these utility taxes.

**Hotel and Motel Tax** This state tax is 6 percent of the hotel and motel occupancy bill paid by the occupant. In 2011, $348,796,113 was collected through the hotel and motel tax, approximately .4 percent of total state revenues.

**Inheritance Tax** This state tax is equal to the amount of the federal credit that is imposed on the transfer of property at death. In 2011, the state inheritance tax accounted for only $1,806,641.

## The Question of the Income Tax in Texas

**regressive/progressive taxation** taxation that hits upper income brackets more heavily (progressive) or lower income brackets more heavily (regressive)

Many commentators have complained that the tax system in Texas is too **regressive**.[8] By this they mean that the tax burden in the state falls more heavily on lower-income individuals. Sales and use taxes such as those found in Texas are generally considered to be regressive. There have been occasional calls for the institution of a state income tax in Texas. Supporters argue that not only is the income tax a more reliable source of revenue for the state, it can also be made fairer. Unlike sales and use taxes, which are applied equally to everyone whatever their income, income taxes can be made **progressive**. With a progressive income tax, people with lower income pay a lower tax rate than people of higher income. Progressive income taxes thus place a higher tax burden on the rich than on the poor.

For the past 40 years, few politicians were willing to support an income tax. One of the attractive features of Texas to business had always been the absence of an income tax. But in the early 1990s, the first serious attempt to put a state income tax in place was undertaken. Responding to mounting budgetary pressures, the retiring lieutenant governor, Bill Hobby, came out in favor of an income tax in late 1989. Bob Bullock, Hobby's successor, announced in early 1991 that he would actively campaign for an income tax. A blue-ribbon panel chaired by John Connally, a former governor, was charged with looking into new revenue sources for the state. The committee ended up recommending to the legislature both a corporate and a personal income tax, but not without generating an enormous amount of controversy.

**for critical analysis**

Is the current tax system in Texas fair? Why or why not? How would the proposals for new forms of taxation affect the majority of Texans? What concerns should be kept in mind when proposing changes to the tax system?

Chairman Connally himself opposed the income-tax recommendations, as did Governor Ann Richards. By the 1993 legislative session, Lieutenant Governor Bullock was backing off. Bullock proposed a constitutional amendment requiring voter approval of any personal income tax. Moreover, it specified that funds raised under the personal income tax be used to support public education. The amendment quickly passed the 73rd legislature and was overwhelmingly approved by voters on November 2, 1993. Because the amendment effectively gave the electorate a veto over any proposal for an income tax, it is unlikely that Texans will have a personal income tax in the foreseeable future.[9]

# Who Pays the Highest State Taxes?

Texas has one of the lowest tax rates in the country. One reason taxes are so low in the state is that Texas is one of only nine states with no income tax on wages, as shown on the map. This keeps the overall tax rates down, but also means that the state's tax revenues come primarily from sales and property taxes. As the second chart below shows, these taxes are regressive—those with less income pay a higher share of their income in taxes; those with higher incomes pay a lower share of their income in taxes.

## Top State Income Tax Rates

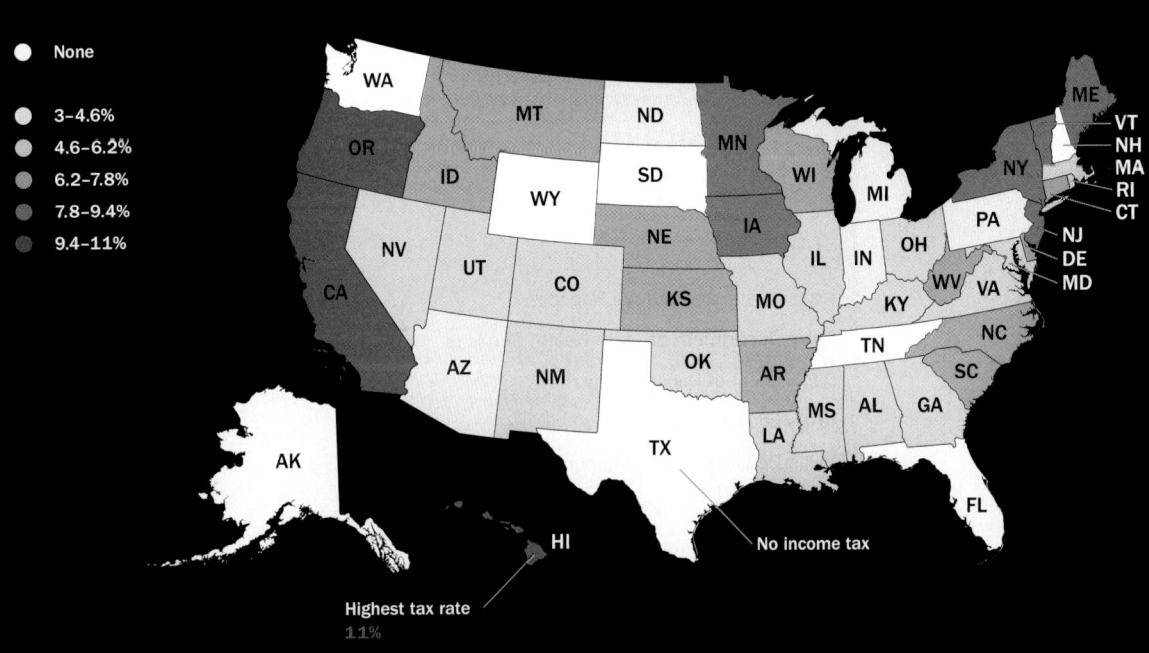

Legend:
- None
- 3–4.6%
- 4.6–6.2%
- 6.2–7.8%
- 7.8–9.4%
- 9.4–11%

No income tax (TX)

Highest tax rate 11% (HI)

## Taxes as a Percentage of Income in Texas

Sales tax   Property tax

| Annual Income | | | | |
|---|---|---|---|---|
| < $29,233 | $29,233–$52,960 | $52,960–$80,882 | $80,882–$126,460 | > $126,460 |
| 6%  $1,473 | 3.4%  $2,177 | 2.9%  $2,989 | 2.5%  $4,089 | 1.3%  $6,507 |
| 5.3%  $1,273 | 2.9%  $1,809 | 2.4%  $2,462 | 2.2%  $3,652 | 1.6%  $7,555 |

## for critical analysis

1. What are the advantages of not having an income tax in the state of Texas?

2. How would an income tax provide a method for the well-off to pay more in taxes than the poor? Where do you stand on this issue? Why?

SOURCES: The Tax Foundation, "Top Marginal State Income Tax Rates, Tax Year 2011," http://taxfoundation.org/article/map-top-marginal-state-income-tax-rates-tax-year-2011 (accessed 11/30/12).

## Other State Revenue

Next to taxes, the second-largest source of revenue for Texas is the federal government (see Table 27.2). Historically, Texas spends relatively little, compared with other states, for state-federal programs. As a result, the federal **matching funds** (federal monies going to a state based on state spending for a program) also have been relatively low. Nevertheless, federal aid to Texas skyrocketed in the 1980s because of the expansion of transportation and human-services programs. For the 2010–11 biennium, federal funds accounted for $33.8 billion, or about 57 percent of the total appropriations for health and human services in Texas. Of this amount, $25.9 billion was for Medicaid.[10]

In addition to federal monies, there are a number of other revenue sources, including interest income, licenses and fees, the sales of goods and services provided by the state, and land income. Two other sources in recent years have had a major impact on monies flowing into the state budget. A state lottery was passed

### TABLE 27.2

### Federal Revenue by State Agency, 2011 (Millions of Dollars)

| STATE AGENCY | |
|---|---:|
| Texas Health and Human Services | $21,571 |
| Texas Department of State Health Services | 1,070 |
| Department of Public Safety | 554 |
| Texas Education Agency | 7,222 |
| Texas Department of Transportation | 3,012 |
| Texas Workforce Commission | 1,075 |
| Family and Protective Services | 436 |
| Texas Rehabilitation Commission | 470 |
| Texas Department of Housing and Community Affairs | 1,136 |
| Department of Assistive and Rehabilitative Services | 470 |
| Department of Agriculture | 400 |
| Texas Department of Rural Affairs | 310 |
| Attorney General | 237 |
| Texas Higher Education Coordinating Board | 204 |
| Comptroller-State Energy Conservation Office | 137 |
| Department of Aging and Disability Services | 132 |
| Adjunct General's Department | 109 |
| All other agencies | 354 |
| Total all agencies | $38,430 |

SOURCE: Texas Comptroller of Public Accounts, 2011 State of Texas Annual Cash Report.

*The lottery, approved by Texas voters in 1991, generates over $1 billion in state revenue every year.*

by the state legislature in July 1991 and approved by the voters that November. Although the lottery was passed by voters overwhelmingly, attitudes about the appropriateness of gambling as a source of state revenues are mixed. Some argue that the lottery unfairly takes money from people who can least afford to give it up by fooling them into thinking that they, too, can strike it rich if only they have a little luck. Large numbers of people from all social classes continue to play the lottery. In 2009, 42 percent of Texans claimed that they had played a lottery game in the previous year. The average monthly dollar amount spent on any lottery game was $45.21.[11] Despite the lottery's popularity, revenues generated by it were still only 1.8 percent of total state revenue in 2010.[12]

A second major source of nontax revenue is a result of the settlement the state reached with tobacco companies in 1999. Under the settlement, Texas would receive over $17.3 billion over the next 25 years, and an additional $580 million every year thereafter, from the tobacco industry. The largest payment—$3.3 billion—came up front, while the remainder was spread out over the remaining 25 years. Nationwide, states received a total of $246 billion in the final settlement reached with the tobacco industry. The Texas Comptroller's Office projects that Texas tobacco settlement receipts will total $867 million in 2012–13, an 8 percent decline from the $950 million in 2010–11.[13]

## Expenditures in Texas

In 2011, Texas government spent $90.4 billion (see Table 27.3). The largest expenditure was on health and human services programs, which spent $38.7 billion, or 42.8 percent of the state budget. In addition, $33.6 billion, or 37.1 percent of the state budget, went to education programs. Transportation was the third-largest expenditure, receiving over $6.7 billion, or 7.4 percent of the state budget. Public safety and corrections programs were the fourth-largest in terms of expenditures, taking up almost $4.5 billion, or a little less than 5 percent of the state budget.

## TABLE 27.3

## Texas Net Expenditures by Function, Fiscal 2011 (All Funds, Excluding Trust)

| GOVERNMENT FUNCTION | AMOUNT | PERCENT OF TOTAL | PERCENT CHANGE FROM PRIOR FISCAL YEAR |
|---|---|---|---|
| General government | | | |
| Executive | $3,924,487,295 | 4.3 | 22.2 |
| Departments | | | |
| Legislative | 138,916,998 | .16 | 5.9 |
| Judicial | 278,932,076 | .3 | 1.4 |
| Education | 33,558,059,096 | 37.1 | 3.5 |
| Employee benefits | 3,410,640,368 | 3.7 | 2.0 |
| Health and human services | 38,718,145,379 | 42.8 | 6.7 |
| Public safety and corrections | 4,549,016,677 | 5.0 | (3.3) |
| Transportation | 6,706,420,175 | 7.4 | 12.3 |
| Natural resources/recreation services | 1,808,419,674 | 2.3 | (0.3) |
| Regulatory services | 312,396,315 | .3 | (6.1) |
| Lottery winnings paid* | 541,356,469 | .6 | 11.2 |
| Debt service | 979,692,074 | 1.1 | 11.2 |
| Capital outlay | 532,373,550 | .6 | (5.9) |
| Total net expenditures | $90,434,143,170 | | 5.6 |

Totals may not sum because of rounding.
*Lottery winnings paid does not include payments made by retailers.
SOURCE: Texas Comptroller of Public Accounts.

## The 2011 Budget Crisis in Texas

The financial crisis of 2008 and the accompanying Great Recession sparked budget crises in state governments across the nation. Higher levels of unemployment and a slowing economy led to declining revenue from various tax sources and to increased demands on public services in health, welfare, and education. Some states, such as California, plunged into serious political crises as state political leaders had difficulty reaching a consensus on how to balance the budget.

At first, Texas appeared to have escaped the budgetary woes of other states.[14] The economic slowdown in Texas did not appear to be as bad as in other states. The budget passed by the 2009 Texas Legislature was a modest one built upon rosy assumptions about future trends. By 2010, concerns began to mount that the Texas budget was in trouble. Initial revenue projections for the 2010–11 budget cycle were found to be too optimistic by up to $2 billion. Although some budget cuts were put into place by state agencies in spring 2010, Comptroller Susan Combs refused to alter revenue estimates made in January 2009. In May 2010 the chief budget writer for the Texas House, Representative Jim Pitts from Waxahachie, speculated that the budget deficit for the next two years might reach $15 to $18 billion. Pitts's projections were summarily rejected by Governor Perry as being "pulled out of the air." Leaders in neither party wanted to confront the intensifying budget crisis until after the election. The two gubernatorial candidates in 2010 seemed to offer little more than vague platitudes about how they would put into place either substantive spending cuts or tax increases to make up a growing budget deficit.

As the fall campaign progressed, it became increasingly difficult to ignore the intensifying budget problems. In early September 2010 the Democratic chairman of the House Ways and Means Committee, Representative Rene Olivera, warned of the disconnect between the budget and the state of the economy. The projected budget deficit was now estimated at $20.6 billion. On September 9, 2010, Perry finally conceded that the state was in trouble. "You'd have to be deaf, dumb, and blind not to understand that we have a major financial crisis on our hands," he told reporters. Yet he remained confident that the budget would be balanced without substantially raising taxes. His Democratic opponent, Bill White, criticized the Perry administration for financial mismanagement. But White remained consistently unclear as to how he would cut the budget deficit if elected. In late October, state leaders were warned that the projected budget deficit had ballooned to almost $25 billion, about 25 percent of current spending. The gap was proportionally bigger than the one that California was experiencing.

There were many factors behind the budget crisis. On the revenue side, sales and business tax receipts were down. On the expenditure side, state obligations were increasing as the demand for welfare, unemployment insurance, and health care intensified with the recession. The state's obligation to fund public schooling also rose.

Numerous proposals began to circulate for how to deal with the impending budget crisis in the 2011 legislative session. Among these were proposals to

- tap the state's $9.7 billion rainy day fund
- close loopholes in the sales tax
- sell unused state land
- eliminate various regulatory agencies involved with overseeing business and environmental regulations
- eliminate various state agencies, including agriculture, the attorney general's office, Parks and Wildlife, and the Workforce Commission
- curtail various business and economic programs in the state
- cut funding to elementary and secondary education
- raise tuition at community colleges and state universities
- curtail or even eliminate funds going to the poor through the Medicaid Program or the Temporary Assistance for Needy Families Program

Significantly, no prominent political leader in the state called for any substantial tax increase prior to the 2010 election. Even after Election Day, triumphant Republican leaders remained quiet as to what might actually be proposed to address the yawning budget deficit in the upcoming legislative session. At least publicly, most were waiting for January 2011 when the comptroller would release her final budgetary projections.

The legislative session of 2011 was a difficult one. Against the expectations of many, Republican leaders were able to put together a balanced budget that sidestepped many of the harsher measures proposed for addressing the deficit at the beginning of the session. The final two-year budget that passed at the end of the session in late May approved $172.3 billion in spending while cutting state spending by $15.2 billion. Spending cuts were concentrated in education and health care. Cuts also were put into place in the state workforce, where 5,727 jobs were eliminated. Significantly, no new taxes were proposed. Resisting Democratic calls to solve the deficit by dipping into the state's rainy day fund of $9.7 billion, the Republican-dominated legislature agreed to draw down the fund by $3.1 billion to balance the portion of the deficit that had emerged in the previous biennium budget. Only five Republicans voted against the budget bill in the House. Only two Democrats supported it. The 2012–13 budget was a triumph of a growingly confident Republican majority in the state.

Although the budget had been passed, a special session had to be called by the governor to deal with some supplemental issues. Among these was a school finance plan to distribute $4 billion in cuts to school districts statewide and to accelerate some tax payments. By the late fall, the Texas economy appeared to be recovering at last from the effects of the Great Recession. As economic indicators in the state started to turn around, lawmakers began to talk about a supplemental appropriations bill of $6.2 billion to address programs such as Medicaid that had been underfunded by the state legislature for the state portion during the regular session in 2011. The LBB executive director noted in February 2012 that the Health and Human Services Commission might actually run out of money for Medicaid and other health care programs for the poor if new funds were not found.

# ● Crime and Corrections Policy

**Describe the major issues in corrections policy in Texas**

It has long been claimed that Texas does things in a big way. That is certainly true of its levels of crime and the way it deals with criminals. In Chapter 25, we considered aspects of the criminal justice systems such as the death penalty. In this section we take a closer look at policies related to the prison system in Texas.

## History of the Prison System

Shortly after Texas joined the Union, construction was authorized for a state penitentiary in Huntsville. The 225-cell facility opened in 1849. It confined prisoners in single cells at night and congregated inmates during the day to work in silence. From 1870 to 1883, the entire prison system was leased to private contractors who used the labor of inmates in exchange for providing maintenance and security for prisoners. After 1883, convicts in the Texas prison system were leased to railroads, planters, and others who provided the prisoners with food and clothing and paid a stipend to the state. These leasing arrangements were abandoned in 1910 because of scandals and abuses of the system.[15]

Although Texas moved to a state-run system, abuses continued. In 1924 an investigation of the system found cruel and brutal treatment of prisoners, inefficient management, and inadequate care of inmates. That investigation led to the creation of a state prison board, which supervised the work of a general prison manager. Nevertheless the abuses continued. By the mid-1940s, the Texas prison system was considered one of the worst in the United States. In 1974 the Joint Committee on Prison Reform submitted findings to the legislature that were very critical of the Texas prison system. It found fault with numerous aspects of the prison system's operation—from living and working conditions for inmates to classification of inmates to medical care to staff training. Still, little was done to remedy the situation.[16]

The event that had the most dramatic effect on the operation of the Texas prison system in modern times was a federal court case, *Ruiz v. Estelle*.[17] Lawsuits filed by prisoners are nothing new. During the tenure of W. J. Estelle Jr., the prison director from 1973–83 and the defendant in the *Ruiz* case, prisoners filed 19,696 cases in the federal courts in Texas, a caseload amounting to about 20 percent of the federal court docket in Texas during that period.[18] However, the *Ruiz* case was exceptional. It was a class-action suit on behalf of inmates that began in 1972, and it focused on issues of crowding in the system, security and supervision, health care, discipline, and access to the courts. In 1980, the federal court concluded that inmates' constitutionally guaranteed rights had been violated. Texas joined several other states in having its prison system declared unconstitutional.

The result was the appointment by the court of a special master, a court officer, to oversee the Texas prison system to eliminate the constitutional problems such as overcrowding and improper care and supervision of inmates. There was a massive reform of the system, one that had to be imposed from outside—from the federal courts—because the state seemed unwilling or unable to reform its own prison system.

For a long time, many in Texas government were resistant to federal court supervision of the prison system, arguing, for example, that the *Ruiz* decision involved federal court judicial activism and interfered with the rights of the state. In order to reduce the overcrowding in state prisons to comply with *Ruiz*, the state also encouraged the early release of prisoners, some of whom reentered society and committed more crimes. *Ruiz* did, however, help to turn the criminal justice system into a major public policy issue in Texas. Federal court supervision of the prison system ended in 2002.

## Texas Crime and Corrections

As of August 31, 2010, 154,795 offenders were incarcerated in the state's correctional institutions.[19] These numbers exclude those incarcerated in municipal and county facilities. In 2010, the average cost per day for each bed in the state's correctional facilities was $50.79.[20] As shown in Figure 27.1, units of the Texas Department of Criminal Justice are now located throughout the state.[21]

There have been dramatic increases in the costs of prison construction and prison maintenance in Texas over time. Operating costs of Texas prisons rose from $147 million in 1982 to $609 million in 1990 to nearly $1.5 billion in 1996 and over $2.8 billion in 2008. In 2011, the total operating budget for the Texas Department of Criminal Justice was $3.06 billion. Despite a steady increase in prison operating costs, prison construction costs have varied from year to year. In 1982, $126 million was spent on prison construction, but in 1990 only $24 million was spent. The greatest period of prison construction was from 1991 through 1995. During those years, nearly $1.4 billion was spent on prison construction. In 2011, prison construction costs were $62.4 million.[22] In the wake of estimates in 2007 that Texas would need 17,000 new prison beds costing $1 billion by 2012, in 2007 the Texas Legislature increased the capacity of prison alternatives such as drug treatment centers and halfway homes, much cheaper alternatives to prison.[23]

**for critical analysis**

What are the important issues and trends regarding the incarceration of criminals in Texas?

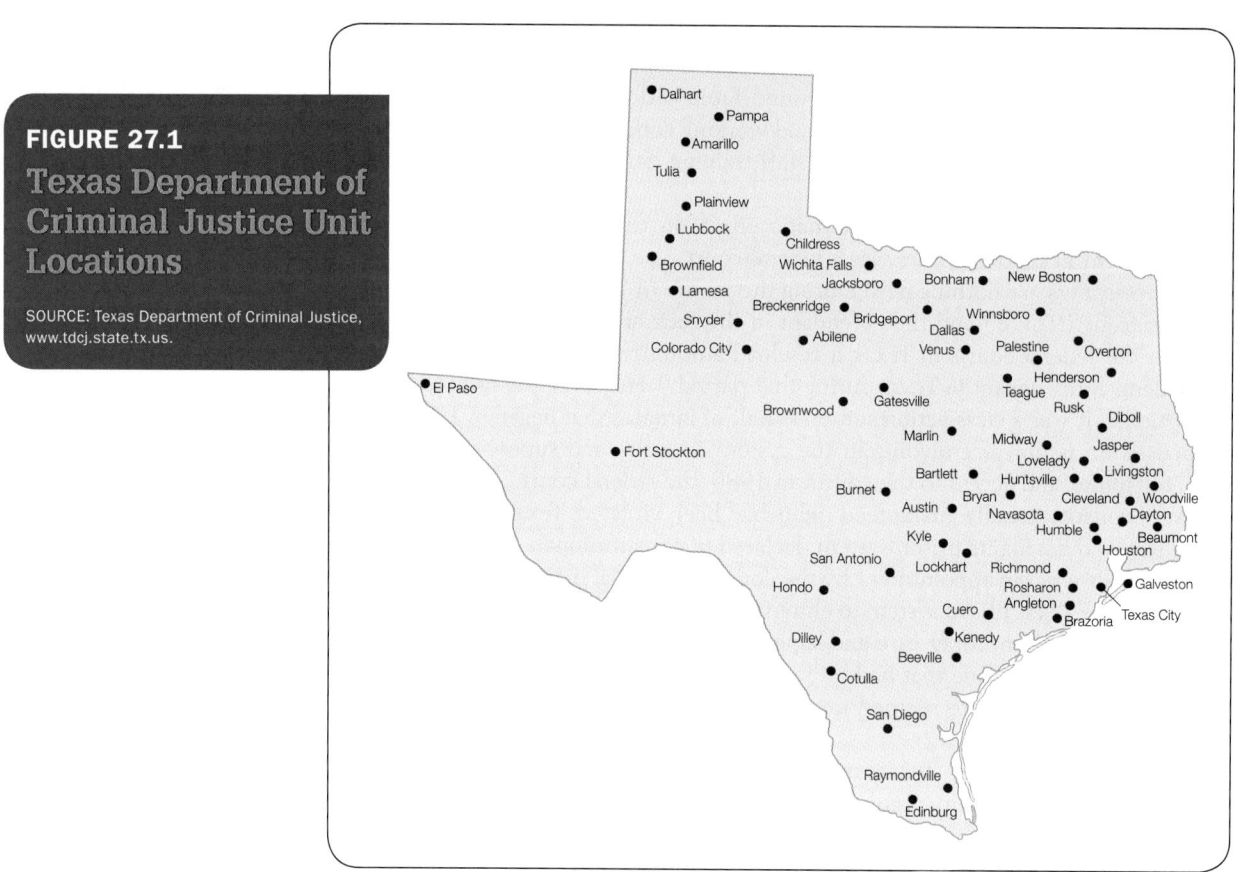

**FIGURE 27.1**

Texas Department of Criminal Justice Unit Locations

SOURCE: Texas Department of Criminal Justice, www.tdcj.state.tx.us.

Until 2007, when the Texas Legislature began to seriously address alternatives to prison, the state government had significantly increased the incarceration of offenders by building more prisons. In 2011, however, for the first time in Texas history, the state actually closed a prison—the century-old Central Unit in Sugarland, Texas. It will also close three juvenile detention centers with its move toward rehabilitation, crime prevention, and cost-cutting.

From 1976 to 1990, the rate of property crime in Texas rose 38 percent, and the violent crime rate rose 113 percent. During the same time period, prison expansion did not keep up with the increase in the crime rate. Instead, generous early-release policies were used to move prisoners out of jail to allow room for newly convicted inmates. With prison expansion, however, early-release polices were reduced. In 1990, for example, 38,000 prisoners were given early release from prison; however, even with a much larger prison population in 1997, only slightly more than 28,000 prisoners were given early release.[24] The steady lengthening of sentences is shown in Figure 27.2. In 1994, prisoners on average were released after serving one-third of their sentences. In 2010 prisoners were serving about 58 percent of their sentences before being released.[25]

As is shown in Figure 27.3, the Texas prison population has soared, especially since about 1992. In 1980, at the time of the *Ruiz* decision, the Texas prison population consisted of fewer than 30,000 inmates. A decade later, in 1990, there were slightly more than 49,000 inmates in Texas prisons. Only seven years later, there were almost 130,000 inmates in state prisons. In 2000 the number of inmates in state prisons had jumped to more than 150,000, dropping back to about 145,000

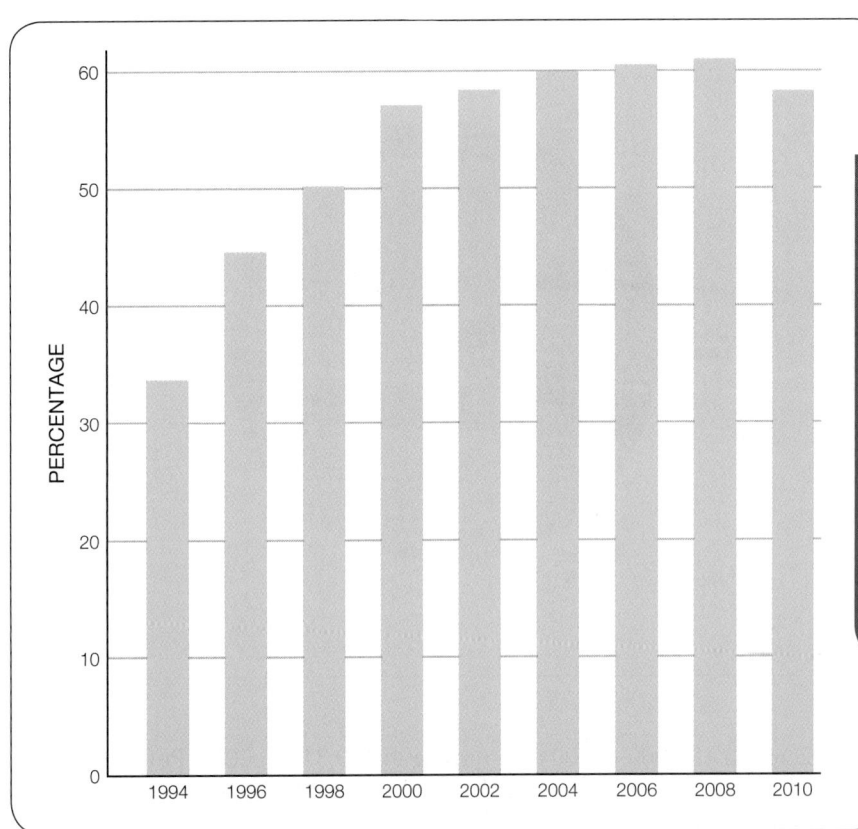

**FIGURE 27.2**

**Percentage of Prison Sentence Served by Texas Inmates**

SOURCES: Criminal Justice Policy Council, "Percentage of Prison Sentence Served for All Release Types, Fiscal Years 1994–2004"; Texas Department of Criminal Justice, Fiscal Year 2006 Statistical Report; Texas Department of Criminal Justice, Fiscal Year 2008 Statistical Report; Texas Department of Criminal Justice, "Fiscal Year 2011 Operating Budget and Fiscal Years 2012–2013 Legislative Appropriations Request," August 16, 2010.

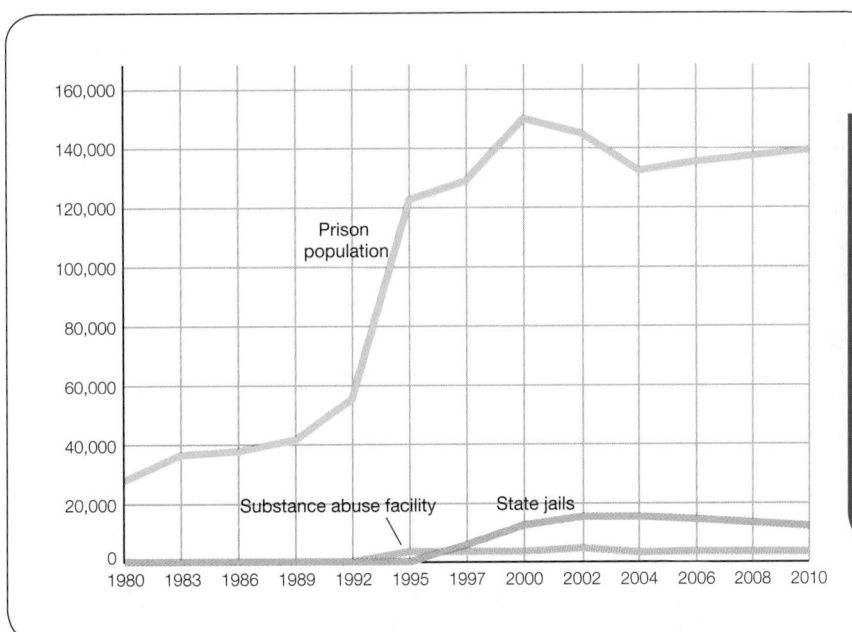

**FIGURE 27.3**

**Texas Inmate Population, 1980–2010**

SOURCES: Associated Texans Against Crime Annual Report, 1998; Texas Department of Criminal Justice, "Fiscal Year 2004 Statistics"; Criminal Justice Policy Council, "Texas Department of Criminal Justice State Incarcerated Population, Fiscal Years 1988–2002"; and Texas Department of Criminal Justice, 2006, 2008, and 2010 Statistical Report.

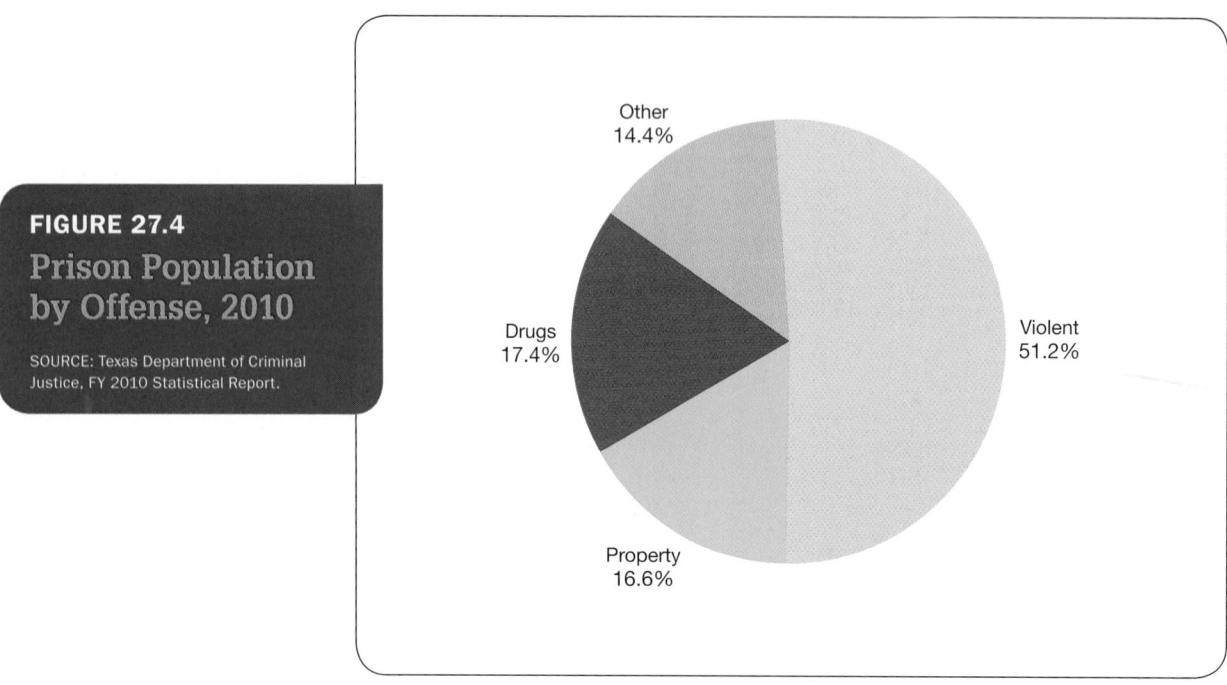

**FIGURE 27.4**

Prison Population by Offense, 2010

SOURCE: Texas Department of Criminal Justice, FY 2010 Statistical Report.

Other
14.4%

Drugs
17.4%

Violent
51.2%

Property
16.6%

in 2002 and to 132,000 in 2004, then rising to 139,316 in 2010. Put another way, there were more than 4.5 inmates in state prisons in 2010 for every inmate in state correctional facilities in 1980.[26]

By the mid-1990s, property and violent crime rates had dropped. It may be argued that the crime rate was reduced by the increased incarceration of offenders.[27] There may also be other causes, however. Others have suggested that demographic change determines the size of the prison population. The most prison-prone group in society is males between the ages of 20 and 29. If that demographic group is large, then we would expect the prison population also to be large.[28] Indeed, 94 percent of Texas prisoners are male, and the average age of prisoners is only 37 years.[29] Of course, changes in laws and treatment practices also affect the crime rate and the incarceration rate. Long sentences for habitual criminals, for example, are relatively new, as are long sentences for the use of a firearm in the commission of a crime.[30] At the end of 2009, the number of prison inmates per 100,000 population in Texas was 648. The national average was 502. California and New York, the closest states in population to Texas, incarcerate 458 per 100,000 population and 298 per 100,000, respectively.[31] Only Louisiana, Mississippi, and Oklahoma have a higher rate of incarceration than Texas.[32] In spite of its high rate of incarceration, Texas ranked high in crime. A study of crime rates nationwide found Texas ranked 37 in the United States in crime where a ranking of 1 is the lowest and 50 is the highest crime rate.[33]

As Figure 27.4 shows, Texas imprisons mostly violent offenders. In 2010, 51.2 percent of Texas inmates had been convicted of violent offenses and 16.6 percent had been convicted of property offenses. Nearly 18 percent of the inmate population were convicted of drug offenses.[34] Whether imprisonment for drug offenses is an appropriate remedy for the drug problem is, of course, debatable, but it is interesting that about one in five people in Texas prisons are there because of drugs.

During the administration of Governor Ann Richards, there was recognition that very large proportions of prisoners were involved with alcoholism, drug addiction, and drug-related crimes.[35] Some effort was made to create alcohol- and drug-abuse treatment programs within the prison system to help alleviate these problems, although the problems remain severe. In 2007, the Texas Legislature again spent resources on prison alternatives, which have greatly reduced the need for prison construction. Indeed, not only have those prison alternative programs led to the closure of one prison, but plans for building three new prisons have been scrapped.[36]

# ● Education Policy in Texas

**Describe the major issues in education policy in Texas**

The debate over public education in Texas extends back to the break with Mexico.[37] One of the indictments of the Mexican regime contained in the Texas Declaration of Independence was that the government had failed to establish a public system of education. Later, the Constitution of the Republic of Texas required a public system of education, but a bill actually establishing a public school system did not pass the legislature until 1854.

Public education was to be financed with a special school fund that would use $2 million of the $10 million given to Texas by the U.S. government on Texas's admission to the Union to settle outstanding land claims in parts of what are now New Mexico, Colorado, and Oklahoma. Unfortunately, the fund was used for a variety of other purposes in the following years, including the purchase of railroad stock and the building of prisons. When Democrats returned to power following Reconstruction, an effort was made to protect the fund and commit its use solely to education. Under the Constitution of 1876, the Special School Fund became the Permanent School Fund, and restrictions were placed on how the money could be used and invested.[38] The Constitution of 1876 also had provisions to support public education through one-quarter of the occupation tax, a $1 poll tax, and local taxation.

Throughout much of the late nineteenth and early twentieth centuries, public education remained largely a local affair. Many of the school systems were chronically short of funds, facing such problems as a shortage of supplies and textbooks, inadequate facilities, and poorly trained teachers. In 1949, the state legislature tried to address some of these problems by passing the **Gilmer-Aikin Laws**, under which school districts were consolidated into 2,900 administrative units, state equalization funding was provided to supplement local taxes, teacher salaries were raised, and a minimum school year was established. In addition, the laws established the Texas Education Agency (TEA) to supervise public education in the state.

The Gilmer-Aikin Laws also established bureaucratic institutions responsible for public education in the state. Previously, public education had been run by a State Board of Education, whose 9 members were appointed by the governor for six-year terms, and an elected state superintendent of public instruction. This was replaced by an elected 21-member board from each of the congressional districts in Texas. The State Board of Education became the policy-making body for public education in the state, selecting budgets, establishing regulations for school accreditation, executing contracts for the purchase of textbooks, and investing in the Permanent School Fund. The board also had the power to appoint a commissioner of education, subject to confirmation by the Texas Senate. The commissioner of education served a four-year term and became the chief executive officer for the

**Gilmer-Aikin Laws** education reform legislation passed in 1949 that supplemented local funding of education with state monies, raised teachers' salaries, mandated a minimum length for the school year, and provided more state supervision of public education

TEA (originally known as the State Department of Education). The TEA was responsible for setting standards for public schools, for supervising the public schools of the state, and for handling federal funds related to public education. For the next 50 years, educational policy in the state would work through the institutional framework established by the Gilmer-Aikin Laws.[39]

Since 1949, the State Board of Education has undergone occasional restructuring. Membership was expanded to 24 in 1973 and to 27 in 1981. Following a special legislative session, the board became a 15-member appointed body in 1984. But in 1988, it reverted to an elected body composed of 15 members serving four-year terms.

Three issues have played a major role in shaping educational policy over the last 50 years: desegregation, equity in funding, and the search for educational excellence.

**for critical analysis**

What are the most important issues that have shaped education policy in Texas over the past 50 years? Have these issues been resolved?

## Desegregation

Few issues have troubled educational policy in Texas as much as desegregation. Segregation of the races was provided for under the Texas Constitution of 1876. In *Plessy v. Ferguson* (1896), the U.S. Supreme Court upheld the validity of segregated schools through the now infamous "separate but equal" doctrine. In Texas, as elsewhere across the South, segregated schools may have been separate, but they were far from equal. In the 1920s and 1930s, for example, the length of the school term for black schools was only about four days shorter than that for white schools, but Texas spent an average of $3.39 less per student per year (about one-third less) on the education of African American students than on white students.[40]

The U.S. Supreme Court overturned *Plessy v. Ferguson* in the 1954 case *Brown v. Board of Education*, ruling that segregated schools violated the equal protection clause of the Fourteenth Amendment. School districts were ordered to desegregate their school systems "with all deliberate speed."[41] In some cases, "all deliberate speed" was quite quick. The San Antonio school district, for example, became one of the first school districts in the nation to comply with the Supreme Court's order. Other school districts in the state, such as Houston's, were much slower in implementing the Court's desegregation ruling.

The desegregation of public schools was hampered further by political opposition at both the local and state levels. In 1957, the Texas state legislature passed laws encouraging school districts to resist federally ordered desegregation, although the current governor, Price Daniel Sr., chose to ignore such laws.[42] By the 1960s, legally segregated schools were a thing of the past. Nevertheless, de facto segregation remained a problem, particularly in urban areas with large minority populations. As in many other urban areas across the country, a large number of middle- and upper-income whites in Texas abandoned urban public school systems for suburban public schools or private schools.

## Equity in the Public School System

Federal court cases such as *Brown v. Board of Education* played a major role in shaping educational policy regarding the desegregation of schools. Two other important court cases have affected education policy and politics in Texas over the last 30 years: *San Antonio ISD v. Rodríguez* and *Edgewood ISD v. Kirby*.

**San Antonio ISD v. Rodríguez** *San Antonio ISD v. Rodríguez* was a landmark case involving the constitutionality of using property taxes to fund public schools.[43] At the heart of the case lay the question of the equitable funding of public schools. The case involved several school districts, including the Edgewood and Alamo Heights independent school districts (ISD). Lawyers for Rodríguez and seven other children in the poor Edgewood ISD argued that the current system of financing public schools in Texas was unfair. The Edgewood school district had one of the highest property tax rates in the country but could raise only $37 per pupil each year. Meanwhile the neighboring school district of Alamo Heights was able to raise $413 per pupil annually with a much lower property tax rate. The difference was that the value of the property subject to taxation in Alamo Heights far exceeded that in Edgewood. Equalizing educational funding would require Edgewood to tax at the rate of $5.76 per $100 property value while Alamo Heights could tax at a rate of $0.68 per $100 property value.

A three-judge federal district court was impaneled to hear the case in January 1969. The district court initially delayed action, giving the 1971 Texas Legislature time to address the funding issue. When the legislature failed to act during its regular session, the court took action. On December 23, 1971, it ruled that the Texas school finance system was unconstitutional under the **equal protection clause** of the Fourteenth Amendment of the U.S. Constitution. However, on appeal to the U.S. Supreme Court, the decision was overturned. On March 21, 1973, the Supreme Court ruled 5–4 that states such as Texas were not required to subsidize poorer school districts under the equal protection clause of the Constitution. The question of equity in public school funding would have to be addressed later in terms of Texas's state constitution and in Texas courts.

> **equal protection clause** provision of the Fourteenth Amendment of the U.S. Constitution guaranteeing citizens "the equal protection of the laws." This clause has been the basis for the civil rights of African Americans, women, and other groups

***Edgewood ISD v. Kirby*** The second landmark case involving the financing of public schools was *Edgewood ISD v. Kirby*. Unlike *Rodríguez*, *Edgewood* considered the equity of funding public schools by the existing property tax system in terms of the Texas state constitution. Much of the litigation over the next few years would center on Article VII, Section 1, of the 1876 Constitution, which read:

> A general diffusion of knowledge being essential to the preservation of the liberties and rights of the people, it shall be the duty of the Legislature of the State to

*When schools are funded through local property taxes, schools in poor districts (such as the one pictured here) can't afford the same facilities and resources as schools in wealthier districts, where there is more tax revenue. The* Edgewood *cases challenged this system as discriminatory and unconstitutional.*

establish and make suitable provision for the support and maintenance of an efficient system of free public schools.

A key constitutional issue would be exactly what constituted an "efficient system of free public schools."

On behalf of the Edgewood ISD, the Mexican American Legal Defense and Education Fund (MALDEF) sued William Kirby, the state commissioner of education, on May 23, 1984. Initially only 8 districts were represented in the case. By the time the case was finally decided, 67 other school districts had joined the original plaintiffs. The plaintiffs argued that the state's reliance on local property taxes to fund public education discriminated against poor children by denying them equal opportunities in education. A month after the original case was filed, the legislature passed House Bill 72, a modest reform measure that increased state aid to poor districts. In 1985, plaintiffs filed an amended lawsuit, arguing that the legislature's action was far from satisfactory.

The amended case was heard early in 1987 by a state district judge, who ruled on April 29, 1987, in favor of the plaintiffs. He found the state's system for financing public education unconstitutional, violating both the "equal protection" (Article I, Section 3) and "efficient system" (Article VII, Section 1) clauses of the Texas Constitution. The judge called for the institution of a new system of public school funding by September 1989.

In a 2-to-1 vote, a state appeals court reversed this decision in December 1988, finding that the funding system was constitutional. Appealing this decision to the Texas Supreme Court, plaintiffs finally won on July 5, 1989. In a 9–0 decision, the Texas Supreme Court held that the funding system was, indeed, in violation of the state constitution. The court held that education was a fundamental right under the Texas Constitution and that the "glaring disparities" between rich and poor schools violated the efficiency clause of the constitution. In its ruling, the court did not demand "absolute equality" in per pupil spending. But it did require a standard of "substantially equal access to similar revenues per pupil at similar levels of tax effort."[44] It ordered the legislature to implement an equitable system by the 1990–91 school year.

The Texas Supreme Court's ruling touched off a political firestorm that swept through Texas politics throughout the early 1990s. The legislature failed to pass appropriate legislation in four special sessions called to address the funding problem. Finally, on June 1, 1990, a master appointed by the Texas Supreme Court announced an equity financing plan that would be implemented if the legislature failed to develop one of its own. Essentially, the plan called for wealthy school districts to transfer funds to poorer districts in order to equalize funds available to all public schools across the state. The so-called Robin Hood plan finally shook the legislature into action. During a sixth special session, the legislature passed Senate Bill 1 (SB 1), which, among other things, implemented funding adjustments to further assist poor school districts. Significantly, the bill did not restrict the ability of wealthier districts to enrich themselves through their higher property tax bases.

The new system of funding was found to be unconstitutional by a state district court in a case that came to be known as *Edgewood II*. The state supreme court upheld the lower court ruling, arguing that SB 1 failed to restructure the overall funding system. The court was particularly critical of the ability of wealthy school systems to accumulate funds outside the system and hinted that a solution might lie in the creation of consolidated countywide tax bases. The legislature responded by passing Senate Bill 351 (SB 351), creating 188 "county education districts," which would equalize wealth across districts by broadening the tax base. Property taxes funding schools were to be collected by both the county education district and the local school district.

This time wealthier districts challenged the legislative initiatives to settle the equity problem in public schools. In January 1992, the state supreme court held 7–2 in *Edgewood III* that SB 351 violated two constitutional provisions: first, it had failed to get the required local voter approval of school property tax levies (Article VII, Section 3). Second, it had violated Article VII, Sections 1–3, which had prohibited a state property tax since 1980. Interestingly, the court did not rule on the nature of the tax itself or whether it adequately addressed the equity question. The state was given until June 1993 to devise a new system for funding public education that was equitable and constitutional.

The legislature met in special session and during regular session in an attempt to meet the court-imposed deadline. A constitutional amendment to allow for a statewide property tax was put before the voters on May 1, 1993, and soundly defeated. The legislature responded by quickly passing SB 7. The key difference between SB 7 and earlier attempts to address the equity issue was its equalization and recapture provisions. Intended to redress the imbalance between wealthier and poorer districts, the bill set a $280,000 cap on the per student taxable property value base in all districts. Districts with property values exceeding this limit had to choose one of a variety of methods to reduce their taxable wealth. Among these methods were consolidating with a poorer district, ceding property tax base to another poorer district, writing a check to the state, partnering with a poorer district, and consolidating with one or more other districts.

SB 7 was challenged in *Edgewood IV*, but it was upheld as being constitutional by the state supreme court. The court noted that additional work was needed on equalizing and improving school facilities across the state. Unfortunately, not enough was done in a timely manner to address the problem. In November 2005, the Texas Supreme Court upheld a lower court ruling that the school districts lacked "meaningful discretion" in setting local maintenance and operation tax rates. In the court's opinion, too many districts were being forced to set tax rates at the maximum $1.50 per $100 valuation. Essentially, this meant that the school system was being financed by an unconstitutional state property tax. The court gave the legislature until June 1, 2006, to address the matter or it would enjoin the state from distributing funding to the public school system.

It took three special sessions of the state legislature to craft a compromise and finally put constitutional concerns over the financing of public schools brought on by Robin Hood to rest. The final proposal cut property taxes by a third and replaced lost revenues with money raised statewide by an expanded business tax and a new $1-per-pack tax on cigarettes. General revenue monies are now used to address some of the inequities of the property tax system.[45]

The struggle to rework the funding mechanism for public education was only one dimension of educational policy in Texas in the 1980s and 1990s. Concerns over the quality of education in the state and how best to promote educational excellence will continue to redefine educational policy in the early twenty-first century.

## Educational Excellence and Accountability in Texas

The equity issue in public education had been touched off by litigation. Only when forced by the courts to rethink how schools were being funded was the legislature finally willing to act. A different set of factors has driven the debate over educational excellence and accountability.

The issue of education reform came to a head in the early 1980s in Texas. The Texas debate was actually part of a larger national debate over the state of education in the United States.[46] A 1983 report by the National Commission on Excellence in Education, *A Nation at Risk*, identified a number of crises that were beginning to grip the nation's educational system. Test scores were declining and functional illiteracy was on the rise. Students were simply not equipped with the intellectual skills that were required in the modern world. If something were not done soon to reform education in the United States, the report argued, the nation was at risk of falling behind other countries in the rapidly changing world of international competition.[47]

Educational reform was put on the state agenda when, at the end of the 1983 regular session, the legislature established the Select Committee on Public Education (SCOPE). Earlier in the session, the Democratic governor Mark White had hoped to appoint a commission concerned with the narrow issue of pay raises for teachers. What he got was something very different. SCOPE was created as a 22-member committee to which the governor would have only five appointments.[48] The remaining seats were filled by appointments made by the House and Senate leadership and by three members of the State Board of Education. The intent of the legislature in creating SCOPE was not just to figure out how to fund pay raises for teachers, but to evaluate the entire system of public education in the state.

*Another means of encouraging educational excellence has been to allow students to transfer from low-performing to high-performing schools, thus promoting competition among the schools and allowing parents more choices.*

One of the most important decisions made by Governor White was appointing the Dallas businessman Ross Perot to chair the committee. Perot had supported White's opponent in the 1982 gubernatorial race. White hoped that Perot's participation in the process would broaden support for the committee across party lines as well as bring in needed support from the business community. At the time of his selection, however, few knew how important Perot would be to the process of educational reform. To the surprise of many, Perot took an active role in SCOPE, mobilizing the committee in private and public to take on what he considered abuses in the public education system.

Perot was particularly scornful of athletic programs and what he considered the misplaced priorities of the existing educational system. In the end, SCOPE presented 140 recommendations for reforming the Texas education system in its final report on April 19, 1984. Among the most controversial of the proposed reforms was "no pass, no play." Students who failed to earn a passing grade of 70, which was raised from 60, would be unable to participate in any extracurricular activities for the next grading period of six weeks. But "no pass, no play" was only the tip of the iceberg. Other reform proposals set new standards for students' attendance and performance; annual school performance reports and tighter accreditation standards, with schools that did not meet these higher standards losing state funds; a longer school year—from 175 to 180 days; and a professional career ladder for teachers, tying pay raises to performance.[49] In early July 1984, many of the reform proposals were put into place in a 266-page education reform bill, along with the necessary accompanying tax increases.

The so-called Perot reforms were but the first round in the debate over excellence and accountability in the public school system. A second round opened during the 1995 legislative session. There were some important differences in the reform package finally signed by Republican governor George W. Bush. The Perot reforms had generally tended to centralize control over education policy in the state. The Bush reforms, in contrast, gave more discretion to local school districts to achieve the educational goals the state was mandating. Some of the reforms put through were symbolic. The controversial "no pass, no play" rule was relaxed, cutting the period of nonparticipation from six to three weeks and lifting a ban on practicing while on scholastic probation. But other changes were more substantive. Local control of public schools was increased by limiting the power of the TEA. Local voters were empowered to adopt home charters that could free their school districts from many state requirements, including class-size caps at lower grades. The 1995 reforms also enabled students, under certain circumstances, to transfer from low-performing schools to high-performing schools in their districts, thus promoting competition among the schools by holding them accountable for the performance of their students.[50]

## Education Policy in Perspective

It is difficult to judge whether the reforms instituted in the 1980s and 1990s have been successful in improving the overall equity and excellence of public education in Texas. Recent statistics suggest that the state still has a long way to go in turning its public school system into one of the best in the nation. Despite the efforts of recent administrations to raise them, teachers' salaries and overall state and local spending on public education remained low compared with those in other states. In 2009 the high school graduation rate in Texas was 80.6 percent (ranging from 73.5 percent for Latinos to 93.5 percent for Asians/Pacific Islanders), ranking the state thirty-sixth in the nation. In 2010, the average SAT scores in Texas were 481 in reading and 504 in math, compared with a national average of 1017 for the two tests together.[51] These scores represented a slight but ongoing fall in Texas test scores in the first decade of the twenty-first century.

Although the dropout rate in grades 7 through 12 has been declining since the 1990s, it is still high among minorities. At the same time, scores on standardized tests such as the TAAS (Texas Assessment of Academic Skills) test improved across the state, sparking calls for the development of new assessment tests to hold teachers and schools accountable. The TAKS (Texas Assessment of Knowledge and Skills) test replaced TAAS in 2003 and expanded the number of subjects assessed from grades 3 through 11. Despite such efforts to increase oversight and accountability in the classroom, concerns were mounting that too much time was spent "teaching to the test." Reforms passed during the 2007 legislative session limited TAKS to grades 3 through 8. In high school TAKS was replaced by new subject tests given at the end of a course.[52]

One of the ways that the 2011 legislature balanced the budget without raising taxes was by making severe cuts in elementary and secondary education funding. The cuts jeopardized many of the reform initiatives of the previous 20 years. Whether the cuts will be reduced or expanded in coming legislative sessions will be determined by

**for critical analysis**

In most categories of educational achievement, Texas's public schools rank poorly, despite the fact that the state budget allocates more for education than for any other item. Call on your experience as a public or private school student, textbook readings, class discussion, and current events to propose a series of changes to enhance the state's educational system.

the overall economic health of the state and the political commitments of the state's leaders. Reforming education with a concern for equity and excellence will continue to be a major policy issue in the state for many years to come.

# Welfare Policy

**Trace how welfare policy has evolved in Texas**

Another major policy area that has been controversial in Texas, and throughout the country, is welfare policy. Especially since the 1930s, the state and national governments have offered various forms of assistance to low-income citizens, often sharing responsibility for these programs.

## Poverty in Texas

Poverty has never been a popular subject in Texas. The idea that some individuals have trouble taking care of themselves or meeting the basic needs of their families seems to fly in the face of Texas's individualistic culture. In light of the booming Texas economy of the late 1990s, many may have hoped that the poverty problem would go away. It hasn't. Between 1990 and 1999, the percentage of Texans living in poverty fell from 15.9 percent to 15.0 percent, but rose again in 2008 to 15.8 percent. According to the U.S. Census Bureau, 4,143,077 people in Texas lived at or below the poverty line in 2009. In November 2010, 3,498,992 people were enrolled in Medicaid, the federally financed, state-operated program providing medical services to low-income people.[53] Despite the economic boom fostered by the age of high tech, poverty remains one of the most intractable problems facing the state.

Policy makers define poverty in very specific terms. Poverty is the condition under which individuals or families do not have the resources to meet their basic needs, including food, shelter, health care, transportation, and clothing. The U.S. Department of Health and Human Services developed a "poverty index" in 1964. This index was revised in 1969 and 1980. The index calculates the consumption requirements of families based on their size and composition. The poverty index is adjusted every year to account for the rate of inflation. Although there is considerable controversy as to whether it adequately measures the minimal needs of a family, the poverty index is the generally accepted standard against which poverty is measured.

In 2011, the federal poverty guideline was $10,890 a year for one person and $3,820 a year for each additional person in the family. In 2008, Texas had 4,143,077 people in poverty or 17.1 percent of its population compared with 14.3 percent nationally. Almost one out of four Latinos and African Americans in Texas are poor. Slightly more than 12 percent of persons over 65 years of age in Texas are poor compared with 9.9 percent in the nation as a whole. Poverty among children, especially young children, is much higher than in the United States as a whole. Fifty-eight percent of poor families in Texas have a worker at the head of the family. More than one in four Texans (26.6 percent) are at 150 percent of the poverty level or less and 36.5 percent are at 200 percent of the poverty level or less. One hundred and fifty percent of the poverty level is $26,400 a year for a family of three and 200 percent of the federal poverty level is $35,200 a year for a family of three.

Texas uses these federal poverty guidelines to determine eligibility for a variety of social programs. For example, a family of three is eligible for reduced price school meals if they are at no more than 185 percent of the poverty level. A family of three is eligible for free school meals if they are at no more than 130 percent of the poverty level and they are eligible for food stamps if they are at no more than 130 percent of the poverty level.[54]

## Welfare in Texas, 1935–96

The origins of modern welfare policy lie in President Franklin Delano Roosevelt's **New Deal**.[55] Prior to the 1930s, welfare was considered to be a state and local responsibility. The Great Depression overwhelmed many state and local welfare arrangements, causing the federal government to expand its role in addressing the needs of the poor and the unemployed. The Social Security Act of 1935 transformed the way in which welfare policy was implemented in the United States. Along with two social insurance programs (Old Age Insurance and Unemployment Insurance), the Social Security Act established a number of state-federal public assistance programs: Aid for Dependent Children (ADC, later **Aid to Families with Dependent Children** or AFDC), Old Age Assistance (OAA), and Aid for the Blind (AB). States administered and determined the benefit levels for these programs. In exchange for federal assistance in funding, state programs had to meet certain minimum federal guidelines.

The Department of Public Welfare was established in Texas in 1939 to run the state's various public assistance programs. It was to be supervised by a state board of welfare, composed of three members appointed by the governor for six-year terms. The board appointed an executive director who, in turn, was the chief administrative officer of the department.[56]

**New Deal** President Franklin Delano Roosevelt's 1930s program to stimulate the national economy and provide relief to victims of the Great Depression

**Aid to Families with Dependent Children (AFDC)** a federally and state-financed program for children living with parents or relatives who fell below state standards of need. Replaced in 1996 by TANF

*The Texas Department of Public Welfare was established in 1939 during the New Deal. This photo shows farmers receiving support from the government at the time.*

Through the early 1960s, the basic strategy adopted by welfare policy makers in Texas was to minimize the cost to the state while maximizing federal dollars. Some programs were expanded during these years. In 1950, ADC became AFDC as mothers were included in the program. Other new social-service programs were added. Much of the initiative for the expansion of welfare came from the federal government. One of the major issues in Texas was the problem of the constitutional ceiling on welfare spending. This had to be raised from $35 million in 1945 to $52 million in 1961, and again to $60 million in 1963.[57]

Welfare policy in Texas was transformed fundamentally in the 1960s. Federal court decisions between 1968 and 1971 effectively ended a series of practices such as man-in-the-house rules and residency requirements, which had been used by states to keep welfare rolls low. In 1965, Congress established **Medicaid**, a state-federal program to finance health care for the poor. President Lyndon Johnson's "War on Poverty" also expanded the number of social service programs available to the poor. Increasingly, it was argued, the solution to alleviating poverty was through expanded federal control over welfare programs.

In 1965, the Department of Public Welfare was authorized to work with the federal government's new antipoverty programs. The welfare ceiling was raised to $80 million in 1969. Among the welfare programs administered by the department were four public assistance programs: AFDC, Aid for the Blind, Aid to the Permanently and Totally Disabled, and Old Age Assistance. The latter three programs were taken over by the federal government in 1972 in the form of the new national Supplemental Security Income program. Along with these programs, the department ran the Texas Medical Assistance Program (Medicaid), the national food stamp program, and a series of social-service programs.

In 1977, the Department of Public Welfare became the Department of Human Resources. It was renamed again in 1985 as the Texas Department of Human Services and then as the Health and Human Services Commission in 2003. The name reflected an ongoing desire on the part of policy makers to think of the agency less as a welfare agency and more as a service agency to the poor. By 1980 the department was reorganized to focus on the major client groups it served: families with children and elderly and disabled people. In 1981 the constitutional ceiling on welfare spending was replaced with a more flexible standard. Instead of a flat cap of $80 million, welfare expenditures could not exceed 1 percent of the total state budget. In 1989 the state board of welfare was expanded from three to six members.[58]

Between 1967 and 1973, participation rates and welfare expenditures in Texas exploded. The number of children on AFDC during this time rose from 79,914 to 325,244, while the number of families on AFDC went from 23,509 to 120,254. Rates leveled off in the late 1970s, but they began to push upward again in the 1980s. Liberal attempts to reform welfare by nationalizing AFDC (turning the state-federal program into a national program like Supplemental Security Income) failed throughout the 1970s. Conservative attempts to compel welfare recipients to participate in job-training programs, such as the Work Incentive

**Medicaid** a federally and state-financed, state-operated program providing medical services to low-income people

*In 2012, 3.6 million Texans participated in the food stamps program (now called SNAP), which allows low-income people to buy groceries with a special debit card. SNAP benefits are paid by the federal government, but the state and federal governments share administrative costs.*

Program of 1967, had limited success. A frustrating political stalemate set in. Few were happy with welfare policy as then conducted, but no consensus had emerged as to what would be a better alternative. Meanwhile, welfare rolls expanded and expenditures continued to increase in both Texas and the nation.

## The Idea of Dependency and Welfare Reform

By the mid-1980s, a new critique of welfare programs had begun to emerge. At its heart lay the idea that the well-intentioned policies of the 1960s had backfired, creating a dysfunctional underclass of people dependent on welfare. Welfare programs such as AFDC may have helped people financially in the short run, but in the long run they had robbed people of the character traits and the moral values that would enable them to succeed in a market economy.[59] Skyrocketing illegitimacy rates, particularly among minorities and the poor, were seen as the partial result of a perverse set of incentives put into place by the state supposedly to help the poor. Under the existing welfare system, the more children you had, the higher the welfare check. Because some states did not provide welfare to families with fathers in the home, fathers were actually being encouraged to abandon their families so that they might qualify for welfare. According to critics, the poor needed the encouragement and proper incentives to become independent workers rather than having a permanent source of income from the state.

At the national level, the deadlock over welfare reform was broken with the passage of the Family Support Act in 1988. In the attempt to stem the rising tide of illegitimacy rates and single-parent families among the poor, the act mandated two-parent coverage for all state AFDC programs. It also established a number of new "workfare" programs whose goals were to get people off welfare and into the workforce. New standards were also developed requiring parents to participate in these workfare programs or lose their benefits.[60]

Much hyperbole surrounded the passage of the Family Support Act. Although the act did break new ground in formulating programs to help people make the transition from welfare to work, it also was an important expansion of the existing AFDC system. Far from declining, welfare roll expansion was unabated in the early 1990s. In Texas, this expansion was especially rapid. By 1994, an average 786,400 people were receiving AFDC in Texas. Total federal and state expenditures rose from $188.3 million in 1984 to $544.9 million in 1994. Food stamp costs also rose rapidly during this period, from $664.9 million to $2.2 billion. But AFDC and food stamps were only part of the problem. Medicaid was escalating at a rate of more than 20 percent a year. During the 1994–95 biennium, $18.6 billion in state and federal funds was being spent on Medicaid. This was 13 percent of the state budget, or $6.7 billion. Escalating costs of AFDC, food stamps, and Medicaid provided the backdrop to the welfare reforms that would be put into place by Texas policy makers in 1995.

Growing discontent over welfare policy across the country encouraged many states to seek **waivers** from federal regulations so that they, too, might experiment with welfare reform.[61] Some states sought to modify AFDC rules to eliminate some of the perverse incentive structures in the welfare system. Other states set caps on benefits and how long one could continue to receive welfare. Welfare became a state issue during the 1994 elections. As governor of Texas, George W. Bush echoed the ideas of conservative critics of the welfare system, arguing that

**waiver** an exemption from a federal requirement

*Though poverty in Texas afflicts many different social groups, Latinos currently make up the majority of Texans living below the poverty line. The border counties in west Texas are by far the poorest in the state.*

the existing system was robbing people of their independence. Among the changes that he called for were

- strengthening child-support procedures and penalties
- imposing a two-year limit on benefits for recipients able to work
- requiring individuals receiving welfare to accept a state-sponsored job if after two years they were unable to find work
- creating new child-care and job-training programs
- requiring unwed mothers to live with their parents or grandparents
- moving family support systems from the state to the local level

Data released by the comptroller's office lent support to the Bush contention that there were serious problems with the existing system of welfare in Texas. More than one-quarter of all welfare recipients in 1993 were "long-term" recipients who had remained on the rolls for five years or more. The publication of *A Partnership for Independence: Welfare Reform in Texas*, by the office of the comptroller, John Sharp, a Democrat, helped set the legislative agenda for the debate over welfare policy. Supporting critics across the nation who were unhappy with the current state of welfare policy, the report documented how welfare often failed to help those most in need or to encourage those dependent on welfare to become independent of government largesse. Among the report's 100 proposals were many of the reforms that had been put into place by conservative reformers in other states or by the Bush gubernatorial administration.

A bipartisan legislative coalition ultimately supported major welfare reform in Texas. On May 26, 1995, the vote on House Bill 1863 was 128 to 9 in the House and 30 to 1 in the Senate. The law provided a number of "carrot and stick" incentives that sought to mold the character of welfare recipients in positive ways and wean them off welfare. Among the carrots were expanded education and job-training programs, as well as a select number of pilot studies involving transitional child care and medical benefits. Among the sticks were a limitation on benefits to

Kayla Nikole

36 months, alimony for spouses who couldn't support themselves, and the institution of a five-year ban on reapplying for benefits once benefits ran out. To implement the state reforms, Texas secured a waiver from the federal government that freed the state from various federal regulations regarding welfare programs. In granting the waivers to Texas and other states, the Clinton administration hoped to stimulate innovative reforms that might be duplicated elsewhere.

Texas was ahead of the welfare reform curve in 1995. In 1996, President Bill Clinton signed into law the most important reform in federal welfare policy since the New Deal. The Personal Responsibility and Work Opportunity Reconciliation Act essentially rethought the assumptions that had guided the expansion of welfare programs for 60 years. Under the legislation, AFDC, JOBS (a work-related training program), and the Emergency Assistance Program were combined into one block grant entitled **Temporary Assistance for Needy Families (TANF)**. As with the welfare reforms instituted in Texas and in other states across the country, the primary purpose of TANF was to make families self-sufficient by ending the cycle of dependency on government benefits. States such as Texas were given great flexibility in setting benefit levels, eligibility requirements, and other program details.

**Temporary Assistance for Needy Families (TANF)** a federal block grant that replaced the AFDC program in 1996

Today in Texas TANF provides temporary financial assistance to families with needy children when one or both of the parents are missing or disabled.[62] The TANF program provides a onetime $1,000 payment to individuals in certain crisis situations. To qualify, a recipient's income must be below 17 percent of the poverty income limit based on family size. In addition, the combined equity of the family may not exceed $2,000 ($3,000 for the elderly and disabled). People participating in TANF receive a monthly assistance payment based on the size of their family. They cannot receive benefits for more than 36 months. They are also eligible for Medicaid benefits, food stamps, and child day-care services. Unless legally exempt, recipients are also required to participate in an employment services program.

## Evaluating Welfare Reform

The welfare reforms in Texas will probably be evaluated along two dimensions. First, they will be measured in terms of the number of people receiving welfare assistance from the state. Success will be determined by the degree to which the reforms help lower the number of welfare recipients in Texas. If the reforms do not decrease the welfare rolls, they likely will be considered a failure. A second measure of success will be the degree to which the reforms help take people off welfare and move them into the workforce as productive, independent members of society.

Judged by changes in the number of people on welfare, the reforms appear to be a success. The average monthly number of people on welfare in Texas rose from a little over half a million in 1989 to a peak of more than three-quarters of a million in 1994 but then began to fall in 1995. Time limits and work requirements were put into place by the state legislature in 1995, one year before similar measures were passed nationally by the U.S. Congress. The decline in the number of people on welfare continued over the next decade, falling to 155,895 people in 2006 and to 103,110 in 2011.[63]

By the second measure—the number of people moving from welfare to work—preliminary indications are that the welfare reforms of 1995 are accomplishing their objectives. Texas ranks among the top 10 states in moving families from welfare to work. The welfare rolls have decreased by 365,000 since 1995. There has been a caseload reduction of 68 percent.[64]

One qualifier must be made before we trumpet the success of welfare reform in the 1990s. Current reforms took place under conditions of a booming economy and a rising demand for all types of labor. Jobs seemed to be available for people who were willing and able to work. But how will the new welfare policies respond to the economic problems of the second decade of the twenty-first century? Now that labor markets have tightened and jobs are difficult to find, will Texas policy makers be satisfied with the welfare reforms in place? How far will unemployment be allowed to go before policy makers demand that we reconsider the incentive structure created to get people off the public dole? These are questions that policy makers concerned with welfare reform will have to consider one day. Only then will we be able to have an exact evaluation of the welfare reforms of the mid-1990s.

## ● Thinking Critically about Public Policy in Texas

In this chapter, we examined various aspects of public-policy making in Texas. We focused attention on the complex tax and spending issues surrounding the budget and the issues that have driven policy making in crime and corrections, public education, and welfare. In earlier chapters, we saw how the high-tech revolution transformed Texas's economy in the 1980s and 1990s. We also traced how social and political changes have restructured the political party system in the state and the increasing power of the Republican Party. In this chapter, we have seen how many of these shifts resulted in important changes in public policy in the 1990s. The reforms in budgetary policy as well as crime and corrections, public education, and welfare are part of a larger shift in the Texas political economy away from an oil, cattle, and cotton economy into an era of computers, high technology, and globalization. We can't be sure exactly where public policy in Texas will go in the next decade. We can be sure that new solutions will be required as the Texas political system tries to meet the challenges and opportunities of the twenty-first century.

# study guide

 **Practice online with:** Chapter 27 Diagnostic Quiz ▪ Chapter 27 Key Term Flashcards

## Taxing and Spending in Texas

■ **Explain why Texas is considered a "low-tax, low-service" state (pp. 1005–16)**

Texas is a low-tax, low-service state. It relies heavily on regressive sales taxes to fund the state's operations and has refused to implement a state income tax. It also has a balanced budget requirement under the state constitution, which has led in recent years to significant spending cuts in education.

### Key Terms

**biennial** (p. 1005)

**dedicated funds** (p. 1006)

**appropriations** (p. 1006)

**pay-as-you-go limit** (p. 1006)

**debt service** (p. 1007)

**regressive/progressive taxation** (p. 1010)

**matching funds** (p. 1012)

### Practice Quiz

1. One result of the low taxes in Texas is that *(p. 1005)*
   a) the state is continually in need of more money.
   b) businesses avoid setting up offices in Texas.
   c) it is also a low-service state.
   d) the state continually asks businesses to assess their taxes.
   e) citizens never lack for services.

2. The Texas Constitution requires that the Texas budget be *(p. 1006)*
   a) balanced
   b) approved by the governor's cabinet
   c) funded only from sales taxes
   d) approved by the governor, the legislature, and the state treasurer
   e) funded only from federal grants

3. What is the major source of tax revenue for the state? *(p. 1009)*
   a) federal funds.
   b) selective sales tax on motor fuel.
   c) selective sales tax on alcoholic beverages.
   d) general sales tax.
   e) taxes on cigarettes and other tobacco products.

4. A progressive tax *(p. 1010)*
   a) frees everyone from a state income tax.
   b) hits upper-income groups more heavily than lower-income groups.
   c) hits lower-income groups more heavily than upper-income groups.
   d) hits all income groups equally.
   e) is increased slightly every year.

5. The most costly item in the Texas budget is *(p. 1013)*
   a) public safety and corrections.
   b) higher education.
   c) flood control.
   d) transportation.
   e) health and human services.

6. Among the factors behind the budget crisis were *(p. 1014)*
   a) military cuts.
   b) declining oil revenues.
   c) smaller than expected income tax receipts.
   d) the Great Recession.
   e) Obamacare.

 **Practice Online**
"Exploring Texas Politics" exercise: *Tax Policy and Health Care*

## Crime and Corrections Policy

■ **Describe the major issues in corrections policy in Texas (pp. 1016–21)**

One of the state's key functions is to keep law and order, and the state's extensive prison system is one example of how much the state spends on the criminal justice system. The state's prison system traditionally has focused on penalizing wrongdoing.

### Practice Quiz

7. The *Ruiz* case was *(p. 1017)*
   a) a class action suit brought on behalf of inmates.
   b) a class action suit brought on behalf of prison guards.
   c) a case that concluded state spending in education was unfair.
   d) a case that led to increased spending on AFDC.

e) a case brought by private companies that run prisons.

f) a case filed against the State Board of Education.

8. The Texas prison system *(p. 1020)*

a) is considered a model of an effective and efficient state prison system.

b) has space for at least 10,000 more inmates.

c) incarcerates mostly violent offenders.

d) is the most costly part of the state budget.

e) has never been reformed.

9. Which of the following best describes today's corrections policy in Texas? *(p. 1021)*

a) Spare no expense to rehabilitate those in prison.

b) Build more prisons.

c) Increase drug and alcohol abuse rehabilitation and educational programs.

d) Rely on private prisons.

e) Send as many prisoners as possible out of state.

# Education Policy in Texas

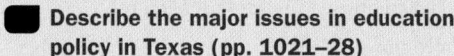 **Describe the major issues in education policy in Texas (pp. 1021–28)**

Texas has an extensive network of public schools, which are largely funded by property taxes. Because of some court rulings, the so-called Robin Hood system redistributes monies from wealthy school districts to poorer school districts. Higher education is also partially funded by the state, but budget cuts in recent years have reduced spending on all levels of education, especially at the higher level.

## Key Terms

**Gilmer-Aikin Laws** (p. 1021)

**equal protection clause** (p. 1023)

## Practice Quiz

10. Primary responsibility for public education in Texas belongs to *(p. 1021)*

a) the State Board of Education.

b) local school boards.

c) county government.

d) federal government.

e) the state and the federal government.

11. The Gilmer-Aikin Laws *(p. 1021)*

a) amended the Texas Constitution and provided free public education to all children under the age of seventeen.

b) established institutions responsible for public education in Texas.

c) established the Medicaid program in Texas.

d) ended segregation in Texas schools.

e) dissolved the Texas Education Agency.

12. Which of the following is *not* one of the most important education policy issues of the last 50 years? *(p. 1022)*

a) desegregation

b) equity in funding

c) no pass, no play

d) excellence in education and accountability

e) None of the above have been important policy issues.

13. In *Edgewood v. Kirby* (p. 1024)

a) the Texas Supreme Court ordered the state legislature to implement an equitable public education system.

b) the U.S. Supreme Court ended segregation in Texas schools.

c) the U.S. Supreme Court ended property tax funding of public schools in Texas.

d) The Texas Supreme Court eliminated the income tax as a way to fund higher education in Texas.

e) the Texas Supreme Court ruled that public education must be free.

 **Practice Online**
Interactive simulation: *Public Policy in Texas*

# Welfare Policy

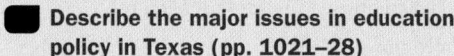 **Trace how welfare policy has evolved in Texas (pp. 1028–34)**

Texas is not as generous in its welfare benefits as most other states, such as California. The federal government provides matching funds for some programs, such as Medicaid, but laws limit how long welfare recipients can receive benefits and require able-bodied people to work.

## Key Terms

**New Deal** (p. 1029)

**Aid to Families with Dependant Children (AFDC)** (p. 1029)

**Medicaid** (p. 1030)

**waiver** (p. 1031)

**Temporary Assistance for Needy Families (TANF)** (p. 1033)

## Practice Quiz

**14.** Which of the following statements is *true* about welfare policy in Texas? *(p. 1030)*
   a) The New Deal programs from the 1930s were expanded in Texas in the 1960s.
   b) In the 1990s, Texas abandoned all poverty programs.
   c) AFDC has replaced the TANF program.
   d) There are more people on welfare in Texas in 2005 than in 1995.
   e) Texas has one of the most generous welfare programs in the country.

**15.** One of the effects of the welfare reforms of the late 1990s is that *(p. 1033)*
   a) welfare rolls have doubled in size in Texas.
   b) welfare rolls have significantly decreased in size in Texas.
   c) welfare programs providing temporary income to poor people have been completely eliminated from Texas.
   d) poverty has been eliminated in Texas.
   e) unemployment is no longer a concern.

# Recommended Websites

**Texas Department of Criminal Justice**
www.tdcj.state.tx.us

**Texas Education Agency**
www.tea.state.tx.us

**Texas Health and Human Service Commission**
www.hhsc.state.tx.us

**Texas Workforce Commission**
www.twc.state.tx.us

**Window on State Government**
www.window.state.tx.us

# appendix

# The Declaration of Independence

In Congress, July 4, 1776

The unanimous Declaration of the thirteen united States of America,

When in the Course of human events, it becomes necessary for one people to dissolve the political bands which have connected them with another, and to assume among the powers of the earth, the separate and equal station to which the Laws of Nature and of Nature's God entitle them, a decent respect to the opinions of mankind requires that they should declare the causes which impel them to the separation.

We hold these truths to be self-evident, that all men are created equal, that they are endowed by their Creator with certain unalienable Rights, that among these are Life, Liberty and the pursuit of Happiness.—That to secure these rights, Governments are instituted among Men, deriving their just powers from the consent of the governed.—That whenever any Form of Government becomes destructive of these ends, it is the Right of the People to alter or to abolish it, and to institute new Government, laying its foundation on such principles and organizing its powers in such form, as to them shall seem most likely to effect their Safety and Happiness. Prudence, indeed, will dictate that Governments long established should not be changed for light and transient causes; and accordingly all experience hath shewn, that mankind are more disposed to suffer, while evils are sufferable, than to right themselves by abolishing the forms to which they are accustomed. But when a long train of abuses and usurpations, pursuing invariably the same Object evinces a design to reduce them under absolute Despotism, it is their right, it is their duty, to throw off such Government, and to provide new Guards for their future security.—Such has been the patient sufferance of these Colonies; and such is now the necessity which constrains them to alter their former Systems of Government. The history of the present King of Great Britain is a history of repeated injuries and usurpations, all having in direct object the establishment of an absolute Tyranny over these States. To prove this, let Facts be submitted to a candid world.

He has refused his Assent to Laws, the most wholesome and necessary for the public good.

He has forbidden his Governors to pass Laws of immediate and pressing importance, unless suspended in their operation till his Assent should be obtained; and when so suspended, he has utterly neglected to attend to them.

He has refused to pass other Laws for the accommodation of large districts of people, unless those people would relinquish the right of Representation in the Legislature, a right inestimable to them and formidable to tyrants only.

He has called together legislative bodies at places unusual, uncomfortable, and distant from the depository of their public Records, for the sole purpose of fatiguing them into compliance with his measures.

He has dissolved Representative Houses repeatedly, for opposing with manly firmness his invasions on the rights of the people.

He has refused for a long time, after such dissolutions, to cause others to be elected; whereby the Legislative powers, incapable of Annihilation, have returned to the People at large for their exercise; the State remaining in the mean time exposed to all the dangers of invasion from without, and convulsions within.

He has endeavoured to prevent the population of these States; for that purpose obstructing the Laws for Naturalization of Foreigners; refusing to pass others to encourage their migrations hither, and raising the conditions of new Appropriations of Lands.

He has obstructed the Administration of Justice, by refusing his Assent to Laws for establishing Judiciary powers.

He has made Judges dependent on his Will alone, for the tenure of their offices, and the amount and payment of their salaries.

He has erected a multitude of New Offices, and sent hither swarms of Officers to harrass our people, and eat out their substance.

He has kept among us, in times of peace, Standing Armies without the Consent of our legislatures.

He has affected to render the Military independent of and superior to the Civil power.

He has combined with others to subject us to a jurisdiction foreign to our constitution, and unacknowledged by our laws; giving his Assent to their Acts of pretended Legislation:

For Quartering large bodies of armed troops among us:

For protecting them, by a mock Trial, from punishment for any Murders which they should commit on the Inhabitants of these States:

For cutting off our Trade with all parts of the world:

For imposing Taxes on us without our Consent:

For depriving us in many cases, of the benefits of Trial by Jury:

For transporting us beyond Seas to be tried for pretended offences:

For abolishing the free System of English Laws in a neighboring Province, establishing therein an Arbitrary government, and enlarging its Boundaries so as to render it at once an example and fit instrument for introducing the same absolute rule into these Colonies:

For taking away our Charters, abolishing our most valuable Laws, and altering fundamentally the Forms of our Governments:

For suspending our own Legislatures, and declaring themselves invested with power to legislate for us in all cases whatsoever.

He has abdicated Government here, by declaring us out of his Protection and waging War against us.

He has plundered our seas, ravaged our Coasts, burnt our towns, and destroyed the lives of our people.

He is at this time transporting large Armies of foreign Mercenaries to compleat the works of death, desolation and tyranny, already begun with circumstances of Cruelty & perfidy scarcely paralleled in the most barbarous ages, and totally unworthy the Head of a civilized nation.

He has constrained our fellow Citizens taken Captive on the high Seas to bear Arms against their Country, to become the executioners of their friends and Brethren, or to fall themselves by their Hands.

He has excited domestic insurrections amongst us, and has endeavoured to bring on the inhabitants of our frontiers, the merciless Indian Savages, whose known rule of warfare, is an undistinguished destruction of all ages, sexes and conditions.

In every stage of these Oppressions We have Petitioned for Redress in the most humble terms: Our repeated Petitions have been answered only by repeated injury. A Prince whose character is thus marked by every act which may define a Tyrant, is unfit to be the ruler of a free people.

Nor have We been wanting in attentions to our Brittish brethren. We have warned them from time to time of attempts by their legislature to extend an unwarrantable jurisdiction over us. We have reminded them of the circumstances of our emigration and settlement here. We have appealed to their native justice and magnanimity, and we have conjured them by the ties of our common kindred to disavow these usurpations, which, would inevitably interrupt our connections and correspondence. They too have been deaf to the voice of justice and of consanguinity. We must, therefore, acquiesce in the necessity, which denounces our Separation, and hold them, as we hold the rest of mankind, Enemies in War, in Peace Friends.

We, Therefore, the Representatives of the United States of America, in General Congress, Assembled, appealing to the Supreme Judge of the world for the rectitude of our intentions, do, in the Name, and by Authority of the good People of these Colonies, solemnly publish and declare, That these United Colonies are, and of Right ought to be Free and Independent States; that they are Absolved from all Allegiance to the British Crown, and that all political connection between them and the State of Great Britain, is and ought to be totally dissolved; and that as Free and Independent States, they have full Power to levy War, conclude Peace, contract Alliances, establish Commerce, and to do all other Acts and Things which Independent States may of right do. And for the support of this Declaration, with a firm reliance on the protection of divine Providence, we mutually pledge to each other our Lives, our Fortunes and our sacred Honor.

The foregoing Declaration was, by order of Congress, engrossed, and signed by the following members:

*John Hancock*

**NEW HAMPSHIRE**
*Josiah Bartlett*
*William Whipple*
*Matthew Thornton*

**MASSACHUSETTS BAY**
*Samuel Adams*
*John Adams*
*Robert Treat Paine*
*Elbridge Gerry*

**RHODE ISLAND**
*Stephen Hopkins*
*William Ellery*

**CONNECTICUT**
*Roger Sherman*
*Samuel Huntington*
*William Williams*
*Oliver Wolcott*

**NEW YORK**
*William Floyd*
*Philip Livingston*
*Francis Lewis*
*Lewis Morris*

**NEW JERSEY**
*Richard Stockton*
*John Witherspoon*
*Francis Hopkinson*
*John Hart*
*Abraham Clark*

**PENNSYLVANIA**
*Robert Morris*
*Benjamin Rush*
*Benjamin Franklin*
*John Morton*
*George Clymer*
*James Smith*
*George Taylor*
*James Wilson*
*George Ross*

**DELAWARE**
*Caesar Rodney*
*George Read*
*Thomas M'Kean*

**MARYLAND**
*Samuel Chase*
*William Paca*
*Thomas Stone*
*Charles Carroll,*
*of Carrollton*

**VIRGINIA**
*George Wythe*
*Richard Henry Lee*
*Thomas Jefferson*
*Benjamin Harrison*
*Thomas Nelson, Jr.*
*Francis Lightfoot Lee*
*Carter Braxton*

**NORTH CAROLINA**
*William Hooper*
*Joseph Hewes*
*John Penn*

**SOUTH CAROLINA**
*Edward Rutledge*
*Thomas Heyward, Jr.*
*Thomas Lynch, Jr.*
*Arthur Middleton*

**GEORGIA**
*Button Gwinnett*
*Lyman Hall*
*George Walton*

*Resolved,* That copies of the Declaration be sent to the several assemblies, conventions, and committees, or councils of safety, and to the several commanding officers of the continental troops; that it be proclaimed in each of the United States, at the head of the army.

# The Articles of Confederation

Agreed to by Congress November 15, 1777;
ratified and in force March 1, 1781

To all whom these Presents shall come, we the undersigned Delegates of the States affixed to our Names, send greeting. Whereas the Delegates of the United States of America, in Congress assembled, did, on the fifteenth day of November, in the Year of Our Lord One thousand Seven Hundred and Seventy seven, and in the Second Year of the Independence of America, agree to certain articles of Confederation and perpetual Union between the States of Newhampshire, Massachusetts-bay, Rhodeisland and Providence Plantations, Connecticut, New-York, New-Jersey, Pennsylvania, Delaware, Maryland, Virginia, North-Carolina, South-Carolina and Georgia in the words following, viz. "Articles of Confederation and perpetual Union between the states of Newhampshire, Massachusettsbay, Rhodeisland and Providence Plantations, Connecticut, New-York, New-Jersey, Pennsylvania, Delaware, Maryland, Virginia, North-Carolina, South-Carolina and Georgia.

Art. I. The Stile of this confederacy shall be "The United States of America."

Art. II. Each state retains its sovereignty, freedom and independence, and every Power, Jurisdiction and right, which is not by this confederation expressly delegated to the United States, in Congress assembled.

Art. III. The said states hereby severally enter into a firm league of friendship with each other, for their common defence, the security of their Liberties, and their mutual and general welfare, binding themselves to assist each other, against all force offered to, or attacks made upon them, or any of them, on account of religion, sovereignty, trade, or any other pretence whatever.

Art. IV. The better to secure and perpetuate mutual friendship and intercourse among the people of the different states in this union, the free inhabitants of each of these states, paupers, vagabonds and fugitives from Justice excepted, shall be entitled to all privileges and immunities of free citizens in the several states; and the people of each state shall have free ingress and regress to and from any other state, and shall enjoy therein all the privileges of trade and commerce, subject to the same duties, impositions and restrictions as the inhabitants thereof respectively, provided that such restriction shall not extend so far as to prevent the removal of property imported into any state, to any other state, of which the Owner is an inhabitant; provided also that no imposition, duties or restriction shall be laid by any state, on the property of the united states, or either of them.

If any Person guilty of, or charged with treason, felony, or other high misdemeanor in any state, shall flee from Justice, and be found in any of the united states, he shall, upon demand of the Governor or executive power, of the state from which he fled, be delivered up and removed to the state having jurisdiction of his offence.

Full faith and credit shall be given in each of these states to the records, acts and judicial proceedings of the courts and magistrates of every other state.

Art. V. For the more convenient management of the general interests of the united states, delegates shall be annually appointed in such manner as the legislature of each state shall direct, to meet in Congress on the first Monday in November, in every year, with a power reserved to each state, to recall its delegates, or any of them, at any time within the year, and to send others in their stead, for the remainder of the Year.

No state shall be represented in Congress by less than two, nor by more than seven Members; and no person shall be capable of being a delegate for more than three years in any term of six years; nor shall any person, being a delegate, be capable of holding any office under the united states, for which he, or another for his benefit receives any salary, fees or emolument of any kind.

Each state shall maintain its own delegates in a meeting of the states, and while they act as members of the committee of the states.

In determining questions in the united states, in Congress assembled, each state shall have one vote.

Freedom of speech and debate in Congress shall not be impeached or questioned in any Court, or place out of Congress, and the members of congress shall be protected in their persons from arrests and imprisonments, during the time of their going to and from, and attendance on congress, except for treason, felony, or breach of the peace.

Art. VI. No state without the Consent of the united states in congress assembled, shall send any embassy to, or receive any embassy from, or enter into any conference, agreement, or alliance or treaty with any King, prince or state; nor shall any person holding any office or profit or trust under the united states, or any of them, accept of any present, emolument, office or title of any kind whatever from any king, prince or foreign state; nor shall the united states in congress assembled, or any of them, grant any title of nobility.

No two or more states shall enter into any treaty, confederation or alliance whatever between them, without the consent of the united states in congress assembled, specifying accurately the purposes for which the same is to be entered into, and how long it shall continue.

No state shall lay any imposts or duties, which may interfere with any stipulations in treaties, entered into by the united states in congress assembled, with any king, prince or state, in pursuance of any treaties already proposed by congress, to the courts of France and Spain.

No vessels of war shall be kept up in time of peace by any state, except such number only, as shall be deemed necessary by the united states in congress assembled, for the defence of such state, or its trade; nor shall any body of forces be kept up by any state, in time of peace, except such number only, as in the judgment of the united states, in congress assembled, shall be deemed requisite to garrison the forts necessary for the defence of such state; but every state shall always keep up a well regulated and disciplined militia, sufficiently armed and accoutred, and shall provide and constantly have ready for use, in public stores, a due number of field pieces and tents, and a proper quantity of arms, ammunition and camp equipage.

No state shall engage in any war without the consent of the united states in congress assembled, unless such state be actually invaded by enemies, or shall have received certain advice of a resolution being formed by some nation of Indians to invade such state, and the danger is so imminent as not to admit of a delay, till the united states in congress asssembled can be consulted; nor shall any state grant commissions to any ships or vessels of war, nor letters of marque or reprisal, except it be after a declaration of war by the united states in congress assembled, and then only against the kingdom or state and the subjects thereof, against which war has been so declared, and under such regulations as shall be established by the united states in congress assembled, unless such state be infested by pirates; in which case vessels of war may be fitted out for that occasion, and kept so long as the danger shall continue, or until the united states in congress assembled shall determine otherwise.

Art. VII. When land-forces are raised by any state for the common defence, all officers of or under the rank of colonel, shall be appointed by the legislature of each state respectively, by whom such forces shall be raised, or in such manner as such state shall direct, and all vacancies shall be filled up by the state which first made the appointment.

Art. VIII. All charges of war, and all other expences that shall be incurred for the common defence or general welfare, and allowed by the united states in congress assembled, shall be defrayed out of a common treasury, which shall be supplied by the several states in proportion to the value of all land within each state, granted to or surveyed for any Person, as such land and the buildings and improvements thereon shall be estimated according to such mode as the united states in congress assembled, shall from time to time direct and appoint.

The taxes for paying that proportion shall be laid and levied by the authority and direction of the legislatures of the several states within the time agreed upon by the united states in congress assembled.

Art. IX. The united states in congress assembled, shall have the sole and exclusive right and power of determining on peace and war, except in the cases mentioned in the sixth article—of sending and receiving ambassadors—entering into treaties and alliances, provided that no treaty of commerce shall be made whereby the legislative power of the respective states shall be restrained from imposing such imposts and duties on foreigners, as their own people are subjected to, or from prohibiting the exportation of any species of goods or commodities whatsoever—of establishing rules for deciding in all cases, what captures on land or water shall be legal, and in what manner prizes taken by land or naval forces in the service of the united states shall be divided or appropriated—of granting letters of marque and reprisal in times of peace—appointing courts for the trial of piracies and felonies committed on the high seas and establishing courts for receiving and determining finally appeals in all cases of captures, provided that no member of congress shall be appointed a judge of any of the said courts.

The united states in congress assembled shall also be the last resort on appeal in all disputes and differences now subsisting or that hereafter may arise between two or more states concerning boundary, jurisdiction or any other cause whatever; which authority shall always be exercised in the manner following. Whenever the legislative or executive authority or lawful agent of any state in controversy with another shall present a petition to congress stating the matter in question and praying for a hearing, notice thereof shall be given by order of congress to the legislative or executive authority of the other state in controversy, and a day assigned for the appearance of the parties by their lawful agents, who shall then be directed to appoint by joint consent, commissioners or judges to constitute a court for hearing and determining the matter in question: but if they cannot agree, congress shall name three persons out of each of the united states, and from the list of such persons each party shall alternately strike out one, the petitioners beginning, until the number shall be reduced to thirteen; and from that number not less than seven, nor more than nine names as congress shall direct, shall in the presence of congress be drawn out by lot, and the persons whose names shall be so drawn or any five of them, shall be commissioners or judges, to hear and finally determine the controversy, so always as a major part of the judges who shall hear the cause shall agree in the determination: and if either party shall neglect to attend at the day appointed, without shewing reasons, which congress shall judge sufficient, or being present shall refuse to strike, the congress shall proceed to nominate three persons out of each state, and the secretary of congress shall strike in behalf of such party absent or refusing; and the judgment and sentence of the court to be appointed, in the manner before prescribed, shall be final and conclusive; and if any of the parties shall refuse to submit to the authority of such court, or to appear to defend their claim or cause, the court shall nevertheless proceed to pronounce sentence, or judgment, which shall in like manner be final and decisive, the judgment or sentence and other proceedings being in either case transmitted to congress, and lodged among the acts of congress for the security of the parties concerned: provided that every commissioner, before he sits in judgment, shall take an oath to be administered by one of the judges of the supreme or superior court of the state, where the cause shall be tried, "well and truly to hear and determine the matter in question, according to the best of his judgment, without favour, affection or hope of reward:" provided also, that no state shall be deprived of territory for the benefit of the united states.

All controversies concerning the private right of soil claimed under different grants of two or more states, whose jurisdictions as they may respect such lands, and the states which passed such grants are adjusted, the said grants or either of them being at the same time claimed to have originated antecedent to such settlement of jurisdiction, shall on the petition of either party to the congress of the united states, be finally determined as near as may be in the same manner as is before prescribed for deciding disputes respecting territorial jurisdiction between different states.

The united states in congress assembled shall also have the sole and exclusive right and power of regulating the alloy and value of coin struck by their own authority, or by that of the respective states—fixing the standard of weights and measures throughout the united states—regulating the trade and managing all affairs with the Indians, not members of any of the states, provided that the legislative right of any state within its own limits be not infringed or violated—establishing and regulating post-offices from one state to another, throughout all the united states, and exacting such postage on the papers passing thro' the same as may be requisite to defray the expences of the said office—appointing all officers of the land forces, in the service of the united states, excepting regimental officers—appointing all the officers of the naval forces, and commissioning all officers whatever in the service of the united states—making rules for the government and regulation of the said land and naval forces, and directing their operations.

The united states in congress assembled shall have authority to appoint a committee, to sit in the recess of congress, to be denominated "A Committee of the States," and to consist of one delegate from each state; and to appoint such other committees and civil officers as may be necessary for managing the general affairs of the united states under their direction—to appoint one of their number to preside, provided that no person be allowed to serve in the office of president more than one year in any term of three years; to ascertain the necessary sums of Money to be raised for the service of the united states,

and to appropriate and apply the same for defraying the public expenses—to borrow money, or emit bills on the credit of the united states, transmitting every half year to the respective states an account of the sums of money so borrowed or emitted,—to build and equip a navy—to agree upon the number of land forces, and to make requisitions from each state for its quota, in proportion to the number of white inhabitants in such state; which requisition shall be binding, and thereupon the legislature of each state shall appoint the regimental officers, raise the men and cloath, arm and equip them in a soldier like manner, at the expense of the united states; and the officers and men so cloathed, armed and equipped shall march to the place appointed, and within the time agreed on by the united states in congress assembled: But if the united states in congress assembled shall, on consideration of circumstances judge proper that any state should not raise men, or should raise a smaller number than its quota, and that any other state should raise a greater number of men than the quota thereof, such extra number shall be raised, officered, cloathed, armed and equipped in the same manner as the quota of such state, unless the legislature of such state shall judge that such extra number cannot be safely spared out of the same, in which case they shall raise officer, cloath, arm and equip as many of such extra number as they judge can be safely spared. And the officers and men so cloathed, armed and equipped, shall march to the place appointed, and within the time agreed on by the united states in congress assembled.

The united states in congress assembled shall never engage in a war, nor grant letters of marque and reprisal in time of peace, nor enter into any treaties or alliances, nor coin money, nor regulate the value thereof, nor ascertain the sums and expenses necessary for the defence and welfare of the united states, or any of them, nor emit bills, nor borrow money on the credit of the united states, nor appropriate money, nor agree upon the number of vessels of war, to be built or purchased, or the number of land or sea forces to be raised, nor appoint a commander in chief of the army or navy, unless nine states assent to the same: nor shall a question on any other point, except for adjourning from day to day be determined, unless by the votes of a majority of the united states in congress assembled.

The congress of the united states shall have power to adjourn to any time within the year, and to any place within the united states, so that no period of adjournment be for a longer duration than the space of six Months, and shall publish the Journal of their proceedings monthly, except such parts thereof relating to treaties, alliances or military operations, as in their judgment require secrecy; and the yeas and nays of the delegates of each state on any question shall be entered on the Journal, when it is desired by any delegate; and the delegates of a state, or any of them, at his or their request shall be furnished with a transcript of the said Journal, except such parts as are above excepted, to lay before the legislatures of the several states.

Art. X. The committee of the states, or any nine of them, shall be authorised to execute, in the recess of congress, such of the powers of congress as the united states in congress assembled, by the consent of nine states, shall from time to time think expedient to vest them with; provided that no power be delegated to the said committee, for the exercise of which, by the articles of confederation, the voice of nine states in the congress of the united states assembled is requisite.

Art. XI. Canada acceding to this confederation, and joining in the measures of the united states, shall be admitted into, and entitled to all the advantages of this union: but no other colony shall be admitted into the same, unless such admission be agreed to by nine states.

Art. XII. All bills of credit emitted, monies borrowed and debts contracted by, or under the authority of congress, before the assembling of the united states, in pursuance of the present confederation, shall be deemed and considered as a charge against the united states, for payment and satisfaction whereof the said united states and the public faith are hereby solemnly pledged.

Art. XIII. Every state shall abide by the determinations of the united states in congress assembled, on all questions which by this confederation are submitted to them. And the Articles of this confederation shall be inviolably observed by every state, and the union shall be perpetual; nor shall any alteration at any time hereafter be made in any of them; unless such alteration be agreed to in a congress of the united states, and be afterwards confirmed by the legislatures of every state.

And Whereas it hath pleased the Great Governor of the World to incline the hearts of the legislatures we respectively represent in congress, to approve of, and to authorize us to ratify the said articles of confederation and perpetual union. Know Ye that we the undersigned delegates, by virtue of the power and authority to us given for that purpose, do by these presents, in the name and in behalf of our respective constituents, fully and entirely ratify and confirm each and every of the said articles of confederation and perpetual union, and all and singular the matters and things therein contained: And we do further solemnly plight and engage the faith of our respective constituents, that they shall abide by the determinations of the united states in congress assembled, on all questions, which by the said confederation are submitted to them. And that the articles thereof shall be inviolably observed by the states we respectively represent, and that the union shall be perpetual. In Witness whereof we have hereunto set our hands in Congress. Done at Philadelphia in the state of Pennsylvania the ninth day of July, in the Year of our Lord one Thousand seven Hundred and Seventy-eight, and in the third year of the independence of America.

# The Constitution of the United States of America

[PREAMBLE]
We the People of the United States, in Order to form a more perfect Union, establish Justice, insure domestic Tranquility, provide for the common defence, promote the general Welfare, and secure the Blessings of Liberty to ourselves and our Posterity, do ordain and establish this Constitution for the United States of America.

## Article I

### SECTION 1

[LEGISLATIVE POWERS]
All legislative Powers herein granted shall be vested in a Congress of the United States, which shall consist of a Senate and House of Representatives.

### SECTION 2

[HOUSE OF REPRESENTATIVES, HOW CONSTITUTED, POWER OF IMPEACHMENT]
The House of Representatives shall be composed of Members chosen every second Year by the People of the several States, and the Electors in each State shall have the Qualifications requisite for Electors of the most numerous Branch of the State Legislature.

No Person shall be a Representative who shall not have attained to the Age of twenty five Years, and been seven Years a Citizen of the United States, and who shall not, when elected, be an Inhabitant of that State in which he shall be chosen.

Representatives and *direct Taxes*[1] shall be apportioned among the several States which may be included within this Union, according to their respective Numbers, *which shall be determined by adding to the whole Number of free Persons, including those bound to Service for a Term of Years, and excluding Indians not taxed, three fifths of all other Persons.*[2] The actual Enumeration shall be made within three Years after the first Meeting of the Congress of the United States, and within every subsequent Term of ten Years, in such Manner as they shall by Law direct. The Number of Representatives shall not exceed one for every thirty Thousand, but each State shall have at Least one Representative; *and until such enumeration shall be made, the State of New Hampshire shall be entitled to chuse three, Massachusetts eight, Rhode-Island and Providence Plantations one, Connecticut five, New-York six, New Jersey four, Pennsylvania eight, Delaware one, Maryland six, Virginia ten, North Carolina five, South Carolina five, and Georgia three.*[3]

When vacancies happen in the Representation from any State, the Executive Authority thereof shall issue Writs of Election to fill such Vacancies.

The House of Representatives shall chuse their Speaker and other Officers; and shall have the sole Power of Impeachment.

### SECTION 3

[THE SENATE, HOW CONSTITUTED, IMPEACHMENT TRIALS]
The Senate of the United States shall be composed of two Senators from each State, *chosen by the Legislature thereof,*[4] for six Years; and each Senator shall have one Vote.

Immediately after they shall be assembled in Consequence of the first Election, they shall be divided as equally as may be into three Classes. The Seats of the Senators of the first Class shall be vacated at the Expiration of the second Year, of the second Class at the Expiration of the fourth Year, and of the third Class at the Expiration of the sixth Year, so that one third may be chosen every second Year; *and if Vacancies happen by Resignation, or otherwise, during the Recess of the Legislature of any State, the Executive thereof may make temporary Appointments until the next Meeting of the Legislature, which shall then fill such Vacancies.*[5]

No Person shall be a Senator who shall not have attained to the Age of thirty Years, and been nine Years a Citizen of the United States, and who shall not, when elected, be an Inhabitant of that State for which he shall be chosen.

The Vice President of the United States shall be President of the Senate, but shall have no Vote, unless they be equally divided.

The Senate shall chuse their other Officers, and also a President pro tempore, in the Absence of the Vice President, or when he shall exercise the Office of President of the United States.

---

[1]Modified by Sixteenth Amendment.

[2]Modified by Fourteenth Amendment.

[3]Temporary provision.

[4]Modified by Seventeenth Amendment.

[5]Modified by Seventeenth Amendment.

The Senate shall have the sole Power to try all Impeachments. When sitting for that Purpose, they shall be on Oath or Affirmation. When the President of the United States is tried, the Chief Justice shall preside: And no Person shall be convicted without the Concurrence of two thirds of the Members present.

Judgment in Cases of Impeachment shall not extend further than to removal from Office, and disqualification to hold and enjoy any Office of honor, Trust or Profit under the United States: but the Party convicted shall nevertheless be liable and subject to Indictment, Trial, Judgment and Punishment, according to Law.

## SECTION 4
[ELECTION OF SENATORS AND REPRESENTATIVES]
The Times, Places and Manner of holding Elections for Senators and Representatives, shall be prescribed in each State by the Legislature thereof; but the Congress may at any time by Law make or alter such Regulations, except as to the Places of chusing Senators.

*The Congress shall assemble at least once in every Year, and such Meeting shall be on the first Monday in December, unless they shall by Law appoint a different Day.*[6]

## SECTION 5
[QUORUM, JOURNALS, MEETINGS, ADJOURNMENTS]
Each House shall be the Judge of the Elections, Returns and Qualifications of its own Members, and a Majority of each shall constitute a Quorum to do Business; but a smaller Number may adjourn from day to day, and may be authorized to compel the Attendance of absent Members, in such Manner, and under such Penalties as each House may provide.

Each House may determine the Rules of its Proceedings, punish its Members for disorderly Behaviour, and, with the Concurrence of two thirds, expel a Member.

Each House shall keep a Journal of its Proceedings, and from time to time publish the same, excepting such Parts as may in their Judgment require Secrecy; and the Yeas and Nays of the Members of either House on any questions shall, at the Desire of one fifth of those Present, be entered on the Journal.

Neither House, during the Session of Congress, shall, without the Consent of the other, adjourn for more than three days, nor to any other Place than that in which the two Houses shall be sitting.

## SECTION 6
[COMPENSATION, PRIVILEGES, DISABILITIES]
The Senators and Representatives shall receive a Compensation for their Services, to be ascertained by Law, and paid out of the Treasury of the United States. They shall in all Cases, except Treason, Felony and Breach of the Peace, be privileged

from Arrest during their Attendance at the Session of their respective Houses, and in going to and returning from the same; and for any Speech or Debate in either House, they shall not be questioned in any other Place.

No Senator or Representative shall, during the Time for which he was elected, be appointed to any civil Office under the Authority of the United States, which shall have been created, or the Emoluments whereof shall have been encreased during such time; and no Person holding any Office under the United States, shall be a Member of either House during his Continuance in Office.

## SECTION 7
[PROCEDURE IN PASSING BILLS AND RESOLUTIONS]
All Bills for raising Revenue shall originate in the House of Representatives; but the Senate may propose or concur with Amendments as on other Bills.

Every Bill which shall have passed the House of Representatives and the Senate, shall, before it become a Law, be presented to the President of the United States: If he approve he shall sign it, but if not he shall return it, with his Objections to that House in which it shall have originated, who shall enter the Objections at large on their Journal, and proceed to reconsider it. If after such Reconsideration two thirds of that House shall agree to pass the Bill, it shall be sent, together with the Objections, to the other House, by which it shall likewise be reconsidered, and if approved by two thirds of that House, it shall become a Law. But in all such Cases the Votes of both Houses shall be determined by yeas and Nays, and the Names of the Persons voting for and against the Bill shall be entered on the Journal of each House respectively. If any Bill shall not be returned by the President within ten Days (Sundays excepted) after it shall have been presented to him, the Same shall be a Law, in like Manner as if he had signed it, unless the Congress by their Adjournment prevent its Return, in which Case it shall not be a Law.

Every Order, Resolution, or Vote to which the Concurrence of the Senate and House of Representatives may be necessary (except on a question of Adjournment) shall be presented to the President of the United States; and before the Same shall take Effect, shall be approved by him, or being disapproved by him, shall be repassed by two thirds of the Senate and House of Representatives, according to the Rules and Limitations prescribed in the Case of a Bill.

## SECTION 8
[POWERS OF CONGRESS]
The Congress shall have Power

To lay and collect Taxes, Duties, Imposts and Excises, to pay the Debts and provide for the common Defence and general Welfare of the United States; but all Duties, Imposts and Excises shall be uniform throughout the United States;

To borrow Money on the credit of the United States;

---

[6]Modified by Twentieth Amendment.

To regulate Commerce with foreign Nations, and among the several States, and with the Indian Tribes;

To establish an uniform Rule of Naturalization, and uniform Laws on the subject of Bankruptcies throughout the United States;

To coin Money, regulate the Value thereof, and of foreign Coin, and fix the Standard of Weights and Measures;

To provide for the Punishment of counterfeiting the Securities and current Coin of the United States;

To establish Post Offices and post Roads;

To promote the Progress of Science and useful Arts, by securing for limited Times to Authors and Inventors the exclusive Right to their respective Writings and Discoveries;

To constitute Tribunals inferior to the supreme Court;

To define and punish Piracies and Felonies committed on the high Seas, and Offences against the Law of Nations;

To declare War, grant Letters of Marque and Reprisal, and make Rules concerning Captures on Land and Water;

To raise and support Armies, but no Appropriation of Money to that Use shall be for a longer Term than two Years;

To provide and maintain a Navy;

To make Rules for the Government and Regulation of the land and naval Forces;

To provide for calling forth the Militia to execute the Laws of the Union, suppress Insurrections and repel Invasions;

To provide for organizing, arming, and disciplining, the Militia, and for governing such Part of them as may be employed in the Service of the United States, reserving to the States respectively, the Appointment of the Officers, and the Authority of training the Militia according to the discipline prescribed by Congress;

To exercise exclusive Legislation in all Cases whatsoever, over such District (not exceeding ten Miles square) as may, by Cession of particular States, and the Acceptance of Congress, become the Seat of the Government of the United States, and to exercise like Authority over all Places purchased by the Consent of the Legislature of the State in which the Same shall be, for the Erection of Forts, Magazines, Arsenals, dock-Yards, and other needful Buildings;—And

To make all Laws which shall be necessary and proper for carrying into Execution the foregoing Powers, and all other Powers vested by this Constitution in the Government of the United States, or in any Department or Officer thereof.

## SECTION 9

[SOME RESTRICTIONS ON FEDERAL POWER]

*The Migration or Importation of such Persons as any of the States now existing shall think proper to admit, shall not be prohibited by the Congress prior to the Year one thousand eight hundred and eight, but a Tax or duty may be imposed on such Importation, not exceeding ten dollars for each Person.*[7]

The Privilege of the Writ of Habeas Corpus shall not be suspended, unless when in Cases of Rebellion or Invasion the public Safety may require it.

No Bill of Attainder or ex post facto Law shall be passed.

*No Capitation, or other direct, Tax shall be laid, unless in Proportion to the Census or Enumeration herein before directed to be taken.*[8]

No Tax or Duty shall be laid on Articles exported from any State.

No Preference shall be given by any Regulation of Commerce or Revenue to the Ports of one State over those of another; nor shall Vessels bound to, or from, one State, be obliged to enter, clear, or pay Duties in another.

No Money shall be drawn from the Treasury, but in Consequence of Appropriations made by Law; and a regular Statement and Account of the Receipts and Expenditures of all public Money shall be published from time to time.

No Title of Nobility shall be granted by the United States: And no Person holding any Office of Profit or Trust under them, shall, without the Consent of the Congress, accept of any present, Emolument, Office, or Title, of any kind whatever, from any King, Prince, or foreign State.

## SECTION 10

[RESTRICTIONS UPON POWERS OF STATES]

No State shall enter into any Treaty, Alliance, or Confederation; grant Letters of Marque and Reprisal; coin Money; emit Bills of Credit; make any Thing but gold and silver Coin a Tender in Payment of Debts; pass any Bill of Attainder, ex post facto Law, or Law impairing the Obligation of Contracts, or grant any Title of Nobility.

No State shall, without the Consent of the Congress, lay any Imposts or Duties on Imports or Exports, except what may be absolutely necessary for executing its inspection Laws: and the net Produce of all Duties and Imposts, laid by any State on Imports or Exports, shall be for the Use of the Treasury of the United States; and all such Laws shall be subject to the Revision and Control of the Congress.

No State shall, without the Consent of Congress, lay any Duty of Tonnage, keep Troops, or Ships of War in time of Peace, enter into any Agreement or Compact with another State, or with a foreign Power, or engage in War, unless actually invaded, or in such imminent Danger as will not admit of delay.

## Article II

### SECTION 1

[EXECUTIVE POWER, ELECTION, QUALIFICATIONS OF THE PRESIDENT]

The executive Power shall be vested in a President of the United States of America. *He shall hold his Office during the*

---

[7]Temporary provision.

[8]Modified by Sixteenth Amendment.

Term of four Years, and, together with the Vice President, chosen for the same Term, be elected, as follows[9]

Each State shall appoint, in such Manner as the Legislature thereof may direct, a Number of Electors, equal to the whole Number of Senators and Representatives to which the State may be entitled in the Congress: but no Senator or Representative, or Person holding an Office of Trust or Profit under the United States, shall be appointed an Elector.

*The electors shall meet in their respective States, and vote by ballot for two Persons, of whom one at least shall not be an Inhabitant of the same State with themselves. And they shall make a List of all the Persons voted for, and of the Number of Votes for each; which List they shall sign and certify, and transmit sealed to the Seat of the Government of the United States, directed to the President of the Senate. The President of the Senate shall, in the Presence of the Senate and House of Representatives, open all the Certificates, and the Votes shall then be counted. The Person having the greatest Number of Votes shall be the President, if such Number be a Majority of the whole Number of Electors appointed; and if there be more than one who have such Majority, and have an equal Number of Votes, then the House of Representatives shall immediately chuse by Ballot one of them for President; and if no Person have a Majority, then from the five highest on the List the said House shall in like Manner chuse the President. But in chusing the President, the Votes shall be taken by States, the Representation from each State having one Vote; A quorum for this Purpose shall consist of a Member or Members from two thirds of the States, and a Majority of all the States shall be necessary to a Choice. In every Case, after the Choice of the President, the person having the greatest Number of Votes of the Electors shall be the Vice President. But if there should remain two or more who have equal Votes, the Senate shall chuse from them by Ballot the Vice President.[10]*

The Congress may determine the Time of chusing the Electors, and the Day on which they shall give their Votes; which Day shall be the same throughout the United States.

No Person except a natural born Citizen, or a Citizen of the United States, at the time of the Adoption of this Constitution, shall be eligible to the Office of President; neither shall any Person be eligible to that Office who shall not have attained to the Age of thirty five Years, and been fourteen Years a Resident within the United States.

In Case of the Removal of the President from Office, or his Death, Resignation, or Inability to discharge the Powers and Duties of the said Office, the Same shall devolve on the Vice President, and the Congress may by Law provide for the Case of Removal, Death, Resignation or Inability, both of the President and Vice President, declaring what Officer shall then act as President, and such Officer shall act accordingly, until the Disability be removed, or a President shall be elected.

---

[9]Number of terms limited to two by Twenty-Second Amendment.

[10]Modified by Twelfth and Twentieth Amendments.

The President shall, at stated Times, receive for his Services, a Compensation, which shall neither be increased nor diminished during the Period for which he shall have been elected, and he shall not receive within that Period any other Emolument from the United States, or any of them.

Before he enter on the Execution of his Office, he shall take the following Oath or Affirmation:—"I do solemnly swear (or affirm) that I will faithfully execute the Office of President of the United States, and will to the best of my Ability, preserve, protect and defend the Constitution of the United States."

## SECTION 2
[POWERS OF THE PRESIDENT]
The President shall be Commander in Chief of the Army and Navy of the United States, and of the Militia of the several States, when called into the actual Service of the United States; he may require the Opinion, in writing, of the principal Officer in each of the executive Departments, upon any Subject relating to the Duties of their respective Offices, and he shall have Power to grant Reprieves and Pardons for Offences against the United States, except in Cases of Impeachment.

He shall have Power, by and with the Advice and Consent of the Senate, to make Treaties, provided two thirds of the Senators present concur; and he shall nominate, and by and with the Advice and Consent of the Senate, shall appoint Ambassadors, other public Ministers and Consuls, Judges of the supreme Court, and all other Officers of the United States, whose Appointments are not herein otherwise provided for, and which shall be established by Law: but the Congress may by Law vest the Appointment of such inferior Officers, as they think proper, in the President alone, in the Courts of Law, or in the Heads of Departments.

The President shall have Power to fill up all Vacancies that may happen during the Recess of the Senate, by granting Commissions which shall expire at the End of their next Session.

## SECTION 3
[POWERS AND DUTIES OF THE PRESIDENT]
He shall from time to time give to the Congress Information of the State of the Union, and recommend to their Consideration such Measures as he shall judge necessary and expedient; he may, on extraordinary Occasions, convene both Houses, or either of them, and in Case of Disagreement between them, with Respect to the Time of Adjournment, he may adjourn them to such Time as he shall think proper; he shall receive Ambassadors and other public Ministers; he shall take Care that the Laws be faithfully executed, and shall Commission all the Officers of the United States.

## SECTION 4
[IMPEACHMENT]
The President, Vice President and all civil Officers of the United States, shall be removed from Office on Impeachment

for, and Conviction of, Treason, Bribery, or other high Crimes and Misdemeanors.

## Article III

### SECTION 1

[JUDICIAL POWER, TENURE OF OFFICE]

The judicial Power of the United States, shall be vested in one supreme Court, and in such inferior Courts as the Congress may from time to time ordain and establish. The Judges, both of the supreme and inferior Courts, shall hold their Offices during good Behaviour, and shall, at stated Times, receive for their Services, a Compensation, which shall not be diminished during their Continuance in Office.

### SECTION 2

[JURISDICTION]

The judicial Power shall extend to all Cases, in Law and Equity, arising under this Constitution, the Laws of the United States, and Treaties made, or which shall be made, under their Authority;—to all Cases affecting Ambassadors, other public Ministers and Consuls;—to all Cases of admiralty and maritime Jurisdiction;—to Controversies to which the United States shall be a Party;—to Controversies between two or more States;—*between a State and Citizens of another State;*—between Citizens of different States,—between Citizens of the same State claiming Lands under Grants of different States, *and between a State*, or the Citizens thereof, *and foreign States, Citizens or Subjects.*[11]

In all Cases affecting Ambassadors, other public Ministers and Consuls, and those in which a State shall be Party, the supreme Court shall have original Jurisdiction. In all the other Cases before mentioned, the supreme Court shall have appellate Jurisdiction, both as to Law and Fact, with such Exceptions, and under such Regulations as the Congress shall make.

The Trial of all Crimes, except in Cases of Impeachment, shall be by Jury; and such Trial shall be held in the State where the said Crimes shall have been committed; but when not committed within any State, the Trial shall be at such Place or Places as the Congress may by Law have directed.

### SECTION 3

[TREASON, PROOF, AND PUNISHMENT]

Treason against the United States, shall consist only in levying War against them, or in adhering to their Enemies, giving them Aid and Comfort. No Person shall be convicted of Treason unless on the Testimony of two Witnesses to the same overt Act, or on Confession in open Court.

The Congress shall have Power to declare the Punishment of Treason, but no Attainder of Treason shall work Corruption of Blood, or Forfeiture except during the Life of the Person attainted.

## Article IV

### SECTION 1

[FAITH AND CREDIT AMONG STATES]

Full Faith and Credit shall be given in each State to the public Acts, Records, and judicial Proceedings of every other State. And the Congress may by general Laws prescribe the Manner in which such Acts, Records and Proceedings shall be proved, and the Effect thereof.

### SECTION 2

[PRIVILEGES AND IMMUNITIES, FUGITIVES]

The Citizens of each State shall be entitled to all Privileges and Immunities of Citizens in the several States.

A Person charged in any State with Treason, Felony or other Crime, who shall flee from Justice, and be found in another State, shall on Demand of the executive Authority of the State from which he fled, be delivered up, to be removed to the State having Jurisdiction of the Crime.

*No person held to Service or Labour in one State, under the Laws thereof, escaping into another, shall, in Consequence of any Law or Regulation therein, be discharged from such Service or Labour, but shall be delivered up on Claim of the Party to whom such Service or Labour may be due.*[12]

### SECTION 3

[ADMISSION OF NEW STATES]

New States may be admitted by the Congress into this Union; but no new State shall be formed or erected within the Jurisdiction of any other State; nor any State be formed by the Junction of two or more States, or Parts of States, without the Consent of the Legislatures of the States concerned as well as of the Congress.

The Congress shall have Power to dispose of and make all needful Rules and Regulations respecting the Territory or other Property belonging to the United States; and nothing in this Constitution shall be so construed as to Prejudice any Claims of the United States, or of any particular State.

### SECTION 4

[GUARANTEE OF REPUBLICAN GOVERNMENT]

The United States shall guarantee to every State in this Union a Republican Form of Government, and shall protect each of them against Invasion; and on Application of the Legislature, or of the Executive (when the Legislature cannot be convened), against domestic Violence.

## Article V

[AMENDMENT OF THE CONSTITUTION]

The Congress, whenever two thirds of both Houses shall deem it necessary, shall propose Amendments to this Constitution, or, on the Application of the Legislatures of two thirds of the

---

[11]Modified by Eleventh Amendment.

[12]Repealed by the Thirteenth Amendment.

several States, shall call a Convention for proposing Amendments, which, in either Case, shall be valid to all Intents and Purposes, as Part of this Constitution, when ratified by the Legislatures of three fourths of the several States, or by Conventions in three fourths thereof, as the one or the other Mode of Ratification may be proposed by the Congress; *Provided that no Amendment which may be made prior to the Year One thousand eight hundred and eight shall in any Manner affect the first and fourth Clauses in the Ninth Section of the first Article;*[13] and that no State, without its Consent, shall be deprived of its equal Suffrage in the Senate.

## Article VI

[DEBTS, SUPREMACY, OATH]

All Debts contracted and Engagements entered into, before the Adoption of this Constitution, shall be as valid against the United States under this Constitution, as under the Confederation.

This Constitution, and the Laws of the United States which shall be made in Pursuance thereof; and all Treaties made, or which shall be made, under the Authority of the United States, shall be the supreme Law of the Land; and the Judges in every State shall be bound thereby, any Thing in the Constitution or Laws of any State to the Contrary notwithstanding.

The Senators and Representatives before mentioned, and the Members of the several State Legislatures, and all executive and judicial Officers, both of the United States and of the several States, shall be bound by Oath or Affirmation, to support this Constitution; but no religious Test shall be required as a Qualification to any Office or public Trust under the United States.

## Article VII

[RATIFICATION AND ESTABLISHMENT]

The Ratification of the Conventions of nine States, shall be sufficient for the Establishment of this Constitution between the States so ratifying the Same.[14]

Done in Convention by the Unanimous Consent of the States present the Seventeenth Day of September in the Year of our Lord one thousand seven hundred and Eighty seven and of the Independence of the United States of America the Twelfth. *In Witness* whereof We have hereunto subscribed our Names,

---

[13]Temporary provision.

[14]The Constitution was submitted on September 17, 1787, by the Constitutional Convention, was ratified by the conventions of several states at various dates up to May 29, 1790, and became effective on March 4, 1789.

G:0 WASHINGTON—
*Presidt. and deputy from Virginia*

**NEW HAMPSHIRE**
*John Langdon*
*Nicholas Gilman*

**MASSACHUSETTS**
*Nathaniel Gorham*
*Rufus King*

**CONNECTICUT**
*Wm. Saml. Johnson*
*Roger Sherman*

**NEW YORK**
*Alexander Hamilton*

**NEW JERSEY**
*Wil: Livingston*
*David Brearley*
*Wm. Paterson*
*Jona: Dayton*

**PENNSYLVANIA**
*B Franklin*
*Thomas Mifflin*
*Robt. Morris*
*Geo. Clymer*
*Thos. FitzSimons*
*Jared Ingersoll*
*James Wilson*
*Gouv Morris*

**DELAWARE**
*Geo: Read*
*Gunning Bedford jun*
*John Dickinson*
*Richard Bassett*
*Jaco: Broom*

**MARYLAND**
*James McHenry*
*Dan of St Thos. Jenifer*
*Danl. Carroll*

**VIRGINIA**
*John Blair—*
*James Madison Jr.*

**NORTH CAROLINA**
*Wm. Blount*
*Richd. Dobbs Spaight*
*Hu Williamson*

**SOUTH CAROLINA**
*J. Rutledge*
*Charles Cotesworth Pinckney*
*Charles Pinckney*
*Pierce Butler*

**GEORGIA**
*William Few*
*Abr Baldwin*

# Amendments to the Constitution

Proposed by Congress and Ratified by the Legislatures of the Several States, Pursuant to Article V of the Original Constitution.

Amendments I–X, known as the Bill of Rights, were proposed by Congress on September 25, 1789, and ratified on December 15, 1791.

## Amendment I

[FREEDOM OF RELIGION, OF SPEECH, AND OF THE PRESS]
Congress shall make no law respecting an establishment of religion, or prohibiting the free exercise thereof; or abridging the freedom of speech, or of the press; or the right of the people peaceably to assemble, and to petition the Government for a redress of grievances.

## Amendment II

[RIGHT TO KEEP AND BEAR ARMS]
A well regulated Militia, being necessary to the security of a free State, the right of the people to keep and bear Arms, shall not be infringed.

## Amendment III

[QUARTERING OF SOLDIERS]
No Soldier shall, in time of peace be quartered in any house, without the consent of the Owner, nor in time of war, but in a manner to be prescribed by law.

## Amendment IV

[SECURITY FROM UNWARRANTABLE SEARCH AND SEIZURE]
The right of the people to be secure in their persons, houses, papers, and effects, against unreasonable searches and seizures, shall not be violated, and no Warrants shall issue, but upon probable cause, supported by Oath or affirmation, and particularly describing the place to be searched, and the persons or things to be seized.

## Amendment V

[RIGHTS OF ACCUSED PERSONS IN CRIMINAL PROCEEDINGS]
No person shall be held to answer for a capital, or otherwise infamous crime, unless on a presentment or indictment of a Grand Jury, except in cases arising in the land or naval forces, or in the Militia, when in actual service in time of War or in public danger; nor shall any person be subject for the same offence to be twice put in jeopardy of life or limb; nor shall be compelled in any criminal case to be a witness against himself, nor be deprived of life, liberty, or property, without due process of law; nor shall private property be taken for public use, without just compensation.

## Amendment VI

[RIGHT TO SPEEDY TRIAL, WITNESSES, ETC.]
In all criminal prosecutions, the accused shall enjoy the right to a speedy and public trial, by an impartial jury of the State and district wherein the crime shall have been committed, which district shall have been previously ascertained by law, and to be informed of the nature and cause of the accusation; to be confronted with the witnesses against him; to have compulsory process for obtaining witnesses in his favor, and to have the Assistance of Counsel for his defence.

## Amendment VII

[TRIAL BY JURY IN CIVIL CASES]
In suits at common law, where the value in controversy shall exceed twenty dollars, the right of trial by jury shall be preserved, and no fact tried by a jury, shall be otherwise reexamined in any Court of the United States, than according to the rules of the common law.

## Amendment VIII

[BAILS, FINES, PUNISHMENTS]
Excessive bail shall not be required, nor excessive fines imposed, nor cruel and unusual punishments inflicted.

## Amendment IX

[RESERVATION OF RIGHTS OF PEOPLE]
The enumeration in the Constitution, of certain rights, shall not be construed to deny or disparage others retained by the people.

## Amendment X

[POWERS RESERVED TO STATES OR PEOPLE]
The powers not delegated to the United States by the Constitution, nor prohibited by it to the States, are reserved to the States respectively, or to the people.

## Amendment XI

[*Proposed by Congress on March 4, 1794;
declared ratified on January 8, 1798.*]

[RESTRICTION OF JUDICIAL POWER]

The Judicial power of the United States shall not be construed to extend to any suit in law or equity, commenced or prosecuted against one of the United States by Citizens of another State, or by Citizens or Subjects of any Foreign State.

## Amendment XII

[*Proposed by Congress on December 9, 1803;
declared ratified on September 25, 1804.*]

[ELECTION OF PRESIDENT AND VICE PRESIDENT]

The Electors shall meet in their respective states and vote by ballot for President and Vice-President, one of whom, at least, shall not be an inhabitant of the same state with themselves; they shall name in their ballots the person voted for as President, and in distinct ballots the person voted for as Vice-President, and they shall make distinct lists of all persons voted for as President, and of all persons voted for as Vice-President, and of the number of votes for each, which lists they shall sign and certify, and transmit sealed to the seat of the government of the United States, directed to the President of the Senate;—the President of the Senate shall, in presence of the Senate and House of Representatives, open all the certificates and the votes shall then be counted;—The person having the greatest number of votes for President, shall be the President, if such number be a majority of the whole number of Electors appointed; and if no person have such majority, then from the persons having the highest numbers not exceeding three on the list of those voted for as President, the House of Representatives shall choose immediately, by ballot, the President. But in choosing the President, the votes shall be taken by states, the representation from each state having one vote; a quorum for this purpose shall consist of a member or members from two-thirds of the states, and a majority of all the states shall be necessary to a choice. And if the House of Representatives shall not choose a President whenever the right of choice shall devolve upon them, before the fourth day of March next following, then the Vice-President shall act as President, as in the case of the death or other constitutional disability of the President.—The person having the greatest number of votes as Vice-President, shall be the Vice-President, if such number be a majority of the whole number of Electors appointed, and if no person have a majority, then from the two highest numbers on the list, the Senate shall choose the Vice-President; a quorum for the purpose shall consist of two-thirds of the whole number of Senators, and a majority of the whole number shall be necessary to a choice. But no person constitutionally ineligible to the office of President shall be eligible to that of Vice-President of the United States.

## Amendment XIII

[*Proposed by Congress on January 31, 1865;
declared ratified on December 18, 1865.*]

### SECTION 1

[ABOLITION OF SLAVERY]

Neither slavery nor involuntary servitude, except as a punishment for crime whereof the party shall have been duly convicted, shall exist within the United States, or any place subject to their jurisdiction.

### SECTION 2

[POWER TO ENFORCE THIS ARTICLE]

Congress shall have power to enforce this article by appropriate legislation.

## Amendment XIV

[*Proposed by Congress on June 13, 1866;
declared ratified on July 28, 1868.*]

### SECTION 1

[CITIZENSHIP RIGHTS NOT TO BE ABRIDGED BY STATES]

All persons born or naturalized in the United States, and subject to the jurisdiction thereof, are citizens of the United States and of the State wherein they reside. No State shall make or enforce any law which shall abridge the privileges or immunities of citizens of the United States; nor shall any State deprive any person of life, liberty, or property, without due process of law; nor deny to any person within its jurisdiction the equal protection of the laws.

### SECTION 2

[APPORTIONMENT OF REPRESENTATIVES IN CONGRESS]

Representatives shall be apportioned among the several States according to their respective numbers, counting the whole number of persons in each State, excluding Indians not taxed. But when the right to vote at any election for the choice of electors for President and Vice-President of the United States, Representatives in Congress, the Executive and Judicial officers of a State, or the members of the Legislature thereof, is denied to any of the male inhabitants of such State, being twenty-one years of age, and citizens of the United States, or in any way abridged, except for participation in rebellion, or other crime, the basis of representation therein shall be reduced in the proportion which the number of such male citizens shall bear to the whole number of male citizens twenty-one years of age in such State.

### SECTION 3

[PERSONS DISQUALIFIED FROM HOLDING OFFICE]

No person shall be a Senator or Representative in Congress, or elector of President and Vice-President, or hold any office, civil or military, under the United States, or under any State, who, having previously taken an oath, as a member of Congress, or as an officer of the United States, or as a member of any State legislature, or as an executive or judicial officer of any State, to support the Constitution of the United States, shall have engaged in insurrection or rebellion against the same, or given aid or comfort to the enemies thereof. But Congress may by a vote of two-thirds of each House, remove such disability.

## SECTION 4
[WHAT PUBLIC DEBTS ARE VALID]
The validity of the public debt of the United States, authorized by law, including debts incurred for payment of pensions and bounties for services in suppressing insurrection or rebellion, shall not be questioned. But neither the United States nor any State shall assume or pay any debt or obligation incurred in aid of insurrection or rebellion against the United States, or any claim for the loss or emancipation of any slave; but all such debts, obligations and claims shall be held illegal and void.

## SECTION 5
[POWER TO ENFORCE THIS ARTICLE]
The Congress shall have power to enforce, by appropriate legislation, the provisions of this article.

## Amendment XV
[*Proposed by Congress on February 26, 1869;
declared ratified on March 30, 1870.*]

## SECTION 1
[NEGRO SUFFRAGE]
The right of citizens of the United States to vote shall not be denied or abridged by the United States or by any State on account of race, color, or previous condition of servitude.

## SECTION 2
[POWER TO ENFORCE THIS ARTICLE]
The Congress shall have power to enforce this article by appropriate legislation.

## Amendment XVI
[*Proposed by Congress on July 2, 1909;
declared ratified on February 25, 1913.*]
[AUTHORIZING INCOME TAXES]
The Congress shall have power to lay and collect taxes on incomes, from whatever source derived, without apportionment among the several States, and without regard to any census or enumeration.

## Amendment XVII
[*Proposed by Congress on May 13, 1912;
declared ratified on May 31, 1913.*]
[POPULAR ELECTION OF SENATORS]
The Senate of the United States shall be composed of two Senators from each State, elected by the people thereof, for six years; and each Senator shall have one vote. The electors in each State shall have the qualifications requisite for electors of the most numerous branch of the State legislatures.

When vacancies happen in the representation of any State in the Senate, the executive authority of such State shall issue writs of election to fill such vacancies: *Provided,* That the legislature of any State may empower the executive thereof to make temporary appointments until the people fill the vacancies by election as the legislature may direct.

This amendment shall not be so construed as to affect the election or term of any Senator chosen before it becomes valid as part of the Constitution.

## Amendment XVIII
[*Proposed by Congress December 18, 1917;
declared ratified on January 29, 1919.*]

## SECTION 1
[NATIONAL LIQUOR PROHIBITION]
*After one year from the ratification of this article the manufacture, sale, or transportation of intoxicating liquors within, the importation thereof into, or the exportation thereof from the United States and all territory subject to the jurisdiction thereof for beverage purposes is hereby prohibited.*

## SECTION 2
[POWER TO ENFORCE THIS ARTICLE]
*The Congress and the several States shall have concurrent power to enforce this article by appropriate legislation.*

## SECTION 3
[RATIFICATION WITHIN SEVEN YEARS]
*This article shall be inoperative unless it shall have been ratified as an amendment to the Constitution by the legislatures of the several States, as provided in the Constitution, within seven years from the date of the submission hereof to the States by the Congress.*[1]

## Amendment XIX
[*Proposed by Congress on June 4, 1919;
declared ratified on August 26, 1920.*]
[WOMAN SUFFRAGE]
The right of citizens of the United States to vote shall not be denied or abridged by the United States or by any State on account of sex.

Congress shall have power to enforce this article by appropriate legislation.

---

[1]Repealed by the Twenty-First Amendment.

## Amendment XX

[*Proposed by Congress on March 2, 1932;*
*declared ratified on February 6, 1933.*]

### SECTION 1
[TERMS OF OFFICE]
The terms of the President and Vice President shall end at noon on the 20th day of January, and the terms of Senators and Representatives at noon on the 3d day of January, of the years in which such terms would have ended if this article had not been ratified; and the terms of their successors shall then begin.

### SECTION 2
[TIME OF CONVENING CONGRESS]
The Congress shall assemble at least once in every year, and such meeting shall begin at noon on the 3d day of January, unless they shall by law appoint a different day.

### SECTION 3
[DEATH OF PRESIDENT-ELECT]
If, at the time fixed for the beginning of the term of the President, the President elect shall have died, the Vice President elect shall become President. If a President shall not have been chosen before the time fixed for the beginning of his term, or if the President elect shall have failed to qualify, then the Vice President elect shall act as President until a President shall have qualified; and the Congress may by law provide for the case wherein neither a President elect nor a Vice President elect shall have qualified, declaring who shall then act as President, or the manner in which one who is to act shall be selected, and such person shall act accordingly until a President or Vice President shall have qualified.

### SECTION 4
[ELECTION OF THE PRESIDENT]
The Congress may by law provide for the case of the death of any of the persons from whom the House of Representatives may choose a President whenever the right of choice shall have devolved upon them, and for the case of the death of any of the persons from whom the Senate may choose a Vice President whenever the right of choice shall have devolved upon them.

### SECTION 5
[AMENDMENT TAKES EFFECT]
Sections 1 and 2 shall take effect on the 15th day of October following the ratification of this article.

### SECTION 6
[RATIFICATION WITHIN SEVEN YEARS]
This article shall be inoperative unless it shall have been ratified as an amendment to the Constitution by the legislatures of three-fourths of the several States within seven years from the date of its submission.

## Amendment XXI

[*Proposed by Congress on February 20, 1933;*
*declared ratified on December 5, 1933.*]

### SECTION 1
[NATIONAL LIQUOR PROHIBITION REPEALED]
The eighteenth article of amendment to the Constitution of the United States is hereby repealed.

### SECTION 2
[TRANSPORTATION OF LIQUOR INTO "DRY" STATES]
The transportation or importation into any State, Territory, or Possession of the United States for delivery or use therein of intoxicating liquors, in violation of the laws thereof, is hereby prohibited.

### SECTION 3
[RATIFICATION WITHIN SEVEN YEARS]
This article shall be inoperative unless it shall have been ratified as an amendment to the Constitution by conventions in the several States, as provided in the Constitution, within seven years from the date of the submission hereof to the States by the Congress.

## Amendment XXII

[*Proposed by Congress on March 21, 1947;*
*declared ratified on February 27, 1951.*]

### SECTION 1
[TENURE OF PRESIDENT LIMITED]
No person shall be elected to the office of President more than twice, and no person who has held the office of President or acted as President, for more than two years of a term to which some other person was elected President shall be elected to the office of the President more than once. But this Article shall not apply to any person holding the office of President when this Article was proposed by the Congress, and shall not prevent any person who may be holding the office of President, or acting as President, during the term within which this Article becomes operative from holding the office of President or acting as President during the remainder of such term.

### SECTION 2
[RATIFICATION WITHIN SEVEN YEARS]
This article shall be inoperative unless it shall have been ratified as an amendment to the Constitution by the legislatures of three-fourths of the several States within seven years from the date of its submission to the States by the Congress.

## Amendment XXIII

[*Proposed by Congress on June 16, 1960;*
*declared ratified on March 29, 1961.*]

### SECTION 1

[ELECTORAL COLLEGE VOTES FOR THE DISTRICT OF COLUMBIA]
The District constituting the seat of Government of the United States shall appoint in such manner as the Congress may direct:

A number of electors of President and Vice President equal to the whole number of Senators and Representatives in Congress to which the District would be entitled if it were a State, but in no event more than the least populous State; they shall be in addition to those appointed by the States, but they shall be considered, for the purposes of the election of President and Vice President, to be electors appointed by a State; and they shall meet in the District and perform such duties as provided by the twelfth article of amendment.

### SECTION 2

[POWER TO ENFORCE THIS ARTICLE]
The Congress shall have power to enforce this article by appropriate legislation.

## Amendment XXIV

[*Proposed by Congress on August 27, 1962;*
*declared ratified on January 23, 1964.*]

### SECTION 1

[ANTI-POLL TAX]
The right of citizens of the United States to vote in any primary or other election for President or Vice President, for electors for President or Vice President, or for Senator or Representative of Congress, shall not be denied or abridged by the United States or any State by reason of failure to pay any poll tax or other tax.

### SECTION 2

[POWER TO ENFORCE THIS ARTICLE]
The Congress shall have power to enforce this article by appropriate legislation.

## Amendment XXV

[*Proposed by Congress on July 6, 1965;*
*declared ratified on February 10, 1967.*]

### SECTION 1

[VICE PRESIDENT TO BECOME PRESIDENT]
In case of the removal of the President from office or his death or resignation, the Vice President shall become President.

### SECTION 2

[CHOICE OF A NEW VICE PRESIDENT]
Whenever there is a vacancy in the office of the Vice President, the President shall nominate a Vice President who shall take the office upon confirmation by a majority vote of both houses of Congress.

### SECTION 3

[PRESIDENT MAY DECLARE OWN DISABILITY]
Whenever the President transmits to the President pro tempore of the Senate and the Speaker of the House of Representatives his written declaration that he is unable to discharge the powers and duties of his office, and until he transmits to them a written declaration to the contrary, such powers and duties shall be discharged by the Vice President as Acting President.

### SECTION 4

[ALTERNATE PROCEDURES TO DECLARE AND
TO END PRESIDENTIAL DISABILITY]
Whenever the Vice President and a majority of either the principal officers of the executive departments, or of such other body as Congress may by law provide, transmit to the President pro tempore of the Senate and the Speaker of the House of Representatives their written declaration that the President is unable to discharge the powers and duties of his office, the Vice President shall immediately assume the powers and duties of the office as Acting President.

Thereafter, when the President transmits to the President pro tempore of the Senate and the Speaker of the House of Representatives his written declaration that no inability exists, he shall resume the powers and duties of his office unless the Vice President and a majority of either the principal officers of the executive department, or of such other body as Congress may by law provide, transmit within four days to the President pro tempore of the Senate and the Speaker of the House of Representatives their written declaration that the President is unable to discharge the powers and duties of his office. Thereupon Congress shall decide the issue, assembling within forty eight hours for that purpose if not in session. If the Congress, within twenty one days after receipt of the latter written declaration, or, if Congress is not in session, within twenty one days after Congress is required to assemble, determines by two-thirds vote of both Houses that the President is unable to discharge the powers and duties of his office, the Vice President shall continue to discharge the same as Acting President; otherwise, the President shall resume the powers and duties of his office.

## Amendment XXVI

[*Proposed by Congress on March 23, 1971;
declared ratified on July 1, 1971.*]

### SECTION 1

[EIGHTEEN-YEAR-OLD VOTE]

The right of citizens of the United States, who are eighteen years of age or older, to vote shall not be denied or abridged by the United States or by any State on account of age.

### SECTION 2

[POWER TO ENFORCE THIS ARTICLE]

The Congress shall have power to enforce this article by appropriate legislation.

## Amendment XXVII

[*Proposed by Congress on September 25, 1789;
declared ratified on May 8, 1992.*]

[CONGRESS CANNOT RAISE ITS OWN PAY]

No law varying the compensation for the services of the Senators and Representatives, shall take effect, until an election of representatives shall have intervened.

# The Federalist Papers

## No. 10: Madison

Among the numerous advantages promised by a well constructed Union, none deserves to be more accurately developed than its tendency to break and control the violence of faction. The friend of popular governments never finds himself so much alarmed for their character and fate, as when he contemplates their propensity to this dangerous vice. He will not fail therefore to set a due value on any plan which, without violating the principles to which he is attached, provides a proper cure for it. The instability, injustice, and confusion introduced into the public councils have, in truth, been the mortal diseases under which popular governments have everywhere perished, as they continue to be the favorite and fruitful topics from which the adversaries to liberty derive their most specious declamations. The valuable improvements made by the American constitutions on the popular models, both ancient and modern, cannot certainly be too much admired; but it would be an unwarrantable partiality to contend that they have as effectually obviated the danger on this side, as was wished and expected. Complaints are everywhere heard from our most considerate and virtuous citizens, equally the friends of public and private faith and of public and personal liberty, that our governments are too unstable, that the public good is disregarded in the conflicts of rival parties, and that measures are too often decided, not according to the rules of justice and the rights of the minor party, but by the superior force of an interested and overbearing majority. However anxiously we may wish that these complaints had no foundation, the evidence of known facts will not permit us to deny that they are in some degree true. It will be found, indeed, on a candid review of our situation, that some of the distresses under which we labor have been erroneously charged on the operation of our governments; but it will be found, at the same time, that other causes will not alone account for many of our heaviest misfortunes; and, particularly, for that prevailing and increasing distrust of public engagements and alarm for private rights which are echoed from one end of the continent to the other. These must be chiefly, if not wholly, effects of the unsteadiness and injustice with which a factious spirit has tainted our public administration.

By a faction I understand a number of citizens, whether amounting to a majority or minority of the whole, who are united and actuated by some common impulse of passion, or of interest, adverse to the rights of other citizens, or to the permanent and aggregate interests of the community.

There are two methods of curing the mischiefs of faction: the one, by removing its causes; the other, by controlling its effects.

There are again two methods of removing the causes of faction: the one, by destroying the liberty which is essential to its existence; the other, by giving to every citizen the same opinions, the same passions, and the same interests.

It could never be more truly said than of the first remedy, that it is worse than the disease. Liberty is to faction what air is to fire, an aliment without which it instantly expires. But it could not be a less folly to abolish liberty, which is essential to political life, because it nourishes faction, than it would be to wish the annihilation of air, which is essential to animal life, because it imparts to fire its destructive agency.

The second expedient is as impracticable, as the first would be unwise. As long as the reason of man continues fallible, and he is at liberty to exercise it, different opinions will be formed. As long as the connection subsists between his reason and his self-love, his opinions and his passions will have a reciprocal influence on each other; and the former will be objects to which the latter will attach themselves. The diversity in the faculties of men, from which the rights of property originate, is not less an insuperable obstacle to a uniformity of interests. The protection of these faculties is the first object of Government. From the protection of different and unequal faculties of acquiring property, the possession of different degrees and kinds of property immediately results; and from the influence of these on the sentiments and views of the respective proprietors, ensues a division of the society into different interests and parties.

The latent causes of faction are thus sown in the nature of man; and we see them everywhere brought into different degrees of activity, according to the different circumstances of civil society. A zeal for different opinions concerning religion, concerning Government, and many other points, as well of speculation as of practice; an attachment to different leaders ambitiously contending for pre-eminence and power; or to persons of other descriptions whose fortunes have been interesting to the human passions, have in turn divided mankind into parties, inflamed them with mutual animosity, and rendered them much more disposed to vex and oppress each other, than to co-operate for their common good. So strong is this propensity of mankind to fall into mutual animosities, that where no substantial occasion presents itself, the most frivolous and fanciful distinctions have been sufficient to kindle their unfriendly passions, and excite their most violent conflicts. But the most common and durable source of factions has been the various and unequal distribution of property. Those who hold and those who are without property have ever formed distinct interests in society. Those who are creditors, and those who are debtors, fall under a like discrimination. A landed interest, a manufacturing interest, a mercantile interest, a moneyed interest, with many lesser interests, grow up of necessity in civilized nations, and divide them into different classes, actuated by different sentiments and views. The regulation of these various and interfering interests forms the principal task of modern Legislation, and involves the spirit of party and faction in the necessary and ordinary operations of Government.

No man is allowed to be judge in his own cause, because his interest would certainly bias his judgment and, not improbably, corrupt his integrity. With equal, nay with greater reason, a body of men are unfit to be both judges and parties at the same time; yet what are many of the most important acts of legislation but so many judicial determinations, not indeed concerning the rights of single persons, but concerning the rights of large bodies of citizens; and what are the different classes of legislators but advocates and parties to the causes which they determine? Is a law proposed concerning private debts? It is a question to which the creditors are parties on one side and the debtors on the other. Justice ought to hold the balance between them. Yet the parties are, and must be, themselves the judges; and the most numerous party, or in other words, the most powerful faction must be expected to prevail. Shall domestic manufacturers be encouraged, and in what degree, by restrictions on foreign manufacturers? are questions which would be differently decided by the landed and the manufacturing classes, and probably by neither with a sole regard to justice and the public good. The apportionment of taxes on the various descriptions of property is an act which seems to require the most exact impartiality; yet there is, perhaps, no legislative act in which greater opportunity and temptation are given to a predominant party to trample on the rules of justice. Every shilling with which they overburden the inferior number is a shilling saved to their own pockets.

It is in vain to say that enlightened statesmen will be able to adjust these clashing interests and render them all subservient to the public good. Enlightened statesmen will not always be at the helm. Nor, in many cases, can such an adjustment be made at all without taking into view indirect and remote considerations, which will rarely prevail over the immediate interest which one party may find in disregarding the rights of another or the good of the whole.

The inference to which we are brought is that the *causes* of faction cannot be removed and that relief is only to be sought in the means of controlling its *effects*.

If a faction consists of less than a majority, relief is supplied by the republican principle, which enables the majority to defeat its sinister views by regular vote. It may clog the administration, it may convulse the society; but it will be unable to execute and mask its violence under the forms of the Constitution. When a majority is included in a faction, the form of popular government, on the other hand, enables it to sacrifice to its ruling passion or interest both the public good and the rights of other citizens. To secure the public good and private rights against the danger of such a faction, and at the same time to preserve the spirit and the form of popular government, is then the great object to which our enquiries are directed. Let me add that it is the great desideratum by which alone this form of government can be rescued from the opprobrium under which it has so long labored and be recommended to the esteem and adoption of mankind.

By what means is this object attainable? Evidently by one of two only. Either the existence of the same passion or interest in a majority at the same time must be prevented, or the majority, having such co-existent passion or interest, must be rendered, by their number and local situation, unable to concert and carry into effect schemes of oppression. If the impulse and the opportunity be suffered to coincide, we well know that neither moral nor religious motives can be relied on as an adequate control. They are not found to be such on the injustice and violence of individuals, and lose their efficacy in proportion to the number combined together, that is, in proportion as their efficacy becomes needful.

From this view of the subject it may be concluded that a pure Democracy, by which I mean a Society consisting of a small number of citizens, who assemble and administer the Government in person, can admit of no cure for the mischiefs of faction. A common passion or interest will, in almost every case, be felt by a majority of the whole; a communication and concert results from the form of Government itself; and there is nothing to check the inducements to sacrifice the weaker party or an obnoxious individual. Hence it is that such Democracies have ever been spectacles of turbulence and contention; have ever been found incompatible with personal security or the rights of property; and have in general been as short in their lives as they have been violent in their deaths. Theoretic politicians, who have patronized this species of Government, have erroneously supposed that by reducing mankind to a perfect equality in their political rights, they would at the same time be perfectly equalized and assimilated in their possessions, their opinions, and their passions.

A Republic, by which I mean a Government in which the scheme of representation takes place, opens a different prospect and promises the cure for which we are seeking. Let us examine the points in which it varies from pure Democracy, and we shall comprehend both the nature of the cure and the efficacy which it must derive from the Union.

The two great points of difference between a Democracy and a Republic are: first, the delegation of the Government, in the latter, to a small number of citizens elected by the rest; secondly, the greater number of citizens and greater sphere of country over which the latter may be extended.

The effect of the first difference is, on the one hand, to refine and enlarge the public views by passing them through the medium of a chosen body of citizens, whose wisdom may best discern the true interest of their country and whose patriotism and love of justice will be least likely to sacrifice it to temporary or partial considerations. Under such a regulation it may well happen that the public voice, pronounced by the representatives of the people, will be more consonant to the public good than if pronounced by the people themselves, convened for the purpose. On the other hand, the effect may be inverted. Men of factious tempers, of local prejudices, or of sinister designs, may, by intrigue, by corruption, or by other means, first obtain the suffrages, and then betray the interests of the people. The question resulting is, whether small or extensive Republics are most favorable to the election of proper guardians of the public weal; and it is clearly decided in favor of the latter by two obvious considerations.

In the first place it is to be remarked that however small the Republic may be, the Representatives must be raised to a certain number in order to guard against the cabals of a few; and that however large it may be they must be limited to a certain number in order to guard against the confusion of a multitude. Hence, the number of Representatives in the two cases not being in proportion to that of the Constituents, and being proportionally greatest in the small Republic, it follows that if the proportion of fit characters be not less in the large than in the small Republic, the former will present a greater option, and consequently a greater probability of a fit choice.

In the next place, as each Representative will be chosen by a greater number of citizens in the large than in the small Republic, it will be more difficult for unworthy candidates to practise with success the vicious arts by which elections are too often carried; and the suffrages of the people being more free, will be more likely to centre on men who possess the most attractive merit and the most diffusive and established characters.

It must be confessed that in this, as in most other cases, there is a mean, on both sides of which inconveniencies will be found to lie. By enlarging too much the number of electors, you render the representative too little acquainted with all their local circumstances and lesser interests; as by reducing it too much, you render him unduly attached to these, and too little fit to comprehend and pursue great and national objects. The Federal Constitution forms a happy combination in this respect; the great and aggregate interests being referred to the national, the local and particular to the State legislatures.

The other point of difference is the greater number of citizens and extent of territory which may be brought within the compass of Republican than of Democratic Government; and it is this circumstance principally which renders factious combinations less to be dreaded in the former than in the latter. The smaller the society, the fewer probably will be the distinct parties and interests composing it; the fewer the distinct parties and interests, the more frequently will a majority be found of the same party; and the smaller the number of individuals composing a majority, and the smaller the compass within which they are placed, the more easily will they concert and execute their plans of oppression. Extend the sphere and you take in a greater variety of parties and interests; you make it less probable that a majority of the whole will have a common motive to invade the rights of other citizens; or if such a common motive exists, it will be more difficult for all who feel it to discover their own strength and to act in unison with each other. Besides other impediments, it may be remarked, that where there is a consciousness of unjust or dishonorable purposes, communication is always checked by distrust in proportion to the number whose concurrence is necessary.

Hence, it clearly appears that the same advantage which a Republic has over a Democracy in controlling the effects of faction is enjoyed by a large over a small republic—is enjoyed by the Union over the States composing it. Does this advantage consist in the substitution of representatives whose enlightened views and virtuous sentiments render them superior to local prejudices and to schemes of injustice? It will not be denied that the representation of the Union will be most likely to possess these requisite endowments. Does it consist in the greater security afforded by a greater variety of parties, against the event of any one party being able to outnumber and oppress the rest? In an equal degree does the increased variety of parties comprised within the Union increase this security? Does it, in fine, consist in the greater obstacles opposed to the concert and accomplishment of the secret wishes of an unjust and interested majority? Here again the extent of the Union gives it the most palpable advantage.

The influence of factious leaders may kindle a flame within their particular States but will be unable to spread a general conflagration through the other States: a religious sect may degenerate into a political faction in a part of the Confederacy; but the variety of sects dispersed over the entire face of it must secure the national Councils against any danger from that source: a rage for paper money, for an abolition of debts, for an equal division of property, or for any other improper or wicked project, will be less apt to pervade the whole body of the Union than a particular member of it; in the same proportion as such a malady is more likely to taint a particular county or district than an entire State.

In the extent and proper structure of the Union, therefore, we behold a republican remedy for the diseases most incident to Republican Government. And according to the degree of pleasure and pride we feel in being republicans ought to be our zeal in cherishing the spirit and supporting the character of federalist.

PUBLIUS

## No. 51: Madison

To what expedient, then, shall we finally resort, for maintaining in practice the necessary partition of power among the several departments as laid down in the constitution? The only answer that can be given is that as all these exterior provisions are found to be inadequate the defect must be supplied, by so contriving the interior structure of the government as that its several constituent parts may, by their mutual relations, be the means of keeping each other in their proper places. Without presuming to undertake a full development of this important idea I will hazard a few general observations which may perhaps place it in a clearer light, and enable us to form a more correct judgment of the principles and structure of the government planned by the convention.

In order to lay a due foundation for that separate and distinct exercise of the different powers of government, which to a certain extent is admitted on all hands to be essential to the preservation of liberty, it is evident that each department should have a will of its own; and consequently should be so constituted that the members of each should have as little agency as possible in the appointment of the members of the others. Were this principle rigorously adhered to, it would require that all the appointments for the supreme executive, legislative, and judiciary magistracies should be drawn from the same fountain of authority, the people, through channels having no communication whatever with one another. Perhaps such a plan of constructing the several departments would be less difficult in practice than it may in contemplation appear. Some difficulties, however, and some additional expense would attend the execution of it. Some deviations, therefore, from the principle must be admitted. In the constitution of the judiciary department in particular, it might be inexpedient to insist rigorously on the principle: first, because peculiar qualifications being essential in the members, the primary consideration ought to be to select that mode of choice which best secures these qualifications; second, because the permanent tenure by which the appointments are held in that department must soon destroy all sense of dependence on the authority conferring them.

It is equally evident that the members of each department should be as little dependent as possible on those of the others for the emoluments annexed to their offices. Were the executive magistrate, or the judges, not independent of the legislature in this particular, their independence in every other would be merely nominal.

But the great security against a gradual concentration of the several powers in the same department consists in giving to those who administer each department the necessary constitutional means and personal motives to resist encroachments of the others. The provision for defence must in this, as in all other cases, be made commensurate to the danger of attack. Ambition must be made to counteract ambition. The interest of the man must be connected with the constitutional rights of the place. It may be a reflection on human nature that such devices should be necessary to control the abuses of government. But what is government itself but the greatest of all reflections on human nature? If men were angels, no government would be necessary. If angels were to govern men, neither external nor internal controls on government would be necessary. In framing a government which is to be administered by men over men, the great difficulty lies in this: You must first enable the government to control the governed; and in the next place

oblige it to control itself. A dependence on the people is, no doubt, the primary control on the government; but experience has taught mankind the necessity of auxiliary precautions.

This policy of supplying, by opposite and rival interests, the defect of better motives, might be traced through the whole system of human affairs, private as well as public. We see it particularly displayed in all the subordinate distributions of power, where the constant aim is to divide and arrange the several offices in such a manner as that each may be a check on the other; that the private interest of every individual may be a sentinel over the public rights. These inventions of prudence cannot be less requisite in the distribution of the supreme powers of the State.

But it is not possible to give to each department an equal power of self-defense. In republican government, the legislative authority necessarily predominates. The remedy for this inconveniency is to divide the legislature into different branches; and to render them, by different modes of election and different principles of action, as little connected with each other as the nature of their common functions and their common dependence on the society will admit. It may even be necessary to guard against dangerous encroachments by still further precautions. As the weight of the legislative authority requires that it should be thus divided, the weakness of the executive may require, on the other hand, that it should be fortified. An absolute negative on the legislature appears, at first view, to be the natural defense with which the executive magistrate should be armed. But perhaps it would be neither altogether safe nor alone sufficient. On ordinary occasions it might not be exerted with the requisite firmness, and on extraordinary occasions it might be perfidiously abused. May not this defect of an absolute negative be supplied by some qualified connection between this weaker branch of the stronger department, by which the latter may be led to support the constitutional rights of the former, without being too much detached from the rights of its own department?

If the principles on which these observations are founded be just, as I persuade myself they are, and they be applied as a criterion to the several State constitutions, and to the federal Constitution, it will be found that if the latter does not perfectly correspond with them, the former are infinitely less able to bear such a test.

There are, moreover, two considerations particularly applicable to the federal system of America, which place that system in a very interesting point of view.

*First.* In a single republic, all the power surrendered by the people is submitted to the administration of a single government; and usurpations are guarded against by a division of the government into distinct and separate departments. In the compound republic of America, the power surrendered by the people is first divided between two distinct governments, and then the portion allotted to each subdivided among distinct and separate departments. Hence a double security arises to the rights of the people. The different governments will control each other, at the same time that each will be controlled by itself.

*Second.* It is of great importance in a republic not only to guard the society against the oppression of its rulers, but to guard one part of the society against the injustice of the other part. Different interests necessarily exist in different classes of citizens. If a majority be united by a common interest, the rights of the minority will be insecure. There are but two methods of providing against this evil: The one by creating a will in the community independent of the majority—that is, of the society itself; the other, by comprehending in the society so many separate descriptions of citizens as will render an unjust combination of a majority of the whole very improbable, if not impracticable. The first method prevails in all governments possessing an hereditary or self-appointed authority. This, at best, is but a precarious security; because a power independent of the society may as well espouse the unjust views of the major as the rightful interests of the minor party, and may possibly be turned against both parties. The second method will be exemplified in the federal republic of the United States. Whilst all authority in it will be derived from and dependent on the society, the society itself will be broken into so many parts, interests and classes of citizens, that the rights of individuals, or of the minority, will be in little danger from interested combinations of the majority. In a free government the security for civil rights must be the same as that for religious rights. It consists in the one case in the multiplicity of interests, and in the other in the multiplicity of sects. The degree of security in both cases will depend on the number of interests and sects; and this may be presumed to depend on the extent of country and number of people comprehended under the same government. This view of the subject must particularly recommend a proper federal system to all the sincere and considerate friends of republican government: Since it shows that in exact proportion as the territory of the Union may be formed into more circumscribed Confederacies, or States, oppressive combinations of a majority will be facilitated; the best security, under the republican form, for the rights of every class of citizens, will be diminished; and consequently the stability and independence of some member of the government, the only other security, must be proportionally increased. Justice is the end of government. It is the end of civil society. It ever has been and ever will be pursued until it be obtained, or until liberty be lost in the pursuit. In a society under the forms of which the stronger faction can readily unite and oppress the weaker, anarchy may as truly be said to reign as in a state of nature, where the weaker individual is not secured against the violence of the stronger: And as, in the latter state, even the stronger individuals are prompted, by the uncertainty of their condition, to submit to a government which may protect the weak as well as themselves: So, in the former state, will the more powerful factions or parties be gradually induced, by a like motive, to wish for a government which will protect all parties, the weaker as well as the more powerful. It can be little doubted that if the State of Rhode Island was separated from the Confederacy and left to itself, the insecurity of rights under the popular form of government within such narrow limits would be displayed by such reiterated oppressions of factious majorities that some power altogether independent of the people would soon be called for by the voice of the very factions whose misrule had proved the necessity of it. In the extended republic of the United States, and among the great variety of interests, parties, and sects which it embraces, a coalition of a majority of the whole society could seldom take place on any other principles than those of justice and the general good; and there being thus less danger to a minor from the will of the major party, there must be less pretext, also, to provide for the security of the former, by introducing into the government a will not dependent on the latter, or, in other words, a will independent of the society itself. It is no less certain than it is important, notwithstanding the contrary opinions which have been entertained, that the larger the society, provided it lie within a practicable sphere, the more duly capable it will be of self-government. And happily for the *republican cause*, practicable sphere may be carried to a very great extent by a judicious modification and mixture of the *federal principle*.

PUBLIUS

# Presidents and Vice Presidents

| | PRESIDENT | VICE PRESIDENT | | PRESIDENT | VICE PRESIDENT |
|---|---|---|---|---|---|
| 1 | George Washington *(Federalist 1789)* | John Adams *(Federalist 1789)* | 12 | Zachary Taylor *(Whig 1849)* | Millard Fillmore *(Whig 1849)* |
| 2 | John Adams *(Federalist 1797)* | Thomas Jefferson *(Dem.-Rep. 1797)* | 13 | Millard Fillmore *(Whig 1850)* | |
| 3 | Thomas Jefferson *(Dem.-Rep. 1801)* | Aaron Burr *(Dem.-Rep. 1801)* | 14 | Franklin Pierce *(Democratic 1853)* | William R. D. King *(Democratic 1853)* |
| | | George Clinton *(Dem.-Rep. 1805)* | 15 | James Buchanan *(Democratic 1857)* | John C. Breckinridge *(Democratic 1857)* |
| 4 | James Madison *(Dem.-Rep. 1809)* | George Clinton *(Dem.-Rep. 1809)* | 16 | Abraham Lincoln *(Republican 1861)* | Hannibal Hamlin *(Republican 1861)* |
| | | Elbridge Gerry *(Dem.-Rep. 1813)* | | | Andrew Johnson *(Unionist 1865)* |
| 5 | James Monroe *(Dem.-Rep. 1817)* | Daniel D. Tompkins *(Dem.-Rep. 1817)* | 17 | Andrew Johnson *(Unionist 1865)* | |
| 6 | John Quincy Adams *(Dem.-Rep. 1825)* | John C. Calhoun *(Dem.-Rep. 1825)* | 18 | Ulysses S. Grant *(Republican 1869)* | Schuyler Colfax *(Republican 1869)* |
| 7 | Andrew Jackson *(Democratic 1829)* | John C. Calhoun *(Democratic 1829)* | | | Henry Wilson *(Republican 1873)* |
| | | Martin Van Buren *(Democratic 1833)* | 19 | Rutherford B. Hayes *(Republican 1877)* | William A. Wheeler *(Republican 1877)* |
| 8 | Martin Van Buren *(Democratic 1837)* | Richard M. Johnson *(Democratic 1837)* | 20 | James A. Garfield *(Republican 1881)* | Chester A. Arthur *(Republican 1881)* |
| 9 | William H. Harrison *(Whig 1841)* | John Tyler *(Whig 1841)* | 21 | Chester A. Arthur *(Republican 1881)* | |
| 10 | John Tyler *(Whig and Democratic 1841)* | | 22 | Grover Cleveland *(Democratic 1885)* | Thomas A. Hendricks *(Democratic 1885)* |
| 11 | James K. Polk *(Democratic 1845)* | George M. Dallas *(Democratic 1845)* | 23 | Benjamin Harrison *(Republican 1889)* | Levi P. Morton *(Republican 1889)* |

| | PRESIDENT | VICE PRESIDENT | | PRESIDENT | VICE PRESIDENT |
|---|---|---|---|---|---|
| 24 | Grover Cleveland *(Democratic 1893)* | Adlai E. Stevenson *(Democratic 1893)* | 34 | Dwight D. Eisenhower *(Republican 1953)* | Richard M. Nixon *(Republican 1953)* |
| 25 | William McKinley *(Republican 1897)* | Garret A. Hobart *(Republican 1897)* | 35 | John F. Kennedy *(Democratic 1961)* | Lyndon B. Johnson *(Democratic 1961)* |
| | | Theodore Roosevelt *(Republican 1901)* | 36 | Lyndon B. Johnson *(Democratic 1963)* | Hubert H. Humphrey *(Democratic 1965)* |
| 26 | Theodore Roosevelt *(Republican 1901)* | Charles W. Fairbanks *(Republican 1905)* | 37 | Richard M. Nixon *(Republican 1969)* | Spiro T. Agnew *(Republican 1969)* |
| 27 | William H. Taft *(Republican 1909)* | James S. Sherman *(Republican 1909)* | | | Gerald R. Ford *(Republican 1973)* |
| 28 | Woodrow Wilson *(Democratic 1913)* | Thomas R. Marshall *(Democratic 1913)* | 38 | Gerald R. Ford *(Republican 1974)* | Nelson Rockefeller *(Republican 1974)* |
| 29 | Warren G. Harding *(Republican 1921)* | Calvin Coolidge *(Republican 1921)* | 39 | James E. Carter *(Democratic 1977)* | Walter Mondale *(Democratic 1977)* |
| 30 | Calvin Coolidge *(Republican 1923)* | Charles G. Dawes *(Republican 1925)* | 40 | Ronald Reagan *(Republican 1981)* | George H. W. Bush *(Republican 1981)* |
| 31 | Herbert Hoover *(Republican 1929)* | Charles Curtis *(Republican 1929)* | 41 | George H. W. Bush *(Republican 1989)* | J. Danforth Quayle *(Republican 1989)* |
| 32 | Franklin D. Roosevelt *(Democratic 1933)* | John Nance Garner *(Democratic 1933)* | 42 | William J. Clinton *(Democratic 1993)* | Albert Gore, Jr. *(Democratic 1993)* |
| | | Henry A. Wallace *(Democratic 1941)* | 43 | George W. Bush *(Republican 2001)* | Richard Cheney *(Republican 2001)* |
| | | Harry S. Truman *(Democratic 1945)* | 44 | Barack H. Obama *(Democratic 2009)* | Joseph R. Biden, Jr. *(Democratic 2009)* |
| 33 | Harry S. Truman *(Democratic 1945)* | Alben W. Barkley *(Democratic 1949)* | | | |

# glossary

**action by the governor** the final step in the legislative process, during which the governor signs, vetoes, or refuses to sign a bill

**affirmative action** government policies or programs that seek to redress past injustices against specified groups by making special efforts to provide members of those groups with access to educational and employment opportunities

**agency representation** the type of representation in which a representative is held accountable to a constituency if he or she fails to represent that constituency properly. This is incentive for good representation when the personal backgrounds, views, and interests of the representative differ from those of his or her constituency

**agenda setting** the power of the media to bring public attention to particular issues and problems

**agents of socialization** social institutions, including families and schools, that help to shape individuals' basic political beliefs and values

**agricultural commissioner** elected state official who is primarily responsible for enforcing agricultural laws

**Aid to Families with Dependent Children (AFDC)** a federally and state-financed program for children living with parents or relatives who fell below state standards of need. Replaced in 1996 by TANF

**amendment** a change added to a bill, law, or constitution

**amicus curiae** literally, "friend of the court"; individuals or groups who are not parties to a lawsuit but who seek to assist the Supreme Court in reaching a decision by presenting additional briefs

**answer** the presentation of a defendant's defense against an allegation in a civil case

**Antifederalists** those who favored strong state governments and a weak national government and who were opponents of the Constitution proposed at the American Constitutional Convention of 1787

**antitrust policy** government regulation of large businesses that have established monopolies

**appeasement** the effort to forestall war by giving in to the demands of a hostile power

**appointment** the power of the chief executive, whether the president of the United States or the governor of a state, to appoint persons to office

**apportionment** the process, occurring after every decennial census, that allocates congressional seats among the 50 states

**appropriations** the amounts of money approved by Congress in statutes (bills) that each unit or agency of government can spend

**appropriations (Texas)** the amounts of money approved by the state legislature in statutes that each unit or agency of government can spend

**Articles of Confederation** America's first written constitution; served as the basis for America's national government until 1789

**at-large election** an election in which officials are selected by voters of the entire geographical area, rather than from smaller districts within that area

**attitude (or opinion)** a specific preference on a particular issue

**attorney general** elected state official who serves as the state's chief civil lawyer

**authoritarian government** a system of rule in which the government recognizes no formal limits but may nevertheless be restrained by the power of other social institutions

**autocracy** a form of government in which a single individual—a king, queen, or dictator—rules

**ballot initiative** a proposed law or policy change that is placed on the ballot by citizens or interest groups for a popular vote

**bandwagon effect** a shift in electoral support to the candidate whom public opinion polls report as the front-runner

**bench trial** a trial held without a jury and before only a judge

**beyond a reasonable doubt** the legal standard in criminal cases, which requires the prosecution to prove that a reasonable doubt of innocence does not exist

**bicameral** having a legislative assembly composed of two chambers or houses; distinguished from *unicameral*

**biennial** occurring every two years

**bilateral treaties**   treaties made between two nations

**bill**   a proposed law that has been sponsored by a member of Congress and submitted to the clerk of the House or Senate

**bill of attainder**   a law that declares a person guilty of a crime without a trial

**Bill of Rights**   the first 10 amendments to the U.S. Constitution, ratified in 1791; they ensure certain rights and liberties to the people

**block grants**   federal grants-in-aid that allow states considerable discretion in how the funds are spent

**briefs**   written documents in which attorneys explain, using case precedents, why the court should find in favor of their client

**broadcast media**   television, radio, or other media that transmit audio and/or video content to the public

***Brown v. Board of Education***   the 1954 Supreme Court decision that struck down the "separate but equal" doctrine as fundamentally unequal. This case eliminated state power to use race as a criterion of discrimination in law and provided the national government with the power to intervene by exercising strict regulatory policies against discriminatory actions

**budget deficit**   amount by which government spending exceeds government revenue in a fiscal year

**bundling**   the interest-group practice of combining campaign contributions from several sources into one larger contribution from the group, so as to increase the group's impact on the candidate

**bureaucracy**   the complex structure of offices, tasks, rules, and principles of organization that are employed by all large-scale institutions to coordinate the work of their personnel

**Bush Doctrine**   foreign policy based on the idea that the United States should take preemptive action against threats to its national security

**Cabinet**   the secretaries, or chief administrators, of the major departments of the federal government. Cabinet secretaries are appointed by the president with the consent of the Senate

**campaign**   an effort by political candidates and their supporters to win the backing of donors, political activists, and voters in their quest for political office

**capital case**   a criminal case that calls for the death penalty

**categorical grants**   congressional grants given to states and localities on the condition that expenditures be limited to a problem or group specified by law

**caucus (political)**   a normally closed political party business meeting of citizens or law makers to select candidates, elect officers, plan strategy, or make decisions regarding legislative matters

**caucuses (congressional)**   associations of members of Congress based on party, interest, or social group, such as gender or race

**checks and balances**   mechanisms through which each branch of government is able to participate in and influence the activities of the other branches; major examples include the presidential veto power over congressional legislation, the power of the Senate to approve presidential appointments, and judicial review of congressional enactments

**chief justice**   justice on the Supreme Court who presides over the Court's public sessions and whose official title is chief justice of the United States

**citizen journalism**   news reported and distributed by citizens, rather than professional journalists and for-profit news organizations

**citizenship**   informed and active membership in a political community

**civil law**   a branch of law that deals with disputes that do not involve criminal penalties

**civil liberties**   areas of personal freedom with which governments are constrained from interfering

**civil rights**   obligation imposed on government to take positive action to protect citizens from any illegal action of government agencies and of other private citizens

**class-action suit**   a legal action by which a group or class of individuals with common interests can file a suit on behalf of everyone who shares that interest

**"clear and present danger" test**   test to determine whether speech is protected or unprotected, based on its capacity to present a "clear and present danger" to society

**closed primary**   a primary election in which voters can participate in the nomination of candidates, but only of the party in which they are enrolled for a period of time prior to primary day

**closed rule**   a provision by the House Rules Committee limiting or prohibiting the introduction of amendments during debate

**cloture**   a rule allowing a majority of two-thirds or three-fifths of the members of a legislative body to set a time limit on debate over a given bill. In the U.S. Senate, 60 senators (three-fifths) must agree in order to impose such a limit.

**coattail effect**   the result of voters casting their ballot for president or governor and "automatically" voting for the remainder of the party's ticket

**Cold War**   the period of struggle between the United States and the former Soviet Union lasting from the late 1940s to about 1990

**collective goods**   benefits, sought by groups, that are broadly available and cannot be denied to nonmembers

**commander in chief**   the role of the president as commander of the national military and the state National Guard units (when called into service)

**commerce clause**   Article I, Section 8, of the Constitution, which delegates to Congress the power "to regulate commerce with foreign nations, and among the several States and with the Indian tribes." This clause was interpreted by the Supreme Court in favor of national power over the economy

**commissioner form of government**   a form of city government in which the city is run by a small group of elected commissioners who act in both legislative and executive capacities

**committee markup** the session in which a congressional committee rewrites legislation to incorporate changes discussed during hearings on the bill

**common law** law made through court precedent rather than legislative enactments

**complaint** the presentation of a grievance by the plaintiff in a civil case

**comptroller** elected state official who directs the collection of taxes and other revenues

**concurrent powers** authority possessed by *both* state and national governments, such as the power to levy taxes

**concurrent resolution** a resolution of interest to both chambers of the legislature and which must pass both the House and Senate and generally be signed by the governor

**Confederacy** the Confederate States of America, those southern states that seceded from the United States in late 1860 and 1861 and argued that the power of the states was more important than the power of the central government

**confederation** a system of government in which states retain sovereign authority except for the powers expressly delegated to the national government

**conference** a gathering of House Republicans every two years to elect their House leaders. Democrats call their gathering the caucus

**conference committee** a joint committee created to work out a compromise on House and Senate versions of a piece of legislation

**conservative** today this term refers to those who generally support the social and economic status quo and are suspicious of efforts to introduce new political formulae and economic arrangements. Conservatives believe that a large and powerful government poses a threat to citizens' freedom

**consideration by standing committee** the third step in the legislative process, during which a bill is killed, amended, or heard by a standing committee

**constable** precinct-level county official involved with serving legal papers and, in some counties, enforcing the law

**constituency** the residents in the area from which an official is elected

**constituent** a person living in the district from which an official is elected

**constitution** the legal structure of a government, which establishes its power and authority as well as the limits on that power

**constitutional county courts** the courts that exist in some counties that are presided over by county judges

**constitutional government** a system of rule in which formal and effective limits are placed on the powers of the government

**contingent fee** a fee paid to the lawyer in a civil case and which is contingent on winning the case

**contracting power** the power of government to set conditions on companies seeking to sell goods or services to government agencies

**contributory programs** social programs financed in whole or in part by taxation or other mandatory contributions by their present or future recipients

**cooperative federalism** a type of federalism existing since the New Deal era in which grants-in-aid have been used strategically to encourage states and localities (without commanding them) to pursue nationally defined goals. Also known as "intergovernmental cooperation"

**cost-of-living adjustments (COLAs)** changes made to the level of benefits of a government program based on the rate of inflation

**council of government (COG)** a regional planning board composed of local elected officials and some private citizens from the same area

**council-manager form of government** a form of city government in which public policies are developed by the city council and executive and administrative functions are assigned to a professional city manager

**county attorney** county official who prosecutes lesser criminal cases in the county court

**county auditor** public official, appointed by the district judges, who receives and disburses county funds; in large counties, this official also prepares the county budget

**county chair** the county party official, who heads the county executive committee

**county clerk** public official who is the main record-keeper of the county

**county commissioner** government official (four per county) on the county commissioners court whose main duty is the construction and maintenance of roads and bridges

**county commissioners court** the main governing body of each county; has the authority to set the county tax rate and budget

**county convention** a meeting held by a political party following its precinct conventions, for the purpose of electing delegates to its state convention

**county executive committee** the party group, made up of a party's county chair and precinct chairs, that is responsible for running a county's primary elections and planning county conventions

**county judge** the person in each of Texas's 254 counties who presides over the constitutional county court and the county commissioners court, with responsibility for the administration of county government; only constitutional some county judges carry out judicial responsibilities

**county tax assessor-collector** public official who maintains the county tax records and collects the taxes owed to the county

**court of appeals** a court that hears appeals of trial court decisions

**courts of appeal (Texas)** the fourteen intermediate-level appellate courts that hear appeals from district and county courts to determine whether the decisions of these lower courts followed legal principles and court procedures

**criminal law** the branch of law that regulates the conduct of individuals, defines crimes, and specifies punishment for criminal acts

**de facto** literally, "by fact"; refers to practices that occur even when there is no legal enforcement, such as school segregation in much of the United States today

**de jure** literally, "by law"; refers to legally enforced practices, such as school segregation in the South before the 1960s

**debt service** the amount of a budget spent by a government on paying interest on its debt

**dedicated funds** a portion of the state budget that is dedicated to mandatory spending on programs such as health care for the poor

**defendant** the one against whom a complaint is brought in a criminal or civil case

**deficit** the total amount the government owes its creditors

**delegate** a representative who votes according to the preferences of his or her constituency

**delegated powers** constitutional powers that are assigned to one governmental agency but that are exercised by another agency with the express permission of the first

**democracy** a system of rule that permits citizens to play a significant part in the governmental process, usually through the election of key public officials

**department** the largest subunit of the executive branch. The secretaries of the 15 departments form the Cabinet.

**deregulation** a policy of reducing or eliminating regulatory restraints on the conduct of individuals or private institutions

**deterrence** the development and maintenance of military strength as a means of discouraging attack

**devolution** a policy to remove a program from one level of government by delegating it or passing it down to a lower level of government, such as from the national government to the state and local governments

**digital citizen** a daily Internet user with regular access to high-speed Internet connections and the technology and literacy skills to participate online for employment, news, politics, entertainment, commerce, and other activities

**diplomacy** the representation of a government to other governments

**direct democracy** a system of rule that permits citizens to vote directly on laws and policies

**directive and supervisory power** the legislature's power over the executive branch; for example, the legislature determines the size of appropriations for state agencies

**discretionary spending** federal spending on programs that are controlled through the regular budget process

**discrimination** the use of any unreasonable and unjust criterion of exclusion

**dissenting opinion** a decision written by a justice in the minority in a particular case in which the justice wishes to express his or her reasoning in the case

**district attorney** public official who prosecutes the more serious criminal cases in the district court

**district clerk** public official who is the main record-keeper of the district court

**district courts** the major trial courts in Texas, which usually have general jurisdiction over a broad range of civil and criminal cases

**divided government** the condition in American government wherein the presidency is controlled by one party while the opposing party controls one or both houses of Congress

**double jeopardy** the Fifth Amendment right providing that a person cannot be tried twice for the same crime

**dual federalism** the system of government that prevailed in the United States from 1789 to 1937, in which most fundamental governmental powers were shared between the federal and state governments

**due process of law** the right of every citizen against arbitrary action by national or state governments

**early registration** the requirement that a voter register long before the general election; in effect in Texas until 1971

**early voting** the option in some states to cast a vote at a polling place or by mail before the election

**early voting (Texas)** a procedure that allows voters to cast ballots during the two-week period before the regularly scheduled election date

**elastic clause** Article I, Section 8, of the Constitution (also known as the necessary and proper clause), which enumerates the powers of Congress and provides Congress with the authority to make all laws "necessary and proper" to carry them out

**Election-Day registration** the option in some states to register on the day of the election, at the polling place, rather than in advance of the election

**electoral college** the presidential electors from each state who meet after the popular election to cast ballots for president and vice president

**electoral power** the legislature's mandated role in counting returns in the elections for governor and lieutenant governor

**electoral realignment** the point in history when a new party supplants the ruling party, becoming in turn the dominant political force; in the United States, this has tended to occur roughly every 30 years

**elite** a small group of people that dominates the political process

**eminent domain** the right of government to take private property for public use

**en banc** referring to an appellate hearing with all judges participating

**entitlement** a legal obligation of the federal government to provide payments to individuals, or groups of individuals, according to eligibility criteria or benefit rules

**equal protection clause** provision of the Fourteenth Amendment guaranteeing citizens "the equal protection of the laws." This clause has been the basis for the civil rights of African Americans, women, and other groups

**equal time rule** the requirement that broadcasters provide candidates for the same political office equal opportunities to communicate their messages to the public

**equality of opportunity** a widely shared American ideal that all people should have the freedom to use whatever talents and wealth they have to reach their fullest potential

**establishment clause** the First Amendment clause that says that "Congress shall make no law respecting an establishment of religion." This law means that a "wall of separation" exists between church and state

**ex post facto laws** laws that declare an action to be illegal after it has been committed

**exclusionary rule** the ability of courts to exclude evidence obtained in violation of the Fourth Amendment

**executive agreement** an agreement, made between the U.S. president and another country, that has the force of a treaty but does not require the Senate's "advice and consent"

**executive budget** the state budget prepared and submitted by the governor to the legislature, which indicates the governor's spending priorities. The executive budget is overshadowed in terms of importance by the legislative budget

**Executive Office of the President (EOP)** the permanent agencies that perform defined management tasks for the president. Created in 1939, the EOP includes the OMB, the CEA, the NSC, and other agencies

**executive order** a rule or regulation issued by the president that has the effect and formal status of legislation

**executive privilege** the claim that confidential communications between a president and close advisers should not be revealed without the consent of the president

**expressed powers** specific powers granted by the Constitution to Congress (Article I, Section 8) and to the president (Article II)

**fairness doctrine** a Federal Communications Commission requirement for broadcasters who air programs on controversial issues to provide time for opposing views; the FCC ceased enforcing this doctrine in 1985

**federal funds rate** the interest rate on loans between banks that the Federal Reserve Board influences by affecting the supply of money available

**Federal Reserve System** a system of 12 Federal Reserve banks that facilitates exchanges of cash, checks, and credit; regulates member banks; and uses monetary policies to fight inflation and deflation

**federal system** a system of government in which the national government shares power with lower levels of government, such as states

**federalism** a system of government in which power is divided, by a constitution, between a central government and regional governments

**Federalist Papers** a series of essays written by Alexander Hamilton, James Madison, and John Jay supporting ratification of the Constitution

**Federalists** those who favored a strong national government and supported the Constitution proposed at the American Constitutional Convention of 1787

**felony** a serious criminal offense, punishable by a prison sentence or a fine. A capital felony is punishable by death.

**Fifteenth Amendment** one of three Civil War amendments; it guaranteed voting rights for African American men

**fighting words** speech that directly incites damaging conduct

**filibuster** a tactic used by members of the Senate to prevent action on legislation they oppose by continuously holding the floor and speaking until the majority backs down. Once given the floor, senators have unlimited time to speak, and it requires a vote of three-fifths of the Senate to end a filibuster

**fiscal policy** the government's use of taxing, monetary, and spending powers to manipulate the economy

**501c(4) committees** nonprofit groups that also engage in issue advocacy. Under Section 501c(4) of the federal tax code such a group may spend up to half its revenue for political purposes

**527 committees** nonprofit independent groups that receive and disburse funds to influence the nomination, election, or defeat of candidates. Named after Section 527 of the Internal Revenue Code, which defines and grants tax-exempt status to nonprofit advocacy groups

**floor action** the fourth step in the legislative process, during which a bill referred by a standing committee is scheduled for floor debate by the Calendars Committee

**formula grants** grants-in-aid in which a formula is used to determine the amount of federal funds a state or local government will receive

**Fourteenth Amendment** one of three Civil War amendments; it guaranteed equal protection and due process

**framing** the power of the media to influence how events and issues are interpreted

**free exercise clause** the First Amendment clause that protects a citizen's right to believe and practice whatever religion he or she chooses

**free riders** those who enjoy the benefits of collective goods but did not participate in acquiring them

**full faith and credit clause** provision, from Article IV, Section 1, of the Constitution, requiring that the states normally honor the public acts and judicial decisions that take place in another state

**gender gap** a distinctive pattern of voting behavior reflecting the differences in views between women and men

**General Agreement on Tariffs and Trade (GATT)** international trade organization, in existence from 1947 to 1995, that set many of the rules governing international trade

**general bill** a bill that applies to all people and/or property in the state

**general election** a regularly scheduled election involving most districts in the nation or state, in which voters select officeholders; in the United States, general elections for national office and most state and local offices are held on the first Tuesday following the first Monday in November in even-numbered years (every four years for presidential elections)

**general election (Texas)** a decisive election that determines who is elected to office

**gerrymandering** the apportionment of voters in districts in such a way as to give unfair advantage to one racial or ethnic group or political party

**Gilmer-Aikin Laws** education reform legislation passed in 1949 that supplemented local funding of education with state monies, raised teachers' salaries, mandated a minimum length for the school year, and provided more state supervision of public education

**government** institutions and procedures through which a territory and its people are ruled

**government corporation** government agency that performs a service normally provided by the private sector

**grand jury** jury that determines whether sufficient evidence is available to justify a trial; grand juries do not rule on the accused's guilt or innocence

**Grange** a militant farmers' movement of the late nineteenth century that fought for improved conditions for farmers

**grants-in-aid** programs through which Congress provides money to state and local governments on the condition that the funds be employed for purposes defined by the federal government

**grassroots mobilization** a lobbying campaign in which a group mobilizes its membership to contact government officials in support of the group's position

**Great Compromise** the agreement reached at the Constitutional Convention of 1787 that gave each state an equal number of senators regardless of its population, but linked representation in the House of Representatives to population

**gross domestic product (GDP)** the total value of goods and services produced within a country

**habeas corpus** a court order demanding that an individual in custody be brought into court and shown the cause for detention

**hidden government** a term that refers to special districts of which many citizens are unaware

**home rule** power delegated by the state to a local unit of government to manage its own affairs

**home-rule charter** the rules under which a city operates

**impeachment** the formal charge by the House of Representatives that a government official has committed "Treason, Bribery, or other high Crimes and Misdemeanors"

**impeachment (Texas)** according to the Texas Constitution, the formal charge by the House of Representatives that leads to a trial in the Senate and possibly to the removal of a state official

**implementation** the efforts of departments and agencies to translate laws into specific bureaucratic rules and actions

**implied powers** powers derived from the necessary and proper clause of Article I, Section 8, of the Constitution. Such powers are not specifically expressed, but are implied through the expansive interpretation of delegated powers

**incumbency** holding a political office for which one is running

**incumbent** a candidate running for reelection to a position that he or she already holds

**independent agency** agency that is not part of a cabinet department

**indexing** periodic process of adjusting social benefits or wages to account for increases in the cost of living

**indictment** a written statement issued by a grand jury that charges a suspect with a crime and states that a trial is warranted

**individualistic political culture** the belief that government should limit its role to providing order in society, so that citizens can pursue their economic self-interests

**inflation** a consistent increase in the general level of prices

**informational benefits** special newsletters, periodicals, training programs, conferences, and other information provided to members of groups to entice others to join

**inherent powers** powers claimed by a president that are not expressed in the Constitution but are inferred from it

**in-kind benefits** noncash goods and services provided to needy individuals and families by the federal government

**institutional advertising** advertising designed to create a positive image of an organization

**interest group** individuals who organize to influence the government's programs and policies

**intermediate scrutiny** a test used by the Supreme Court in gender discrimination cases that places the burden of proof partially on the government and partially on the challengers to show that the law in question is unconstitutional

**International Monetary Fund (IMF)** an institution established in 1944 that provides loans and facilitates international monetary exchange

**introduction** the first step in the legislative process, during which a member of the legislature gets an idea for a bill and files a copy of it with the clerk of the House or secretary of the Senate

**investigative power** the power, exercised by the House, the Senate, or both chambers jointly, to investigate problems facing the state

**iron triangle** the stable, cooperative relationship that often develops among a congressional committee, an administrative agency, and one or more supportive interest groups. Not all of these relationships are triangular, but the iron triangle is the most typical

**isolationism** avoidance of involvement in the affairs of other nations

**issue advocacy** independent spending by individuals or interest groups on a campaign issue but not directly tied to a particular candidate

**issue network** a loose network of elected leaders, public officials, activists, and interest groups drawn together by a specific policy issue

**Jim Crow laws** laws enacted by southern states following Reconstruction that discriminated against African Americans

**joint committees** legislative committees formed of members of both the House and Senate

**joint resolution** a resolution, commonly a proposed amendment to the Texas Constitution or ratification of an amendment to the U.S. Constitution, that must pass both the

House and Senate but which does not require the governor's signature

**judicial activism** judicial philosophy that posits that the Court should go beyond the words of the Constitution or a statute to consider the broader societal implications of its decisions

**Judicial Campaign Fairness Act** a judicial reform under which campaign contributions are limited

**judicial power** the power of the House to impeach and of the Senate to convict members of the executive and judicial branches of state government

**judicial restraint** judicial philosophy whose adherents refuse to go beyond the clear words of the Constitution in interpreting the document's meaning

**judicial review** the power of the courts to review and, if necessary, declare actions of the legislative and executive branches invalid or unconstitutional; the Supreme Court asserted this power in *Marbury v. Madison*

**jurisdiction** the sphere of a court's power and authority

**justice of the peace courts** local trial courts with limited jurisdiction over small claims and very minor criminal misdemeanors

**Keynesians** followers of the economic theories of John Maynard Keynes, who argued that the government can stimulate the economy by increasing public spending or by cutting taxes

**Kitchen Cabinet** an informal group of advisers to whom the president turns for counsel and guidance. Members of the official Cabinet may or may not also be members of the Kitchen Cabinet

**laissez-faire capitalism** an economic system in which the means of production and distribution are privately owned and operated for profit with minimal or no government interference

**land commissioner** elected state official who is the manager of most publicly owned lands

**leak** a disclosure of confidential information to the news media

**legislative budget** the state budget that is prepared and submitted by the Legislative Budget Board (LBB) and that is fully considered by the House and Senate

**legislative initiative** the president's inherent power to bring a legislative agenda before Congress

***Lemon* test** a rule articulated in *Lemon v. Kurtzman* that government action toward religion is permissible if it is secular in purpose, neither promotes nor inhibits the practice of religion, and does not lead to "excessive entanglement" with religion

**libel** a written statement made in "reckless disregard of the truth" that is considered damaging to a victim because it is "malicious, scandalous, and defamatory"

**liberal** today this term refers to those who generally support social and political reform; extensive governmental intervention in the economy; the expansion of federal social services; more vigorous efforts on behalf of the poor, minorities, and women; and greater concern for consumers and the environment

**libertarianism** a political ideology that emphasizes freedom and voluntary association with small government

**liberty** freedom from governmental control

**lieutenant governor** the second-highest elected official in the state and president of the state Senate

**limited government** a principle of constitutional government; a government whose powers are defined and limited by a constitution

**line-item veto** the power of the executive to veto specific provisions (lines) of an appropriations bill passed by the legislature

**lobbying** a strategy by which organized interests seek to influence the passage of legislation by exerting direct pressure on members of the legislature

**lobbyist** an individual employed by an interest group who tries to influence governmental decisions on behalf of that group

**local bill** a bill affecting only units of local government, such as a city, county, or special district

**logrolling** a legislative practice whereby agreements are made between legislators in voting for or against a bill; vote trading

**loophole** incentive to individuals and businesses to reduce their tax liabilities by investing their money in areas the government designates

**machines** strong party organizations in late-nineteenth- and early-twentieth-century American cities. These machines were led by "bosses" who controlled party nominations and patronage

**majority leader** the elected leader of the majority party in the House of Representatives or in the Senate. In the House, the majority leader is subordinate in the party hierarchy to the Speaker of the House

**majority party** the party that holds the majority of legislative seats in either the House or the Senate

**majority rule, minority rights** the democratic principle that a government follows the preferences of the majority of voters but protects the interests of the minority

**majority system** a type of electoral system in which, to win a seat in the parliament or other representative body, a candidate must receive a majority of all the votes cast in the relevant district

**majority-minority district** a gerrymandered voting district that improves the chances of minority candidates by making selected minority groups the majority within the district

**mandatory spending** federal spending that is made up of "uncontrollables," budget items that cannot be controlled through the regular budget process

**marketplace of ideas** the public forum in which beliefs and ideas are exchanged and compete

**matching funds** federal monies given to a state to match the state's funding on a joint program

**material benefits** special goods, services, or money provided to members of groups to entice others to join

**mayor-council form of government** a form of city government in which the mayor is the chief executive and the city council is the legislative body; in the *strong mayor-council* variation, the mayor's powers enable him or her to control executive departments and the agenda of the city council; in the *weak mayor-council* variation, the mayor's power is more limited

**means testing** a procedure by which potential beneficiaries of a public-assistance program establish their eligibility by demonstrating a genuine need for the assistance

**media monopoly** the ownership and control of the media by a few large corporations

**median voter theorem** a proposition predicting that when policy options can be arrayed along a single dimension, majority rule will pick the policy most preferred by the voter whose ideal policy is to the left of half of the voters and to the right of exactly half of the voters

**Medicaid** a federally and state-financed, state-operated program providing medical services to low-income people

**Medicare** a form of national health insurance for the elderly and the disabled

**membership association** an organized group in which members actually play a substantial role, sitting on committees and engaging in group projects

**merit selection** a judicial reform under which judges would be nominated by a blue-ribbon committee, would be appointed by the governor, and, after a brief period in office, would run in a retention election

**merit system** a product of civil service reform, in which appointees to positions in public bureaucracies must objectively be deemed qualified for those positions

**midterm elections** congressional elections that do not coincide with a presidential election; also called off-year elections

**minority leader** the elected leader of the minority party in the House or Senate

**minority party** the party that holds a minority of legislative seats in either the House or the Senate

**Miranda rule** the requirement, articulated by the Supreme Court in *Miranda v. Arizona*, that persons under arrest must be informed prior to police interrogation of their rights to remain silent and to have the benefit of legal counsel

**misdemeanor** a minor criminal offense, usually punishable by a small fine or a short jail sentence

**mobilization** the process by which large numbers of people are organized for a political activity

**monetarists** followers of economic theories that contend that the role of the government in the economy should be limited to regulating the supply of money

**monetary policies** efforts to regulate the economy through the manipulation of the supply of money and credit. America's most powerful institution in this area of monetary policy is the Federal Reserve Board

**monopoly** a single firm in a market that controls all the goods and services of that market; absence of competition

**mootness** a criterion used by courts to screen cases that no longer require resolution

**moralistic political culture** the belief that government should be active in promoting the public good and that citizens should participate in politics and civic activities to ensure that good

**most favored nation status** agreement to offer a trading partner the lowest tariff rate offered to other trading partners

**motor voter law** a national act, passed in 1993, that requires states to allow people to register to vote when applying for a driver's license

**municipal courts** local trial courts with limited jurisdiction over violations of city ordinances and very minor criminal misdemeanors; municipal courts are located in each of Texas's incorporated cities and towns

**municipal utility district (MUD)** a special district that offers services such as electricity, water, sewage, and sanitation outside the city limits

**national convention** a national party political institution that nominates the party's presidential and vice presidential candidates, establishes party rules, and writes and ratifies the party's platform

**national debt** the amount that government spending exceeds the government's revenue in any year

**National Security Council (NSC)** a presidential foreign policy advisory council composed of the president, the vice president, the secretary of state, the secretary of defense, and other officials invited by the president

**nation-states** political entities consisting of a people with some common cultural experience (nation) who also share a common political authority (state), recognized by other sovereignties (nation-states)

**necessary and proper clause** Article I, Section 8, of the Constitution, which provides Congress with the authority to make all laws "necessary and proper" to carry out its expressed powers

**New Deal** President Franklin Delano Roosevelt's 1930s program to stimulate the national economy and provide relief to victims of the Great Depression

**New Federalism** attempts by Presidents Nixon and Reagan to return power to the states through block grants

**New Jersey Plan** a framework for the Constitution, introduced by William Paterson, that called for equal state representation in the national legislature regardless of population

**New Politics movement** a political movement that began in the 1960s and '70s, made up of professionals and intellectuals for whom the civil rights and antiwar movements were formative experiences. The New Politics movement strengthened public interest groups

**nomination** the process by which political parties select their candidates for election to public office

**noncontributory programs** social programs that provide assistance to people on the basis of demonstrated need rather than any contribution they have made

**nonschool special district** any special district other than a school district; examples include municipal utility districts (MUDs) and hospital districts

**non-state actors** groups other than nation-states that attempt to play a role in the international system. Terrorist groups are one type of non-state actor

**North American Free Trade Agreement (NAFTA)** trade treaty among the United States, Canada, and Mexico to lower and eliminate tariffs among the three countries

**North Atlantic Treaty Organization (NATO)** an organization, comprising the United States, Canada, and most of Western Europe, formed in 1948 to counter the perceived threat from the Soviet Union

**oligarchy** a form of government in which a small group—landowners, military officers, or wealthy merchants—controls most of the governing decisions

**one-person, one-vote principle** the principle that all districts should have roughly equal populations

**online political participation** activities designed to influence government using the Internet, including visiting a candidate's website, organizing events online, or signing an online petition

**open primary** a primary election in which the voter can wait until the day of the primary to choose which party to enroll in to select candidates for the general election

**open rule** a provision by the House Rules Committee that permits floor debate and the addition of new amendments to a bill

**open-market operations** methods by which the Open Market Committee of the Federal Reserve System buys and sells government securities and other investment instruments to help finance government operations and to reduce or increase the total amount of money circulating in the economy

**opinion** the written explanation of the Supreme Court's decision in a particular case

**oral argument** the stage in Supreme Court procedure in which attorneys for both sides appear before the Court to present their positions and answer questions posed by justices

**ordinance** a regulation enacted by a city government

**original jurisdiction** the authority to initially consider a case. Distinguished from appellate jurisdiction, which is the authority to hear appeals from a lower court's decision.

**oversight** the effort by Congress, through hearings, investigations, and other techniques, to exercise control over the activities of executive agencies

**party activists** partisans who contribute time, energy, and effort to support their party and its candidates

**party identification** an individual voter's psychological ties to one party or another

**party organization** the formal structure of a political party, including its leadership, election committees, active members, and paid staff

**party polarization** the division between the two major parties on most policy issues, with members of each party unified around their party's positions with little crossover

**party unity vote** a roll-call vote in the House or Senate in which at least 50 percent of the members of one party take a particular position and are opposed by at least 50 percent of the members of the other party

**patronage** the resources available to higher officials, usually opportunities to make partisan appointments to offices and to confer grants, licenses, or special favors to supporters

**pay-as-you-go limit** a rule in the Texas Constitution that requires the state to balance its budget

**penny press** cheap, tabloid-style newspaper produced in the nineteenth century, when mass production of inexpensive newspapers first became possible due to the steam-powered printing press; a penny press cost one cent compared to other papers, which cost more than five cents

**news aggregator** an application or feed that collects Web content such as news headlines, blogs, podcasts, and online videos in one location for easy viewing

**niche journalism** news reporting devoted to a targeted portion (subset) of a journalism market sector or for a portion of readers/viewers based on content or ideological presentation

*per curiam* a brief, unsigned decision by an appellate court, usually rejecting a petition to review the decision of a lower court

**per diem** daily payment to a public official engaged in state business

**permanent absentee ballots** the option in some states to have a ballot sent automatically to your home for each election, rather than having to request an absentee ballot each time

**pigeonholing** a step in the legislative process during which a bill is killed by the chair of the standing committee to which it was referred, as a result of his or her setting the bill aside and not bringing it before the committee

**plaintiff** the individual or organization that brings a complaint in court

**platform** a party document, written at a national convention, that contains party philosophy, principles, and positions on issues

**plea bargain** a negotiated agreement in a criminal case in which a defendant agrees to plead guilty in return for the state's agreement to reduce the severity of the criminal charge or prison sentence the defendant is facing

**plural executive** an executive branch in which power is fragmented because the election of statewide officeholders is independent of the election of the governor

**pluralism** the theory that all interests are and should be free to compete for influence in the government; the outcome of this competition is compromise and moderation

**plurality system** a type of electoral system in which, to win a seat in the parliament or other representative body, a candidate need only receive the most votes in the election, not necessarily a majority of votes cast

**pocket veto** a presidential veto that is automatically triggered if the president does not act on a given piece of legislation passed during the final 10 days of a legislative session

**police power** power reserved to the state government to regulate the health, safety, and morals of its citizens

**policy entrepreneur** an individual who identifies a problem as a political issue and brings a policy proposal into the political agenda

**political action committee (PAC)** a private group that raises and distributes funds for use in election campaigns

**political culture** broadly shared values, beliefs, and attitudes about how the government should function. American political culture emphasizes the values of liberty, equality, and democracy

**political economy** the complex interrelations between politics and the economy, as well as their effect on one another

**political efficacy** the ability to influence government and politics

**political equality** the right to participate in politics equally, based on the principle of "one person, one vote"

**political ideology** a cohesive set of beliefs that forms a general philosophy about the role of government

**political parties** organized groups that attempt to influence the government by electing their members to important government offices

**political socialization** the induction of individuals into the political culture; learning the underlying beliefs and values on which the political system is based

**politics conflict** over the leadership, structure, and policies of governments

**poll tax** a state-imposed tax on voters as a prerequisite for registration. Poll taxes were rendered unconstitutional in national elections by the Twenty-Fourth Amendment, and in state elections by the Supreme Court in 1966

**popular sovereignty** a principle of democracy in which political authority rests ultimately in the hands of the people

**pork barrel (or pork)** appropriations made by legislative bodies for local projects that are often not needed but that are created so that local representatives can win re-election in their home districts

**post-adjournment veto** a veto of a bill that occurs after the legislature adjourns, thus preventing the legislature from overriding it

**power** influence over a government's leadership, organization, or policies

**precedent** prior case whose principles are used by judges as the basis for their decision in a present case

**precinct** a local voting district

**precinct chair** the local party official, elected in the party's primary election, who heads the precinct convention and serves on the party's county executive committee

**precinct convention** a meeting held by a political party to select delegates for the county convention and to submit resolutions to the party's state platform; precinct conventions are held on the day of the party's primary election and are open to anyone who voted in that election

**preemption** the principle that allows the national government to override state or local actions in certain policy areas; in foreign policy, the willingness to strike first in order to prevent an enemy attack

**preponderance of the evidence** the standard of proof in a civil jury case, by which the plaintiff must show that the defendant is more likely than not the cause of the harm suffered by the plaintiff

**presidential Republicanism** a voting pattern in which conservatives vote Democratic for state offices, but Republican for presidential candidates

**preventive war** policy of striking first when a nation fears that a foreign foe is contemplating hostile action

**primary elections** elections held to select a party's candidate for the general election

**priming** process of preparing the public to take a particular view of an event or political actor

**prior restraint** an effort by a governmental agency to block the publication of material it deems libelous or harmful in some other way; censorship. In the United States, the courts forbid prior restraint except under the most extraordinary circumstances

**private bill** a proposal in Congress to provide a specific person with some kind of relief, such as a special exemption from immigration quotas

**privatization** the transfer of all or part of a program from the public sector to the private sector

**privileges and immunities clause** provision, from Article IV, Section 2, of the Constitution, that a state cannot discriminate against someone from another state or give its own residents special privileges

**probability sampling** a method used by pollsters to select a representative sample in which every individual in the population has an equal probability of being selected as a respondent

**progressive taxation** taxation that hits upper income brackets more heavily

**project grants** grant programs in which state and local governments submit proposals to federal agencies and for which funding is provided on a competitive basis

**property tax** a tax based on an assessment of the value of one's property, which is used to fund the services provided by local governments, such as education

**proportional representation** a multiple-member district system that allows each political party representation in proportion to its percentage of the total vote

**prospective voting** voting based on the imagined future performance of a candidate or political party

**protest** participation that involves assembling crowds to confront a government or other official organization

**provincialism** a narrow, limited, and self-interested view of the world

**public goods** goods or services that are provided by the government because they either are not supplied by the market or are not supplied in sufficient quantities

**public interest groups** groups that claim they serve the general good rather than only their own particular interest

**public opinion** citizens' attitudes about political issues, leaders, institutions, and events

**public-opinion polls** scientific instruments for measuring public opinion

**public policy** a law, rule, statute, or edict that expresses the government's goals and provides for rewards and punishments to promote those goals' attainment

**purposive benefits** selective benefits of group membership that emphasize the purpose and accomplishments of the group

**push polling** a polling technique in which the questions are designed to shape the respondent's opinion

**Radical Republicans** a bloc of Republicans in the U.S. Congress who pushed through the adoption of black suffrage as well as an extended period of military occupation of the South following the Civil War

**random digit dialing** a polling method in which respondents are selected at random from a list of ten-digit telephone numbers, with every effort made to avoid bias in the construction of the sample

**recall** a procedure to allow voters to remove state officials from office before their terms expire by circulating petitions to call a vote

**recognition** the power to control floor debate by recognizing who can speak before the House and Senate

**redistribution** a policy whose objective is to tax or spend in such a way as to reduce the disparities of wealth between the lowest and the highest income brackets

**redistributive programs** economic policies designed to control the economy through taxing and spending, with the goal of benefiting the poor

**redistricting** the process of redrawing election districts and redistributing legislative representatives in the Texas House, Texas Senate, and U.S. House. This usually happens every 10 years to reflect shifts in population or in response to legal challenges in existing districts

**redlining** a practice in which banks refuse to make loans to people living in certain geographic locations

**referendum** the practice of referring a proposed law passed by a legislature to the vote of the electorate for approval or rejection

**referral** the second step in the legislative process, during which a bill is assigned to the appropriate standing committee by the Speaker (for House bills) or the lieutenant governor (for Senate bills)

**regressive taxation** taxation that hits lower income brackets more heavily

**regular session** the 140-day period during which the Texas Legislature meets to consider and pass bills; occurs only in odd-numbered years

**regulated federalism** a form of federalism in which Congress imposes legislation on states and localities, requiring them to meet national standards

**regulatory agency** a department, bureau, or independent agency whose primary mission is to impose limits, restrictions, or other obligations on the conduct of individuals or companies in the private sector

**representative democracy/republic** a system of government in which the populace selects representatives, who play a significant role in governmental decision making

**republican government** a representative democracy, a system of government in which power is derived from the people

**reserve requirement** the amount of liquid assets and ready cash that banks are required to hold to meet depositors' demands for their money

**reserved powers** powers, derived from the Tenth Amendment to the Constitution, that are not specifically delegated to the national government or denied to the states

**resolution** an expression of opinion on an issue by a legislative body

**retention election** an election in which voters decide "yes" or "no" regarding whether to keep an incumbent in office

**retrospective voting** voting based on the past performance of a candidate or political party

**revenue agency** an agency responsible for collecting taxes. Examples include the Internal Revenue Service for income taxes, the U.S. Customs Service for tariffs and other taxes on imported goods, and the Bureau of Alcohol, Tobacco, Firearms and Explosives for collection of taxes on the sale of those particular products

**revenue sharing** the process by which one unit of government yields a portion of its tax income to another unit of government, according to an established formula. Revenue sharing typically involves the national government providing money to state governments

**right of rebuttal** a Federal Communications Commission regulation giving individuals the right to have the opportunity to respond to personal attacks made on a radio or television broadcast

**right to privacy** the right to be left alone, which has been interpreted by the Supreme Court to entail individual access to birth control and abortion

**roll-call vote** a vote in which each legislator's yes or no vote is recorded as the clerk calls the names of the members alphabetically

**runoff election** a "second round" election in which voters choose between the top two candidates from the first round

**runoff primary** where no candidate received a majority, a second primary election is held between the two candidates who received the most votes in the first primary election

**sample** a small group selected by researchers to represent the most important characteristics of an entire population

**sampling error** polling error that arises based on the small size of the sample

**secretary of state** state official, appointed by the governor, whose primary responsibility is administering elections

**select committees** (usually) temporary legislative committees set up to highlight or investigate a particular issue or address an issue not within the jurisdiction of existing committees

**selection bias (news)** the tendency to focus news coverage on only on aspect of an event or issue, avoiding coverage of over aspects

**selection bias (surveys)** polling error that arises when the sample is not representative of the population being studied, which creates errors in overrepresenting or underrepresenting some opinions

**selective incorporation** the process by which different protections in the Bill of Rights were incorporated into the Fourteenth Amendment, thus guaranteeing citizens protection from state as well as national governments

**senatorial courtesy** the practice whereby the president, before formally nominating a person for a federal judgeship, seeks the indication that senators from the candidate's own state support the nomination; in Texas, the practice whereby the governor seeks the indication that the senator from the candidate's home supports the nomination

**seniority** the ranking given to an individual on the basis of length of continuous service on a committee in Congress

**"separate but equal" rule** doctrine that public accommodations could be segregated by race but still be considered equal

**separation of powers** the division of governmental power among several institutions that must cooperate in decision making

**Shivercrat movement** a movement led by the Texas governor Allan Shivers during the 1950s in which conservative Democrats in Texas supported the Republican presidential ticket of Eisenhower and Nixon in 1952 and 1956; they believed that the national Democratic Party had become too liberal

**signing statements** announcements made by the president when signing bills into law, often presenting the president's interpretation of the law

**simple resolution** a resolution that concerns only the Texas House or Senate, such as the adoption of a rule or the appointment of an employee, and which does not require the governor's signature

**single-member district** an electorate that is allowed to elect only one representative for each district

**slander** an oral statement made in "reckless disregard of the truth" that is considered damaging to the victim because it is "malicious, scandalous, and defamatory"

**social desirability effect** the effect that results when respondents in a survey report what they expect the interviewer wishes to hear rather than what they believe

**social media** Web-based and mobile-based technologies that are used to turn communication into interactive dialogue between organizations, communities, and individuals; social media technologies take on many different forms including blogs, Wikis, podcasts, pictures, video, Facebook, and Twitter

**Social Security** a contributory welfare program into which working Americans contribute a percentage of their wages and from which they receive cash benefits after retirement

**socialism** a political ideology that emphasizes social ownership or collective government ownership and strong government

**socioeconomic status** status in society based on level of education, income, and occupational prestige

**sociological representation** a type of representation in which representatives have the same racial, gender, ethnic, religious, or educational backgrounds as their constituents. It is based on the principle that if two individuals are similar in background, character, interests, and perspectives, then one could correctly represent the other's views

**soft money** money contributed directly to political parties and other organizations for political activities that is not regulated by federal campaign spending laws; in 2002 federal law prohibited unregulated donations to national party committees

**solicitor general** the top government lawyer in all cases before the Supreme Court where the government is a party

**solidary benefits** selective benefits of group membership that emphasize friendship, networking, and consciousness raising

**school district** a specific type of special district that provides public education in a designated area

**Speaker of the House** the chief presiding officer of the House of Representatives. The Speaker is the most important party and House leader, and can influence the legislative agenda, the fate of individual pieces of legislation, and members' positions within the House

**special bill** a bill that gives an individual or corporation a special exemption from state law

**special district** a unit of local government that performs a single service, such as education or sanitation, within a limited geographical area

**special election** an election that is not held on a regularly scheduled basis; in Texas, a special election is called to fill a vacancy in office, to give approval for the state government to borrow money, or to ratify amendments to the Texas Constitution

**special session** a legislative session called by the governor that addresses an agenda set by him or her and that lasts no longer than 30 days

**"speech plus"** speech accompanied by conduct such as sit-ins, picketing, and demonstrations. Protection of this form of speech under the First Amendment is conditional, and restrictions imposed by state or local authorities are acceptable if properly balanced by considerations of public order

**spot (advertisement)** a 15-, 30-, or 60-second television campaign commercial that permits a candidate's message to be delivered to a target audience

**staff agencies** legislative support agencies responsible for policy analysis

**staff organization** a type of membership group in which a professional staff conducts most of the group's activities

**standing committee**   a permanent committee with the power to propose and write legislation that covers a particular subject, such as finance or agriculture

**standing**   the right of an individual or organization to initiate a court case, on the basis of their having a substantial stake in the outcome

***stare decisis***   literally, "let the decision stand." The doctrine that a previous decision by a court applies as a precedent in similar cases until that decision is overruled

**state chair** and **vice chair**   the top two state-level leaders in the party

**state convention**   a party meeting held every two years for the purpose of nominating candidates for statewide office, adopting a platform, electing the party's leadership, and in presidential election years selecting delegates for the national convention and choosing presidential electors

**state executive committee**   the committee responsible for governing a party's activities throughout the state

**states' rights**   the principle that the states should oppose the increasing authority of the national government. This principle was most popular in the period before the Civil War

**statutory county courts at law**   courts that tend to hear less serious cases than those heard by district courts

**statutory probate courts**   specialized courts whose jurisdiction is limited to probate and guardianship matters

**straight-ticket voting**   selecting candidates from the same political party for all offices on the ballot

**strict scrutiny**   a test used by the Supreme Court in racial discrimination cases and other cases involving civil liberties and civil rights that places the burden of proof on the government rather than on the challengers to show that the law in question is constitutional

**subsidies**   government grants of cash or other valuable commodities, such as land, to an individual or an organization; used to promote activities desired by the government, to reward political support, or to buy off political opposition

**suffrage**   the right to vote; also called *franchise*

**Sunset Advisory Commission (SAC)**   a commission created in 1975 for the purpose of reviewing the effectiveness of state agencies

**superdelegate**   a convention delegate position, in Democratic conventions, reserved for party officials

**Supplemental Nutrition Assistance Program (SNAP)**   the largest anti-poverty program, which provides recipients with a debit card for food at most grocery stores; formerly known as *food stamps*

**supply-side economics**   a social science that posits that reducing the marginal rate of taxation will create a productive economy by promoting levels of work and investment that would otherwise be discouraged by higher taxes

**supremacy clause**   Article VI of the Constitution, which states that laws passed by the national government and all treaties are the supreme law of the land and superior to all laws adopted by any state or any subdivision

**supreme court**   the highest court in a particular state or in the United States. This court primarily serves an appellate function

**tariff**   a tax on imported goods

**tax expenditures**   government subsidies provided to employers and employees through tax deductions for amounts spent on health insurance and other benefits

**Temporary Assistance for Needy Families (TANF)**   a federal block grant that replaced the AFDC program in 1996

**term limits**   legally prescribed limits on the number of terms an elected official can serve

**Texas Court of Criminal Appeals**   the highest criminal court in Texas; consists of nine justices and has final state appellate authority over criminal cases

**Texas Supreme Court**   the highest civil court in Texas; consists of nine justices and has final state appellate authority over civil cases

**third parties**   parties that organize to compete against the two major American political parties

**Thirteenth Amendment**   one of three Civil War amendments; it abolished slavery

**Three-Fifths Compromise**   the agreement reached at the Constitutional Convention of 1787 that stipulated that for purposes of the apportionment of congressional seats, every slave would be counted as three-fifths of a person

**totalitarian government**   a system of rule in which the government recognizes no formal limits on its power and seeks to absorb or eliminate other social institutions that might challenge it

**town hall meeting**   an informal public meeting in which candidates meet with ordinary citizens. Allows candidates to deliver messages without the presence of journalists or commentators

**traditional political participation**   activities designed to influence government including voting and face-to-face activities such as protesting or volunteering for a campaign

**traditionalistic political culture**   the belief that government should be dominated by political elites and guided by tradition

**trial court**   the first court to hear a criminal or civil case

**trustee**   a representative who votes based on what he or she thinks is best for his or her constituency

**turnout**   the percentage of eligible individuals who actually vote

**two-party system**   a political system in which only two parties have a realistic opportunity to compete effectively for control

**tyranny**   oppressive government that employs cruel and unjust use of power and authority

**uncontrollables**   budgetary items that are beyond the control of budgetary committees and can be controlled only by substantive legislative action in Congress. Some uncontrollables, such as interest on the debt, are beyond the power of Congress, because the terms of payments are set in contracts

**unfunded mandates**   regulations or conditions for receiving grants that impose costs on state and local governments for which they are not reimbursed by the federal government

**unicameral**   comprising one body or house, as in a one-house legislature

**unitary system**   a centralized government system in which lower levels of government have little power independent of the national government

**United Nations (UN)**   an organization of nations founded in 1945 to be a channel for negotiation and a means of settling international disputes peaceably. The UN has had frequent successes in providing a forum for negotiation and, on some occasions, a means of preventing international conflicts from spreading. On a number of occasions, the UN has been a convenient cover for U.S. foreign policy goals

**urbanization**   the process by which people move from rural areas to cities

**user fee**   a fee paid for public goods and services, such as water or sewage service

**values (or beliefs)**   basic principles that shape a person's opinions about political issues and events

**veto**   the president's constitutional power to turn down acts of Congress. A presidential veto may be overridden by a two-thirds vote of each house of Congress

**veto (Texas)**   according to the Texas Constitution, the governor's power to turn down legislation; can be overridden by a two-thirds vote of both the House and Senate

**Virginia Plan**   a framework for the Constitution, introduced by Edmund Randolph, that called for representation in the national legislature based on the population of each state

**waiver**   an exemption from a federal requirement

**War Powers Resolution**   a resolution of Congress that the president can send troops into action abroad only by authorization of Congress, or if American troops are already under attack or serious threat

**whip**   a party member in the House or Senate responsible for coordinating the party's legislative strategy, building support for key issues, and counting votes

**White House staff**   analysts and advisers to the president, each of whom is often given the title "special assistant"

**white primary**   primary election in which only white voters are eligible to participate

**Word Trade Organization (WTO)**   international organization promoting free trade that grew out of the General Agreement on Tariffs and Trade

**writ of *certiorari***   a decision of at least four of the nine Supreme Court justices to review a decision of a lower court; *certiorari* is Latin, meaning "to make more certain"

**writ of *habeas corpus***   a court order that the individual in custody be brought into court and shown the cause for detention. *Habeas corpus* is guaranteed by the Constitution and can be suspended only in cases of rebellion or invasion

# endnotes

## Chapter 1

1. Theda Skocpol and Vanessa Williamson, *The Tea Party and the Making of Republican Conservatism* (New York: Oxford University Press, 2012), pp. 59–64.
2. The ANES Guide to Public Opinion and Electoral Behavior, "Trust the Federal Government, 1958–2008," www.electionstudies.org/nesguide/toptable/tab5a_1.htm (accessed 6/8/12).
3. Pew Research Center for the People and the Press, "Distrust, Discontent, Anger, and Partisan Rancor," April 18, 2010, www.people-press.org/2010/04/18/section-1-trust-in-government-1958-2010/ (accessed 10/14/2011).
4. ANES Guide to Public Opinion and Electoral Behavior, "Trust the Federal Government."
5. ANES Guide to Public Opinion and Electoral Behavior, "Trust the Federal Government."
6. The New York Times/CBS News Poll, "Americans' Approval of Congress Drops to Single Digits," October 25, 2011, www.nytimes.com/interactive/2011/10/25/us/politics/approval-of-congress-drops-to-single-digits.html?ref=politics (accessed 6/8/12).
7. Joseph S. Nye Jr., "Introduction: The Decline of Confidence in Government," in *Why People Don't Trust Government*, ed. Joseph S. Nye Jr., Philip D. Zelikow, and David C. King (Cambridge, MA: Harvard University Press, 1997), p. 4.
8. The Pew Research Center for the People and the Press, "Partisan Polarization Surges in Bush, Obama Years; Trends in American Values: 1987–2012, Section 4: Values about Government and the Social Safety Net," www.people-press.org/2012/06/04/section-4-values-about-government-and-the-social-safety-net/ (accessed 6/8/12).
9. This definition is taken from Norman H. Nie, Jane Junn, and Kenneth Stehlik-Barry, *Education and Democratic Citizenship in America* (Chicago: University of Chicago Press, 1996).
10. Freedom House, "Freedom in the World Report, 2011, Tables and Charts," www.freedomhouse.org/images/File/fiw/Tables%2C%20Graphs%2C%20etc%2C%20FIW%202011_Revised%201_11_11.pdf (accessed 10/10/11).
11. See Eugen Weber, *Peasants into Frenchmen: The Modernization of Rural France, 1870–1914* (Stanford, CA: Stanford University Press, 1976), chap. 5.
12. See V. O. Key, *Politics, Parties, and Pressure Groups* (New York: Crowell, 1964), p. 201.
13. Harold Lasswell, *Politics: Who Gets What, When, How* (New York: Meridian Books, 1958).
14. Susan B. Carter, Scott Sigmund Gartner, Michael R. Haines, Alan L. Olmstead, Richard Sutch, and Gavin Wright, eds., *Historical Statistics of the United States: Millennial Edition Online*, Table Aa145-184, Population, by Sex and Race: 1790–1990 (New York: Cambridge University Press, 2006). Data from 2012 available at U.S. Census Bureau, www.census.gov (accessed 2/25/12).
15. Carter et al., *Historical Statistics of the United States*, Table Aa145-184, Population, by Sex and Race: 1790–1990.
16. Carter et al., *Historical Statistics of the United States*, Table Aa145-184, Population, by Sex and Race: 1790–1990; Table Aa2189-2215, Hispanic Population Estimates.
17. U.S. Census Bureau, www.census.gov; Claude S. Fischer and Michael Hout, *A Century of Difference: How America Changed in the Last One Hundred Years* (New York: Russell Sage Foundation, 2006), p. 36.
18. Carter et al., *Historical Statistics of the United States*, Table Aa22-35, Selected Population Characteristics.
19. Fischer and Hout, *A Century of Difference*, p. 24.
20. Michael B. Katz and Mark J. Stern, *One Nation Divisible: What America Was and What It Is Becoming* (New York: Russell Sage Foundation, 2006), p. 16.
21. Carter et al., *Historical Statistics of the United States*, Table Aa145-184, Population, by Sex and Race: 1790–1990, p. 23. Karen R. Humes, Nicholas A. Jones, and Roberto R. Ramirez, "Overview of Race and Hispanic Origin: 2010," *2010 Census Briefs*, Number C210BR-02 (Washington, DC: U.S. Census Bureau, March 2011), p. 4, www.census.gov/prod/cen2010/briefs/c2010br-02.pdf (accessed 10/14/2011).
22. Karen R. Humes, Nicholas A. Jones, and Roberto R. Ramirez, "Overview of Race and Hispanic Origin: 2010," U.S. Census Bureau, March 2010, Table 2 (accessed 6/9/12).

23. U.S. Census, "Table 1.1. Population by Sex, Age, Nativity, and U.S. Citizenship Status: 2010," www.census.gov/population/foreign/data/cps2010.html (accessed 10/14/11).

24. Yesenia D. Acosta and D. Patricia de la Cruz, "The Foreign Born from Latin America and the Caribbean: 2010," *American Community Survey Briefs*, Number ACSBR/10-15 (Washington DC: U.S. Census Bureau, September 2011), p. 2, www.census.gov/prod/2011pubs/acsbr10-15.pdf (accessed 10/14/11).

25. Michael Hoefer, Nancy Rytina, and Bryan C. Baker, "Estimates of the Unauthorized Immigrant Population Residing in the United States: January 2010, *Population Estimates*, Office of Immigration Statistics, Department of Homeland Security, February 2011, www.dhs.gov/xlibrary/assets/statistics/publications/ois_ill_pe_2010.pdf (accessed 10/14/11).

26. Anthony Faiola, "States' Immigrant Policies Diverge," *Washington Post*, October 15, 2007, p. A1.

27. *Plyer v. Doe*, 457 U.S. 202 (1982).

28. Fischer and Hout, *A Century of Difference*, p. 187. "U.S. Census Bureau, *The 2012 Statistical Abstract: Population*, Table 75: Self-Described Religious Identification of Adult Population, 1990, 2001, and 2008," www.census.gov/compendia/statab/cats/population.html (accessed 10/14/11).

29. U.S. Census Bureau, *The 2012 Statistical Abstract: Population*, Table 75: Self-Described Religious Identification of Adult Population, 1990, 2001, and 2008, www.census.gov/compendia/statab/cats/population.html (accessed 10/14/2011).

30. Lindsay M. Howden and Julie A. Meyer, "Age and Sex Composition: 2010 Census Briefs, Number C2010BR-03" (Washington, DC: U.S. Census Bureau, May 2011), pp. 4, 2, www.census.gov/prod/cen2010/briefs/c2010br-03.pdf (accessed 10/14/11).

31. Eurostat, "Population Structure and Ageing," October 2010, http://epp.eurostat.ec.europa.eu/statistics_explained/index.php/Population_structure_and_ageing (accessed 10/14/11).

32. U.S. Census, "Apportionment Population and Number of Representatives, by State: 2010 Census," http://2010.census.gov/news/pdf/apport2010_table1.pdf (accessed 6/22/12).

33. Constitution of the United States of America, Article I, Section 2; U.S. Census, "Congressional Apportionment: 2010 Apportionment Results," www.census.gov/population/apportionment/data/2010_apportionment_results.html (accessed 6/9/12).

34. See Judith N. Shklar, *American Citizenship: The Quest for Inclusion* (Cambridge, MA: Harvard University Press, 1991).

35. Herbert McClosky and John Zaller, *The American Ethos: Public Attitudes toward Capitalism and Democracy* (Cambridge, MA: Harvard University Press, 1984), p. 19.

36. Gardiner Harris, "Flavors Banned from Cigarettes to Deter Youths," *New York Times*, September 22, 2009, www.nytimes.com/2009/09/23/health/policy/23fda.html (accessed 9/24/09).

37. J. R. Pole, *The Pursuit of Equality in American History* (Berkeley: University of California Press, 1978), p. 3.

38. *Plessy v. Ferguson*, 163 U.S. 537 (1896).

39. *Brown v. Board of Education*, 347 U.S. 483 (1954).

40. See Rogers M. Smith, *Liberalism and American Constitutional Law* (Cambridge, MA: Harvard University Press, 1985), chap. 6.

41. The case was *San Antonio Independent School District v. Rodriguez*, 411 U.S. 1 (1973). See the discussion in Smith, *Liberalism and American Constitutional Law*, pp. 163–64.

42. See the discussion in Eileen McDonagh, "Gender Political Change," in *New Perspectives on American Politics*, ed. Lawrence C. Dodd and Calvin C. Jillson (Washington, DC: CQ Press, 1994), pp. 58–73. The argument for moving women's issues into the public sphere is made by Jean Bethke Elshtain, *Public Man, Private Woman* (Princeton, NJ: Princeton University Press, 1981).

43. Roger Lowenstein, "The Way We Live Now: The Inequality Conundrum," *New York Times Magazine*, June 10, 2007, p. 11.

44. Associated Press, "Obama: Tax Cuts Will Be Felt by April 1," February 21, 2009, www.msnbc.msn.com/id/29314485/ (accessed 9/28/09).

45. Reuters, "Obama to Allow Bush Tax Cuts to Expire on Schedule," February 21, 2009, www.reuters.com/article/topNews/idUSTRE51K1ZF20090221 (accessed 9/28/09); Pew Research Center for the People and the Press and for the Public, "Trends in American Values, 1987–2012, Partisan Polarization Surges in Bush, Obama Years," June 4, 2012, www.people-press.org/2012/06/04/partisan-polarization-surges-in-bush-obama-years p. 89 (accessed 6/9/12).

46. Kevin Phillips, *Arrogant Capital: Washington, Wall Street, and the Frustration of American Politics* (Boston: Little, Brown, 1994).

47. United States Election Project, "Voter Turnout: Turnout 1980–2008," http://elections.gmu.edu/voter_turnout.htm (accessed 9/29/09).

48. Center for the Study of the American Electorate, "2008 Turnout Report: African-Americans, Anger, Fear and Youth Propel Turnout to Highest Level since 1960," news release, December 17, 2008, www.american.edu/ia/cdem/csae/pdfs/2008pdfoffinaledited.pdf (accessed 9/29/09).

## Chapter 2

1. Michael Kammen, *A Machine That Would Go of Itself* (New York: Vintage, 1986), p. 22.

2. The social makeup of colonial America and some of the social conflicts that divided colonial society are discussed in Jackson Turner Main, *The Social Structure of Revolu-*

*tionary America* (Princeton, NJ: Princeton University Press, 1965).

3. George B. Tindall and David E. Shi, *America: A Narrative History*, 8th ed. (New York: W.W. Norton, 2010), p. 202.

4. For a discussion of events leading up to the Revolution, see Charles M. Andrews, *The Colonial Background of the American Revolution* (New Haven, CT: Yale University Press, 1924).

5. See Carl Becker, *The Declaration of Independence* (New York: Knopf, 1942).

6. An excellent and readable account of the development from the Articles of Confederation to the Constitution will be found in Alfred H. Kelly, Winfred A. Harbison, and Herman Belz, *The American Constitution: Its Origins and Development*, 7th ed. (New York: W.W. Norton, 1991), vol. 1, chap. 5.

7. Reported in Samuel E. Morrison, Henry Steele Commager, and William Leuchtenberg, *The Growth of the American Republic* (New York: Oxford University Press, 1969), vol. 1, p. 244.

8. Quoted in Morrison et al., *The Growth of the American Republic*, vol. 1, p. 242.

9. Charles A. Beard, *An Economic Interpretation of the Constitution of the United States* (New York: Macmillan, 1913).

10. Madison's notes, along with the somewhat less complete records kept by several other participants in the convention, are available in a four-volume set. See Max Farrand, ed., *The Records of the Federal Convention of 1787*, 4 vols., rev. ed. (New Haven, CT: Yale University Press, 1966).

11. Farrand, ed., *The Records of the Federal Convention of 1787*, vol. 1, p. 476.

12. Alexander Hamilton, James Madison, and John Jay, *The Federalist Papers*, ed. Clinton L. Rossiter (New York: New American Library, 1961), no. 71.

13. *The Federalist Papers*, no. 62.

14. *The Federalist Papers*, no. 70.

15. Max Farrand, *The Framing of the Constitution of the United States* (New Haven, CT: Yale University Press, 1962), p. 49.

16. Melancthon Smith, quoted in Herbert J. Storing, *What the Anti-Federalists Were For* (Chicago: University of Chicago Press, 1981), p. 17.

17. "Essays of Brutus," no. 1, in *The Complete Anti-Federalist*, ed. Herbert Storing (Chicago: University of Chicago Press, 1981).

18. *The Federalist Papers*, no. 57.

19. "Essays of Brutus," no. 15, in Storing, ed., *The Complete Anti-Federalist*.

20. *The Federalist Papers*, no. 10.

21. "Essays of Brutus," no. 7, in Storing, ed., *The Complete Anti-Federalist*.

22. "Essays of Brutus," no. 6, in Storing, ed., *The Complete Anti-Federalist*.

23. Storing, *What the Anti-Federalists Were For*, p. 28.

24. *The Federalist Papers*, no. 51.

25. Quoted in Storing, *What the Anti-Federalists Were For*, p. 30.

26. *The Federalist Papers*, no. 10.

# Chapter 3

1. *National Federation of Independent Business v. Sebeilus*, 11–393 (2012).

2. Adam Liptak, "Bans on Interracial Unions Offer Perspective on Gay Ones," *New York Times*, March 17, 2004, p. A22.

3. National Conference of State Legislators, Same Sex Marriage, Civil Unions and Domestic Partnerships, Last Update: August, 2009, www.ncsl.org/IssuesResearch/Human-Services/SameSexMarriage/tabid/16430/Default.aspx (accessed 10/16/09); "California Bill to Recognize Some Same-Sex Marriages," www.cnn.com/2009/US/10/12/california.samesex.marriage (accessed 10/16/09).

4. Ken I. Kersch, "Full Faith and Credit for Same-Sex Marriages?" Political Science Quarterly 112 (Spring 1997): 117–36; Joan Biskupic, "Once Unthinkable, Now under Debate," *Washington Post*, September 3, 1996, p. A1.

5. Barbara Hoberock, "State Won't Fight Same-Sex Adoption Ruling," *Tulsa World*, August 17, 2007, p. A9.

6. *Hicklin v. Orbeck*, 437 U.S. 518 (1978).

7. *Sweeny v. Woodall*, 344 U.S. 86 (1953).

8. Raphael Minder, "Court Refuses to Extradite Killer Wanted in Hijacking," *New York Times*, November 18, 2011, p. A29.

9. Patricia S. Florestano, "Past and Present Utilization of Interstate Compacts in the United States," *Publius* 24 (Fall 1994): 13–26.

10. See the discussion in www.nationalpopularvote.com (accessed 11/21/11); for a critique of the effort, see David Gringer, "Note: Why the National Popular Vote Is the Wrong Way to Abolish the Electoral College," 108 *Columbia Law Review* (January 2008), 182–230.

11. A good discussion of the constitutional position of local governments is in Richard Briffault, "Our Localism: Part I, The Structure of Local Government Law," 90 *Columbia Law Review*, no. 1 (January 1990), 1–115. For more on the structure and theory of federalism, see Larry N. Gerston, *American Federalism: A Concise Introduction* (Armonk, NY: M.E. Sharpe, 2007), and Martha Derthick, "Up-to-Date in Kansas City: Reflections on American Federalism" (1992 John Gaus Lecture), *PS: Political Science & Politics* 25 (December 1992): 671–5.

12. For a good treatment of the contrast between national political stability and social instability, see Samuel P. Huntington, *Political Order in Changing Societies* (New Haven, CT: Yale University Press, 1968), chap. 2.

13. *McCulloch v. Maryland*, 4 Wheaton 316 (1819).

14. *Gibbons v. Ogden*, 9 Wheaton 1 (1824).

15. The Sherman Antitrust Act, adopted in 1890, for example, was enacted not to restrict commerce, but rather to protect it from monopolies, or trusts, in order to prevent unfair trade practices and to enable the market again to become self-regulating. Moreover, the Supreme Court sought to uphold liberty of contract to protect businesses.

For example, in *Lochner v. New York*, 198 U.S. 45 (1905), the Court invalidated a New York law regulating the sanitary conditions and hours of labor of bakers on the grounds that the law interfered with liberty of contract.

16. The key case in this process of expanding the power of the national government is generally considered to be *NLRB v. Jones & Laughlin Steel Corporation*, 301 U.S. 1 (1937), in which the Supreme Court approved federal regulation of the workplace and thereby virtually eliminated interstate commerce as a limit on the national government's power.

17. *United States v. Darby Lumber Co.*, 312 U.S. 100 (1941).

18. W. John Moore, "Pleading the 10th," *National Journal*, July 29, 1995, p. 1940.

19. *United States v. Lopez*, 14 U.S. 549 (1995).

20. *Printz v. United States*, 521 U.S. 98 (1997).

21. See the poll reported in Guy Gugliotta, "Scaling Down the American Dream," *Washington Post*, April 19, 1995, p. A21. See also John Kincaid and Richard L. Cole, "Citizens' Attitudes toward Issues of Federalism in Canada, Mexico and the United States," *Publius: The Journal of Federalism* 41, no. 1 (2011): 53–75.

22. Kenneth T. Palmer, "The Evolution of Grant Policies," in *The Changing Politics of Federal Grants*, ed. Lawrence D. Brown, James W. Fossett, and Kenneth T. Palmer (Washington, DC: Brookings Institution Press, 1984), p. 15.

23. Palmer, "The Evolution of Grant Policies," p. 6.

24. Morton Grodzins, *The American System*, ed. Daniel J. Elazar (Chicago: Rand McNally, 1966).

25. See Terry Sanford, *Storm over the States* (New York: McGraw-Hill, 1967).

26. James L. Sundquist, with David W. Davis, *Making Federalism Work* (Washington, DC: Brookings Institution Press, 1969), p. 271. George Wallace was mistrusted by the architects of the War on Poverty because he was a strong proponent of racial segregation and "states' rights."

27. See Donald F. Kettl, *The Regulation of American Federalism* (Baton Rouge: Louisiana State University Press, 1983).

28. Cindy Skrzycki, "Trial Lawyers on the Offensive in Fight against Preemptive Rules," *Washington Post*, September 11, 2007, p. D2.

29. *Gonazales v. Oregon*, 546 U.S. 243 (2006).

30. *Wyeth v. Levine*, 555 U.S. 555 (2009).

31. Philip Rucker, "Obama Curtails Bush's Policy of 'Preemption,'" *Washington Post*, May 22, 2009, p. A3.

32. See U.S. Advisory Commission on Intergovernmental Relations, *Federal Regulation of State and Local Governments: The Mixed Record of the 1980s* (Washington, DC: Advisory Commission on Intergovernmental Relations, July 1993).

33. U.S. Advisory Commission on Intergovernmental Relations, *Federal Regulation of State and Local Governments*, p. iii.

34. Adam Liptak, "Justices to Hear Health Care Case as Race Heats Up," *New York Times*, November 15, 2011, p. A1.

35. Quoted in Timothy Conlon, *New Federalism: Intergovernmental Reform from Nixon to Reagan* (Washington, DC: Brookings Institution Press, 1988), p. 25.

36. For the emergence of complaints about federal categorical grants, see Palmer, "The Evolution of Grant Policies," pp. 17–8. On the governors' efforts to gain more control over federal grants after the 1994 congressional elections, see Dan Balz, "GOP Governors Eager to Do Things Their Way," *Washington Post*, November 22, 1994, p. A4.

37. U.S. Advisory Commission on Intergovernmental Relations, *Federal Regulation of State and Local Governments*.

38. For an assessment of the achievements of the 104th and 105th Congresses, see Timothy Conlan, *From New Federalism to Devolution: Twenty-Five Years of Intergovernmental Reform* (Washington, DC: Brookings Institution Press, 1998).

39. Robert Frank, "Proposed Block Grants Seen Unlikely to Cure Management Problems," *Wall Street Journal*, May 1, 1995, p. 1.

40. Sarah Kershaw, "U.S. Rule Limits Emergency Care for Immigrants," *New York Times*, September 22, 2007, p. A1.

41. U.S. Committee on Federalism and National Purpose, *To Form a More Perfect Union* (Washington, DC: National Conference on Social Welfare, 1985). See also the discussion in Paul E. Peterson, *The Price of Federalism* (Washington, DC: Brooking Institution Press, 1995), esp. chap. 8.

42. Malcolm Gladwell, "Remaking Welfare: In States' Experiments, a Cutting Contest," *Washington Post*, March 10, 1995, p. 6.

43. The phrase "laboratories of democracy" was coined by Supreme Court Justice Louis Brandeis in his dissenting opinion in *New State Ice Co. v. Liebman*, 285 U.S. 262 (1932).

44. "Motor Vehicle Fatalities in 1996 Were 12 Percent Higher on Interstates, Freeways in 12 States That Raised Speed Limits," Insurance Institute for Highway Safety, press release, October 10, 1997.

45. William Yardley, "New Federal Crackdown Confounds States That Allow Medical Marijuana," *New York Times*, May 8, 2011, p. A13.

46. *Gonzales v. Oregon* (2006).

47. National Conference of State Legislatures, "2011 State Immigration-Related Bills," www.ncsl.org/default.aspx?TabID=756&tabs=951,102#951 (accessed 11/27/11).

48. Associated Press, "Justice Department Sues Utah over State's Illegal Immigration Enforcement Law," *Washington Post*, November 22, 2011, www.washingtonpost.com/national/us-department-of-justice-sues-utah-over-immigration-enforcement-law/2011/11/22/gIQAJeJEmN_story.html (accessed 11/27/11).

49. *Arizona v. United States*, 11–182 (2012).

50. David Nasaw, "Toughest US Sheriff Loses Power to Arrest Illegal Immigrants: Stripping of Federal Duties Political Move, Says Officer: Female Chain Gangs among Criti-

cized Tactics," *The Guardian*, October 10, 2009, p. 27; Anna Gorman, "ICE-Local Alliance to Stay; but the Immigration Enforcement Will Be Subject to More Federal Oversight, Officials Say," *Los Angeles Times*, October 17, 2009, p. A16.

51. Julia Preston, "States Resisting Program Central to Obama's Immigration Strategy," *New York Times*, May 6, 2011, p. A18; Gretchen Gavett, "Why Three Governors Challenged Secure Communities," PBS *Frontline*, October 18, 2011, www.pbs.org/wgbh/pages/frontline/race-multicultural/lost-in-detention/why-three-governors-challenged-secure-communities/ (accessed 11/27/11).

52. Kate Phillips, "South Carolina Governor Rejects Stimulus Money," *New York Times*, March 20, 2009, http://thecaucus.blogs.nytimes.com/2009/03/20/round-2-omb-rejects-sc-governors-stimulus-plan/ (accessed 10/6/09).

53. Robert Pear and J. David Goodman, "Governors' Fight over Stimulus May Define G.O.P.," *New York Times*, February 22, 2009, www.nytimes.com/2009/02/23/us/politics/23governors.html (accessed 10/7/09).

54. The White House, Office of the Press Secretary, Memorandum for the Heads of Executive Departments and Agencies, Subject: Preemption, May 20, 2009, http://theusconstitution.org/blog.history/wp-content/uploads/2009/05/obama-preemption-memo-5202009.pdf (accessed 10/17/09).

55. Adam Liptak, "In Health Law, Asking Where U.S. Power Stops," *New York Times*, November 14, 2011, p. A1.

56. This was a comment from Walter E. Dellinger, President Clinton's acting solicitor general. Linda Greenhouse, "Will the Court Reassert National Authority?" *New York Times*, September 30, 2001, Week in Review, p. 14.

57. Jeff Zeleny and Megan Thee-Brenan, "New Poll Finds a Deep Distrust of Government," *New York Times*, October 26, 2011, p. A1.

58. The Pew Research Center for People and the Press, "Growing Gap in Favorable Views of Federal, State Governments," April 26, 2012, www.people-press.org/2012/04/26/growing-gap-in-favorable-views-of-federal-state-governments/ (accessed 6/10/12).

# Chapter 4

1. Alexander Hamilton, James Madison, and John Jay, *The Federalist Papers*, ed. Clinton Rossiter (New York: New American Library, 1961), no. 84, p. 513.

2. *The Federalist Papers*, no. 84, p. 513.

3. Clinton Rossiter, *1787: The Grand Convention* (New York: W.W. Norton, 1987), 302.

4. Rossiter, *1787*, p. 303. Rossiter also reports that "in 1941 the States of Connecticut, Massachusetts, and Georgia celebrated the sesquicentennial of the Bill of Rights by giving their hitherto withheld and unneeded assent."

5. *Barron v. Baltimore*, 7 Peters 243, 246 (1833).

6. The Fourteenth Amendment also seems designed to introduce civil rights. The final clause of the all-important Section 1 provides that no state can "deny to any person within its jurisdiction the equal protection of the laws." It is not unreasonable to conclude that the purpose of this provision was to obligate the state governments as well as the national government to take positive actions to protect citizens from arbitrary and discriminatory actions, at least those based on race. This will be explored in Chapter 5.

7. For example, *The Slaughterhouse Cases*, 16 Wallace 36 (1883).

8. *Chicago, Burlington and Quincy Railroad Company v. Chicago*, 166 U.S. 226 (1897).

9. *Gitlow v. New York*, 268 U.S. 652 (1925).

10. *Near v. Minnesota*, 283 U.S. 697 (1931); *Hague v. C.I.O.*, 307 U.S. 496 (1939).

11. *Palko v. Connecticut*, 302 U.S. 319 (1937).

12. All of these were implicitly included in the *Palko* case as "not incorporated" into the Fourteenth Amendment as limitations on the powers of the states.

13. There is one interesting exception, which involves the Sixth Amendment right to public trial. In the 1948 case *In re Oliver*, 33 U.S. 257, the right to the public trial was, in effect, incorporated as part of the Fourteenth Amendment. However, the issue in that case was put more generally as "due process," and public trial itself was not actually mentioned in so many words. Later opinions, such as *Duncan v. Louisiana*, 391 U.S. 145 (1968), cited the *Oliver* case as the precedent for more explicit incorporation of public trials as part of the Fourteenth Amendment.

14. *McDonald v. Chicago*, 561 U.S. 3025 (2010).

15. *Abington School District v. Schempp*, 374 U.S. 203 (1963).

16. *Engel v. Vitale*, 370 U.S. 421 (1962).

17. *Wallace v. Jaffree*, 472 U.S. 38 (1985).

18. *Lynch v. Donnelly*, 465 U.S. 668 (1984).

19. *Lemon v. Kurtzman*, 403 U.S. 602 (1971). The *Lemon* test is still good law, but as recently as the 1994 Court term, four justices have urged that the test be abandoned. Here is a settled area of law that may soon become unsettled.

20. *Rosenberger v. Rector and Visitors of the University of Virginia*, 515 U.S. 819 (1995).

21. *Van Orden v. Perry*, 545 U.S. 677 (2005).

22. *McCreary v. ACLU*, 545 U.S. 844 (2005).

23. *West Virginia State Board of Education v. Barnette*, 319 U.S. 624 (1943). The case it reversed was *Minersville School District v. Gobitus*, 310 U.S. 586 (1940).

24. *Cantwell v. Connecticut*, 310 U.S. 296 (1940).

25. *Employment Division, Department of Human Resources of Oregon v. Smith*, 494 U.S. 872 (1990).

26. *City of Boerne v. Flores*, 521 U.S. 507 (1997).

27. *Abrams v. U.S.*, 250 U.S. 616 (1919).

28. *U.S. v. Carolene Products Company*, 304 U.S. 144 (1938), note 4. This footnote is one of the Court's most important doctrines. See Alfred H. Kelly, Winfred A. Harbison, and Herman Belz, *The American Constitution: Its Origins and Development*, 7th ed. (New York: W.W. Norton, 1991), vol. 2, 519–23.

29. *Schenk v. United States*, 249 U.S. 47 (1919).
30. *Brandenburg v. Ohio*, 395 U.S. 444 (1969).
31. *McConnell v. Federal Election Committee*, 540 U.S. 93 (2003).
32. *Federal Election Commission v. Wisconsin Right to Life*, 551 U.S. 449 (2007).
33. *Davis v. Federal Election Commission*, 554 U.S. 724 (2008).
34. *Citizens United v. Federal Election Commission*, 558 U.S. 50 (2010).
35. Arthur Delaney, "Supreme Court Rolls Back Campaign Finance Restrictions," *Huffington Post*, updated May 25, 2011, www.huffingtonpost.com/2010/01/21/supreme-court -rolls-back_n_431227.html (accessed 7/9/12).
36. *Hague v. Committee for Industrial Organization*, 307 U.S. 496 (1939).
37. *Stromberg v. California*, 283 U.S. 359 (1931).
38. *Texas v. Johnson*, 488 U.S. 884 (1989).
39. *United States v. Eichman*, 496 U.S. 310 (1990).
40. Lizette Alvarez, "Measure to Ban Flag Burning Falls 4 Votes Short in the Senate," *New York Times*, March 30, 2000, p. A24; Adam Clymer, "House, in Ritual Vote, Opposes Flag Burning," *New York Times*, July 18, 2001, p. A20.
41. *Virginia v. Black*, 528 U.S. 343 (2003).
42. *Snyder v. Phelps*, 09–751 (2011).
43. For a good general discussion of speech plus, see Louis Fisher, *American Constitutional Law* (New York: McGraw-Hill, 1990), 544–6. The case upholding the buffer zone against the abortion protesters is *Madsen v. Women's Health Center*, 512 U.S. 753 (1994).
44. *Rumsfeld v. Forum for Academic and Institutional Rights*, 547 U.S. 47 (2006).
45. *Near v. Minnesota*, 283 U.S. 697 (1931).
46. *New York Times v. United States*, 403 U.S. 731 (1971).
47. *Cable News Network, Inc., v. Noriega*, 498 U.S. 976 (1990).
48. *Branzburg v. Hayes*, 408 U.S. 656 (1972).
49. *New York Times v. Sullivan*, 376 U.S. 254 (1964).
50. Shannon Hutzler, "Protecting Informed Public Participation," 41 *Valparaiso University Law Review*, no. 3 (Spring 2007), 1235–84.
51. *Hustler Magazine v. Falwell*, 485 U.S. 46 (1988).
52. See *Zeran v. America Online*, 129 F3d 327 (4th Cir. 1977).
53. *Roth v. United States*, 354 U.S. 476 (1957).
54. Concurring opinion in *Jacobellis v. Ohio*, 378 U.S. 184 (1964).
55. *Miller v. California*, 413 U.S. 15 (1973).
56. *Reno v. American Civil Liberties Union*, 521 U.S. 844 (1997).
57. *United States v. American Library Association*, 539 U.S. 194 (2003).
58. *United States v. Williams*, 553 U.S. 285 (2008).
59. *United States v. Playboy Entertainment Group*, 529 U.S. 803 (2000).
60. *Brown v. Entertainment Merchants Association*, 08-1448 (2011).
61. *Chaplinsky v. State of New Hampshire*, 315 U.S. 568 (1942).
62. *Dennis v. United States*, 341 U.S. 494 (1951), which upheld the infamous Smith Act of 1940, which provided criminal penalties for those who "willfully and knowingly conspire to teach and advocate the forceful and violent overthrow and destruction of the government."
63. *Capital Broadcasting Company v. Acting Attorney General*, 405 U.S. 1000 (1972).
64. *R.A.V. v. City of St. Paul*, 506 U.S. 377 (1992)
65. *Bethel School District No. 403 v. Fraser*, 478 U.S. 675 (1986).
66. *Hazelwood School District v. Kuhlmeier*, 484 U.S. 260 (1988).
67. *Morse v. Frederick*, 551 U.S. 393 (2007).
68. *Meritor Savings Bank v. Vinson*, 477 U.S. 57 (1986).
69. *City Council v. Taxpayers for Vincent*, 466 U.S. 789 (1984).
70. *Posadas de Puerto Rico Associates v. Tourism Company of Puerto Rico*, 479 U.S. 328 (1986).
71. Fisher, *American Constitutional Law*, p. 546.
72. *Bigelow v. Virginia*, 421 U.S. 809 (1975).
73. *Virginia State Board of Pharmacy v. Virginia Citizens Consumer Council*, 425 U.S. 748 (1976). Later cases restored the rights of lawyers to advertise their services.
74. *44 Liquormart, Inc. and Peoples Super Liquor Stores Inc., Petitioners v. Rhode Island and Rhode Island Liquor Stores Association*, 517 U.S. 484 (1996).
75. *Lorillard Tobacco v. Reilly*, 533 U.S. 525 (2001).
76. *Presser v. Illinois*, 116 U.S. 252 (1886).
77. *District of Columbia v. Heller*, 554 U.S. 570 (2008).
78. *McDonald v. Chicago*, 561 U.S. 3025 (2010).
79. *In re Winship*, 397 U.S. 361 (1970). An outstanding treatment of due process in issues involving the Fourth through Seventh amendments will be found in Fisher, *American Constitutional Law*, chap. 13.
80. *Horton v. California*, 496 U.S. 128 (1990).
81. *Mapp v. Ohio*, 367 U.S. 643 (1961). Although Mapp went free in this case, she was later convicted in New York on narcotics trafficking charges and served 9 years of a 20-year sentence.
82. For a good discussion of the issue, see Fisher, *American Constitutional Law*, pp. 884–9.
83. *United States v. Grubbs*, 547 U.S. 90 (2006).
84. *National Treasury Employees Union v. Von Raab*, 39 U.S. 656 (1989).
85. *Skinner v. Railroad Labor Executives' Association*, 489 U.S. 602 (1989).
86. *Vernonia School District 47J v. Acton*, 515 U.S. 646 (1995).
87. *Indianapolis v. Edmund*, 531 U.S. 32 (2000), 531 U.S. 32 (2000).
88. *Chandler v. Miller*, 520 U.S. 305 (1997).
89. *Brendlin v. California*, 551 U.S. 249 (2007).
90. *Ferguson v. Charleston*, 532 U.S. 67 (2001).
91. *Kyllo v. United States*, 533 U.S. 27 (2001).
92. *Safford Unified School District No. 1 v. No. Redding*, 08–477 (2009).

93. Edwin S. Corwin and J. W. Peltason, *Understanding the Constitution* (New York: Holt, 1967), p. 286.
94. *Miranda v. Arizona*, 348 U.S. 436 (1966).
95. *Berghuis v. Thompkins*, 08–1470 (2010).
96. *Berman v. Parker*, 348 U.S. 26 (1954). For a thorough analysis of the case, see Benjamin Ginsberg, "*Berman v. Parker*: Congress, the Court, and the Public Purpose," *Polity* 4 (1971): 48–75. For a later application of the case that suggests that "just compensation"—defined as something approximating market value—is about all a property owner can hope for protection against a public taking of property, see Theodore Lowi et al., *Poliscide: Big Government, Big Science, Lilliputian Politics*, 2nd ed. (Lanham, MD: University Press of America, 1990), pp. 267–70.
97. *Kelo v. City of New London*, 545 U.S. 469 (2005).
98. *Gideon v. Wainright*, 372 U.S. 335 (1963).
99. *Wiggins v. Smith*, 539 U.S. 510 (2003).
100. For further discussion of these issues, see Corwin and Peltason, *Understanding the Constitution*, pp. 319–23.
101. *United States v. Gonzalez-Lopez*, 548 U.S. 140 (2006).
102. *Furman v. Georgia*, 408 U.S. 238 (1972).
103. *Gregg v. Georgia*, 428 U.S. 153 (1976).
104. *Kennedy v. Louisiana*,, 554 U.S. 407 (2008).
105. *Snyder v. Louisiana*, 552 U.S. 472 (2008).
106. *Medellin v. Texas*, 552 U.S. 491 (2008).
107. *Baze v. Rees*, 553 U.S. 35 (2008).
108. *Olmstead v. United States*, 227 U.S. 438 (1928). See also David M. O'Brien, *Constitutional Law and Politics*, 6th ed. (New York: W.W. Norton, 2005), vol. 1, pp. 76–84.
109. *West Virginia State Board of Education v. Barnette* (1943).
110. *NAACP v. Alabama ex rel. Patterson*, 357 U.S. 447 (1958).
111. *Griswold v. Connecticut*, 381 U.S. 479 (1965).
112. *Griswold v. Connecticut*, concurring opinion. In 1972 the Court extended the privacy right to unmarried women: *Eisenstadt v. Baird*, 405 U.S. 438 (1972).
113. *Roe v. Wade*, 410 U.S. 113 (1973).
114. *Webster v. Reproductive Health Services*, 492 U.S. 490 (1989), which upheld a Missouri law that restricted the use of public medical facilities for abortion. The decision opened the way for other states to limit the availability of abortion.
115. *Planned Parenthood of Southeastern Pennsylvania v. Casey*, 505 U.S. 833 (1992).
116. *Stenberg v. Carhart*, 530 U.S. 914 (2000).
117. *Ayotte v. Planned Parenthood*, 546 U.S. 320 (2006).
118. *Gonzales v. Carhart*, 550 U.S. 124 (2007).
119. *Bowers v. Hardwick*, 478 U.S. 186 (1986).
120. *Lawrence v. Texas*, 539 U.S. 558 (2003).
121. *Lawrence v. Texas* (2003).
122. It is worth recalling here the provision of the Ninth Amendment: "The enumeration in the Constitution, of certain rights, shall not be construed to deny or disparage others retained by the people."
123. *Gonzales v. Oregon*, 546 U.S. 243 (2006).
124. *Hamdi v. Rumsfeld*, 542 U.S. 507 (2004).
125. *Hamdan v. Rumsfeld*, 548 U.S. 557 (2006).
126. *ACLU v. NSA*, 06-2095 (6th Cir. 2007).

## Chapter 5

1. See Julia Preston, "Immigration Crackdown Also Snares Americans," *New York Times*, December 14, 2011, p. A20; on the charges against the Maricopa County Sheriff's Office, see "Assistant Attorney General Thomas E. Perez Speaks at the Maricopa County Sheriff's Office Investigative Findings Announcement," December 15, 2011, www.justice.gov/crt/opa/pr/speeches/2011/crt-speech -111215.html (accessed 12/15/11).
2. Paula Baker, "The Domestication of Politics: Women and American Political Society, 1780–1920," *American Historical Review* 89 (June 1984): 620–47.
3. Oscar Handlin, *America—A History* (New York: Holt, Rinehart and Winston, 1968), p. 474.
4. *Dred Scott v. Sandford*, 19 Howard 393 (1857).
5. August Meier and Elliot Rudwick, *From Plantation to Ghetto* (New York: Hill and Wang, 1976), pp. 184–8.
6. Jill Dupont, "Susan B. Anthony," *New York Notes* (Albany: New York State Commission on the Bicentennial of the U.S. Constitution, 1988), p. 3.
7. *Plessy v. Ferguson*, 163 U.S. 537 (1896).
8. Dupont, "Susan B. Anthony," p. 4.
9. The prospect of a "fair employment practices" law tied to the commerce power produced the Dixiecrat break with the Democratic Party in 1948. The Democratic Party organization of the States of the Old Confederacy seceded from the national party and nominated its own candidate, the then-Democratic governor of South Carolina, Strom Thurmond, who later became a Republican senator. This almost cost President Truman the election.
10. This was based on the provision in Article VI of the Constitution that "all treaties made, . . . under the Authority of the United States" shall be the "supreme Law of the Land." The commission recognized that if the U.S. Senate ratified what became the Universal Declaration of Human Rights (a treaty), then that power could be used as the constitutional umbrella for effective civil rights legislation. The Supreme Court had recognized in *Missouri v. Holland*, 252 U.S. 416 (1920), that a treaty could enlarge federal power at the expense of the states.
11. *Missouri ex rel. Gaines v. Canada*, 305 U.S. 337 (1938).
12. *Sweatt v. Painter*, 339 U.S. 629 (1950).
13. *Smith v. Allwright*, 321 U.S. 649 (1944).
14. *Shelley v. Kraemer*, 334 U.S. 1 (1948).
15. Kermit L. Hall, *The Magic Mirror: Law in American History* (New York: Oxford University Press, 1989), pp. 322–4. See also Richard Kluger, *Simple Justice* (New York: Random House, Vintage Edition, 1977), pp. 530–7.
16. The District of Columbia case came up, too, but since the District of Columbia is not a state, this case did not directly involve the Fourteenth Amendment and its

equal protection clause. The plaintiffs confronted the Court on the same grounds, however—that segregation is inherently unequal. Their victory in effect was "incorporation in reverse," with equal protection moving from the Fourteenth Amendment to become part of the Bill of Rights. See *Bolling v. Sharpe*, 347 U.S. 497 (1954).

17. *Brown v. Board of Education of Topeka, Kansas*, 347 U.S. 483 (1954).

18. The Supreme Court first declared that race was a suspect classification requiring strict scrutiny in the decision *Korematsu v. United States*, 323 U.S. 214 (1944). In this case, the Court upheld President Roosevelt's executive order of 1941 allowing the military to exclude persons of Japanese ancestry from the West Coast and to place them in internment camps. It is one of the few cases in which classification based on race survived strict scrutiny.

19. The two most important cases were *Cooper v. Aaron*, 358 U.S. 1 (1958), which required Little Rock, Arkansas, to desegregate, and *Griffin v. Prince Edward County School Board*, 377 U.S. 218 (1964), which forced all the schools of that Virginia county to reopen after five years of closing to avoid desegregation.

20. In *Cooper v. Aaron*, the Supreme Court ordered immediate compliance with the lower court's desegregation order and went beyond that with a stern warning that it is "emphatically the province and duty of the judicial department to say what the law is."

21. *Shuttlesworth v. Birmingham Board of Education*, 358 U.S. 101 (1958), upheld a "pupil placement" plan purporting to assign pupils on various bases, with no mention of race. This case interpreted *Brown* to mean that school districts had to stop explicit racial discrimination but were under no obligation to take positive steps to desegregate. For a while black parents were doomed to case-by-case approaches.

22. For good treatments of this long stretch of the struggle of the federal courts to integrate the schools, see Paul Brest and Sanford Levinson, *Processes of Constitutional Decision-Making: Cases and Materials*, 2nd ed. (Boston: Little, Brown, 1983), pp. 471–80; and Alfred Kelly et al., *The American Constitution: Its Origins and Development*, 6th ed. (New York: W.W. Norton, 1983), pp. 610–6.

23. Pierre Thomas, "Denny's to Settle Bias Cases," *Washington Post*, May 24, 1994, p. A1.

24. See Hamil Harris, "For Blacks, Cabs Can Be Hard to Get," *Washington Post*, July 21, 1994, p. J1.

25. For a thorough analysis of the Office for Civil Rights, see Jeremy Rabkin, "Office for Civil Rights," in James Q. Wilson, ed., *The Politics of Regulation* (New York: Basic Books, 1980).

26. This was an accepted way of using quotas or ratios to determine statistically that blacks or other minorities were being excluded from schools or jobs, and then, on the basis of that statistical evidence, to authorize the Justice Department to bring suits in individual cases and class-action suits. In most segregated situations outside the South, it is virtually impossible to identify and document an intent to discriminate.

27. *Swann v. Charlotte-Mecklenburg Board of Education*, 402 U.S. 1 (1971).

28. *Milliken v. Bradley*, 418 U.S. 717 (1974).

29. For a good evaluation of the Boston effort, see Gary Orfield, *Must We Bus? Segregated Schools and National Policy* (Washington, DC: Brookings Institution, 1978), pp. 144–6. See also Bob Woodward and Scott Armstrong, *The Brethren: Inside the Supreme Court* (New York: Simon and Schuster, 1979), pp. 426–7; and J. Anthony Lukas, *Common Ground* (New York: Random House, 1986).

30. *Board of Education v. Dowell*, 498 U.S. 237 (1991).

31. *Missouri v. Jenkins*, 515 U.S. 70 (1995).

32. John A. Powell, "Segregated Schools Ruling Not All Bad: In Rejecting Seattle's Integration Bid, Top Court Majority Also Held that Avoiding Racial Isolation Is a Legitimate Public Goal," *Newsday*, July 16, 2007, p. A33.

33. See especially *Katzenbach v. McClung*, 379 U.S. 294 (1964). Almost immediately after passage of the Civil Rights Act of 1964, a case was brought challenging the validity of Title II, which covered discrimination in public accommodations. Ollie's Barbecue was a neighborhood restaurant in Birmingham, Alabama. It was located 11 blocks away from an interstate highway and even farther from railroad and bus stations. Its table service was for whites only; there was only a take-out service for blacks. The Supreme Court agreed that Ollie's was strictly an intrastate restaurant, but since a substantial proportion of its food and other supplies was bought from companies outside the state of Alabama, there was a sufficient connection to interstate commerce; therefore, racial discrimination at such restaurants would "impose commercial burdens of national magnitude upon interstate commerce." Although this case involved Title II, it had direct bearing on the constitutionality of Title VII.

34. *Griggs v. Duke Power Company*, 401 U.S. 24 (1971). See also Allan Sindler, *Bakke, DeFunis, and Minority Admissions* (New York: Longman, 1978), pp. 180–9.

35. For a good treatment of these issues, see Charles O. Gregory and Harold A. Katz, *Labor and the Law* (New York: W.W. Norton, 1979), chap. 17.

36. In 1970 this act was amended to outlaw for five years literacy tests as a condition for voting in all states.

37. Joint Center for Political Studies, *Black Elected Officials: A National Roster—1988* (Washington, DC: Joint Center for Political Studies Press, 1988), pp. 9–10. For a comprehensive analysis and evaluation of the Voting Rights Act, see Bernard Grofman and Chandler Davidson, eds., *Controversies in Minority Voting: The Voting Rights Act in Perspective* (Washington, DC: Brookings Institution Press, 1992).

38. Ford Fessenden, "Ballots Cast by Blacks and Older Voters Were Tossed in Far Greater Numbers," *New York Times*, November 12, 2001, p. A17.

39. Aaron Blake, "Texas Redistricting Case: Five Things You Need to Know," *Washington Post*, December 13, 2011, www

.washingtonpost.com/blogs/the-fix/post/texas -redistricting-case-five-things-you-need-to-know/2011/ 12/13/gIQAdowHsO_blog.html (accessed 6/22/12); Manny Fernandez, "Federal Judges Approve Final Texas Redistricting Maps," *New York Times*, February 28, 2012, www.nytimes.com/2012/02/29/US/final-texas -redistricting-maps-approved.html (accessed 6/22/12).

40. See Douglas S. Massey and Nancy A. Denton, *American Apartheid: Segregation and the Making of the Underclass* (Cambridge, MA: Harvard University Press, 1993), chap. 7.

41. Michael Powell, "Bank Accused of Pushing Mortgage Deals on Blacks," *New York Times*, June 6, 2009; Charlie Savage, "Countrywide Will Settle a Bias Suit," *New York Times*, December 22, 2011, p. B1.

42. *Loving v. Virginia*, 388 U.S. 1. (1967).

43. See Jane J. Mansbridge, *Why We Lost the ERA* (Chicago: University of Chicago Press, 1986), and Gilbert Steiner, *Constitutional Inequality* (Washington, DC: Brookings Institution Press, 1985).

44. See *Frontiero v. Richardson*, 411 U.S. 677 (1973).

45. See *Craig v. Boren*, 423 U.S. 1047 (1976).

46. *Franklin v. Gwinnett County Public Schools*, 503 U.S. 60 (1992).

47. Jennifer Halperin, "Women Step Up to Bat," *Illinois Issues* 21 (September 1995): 11–14.

48. Joan Biskupic and David Nakamura, "Court Won't Review Sports Equity Ruling," *Washington Post*, April 22, 1997, p. A1.

49. Debra DeMeis and Rosanna Hertz, "Sex, Sports, and Title IX on Campus: The Triumphs and Travails," *Daily Beast*, June 22, 2012, www.dailybeast.com/articles/2012/06 /22/sex-sports-and-title-ix-on-campus-the-triumphs-and -travails.html (accessed 6/22/12).

50. *United States v. Virginia*, 518 U.S. 515 (1996).

51. Judith Havemann, "Two Women Quit Citadel over Alleged Harassment," *Washington Post*, January 13, 1997, p. A1.

52. *Meritor Savings Bank v. Vinson*, 477 U.S. 57 (1986). See also Gwendolyn Mink, *Hostile Environment—The Political Betrayal of Sexually Harassed Women* (Ithaca, NY: Cornell University Press, 2000), pp. 28–32.

53. *Harris v. Forklift Systems, Inc.*, 510 U.S. 17 (1993).

54. *Burlington Industries v. Ellerth*, 524 U.S. 742 (1998); *Faragher v. City of Boca Raton*, 524 U.S. 775 (1998).

55. *United States v. Morrison*, 529 U.S. 598 (2000).

56. *Ledbetter v. Goodyear Tire and Rubber Co.*, 550 U.S. 618 (2007).

57. New Mexico had a different history because not many Anglos settled there initially. (*Anglo* is the term for a non-Hispanic white, generally of European background.) Mexican Americans had considerable power in territorial legislatures between 1865 and 1912. See Lawrence H. Fuchs, *The American Kaleidoscope* (Hanover, NH: University Press of New England, 1990), pp. 239–40.

58. *Salvatierra v. Del Rio Independent School District*, 1931 (Texas).

59. On the United Farm Workers and César Chávez, see Marshall Ganz, *Why David Sometimes Wins: Leadership, Organization, and Strategy in the California Farm Worker Movement* (New York: Oxford University Press, 2009); Miriam Pawel, *The Union of Their Dreams: Power, Hope and Struggle in Cesar Chavez's Farm Worker Movement* (New York: Bloomsbury Press, 2010); and Jacques E. Levy, *Cesar Chavez: Autobiography of La Causa* (Minneapolis: University of Minnesota Press, 2007).

60. On La Raza Unida Party, see "La Raza Unida Party and the Chicano Student Movement in California," in *Latinos in the American Political System* ed. F. Chris Garcia (Notre Dame, IN: University of Notre Dame Press, 1988), pp. 213–35.

61. Dick Kirschten, "Not Black and White," *National Journal*, March 2, 1991, p. 497.

62. Krissah Thompson, "Justice Department to Address Backlog of Civil Rights Complaints," September 25, 2009, www.washingtonpost.com/wp-dyn/content/article/ 2009/09/25/AR2009092502151.html?nav=emailpage (accessed 10/27/09).

63. Anna Gorman, "ICE-Local Alliance to Stay; but Immigration Enforcement Will Be Subject to More Federal Oversight, Officials Say," *Los Angeles Times*, October 17, 2009, p. 16. For recent criticism, see Preston, "Immigration Crackdown Also Snares Americans," and the PBS *Frontline* documentary "Lost in Detention," available at www.pbs.org/wgbh/pages/frontline/lost-in-detention (accessed 12/15/11). On the charges against the Maricopa County Sheriff's Office, see Marc Lacey, "U.S. Says Arizona Sheriff Shows Pervasive Bias against Latinos," *New York Times*, December 16, 2011, p. A1.

64. *Arizona v. United States*, 567 U.S.___ (2012); Robert Barnes and N. C. Aizenmann, "Supreme Court Rejects Much of Arizona Immigration Law," *Washington Post*, June 25, 2012, www.washingtonpost.com/politics/supreme -court-rules-on-arizona-immigration-law/2012/06/25/ gJQA0Nrm1V_story.html?hpid=zl (accessed 6/25/12).

65. *United States v. Wong Kim Ark*, 169 U.S. 649 (1898).

66. *Korematsu v. United States*, 323 U.S. 214 (1944).

67. Children of the Camps, "Historical Documents: The Civil Liberties Act of 1988," http://pbs.org/childofcamp/ history/civilact.html (accessed 2/17/08).

68. *Lau v. Nichols*, 414 U.S. 563 (1974).

69. Not all Native American tribes agreed with this, including the Navajos. See Ronald Takaki, *A Different Mirror: A History of Multicultural America* (Boston: Little, Brown: 1993), pp. 238–45.

70. On the resurgence of Native American political activity, see Stephen Cornell, *The Return of the Native: American Indian Political Resurgence* (New York: Oxford University Press, 1990); and Dee Brown, *Bury My Heart at Wounded Knee* (New York: Holt, Rinehart, 1971).

71. See the discussion in Robert A. Katzmann, *Institutional Disability: The Saga of Transportation Policy for the Disabled* (Washington, DC: Brookings Institution Press, 1986).

72. For example, after pressure from the Justice Department, one of the nation's largest rental-car companies agreed to make special hand controls available to any customer requesting them. See "Avis Agrees to Equip Cars for Disabled," *Los Angeles Times*, September 2, 1994, p. D1.

73. The case and the interview with Stephen Bokat were reported in Margaret Warner, "Expanding Coverage," *The NewsHour with Jim Lehrer*, July 1, 1998, www.pbs.org/newshour/bb/law/jan-june98/hiv_6-30.html (accessed 2/18/08).

74. *Gross v. FBL Financial Services, Inc.*, 557 U.S.___(2009).

75. *Bowers v. Hardwick*, 478 U.S. 186 (1986).

76. Quoted in Joan Biskupic, "Gay Rights Activists Seek a Supreme Court Test Case," *Washington Post*, December 19, 1993, p. A1.

77. *Romer v. Evans*, 517 U.S. 620 (1996).

78. *Lawrence v. Texas*, 539 U.S. 558 (2003).

79. From Lyndon B. Johnson, *The Vantage Point* (New York: Holt, Rinehart, and Winston, 1971), p. 166.

80. The Department of Health, Education, and Welfare (HEW) was the cabinet department charged with administering most federal social programs. In 1980, when education programs were transferred to the newly created Department of Education, HEW was renamed the Department of Health and Human Services.

81. *Regents of the University of California v. Bakke*, 438 U.S. 265 (1978).

82. See, for example, *United Steelworkers v. Weber*, 443 U.S. 193 (1979), and *Fullilove v. Klutznick*, 448 U.S. 448 (1980).

83. *Wards Cove v. Atonio*, 490 U.S. 642 (1989).

84. *Adarand Constructors v. Peña*, 515 U.S. 200 (1995).

85. *Gratz v. Bollinger*, 539 U.S. 244 (2003).

86. *Grutter v. Bollinger*, 539 U.S. 306 (2003).

87. *Fisher v. University of Texas*, 11–345 (2012).

88. Michael A. Fletcher, "Opponents of Affirmative Action Heartened by Court Decision," *Washington Post*, April 13, 1997, p. A21.

89. See Sam Howe Verhovek, "Houston Vote Underlined Complexity of Rights Issue," *New York Times*, November 6, 1997, p. A1.

90. Frank Newport, "Little 'Obama Effect' on Views about Race Relations; Attitudes toward Race Not Significantly Improved from Previous Years," October 29, 2009, www.gallup.com/poll/123944/Little-Obama-Effect-Views-Race-Relations.aspx (accessed 10/30/09).

91. There are still many genuine racists in America, but with the exception of a lunatic fringe, made up of neo-Nazis and members of the Ku Klux Klan, most racists are too ashamed or embarrassed to take part in normal political discourse. They are not included in either category here.

92. *Slaughterhouse Cases*, 16 Wallace 36 (1873).

93. See Paul M. Sniderman and Edward G. Carmines, *Reaching beyond Race* (Cambridge, MA: Harvard University Press, 1997).

# Chapter 6

1. See, for example, John H. Aldrich, Christopher Gelpi, Peter Feaver, Jason Reifler, and Kristin Thompson Sharp, "Foreign Policy and the Electoral Connection" *Annual Review of Political Science* 9: 477–502 (2006). John H. Aldrich, John L. Sullivan, and Eugene Borgida "Foreign Affairs and Issue Voting: Do Presidential Candidates 'Waltz before a Blind Audience'?" *American Political Science Review* 81: 123–41 (1989).

2. Pew Research Center, "No Decline in Belief That Obama Is a Muslim: Nearly One-in-Five White Evangelicals Think So" April 1, 2009, http://pewresearch.org/pubs/1176/obama-muslim-opinion-not-changed (accessed 9/7/12). The same survey also found that 28 percent of Americans think Muslims should not be eligible to sit on the Supreme Court, while fully one-third believe that Muslims should be barred from running for president. See also David Redlawsk, "A Matter of Motivated Reasoning," *New York Times*, April 22, 2011, www.nytimes.com/roomfordebate/2011/04/21/barack-obama-and-the-psychology-of-the-birther-myth/a-matter-of-motivated-reasoning (accessed 9/7/12).

3. www.whitehouse.gov/sites/default/files/rss_viewer/birth-certificate-long-form.pdf (accessed 9/7/12).

4. A July 15, 2008, Pew Research Center survey found that about 12 percent of voters nationwide thought Obama was Muslim (http://pewresearch.org/pubs/898/belief-that-obama-is-muslim-is-bipartisan-but-most-likely-to-sway-democrats, accessed 9/7/12). A November 2008 Pew survey reports that even after the election, about 12 percent of American still believed Obama to be Muslim (http://pewresearch.org/pubs/1176/obama-muslim-opinion-not-changed, accessed 9/7/12). An October 2008 University of Iowa Hawkeye Poll, using an open-ended question, asked a national sample of respondents to name both McCain and Obama's religions. For Obama's religion, 37.9 percent of likely voters said they did not know, somewhat higher than Pew's 25 percent. The difference likely stems from Pew's use of a closed-ended question, where options were given to the respondent, compared to an open-ended one, for which the respondent must come up with an answer.

5. Matt Barreto and Dino Bozonelos, "Democrat, Republican, or None of the Above? The Role of Religiosity in Muslim American Party Identification" *Politics and Religion* 2 (2009): 200–29. Jaihyun Park, Karla Felix, and Grace Lee, "Implicit Attitudes toward Arab-Muslims and the Moderating Effects of Social Information" *Basic and Applied Social Psychology* 29, no. 1 (2007): 35–45.

6. Tali Mendelberg, *The Race Card: Campaign Strategy, Implicit Messages, and the Norm of Equality* (Princeton, NJ: Princeton University Press, 2001).

7. Redlawsk, "A Matter of Motivated Reasoning."

8. David Redlawsk, "Hot Cognition or Cool Consideration? Testing the Effects of Motivated Reasoning on

Political Decision Making," *Journal of Politics* 64 (2002): 1021–44. See also David Redlawsk, Andrew Civettini, and Karen Emmerson, "The Affective Tipping Point: Do Motivated Reasoners Ever 'Get It'?" *Political Psychology* 31, no. 4 (2010).

9. M. Lodge and C. S. Taber, "Three Steps toward a Theory of Motivated Political Reasoning," in A. Lupia, M. McCubbins, and S. Popkin, eds., *Elements of Reason: Cognition, Choice, and the Bounds of Rationality* (London: Cambridge University Press, 2000). George E. Marcus, W. Russell Neuman, and Michael MacKuen, *Affective Intelligence and Political Judgment* (Chicago: University of Chicago Press, 2000); Redlawsk, "Hot Cognition or Cool Consideration?"; Redlawsk, Civettini, and Emmerson, "The Affective Tipping Point."

10. Marcus, Neuman, and MacKuen, *Affective Intelligence and Political Judgment.*

11. ACLU Statement on Obama's Signing of NDAA, "President Obama Signs Indefinite Detention Bill into Law," GG Drafts, December 31, 2011, http://ggdrafts.blogspot.com/2011/12/aclu-statement-on-obamas-signing-of.html?spref=fb (accessed 9/7/12).

12. See Karen Mossberger, Caroline Tolbert, and Ramona McNeal, *Digital Citizenship: The Internet, Society and Participation* (Cambridge: MIT Press, 2008).

13. See Harry Holloway and John George, *Public Opinion* (New York: St. Martin's, 1986). See also Paul R. Abramson, *Political Attitudes in America* (San Francisco: Freeman, 1983).

14. See Paul M. Sniderman and Edward G. Carmines, *Reaching beyond Race* (Cambridge, MA: Harvard University Press, 1997).

15. Douglas R. Oxley, Kevin B. Smith, John R. Alford, Matthew V. Hibbing, Jennifer L. Miller, Mario Scalora, Peter K. Hatemi, and John R. Hibbing, "Political Attitudes Vary with Physiological Traits," *Science* 321, no. 5896 (September 19, 2008): 1667–70. See also Jeffrey Mondak, *Personality and the Foundation of Political Behavior* (Cambridge, UK: Cambridge University Press, 2010).

16. See Angus Campbell et al., *The American Voter* (New York: Wiley, 1960), p. 147.

17. Betsy Sinclair, *The Social Citizen: Peer Networks and Political Behavior* (Chicago: University of Chicago Press, 2012).

18. CNN Poll, 2009.

19. CBS News/New York Times Poll, 2008.

20. Donald Green, Bradley Palmquist, and Eric Schickler, *Partisan Hearts and Minds: Political Parties and the Social Identities of Voters* (New Haven, CT: Yale University Press, 2002).

21. See Richard Lau and David Redlawsk, *How Voters Decide: Information Processing during an Election Campaign* (New York: Cambridge University Press, 2006).

22. David S. Broder, "Partisan Gap Is at a High, Poll Finds," *Washington Post*, November 9, 2003, p. A6.

23. Broder, "Partisan Gap Is at a High, Poll Finds." See also Thomas E. Mann and Norman J. Ornstein, *It's Even Worse Than It Looks: How the American Constitutional System Collided with the New Politics of Extremism* (New York: Basic Books, 2012).

24. Morris Fiorina, Samuel Abrams, and Jeremy Pope, *Culture War? The Myth of a Polarized America* (New York: Longman Publishers, 2004).

25. Pew Research Center, The Complicated Politics of Abortion, August 22, 2012, www.people-press.org/2012/08/22/the-complicated-politics-of-abortion/ (accessed 9/7/12)

26. Pamela Johnston Conover, "The Role of Social Groups in Political Thinking," *British Journal of Political Science* 18 (1988): 51–78.

27. See also Michael C. Dawson, *Behind the Mule: Race, Class, and African American Politics* (Princeton, NJ: Princeton University Press, 1994).

28. Jack Citrin, Donald Green, Christopher Muste, and Cara Wong, "Public Opinion toward Immigration Reform: The Role of Economic Motivations," *Journal of Politics* 59 (1997): 858–81. David Sears and Jack Citrin, *Something for Nothing in California* (Berkeley, CA: University of California Press, 1982).

29. Nathan J. Kelly and Peter K. Enns, "Inequality and the Dynamics of Public Opinion: The Self-Reinforcing Link between Economic Inequality and Mass Preferences," *The American Journal of Political Science* 54, no. 4 (2010): 855–70. Jacob S. Hacker and Paul Pierson, *Winner-Take-All Politics: How Washington Made the Rich Richer—and Turned Its Back on the Middle Class* (New York: Simon and Schuster, 2010).

30. Larry M. Bartels, "Homer Gets a Tax Cut: Inequality and Public Policy in the American Mind," *Perspectives on Politics* 3, no. 1 (2005): 15–31. Larry Bartels, *Unequal Democracy* (Princeton, NJ: Princeton University Press, 2008).

31. O. R. Holsti, "A Widening Gap between the Military and Society? Some Evidence, 1976–1996," *International Security* 23 (Winter 1998/1999): 5–42

32. Jennifer A. Heerwig and Brian J. McCabe, "Education and Social Desirability Bias: The Case of a Black Presidential Candidate," *Social Science Quarterly* 90, no. 3 (2009): 674–86.

33. Raymond E. Wolfinger and Steven J. Rosenstone, *Who Votes?* (New Haven, CT: Yale University Press, 1980). See also Steven J. Rosenstone and John Mark Hansen, *Mobilization, Participation, and Democracy in America* (New York: Macmillan, 1993).

34. Mann and Ornstein, *It's Even Worse Than It Looks.*

35. Shaun Bowler, Gary Segura, and Stephen Nicholson, "Earthquakes and Aftershocks: Race, Direct Democracy, and Partisan Change," *American Journal of Political Science* 50 (2006): 146–59. For a more general discussion of the spillover effects of ballot measures on public opinion, see Stephen Nicholson, *Voting the Agenda: Candidates*

*Elections and Ballot Propositions* (Princeton, NJ: Princeton University Press, 2005).

36. Paul Davidson, "Fannie, Freddie Bailout to Cost Taxpayers $154 Billion," *USA Today*, October, 22, 2010.

37. John R. Zaller, *The Nature and Origins of Mass Opinion* (New York: Cambridge University Press, 1992).

38. Benjamin I. Page and Robert Y. Shapiro, *The Rational Public: Fifty Years of Trends in Americans' Policy Preferences* (Chicago: University of Chicago Press, 1995); Eugene Wittkopf, *Faces of Internationalism: Public Opinion and Foreign Policy* (Durham, NC: Duke University Press, 1990).

39. Zaller, *Nature and Origins of Mass Opinion*.

40. Carol Glynn et al., *Public Opinion*, 2nd ed. (Boulder, CO: Westview, 2004), p. 293. See also Michael X. Delli Carpini and Scott Keeter, *What Americans Know about Politics and Why It Matters* (New Haven, CT: Yale University Press, 1996).

41. Adam J. Berinsky, "The Two Faces of Public Opinion,"*American Journal of Political Science* 43, no. 4 (1999): 1209–30.

42. Delli Carpini and Keeter, *What Americans Know about Politics and Why It Matters*.

43. Michael Lewis Beck, *Economics and Elections: The Major Western Democracies* (Ann Arbor: University of Michigan Press, 1990).

44. Matt Barreto, "Watch for 'Si Se Puede' Signs at Obama Rallies," *New York Times*, May 23, 2012, www.nytimes.com/roomfordebate/2012/05/23/securing-the-hispanic-vote/watch-for-si-se-puede-signs-at-obama-rallies (accessed 6/6/12).

45. Pilar Marrero, "June Tracking Poll: Immigration Is a Critical Issue for Voters," *Latino Decisions*, June 10, 2011, www.latinodecisions.com/blog/2011/06/10/june-tracking-poll-immigration-is-a-critical-issue-for-voters/ (accessed 6/6/12).

46. Adam J. Berinsky, "Assuming the Costs of War: Events, Elites and American Support for Military Conflict," *The Journal of Politics* 69, no. 4 (2007): 975–97; Zaller, *Nature and Origins of Mass Opinion*.

47. Richard R. Lau and David P. Redlawsk, "Advantages and Disadvantages of Cognitive Heuristics in Political Decision Making," *American Journal of Political Science* 45 (October 2001): 951–71. Lau and Redlawsk, *How Voters Decide*.

48. For a discussion of the role of information politics, see Arthur Lupia and Matthew D. McCubbins, *The Democratic Dilemma: Can Citizens Learn What They Need to Know?* (New York: Cambridge University Press, 1998). See also Shaun Bowler and Todd Donovan, *Demanding Choices: Opinion and Voting in Direct Democracy* (Ann Arbor: University of Michigan Press, 1998). See also Samuel Popkin, *The Reasoning Voter: Communication and Persuasion in Presidential Campaigns* (Chicago: University of Chicago Press, 1991); Arthur Lupia, "Shortcuts Versus Encyclopedias: Information and Voting Behavior in California Insurance Reform Elections," *American Political Science Review* 88 (1994): 63–76; and Wendy

Rahn, "The Role of Partisan Stereotypes in Information Processing about Political Candidates," *American Journal of Political Science* 37 (1993): 472–96.

49. Bartels, *Unequal Democracy*.

50. Benjamin Ginsberg, *The American Lie: Government by the People and Other Political Fables* (Boulder, CO: Paradigm, 2007).

51. Gerald F. Seib and Michael K. Frisby, "Selling Sacrifice," *Wall Street Journal*, February 5, 1993, p. 1.

52. Peter Marks, "Adept in Politics and Advertising, 4 Women Shape a Campaign," *New York Times*, November 11, 2001, p. B6.

53. Facebook pages accessed May 2012.

54. *Roe v. Wade*, 410 U.S. 113 (1973).

55. See Gillian Peele, *Revival and Reaction* (Oxford, UK: Clarendon, 1985). Also see Connie Paige, *The Right-to-Lifers* (New York: Summit, 1983).

56. For example, see the poll conducted for the Des Register by Selzer and Co. Inc. of Des Moines, October 26–29. The sample includes 1,093 Iowans 18 and older, with a margin of error of 3.5 percent.

57. Caroline Tolbert and Amanda Keller, "Iowa's 2010 Gubernatorial Race: Money, the Economy and Same-Sex Marriage," in *Pendulum Swing*, ed. Larry J. Sabato (New York: Longman Publishers, 2011). See also Daniel A. Smith and Caroline Tolbert, *Educated by Initiative: The Effects of Direct Democracy on Citizens and Political Organizations in the American States* (Ann Arbor: University of Michigan Press, 2004).

58. See David Vogel, "The Power of Business in America: A Reappraisal," *British Journal of Political Science* 13 (January 1983): 19–44.

59. See David Vogel, "The Public Interest Movement and the American Reform Tradition," *Political Science Quarterly* 96 (Winter 1980): 607–27.

60. Frank Newport, "Congress Ends 2011 with Record-Low 11% Approval," Gallup Politics, December 19, 2011, www.gallup.com/poll/151628/Congress-Ends-2011-Record-Low-Approval.aspx (accessed 6/6/12).

61. Mann and Ornstein, *It's Even Worse Than It Looks*.

62. See Shanto Iyengar, *Is Anyone Responsible? How Television Frames Political Issues* (Chicago: University of Chicago Press, 1991); and Shanto Iyengar, *Do the Media Govern?* (Thousand Oaks, CA: Sage, 1997).

63. David Redlawsk, Caroline Tolbert, and Todd Donovan. *Why Iowa? How Caucuses and Sequential Elections Improve the Presidential Nominating Process* (Chicago: University of Chicago Press, 2011).

64. Redlawsk, Tolbert, and Donovan, *Why Iowa?*

65. Herbert Asher, *Polling and the Public* (Washington, DC: CQ Press, 2001), 64.

66. Michael Kagay and Janet Elder, "Numbers Are No Problem for Pollsters, Words Are," *New York Times*, August 9, 1992, p. E6.

67. Lynn Vavreck and Douglas Rivers, "The 2006 Cooperative Congressional Election Study," *Journal of Elections,*

*Public Opinion and Parties* 18, no. 4 (2008): 355–66. See also Simon Jackman and Lynn Vavreck, "Primary Politics: Race, Gender, and Age in the 2008 Democratic Primary," *Journal of Elections, Public Opinion and Parties* 20, no. 2 (2010): 153–86.

68. Dennis Chong and James N. Druckman, "A Theory of Framing and Opinion Formation in Competitive Elite Environments," *Journal of Communication* 57 (2007): 99–118. See also Stephen P. Nicholson and Robert M. Howard, "Framing Support for the Supreme Court in the Aftermath of Bush v. Gore," *Journal of Politics* 65, no. 3 (2003): 676–95; and Dennis Chong and James N. Druckman, "Framing Public Opinion in Competitive Democracies" *American Political Science Review* 101, no. 4 (2007): 637–55.

69. John R. Zaller, *The Nature and Origins of Mass Opinion* (New York: Cambridge University Press, 1992).

70. See Adam Berinsky, "The Two Faces of Public Opinion," *American Journal of Political Science* 43, no. 4 (1999): 1209–30. See also Adam Berinsky, "Political Context and the Survey Response: The Dynamics of Racial Policy Opinion," *Journal of Politics* 64, no. 2 (2002): 567–84.

71. Jennifer A. Heerwig and Brian J. McCabe, "Education and Social Desirability Bias: The Case of a Black Presidential Candidate," *Social Science Quarterly* 90, no. 3 (2009): 674–86.

72. David Redlawsk, Caroline Tolbert, and William Franko, "Voters, Emotions, and Race in 2008: Obama as the First Black President," *Political Research Quarterly* 63, no. 3 (2010): 875–89.

73. Michael Tesler and David O. Sears, *Obama's Race: The 2008 Election and the Dream of a Post-Racial America* (Chicago: University of Chicago Press, 2010).

74. See James H. Kuklinski, Michael D. Cobb, and Martin Gilens, "Racial Attitudes and the 'New South,'" *Journal of Politics* 59, no. 2 (1997): 323–49; and James H. Kuklinski, Paul M. Sniderman, Kathleen Knight, Thomas Piazza, Philip E. Tetlock, Gordon R. Lawrence, and Barbara Mellers, "Racial Prejudice and Attitudes Toward Affirmative Action," *American Journal of Political Science* 41, no. 2 (1997): 402–19. See also Jeffrey A. Karp and David Brockington, "Social Desirability and Response Validity: A Comparative Analysis of Overreporting Voter Turnout in Five Countries," *Journal of Politics* 67, no. 3 (2005): 825–40; and Matthew J. Streb, Barbara Burrell, Brian Frederick, and Michael A. Genovese, "Social Desirability Effects and Support for a Female American President," *Public Opinion Quarterly* 72, no. 1 (2008): 76–89.

75. Carl Cannon, "A Pox on Both Our Parties," in *The Enduring Debate*, ed. David C. Canon et al. (New York: W.W .Norton, 2000), p. 389.

76. "Dial S for Smear," *Memphis Commercial Appeal*, September 22, 1996.

77. Amy Keller, "Subcommittee Launches Investigation of Push Polls," *Roll Call*, October 3, 1996.

78. For a discussion of the growing difficulty of persuading people to respond to surveys, see John Brehm, *Phantom Respondents* (Ann Arbor: University of Michigan Press, 1993).

79. Redlawsk, Tolbert and Donovan, *Why Iowa?*

80. Angus Campbell et al. *The American Voter* (New York: Wiley, 1960).

81. Benjamin I. Page and Robert Y. Shapiro, "Effects of Public Opinion on Policy," *American Political Science Review* 77, no. 1 (1983): 175–90.

82. Gerald C. Wright, Rober S. Erikson, and John P. McIver, "Public Opinion and Policy Liberalism in the American States," *American Journal of Political Science* 31, no. 4 (November 1987): 980–1001.

83. Richard F. Fenno, *Home Style: House Members in Their Districts* (Boston: Little, Brown and Co., 1978); and Lawrence R. Jacobs and Robert Y Shapiro, *Politicians Don't Pander: Political Manipulation and the Loss of Democratic Responsiveness* (Chicago: University of Chicago Press, 2000).

84. Malcolm E. Jewell, *Representation in State Legislatures* (Lexington: University Press of Kentucky, 1982).

85. Jacobs and Shapiro, *Politicians Don't Pander.*

86. John Griffin and Brian Newman, "Are Voters Better Represented?" *Journal of Politics* 67 (2005): 1206–27.

87. Bartels, *Unequal Democracy.*

88. Other authors have endorsed Bartels's view that government policy exacerbates income inequality. See, for example, Jacob S. Hacker and Paul Pierson, *Winner-Take-All Politics: How Washington Made the Rich Richer—And Turned Its Back on the Middle Class* (New York: Simon and Schuster, 2010).

89. Martin Gilens, "Inequality and Democratic Responsiveness," *Public Opinion Quarterly* 69, no. 5 (2005): 778–96; and Martin Gilens, "Preference Gaps and Inequality in Representation," *PS: Political Science and Politics* 42, no. 2 (2009): 335–41.

90. Christopher Wlezien and Stuart Soroka, "The Relationship between Public Opinion and Policy," in Russell Dalton and Hans-Dieter Klingemann, eds., *Oxford Handbook of Political Behavior* (New York: Oxford University Press, 2009), pp. 799–817.

91. Gilens, "Inequality and Democratic Responsiveness"; Bartels, *Unequal Democracy.*

92. Ryan Claassen and Benjamin Highton, "Does Policy Debate Reduce Information Effects in Public Opinion? Analyzing the Evolution of Public Opinion on Health Care," *Journal of Politics* 68, no. 2 (2006): 410–20.

93. Nicholas Carr, *The Shallows: What the Internet Is Doing to Our Brains* (New York: W.W. Norton, 2011).

## Chapter 7

1. Larry M. Bartels, *Presidential Primaries and the Dynamics of Public Choice* (Princeton, NJ: Princeton University Press, 1988).

2. David Redlawsk, Caroline Tolbert and Todd Donovan, *Why Iowa? How Caucuses and Sequential Elections Improve the Presidential Nominating Process* (Chicago: University of Chicago Press, 2011).

3. Karen Mossberger, Caroline Tolbert, and Ramona McNeal, *Digital Citizenship: The Internet, Society and Participation* (Cambridge, MA: MIT Press, 2008). See also J. E. Katz and R. E. Rice, *Social Consequences of Internet Use: Access, Involvement, and Interaction* (Cambridge, MA: MIT Press, 2002).

4. Karen Mossberger, Caroline Tolbert and William Franko, *Digital Cities: The Internet and the Geography of Opportunity* (New York: Oxford University Press, 2012). See also the National Telecommunications and Information Administration, *Digital Nation: 21st Century America's Progress toward Universal Broadband Access* (Washington, DC: U.S. Department of Commerce, 2011).

5. Pew Internet and American Life, "Trend Data (Adults): What Internet Users Do Online," February 2012, http://pewinternet.org/Static-Pages/Trend-Data-(Adults)/Online-Activites-Total.aspx (accessed 6/12/12).

6. Caroline Tolbert and Ramona McNeal, "Unraveling the Effects of the Internet on Political Participation," *Political Research Quarterly* 56, no. 2 (2003): 175–85. See also Bruce Bimber, "Information and Political Engagement in America: The Search for Effects of Information Technology at the Individual Level," *Political Research Quarterly* 54 (2001): 53–67; Bruce Bimber, *Information and American Democracy: Technology in the Evolution of Political Power* (Cambridge, UK: Cambridge University Press, 2003); and Brian S. Krueger, "Assessing the Potential of Internet Political Participation in the United States," *American Politics Research* 30 (2002): 476–98.

7. Pew Research Center Publications, "The Internet's Broader Role in Campaign 2008," January 11, 2008, http://pewresearch.org/pubs/689/the-internets-broader-role-in-campaign-2008, and "*The Daily Show*: Journalism, Satire or Just Laughs?" May 8, 2008, http://pewresearch.org/pubs/829/the-daily-show-journalism-satire-or-just-laughs (accessed 9/7/12).

8. Robert McChesney and John Nichols, *The Death and Life of American Journalism: The Media Revolution that Will Begin the World Again* (New York: Nation Books, 2010).

9. Pew Research Center Publications, "State of the News Media 2010," March 15, 2010, http://pewresearch.org/pubs/1523/state-of-the-news-media-2010 (accessed 9/11/12).

10. Darrell West, *The Next Wave: Using Digital Technology to Further Social and Political Innovation* (Washington, DC: Brookings Institution Press, 2011).

11. West, *The Next Wave*; Edward Glaeser, *Triumph of the City: How Our Greatest Invention Makes Us Richer, Smarter, Greener, Healthier, and Happier* (New York: Penguin Press, 2011).

12. West, *The Next Wave*.

13. Mossberger, Tolbert and McNeal, *Digital Citizenship*.

14. Mossberger, Tolbert and McNeal, *Digital Citizenship*; Brian A. Krueger, "A Comparison of Conventional and Internet Political Mobilization, *American Politics Research* 34, no. 6 (2006): 759–76.

15. Antony Wilhelm, *Digital Nation: Toward an Inclusive Information Society* (Cambridge, MA: MIT Press, 2006). P. DiMaggio, E. Hargittai, et al., "Social Implications of the Internet," *Annual Review of Sociology* 27, no. 1 (2001): 307–36.

16. Karen Mossberger, Caroline Tolbert, and Mary Stansbury, *Virtual Inequality: Beyond the Digital Divide* (Washington, DC: Georgetown University Press, 2003); Pippa Norris, *Digital Divide: Civic Engagement, Information Poverty, and the Internet Worldwide* (New York: Cambridge University Press, 2001).

17. National Telecommunications and Information Administration, *Digital Nation: 21st Century America's Progress Toward Universal Broadband Access* (Washington, DC: U.S. Department of Commerce, 2011).

18. Eric R. A. N. Smith, *The Unchanging American Voter* (Berkeley: University of California Press, 1989), chap. 4.

19. See Pew Internet and American Life, "Trend Data (Adults): Online Activities, 2000-2009," February 2012, http://pewinternet.org/Static-Pages/Trend-Data-(Adults)/Online-Activites-Total.aspx (accessed 6/28/12). See also Kathryn Zickuhr and Aaron Smith, "Digital Differences," Pew Internet and American Life, April 13, 2012, www.pewinternet.org/Reports/2012/Digital-differences.aspx (accessed 6/28/12).

20. June Kronholz and Amy Schatz, "How Conservatives Enhanced Online Voice," *Wall Street Journal*, July 3, 2007, p. A5.

21. Richard Davis, "Interplay: Political Blogging and Journalism," in *iPolitics: Citizens, Elections, and Governing in the New Media Era*, ed. Richard L. Fox and Jennifer M. Ramos (Cambridge, UK: Cambridge University Press, 2012), pp. 76–99.

22. Zoe M. Oxley, "More Sources, Better Informed Public? New Media and Political Knowledge," in *iPolitics*, ed. Fox and Ramos, pp. 25–47. James Fallows, "Bit by Bit It Takes Shape: Media Evolution from the 'Post-Truth' Age." *The Atlantic*, August 29, 2012, www.theatlantic.com/politics/archive/2012/08/bit-by-bit-it-takes-shape-media-evolution-for-the-post-truth-age/261741/ (accessed 9/10/12).

23. Pew Research Center, "State of the Media, 2010"; West, *The Next Wave*.

24. Aaron Smith and Joanna Brenner, "Social Networking: Twitter Use 2012." Pew Internet and American Life Project, May 31, 2012, http://pewinternet.org/topics/Social-Networking.aspx?typeFilter=5 (accessed 6/28/12).

25. Amy Schatz, "BO, UR So Gr8: How a Young Tech Entrepreneur Translated Barack Obama into the Idiom of Facebook," *Wall Street Journal*, May 26, 2007, p. 1.

26. Karen Mossberger and Caroline Tolbert, "Digital Democracy," in *Oxford Handbook of American Elections*

*and Political Behavior*, ed. Jan Leighley (New York: Oxford University Press, 2010).

27. Tolbert and McNeal, "Unraveling the Effects of the Internet."

28. Mossberger, Tolbert, and McNeal, *Digital Citizenship*. See Richard L. Fox and Jennifer M. Ramos, eds., *iPolitics: Citizens, Elections, and Governing in the New Media Era* (Cambridge, UK: Cambridge University Press, 2011).

29. W. R. Neuman, M. R. Just, A. N. Crigler, *Common Knowledge: News and the Construction of Political Meaning* (Chicago: University of Chicago Press, 1992).

30. A. Healy and D. McNamara, "Verbal Learning and Memory: Does the Modal Model Still Work?" in *Annual Review of Psychology*, Vol. 47, ed. J. Spense, J. Darley, and D. Foss (Palo Alto, CA: Annual Reviews, 1996), pp. 143–72.

31. Cass Sunstein, *Republic.com* (Princeton, NJ: Princeton University Press, 2001). See also Mossberger and Tolbert "Digital Democracy."

32. Michael Margolis and David Resnick *Politics as Usual: The Cyberspace "Revolution"* (Thousand Oaks, CA: Sage, 2000).

33. West, *The Next Wave*.

34. See Pew Internet and American Life, "Trend Data (Adults): What Internet Users Do Online." See also Karen Mossberger, Caroline Tolbert and Allison Hamilton, "Measuring Digital Citizenship: Mobile Access and Broadband." *International Journal of Communication* 6 (2012): 2492–528.

35. West, *The Next Wave*; McChesney and Nichols, *The Death and Life of American Journalism*.

36. Dianne Bystrom, "Advertising, Web Sites, and Media Coverage: Gender and Communication along the Campaign Trail," in *Gender and Elections: Shaping the Future of American Politics*, 2nd ed., ed. Susan J. Carroll and Richard L. Fox (Cambridge, UK: Cambridge University Press, 2010), pp. 239–62.

37. Regina G. Lawrence and Melody Rose, *Hillary Clinton's Race for the White House: Gender Politics and Media on the Campaign Trail* (Boulder, CO: Lynne Reinner Publishers, 2010).

38. Joe Sterling and Phil Gast, "Assistant Coach Who Reported Penn State Incident Threatened, Won't Be at Game," *CNN*, November 10, 2011, www.cnn.com (accessed 10/22/12).

39. Oxley, "More Sources, Better Informed Public?"

40. Matthew A. Baum, "Preaching to the Choir or Converting the Flock: Presidential Communication Strategies in the Age of Three Medias," in *iPolitics*, ed. Fox and Ramos, pp. 183–205.

41. Ann Crigler, Marion Just, Lauren Hume, Jesse Mills, and Parker Hevron, "YouTube and TV Advertising Campaigns: Obama versus McCain in 2008," in *iPolitics*, ed. Fox and Ramos, pp. 103–24.

42. Eli Pariser, *The Filter Bubble: What the Internet Is Hiding from You* (New York: Penguin Press, 2011).

43. Karen Mossberger, Caroline Tolbert, and Mary Stansbury, *Virtual Inequality: Beyond the Digital Divide* (Washington, DC: Georgetown University Press, 2003).

44. For a criticism of the increasing consolidation of the media, see the essays in Patricia Aufderheide et al., *Conglomerates and the Media* (New York: New Press, 1997).

45. Jonathan M. Ladd, *Why Americans Hate the Media and How It Matters* (Princeton, NJ: Princeton University Press, 2012).

46. David J. Garrow, *Protest at Selma: Martin Luther King, Jr., and the Voting Rights Act of 1965* (New Haven, CT: Yale University Press, 2001).

47. See Todd Gitlin, *The Whole World Is Watching* (Berkeley: University of California Press, 1980).

48. Tim Groseclose, *Left Turn: How Liberal Media Bias Distorts the American Mind* (New York: St. Martin's Press, 2011).

49. Pew Research Center Publications, "How Journalists See Journalists in 2004: Views on Profits, Performance and Politics," May 2004, http://people-press.org/http://people-press.org/files/legacy-pdf/214.pdf (accessed on 9/7/2012)

50. Doris Graber, ed., *Media Power in American Politics*, 5th ed. (Washington, DC: CQ Press, 2006).

51. Larry Bartels, *Unequal Democracy* (Princeton, NJ: Princeton University Press, 2008).

52. Michael Tesler and David O. Sears, *Obama's Race: The 2008 Election and the Dream of a Post-Racial America.* (Chicago: University of Chicago Press, 2010). See also Redlawsk, Tolbert, and Donovan, *Why Iowa?*

53. Iyengar Shanto and Donald R. Kinder, *News That Matters: Television and American Opinion* (Chicago: University of Chicago Press, 1987), p. 63.

54. Redlawsk, Donovan, and Tolbert, *Why Iowa?*

55. Todd Donovan, Caroline Tolbert, and Daniel Smith, "Priming Presidential Votes with Direct Democracy," *Journal of Politics* 70, no. 4 (2008): 1217–31.

56. Daniel Smith and Caroline Tolbert, "Direct Democracy, Public Opinion, and Candidate Choice," *Public Opinion Quarterly* 74 (1 (2010): 85–108.

57. *New York Times v. United States*, 403 U.S. 713 (1971).

58. Michael Massing, "The Press: The Enemy Within," *New York Review of Books*, December 15, 2005, p. 6.

59. *Red Lion Broadcasting Company v. FCC*, 395 U.S. 367 (1969).

60. United Nations General Assembly, "Report of the Special Rapporteur on the Promotion and Protection of the Right to Freedom of Opinion and Expression," 2011.

61. Andrew Chadwick, *Internet Politics: States, Citizens, and New Communication Technologies* (Oxford, UK: Oxford University Press, 2006).

62. See Martin Linsky, *Impact: How the Press Affects Federal Policymaking* (New York: W.W. Norton, 1986).

## Chapter 8

1. Douglas R. Hess and Jody Herman, "Representational Bias in the 2008 Electorate, November 2009," www.projectvote.org/reports-on-the-electorate-/440.html (accessed 11/21/09).

Alonoo

2. Angus Campbell, Philip E. Converse, Warren E. Miller, and Donald E. Stokes, *The American Voter* (New York: Wiley, 1960); Raymond E. Wolfinger and Steven J. Rosenstone, *Who Votes?* (New Haven, CT: Yale University Press, 1980); Frances Fox Piven and Richard A. Cloward, *Why Americans Don't Vote* (New York: Pantheon, 1988).

3. Joanne Laucius, "Vote or Die?" *Ottawa Citizen*, November 4, 2004, p. A8.

4. Bruce E. Cain, Todd Donovan, and Caroline J. Tolbert, *Democracy in the States: Experiments in Election Reform* (Washington, DC: Brookings Institution Press, 2008).

5. Pew Research Center for the People and the Press, "No Consensus about Whether Nation Is Divided Into 'Haves' and 'Have-Nots,'" September 29, 2011, http://pewresearch.org/pubs/2109/haves-have-nots-economic-divisions (accessed 9/14/12).

6. The American National Election Studies (ANES), "American National Election Study, 2008: Pre- and Post-Election Survey" [computer file], ICPSR25383-v1, Ann Arbor, MI: Inter-university Consortium for Political and Social Research [distributor], 2009-06-10. doi:10.3886/ICPSR25383 (accessed 12/4/09).

7. Sidney Verba, Kay Lehman Schlozman, and Henry E. Brady, *Voice and Equality: Civic Voluntarism in American Politics* (Cambridge, MA: Harvard University Press, 2005), chap. 3, for kinds of participation, and pp. 66–7 for prevalence of local activity.

8. Karen Mossberger, Caroline Tolbert, and Ramona McNeal, *Digital Citizenship: The Internet, Society, and Participation* (Cambridge, MA: MIT Press, 2008).

9. Pew Internet and American Life Project, "Trend Data (Adults): What Internet Users Do Online," April 2012, http://pewinternet.org/Trend-Data-%28Adults%29/Online-Activites-Total.aspx (accessed 7/26/12).

10. Aaron Smith, "The Internet's Role in Campaign 2008," Pew Research Center for the People and the Press, November 2008.

11. David Redlawsk, Caroline Tolbert, and Todd Donovan, *Why Iowa? How Caucuses and Sequential Elections Improve the Presidential Nominating Process* (Chicago: University of Chicago Press, 2011). See also Karen Mossberger and Caroline Tolbert, "Digital Democracy," in *The Oxford Handbook of American Elections and Political Behavior*, ed. Jan Leighley (New York: Oxford University Press, 2010).

12. Mossberger, Tolbert, and McNeal, *Digital Citizenship*; B. S. Krueger, "Assessing the Potential of Internet Political Participation in the United States," *American Politics Research* 30 (2002): 476–98; B. S. Krueger, "A Comparison of Conventional and Internet Political Mobilization," *American Politics Research* 34, no. 6 (2006): 759–76; Andrew Chadwick, *Internet Politics: States, Citizens, and New Communication Technologies* (Oxford, UK: Oxford University Press, 2006); Bruce Bimber, *Information and American Democracy: Technology in the Evolution of Political Power* (Cambridge, UK: Cambridge University Press, 2003); and

Rachel Gibson, Wainer Lusoli, and Steven Ward, "Online Participation in the UK: Testing a 'Contextualized' Model of Internet Effects," *British Journal of Politics and International Relations* 7, no. 4 (2006): 561–83.

13. Karen Mossberger, Allison Hamilton, and Caroline Tolbert, "Measuring Digital Citizenship: Mobile Access and the Less Connected," *International Journal of Communication*, forthcoming.

14. Verba, Schlozman, and Brady, *Voice and Equality*.

15. Caroline Tolbert and Ramona McNeal, "Unraveling the Effects of the Internet on Political Participation." *Political Research Quarterly* 56, no. 2 (2003): 175–85; see also Bruce Bimber, "Information and Political Engagement in America: The Search for Effects of Information Technology at the Individual Level," *Political Research Quarterly* 54 (2001): 53–67; Bruce Bimber, *Information and American Democracy: Technology in the Evolution of Political Power* (Cambridge, UK: Cambridge University Press, 2003); and Brian Krueger, "Assessing the Potential of Internet Political Participation in the United States," *American Politics Research* 30 (2002): 476–98. Thomas, J. and G. Streib, "The New Face of Government: Citizen-Initiated Contacts in the Era of E-Government," *Journal of Public Administration Theory and Research* 13, no. 1(2003): 83–102; D. V. Shah, J. Cho, William P. Eveland, and N. Kwak, "Information and Expression in a Digital Age: Modeling Internet Effects on Civic Participation," *Communication Research* 32, no. 5 (2005): 531–65; K. Kenski and N. J. Stroud, "Connections Between Internet Use and Political Efficacy, Knowledge, and Participation," *Journal of Broadcasting and Electronic Media* 50, no. 2 (2006): 173–92; Arthur Lupia and G. Sin, "Which Public Goods Are Endangered? How Evolving Communication Technologies Affect the Logic of Collective Action," *Public Choice* 117 (2003): 315–31.

16. Smith, "Internet's Role in Campaign 2008." See also Darrell West, *The New Wave* (Washington DC: Brookings Institution Press, 2011).

17. Pew Internet and American Life Project, "Post-Election 2004 Tracking Survey," November 22, 2004, www.pewinternet.org/Shared-Content/Data-Sets/2004/PostElection-2004-Tracking-Survey.aspx (accessed 12/29/08).

18. Doris Graber, *Processing the News: How People Tame the Information Tide*, 2nd ed. (New York: Longman, 1988).

19. Mossberger and Tolbert, "Digital Democracy."

20. Caroline Tolbert and Allison Hamilton, "Political Engagement and the Internet in the 2008 U.S. Presidential Election: A Panel Survey," in Eva Anduiza, Mike Jensen, and Laia Jorba, eds., *Digital Media and Political Engagement Worldwide: A Comparative Study* (Cambridge, UK: Cambridge University Press, 2012).

21. Sunshine Hillygus and Todd Shields, *The Persuadable Voter: Wedge Issues in Presidential Campaigns* (Princeton, NJ: Princeton University Press, 2008).

22. Karen Mossberger and Caroline Tolbert, "Digital Democracy," in *Oxford Handbook of American Elections*

*and Political Behavior*, ed. Jan Leighley (New York: Oxford University Press, 2010).

23. W. R. Neuman, M. R. Just, and A. N. Crigler, *Common Knowledge: News and the Construction of Political Meaning* (Chicago: University of Chicago Press, 1992).

24. David P. Redlawsk, "Hot Cognition or Cool Consideration: Testing the Effects of Motivated Reasoning," *Journal of Politics* 64 (2002): 1021–44.

25. Michael Margolis and D. Resnick, *Politics as Usual: The Cyberspace "Revolution"* (Thousand Oaks, CA: Sage, 2000).

26. Pew Internet and American Life Project, "Post-Election 2004 Tracking Survey."

27. Manuel Castells, *The Rise of the Network Society: The Information Age: Economy, Society, and Culture* (Oxford, UK: Blackwell, 1997).

28. Bimber, *Information and American Democracy*; Bruce Bimber and Richard Davis, *Campaigning Online: The Internet in U.S. Elections* (Cambridge, UK: Cambridge University Press, 2003).

29. D. Stolle and M. Micheletti, "The Expansion of Political Action Repertoires: Theoretical Reflections on Results from the Nike Email Exchange Internet Campaign," American Political Science Association, Washington, D.C., 2005.

30. Joseph Graf, "The Audience for Political Blogs: New Research on Blog Readership," Institute for Politics, Democracy & the Internet, October 2006.

31. Russell Dalton, *The Good Citizen: How a Younger Generation Is Reshaping American Politics* (Washington, DC: CQ Press, 2008).

32. Robert Putnam. *Bowling Alone: The Collapse and Revival of American Community* (New York: Simon and Schuster, 2000).

33. Mossberger, Tolbert, and McNeal, *Digital Citizenship*; Pippa Norris, *Digital Divide: Civic Engagement, Information Poverty, and the Internet Worldwide* (New York: Cambridge University Press, 2001); Benjamin Barber, "The New Telecommunications Technology: Endless Frontier or the End of Democracy?" *Constellations* 4, no. 2 (2011): 208–28; Tolbert and McNeal, "Unraveling the Effects of the Internet"; H. Rheingold, *The Virtual Community: Homesteading on the Electronic Frontier* (Reading, MA: Addison-Wesley, 1993).

34. Acronyms for the Stop Online Piracy Act (SOPA) and the PROTECT IP Act (Preventing Real Online Threats to Economic Creativity and Theft of Intellectual Property Act, or PIPA).

35. "A Political Coming of Age for the Tech Industry" *New York Times*, January 18, 2012.

36. "Public Outcry over Antipiracy Bills Began as Grass-Roots Grumbling: Suddenly, Hollywood Wants to Sit Down and Talk," *New York Times*, January 20, 2012, p. B1.

37. Mossberger, Tolbert, and McNeal, *Digital Citizenship*.

38. Pippa Norris, *Digital Divide: Civic Engagement, Information Poverty, and the Internet Worldwide* (New York: Cambridge University Press, 2001). See also Karen Mossberger, Caroline Tolbert, and May Stansbury. *Virtual Inequality:*

*Beyond the Digital Divide* (Washington, DC: Georgetown University Press, 2003).

39. U.S. Department of Commerce. "Digital Nation," National Telecommunications and Information Administration, Washington, DC, 2011.

40. Karen Mossberger, Caroline Tolbert, and William Franko, *Digital Cities: The Internet and the Geography of Opportunity* (New York: Oxford University Press, 2012).

41. *Citizens United v. Federal Election Commission*, 558 U.S. 50 (2010).

42. Michael P. McDonald, "American Voter Turnout in Historical Perspective," in *The Oxford Handbook of American Elections and Political Behavior*, pp. 125–43.

43. Todd Donovan and Shaun Bowler, *Reforming the Republic: Democratic Institutions for the New America* (Upper Saddle River, NJ: Pearson Education, 2004).

44. For a discussion of the decline in voter turnout over time, see Ruy A. Teixeira, *The Disappearing American Voter* (Washington, DC: Brookings Institution Press, 1992). See also Michael McDonald and Samuel Popkin, "The Myth of the Vanishing Voter" *American Political Science Review*, 95 (2001): 963–74, and Michael McDonald, "Voter Turnout," *United States Election Project*, http.//elections.gmu.edu/voter_turnout.htm (accessed 9/14/12).

45. Robert Jackman, "Political Institutions and Voter Turnout in the Democracies," *American Political Science Review* 81 (June 1987): 420.

46. Anthony Downs, *An Economic Theory of Democracy* (New York: Harper and Row, 1957); William H. Riker and Peter C. Ordeshook, "A Theory of the Calculus of Voting," *American Political Science Review* 62, no. 1 (1968): 25–42.

47. Angus Campbell, Philip E. Converse, Warren E. Miller, and Donald E. Stokes, *The American Voter* (New York: Wiley, 1960); Steven Rosenstone and John Mark Hansen, *Mobilization, Participation, and Democracy in America* (New York: Macmillan, 1993).

48. Sidney Verba and Norman H. Nie, *Participation in America: Political Democracy and Social Equality* (New York: Harper and Row, 1972).

49. Douglas R. Hess and Jody Herman, "Representational Bias in the 2008 Electorate," November 2009, www.projectvote.org/reports-on-the-electorate-/440.html (accessed 11/21/09).

50. Jan E. Leighley and Jonathan Nagler, "Socioeconomic Class Bias in Turnout, 1964–1988: The Voters Remain the Same," *American Political Science Review* 86, no. 3 (1992): 725–36.

51. See Richard A. Brody, "The Puzzle of Political Participation in America," in *The New American Political System*, ed. Anthony King (Washington, DC: American Enterprise Institute, 1978), chap. 8.

52. Rosenstone and Hansen, *Mobilization, Participation, and Democracy*, p. 59.

53. Alan S. Gerber and Donald P. Green, "The Effects of Canvassing, Telephone Calls, and Direct Mail on Voter

Turnout: A Field Experiment," *American Political Science Review* 94, no. 3 (September 2000): 660.

54. Donald P. Green and Alan S. Gerber, "Getting Out the Youth Vote: Results from Randomized Field Experiments," December 29, 2001, pp. 26–7, www.youngvoterstrategies .org (accessed 3/8/08).

55. Student PIRGs New Voter Project, "Text Reminders Increase Primary Youth Turnout," October 2008, www .newvotersproject.org/research/text-messaging (accessed 11/30/09).

56. Erik Austin and Jerome Chubb, *Political Facts of the United States since 1789* (New York: Columbia University Press, 1986), pp. 378–9.

57. Michael P. McDonald and John Samples, eds., *The Marketplace of Democracy: Electoral Competition and American Politics* (Washington, DC: Brookings Institution Press, 2006).

58. Mark N. Franklin, "Electoral Participation," in *Comparing Democracies: Elections and Voting in Global Perspective*, ed. Lawrence LeDuc, Richard G. Niemi, and Pippa Norris (Thousand Oaks, CA: Sage, 1996), pp. 216–35; G. Bingham Powell, "American Voter Turnout in Comparative Perspective," *American Political Science Review* 80, no. 1 (1986): 17–43.

59. Todd Donovan, "A Goal for Reform: Make Elections Worth Stealing," *PS: Political Science and Politics* 40, no. 4 (2007): 681–6.

60. Donovan, "A Goal for Reform"; Gary W. Cox and Michael C. Munger, "Closeness, Expenditures, and Turnout in the 1982 U.S. House Elections," *American Political Science Review* 83, no. 1 (1989): 217–31; James G. Gimpel, Karen M. Kaufmann, and Shanna Pearson-Merkowitz, "Battleground States versus Blackout States: The Behavioral Implications of Modern Presidential Campaigns," *Journal of Politics* 69, no. 3 (2007): 786–97.

61. Donovan and Bowler, *Reforming the Republic*; McDonald and Samples, *Marketplace of Democracy*; Gary Jacobson, *The Politics of Congressional Elections*, 7th ed. (New York: Longman, 2008).

62. Samuel C. Patterson and Gregory A. Caldeira, "Getting Out the Vote: Participation in Gubernatorial Elections," *American Political Science Review* 77, no. 3 (1983): 675–89; Gregory A. Caldeira and Samuel C. Patterson, "Contextual Influences on Participation in U.S. State Legislative Elections," *Legislative Studies Quarterly* 7, no. 3 (1982): 359–81; Cox and Munger, "Closeness, Expenditures, and Turnout"; Gary W. Copeland, "Activating Voters in Congressional Elections," *Political Behavior* 5, no. 4 (1983): 391–401; Robert A. Jackson, "The Mobilization of U.S. State Electorates in the 1988 and 1990 Elections," *Journal of Politics* 59, no. 2 (1997): 520–37; Thomas M. Holbrook and Scott D. McClurg, "The Mobilization of Core Supporters: Campaigns, Turnout, and Electoral Composition in United States Presidential Elections," *American Journal of Political Science* 49, no. 4 (2005):

689–703; Andre Blais, "What Affects Voter Turnout?" *Annual Review of Political Science* 9 (2006): 111–25; Andre Blais and Agnieszka Dobrzynska, "Turnout in Electoral Democracies," *European Journal of Political Research* 33, no. 2 (2003): 239–61.

63. Caroline Tolbert, Daniel C. Bowen, and Todd Donovan, "Initiative Campaigns: Direct Democracy and Voter Mobilization," *American Politics Research* 37, no. 1 (2009): 155–92.

64. Caroline Tolbert, John A. Grummel, and Daniel A. Smith, "The Effects of Ballot Initiatives on Voter Turnout in the American States," *American Politics Research* 29, no. 6 (2001): 625–48; Mark A. Smith, "The Contingent Effects of Ballot Initiatives and Candidate Races on Turnout," *American Journal of Political Science* 45, no. 3 (2001): 700–706; Caroline J. Tolbert and Daniel A. Smith, "The Educative Effects of Ballot Initiatives on Voter Turnout," *American Politics Research* 33, no. 2 (2005): 283–309; Daniel A. Smith and Caroline J. Tolbert, *Educated by Initiative: The Effects of Direct Democracy on Citizens and Political Organizations in the American States* (Ann Arbor: University of Michigan Press, 2004).

65. Stephen Nicholson, *Voting the Agenda: Candidates, Elections, and Ballot Propositions* (Princeton, NJ: Princeton University Press, 2005).

66. Todd Donovan, Caroline Tolbert, and Daniel Smith, "Priming Presidential Votes with Direct Democracy, *Journal of Politics* 70, no. 4 (2008): 1217–31.

67. Jeffrey Karp and Caroline Tolbert, "Support for Nationalizing Presidential Elections," *Presidential Studies Quarterly* 40, no. 4 (2010): 771–93; Daron Shaw, *The Race to 270: The Electoral College and the Campaign Strategies of 2000 and 2004* (Chicago: University of Chicago Press, 2006).

68. Gimpel, Kaufmann, Pearson-Merkowitz, "Battleground States versus Blackout States"; Julianna Sandell Pacheco, "Political Socialization in Context: The Effect of Political Competition on Youth Voter Turnout," *Political Behavior* 30, no. 4 (2008): 415–36; Keena Lipsitz, "The Consequences of Battleground and 'Spectator' State Residency for Political Participation," *Political Behavior* 31, no. 2 (2009): 187–209.

69. Redlawsk, Tolbert, and Donovan, *Why Iowa?*

70. Cain, Donovan, and Tolbert, *Democracy in the States.*

71. The data in this paragraph are drawn from the Sentencing Project and Human Rights Watch, "Losing the Vote: The Impact of Felony Disenfranchisement Laws in the United States" (October 1998), www.sentencingproject.org/ tmp/File/FVR/fd_losingthevote.pdf (accessed 2/22/08).

72. Sentencing Project, "Expanding the Vote: State Felony Disenfranchisement Reform, 1997–2008," September 25, 2008, www.sentencingproject.org/detail/news/cfm?news _id=492 (accessed 11/30/09).

73. Ryan S. King, "Expanding the Vote: State Felony Disenfranchisement Reform, 1997–2008" (Sentencing Project, Septem-

ber 2008), www.sentencingproject.org/doc/publications/fd_statedisenfranchisement.pdf (accessed 12/5/09).

74. Chris Uggen and Jeffrey Manza, "Democratic Contraction: Political Consequences of Felon Disenfranchisement in the United States," *American Sociological Review 2002* 67, no. 6 (2002): 777–803.

75. Matt Barreto, Stephen Nuño, and Gabriel Sanchez, "The Disproportionate Impact of Voter-ID Requirements on the Electorate—New Evidence from Indiana," *PS: Political Science & Politics* 42 (2009): 111–16.

76. Benjamin Highton, "Easy Registration and Voter Turnout," *Journal of Politics* 59 (1997): 565–75; Benjamin Highton, "Voter Registration and Turnout in the United States," *Perspectives on Politics* 2, no. 3 (2004): 507–15; Michael J. Hanmer, *Discount Voting: Voter Registration Reforms and Their Effects* (New York: Cambridge University Press, 2009); Cain, Donovan, and Tolbert, *Democracy in the States*.

77. Cain, Donovan, and Tolbert, *Democracy in the States*.

78. Robert A. Jackson, Robert D. Brown, and Gerald C. Wright, "Registration, Turnout and the Electoral Representativeness of U.S. State Electorates," *American Politics Quarterly* 26, no. 3 (July 1998): 259–87. See also Benjamin Highton, "Easy Registration and Voter Turnout," *Journal of Politics* 59, no. 2 (April 1997): 565–87.

79. Highton "Easy Registration and Voter Turnout"; Stephen Knack and James White, "Election-Day Registration and Turnout Inequality," *Political Behavior* 22, no. 1 (2000): 29–44; Craig Leonard Brians and Bernard Grofman, "When Registration Barriers Fall, Who Votes? An Empirical Test of a Rational Choice Model," *Public Choice* 99 (1999): 161–76; Michael J. Hanmer, *Discount Voting: Voter Registration Reforms and Their Effects* (New York: Cambridge University Press, 2009); Mary Fitzgerald, "Greater Convenience But Not Greater Turnout: The Impact of Alternative Voting Methods on Electoral Participation in the United States," *American Politics Research* 33, no. 6 (2005): 842–67; Caroline J. Tolbert, Todd Donovan, Bridgett King, and Shaun Bowler, "Election Day Registration, Competition, and Voter Turnout," in *Democracy in the States: Experiments in Election Reform*, ed. Bruce E. Cain, Todd Donovan, and Caroline J. Tolbert (Washington, DC: Brookings Institution Press, 2008), pp. 83–98.

80. Hanmer, *Discount Voting*; Robert A. Jackson, Robert D. Brown, and Gerald C. Wright, "Registration, Turnout, and the Electoral Representativeness of U.S. State Electorates," *American Politics Quarterly* 26, no. 3 (1998): 259–87; Robert D. Brown, Robert A. Jackson, and Gerald C. Wright, "Registration, Turnout, and State Party Systems," *Political Research Quarterly* 52, no. 3 (1999): 463–79.

81. Michael P. McDonald, 2008. "Portable Voter Registration," *Political Behavior* 30, no. 4 (2008): 491–501.

82. Cain, Donovan, and Tolbert, *Democracy in the States*.

83. Michael McDonald, "2008 Early Voting Statistics," *United States Election Project*, http://elections.gmu.edu/early vote 2008.html (accessed 11/20/09).

84. Paul Gronke, Eva Galanes-Rosenbaum, and Peter Miller, "Early Voting and Turnout," *PS: Political Science and Politics* 40, no. 4 (October 2007): 639–45; Fitzgerald "Greater Convenience but Not Greater Turnout"; Adam J. Berinsky, "The Perverse Consequences of Electoral Reform in the United States," *American Politics Research* 33, no. 4 (2005): 471–91.

85. Jeffrey Karp and Susan Banducci, "Going Postal: How All-Mail Elections Influence Turnout," *Political Behavior* 22, no. 3 (2000): 223–39.

86. Connie Cass, "'Motor Voter' Impact Slight," *Chattanooga News-Free Press*, June 20, 1997, p. A5. On the need to motivate voters, see Marshall Ganz, "Motor Voter or Motivated Voter?" *American Prospect* 28 (September–October 1996): 41–9. On the hopes for Motor Voter, see Frances Fox Piven and Richard A. Cloward, "Northern Bourbons: A Preliminary Report on the National Voter Registration Act," *PS: Political Science and Politics* 29, no. 1 (March 1996): 39–42. On turnout in the 1996 election, see Barbara Vobejda, "Just under Half of Possible Voters Went to the Polls," *Washington Post*, November 7, 1996, p. A3.

87. Elizabeth Rigby and Melanie J. Springer, "Does Electoral Reform Increase (or Decrease) Political Equality?" *Political Research Quarterly* (2010): 1–15.

88. Democracy Corps, "The 2008 Early Voting Statistics," *United States Election Project*, http://elections.gmu.edu/early vote 2008.html (accessed 11/20/09).

89. "Voting by Mail and Turnout: A Replication and Extension," Early Voting Information Center, www.earlyvoting.net/blog/node/155 (accessed 12/5/09); Paul Gronke, Eva Galanes-Rosenbaum, and Peter Miller, "Early Voting and Turnout," *PS: Political Science and Politics* 40, no. 4 (October 2007): 639–45.

90. Lawrence Bobo and Franklin D. Gilliam, "Race, Sociopolitical Participation, and Black Empowerment," *American Political Science Review* 24, no. 2 (June 1990): 377–93.

91. Rene Rocha, Caroline Tolbert, Daniel Bowen, and Chris Clark, "Race and Turnout: Does Descriptive Representation in State Legislatures Increase Minority Voting?" *Political Research Quarterly* 63, no. 3 (2010): 890–907.

92. Susan Banducci, Todd Donovan, and Jeffrey Karp, "Minority Representation, Empowerment and Participation," *Journal of Politics* 66, no. 2 (2004): 34–556.

93. Matt Barreto, Gary Segura, and Nathan Woods, "The Mobilizing Effect of Majority—Minority Districts on Latino Turnout," *American Political Science Review* 98 (2004): 65–75.

94. Adrian Pantoja and Gary Segura, "Does Ethnicity Matter? Descriptive Representation in the Statehouse and Political Alienation Among Latinos," *Social Science Quarterly* 84 (2003): 441–60.

95. Ryan Claassen, "Political Opinion and Distinctiveness: The Case of Hispanic Ethnicity," *Political Research Quarterly* 57 (2004): 609–20.

96. Connie Cass, "'Motor Voter' Impact Slight," *Chattanooga News-Free Press*, June 20, 1997, p. A5. On the need to motivate voters see Marshall Ganz, "Motor Voter or Motivated Voter?" *American Prospect*, no. 28 (September–October 1996): 41–49. On the hopes for Motor Voter, see Fox Piven and Cloward, "Northern Bourbons." On turnout in the 1996 election, see Barbara Vobejda, "Just under Half of Possible Voters Went to the Polls," *Washington Post*, November 7, 1996, p. A3.

97. See William Julius Wilson, *The Truly Disadvantaged: The Inner City, the Underclass, and Public Policy* (Chicago: University of Chicago Press, 1987); and Douglas Massey and Nancy Denton, *American Apartheid: Segregation and the Making of the American Underclass* (Cambridge, MA: Harvard University Press, 1993).

98. See Michael C. Dawson, *Behind the Mule: Race and Class in African-American Politics* (Princeton, NJ: Princeton University Press, 1994), chaps. 5 and 6.

99. Dawson, *Behind the Mule*.

100. Mark Hugo Lopez and Paul Taylor, "Dissecting the 2008 Electorate: Most Diverse in U.S. History," Pew Research Center, April 30, 2009, www.pewhispanic .org/2009/04/30/dissecting-the-2008-electorate-most -diverse-in-us-history/ (accessed 9/14/12).

101. Barreto, Nuño, and Sanchez, "The Disproportionate Impact of Voter ID Requirements."

102. U.S. Census Bureau, "Resident Population by Race, Hispanic Origin Status, and Age—Projections," www .census.gov/compendia/statab/cats/population/ estimates_and_projections_by_age_sex_raceethnicity .html (accessed 11/25/09).

103. Douglas R. Hess and Jody Herman, "Representational Bias in the 2008 Electorate, November 2009," www.project vote.org/reports-on-the-electorate-/440.html (accessed 11/21/09). The 2012 data are from exit polls available at http://elections.nytimes.com (accessed 11/11/12).

104. Center for Health Policy, University of New Mexico, "New Survey Shows Overwhelming Support among Latinos for Health Care Reform That Includes Public Option," November 30, 2009, http://healthpolicy.unm .edu/resources/new-survey-shows-overwhelming -support-among-latinos-health-care-reform-includes -public-opt (accessed 12/1/09).

105. Liz Sidoti, "Keeping Latino Support a Big Challenge for Obama," *Associated Press*, November 29, 2009, www .chron.com/disp/story.mpl/nation/6743401.html (accessed 11/29/09).

106. U.S. Census Bureau, "Resident Population by Race, Hispanic Origin Status, and Age—Projections," www .census.gov/compendia/statab/cats/population/ estimates_and_projections_by_age_sex_raceethnicity .html (accessed 11/24/09).

107. U.S. Census Bureau, "Reported Voting and Registration by Race, Hispanic Origin, Sex, and Age Groups: November 1964 to 2008"; "Reported Voting and Regis- tration by Region, Educational Attainment, and Labor Force: November 1964 to 2008," CNN National Exit Poll 2008, www.cnn.com/ELECTION/2008/results/ polls/#USP00p1 (accessed 11/22/09).

108. Anne E. Kornblut, "Bush Plan to Win Over Democratic Voters Lags," *Boston Globe*, April 27, 2003, p. A1.

109. CNN.com, "America Votes, 2006."

110. Dan Balz and Jon Cohen, "Majority in Poll Favor Deadline for Iraq Pullout," *Washington Post*, February 27, 2007, p. A1.

111. Gallup Poll, January 2003.

112. Center for American Women and Politics, "Gender Gap in 2004 Presidential Race Is Widespread" (November 10, 2004), www.cawp.rutgers.edu/Facts/Elections/ GG2004widespread.pdf (accessed 2/22/08).

113. National Conference of State Legislatures, "Women in State Legislatures: 2009 Legislative Session," www.ncsl.org/default.aspx?tabid=15398 (accessed 11/25/09).

114. Kira Sanbonmatsu, "Political Parties and the Recruit- ment of Women to State Legislatures," *Journal of Poli- tics* 64, no. 3 (August 2002): 791–809; Jennifer L. Lawless and Richard L. Fox, *Why Are Women Still Not Running for Public Office?* (Washington, DC: Brookings Institution Press, 2008).

115. Center for American Women and Politics, "The Impact of Women in Public Office: Findings at a Glance" (New Brunswick, NJ: Rutgers University Press, n.d.).

116. Paul Taylor, Rich Morin, D'Vera Cohn, April Clark, and Wendy Wang, "A Paradox in Public Attitudes: Men or Women: Who's the Better Leader?" Pew Research Cen- ter, Washington, DC, August 25, 2008, p. 25, http:// pewsocialtrends.org/assets/pdf/gender-leadership.pdf (accessed 12/6/09).

117. Emily Hoban Kirby and Kei Kawashima-Ginsberg, "The Youth Vote in 2008," Center for Information and Research on Civic Learning and Engagement, August 17, 2009, www.civicyouth.org/?page_id=241 (accessed 11/25/09).

118. Michael DeCourcy Hinds, "Youth Vote 2000: They'd Rather Volunteer," *Carnegie Reporter* 1, no. 2 (Spring 2001): 2.

119. Kirby and Kei Kawashima-Ginsberg, "The Youth Vote in 2008," *The Center for Information & Research on Civic Learning & Engagement*, August 17, 2009, www.civicyouth .org/?page_id=241 (accessed 11/25/09).

120. CNN National Exit Poll 2008, www.cnn.com/ ELECTION/2008/results/polls/#UPS00p1 (accessed 11/22/09).

121. The OnLine NewsHour, Generation Next: Speak Up Be Heard, "Iraq, Economy Weigh on Minds of Young Voters," August 31, 2007, www.pbs.org/newshour/ generation-next/demographic/youthvote_08-31.html (accessed 2/21/08).

122. Emily Hoban Kirby, Karlo Barrios Marcelo, and Kei Kawashima-Ginsberg, "Volunteering and the College

Experience," Center for Information and Research on Civic Learning and Engagement, August 2009, www.civicyouth.org/?page_id=237 (accessed 11/25/09).

123. The Center of Information and Research on Civic Learning and Engagement, "Millennials Talk Politics: A Study of College Student Political Engagement," 2007, www.civicyouth.org/?page_id=250 (accessed 11/29/09).

124. *Engel v. Vitale*, 370 U.S. 421 (1962); *Abington School District v. Schempp*, 374 U.S. 203 (1963).

125. Laurie Goodstein, "Bush's Charity Plan Is Raising Concerns for Religious Right," *New York Times*, March 3, 2001, p. A1.

126. John Griffin, and Michael Keane, "Are Voters Better Represented?" *Journal of Politics* 67, no. 4 (2005): 1206–27.

127. Larry Bartels, *Unequal Democracy: The Political Economy of the New Gilded Age* (Princeton, NJ: Princeton University Press, 2008).

128. *Buckley v. Valeo*, 424 U.S. 1 (1976).

129. *Citizens United v. Federal Election Commission*.

## Chapter 9

1. Todd Donovan and Shaun Bowler, *Reforming the Republic: Democratic Institutions for the New America* (Upper Saddle River, NJ: Prentice Hall, 2003).

2. Morris Fiorina, Samuel Abrams, and Jeremy Pope. *Culture War? The Myth of a Polarized America* (New York: Pearson Longman, 2004).

3. E. E. Schattschneider, *The Semi-Sovereign People: A Realist's View of Democracy in America* (New York: Holt, Rinehart, Winston, 1960).

4. Donovan and Bowler, *Reforming the Republic.*

5. James Madison, *The Federalist Papers*, no. 10: "The Same Subject Continued: The Union as a Safeguard against Domestic Faction and Insurrection. The New York Packet. Friday, November 23, 1787," http://thomas.loc.gov/home/histdox/fed_10.html (accessed 11/11/12).

6. See Matthew Crenson and Benjamin Ginsberg, *Downsizing Democracy* (Baltimore: Johns Hopkins University Press, 2002).

7. Jacob S. Hacker and Paul Pierson, *Winner-Take-All Politics: How Washington Made the Rich Richer—and Turned Its Back on the Middle Class* (New York: Simon & Schuster, 2010).

8. Larry Bartels, *Unequal Democracy: The Political Economy of the New Guilded Age* (Princeton, NJ: Princeton University Press, 2008).

9. Benjamin Ginsberg, *The Consequences of Consent* (New York: Random House, 1982), chap. 4.

10. Nolan McCarty, Keith T. Poole, and Howard Rosenthal. *Polarized America: The Dance of Ideology and Unequal Riches.* Cambridge, MA: MIT Press, 2006. For 2010 data, see Voteview.com, http://voteview.com/polarized_america.htm#POLITICALPOLARIZATION.

11. Donovan and Bowler, *Reforming the Republic.*

12. Frank Newport, "Congress Ends 2011 with Record-Low 11% Approval," Gallup Politics, December 19, 2011, www.gallup.com/poll/151628/Congress-Ends-2011-Record-Low-Approval.aspx (accessed 9/16/12)

13. Fiorina, Abrams, and Pope. *The Myth of a Polarized America.*

14. For a discussion of third parties in the United States, see Daniel Mazmanian, *Third Parties in Presidential Elections* (Washington, DC: Brookings Institution Press, 1974).

15. See Maurice Duverger, *Political Parties* (New York: Wiley, 1954).

16. Alex Isenstadt, "Tea Party Candidates Falling Short," *Politico*, March 7, 2010, www.politico.com/news/stories/0310/34041.html (accessed 3/11/10).

17. Donovan and Bowler, *Reforming the Republic.*

18. Andri Blais. *To Keep or To Change First Past the Post? The Politics of Election Reform* (New York: Oxford University Press, 2008).

19. Glen Justice, "F.E.C. Declines to Curb Independent Fund Raisers," *New York Times*, May 14, 2004, p. A16.

20. Jim Rutenberg and David D. Kirkpatrick, "A New Channel for Soft Money Appears in Race," *New York Times*, November 12, 2007, p. A1.

21. *Citizens United v. Federal Election Commission*, 558 U.S. 50 (2010).

22. See Harold Gosnell, *Machine Politics Chicago Model*, rev. ed. (Chicago: University of Chicago Press, 1968).

23. For a useful discussion, see John Bibby and Thomas Holbrook, "Parties and Elections," in *Politics in the American States*, ed. Virginia Gray and Herbert Jacob (Washington, DC: CQ Press, 1996), pp. 78–121.

24. Kyle L. Saunders and Alan I. Abramowitz, "Ideological Realignment and Active Partisans in the American Electorate," *American Politics Research* 32 (May 2004): 285–309.

25. Based on exit polls available at http://elections.nytimes.com/2012/results/president/exit-polls (accessed 11/12/12).

26. The Pew Forum on Religion and Public Life, "How the Faithful Voted: 2012 Preliminary Analysis," www.pewforum.org/Politics-and-Elections/How-the-Faithful-Voted-2012-Preliminary-Exit-Poll-Analysis.aspx#rr (accessed 11/12/12).

27. Christopher Shea, "Who Are You Calling Working Class?" *Boston Globe*, February 12, 2006, www.boston.com/news/globe/ideas/articles/2006/02/12/who_are_you_calling_working_class/ (accessed 2/24/08).

28. Shaun Bowler, Gary Segura, and Stephen Nicholson. "Earthquakes and Aftershocks: Race, Direct Democracy, and Partisan Change," *American Journal of Political Science* 50 (January 2006): 146–59.

29. See Morris Fiorina, "Parties and Partisanship: A Forty Year Retrospective," *Political Behavior* 24, no. 2 (June 2002): 93–115.

30. On the limited polarization among ordinary voters, see Fiorina, Abrams, and Pope, *Culture War?*; on growing partisan attachment among a subset of voters, see Alan Abramowitz and Kyle Saunders, "Why Can't We Just Get Along? The Reality of a Polarized America," *The Forum* 3, no. 2 (2005): 1–22.

31. Raymond J. La Raja, "Political Parties in the Era of Soft Money," in *The Parties Respond: Changes in American Parties and Campaigns*, 4th ed., ed. Sandy L. Maisel (Boulder, CO: Westview Press, 2002), pp. 163–88.

32. For an excellent analysis of the parties' role in recruitment, see Paul Herrnson, *Congressional Elections: Campaigning at Home and in Washington* (Washington, DC: CQ Press, 1995).

33. Daniel Galvin, *Presidential Party Building: Dwight D. Eisenhower to George W. Bush* (Princeton, NJ: Princeton University Press, 2009).

34. Stanley Kelley Jr., Richard E. Ayres, and William Bowen, "Registration and Voting: Putting First Things First," *American Political Science Review* 61 (June 1967): 359–70.

35. David H. Fischer, *The Revolution of American Conservatism* (New York: Harper & Row, 1965), p. 93.

36. Henry Jones Ford, *The Rise and Growth of American Politics: A Sketch of Constitutional Development* (1898 reprint; New York: Da Capo Press, 1967 edition), chap. 9.

37. Ford, *The Rise and Growth of American Politics*, p. 125.

38. Ford, *The Rise and Growth of American Politics*, p. 125.

39. Ford, *The Rise and Growth of American Politics*, p. 126.

## Chapter 10

1. *Gray v. Sanders*, 372 U.S. 368 (1963); *Wesberry v. Sanders*, 376 U.S. 1 (1964); *Reynolds v. Sims*, 377 U.S. 533 (1964).

2. *Thornburg v. Gingles*, 478 U.S. 613 (1986).

3. *Shaw v. Reno*, 509 U.S. 113 (1993).

4. Daron Shaw, *The Race to 270: The Electoral College and the Campaign Strategies of 2000 and 2004* (Chicago: University of Chicago Press, 2006).

5. State legislatures determine the system by which electors are selected. Almost all states use this "winner-take-all" system. Maine and Nebraska, however, provide that one electoral vote goes to the winner in each congressional district and two electoral votes go to the winner statewide.

6. *Bush v. Gore*, 531 U.S. 98 (2000).

7. Jeffrey Karp and Caroline J. Tolbert, "Explaining Support for Nationalizing Presidential Elections," Midwest Political Science Association (2009)

8. See www.nationalpopularvote.com for details (accessed 9/26/12).

9. Karp and Tolbert, *Explaining Support*; Shaw, *Race to 270.*

10. David Redlawsk, Caroline J. Tolbert, and Todd Donovan, *Why Iowa? How Caucuses and Sequential Elections Improve the Presidential Nomination Process* (Chicago: University of Chicago Press, 2011).

11. Redlawsk, Tolbert, and Donovan, *Why Iowa?*

12. Adam Nagourney, "Court Strikes Down Ban on Gay Marriage in California," *New York Times*, February 7, 2012, www.nytimes.com/2012/02/08/us/marriage-ban-violates-constitution-court-rules.html (accessed 8/21/12).

13. Daniel Smith and Caroline J. Tolbert, *Educated by Initiative: The Effects of Direct Democracy on Citizens and Political Organizations in the American States* (Ann Arbor: University of Michigan Press, 2004).

14. Shaun Bowler, Todd Donovan, and Caroline J. Tolbert. *Citizens as Legislators: Direct Democracy in the United States* (Columbus: Ohio State University Press, 1998).

15. Caroline Tolbert, Daniel Bowen, and Todd Donovan, "Initiative Campaigns; Direct Democracy and Voter Mobilization," *American Politics Research* 37, no.1 (2009): 155–192.

16. Caroline Tolbert, Daniel Bowen and Todd Donovan, "Initiative Campaigns: Direct Democracy and Voter Mobilization," American *Politics Research 37*, no. 1 (2009): 155–92.

17. Stephen Nicholson, *Voting the Agenda: Candidates, Elections, and Ballot Propositions* (Princeton, NJ: Princeton University Press, 2005).

18. Stephen Ansolabehere and James Snyder, "Campaign War Chests and Congressional Elections," *Business and Politics* 2 (2000): 9–34.

19. Gary W. Cox and Eric Magar, "How Much Is Majority Status in the U.S. Congress Worth?" *American Political Science Review* 93 (1999): 299–309.

20. John Greer, *In Defense of Negativity: Attack Ads in Presidential Campaigns* (Chicago: University of Chicago Press, 2006).

21. *Federal Election Commission v. Wisconsin Right to Life, Inc.*, 551 U.S. 449 (2007).

22. Redlawsk, Tolbert, and Donovan, *Why Iowa?*

23. Amy Schatz, "BO, UR So Gr8," *Wall Street Journal*, May 26, 2007.

24. M. Ostrogorski, *Democracy and the Organization of Political Parties* (New York: Macmillan, 1902).

25. Timothy Clark, "The RNC Prospers, the DNC Struggles as They Face the 1980 Election," *National Journal*, October 27, 1980, p. 1619.

26. For discussions of the consequences of this, see Thomas Edsall, *The New Politics of Inequality* (New York: W.W.Norton, 1984). Also see Thomas Edsall, "Both Parties Get the Company's Money—but the Boss Backs the GOP," *Washington Post*, National Weekly Edition, September 16, 1986, p. 14; and Benjamin Ginsberg, "Money and Power: The New Political Economy of American Elections," in *The Political Economy*, ed. Thomas Ferguson and Joel Rogers (Armonk, NY: M.E. Sharpe, 1984).

27. Michael Luo and Jeff Zeleny, "Straining to Reach Money Goal, Obama Presses Donors" *New York Times*, September 9, 2008, p. 1.

28. *Citizens United v. Federal Election Commission*, 558 U.S. 50 (2010).

29. *Citizens United v. Federal Election Commission.*

30. *Citizens United v. Federal Election Commission.*

31. *Buckley v. Valeo*, 424 U.S. 1 (1976).

# Chapter 11

1. Alexander Hamilton, James Madison, and John Jay, *The Federalist Papers*, ed. Clinton L. Rossiter (New York: New American Library, 1961), no. 10, p. 83.

2. *The Federalist Papers*, no. 10.

3. The best statement of the pluralist view is in David Truman, *The Governmental Process* (New York: Knopf, 1951), chap. 2.

4. Erika Falk, Erin Grizard, and Gordon McDonald, "Legislative Issue Advertising in the 108th Congress: Pluralism or Peril?" *Harvard International Journal of Press/Politics* 11, no. 4 (Fall 2006): 148–64, http://hij.sagepub.com/cgi/reprint/11/4/148 (accessed 3/2/08).

5. Betsy Wagner and David Bowermaster, "B.S. Economics," *Washington Monthly*, November 1992, pp. 19–21.

6. Truman, *The Governmental Process*.

7. Kay Lehman Schlozman and John T. Tierney, *Organized Interests and American Democracy* (New York: Harper and Row, 1986), p. 60.

8. Mancur Olson, *The Logic of Collective Action* (Cambridge, MA: Harvard University Press, 1965).

9. Timothy Penny and Steven Schier, *Payment Due: A Nation in Debt, a Generation in Trouble* (Boulder, CO: Westview, 1996), pp. 64–5.

10. John Herbers, "Special Interests Gaining Power as Voter Disillusionment Grows," *New York Times*, November 14, 1978.

11. Center for Responsive Politics, "Lobbying Database," www.opensecrets.org/lobby/index.php (accessed 11/6/12).

12. See Frank Baumgartner and Beth Leech, *Basic Interests* (Princeton, NJ: Princeton University Press, 1998).

13. For discussions of lobbying, see Allan J. Cigler and Burdett A. Loomis, eds., *Interest Group Politics* (Washington, DC: CQ Press, 1983). See also Jeffrey M. Berry, *Lobbying for the People* (Princeton, NJ: Princeton University Press, 1977).

14. Daniel Franklin, "Tommy Boggs and the Death of Health Care Reform," *Washington Monthly*, April 1995, p. 36.

15. "The Swarming Lobbyists," *Time*, August 7, 1978, p. 15

16. "Top Lobbyists: Hired Guns," *The Hill*, May 14, 2009, p. 1.

17. Brody Mullins, "Growing Role for Lobbyists: Raising Funds for Lawmakers," *Wall Street Journal*, January 27, 2006, p. 1.

18. Eliza Carney, "Cleaning House," *National Journal*, January 28, 2006, p. 36.

19. Jonathan Weisman and Charles H. Babcock, "K Street's New Ways Spawn More Pork," *Washington Post*, January 27, 2006, p. 1.

20. Marie Jojnacki, "Interest Groups' Decisions to Join Alliances or Work Alone," *American Journal of Political Science* 41 (1997): 61–87; Kevin W. Hula, *Lobbying Together: Interest Groups Coalitions in Legislative Politics* (Washington, DC: Georgetown University Press, 1999).

21. Peter H. Stone, "Follow the Leaders," *National Journal*, June 24, 1995, p. 1641.

22. Common Cause, "The Microsoft Playbook: A Report from Common Cause," September 25, 2000.

23. Michael Barbaro, "A New Weapon for Wal-Mart: A War Room," *New York Times*, November 1, 2005, p. 1.

24. *The Washington Times*, "Editorial: Obama's Lobbyists," May 7, 2009, www.washingtontimes.com/news/2009/may/07/obamas-lobbyists (accessed 9/6/12).

25. For an excellent discussion of the political origins of the Administrative Procedure Act, see Martin Shapiro, "APA: Past, Present, Future," 72 *Virginia Law Review*, no. 477 (March 1986), 447–92.

26. David Kirkpatrick, "Congress Finds Ways of Avoiding Lobbyist Limits," *Washington Post*, February 11, 2007, p. 1.

27. *Brown v. Board of Education of Topeka, Kansas*, 347 U.S. 483 (1954).

28. *Roe v. Wade*, 410 U.S. 113 (1973).

29. *Webster v. Reproductive Health Services*, 492 U.S. 490 (1989).

30. E. Pendleton Herring, *Group Representation before Congress* (New York: McGraw-Hill, 1936).

31. Michael Weisskopf, "Energized by Pulpit or Passion, the Public Is Calling," *Washington Post*, February 1, 1993, p. 1.

32. Julia Preston, "Grass Roots Roared and Immigration Bill Collapsed," *New York Times*, June 10, 2007, p. 1.

33. *Citizens United v. Federal Election Commission*, 558 U. S. 50 (2010).

34. Richard L. Burke, "Religious-Right Candidates Gain as GOP Turnout Rises," *New York Times*, November 12, 1994, p. 10.

35. Elisabeth R. Gerber, *The Populist Paradox* (Princeton, NJ: Princeton University Press, 1999).

36. *The Federalist Papers*, no. 10.

37. Olson, *The Logic of Collective Action*.

# Chapter 12

1. Tim Walker, "WWW: World without Wikipedia," *The Independent*, January 19, 2012, www.independent.co.uk/life-style/gadgets-and-tech/news/www-world-without-wikipedia-6291597.html (accessed 1/23/12).

2. Rebecca MacKinnon, "Why Doesn't Washington Understand the Internet?" *Washington Post*, January 20, 2012, www.washingtonpost.com/opinions/why-doesnt-washington-understand-the-internet/2012/01/17/gIQAGPzWEQ_story.html (accessed 1/23/12).

3. Mildred Amer and Jennifer E. Manning, *Membership of the 112th Congress: A Profile*, Congressional Research Service 7-5700, September 20, 2011, pp. 5–6, fpc.state.gov/documents/organization/174246.pdf (accessed 1/23/12).

4. Amer and Manning, *Membership of the 112th Congress*, p. 2.

5. Amer and Manning, *Membership of the 112th Congress*, p. 3.

6. For a discussion, see Benjamin Ginsberg, *The Consequences of Consent* (New York: Random House, 1982), chap. 1.

7. See Kristen D. Burnett, "Congressional Apportionment" (Washington, DC: U.S. Census Bureau, November 2011),

www.census.gov/prod/cen2010/briefs/c2010br-08 .pdf (accessed 1/23/12). For some interesting empirical evidence, see Angus Campbell, Philip Converse, Warren Miller, and Donald Stokes, *Elections and the Political Order* (New York: Wiley, 1966), chap. 11; for more recent considerations about the relationship between members of Congress and their constituents, see Lawrence Jacobs and Robert Y. Shapiro, *Politicians Don't Pander: Political Manipulation and the Loss of Democratic Responsiveness* (Chicago: University of Chicago Press, 2000), and Larry M. Bartels, *Unequal Democracy: The Political Economy of the New Gilded Age* (Princeton, NJ: Princeton University Press, 2008).

8. Congressional Management Foundation, *Communicating with Congress: How Citizen Advocacy Is Changing Mail Operations on Capitol Hill* (Washington, DC: Partnership for a More Perfect Union at the Congressional Management Foundation, 2011), http://congressfoundation.org/ storage/documents/CMF_Pubs/cwc-mail-operations .pdf (accessed 1/23/12).

9. Norman J. Ornstein, Thomas E. Mann, and Michael J. Malbin, *Vital Statistics on Congress 2008* (Washington, DC: Brookings Institution, 2009), pp. 111–2.

10. See Linda Fowler and Robert McClure, *Political Ambition: Who Decides to Run for Congress* (New Haven, CT: Yale University Press, 1989); and Alan Ehrenhalt, *The United States of Ambition: Politicians, Power, and the Pursuit of Office* (New York: Three Rivers Press, 1992).

11. Barbara Palmer and Denise Simon, *Breaking the Political Glass Ceiling: Women and Congressional Elections*, 2nd ed. (New York: Routledge, 2008); Jennifer L. Lawless and Kathryn Pearson, "The Primary Reason for Women's Underrepresentation? Reevaluating the Conventional Wisdom," *Journal of Politics* 70 (2008): 67–82.

12. Michael Leahy, "House Rules," *Washington Post*, June 10, 2007, p. W12.

13. See Barbara C. Burrell, *A Woman's Place Is in the House: Campaigning for Congress in the Feminist Era* (Ann Arbor: University of Michigan Press, 1994), and David Broder, "Key to Women's Political Parity: Running," *Washington Post*, September 8, 1994, p. A17.

14. Dan Balz, "Dodd, Dorgan, and Ritter to Retire as Democrats Face a Difficult Mid-Term Year," *Washington Post*, January 7, 2010.

15. U.S. Census Bureau, "Map: Apportionment of the U.S. House of Representatives Based on the 2010 Census," *U.S. Census Bureau Congressional Apportionment*, www .census.gov/population/apportionment/data/2010 _apportionment_results.html (accessed 02/6/12).

16. Aaron Blake, "GOP's Redistricting Advantage, Muted but Real," *Washington Post*, June 15, 2011, www.washingtonpost .com/blogs/the-fix/post/gops-redistricting-advantage -is-real-but-muted/2011/06/14/AGwaQDWH_blog .html (accessed 1/23/12).

17. "Did Redistricting Sink the Democrats?" *National Journal*, December 17, 1994, p. 2984.

18. *Miller v. Johnson*, 515 U.S. 900 (1995).

19. Bernie Becker, "Reapportionment Roundup," *New York Times*, December 24, 2009, http://thecaucus.blogs .nytimes.com/2009/12/24/reapoortionment-roundup/ (accessed 1/31/10).

20. Tom Hamburger and Richard Simon, "Everybody Will Know if It's Pork," *Los Angeles Times*, January 6, 2007, p. A1.

21. Jared Allen, "Lawmakers Pushing for Earmark Reform Think Obama Boosted Their Chances," *The Hill*, January 30, 2010, http://thehill.com/homenews/house/78869 -lawmakers-think-obama-boosted-earmark-reform- (accessed 1/31/10); David S. Fallis, Scott Higham and Kimberly Kindy, "Congressional Earmarks Sometimes Used to Fund Projects Near Lawmakers' Properties," *Washington Post*, February 6, 2012, p. 1.

22. Congressman Tom Petri, "Constituent Services," http:// petrihouse.gov/serving-you/help-federal-agency (accessed 7/4/12).

23. Associated Press, "Congress Passes Rare Private Immigration Bills," Associated Press, December 15, 2010, www .aolnews.com/2010/12/15/congress-passes-rare-private -immigration-bills/ (accessed 2/1/12).

24. Richard Fenno Jr., *Home Style: House Members in Their Districts* (Boston: Little, Brown, 1978).

25. Edward Epstein, "Dusting Off Deliberation," CQ *Weekly*, June 14, 2010, pp. 1436–42. Sarah Binder, "Where Have All the Conference Committees Gone?" *The Monkey Cage* (blog), December 21, 2011, themonkeycage.org/ blog/2011/12/21/where-have-all-the-conference -committees-gone/ (accessed 2/7/12).

26. Derek Willis, "Republicans Mix It Up When Assigning House Chairmen for the 108th," *Congressional Quarterly Weekly*, January 11, 2003, p. 89.

27. Rebecca Kimitch, "CQ Guide to the Committees: Democrats Opt to Spread the Power," *Congressional Quarterly Weekly*, April 16, 2007, p. 1080.

28. Richard E. Cohen, "Crackup of the Committees," *National Journal*, July 31, 1999, pp. 2210–16.

29. David W. Rohde, "Committees and Policy Formulation," in *Institutions of American Democracy: The Legislative Branch*, ed. Paul J. Quirk and Sarah A. Binder (New York: Oxford University Press, 2005), pp. 201–23.

30. U.S. Senate, "Cloture Motions—111th Congress," www .senate.gov/pagelayout/reference/cloture_motions/ 111.htm (accessed 2/1/12); U.S. Senate, "Cloture Motions— 112th Congress," www.senate.gov/pagelayout/reference/ cloture_motions/112.shtml (accessed 2/1/12). For Obama's 2010 speech, see Matt Negrin, "Comparing the 1950s with 2009," *Politico*, February 4, 2010, www .politico.com/politico44/perm/0210/about_those_ filibusters_ac215c69-38c3-4ad8-ad44-183d81490ce2 .html (accessed 2/9/12).

31. See Robert Pear, "Senator X Kills Measure on Anonymity," *New York Times*, November 11, 1997, p. 12.

32. Jonathan Weisman, "House Votes 411–18 to Pass Ethics Overhaul," *Washington Post*, August 1, 2007, p. A1.

33. Kate Phillips and Jeff Zeleny, "White House Blasts Shelby Hold on Nominees," *New York Times*, February 5, 2010, http://thecaucus.blogs.nytimes.com/2010/02/05/white-house-blasts-shelby-hold-on-nominees/ (accessed 2/5/10).

34. Carl Hulse and David M. Herszenhorn, "Defiant House Rejects Huge Bailout; Next Step Is Uncertain," *New York Times*, September 29, 2008, www.nytimes.com/2008/09/30/business/30cong.html?pagewanted=1&_r=1 (accessed 2/4/10); Reuters. "House Passes Bailout, Focus Shifts to Fallout," October 3, 2008, www.reuters.com/article/idUSTRE49267J20081003 (accessed 2/4/10).

35. See John W. Kingdon, *Congressmen's Voting Decisions* (New York: Harper and Row, 1973), chap. 3; and R. Douglas Arnold, *The Logic of Congressional Action* (New Haven, CT: Yale University Press, 1990).

36. Jane Fritsch, "The Grass Roots, Just a Free Phone Call Away," *New York Times*, June 23, 1995, p. A1.

37. Robert Pear, "In House, Many Spoke with One Voice: Lobbyists," *New York Times*, November 14, 2009, p. A1.

38. Eliza Newlin Carney, "For Ethics Hawks, Congress Could Be Next," *National Journal Online*, February 17, 2009, www.nationaljournal.com/njonline/rg_20090217_2426.php (accessed 2/5/10).

39. Dan Eggen, "SuperPACs Target Congressional Races," *Washington Post*, January 29, 2012, www.washingtonpost.com/politics/super-pacs-target-congressional-races/2012/01/26/gIQAyRfnaQ_story.html (accessed 2/9/12).

40. Holly Idelson, "Signs Point to Greater Loyalty on Both Sides of the Aisle," *Congressional Quarterly Weekly Report*, December 19, 1992, p. 3849.

41. "Vote Studies 2011," in Graphics, CQ.com, http://media.cq.com/media/2011/votestudy_2011/graphics/ (accessed 2/1/12).

42. Alexander Bolton, "DeMint's Leadership PAC Battles Leaders in Fight for the Future of Senate GOP Caucus," *The Hill*, August 4, 2011, http://thehill.com/homenews/senate/175397-demints-leadership-pac-battles-leaders-in-fight-for-future-of-senate (accessed 1/23/12); for a list of leadership PACs, see the Open Secrets website, www.opensecrets.org/industries/indus.php?Ind=Q03 (accessed 1/23/12).

43. Kimitch, "CQ Guide to the Committees," p. 1080.

44. Leahy, "House Rules," p. W12; Marin Cogan, "Freshmen Jump Line for Floor Speeches," *Politico*, January 18, 2011, www.politico.com/news/stories/0111/47791.html (accessed 2/9/12).

45. Robert Draper, "How Kevin McCarthy Wrangles the Tea Party in Washington," *New York Times*, July 13, 2011, www.nytimes.com/2011/07/17/magazine/how-kevin-mccarthy-wrangles-the-tea-party.html?pagewanted=all (accessed 2/1/12).

46. James J. Kilpatrick, "Don't Overlook Corn for Porn Plot," *Chicago Sun-Times*, January 3, 1992, p. 23.

47. Dennis McDougal, "Cattle Are Bargaining Chip of the NEA," *Los Angeles Times*, November 2, 1991, p. F1.

48. Frank Newport, "Congress' Job Approval at New Low of 10%," Gallup Politics, www.gallup.com/poll/152528/ Congress-Job-Approval-New-Low.aspx (accessed 2/10/12).

49. Pew Research Center for the People and the Press, "Frustration with Congress Could Hurt Republican Incumbents, GOP Base Critical of Party's Washington Leadership," December 15, 2011, www.people-press.org/2011/12/15/section-1-congress-the-parties-and-the-anti-incumbent-mood/ (accessed 2/10/11).

50. Rasmussen Reports, "New High: 48% Say Most Members of Congress Are Corrupt," December 31, 2011, www.rasmussenreports.com/public_content/politics/general_politics/december_2011/new_high_48_say_most_members_of_congress_are_corrupt (accessed 2/10/12).

51. *Citizens United v. Federal Election Commission*, 558 U.S. 50 (2010).

52. Susan Milligan, "Congress Reduces Its Oversight Role; Since Clinton, a Change in Focus," *Boston Globe*, November 20, 2005, p. A1; Bill Shaikin, "Clemens Is Star Attraction at Hearing," *Los Angeles Times*, February 12, 2008, p. D1.

53. Elizabeth Williamson, "Revival of Oversight Role Sought; Congress Hires More Investigators, Plans Subpoenas," *Washington Post*, April 25, 2007, p. A1.

54. Thomas E. Mann, Molly Reynolds, and Peter Hoey, "A New, Improved Congress?" *New York Times*, August 26, 2007, p. 11.

55. John Stanton and Daniel Newhowser, "House GOP Uses Retreat to Lay 2012 Plans," *The Hill*, January 23, 2012, www.rollcall.com/issues/57_82/house_gop_uses_retreat_lay_2012_plans-211670-1.html (accessed 2/9/12).

56. *United States v. Pink*, 315 U.S. 203 (1942). For a good discussion of the problem, see James W. Davis, *The American Presidency* (New York: Harper and Row, 1987), chap. 8.

57. Carroll J. Doherty, "Impeachment: How It Would Work," *Congressional Quarterly Weekly Report*, January 31, 1998, p. 222.

58. See Kenneth A. Shepsle, "Representation and Governance: The Great Legislative Trade-off," *Political Science Quarterly* 103, no. 3 (1988): 461–84.

59. John R. Hibbing and Elizabeth Theiss-Morse, *Congress as Public Enemy: Public Attitudes toward American Political Institutions* (New York: Cambridge University Press, 1996), p. 105.

## Chapter 13

1. *In re Neagle*, 135 U.S. 1 (1890).

2. James G. Randall, *Constitutional Problems under Lincoln* (New York: Appleton, 1926), chap. 1.

3. Edward S. Corwin, *The President: Office and Powers*, 4th rev. ed. (New York: New York University Press, 1957), p. 229.

4. These statutes are contained mainly in Title 10 of the United States Code, Sections 331, 332, and 333.

5. The best study covering all aspects of the domestic use of the military is that of Adam Yarmolinsky, *The Military Establishment* (New York: Harper and Row, 1971). Probably the most famous instance of a president's unilateral use of the power to protect a state "against domestic violence" was President Grover Cleveland's dealing with the Pullman Strike of 1894. The famous Supreme Court case that ensued was *In re Debs*, 158 U.S. 564 (1895).

6. In *United States v. Pink*, 315 U.S. 203 (1942), the Supreme Court confirmed that an executive agreement is the legal equivalent of a treaty, despite the absence of Senate approval. This case approved the executive agreement that was used to establish diplomatic relations with the Soviet Union in 1933. An executive agreement, not a treaty, was used in 1940 to exchange "fifty over-age destroyers" for 99-year leases on some important military bases.

7. *United States v. Nixon*, 418 U.S. 683 (1974).

8. For a different perspective, see William F. Grover, *The President as Prisoner: A Structural Critique of the Carter and Reagan Years* (Albany: State University of New York Press, 1988).

9. A third source of presidential power is implied from the provision for "faithful execution of the laws." This is the president's power to impound funds—that is, to refuse to spend money Congress has appropriated for certain purposes. One author referred to this as a "retroactive veto power" (Robert E. Goosetree, "The Power of the President to Impound Appropriated Funds," *American University Law Review* [January 1962]). This impoundment power has been used freely and to considerable effect by many modern presidents, and Congress has occasionally delegated such power to the president by statute. But in reaction to the Watergate scandal, Congress adopted the Congressional Budget and Impoundment Control Act of 1974, which was designed to circumscribe the president's ability to impound funds by requiring that the president must spend all appropriated funds unless both houses of Congress consented to an impoundment within 45 days of a presidential request. Therefore, since 1974, the use of impoundment has declined significantly. Presidents have had either to bite their tongues and accept unwanted appropriations or to revert to the older and more dependable but politically limited method of vetoing the entire bill.

10. For more on the veto, see Robert J. Spitzer, *The Presidential Veto: Touchstone of the American Presidency* (Albany: State University of New York Press, 1989).

11. Dan Eggen, "Bush Announces Veto of Waterboarding Ban," WashingtonPost.com, March 8, 2008, www.washingtonpost.com/wp-dyn/content/article/2008/03/08AR2008030800304.html (accessed 6/10/10).

12. For a good review of President Clinton's legislative leadership in the first session of his last Congress, see *Congressional Quarterly Weekly*, November 13, 1999, especially the cover story by Andrew Taylor, "Clinton Gives Republicans a Gentler Year-End Beating," pp. 2698–700.

13. Kenneth F. Warren, *Administrative Law*, 3rd ed. (Upper Saddle River, NJ: Prentice-Hall, 1996), p. 250.

14. Theodore J. Lowi, *The End of Liberalism*, 2nd ed. (New York: W.W. Norton, 1979), pp. 117–8.

15. *J. W. Hampton & Co. v. United States*, 276 U.S. 394 (1928).

16. 48 Stat. 200.

17. David Schoenbrod, *Power without Responsibility: How Congress Abuses the People through Delegation* (New Haven, CT: Yale University Press, 1993), pp. 49–50.

18. Lowi, *The End of Liberalism*, p. 117.

19. Adam Clymer, "The Transition: Push for Diversity May Cause Reversal on Interior Secretary," *New York Times*, December 23, 1992, p. 1.

20. A substantial portion of this section is taken from Theodore J. Lowi, *The Personal President* (Ithaca, NY: Cornell University Press, 1985), pp. 141–50.

21. All the figures since 1967, and probably 1957, are understated, because additional White House staff members were on "detail" service from the military and other departments (some secretly assigned) and are not counted here because they were not on the White House payroll.

22. The actual number is difficult to estimate because, as with White House staff, some EOP personnel, especially in national security work, are detailed to the EOP from outside agencies.

23. Article I, Section 3, provides that "The Vice-President . . . shall be President of the Senate, but shall have no Vote, unless they be equally divided." This is the only vote the vice president is allowed.

24. David Ignatius, "A Skeptical Biden's Role," RealClearPolitics.com, November 26, 2009, www.realclearpolitics.com/articles/2009/11/26/a_skeptical_bidens_role_99320.html (accessed 5/12/09).

25. Samuel Kernell, *Going Public: New Strategies of Presidential Leadership*, 3rd ed. (Washington, DC: CQ Press, 1997); also Jeffrey K. Tulis, *The Rhetorical Presidency* (Princeton, NJ: Princeton University Press, 1987).

26. Tulis, *The Rhetorical Presidency*, p. 91.

27. Sidney M. Milkis, *The President and the Parties* (New York: Oxford University Press, 1993), p. 97.

28. James MacGregor Burns, *Roosevelt: The Lion and the Fox* (New York: Harcourt, Brace, 1956), p. 317.

29. Burns, *Roosevelt*, p. 317.

30. Kernell, *Going Public*, p. 79.

31. Tulis, *The Rhetorical Presidency*, p. 161.

32. Lowi, *The Personal President*.

33. Lowi, *The Personal President*, p. 11.

34. Harold W. Stanley and Richard G. Niemi, *Vital Statistics on American Politics, 2001–2002* (Washington, DC: CQ Press, 2001), pp. 250–1.

35. Milkis, *The President and the Parties*, p. 128.

36. Milkis, *The President and the Parties*, p. 160.

37. The classic critique of this process is Lowi, *The End of Liberalism*.

38. Kenneth Culp Davis, *Administrative Law Treatise* (St. Paul, MN: West Publishing, 1958), p. 9.

39. For example, Douglas W. Kmiec, "Expanding Power," in *The Rule of Law in the Wake of Clinton*, ed. Roger Pilon (Washington, DC: Cato Institute Press, 2000), pp. 47–68.

40. John M. Broder, "Powerful Shaper of U.S. Rules Quits, Leaving Critics in Wake," *New York Times*, August 4, 2012, p. A1.

41. A complete inventory is provided in Harold C. Relyea, "Presidential Directives: Background and Review," Congressional Research Service Report 98–611 (Washington, DC: Library of Congress, November 9, 2001).

42. Terry M. Moe and William G. Howell, "The Presidential Power of Unilateral Action," *Journal of Law, Economics and Organization* 15, no. 1 (January 1999): 133–4.

43. Moe and Howell, "The Presidential Power of Unilateral Action," p. 164.

44. *Youngstown Sheet & Tube Co. v. Sawyer*, 346 U.S. 579 (1952).

45. Todd Gaziano, "The New 'Massive Resistance,'" *Policy Review* (May–June 1998): 283.

46. Mark Killenbeck, "A Matter of Mere Approval: The Role of the President in the Creation of Legislative History," 48 *University of Arkansas Law Review*, no. 239 (1995).

47. Philip Cooper, *By Order of the President* (Lawrence: University Press of Kansas, 2002), p. 201.

48. Corwin, *The President*, p. 283.

49. Cooper, *By Order of the President*, p. 201.

50. Cooper, *By Order of the President*, p. 203.

51. Cooper, *By Order of the President*, p. 216.

52. Peter Baker, "Obama Is Making Plans to Use Executive Power for Action on Several Fronts," *New York Times*, February 13, 2010, p. A12.

53. Baker, "Obama Is Making Plans," p. A12.

54. Alexander Hamilton, James Madison, and John Jay, *The Federalist Papers*, ed. Clinton Rossiter (New York: New American Library, 1961), no. 70, pp. 423–30.

55. Terry Moe, "The Presidency and the Bureaucracy: The Presidential Advantage," in *The Presidency and the Political System*, ed. Michael Nelson (Washington, DC: CQ Press, 2002), pp. 416–20.

# Chapter 14

1. "Obama's Health Care Speech to Congress," *New York Times*, September 9, 2009, www.nytimes.com/2009/09/10/us/politics/10obama.text.html (accessed 2/10/10).

2. U.S. Census Bureau, "Federal Civilian Employment and Annual Payroll by Branch: 1970 to 2010," *Statistical Abstract of the United States 2012*, Table 496, www.census.gov/compendia/statab/2012/tables/12s0496.pdf (accessed 1/2/12); U.S. Census Bureau, "Department of Defense Personnel: 1960–2010," *Statistical Abstract of the United States 2010*, Table 510, www.census.gov/compendia/statab/2012/tables/12s0510.pdf (accessed 1/2/12).

3. U.S. Census Bureau, Table 461, "Government Employment and Payrolls, 1982–2009," *Statistical Abstract of the United States 2012*, www.census.gov/compendia/statab/2012/tables/12s0462.pdf (accessed 1/2/12), and Table 602, "Employed Civilians and Weekly Hours 1980 to 2010, www.census.gov/compendia/statab/2012/tables/12s0602.pdf (accessed 1/2/12).

4. Arnold Brecht and Comstock Glaser, *The Art and Techniques of Administration in German Ministries* (Cambridge, MA: Harvard University Press, 1940), p. 6.

5. Linda Greenhouse, "Justices Say E.P.A. Has Power to Act on Harmful Gases," *New York Times*, April 3, 2007, www.nytimes.com/2007/04/03/washington/03scotus.html?ex=1333339200&en=e0d0a1497263d879&ei=5124&partner=permalink&exprod=permalink (accessed 2/15/10).

6. Environmental Protection Agency, "Endangerment and Cause or Contribute Findings for Greenhouse Cases under Section 202(a) of the Clean Air Act," epa.gov/climatechange/endangerment.html (accessed 2/16/10).

7. Environmental Protection Agency, "Regulations and Standards: Vehicles/Engines," www.epa.gov/oms/climate/regulations.htm (accessed 2/16/10).

8. Juliet Eilperin, "EPA Needed More Data before Ruling on Greenhouse Gas Emissions, Report Says," *Washington Post* September 28, 2011, www.washingtonpost.com/national/health-science/epa-needed-more-data-before-ruling-on-greenhouse-gas-emissions-report-says/2011/09/28/gIQABs2X5K_story.html (accessed 1/2/12).

9. Federal Trade Commission, "Facebook Settles FTC Charges That It Deceived Consumers by Failing to Keep Privacy Promises," November 29, 2011, http://ftc.gov/opa/2011/11/privacysettlement.shtm (accessed 7/4/12)

10. Greg Gardner, "U.S. Probes Toyota Recall, Could Levy $16.4M Fine If Carmaker Acted Too Slowly," *Detroit Free Press*, www.freep.com/article/20100216/BUSINESS01/100216030/1318/U.S.-probes-Toyota-recall-could-levy-16.4M-fine-if-carmaker-acted-too-slowly (accessed 2/16/10); Ralph Vartabedian, "Sudden Acceleration in Toyota Vehicles Not an Electronic Issue, U.S. Study Finds," *Los Angeles Times* February 9, 2011, articles.latimes.com/2011/feb/09/business/la-fi-toyota-nasa-20110209 (accessed 1/3/12).

11. Gary Bryner, *Bureaucratic Discretion* (New York: Pergamon Press, 1987).

12. This account is drawn from Alan Stone, *How America Got On-Line: Politics, Markets, and the Revolution in Telecommunications* (Armonk, NY: M.E. Sharpe, 1997), pp. 184–7.

13. There are historical reasons that American cabinet-level administrators are called "secretaries." During the Second Continental Congress and the subsequent confederal government, standing committees were formed to deal with executive functions related to foreign affairs, military and maritime issues, and public financing. The heads of those committees were called "secretaries" because their primary task was to handle all correspondence and documentation related to their areas of responsibility.

14. Rob Margetta, "Homeland Security for Hire," *Congressional Quarterly Weekly*, November 12, 2007, pp. 3392–9, http://library.cqpress.com/cqweekly/weeklyreport 110 -000002625610 (accessed 11/14/07).

15. Julia Preston, "States Resisting Program Central to Obama's Immigration Strategy," *New York Times*, May 5, 2011, p. A18.

16. U.S. Department of State, "Department Organization Chart," www.state.gov/r/pa/ei/rls/dos/99494.htm (accessed 2/16/10).

17. For more details, consult John E. Harr, *The Professional Diplomat* (Princeton, NJ: Princeton University Press, 1972), p. 11; and Nicholas Horrock, "The CIA Has Neighbors in the 'Intelligence Community,'" *New York Times*, June 29, 1975, sec. 4, p. 2. See also Morton H. Halperin and Priscilla Clapp, with Arnold Kanter, *Bureaucratic Politics and Foreign Policy*, 2nd ed. (Washington, DC: Brookings Institution Press, 2007).

18. *The 9/11 Commission Report: Final Report of the National Commission on Terrorist Attacks upon the United States* (New York: W.W. Norton, 2004).

19. Daniel Patrick Moynihan, "The Culture of Secrecy," *Public Interest* (Summer 1997): 55–71.

20. Charlie Savage, "Obama Curbs Secrecy of Classified Documents," *New York Times*, December 30, 2009, p. A19. See the comprehensive evaluation in Citizens for Responsibility and Ethics in Washington, OpenTheGovernment.org, "Measuring Transparency under the FOIA: The Real Story behind the Numbers, December 2011, crew.3cdn.net/591 1487fbaaa8cb0f8_9xm6bgari.pdf (accessed 1/3/12).

21. Scott Shane, "Cost to Protect U.S. Secrets Doubles to Over $11 Billion," *New York Times*, July 3, 2012, p. A11. The official figure was $11 billion, but that did not include the expenses of the Central Intelligence Agency and the National Security Agency, which were estimated at $2 billion.

22. U.S. Department of the Treasury, "The Debt to the Penny and Who Holds It," www.treasurydirect.gov/NP/ BPDLogin?application=np (accessed 2/18/10).

23. For an excellent political analysis of the Fed, see Donald Kettl, *Leadership at the Fed* (New Haven, CT: Yale University Press, 1986).

24. Annie Lowrey, "Regulators Move Closer to Oversight of Nonbanks," *New York Times*, April 4, 2012, p. B3, www.nytimes.com/2012/04/04/business/economy/ regulators-move-closer-to-scrutinizing-nonbanks.html (accessed 7/3/12).

25. For an account of the Financial Stability Oversight Council and passage of the Dodd-Frank financial regulatory legislation, see John T. Woolley and J. Nicholas Ziegler, "The Two-Tiered Politics of Financial Reform in the United States," in *Crisis and Control. Institutional Change in Financial Market Regulation*, ed. Renate Mayntz (Frankfurt: Campus/MPIfG, 2012); the council's early activities are described in Financial Stability Oversight Council, Annual Report 2011, www .treasury.gov/initiatives/fsoc/Documents/FSOCAR2011 .pdf (accessed 1/3/12), and in Edward V. Murphy and Michael B. Bernier, "Financial Stability Oversight Council: A Framework to Mitigate Systemic Risk," (Washington DC: Congressional Research Service, November 15, 2011), www.llsdc.org/attachments/wysiwyg/544/CRS-R42083. pdf (accessed 1/3/2012).

26. George E. Berkley, *The Craft of Public Administration* (Boston: Allyn and Bacon, 1975), p. 417.

27. OMB Watch, "IRS Gets Serious about Tax Enforcement," November 24, 2009. www.ombwatch.org/node/10583 (accessed 2/18/10).

28. On the Swiss banks, see "U.S. Charges 3 Swiss Bank Employees with Aiding Tax Evasion," *New York Times*, January 4, 2012, http://dealbook.nytimes.com/2012/01/04/ u-s-charges-swiss-bank-employees-with-tax-evasion/ (accessed 1/4/12); David Kocieniewski, "Senate Bill Seeks to Raise Revenue by Closing Tax Havens," *New York Times*, July 13, 2011, p. B12.

29. Eric Schmitt, "Washington Talk: No $435 Hammers, but Questions," *New York Times*, October 23, 1990, p. A16; Jerry Markon, "A $16 Muffin? Justice Dept. Audit Finds 'Wasteful' and Extravagant Spending, *Washington Post*, September 20, 2011, www.washingtonpost.com/politics/ a-16-muffin-justice-dept-audit-finds-wasteful-and -extravagant-spending/2011/09/20/gIQAXKyhiK_story. html (accessed 1/3/12); and Charlie Savage, "The $16 Muffin That Wasn't," *New York Times*, October 29, 2011, p. A14.

30. Vice President Gore's National Partnership for Reinventing Government, "Appendix F, History of the National Partnership for Reinventing Government Accomplishments, 1993–2000, A Summary," http://govinfo.library.unt.edu/ npr/whoweare/appendixf.html (accessed 3/28/08).

31. Public Law 101–510, Title XXIX, Sections 2,901 and 2,902 of Part A (Defense Base Closure and Realignment Commission); see the 2005 commission's Web site, Defense Base Closure and Realignment Commission, www .brac.gov (accessed 1/3/12).

32. *National Federation of Independent Business v. Sebelius*, 567 U.S.__(2012).

33. Robert Pear, "Republican Governor of Florida Says State Won't Expand Medicaid," *New York Times*, July 3, 2012, p. A10.

34. Sheila Zedlewski and Pamela Loprest with Erika Huber, "What Role Is Welfare Playing in This Period of High Unemployment?" Urban Institute, Fact Sheet 3, August 2011, www.urban.org/UploadedPDF/412378- Role-of-Welfare-in-this-Period-of-High-Unemployment .pdf (accessed 7/4/12)

35. Sabrina Tavernise, "Food Stamps Helped Reduced Poverty Rate, Study Says," *New York Times*, April 10, 2012, A16.

36. Paul C. Light, "The New True Size of Government," Organizational Performance Initiative, Research Brief no. 2, p. 8, Wagner School of Public Service, New York University, http://wagner.nyu.edu/performance/files/ True_Size.pdf (accessed 3/11/08).

37. OMB Watch, "Total Spending by Year," FedSpending.org, www.fedspending.org/fpds/chart_total.php (accessed 1/2/12).

38. Scott Shane and Ron Nixon, "In Washington, Contractors Take on Biggest Role Ever," *New York Times*, February 4, 2007, p. A1.

39. Shane and Nixon, "In Washington, Contractors Take on Biggest Role Ever."

40. Matt Kelley, "GAO Challenges $150B Contract Awarded by Army," *USA Today*, October 31, 2007, p. 5A.

41. Commission on Wartime Contracting in Iraq and Afghanistan, *Transforming Wartime Contracting: Controlling Costs, Reducing Risks: Final Report to Congress*, p.18, August 2011, www.wartimecontracting.gov (accessed 1/4/12); Congressional Research Service, "The Department of Defense's Use of Private Contractors in Iraq and Afghanistan: Background, Analysis, and Options for Congress," September 29, 2009, fpc.state.gov/documents/organization/130803.pdf (accessed 2/18/10).

42. Committee on Oversight and Government Reform, Hearings on Blackwater USA, preliminary transcript, October 2, 2007, http://oversight.house.gov/documents/20071127131151.pdf (accessed 3/10/08).

43. Committee on Oversight and Government Reform, Hearings on Blackwater USA.

44. Shane and Nixon, "In Washington, Contractors Take on Biggest Role Ever."

45. Shane and Nixon, "In Washington, Contractors Take on Biggest Role Ever."

46. General Accountability Office, *Federal Contractors: Better Performance Information Needed to Support Agency Contract Award Decisions*, April 2009, GAO-09-374; www.gao.gov/new.items/d09374.pdf (accessed 2/26/10).

47. Neil Gordon, "Move Over FCMD, Make Way for FAPI-IS," Project on Government Oversight, http://pogoblog.typepad.com/pogo/2009/09/move-over-fcmd-make-way-for-fapiis.html (accessed 2/26/10).

48. For the estimates on waste, see Commission on Wartime Contracting in Iraq and Afghanistan, *Transforming Wartime Contracting*.

49. Dan Egan, "Democrats Proposing New Limits on Corporate Campaign Donations," *Boston Globe*, February 12, 2010, www.boston.com/news/nation/washington/articles/2010/02/12/democrats proposing new limits on corporate campaign donations/ (accessed 2/27/10).

50. Joe Davidson, "OMB Moves to Cut Outside Contractors," *Washington Post*, July 29, 2009, www.washingtonpost.com/wp-dyn/content/article/2009/07/28/AR2009072802812.html (accessed 2/18/10)

51. Joe Davidson, "Deficit-Cutters Must Also Weigh the Cost of Contractors," *Washington Post*, February 4, 2011, www.washingtonpost.com/wp-dyn/content/article/2011/02/03/AR2011020306809.html?nav=emailpage (accessed 1/2/12).

52. Alexander Hamilton, James Madison, and John Jay, *The Federalist Papers*, ed. Clinton Rossiter (New York: New American Library, 1961), no. 51, p. 322.

53. The title of this section was inspired by Peri Arnold, *Making the Managerial Presidency* (Princeton, NJ: Princeton University Press, 1986).

54. For more details and evaluations, see David Rosenbloom, *Public Administration* (New York: Random House, 1986), pp. 186–221; Charles H. Levine, with the assistance of Rosslyn S. Kleeman, *The Quiet Crisis of the Civil Service: The Federal Personnel System at the Crossroads* (Washington, DC: National Academy of Public Administration, 1986).

55. Lester Salamon and Alan Abramson, "Governance: The Politics of Retrenchment," in *The Reagan Record*, ed. John Palmer and Isabel Sawhill (Cambridge, MA: Ballinger, 1984), p. 40.

56. Colin Campbell, "The White House and the Presidency under the 'Let's Deal' President," in *The Bush Presidency: First Appraisals*, ed. Colin Campbell and Bert A. Rockman (Chatham, NJ: Chatham House, 1991), pp. 185–222.

57. See John Micklethwait, "Managing to Look Attractive," *New Statesman* 125, November 8, 1996, p. 24.

58. Quoted in I. M. Destler, "Reagan and the World: An 'Awesome Stubborness,'" in *The Reagan Legacy: Promise and Performance*, ed. Charles O. Jones, (Chatham, NJ: Chatham House, 1988), pp. 244–57. The source of the quote is *Report of the President's Special Review Board* (Washington, DC: Government Printing Office, 1987).

59. Thomas E. Mann and Norman J. Ornstein. *The Broken Branch: How Congress Is Failing America and How to Get It Back on Track* (New York: Oxford University Press, 2006), p. 155.

60. The Office of Technology Assessment (OTA) was a fourth research agency serving Congress until 1995. It was one of the first agencies scheduled for elimination by the 104th Congress. Until 1983, Congress had still another tool of legislative oversight: the legislative veto. Each agency operating under such provisions was obliged to submit to Congress every proposed decision or rule, which would then lie before both chambers for 30 to 60 days. If Congress took no action by one-house or two-house resolution explicitly to veto the proposed measure during the prescribed period, the measure became law. The legislative veto was declared unconstitutional by the Supreme Court in 1983 on the grounds that it violated the separation of powers—the resolutions Congress passed to exercise its veto were not subject to presidential veto, as required by the Constitution. See *Immigration and Naturalization Service v. Chadha*, 462 U.S. 919 (1983).

## Chapter 15

1. *Morse v. Frederick*, 551 U.S. 393 (2007).

2. Charles Lane, "Court Backs School on Speech Curbs," *Washington Post*, June 26, 2007, p. A6.

3. *Hosanna-Tabor Evangelical Lutheran Church and School v. Equal Employment Opportunity Commission*, 565 U.S. ___ (2012).

4. U.S. Bureau of the Census, *Statistical Abstract of the United States* (Washington, DC: Government Printing Office, 2012).

5. Michael A. Fletcher, "Obama Criticized as Too Cautious on Judicial Posts," *Washington Post*, October 15, 2009, www.washingtonpost.com/wp-dyn/content/article/2009/10/15/AR2009101504083.html (accessed 3/1/10).

6. Russell Wheeler, "Judicial Nominations and Confirmations after Three Years—Where Do Things Stand?" Governance Studies at Brookings, January 13, 2012. [give URL and date accessed]

7. *Arizona v. United States*, 11–182 (2012).

8. *National Federation of Independent Business v. Sebelius*, 11–393 (2012).

9. Peter Wallsten and Richard Simon, "Sotomayor Nomination Splits GOP," *Los Angeles Times*, May 27, 2009, http://articles.latimes.com/2009/may/27/nation/na-court-access27 (accessed 3/1/10).

10. C. Herman Pritchett, *The American Constitution* (New York: McGraw-Hill, 1959), p. 138.

11. *Marbury v. Madison*, 1 Cr. 137 (1803).

12. *Federal Election Commission v. Wisconsin Right to Life*, 551 U.S. 449 (2007).

13. This review power was affirmed by the Supreme Court in *Martin v. Hunter's Lessee*, 1 Wheat. 304 (1816).

14. *Brown v. Board of Education*, 347 U.S. 483 (1954).

15. *Loving v. Virginia*, 388 U.S. 1 (1967).

16. *Griswold v. Connecticut*, 381 U.S. 479 (1965).

17. *Brandenburg v. Ohio*, 395 U.S. 444 (1969).

18. *United States v. Jones*, 10-1259 (2012).

19. Theodore J. Lowi, *The End of Liberalism*, 2nd ed. (New York: W.W. Norton, 1979); also David Schoenbrod, *Power without Responsibility: How Congress Abuses the People through Delegation* (New Haven, CT: Yale University Press, 1993).

20. Kenneth Culp Davis, *Discretionary Justice* (Baton Rouge: Louisiana State University Press, 1969), pp. 15–21.

21. Emergency Price Control Act, 56 Stat. 23 (January 30, 1942).

22. *Hamdi v. Rumsfeld*, 542 U.S. 507 (2004).

23. *Hamdan v. Rumsfeld*, 548 U.S. 557 (2006).

24. *Boumediene v. Bush*, 553 U.S. 723 (2008).

25. *Shelley v. Kraemer*, 334 U.S. 1 (1948).

26. *Burlington Northern v. White*, 548 U.S. 53 (2006).

27. *Engel v. Vitale*, 370 U.S. 421 (1962).

28. *Gideon v. Wainwright*, 372 U.S. 335 (1963).

29. *Escobedo v. Illinois*, 378 U.S. 478 (1964).

30. *Miranda v. Arizona*, 384 U.S. 436 (1966).

31. *Dickerson v. United States*, 530 U.S. 428 (2000).

32. *Baker v. Carr*, 369 U.S. 186 (1962).

33. Walter F. Murphy, "The Supreme Court of the United States," in *Encyclopedia of the American Judicial System*, ed. Robert J. Janosik (New York: Scribner's, 1987).

34. *Roe v. Wade*, 410 U.S. 113 (1973).

35. *Ricci v. DeStefano*, 200 U.S. 321 (2009).

36. Robert Scigliano, *The Supreme Court and the Presidency* (New York: Free Press, 1971), p. 162. For an interesting critique of the solicitor general's role during the Reagan administration, see Lincoln Caplan, "Annals of the Law," *New Yorker*, August 17, 1987, pp. 30–62.

37. Edward Lazarus, *Closed Chambers* (New York: Times Books, 1998), p. 6.

38. *NAACP v. Button*, 371 U.S. 415 (1963). The quotation is from the opinion in this case.

39. *Smith v. Allwright*, 321 U.S. 649 (1994).

40. *Griswold v. Connecticut*, 381 U.S. 479 (1965).

41. R. W. Apple Jr., "A Divided Government Remains, and with It the Prospect of Further Combat," *New York Times*, November 7, 1996, p. B6.

42. For limits on judicial power, see Alexander Bickel, *The Least Dangerous Branch* (Indianapolis: Bobbs-Merrill, 1962).

43. *Worcester v. Georgia*, 6 Pet. 515 (1832).

44. See Walter Murphy, *Congress and the Court* (Chicago: University of Chicago Press, 1962).

45. Robert Dahl, "The Supreme Court and National Policy Making," *Journal of Public Law* 6 (1958): 279.

46. Martin Shapiro, "The Supreme Court: From Warren to Burger," in *The New American Political System*, ed. Anthony King (Washington, DC: American Enterprise Institute, 1978).

47. *Citizens to Preserve Overton Park v. Volpe*, 401 U.S. 402 (1971).

48. Toni Locy, "Bracing for Health Care's Caseload," *Washington Post*, August 22, 1994, p. A15.

49. See "Developments in the Law—Class Actions," 89 *Harvard Law Review* (1976), 1318.

50. *In re Agent Orange Product Liability Litigation*, 100 F.R.D. 718 (D.C.N.Y. 1983).

51. See Donald Horowitz, *The Courts and Social Policy* (Washington, DC: Brookings Institution Press, 1977).

52. *Moran v. McDonough*, 540 F2d 527 (1 Cir., 1976; *cert. denied*, 429 U.S. 1042 [1977]).

53. Alexander Hamilton, James Madison, and John Jay, *The Federalist Papers*, ed. Clinton Rossiter (New York: New American Library, 1961), no. 10, p. 78.

## Chapter 16

1. Robert Nozick, *Anarchy, State and Utopia* (New York: Basic Books, 1974; reprint, Oxford: Blackwell, 2003).

2. Compare with Gabriel Kolko, *The Triumph of Conservatism* (New York: Free Press, 1963), chap. 6.

3. Bureau of Economic Analysis, "Percent Change from Preceding Period in Real Gross Domestic Product," www.bea.gov/national/nipaweb/SelectTable.asp?Popular=Y (accessed 3/5/10).

4. "Times Topics: Financial Regulatory Reform," *New York Times*, updated September 20, 2011, http://topics.nytimes.com/topics/reference/timestopics/subjects/c/credit_crisis/financial_regulatory_reform/index.html (accessed 5/16/12).

5. See David M. Hart, *Forged Consensus: Science, Technology and Economic Policy in the United States, 1921–1953* (Princeton, NJ: Princeton University Press, 1998).

6. See Margaret Weir, *Politics and Jobs: The Boundaries of Employment Policy in the United States* (Princeton, NJ: Princeton University Press, 1992).

7. Bradford DeLong, "America's Only Peacetime Inflation: The 1970s" (University of California at Berkeley and National Bureau of Economic Research, December 19, 1995), www.j-bradford-delong.net/pdf_files/Peacetime_Inflation.pdf (accessed 3/18/08).

8. The act of 1955 officially designated the interstate highways as the National System of Interstate and Defense Highways. It was indirectly a major part of President Dwight Eisenhower's defense program. But it was just as obviously a "pork barrel" policy as any rivers and harbors legislation.

9. The members were AMD, Digital, Hewlett-Packard, IBM, Intel, Lucent, Motorola, National Semiconductor, Rockwell, and Texas Instruments.

10. U.S. Department of Defense Small Business Innovation Research and Small Business Technology Transfer Programs, www.acq.osd.mil/osbp/sbir/ (accessed 3/7/10).

11. U.S. Consumer Product Safety Commission, *2009 Annual Performance and Accountability Report*, www.cpsc.gov/about/budperf.html (accessed 3/7/10).

12. Kevin G. Hall, "Bernanke to Stay on Greenspan Path, but Not All the Way," *Seattle Times*, November 16, 2005, p. C1.

13. The Federal Reserve Board, *Intended Federal Funds Rate, 1990 to Present*, www.federalreserve.gov/fomc/fundsrate.htm (accessed 3/8/10).

14. As a rule of thumb, in a growing economy where there is demand for credit, and assuming a reserve requirement of 20 percent, a deposit of $100 will create nearly $500 of new credit. This is called the "multiplier effect," because the bank can lend out $80 of the original $100 deposit to a new borrower; that becomes another $80 deposit, 20 percent of which ($64) can be lent to another borrower, and so on, until the original $100 grows to approximately $500 of new credit.

15. Good treatments of the Federal Reserve System and monetary policy can be found in Donald Kettl, *Leadership at the Fed* (New Haven, CT: Yale University Press, 1986); and Albert T. Sommers, *The U.S. Economy Demystified* (Lexington, MA: Lexington Books, 1988), especially chap. 5.

16. Donna S. Robinson, "NY Fed Estimates Millions More Foreclosures Possible" *Realty Biz News*, January 13, 2012. http://realtybiznews.com/ny-fed-estimates-millions-more-foreclosures-possible-in-2012-and-2013/9878531/ (accessed 9/26/12).

17. Steven R. Weisman, "Bernanke Faces Bear Stearns Queries," *New York Times*, April 2, 2008, p. C1.

18. John Ydstie, "Federal Reserve Mulls Its Role One Year after Crisis," National Public Radio, September 14, 2009, www.npr.org/templates/story/story.php?storyId=112767144 (accessed 3/8/10).

19. Executive Office of the President of the United States, GPO Access, "Budget of the United States Government: Historical Tables Fiscal Year 2009," Table 2.2—Percentage Composition of Receipts by Source: 1934–2013, http://origin.www.gpoaccess.gov/usbudget/fy09/hist.html (accessed 5/9/08).

20. For a systematic account of the role of government in providing incentives and inducements to business, see C. E. Lindblom, *Politics and Markets* (New York: Basic Books, 1977), chap. 13. For a detailed account of the dramatic Reagan tax cuts and reforms, see Jeffrey Birnbaum and Alan Murray, *Showdown at Gucci Gulch: Lawmakers, Lobbyists, and the Unlikely Triumph of Tax Reform* (New York: Random House, 1987).

21. For further background, see David E. Rosenbaum, "Cutting the Deficit Overshadows Clinton's Promise to Cut Taxes," *New York Times*, January 12, 1993, p. A1; and "Clinton Weighing Freeze or New Tax on Social Security," *New York Times*, January 31, 1993, p. A1.

22. Center on Budget and Policy Priorities, "Tax Cuts, Myths and Realities," November 16, 2007, www.cbpp.org/9-27-06tax.htm (accessed 3/20/08).

23. Jay Heflin, "House Dems Want Bush Tax Cuts to Expire, but Say It's Tough Sell," *The Hill*, February 8, 2010, http://thehill.com/homenews /house/80133-democrats-supporting-ending-tax-cut-but-see-it-as-tough-sell (accessed 3/8/10).

24. Adam Levine, "Senate Rejects Additional F-22 Funding," *CNN Politics*, July 21, 2009, www.cnn.com/2009/POLITICS/07/21/se nate.f22/index.html (accessed 3/8/10).

25. For an account of the relationship between mechanization and law, see Lawrence Friedman, *A History of American Law* (New York: Simon & Schuster, 1973), 409–29.

26. The *Federal Register* is the daily publication of all official acts of Congress, the president, and the administrative agencies. A law or executive order is not legally binding until it is published in the *Federal Register*.

27. Veronique de Rugy, "Hold On to Your Wallet: The Cost of Corporate Welfare and Rent-Seeking," *National Review Online*, July 25, 2012, www.nationalreview.com/corner/312251/hold-your-wallet-cost-corporate-welfare-and-rent-seeking-veronique-de-rugy# (accessed 9/26/12).

28. James Dao, "The Nation; Big Bucks Trip Up the Lean New Army," *New York Times*, February 10, 2002, sec. 4, p. 5, www.nytimes.com/2002/02/10/weekinreview/the-nation-big-bucks-trip-up-the-lean-new-army.html?pagewanted=all (accessed 9/26/12).

29. See Samuel P. Hays, *Beauty, Health, and Permanence: Environmental Politics in the United States, 1955–1985* (Cambridge: Cambridge University Press, 1987).

30. Pew Center on Global Climate Change, "Climate Change 101: The Science and Impacts," www.pewclimate.org/docUploads/101_Science_Impacts.pdf (accessed 3/21/08).

31. See the discussion in Peter R. Orszag, "Issues in Climate Change," Congressional Budget Office, November 16, 2007, www.cbo.gov/ftpdocs/88xx/doc8819/11-16-ClimateChangeConf.pdf (accessed 3/21/08).

32. Energy Information Administration, "Greenhouse Gases, Climate Change, and Energy," www.eia.doe.gov/oiaf/1605/ggccebro/chapter1.html (accessed 3/21/08).

33. John M. Broder and Marjorie Connelly, "Public Says Warming Is a Problem, but Remains Split on Response," *New York Times*, April 27, 2007, www.nytimes.com/2007/04/27/world/americas/27iht-27poll.5466260.html (accessed 7/3/12).

34. Tam Hunt, "The Good News: Climate Change Doesn't Matter Anymore," May 31, 2011, www.renewableenergyworld.com/rea/news/article/2011/05/the-good-news-climate-change-doesnt-matter-anymore (accessed 7/2/12).

35. Hunt, "The Good News."

36. Associated Press, "Obama Proposes Agency on Climate Change," February 8, 2010, www.cbsnews.com/stories/2010/02/08/tech/main6186608.shtml (accessed 3/8/10).

37. Michael Austin, "Breaking Down the New 2016 Fuel Economy Standards," *Car and Driver*, April 2, 2010, http://blog.caranddriver.com/breaking-down-the-new-2016-fuel-economy-standards/ (accessed 9/26/12)

38. Survey by Cable News Network, conducted by Opinion Research Corporation, November 2–4, 2007, and based on telephone interviews with a national adult sample of 1,024, USORC.110707.R05L.

39. Environmental Defense Fund, "Coalition Defines Clear Path for Climate Action," www.edf.org/climate/coalition-defines-clear-path-climate-action (accessed 7/2/12).

40. Juliet Eilperin and Steven Mufson, "Senators to Propose Abandoning Cap-and-Trade," *Washington Post*, February 27, 2010, www.washingtonpost.com/wp-dyn/content/article/2010/02/26/AR2010022606084.html?hpid=topnews (accessed 3/5/10).

41. Associated Press, "Obama Proposes Agency on Climate Change," February 8, 2010, www.cbsnews.com/stories/2010/02/08/tech/main6186608.shtml (accessed 3/8/10).

42. Hendrik Hertzberg, "Cooling on Warming," *The New Yorker*, February 7, 2011, p. 21.

43. Orszag, "Issues in Climate Change."

44. Joe Palca, "California Turns to Holland for Flood Expertise," National Public Radio, January 14, 2008. www.npr.org/templates/story/story.php?storyId=18080442 (accessed 3/21/08).

45. For a good summary of Keynes's ideas, see Robert Lekachman, *The Age of Keynes* (New York: McGraw-Hill, 1966).

46. David Sanger, David Herszenhorn, and Bill Vlasic, "Bush Aids Detroit, but Hard Choices Await Obama," *New York Times*, December 19, 2008, www.nytimes.com/2008/12/20/business/20auto.html?r=3&hp (accessed 3/7/10).

47. Matthew L. Wald, "'Cash for Clunkers' Car-Rebate Plan Sells Out in Days," *The New York Times*, July 30, 2009, p. B1.

48. Reuters, "CBO Raises TARP Cost Estimate to $34 Billion," December 16, 2011, www.reuters.com/article/2011/12/16/us-usa-tarp-cost-idUSTRE7BF1W920111216 (accessed 7/3/12).

49. Bureau of Labor Statistics, "United States Unemployment Rate," www.tradingeconomics.com/united-states/unemployment-rate (accessed 7/3/12).

50. Congressional Budget Office, February 22, 2012, http://cbo.gov/publications/43014 (accessed 7/3/12).

51. Ben Pershing, "House Passes $15 Billion Jobs Bill," *Washington Post*, March 5, 2010, www.washingtonpost.com/wp-dyn/content/article/2010/03/04/AR2010030402757.html (accessed 3/5/10).

52. Congressional Budget Office, June 22, 2011, http://cbo.gov/publications/414816 (accessed 7/3/12).

53. U.S. Treasury, "Interest Expense on the Debt Outstanding," www.treasurydirect.gov/govt/reports/ir/ir_expense.htm (accessed 7/3/12).

54. Chad Stone, "The Misconceptions about Where Our Tax Dollars Go," *U.S. News and World Report*, April 11, 2012, www.usnews.com/opinion/blogs/economic-intelligence/2012/04/11/0411econ.stone (accessed 7/3/12).

55. Megan Garvey, "Company Town; SAG Says Canada Film Policies Illegal, Seeks Federal Inquiry," *Los Angeles Times*, August 22, 2001, part 3, p. 5.

56. Robert H. Frank, *Falling Behind: How Rising Inequality Harms the Middle Class* (Berkeley: University of California Press, 2007).

57. Thomas Piketty and Emmanuel Saez credit the progressive income tax with reducing income inequality in the United States since the 1930s. See their argument in "Income Inequality in the United States, 1913–1998," *Quarterly Journal of Economics* 118, no. 1 (February 2003): 1–39.

58. Tax Policy Center, Table T06-0279 Combined Effect of the 2001–2006 Tax Cuts, Distribution of Federal Tax Change by Cash Income Percentile, 2006, November 13, 2006, www.taxpolicycenter.org/numbers/displayatab.cfm?DocID=1361 (accessed 3/22/08).

59. For a classic statement, see Milton Friedman and Rose Friedman, *Free to Choose* (New York: Harvest Books, 1990). See also Bruce Bartlett, "Is Income Inequality Really a Problem?" *New York Times*, January 24, 2007, http://bartlett.blogs.nytimes.com/2007/01/24/is-income-inequality-really-a-problem/ (accessed 3/22/08).

60. Larry M. Bartels, "Homer Gets a Tax Cut: Inequality and Public Policy in the American Mind," paper prepared for presentation at the Annual Meeting of the American Political Science Association, Philadelphia, August 2003.

## Chapter 17

1. The Henry J. Kaiser Family Foundation, Kaiser Health Tracking Poll, "Early Reaction to Supreme Court Decision on the ACA," p.1, www.kff.org/kaiserpolls/upload/8329-F.PDF (accessed 7/6/12).

2. A good source of pre-1930s welfare history is James T. Patterson, *America's Struggle against Poverty, 1900–1994*

(Cambridge, MA: Harvard University Press, 1994), chap. 2.

3. Quoted in Patterson, *America's Struggle against Poverty*, p. 26.

4. Patterson, *America's Struggle against Poverty*, p. 26.

5. Patterson, *America's Struggle against Poverty*, p. 27

6. This figure is based on a WPA study by Ann E. Geddes, reported in Merle Fainsod et al., *Government and the American Economy*, 3rd ed. (New York: W.W. Norton, 1959), p. 769.

7. Social Security Online, "Contribution and Benefit Base," www.socialsecurity.gov/OACT/COLA/cbb.html (accessed 2/10/12).

8. Edward J. Harpham, "Fiscal Crisis and the Politics of Social Security Reform," in *The Attack on the Welfare State*, ed. Anthony Champagne and Edward Harpham (Prospect Heights, IL: Waveland, 1984), p. 13.

9. Liz Schott and Ife Finch, "Tax Benefits Are Low and Have Not Kept Pace with Inflation: Benefits Are Not Enough to Meet Families' Basic Needs. Appendix 1: Changes in State TANF Benefit Levels (Single-Parent Family of Three)," *Center on Budget and Policy Priorities*, October 14, 2010, www.cbpp.org/files/10-14-10tanf.pdf (accessed 2/19/12).

10. This poverty threshold is for a household of 3 persons that includes two children, U.S. Census Bureau, Poverty Thresholds, www.census.gov/hhes/www/poverty/data/treshld/index.html (accessed 7/6/12).

11. *Goldberg v. Kelly*, 397 U.S. 254 (1970).

12. Henry J. Kaiser Family Foundation, Statehealthfacts. org, "Distribution of Medicaid Payments by Enrollment Group (in millions), FY2005," www.statehealthfacts.org/comparetable.jsp?ind=182&cat=4 (accessed 4/9/08).

13. See Martin Gilens, *Why Americans Hate Welfare* (Chicago: University of Chicago Press, 1999), chaps. 3, 4.

14. Gilens, *Why Americans Hate Welfare*.

15. Center for Law and Social Policy, "Analysis of Fiscal Year 2006 TANF and MOE Spending by States," http://clasp.org/WelfarePolicy/pdf/map100907us.pdf (accessed 4/9/08).

16. See the discussion of the law and the data presented in House Ways and Means Committee Print, WMCP: 106-14, 2000 Green Book, Section 7, Temporary Assistance for Needy Families (TANF), http://frwebgate.access.gpo.gov/cgi-bin/useftp.cgi?IPaddress=162.140.64.181&filename=wm014_07.wais&directory=/data/wais/data/106_green_book (accessed 3/26/08); Rebecca M. Blank, "Evaluating Welfare Reform in the United States," *Journal of Economic Literature* 40 (December 2002): 1105–66.

17. LaDonna Pavetti and Liz Schott, "TANF's Inadequate Response to Recession Highlights Weakness of Block-Grant Structure," (Washington, DC: Center on Budget and Policy Priorities), July 14, 2011, www.cbpp.org/cms/?fa=view&id=3534 (accessed 2/10/12).

18. Center for Budget and Policy Priorities, "Chartbook: SNAP Helps Struggling Families Put Food on the Table," April 18, 2012, www.cbpp.org/cms/?fa=view&id=3744#part5 (accessed 7/6/12); U.S. Department of Agriculture, Food and Nutrition Service, Supplemental Nutrition Assistance Program, www.fns.usda.gov/snap/ (accessed 7/6/12).

19. Center for Budget and Policy Priorites, "Chartbook:SNAP Helps Struggling Families Put Food On the Table," April 18, 2012, www.cbpp.org/cms/?fa=view&id=37443part5 (accessed 7/612); U.S. Department of Agriculture, Food and Nutrition Service, Supplemental Nutrition Assistance Program, www.fns.usda.gov/snap/ (accessed 7/6/12). Data for 2012 are estimates. Office of Management and Budget, "Table 8.3, Percentage Distribution of Outlays by Budget Enforcement Act Category: 1962–2015," www.whitehouse.gov/omb/budget/Historicals (accessed 2/19/12); Office of Management and Budget, "The President's Budget, Historical Tables: Table 2.2, Percentage Composition of Receipts by Source: 1934–2017," www.whitehouse.gov/omb/budget/Historicals (accessed 2/19/12).

20. President's Commission to Strengthen Social Security, "Strengthening Social Security and Creating Personal Wealth for All Americans," December 21, 2001, 5, www.csss.gov/reports/Final_report.pdf (accessed 3/26/08).

21. President's Commission to Strengthen Social Security, "Strengthening Social Security."

22. Alicia H. Munnell, "Are the Social Security Trust Funds Meaningful?" Center for Retirement Research, Boston College, May 2005, no. 30, p. 4, http://crr.bc.edu/images/stories/Briefs/ib_30.pdf (accessed 3/25/08); see also Social Security Online, Summary of P.L. 98-21, (H.R. 1900) Social Security Amendments of 1983—Signed on April 20, 1983, www.ssa.gov/history/1983amend.html (accessed 3/25/08).

23. Christian E. Weller, "Undermining Social Security with Private Accounts," Economic Policy Institute Issue Brief, December 11, 2001, www.epi.org/content.cfm/issuebriefs_ib172 (accessed 3/26/08); Robert Greenstein, "Social Security Commission Proposals Contain Serious Weaknesses but May Improve the Debate in an Important Respect," Center on Budget and Policy Priorities, December 26, 2001, www.centeronbudget.org/12-11-01socsec.htm (accessed 3/26/08).

24. Quoted in Jill Quadragno, "Social Security Policy and the Entitlement Debate," in *Social Policy and the Conservative Agenda*, eds. Clarence Y. H. Lo and Michael Schwartz (Malden, MA: Blackwell, 1998), p. 111.

25. "Estimated Sources of Medicare Revenue," facts.kff.org/chart.aspx?ch=1807 (accessed 3/1/12).

26. Congressional Budget Office, "Long Term Analysis of a Budget Proposal by Chairman Ryan," April 5, 2011, www.cbo.gov/publication/22085 (accessed 7/6/12); See also the discussion in Kaiser Family Foundation Program on Medicare Policy, "Proposed Changes to Medicare in the 'Path to Prosperity,'" April 2011, www.kff.org/medicare/upload/8179.pdf (accessed 3/1/12).

27. There were a couple of minor precedents. One was the Smith-Hughes Act of 1917, which made federal funds available to the states for vocational education

at the elementary and secondary levels. Second, the Lanham Act of 1940 made federal funds available to schools in "federally impacted areas," that is, areas with an unusually large number of government employees and/or where the local tax base was reduced by large amounts of government-owned property.

28. Office of Management and Budget, *Budget of the United States Government, Fiscal Year 1982* (Washington, DC: Government Printing Office, 1981), p. 427.

29. Motoko Rich, "'No Child' Law Whittled Down by White House," *New York Times*, July 6, 2012, p. A1.

30. Veronica DeVore, "'Race to the Top' Education Funds Awarded to 9 States and D.C.," August 24, 2010, www.pbs.org/newshour/rundown/2010/08/round-two-results-announced-for-race-to-the-top.html (accessed 7/6/12).

31. Morton Keller, *Affairs of State: Public Life in Nineteenth Century America* (Cambridge, MA: Belknap Press, 1977), p. 500.

32. Data for 2012 are estimates. Office of Management and Budget, "Table 16.1—Total Outlays for Health Programs: 1962–2017," www.whitehouse.gov/omb/budget/Historicals (accessed 2/19/12).

33. Noam N. Levey, "Obama's HIV/AIDS Policy Hailed for Targeting Spread of Disease," *Los Angeles Times*, July 14, 2010, articles.latimes.com/2010/jul/14/nation/la-na-obama-aids-20100714 (accessed 3/1/12).

34. For a comparison of opinion in 1993 when the Clinton plan was considered and opinion in 2009 as reform was just beginning again, see Pew Research Center for the People and the Press, "Obama's Ratings Remain High Despite Some Policy Concerns," www.people-press.org/2009/06/18/obamas-ratings-remain-high-despite-some-policy-concerns/ (accessed 7/6/12).

35. Sarah Kliff, "Americans Still Don't Know What's in the Health Reform Law. They May Not Care Either," *Washington Post*, November 30, 2011, www.washingtonpost.com/blogs/ezra-klein/post/americans-still-dont-know-whats-in-the-health-reform-law-they-may-not-care-either/2011/11/29/gIQAh5Z89N_blog.html (accessed 3/1/12).

36. "June Kaiser Health Tracking Poll: Americans Still Divided on Health Reform Law," June 30, 2011, http://healthreform.kff.org/scan.aspx?tag=KFF+Tracking+Polls&page=2 (accessed 3/1/12).

37. The Henry J. Kaiser Family Foundation, Kaiser Health Tracking Poll, "Early Reaction to Supreme Court Decision on the ACA," p. 3.

38. "February Kaiser Health Tracking Poll," March 1, 2012, healthreform.kff.org/scan.aspx?tag=Public+Opinion (accessed 3/1/12).

39. *National Federation of Independent Business v. Sebelius*, 567 U.S. ___ (2012).

40. John E. Schwarz, *America's Hidden Success*, 2nd ed. (New York: W.W. Norton, 1988), pp. 41–2.

41. "Atlanta Housing Shortage Sparks Desperation, Chaos," www.npr.org/templates/story/story.php?storyId=129179066 (accessed 3/1/12).

42. See, for example, Lawrence Vale, "Housing Chicago: Cabrini-Green to Parkside of Old Town," places.designobserver.com/feature/housing-chicago-cabrini-green-to-parkside-of-old-town/32298/ (accessed 3/1/12).

43. "Foreclosures, 2012 Robosigning and Foreclosure Abuse Settlement," *New York Times*, updated February 16, 2012, topics.nytimes.com/top/reference/timestopics/subjects/f/foreclosures/index.html (accessed 7/7/12).

44. Theda Skocpol and Vanessa Williamson, *The Tea Party and the Remaking of Republican Conservatism* (New York: Oxford University Press, 2012), chapter 1.

45. Julie Schmitt, "Homeownership Rates Fall to 66% as Downturn Nears a Bottom," *USA Today*, February 1, 2012, www.usatoday.com/money/economy/housing/story/2012-01-31/home-prices-ownership/52907436/1 (accessed 3/1/12).

46. U.S. Census Bureau, "Table 4: People and Families in Poverty by Selected Characteristics: 2009 and 2010," www.census.gov/hhes/www/poverty/data/incpovhlth/2010/table4.pdf (accessed 2/19/12).

47. See, for example, Theodore R. Marmor, Jerry L. Mashaw, and Philip L. Harvey, *America's Misunderstood Welfare State* (New York: Basic Books, 1990), 156.

48. U.S. Census Bureau, "Income, Households: Table H-10. Age of Head of Household by Median and Mean Income," www.census.gov/hhes/www/income/data/historical/household/ (accessed 2/19/2012)

49. See U.S. Census Bureau, "Age and Sex in the United States: 2010: Table 1. Population by Age and Sex: 2010," www.census.gov/population/www/socdemo/age/age_sex_2010.html (accessed 2/19/12); on AARP, see Frederick R. Lynch, "How AARP Can Get Its Groove Back," *New York Times*, June 23, 2011, www.nytimes.com/2011/06/24/opinion/24lynch.html (accessed 2/20/212), and "Influence and Lobbying: AARP Lobbyists, 2011," www.opensecrets.org/lobby/clientlbs.php?id=D000023726&year=2011 (accessed 2/20/2012).

50. See Andrea Louise Campbell, *How Policies Make Citizens: Senior Political Activism and the American Welfare State* (Princeton, NJ: Princeton University Press, 2005).

51. Christopher Howard, *The Hidden Welfare State: Tax Expenditures and Social Policy in the United States* (Princeton, NJ: Princeton University Press, 1999); Jacob S. Hacker, *The Divided Welfare State: The Battle over Public and Private Benefits in the United States* (New York: Cambridge University Press, 2002).

52. Office of Management and Budget, "Table 17-1: Estimates of Total Income Tax Expenditures for Fiscal Years 2010–2016," *Analytical Perspectives: Budget of the U.S. Government* (2010), www.whitehouse.gov/sites/default/files/omb/budget/fy2012/assets/spec.pdf (accessed 2/20/12)

53. Raymond Hernandez, "Federal Welfare Overhaul Allows Albany to Shift Money Elsewhere," *New York Times*, April 23, 2000, p. 1.

54. Frances Fox Piven and Richard Cloward, *Poor People's Movements* (New York: Pantheon, 1977), chap. 5.

55. Department of Agriculture Supplemental Nutrition Assistance Program (SNAP), www.fns.usda.gov/snap/ (accessed 3/1/12).

56. U.S. Census Bureau, "Table 4: People and Families in Poverty by Selected Characteristics: 2009 and 2010," www.census.gov/hhes/www/poverty/data/incpovhlth/2010/tables.html (accessed 2/20/12).

57. Carmen DeNavas-Walt, Bernadette D. Proctor, and Jessica C. Smith, "Income Poverty and Health Insurance Coverage in the United States," U.S. Census Bureau, September 2011, www.census.gov/prod/2011pubs/p60-239.pdf, p. 10 (accessed 7/7/12).

58. See, for example, Sharon Hayes, *Flat Broke with Children: Women in the Age of Welfare Reform* (New York: Oxford University Press, 2004).

59. U.S. Census Bureau, "Poverty: Historical Poverty Tables—People: Table 2: Poverty Status of People by Family Relationship, Race, And Hispanic Origin: 1959 to 2010," www.Census.Gov/Hhes/Www/Poverty/Data/Historical/People.Html (Accessed 2/20/12). For An Argument That Children Should Be Given The Vote, See Paul E. Peterson, "An Immodest Proposal," *Daedalus* 121, no.4 (Fall 1992): 151–74.

60. On the relationship between education and democracy in the United States, see Ira Katznelson and Margaret Weir, *Schooling for All: Race, Class, and the Democratic Ideal* (New York: Basic Books, 1985).

61. See L. Free and Hadley Cantril, *The Political Beliefs of Americans* (New York: Simon and Schuster, 1968).

62. See Fay Lomax Cook and Edith Barrett, *Support for the American Welfare State* (New York: Columbia University Press, 1992); and Hugh Heclo, "The Political Foundations of Antipoverty Policy," in *Fighting Poverty: What Works and What Doesn't*, ed. Sheldon H. Danziger and Daniel H. Weinberg (Cambridge, MA: Harvard University Press, 1986), pp. 312–40.

## Chapter 18

1. Geoffrey Perret, *A Country Made by War* (New York: Random House, 1989), p. 558.

2. Alexis de Tocqueville, *Democracy in America*, trans. Phillips Bradley, 2 vols. (1835; New York: Vintage, 1945), vol. 1, p. 243.

3. Rupert Smith, *The Utility of Force: The Art of War in the Modern World* (New York: Vintage, 2008).

4. D. Robert Worley, *Shaping U.S. Military Forces: Revolution or Relevance in a Post–Cold War World* (Westport, CT: Praeger Security International, 2006).

5. This was done quietly in an amendment to the Internal Revenue Service Reform Act (PL 105–206), June 22, 1998. But it was not accomplished easily. See Bob Gravely, "Normal Trade with China Wins Approval," *Congressional Quarterly Weekly Report*, July 25, 1998; and Richard Dunham, "MFN by Any Other Name Is . . . NTR?," Business Week online news flash, June 19, 1997, www.businessweek.com/bwdaily/dnflash/june/lf70619b.htm (accessed 9/26/12).

6. Matthew Crenson and Benjamin Ginsberg, *Presidential Power: Unchecked and Unbalanced* (New York: W.W. Norton, 2007).

7. Benjamin Ginsberg, *The American Lie: Government by the People and Other Political Fables* (Boulder, CO: Paradigm, 2007).

8. Paul R. Pillar, *Terrorism and American Foreign Policy* (Washington, DC: Brookings Institution Press, 2003).

9. Raymond A. Bauer, Ithiel de Sola Pool, and Lewis Anthony Dexter, *American Business and Public Policy: The Politics of Foreign Trade*, 2nd ed. (Chicago: Aldine-Atherton, 1972).

10. For a good treatment of this in regard to Irish-Catholics and Catholics in general, see Timothy Byrnes, *Catholic Bishops and American Politics* (Princeton, NJ: Princeton University Press, 1991). For a (controversial) discussion of the role of Jewish groups, see John J. Mearsheimer and Stephen M. Walt, *The Israel Lobby and U.S. Foreign Policy* (New York: Farrar, Straus and Giroux, 2007).

11. This felicitous term is from David R. Mayhew, *Congress: The Electoral Connection* (New Haven, CT: Yale University Press, 1974).

12. John H. Aldrich, *Why Parties? The Origin and Transformation of Political Parties in America* (Chicago: University of Chicago Press, 1995), 278.

13. A very good brief outline of the centrality of the president in foreign policy is found in Paul E. Peterson, "The President's Dominance in Foreign Policy Making," *Political Science Quarterly* 109 (Summer 1994): 215–34.

14. One confirmation of this is found in Theodore Lowi, *The End of Liberalism: The Second Republic of the United States*, 2nd ed. (New York: W.W. Norton, 1979), pp. 127–30; another is found in Stephen Krasner, "Are Bureaucracies Important?" *Foreign Policy* 7 (Summer 1972): 159–79. However, it should be noted that Krasner was writing his article in disagreement with Graham T. Allison, "Conceptual Models and the Cuban Missile Crisis," *American Political Science Review* 63, no. 3 (September 1969): 689–718.

15. Peterson, "The President's Dominance in Foreign Policy Making," p. 232.

16. Hans Morgenthau, *Politics among Nations*, 2nd ed. (New York: Knopf, 1956), p. 505.

17. See Theodore Lowi, *The Personal President: Power Invested, Promise Unfulfilled* (Ithaca, NY: Cornell University Press, 1985), pp. 167–9.

18. "IMF: Sleeve-Rolling Time," *The Economist*, May 2, 1992, pp. 98–9.
19. James Dao and Patrick E. Tyler, "U.S. Says Military Strikes Are Just a Part of Big Plan," *The Alliance*, September 27, 2001; and Joseph Kahn, "A Nation Challenged: Global Dollars," *New York Times*, September 20, 2001, p. B1.
20. Turkey was desperate for help extricating its economy from its worst recession since 1945. The Afghanistan crisis was going to hurt Turkey all the more; Turkey's strategic location helped its case with the IMF. "Official Says Turkey Is Advancing in Drive for I.M.F. Financing," *New York Times*, October 6, 2001, p. A7.
21. George Quester, *The Continuing Problem of International Politics* (Hinsdale, IL: Dryden Press, 1974), p. 229.
22. The Warsaw Pact was signed in 1955 by Albania, Bulgaria, Czechoslovakia, Hungary, the German Democratic Republic (East Germany), Poland, Romania, and the Soviet Union. Albania later dropped out. The Warsaw Pact was terminated in 1991.
23. Ginsberg, *The American Lie*, p. 3.

## Chapter 19

1. Alan Rosenthal, "On Analyzing States," in *The Political Life of the American States*, ed. Alan Rosenthal and Maureen Moakley (New York: Praeger, 1984), pp. 11–2.
2. Daniel Elazar, *American Federalism: A View from the States*, 2nd ed. (New York: Crowell, 1971), pp. 84–126. See also John Kincaid, "Introduction," in *Political Culture, Public Policy and the American States*, ed. John Kincaid (Philadelphia: Center for the Study of Federalism, Institute for the Study of Human Issues, 1982), pp. 1–24.
3. Rosenthal, "On Analyzing States," p. 13.
4. U.S. Census Bureau, 2010 Census.
5. The following is drawn from Dallas Morning News, *Texas Almanac 2000–2001* (Dallas: Dallas Morning News, 1999), pp. 55–8.
6. American Ground Water Trust, "What Have We Done to the Ogallala Aquifer," The American Well Owner (2002).
7. See Joseph A. Schumpeter, *Capitalism, Socialism, and Democracy*, 3rd ed. (New York: Harper & Brothers, 1950), chap. 6.
8. The following is drawn from Karen Gerhardt Britton, Fred C. Elliott, and E. A. Miller, "Cotton Culture," *Handbook of Texas Online*.
9. See Dallas Morning News, *Texas Almanac 2000–2001*, p. 51.
10. Dallas Morning News, *Texas Almanac 2000–2001*, p. 567–8.
11. See "Ranching" in *Handbook of Texas Online*.
12. U.S. Department of Agriculture, National Agricultural Statistics Service, "Texas Upland Cotton Production Estimated at 8.05 Million Bales," News Release, December 10, 2010.
13. The following is drawn from Mary G. Ramos, "Oil and Texas: A Cultural History," Dallas Morning News, *Texas Almanac 2000–2001*, pp. 29–35; and Roger M. Olien, "Oil and Gas Industry," *Handbook of Texas Online*.
14. Ramos, "Oil and Texas," p. 31.
15. Olien, "Oil and Gas Industry."
16. Texas State Comptroller, "Where the Money Comes From: Texas Budget Source," August 2, 2011.
17. Financial Statements and Independent Auditors' Report Permanent, University Fund, Years Ended August 31, 2010 and 2009.
18. The following is drawn from Anthony Champagne and Edward J. Harpham, "The Changing Political Economy of Texas," in *Texas Politics: A Reader*, 2nd ed., ed. Anthony Champagne and Edward J. Harpham (New York: W.W. Norton, 1998), pp. 4–6. Production figures are drawn from Dallas Morning News, *Texas Almanac 1994–95* (Dallas: Belo, 1993); John Sharp, *Forces of Change: Shaping the Future of Texas* (Austin: Texas Comptroller of Public Accounts, 1993).
19. Texas State Comptroller, "Texas Gross State Product Detail—Calendar Years 1990–2040."
20. Texas Wide Open for Business, "Overview of the Texas Economy."
21. Anil Kumar, "Did NAFTA Spur Texas Exports?" *Southwest Economy* 2 (March–April 2006), www.dallasfed.org/research/swe/2006/swe0602b.html (accessed 3/28/08); U.S. Department of Labor Employment & Training Administration, "Trade Adjustment Assistance: Number of Certified Workers by State"; Robert E. Scott, "Heading South: U.S.-Mexico Trade and Job Displacement after NAFTA," Economic Policy Institute (May 3, 2011).
22. U.S. Census Bureau. "State Exports for Texas" and "State Imports for Texas." See also Texas Economy Online Report from the Office of the Governor, "Overview of the Texas Economy."
23. Daniel Gross, "Lone Star: Why Texas Is Doing So Much Better Than the Rest of the Nation," *Slate*, April 19, 2010, www.slate.com/id/2250999 (accessed 7/7/10).
24. Bruce Wright, "Weathering the Storm," *Fiscal Notes*, March 2009; D'Ann Petersen and Laila Assanie, "Texas Dodges Worst of Foreclosure Wars," Federal Reserve of Dallas.
25. Federal Reserve Bank of Dallas, Texas Leading Economic Indicators, May 2010. See also Texas Wide Open for Business, "Overview of the Texas Economy."
26. See "Estimated Population by Year for Texas, 1980–94."
27. Office of the State Demographer, "Changing Demographics in Texas," presented at the 2011 Texas Labor Management Conference, June 22, 2011, San Antonio, Texas.
28. See Arnoldo De León, "Mexican Americans," *Handbook of Texas Online*.
29. U.S. Census Bureau, 2010 Census ; Sharon R. Ennis, Merarys Rios-Vargis, and Nora G. Albert. "The Hispanic Population: 2010," *2010 Census Briefs*, May 2011.

30. Data provided by the National Association of Latino Elected and Appointed Officials (NALEO).

31. See W. Marvin Dulaney, "African Americans," *Handbook of Texas Online*; Chandler Davidson, "African Americans and Politics," *Handbook of Texas Online*.

32. U.S. Census Bureau, "Texas."

33. Bruce H. Webster Jr. and Alemayehu Bishaw, "Income, Earnings, and Poverty Data from the 2006 American Community Survey" (American Community Survey Reports, U.S. Census Bureau, August 2007); U.S. Census Bureau, Poverty 2007 and 2008 American Community Surveys (September 2009); U.S. Census Bureau, *Texas Quick Facts: 2009*.

34. The following is based on David G. McComb, "Urbanization," *Handbook of Texas Online*.

35. The following is drawn from David G. McComb, "Houston, Texas," *Handbook of Texas Online*.

36. Estimates are drawn from the U.S. Census Bureau, American Community Survey 2006–2008.

37. The following is drawn from Jackie McElhaney and Michael V. Hazel, "Dallas, Texas," *Handbook of Texas Online*.

38. The following is drawn from Janet Schmelzer, "Fort Worth, Texas," *Handbook of Texas Online*.

39. The following is drawn from T. R. Fehrenbach, "San Antonio, Texas," *Handbook of Texas Online*.

40. Estimates are drawn from the U.S. Census Bureau, American Community Survey 2006–2008.

## Chapter 20

1. The following is drawn from Proposition 10, Deleting Constitutional References to County Office of Inspector of Hides and Animals, www.hro.house.state.tx.us/focus prop80–10.pdf (accessed 3/31/08); Eric Aasen, "Round 'Em Up: Hide Inspectors Abolished," *Dallas Morning News*, November 8, 2007; John Council, "Richmond Lawyer Has Personal Stake in Hide Inspector Position," *Texas Lawyer*, November 2, 2007; Mark Lisheron, "Prop. 10 Would Abolish Office That No One Holds," *Austin American-Statesman*, October 15, 2007.

2. See Dick Smith, "Inspector of Hides and Animals," *Handbook of Texas Online*.

3. Donald E. Chipman, "Spanish Texas," *Handbook of Texas Online*; Donald E. Chipman, *Spanish Texas, 1519–1821* (Austin: University of Texas Press, 1992).

4. S. S. McKay, "Constitution of 1824," *Handbook of Texas Online*.

5. S. S. McKay, "Constitution of Coahuila and Texas," *Handbook of Texas Online*.

6. See Ralph W. Steen, "Convention of 1836," *Handbook of Texas Online*.

7. The following is drawn from Joe E. Ericson, "Constitution of the Republic of Texas," *Handbook of Texas Online*.

8. Randolph B. Campbell, "Slavery," *Handbook of Texas Online*.

9. For a brief summary of the war, see Eugene C. Barker and James W. Pohl, "Texas Revolution," *Handbook of Texas Online*.

10. S. S. McKay, "Constitution of 1845," *Handbook of Texas Online*.

11. The Texas Ordinance of Secession (February 2, 1861).

12. See Walter L. Buenger, "Secession Convention," *Handbook of Texas Online*; Walter L. Buenger, *Secession and the Union in Texas* (Austin: University of Texas Press, 1984).

13. See Claude Elliott, "Constitutional Convention of 1866," *Handbook of Texas Online*; S. McKay, "Constitution of 1866," *Handbook of Texas Online*; Charles W. Ramsdell, *Reconstruction in Texas* (New York: Columbia University Press, 1970).

14. See S. S. McKay, "Constitution of 1869," *Handbook of Texas Online*; Ramsdell, *Reconstruction in Texas*.

15. See John Walker Mauer, "Constitution Proposed in 1874," *Handbook of Texas Online*; John Walker Mauer, "State Constitutions in a Time of Crisis: The Case of the Texas Constitution of 1876," 68 *Texas Law Review* (June 1990), 1615–46.

16. For a further discussion, see George D. Braden et al., *The Constitution of the State of Texas: An Annotated and Comparative Analysis* (Austin: University of Texas Press, 1977), pp. 707–10.

17. See Sam Kinch Jr., "Sharpstown Stock-Fraud Scandal," *Handbook of Texas Online*; Charles Deaton, *The Year They Threw the Rascals Out* (Austin: Shoal Creek, 1973).

18. CBSDFW.com, "Texas Voters Approve 7 Constitutional Amendments," November 9, 2011.

19. Angela Shah, "Both Sides Claim Victory in Approval of Lawsuit Caps," *Dallas Morning News*, September 15, 2003, pp. 1A, 10A.

20. Terry Maxon, "Prop. 12 Battle Was Costliest Yet," *Dallas Morning News*, January 19, 2004, p. 2D.

21. John Council, "Power and the Prize," *Texas Lawyer*, June 16, 2003, pp. 1, 22.

## Chapter 21

1. Jeffrey M. Jones, "Special Report: Many States Shift Democratic during 2005," Gallup, January 23, 2006.

2. Use of party affiliation as an ideological cue is discussed in Philip L. Dubois, *From Ballot to Bench* (Austin: University of Texas Press, 1980).

3. Quoted in Chandler Davidson, Race and Class in Texas Politics (Princeton, NJ: Princeton University Press, 1990), p. 198.

4. Davidson, *Race and Class in Texas Politics*, pp. 24–5.

5. Jones, "Special Report: Many States Shift Democratic During 2005."

6. Pew Research Center for the People and the Press, "Fewer Voters Identify as Republicans," March 20, 2008.

7. Gallup, "Party ID: Despite GOP Gains, Most States Remain Blue," February 1, 2010.

8. James R. Soukup, Clifton McClesky, and Harry Holloway, *Party and Factional Division in Texas* (Austin: University of Texas Press, 1964), p. 22.

9. Wayne Slater, "Strayhorn Gets Democratic Cash," *Dallas Morning News*, January 26, 2006, pp. 1A, 17A.

10. Pete Slover, "Independents' Day Is a Bid for the Ballot," *Dallas Morning News*, March 8, 2006, p. 14A.

11. Robert T. Garrett, "2 Major GOP Donors Show Rift in Party," *Dallas Morning News*, February 3, 2006, p. 2A.

12. Robert T. Garrett, "PAC's Late Aid Altered Races," *Dallas Morning News*, March 10, 2006, pp. 1A, 16A.

13. Terri Langford, "District Judge Fends off Democratic Rival's Challenge," *Dallas Morning News*, November 9, 2000.

14. Anthony Champagne and Greg Thielemann, "Awareness of Trial Court Judges," 75 *Judicature* (1991): 271–2.

15. Anthony Champagne, "The Selection and Retention of Judges in Texas," 40 *Southwestern Law Journal* (1986): 80.

16. The lone Democratic survivor, Ron Chapman, became an appellate judge. Democratic judges who did not switch to the Republican Party were defeated.

17. Langford, "District Judge Fends Off Democratic Rival's Challenge."

18. Joe Holley, "Are Texas' Hispanics Ready to Go Democrat?" *Houston Chronicle*, April 3, 2010.

19. In 1994 it was estimated that there were between 420,000 and 460,000 illegal immigrants in Texas. Many of those illegal immigrants were Hispanic. See Leon F. Bouvier and John L. Martin, "Shaping Texas: The Effects of Immigration, 1970–2020," Center for Immigration Studies, April 1995. The Federation for American Immigration Reform cites the Immigration and Naturalization Service for a January 2000 estimate that there were 1,041,000 illegal immigrants then in Texas. See their report, "Texas: Illegal Aliens." An April 2006 study by the Pew Hispanic Center estimated that between 1.4 and 1.6 million unauthorized individuals were living in Texas. Pew Hispanic Center, "Estimates of the Unauthorized Migrant Population for States Based on the March 2006 CPS, Fact Sheet: April 26, 2006."

20. Holley, "Are Texas' Hispanics Ready to Go Democrat?"

21. Texas Secretary of State, "Turnout and Voter Registration Figures, 1970–Current." Dallas and Harris counties have more voting precincts than are found in the entire state of New Hampshire.

22. Sam Acheson, *Joe Bailey: The Last Democrat* (New York: Macmillan, 1932), p. 354.

23. Joe Robert Baulch, "James B. Wells: State Economic and Political Leader" (Ph.D. dissertation, Texas Tech University, 1974), pp. 358–9.

24. Sue Tolleson-Rinehart and Jeanie R. Stanley, *Claytie and the Lady* (Austin: University of Texas Press, 1994), pp. 18–9.

25. O. Douglas Weeks, "The Texas-Mexican and the Politics of South Texas 34," *American Political Science Review* (1930): 625–6; Anthony Champagne, "John Nance Garner," in *Masters of the House*, ed. Roger H. Davidson, Susan Webb Hammond, and Raymond W. Smock (Boulder, CO: Westview, 1998), pp. 145–80.

26. *United States v. Texas*, 384 U.S. 155 (1966).

27. *Beare v. Smith*, 321 F. Supp. 1100 (1971).

28. *Kramer v. Union Free School District No. 15*, 395 U.S. 621 (1969); *Hill v. Stone*, 421 U.S. 289 (1975).

29. *Dunn v. Blumstein*, 405 U.S. 330 (1972).

30. *Newberry v. United States*, 256 U.S. 232 (1921).

31. *Nixon v. Herndon*, 273 U.S. 536 (1927).

32. *Nixon v. Condon*, 286 U.S. 73 (1932).

33. *Grovey v. Townsend*, 295 U.S. 45 (1935).

34. *Smith v. Allwright*, 321 U.S. 649 (1944).

35. *Terry v. Adams*, 345 U.S. 461 (1953).

36. Gary Scharrer, "Holder Issues Challenge to Texas on Voter Rights," *Houston Chronicle*, December 13, 2011.

37. National Conference of State Legislatures, "State Requirements for Voter ID."

38. *Houston Chronicle*, Texas Secretary of State, "Turnout and Voter Registration Figures (1970–current)."

39. Texas Secretary of State, "Turnout and Voter Registration Figures (1970–current)."

40. Thomas R. Patterson, *The American Democracy* (New York: McGraw Hill, 1999), p. 188.

41. For this classic in campaign mistakes, see the October 2002 issue of *Texas Monthly* magazine. An example of the negative impact of the ad can be found in a front-page article, Wayne Slater and Pete Slover, "Dewhurst Campaign Ad: The Flag Is Ours, But What's with the German Officer?" *Dallas Morning News*, October 26, 2001.

42. Candidates in Texas Supreme Court races are affected by "friends and neighbors" voting, whereby voters tend to cast ballots for candidates from their home county or from neighboring counties. See Gregory Thielemann, "Local Advantage in Campaign Financing: Friends, Neighbors, and Their Money in Texas Supreme Court Elections," *Journal of Politics* 55 (1993): 472–8.

43. Roy A. Schotland, "Campaign Finance in Judicial Elections," *Loyola of Los Angeles Law Review* (2001), 1508–12.

## Chapter 22

1. *Kelo v. City of New London*, 545 U.S. 469 (2005).

2. James W. Lamare, *Texas Politics: Economics, Power and Policy*, 3rd ed. (St. Paul: West, 1988), p. 82.

3. Kenneth R. Mladenka and Kim Quaile Hill, *Texas Government: Politics and Economics* (Belmont, CA: Wadsworth, 1986), pp. 80–2.

4. Governor Rick Perry's schedule, September 15, 2010.

5. Jason Embry, "The Most Powerful Group in Texas Politics Has Wentworth in Its Sights," *Statesman.com*, December 7, 2011.

6. Texans for Public Justice, "Power Surge: TXU's Patronage Grid Plugs All but Seven Lawmakers," *Lobby Watch*, March 1, 2007.

7. Matt Stiles, "Lobbyist Gives 'Shocking' Gift to Lawmaker," *Texas Tribune*, February 15, 2010.

8. Steve McGonigle, "For Perry, Big Game Means Big Business—Trucking Lobby Paid for Governor's Private Jet to Rose Bowl," *Dallas Morning News*, December 12, 2006.

9. Matt Stiles and Chris Chang, "Texas Lobbying Directory Details Spending, Clients," *Texas Tribune*, March 15, 2011.

10. Emily Ramshaw and Marcus Funk, "For Some Dallas-Area Legislators, Donations Fund the Good Life," *Dallas Morning News*, February 1, 2009.

11. Ross Ramsey, "Legislature Is a Training Ground for Lobbyists," *Texas Tribune*, June 10, 2010.

12. Ramsey, "Legislature Is a Training Ground."

13. Texas for Public Justice, "Ten New Lawmaker Retreads Merge into the 2009 Lobby," *Lobby Watch*, May 20, 2009.

14. "Rick Perry's Former Staffers Made Millions as Lobbyists," *Huffington Post*, December 19, 2011.

15. "Rick Perry's Former Staffers."

16. Ramsey, "Legislature Is a Training Ground."

17. Texans for Public Justice, "Texas Revolvers: Public Officials Recast as Hired Guns" (1999).

18. Texas Ethics Commission.

19. Texans for Public Justice, "Austin's Oldest Profession" (2012).

20. Texans for Public Justice, "Austin's Oldest Profession."

21. Texans for Public Justice, "Austin's Oldest Profession."

22. Texans for Public Justice, "Special-Interests Spend Up to $180 Million on Lobby Services in 1999 Legislative Session," May 24, 1999.

23. Texans for Public Justice, "Money in Politex" (2008).

24. Anthony Champagne, "Campaign Contributions in Texas Supreme Court Races," *Crime, Law & Social Change* 17 (1992): 91–106.

25. Texans for Public Justice, "Texans for Lawsuit Reform Sustains Pricey Primary Hits," *Lobby Watch*, March 5, 2010; Julian Aguilar, "Primary Color: HD-43," *Texas Tribune*, February 26, 2010.

26. Embry, "Most Powerful Group."

27. National Institute on Money in State Politics.

28. Kristen Mack, "New Lawmakers Learn to Juggle Hectic Lives; Everybody—Lobbyists, Family—Wants a Moment of Their Time," *Houston Chronicle*, February 6, 2005, p. 1B.

29. Texans for Public Justice, "Texans for Lawsuit Reform."

30. Embry, "Most Powerful Group." John W. Gonazalez, "Campbell Upsets Wentworth for Texas Senate," *San Antonio Express-News*, August 1, 2012.

31. Texans for Public Justice, "Operation Vouchsafe: Dr. Leininger Injects $5 Million into Election; Many Candidates Fail on His Life Support," *Lobby Watch*, n.d.

32. Emily Ramshaw, "Fighting for Fair Warning—Man Who Lost Wife, Kids in Blaze Seeks Visual Smoke Alarms for Deaf," *Dallas Morning News*, April 17, 2009; "Tragedy Leads to Improved Fire Safety in Texas," National Association of the Deaf, July 1, 2009.

# Chapter 23

1. The preceding is drawn from S. C. Gwynne, "Tom Craddick: How Did Tom Craddick Become the Most Powerful Speaker Ever—and the Most Powerful Texan Today? Let Us Count the Ways," *Texas Monthly*, February 2005; R. G. Ratcliffe and Gary Scharrer, "Craddick Safe as Session Ends, but '08 Race Is Ahead," *Houston Chronicle*, May 28, 2007; Dan Collins, "Chaos in Texas House over Speaker Fight," CBSNEWS, May 26, 2007; Karen Brooks and Christy Hoppe, "Craddick Quits House Speaker's Race; Straus Poised to Take Over," *Dallas Morning News*, January 5, 2009; Karen Brooks, "GOP Bloc Backs Joe Straus to Topple House Speaker Tom Craddick," *Dallas Morning News*, January 3, 2009.

2. "Senate Gives Tentative OK to Guns on Campuses," *Dallas Morning News*, May 20, 2009.

3. "Texas Bill to Allow Guns on Campus Rejected for Violating Constitutional Requirement," *Security Director News*, June 7, 2011.

4. Ann Marie Kilday, "Equal Measure," *Dallas Morning News*, May 24, 2001, p. 31A.

5. Anthony Champagne and Rick Collis, "Texas," in *The Political Life of the American States*, ed. Alan Rosenthal and Maureen Moakley (New York: Praeger, 1984), p. 138.

6. Ross Ramsey, "Will Texas Lawmakers Cut Their Own Benefits?," *Texas Tribune*, March 11, 2011.

7. Ramsey, "Will Texas Lawmakers Cut."

8. "State Rep. Joe Driver of Garland Double-Billed for Travel," *Dallas Morning News*, August 16, 2010; "Garland Republican Joe Driver Pleads Guilty to Double-Dipping on Travel Reimbursements," *Dallas Morning News*, November 22, 2011.

9. Kelley Shannon, "Doctor Twice Honored by the Texas Legislature Registered as Sex Offender," *Sulphur Springs News-Telegram*, June 22, 2007, p. 1.

10. Frank M. Stewart, "Impeachment in Texas," 24 *American Political Science Review*, no. 3 (August 1930), 652–8; George D. Braden et al., *The Constitution of the State Texas: An Annotated and Comparative Analysis* (Austin: University of Texas Press, 1977), pp. 707–18.

11. Legislative Reference Library of Texas, "Bill Statistics."

12. Lisa Falkenberg, "Texas Lawmakers Scramble to Finish Last-Minute Bills," *Dallas Morning News*, March 10, 2001, p. 38A.

13. Office of Governor Rick Perry, "Press Release," June 19, 2009.

14. Mike Ward, "Perry Vetoes Texting while Driving Ban, 22 Other Bills," *Statesman.com*, June 17, 2011.

15. Karen Brooks, "Craddick's Win May Cost Him," *Dallas Morning News*, May 27, 2007, p. 1.

16. Karen Brooks, "In 1877, Lawmakers Ran Republican Out of the Chair," *Dallas Morning News*, May 27, 2007, p. 26A.

17. John W. Gonzalez, "Texas Legislature; Jobs Well Done; Laney, Lauded for Maintaining Order and Fairness, Ends

3rd Term as Speaker," *Houston Chronicle*, June 6, 1999, p. State 1.

18. Vince Leibowitz, "Texas Senate Republicans Trying to Dump Two-Thirds Voting Rule," *Capitol Annex*, January 14, 2009.

19. Terrence Stutz, "Texas Senate at Odds over Voter ID Legislation, Two-Thirds Rule," *Dallas Morning News*, January 14, 2009.

20. *Baker v. Carr*, 369 U.S. 186 (1962); *Reynolds v. Sims*, 377 U.S. 533 (1964).

21. *Wesberry v. Sanders*, 376 U.S. 1 (1964).

22. Sam Attlesey, "Panel OKs Map Favoring GOP," *Dallas Morning News*, December 7, 2001.

23. The preceding is drawn from Sam Attlesey, "Taking Stock of the Fallout from Redistricting," *Dallas Morning News*, December 11, 2001; Terrance Stutz, "GOP Expecting to Grab the House," *Dallas Morning News*, January 3, 2002; Sam Attlesey, "Before Election, House Democrats Seeing Losses," *Dallas Morning News*, December 11, 2001.

24. Medill School of Journalism, "On the Docket: *League of United Latin American Citizens, Travis County, Jackson, Eddie and GI Forum of Texas v. Perry, Rick (Texas Gov.).*"

25. State Appellants' Brief in the Supreme Court of the United States, *LULAC v. Perry*.

26. Medill School of Journalism, "On the Docket."

27. Appellants' Brief on the Merits, *LULAC v. Perry*.

28. See, generally, Steve Bickerstaff, *Lines in the Sand: Congressional Redistricting in Texas and the Downfall of Tom DeLay* (Austin: University of Texas Press, 2007).

## Chapter 24

1. The next two paragraphs rely on James C. McKinley Jr., "Re-elected Texas Governor Sounding Like a Candidate," *New York Times*, November 5, 2010, p. A18.

2. See the discussion of gubernatorial power in Cheryl D. Young and John J. Hindera, "The Texas Governor: Weak or Strong?" in *Texas Politics: A Reader*, ed. Anthony Champagne and Edward J. Harpham (New York: W. W. Norton, 1998), p. 53.

3. Sam Kinch, in *Government by Consent—Texas, A Telecourse* (Dallas: Dallas County Community College District, 1990).

4. Brian McCall, *The Power of the Texas Governor: Connally to Bush* (Austin: University of Texas Press, 2009).

5. McCall, *Power of the Texas Governor*, p. 120.

6. Christy Hoppe and Robert T. Garrett, "How Deep Does Governor Dig into Issues?" *Dallas Morning News*, November 27, 2011, pp. 1, 30A.

7. Kinch, *Government*.

8. Polly Ross Hughes, "Farewell to a Yalie, Howdy to an Aggie," *Houston Chronicle*, December 14, 2000, p. 1A.

9. Hughes, "Farewell to a Yalie," p. 26A.

10. George Kuempel, "The Tab Texas Taxpayers Are Picking up for Security Protection," *Dallas Morning News*, February 2, 2000, p. 25A.

11. William P. Hobby, in *Government by Consent—Texas, A Telecourse* (Dallas: Dallas County Community College District, 1990).

12. Christy Hoppe, "Lt. Gov. Rick Perry, Honoring the Economic Generators of Texas Tourism," *Dallas Morning News*, February 28, 2000, p. 13A.

13. Hoppe, "Lt. Gov. Rick Perry."

14. Hoppe and Garrett, "How Deep Does Governor Dig," p. 30A.

15. Steve McGonigle and James Drew, "Perry Stocks State Boards with Allies," *Dallas Morning News*, December 4, 2011, pp. 1, 32A.

16. Young and Hindera, "Texas Governor: Weak or Strong?" p. 62.

17. Legislative Reference Library of Texas, "Bill Statistics."

18. Richard Whittaker, "Gov. Perry's Ham-Fisted Veto Pen Strikes Again," *Austin Chronicle*, June 22, 2007.

19. Office of Governor Rick Perry, "Governor Perry Signs State Budget That Reduces GR by $1.6 Billion," Press Release, June 19, 2009.

20. Texas Legislative Library, Special Sessions of the Texas Legislature (2010).

21. Young and Hindera, "Texas Governor: Weak or Strong?" p. 61.

22. Young and Hindera, "Texas Governor: Weak or Strong?" p. 61.

23. The above discussion was taken from Jim Yardley, "Public Lives: This Texan, Too, Has a Lot Riding on Bush's Campaign," *New York Times*, October 7, 2000, p. 9; Kathy Walt, "Texas Legislature; Jobs Well Done; Senators Give Perry High Marks after Starting out with Low Expectation," *Houston Chronicle*, June 6, 1999, p. State 1.

24. Jim Yardley, "Public Lives: A Power in Texas Governing Finds Fault in Texas Politics," *New York Times*, June 9, 2001, p. A7.

25. Much of this material on the attorney general's office is taken from the website of the Attorney General of Texas Greg Abbott.

26. Much of this material on the Texas General Land Office is taken from the website of the Texas General Land Office.

27. Christy Hoppe, "Perry's Appointees Give Him Unprecedented Hold on Texas—Longest-Serving Governor Spreads Pro-Business View," *Dallas Morning News*, December 19, 2008.

28. Christy Hoppe, "Perry Ousts Officials before Arson Hearing—He's Assailed as New Chair Delays Session on Flawed Case That Led to Execution," *Dallas Morning News*, October 1, 2009.

29. William McKenzie, "Rick Perry's Curious Ways—Governor's Strongman Tactics Are Hard to Comprehend amid a Heated Campaign, Says William McKenzie," *Dallas Morning News*, October 20, 2009.

30. Terrence Stutz, "Senate Rejects Perry Appointee to Parole Board—Activist Faulted on Credentials; Governor Stands by Nominee," *Dallas Morning News*, May 14, 2009.

31. Texas Department of Insurance, "Texas Department of Insurance History."

32. Bill Peacock, "Policy Perspective: Is the Free Market Working for the Texas Homeowners' Insurance Market?" Texas Public Policy Foundation, February 28, 2006.

33. Terrence Stutz, "State Farm Stiff-Arming Regulators," *Dallas Morning News*, April 14, 2010; Terrence Stutz, "State Farm Near Top in Rates," *Dallas Morning News*, September 7, 2011, p. 1.

34. Terrence Stutz, "Legal Tactics Stall Insurance Reform," *DallasNews.com*, September 16, 2007.

35. Russell Shorto, "How Christian Were the Founders?" *New York Times*, February 14, 2010; Terrence Stutz, "Debate Continues over Social Studies," *Dallas Morning News*, March 11, 2010.

36. Morgan Smith, "Texas State Board of Education Races Could Get Ugly," *Texas Tribune*, November 7, 2011; Dan, "Another Big Setback for the Far Right on Texas State Board of Education," TFN Insider, November 7, 2012, tfninsider.org/2012/11/07/another-big-setback-for-the-far-right-on-texas-state-board-of-eduction/.

# Chapter 25

1. The discussion of the Michael Richard case and its aftermath is from Ralph Blumenthal, "Texas Judge Draws Outcry for Allowing an Execution," *New York Times*, October 25, 2007; Christy Hoppe, "Criminal Appeals Court Creates Emergency Filing System," *DallasNews.com*. November 6, 2007; "Texas Judge Fosters Tough-on-Crime Reputation," MSNBC, October 23, 2007; State Commission on Judicial Conduct, Special Master's Findings of Fact, In Re: Honorable Sharon Keller, Presiding Judge of the Texas Court of Criminal Appeals, January 20, 2010. Judge Keller's problems with financial disclosure are from Chuck Lindell, "Judge Keller Fined $100,000 for Disclosure Lapses," *Statesman.com*, May 1, 2010, www.statesman.com/news/local/judge-keller-fined-100-000-for-disclosure-lapses-654591.html (accessed 5/9/12).

2. Texas Office of Court Administration, "Activity Report for Justice Courts, September 1, 2009 to August 31, 2010."

3. Barbara Kirby, "Neighborhood Justice: Campaign Funding and Texas Justice of the Peace Courts," paper presented at the annual meeting of the Southern Political Science Association, New Orleans, Louisiana, January 3, 2007.

4. Ed Housewright, "Emotional Issues, Historical Pedigree," *Dallas Morning News*, April 9, 2001, p. 10A.

5. Texas Office of Court Administration, "Activity Report for Municipal Courts, September 1, 2008 to August 31, 2009."

6. Texas Office of Court Administration, "Activity Report for Municipal Courts, September 1, 2009 to August 31, 2010."

7. Thomas Petzinger Jr., *Oil and Honor: The Texaco-Pennzoil Wars* (New York: Putnam, 1987).

8. Task Force on Indigent Defense, "Evidence for the Feasibility of Public Defender Offices in Texas."

9. Mary Alice Robbins, "West Texas Plans Public Defender Office for Capital Cases," *Texas Lawyer*, August 20, 2007, pp. 1, 19; "New Public Defender for Capital Cases," Tex Parte Blog, October 16, 2007.

10. Ken Anderson, *Crime in Texas* (Austin: University of Texas Press, 1997), p. 40.

11. Anderson, *Crime in Texas*, p. 44. Nationally, 95 percent of felonies are plea-bargained.

12. Of the 79 judicial appointments made by Governor William Clements, only 6 were either African American or Hispanic. In contrast, one-third of Governor Ann Richards's judicial appointees were minorities. See Michael Totty, "Is This Any Way to Choose a Judge?" *Wall Street Journal*, August 3, 1994, pp. T1, T4.

13. Texas Office of Court Administration, "Profile of Appellate and Trial Judges as of September 1, 2009."

14. Anthony Champagne, "The Selection and Retention of Judges in Texas," *Southwestern Law Journal* 40 (1986), 78–9.

15. Texans for Public Justice, "Payola Justice: How Texas Supreme Court Justices Raise Money from Court Litigants."

16. Texans for Public Justice, "Judging Texas Justice in the Court of Opinion."

17. L. Douglas Kiel, Carole Funk, and Anthony Champagne, "Two-Party Competition and Trial Court Elections in Texas," 77 *Judicature* (1994), 291.

18. Linda Campbell, " 'H' as in Herasimchuk," *Fort Worth Star-Telegram*, December 6, 2001.

19. Mary Flood and Brian Rogers, "Why Some Harris County Judges Lost Not Entirely Clear," *Houston Chronicle*, November 6, 2008.

20. Elliott Slotnik, "Gender, Affirmative Action, and Recruitment to the Federal Bench," 14 *Golden Gate University Law Review* (1984), 524.

21. Texas Office of Court Administration, "Profile of Appellate and Trial Judges as of March 1, 2011."

22. Barbara L. Graham, "Toward an Understanding of Judicial Diversity in American Courts," 10 *Michigan Journal of Race and Law* (2004), 178.

23. One report is that 90 percent of African American voters and 60 to 79 percent of Hispanic voters vote Democratic. See Ronald W. Chapman, "Judicial Roulette: Alternatives to Single-Member Districts as a Legal and Political Solution to Voting-Rights Challenges to At-Large Judicial Elections," 48 *SMU Law Review* (1995), 182.

24. The trial court opinion was unpublished.

25. *League of United Latin American Citizens v. Clements*, 902 F2d 293 (1990), and *League of United Latin American Citizens v. Clements*, 914 F2d 620 (1990).

26. *Houston Lawyers' Association v. Attorney General of Texas*, 501 U.S. 419 (1991).

27. *League of United Latin American Citizens Council v. Clements*, 999 F2d 831 (1993).

28. A discussion of the Bullock plan and the politics surrounding it is in Anthony Champagne, "Judicial Selection in Texas," *Texas Politics: A Reader*, 2nd ed., ed. Anthony Champagne and Edward J. Harpham (New York: W.W. Norton, 1998), pp. 99–103.

29. Susan Carbon and Larry Berkson, *Judicial Retention Elections in the United States* (Chicago: American Judicature Society, 1980), p. 21.

30. A discussion of these general systems of selection is found in Champagne, "Judicial Selection in Texas," pp. 88–104.

31. Daniel Becker and Malia Reddick, *Judicial Selection Reform: Examples from Six States* (Chicago: American Judicature Society, 2003), pp. 1–10.

32. Bill Jeffreys, "Death, Simplified," *Texas Lawyer*, October 23, 2000, p. 1.

33. Pete Slover, "Attorney's Inexperience No Barrier," *Dallas Morning News*, September 11, 2000, p. 12A.

34. Texas Department of Criminal Justice, "Death Row Information."

35. Texas Department of Criminal Justice, "Death Row Information."

36. Texas Department of Criminal Justice, "Death Row Information."

37. Texas Department of Criminal Justice, "Executions, December 7, 1982 through March 16, 2010"; Texas Department of Criminal Justice, "Gender and Racial Statistics of Death Row Offenders," *McClesky v. Kemp*, 481 U.S. 279 (1987).

38. Erica C. Barnett, "No Sunshine on Clemency," *Austin Chronicle*, January 1, 1999.

39. "Gov. Perry Commutes Sentences of Man Scheduled to Die Thursday," ABC 13, August 30, 2007.

40. David McCord, "What's Messing with Texas Death Sentences?" 43 *Texas Tech Law Review* (2011), 601–12.

41. The Pew Center on the States, "Prison Count 2010" (March 2010), p. 7.

42. The Innocence Project of Texas, "Facts on Post-Conviction DNA Exonerations."

43. "DNA Proving to Cut Both Ways on Death Penalty," *Dallas Morning News*, January 14, 2006, p. 10A.

44. See Nate Blakeslee, *Tulia: Race, Cocaine, and Corruption in a Small Texas Town* (New York: Public Affairs, 2005).

45. Paul Duggan, " 'Sheetrock Scandal' Hits Dallas Police," *Washington Post*, January 18, 2002, p. 12.

46. Michael Hall, "Why Can't Steven Phillips Get a DNA Test?" *Texas Monthly*, January 2006.

47. The Innocence Project of Texas, "Texas Exonerations."

48. Radley Balke, "The 250th DNA Exoneration," *Reason*, February 4, 2010.

49. Steve McGonigle, "Righting Wrongs," *Dallas Morning News*, January 22, 2007, p. 1; Jennifer Emily, "DA: Man Didn't Do '82 Rape," *Dallas Morning News*, September 17, 2007, p. 1B.

50. David Grann, "Trial by Fire," *The New Yorker*, September 7, 2009.

51. Jeff Carleton, "Cameron Todd Willingham: Texas Governor Dismisses 3 Commission Members Just 48 Hours before Arson Review," *Huffington Post*, September 30, 2009.

52. Allan Turner, "Abbott Ruling Limits Probe of Arson Case," *Houston Chronicle*, July 29, 2011.

53. Jeff Blackburn, "Dog Scent Lineups: A Junk Science Injustice," special report by the Innocence Project of Texas, September 21, 2009.

54. Pamela Colloff, "Innocence Lost," *Texas Monthly*, October 2010; Pamela Colloff, "Innocence Found," *Texas Monthly*, January 2011.

55. Phil Hardberger, "Juries under Siege," 30 *St. Mary's Law Journal* (1998), 6–7.

56. "High Court Voting Patterns," *Texas Lawyer*, September 6, 1999, p. 5.

57. David A. Anderson, "Judicial Tort Reform in Texas," 26 *Review of Litigation*, (2007), 7.

## Chapter 26

1. This discussion of the office of constable is taken from Ed Timms and Kevin Krause, "Constables' Tickets Collect Funds, Critics," *Dallas Morning News*, October 25, 2009; Kevin Krause, "Commissioners OK Hiring Own Lawyer," *Dallas Morning News*, September 30, 2009; Kevin Krause, "Towed Cars Remain on Road to Nowhere," *Dallas Morning News*, September 18, 2009; Ed Timms and Kevin Krause, "Constables' Mission Has Changed," *Dallas Morning News*, October 26, 2009.

2. This discussion of the Hill corruption case is from Gromer Jeffers Jr., "Political Star Tainted by Liabilities—Dallas: Hill's Successes Slowed by Sanctions, FBI Investigation," *Dallas Morning News*, July 23, 2005; Jason Trahan, "Hill's Trial Opens Today—Third Corruption Case Involving a Councilman Is Wide in Scope," *Dallas Morning News*, June 29, 2009; Jason Trahan and Diane Jennings, "Three Sentenced in 'Betrayal of Our City,' " *Dallas Morning News*, February 27, 2010.

3. Dallas Morning News, *Texas Almanac 2009–2010* (Dallas: Dallas Morning News, 2008), p. 500; U.S. Census Bureau, *Lists & Structure of Government*; www.texasalmanac.com/topics/government. Different sources provide varying numbers regarding municipal governments in Texas.

4. The two states that don't use counties as units of local government are Connecticut and Rhode Island. See Rich-

ard L. Cole and Delbert A. Taebel, *Texas: Politics and Public Policy* (Fort Worth: Harcourt Brace Jovanovich, 1987), p. 151.

5. Texas Association of Counties, "About Counties: County Government."

6. Texas Association of Counties, "About Counties."

7. Cole and Taebel, *Texas Politics and Public Policy*, p. 152.

8. *Avery v. Midland County*, 390 U.S. 474 (1968).

9. Anthony Champagne and Rick Collis, "Texas," in *The Political Life of the American States*, ed. Alan Rosenthal and Maureen Moakley (Washington, DC: CQ Press, 1984), p. 140.

10. Texas State Data Center.

11. Brenda Rodriguez, "Loving and Losing in West Texas," *Dallas Morning News*, March 14, 2001, p. 21A.

12. Russell Gold, "Counties Struggle with High Cost of Prosecuting Death-Penalty Cases," *Wall Street Journal*, January 9, 2002, p. B1.

13. "Capital Trial Could Be Costly for Franklin Co.," *Sulphur Springs News-Telegram*, June 27, 2007, p. 4.

14. Adam M. Gershowitz, "Statewide Capital Punishment: The Case for Eliminating Counties' Role in the Death Penalty," 63 *Vanderbilt Law Review* (2010), 8–9.

15. Cole and Taebel, *Texas: Politics and Public Policy*, p. 155.

16. Lawrence M. Crane, Nat Pinnoi, and Stephen W. Fuller, "Private Demand for Publicly Provided Goods: A Case Study of Rural Roads in Texas," *TAMRC Contemporary Market Issues Report No. CI-1-92* (1992).

17. Texas Association of Counties, "Debate Goes Back and Forth, Just Like Overweight Trucks," www.county.org/resources/library/county-mag/county/124/bridgedebate.html.

18. Texas Commission on Jail Standards, "Abbreviated Population Report," August 1, 2011.

19. "Knock! Knock! Smith County Sheriff's Office Goes Armored," *County Magazine*, July–August 1997.

20. Article XI, Section 5, of the Texas Constitution is concerned with home rule. For a further discussion of home rule in Texas, see Terrell Blodgett, *Texas Home Rule Charters* (Austin: Texas Municipal League, 1994); Terrell Blodgett, "Home Rule Charters," *Handbook of Texas Online*, www.tshaonline.org/handbook/online/articles/HH/mvhek.html (accessed 4/17/08).

21. Correspondence with Terrell Blodgett, Wednesday, February 3, 2000; *Texas Almanac 2009–2010*, 500–510.

22. The following is drawn from Bradley R. Rice, "Commission Form of City Government," *Handbook of Texas Online*.

23. Dallas Morning News, *Texas Almanac 1996–97* (Dallas: Dallas Morning News, 1995), p. 513.

24. Correspondence with Terrell Blodgett, Wednesday, February 3, 2000.

25. For a further discussion, see Terrell Blodgett, "Council-Manager Form of City Government," *Handbook of Texas Online*; Blodgett, *Texas Home Rule Charters*.

26. For a history of the Office of Controller in Houston, see "Office History."

27. Jack C. Plano and Milton Greenberg, *The American Political Dictionary*, 10th ed. (Fort Worth: Harcourt, Brace, 1997).

28. *Texas Almanac and State Industrial Guide, 2000–2001* (Dallas: Dallas Morning News, I.P 1999), p. 533; *Statistical Abstract of the United States* (Washington, DC: Bureau of the Census, 1998), p. 496.

29. Brooks Egerton and Reese Dunklin, "Government by Developer," *Dallas Morning News*, June 10, 2001, p. 1A.

30. Peggy Heinkel-Wolfe, "Developers Still Using Renters to Create Special Tax Districts," *Dallas Morning News*, November 1, 2006, p. 1B.

31. Peggy Heinkel-Wolfe, "Bonds Approved with Blessing of 2 Voters," *Dallas Morning News*, November 22, 2010, p. B6.

32. Sara C. Galvan, "Wrestling with MUDs to Pin Down the Truth about Special Districts," 75 *Fordham Law Review* (2007), 3041–80.

33. See Texas Association of Regional Councils, "About TARC."

## Chapter 27

1. The following is drawn from Brandon Formby, "Schools Wrestling with Policies under New Religious Liberties Act," *Dallas Morning News*, August 27, 2007; Jenny Lacoste-Caputo, "Law on Religion in School Spurs Fear," *San Antonio Express-News*, July 25, 2007; Kelly Coghlan, "Religion Gets Equal Treatment," *Dallas Morning News*, September 6, 2007; Karen Brooks, "One State under God," *Dallas Morning News*, April 22, 2007; Wendy Gragg, "New State Law on Religious Expression in Schools Draws Mixed Reactions," *Waco Tribune-Herald*, August 9, 2007. The text of HB 3678 is available at www.capitol.state.tx.us/tlodocs/80R/billtext/html/HB03678F.htm (accessed 4/21/08).

2. See Texas Association of School Boards, "Legal Notes: An Open Mike."

3. See data provided by Federation of Tax Administrators at www.taxadmin.org. and Texas Public Policy Foundation at www.texasbudgetsource.com. Other ranking information is available from Lisele Zavala, Revenue Estimate Division, Texas Comptroller of Public Accounts. See also tax burden rankings provided by the Tax Foundation at www.taxfoundation.org.

4. The above data on Texas are from the Tax Foundation.

5. See Bernard L. Weinstein, "Taxes in Texas," in *Texas Politics: A Reader*, ed. Anthony Champagne and Edward J. Harpham (New York: W. W. Norton, 1998), chap. 12.

6. The following discussion is drawn from Texas Legislative Budget Board, *Texas Facts Book* (Austin: State of Texas, 1998).

7. For a discussion of the budgetary process, see Texas Comptroller of Public Accounts, *Disturbing the Peace*, Appendix I (Austin: State of Texas, 1996), www.window.state.tx.us/tpr/tpr4/vol1/v13app12.html (accessed 4/21/08).

8. For a discussion of these issues, see Weinstein, "Taxes in Texas."

9. See Kim Quaile Hill and Kenneth R. Mladenka, *Texas Government* (Belmont, CA: Wadsworth, 1993), 269–70; James MacGregor Burns et al., *Government by the People: Texas Version* (Englewood Cliffs, NJ: Prentice Hall, 1995), pp. 746–8.

10. See Texas Health and Human Services Commission, "Medicaid Spending from All Angles." At www.hhsc.state.tx.us/medicaid/reports/PB8/PDF/Chp-7.pdf.

11. Texas Lottery Commission, Demographic Survey of Texas Lottery Players 2009, December 1, 2009.

12. See Office of the Texas Comptroller, Window on State Government: Revenue by Source for Fiscal Year 2011. See also Texas Lottery Commission, Demographic Survey of Texas Lottery Players 2009, December 1, 2009, p. 11.

13. See James LeBas, "Who Wants to Be a Billionaire? Texas Spending Tobacco Money on Health Care, Endowments," Texas Comptroller of Public Accounts, *Fiscal Notes* (January 2000); Texas House of Representatives, House Research Organization. State Finance Report No. 82-3, March 11, 2011.

14. The following is drawn largely from Robert T. Garrett, "Many Texas Politicians, including Perry and White, Talk Little of $21 Billion Budget Gap," *Dallas Morning News*, September 12, 2010; Robert T. Garrett, "Budget Likely to Cut Deep," *Dallas Morning News*, October 24, 2010; Emily Ramshaw, "Legislators Consider Medicaid Withdrawal," *Texas Tribune* for *New York Times*, November 7, 2010. See also Dave Montgomery and Anna M. Tinsley, "Texas Budget with $15 Billion in Cuts Clears Legislature," *Ft. Worth Star Telegram*, May 28, 2011; Eugenio Aleman and Tyler B. Kruse, "Texas Budget: 2012–2013 Biennium," Wells Fargo Securities, June 24, 2011.

15. Harry Mika and Lawrence J. Redlinger, "Crime and Correction," in *Texas at the Crossroads*, ed. Anthony Champagne and Edward J. Harpham (College Station: Texas A&M University Press, 1987), pp. 245–6.

16. Mika and Redlinger, "Crime and Correction," pp. 245–6.

17. *Ruiz v. Estelle*, 503 F. Supp. 1265 (1980).

18. Mika and Redlinger, "Crime and Correction," p. 247.

19. Texas Department of Criminal Justice, "Fiscal Year 2010 Statistical Report."

20. Legislative Budget Board, "Criminal Justice Uniform Cost Report Fiscal Years 2008–2010" (January 2011), p. 3.

21. Texas Department of Criminal Justice, "Fiscal Year 2005 Operating Budget and Fiscal Years 2006–2007 Legislative Appropriations Request," August 23, 2004, www.tdcj.state.tx.us/Publications/Finance/LAR-FY2006-7-Short.pdf (accessed 4/21/08).

22. See Associated Texans against Crime, Annual Report, 1998; Texas Department of Criminal Justice, "Fiscal Year 2011 Operating Budget and Fiscal Years 2010–2013 Legislative Appropriations Request," August 16, 2010.

23. Marc A. Levin, 2009–2010 Legislators Guide to the Issues (November, 2008), p. 1.

24. See Associated Texans against Crime, Annual Report, 1998.

25. Texas Department of Criminal Justice, "Fiscal Year 2010 Statistical Report"; Mika and Redlinger, "Crime and Correction," p. 245.

26. Mika and Redlinger, "Crime and Correction," p. 245.

27. See Associated Texans against Crime, Annual Report, 1998.

28. Texas Department of Criminal Justice, Fiscal Year 2006 Statistical Summary, December 2006.

29. Texas Department of Criminal Justice, Fiscal Year 2010 Statistical Reports.

30. Mika and Redlinger, "Crime and Correction," p. 245.

31. U.S. Department of Justice, Bureau of Justice Statistics Bulletin, Prisoners in 2009, December 2010, p. 24.

32. Scott Morgan and Kathleen O'Leary Morgan, eds., *Crime State Rankings 2009* (Washington, DC: CQ Press, 2009), p. xxi.

33. Morgan and O'Leary Morgan, *Crime State Rankings 2009*, p. xxi.

34. Texas Department of Criminal Justice, Fiscal Year 2010 Statistical Report.

35. L. Tucker Gibson Jr. and Clay Robinson, *Government and Politics in the Lone Star State*, 2nd ed. (Upper Saddle River, NJ: Prentice Hall, 1995).

36. Marc A. Levin, *2009–2010 Legislators Guide to the Issues* 1 (Washington, DC: CQ Press, 2009).

37. For a discussion of the history of public education in Texas from which the following is drawn, see Max Berger and Lee Wilborn, "Education," *Texas Handbook Online*, www.tshaonline.org/handbook/online/articles/EE/khel.html (accessed 4/21/08); Dallas Morning News, "Public Schools," *Texas Almanac 2000–2001*, Millennium Edition (Dallas: Dallas Morning News, 1999), pp. 533–4.

38. See Lewis B. Cooper, *The Permanent School Fund of Texas* (Fort Worth: Texas State Teachers Association, 1934); Michael E. McClellan, "Permanent School Fund," *Handbook of Texas Online*, www.tshaonline.org/handbook/online/articles/PP/khpl.html (accessed 4/21/08).

39. See Oscar Mauzy, "Gilmer-Aikin Laws," *Handbook of Texas Online*, www.tshaonline.org/handbook/online/articles/GG/mlgl.html (accessed 4/21/08); Dick Smith and Richard Allen Burns, "Texas Education Agency," *Handbook of Texas Online*, www.tshaonline.org/handbook/online/articles/TT/met2.html (accessed 4/21/08); Berger and Wilborn, "Education."

40. See Anna Victoria Wilson, "Education for African Americans," *Handbook of Texas Online*, www.tshaonline.org/handbook/online/articles/EE/kde2.html (accessed 4/21/08).

41. *Brown v. Board of Education of Topeka, Kansas,* 347 U.S. 483 (1954).
42. Arnoldo De León and Robert A. Calvert, "Segregation," *Handbook of Texas Online,* www.tshaonline.org/handbook/online/articles/SS/pksl.html (accessed 4/21/08).
43. The following discussion of the *Rodríguez* and *Edgewood* cases is drawn from Legislative Budget Board Staff, "Financing Public Education in Texas: Kindergarten through Grade 12," *Legislative Handbook* (February 1999); Berger and Wilborn, "Education"; Cynthia E. Orozco, *"Rodríguez v. San Antonio ISD," Handbook of Texas Online,* www.tshaonline.org/handbook/online/articles/RR/jrrht.html (accessed 4/21/08); Teresa Palomo Acosta, *"Edgewood ISD v. Kirby," Handbook of Texas Online,* www.tshaonline.org/handbook/online/articles/EE/jre2.html (accessed 4/21/08).
44. See Legislative Budget Board Staff, "Financing Public Education in Texas: Kindergarten through Grade 12," *Legislative Handbook* (February 1999), pp. 26–7.
45. See Texas House of Representatives, House Research Organization, "Focus Report: Schools and Taxes," May 25, 2007, www.house.state.tx.us/featured/schools&taxes79–13.pdf (accessed 4/21/08); Jason Embry, "Session Ends with Property Tax Cut," *Austin American-Statesman,* May 26, 2006.
46. See Clark D. Thomas, "Education Reform in Texas," in *Texas Politics,* ed. Champagne and Harpham, chap. 13.
47. National Commission on Excellence in Education, *A Nation at Risk: The Imperative for Educational Reform* (Washington, DC: Department of Education, 1983).
48. See Thomas, "Education Reform in Texas," p. 218.
49. See Thomas, "Education Reform in Texas," p. 221.
50. See Thomas, "Education Reform in Texas," p. 231; Dallas Morning News, "Public Schools," *Texas Almanac 2000–2001,* Millennium Edition (Dallas: Dallas Morning News, 1999), p. 533. See also Terrence Stutz, "State's List Cites Sub-par Schools in Transfer Plan," *Dallas Morning News,* December 24, 1999, p. 1.
51. Commonwealth Foundation, *Texas Fact Book* (2009), p. 19; College Board, Mean 2009 SAT Scores by State; College Board, 2009 College-Bound Seniors Total Group Profile Report (2009), p. 3. See also Texas Education Agency, College Admissions Testing of Graduating Seniors in Texas High Schools, Class of 2010 (October 2011) and *2010 Comprehensive Annual Report on Texas Public Schools.*
52. See Joshua Benton, "Legislators Left Unanswered Questions on New State Tests," *Dallas Morning News,* June 11, 2007, p. B1. See also Terrence Stutz, "Failing Tests, Passing Grades," *Dallas Morning News,* March 8, 2012, p. A1.
53. Data from U.S. Bureau of the Census and Texas Health and Human Services Commission.
54. Center for Public Policy Priorities, Policy Point, Policy 101, September 2009.
55. The following is drawn from Edward J. Harpham, "Welfare Reform and the New Paternalism in Texas," in *Texas Politics,* ed. Champagne and Harpham, chap. 14.
56. See Vivian Elizabeth Smyrl, "Texas Department of Human Services," *Handbook of Texas Online,* www.tshaonline.org/handbook/online/articles/TT/mct6.html (accessed 4/23/08).
57. Harpham, "Welfare Reform and the New Paternalism," p. 238.
58. See Smyrl, "Texas Department of Human Services."
59. See Charles Murray, *Losing Ground* (New York: Basic Books, 1984).
60. For a discussion of these programs, see Lawrence Mead, *The New Politics of Poverty: The Nonworking Poor in America* (New York: Basic Books, 1992).
61. The following paragraphs are drawn from Harpham, "Welfare Reform and the New Paternalism," 244–7.
62. See Texas Health and Human Services Commission, "Temporary Assistance for Needy Families (TANF): Frequently Asked Questions," www.hhsc.state.tx.us/programs/TexasWorks/TANF-FAQ.html (accessed 4/23/08).
63. See Texas Workforce Investment Council, "Issues in Welfare to Work: A State of the Workforce Report on State Issues Arising from TANF Reauthorization," December 2006, p. 11, www.governor.state.tx.us/divisions/twic/files/wfwissues.pdf (accessed 4/23/08). Texas Health and Human Services Commission, Texas TANF and SNAP Enrollment Statistics, March 2010, www.hhsc.state.tx.us (accessed 4/23/10). See also www.hhsc.state.tx.us/research/TANF-Statewide.asp.
64. Texas Workforce, "Welfare Reform Initiatives, 2005."

# answer key

**Chapter 1**
1. e
2. b
3. c
4. a
5. c
6. c
7. c
8. b
9. e
10. a
11. c
12. e
13. e
14. a
15. a

**Chapter 2**
1. a
2. b
3. b
4. c
5. e
6. c
7. a
8. d
9. b
10. e
11. e
12. b
13. e
14. a

**Chapter 3**
1. c
2. c
3. b
4. e
5. a
6. d

7. d
8. b
9. a
10. c
11. b
12. b
13. d
14. d

**Chapter 4**
1. a
2. e
3. b
4. b
5. e
6. e
7. b
8. e
9. b
10. d
11. b
12. a
13. c
14. a
15. d

**Chapter 5**
1. b
2. e
3. a
4. c
5. a
6. b
7. d
8. a
9. b
10. d
11. a
12. a
13. c

14. a
15. b

**Chapter 6**
1. c
2. a
3. e
4. d
5. c
6. b
7. c
8. a
9. b
10. b
11. a
12. b
13. b

**Chapter 7**
1. b
2. e
3. c
4. e
5. c
6. c
7. e
8. b
9. b
10. c
11. b
12. e
13. c
14. c

**Chapter 8**
1. e
2. b
3. d
4. d
5. a

6. c
7. a
8. d
9. b
10. d
11. c
12. b
13. e
14. d
15. b

**Chapter 9**
1. a
2. d
3. a
4. c
5. e
6. c
7. d
8. d
9. b
10. c
11. a
12. e
13. a
14. e
15. d

**Chapter 10**
1. b
2. a
3. d
4. c
5. d
6. a
7. b
8. d
9. d
10. b
11. c

12. b
13. a
14. c

**Chapter 11**
1. a
2. e
3. c
4. e
5. a
6. b
7. e
8. d
9. a
10. e
11. c
12. b
13. a
14. e

**Chapter 12**
1. d
2. a
3. d
4. c
5. a
6. c
7. a
8. a
9. b
10. a
11. e
12. c
13. a
14. a

**Chapter 13**
1. b
2. d
3. b

4. e
5. a
6. c
7. b
8. b
9. c
10. a
11. c
12. b
13. b
14. a

**Chapter 14**
1. b
2. b
3. b
4. e
5. b
6. e
7. d
8. d
9. d
10. d
11. d
12. b
13. a
14. a

**Chapter 15**
1. a
2. c
3. a
4. a
5. d
6. e
7. a
8. d
9. c
10. b
11. e
12. a
13. c
14. a
15. c

**Chapter 16**
1. a
2. b
3. c
4. c

5. d
6. d
7. b
8. e
9. a
10. c
11. d
12. e
13. a
14. c
15. c

**Chapter 17**
1. c
2. b
3. d
4. c
5. e
6. a
7. c
8. d
9. d
10. a
11. d
12. c
13. e
14. d
15. c

**Chapter 18**
1. b
2. d
3. c
4. a
5. e
6. c
7. c
8. c
9. e
10. c
11. a
12. d
13. b
14. b

**Chapter 19**
1. b
2. a
3. c
4. b

5. b
6. d
7. c
8. a
9. e
10. c
11. b
12. c
13. a
14. a

**Chapter 20**
1. a
2. c
3. d
4. c
5. e
6. d
7. d
8. a
9. d
10. c
11. a
12. a
13. d
14. d
15. d

**Chapter 21**
1. b
2. b
3. a
4. c
5. e
6. a
7. d
8. c
9. d
10. c
11. b
12. a
13. a
14. a
15. e

**Chapter 22**
1. b
2. e
3. e
4. e

5. e
6. a
7. d
8. e
9. a
10. c
11. c
12. e
13. b
14. d
15. a

**Chapter 23**
1. a
2. a
3. d
4. b
5. c
6. b
7. d
8. a
9. d
10. c
11. d
12. a
13. d
14. a

**Chapter 24**
1. d
2. e
3. e
4. b
5. d
6. a
7. a
8. b
9. b
10. b
11. e
12. a
13. c
14. a
15. e

**Chapter 25**
1. c
2. c
3. c
4. b

5. b
6. a
7. d
8. d
9. d
10. d
11. e
12. a
13. e
14. d
15. a

**Chapter 26**
1. b
2. d
3. d
4. d
5. c
6. a
7. b
8. b
9. d
10. e
11. a
12. a
13. c
14. a
15. b

**Chapter 27**
1. c
2. a
3. d
4. b
5. e
6. d
7. a
8. c
9. c
10. a
11. b
12. c
13. a
14. a
15. b

# photo credits

# index

Alonzo is always sad

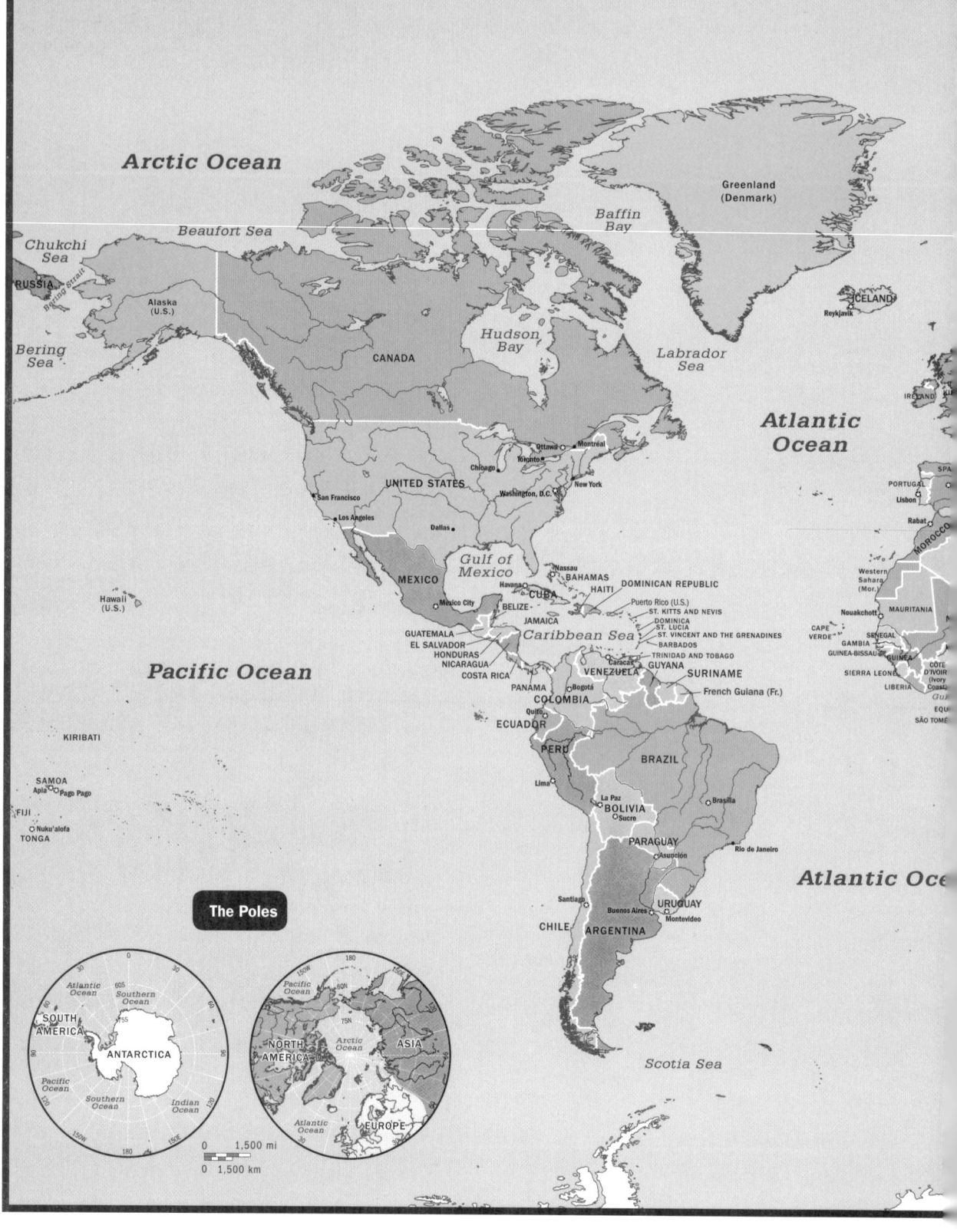

Arctic Ocean

Chukchi Sea

RUSSIA

Bering Strait

Bering Sea

Alaska (U.S.)

Beaufort Sea

CANADA

Hudson Bay

Greenland (Denmark)

Baffin Bay

Labrador Sea

ICELAND

Reykjavik

Atlantic Ocean

IRELAND

Hawaii (U.S.)

San Francisco

Los Angeles

UNITED STATES

Chicago

Ottawa  Montréal
Toronto

Washington, D.C.  New York

SPA

PORTUGAL

Lisbon

Rabat

MOROCCO

Dallas

Gulf of Mexico

MEXICO

Mexico City

Nassau  BAHAMAS
Havana  CUBA
BELIZE

DOMINICAN REPUBLIC
HAITI

Puerto Rico (U.S.)
ST. KITTS AND NEVIS
DOMINICA
ST. LUCIA
ST. VINCENT AND THE GRENADINES
BARBADOS
TRINIDAD AND TOBAGO

Western Sahara (Mor.)

Nouakchott  MAURITANIA

CAPE VERDE  SENEGAL
GAMBIA
GUINEA-BISSAU  GUINEA

Pacific Ocean

JAMAICA

GUATEMALA
EL SALVADOR
HONDURAS
NICARAGUA
COSTA RICA

Caribbean Sea

PANAMA

Caracas
VENEZUELA  GUYANA

SURINAME

French Guiana (Fr.)

SIERRA LEONE

LIBERIA

CÔTE D'IVOIR
(Ivory Coast)

Gu

Bogotá
COLOMBIA

Quito
ECUADOR

PERU

Lima

EQU
SÃO TOMÉ

KIRIBATI

BRAZIL

Brasília

La Paz
BOLIVIA
Sucre

SAMOA
Apia  Pago Pago

FIJI

Nuku'alofa
TONGA

PARAGUAY

Asunción

Rio de Janeiro

Atlantic Oce

URUGUAY

Santiago

Buenos Aires
Montevideo

CHILE  ARGENTINA

Scotia Sea

**The Poles**

Atlantic Ocean

0

60S

Southern Ocean

30

SOUTH AMERICA

75S

ANTARCTICA

Pacific Ocean

Southern Ocean

Indian Ocean

150W  180  150E

180

Pacific Ocean

150W  180

60N

NORTH AMERICA

75N

Arctic Ocean

ASIA

Atlantic Ocean

EUROPE

0  1,500 mi

0  1,500 km

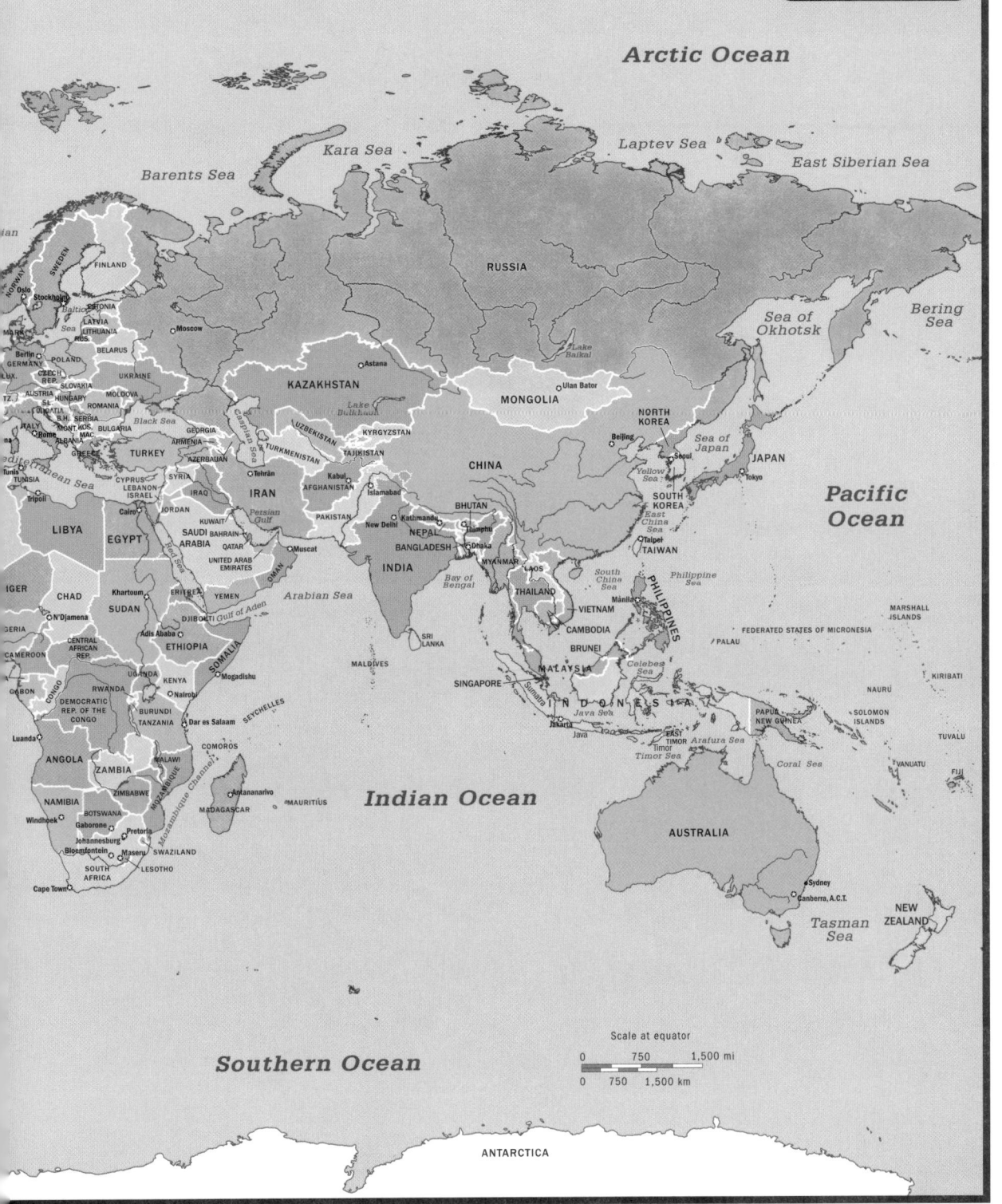

# The World

**Arctic Ocean**

Kara Sea

Laptev Sea

East Siberian Sea

Barents Sea

RUSSIA

Bering Sea

Sea of Okhotsk

SWEDEN

FINLAND

NORWAY

Oslo

Stockholm

ESTONIA

Baltic Sea

LATVIA

LITHUANIA

RUSS.

Moscow

Berlin

GERMANY

POLAND

BELARUS

CZECH REP.

SLOVAKIA

UKRAINE

KAZAKHSTAN

Astana

MONGOLIA

Ulan Bator

Lake Baikal

NORTH KOREA

Beijing

Sea of Japan

JAPAN

Tokyo

LUX.

AUSTRIA

HUNGARY

MOLDOVA

TZ.

SL.

CROATIA

ROMANIA

B.H.

SERBIA

Lake Balkhash

KYRGYZSTAN

SOUTH KOREA

Seoul

ITALY

MONT.

KOS.

BULGARIA

Black Sea

GEORGIA

UZBEKISTAN

Yellow Sea

Rome

MAC.

ALBANIA

GREECE

TURKEY

ARMENIA

AZERBAIJAN

TURKMENISTAN

TAJIKISTAN

CHINA

East China Sea

Taipei

TAIWAN

Tunis

Mediterranean Sea

CYPRUS

LEBANON

ISRAEL

SYRIA

Tehrān

Kabul

Islamabad

BHUTAN

Thimphu

TUNISIA

Tripoli

Cairo

JORDAN

IRAQ

IRAN

AFGHANISTAN

New Delhi

Kathmandu

NEPAL

Dhaka

South China Sea

Philippine Sea

KUWAIT

PAKISTAN

BANGLADESH

LIBYA

EGYPT

SAUDI ARABIA

BAHRAIN

QATAR

Persian Gulf

Muscat

INDIA

MYANMAR

LAOS

Manila

PHILIPPINES

MARSHALL ISLANDS

NIGER

CHAD

UNITED ARAB EMIRATES

OMAN

Arabian Sea

THAILAND

VIETNAM

FEDERATED STATES OF MICRONESIA

PALAU

N'Djamena

SUDAN

Khartoum

ERITREA

YEMEN

Bay of Bengal

CAMBODIA

KIRIBATI

NGERIA

CENTRAL AFRICAN REP.

Adis Ababa

DJIBOUTI

Gulf of Aden

SRI LANKA

BRUNEI

Celebes Sea

NAURU

CAMEROON

ETHIOPIA

MALDIVES

MALAYSIA

SINGAPORE

Sumatra

I N D O N E S I A

SOLOMON ISLANDS

GABON

UGANDA

KENYA

Nairobi

SOMALIA

Mogadishu

TUVALU

CONGO

RWANDA

BURUNDI

SEYCHELLES

Java Sea

Jakarta

PAPUA NEW GUINEA

Luanda

DEMOCRATIC REP. OF THE CONGO

TANZANIA

Dar es Salaam

Java

EAST TIMOR

Arafura Sea

VANUATU

ANGOLA

ZAMBIA

MALAWI

COMOROS

Timor Sea

Coral Sea

FIJI

MOZAMBIQUE

ZIMBABWE

Antananarivo

MAURITIUS

Indian Ocean

NAMIBIA

BOTSWANA

MADAGASCAR

Mozambique Channel

Windhoek

Gaborone

Pretoria

Johannesburg

AUSTRALIA

Bloemfontein

Maseru

SWAZILAND

SOUTH AFRICA

LESOTHO

Cape Town

Sydney

Canberra, A.C.T.

Pacific Ocean

NEW ZEALAND

Tasman Sea

**Southern Ocean**

Scale at equator

0     750     1,500 mi

0     750     1,500 km

ANTARCTICA